P9-DFT-607

Third Edition

A Diagnostic Approach to Organizational Behavior

JUDITH R. GORDON
Carroll School of Management
BOSTON COLLEGE

ALLYN AND BACON
Boston / London / Toronto / Sydney / Tokyo / Singapore

SERIES EDITOR: Jack Peters
SENIOR EDITORIAL ASSISTANT: Carol Alper
PRODUCTION ADMINISTRATOR: Rowena Dores
EDITORIAL-PRODUCTION SERVICE: Helyn Pultz
TEXT DESIGNER: Karen Mason
COMPOSITION BUYER: Linda Cox
MANUFACTURING BUYER: Megan Cochran
COVER ADMINISTRATOR: Linda Dickinson

Library of Congress Cataloging-in-Publication Data
Gordon, Judith R.
A diagnostic approach to organizational behavior / Judith R. Gordon.—3rd ed.
p. cm.
Includes bibliographical references and indexes.
ISBN 0-205-12090-3
1. Organizational behavior. I. Title.
HD58.7.G67 1991
658.3—dc20 90-38759
CIP

PHOTO CREDITS

Chapter 1: Courtesy of Atari Corporation
Chapter 2: Goodyear News Bureau
Chapter 3: © Susan Lapides. All rights reserved.
Chapter 4: © Susan Lapides. All rights reserved.
Chapter 5: The Christian Science Monitor/Melanie Stetson
Chapter 6: Copyright Frank Siteman 1990
Chapter 7: Copyright Frank Siteman 1990
Chapter 8: © Susan Lapides 1984. All rights reserved.
Chapter 9: The Christian Science Monitor © Robert Harbison
Chapter 10: Courtesy of Honeywell Inc.
Chapter 11: Copyright Frank Siteman 1990
Chapter 12: © Jim Pickerell 1985
Chapter 13: Courtesy of Volvo
Chapter 14: © Jim Pickerell 1986
Chapter 15: © Susan Lapides 1983. All rights reserved.

PRINTED IN THE UNITED STATES OF AMERICA
10 9 8 7 6 5 4 3 2 95 94 93 92 91

In Loving Memory of My Father
and in Honor of His Namesake, Michael

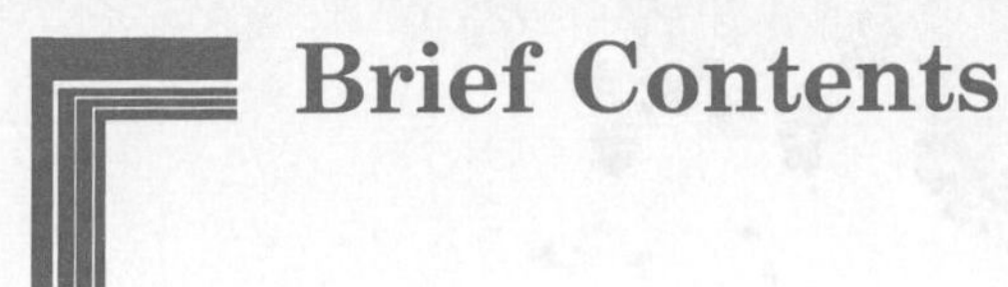

Brief Contents

Complete Contents

PART ONE INTRODUCING ORGANIZATIONAL BEHAVIOR

PART TWO DIAGNOSING INDIVIDUAL BEHAVIOR

PART THREE DIAGNOSING GROUP BEHAVIOR

PART FOUR DIAGNOSING BEHAVIOR AT THE ORGANIZATIONAL LEVEL

Preface

The third edition of *A Diagnostic Approach to Organizational Behavior,* like the previous two editions, has a dual emphasis. First, it focuses on *diagnosis:* describing, understanding, and explaining behavior in organizations. Second, it considers *action:* controlling, managing, or influencing behavior. The diagnostic approach combines theory and practice by encouraging students to learn organizational theories, experience behavior in organizations, and then apply the theories to the analysis of their experiences. Taking this approach should stimulate effective employee performance, as well as facilitate effective managerial action.

This book includes text, readings, cases, exercises, and numerous examples of organizational situations. It is designed for students of organizational behavior at all levels. Undergraduate students, graduate students, and practitioners can enrich their understanding of human behavior and consequently improve their action effectiveness as organizational members. This edition differs from previous editions in its expanded treatment of many of the topics as well as extensive consideration of international issues and discussion of organizational ethics.

The diagnostic approach encourages the application of diverse conceptual and theoretical frameworks to a situational analysis. The complexity of organizations and their environments makes it unlikely that any one theory can provide a definitive answer to all questions about how people in organizations act. Transformational leadership complements but differs from contingency approaches to leadership effectiveness. Reinforcement theories of motivation differ from equity theories. Likewise there are various ways of classifying organizational structure—mechanistic and organic, or functional and integrated, for example. Taking an international perspective enriches our understanding of organizations in both the United States and abroad. The various theories complement each other, and each can provide insight into behavior in organizations, leading to more effective managerial behavior. Understanding theories of communication, group development, individual needs, conflict, leadership, and power, among others, improves the understanding of group problem solving. Knowing theories of motivation, learning, and communication, helps the identification of issues of work design. Focusing on diverse facets of behavior also improves diagnosis and ultimately action.

Thus the understanding of any organizational situation includes the ability to analyze it in a number of ways, rather than to assume that any one explanation is adequate. The use of triangulation, or a multiperspective viewpoint, to more completely understand a situation and to reinforce the accuracy of a diagnosis is a significant feature of the diagnostic approach. More effective action follows more accurate diagnosis. The viewpoint of this book assumes that more than one perspective can be right. Students are encouraged to view a situation from a variety of theoretical perspectives, as a way of increasing their understanding of behavior and using this enriched understanding to improve action. The thorough internalization of new theories and concepts for regular use in observing and understanding behavior is the result of practice in diagnosis. More effective action can then occur. Of course, experienced managers do not try all approaches in each situation: they choose the tools that fit and help. As students become more practiced in using the diagnostic approach, they too become more adept in selecting the appropriate frameworks to apply.

This book presents several processes for viewing the same situation from different perspectives. First, students are asked to analyze a situation using various theoretical perspectives, one at a time. Next, they are presented with an ambiguous case study and asked to identify diverse perspectives that contribute to effective diagnosis. They analyze the situation from the various perspectives, then suggest action on the basis of the perspectives. Finally, students are asked to observe their own and others' behavior in organizational simulations, analyze it from diverse perspectives, and consider the implications for action. The book encourages the use of a multifaceted pedagogy, where materials presented in text, cases, and exercises provide mutual reinforcement and practice in using the diagnostic approach.

The book begins with an introductory chapter that describes the diagnostic approach and illustrates it using numerous historical perspectives of organizational behavior. The book next discusses individual behavior. It then moves to an examination of interactions among individuals in groups, which builds on knowledge of individual behavior and individual interactions. Finally, the book presents organizational issues, which discussion incorporates knowledge of both individuals and groups. Thus, the organization of the book reflects a key feature of the diagnostic approach: viewing behavior from an increasing number of different but complementary, more complex but elaborating, perspectives.

More specifically, in Chapter 1, the stage is set by defining the diagnostic approach. The first chapter also details various historical perspectives on behavior in organizations, including a discussion of the systems and contingency perspectives.

Chapter 2 begins Part Two, which focuses on individual behavior by describing perception, attribution, learning, and attitudes. Chapter 3 introduces perspectives related to individual personality differences and variations in personal development. Chapter 4 presents various theories of motivation.

Chapter 5, which begins Part Three, discusses specific group issues, including group formation, development, norms, roles, goals, and structure. Chapter 6 examines decision making. Chapter 7 looks at communication. In Chapter 8, the role of leadership and management in dealing with groups is discussed. Chapter 9 considers the roles of power in organizations; it also discusses the process of negotiation. Chapter 10 concludes the discussion of group behavior by describing conflict management and intergroup behavior, providing a transition to organizational issues.

In Part Four, large-scale organizational issues are discussed and prescriptions for changing organizations are emphasized. Chapters 11 and 12 investigate the structures of organizations and the factors that influence their design. Chapter 13 integrates individual, group, and organizational issues by considering work design.

Part Five includes Chapter 14, which discusses organizational change. The book concludes with Chapter 15, which examines the nature of organizational effectiveness, the role of the diagnostic approach in increasing such effectiveness, and long-lasting organizational transformations.

This book provides an integrated presentation of each topic, using text, readings, case analyses, and exercises to apply the diagnostic approach. The book is designed to be versatile in its use. Each chapter includes a presentation of key theories or concepts regarding a particular topic and cases and exercises that allow the application of the theoretical perspectives to diverse situations. Most also include a reading that examines specific issues in greater depth. Each chapter includes a summary of the textual material, as well as concluding comments intended to integrate the text and readings with the outcomes of the case discussions and exercises.

Readings are an integral part of the book because they present the thinking of current writers and researchers in the field of organizational behavior. The readings have been selected to provide critical elaborations of core concepts and to consider organizational issues from diverse approaches. They include theoretical formulations, research reports, descriptions of organizational programs, and commentaries on organizational issues. Discussion questions following each reading highlight these concepts and their contribution to diagnosing organizational behavior and acting effectively in organizations.

Cases offer the unique advantage of allowing students to experience a real-life situation without leaving the classroom. They can analyze the behavior that occurs and offer solutions for improving individual, group, and/or organizational effectiveness without suffering the consequences of inaccurate diagnosis or inappropriate recommendations. But, just as in real-life situations, the complexity of the human actions involved provides a significant challenge to students' diagnostic skills. Students are encouraged first to list the facts of a case; then to identify the key managerial and behavioral issues in the situation. In problem situations they next specify the symptoms that indicate problems exist, as well as describe and show other evidence of the problems in the case. In all situations they then apply relevant theoretical models to diagnose each situation more thoroughly. They conclude by offering a prescription or plan for managerial action, directed at acting effectively or remedying a problem situation.

Finally, *exercises* give students practice in responding to situations similar to those they might experience as members of organizations. The exercises call for students to make certain decisions, redesign jobs, or plan ways to correct dysfunctional situations. Students are encouraged to participate in role plays, where each acts the part of a character in a work situation; to complete self-assessment questionnaires or interviews; and to participate in other activities that encourage the description and diagnosis of their own and others' behavior as a prerequisite to effective action.

The development of this book has been influenced by the contributions of many individuals. First, I would like to thank the adopters of *A Diagnostic Approach to Organizational Behavior,* as well as the reviewers of the first two editions. Second, I would like to thank the reviewers of this edition: James McElroy, Iowa State University; Joanna Banthin, New Jersey Institute of Technology; James Daily, Wright State University; Cynthia Fukami, University of Denver; Robert Goddard, Appalachian State University; George Jacobs,

Middle Tennessee State University; Vicki LaFarge, Bentley College; George Lyne, Appalachian State University; Elizabeth Ravlin, University of North Carolina; Richard Sebastian, St. Cloud State University; and Mary Anne Watson, University of Tampa. Third, I would like to thank my colleagues at the Boston College School of Management for their enthusiastic adoption of the book and their suggestions for its improvement. I also wish to thank the Dean of the School of Management, John J. Neuhauser III, for his support. My deepest thanks go to my extended family, whose support and enthusiasm have been greatly appreciated. Most of all, I would like to thank my husband and children, who are my mainstay and my inspiration.

A Diagnostic Approach to Organizational Behavior

1

Setting the Stage

CHAPTER OUTLINE

Organizational Behavior in the Decision Support Group
The Importance of Organizational Behavior to Managers
Organizational Behavior Defined and Studied
The Diagnostic Approach
Description
Diagnosis
Prescription
Action
Applying the Diagnostic Approach
Historical Perspectives
Structural Perspectives
Behavioral Perspectives
Integrative Perspectives
Organization of This Book
SUMMARY
ENDNOTES
RECOMMENDED READINGS

LEARNING OBJECTIVES

After completing the reading in Chapter 1, students will be able to

- discuss organizational behavior as a field of study;
- describe the diagnostic approach;
- compare and contrast four ways of collecting data for use in description;
- describe three types of research designs and cite their advantages and disadvantages;
- identify, compare, and contrast the major periods and perspectives in the history of organizational thought;
- apply theoretical perspectives one at a time to diagnosing an organizational situation and describe their advantages and limitations for understanding behavior and attitudes;
- apply the systems model to analyze an organizational decision; and
- comment on the way contingency theory addresses shortcomings of previous theories and meshes with the diagnostic approach.

Organizational Behavior in the Decision Support Group

Ellen Mitchell manages the Decision Support Group in the Development Division of Applied Computations, Inc., better known as ACI. She had held a similar position for a competitor for three years prior to joining ACI. The position as manager of the Decision Support Group had been vacant for eight months before Ellen was hired. The Group develops a line of software products, called Dataworks, that enable users to manipulate data quickly. The products consist of a spread sheet, data table processor, charting component, screen manager, and report writer. The Dataworks package is updated and revised on an ongoing basis, with new components released at least once a year. Dataworks is well known, and company employees feel great pride in working for Applied Computations on this product.

Ellen supervises five project leaders, each responsible for one of the components of the software. Each leader in turn manages a three- to five-person product team that develops and maintains its component of the software package. None of the project leaders has the formal engineering degree or official title that corresponds to his or her responsibility. Each has worked his or her way into the position because of quality performance as a team member.

The most recent revision of the software began six months before Ellen's arrival at ACI. Two weeks after Ellen joined the firm she asked the project leaders for a detailed schedule of the time and resources they required to complete the revision as designed and scheduled. She asked them to report any slips in the schedule and update her on their progress daily. She scheduled formal meetings with each project leader twice a week. During these meetings she asked them to describe their progress in detail and outline the specific activities of each team member for the next two to three days. Often she gave them specific directives about how they should allocate their staff's time.

Four weeks after Ellen joined the firm, the Vice President of Marketing and the Vice President of Development agreed to a release date for the revised version of Dataworks without any discussion with members of the Decision Support Group. Ellen announced this date during the next regularly scheduled weekly status meeting, which all project leaders attended. Leaders and members of the project teams uniformly reacted with shock and anger. They knew that meeting this deadline would require them to cut many new and important features from the revision. They had spent many hours with Ellen's predecessor agreeing to the scope of the revision and now felt betrayed by top management. They said that a quality product was important to them because they had always felt proud to be employees of ACI.

The project leaders asked Ellen for more staff and resources as a way of meeting the original specifications. Ellen denied their requests and offered no explanation for her denial. To make matters worse, management had recently implemented a new policy that called for the evaluation of project leaders' ability to meet schedules (decided by management) as part of their annual performance reviews.

Members of the Decision Support Group began to express concern about Ellen. They said that she ignored their requests, interfered with their work, and failed to stand up to top management when it set impossible demands. They argued that the schedule would slip, as it always had in the past, because it was unrealistic, and the group leader was unwilling to provide additional support to ensure its accomplishment. Staff members seemed irritable. One team member was heard refusing to help another when a new problem arose because "it wasn't in the schedule." Team members complained constantly. Morale declined. Overtime work increased, but productivity declined.

Ellen called a meeting of the entire Decision Support Group. It became a gripe session. Many workers repeated their litany of complaints. At the end of the meeting Ellen told the team members that the problem was simple: the project leaders could not create appropriate schedules. She planned to ask another manager to conduct a seminar on the importance of schedules. She also began to meet with individuals to learn their plans for work after the revision was released. Within the next month four of the project leaders requested a transfer. One-third of the team members began active job hunting.[1]

Like Ellen Mitchell and the members of the Decision Support Group, we all belong to organizations. We work in organizations, are educated in organizations, and have our needs for such things as food, clothing, and recreation met by organizations. Often we find that our identity is tightly bound up with the organizations to which we belong. The project team members considered themselves as representatives of ACI and felt proud to be part of the company.

THE IMPORTANCE OF ORGANIZATIONAL BEHAVIOR TO MANAGERS

As members of organizations, especially work organizations, we are likely to face situations similar to the ones Ellen and her subordinates encountered. Managers must understand organizational behavior to ensure their own and others' performance and satisfaction. Why did morale decline? Why did complaints increase? Why did productivity decrease? Why was more overtime required? What can be done about the employees' attitude toward the schedule? What should be done? How can the relationship between members of the Decision Support Group and Ellen Mitchell be improved? How can Ellen become a more effective manager?

This case describes a situation neither new nor unique to Applied Computations. Many managers have employees who do not produce in the way that manager expects. The team members, for example, do not docilely comply with Ellen's directive to meet the release date announced by the vice presidents. Other employees who are initially very active and involved in their organizations and committed to its goals and products become progressively less supportive. The Decision Support Group seems unwilling (and probably unable), for example, to complete the task without additional resources and staff. Still other employees may lack the skills a manager expected them to have when they were hired. The project leaders may in fact lack the ability to construct a proper schedule, or their lack of engineering training may cause them to require more time for some development tasks. Still others may react to a manager's leadership with disgust, anger, or ambivalence. Clearly, members of the Decision Support Group respond negatively to Ellen's controlling style. Ultimately such situations affect the company's productivity and the workers' satisfaction and performance.

How do situations such as these occur? Changes in the external environment of the work situation, such as increased competition, requirements for new products, or increased pressures from customers for early delivery, may cause positive or negative reactions from workers. Changes in the resources available for a project, such as the alteration of the work force through hirings, layoffs, resignations, or terminations; the reduction of financial resources available for a project; or changes in scheduled due dates or completion schedules, may affect workers' satisfaction, involvement, performance, and attendance. Does the situation of the Decision Support Group describe such changes? Or does it describe ineffective leadership, lack of employee motivation, intergroup conflict, or inappropriate organizational structure? The situation could result from any of these problems or, more likely, from several of them.

Insights from the field of organizational behavior help us to better understand the situation faced by Ellen Mitchell and her coworkers. These insights help us to not only describe organizational situations and problems but also diagnose them and determine reasons the situations exist as they do, to develop prescriptions for effective action, and to take action as appropriate to deal with the situations faced.

ORGANIZATIONAL BEHAVIOR DEFINED AND STUDIED

Organizational behavior is defined as the actions and attitudes of people in organizations. It is also a body of knowledge and a field of study about organizations and their members. Organizational behavior has its roots in several social science disciplines—psychology, sociology, anthropology, economics, political science, and management—and it applies models, or ways of thinking, from these areas to the study of people's behavior in organizations. For example, it addresses the following issues that may be relevant to the case:

- What facilitates accurate perception and attribution?
- What influences individual, group, and organizational learning and the development of individual attitudes toward work?
- What motivates people to work, and how does the organization's reward system influence worker behavior and attitudes?
- What contributes to effective decision making?
- What constitutes effective communication?
- What characterizes effective leadership?
- How can groups of employees be encouraged to work together productively?
- How can power be secured and used productively?
- What increases stress and how can it be managed?
- How can conflict (between groups or between a manager and subordinates) be resolved or managed?
- How can jobs and organizations be effectively designed?
- How can managers help workers deal effectively with change?

Organizational behavior as a field of study represents more than a mere collection of separate theories and models. Rather, the field offers the opportunity to apply simultaneously several different perspectives to the understanding of specific, concrete events such as those faced by Ellen and her subordinates. Thus it offers the chance to understand some of the *complexity* of organizations and organizational dilemmas and situations, and to understand that most organizational problems have several causes. The more fully we understand all the reasons for specific organizational events or problems, the more we can respond appropriately to them. The better Ellen Mitchell understands the causes of the declining performance and increasing turnover in the Decision Support Group, the more easily she can determine appropriate actions for correcting the problems that cause this situation. Organizational behavior principles play an essential role in determining *organizational effectiveness,* which is a central responsibility and focus for all managers.

The primary objective of this book is to make use of this capacity of organizational behavior: to develop the ability to *understand* organizational events as fully as possible. We are defining the application of knowledge and skill to a real situation as *diagnosis*. Accurate diagnosis forms the basis for effective *action*.

THE DIAGNOSTIC APPROACH

What is the first step Ellen Mitchell and her superiors (the vice presidents) should take to address the problems they face? They could just pick a quick solution: Ellen could hire more staff or extend the schedule; she could take a leadership-training course; she could replace her staff with engineers who could make the deadline without complaining; Ellen's boss could fire her; Ellen could reduce the pay of any team member who complains; the workers could file a petition of complaint with top management; the team members could all quit; or they could unionize.

Would any of these actions be effective? Which would be the most effective? How do we know? Responding to a problem with the wrong solution may cause no improvement—or even seriously magnify existing problems. Before a person responds to or acts in a given situation, he or she must first understand, as fully as possible, what is happening. Ellen Mitchell should *diagnose* the present situation. After a complete diagnosis, she can *act*—prescribe and implement appropriate solutions.

We diagnose when we first describe a situation, behavior, or attitude, and then identify its components and causes. In examining the case of Ellen Mitchell and the Decision Support Group project teams, for example, we must first identify the key elements of the situation: Ellen has recently joined the department; she closely monitors her subordinates' activities and progress; top management has tightened the schedule for releasing the new version of Dataworks, and Ellen has imposed this deadline without providing more resources or consulting with her project teams. We also know that several symptoms exist—indicators that there is a problem situation: morale and performance have declined, and requests for transfer have increased.

Second, we can identify several problems or potential causes of these behaviors and attitudes. Ellen uses an autocratic style of management, which contrasts greatly with the leadership void that existed prior to her arrival. She also replaces much of the autonomy previously experienced by the team leaders with close monitoring of their activities; she does not involve them in decision making. Ellen does not financially or psychologically reward the extra effort of the workers. She overlooks any group spirit that existed prior to her arrival and may violate norms that provided for more resources when tight deadlines were set. She fails to communicate effectively with her subordinates and creates a defensive climate by suggesting that team leaders are incompetent at scheduling. Complete diagnosis would involve a full specification of all relevant aspects of a given situation. Often this requires collecting additional information or describing the situation more fully. Hypothesizing links between various facets of the situation may be required to complete the diagnosis; for example, testing the implications of leadership style for employees' behavior, organizational structure for management's actions, or sources of power for subordinates' responses to management directives may be essential for Ellen Mitchell to diagnose the problems in the Decision Support Group. After identifying all possible causes of the situation, we can determine the likelihood that each of these potential causes affects the situation described. Ineffective leadership seems a likely problem in the opening case; intergroup conflict between project teams seems less likely. We can use the various theories presented in this book to help us evaluate the relevance of each potential cause to the situation.

Then we can plan a course of action for correcting the situation. Such a course of action, based on a strong diagnosis, should be more effective than action based on very little understanding of the problem. Correcting defective leadership calls for different strategies than improving an inefficient organizational design; changing group norms calls for different approaches than building new bases of power. Throughout this book you are encouraged to understand organizational events or problems as fully as you can before deciding how you wish to respond to them; diagnosis precedes action. Even if no problem currently exists, applying the diagnostic approach allows managers to anticipate difficulties that might occur later and to prevent their happening by early, effective action. Diagnosis is a key skill for effective managers.

Figure 1–1 shows the diagnostic approach proposed in this book for use by managers and other organizational members. This approach includes four phases: (1) description, (2) diagnosis, (3) prescription, and (4) action.

Description

Phase 1, description, is simply that: a reporting of concrete aspects of or events in a specific situation without any attempt to explain the reasons for the events, or to make inferences about a person's motives or purposes.

The Process of Description In the Decision Support Group at ACI, for example, we can describe a number of concrete occurrences. Requests for transfers and job-hunting activities have increased. Employee satisfaction has decreased. Project team members complain about tighter deadlines. Ellen Mitchell has not allocated additional resources to the current projects. Each of these is directly observable.

In analyzing any situation—live or written in a case format—you can begin by listing the facts. At Applied Computations, for example, we know that Ellen

Figure 1–1 THE DIAGNOSTIC APPROACH

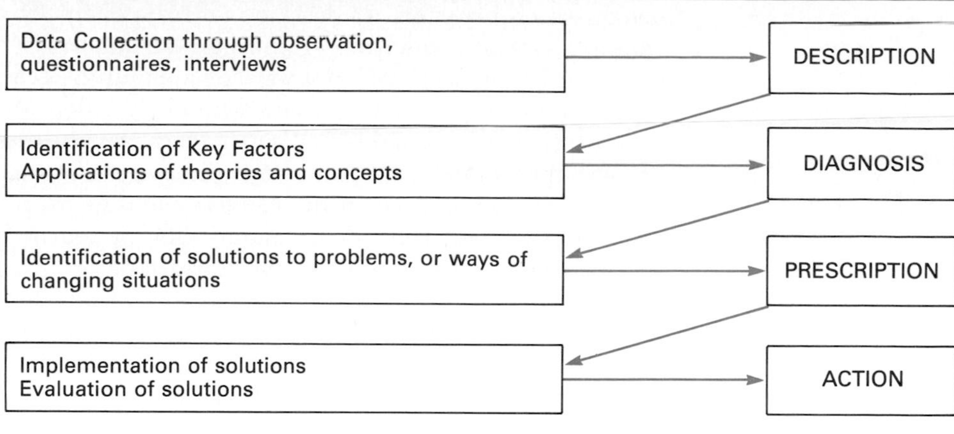

called a meeting of the entire group, and it became a gripe session. We also know she appeared to accept without challenge the release date set by the vice presidents. We also know that she met with each team leader formally at least twice a week. In analyzing this or other situations you might also specify any assumptions you are making about the events; for example, you might assume that the gripe session signals the existence of a problem situation or that effective managers respond to employees' complaints. As much as possible you should test these assumptions to identify any that can be added to the list of facts.

The process of simple description is much more difficult than it looks; sometimes it is not easy to separate facts from assumptions. Most of us have little practice in making such a separation. Yet effective diagnosis and understanding of the situation depend on a valid and factual description of it. The better we can describe situations, the better we understand them. So throughout this book you are given opportunities to describe what you have read or seen.

In the case of the Decision Support Group, we base our description primarily on the summary of the situation presented in the introduction to this chapter. This description is probably not complete; nuances of attitudes and seemingly insignificant behaviors may be excluded. Nor does description completely recount the views of the vice presidents or even Ellen Mitchell. In dealing with real organizational situations, we would attempt to secure a full description of the actual organizational events as they occur. What methods can we use to gain information that allows us to accurately describe events, behaviors, and attitudes?

Sources of Information Managers and organizational researchers primarily use four sources of information about situations they face or analyze: direct observation, questionnaires, interviews, and written documents. Each of these methods helps us first to report events, not to diagnose their deeper implications. Together these methods help us to validate our perceptions of the events (described in greater detail in Chapter 2)

Direct observation When we as managers or organizational researchers use direct observation, we describe concrete events that we see. We might, for example, spend some time attending staff meetings of the Decision Support Group and then describe what we see happening, such as who talks most often, what topics they discuss, or how frequently Ellen Mitchell asks for her subordinates' views on a subject. We can also observe everyday events in everyday places[2]: for example, we can watch the actions of the team members as they wait for an elevator, sit in the company lounge, or meet in the hallways. We can listen to their conversations and thereby learn their expressed attitudes toward their supervisor, job, or organization.

Questionnaires When we use questionnaires, we write questions designed to elicit organization members' opinions. We might develop a questionnaire that we distribute to all members of the Decision Support Group to help determine their attitudes toward their jobs and their supervisor. We could then describe the attitudes expressed in the questionnaire without determining the reasons behind these attitudes.[3] A questionnaire used at Applied Computations might show the workers' increasing dissatisfaction; repeated administration of such a questionnaire might indicate changes over time in their attitude toward the organization.

Interviews We could also ask organization members a series of questions in person to explore their attitudes and opinions in depth. Managers often "interview" employees informally, chatting with them about their views of a particular situation. We might, for example, interview several team leaders to discuss their experiences in the Decision Support Group. We might talk with Ellen Mitchell to gain her viewpoint on the scheduling issue. We might interview the two vice presidents to learn the rationale behind their decision about the release date and whether they prohibited the allocation of additional resources to the teams for completing the present version. We would then describe these experiences and attitudes as part of the first step in the diagnostic approach.

Written documents Finally, we could gather data about past performance, work-team behavior, or other aspects of individual, group, and organizational functioning from the firm's records, such as annual reports, departmental evaluations, memoranda, or nonconfidential personnel files. Then we would analyze the content of these documents. At ACI, for example, an examination of transfer requests or performance data should suggest that a problem situation exists. We might review additional records, such as all internal memoranda or performance reviews, to identify the nature of performance problems, the nature of supervisory activities, or other possible reasons for the Decision Support Group's inability to meet the release date specified by the vice presidents. We could then summarize the issues raised by these data.

Diagnosis

The next phase, diagnosis, involves attempting to explain the reasons for, or causes of, the behaviors and attitudes described. We could simply develop our own theories or reasons for the event. In the case of the Decision Support Group, we might believe that Ellen's leadership style is the major reason for the declining performance and increasing dissatisfaction; or we might argue that Ellen has failed to communicate her rationale for not allocating additional resources to help the project teams meet the release deadline and still release a high-quality product. This book offers and describes a number of theories people studying organizational behavior have developed to explain why events such as these occur. You can use these theories to diagnose any situations or problems that exist. You can apply them in sequence and test whether they help you understand the situation better. Once you know and understand the theories you can choose the most appropriate ones to use in diagnosis.

Focusing on motivation as a cause of poor performance and dissatisfaction in the Decision Support Group, for example, we might apply a series of theories that direct us to assess whether people's needs are being met, whether good performance is recognized and rewarded, and whether the group members feel that their effort will result in high-level performance. Or, focusing on leadership as a problem, we might explore whether Ellen's style fits with the requirements of the situation, whether she demonstrates transformational leadership, or whether her leadership behavior is reinforced. Needs theory, goal-setting theory, expectancy theory, trait theory, and the contingency theory of leadership help us gain greater understanding of the reasons people such as Ellen and her subordinates act as they do, and the reasons our behavior is more effective in some circumstances than in others.

Research Methods Organizational researchers and occasionally other organizational members use more systematic research methods to determine the causes of events, behaviors, or attitudes.[4] Laboratory experiments, field studies, or even simulations (often computerized) of organizational situations can assist in the diagnosis of the causes of certain behaviors and attitudes.

Laboratory experiments In laboratory experiments, researchers choose a phenomenon to study, such as obedience to authority, risk taking in decision making, or conflict in negotiations. They attempt to control all extraneous stimuli so that they can reliably pinpoint the causes of a specific behavioral phenomenon. Although individual studies do not capture the complexity of organizational life, a set of these studies about a particular topic, considered together, may explain behavior outside the laboratory. No laboratory study acknowledges, for example, that risk behavior is a function of the interaction of such factors as individual personality, characteristics of the organization, and pressures exerted by group membership. Considering all laboratory studies about risk behavior together may result in identifying, without validating it, a set of interactive causes. The rigorous controls imposed to identify the "real cause" of the observed phenomenon often result in laboratory behavior that differs from the behavior obtained in real organizational situations. The type of risk individuals take in spending money in a laboratory may differ significantly from the risk they take when their own or their employer's resources are at stake. In laboratory studies researchers simplify organizational phenomena in order to determine the causes of behavior or attitudes precisely.

Field studies To study behavior in more realistic settings and as it occurs naturally, researchers conduct field studies.[5] This approach differs from laboratory studies in the amount of control exerted over behavior and the circumstances in which the behavior occurs. Here, many factors can explain an observed phenomenon. Low performance might be attributed to changes in incentives, the personality of the subject, new organizational policies, or merely the weather. Thus researchers can be more certain that they are observing "true" behavior but less certain of the correct explanation of the behavior or attitudes observed. Because field studies acknowledge the complexity of real-life situations, researchers are increasingly relying on this approach rather than the more controlled laboratory testing.

Simulations Organizational simulations attempt to combine the advantages of both laboratory and field studies. An organizational simulation is a computerized or noncomputerized facsimile of an organization. It prescribes the rules and regulations of the organization, specifies the actions and interactions of organization members, and defines the impact of various inputs and processes on the organization's functioning. Researchers manipulate the behavior or attitudes being studied as well as the circumstances in which they occur by providing diverse inputs and examining their effects. Using this approach, researchers can study complex behavior while at the same time controlling it. The challenge is modeling affective and behavioral responses, such as worker satisfaction and productivity, as accurately as organizational outcomes such as return on investment or market share. Because of the artificiality involved in manipulating the factors being studied, some argue that this research approach lacks realism and thus yields useless results. Using this method in conjunction with the other two, or with the analyses described in the next sections, may overcome some of its limitations.

A Three-Step Approach to Diagnosis Managers and other organizational members frequently rely on a more ad hoc, less controlled approach to diagnosis. By applying the diagnostic approach, they can use the research results obtained by organizational scholars to enrich their diagnoses.

In this book, we take a specific approach to diagnosis: we assume that events, behaviors, and attitudes that occur in organizations typically have more than one cause, and that it is important to try to understand the causes as fully as possible. The more completely we understand the causes, the more appropriately we can act in organizational situations.

This approach develops diagnostic abilities in three steps. The first is to study a number of theories by themselves, without applying them to concrete situations. Students learn theories of motivation and leadership, models of effective communication and decision making, for example. The second is to indicate the ways in which the different theories help explain the reasons the situation exists as it does—how a particular theory of leadership, motivation, or organizational design, for example, might help to explain the situation faced by Ellen Mitchell. The third is to develop connections between the different theoretical perspectives, to see how motivation, leadership, and organizational design theories, as well as other areas addressed by the field of organizational behavior, complement each other and help to provide a richer description of organizational events.

You should begin the diagnosis phase by specifying the problem or issues in the situation. To identify the problems, for example, you must first list the evidence that a problem exists. You might list, for example, the symptoms—increased complaints and decreased productivity in the Decision Support Group. Or you might note the requests for transfers and initiation of job-hunting activities. Then, reviewing these symptoms together with the facts of the case and your assumptions, you should specify the problem(s) in as much detail as possible. Where more than one problem exists, you should specify the relationships among the problems. For example, Ellen Mitchell's leadership style together with the Decision Support Group's lack of participation in the decision about the release date and the introduction of a new performance evaluation criterion—the project leader's ability to meet the schedule—may contribute to the staff's declining performance and morale.

In this phase of the diagnostic approach you should also apply the relevant theoretical models to the problems to increase the completeness and accuracy of your diagnosis. If, for example, the problem is ineffective leadership, you should apply several leadership theories in sequence to determine the precise deficiency in Ellen's leadership. Does she lack the traits of an effective leader? Does she choose the wrong style for this situation? Does she fail to perform the diverse roles of an effective manager? If the problem is lack of worker motivation, you should similarly and sequentially apply diverse motivation theories. As you grow in experience and competence you will learn better which theories to use. Diagnosis concludes when there is sufficient understanding for appropriate decision making and action.

Keep in mind that not all organizational problems and events can be understood by *all* organizational behavior models and theories. At best they only facilitate and enhance understanding; they do not produce it. The life-cycle theory of leadership (described in Chapter 8) may help explain the situation faced by Ellen Mitchell and her subordinates, but the attribution theory of leadership may not. Looking at group norms may offer new insights into the situation, but looking at Ellen's cognitive style may not. The ability to diagnose includes the ability to critically evaluate different perspectives and theories, and to determine whether they apply to each specific case. By examining the degree of fit between the theories and the key aspects of each situation, you can identify the most likely causes of specific behaviors and attitudes. You can also determine how well different perspectives apply. And, throughout the process of diagnosis, you are continually encouraged to develop your own explanations for the events you describe.

Prescription

Phase 3, prescription, involves identification, review, and evaluation of, and then a decision on, a desired course of action for particular circumstances based on the foregoing diagnosis. Prescription is the first part of translating diagnosis—your understanding of a situation—into action. Managers and other organization members must *act* in problem situations; they do not have the luxury of simply understanding them, although understanding alone can have value and relevance too. In this step, the manager or other organizational member must propose ways of correcting the problems identified in the diagnosis phase. If, for example, you believe from your diagnosis that the subordinates' needs are not being met, you might determine ways in which Ellen Mitchell could better meet those needs. If your diagnosis showed that Ellen's leadership is too directive, you might determine whether she should use a more supportive, achievement-oriented, or participative style. If top management's making the decision about the release date is inappropriate, you might determine whether more decentralized decision making would be more effective.

Most problem situations have no single correct response, in part because the problems are complex. Thus we should begin the prescription phase by proposing multiple solutions to diagnosed problems. We might recommend redesigning work, modifying the reward system, or ensuring direct communication as ways of addressing motivation problems. We might propose organizational restructuring, development of superordinate goals, or the introduction of new jobs as ways of dealing with conflict between work groups.

In this book you are asked to suggest solutions to problems; to develop specific courses of action for different situations. You then have the opportunity to evaluate the solutions proposed in terms of the models and theories discussed, and to test whether the recommended changes should result in the desired consequences. In the case of Ellen Mitchell, for example, you probably would prescribe a different leadership style. By comparing the style you choose to the style suggested by various leadership theories, you can predict the effectiveness of your prescription before it is implemented. Knowing what type of reward system the research about effective motivation would suggest, you can prescribe better ways to meet the staff's needs.

You should consider as many reasonable, feasible, and practical alternative solutions to each problem or behavioral concern diagnosed as possible. Evaluate these alternatives and their effectiveness by using the relevant theoretical models to predict outcomes of various actions. Determine the costs and benefits of each alternative. Then select the alternative with the relatively lowest costs and highest benefits. For example, Ellen Mitchell can quantitatively and qualitatively assess the costs of training, recruitment, selection, or lost time associated with changing her leadership style, redesigning her organization's structure, or even replacing many of her subordinates. She can similarly assess the likely benefits of each prescription in terms of reducing turnover or increasing productivity. Such an assessment might indicate that in Ellen's situation, changing to a more achievement-oriented leadership style may be the best alternative, the one that has the relatively lowest costs and greatest benefits.

Action

The final phase, action, is the implementation of the solutions you propose. Often we know the correct solution, but cannot apply it. We might know, for example, that Ellen should find a way to meet the employees' needs. We might even prescribe a new compensation system or ask top management to change the performance evaluation criteria. But how do they actually do that? What pitfalls will they encounter in trying to translate solutions into behavior?

Action might involve testing the prescription in a limited part of the organization. Pilot programs are frequently used to implement change in organizations in measured, observable ways. Top management might introduce a bonus program or a new performance evaluation instrument. Or the executives may provide Ellen with consultation or training about how to alter her leadership style. Experimentation might accompany effective action. Or we might simulate the action we propose using facsimiles of the organization.

Action involves a careful scrutiny of all individuals and other systems in the organization to plan for the impact of the changes. It means determining where possible resistances to change exist and planning strategies and activities to overcome them. Implementing staffing or policy changes might require the introduction of new education programs, and new resources might be necessary to support the new programs. The effects of action may cascade throughout the organization.

In this book you are given opportunities to test your ideas to see how they work in different problem situations. You can act as a manager would act in a given situation. You then have the opportunity to evaluate these actions and consider ways of improving managerial action.

And so the cycle can start again: as part of the evaluation you can describe your own and others' behavior and attitudes. Then you can diagnose the reasons the behavior succeeded or failed, offer new prescriptions, and once more act.

APPLYING THE DIAGNOSTIC APPROACH

Diagnosis is the cornerstone of effective behavior in organizations. If organization members can understand the factors affecting themselves and others in a work situation, they have taken an important step toward effective behavior. But effective action complements quality diagnosis. Stopping at understanding a situation is insufficient. Prescribing and implementing good solutions must also occur.

What advantages does the diagnostic approach offer over others? It encourages managers and other organizational members to take time before they jump into prescriptions or implement action. It encourages them to spend time on describing the situation in detail and completely diagnosing its problems. It requires them to spend some time trying to understand what is really occurring in an organizational situation. It offers a systematic procedure for analyzing organizational functions; individuals must devote time to describing and diagnosing a situation before they prescribe and implement solutions to the problems they encounter. The diagnostic approach also encourages employers and employees to carefully evaluate the costs and benefits of various prescriptions for change. It requires them to assess the likely impact of proposed solutions. It encourages them to test the fit between diagnosis and action.

This approach also offers a means of applying diverse theoretical knowledge to organizational behavior and attitudes. It requires you to use and apply a range of theories to help understand in more depth a given situation or series of events. When applied carefully and completely, the diagnostic approach should improve the quality of management practices. Managers can use their extensive knowledge of theories to understand a situation better and thus respond more effectively. Using this approach also prevents their responding too quickly and without sufficient thought to organizational dilemmas.

Tracing the history of organizational behavior provides a context for understanding the evolution of organizational behavior and effective management. It offers diverse views of the same phenomena, much in line with the basic premise of the diagnostic approach. It also provides one set of perspectives for viewing managerial and worker actions and attitudes. In applying these and other perspectives described later in this book, we must recognize both their value and their limitations. It is essential that we recognize the complexity of organizations when applying a perspective. We must also note that most perspectives address only some of the aspects of any particular situation. Because of this, we must apply multiple perspectives to obtain a complete understanding. In the Decision Support Group, for example, we can use the classical, human relations, and contingency perspectives, among others, to better understand the situation. Or we can use motivation, leadership, or decision-making theories to help us understand a situation. Other perspectives may be less useful for this particular situation: considering issues of work design or career development may not be helpful in this case.

Human behavior in organizations is complex, and no single perspective provides a definitive answer to all questions about how people act. But the application of a number of theories, none complete in itself, should increase your understanding of behavior and attitudes. In the next section we illustrate the process of diagnosis using the major theoretical perspectives that have emerged in this century.

Historical Perspectives

Earlier viewpoints, philosophies, and schools of thought remain applicable and relevant today and can provide useful tools for description, diagnosis, prescription, and action. By using these different perspectives concurrently—considering both the structural and behavioral aspects—we can enrich our understanding of organizational situations.

We can take the perspectives that dominated management and organizational thought at different times during this century as a first step to understanding and identifying the key issues in particular organizational situations. These perspectives remain current and relevant to organizational diagnosis in many respects. They also provide a backdrop for the development of current organizational thought. Management theory and principles continuously change and evolve; having a historical perspective is essential for understanding their significance.

We now look at the major schools of organizational thought during this century and show how they help us to diagnose and understand problem situations such as the one Ellen Mitchell faced in the Decision Support Group. The book presents both the different diagnostic questions that people taking a particular perspective have asked and some of the effects of applying each one. In recounting the history of organizational theory, this chapter presents selected representative perspectives, as shown in the timeline of Figure 1–2, and groups them into schools, shown in Table 1–1.

Figure 1–2 TIMELINE OF ORGANIZATIONAL THOUGHT

Scientific Management	Classical School	Human Relations School	Bureaucracy	Classical School Revisited	Group Dynamics	Leadership	Decision Making	Sociotechnical School	Systems Theory	Contingency Theory
1910	1920			1930	1940	1950		1960		1980

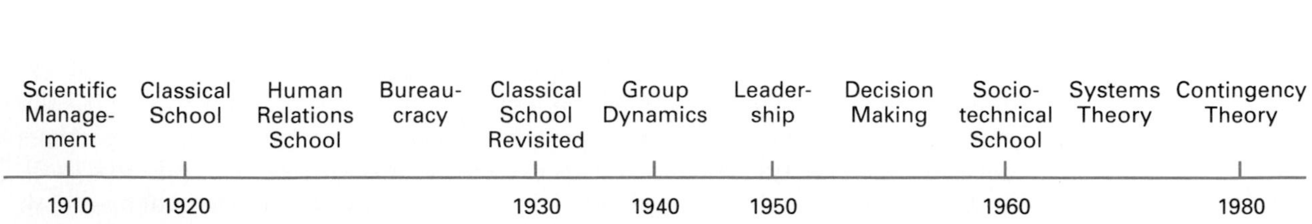

Table 1–1 HISTORICAL SCHOOLS OF THOUGHT AND THEIR COMPONENTS (BY DECADE)

School	Decade	Perspective	Description
Organizational theory prior to 1900	Before 1900	Structural	Emphasized the division of labor and the importance of machinery to facilitate labor
Scientific Management	1910s	Structural	Described management as a science, with employees having specific but different responsibilities; encouraged the scientific selection, training, and development of workers and the equal division of work between workers and management
Classical School	1910s	Structural	Listed the duties of a manager as planning, organizing, commanding employees, coordinating activities, and controlling performance; basic principles called for specialization of work, unity of command, scalar chain of command, and coordination of activities
Bureaucracy	1920s	Structural	Emphasized order, system, rationality, uniformity, and consistency in management; these attributes led to equitable treatment for all employees by management
Human Relations	1920s	Behavioral	Focused on the importance of the attitudes and feelings of workers; informal roles and norms influenced performance
Classical School Revisited	1930s	Structural	Reemphasis on the classical principles described above
Group Dynamics	1940s	Behavioral	Encouraged individual participation in decision making; noted the impact of the work group on performance
Leadership	1950s	Behavioral	Stressed the importance of groups having both social and task leaders; differentiated between Theory X and Theory Y management
Decision Theory	1960s	Behavioral	Suggested that individuals "satisfice" when they make decisions
Sociotechnical School	1960s	Integrative	Called for considering technology and work groups when understanding a work system
Systems Theory	1960s	Integrative	Represented an organization as an open system with inputs, transformations, output, and feedback; systems strive for equilibrium and experience equifinality
Environmental and Technological Analysis	1960s	Integrative	Described the existence of mechanistic and organic structures and stated their effectiveness with specific types of environmental conditions and technological types
Contingency Theory	1980s	Integrative	Emphasized the fit between organizational processes and characteristics of the situation; called for fitting the organization's structure to various contingencies

Structural Perspectives

The earliest theorists were concerned primarily about the structuring and design of work and organizations. Organizational theory prior to 1900, scientific management, classical theory, and bureaucracy each addressed issues of structure in organizations.

Organizational Theory Prior to 1900 Prior to 1900, very little formal management or organizational theorizing occurred. In addition, few industrial organizations of the types we know today existed; the basic organizational models were the military and the Roman Catholic Church. But the factory system had developed and was creating strong demands for theories of management.

Despite the lack of formal theory, economists such as Adam Smith sowed the seeds of later theory. In his famous book, *An Inquiry into the Nature and Cause of the Wealth of Nations,*[6] published in the early eighteenth century, Smith included a chapter on the division of labor which laid the groundwork for the later introduction of assembly-line processes. In this chapter Smith spoke approvingly of a pin manufacturer that divided the work into a number of "branches," causing the separation of pin making into eighteen different operations. The separation of operations radically increased the quantity of pins manufactured in a day, since the workers had only to concentrate on one task. Smith also emphasized the importance of proper machinery to facilitate labor. Smith's perspective provided a basis for the concern with the structure of organizations and work and the development in the nineteenth century of theories that emphasized a structural perspective.

Obviously, Applied Computations could not have existed prior to 1900. Nevertheless, could we use Adam Smith's perspective to understand the present situation in the Decision Support Group? Is it possible that the division of labor is not appropriate and that it contributes to the workers' poor performance and dissatisfaction? Certainly we can ask whether the tasks performed by various teams and their members are sufficiently specialized. The workers' performance of multiple tasks may inhibit their efficiency.

Scientific Management Not until the early twentieth century did management emerge as a field of study per se. One of the earlier people to construct a formal management theory was Frederick W. Taylor, a foreman at the Bethlehem Steel Works in Bethlehem, Pennsylvania. Taylor's observations about industrial efficiency offered prescriptions for effective organizations and focused management theory on manufacturing organizations, which had become more common after 1900. He described management as a science, with managers and employees having clearly specified yet different responsibilities. His theory focused on the structure and design of management activities.

Taylor characterized a manager's responsibility in four ways:

> First. Managers develop a science for each element of a man's work, which replaces the old rule of thumb method.
>
> Second. Managers scientifically select and then train, teach, and develop the worker, whereas in the past he chose his own work and trained himself as best he could.
>
> Third. Managers heartily cooperate with the men so as to insure all of the work being done in accordance with the principles of the science which has been developed.

> Fourth. There is almost equal division of the work and the responsibility between the management and the workers. The management take over all the work for which they are better fitted than the workers, while in the past almost all of the work and the greater part of the responsibility were thrown upon the men.[7]

In the report of his classic experiment,[8] Taylor showed that a pig-iron handler, who formerly loaded 12½ tons per day, loaded 47½ tons after application of the principles of scientific management. Imagine, if you can, someone shoveling iron ore into a furnace. An observer, the equivalent of a modern-day industrial engineer, times how long it takes a worker to pick up a shovel, move it and the ore into a car, drop off the ore, and then prime the shovel for the next load. At the same time another observer records the precise physical movements the worker makes, such as whether he picks up the shovel with his right hand or his left (no women handled iron ore at the Bethlehem Steel Works), whether he switches hands before moving it, how far apart he places his feet, and so on. With these data, Taylor determined the physical positions that led to the fastest time for shoveling ore and developed the "science" of shoveling. Although Taylor's principles seem reasonable and useful, they had their greatest impact when applied to increasing productivity on a relatively simple task.

Do you think that applying scientific management principles to the jobs of Decision Support team members would improve the situation at Applied Computations? The training of workers might need to be changed so that it more systematically prepares them for their jobs. Or Ellen Mitchell might need to analyze the tasks being performed in the office and change the work process to maximize performance. It is possible, for example, that the software development task should be fragmented, and that team members should be given only a fraction of the types of work they have been performing.

Classical School Henri Fayol was a French manager who wrote at about the same time as Taylor, though his works did not have a widely read English translation until 1949. Even at this early date we see the influence of management thinking abroad on the view of organizational behavior in the United States and abroad. Once translated, Fayol's works became very popular in the United States. Fayol's comments typified the *classical* view of administration.[9] Fayol listed the duties of a manager as planning, organizing, commanding employees, coordinating activities, and controlling performance. He also specified fourteen principles of management,[10] shown in Figure 1–3.

Organizational theorists have identified four features of organizations based on these structural elements and principles.[11] First, organizations should specialize. This means they should organize workers according to logical groupings, such as client, place of work, product, expertise, or functional area. At Applied Computations, for example, all development staff for a particular piece of software are placed on a single team. Second, unity of command dictates that each organizational member should have exactly one direct supervisor. In the Decision Support Group, for example, the software developers should report directly to their team leader, and each team leader reports to Ellen Mitchell. Third, reporting relationships should be clearly defined within a formal organizational structure, beginning with the chief administrator and extending to the least skilled employee. The scalar chain of command at ACI begins with the Vice President of Development, continues through Ellen Mitch-

Figure 1–3 FAYOL'S PRINCIPLES OF MANAGEMENT

1. Division of work—the specialization of work
2. Authority—"the right to give orders, and power to exact obedience"
3. Discipline—"obedience, application, energy, behavior, and outward marks of respect"
4. Unity of command—"an employee should receive orders from one superior only"
5. Unity of direction—"one head and one plan for a group of activities having the same objective"
6. Subordination of individual interests to the general interest—the interest of an individual or group should not supercede the organization's concerns
7. Remuneration—fair payment for services
8. Centralization—degree of consolidation of management functions
9. Scalar chain (line of authority)—"the chain of superiors ranging from the ultimate authority to the lower ranks"
10. Order—all materials and people should be in an appointed place
11. Equity—equality of (although not necessarily identical) treatment
12. Stability of tenure of personnel—limited turnover of personnel
13. Initiative—"thinking out a plan and ensuring its success"
14. Esprit de corps—"harmony, union among the personnel of a concern"

Adapted and excerpted from H. Fayol, *General and Industrial Management,* Trans. C. Storrs (London: Pitman, 1949).

ell, extends to the project team leaders, and ends with the development staff. Fourth and finally, managers must coordinate activities through the use of mechanisms that ensure communication among specialized groups. For example, Ellen Mitchell conducts weekly staff meetings and more frequent informal meetings with team leaders to expedite the efficient implementation and coordination of activities in the Decision Support Group.

Does Ellen Mitchell operate according to classical principles? The description presented in the introduction suggests that limited unity of command is implemented, although both a scalar chain of authority and coordination of activities among teams exist. Fayol might suggest, however, that problems exist with specialization, stability of tenure of personnel, initiative, and esprit de corps.

Bureaucracy Max Weber, a German sociologist, addressed the issue of organizational administration in a somewhat different fashion.[12] Studying European organizations he described what he considered to be a prototypical form of organization—the bureaucracy—early in the twentieth century. Although his principles were well known in the United States through spokespersons and interpreters, his writings were not translated into English until the 1940s.[13] Here, too, international thought influenced management in the United States. Figure 1–4 summarizes Weber's principles of bureaucracy, which also offered prescriptions for the best structure of an organization.

For many people, the word *bureaucracy* conjures up images of massive red tape and endless, unneeded details. For Weber, however, the major assets of bureaucracy were its emphasis on order, system, rationality, uniformity, and

Figure 1–4 SUMMARY OF WEBER'S PRINCIPLES OF BUREAUCRACY

- Specified and official areas of responsibility based on knowledge
- Orderly system of supervision and subordination
- Unity of command
- Extensive use of written documents
- Extensive training in job requirements
- Application of consistent and complete rules

Based on M. Weber, *Essays on Sociology,* trans. and ed. H.H. Gerth and C.W. Mills (New York: Oxford University Press, 1946).

consistency. These primary attributes, in his view, led to equitable treatment for all employees by management. To this end, bureaucratic organizations emphasize impersonality and strict rules. Weber defined bureaucracies as having characteristics that ensure this impersonality and fairness.[14]

In bureaucracies, each employee has specified and official areas of responsibility that are assigned on the basis of competence and expertise. Applying the bureaucratic model to understanding the situation at ACI, we could first assess whether the software developers and Ellen are competent to handle their roles. Like the classical school, bureaucracy also calls for an orderly system of supervision and subordination, a unity of command specifying that each subordinate has a single supervisor.

In a bureaucracy, managers use written documents extensively in managing employees. Not only do rules and regulations exist, but these are translated into detailed employment manuals. Managers of offices or other work groups also receive extensive training in their job requirements. Finally, office management must use rules that are consistent, complete, and can be learned. We can ask whether a lack of specified areas of responsibility, absence of a clearly ordered system of supervision, limited use of written documents, unavailability of expert training, lack of management dedication and devotion to the job, and failure to establish general rules explain the problems experienced by the Decision Support Group.

Behavioral Perspectives

While the scientific management, classical, and bureaucratic perspectives emphasize the structure and design of organizations, such a viewpoint does not adequately diagnose the problems in the Decision Support Group. Reviewing the situation there reveals numerous references to the workers' dissatisfaction, low morale, and negative reactions to the new boss's initiatives, issues not addressed by these theories. The human relations, group dynamics, decision theory, and leadership researchers explicitly considered this human side of organizations. They offered a different explanation from the structural one presented previously, which they found to inadequately explain various organizational phenomena.

Human Relations School Beginning in 1924, the Western Electric Company, in conjunction with the National Academy of Sciences, performed five studies of various work groups at Western Electric's Hawthorne plant.[15] The first study looked at the effects of lighting on the productivity of workers in different departments of the company. In the tradition of scientific management, it considered whether certain illumination levels affected output positively or adversely. Essentially, the researchers first increased the lighting to an extreme brightness and then decreased the light until the work area was so dim that assembly material could hardly be seen. What happened to employee output? Did it increase, decrease, or remain at normal levels? Regardless of whether researchers increased or decreased illumination, the workers maintained or even exceeded their normal output. What explains this behavior?

Subsequent studies by Elton Mayo, Fritz Roethlisberger, William Dickson, and their colleagues attempted to answer this question by introducing a variety of changes in the workplace. They examined the impact of rest pauses, shorter working days and weeks, wage incentives, and the nature of supervision on output.[16] They also suggested that something other than the physical work environment (which Taylor would have suggested) or the organizational structure (which Fayol would have suggested) resulted in improved productivity among workers. In observing and interviewing the employees, the researchers discovered that during the experiments the employees felt that someone was paying attention to them, so their morale improved and they produced more. This so-called Hawthorne Effect offered the first dramatic indication that the attitudes and feelings of workers could significantly influence productivity.

Consequently, Western Electric instituted a program where interviewers questioned workers regarding their feelings about work. The interviewing program suggested even more strongly the close relationship between morale and the quality of supervision, and resulted in the creation of a new training program for supervisors.

In the final experiments of the Hawthorne series, the researchers identified one other human feature of organizations: the informal groups that workers develop among themselves. In these experiments, the researchers observed the way a group from the bank-wiring room worked. They found that the workers set up informal roles and norms (expected standards of behavior) among themselves and that through these norms they controlled and restricted their productivity level. For example, workers could be identified as leaders and followers. "Rate-busters"—those who produced more than the level acceptable to the leaders—were ostracized by the group; likewise, "deviants"—those who produced too little—were also ostracized.

If you were one of the Hawthorne researchers, what would you suggest are the major problems in the Decision Support Group? Clearly, the quality of supervision affected morale. In addition, Ellen Mitchell's failure to consider the group and its expectations with regard to schedules and decision making may have hindered both her effectiveness and the group's performance.

Group Dynamics Later in the century, during World War II, Kurt Lewin, a social psychologist at the University of Iowa, was asked to study methods of changing housewives' food habits away from meat consumption, since there was a shortage of meat.[17] Lewis believed that the housewives were expected by their families, parents, and other housewives not to serve other kinds of food, and that this norm created a significant barrier to change. He suggested that the primary way to break down this barrier was to give the housewives the opportunity to discuss and make decisions themselves about the types of foods to serve. He and his associates conducted experiments, the results of which supported Lewin's ideas about participation: housewives who joined in group discussions were ten times more likely to change their food habits than were housewives who received lectures on the subject.[18]

Lewin's associates later extended these experiments to industrial settings. For example, Lester Coch and John R.P. French found that employees at the Harwood pajama plant in Marion, Virginia, were much more likely to learn new work methods if they had the opportunity to discuss the methods and influence how to apply them to their jobs.[19] Studies such as Lewin's and Coch and French's led to a greatly expanded awareness of the impact of the work group and spawned research on the relationship between organizational effectiveness and group formation, development, behavior, and attitudes.[20]

Thus researchers in the group-dynamics tradition might believe the problem in the Decision Support Group to be decreased involvement of the team members in discussions and decision making about the release date. This lack of involvement could contribute to their decreased productivity and increased dissatisfaction.

Decision Theory In the 1950s, Herbert Simon and James March introduced the decision-making framework for understanding organizational behavior.[21] In many ways Simon and March elaborated on the bureaucratic model by emphasizing that individuals work in rational organizations and thus behave rationally. But their model (which eventually won Simon the Nobel prize for economics) added a new dimension: the idea that a human being's rationality is limited. This model offered a more realistic alternative to classical assumptions of rationality in decision making, therefore it had a behavioral focus. The model suggested that when individuals make decisions, they examine a limited set of possible alternatives rather than all available options. In doing this search, they follow rules and programs. For example, in deciding the best way to schedule software development, the team leaders might use certain rules-of-thumb. The vice presidents might follow different rules and programs, thereby creating conflict at Applied Computations.

Individuals also "satisfice"; that is, they accept satisfactory or "good enough" choices, rather than insist on optimal choices. They make choices that are good enough because they do not search until they find perfect solutions to problems. For example, the vice presidents might construct and Ellen Mitchell might agree to a work schedule that results in an acceptable, but not the best, product. To analyze this decision making for the introductory case we could ask whether Ellen generates alternative solutions to problems, how she chooses the final solution, and whether she optimizes or satisfices.

Leadership The 1950s saw the beginning of concentrated research in the area of leadership. Researchers and theorists such as Robert Bales and Douglas McGregor, among others, studied the roles of managers and leaders in organizations.[22] Bales postulated the importance of groups' having both task and social leaders. A task leader helps the group achieve its goals by clarifying and summarizing member comments and focusing on the group's tasks. A social leader maintains the group and helps it develop cohesiveness and collaboration by encouraging group members' involvement.

McGregor described two types of managers (among others).[23] Those who believe "Theory X" hold the following assumptions: that workers have an inherent dislike for work, that they must be controlled and threatened with punishment if they are to put forth adequate effort, and that they prefer to avoid responsibility. Managers who believe "Theory Y," on the other hand, believe that people feel work is as natural as play or rest, that people will exercise self-direction toward the objectives to which they are committed (so they do not need strict control), and that the average human being can learn to seek responsibility. McGregor, together with other researchers of the human relations school, postulated that the assumptions managers hold affect the way they treat their employees and also affect the employees' productivity.

To diagnose the situation at ACI, we can ask whether Decision Support Group teams include both task and social leaders; in particular, whether Ellen Mitchell shows both types of leadership behavior. We can also ask what assumptions she has regarding the software developers: does she hold Theory X or Theory Y assumptions? We can further diagnose whether her actual leadership style fits with various dimensions of the situation.

Integrative Perspectives

In contrast to an emphasis on either structure or the human side of organizations, organizational thought in the past few decades has emphasized the integration of these two perspectives, along with more specific consideration of environmental or external influences. More recently, contingency theory has added an emphasis on fitting managerial and organizational features to the work situation. The contingency perspective is the foundation of the diagnostic approach presented in this book, which means that effective diagnosis is situational in nature.

Sociotechnical School In the first half of the twentieth century theorists focused on either a structural or behavioral perspective but not on both. In the 1950s several theorists changed this trend; they studied technology as a key influence on structure and emphasized its interaction with functioning work groups, an element of the human perspective. As members of the sociotechnical school, studying organizations in England, India, and Norway, Trist and Bamforth, Rice, and Emery and Trist recognized that managers could exclude neither technology nor work groups when understanding a work system.[24]

Trist and Bamforth, for example, described a change in technology in a British coal mine.[25] In the mine, workers were used to working independently in small, self-contained units in which they organized the work themselves. But the technology for mining coal improved in a way that required management to increase job specialization and decrease the workers' participation in job assignments. This greater job specialization followed from the scientific management and classical management traditions, and was expected to increase productivity. But the coal miners hated the specialization. They much preferred working with each other and performing a variety of tasks.

Trist and Bamforth compared the performance of work groups whose jobs had become specialized by the new technology, causing a different social interaction, to work groups that retained the same pattern of social interactions after the new technology was introduced. They found that absenteeism in the specialized groups was several times greater and productivity much lower than in the groups that had maintained their original interrelationships. After a number of studies such as these, the sociotechnical systems researchers concluded that technological changes must be made in conjunction with a strong social system; that both social *and* technical/structural aspects of jobs must be considered simultaneously.

How would these researchers assess the problems in the Decision Support Group? What effect did the work process have on the staff's performance and attitudes? How did the work process and constraints on it, such as time and human resources, influence the group's behavior? Clearly the craft nature of software development influences the ability to expedite its development. While an assembly-line technology might be applied, its disadvantages for the task clearly outweigh any benefits that would result. In addition, the workers might perceive that the new deadlines could only be met by imposing such an (undesirable) assembly-line technology. The time and staffing constraints imposed under the new deadlines hindered the completion of the product. A manager who views the work situation as a technical system alone is likely to have different concerns from a manager who views it more as a human system.

Certainly a consideration of both structural and human issues should provide a more complete diagnosis of the situation at ACI.

Systems Theory Systems theory offers an integrated and comprehensive view of organizational functioning. It evolved from economic, sociological, psychological, and natural science theories and includes human, structural, environmental, technological, and other concerns.

Characteristics of systems The general systems model, described by Katz and Kahn, among others, represents an organization as an open system, one that interacts with environmental forces and factors, akin to physical systems such as the human body, a microscopic organism, or a cell.[26] First, this system comprises a number of interrelated, interdependent, and interacting subsystems. Second, the organization is open and dynamic. Third, it strives for equilibrium. And fourth, it has multiple purposes, objectives, and functions, some of which are in conflict.

The Decision Support Group of Applied Computations is a subsystem of an organizational system; so is each project team; so is each individual worker; so is the group of project leaders; so is the management of the Decision Support Group and the company—Ellen Mitchell and the Vice Presidents of Development and Marketing. Of course, each subsystem is also a system itself, composed of other subsystems; each system is also a subsystem in a larger or superordinate system. Subsystems vary in size from a single cell in an organism to a major division in an organization. To trace subsystems in organizations, the observer generally specifies significant individuals and groups of organizations and examines their interdependence. Typical subsystems of interest include individual employees, work teams, departments, and management groups.

How are subsystems such as two members of the Decision Support Group interdependent and interrelated? How are the development and marketing divisions interdependent and interrelated? Their tasks might be sequential, or they might depend on each other to meet their social needs. How is the Decision Support Group related to the rest of Applied Computations? Pause for a moment and jot down as many subsystems at ACI as you can think of. Now briefly describe some ways each pair is interdependent and interrelated. Interactions such as the ones you described contribute to the complexity of organizations and make effective diagnosis and action more challenging.

An organization, as a system, is also open and dynamic; that is, it continually receives new energy. This energy may be added in the form of new resources (people, materials, and money) or information (concerning strategy, environment, and history) from the environment, called *inputs*. For example, the new manager, Ellen Mitchell, is an input into the Decision Support Group. So is the new release date. The new energy can also alter the *transformation* of the inputs into new *outputs*.

The inputs described in the case center on the company's addition of a new staff member and the specification of a release date for the software product. But the inputs are not limited to these. Other inputs include the current employees, the raw materials, management's goals, and the feedback the company receives about the workers' performance.

Transformation processes refer to key organizational components that change inputs into outputs. Ellen Mitchell's leadership or the reward system of the organization are influences that help change the employees into productive organizational members. Ellen perceives that training activities would transform the project team leaders into more competent schedulers. The organization itself, composed of task characteristics, characteristics of individuals, the formal organizational arrangements, and the informal organization, transforms inputs into outputs.[27]

Task characteristics include the degree of specialization, amount of feedback, and extent of autonomy involved in performing work activities. The Decision Support Group develops software products and provides customer support in using those products. The team members primarily work independently, although they rely on other team members for information and the provision of related computer code.

Individual characteristics include the needs, knowledge, expectations, and experiences of organizational members. The case tells us little about the individuals (with the exception of Ellen Mitchell). We do not know anything definite about their age, education, personality, sex, or background.

Formal organizational processes encompass the organization's structure, job design, reward system, performance evaluation system, and other human resources management practices. Among the organizational arrangements are the rules and procedures of Applied Computations, including the new performance appraisal system assessing team leaders on how well they meet schedules and affecting the rewards given to employees. Ellen's allocation of resources is also part of the organizational arrangements.

The *informal elements* refer to leader behavior, group and intergroup relations, and power behavior outside the formal hierarchy. The cohesive informal organization that existed prior to Ellen's arrival has changed. She has reduced the autonomy of team leaders. Attempts to control the workers have failed. The new organizational arrangements seem to interfere with the group dynamics that existed previously.

The transformation of inputs alters individual, group, and organizational behaviors and attitudes, resulting in *outputs*. Changes in performance, satisfaction, morale, turnover, and absenteeism, as well as other indicators of effective functioning, may occur. For example, Ellen's filling the vacant managerial position altered the software developers' behavior and attitudes. Changes in the evaluation system to include effective scheduling as a criterion altered the project team leaders' attitudes.

When organizations receive new inputs or experience certain transformations, they simultaneously seek stability, balance, or *equilibrium*. When organizations become unbalanced or experience disequilibrium, such as when changes in the environment or organizational practices make current resources inadequate, the organizations attempt to return to a steady state, which may mirror or significantly differ from the original state of equilibrium. They use information about their outputs, called *feedback* or *exchange,* to modify their inputs or transformations to result in more desirable outcomes and equilibrium, as shown in Figure 1–5. Let us assume, for example, in the case of the Decision Support Group, that worker performance has declined significantly. This information cues the organization to examine the nature of its inputs and transformations for a cause. The feedback may subsequently pinpoint changes needed in inputs, such as employees' skills, or transformations, such as a new leadership style or reward system.

Figure 1–5 THE BASIC SYSTEMS MODEL

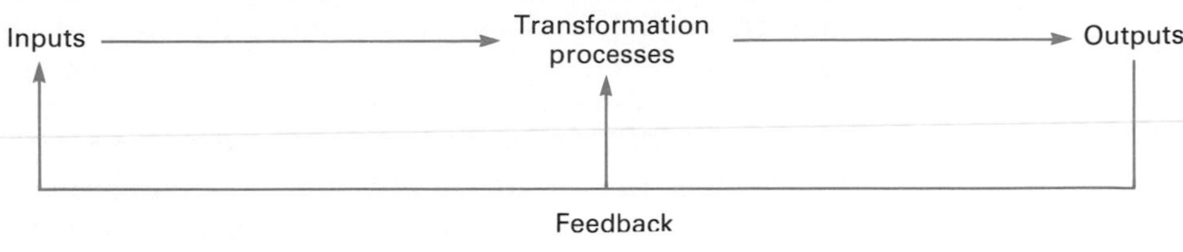

Feedback may also indicate which subsystems have similar goals and which have different or even conflicting goals. Various parts of organizations—individuals, managers, work groups, departments, or divisions—have multiple purposes, functions, and objectives, some of which may conflict. For example, Ellen Mitchell might aim for consistency among work assignments, whereas workers might aspire to jobs that respond to their unique needs and talents. Top management might want adherence to a schedule and budget at the expense of optimal product quality. Workers might wish to craft the best product possible even if it requires more resources than budgeted.

What goals does the management of Applied Computations have? What goals does Ellen Mitchell have? What goals do the project team leaders have? What goals do the team members have? Which goals are the same? Which are different? How similar are the goals of the managers and employees? Certainly the vice presidents and the team members differ in the value they attach to an earlier release date. They also appear to differ in the value they attach to expanded content for the revised software.

Finally, organizations as open systems demonstrate *equifinality,* which suggests that organizations may employ a variety of means to achieve their desired objectives. For example, McDonald's Restaurants achieves its objectives of growth and profitability by employing a highly specialized system for producing its hamburgers. Digital Equipment Corporation, on the other hand, employs a more flexible and adaptive operation to achieve the same objective. No single structure results in a predetermined set of inputs, outputs, and transformations. For example, introducing an adaptive structure does not necessarily result in increased productivity; likewise, increasing the amount of individual involvement in decision making does not necessarily change worker attitudes. Thus organizations that survive *adapt* to a particular situation. They respond to changes in the environment with appropriate changes in the system. Ellen Mitchell responded with certain changes that were not effective; she must now respond with different adjustments. Some organizations may be unable to adapt or change. In an extreme situation, *entropy* may occur. In this situation a lack of new inputs or transformations may result in the system's decay and ultimate demise.

Contingency Theory Contingency theory currently emphasizes the fit between organizational processes and characteristics of the situation. Early contingency research looked at the fit between the organization's structure and its environment.

Burns and Stalker, for example, described two radically different types of management systems: mechanistic (machinelike) and organic (living, human, and flexible).[28] Mechanistic systems have characteristics such as those described by people in the scientific and classical management traditions. Organic systems are much more flexible and loosely structured, and allow more employee influence over decisions than do mechanistic systems. If we look at the changes Ellen Mitchell initiated for the Decision Support Group, we note that the project teams functioned in an organic structure, but Ellen's frequent monitoring and control added a strong mechanistic element. Burns and Stalker described mechanistic systems as appropriate to stable environmental conditions and organic systems as appropriate to changing organizations. Does Ellen Mitchell choose the appropriate structure for the changing conditions typical of her industry? Her formal control and removal of accountability from the teams probably would cause the Decision Support Group, with workers in a highly volatile industry, to experience problems in the long run.

Joan Woodward found that the type of structure the organization develops (and should develop) is influenced by the organization's technology: whether unit, mass production, or continuous process.[29] She suggested that a mechanistic type of organization fits best with a mass production technology (e.g., producing pins, lifting pig iron, or manufacturing heavy equipment). A more organic form of organization responds best to a unit (craft) or continuous process (e.g., a gas refinery) technology.

Researchers in this tradition would want to know about technology at Applied Computations. Is the technology increasingly automated and sophisticated? Is the lack of fit between technology and structure the problem? We might conjecture, for example, that Ellen Mitchell's introduction of a more mechanistic structure does not fit well with the more expertise-based, team-based technology used by the Decision Support Group.

Recent thinking in organization design has reemphasized the importance of fitting organizational structure to various contingencies.[30] Managers in the United States have borrowed Japanese management principles, in addition to those from Western Europe, and applied them to organizational issues. Contingency theory has also extended to leadership, group dynamics, power relations, and work design, as described later in this book.

ORGANIZATION OF THIS BOOK

This book includes five parts. Each emphasizes one or more phases of the diagnostic approach. Part One sets the stage in this chapter and, together with the first chapter of Part Two, examines in detail the descriptive phase of the diagnostic approach. Throughout Part Two, diagnostic perspectives that focus on individual issues are introduced. Beginning with Chapter 2 and continuing through the rest of the book, prescriptions for increasing the effectiveness of organizations and approaches to managerial action are introduced. Part Three emphasizes frameworks for dealing with group issues. Part Four emphasizes the use of organization-level theories. Part Five concludes the book with a discussion of change and organizational transformation.

SUMMARY

Where do we find organizational behavior? What kinds of events should we seek to describe and understand? Clearly, organizational behavior does not occur only in large profit-making, private-sector organizations such as Applied Computations. Government, universities, hospitals, baseball teams, pet stores, and families are all organizations. Thus this book presents organizational behavior in diverse contexts, encouraging you to examine organizational behavior in Fortune 500 companies as well as situations you confront every day.

Understanding organizational behavior is essential for the manager. Knowing the causes of behavioral and attitudinal problems allows the manager to prescribe changes in the work situation and act in more effective ways. But other employees can also benefit from a knowledge of organizational behavior. They can act as advocates for improvements or fine-tune their own responses to new inputs and transformational processes.

We have recounted several of the most influential perspectives used to explain organizational behavior during the twentieth century. At the same time, we have taken each perspective and used it to diagnose, as far as possible, the events of the Decision Support Group of ACI. The application of each perspective in this way has suggested that people taking different perspectives would ask radically different questions and would thus attempt to correct very different problems.

We must also recall, however, that in some cases empirical data may question the validity of particular perspectives. For example, research has seriously questioned the validity of both Taylor's pig-iron experiments and the Hawthorne illumination experiments.[31] Organizational researchers will continue to find evidence that contradicts other evidence about the value of particular theories. Others will continue to find evidence that supports them (e.g., some researchers support the validity and pervasiveness of Taylor's theory today[32]). Must we ignore early perspectives and rule them out as invalid? Should we never use the results of these early theories for understanding behavior? Or can we learn something by applying such perspectives while recognizing their limitations?

Some questions we could ask apply much more clearly to the case of the Decision Support Group at Applied Computations than do others. In many situations, appropriate action would depend on asking questions that come from a number of different perspectives, since each perspective alone has a fairly narrow view and does not address the complexity of the behavior being considered. But considering the diagnostic questions from each perspective together, as shown in Figure 1–6, we can make a fairly complete problem diagnosis:

- Inappropriate division of labor and decision making among managers (Adam Smith)
- The science of software design does not fit with schedule demands, and project leaders have not been sufficiently trained in scheduling (scientific management).
- Failure to recognize changes in leadership style and to continue a team spirit throughout the Decision Support Group (human relations)
- Inappropriate specialization of functions (classical)
- Decreased worker participation in decision making (group dynamics)

Figure 1–6 DIAGNOSTIC QUESTIONS FOR ACI USING THE HISTORICAL PERSPECTIVES

- Is there an appropriate division of labor?
- Is work done efficiently, and are workers sufficiently trained to do their jobs?
- Do employees have specified areas of responsibility?
- Is the work defined effectively?
- Do work groups operate effectively?
- Do managers perform organizing roles and have an appropriate span of control?
- Does the group have effective task and social leadership?
- Does management work with the correct assumptions about employees?
- Is decision making effective?
- Is the interface of technology and individual workers effective?
- Does the organization's structure respond to the environmental contingencies?
- Is there a good fit between inputs and transformations?
- Are there good fits between individuals, tasks, organizational arrangements, and the informal organization?

- Lack of sufficient training and appropriate reward system (bureaucracy)
- Insufficient task and social leaders (leadership)
- Management with Theory X rather than Theory Y assumptions (leadership)
- Ineffective decision making (decision making)
- Introduction of schedule changes without considering social implications (sociotechnical)
- Organizational structure that does not respond to the environment (environmental analysis)
- Lack of fit between individuals, task characteristics, the informal organization, and organizational arrangements (systems theory).

ENDNOTES

[1]This case was based on one prepared by Kristi Lagerstrom at the Boston College School of Management.

[2]K.E. Weick, Amendments to organizational theorizing, *Academy of Management Journal* 17 (1974): 487–502.

[3]R. Dubin, Management: Meanings, methods, and moxie, *Academy of Management Review* 7 (1982): 372–379; and C.A. Schriesheim and S. Kerr, Theories and measures of leadership: A critical appraisal of current and future directions. In J.G. Hunt and L.L. Larson (eds.), *Leadership: The Cutting Edge* (Carbondale: Southern Illinois University Press, 1977), pp. 9–45 have criticized the use of questionnaires in organizational research.

[4]Extensive writings exist regarding research methodology. Some good examples include A. Strauss, *Qualitative Analysis for Social Scientists* (New York: Cambridge University Press, 1987); H.M. Blalock Jr. *Causal Models in the Social Sciences* (New York: Aldine, 1985); and F.N. Kerlinger, *Behavioral Research* 3d ed. (New York: Holt, Rinehart, & Winston, 1986).

[5] T.R. Mitchell, An evaluation of the validity of correlational research conducted in organizations, *Academy of Management Review* 10 (1985): 192–205, discusses some of the drawbacks of correlational research as compared to experimental research; K.M. Borman, M.D. LeCompte, and J.P. Goetz, Ethnographic and qualitative research design and why it doesn't work, *American Behavioral Scientist* 30 (1986), 42–57, suggests ways of overcoming the limitations of qualitative research.

[6]Adam Smith, *An Inquiry into the Nature and Cause of the Wealth of Nations,* 1776.

[7]F.W. Taylor, *The Principles of Scientific Management* (New York: Harper and Brothers, 1911), pp. 36–37.

[8]C.D. Wrege and A.G. Perroni, Taylor's pig-tale: A historical analysis of Frederick W. Taylor's pig-iron experiments, *Academy of Management Journal* 17 (1974): 6–17, shows that Taylor's story and the facts of the situation have little in common.

[9]H. Fayol, *General and Industrial Management,* trans. C. Storrs (London: Pitman, 1949).

[10]*Ibid.*

[11]L. Gulick and L. Urwick, eds., *Papers on the Science of Administration* (New York: Columbia University Institute of Public Administration, 1937); and J.D. Mooney and A.C. Reiley, *Onward Industry* (New York: Harper, 1931) offered complementary views of management. F.B. Gilbreth and L.M. Gilbreth, *Applied Motion Study* (New York: Sturgis and Walton, 1917) earlier offered a similar view.

[12]M. Weber, *The Theory of Social and Economic Organization,* trans. and ed. A.M. Henderson and T. Parsons (New York: Oxford University Press, 1947).

[13]R.M. Weiss, Weber on bureaucracy: Management consultant or political theorist?, *Academy of Management Review* 8 (1983): 242–248, argues that Weber was not concerned with prescribing the characteristics of an efficient organization but rather was solely offering political theory.

[14]M. Weber, *Essays on Sociology,* trans. and ed. H.H. Gerth and C.W. Mills (New York: Oxford University Press, 1946), pp. 196–198.

[15]C.E. Snow, A discussion of the relation of illumination intensity to productive efficiency, *The Tech Engineering News,* November, 1927. Cited in E.J. Roethlisberger and W.J. Dickson, *Management and the Worker* (Cambridge, Mass.: Harvard University Press, 1939).

[16]Roethlisberger and Dickson, *op. cit.*

[17]K. Lewin, Forces behind food habits and methods of change, *Bulletin of the National Research Council* 108 (1943): 35–65.

[18]M. Radke and D. Klisurich, Experiments in changing food habits, *Journal of the American Dietetics Association* 23 (1947): 403–409.

[19]L. Coch and J.R.P. French, Jr., Overcoming resistance to change, *Human Relations* 1 (1948): 512–533.

[20]See C.S. Bartlem and E.A. Locke, The Coch and French study: A critique and reinterpretation, *Human Relations* 34 (1981): 555–566, for another view of the significance of research on participation.

[21]H. Simon, *Administrative Behavior* 2d ed. (New York: Macmillan, 1957); and J.G. March and H.A. Simon, *Organizations* (New York: John Wiley, 1958).

[22]R.F. Bales, Task roles and social roles in problem-solving groups. In *Readings in Social*

Psychology 3d ed., ed. E. Maccoby, T.M. Newcomb, and E.L. Hartley (New York: Holt, Rinehart, and Winston, 1958), pp. 437–447; D. McGregor, *The Human Side of Enterprise* (New York: McGraw-Hill, 1960).

[23]McGregor, *op. cit.;* E.H. Schein, The Hawthorne group studies revisited: A defense of Theory Y (Cambridge, Mass.: M.I.T. Sloan School of Management Working Paper #756-74, December, 1974).

[24]E.K. Trist and K.W. Bamforth, Some social and psychological consequences of the long-wall method of coal getting, *Human Relations* 4 (1951): 3–38; A.K. Rice, *The Enterprise and Its Environment* (London: Tavistock, 1963); F.E. Emery and I.L. Trist, Sociotechnical systems, *Management Science: Models and Techniques vol. 2* (London: Pergamom, 1960).

[25]Trist and Bamforth, *op. cit.*

[26]D. Katz and R.L. Kahn, *The Social Psychology of Organizations* 2d ed. (New York: John Wiley & Sons, 1978).

[27]D.A. Nadler and M.L. Tushman, A diagnostic model for organizational behavior. In *Perspectives on Behavior in Organizations,* ed. J.R. Hackman, L.W. Porter, and E.E. Lawler III (New York: McGraw-Hill, 1977).

[28]T. Burns and G.M. Stalker, *The Management of Innovation* (London: Tavistock, 1961).

[29]J. Woodward, *Industrial Organization: Theory and Practice* (London: Oxford University Press, 1965); P. Lawrence and J. Lorsch, *Organization and Environment* (Boston: Harvard Business School Division of Research, 1967).

[30]H. Mintzberg, *Structure in Fives: Designing Effective Organizations* (Englewood Cliffs, N.J.: Prentice-Hall, 1983) summarizes the fit between structure and the contingencies of technology, environment, goals, work force, age, and size of the organization.

[31]Wrege and Perroni, *op. cit.;* R.H. Franke and J.D. Kaul, The Hawthorne experiments: First statistical interpretation, *American Sociological Review* 43 (1978): 623–643.

[32] E.A. Locke, The ideas of Frederick W. Taylor: An evaluation, *Academy of Management Review* 7 (1982): 14–24.

RECOMMENDED READINGS

Babbie, E.R. *The Practice of Social Research.* Belmont, Calif.: Wadsworth, 1989.

Davis, D., and Cosenza, R.M. *Business Research for Decision Making*. Boston: Kent, 1988.

Kerlinger, F.N. *Foundations of Behavioral Research* 3rd ed. New York: Holt, Rinehart, and Winston, 1986.

Singleton, R., Sr. *Approaches to Social Research.* New York: Oxford University Press, 1988.

Van Maanen, J. (Ed.) *Qualitative Research Methods Series.* Newbury Park, Calif.: Sage, 1987.

Wren, D.A. *The Evolution of Management Thought* 2d ed. New York: Wiley, 1979.

Zikmund, W.G. *Business Research Methods.* Chicago: Dryden, 1988.

2

Understanding Perception, Attribution, Learning, and Attitude Formation

CHAPTER OUTLINE

LEARNING OBJECTIVES

After completing the reading and activities in Chapter 2, students will be able to

- describe the process of perception;
- identify and give examples of four perceptual biases and show how they affect effective action;
- describe the process of attribution;
- describe and illustrate the types of attributional biases and show how they affect effective action;
- differentiate among and identify the key factors of three models of learning;
- describe the barriers to effective learning; and
- illustrate the process of attitude formation and cite two strategies for influencing attitudes.

Introduction of a New Manufacturing Process at Ford Motor Company's Dagenham Plant

Dagenham, East London—Ten years ago, Jim Collyer spent his workday in the body shop of Ford Motor Co.'s huge plant here, filing and hammering defects out of door panels.

Now, the 47-year-old metal finisher stands in the same spot along the production line, pressing buttons that operate a machine that automatically finishes door panels. "It's purgatory," he complains. "I'm nothing but a zombie on the line."

But while his satisfaction plunged, Ford's surged. New manufacturing methods helped raise productivity at the company's British plants to an estimated 12 cars per employee last year, from 6.4 in 1984. British car sales are a crucial part of Ford's European operations, which have been solidly profitable in recent years.

But these corporate gains appear more like personal setbacks to Mr. Collyer and many of the other 32,500 British workers who struck Ford's British plants eight days ago. Huddling with five other strikers around a brazier outside the Dagenham plant, Mr. Collyer accuses Ford of wanting him to "work like (the) Japanese." . . .

That attitude goes far toward explaining why Ford's British workers walked off the job last week for the first time in a decade. Money is an issue, of course. But running through this strike, where picketers displayed banners with racist slurs . . . until union officials requested their removal, are deeper strains involving flexible work practices, which would break down strict demarcation lines in workers' roles.

Ford and union officials agreed to reconvene talks today. But that decision comes amid reports the company will drop some of its demands for work-practice changes. Both Ford and union leaders declined comment on the reports.

Analysts estimate that the walkout is costing Ford about 1 million pounds ($1.8 million) a day in profit, while the 12 unions representing Ford's British workers are paying their members about 650,000 pounds a week in strike pay.

For Ford's British workers, flexibility is tough to accept. Britain's class system so pervades the shop-room floor that skilled workers resent even short stints on the production line. Workers so distrust government statistics that any idea of linking future wage increases to the inflation rate—a benefit eagerly sought by American workers—is out of the question.

But most important, Ford workers bitterly reject anything associated with Japanese-style management. For them, factory flexibility conjures up derisive stereotypes of work-crazed Japanese.

For Ford, however, flexibility is vital and the stakes are high. The company faces serious competition from Nissan Motor Co.'s new plant in Sunderland, in northeast England. Last year, that plant produced about 26 vehicles per employee; the company's target for 1992 is 57. By then, Nissan plans to produce 200,000 cars a year, up from 29,000 last year.

Ford "is scared to death of what Nissan" is doing in England, says Richard Whipp, a research assistant at Warwick University.

"It is obviously vital" that Ford boost its productivity and efficiency in Britain, a British company spokesman says. "Some of us (European car makers) aren't going to be here 10 years from now. Ford hopes to survive."

Against that background, Ford on Jan. 31 sweetened its contract offer to a 7% pay increase in the first year, followed by raises of 2.5 percentage points above the inflation rate for the following two years. In return, Ford insisted on work-practice changes to boost productivity. Union leaders hailed the package as "historic" and recommended members accept it.

But four days later, about 62% of union members rejected the offer, prompting the nationwide strike that began Feb. 8. The repercussions spread quickly, with Ford closing its factory at Ghent, Belgium, because it ran out of Dagenham-manufactured engines.

Ford workers have been "stung" by "this whole Japanization," Mr. Whipp says. Work-practice changes over the past decade already "have been quite destabilizing" for auto workers, he adds. "The prospect of adding another bout of change on the Japanese model is quite threatening indeed."

Certainly, the Dagenham picketers consider themselves different from Japanese autoworkers. For many Britons in both the laboring and upper classes, work ranks far down the list of what is important in life. "The Japanese live to work; we work to live," Ford truck driver Mick Grant says as he tosses wood onto a brazier.

The fact that some 1,100 British workers have accepted flexibility at Nissan's Sunderland plant doesn't diminish Ford workers' resistance. Auto workers here in the Southeast pity their counterparts on the other side of the North-South property divide.

Des Heemskerk, a bespectacled production worker sipping tea on the Dagenham picket line, earnestly recounts a story he says he read in a national tabloid newspaper: "One of those blokes at Nissan lost three stone (42 pounds) in weight and had to retire because of the pressure," he says.

Another factor blocking change is class-consciousness. To Ford, flexibility involves such things as occasionally moving skilled workers to the production line to test machinery they've repaired. But for British craftsmen whose training has boosted them up the social hierarchy, the very suggestion touches a raw nerve.

"If the new work practices are forced through, I would leave Ford Motor Co.," says Harry Scott, an electrician who was the first in his family to go to college. "When I was hired, they said they wanted an electrician. Now, they want an electrician who is prepared to work on the production line. There's no pride."

As for index-linked pay, these men consider it a much bigger gamble than a straight pay raise. Munching a sausage plucked from the brazier, Mr. Collyer says Margaret Thatcher's Conservative government "jiggles figures" to arrive at an official inflation rate that underestimates the true number. "We don't want to be tied to a government fiddle," he says.

A fellow picketer agrees. "How do we know we aren't going to get wrong figures from the government? There could be a conspiracy between government and employers. You don't know," he shrugs.[1]

Ford Company management and their workers disagree about the value of the changes in the manufacturing at Ford's British plants. The corporate leaders view the new manufacturing methods favorably because they have resulted in corporate gains, whereas the workers view the new methods negatively, as personal setbacks. Why did the perceptions of the two groups differ? What did each group perceive as the causes for the strike? What happened when the union recommended accepting management's offer? What happened when union and management tried to talk about the situation and determine how to correct it? How did the previous experiences of management and workers—their learned behaviors and attitudes—influence the events described here? How did the workers form their attitudes about Japanese methods? What impact did these attitudes have on the situation?

Questions such as these are fundamental to the diagnostic approach, since they deal with the description of and the reasons given for the events. As the case suggests, different observers of an incident may describe and diagnose it very differently. In this and similar situations, for example, union and management differ in their attitudes about work methods and their responses to change. They in turn would act based on their different understandings of the situation.

In this chapter we explore areas of organizational behavior that deal with the way we perceive (and thus describe) events or other people; the way we understand (and thus analyze or diagnose) the events and people we perceive; the way our past experiences and acquisition of knowledge and information influence this description and diagnosis; and the way we form attitudes about the situations based on our perceptions, understanding, and experience. These four processes are referred to as *perception, attribution, learning,* and *attitude formation.* They comprise the basic processes that underlie the description and diagnosis of organizational behavior. In this chapter we address

- why people viewing the same stimulus "see" it differently;
- how people viewing the same stimulus differ in their organization of it;
- how people viewing the same stimulus may distort their interpretation of it;
- why people viewing the same stimulus give different reasons for its occurrence;
- how individuals can increase the accuracy of their perceptions and attributions;
- how individuals' past learning influences their behavior in organizations;
- how individuals form attitudes about various aspects of their jobs;
- how individuals' perceptions, attributions, and learning influence their attitudes and behavior; and
- how individuals' attitudes influence their behavior.

THE PERCEPTION PROCESS

We begin our discussion by considering the situation at the Ford Motor Company. Let's view the introduction of new manufacturing processes from several different perspectives. First, think of yourself as the Vice President for European Operations at Ford. What do you notice about the new processes? Which features of the situation stand out to you? What thoughts come to your mind? You might notice the smooth functioning of the new manufacturing methods.

You might note the increased productivity of the British plants. You might view the "Japanization" of methods as vital because it offers a means to increase productivity and efficiency. You might commend the Japanese approach to manufacturing. Now think of yourself as Jim Collyer. What do the events feel like to you? What features of them do you notice? What thoughts come to your mind? You experience the new methods as "purgatory." You state, "I'm nothing but a zombie on the line." You feel stressed and pressured to produce more than you feel capable of doing. You might feel demeaned because your job has become repetitive and boring. You might criticize the Japanese for developing these methods that threaten British workers' basic beliefs. Finally, think of yourself as Richard Whipp, a research assistant at Warwick University. Which features of the situation stand out to you? What thoughts come to your mind? Mr. Whipp reconciles the two views. He validates part of the workers' views by agreeing that they have been "stung by this wholesale Japanization." But he also notes that Ford must compete with Nissan in Great Britain, and that increasing the efficiency of work practices is essential.

When you put yourself in these different positions, you probably notice different features of the situation and think about the introduction of the new manufacturing methods and the Japanese approach to production in different ways. Even though objectively this situation was a single event, your experience of it—your perception—varies when you put yourself in the position of different observers of the event. You then act based on your perception.

Perception is the process of sensing reality and the resulting understanding or view people have of it. As the introductory case illustrates, different people are likely to have somewhat different, and sometimes contradictory, views or understandings of the same event or person. Rarely do different observers describe events or persons in exactly the same way. Often managers and their subordinates, coworkers, or supervisors see and describe the same situation differently. For this reason, presenting a clear, well-documented, agreed-upon description of a situation is the first step in the diagnostic approach. Because our perceptions have a strong impact on our descriptions, our diagnoses of events, and our subsequent behavior, it is important to examine the perceptual process and some of the factors that affect it.

Basically, the perceptual process takes place in two stages, as shown in Figure 2–1. The first is *selection;* the second is *organization.*[2]

Selection

In the situation at Ford Motor Company, the workers and top executives *select* certain features of the event to notice. Quite possibly, because of their different concerns, perspectives, unconscious biases, and vantage points, they would select quite different features. For example, corporate leaders focused on the efficiency of the new methods, while Collyer and other employees emphasized its dehumanizing effects. Managers cited the assets of Japanese management; workers cited its deficits.

So many stimuli bombard us that we have difficulty taking full account of them all. We continually face a mélange of sounds and sights. If we observed Jim Collyer on the production line, for example, we might see him pressing buttons that operate a machine that automatically finishes door panels; we might see him and other workers talking loudly among themselves; we might hear the workers complaining about the new methods. What else might we

Figure 2–1 THE PERCEPTUAL PROCESS

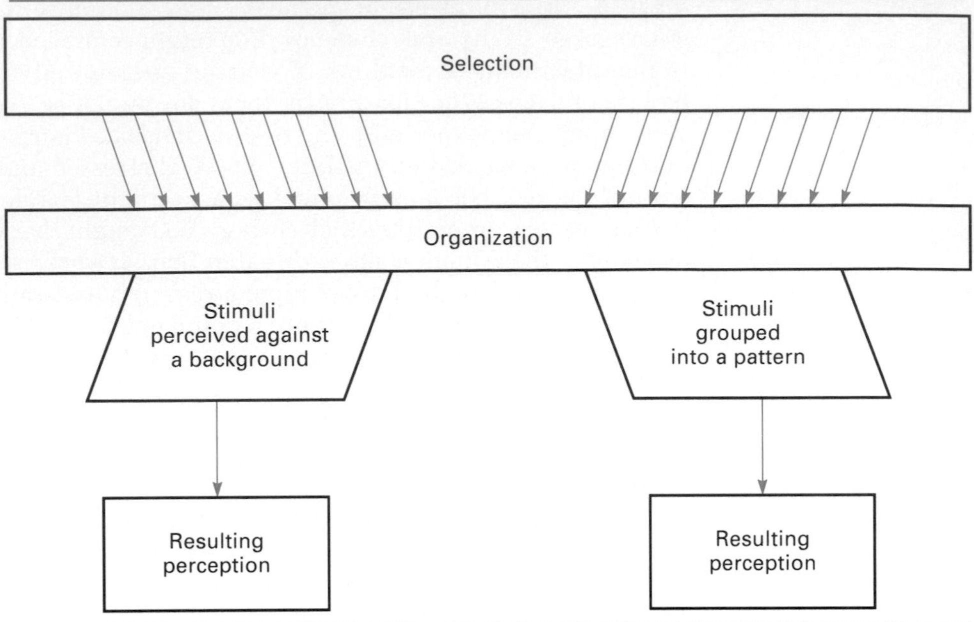

see in that situation? We might see a supervisor or union steward conversing with certain workers. A different observer might select a different set of stimuli to pay attention to.

We tend to select and attend to only some features present in any situation; thus we may pay attention to only certain workers' actions and conversations. We also attend to only some characteristics of the people we meet; thus we might be alert to a worker's experience with a particular piece of machinery, or the worker's age or sex. This selection process helps us avoid dealing with information that seems to be irrelevant to us. It also helps us avoid information overload by focusing on the most relevant information in a particular situation. In some cases, however, individuals may overlook important stimuli. The metal finishers may not see the higher quality of products resulting from the new processes. Or the supervisors might overlook the pressure created by the high-speed assembly lines.

Characteristics of the Stimuli Certain characteristics of the stimuli themselves influence what we attend to. We tend to select stimuli that are larger, more intense, in motion, repetitive, either novel or very familiar, or in contrast to their background.[3] We tend to overlook stimuli that are small, less intense, stationary, or blend in with their backgrounds.

Consider, for example, an error in bookkeeping: a manager is more likely to see a large error than a small one. Consider next a salesperson's response to a ringing telephone, a relatively intense stimulus: a salesperson frequently answers a phone before helping a customer waiting in person, because that individual—unless he or she is very vocal or demanding—offers a less intense stimulus.

Now consider two workers who come to work late: one worker has been late three times already during the week; the second has not been late for two months. Which tardiness is the manager likely to notice? Some perceptual research suggests the manager would notice the first worker's tardiness because of the stimulus's (tardy behavior) repetitiveness; other research would indicate that the manager would notice the second worker's tardiness because it is a novel stimulus. The specific interpretation given to these two situations would depend on additional information the observer has about the individual involved and the specific situation. In another work situation, employees may not hear (or select) the voice of a supervisor who continually complains about the quality of their work; the voice may lack sufficient intensity, novelty, or contrast.

Which characteristics of the stimuli in the case of Ford's introduction of new manufacturing methods and subsequent strike attracted the attention of the workers and management? Both groups seem to note the "Japanization" of the work methods, perhaps because they are novel or in contrast to the cultural backdrop of the British factory and British society. Not surprisingly, one of the workers noticed the comment about Nissan's worker in the national newspaper; this comment may have attracted attention because it contrasted with the background or was new and novel.

Characteristics of Selectors We also select stimuli according to our internal state and cultural experiences. Such states evolve from the individual's experiences, motivation, and personality. Figure 2–2 illustrates the role learning plays in our perceptions. In (a) you initially see an old lady or a young lady, based on your cultural experiences. Parts (b) and (c) are optical illusions. In (d), (e), (f), and (g), lengths you perceive to differ are in fact identical. In (h) all three men are the same height.

In organizations we might "see" an employee's tardiness, for example, in terms of our own education or experience in viewing key events—as a function of the person's social class, educational background, or job history. We might see it in terms of our own physiological requirements for sleep. Or we might see it in terms of our own personality, such as our aggressiveness, enthusiasm, or introversion. Similarly, we "see" advertisements for a new restaurant one way if we have experience with that type of restaurant. We might see them differently if a need for food motivates us, rather than if a need for security or esteem motivates us.

Think of the situation that opened this chapter. Which stimuli in Ford's situation did the workers select? Why did they select those? Why, for example, did they see the new production methods as the company's wanting them to work like Japanese? Why did they overlook the competition provided by Nissan? Which stimuli did management select? Why did management select those? Both groups likely were influenced by their learning processes, motivation, and personality in selecting the stimuli to see or hear. Different experiences, needs, or personalities might have resulted in different perceptions of the situation. These different perceptions in turn result in different actions by various organizational members.

Cultural Influences on Perception Cultural background can particularly influence perceptions. It affects the stimuli we select to perceive, the way we organize them, and how we interpret them. It may cause us to distort our perceptions in predictable or unpredictable ways. Our cultural heritage, for example, may cause us to ignore certain stimuli and focus on others; an Amer-

Figure 2–2 INFLUENCE OF LEARNING ON PERCEPTION

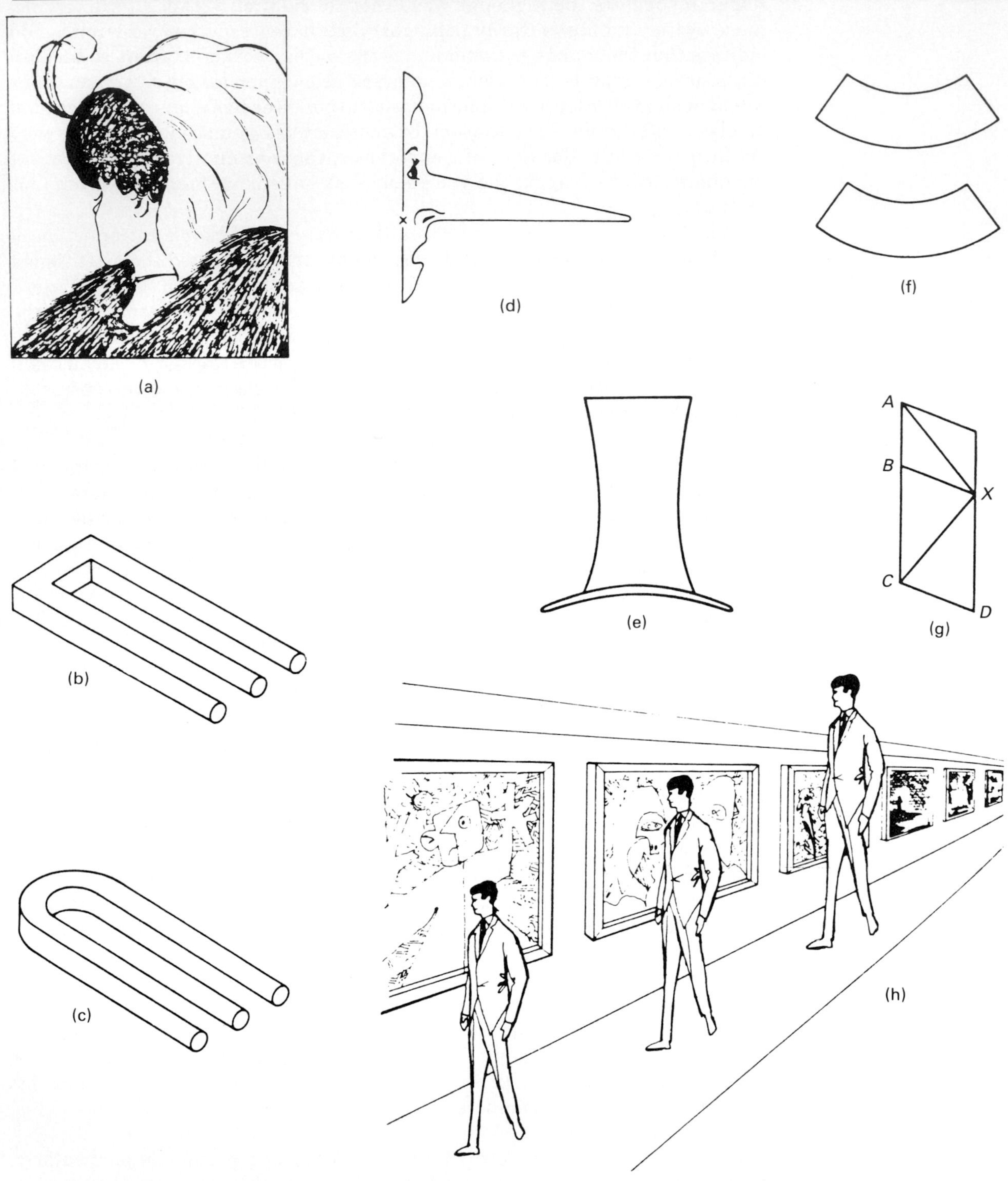

SOURCES: (a) W.E. Hill, *Puck*, 6 November 1915; (d) E.P. Johnson, *Student's Manual to Accompany Psychology* 2d ed. Boston: Houghton Mifflin, 1951; (h) F. Luthans, *Organizational Behavior* 4th ed. New York: McGraw Hill, 1985, p. 166. Reproduced by permission.

ican may ignore certain gestures as part of normal conversation, whereas a Japanese business person might find them offensive.

Consider the intensity of the workers' reactions to what they view as the Japanization of management. Could their country's historic view of the Japanese affect their perceptions? Could the dramatic cultural differences also affect their perceptions of the new production methods? Cultural biases certainly exist and affect perceptions and ultimately behavior and attitudes.

According to one researcher, national cultures differ on four dimensions, which he labels power distance, uncertainty avoidance, individualism, and masculinity.[4] These dimensions are as follows:

Power distance—the extent to which a society accepts the fact that power in institutions and organizations is distributed unequally

Uncertainty avoidance—the extent to which a society responds to the potential occurrence of uncertain and ambiguous situations by providing career stability, establishing formal rules, not tolerating deviant ideas and behaviors, and believing in absolute truths and the attainment of expertise.

Individualism—implies a loosely knit social framework in which people are supposed to take care of themselves and their immediate families only. The opposite, **collectivism,** is characterized by a tight social framework in which people distinguish between in-groups and out-groups and expect their in-group (relatives, clan, or organizations) to look after them, for which they feel they owe absolute loyalty to the in-group in exchange.

Masculinity—the extent to which the dominant values in society reflect traditionally masculine behaviors, such as assertiveness and the acquisition of money and things, and a lesser concern for relationships.

As a result of variations on these dimensions, interpersonal processes, group behavior, and organizational structure vary in different cultures. How might these differences influence perception?

Organization

Once we have selected stimuli, we categorize and organize them so that the new material makes sense to us. If possible, we make the new stimuli fit in with the ways we already understand and know the world. If we as managers, for example, see our current employees as being lazy, we likely will see new employees as lazy, too. We tend not to notice disconfirming evidence.

We organize stimuli in two basic ways. First, we perceive stimuli as figures standing out against a background. A plant manager sees, for example, assembly-line workers against a background of the plant's equipment, or sees the actions of one worker against the entire group of workers. The distinctions made between figure and background influence the attitudes and behaviors on which the plant manager ultimately focuses.

Such distinctions are particularly influential in performance evaluations. If someone is being interviewed for a job, the people whose interviews are immediately before that person's affect the way in which the interviewer perceives him or her; the previous interviews act as background against which the current interviewee is assessed. In one study, interviewees who had average qualifications were judged differently depending on whether their employment interviews followed those of a person of very high or very low qualifications.[5] As might be expected, the average interviewees were rated much higher when they followed people with low qualifications; their "better" features stood out. When the average interviewees followed people with high qualifications, their "worse" features were noted, so they were rated as poor.

In addition to perceiving figures against a background, we group discrete stimuli into a pattern.[6] For example, we try to create closure, "the tendency to form a complete mental image out of incomplete data,[7] among related stimuli. Figure 2–3 illustrates closure for physical stimuli. Notice that you tend to complete the square and ignore the duplication of words in the three sayings. How does this principle apply to behavior in organizations? The supervisor who has thirty subordinates has a complete mental picture of each worker, generally based on just a few details. The workers have a mental picture of their coworkers' jobs, often based on a few tasks. Either may draw factual or erroneous conclusions about the other based on limited information.

Grouping of stimuli occurs when they are similar, near other stimuli, form a continuous pattern, or create a completed pattern. For example, a vice president in an insurance firm may have difficulty distinguishing between the performance of two actuaries who have adjacent offices. An office manager may consider all the women as interchangeable and all the men as interchangeable. A headmaster in a high school may mentally group all tardy students and have difficulty differentiating among them, regardless of the legitimacy of their tardiness. Grouping of stimuli underlies the interpretation of stimuli and contributes to the distortions of perceptions, which are described in the next section.

Cultural Influences We may miscategorize certain perceptions because we fail to view them in their cultural context. In a hospital setting many Americans call any female in a white uniform a nurse, not considering that the woman could also be a doctor. In the Soviet Union this automatic categorization rarely occurs because of the large number of female physicians. Tardiness in coming to work may have different significance in Western and Eastern cultures because of different views of work vis-à-vis nonwork activities.

Figure 2–3 CLOSURE FOR PHYSICAL STIMULI

Hear all who
come to
to speak

Walk softly and
and carry a
big stick

Down by the
the old mill
stream

PERCEPTUAL DISTORTIONS

In reality, both selection and organization generally suffer from inaccuracies or distortions. Although such biases are normal and human, they can have significant consequences when managers or other organizational members base action on potentially invalid distortions. Distortions include (1) stereotyping, (2) the halo effect, (3) projection, and (4) expectancy.

Stereotyping

Stereotyping occurs when an individual attributes behaviors or attitudes to a person on the basis of the group or category to which that person belongs. "Blondes have more fun" and "all managers are smart" illustrate stereotyping. Can you think of a situation in which you experienced stereotyping? Can you think of one in which you stereotyped another person? What behaviors or attitudes did you associate with that person's group membership? Was this description accurate?

We frequently stereotype members of ethnic groups, women, managers, white-collar workers, and blue-collar workers. What stereotypes do you think existed at the Dagenham plant? The British workers stereotyped the Japanese as "living to work" and the British as "working to live." The crafts workers stereotyped the production workers as lower class. While the stereotypes may be accurate, they often result in uninformed action.

Why does stereotyping occur? Often individuals do not gather sufficient data about others to describe their behaviors or attitudes accurately. They may look for short-cut ways of describing certain phenomena without spending the time to completely analyze them. Alternatively, some individuals have personal biases against certain groups of individuals. Historical attitudes toward certain cultural groups may result in stereotypes. The British, for example, may have certain views of the Japanese based on their experiences during World War II. Using stereotypes reduces the accuracy of our perceptions about these groups. Even when overwhelming disconfirming evidence should cause the perceiver to admit that a person or thing does not conform to the stereotype, the perceiver often maintains the stereotype and misviews the exception.[8]

How can we reduce dysfunctional stereotyping in organizations? First, individuals must gather sufficient information about other people's behavior and attitudes to encourage more realistic perceptions. Managers, for example, must judge an individual's performance on his or her observed behavior, rather than on the behavior of a group to which the person belongs. Second, they must check the conclusions they draw to ensure their validity. Ford workers, for example, should not automatically reject anything associated with Japanese-style management. Third, they must differentiate between facts and assumptions in determining the basis of their perceptions. Ford workers cannot know, for example, that Nissan workers are losing weight because of the pressure created by the new job methods.

Halo Effect

The halo effect refers to an individual's letting one salient feature of a person dominate the whole evaluation of that individual. Working overtime, for example, can lead a supervisor to evaluate someone as highly cooperative and productive as well. A neat personal appearance can cause someone to be judged precise in his or her work, reliable, and a good employee. A talkative person may be judged less responsible and effective than a quieter, seemingly pensive individual.

The halo effect frequently occurs in assessments of employee performance. Individuals may be judged on the basis of one trait—promptness, neatness, or enthusiasm, for example—rather than on a composite of traits over a period of time. Research suggests that a supervisor who has information suggesting identical performance from two female subordinates gives them different evaluations according to their attractiveness.[9] Attractiveness increased the performance evaluations, pay raises, and promotions of women in nonmanagerial positions, but decreased these same outcomes for women in managerial positions. In that study, no differences based on attractiveness occurred in the evaluations or compensation of men.

What incidents illustrating the halo effect have you observed in daily life? How can you reduce these? As individuals gather more complete data about an individual they can assess behavior more accurately. In addition, distinguishing among various aspects of an individual's behavior, rather than grouping even superficially related aspects, should reduce the influence of the halo effect. Managers must separate appearance from performance, productivity from attendance, personality from creativity. They must know what behaviors and attitudes result in better performance.

Projection

Projection refers to an individual's attributing his or her own attitudes or feelings to another person. Individuals use projection as a defense mechanism, to transfer blame to another person, or to provide protection from their own unacceptable feelings. Individuals frequently attribute their own prejudices against minorities, managers, or employees, for example, to another party.

Have you ever heard someone say, My boss is prejudiced; my boss doesn't like women; my boss doesn't like minority workers; my boss doesn't trust workers over forty? While these observations about the boss may be accurate, they may also be a reflection of the worker's own prejudices. The speaker, rather than the boss, may not like women, minority workers, or workers over forty. Consider a salesperson who hesitantly approaches a prospective customer, feeling that the customer will consider the product shoddy. The salesperson may be seeing his or her own attitudes about the product in the customer's response, whether or not the customer really feels that way.

Projection involves an emotional biasing of perceptions. Fear, hatred, uncertainty, anger, love, deceit, or distrust may influence an individual's perceptions. An older worker who fears that his skills are becoming obsolete may translate this fear to a dislike or distrust of younger workers, which may in turn be reflected in his perceptions of their attitudes and behaviors; he may even state that the new recruits don't like the experienced employees. Thus projection decreases perceptual accuracy.

Projection frequently occurs in union–management relations. Each side attributes feelings of mistrust (its own) to the other side. Management might state that the union mistrusts them, when, in fact, it is management that mistrusts the union. They project their own feelings onto the other group, representing them as that group's feelings. Isn't it likely that union and management had such attitudes at the Dagenham plant?

Can you think of other examples of projection? How could the boss, salesperson, or union members described above have avoided their perceptual distortions? How can a person diagnose projection and act to reduce it? To eliminate or reduce projection, you must first identify your true feelings. Do you feel anger, uncertainty, distrust? Once you recognize these feelings, then you must repeatedly assess whether and how they are influencing your perceptions of others. Further, in situations where projection is common, such as in union–management relations, you must carefully evaluate the accuracy of your perceptions.

Self-fulfilling Prophecy

In many situations, participants expect certain behaviors from other participants. They then see these behaviors as occurring whether or not they actually do. Their expectations become self-fulfilling prophecies. They may expect workers to be lazy, bossy, or tardy, then they perceive the workers actually are lazy, bossy, or tardy. These expectations may be associated with the participants' anticipating certain types of behavior from different groups of workers (stereotyping), from workers who demonstrate specific good or bad behavior (halo effect), or from workers onto whom they project their own attitudes (projection). Thus, these expectations, and the resulting self-fulfilling prophecies, underlie the other three types of perceptual distortions.

Assume you are a marketing manager with two subordinates. The first subordinate has demonstrated great creativity and productivity in the advertising campaigns she has developed. The second subordinate follows the directions given by you to the letter, but has demonstrated neither initiative nor enthusiasm for special projects. You have just found an innovative marketing plan on your desk. Which subordinate do you congratulate for the excellent work? If the self-fulfilling prophecy is operating, you would approach the first subordinate, whom you expect to demonstrate creativity because she has in the past. Could you be in error? Of course; either subordinate could have developed the plan. Our expectations influence and bias our perceptions of others, reducing their accuracy; they have also been shown to influence the performance of those of whom we have expectations.

How did the union's leadership in the introductory case expect the workers to behave after they "hailed the package as 'historic' "? How did they actually behave? How did Mr. Collyer expect the government to behave? What influence did this expectation have on his and other workers' behaviors? To reduce the distortions that result from expectancy, we must carefully test the assumptions we make about behavior in organizational situations.

Cross-Cultural Misperceptions

To reiterate one point made above: Because of our perceptual processes, rarely is the description we give of any particular event or person totally objective or accurate. Rather, many factors color our descriptions and cause them to differ from another person's descriptions.

Cross-cultural misperceptions occur for four reasons.[10] First, we have subconscious cultural blinders that cause us to interpret events in other countries as if they were occurring in our own. Second, we lack a complete understanding of our own culture and its influence on our behavior. Third, we assume people are more similar to us than they are. Finally, in general, our parochialism and lack of knowledge about other cultures contribute to our misperceptions.

An awareness of these differences can help us consider and represent the perspectives of several different observers when we describe events or people. If we can incorporate many people's perceptions into an account of a person or event, our description should be more accurate than if we attend only to our own perceptions. To obtain an accurate account of the situation at Ford Motor Company, we need to be conscious of the perceptions of the different people involved.

THE ATTRIBUTION PROCESS

But is perception enough? Is it sufficient simply to describe different events or people? Would the stockholders or corporate management of Ford be content with a simple description of the decision to strike? Most likely they would move to the next step, which involves determining the cause of the situation. In fact, as you read the case description, most likely you too pinpointed the cause or causes for the decision to strike.

The need to determine why events occur is a common one and is inherent in the diagnostic approach. Many of us, whether consciously or not, first ponder the reasons for many events and then decide *why* the events occurred. In this way, we *attribute causes* to the events. We move from description to diagnosis. As might be expected, different people often attribute different causes to the same event. In this book, we present a wide range of explanations for various phenomena so that individuals can attribute causes as accurately and *completely* as possible. They can then act on the basis of correct causal attributions.

Think again of the strike by the Dagenham employees. How would the workers and management explain the reasons for the strike? The workers likely would attribute it to the work-practice changes that had occurred and would continue under the new contract. Management likely would attribute the strike to workers' petulance, greed, or unwillingness to compromise. Why would these reasons differ? How would the workers' and management's subsequent actions likely differ, given these attributions? Put yourself in the position of an observer of the situation. Why do you think the strike occurred? We can similarly assess differences in attributions for the workers' dissatisfaction with and resistance to the new work methods, or Nissan's relatively high productivity.

Relevant Theory

Kurt Lewin defined behavior as being a function of both an individual's personality and the environment.[11] He suggested that any time a person acts, the action probably results from both the individual's personal characteristics and situational influences. He added that it is inaccurate to assume that behavior results from just one of these causes.

When people try to understand reasons for behavior, however, they often ignore one of these types of causes. They either focus on personal causes, such as habits, needs, abilities, or interests, or emphasize situational factors, such as increases in competition, poor supervision, shortages of resources, or the nature of the work itself. They tend to overestimate the influence of either an individual's personality characteristics or environmental influences and typically discount the other factor. Some managers always attribute an individual's performance to his or her effort; others discount this and attribute performance to rewards or punishments given. Thus, in the Ford example, people who blame the union for the strike likely discount the impact of new work methods and see an overconcern for efficiency as possible causes. People who blame management's traits likely discount the critical need for flexibility to Ford's survival and the strong competition by Nissan as significant in causing the strike. In part through the introduction of behavioral theories in this text, we hope to increase the accuracy of attributions you make and improve your diagnosis of organizational phenomena.

The Steps in Attribution

Attribution theorists and researchers have studied the process of determining the causes of specific events, the responsibility for particular outcomes, and the personal qualities of individuals participating in the situation.[12] They have also studied the process by which we come to attribute people's behavior primarily to personality or situational causes.[13] One researcher has suggested that this process occurs in three stages (shown in Figure 2–4): a person (1) observes another person's action; (2) determines whether the behavior was intended; and (3) assigns a reason for the behavior.[14] More specifically, the process takes place as follows:

Stage 1. First, we observe or are told about some action; for example, the walkout by the Ford employees. We are told that 62 percent of the union members rejected Ford's contract offer and began a nationwide strike.

Stage 2. Having identified the action, we move to the second stage, where we determine if the behavior we observed was intended or accidental. Did the strike occur on purpose, or did it just happen by accident? By answering this question, we make a first-level determination of the cause of the behavior. If we assume that the strike occurred accidentally, we do not determine its causes. We attribute it to fate, luck, accident, or a similar uncontrollable phenomenon. If, however, we

Figure 2–4 THE ATTRIBUTION PROCESS

In General:	*Stage 1*	*Stage 2*	*Stage 3*
Behavior occurs	Observation of behavior	Determination of intent by observer or actor	Assignment of reason for the behavior
At the Dagenham Plant:			
Strike occurs	Union, management, the media, and other constituencies observe the strike	A person (observer or participant) determines if the strike was accidental or intentional	Assuming the strike was intended, that person attributes its cause to personal or situational characteristics

assume that the strike was intended, that the workers chose to walk off their jobs, we then move to stage 3, in which we attempt to assign a more specific reason for the behavior.

Stage 3. We question whether situational causes or personal characteristics explain the behavior. We might consider, for example, whether the new work practices were the main impetus for the strike; if so, we attribute the workers' walk-out to situational factors. If, on the other hand, we feel that the workers' personalities influenced their decision to strike, that they were tired of their jobs and saw the strike as a way to get an unscheduled vacation, then we are likely to conclude that personal dispositions motivated the strike. Can you perform a similar analysis for top management's introduction of the new work rules? If we attribute the introduction of new work rules to competitive pressure, then situational factors are their main cause; if we attribute the introduction to the desire to punish the workers, then the personal dispositions of management caused the change.

In cross-cultural situations similar patterns of attributions can occur. Behaviors can be attributed to the situation, that is, the cultural differences, or to the personal characteristics of the individual, such as arrogance, laziness, or disrespect. To make accurate attributions in such situations it is essential that we be familiar with the culture in which the situation occurs; in the Dagenham situation, for example, with the nature of labor–management relations in the British culture.

While both situational and personal factors may have influenced the decision to strike, we generally try to simplify our understanding and so attend primarily to only one of these types of causes rather than to both types. Recognizing this tendency to simplify understanding, this book encourages students to identify multiple possible causes of behaviors and attitudes by systematically applying a series of behavioral perspectives to understanding a situation and attributing causes to it. The diagnostic approach emphasizes the complexity of organizational situations and the value of using diverse theories and perspectives to understand them.

ATTRIBUTIONAL BIASES

We not only attribute the reasons for behavior to either situational or personal factors, but we make these attributions in predictable ways, based on both our point of view and the effectiveness of the behavior.

Point of View

An individual can participate in a situation as an *actor* or an *observer*. In looking at the Ford situation, we can view Jim Collyer, the metal finisher, as an actor in the situation and Ford corporate management as the observers. Whom we designate as the actor and observer depends on the behavior to which we are attributing causes. If we look instead at top management's behavior with regard to introducing new work rules, then top corporate managers become the actors and the production-line workers become the observers.

Research about such attributions indicates that an actor in a given situation emphasizes the situational causes of a behavior and deemphasizes the personal factors to protect his or her self-image and ego.[15] For example, Jim Collyer as the actor, would emphasize the economic conditions, including labor's position, and deemphasize his personal attitudes as contributing to the strike. Top management, as the observer, would emphasize the personal factors of the actor, such as Collyer's perceived laziness, antagonism, or stubbornness, and deemphasize situational factors, such as poor working conditions or unsatisfactory rewards, as explanations of the situation.[16]

Consider the worker who arrives at work late. Does the worker attribute the cause of the tardiness to his or her personal characteristics or to situational factors such as traffic, a malfunctioning alarm clock, or changed work rules? To what does the worker's boss attribute the cause of the tardiness? According to the attributional biases we have just discussed, the worker attributes his or her behavior to the situation, a delayed subway, for example; and the boss attributes the worker's behavior to his or her personal characteristics, perhaps laziness. Misattributions of these kinds can be particularly significant in the conduct of performance reviews, but recognizing such bias should alert individuals to possible inaccuracies in their attributions and diagnoses.

Two other factors moderate the effect of point of view on attributions: the appropriateness of the behavior and the belief that the behavior was meant to affect the observer.[17] An observer who views a person acting in a way that is not considered socially desirable attributes the actor's behavior to personality characteristics. If an assembly-line worker is observed sabotaging the product, top management would attribute this action to the worker's personality. An observer who believes that a person has acted in a way to specifically influence the observer also attributes the actor's behavior to his or her personality traits. If top management felt that Jim Collyer and other workers walked off the job to "get back at management's Japanization of work practices," they likely would attribute the cause of the strike to the workers' personalities.

Effectiveness of the Behavior

The perceived success or failure of a behavior complicates the attribution of its cause, as shown in Table 2–1. By *successful behavior* we mean actions that are viewed as effective and in line with the organization's goals. For actors, increases in performance and efficiency, or following work rules are considered successful behaviors. Failures include increased turnover or absenteeism, declining productivity or morale, or performance of more specific unacceptable behaviors. Although research results are somewhat mixed, the weight of evidence suggests that actors tend to attribute successes to personal factors, and failures to situational factors.[18] For observers the reverse is true: they tend to attribute successes to situational factors and failures to personal factors.[19]

Consider the case of a student who has just completed a final examination. If the student obtains an A on the exam, how will he or she explain the excellent performance? If that student obtains an F on the exam, how will he or she explain the poor performance? To what will the professor attribute the student's performance? The student, as an actor, will attribute an A (success) to personal factors, such as his or her knowledge or effort, but an F (failure), to situational factors, such as poor teaching or noise in the examination room. The professor,

Table 2–1 SUMMARY OF ATTRIBUTIONS

Person Making Attributions	Behavior as Focus of Evaluation	Quality of Actions	
		Success	Failure
Actor	Actor's Actions	Personal	Situational
	Observer's Actions	Situational	Personal
Observer	Actor's Actions	Situational	Personal
	Observer's Actions	Personal	Situational

as an observer of the student's behavior, will make the reverse attributions: he or she will attribute an A to his or her excellent teaching (aspects of the situation) and an F to the student's laziness or low IQ. If the professor views himself or herself as an actor rather than an observer in the situation the attributions likely change. As an actor, the professor sees productivity (the "A") as a result of effort (teaching), which is a personal, not a situational, explanation. Which of these attributions is correct? The correct attribution depends on the specific situation. And of course any of these attributions probably represents an oversimplification of the causes.

In some cases, the tendencies for a manager to make the easiest response and to maintain his or her self-esteem cause different attributions.[20] A manager more easily assumes, for example, that a worker is responsible for a problem, rather than the situation. To determine the situational impact typically requires that the manager spend time investigating the situation in great detail. Correcting the situation is also more difficult than dealing with or removing the individual seen as responsible. A manager can more easily assume that a subordinate is responsible and might need to be replaced than he or she can alter organizational or environmental influences. Further, managers often view their subordinates' behavior as a reflection of themselves; in order to maintain their own self-esteem, then, managers are more likely to attribute subordinates' successes to the external situation, such as the manager's contributions, and failures to subordinates' personalities.

Consider the case of Ford again. If top management views the Japanization of management as successful behavior, they would attribute its cause to their personal skill or ability to recognize and introduce quality management processes. They would continue to act in accord with this understanding. If they view it as a mistake or failure, they likely attribute its introduction to the situation, such as economic pressures, competition from Nissan, or requirements of their Board of Directors, all outside of their control.

Rectifying Attributional Problems

Testing the nature of attributions in a problem situation should be an early and recurring step of diagnosis. As much as possible, individuals should be involved in processing information about the situation *actively* rather than passively.[21] Individuals can learn reasonable causes for various behaviors as well as methods for testing their assumptions. By knowing the typical attributional biases, individuals can be alert to them in their own attributions and verify the accuracy of the causes they identify. They can then act on the basis of correct causal attributions.

Although little research has been done about multicultural biases in attribution, managers should be alert to this possibility. Differences in personal responsibility assumed, as opposed to situational responsibility, may be a function of cultural dimensions such as individualism or power distance.

THE LEARNING PROCESS

In addition to perception and attribution, learning influences both description and diagnosis of organizational behavior. *Learning* refers to the acquisition of skills, knowledge, ability, or attitudes.

Individuals learn in a variety of ways. Behaviorists emphasize external influences and the power of rewards. Cognitive psychologists emphasize the internal mental processes involved in gaining new insights. Social learning theorists integrate both behaviorist and cognitive approaches with the idea of behavior modeling or imitative behavior.

Behaviorist Approach

Beginning with research on animal responses, the behaviorist theorists emphasized the link between a given stimulus and response. Recall Pavlov's work with dogs.[22] He noted that, on presentation of powdered meat blown through a tube (unconditioned stimulus) to a dog, the dog salivated (unconditioned response). The ringing of a bell (neutral stimulus) initially yielded no salivation responses. After pairing the ringing bell with the powdered meat several times, Pavlov then rang the bell without the meat. The dogs salivated (conditioned response). In classical conditioning, after the repeated pairing of neutral and unconditioned stimuli, presentation of the neutral stimulus alone led to a conditioned response, as illustrated in Figure 2–5. Another example: (1) the telephone rings and a salesclerk jumps; (2) flashing a light when the telephone rings leads to the salesclerk's jumping; (3) the light flashing alone leads to the salesclerk's jumping.

Operant conditioning extends classical conditioning to focus on the consequences of a behavior (Figure 2–5).[23] While a stimulus can still cue a response behavior, what happens after the behavior—e.g., a desired or undesired consequence—determines whether the behavior will recur. For example, an individual who receives a bonus (a positive consequence) after creative performance (behavior) on a work assignment (stimulus) is more likely to repeat the creative behavior than if his or her performance is ignored (a negative consequence). Continuation of the workers' strike at Ford may depend on the consequences associated with it. If the workers cannot afford food or shelter (negative consequences) they are less likely to continue the strike than if a strike fund meets the workers' basic needs. Similarly, the learned, new behaviors of assembly-line work would more likely continue if the workers received higher pay (positive consequences) than if they received the same pay

Figure 2–5 BEHAVIORAL LEARNING MODELS

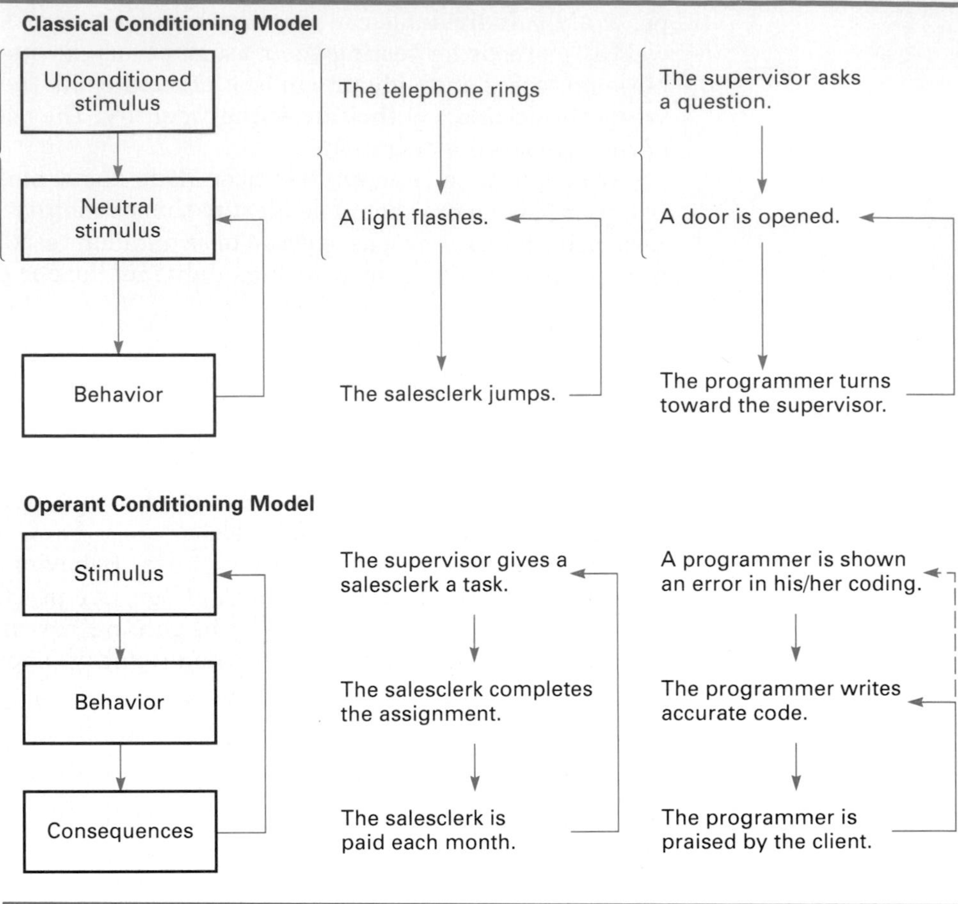

(negative consequences). Chapter 4 examines the significance of operant conditioning for motivation in organizations.

Cognitive Approach

In contrast to the behavior-reinforcement links that are central to behaviorist theories, cognitive theorists viewed learning as resulting from the joining of various cues in the environment into a mental map.[24] In Edward Tolman's early experiments, rats learned to run through a maze to reach a goal of food. Repeated trials caused the rat to develop cognitive connections that identified the correct path to the goal. Each time the rat reached its goal, the connections between the cognitive cues and the expectancies of reaching the goal were strengthened. According to Tolman, the rat developed a cognitive map of the path to the goal. Employees, too, can develop a cognitive map that shows the path to a specific goal, as illustrated in Figure 2–6. Here, the cognitive processes join (and act on) the stimulus to result in a given behavior. At the Ford plant, on-the-job training in the new assembly lines should result in a new cognitive map of job performance for the workers. Collyer's calling the new

Figure 2–6 COGNITIVE LEARNING MODEL

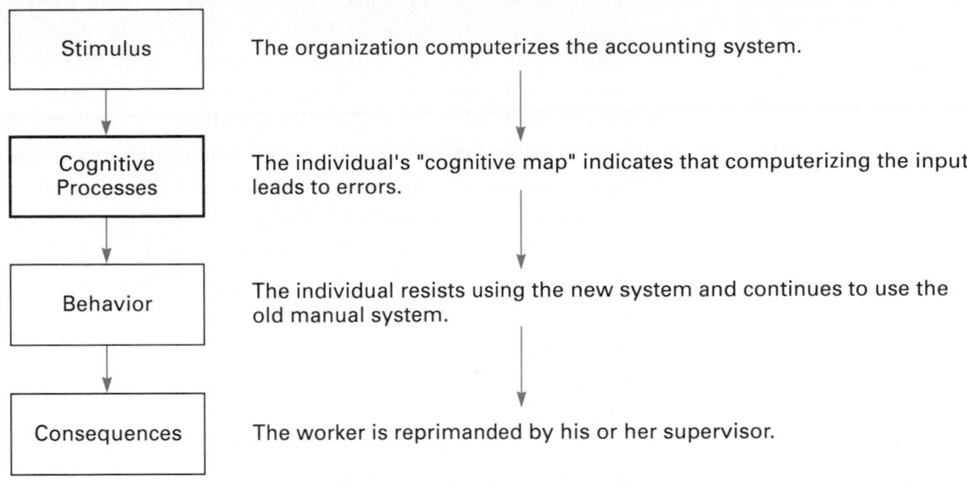

work processes the "Japanization of management" may also result from his cognitive map of that type of behavior and job design.

Cognitive learning theories have since been integrated into expectancy and goal-setting theories (described in Chapter 4). For example, programs that link job and organizational rules, regulations, and activities with worker expectations about the goals associated with them emphasize the cognitive connections between environmental cues, worker expectancies, and goals.[25]

Social Learning Approach

Extending beyond both behavioral and cognitive learning theories, social learning theory suggests that learning results from modeling behaviors. Using observations to gather information, learners imitate the behavior of others.[26] According to Albert Bandura, learners first watch others who act as models and then develop a mental picture of the behavior and its consequences.[27] The observer then tries out the behavior; if positive consequences result he or she repeats the behavior; if negative consequences occur, no repetition occurs. This assessment of response consequences parallels behaviorist theories. The learning impact occurs when the subject tries the behavior and experiences a favorable result. The learner's development of a cognitive image of the situation incorporates one of the basic aspects of cognitive learning.

Applications of modeling theory to understanding and improving behavior in organizations are increasing.[28] Fred Luthans and Robert Kreitner suggest the following modeling strategy for a manager. First, the manager should identify the goal or target behavior(s) that will lead to improved performance. Ford, for example, may have identified participation in the new production line as such a target behavior. Second, the manager must select the appropriate model. He or she should also determine the media with which to present the model, such as live demonstrations, training films, or videotapes. At Ford, top management might conduct a live demonstration of the new production techniques, show training films to the workers, or provide them with videotapes to view. Third, managers must make sure the employee is capable of meeting the technical skill requirements of the target behaviors. Clearly the Ford workers have the skills to perform effectively on the assembly line. Fourth, the managers must structure a favorable and positive learning environment to increase the likelihood that workers will learn the new behaviors and act in the desired way. Ford did not construct a completely positive environment since the workers' motivation to learn and improve was deflated by their attitude toward Japanese management. Fifth, management must model the target behavior and carry out supporting activities such as role playing. They must clearly demonstrate the positive consequences of engaging in the modeled target behaviors. Sixth, they must positively reinforce reproduction of the target behaviors, both in training and back on the job. It is unclear whether Ford adjusted the reward system to fit the new behaviors. Bonuses for improved productivity or praise for a job well done clearly would encourage the desired behaviors. Finally, once the target behaviors are reproduced, management must maintain and strengthen them, first with a continuous schedule of reinforcement (see Chapter 4) and later with an intermittent schedule.[29] Ford must reward the increased productivity with money and other incentives that meet the workers' needs.

How effectively did Ford apply such a modeling strategy? Clearly the workers learned the desired behaviors, since productivity increased significantly. But learning the behaviors was not enough: motivation lagged, in large part because of the workers' attitudes.

Managerial Implications of Learning

How can managers encourage their own and others' learning in the workplace? They can ensure that appropriate conditions for learning exist; providing appropriate stimuli (e.g., complete and understandable information or material) should facilitate acquisition of skills, knowledge, or attitudes. Managers should reinforce desired learned behaviors. They should also provide environmental cues that encourage learning; structuring a context (e.g., a physical and emotional climate) that supports learning is essential. Finally, managers should provide individuals who can model desired behaviors. Reproduction of desired behaviors should be encouraged and reinforced. Reading 2–1, "Varieties of Managerial Learning," by Gib Akin, incorporates these models in seven specific learning themes for managers.

Reproduction of desired attitudes should also be stimulated. But the process of attitude formation is more complicated than can be explained by learning theory alone.

DEVELOPING PRODUCTIVE ATTITUDES

An attitude is a consistent predisposition to respond to various aspects of people, situations, or objects. Since an attitude is a hypothetical construct and cannot be observed, we only infer it from a person's behavior or verbal expression. We might, for example, determine an individual's job satisfaction by inferring it from his or her general demeanor on the job or by asking the person to describe this attitude. The strength of an attitude depends first on the type of experience the individual has had with the person, object, or situation: the more direct the experience, the stronger the attitude.[30] Second, the attitude's strength increases along with the number of times it has been expressed[31]: the more often a worker expresses dissatisfaction with his or her job, the stronger that attitude becomes. Determining attitudes should be part of the description phase of the diagnostic approach. How do attitudes form in organizations? What effect do they have on worker behaviors and organizational performance?

Components of Attitudes

Research has suggested that attitudes have three components (shown in Table 2–2): (1) cognitive, (2) affective, and (3) behavioral.[32] The *cognitive* component is the beliefs an individual has about a certain person, object, or situation. These beliefs serve as an antecedent to specific attitudes. Individuals consider beliefs, such as "You need to work long hours to get ahead in this job," to be true; to be "what is." Beliefs are learned in the ways described in the last sections—through modeling, the association of cognitive cues, or reinforcement. Although we have many beliefs, not all of them are important enough to lead to significant attitudes. Can you think of a belief you hold that has a work-related attitude associated with it? Can you think of a belief that does not have an associated attitude?

The *affective* component refers to the individual's feeling that results from his or her view of a person, object, or situation. An individual might have a negative feeling about his or her job because of the beliefs held about promotion. A person may feel anger or frustration because he or she believes hard work deserves promotion, and the person has worked hard but has not been promoted.

Finally, the *behavioral* component is the individual's behavior that occurs as a result of his or her feeling about the focal person, object, or situation. The relationship between attitudes and behaviors is stronger the more active a person's attitude when he or she is behaving.[33] Thus the more often an individual expresses dissatisfaction with his or her job, the more likely that person is to demonstrate such negative consequences as lowered productivity, requests for transfer, sabotage, or other dysfunctional behavior. The individual dissatisfied with promotion opportunities on the job may plan to leave, intend to

Table 2–2 THE COMPONENTS OF ATTITUDES

Components	Definition	Example
Cognitive	Beliefs, knowledge, understanding	The workers' understanding about the quality of life in Japan and the role of work there
Affective	Favorable or unfavorable feelings	The workers' feelings about the work processes used in Japan and their translation into British practices
Behavioral	Human actions	The workers' decision to strike and the strike itself

work fewer hours, or decide to complain to management about promotion policies. Behavioral intentions are significant because in many cases they are positively associated with actual behaviors.[34]

The situation at Ford illustrates the three components of attitudes. Clearly the workers have a series of beliefs and values about the Japanization of work. These result in negative feelings toward the new assembly-line procedures. These attitudes in turn result in the behavioral actions of leaving the job or being uncooperative with management. In this case, a work stoppage resulted.

Job Satisfaction

Job satisfaction is an emotional reaction that "results from the perception that one's job fulfills or allows the fulfillment of one's important job values, providing and to the degree that those values are congruent with one's needs."[35] A variety of job-related factors such as autonomy, flexibility, and responsibility, as well as organization-related factors such as pay, advancement opportunities, and company policies, can influence job satisfaction. Individuals may have different amounts of satisfaction with various facets of their jobs. Some factors, such as satisfaction with pay, with the work itself, and with supervision, contribute most significantly to overall satisfaction.[36] Most managers should be concerned about an individual's job satisfaction because it has consequences for performance, absenteeism, and turnover.[37]

Managerial Implications of Attitude Formation

Managers should recognize that there are links between attitudes and behavior, thus they should encourage positive attitudes, typically by influencing a worker's beliefs and feelings. Influencing an attitude requires altering both a belief and its related feelings. At Ford, changing the attitude toward the new work procedures requires first altering the beliefs and values of the workers. Ford might need to show the British laborers, for example, that their belief that only certain classes of workers belong on the assembly line is erroneous. Of course, such attitude change does not occur easily. Dissemination of factual information may eventually change some beliefs, but more emotion-oriented persuasive techniques and longer term educational efforts may be needed to alter attitudes.

SUMMARY

In this chapter we focused on four basic individual processes: perception, attribution, learning, and attitude formation. Figure 2–7 offers a set of diagnostic questions for these. Perception, or the selection and organization of stimuli, influences the way we describe organizational situations. Because organizational phenomena are not totally objective, characteristics of the perceiver and the object being perceived influence what aspects become important; these aspects are then incorporated into a description. Often we distort perceptions through stereotyping, the halo effect, projection, and expectancy. These distortions may cause inaccurate descriptions or diagnoses.

We not only attend to and organize certain stimuli in predictable, although not necessarily objective, ways but we also attribute reasons for behavior in

Figure 2–7 DIAGNOSTIC QUESTIONS FROM THE PERCEPTION, ATTRIBUTION, LEARNING, AND ATTITUDE-FORMATION PERSPECTIVES

- What factors influence the perceptions of organizational members?
- What distortions of perception occur?
- What factors influence the attributions of organizational members?
- What biases exist in these attributions?
- What behaviors are reinforced as part of the learning process?
- What cues encourage learning?
- What learning themes exist in the organization?
- How are these learning themes supported in the organization?
- What beliefs and values do individuals hold?
- How do these beliefs and values influence the individuals' attitudes?
- What functional and dysfunctional behavioral intentions result from the individuals' attitudes?

predictable ways. Attribution specifies the causes of organizational phenomena. Individuals assign reasons according to whether they are actors or observers of the behavior, and also based upon the effectiveness of the behavior. We must recognize the biases in such attributions and attempt to identify precise causes.

We discussed the role of learning as another significant form of organizational behavior. Behaviorist, cognitive, and social learning theories differ in the emphases they place on external rewards, psychological processes, and behavior modeling. The behaviorists emphasize the links between behaviors and their consequences. Cognitive theories focus on attempts to understand and predict the functioning of the human mind. Social learning theorists encourage the development of a mental map of the situation, to be built on with the use of imitation in learning.

Finally, we discussed the nature of attitude formation in organizations. Attitudes have cognitive, affective, and behavioral components, the sequencing of which affects attitude formation and resulting behaviors. Individuals have certain beliefs and values that result in specific attitudes. The resulting attitudes in turn influence behaviors.

READING

Reading 2–1: VARIETIES OF MANAGERIAL LEARNING

Gib Akin

The list of books and articles revealing the secrets of how to manage well seems endless. Do this, or think this way, or apply this technique, and you will be a better manager, the writers say. The books and articles keep coming along; some with truly new ideas, many with new presentations of old ideas. With all this good information available about how to manage well, you would think that managers would learn. All of us have probably been affected from time to time by reading others' prescriptions for success, but exhortation to do what others have found to be effective is insufficient to reliably transform actual practice. What, then, does it take?

Although much is known about what successful managers are like, not as much is known about how they became that way. We know what successful managers do but not how they came to be doing it. Most of the how-to books suggest that the reader begin to act like the exemplar manager—to emulate the techniques and approaches associated with management "excellence." Yet the writers never explain what the exemplar managers did to learn their effective practices. Since an exemplar manager did not become that way by reading a book about himself or herself, readers might be better off emulating the learning experiences of an effective manager rather than emulating the learned technique.

Theories and models of managerial practice are quite elaborate, whereas theories of managerial learning are often quite simplistic. In a review of the literature on supervision in social work, I looked for the assumptions that the authors made about how supervisors might learn the techniques and practices that were being presented. Most often, the authors assumed that people would learn by being told—emphatically—to do the right thing (whatever that might be for a particular writer). I believe that systematic analysis of management literature in general would reveal a similar primitive approach to management learning.

To develop effective managers, we not only have to know what skills, knowledge, and attitudes are associated with excellent management, but also how those things can be learned. Training and development professionals in organizations and in academia have not been unconcerned about this dilemma; they have focused on their own technology of teaching. For the most part, their work has been influenced by research and practice in psychology and education, and a lively discussion of theory and practice for management training can be found in both academic and practitioner journals. One encouraging sign is that most modern training is guided by more advanced theories of learning than is found in some of the more popular books on effective management.

Unfortunately, application of learning theories often does not produce the intended results. Most management development programs are beset by the "transfer of training" problem: Will managers be able to use what they have learned when they leave the classroom and return to their jobs? This question, of course, begs the real question of whether anything is learned at all if it cannot be used elsewhere. Perhaps the problem is not really a "transfer of training" problem but more fundamentally a learning problem.

From my own experience in training and teaching (using learning theories developed in psychology and education), I have found that people do not always learn what or in ways that they are expected to but that they almost always learn something. What seems to be missing from most of the learning models is the learner and his or her actual experience of learning as he or she understands it. To build a useful model of how successful managers learn, we need to explore their actual learning experiences. For me, then, the really interesting question is, *What are the varieties of learning experiences that account for managerial excellence?*

HOW MANAGERS LEARN

To find out about managers' learning experiences, I talked with 60 managers for more than two hours each on average. The managers were seasoned veterans in a variety of fields (insurance, manufacturing, social service, education, government, and retailing), and the positions they held represented all organizational levels. Although not necessarily stars in their organizations, the managers had achieved some success. The point of my investigation was to identify the learning experiences tied to their success.

First, I asked each manager to reflect on which skills, knowledge, or attitudes had been most important for achieving whatever success he or she had achieved. The managers' answers reflected their own image of themselves at their best—the learnings they relied on to manage well.

The heart of each interview was a joint inquiry by the interviewer and the manager into how those personal determinants of managerial success had been learned. For each determinant named, I asked the following questions: Where did you learn that? How? What did you do? What was it like? How did you know that you had learned it? What prompted you to pursue such learning in the first place? In other words, I asked each participant in the study to describe in as much detail as possible their most significant managerial learning experiences.

In the following discussion, I will present a model of managerial learning based on analysis and interpretation of the learning experiences of the 60 managers as revealed through my interviews with them. My research shows a remarkable similarity in the way that learning is triggered and how important learning is experienced by the learner. It also shows a rich variety in the learning activities that managers pursue and in the ways that pursuit is personally organized.

How Learning Is Known

To be able to describe learning experiences, a person must first be able to identify them. This seemed to be no problem for the managers I interviewed. They described powerful and vivid learning experiences that were distinct from any other type of experience. Their descriptions were surprisingly congruous. Apparently, the experience of learning and how it is known is quite similar for different people and in different settings.

Learning is experienced as a personal transformation. A person does not gather learnings as possessions but rather becomes a new person with those learnings as a part of his or her new self. To learn is not to have; it is to be.

The managers whom I interviewed knew that they had learned—that they had been transformed—because they experienced a different world from the one they had experienced before the learning occurred. They found their reality reshaped, that they literally were living in a new world. Furthermore, that new world was well known by them, as if they owned a very legible map of it. Effective action in this new world was "automatic," a "part of me." The managers had gained a sense of comfort, whereas before the learning experience they had felt anxiety or uneasiness.

Managers know that they have learned when others see and verify their successes. They are able to solve and even anticipate problems. In general, they sense that "I can do it." For example, the manager of a data processing operation for a university cited as particularly vivid his learning to program computers, the technical ground of his managerial performance. He said:

> Becoming a programmer was extremely important for me. It made me a part of this business. I remember this incredible breakthrough where one day it just all came together and I knew that now I could really do it. I had been programming for a while, but I didn't ever feel really comfortable. Oh, I knew all the rules and could write code and get things to run, but there was something missing. Then one day I was studying this bootstrap routine, trying to understand it, and it all became clear. At that point, I knew I could program anything on any machine. I had written programs before, but now I was a real programmer. I don't program much anymore, but I will always be a programmer. And that's important to get this job [as a manager] done, too.

At some point, as with the manager quoted above, the content of a learning experience may become less relevant. At a deeper level, however, the information that has been learned transforms the learner into a new person.

What Is Learned

The first part of each interview was devoted to finding out what kinds of skills, knowledge, and attitudes a manager relied on to be effective. In effect, I was trying to discover the manager's own model of competency. That model invariably included six categories of managerial competence.

Interpersonal skills, or the general ability to work well with others. The particular skills required by the managers varied, as did the managers' opinions about the nature of "good" interpersonal relations. However, the managers agreed that, whatever the definition, interpersonal skills were important to their success.

Analytical skills, or the ability to successfully solve unstructured problems. Again, the specifics varied with the situation, but the category was important to all of the managers interviewed.

Communication skills, including the ability to effectively present and sell ideas, both orally and in writing. As one manager, director of an agricultural laboratory, said, "If I hadn't had this drama teacher who helped me break loose, I could very well have ended up a wall flower, someone who would never speak up."

Job knowledge, or whatever needs to be known to accomplish a particular job (the technical grounding referred to by the data processing manager). Job knowledge usually is taken for granted. Even though it is critical for success, job knowledge is often overlooked as a significant managerial skill.

Knowledge of organizational and professional norms, or knowing the organization's "culture." However, simply knowing an organization's norms and values is not enough; a manager must embrace and enact those norms and values.

Self-confidence, or the learned attitude toward oneself as a competent person. Self-confidence also refers to seeing oneself as a skilled learner who knows how to gain new knowledge and competencies.

Learning Activities

What do managers do to learn the competencies associated with excellent management? The answers to this question took the form of detailed stories about the events resulting in specific learning experiences. Managers usually had a clear explanation of the process by which they had acquired an important managerial ability.

The original learning experiences to which the managers attributed their current abilities were not always related to the managers' current context. In fact, many managerial abilities had been imported from other domains. For example, a large number of male managers attributed their interpersonal skills and self-confidence, factors critical to their success, to their experience in the Boy Scouts. Many managers attributed their analytical skills to family and early school experiences. Many cited participation in fraternity or sorority governance as a source of interpersonal and communication skills.

The importation of knowledge from other domains may result in the appearance that a successful manager has certain innate personal attributes. However, the managers I interviewed were always able to cite learning experiences to account for what appeared to be personal characteristics. This finding is not surprising if we understand learning as a personal transformation, and it makes the study of the varieties of learning experiences even more fascinating.

THEMES FOR LEARNING

The variety of actual learning activities is enormous. Further, these activities, variously pursued, have different meanings for different people. People may read a book, take a course, or practice a skill with many different things in mind—with different intentions, concerns, interests, or whatever. A person's orientation toward his or her own learning processes organizes and gives meaning to particular learning activities.

Analysis of my interview data reveals that most of the managers had a rather singular way of describing their learning experiences. Their descriptions of how learning happened were similar, transcending particular content or circumstance. The managers seemed to have a general framework that they used to organize, understand, and pursue learning activities. That pattern included the choice of learning activities, the use of resources, the order for the development of complex learning experiences, the role of teachers, and so forth. I call the pattern a *learning theme.*

In choosing the term "theme" as a metaphor for the regularities in the managers' descriptions of their learning experiences, I gave some thought to the implications. A theme is not an attribute of a person. It is not a choice or a goal. Rather, it is both a procedure and a path. I like to think of a learning theme as what learning *means* as a practical action. A learning theme is neither an opinion about learning nor a criterion for learning. Instead, it is what a person *does* about learning. A theme is a taken-for-granted (and obvious, for me at least) structure of a person's practical action, what a person preconsciously uses to organize his or her learning experiences and outcomes. The learner, when in action, does not comprehend the theme itself but rather what the theme reveals. Since they seem to be taken for granted, learning themes probably are not chosen by the learner. In that sense, it is not clear whether the themes themselves are learned in the way that learning is described here. My interpretation of the managers' stories of learning, of their hundreds of specific learning experiences, led me to identify the seven learning themes described below.

Emulation of a Mentor

Some managers described all of their learning experiences in terms of emulating a specific person, a mentor. The mentor was recognized as having a well-developed, coherent world view—in effect, a system for "putting it all together." By acting like this person, seeing the world in his or her way, the managers in this group believed that they would become a skilled and effective manager like the mentor.

A mentor does not actually have to be present in a person's life. Some managers emulated historical figures such as General George Patton or Alfred Sloan. The most central learning activity within this learning theme is to find out as much as possible about how the mentor thinks and does things and then practice those methods in real situations.

For learners enacting the mentor theme, almost any situation is organized in terms of who the exemplar character is and what he or she is doing. Conceptual material and models are used in unique ways. The concepts presented are overlooked in favor of the stories of what some effective manager is said to have done. The elegance or practical utility of management models is less important than the person who is using them. These learners also tend to emulate the mentor (not what he says but what he does) if they like his or her management style.

Role Taking

This learning theme is similar to the mentoring theme in that emulation is a central activity. However, people who learn by role taking use no specific person as a model. Instead, they have a broad conception of what they should be—a competent person in a professional or organizational position. The learner focuses on adopting and behaving the skills and attitudes specified by the role model. People who have learned this way always "look the part."

For managers, the role model adopted may come from almost anywhere: a formal prescription developed by the organization, professional management literature describing the "excellent executive," observation of others, or answers to questions such as, What does it take to make it around here? Whatever the source of the role model to be learned, the manager who learns in this way looks for role models and strives to exemplify them.

Moreover, managers who learn by role taking attend formal management development seminars to get information to elaborate their role models and to practice role behaviors. They consider their learning experience successful if they feel as though they have become whatever the role name is they are attempting to emulate and are treated by others in that way. They believe it is important to feel like and be seen by others as a professional.

Practical Accomplishment

Managers who learn through practical accomplishment focus on problem solving. They are less interested in becoming a particular type of manager and more interested in learning from "doing whatever works to get results." Compared with the two previous learning themes, this theme has a relatively short time horizon for learning.

For managers in this category, the authoritative guide to learning and competence is not a conception of a mentor or a role. Instead, it is found in the outcome of actions taken to solve problems and from others who verify accomplishment. This point is illustrated by the following comment made by a supervisor in field training:

> One of the main problems for me is delegation. I tend not to want to let go; I want to see a job done. But I had to. There was just too much to do. To learn that, you have to be there. Studying won't give it to you.

Managers who learn through practical accomplishment tend to see most problems as opportunities. They say, "Give me a challenge." They learn through the experience of meeting a challenge. This is an active learning mode. Therefore, learning cannot be derived from management concepts and models without concrete application of those concepts and models.

Validation

This learning theme emphasizes the interplay of concepts and practice, the usual assumption made in the design of most formal training programs. The validational theme is longitudinal, the experience of learning not being realized by the learner until usually long after the initial learning activities. The theme is called "validational" because the learner validates what he or she is already reliably and perhaps competently doing. It is a reframing of skills as "right" and of the learner as competent for having those skills. (Recall the student who was surprised to find out that he had been speaking prose all his life!) Learning is based on authoritative information, from either a specific person or a professional source, and reinforces a person's belief that what he or she has been doing all along is right.

I can easily identify validational learners in the management seminars that I conduct. They often bring up examples and situations from their own work experiences and use the concepts I am introducing to explain why they were successful or unsuccessful. "Now I understand. I've actually been using contingency theory all along." This reaction is not just self-congratulation; for the validational learner, this kind of experience is the learning. Through this experience, the transformation that constitutes learning is completed.

Anticipation

This learning theme is similar to validational learning because it also emphasizes the interplay of concept and practice within a longitudinal framework. However, the difference between anticipatory and validational learning is the sequence of events. For validational learners, action precedes conceptualization. For anticipatory learners, conceptualization precedes action. Anticipatory learners tend to focus on learning concepts and models to use in taking action. However, learning is completed only by applying the concepts and models and finding, through practical experience, that "what I thought I knew fell into place." As one hospital administrator commented:

> I learn best when it's not "force fed." When the ideas are presented, I get a chance to take them back, think about them, digest them, and then implement them. I read things, get a good idea, and then try it out. It's a matter of repetition. The first few times, I'm not comfortable with a new concept. I really learn it when I become comfortable with it.

Most formal schooling is designed as if people were anticipatory learners. Have people "learn" theory and concepts first and then put them to use later, usually outside the designated learning situation. (This approach creates the "transfer of training" problem.) However, even for anticipatory learners, the formal learning experience is only the prelude; the real experience of having learned something occurs later when the anticipated practice turns out to be similar to what was predicted by the theory.

Personal Growth

With the previously described themes, learning activities are engaged and organized around accomplishments and competencies. With this theme, the focus is on self-development as a person, perhaps only marginally connected with practical accomplishments. The underlying, fundamental value of learning is self-understanding and personal fulfillment. Learning is the actualization of possibilities. The learner is less concerned about gaining skills and knowledge and more concerned about self-understanding and the transformation of values and attitudes.

People who learn through personal growth seek and organize learning activities around self-development. In formal learning settings, they seek knowledge for its relevance not to getting things done but to understanding who they are and what their activities might mean. In management development workshops, participants who learn through personal growth like to explore the implications of ideas and practices for the kind of world we are constructing and their place in it. They search for insight. One executive, talking about his acquisition and development of the interpersonal and communication skills that he now relies on, commented:

> I think you have certain core abilities. If you are going to be a growing person, you have to build on those core abilities—be willing to analyze yourself, find out where your deficiencies are, and then try to overcome those deficiencies and build your strengths. . . . My best learning experience was the Peace Corps. I left a good job in industry to find out who I really was and what was really important.

Scientific Learning

I call this last learning theme "scientific" because it resembles closely the popular model of scientific endeavor—cool, rational, and objective. The preferred pattern is to observe, conceptualize about the observations, and then experiment to collect new data. The focus is on truth—the facts and the concepts to organize those facts. An executive at the Department of Interior provided a succinct description of this learning theme:

> First you define the problem, the question, or the opportunity; assimilate the information that is relevant; and develop a concept about how it works or get other thoughts about how it works. Then you test that concept and collect data under actual con-

ditions or experience. Next you objectively review what results have occurred by putting the concept into practice. Then you bring that information back into the conceptualization, assimilate it into all the new information others have gathered, set a new base, and go from there around again. To a great extent, I've patterned my whole life in this way—much to the chagrin of my family.

Managers who learn in this way rely on others to stimulate interest in exploring something or inquire into things just because they present themselves. They are not particularly interested in relevant application of learning experiences. They want to know how things work because knowing about things is the preferred way of treating them. One manager I interviewed said that he had studied psychology not because he thought he would become a better manager but because people were always around and he thought he ought to know about them.

Although these are only rough descriptions of the learning themes revealed through my interviews with

Figure 2–8 INTERRELATIONSHIPS BETWEEN THE DIFFERENT COMPONENTS OF LEARNING

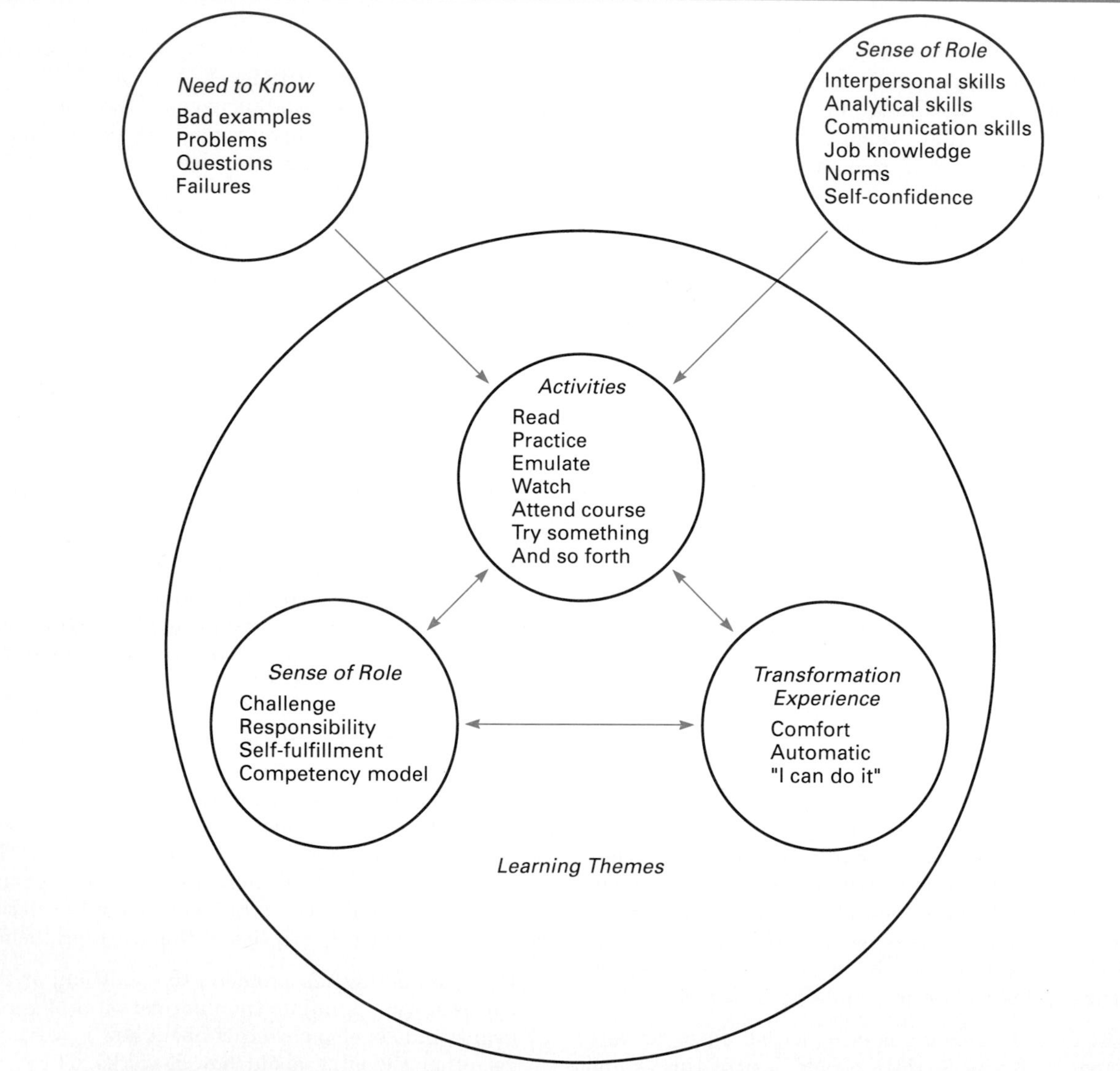

the 60 managers in my study, the work of some of my students supports the validity of these categories. After I had identified the themes from the first sets of interviews, I had four students conduct similar interviews and instructed them as to the characteristics of each emergent theme. When I asked each of the students to categorize the dominant learning theme independently in each interview, both those done by them and those done by me, each student usually designated the same theme. Any differences that arose were easily resolved through discussion. Apparently, the managers studied (and there is no reason to believe that they are particularly different from managers in general) have preferred ways of learning on which they rely in most situations. Those learning methods are readily identifiable using the categories above.

WHAT STARTS THE PROCESS

My description of the varieties of managerial learning experience started at the far end of the process—how learning is known—and proceeded to the activities that lead to the experience of having learned something. But how are these processes started in the first place? What triggers engagement in learning activities? What conditions a manager to treat situations as learning opportunities? These questions were explored next with each of the participants in the study.

I was not looking for the "causes" of learning or for the factors that "motivated" the managers to pursue learning activities. Rather, I was looking for descriptions of the initial and early parts of the experiences that account for a manager's achieving managerial competence. What were the beginnings of the learning process like for the learners?

The learning process invariably started with one or both of two conditions. These conditions were states of being for the learner, usually connected with external conditions but centered in the person. The conditions seemed to dispose the managers to treat situations in terms of learning something and sometimes to engage actively and intentionally in learning activities. When one or both of the conditions exist, learning is sure to follow, whatever else happens or whatever learning theme is being enacted.

The need to know is one of the two prelearning conditions described by the managers in the study. They described the need to know as rather like a thirst or a hunger, gnawing at them, sometimes dominating their attention until satisfied. When a person needs to know something, potential answers are everywhere. The need to know is associated with a variety of experiences, such as encountering poor practice, problems that demand solutions, or questions that have no answers. The most common and powerful experience associated with the need to know, and thus with the start of important learning, is actual failure. Every manager interviewed reported various concrete personal failures as the starting point of learning experiences critical to their managerial success.

Sense of role is the other prelearning condition described by the managers. More explicitly, the feeling that underpins the start of learning is related to a person's perception of the gap between what he or she is and what he or she should be. Wherever it arises, it results from a comparison of current skills, knowledge, and attitudes with those that characterize an ideal role model.

Sense of role is the adoption of a part to be played, which of course must be learned in some way. The role may be taken from any of a variety of sources external to the person, or it may be an internal sense of self to be fulfilled. The sense of role may be related to a challenge or a responsibility to be fulfilled. Whatever the source, some kind of explicit or implicit competency model is used as a standard. Regardless of its content or its source, the message says, "You should be. . . ."

A WAY OF BEING

Even though the descriptions of important learning events were presented in discrete pieces by the managers, the actual experience of learning is a lived whole for the learner. The parts I have described are not strictly separable. Learning is neither the activities nor the outcomes. Learning is exactly what the managers all knew it to be in their own experience.

Figure 2–8 illustrates the interrelationships between the different components of a learning experience. Remember that everything affects everything else in this model. The relevance of events for starting the process is probably affected by a person's preferred learning theme. Success or failure with certain activities probably shapes a person's preference for a learning theme. Depending on the learning theme enacted, outcomes will tend more or less to be the beginnings of new learning experiences.

THE MANAGER AS TEACHER

The managers who participated in this study have helped us understand the nature of effective learning in organizations. This information will help anyone who wants to promote managerial learning in organizations, including management training and development professionals. By knowing what triggers the pursuit of learning, more of the conditioning experiences can be built into organizational life. By understanding that different people learn in different ways, training and development experiences can be tailored to the needs and themes of the learner. This study also makes clear that managerial learners should be involved in the design of their own learning and development.

In *The Human Side of Enterprise* (McGraw-Hill, 1960), Douglas McGregor noted that, as a manager, you are always teaching. "Every encounter between superior and subordinate involves learning of some kind for the subordinate. . . . The day-to-day experience of the job is so much more powerful that it tends to overshadow what the individual may learn in other settings." Thus the manager who has the ability to help employees learn will be of great value.

In a 1916 paper in the *Annals of the American Academy of Political and Social Science,* Frank and Lillian Gilbreth, proteges of Frederick Taylor, introduced "the three-position plan of promotion." The plan is based on the three different roles that an organizational member plays at any one time: performing his or her assigned job, learning the next job in the progression, and *teaching his or her current job to the next occupant.* Organizational advancement and career progression are based on being a good learner *and* a good teacher. Learning itself fuels organizational and personal progress.

More recently, in their book *Managing for Excellence* (Wiley, 1984), David Bradford and Allan Cohen presented the leader as a developer. In part, they meant that a central task for the leader is helping others learn and grow. Part of what a manager has to teach is how to be an effective manager. However, to teach, which entails more than imparting information, a manager must have a model of how people learn and be able to use that model in the everyday practice of his or her job.

Managers can use the discoveries about the varieties of managerial learning to be a better teacher and to foster managerial learning in others. Part of a manager's task is to help others articulate the "need to know" and to help them develop competency models. These two "hooks" get the learning process started. The description of the seven typical learning themes makes it possible to play to a person's preferred way of learning. What will really hook someone to pursue learning? What learning activities will be preferred? What resources will be most helpful? And, what role should the manager play in the process?

Table 2–3 shows, for each learning theme, how to recognize when someone is using it, what is likely to hook the person to actively pursue some significant learning, and what activities and resources will be most useful. Table 2–3 also suggests the role the manager can play. What a manager does to be a developer will differ depending on the learner's preferred learning theme.

CAPITALIZE ON LEARNING STRENGTHS

The development of managerial excellence requires knowing not only what excellence is but also how managers attain it. By studying closely the actual learning experiences that account for how good managers become competent, I have identified seven distinct organizations of those experiences, or learning themes. The seven learning themes are the varieties of managerial learning.

This information can be useful in designing formal management training programs. The first step is to determine learning themes and arrange activities to capitalize on participants' learning strengths. This process will also encourage more active participation by the learner in his or her own learning experience and make it less like a typical classroom. As this study has shown, the most powerful learning experiences rarely happen in a classroom anyway.

Part of a manager's job is the development of managerial competence in others. Knowing how others learn and how to reach them through their own preferred learning theme will help the manager do that job well. For most managers, teaching probably does not happen formally but rather on the job in ongoing, everyday interactions. My findings about the rich variety of managerial learning experiences can be used to guide learners toward their full learning potential.

SELECTED BIBLIOGRAPHY

The analysis of the literature on supervision in social work that revealed the simplistic assumptions about learning originally appeared in an article I coauthored with Marie Weil, "The Prior Question: How Do Supervisors Learn to Supervise" (*Social Casework,* October 1981). In the United States, the most widely used work on management learning is that of David Kolb. His basic theory, including instrumentation, is described in *Learning Style Inventory: Technical Manual,* (McBer & Co., 1976). In England, the Center for the Study of Management Learning has a very robust research and training operation at the University of Lancaster. The Center's foundational work on how managers learn is found in John Burgoyne and Roger Stuart's "The Nature, Use, and Acquisition of Managerial Skills and Other Attributes" (*Personnel Review,* Autumn 1976).

The seminal work on adult, self-directed learning is that of Malcomb Knowles, especially his book *The*

Table 2–3 HOW TO RECOGNIZE AND SUPPORT DIFFERENT LEARNING THEMES

Learning Theme	Hook	Preferred Activities	Resources	How to Recognize	Role of Boss
Emulation of a Mentor	Contact with a guru Success story Competency model (actual person)	Watch Listen Emulate	Actual person to work beside Biographies Anecdotes Demonstrations	Tends to act like mentor Asks mentor what he or she would do if in same situation Justifies action by referring to what someone else has done	Model competencies Live preferred attitudes
Role Taking	Competency model (organizational expectations)	Question role incumbents Watch Get feedback from peers Seek formal, internal training	Job descriptions Company courses (with peers) Explicit professional standards Role models	Asks boss for expectations Emulates high-status peers Is concerned about fitting in Seeks information about "how we do things here"	Role sender Negotiate expectations Joint performance assessment
Practical Accomplish-ment	Problems to be solved; failure	Solve problems Try new situations Apply skills	Tools Skills from other domains Autonomy "An opportunity" Feedback from the task itself	Asks for opportunities to "fix things" Asks for autonomy Focuses on results	Assign problems Get work Delegate
Validation	Questions about failures or bad examples Questions about own practice	Ask expert Read Analyze situations Interpret Apply theory	Concepts Analytic tools Cases Discussion Expert commentator	Asks for feedback Prefers instruction followed by theory Likes to "debrief" situations	Expert commentator
Anticipation	Promise of future opportunities	Read Hear from "those who have been there" Watch examples Practice Predict	Concepts Instructions Practice opportunities Feedback from experts Demonstrations	Asks for concepts before taking on tasks Prefers to read about it before trying it Seeks trends to know how to prepare for the future	Expert instructor/ coach
Personal Growth	Model of the fully functioning person Utopias Questions of principle	Introspect Explore Discuss Extrapolate implications Build systems	Dilemmas Values Normative models Philosophical systems	Focuses on transformation beyond specific situations Asks value questions Wants to think about the "big picture"	Counsel Listen Encourage Show confidence
Scientific Learning	Puzzle Other peoples' problems Questions about the "nature of things"	Experiment Build models Observe Measure Analyze	Theories Scientific method "Facts" Technology Analytic tools	Objective and rational, given to abstraction	Create a dilemma Ask for help Pose a query

Modern Practice of Adult Education, (Association Press, 1970.) Allen Tough's research, reported in *The Adult's Learning Projects* (Learning Concepts, 1979), presents an empirically based theory of self-initiated learning by adults outside of school settings. Although many approaches to leadership imply the educational role for the manager, the idea of the leader as developer is most fully developed in David Bradford and Allan Cohen's *Managing for Excellence* (Wiley, 1984).

DISCUSSION QUESTIONS

1. Describe the six categories of managerial competence.
2. Compare and contrast the seven learning themes.
3. What interrelationships exist between the different components of learning, and what are their significance for managerial practice?

Reprinted, by permission of the publisher, from G. Akin, "Varieties of Managerial Learning," *Organizational Dynamics* (Fall 1987) © 1987. American Management Association, New York.

ACTIVITIES

Activity 2–1: FACTS AND INFERENCES

Step 1: Carefully read the following report and the observations based on it. Indicate whether you think the observations are true, false, or doubtful on the basis of the information presented in the report. Circle **T** if the observation is definitely true, circle **F** if the observation is definitely false, and circle **?** if the observation may be either true or false. Judge each observation in order. Do not re-read the observations after you have indicated your judgment and do not change any of your answers.

A well-liked college teacher had just completed making up the final examinations and had turned off the lights in the office. Just then a tall, dark, broad figure appeared and demanded the examination. The professor opened the drawer. Everything in the drawer was picked up and the individual ran down the corridor. The Dean was notified immediately.

1. The thief was tall, dark, and broad. T F ?
2. The professor turned off the lights. T F ?
3. A tall figure demanded the examination. T F ?
4. The examination was picked up by someone. T F ?
5. The examination was picked up by the professor. T F ?
6. A tall, dark figure appeared after the professor turned off the lights in the office. T F ?
7. The man who opened the drawer was the professor. T F ?
8. The professor ran down the corridor. T F ?
9. The drawer was never actually opened. T F ?
10. In this report three persons are referred to. T F ?

Step 2: In small groups, discuss your answers and then reach consensus about the answers. Write these answers in a separate place.

Step 3: The instructor will read the correct answers. Score the questions, once for you as an individual and again for your group.

Step 4: Discussion. Did your scores change? Why? Why do people answer these questions incorrectly?

This exercise is taken from Joseph A. Devito, *General Semantics: Guide and Workbook,* rev. ed. Deland, Fl.: Everett/Edwards, 1974, p. 55, and is reprinted with permission.

Activity 2–2: ATTRIBUTION EXERCISE

Step 1: Read the following scenario:

TROLLEY CAR CRASH HURTS 30*

About 30 persons were injured, none seriously, when an MBTA light rail vehicle bound for Lechmere derailed and struck a retaining wall on its approach to North Station shortly before 4 p.m. yesterday.

Robert L. Foster, MBTA chairman, said the accident apparently was caused by excessive speed. The trolley took a curve just before the station at 2 to 2½ times the mandated speed of 10–15 miles per hour, according to Foster.

MBTA officials said the retaining wall prevented the car from dropping 35 feet to the ground.

Foster said the vehicle, No. 3509, had been involved in three other derailments. The most recent, three weeks ago, also involved the driver of the trolley in yesterday's crash.

All the other derailments involved difficulties at a switching point in Kenmore Square.

Many of the 40 passengers on the vehicle yesterday were thrown to the floor. Witnesses described screaming and scenes of panic as the occupants tried unsuccessfully to open the door of the trolley and get out.

Passengers said it was "a few minutes" before MBTA officials were able to free them from the wreckage.

Valerie Mitchell, 18, of Somerville, said she closed her eyes when she saw that a crash was inevitable.

"People were screaming, 'stop, stop.' There was panic. A few were trying to calm others down. I was just trying to get out."

The front windshield of the trolley was smashed against the retaining wall, showering passengers with glass, according to passengers, and raining concrete and gravel onto Causeway Street below.

David Grant, manager of a restaurant under the elevated track, said "it rained gravel and concrete when it hit. The windshield was out, and the glass was all over the tracks. . . ."

. . . MBTA chairman Foster, who arrived at the scene about 20 minutes after the car derailed at 3:54 p.m., said that "the evidence at this point indicates that the operator was speeding. In that case, the operator was at error."

Foster said the driver . . . would be suspended from operating if he is found at fault in the accident.

Step 2: Individually or in small groups, as directed by your instructor, answer the following question: According to the article, who or what was responsible for the subway accident?

Step 3: Now read the following account of the same situation:

LRVs BLAMED BY CARMEN FOR CRASH ON GREEN LINE†

Faulty design and poor maintenance on all the light rail vehicles (LRVs) in the MBTA system were at least as likely a cause of Tuesday's trolley car crash as operator error, an official of the Boston Carmen's Union said yesterday.

George Adams, vice president of the union, also warned that "if nothing is done soon, we're not going to run those vehicles."

Adams agreed he did not know the cause "of this specific problem," but said, "We would like management not to be so hasty as to lay blame on human error. The history of these vehicles is faulty."

There have been more than 100 reported derailments of the sleek, articulated cars since they were first installed in January, 1977. Of the 175 cars originally ordered at a cost of $58.5 million, with another $50 million for track work, only 94 are actually in service here now. The rest are in storage.

MBTA spokesman Don Eagles said MBTA engineers had inspected the elevated structure where the crash occurred "and decided it was well within operating tolerances. . . ."

The speed limit at the curve, which is on an elevated structure just before the tracks enter a subway tunnel, is 10 miles per hour. Some passengers and Foster said the car was going perhaps as fast as 35 miles per hour. . . .

One union official, delegate James Slattery, spoke to (the driver) Tuesday night and reported yesterday that the driver said he was not speeding. The driver, a 20-year MBTA employee, was involved in another LRV derailment three weeks ago near Kenmore Station, but Eagles said yesterday, "He was only going 3 to 4 miles per hour. We're certain that speeding had nothing to do with that accident."

Nonetheless, Eagles said that Foster "still feels there was some truth in attributing part of the cause to speeding."

Step 4: Individually or in small groups, as directed by your instructor, answer the following question: According to this article, who or what was responsible for the subway accident?

Step 5: In small groups or with the entire class, answer the following questions:

Description

1. How do the two accounts of the subway accident differ?

Diagnosis

2. Who is responsible for the accident?
3. How does our knowledge of attributional biases allow us to predict the differences between the two versions?
4. What is the most likely cause of the accident?

Prescription

5. How can we and those involved in the situation correctly attribute the cause of the accident?

*"Trolley Car Crash Hurts 30" by Timothy Dwyer and Ben Bradlee, *The Boston Globe,* April 25, 1979. Reprinted courtesy of *The Boston Globe.*

†"LRVs Blamed for Crash on Green Line" by Gary McMillan, *The Boston Globe,* April 26, 1979. Reprinted courtesy of *The Boston Globe.*

Activity 2–3: A-PLUS AERONAUTICS

Step 1: Read the following case. (Your instructor will distribute the performance charts to you.)

A-Plus Aeronautics is an electronics firm that manufactures components for instrument control panels used in commercial jets. The company operates as a large job shop, routing custom-ordered products through the work centers in three major shop areas: Fabrication, Assembly, and Testing. There are several work centers in each shop. The custom-ordered products are manufactured in lots of approximately 100 to 1000, with each item flowing through at least 30 work centers on its way to completion.

Subcomponents such as circuit boards are assembled in the Assembly Shop, where there are 15 different work centers dedicated to particular kinds of technologies and tasks. The 100 employees in this shop are highly skilled and most of them have been with the company for five or more years.

Hanna Yates is a first line supervisor for the employees in Work Center 7 of the Assembly Shop. She was transferred to this position from Testing and has not previously held a strictly supervisory position. There are 15 people reporting to her, 10 of whom are on the day shift, and five of whom are on the night shift. The performance of day-shift employees is the easiest to monitor because it is possible for Hanna to observe them. Performance of night-shift employees is more difficult to monitor, however, and she relies heavily on daily performance charts generated by the company computer as a source of information about this group. Hanna has learned through informal channels that there may be a performance problem, having to do with declining output, during the night shift. She refers to her performance charts to see what the problem might be.

Step 2: Answer the following questions as if you were Hanna, using only the information available to you. Respond to each one by circling the number that best represents your assessment of the situation.

1. How would you rate the seriousness of employee "C's" output decline?

1	2	3	4	5	6	7
not serious			moderately serious			extremely serious

2. What is the likelihood that the problem has something to do with employee "C" him/herself (e.g., effort, ability, attitude)?

1	2	3	4	5	6	7
not likely			moderate likelihood			extremely likely

3. What is the likelihood that the problem has something to do with the work environment (e.g., task difficulty, materials, equipment, available information)?

1	2	3	4	5	6	7
not likely			moderate likelihood			extremely likely

Step 3: Your instructor will direct you in tallying the questionnaire results and displaying them.

Step 4: Discussion. In small groups, with the entire class, or in writing, as directed by your instructor, answer the following questions:

Description

1. How did the ratings of Group A and Group B differ?

Diagnosis

2. Would attribution theory have predicted these differences?
3. How do attributional biases influence supervisors' diagnostic judgments?

Prescription

4. How could we improve their judgments?

This exercise was drawn from Karen Brown and Terence Mitchell, Teaching attribution theory with graphical displays of performance comparisons, *The Organizational Behavior Teaching Journal* 8(3)(1983): 23–28.

Activity 2–4: CREDIT COMES SOUTH CASE

Step 1: Read the Credit Comes South case.

Birmingham Industries is one of the nation's leading producers of textiles for apparel, home furnishings and industrial markets. Their expected sales for the coming year should be in the vicinity of $500 million with a net income of over $20 million. The main headquarters are located in New York City due mainly to the proximity of the apparel and money markets. These offices house the Chairman of the Board, several Vice-Presidents, the Treasurer, Controller, sales functions and Credit department.

The southern headquarters for the corporation is located in Raleigh and is the hub for the over twenty-five plants located in the southeastern United States. These offices are manned by 250 employees, headed by the corporation's president. It functions as a service center and supplies the plants with centralized staff departments such as purchasing, engineering, accounting, information services, industrial engineering, transportation and research and development.

Birmingham Industries deviates somewhat from traditional textile administrative customs, probably due to its diversity of products. Such a deviation is the credit operation which is normally a function factored by most companies in the textile industry.

Until June of this year the entire credit function was handled from the New York office. The various company divisions were spread among three credit managers who reported directly to the treasurer. Each manager had several credit analysts (10 altogether) directly reporting to him, and some of the analysts had assistants with the title of collection men.

At the beginning of the year the decision was made to "consider moving a portion of the credit function to the Raleigh office." The final decision was to be based on the following:

1. The availability of qualified personnel, in the immediate area, to staff the department.
2. The number of experienced workers in the New York department that would move south.
3. The effect, on the remaining staff, of terminating those personnel who would not relocate.
4. The divisions or areas of credit that could be handled as well in the south as in New York.
5. The expenses and savings of such a move.
6. The availability of resources (space, equipment, communication) in the Raleigh office.

Many other criteria were also used in making the final decision, however, it all ultimately culminated in the newly formed "Southern Credit office."

One of the present credit managers in the New York office was offered the top post in the new department, however, he turned it down when the company would not meet his demands for a substantial salary increase (he was subsequently terminated). Jack O'Brian, an aggressive young credit analyst, was then given the opportunity to make this new department work. . . . He accepted.

The staff was to be made up of one manager, four credit analysts, two collection men and three secretaries. Only one other man from the New York credit department accepted the offer to move to North Carolina. The remainder of the staff were recruited and hired by the personnel department in the Raleigh office. The men were interviewed personally by both Jack and Mr. Donivan, the treasurer of the corporation. The secretaries were first screened by personnel and then interviewed by Jack alone.

By June 14th the construction required to expand the new office area was complete and most of the file cabinets and equipment were in place. In a few days the office was buzzing with the sounds of a busy staff trying to get oriented to the new environment. A sketch of the office shows the final layout as designed by the treasurer (Figure 2–9).

Figure 2–9 NEW OFFICE LAYOUT

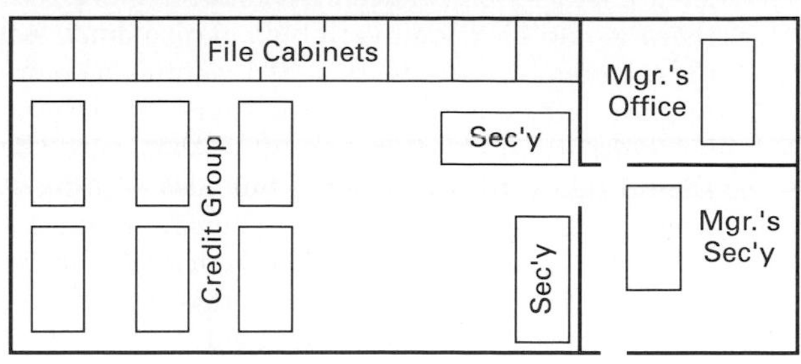

On July 21st, Bobbie Leigh, the manager's secretary, quit after working for just over one month.

This came as quite a surprise to Jack O'Brian as well as the personnel department. There didn't seem to be any problems, then all of a sudden she was handing in her two week notice.

The following is an excerpt from her exit interview:

Q. Why did you quit?

A. So many reasons, it's hard to put in a nut shell.....It's more or less working "for" instead of "with".....I want to feel I'm part of the team.....I want to feel equal.....

Q. Equal to the other girls or the men in the office?

A. The men.....I want to feel equal to the men.....That's terrible isn't it!

Q. What made you feel unequal?

A. I don't know.....I felt he (the manager) didn't trust my judgment.....I feel that this whole corporation is very male oriented.....I can see the men getting special privileges within our department and that doesn't seem right.....They don't work as hard as we do.....yet I'm sure they're paid on a far larger scale.....even their pay checks aren't distributed like ours.....special handled (monthly vs. weekly payroll).....and I guess those things make them appear special.....I'm not really for Women's Lib in the violent, dramatic sort of way, I just feel that a woman can handle a job as equal as any man.....In fact I can see in our office that the women are, more or less, doing the work for the men as far as the actual paperwork involved and they are chatting on the phone.....I'd rather be chatting on the phone than doing paperwork.....I feel I could handle any Credit Analyst's job, with more fineness than I've seen there.....and I don't see any future for me.....you know, in credit.....I'm always looking for a chance for advancement and I can see that there would be none available.....I also don't feel appreciated, I don't mean that I want to be pampered or babied.....but just to be appreciated would be so great.....I think in any office that, sure you should get your work done, but also I think it would be the ideal situation to be able to have a rapport where one can have a friendly conversation with their superior, I think this is good.

Q. Could you talk with your manager?

A. No.....I tried to.....maybe I'm too pushy.

Q. Do you think you're too pushy?

A. Yes.....you should have seen me at my last job at Biscayne (2 year business college).....I was.....well, admission secretary, but just before I left we had new accounts to sell and I took over and that was a man's job.....money started coming in because I was on commission.....it was easy.....of course if someone needed me I would have to be there, even at 8:30 in the evening.....my hours were very flexible because it depended on when I had an appointment.....I could even play tennis for a couple of hours in the day if there were no appointments.....

Q. Why did you leave, was there more money here?

A. Oh no! I was paid better there, however, they were in the process of cutting salaries and tightening their belts to improve profits.....the competition from a local technical school was beginning to hurt them.

Q. That sounds like a selling type of job, have you done pure secretarial work before?

A. Yes.....but what I'm doing now has no challenge, it's a very dull type of atmosphere.....I'm sure it's exciting for the men because they have a little bit of power there.

Q. What kind of power?

A. You know, they can refuse a customer.....decide on how much credit to give him.

Q. Were you given a complete job description before you were hired?

A. No one is going to believe me, no one has believed me, but I swear he just kept saying "my secretary, my secretary".....Peggy (personnel) kept saying "Mr. O'Brian's secretary".....if he had said secretary to me, also to two other people, I'd have said, "hey, this is not enough money".....'cause it isn't.....don't get me wrong, I like to stay busy, I like working hard, in a way, because it keeps the day from dragging.....What bothered me was that on the second week when the men came in it was then that I realized I was working for three instead of one.

Q. How were you told about the other two men?

A. I was so stupid.....Jack told me there was to be some phone switches installed, one to his desk and two more at the rear desks so that if those men were out or busy I could pick up.....but he felt that there would not be much need for that.....I still didn't catch on that I'd be working for them.....I didn't stop to think.....I knew that during the interview he said I would be preparing tickers for some of the other men.....but I still didn't tie it together.....but I think it was a matter of self-importance (the manager's self-importance).....he kept describing himself, his duties, his power, his contacts and things like that.....and how it would relate to me.....being his secretary and all, that I didn't realize that anyone else was involved and he did the same thing to my replacement, Mary. He kept saying as my secretary this, and as my secretary that.....but of course she already knew (about the additional duties).....

Q. How did you get along with the two other men once you realized you'd also be working for them?

A. Well, I don't think it would have mattered that much but.....well, let me give you an example.....I had been working through breaks and after five trying to get my head above water and Fred said, "Tiger, when are you ever going to get my filing done, it's stacking up over my head!".....and he was right, it was piling up.....but then Jack said, "Well, what have you been doing".....I didn't feel I had to stop and tell him what I'd been doing when I had been going as fast as I possibly could.....nothing was said like "you've been doing a good job".....just "what have you been doing?".....there was no appreciation for what you did, just accountability for what you didn't do!.....

Q. Did the other two men give a lot of orders?

A. Well, I heard one of the men say (when they were first organizing the department), "when my secretary gets in she'll be doing everything for me".....and I think this is about the attitude that they have.....when your desk is next to the file cabinets and you need two files pulled, and your secretary is in an entirely different room and it will require you to walk 40 feet to get her, wouldn't it be easier to go to the file cabinet yourself, pull the two folders and return to your desk?.....Well, they would come all the way into my office, give me the ticker and I would follow them back to almost their desk to pull the folders.

Q. Do you work in teams, either with the men or the other secretaries?

A. Mary has a Credit Analyst and a Collection man, so does Lynn, where I have two Credit Analysts and the manager.....you see, this department started from scratch, down to the pencils.....I've bugged purchasing to death.....they hate to see me coming.....my name's mud everywhere, the storeroom, maintenance, engineering.....you know!.....

Jack had to look at a dozen catalogs to buy one ashtray for his office.

Q. Who did you like best in your office and why?

A. Scott (no reporting relationship) because he's cheerful, friendly, very easy to work with and easy to please.....he's businesslike but comfortable to be with.....I think working for him would be fun!

Q. Who did you least like working with and why?

A. Lester (direct reporting relationship).....hey, this is hard to say.....well, for example these files that came down from New York go back years and Lester feels we should go through and update all the files.....I know they're in bad shape, but we're just trying to get started and every night Lester would have 25 or 30 folders to update that would need eight letters for references.....he makes me feel subservient.

Q. Are you training your replacement?

A. Jack called me in to tell me that Mary was going to get my job and the training period will start next Monday and that since both our jobs were so similar that all I would really have to do is show her where I kept the pencils.....it really hurt my feelings because I had worked so hard to accomplish this that.....gee, I really thought I had something.....I have a two year degree in secretarial science, keep house, raise a family, and work all at the same time.....I thought I had really accomplished something. I guess I felt almost as arrogant as he did!.....so I figured here is this person who was a beautician (Mary) for ten years and worked for Sears on the floor.....and she was taking over my job.....Jack had a way of making me feel inadequate.

Q. Is that the main reason you're leaving?

A. No, the main reason I'm leaving is because I'm not happy, I don't feel comfortable.....think about it, most of your waking hours are spent on the job.....then why can't your job be something delightful? People don't realize how much I'm by myself.....my office is separated from the others and the only contact I have is when they bring me some work to put on my desk.....they'll be in the outer credit office talking and laughing and they can enjoy each other, but I can't! Oh, that reminds me of something that happened.....I think Mr. Donivan is a really nice man (The Treasurer of the corporation, whom she has never met).....I really like him.....I liked him immediately as soon as I heard his voice on the phone.....his voice had character.....he would call several times a day.....and he would call me Bobbie and I would say, "Well, how are you?" and he'd say "I'm fine Bobbie, how are you?" and I'd say "Well how's the weather in New York?" and he said "Oh, not too good!" and I'd say something like "Oh it's beautiful here today and what a beautiful view we have out the back window, you should be here" and he'd say "Well I'll be coming down soon" and I'd say "I'm looking forward to meeting you, hurry down".....well, Jack overheard this one day and nearly had a stroke! He said, "Oh, Mr. Donivan is such a professional, I just don't think it would be advisable to chit-chat with him over the phone, he's just too busy!".....I couldn't believe it.....I thought, "well, is he ashamed of me?.....does he feel I'm not capable of carrying on a normal conversation with his superior?".....he may be scared to death of him, but I'm not a bit afraid of him.....I'm just as good as Mr. Donivan!.....You know, people with positions like Mr. Donivan.....they don't feel as important as Jack does!

Q. Did you ever try to make suggestions to Jack which might improve conditions in the Credit department?

A. I tried.....I went in three weeks ago and told him that I just can't seem to get everything done.....keep up my filing, sort mail, get the reports and everything else.....he said "Why is it you can't? You don't seem to realize that everybody has a lot of work to do".....and I thought, well, if you can't talk to him.....if you work your butt off and that's not enough and you go to him for some help.....and it does no good, why bother?

Q. When you told Jack that you planned to quit, did you leave him any options?

A. I went into his office Friday afternoon.....I realize it was a bad time cause he was getting ready to go out of town around six.....this was around four.....Fred had just asked me why I hadn't gotten his filing done and Lester wanted to know why I didn't get his letters sent out.....and I went in to tell Jack that I hadn't had time to get those things done.....and Jack said "What have you been doing?".....I told him that I didn't think that anyone should be on my back wanting to know why I hadn't done something!.....I don't think this is asking too much.....I had been working hard all day!.....I told him that I didn't think the work load was fair.....working for these three men was like working for six.....and the other girls had only two each.....I just don't think it's fair.....and he said, "Actually Lynn and Mary have more paperwork than you do!.....so what's your problem?".....so I said my problem is that I want to leave.....that I'm not happy here.....he said to hold off until we could discuss this on Wednesday when he got back.

Q. Did he discuss it when he got back?

A. He said, "Well, did you decide that you want to leave?".....and I said "Yes".....so that was it!.....he doesn't care, don't ya see, he just doesn't care.....he thinks that I'm stupid!

After the interview someone from the personnel department went to the Credit Department to find out more about Bobbie. His first stop was at Jack's office where the following conversation took place.

Personnel: Jack, did Bobbie get a complete job description on her interview?

O'Brian: Absolutely.....she knew exactly what her job was going to be like.....as best as I knew it at the time! You know this was a completely new department and in the beginning a lot of changes had to be made.....but I definitely told her she'd be working for some other credit men as well as myself.

Personnel: What were your feelings about Bobbie after the initial interview?

O'Brian: She was "gangbusters".....really came on strong.....seemed bright, and with her skills and education she was more than qualified. In fact, I was joking with some of the guys in New York.....that she'd probably have my job in a couple of weeks.

Personnel: Did your feelings about Bobbie change?

O'Brian: Well,.....her work was acceptable, but she wasn't grasping some of the department concepts as rapidly as I first thought she would.....She also started directing the other girls.....so I had to call her in to put a stop to that.....I told her that Mary and Lynn report to their respective credit men and not to her!

Personnel: Was there anything else?

O'Brian: Yes,.....she treated Fred and Lester as though they were a secondary portion of her job.....a nuisance.....it bothered her to do anything for them.....I was afraid this would lead to additional conflicts in the department morale.

Personnel: I guess that's it then!

O'Brian: Another thing bothered me.....she was a "people person".....she would strike up an immediate conversation with a complete stranger.....if a customer came in she'd start right off by telling them about her family life, her vacation.....about anything.....she even did this with the treasurer!.....and she was always too nice!

Personnel: Too nice?

O'Brian: Sounds crazy, doesn't it!.....but she would "please" and "excuse me" and "thank you" and "pardon me" and "I appreciate it" and "you are welcome" me to death!.....with all these adjectives it took her ten minutes to tell me who was holding on my line! (phone)

Personnel: When she quit were you surprised?

O'Brian: Surprised?.....yes, but also somewhat relieved.....I could see some more serious problems developing and this would solve several of them.

Personnel: Do you mind if I talk to some of your men?

O'Brian: No, go right ahead.

The next day in the office cafeteria the man from personnel saw some of the credit men gathered around a table sipping coffee.

Personnel: Mind if I join you all?

Credit Men: No, sit down.

Personnel: I hear Bobbie is leaving!

Lester: Ya, thank God!

Personnel: You didn't like her?

Lester: She was dumb.

Personnel: Oh really.....she seemed pretty bright to me!

Fred: Oh, he doesn't mean that kind of dumb.....she just had no common sense.....she was naive to normal business rapport.

Lester: Last week she addressed a letter to a customer using just the city, in this case it was New York.....so the letter came back today!.....Also, the other day I gave her five "short payment" notices for the same customer.....She wrote five separate letters instead of attaching all five to one letter!.....that's dumb!

Fred: I don't think she ever worked in an office before.....she would interrupt a meeting between Jack and I just to see if it was alright to buy a pair of scissors and if you needed something.....like a tape dispenser.....it would take her three days just to get the order up to the purchasing department.

Personnel: I take it you're glad to see her go?

Lester: You bet!

Fred: To be honest, Lester, you'll have to admit she had a good personality.....and her attitude wasn't that bad.

Lester: She talked too much!

Fred: She did give us more information than we really needed.....like when she took a call she'd tell us who it was, the company, what they wanted, etc.....All I wanted was his name!

Lester: .....and she was too damn nice!

Fred: Ha-Ha!.....he's right you know.....she was so sugary it was sickening.....when she came in the room everything got syrupy.

Lester: I guess that wouldn't be bad under normal conditions but we talk with irate customers and obstinate salesmen all day.....I guess the contrast was too great.

Fred: Ya,.....I think she'd make a good receptionist!

They all got up and went back to the credit department.

Step 2: Prepare the case for class discussion.

Step 3: Answer each of the following questions, individually or in small groups, as directed by your instructor.

Description

1. What was Bobbie Leigh's perception of the situation in the Southern Credit Office?
2. What data influenced her perception?
3. How accurate was her perception?
4. What was Jack O'Brian's perception of the situation in the office?
5. What data influenced his perception?
6. How accurate was his perception?
7. What were the credit men's perceptions?
8. How did Leigh's, O'Brian's, and the credit men's perceptions differ?

Diagnosis

9. What factors influenced these perceptions?
10. What were Leigh's attributions of the reasons for her declining performance?
11. What were O'Brian's attributions of the reasons for her declining performance?
12. What factors explain their attributions?
13. How do their attitudes toward their work situation differ?
14. How did the cultural context of the case affect their perceptions and attributions?

Prescription

15. How could the situation have been improved?

Step 4: Discussion. In small groups, with the class as a whole, or in written form, share your answers to the questions above. Then answer the following questions.

1. What symptoms suggest a problem exists?
2. What problems exist in the case?
3. What theories and concepts help explain those problems?
4. How can the problems be corrected?
5. Are the actions likely to be effective?

Case prepared by Edward F. Mills under the supervision of Professor Virginia Guerin. Available in looseleaf form from Lord Publishing, Inc., One Apple Hill, Natick, Mass. 01760. (508) 651-9955 for information.

Activity 2–5: THE ROAD TO HELL CASE

Step 1: Read the Road to Hell case.

John Baker, Chief Engineer of the Caribbean Bauxite Company of Barracania in the West Indies, was making his final preparations to leave the island. His promotion to production manager of Keso Mining Corporation near Winnipeg—one of Continental Ore's fast-expanding Canadian enterprises—had been announced a month before and now everything had been tidied up except the last vital interview with his successor—the able young Barracanian, Matthew Rennalls. It was vital that this interview be a success and that Rennalls should leave his office uplifted and encouraged to face the challenge of his new job. A touch on the bell would have brought Rennalls walking into the room but Baker delayed the moment and gazed thoughtfully through the window, considering just exactly what he was going to say and, more particularly, how he was going to say it.

John Baker, an English expatriate, was 45 years old and had served his 23 years with Continental Ore in many different places: in the Far East; several countries of Africa; Europe; and, for the last two years, in the West Indies. He hadn't cared much for his previous assignment in Hamburg and was delighted when the West Indian appointment came through. Climate was not the only attraction. Baker had always preferred working overseas (in what were termed the developing countries) because he felt he had an innate knack—better than most other expatriates working for Continental Ore—of knowing just how to get on with regional staff. Twenty-four hours in Barracania, however, soon made him realize that he would need all of this "innate knack" if he was to deal effectively with the problems in this field that now awaited him.

At his first interview with Hutchins, the production manager, the whole problem of Rennalls and his future was discussed. There and then it was made quite clear to Baker that one of his most important tasks would be the "grooming" of Rennalls as his successor. Hutchins had pointed out that, not only was Rennalls one of the brightest Barracanian prospects on the staff of Caribbean Bauxite—at London University he had taken first-class honours in the B.Sc. Engineering degree—but, being the son of the Minister of Finance and Economic Planning, he had no small political pull.

The company had been particularly pleased when Rennalls decided to work for them rather than for the Government in which his father had such a prominent post. They ascribed his action to the effect of their vigorous and liberal regionalisation programme which, since the Second World War, had produced eighteen Barracanians at mid-management level and given Caribbean Bauxite a good lead in respect over all other international concerns operating in Barracania. The success of this timely regionalisation policy had led to excellent relations with the Government—a relationship which had been given an added importance when Barracania, three years later, became independent—an occasion which encouraged a critical and challenging attitude towards the role foreign interests would have to play in the new Barracania. Hutchins had therefore little difficulty in convincing Baker that the successful career development of Rennalls was of the first importance.

The interview with Hutchins was now two years old and Baker, leaning back in his office chair, reviewed just how successful he had been in the "grooming" of Rennalls. What aspects of the latter's character had helped and hindered? What about his own personality? How had that helped or hindered? The first item to go on the credit side would, without question, be the ability of Rennalls to master the technical aspects of his job. From the start he had shown keenness and enthusiasm and had often impressed Baker with his ability in tackling new assignments and the constructive comments he invariably made in departmental discussions. He was popular with all ranks of Barracanian staff and had an ease of manner which stood him in good stead when dealing with his expatriate seniors. These were all assets, but what about the debit side?

First and foremost, there was his racial consciousness. His four years at London University had accentuated this feeling and made him sensitive to any sign of condescension on the part of expatriates. It may have been to give expression to this sentiment that, as soon as he returned home from London, he threw himself into politics on behalf of the United Action Party who were later to win the preindependence elections and provide the country with its first Prime Minister.

The ambitions of Rennalls—and he certainly was ambitious—did not, however, lie in politics for, staunch nationalist as he was, he saw that he could serve himself and his country best—for was not bauxite responsible for nearly half the value of Barracania's export trade?—by putting his engineering talent to the best use possible. On this account, Hutchins found that he had an unexpectedly easy task in persuading Rennalls to give up his political work before entering the production department as an assistant engineer.

It was, Baker knew, Rennalls' well repressed sense of race consciousness which had prevented their relationship from being as close as it should have been. On the surface, nothing could have seemed more agreeable. Formality between the two men was at a minimum; Baker was delighted to find that his assistant shared his own peculiar "shaggy dog" sense of humour so that jokes were continually being exchanged; they entertained each other at their homes and often played tennis together—and yet the barrier remained invisible, indefinable, but ever present. The existence of this "screen" between them was a constant source of frustration to Baker since it indicated a weakness which he was loath to accept. If successful with all other nationalities, why not with Rennalls?

But at least he had managed to "break through" to Rennalls more successfully than any other expatriate. In fact, it was the young Barracanian's attitude—sometimes overbearing; sometimes cynical—towards other company expatriates that had been one of the subjects Baker had raised last year when he discussed Rennalls' staff report with him. He knew, too, that he would have to raise the same subject again in the forthcoming interview because Jackson, the senior draughtsman, had complained only yesterday about the rudeness of Rennalls. With this thought in mind, Baker leaned forward and spoke into the intercom: "Would you come in, Matt, please? I'd like a word with you," and later, "Do sit down," proffering the box, "have a cigarette." He paused while he held out his lighter and then went on.

"As you know, Matt, I'll be off to Canada in a few days' time, and before I go, I thought it would be useful if we could have a final chat together. It is indeed with some deference that I suggest I can be of help. You will shortly be sitting in this chair doing the job I am now doing, but I, on the other hand, am ten years older, so perhaps you can accept the idea that I may be able to give you the benefit of my longer experience."

Baker saw Rennalls stiffen slightly in his chair as he made this point so added in explanation, "You and I have attended enough company courses to remember those repeated requests by the personnel manager to tell people how they are getting on as often as the convenient moment arises and not just the automatic 'once a year' when, by regulation, staff reports have to be disclosed."

Rennalls nodded his agreement so Baker went on, "I shall always remember the last job performance discussion I had with my previous boss back in Germany. He used what he called the "plus and minus" technique. His firm belief was that when a senior, by discussion, seeks to improve the work performance of his staff, his prime objective should be to make sure that the latter leaves the interview encouraged and inspired to improve. Any criticism must, therefore, be constructive and helpful. He said that one very good way to encourage a man—and I fully agree with him—is to tell him about his good points—the plus factors—as well as his weak ones—the minus factors—so I thought, Matt, it would be a good idea to run our discussion along these lines."

Rennalls offered no comment, so Baker continued: "Let me say, therefore, right away, that, as far as your own work performance is concerned, the plus far outweighs the minus. I have, for instance, been most impressed with the way you have adapted your considerable theoretical knowledge to master the practical techniques of your job—that ingenious method you used to get air down to the fifth-shaft level is a sufficient case in point—and at departmental meetings I have invariably found your comments well taken and helpful. In fact, you will be interested to know that only last week I reported to Mr. Hutchins that, from the technical point of view, he could not wish for a more able man to succeed to the position of chief engineer."

"That's very good indeed of you, John," cut in Rennalls with a smile of thanks, "My only worry now is how to live up to such a high recommendation."

"Of that I am quite sure," returned Baker, "especially if you can overcome the minus factor which I would like now to discuss with you. It is one which I have talked about before so I'll come straight to the point. I have noticed that you are more friendly and get on better with your fellow Barracanians than you do with Europeans. In point of fact, I had a complaint only yesterday from Mr. Jackson, who said you had been rude to him—and not for the first time either.

"There is, Matt, I am sure, no need for me to tell you how necessary it will be for you to get on well with expatriates because until the company has trained up sufficient men of your calibre, Europeans are bound to occupy senior positions here in Barracania. All this is vital to your future interests, so can I help you in any way?"

While Baker was speaking on this theme, Rennalls had sat tensed in his chair and it was some seconds before he replied. "It is quite extraordinary, isn't it, how one can convey an impression to others so at variance with what one intends? I can only assure you once again that my disputes with Jackson—and you may remember also Godson—have had nothing at all to do with the colour of their skins. I promise you that if a Barracanian had behaved in an equally peremptory manner I would have reacted in precisely the same way. And again, if I may say it within these four walls, I am sure I am not the only one who had found Jackson and Godson difficult. I could mention the names of several expatriates who have felt the same. However, I am really sorry to have created this impression of not being able to get on with Europeans—it is entirely a false one—and I quite realise that I must do all I can to correct it as quickly as possible. On your last point, regarding Europeans holding senior positions in the Company for some time to come, I quite accept the situation. I know that Caribbean Bauxite—as they have been doing for many years now—will promote Barracanians as soon as their experience warrants it. And, finally, I would like to assure you, John—and my father thinks the same too—that I am very happy in my work here and hope to stay with the company for many years to come."

Rennalls had spoken earnestly and, although not convinced by what he had heard, Baker did not think he could pursue the matter further except to say, "All right, Matt, my impression *may* be wrong, but I would like to remind you about the truth of that old saying, 'What is important is not what is true but what is believed,' Let it rest at that."

But suddenly Baker knew that he didn't want to "let it rest at that." He was disappointed once again at not being able to "break through" to Rennalls and having yet again to listen to his bland denial that there was any racial prejudice in his make-up. Baker, who had intended ending the interview at this point, decided to try another tack.

"To return for a moment to the 'plus and minus technique' I was telling you about just now, there is another plus factor I forgot to mention. I would like to congratulate you not only on the calibre of your work but also on the ability you have shown in overcoming a challenge which I, as a European, have never had to meet.

"Continental Ore is, as you know, a typical commercial enterprise—admittedly a big one—which is a product of the economic and social environment of the United States and Western Europe. My ancestors have all been brought up in this environment for the past two or three hundred years and I have, therefore, been able to live in a world in which commerce (as we know it today) has been part and parcel of my being. It has not been something revolutionary and new which has suddenly entered my life. In your case," went on Baker, "the situation is different because you and your forebears have only had some fifty or sixty years' experience of this commercial environment. You have had to face the challenge of bridging the gap between fifty and two or three hundred years. Again, Matt, let me congratulate you—and people like you—once again on having so successfully overcome this particular hurdle. It is for this very reason that I think the outlook for Barracania—and particularly Caribbean Bauxite—is so bright."

Rennalls had listened intently and when Baker finished, replied, "Well, once again, John, I have to thank you for what you have said, and for my part, I can only say that it is gratifying to know that my own personal effort has been so much appreciated. I hope that more people will soon come to think as you do."

There was a pause and, for a moment, Baker thought hopefully that he was about to achieve his long awaited "breakthrough," but Rennalls merely smiled back. The barrier remained unbreached. There remained some five minutes' cheerful conversation about the contrast between the Caribbean and Canadian climate and whether the West Indies had any hope of beating England in the Fifth Test before Baker drew the interview to a close. Although he was as far as ever from knowing the real Rennalls, he was nevertheless glad that the interview had run along in this friendly manner and, particularly, that it had ended on such a cheerful note.

This feeling, however, lasted only until the following morning. Baker had some farewells to make, so he arrived at the office considerably later than usual. He had no sooner sat down at his desk than his secretary walked into the room with a worried frown on her face. Her words came fast. "When I arrived this morning I found Mr. Rennalls already waiting at my door. He seemed very angry and told me in quite a peremptory manner that he had a vital letter to dictate which must be sent off without any delay. He was so worked up that he couldn't keep still and kept pacing about the room, which is most unlike him. He wouldn't even wait to read what he had dictated, just signed the page where he thought the letter would end. It has been distributed and your copy is in your 'in tray.' "

Puzzled and feeling vaguely uneasy, Baker opened the "Confidential" envelope and read the following letter:

From: Assistant Engineer

To: The Chief Engineer, Caribbean Bauxite Limited
14th August, 196-

Assessment of Interview Between Messrs. Baker and Rennalls

It has always been my practice to respect the advice given me by seniors, so after our interview, I decided to give careful thought once again to its main points and so make sure that I had understood all that had been said. As I promised you at the time, I had every intention of putting your advice to the best effect.

It was not, therefore, until I had sat down quietly in my home yesterday evening to consider the interview objectively that its main purport became clear. Only then did the full enormity of what you said dawn on me. The more I thought about it, the more convinced I was that I had hit upon the real truth—and the more furious I became. With a facility in the English language which I—a poor Barracanian—cannot hope to match, you had the audacity to insult me (and through me every Barracanian worth his salt) by claiming that our knowledge of modern living is only a paltry fifty years old whilst yours goes back 200–300 years. As if your materialistic commercial environment could possibly be compared with the spiritual values of our culture. I'll have you know that if much of what I saw in London is representative of your most boasted culture, I hope fervently that it will never come to Barracania. By what right do you have the effrontery to condescend to us? At heart, all you Europeans think us barbarians, or, as you say amongst yourselves, we are "just down from the trees."

Far into the night I discussed this matter with my father, and he is as disgusted as I. He agrees with me that any company whose senior staff think as you do is no place for any Barracanian proud of his culture and race—so much for all the company "claptrap" and specious propaganda about regionalisation and Barracania for the Barracanians.

I feel ashamed and betrayed. Please accept this letter as my resignation which I wish to become effective immediately.

cc: Production Manager
Managing Director

Step 2: Prepare the case for class discussion.

Step 3: Answer each of the following questions, individually or in small groups, as directed by your instructor.

Description

1. What was Baker's perception of Rennalls?
2. How did Baker's perception change during the case description?
3. What was Rennalls's perception of Baker?
4. How did Rennalls's perception change during the case description?
5. How did Rennalls's and Baker's perceptions differ?

Diagnosis

6. What factors influenced Baker's perceptions?
7. What were Baker's attributions of the reasons for Rennalls's behavior toward him?
8. What factors influenced Rennalls's perceptions?
9. What were Rennalls's attributions of the reasons for Baker's behavior toward him?
10. What factors explain their attributions?
11. What learning occurred during the case?
12. What factors affected the learning?
13. What were Baker's and Rennalls's attitudes toward the situation?
14. How did they form?
15. How did the cultural setting of Barracania influence the situation?

Prescription

16. How could the situation have been improved?

Step 4: Discussion. In small groups, with the class as a whole, or in written form, share your answers to the questions above. Then answer the following questions:

1. What symptoms suggest a problem exists?
2. What problems exist in the case?
3. What theories and concepts help explain those problems?
4. How can the problems be corrected?
5. Are the actions likely to be effective?

Activity 2–6: LEARNING BY MODELING

Step 1: Select a (target) behavior you wish a fellow student, friend, or coworker to acquire.

Step 2: Develop a social modeling strategy to use to help the other person acquire this behavior.

Step 3: Implement the strategy.

Step 4: Discussion. In small groups or with the entire class, answer the following questions:

1. What target behavior did you specify?
2. What strategies did you implement?
3. Which strategies were effective?
4. What are the characteristics of an effective social learning strategy?
5. How could your strategy or other strategies be improved?

Activity 2–7: ASSESSING ATTITUDES TOWARD WORK

Step 1: Select two individuals who hold jobs. (You may select two classmates and have them use their jobs as students.)

Step 2: Ask each person to complete the following questionnaire.

Please indicate how satisfied you are with your work situation in each of the respects listed below. For each item circle the number that most accurately describes your attitude.

	Very Dissatisfied	Dissatisfied	Neither Satisfied Nor Dissatisfied	Satisfied	Very Satisfied
1) content of my work	1	2	3	4	5
2) challenge provided by my work	1	2	3	4	5
3) variety in my job	1	2	3	4	5
4) autonomy in my job	1	2	3	4	5
5) chance for advancement	1	2	3	4	5
6) salary I receive	1	2	3	4	5
7) opportunity for promotion	1	2	3	4	5
8) opportunity for creativity	1	2	3	4	5
9) opportunity for personal growth	1	2	3	4	5
10) job security	1	2	3	4	5
11) supervision I receive	1	2	3	4	5
12) my relationship to my co-workers	1	2	3	4	5
13) opportunity I have to suggest new ideas	1	2	3	4	5
14) recognition I receive for my work	1	2	3	4	5
15) control I have over my work and assignments	1	2	3	4	5
16) opportunity my job provides for me to remain current in my field	1	2	3	4	5
17) fairness of promotion	1	2	3	4	5
18) consistency of my organization's policies and practices	1	2	3	4	5
19) power I have in my job	1	2	3	4	5
20) opportunity to do work I consider important	1	2	3	4	5
21) involvement in my organization's decision-making	1	2	3	4	5
22) fairness of pay raises	1	2	3	4	5

Step 3: Tabulate the responses for each facet indicated by completing the following questions.

Job Properties: Ratings for questions 1,2,3,8,9,16,20 = ________ Divided by 7 = ________
Organizational Policies and Practices: Ratings for questions 5,6,7,17,22 = ________ Divided by 5 = ________
Power and Control: Ratings for questions 4,13,15,19,21 = ________ Divided by 5 = ________
Relationships with Others: Ratings for questions 11,12 = ________ Divided by 2 = ________
Other Facets of the Work Situation: Ratings for questions 10,14,18 = ________ Divided by 3 = ________

Step 4: Compare the scores of the two respondents. How do the differences in their scores reflect differences in their attitudes?

Step 5: Interview each respondent to determine the causes and consequences of at least one of these attitudes toward their jobs.

1. What beliefs have influenced their attitude toward their jobs?
2. What values have influenced their attitude toward their jobs?
3. What behaviors (intended or actual) resulted from positive attitudes? negative attitudes?
4. How can dysfunctional behaviors be altered?

These questions were drawn from the alumni questionnaire in J.R. Gordon, *The Congruence Between the Job Orientation and Job Content of Management School Alumni,* Doctoral Dissertation, Massachusetts Institute of Technology, 1977.

CONCLUDING COMMENTS

In Chapter 1 we suggested that different theoretical perspectives have been emphasized in the field of organizational behavior during different decades. In this chapter we have looked at the issue of different perspectives in another way. We have focused on the ways in which different people in organizations often have different perceptions of any particular event. Managers and their subordinates, in particular, frequently "see" the same organizational events—or people—differently. A worker may "hear" a performance evaluation differently from the way his or her supervisor "said" it. Thus, they often *describe* events differently. Then they are also likely to assign different causes for the things that happen; they may *diagnose* situations differently.

In the activities of this chapter, Facts and Inferences provided the opportunity to examine factors that influence perception. The Attribution Exercise and A-Plus Aeronautics offered a chance to test attributional biases. Both Credit Comes South and the Road to Hell cases illustrate the role of perceptual and attributional distortions in organizational situations. Learning by Modeling provided practice in developing social learning strategies. Assessing Attitudes toward Work allowed you to compare and contrast workers' job attitudes and their causes and consequences.

When managers and subordinates see things differently, who is "right"? The manager's viewpoint is often taken to have more weight, in part because the manager has more power. In fact, however, neither the manager nor the employee is necessarily "right" or the other "wrong." Rather, the understanding of what is "right" requires understanding of the way both people view the situation. It also requires comprehending the ways individuals learn in organizations. In this book we attempt to expand individuals' perspectives and encourage experimentation as a means of learning.

ENDNOTES

[1]Excerpted from B. Toman, "For the Strikers at Ford's British Plants, Japan Represents Threat to Way of Life," *The Wall Street Journal,* February 16, 1988. Reprinted by permission of *The Wall Street Journal,* © Dow Jones & Company, Inc. 1988. All rights reserved worldwide.

[2]T.R. Mitchell, *People in Organizations: Understanding Their Behavior* (New York: McGraw-Hill, 1978); and H.C. Triandis, *Interpersonal Behavior* (Monterey, Cal.: Brooks/Cole, 1977).

[3]D. Coon, *Introduction to Psychology: Exploration and Application* (St. Paul, Minn.: West, 1977).

[4]G. Hofstede, Motivation, leadership, and organization: Do American theories apply abroad?, *Organizational Dynamics* 9 (Summer 1980), 45–46.

[5]K.N. Wexley, G.A. Yukl, S.Z. Kovacs, and R.E. Sanders, Importance of contrast effects in employment interviews, *Journal of Applied Psychology* 63 (1978): 579–588.

[6]E. Gibson, *Principles of Perceptual Learning and Development* (New York: Appleton-Century-Crofts, 1969).

[7]D. Fisher, *Communication in Organizations* (St. Paul, Minn.: West, 1981).

[8]G. Allport, *The Nature of Prejudice* (Reading, Mass.: Addison-Wesley, 1954).

[9]M.E. Heilman and M.H. Stopeck, Being attractive, advantage or disadvantage? Performance evaluations and recommended personnel actions as a function of appearance, sex, and job type, *Organizational Behavior and Human Decision Processes* 35 (1985): 202–215.

[10]N.J. Adler, *International Dimensions of Organizational Behavior* (Boston: Kent, 1986).

[11]K. Lewin, *Field Theory in Social Science* (New York: Harper, 1951).

[12]H.H. Kelley, The process of causal attribution, *American Psychologist* 28 (1973): 107–128; V.L. Hamilton, Intuitive psychologist or intuitive lawyer: Alternative models of the attribution process, *Journal of Personality and Social Psychology* 39 (1980): 767–772; E.E. Jones and K.E. Davis, From acts to dispositions: The attribution process in person perception. In L. Berkowitz (ed.), *Advances in Experimental Social Psychology vol. 2* (New York: Academic Press, 1965), pp. 219–266.

[13]S.G. Green and T.R. Mitchell, Attributional processes of leaders in leader–member interactions, *Organizational Behavior and Human Performance* 23 (1979): 429–458; D.R. Ilgen and W.A. Knowlton, Jr., Performance attributional effects on feedback from superiors, *Organizational Behavior and Human Performance* 25 (1980): 441–456; W.A. Knowlton, Jr., and T. R. Mitchell, Effects of causal attributions on a supervisor's evaluation of subordinate performance, *Journal of Applied Psychology* 65 (1980): 459–466.

[14]E.K. Shaver, *An Introduction to Attribution Processes* (Cambridge, Mass.: Winthrop, 1975).

[15]E.E. Jones and R.E. Nisbett, *The Actor and The Observer, Divergent Perceptions of the Causes of Behavior* (Morristown, N.J.: General Learning Press, 1971).

[16]*Ibid.*

[17]J. Bartunek, Why did you do that? Attribution theory in organizations, *Business Horizons* 24 (1981): 66–71.

[18]*Ibid.*

[19]H.H. Kelley and J.L. Michela, Attribution theory and research, *Annual Review of Psychology* 31 (1980): 457–501.

[20]Bartunek, *op. cit.*

[21]R.G. Lord and J.E. Smith, Theoretical, information processing, and situational factors affecting attribution theory models of organizational behavior, *Academy of Management Review* 8 (1983): 50–60.

[22]I.P. Pavlov, *Conditioned Reflexes: An Investigation of the Physiological Activity of the Cerebral Cortex,* trans. and ed. G.V. Anrep (London: Oxford University Press, 1927). Comparable work was done in the United States by J.B. Watson and is described in *Behaviorism* (New York: Norton, 1924).

[23]B.F. Skinner, *About Behaviorism* (New York: Knopf, 1974); B.F. Skinner, *The Behavior of Organisms* (New York: Appleton-Century-Crofts, 1938).

[24]E.C. Tolman, *Purposive Behavior in Animals and Men* (New York: Appleton-Century-Crofts, 1932).

[25]F. Luthans, *Organizational Behavior 4th ed* (New York: McGraw-Hill, 1985).

[26]*Ibid.*

[27]A. Bandura, *Social Learning Theory* (Englewood Cliffs, N.J.: Prentice-Hall, 1978).

[28]C.C. Manz and H.P. Sims, Vicarious learning: The influence of modeling on organizational behavior, *Academy of Management Review* 6 (1981): 105–113.

[29]F. Luthans and R. Kreitner, *Organizational Behavior Modification and Beyond* (Glenview, Ill.: Scott, Foresman, 1985), p. 157.

[30]R.H. Fazio, How do attitudes guide behavior? In R.M. Sorrentino and E.T. Higgins (eds.), *Handbook of Motivation and Cognition* (New York: Guilford, 1986), pp. 204–243.

[31]*Ibid.*

[32]M. Fishbein and I. Ajzen, *Beliefs, Attitude, Intention, and Behavior: An Introduction to Theory and Research* (Reading, Mass.: Addison-Wesley, 1975) sequenced an attitude's components identified by H.C. Triandis, *Attitude and Attitude Change* (New York: Wiley, 1971).

[33]Fazio, *op. cit.*

[34]For example, intent to leave a job is one of the best predictors of turnover, as shown in A.I. Kraut, Predicting turnover of employees from measuring job attitudes, *Organizational Behavior and Human Performance* 13 (1975): 233–243.

[35]R. Kreitner, Personal wellness: It's just good business, *Business Horizons* 25 (May-June 1982): 28–35.

[36]E.A. Locke, The nature and causes of job satisfaction. In M.D. Dunnette (ed.), *Handbook of Industrial and Organizational Psychology* (Chicago: Rand McNally, 1976).

[37]E.E. Lawler, III, *Motivation in Work Organizations* (Monterey, Cal.: Brooks/Cole, 1973).

RECOMMENDED READINGS

Advances in Social Cognition, vol. 1. Hillsdale, N.J.: Ehrlbaum Associates, 1988.

Amsel, A. *Behaviorism, Neobehaviorism, and Cognitivism in Learning Theory.* Hillsdale, N.J.: Ehrlbaum Associates, 1989.

Boff, K.R., Kaufman, L., and Thomas, J.P. (eds.) *Handbook of Perception and Human Performance.* New York: Wiley, 1986.

Davey, G., and Cullen, C. (eds.) *Human Operant Conditioning and Behavior Modification.* New York: Wiley, 1987.

Fishbein, M., and Ajzen, I. *Belief, Attitude, Attention, and Behavior: An Introduction to Theory and Research.* Reading, Mass.: Addison-Wesley, 1975.

Harvey, J.H., and Weary, G. (eds.) *Attribution: Basic Issues and Applications.* Orlando, Fla.: Academic, 1985.

Luthans, F., and Kreitner, R. *Organizational Behavior Modification and Beyond.* Glenview, Ill.: Scott, Foresman, 1985.

Upmeyer, A. (ed.) *Attitudes and Behavioral Decisions.* New York: Springer-Verlag, 1988.

3

Dealing with Individual Differences and Role Pressures

CHAPTER OUTLINE

LEARNING OBJECTIVES

After completing the reading and activities of Chapter 3, students will be able to

- define personality and show its significance for personal development and individual behavior in organizations;
- trace the stages of adult, career, and family development and their relationship to individual behavior and attitudes;
- describe organizational socialization and its relationship to organizational behavior and performance;
- diagnose possible sources of role conflict and role ambiguity in organizations; and
- offer strategies for reducing role conflict and role ambiguity.

Reconciling Individual Differences at Investment Management Associates

Roger Anderson, a twenty-three-year-old business school graduate, is a junior analyst at Investment Management Associates, a small, reputable investment counseling firm in Milwaukee, Wisconsin. For the past three years he has been responsible for investing daily cash positions in thirty institutional pension trusts, as well as monitoring stock market developments for his two immediate supervisors, senior analysts Lorna Solari and Donald Lane. Donald has been with the firm for five years and is in his late twenties. Lorna is in her mid-thirties, having joined the firm after receiving her MBA, which she earned as a part-time student. Roger enjoys a solid, professional working relationship with both Lorna and Donald. They often comment on how his knowledge and effort contribute significantly to the overall investment performance of the various portfolios they manage.

Last October, the firm hired an additional senior pension analyst from an outside firm. Edward Kelleher brought with him a proven record of competence, as well as an arrogant and condescending disposition. He had switched to the investment business five years before, at the age of thirty-eight. The president of the firm, Robert Keefe, was largely responsible for hiring both Ed and Roger. Keefe had helped build the firm and was the main force behind its success.

During the afternoon of his second day on the job Ed was meeting with Lorna and Don. Roger poked his head into the room to introduce himself. Ed ignored Roger's outstretched hand, verbally reprimanded him for interrupting, and instructed him to return to his "go-fer work." Roger was embarrassed and shocked, yet restrained, as he left the room. When Lorna and Don informed Ed that Roger was to be his assistant, Ed simply shrugged and continued the conversation at hand.

Roger felt extremely uneasy during the following two weeks. Ed ignored him and never once sought his input or assistance. Ed had a reputation for being very inflexible, reluctant to give praise, a perfectionist, and a stickler for details, whereas the other senior analysts seemed to be more people-oriented and to take a broader, more intuitive view of investment decisions. Roger complained to Lorna and Don about the situation. Lorna said that she spoke to Ed briefly concerning the matter. Her only comment to Roger was, "Apparently, if he needs your help, he'll ask for it." Noticeably disturbed, Roger's daily investment decisions were not as sharp, and his satisfaction declined considerably.[1]

We might identify perceptual, motivational, leadership, or communication issues in this situation. But in this chapter we look at other possible explanations for behavior: the effect of differences in individual personality and personal development, as well as dysfunctional role pressures, on individual behavior and attitudes.

INDIVIDUAL DIFFERENCES IN PERSONALITY

An individual's personality can significantly affect individual behavior in organizations. *Personality* refers to the set of characteristics distinctive to an individual, including his or her motives, emotions, values, interests, attitudes, and competencies. These characteristics frequently are organized into patterns that are influenced by an individual's heredity and social, cultural, and family environments. Thus diagnosing aspects of individual personality may help to explain individual behaviors and attitudes.

Personality Characteristics

Psychological research has identified a wide range of psychological characteristics that compose an individual's personality. As one example, Rotter described the extent to which individuals believe that their behaviors influence what happens to them.[2] Internalizers feel that they control their own lives and actions; externalizers believe others control their lives. Internalizers would believe, for example, that "promotions are earned through hard work and persistence," and "when I am right, I can convince others."[3] Externalizers would believe that "making a lot of money is largely a matter of getting the right breaks," and "it is silly to think that one can really change another person's basic attitudes."[4]

Our researchers have described the dimension called Machiavellianism, or the extent to which an individual tends to manipulate others.[5] Those who score high on this personality trait believe that "anyone who completely trusts anyone else is asking for trouble," and "the best way to handle people is to tell them what they want to hear."[6]

A third personality dimension is Type A or Type B characteristics. Individuals with these two types of personalities differ in their desires for achievement, perfectionism, and competitiveness, and their ability to relax.[7] Type A people tend to feel very competitive, be prompt for appointments, do things quickly, and always feel rushed. Type B individuals tend to be more relaxed, take things one at a time, and express their feelings.[8] We might hypothesize that among the senior analysts, Ed has a Type A personality because he is described as being inflexible and a perfectionist. In contrast, we might hypothesize that Lorna and Don have Type B personalities because they are more relaxed and express their feelings more easily. Of course, a definitive characterization of their personality types would require more detailed observation and precise measurement. Even then, this would only be a single dimension of complex individual behavior.

Jungian psychology identifies two basic personalities: introversion and extroversion.[9] At the extremes, the introverted person is shy and withdrawn, whereas the extroverted person is outgoing, often aggressive, and dominant. These personality patterns are matched by four problem-solving orientations: (1) sensor, (2) intuitor, (3) thinker, and (4) feeler. Figure 3–1 and Table 3–1 describe each type in more detail. How might you characterize the personality of the three senior analysts? Again, we might hypothesize that Lorna and Don have similar personality types, are perhaps intuitor–feelers, but Ed seems to have a different type—possibly he is a sensor–thinker.

Measuring Personality

Personality is assessed primarily in three ways. Individuals can complete inventories—lists of questions that describe the respondent's personality—such as the Myers-Briggs Scale or the Minnesota Multiphasic Personality Inventory

Figure 3–1 PROBLEM-SOLVING ORIENTATIONS

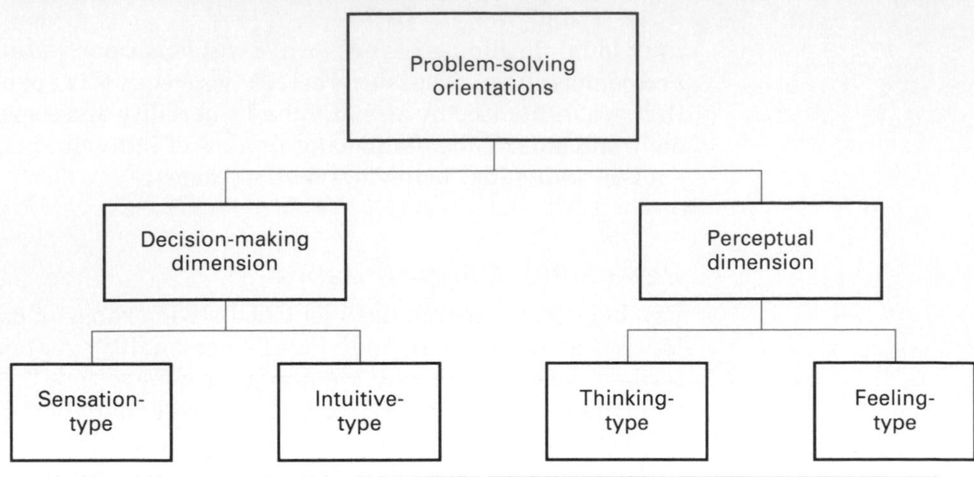

Table 3–1 BEHAVIORAL CLUES OF FOUR PERSONAL STYLES

Perceptual Dimensions

Style Characteristic	Sensor	Intuitor
Emphasis	Action, getting things done, wants to see results of efforts quickly	Ideas, concepts, theory, innovation, long-range thinking
Time orientation	Present	Future
Sources of satisfaction	Likes quick results, enjoys making things happen, likes feedback on efforts, likes to be in charge	Derived from world of possibilities, oriented toward problem solving but not terribly interested in implementing solutions
Strengths	Pragmatic, assertive, directional, results-oriented, objective, competitive, confident	Original, imaginative, creative, idealistic, intellectually tenacious, ideological
Weaknesses (if style is overextended)	Doesn't see long range, acts first then thinks, lacks trust in others, domineering, arrogant	Unrealistic, "far out," fantasy-bound, scattered, devious, out-of-touch, dogmatic, impractical
In clothing	Informal, simple, functional, neat but not fancy	Erratic and hard to predict
In surroundings	Hard-charging, clutter	Futuristic, modern, creative
Typical occupations	Accountants, pilots, bankers, investors, professional athletes, salespeople, models, physicians, land developers	Scientists, researchers, artists, market researchers, writers, corporate planners, "idea" people

(known as the MMPI). The Myers-Briggs Scale assesses the perceptual (sensation–intuition) and decision-making (thinking–feeling) dimensions described in the previous section.[10] The MMPI asks respondents to indicate the truth of over 400 statements about their health, social attitudes, and phobias.[11]

Trained psychologists can also administer projective tests, such as the Thematic Apperception Test (TAT) and the Rorschach Inkblot Test. In these tests the respondent tells the administrator what he or she sees in a picture (the TAT) or in relatively ambiguous inkblots (the Rorschach). This description is then scored using a detailed protocol. The scores describe the individual along a variety of personality dimensions.

The third assessment approach involves individuals in simulations, role-playing exercises, and stress interviews. A participant's behavior is observed and scored along a variety of dimensions. The scoring protocol may assess an individual's adaptability, assertiveness, or dominance, for example. These instruments describe personality by helping to define consistent patterns of psy-

Decision-Making Dimensions

Style Characteristic	Thinker	Feeler
Emphasis	Logic, organization, analysis, systematic inquiry	Human interaction, feelings, emotions
Time orientation	Past, present, future	Past
Sources of satisfaction	Enjoys seeing a problem through to implementing solution; enjoys anything well-organized or methodically thought out	Enjoys "reading between the lines;" social interpersonal contact is sought out
Strengths	Effective communicator, deliberative, prudent, weighs alternatives, stabilizing, objective, rational, analytical	Spontaneous, persuasive, emphatic, grasps traditional values, probing, introspective, draws out feelings of others, loyal
Weaknesses (if style is overextended)	Verbose, indecisive, overly cautious, overanalytical, controlled and controlling, overly serious, rigid	Impulsive, manipulative, over-personalizes, sentimental, postponing, stirs up conflict, subjective
In clothing	Conservative, unassuming, understated, color-coordinated	Colorful, informal, mood-oriented
In surroundings	Correct, nondistracting, tasteful but conventional, organized	Informal, warm, personalized
Typical occupations	Lawyers, engineers, computer programmers, accountants	Entertainers, salespeople, writers, teachers, public relations specialists, nurses, social workers, psychiatrists, psychologists, secretaries, retail business people

chological functioning. They look for repetitive behaviors and attitudes that they can associate with a given personality type. Although reliable and valid measures of personality exist, they should be used in organizational settings relatively infrequently and always carefully. Trained professionals are required to assess personality; and this limits managers' abilities to confidently draw conclusions about personality without a careful psychometric assessment.

Effects of Personality

A description and analysis of an individual's personality or personal style can help us understand the way that individual behaves in organizations and particularly the way that he or she interacts with others. Assume that Roger Anderson is an internalizer and Ed Kelleher is an externalizer. An internalizer may perceive that he determines and is responsible for his own level of performance. An externalizer, in contrast, believes that others control his life and actions and therefore determine his level of performance. How might these two men differ in their views of the best way to advance in an organization? The first might view advancement as being within his control; the second would view it as being out of his control. Similarly, Roger might attribute success to himself rather than to the situation, but Ed might make the reverse attribution. Or Roger might view attaining a new client as being within his control, whereas Ed might consider such an acquisition a matter of luck.

Now consider a male manager with a thinking-type personal style. How would he begin to deal with a poorly performing employee? He likely would perform a logical, systematic inquiry into the situation, focusing on behaviors rather than feelings. Compare this behavior to that of a feeling-type male manager in the same situation. He might begin by conducting a more ad hoc assessment, focusing first on the employee's feelings. Consider how these two managers might deal with a worker experiencing personal problems. We can hypothesize that the first manager would focus on the organizational implications of the personal dilemma, whereas the second would be more concerned with its consequences for the employee. By diagnosing the impact of an individual's personality on an organizational situation, a manager might anticipate the possible consequences and make provisional plans for responding.

Recent research has suggested that the personalities of top executives can help explain dysfunctional organizations.[12] That is, a manager with a neurotic personality is more likely to lead an organization that experiences significant dysfunctions and pathologies. For example, an executive who believes that no one can be trusted often creates an organization in which secrecy and guardedness characterize the culture. Likewise a manager whose compulsive personality reflects a need for control often creates an organization that relies too much on formal controls and direct supervision to accomplish organizational goals.

In considering the implications of personality for individual and organizational performance, we must be careful not to stereotype individuals on the basis of these traits. We should not consider assessing personality dimensions routinely, since their relationship to job performance can be highly variable. In some cases, however, differences in personality type between interacting coworkers can help explain dysfunctional behavior. One explanation for the nature of the interactions between Roger and Ed is a lack of understanding of each other's perspectives of the work situation due to radically different personality types. While personality and personal style are relatively stable dimensions of individuals, their manifestations may differ over the course of an individual's life, as described in the next sections.

INDIVIDUAL DEVELOPMENT

Research has suggested that adults, like children, have clearly defined stages of biological, social, family, and career growth and development.[13] Individuals at any particular stage are likely to have common needs and similar ways of coping with and responding to these situations. Of course these ways may be modified by an individual's personality, causing variations within stages. Individuals at different biological developmental stages, however, may respond differently to requirements for overtime work or supervisory responsibility. Individuals at different family stages, too, may experience dilemmas because of certain features of work situations.

Consider the five people mentioned in the introductory scenario (Table 3–2 provides additional data about them). Do you think these individuals respond to their work the same way? How much do they value their jobs? How involved are they in their work? What outside-of-work issues influence their work behavior? If these individuals differ in their positions in their biosocial, family, and career cycles, they probably would not react to their work situations in the same ways. In the following sections we examine the typical patterns of such reactions.

Table 3–2 PROFILES OF FIVE EMPLOYEES AT INVESTMENT MANAGEMENT ASSOCIATES

	Roger Anderson	Donald Lane	Lorna Solari	Edward Kelleher	Robert Keefe
Age	23	29	33	47	58
Marital Status	single	married	married	divorced	widower, remarried
Number of Children	0	0	2 school-age children	3 teenagers	7 grown children or stepchildren
Education	B.A. three years ago	M.B.A. five years ago	M.B.A. two years ago	B.A. in general studies 20 years ago	B.A. in economics 35 years ago
Number of Jobs Held Previously	0	1	1	3	2
Number of Years at Investment Management Associates	3	5	2	0	15
Number of Years in Current Job	3	5	2	1	10

Biosocial Development

An individual like Roger Anderson is primarily concerned with getting into the adult world, developing a sense of identity, and building a life that reflects his or her personality and personal style. Such individuals can experiment with various combinations of work and nonwork in their lives. At times they may spend seventy or eighty hours at work; at other times they may work only the minimum time required. Roger and others like him typically devote energy to establishing their independence and looking for individuals at work and elsewhere to replace their parents as models of behavior.

Whether individuals in this stage find a mentor or sponsor seems to be particularly important.[14] A mentor can influence movement through the organization and exert a significant influence over an employee's life style.[15] He or she performs diverse functions, as shown in Table 3–3.

Individuals should select a mentor who can help and has the confidence of the young worker; someone the protégé can help and make look good in the eyes of others; and someone who has a successful track record.[16] Recent research suggests that in some situations a worker's peers can act as effective mentors.[17] In one study two-thirds of the executives surveyed had mentors, and these executives received greater compensation than executives without mentors.[18] Thus mentorship seems to be a critical tool for career success for many individuals.[19] The establishment of formal mentoring programs, the

Table 3–3 MENTORING FUNCTIONS

Career Functions	Psychosocial Functions
Sponsorship Opening doors. Having connections that will support the junior's career advancement.	*Role modeling* Demonstrating valued behavior, attitudes and/or skills that aid the junior in achieving competence, confidence, and a clear professional identity.
Coaching Teaching "the ropes." Giving relevant positive and negative feedback to improve the junior's performance and potential.	*Counseling* Providing a helpful and confidential forum for exploring personal and professional dilemmas. Excellent listening, trust, and rapport that enable both individuals to address central developmental concerns.
Protection Providing support in different situations. Taking responsibility for mistakes that were outside the junior's control. Acting as a buffer when necessary.	*Acceptance and confirmation* Providing ongoing support, respect, and admiration, which strengthens self-confidence and self-image. Regularly reinforcing both as highly valued people and contributors to the organization.
Exposure Creating opportunities for the junior to demonstrate competence where it counts. Taking the junior to important meetings that will enhance his or her visibility.	*Friendship* Mutual caring and intimacy that extends beyond the requirements of daily work tasks. Sharing of experience outside the immediate work setting.
Challenging work Delegating assignments that stretch the junior's knowledge and skills in order to stimulate growth and preparation to move ahead.	

Reprinted with permission from K.E. Kram, "Mentoring in the Workplace." In D.T. Hall and Associates (eds.), *Career Development in Organizations* (San Francisco: Jossey-Bass, 1986), p. 162.

conduct of educational programs about mentoring and career development, and the implementation of significant changes in organizational structure, norms, and processes are three strategies that have been used to support mentorship.[20]

Don Lane's energies are probably focused on more diverse arenas. Because of responsibilities outside the work situation, he may be both more economical with his time at work and more committed to achieving. People like Don most likely spend much of their twenties establishing their identities and life styles; for example, they may be part of dual-career families, or they may be "workaholics." As they approach the age of thirty, Don and others like him usually review all past commitments and reappraise their personal and career progress to date. The precise approach they take depends on their personalities. For example, a thinking person takes a more analytical approach to developmental tasks than does a feeling person, who is more likely to emphasize his or her own and others' emotions.

At this point some women (and men), anticipating a need for greater career flexibility if and when they have children (if they haven't already), may consciously emphasize work over nonwork life. They try to make themselves indispensable to their organizations so that later they may have the option of part-time work or more flexible hours.

Lorna Solari has entered her thirties. During this decade individuals typically face different challenges and dilemmas from those they faced in their twenties. At this time, individuals such as Lorna come to terms with both their careers and their family concerns. They may feel pressure to have children if they do not already. If they already have children, they might experience a dilemma about how much time and energy to devote to family versus career. Too, Solari might react differently than others to these family and career demands depending on her perceptual and decision-making style. As an intuitive type how might she respond? How would she react if she were a sensation type? While in the past women frequently have withdrawn from the work force for a period of five to ten years, an increasing number of women with preschool and school-age children are remaining in the work force and juggling work and nonwork responsibilities. In the last decade men, too, have been changing, becoming more involved in family responsibilities. An increasing number share childrearing and housekeeping responsibilities with their spouses.

Ed Kelleher likely has already faced the difficulties encountered at midlife. His career change in his early forties may reflect a *midcareer crisis,* where he questioned the fundamental value, appropriateness, and real accomplishment in his career and family. Individuals at this stage of development must assess their own accomplishments, locate their own life goals and values, and make final decisions about their careers. These midcareer requirements may have temporarily distracted Kelleher from his job responsibilities while he reassessed his commitment to them. Ultimately he chose to switch to another career or job rather than reaffirm his commitment to his original work affiliation.

Men and women such as Robert Keefe basically have two options at their life stage. Keefe can enjoy the relative stability he is experiencing in his life and career. Alternatively, he can focus his energies on retirement, which often is possible at the age of sixty. Planning for the adjustment to reduced status and work role may create both personal and work-related problems for Keefe.

Clearly, then, individuals tend to confront different issues during each decade of their lives. Their abilities to deal with these issues, as well as the organization's success in responding to different needs, influence both individual and organizational performance. Managers can assist employees by helping them to recognize their developmental needs and, where possible, restructuring the work situations to meet these needs. Reading 3–1, "Human Development and Managerial Effectiveness," discusses the managerial implications of development theory.

Family Development

Consider again Roger Anderson, Donald Lane, Lorna Solari, Edward Kelleher, and Robert Keefe. Do you think that the interaction between work and family would be identical or even similar for these five individuals? What issues must each of them face? Are the issues the same for male and female employees with the same family configurations?

Family Stages Table 3–4 shows some representative stages and tasks of family development. While Roger Anderson is getting into the adult world and

Table 3–4 SAMPLE STATES, STAGES, AND TASKS OF THE FAMILY CIRCLE

State or Stage	Issues	Specific Tasks
Dependent child	Learning to adapt to the environment	Getting own needs met
Transition to adulthood	Managing the delicate balance between total and partial independence to allow for some trial and error in an environment of safety and support	
Single adult	Managing relations with other sex	
Married adult	Learning to live with a mate Making a long-term commitment to a family style and financial requirements	Balancing one's own needs and styles with those of another
Parent of young child	Adjusting to parenthood emotionally	Setting up workable schedule of child care
Parent of adolescents	Dealing with the independence needs and rebellion of own children Coming to terms with changing values	Setting reasonable standards and limits Enforcing limits
Parent of grown children	Adjusting to the departure of children Building new relationship with spouse	Developing new work role, hobbies, etc.
Grandparent	Establishing a relationship with a small child Dealing with own children in parent role Assessing own role as a mentor	

SOURCE: Schein, *Career Dynamics: Matching Individual and Organizational Needs,* © 1978, Addison-Wesley Publishing Company, Inc. Adapted from Table 5.1. Reprinted with permission of the publisher.

developing his sense of self, he is also managing the balance between partial and complete independence from his family. Roger and people like him must decide where to live and how much time to spend with their parents. Managing their relations with the opposite sex may also require some time and attention. They must decide whether to date, whether to marry, and how much time to devote to their social lives. Increasingly, professionals are focusing more on their careers than on nonwork issues at this time; many are delaying close involvements until their late twenties or early thirties.

In contrast, Don Lane has had to learn to live with a spouse. Balancing his own needs with those of another may create performance dilemmas for him at this developmental stage. Likewise the work demands of one spouse may require a geographical relocation that would affect the other spouse's career. Or conflicting work schedules may limit the amount of time husband and wife spend together. Clearly, Don's choice of a family style, such as whether he will be part of a dual-career family, influences the nature of his work involvement and commitment.

Lorna Solari may face very real conflicts between her work and home responsibilities. In addition to adjusting emotionally to parenthood, individuals like Solari must resolve the more practical issues of establishing a workable division of responsibilities within their marriages. Work demands may limit the amount of time they can devote to the home. Women at this stage often face the dilemma of whether to continue working. For women with young children who continue to work, their comfort with their decision to do so has an influence on their behavior at work. Feelings of guilt may lead to increased feelings of stress and job dissatisfaction. The quality of child care they arrange, the flexibility of their employers in allowing them to respond to family problems, and the cooperation of their spouses in sharing home responsibilities all influence individual performance.

Ed Kelleher's midcareer crisis may be compounded by difficulties in his family arrangements. Dealing with the independence and possible rebellion of his own children may reinforce his own feelings of inadequacy or dissatisfaction. These feelings may in turn restrict his ability to perform effectively at work. Extra financial demands for support in his own and his former spouse's households may further intensify the stress he feels.

At the same time that Robert Keefe's work requirements could decline, his family requirements are also decreasing. He must adjust to the departure of his children and build a new relationship with a new spouse. In this stage, both men and women may face the decision of whether to withdraw from the work world to accompany spouses who choose to retire.

The family issues faced by Robert Keefe and his colleagues at Investment Management Associates might differ significantly from those in cultures outside the United States. Family size, age of marriage, and the role of extended family, for example, differ in the Soviet Union, China, Japan, and Arab countries. The attitude toward a mix of family and career for women is also culture-specific.

Career Development

A variety of schemes have been used to illuminate career development. Table 3–5 presents three models of career stages and their approximate age correlates. Note, however, that the ages may vary significantly for different careers

Table 3–5 CAREER STAGES ACCORDING TO SEVERAL THEORISTS

Age	Super	Schein	Miller and Form
0			
5		Growth, Fantasy	Preparatory
10	Growth	Exploration	Pre-work
15			
20	Exploration	Entry into work world/training	Initial work period
25			
30		Full membership: early career	Trial work period
35	Establishment	Midcareer	
40		Midcareer crisis	
45			Stable work period
50		Late career/decline and disengagement	
55	Maintenance		
60			
65			
70	Decline	Retirement	Retirement

SOURCES: See D. Super, *The Psychology of Careers* (New York: Harper and Row, 1957); D.C. Miller and W.H. Form, *Industrial Sociology* (New York: Harper, 1951); E.H. Schein, *Career Dynamics* (Reading, Mass.: Addison-Wesley, 1978).

and different individuals. A salesperson can enter the initial work stage at age twenty; but a lawyer must complete law school before entering this stage, typically at the age of twenty-five or twenty-six. Similarly, some individuals retire at age sixty; others never retire. Table 3–6 presents representative career stages and a sample of issues and tasks associated with each.

Recall the five members of Investment Management Associates described at the beginning of this chapter. Are these five department members at the same career stage? What do they expect from their jobs in relation to their careers? Will they react in the same way to the requirements of their jobs and their organization?

Individuals like Roger Anderson try to become effective and accepted members of their organizations while they learn the ropes and routines of their first jobs. They must spend time learning to get along with their boss and coworkers, as well as trying to become an effective member as quickly as possible.

Don Lane strives for full membership in a career. His primary emphasis must be on performing effectively, accepting responsibility, managing subordinates, discharging duties, and developing special skills. Young professionals often experience difficulties in accomplishing these tasks.[21] Superiors, peers,

Table 3–6 SAMPLE STAGES, ISSUES, AND TASKS OF THE CAREER CYCLE

Stages	Issues	Specific Tasks
Growth, fantasy, exploration	Developing a basis for making realistic vocational choices Obtaining education or training	Developing and discovering one's own needs and interests Getting maximum career information
Entry into world of work	Becoming a member of an organization or occupation	Learning how to look for and secure a job
Basic training	Becoming an effective member quickly	Overcoming the insecurity of inexperience Learning to get along with boss and coworkers
Full membership in early career	Accepting the reponsibility and discharging duties Developing and displaying special skills	Performing effectively Accepting subordinate status Developing initiative and realistic expectations
Full membership, midcareer	Choosing a specialty Remaining technically competent Establishing a clear identity	Gaining a measure of independence Assessing own motives, talents Assessing organizational and occupational opportunities
Midcareer crisis	Reassessing own progress relative to ambitions Deciding relative importance of work and family	Becoming aware of career anchor Making specific choices about the present and future
Late career in nonleadership role	Becoming a mentor Broadening interests Deepening skills	Remaining technically competent Developing interpersonal skills Dealing with younger persons
Late career in leadership role	Using skills and talents for organization's welfare Selecting and developing subordinates	Becoming more responsible for organization Handling power Balancing career and family
Decline and disengagement	Learning to accept reduced power and responsibility	Finding new sources of satisfaction
Retirement	Adjusting to more drastic life style changes	Maintaining a sense of identity and self-worth without job

SOURCE: Schein, *Career Dynamics: Matching Individual and Organizational Needs*, © 1978, Addison-Wesley Publishing Company, Inc. Adapted from Table 4.1. Reprinted with permission of the publisher.

and subordinates (if there are any) may have conflicting expectations of these people: some may expect compassion, others, obedience to orders. Incompetent supervisors may limit an individual's acquisition of knowledge and advancement. In addition, young professionals, particularly young managers, may be insensitive to the internal political environment in the organization. Personal passivity and ignorance of real evaluative criteria may prevent an individual from actively improving his or her status and performance. Too, younger employees may not recognize that they must relinquish technical involvement or train successors if they are to advance in the organization. Tensions between older and younger managers, dilemmas about the person to whom the young professional owes loyalty, as well as ethical dilemmas and anxiety about integrity, commitment, and dependence, may contribute to problems experienced by workers such as Donald Lane.

Lorna Solari has similar career tasks. She already has full membership, but has become increasingly autonomous in her job while assuming additional responsibilities. Yet she is concerned with remaining technically competent. She must assess to what extent she wishes to remain technical or advance into a managerial position. Regular assessment of her own motives and talents, as well as organizational and occupational opportunities, must take place.

She must also be concerned with *obsolescence,* or the failure to maintain up-to-date knowledge in her career field.[22] She must ensure that she does not become a *plateaued performer*. "Plateaued individuals are by and large 'solid citizens,' people who are doing their present jobs well but who are seen as having little likelihood of achieving positions at higher levels; they constitute the bulk of the managerial work force in most organizations—those who 'get the work done.' "[23] Effectively performing plateaued managers have opportunities to demonstrate their capabilities and set goals; have clear job duties; perceive their jobs as important to the organization; view their jobs as challenging, interesting, and enjoyable; and receive feedback about their performance.[24]

Ed Kelleher may continue to experience a difficult midlife transition in his career as well as personal life. The midlife transition or midlife decade, which typically (although not always) occurs between ages thirty-five and forty-five, leads individuals to appraise their life's accomplishments to date. *Midcareer* is defined as "the period during one's work in an occupational (career) role after one feels established and has achieved perceived mastery and prior to the commencement of the disengagement process."[25] Sometimes male workers at midcareer experience the need to disrupt their habitual behavior and initiate career exploration.[26] Individuals at this stage ask themselves such questions as "What have I done with my life? What do I really get from and give to my (spouse), children, friends, work, community, and self? What are my real values and how are they reflected in my life?"[27] Feedback and recognition often decrease, reducing feelings of success.[28] In one study of men at midcareer, 80 percent experienced significant struggles over career or family, which frequently resulted in moderate or severe crises where individuals questioned every facet of their lives.[29] To resolve these crises individuals frequently make new choices about career and family or finally accept old choices as appropriate. They may seek and assume new roles within the organization or new jobs outside it. Eventually they come to terms with time, accept that life is finite, and view themselves as stable and accomplished.[30]

Robert Keefe must find a way to continue to contribute to the organization. He might continue to be involved with shaping the direction of the organization by acting as a sponsor for younger workers.[31] Professionals older than forty are considered above-average performers only if they have moved into this stage or one where they train and assume responsibilities for others and act as mentors toward them.[32]

For employers, "the basic challenge is not to weed out deadwood but to maintain the motivation and performance of managers (and other workers) who no longer see the carrot of vertical mobility."[33] Although individuals must assume some responsibility for preventing stagnation, unless organizations can respond with continuous challenges and additional responsibilities, the plateaued performer will probably experience performance problems in most situations.

Recent research has questioned whether the same model of career development applies to both men and women.[34] Because significant social changes have recently altered the career and job opportunities for women, a career model must consider differences in career preparation, opportunities, the role of marriage and pregnancy, and the timing and age of women at various career events.[35] To date no such model seems to exist.

Professional Careers

Professional employees, such as scientists, engineers, teachers, and accountants, bring specialized expertise to organizations, frequently as a result of advanced education or special training. They may face different career and organizational issues than those experienced by managerial or other employees. Managers who do not share the same professional background may have difficulty motivating or supervising these employees. Recognition for the quality of their work may be limited by management's lack of technical knowledge; and professionals often disagree with managers over the technical sophistication required to complete their work. Professionals also frequently demand extensive autonomy in their work. They may be committed more to their specialty and profession than to the organization. Professionals may require more autonomy than their nonprofessional counterparts, or they may insist on professional standards of conduct, both of which may be dysfunctional for the organization.[36]

Too, professional employees may not be able to advance in their organizations without assuming managerial responsibility.[37] Dual ladders, where individuals can assume increasingly higher positions in the organization (with higher pay, status, and greater responsibility) without assuming managerial or supervisory responsibility, as shown in Figure 3–2, are uncommon. Where a dual ladder exists, however, employees have two equivalent routes for increasing their status, work responsibility, and compensation in the workplace.

If professionals experience conflicting expectations with their management about their work, it may result in either deviant or adaptive behaviors, or some of both.[38] Figure 3–3 shows the range of responses professionals can make vis-à-vis management, the job, oneself, or one's career. For example, a professional may show adaptive behavior vis-à-vis management: he or she may seek and obtain freedom from professional constraints, utilize professional privileges such as flexible work hours, demonstrate autonomy, or rely on technology such as computerization of various aspects of his or her job. In contrast, a professional may also demonstrate deviant behaviors, such as failing to keep company secrets or resorting to unethical practices. Behaviors that have both adaptive and deviant elements include refusal to implement management's requests, work-to-rule (that is, following the letter of the professional's contract), or interpersonal sabotage. A similar range of behaviors can occur with regard to the job, oneself, and one's career.

Figure 3–2 EXAMPLE OF "DUAL LADDERS"

Scientific Ladder	Managerial Ladder
Senior Scientist	Vice-President of Engineering
Senior Engineer	Director of Engineering
Staff Engineer	Chief Engineer
Engineer	Engineer

To ensure the productivity of professionals, managers must use accommodative mechanisms, including job redesign, dual ladders, professional reward systems, and mentorship by managers. Likewise, professionals must learn about the organization they enter and evaluate whether it fits with their personal and professional goals.

Career effectiveness, and the individual job effectiveness that accompanies it, often arise from the organization's ability to integrate the employee into the organization and to help that employee make career transitions effectively. Both employees and their managers should assume some career development responsibilities. Employees should know and understand the implications of their own stage of career development for satisfaction and job performance. Managers should provide opportunities to discuss career development issues, give feedback about reasonable expectations for employees, identify employee potential, provide relevant growth opportunities, and link employees to appropriate resources.[39] A lack of such information in addition to the dilemmas experienced at various stages of biosocial, family, and career development may contribute to confusion and conflict in the performance of work and nonwork roles.

INDIVIDUAL ROLE PRESSURES

Each of the professionals described in the introduction has a prescribed set of activities, or potential behavior, that constitute the *role* he or she performs.[40]

Figure 3–3 Four Continua of Professional Deviant/Adaptive Behaviors

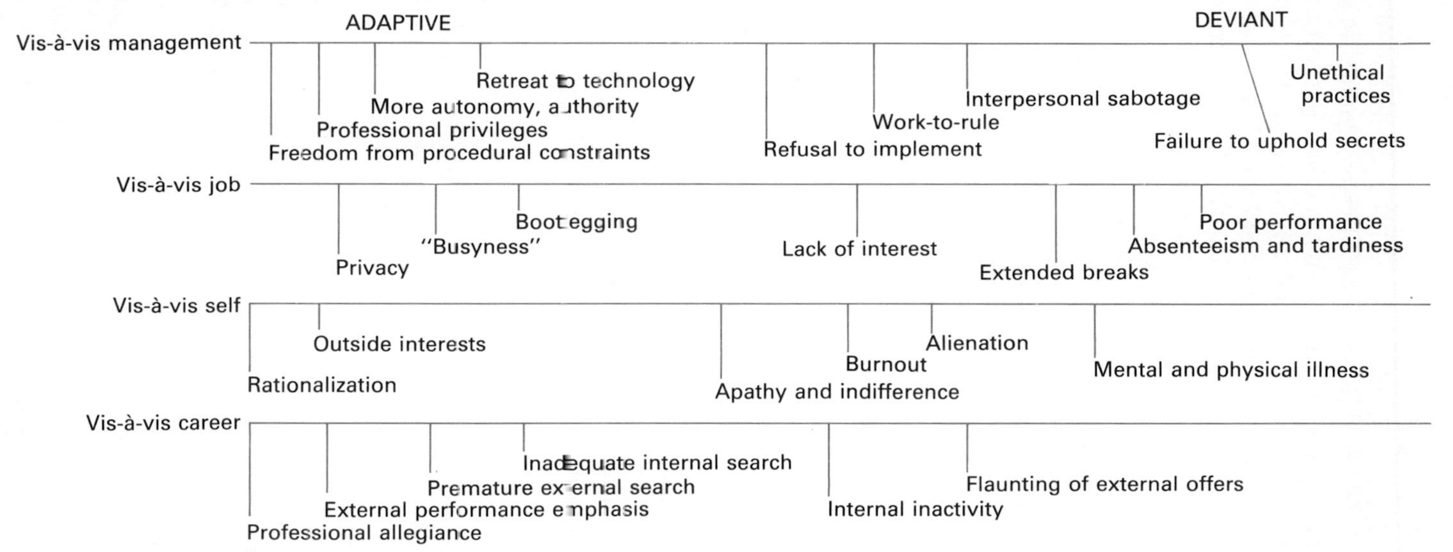

Source: J. Raelin, Examination of deviant/adaptive behaviors in the organizational careers of professionals, *Academy of Management Review* 9 (1984): 413–427. Reprinted with permission.

For example, Roger Anderson's role includes examining changes in the market and investing daily case positions.

Role Set

Typically, an individual who holds a particular role relates to or interacts with others in comparable or related roles, known as the *role set.* A woman may hold the roles of manager, wife, mother, and community participant. A manager may hold the roles of supervisor and subordinate simultaneously. At Investment Management Associates each investment counselor interacts with others in the department, with the department manager, and with clients. These others generally have *expectations* of how a role holder will operate. For example, a supervisor may expect a junior investment analyst to follow his or her specifications precisely and complete the desired transactions as quickly as possible. Senior analysts in the department may expect other senior analysts to act as resources for questions they might have, even if this occasionally distracts them from their own activities. Junior analysts may expect the senior analysts or the company's president to provide training. Clients may ask the analysts to change portfolios in specific ways. The role holder may or may not conform to these expectations. The analysts may conform to the clients' expectations of what constitutes profitability, or they may act contrary to these expectations by seeking stability in the short term, growth in the long term, or vice versa. As in Roger's case, they may meet their boss's requirements for how to handle accounts in normal situations, or they may not.

Generally, an individual operates *in role;* that is, he or she operates according to the general, nonconflicting expectations associated with the role. For example, the factory worker will assemble engines, or the professor will counsel students. On occasion, role holders operate out of role; they perform activities typically not associated with their roles. The factory worker may make heated political oratories during work hours; or the professor may request contributions for a political candidate during class time.

Definition of Role Conflict

You might say, however, that such behaviors are not really out of role. People often have differing expectations about the activities that are appropriate for a role holder. These differences in expectations that pressure a role holder to perform in one way rather than another result in *role conflict,* where compliance with one set of pressures prevents or makes more difficult compliance with a different set. Role conflict and role ambiguity (described below) lead to dysfunctional work-related behaviors, such as tension, stress, job dissatisfaction, propensity to leave the organization, and lowered organizational commitment.[41]

The role of an accountant whom top management expects to perform as a detail person and process as many accounts as possible differs from the role of the accountant whom management expects to sacrifice the quantity of production for its quality and creativity. Look at the situation faced by an individual with strong religious beliefs who is asked to work overtime on a rush project on a religious holiday. Or consider the programmer who is asked to write programs for a project to which he or she has ethical objections. Such situations offer a high possibility of role conflict.

Not only is conflict inherent within a single role, but the multiple roles a person plays often create diverse conflicting expectations. Remember that roles can be both formal and informal, work and nonwork. For example, a manager, who is also a wife and mother, and her husband, who is also a manager and father, might experience role conflict when they must deal with a sick child on the same day as a mandatory meeting for all managers. A lawyer who also serves as a local school committee member may find that work responsibilities infringe on time required to deal with school business or vice versa. A government employee who is expected to make contributions of time or money to the mayor's reelection campaign might also experience role conflict.

Each type of role conflict involves implicit or explicit pressure on the role holder to change to conform to the sender's expectations. For example, a supervisor who creates role conflict pressures a subordinate to act in undesirable or inappropriate ways, such as to make tradeoffs between meeting a deadline and producing the highest quality product possible. Generally, the more extreme the pressure, the more extensive the conflict. Stress (discussed in Chapter 10) often results from such conflicts.

The ability of different individuals to deal with conflict may be linked to their personalities and personal styles. For example, sensation-oriented individuals, who focus more on details than others, may be better able to deal with role overload than those who cannot organize details or diverse activities.

Role conflict can affect both job performance and satisfaction. The more an individual perceives incompatible expectations on the job and feels he or she must respond to them, the greater the frustration the person feels. This increasing frustration often translates into decreasing satisfaction and performance in the work situation.

Types of Role Conflict

Role conflicts are of four general types: (1) intrasender, (2) intersender, (3) interrole, and (4) person-role.

Intrasender Conflict When one person sends a role holder conflicting or inconsistent expectations, intrasender role conflict occurs. A computer programmer whose boss tells him or her, on the one hand, to write as many lines of code as possible, and on the other hand, to write programs that are error-free may experience intrasender conflict. A single person—the boss—sends the role holder—the programmer—conflicting expectations.

Now consider the situation at Investment Management Associates. Who experiences intrasender role conflict? Ed Kelleher may give Roger Anderson conflicting messages: to be his assistant but to provide no input into decision making.

Intersender Conflict When different people with whom the role holder interacts have different expectations of him or her, intersender conflict occurs. Computer programmers may "hear" different expectations about their role from their clients (other departments) and their supervisor. The clients may want the programs as quickly as possible, regardless of the overtime and cost required, but the supervisor may want to maintain a cost ceiling on salaries and overtime on a particular project.

Investment Management Associates' different senior analysts may make diverse and conflicting demands on junior analysts. Lorna Solari and Donald Lane wanted Roger Anderson to monitor stock market developments for them; Ed Kelleher wanted Roger to perform only clerical work for him.

Interrole Conflict When the expectations associated with different roles a person holds come into conflict, interrole conflict occurs. The working mother who has a sick child feels she is expected to perform her job at work and be at home to care for her sick child at the same time.

Work–family conflict is "a form of interrole conflict in which the role pressures from the work and family domains are mutually incompatible in some respect. That is, participation in the work (family) role is made more difficult by virtue of participation in the family (work) role."[42] These conflicts arise from insufficient time to perform one or the other role sufficiently, preoccupation with the role not currently performed, strain caused by one or both roles, and behavior required by one role (e.g., aggressiveness or nurturance) that interferes with the performance of the other role.[43] Research has found that a larger proportion of managerial women than managerial men remain unmarried or childless; in this way they have reduced the possible interrole conflict caused by career advancement.[44]

Organizations are increasingly employing individuals who are members of families in which both partners have professional careers.[45] Both partners in a dual-career family are expected, by society and often themselves, their bosses, and their peers, to be fully committed to both work and family. Such workers often experience conflicts between their work and family responsibilities. For example, which spouse will stay home with a sick child? What will happen if one person's career advancement depends on geographical relocation? Who will perform the social responsibilities that the wife has traditionally performed for a fast-track husband?

Individuals in dual-career families often use one or more of the following five strategies for dealing with role pressures.[46] First, family members can develop a commitment to both careers. Each person agrees to his or her spouse's need and right to pursue a career. Second, they can build in flexibility at home and on the job. Each person must be willing to adjust and revise his or her plans as required. For example, in dual-career families one or both members may forego a particular advancement opportunity if it requires geographical relocation. Where possible they might hold jobs that give them autonomy or other means of adaptability. A university professor, for example, often has greater flexibility in his or her career than the branch manager of a bank. Third, two-career families may use various coping mechanisms that help members negotiate the responsibilities, such as child care. They may change their own attitudes about the priority they attach to certain activities such as eating specific types of meals at regular times. Or they may find better ways to fulfill all their responsibilities, such as through better scheduling of activities. They might, for example, shop for food only once a week or use shop-at-home services. Fourth, members of two-career families must be skilled at time management. They generally employ their energy carefully and pare their lives down to priority activities. Often they limit the number of social activities in which they participate and choose volunteer responsibilities carefully. Fifth and finally, they develop career competencies such as self-assessment, collection of vocational information, goal setting, planning, and problem solving to facilitate their mutual career advancement. Organizations that wish to retain valued workers who are part of dual-career families often assist by securing a job for the spouse.

Organizations must recognize that personal-life transitions often accompany career transitions.[47] They must be concerned with the consequences of major moves within an organization and help individuals develop strategies for managing the accompanying personal changes.

Person–Role Conflict When the activities expected of a role holder violate the individual's values and morals, person–role conflict occurs. The employee who is asked to work on a religious holiday or to participate in activities that contradict his or her moral values may experience this type of conflict. The employee who is asked to distort data in an affirmative action report in order to represent the company favorably may also experience such conflict. Recent emphasis on ethics in organizations suggests that employees should inform management when person–role conflict exists and jointly find ways to eliminate it.

Role Overload

When the expectations sent to a role holder are compatible, but their performance requires more time or knowledge than is available to the person for performing the expected activities, *role overload* occurs. A person who holds a full-time job and has too many tasks to complete in the available time likely experiences role overload. So too does a person who is asked to perform tasks that exceed his or her knowledge, skills, or abilities. Overload typifies top management jobs, where the role holder often has more responsibilities than a single individual can handle.

Role Ambiguity

A role holder for whom expectations of the role are not adequately clear experiences *role ambiguity*. A new employee who receives no orientation to the job often experiences role ambiguity, because he or she lacks complete information about job activities and responsibilities, as well as about the employing organization. (Organizational socialization activities, described in the next sections, address this deficiency.) Likewise, the employee who does not know what activities the organization rewards may also experience role ambiguity. Does a company promote individuals who conform to company policies completely, or those who take some risks and demonstrate creativity? Does the company value a perfect attendance record over productivity? Does the company reward loyalty and encourage long-term employment?

Organizational Socialization "The process of 'learning the ropes,' the process of being indoctrinated and trained, the process of being taught what is important in an organization or subunit thereof," helps reduce role ambiguity for individuals entering new jobs or organizations.[48] Organizational socialization is the process by which a new member learns the organization's (1) basic *goals;* (2) preferred *means* to attain those goals; (3) basic role *responsibilities* of the members; (4) *behavior patterns* required for effective role performance; (5) rules or principles that pertain to maintaining the organization's *identity* and *integrity;* (6) *symbols* and *rituals;* and (7) *meaning of events.*[49] It is a natural organizational behavioral process that occurs in organizations, even without formal procedures. Formal programs for orientation, however, are a management option that is quite useful and typically found in large organizations.

Orientation programs frequently provide the initial socialization of new members. In some organizations, top managers meet with new recruits to discuss their philosophy and vision of the organization. In others, the human resources management department meets with newly hired employees and presents the organization's rules and standard operating procedures. In still other organizations, small groups of new employees meet with managers to discuss their concerns. Individual recruits may also receive orientation from their own managers. Do you think the participants in these various types of orientation sessions will perceive that the same things are important in their organizations? Certainly the formality or informality of orientation provides cues about the operation of the organization; so too does the choice to orient newly hired employees individually or in large groups.

Subsequent on-the-job training and informal interactions with peers and subordinates reinforce the values, norms, and behavior patterns introduced earlier. For example, continued, individualized on-the-job training suggests to a new recruit that the organization values individuality. In contrast, the repetition of rules and procedures reflects a more bureaucratic operating style.

Socialization occurs continually, but the process begins again each time an individual makes a transition by entering a new, often higher, position or a different department. A newly promoted manager must "learn the ropes" of his or her new position and role. Workers whose supervisor has just been replaced also must learn the ways the new boss operates, and this is another form in which socialization occurs.

Socialization Strategies Organizational socialization often occurs unconsciously, with no analysis of the means employed or their likely consequences. Strategies that are associated with transitions in organizations can be described along seven dimensions, and managers should consciously choose strategies that fit with their objectives.[50] Table 3–7 names and defines these strategies, provides a brief example of each, and lists some hypothetical consequences. Using a collective strategy to orient a new employee, for example, a manager sends him or her to training sessions with all the other new em-

Table 3–7 NAMES, DEFINITION, EXAMPLES, AND HYPOTHESIZED CONSEQUENCES OF SOCIALIZATION STRATEGIES

Strategy	Definition	Example
Collective	Puts newcomer through a common set of experiences as part of a group	Freshman orientation
Individual	Processes recruits singly and in isolation from each other	On-the-job training

Table 3–7 CONTINUED

Strategy	Definition	Example
Formal	Segregates newcomers from regular organizational members	Basic military training
Informal	Treats newcomers as undifferentiated from other members	Transferred employees
Sequential steps	Requires entrant to move through a series of discrete and identifiable steps to achieve a defined role	Specialized medical training
Nonsequential steps	Accomplishes achievement of a defined role in one transitional stage	Promotion
Tournament	Separates clusters of recruits into different programs on the basis of presumed differences	Academic tracked programs
Contest	Avoids sharp distinctions between clusters of recruits	Law school
Fixed	Gives the recruit complete knowledge of time required to complete passage	Six-week managerial training program
Variable	Offers a timetable that does not fix the length of socialization	Doctoral program
Serial	Provides experienced members as role models for newcomers about to assume similar positions to follow	Apprentice program
Disjunctive	Has no role models available for newcomers about to assume similar positions to follow	First holder of newly defined job
Investiture	Ratifies and documents the usefulness of personal characteristics of new recruits	New faculty orientation
Divestiture	Seeks to deny and strip away recruits' personal characteristics	Training for the priesthood

Based in part on J. Van Maanen, People processing: Strategies of organizational socialization, *Organizational Dynamics* 7 (1978): 19–36.

ployees, which likely results in conforming rather than innovative responses on the job.

Consider a one-day orientation program for bank tellers in which a group of new recruits views a film about the company, receives a lecture about the benefits they receive, tours the organization, and receives initial classroom training about bank procedures. What types of socialization strategies are incorporated into this orientation? The orientation program uses collective and formal strategies, where newcomers go through a common set of experiences as part of a group that does not include regular organizational members. It also avoids distinctions between recruits, requires them to move through a series of identifiable steps in a prespecified time period, and encourages newcomers to model their behavior on that of previously successful tellers. Assuming that the socialization of the new tellers continues to use similar strategies, such as providing training for all tellers as a group in a formal classroom setting, researchers would hypothesize that most of these strategies would result in conforming behavior[51] and that the tellers would demonstrate limited innovation in their jobs. Of course, this type of outcome may seem appropriate for bank tellers, but would orientation that uses these strategies be appropriate for salespeople or middle managers? What type of orientation should investment counselors at Investment Management Associates receive when they are hired? What would be the consequences of these strategies?

We can hypothesize that a different set of strategies would result in innovative behavior, which might be more desirable for the investment counselors. Training that uses individual and informal strategies, such as apprenticeship and on-the-job training, for example, encourages this outcome. Not only do early learning experiences in the organization and the organization's tactics of socialization influence newcomers' adjustment to the organization, but individual differences and attributions influence performance.[52]

Preventing Role Ambiguity Kahn and his associates suggest that role holders must know six basic types of information about the organization and its reward system to prevent role ambiguity; managers can help workers by providing such information.[53] First, role holders must know the expectations of others. For example, what attitudes and behaviors does a supervisor require of his or her subordinates? What types of interaction do peers and subordinates expect? Clearly Roger Anderson lacked this information about Ed Kelleher, which interfered with the development of a productive working relationship.

Second, they must know the activities that an individual should perform and the interpersonal interactions an individual should demonstrate to fulfill these expectations. How should the analysts complete their work? Must they work at the office or can they work from their homes? How extensively should they consult peers or supervisors? The individuals must also determine the best way to perform the activities. They can gather this information from discussions with supervisors and coworkers as part of the process of becoming socialized.

Third, role holders must know the consequences of performing or not performing the activities or interacting with others in certain ways. If, for example, the senior analysts mishandle their portfolios they may be reprimanded, transferred, demoted, or fired. Never eating lunch with coworkers may result in a worker's isolation on the job. Knowing the precise consequences reduces ambiguity and often the tension that accompanies it.

Fourth, role holders must know the kinds of behaviors or attitudes that will be rewarded or punished. Is tardiness a punishable offense? What happens if other clients complain (justifiably or not) about an analyst's performance? What happens if the worker disregards the advice of others or assumes a competitive attitude toward coworkers? The consequences for Roger Anderson and Ed Kelleher of not resolving difficulties in their relationship are still not clear.

Fifth, role holders must assess the likelihood of receiving rewards and punishments for these types of behaviors and attitudes, as well as the types of rewards and punishments to be given. They might gather this information by asking supervisors or observing past organizational behavior.

Finally, role holders must determine the kinds of behaviors and attitudes that can satisfy or frustrate personal needs. Do the rewards offered meet employees' needs? Do the required behaviors help the individuals accomplish their tasks?

Dealing with Role Pressures

Action first requires determining whether role conflict, role overload, or role ambiguity exists in a given situation, such as the one at Investment Management Associates. To diagnose the nature of role pressures we can ask the following questions:

1. Do any symptoms of role conflict, role overload, or role ambiguity, such as dissatisfaction, confusion, or low productivity, exist? Roger's declining performance and increasing dissatisfaction suggest an affirmative response to this question.
2. How is each person's role defined by the role holder and by relevant others? The senior analysts define Roger's role in two different ways—as a "go fer" and as a portfolio manager.
3. Are the expectations for the role holder clear? Roger understands but disagrees with his responsibilities as Ed defines them.
4. Do any of the role expectations create conflict? The senior analysts' expectations of the junior analyst's role result in conflict.
5. What socialization processes does the organization use? Although these are not explicitly described in the case, they appear to be informal and individual.
6. What are the outcomes of the socialization processes? Are they appropriate to the individuals involved and the situation? The socialization strategies result in innovative behavior, which may not be appropriate in certain situations.

Individuals respond to both role conflict and role ambiguity in a variety of ways. Think about an experience you have had where you experienced role conflict or role ambiguity. How did you handle it?

Some cope by adjusting to the situation, setting priorities, or ignoring certain expectations. For example, members of dual-career families may, at different stages in their careers, attribute priority to one or the other spouse's career. Early in their careers a husband's needs to relocate geographically may take precedence over the wife's career requirements; later, the reverse may be true. Working parents may specify for themselves that family responsibilities (e.g., a sick child or a conference with a child's teacher) have a higher priority than work responsibilities (staff meetings or deadlines) or vice versa. A programmer who is a perfectionist may ignore his or her boss's demands to program quickly even if errors result. Or a project manager who observes certain religious holidays may leave a job that unexpectedly requires work on those days. Other people respond by experiencing anxiety and stress or becoming less satisfied with their jobs.

SUMMARY

Roger Anderson at Investment Management Associates demonstrated performance problems, as did Ed Kelleher. In this chapter we considered the ways individual differences, development, and role pressures can contribute to such problems.

First we defined personality and considered how individuals with different personalities might function in an organization. Those with certain personalities may not fit with the activities or goals of a particular organization, work team, or supervisor. They might also experience difficulties in working with others whose personalities differ from theirs.

Although some aspects of personality remain relatively constant throughout an individual's life, developmental issues and tasks vary according to biosocial, family, and career development stages. The investment analysts at Investment Management Associates vary in age; thus they differ in their most salient developmental tasks. We considered the differences between individuals just entering their careers compared to those facing midlife. We noted the dilemma posed by the interaction of work and family.

We next examined role pressures experienced by organizational members. Intrasender, intersender, interrole, and person–role role conflicts; role overload; and role ambiguity can create dysfunctional behavior and attitudes in organizational members. We also looked at strategies of socialization that can turn individuals into innovative or conforming organizational members. Clearly the analysts at Investment Management Associates experienced role conflict and role ambiguity. These have consequences for their job performance and satisfaction. Figure 3–4 summarizes the issues presented in this chapter, in a series of diagnostic questions related to individual differences, development, and role pressures.

Figure 3–4 DIAGNOSTIC QUESTIONS ABOUT INDIVIDUAL DIFFERENCES AND ROLE PRESSURES

- Do the personality styles of participants fit with the situation?
- Do the personality styles of participants fit with those of other organizational members?
- Do the organizational members experience problems in adult or career development?
- How compatible are the adult and career development stages of various organizational members?
- Do individuals experience role conflict?
- Do individuals experience role overload?
- Are roles clear or ambiguous?
- Do the socialization processes used fit with the situational requirements and help reduce role ambiguity?
- How do managers and other organizational members deal with role pressures?

READING

Reading 3–1: HUMAN DEVELOPMENT AND MANAGERIAL EFFECTIVENESS

Dalmar Fisher, Keith Merron, and William R. Torbert

A management trainer is giving a workshop for computer engineers who are interested in becoming managers. After two days of theory, exercises, cases and role playing, the trainer has the sense that one-fourth of the participants have really understood what it means to be a manager and have demonstrated relatively effective managerial skills, one-half seem to have the ideas, but would not be able to manage effectively without further training and guidance far beyond that provided by the company. The rest believe they understand what it means to be a manager, but do not.

A group of middle managers are in a departmental strategic planning session. Although some of the group are highly invested in coming up with ideas for how the department can be successful in the long run, others have been going along for the ride, participating like good department citizens, but "knowing" all too well how worthless planning really is. One of the latter voices his wish that the group could get on with "real work" instead. Tensions mount as the committed members call their colleague shortsighted, he calls them heady planners who can't act, and the wary others sit and watch the drama, wishing it would end so they can go back to their jobs.

Such events are common. No matter what task and circumstances are faced by a management or employee group, the members almost invariably split several ways in their responses to it. The trainer's methods and results could probably be improved through applications of learning theory, teaching by objectives, or any of a number of techniques of management education. But few management training processes enable trainers to *differentiate* among the learning capacities of their workshop participants, much less act upon this knowledge to adapt their teaching styles. The planning meeting's difficulties could be understood in terms of group dynamics, decision theory, leadership, motivation, or conflict management—bodies of theory that suggest approaches to improving performance. But none of these approaches is guided by a theory of development that suggests both why people respond differently to the same situation and how better informed practice can address these differences. Without such a theory, a current situation may be resolved, but neither individual development nor a shared vision that accommodates individual differences is likely.

This article calls attention to a growing body of theory and research pointing to the importance of viewing human and organizational behavior from a human development point of view. First we summarize structural developmental theory as it applies to adults. We relate this concept of development to theories of decision making and leadership, and review an emerging body of research that confirms the importance of looking at managerial and organizational behavior from a developmental point of view. We conclude by exploring the implications of developmental theory for management education in universities, for the training and development of managers during their careers, and for the practice of organization development.

STRUCTURAL DEVELOPMENTAL THEORY

It is widely accepted that people act on the basis of the meanings things have for them, meanings that are shaped by the person's attitudes, assumptions, values, and beliefs—in short, the person's worldview. Individuals' worldviews are complex and firmly set. Indeed, most structural theorists, including linguist Noam Chomsky and anthropologist Claude Leví-Strauss, believe there are deep universal structures within the human organism that explain how people form meanings, speak, and act, despite the manifest variation of people from different regions and eras.

It is less widely recognized, however, that although these structures are complex and resistant to change, people have the potential to grow, developing new ways of making meaning in their worlds. Recent structural developmental theories, be they theories of interpersonal development (Selman, 1980), moral development (Kohlberg, 1969), ego development (Loevinger, 1976), or of the evolution of meaning making (Kegan, 1982), identify clear, discrete steps along a stairway of human development (Table 3–8). As each step is taken, a new self emerges with a new way of constructing the world, and the new inner experience of the world results in a new way of expressing ideas, feelings, and purposes. At each step, the corresponding worldview deeply influences what the person chooses to see, and how he or she interprets and reacts to what is seen.

As Table 3–8 suggests, most adults inhabit one of four developmental stages, or worldviews. The four principal stages can be named *opportunistic, social, goal-oriented,* and *self-defining*. We have chosen these names in an effort to capture the meanings of several theorists and to avoid judgmental connotations.

Table 3–8 STAGES OF HUMAN DEVELOPMENT AS IDENTIFIED IN SEVERAL DEVELOPMENTAL THEORIES

Developmental Theory	Opportunistic Stage	Social Stage	Goal-Oriented Stage	Self-Defining Stage
Kohlberg (1969)	instrumental orientation	interpersonal concordance orientation	societal orientation	principled orientation
Loevinger (1976)	opportunistic	conformist	conscientious	autonomous
Selman (1980)	unilateral, authoritarian relations	fair weather cooperation	stability; mutual conflict resolution	interdependence
Kegan (1982)	imperial	interpersonal	institutional	interindividual

People in the opportunistic stage of development are primarily predisposed to the use of unilateral power. Their belief is that to get one's way, one must play one's cards close to one's vest, because others are doing the same. Self-criticism is rare, blame being externalized to other people. The world is seen in simple, stereotypical terms: right or wrong, true or false. The focus is on the outside world and on gaining control of it.

In the social worldview, people tend to focus on group norms about appropriate and inappropriate behavior and on gaining control of their own behavior. Adherence to norms and leadership in exemplifying or enforcing norms is seen as the road to approval, status, and happiness. The world is seen in specific, concrete ways. Things are clear and unambiguous. Other people are characterized by a few major features rather than by fine details.

People holding the goal-oriented worldview tend to emphasize the competent execution of rationally interrelated steps leading from the presenting problem to a solution, or, put differently, the interrelated steps leading from strategy, to implementation, to intended outcome. Conscientious planning and hard work are seen as the elements necessary for accomplishment and success, which are viewed as valuable for their own sake. People and events are seen in richer detail. Differences between outward appearances and internal feelings are recognized in self and others, and agreements reached through consensus are valued. Because the focus is on conceptual relationships and because one can relate strategy to one's own behavior and to its effects in the outside world, the goal-oriented worldview encompasses the behavioral and outside worlds as well as the conceptual world itself.

People at the self-defining stage focus on the ability to resolve intrapersonal, interpersonal, and political conflicts involving both ends and means. The person is able to see integrated patternings among seemingly disparate objects, events, and patterns—indeed, among disparate patterns. The view of life is rich in variety of issues and topics, ranging from political, social, or aesthetic concerns to issues relating to others close to oneself. Tolerance for ambiguity, delight in paradox, and open exploration of differences are prized as essential in creating new shared meanings that motivate work and redefine goals. The new meanings sought are shared visions that encourage development, that minimize coercion and conformity, and that make room for the wide range of developmental differences (Cook-Greuter, 1984; Torbert, 1974, 1978).

In addition to inhabiting one of these four stages, persons may, at a given time, be in the midst of a transition between two stages, and such a transition may persist for quite a long time. The transition that occurs most frequently among adults is between the social and goal-oriented stages. Termed the *analytic transition,* it has been found to be the modal position for managers in each of three studies summarized in Table 3–9. Here the person becomes keenly interested in the inner workings of tasks, persons, and self, and in why things and persons work the way they do. Whatever the logic or craft—computer programming, ballet, or sailboating—the person seeks technical perfection. Multiple possibilities, contingencies, and exceptions are seen in situations, but a single position is usually chosen as preferable. Others' positions are attended to closely, but personal views are defended. The focus here is on the internal elegance and logic of ideas. Concern with the behavioral and external worlds is minimized rather than embraced as it will be at the next stage, the goal-oriented position.

A second transition—between the goal-oriented and the self-defining worldviews—we call the *relativistic transition.* Here persons become sharply aware that there are multiple ways of perceiving, valuing, and acting—each of which has merit, and no one of which is in any objective sense "right." They can see that there are different worldviews, but cannot yet commit to con-

Table 3–9 DISTRIBUTION OF MANAGERS BY DEVELOPMENTAL POSITION IN THREE STUDIES

Developmental Positions	Study 1 (Smith, 1980) N = 37	Study 2 (Torbert, 1983) N = 177	Study 3 (Gratch, 1985) N = 66
Opportunistic	0.0%	5.0%	0.0%
Social	24.0	9.0	6.0
Analytic	68.0	43.5	47.0
Goal-oriented	8.0	40.0	33.0
Relativistic	0.0	2.0	14.0
Self-defining	0.0	0.5	0.0
	100.0	100.0	100.0
Sample:	First-Line Supervisors	Junior and Middle Managers	Senior Managers

structing a pattern among these different patterns, as they will at the next (self-defining) position. Tolerance of self and others produces a cherishing of interpersonal relationships, a view of a common humanity, and a concern for social problems.

In theory, it is from the perspectives of the relativistic and self-defining worldviews that the person becomes cognitively capable of and emotionally committed to recognizing and working with people holding different worldviews, as well as willing to redefine presented problems and search for underlying issues when circumstances seem to warrant. To persons inhabiting the other worldviews, ambiguity, paradox, and exploration of implied, underlying meanings are likely to seem like irritating vagueness, overly idealistic, and a waste of time. Because they do not recognize the factors other worldviews define as determining outcomes nor the fact that there are legitimately different worldviews, persons at the opportunistic, social analytic, and goal-oriented positions (the vast majority of managers, according to the results shown in Table 3–9) tend to regard persons at developmental stages other than their own as unrealistic and irrelevant.

An important feature of developmental theory, consistently supported by research, is that there is a natural ordering or progression of these worldviews. As a person grows or matures, his or her worldview tends to go through a predictable sequence of changes (Kegan, 1982; Kohlberg, 1969; Piaget, 1967). In addition, structural developmental theory includes the following key propositions:

1. The order of development implies an invariant hierarchical sequence in which each more evolved worldview represents a more adequate understanding of the world than prior worldviews (Kohlberg, 1969).
2. Individuals holding more evolved worldviews tend to have developed greater cognitive abilities and conceptual complexity than those holding earlier worldviews (Harvey, Hunt, & Schroeder, 1961; Loevinger, 1976).
3. As one matures developmentally, one becomes increasingly able to (a) accept responsibility for the consequences of one's actions, (b) empathize with others who hold conflicting or dissimilar worldviews, and (c) tolerate higher levels of stress and ambiguity (Bartunek, Gordon, & Weathersby, 1983).
4. The person holding a more evolved worldview tends to be more attuned to his or her own inner feelings and outer environment than the person holding an earlier worldview (Loevinger, 1976).

Although structural theories of human development have played a key role in the fields of education and psychotherapy, we believe they hold equally significant implications for management education and training and for understanding and affecting change in organizations. For example, the worldviews managers hold carry implications for the ways they structure their managerial experience. Worldview is likely to influence their conception of what power is, what types of behavior are appropriate in meetings, how tasks are defined and done, and how conflicts are resolved. To understand this better, we will look at two functions central to the practice of management: decision making and leading.

DECIDING AND LEADING: A DEVELOPMENTAL PERSPECTIVE

Some organization theorists view contemporary organizations not as stable entities, operating rationally, but rather as highly changeable "messes." As decision makers, many managers face what Mason and Mitroff (1981) have termed "wicked problems" that become more complicated the more an effort is made to tame them. Decision making in this context requires alternatives to both the classical-rational model, where all factors are known and weighted to give an "optimal" choice, and its polar opposite, simple incrementalism, in which small doable actions are taken on a trial-and-error basis. Decision models alternative to these appear to require the kind of "complicated understanding" typifying the later stages of adult development (Bartunek et al., 1983). For example, the dialectical approach to decision making offered by Mason and Mitroff (1981) is adversarial and participative, based on the assumption that the manager should be exposed to diverse assumptions in a context of opposition. Clearly, this requires that the manager be capable of attending to and drawing from the strengths of differing viewpoints, rather than considering them irrelevant or undesirable. Similarly, Schön's reflection-in-action approach to decision making involves the manager's constantly searching for and experimenting with ways of redefining a problem rather than accepting it as given (Schön, 1983). A high degree of self-insight is required, because the manager's own ends as well as means are continually being reviewed and changed. Each of these skills—ability to appreciate multiple perspectives, to reflect and experiment while in action, and to engage in self-questioning—is a reflection of highly developed organizational sensitivities. According to Argyris and Schön (1974), such reframing is a rare occurrence in organizations. We suggest this is because it requires a relativistic or self-defining worldview, both later developmental positions than those occupied by most managers.

As leaders, many managers experience futility in trying to stimulate excellent performance by others. Some lead "heroically" by relying on their own technical or administrative skills, others "transactionally" by enabling followers to fulfill their goals (Bass, 1985; Bradford & Cohen, 1984). The potentials of these approaches are limited by the manager's abilities or the followers' existing goals. Recent leadership approaches, such as Bradford and Cohen's manager-as-developer and Bass's transformational leadership require highly advanced developmental worldviews. In the former, the manager works to develop subordinates' abilities to share in management. The leader's effort is to find how each problem can be solved in a way that further develops subordinates' commitment and capabilities. In the latter, the leader refuses to accept group and self identities as fixed and leads others, according to Bass, by raising their levels of consciousness about the importance and value of designated outcomes, by inspiring them to transcend their own self-interest, and by altering their need level and expanding their portfolio of needs and wants (1985, p. 20). These approaches to leadership appear to require that the leader be capable not only of reframing situations and understanding others' worldviews but also of being the stimulator and steward of the developmental process in his or her subordinates. In short, the newer theories of decision making and leadership imply the need to understand more about human development. More specifically, they imply that to manage effectively, a manager needs to occupy one of the later developmental stages.

PERSONAL DEVELOPMENT AND EFFECTIVE PERFORMANCE

Recent research has begun to test this proposition. Smith (1980) found, for example, that a person at the goal-oriented state is more likely to form power relationships based on collaboration than a manager at the opportunistic or social stage, who is more likely to try to coerce others. Smith also found that managers at the analytic transition tended to be so ambivalent about how to use power that they were often indecisive.

Lasker (1978) has shown that people with high need for achievement tend to be measured at later developmental positions than people with either high need for control over others or with high need for generating close relationships. Previous research has shown a correlation between need for achievement and leadership effectiveness (Birney, 1968). Lasker's research also shows a strong relationship between worldview and organizational position. The greater one's organizational authority, the more likely one holds a later stage worldview.

Hall and Thompson (1980) have reported findings that different leadership behaviors can be ordered along a continuum of less effective to more effective leadership styles. These range from highly autocratic, at one extreme, to a leadership style able to tap the strengths of others. Their research indicates that those who have a self-defining worldview are more likely to create conditions that support the development of others than managers with an opportunistic or social worldview.

Our own research suggests links between the manager's developmental position and his or her tendencies to employ Schön's reflection-in-action approach to problem solving and to implement actions through collaborative rather than unilateral means (Merron, Fisher, & Torbert, 1986). Subjects were given a managerial task involving deciding and acting under a relatively high degree of uncertainty and ambiguity. Both reflection-in-action and collaboration were more characteristic of persons at later developmental positions.

Organizations, like individuals, are observed to grow

through clearly discrete stages of development, beginning with an entrepreneurial stage, moving into one or more bureaucratic stages, followed in some cases by postbureaucratic stages (Blake, Avis, & Mouton, 1966; Greiner, 1972; Torbert, 1986). Greiner details these stages as birth, direction, delegation, coordination, and collaboration. Decision making and control are centralized in the first two stages, decentralized in the third. Then, in the coordination stage, unlike those preceding, managers must attend simultaneously to the often conflicting goals of their own unit and the organization as a whole. Finally, in the collaboration stage, decisions are made through skillful interpersonal confrontations within a matrix organization structure. The coordination and collaboration stages clearly seem to call for managers who occupy the later stages of adult development. Torbert argues that each organizational stage tends to reward a managerial style and worldview specific to one of the stages of adult development. He contends managers must undergo developmental change if they are to remain effective in an organization that transforms from one stage of growth to another. Moreover, only managers who have already developed beyond the goal-oriented stage can successfully lead individual managers and the organization as a whole through developmental changes.

The theories and research reviewed above suggest that managerial behavior can be understood from a developmental point of view. Table 3–10 shows the relationships we posit between the worldviews associated with different levels of adult development, decision style, leadership style, and organizational growth stage. We propose that earlier worldviews such as opportunistic and social imply a greater preference for classical-rational or simple incremental decision approaches and for heroic or transactional leadership styles. These managerial modes are more appropriate to early stages of one's career, early stages of organizational growth, and to relatively stable organizations. Later stage worldviews, the relativistic and self-defining, imply increased preference for neoclassical decision approaches as well as for postheroic and transformational leadership styles. These managerial modes are more relevant to later stages of one's career, to organizations at later stages of growth, and to leading organizations from one state of development to the next. We suggest the linkage between organization development and human development explains why relatively few organizations reach the highest stages of development. It appears that few people who occupy the later stages of adult development are to be found in organizations. The three recent studies of supervisors and managers by Gratch (1985), Smith (1980), and Torbert (1983) presented in Table 3–9 reveal, respectively, 14%, 0%, and 2.5% to be beyond the goal-oriented stage. This poses a serious challenge to management development and organization development professionals.

IMPLICATIONS FOR THE MANAGEMENT DEVELOPMENT PROFESSIONS

Human development would seem to be a central concern of management educators in universities, management

Table 3–10 RELATIONSHIPS BETWEEN LEVEL OF ADULT DEVELOPMENT, WORLDVIEW, DECISION STYLE, LEADERSHIP STYLE, AND ORGANIZATIONAL MODE

Level of Adult Development	Worldview	Decision Style	Leadership Style	Relevant Organizational Mode
Earlier stages, e.g., opportunistic, social	concreteness, cognitive simplicity, stereotyping, conformity, little empathy, low tolerance for diversity and ambiguity	greater preference for classical-rational or incremental approaches	"heroic" or "transactional" approaches	earlier stage, less complex, more stable
Later stages, e.g., relativistic, self-defining	cognitively complex and abstract, more empathy and social understanding, higher tolerance for diversity and ambiguity	increased use of neoclassical approaches, e.g., dialectical, reflection-in-action	"manager-as-developer," "transformational leadership"	later stage, more complex, transforming

trainers in organizations, and organization development professionals. However, we can locate very few examples from these fields that incorporate into practice what is known about the structural stages of human development. As for universities, we believe there is much truth to the assertion that "management education . . . is largely geared to training students to solve exercises that are predicated on a simple, stable view of the world" (Mitroff & Kilman, 1984). In organizations, management training concerns itself almost exclusively with imparting skills the person needs to perform the present or next job. It results in a first-order change (Watzlawik, Weakland, & Fisch, 1974). It virtually never includes the effort to augment managers' ways of thinking, to teach them how to think rather than what to think, to increase their capacity to acquire new knowledge or skills, and to define problems and tasks that have never been defined before. These mean second-order change, a fundamental transformation of the self-system. This is what development means to the structural development theorists. Given this view, organizations and schools of management would place as much emphasis on creating learning environments conducive to personal development as on teaching specific knowledge and skills. We are convinced that if developmental theory were taken seriously, it would make for substantial differences in management education and development.

MANAGEMENT EDUCATION

In management education, we know of only one MBA program in which the curriculum and administrative support system are designed with explicit reference to developmental theory (Torbert, 1983, 1986). Self-awareness and change are prompted in a new course in which students are instructed in developmental theory, encouraged to examine closely their own practice of management in relation to it, and to develop their own philosophies of management. The process of examining and improving their own action effectiveness is further emphasized (1) through project groups in which each member holds a leadership role, with consultants (advanced students who have had further training in developmental theory) offering feedback; (2) by team field study projects with live clients, with instruction in developing and terminating professional consulting relationships; and (3) by treating the MBA program itself as a live organization in which students not only receive assessments of their own performance but are asked to provide responsible feedback about the program and how to make it more effective. These activities supplement, rather than replace the usual analytical and functional courses. These efforts appear successful in their own right, according to student evaluations, but measured changes in students' developmental stages (measured by administering Loevinger's Sentence Completion Test of Ego Development at entry to and exit from the program) have been few. In a typical class of 90, for example, only 8 students' scores increased. Of these 8, 7 had volunteered to receive the special training required to serve as consultants to project groups, thus focusing on developmental practice for 21 months rather than the 9 months required of all students in the program, a provocative commentary on the kind of commitment to the developmental process needed to bring about change.

The sheer workload and performance pressure in current MBA programs may make them at best potent incubators for development from the analytic to the goal-oriented worldview. If research continues to point to the self-defining worldview as most conducive to effective managerial action, the task of management education would gain significant new definition, and endorsement would be given to efforts along the lines of the above example.

MANAGEMENT DEVELOPMENT

If MBA programs tend to reinforce the goal-oriented worldview, how much more so the pressures in organizations. Reflecting the demands for here-and-now performance, management training and development programs typically aim to impart skills and knowledge needed immediately or in the near future, a short-run rather than a developmental orientation (Johnson, 1976). Furthermore, training is more likely to be offered to junior and middle-level managers than to senior managers, though senior positions especially call for a reframing of the individual's worldview. Again, we know of just one managerial training effort explicitly built around developmental theory. Bartunek, Gordon, and Weathersby (1982) designed a conference for teaching "complicated understanding" to administrators of a women's religious order. In a 10-day residential conference, participants explored ways of understanding career and life development problems in the order from several social science perspectives. The aim was to drill participants in concurrent use of several conceptions of a problem, a way of thinking characteristic of the later developmental stages. Solutions to selected problems were developed, again with simultaneous attention to multiple frames of reference. Among other activities, participants role-played persons at different developmental stages to heighten sensitivity to problems that arise because of differences in worldviews.

No attempt was made to measure changes in developmental stages, but pre- and posttests indicated participants framed problems differently after the training than they had before. The conference was preceded by nine months of preparation in which participants were sent sets of readings and kept logs of the applicability of the readings to organizational and personal issues faced during the year. This plus the 10-day full-time duration of the conference imply that developmentally based training requires an important resource commitment. Clearly, such expenditures will be made only in organizations whose senior managers believe there is a connection between developmental stage and managerial effectiveness, who view training as an investment in the long-term capital formation of the enterprise, and who aim to apply training efforts toward real and lasting developmental change in the participants.

ORGANIZATION DEVELOPMENT

The field of organization development has become well established in the past two decades, yet two concerns are often expressed. OD's heavy reliance on humanistic values is seen to result, first, in a downplaying of power issues by OD practitioners and, second, in the virtual absence of OD interventions in bureaucracies, which, as Schein and Greiner (1977) say, "leads us to question the relevance of the OD movement for the great bulk of U.S. business and public organizations." Second, a preoccupation with human and social explanations is said to typify OD, to the detriment of task, technical, and structural considerations (French & Bell, 1984). Both these critiques imply a need for the use of a broader array of conceptual, interpersonal, and value perspectives—in other words, for the development of later stage worldviews—by OD practitioners and their clients. At present, OD aims to improve the quality of work life, but quality that is better from the standpoint of one worldview may not be from another. OD enriches the job, builds the team, provides survey feedback, but is human development really stimulated? Ironically, although the word "development" is in the name of the OD field, the field has operated virtually without reference to structural developmental theory.

One study of a QWL program in a highly politicized municipal government does suggest the potential usefulness of developmental theory to OD interventions (Krim, 1986). The interventionist, who became a senior city manager, explicitly used developmental theory to understand himself, the other major players, and to set strategy for the program's development.

The interventionist was himself measured at the relativistic transition. Characteristically, he found his ability to understand others' perspectives, as well as to understand the limited validity of his own perspective, led him to systematically "deauthorize" himself in critical action situations. Moreover, perhaps because his worldview was relatively rare, major players criticized him as "lacking political instincts." On the other hand, the interventionist made use of his awareness that different forms of power are recognizable to actors at different developmental stages (opportunistic—unilateral/coercion; social—diplomacy/referent; goal-oriented—logistical/legitimate), as well as the possibility of reframing deteriorating situations. He also struggled to overcome his "self-deauthorizing" tendency and increasingly succeeded in taking appropriate authority during the second year of the program.

After two years, the program had grown in size and had achieved two significant successes. Though viewed as only marginally successful, and not yet endorsed by the city's mayor, the program's record becomes clearer by comparison with other similar efforts. None of the other six municipal QWL programs in that state survived more than one year. Furthermore, fewer than one-third of municipal QWL programs nationally have survived as long as two years.

SUMMARY

The stages of adult development revealed by research based on structural developmental theory illuminate the profound differences between the ways individuals make meaning in the world and then act given these meaning-making systems. These systems are well established and resistant to change, but they can change. As research begins to show a relationship between managerial effectiveness and later stages of adult development, those who educate and train managers and who practice in the field of organization development are offered a potentially powerful framework for giving explicit attention to the structural development "variable." We consider that most training and organization development efforts have emphasized helping people acquire skills rather than build the wider vision that will enable them to increase their skill-acquiring capacity. Only recently have we begun learning what it takes to help adults to move along the developmental ladder. Although no easy task, efforts to foster adult development may be crucial to the attainment of truly meaningful and enduring increases in managerial and organizational effectiveness.

REFERENCES

Argyris, C., & Schön, D. A. (1974). *Theory in practice: Increased professional effectiveness*. San Francisco: Jossey-Bass.

Bartunek, J., Gordon, J., & Weathersby, R. (1982). Teaching for "complicated understanding." *Exchange: The Organizational Behavior Teaching Journal, 7*(4), 7–15.

Bartunek, J., Gordon, J., & Weathersby, R. (1983). Developing complicated understanding in administrators. *Academy of Management Review,* 8(2), 273–284.

Bass, B. M. (1985). *Leadership and performance beyond expectations*. New York: Free Press.

Birney, R. C. (1968). Research on the achievement motive. In E. Borgatta & W. Lambert (Eds.), *Handbook of personality and research*. Chicago: Rand-McNally.

Blake, R. R., Avis, W. E., & Mouton, J. S. (1966). *Corporate Darwinism*. Houston: Gulf.

Bradford, D. L., & Cohen, A. R. (1984). *Managing for excellence*. New York: John Wiley.

Cook-Greuter, S. R. (1985). *Maps for living: Ego-development theory from symbiosis to conscious universal embeddedness*. Unpublished manuscript, Dare Institute, Cambridge, MA.

French, W. L., & Bell, C. H., Jr. (1984). *Organization development*. Englewood Cliffs, NJ: Prentice-Hall.

Gratch, A. (1985). *Managers' prescriptions of decision-making processes as a function of ego development and of the situation*. Unpublished manuscript, Teachers College, Columbia University.

Greiner, L. E. (1972). Evolution and revolution as organizations grow. *Harvard Business Review, 50*(4), 37–46.

Hall, B., & Thompson, H. (1980). *Leadership through values*. New York: Paulist Press.

Harvey, O. J., Hunt, D. E., & Schroder, H. M. (1961). *Conceptual systems and personality organization*. New York: John Wiley.

Johnson, L. (1976). Organization and management of training. In R. L. Craig (Ed.), *Training and development handbook*. New York: McGraw-Hill.

Kegan, R. (1982). *The evolving self.* Cambridge, MA: Harvard.

Kohlberg, L. (1969). Stage and sequence: The cognitive and developmental approach to socialization theory and research. In D. A. Goslin (Ed.), *Handbook of socialization theory and research*. Chicago: Rand-McNally.

Krim, R. M. (1986). *The challenge of creating organizational effectiveness: Labor-management cooperation and learning strategies in the public sector*. Doctoral dissertation, Department of Sociology, Boston College.

Lasker, H. (1978). *Ego development and motivation: A cross-cultural cognitive analysis of an achievement*. Doctoral dissertation, University of Chicago.

Loevinger, J. (1976). Ego development: Conception and theories. San Francisco: Jossey-Bass.

Mason, R., & Mitroff, I. (1981). *Challenging strategic planning assumptions*. New York: John Wiley.

Merron, K., Fisher, D., & Torbert, W. R. (1986). *Meaning making and managerial effectiveness: A developmental perspective*. Paper presented at the national meeting of the Academy of Management, Chicago.

Mitroff, I., & Kilman, R. (1984). Corporate tragedies: Teaching companies to cope with evil. *New Management,* 1(4), 48–53.

Piaget, J. (1967). *Six psychological studies*. New York: Random House.

Schein, V. E., & Greiner, L. E. (1977). Can organization development be fine tuned to bureaucracies? *Organizational Dynamics,* 5(3), 48–61.

Schön, D. A. (1983). *The reflective practitioner*. New York: Basic Books.

Selman, R. L. (1980). *The growth of interpersonal understanding*. New York: Academic Press.

Smith, S. (1980). *Ego development and the problems of power and agreement in organizations*. Doctoral dissertation, School of Business and Public Administration, George Washington University.

Torbert, W. R. (1974). Doing Rawls justice: An essay review of John Rawls's *Theory of Justice*. *Harvard Educational Review,* 44(4), 459–460.

Torbert, W. R. (1978). Educating toward shared purpose, self-direction and quality work: The theory and practice of liberating structure. *The Journal of Higher Education,* 49(2), 109–135.

Torbert, W. R. (1983). *Identifying and cultivating professional effectiveness: "Bureaucratic action" at one professional business school*. Paper presented at the annual meeting of the American Society for Public Administration, New York.

Torbert, W. R. (1986). *Managing the corporate dream*. Homewood, IL: Dow Jones-Irwin.

Watzlawik, P., Weakland, J., & Fisch, R. (1974). *Change: Principles of problem formulation and problem resolution*. New York: W. W. Norton.

DISCUSSION QUESTIONS

1. Describe structural development theory and give an example.
2. Why might an effective manager need to occupy a later developmental stage?
3. What links exist between personal development and effective performance?
4. What are the implications of level of adult development for the management development professions, management education, management development, and organization development?

ACTIVITIES

Activity 3–1: TYPE A–TYPE B SELF-TEST

Step 1: Complete the following questionnaire* by circling the number on the continuum (the verbal descriptions represent endpoints) that best represents your behavior for each dimension.

Am casual about appointments	1	2	3	4	5	6	7	8	Am never late
Am not competitive	1	2	3	4	5	6	7	8	Am very competitive
Never feel rushed, even under pressure	1	2	3	4	5	6	7	8	Always feel rushed
Take things one at a time	1	2	3	4	5	6	7	8	Try to do many things at once; think about what I am going to do next
Do things slowly	1	2	3	4	5	6	7	8	Do things fast (eating, walking, etc.)
Express feelings	1	2	3	4	5	6	7	8	"Sit on" feelings
Have many interests	1	2	3	4	5	6	7	8	Have few interests outside work

Step 2: Score your responses by totaling the numbers circled. Then multiply this total by 3. The interpretation of your score is as follows:

Number of Points	Type of Personality
less than 90	B
90 to 99	B+
100 to 105	A−
106 to 119	A
120 or more	A+

Step 3: Discussion. In small groups or with the class as a whole, answer the following questions:

Description
1. What was your score?
2. What type of personality does this represent?
3. How does this compare to scores of others in the class?

Diagnosis

4. What behaviors and attitudes is each personality type likely to demonstrate?

Step 4: Identify the impact of different personality types in reacting to the following incident:

You have recently become head teller in a branch of a bank. You supervise ten tellers. Your branch has the worst performance record in the bank. You have been told that your job is on the line if you cannot turn the branch around in two months. And you cannot afford to lose this job. Preliminary meetings with your tellers suggest that they resent your presence and will actively resist any changes. How do you cope with this situation?

1. Form into groups of four to six others of the same personality type.
2. Compare your reactions to the situation with other group members. Are they similar? What elements do they share?
3. Offer a plan for coping with the situation.
4. Compare your plans to those of groups with different personalities. How are they the same? different?
5. Do the approaches consider the possible personalities of the head teller?

*Adapted with permission from R.W. Bortner, "A Short Rating Scale as a Potential Measure of Pattern A Behavior," *Journal of Chronic Diseases* 22 (1966): 87–91.

Activity 3–2: LIFELINE EXERCISE

Step 1: Draw a timeline that represents the major events in your life (your lifeline). Represent it in any way you choose, but be sure to identify all key events.

Step 2: Now draw separate lifelines for (1) your career, (2) your family, and (3) your biological development.

1. How do they interface?
2. Identify times of stress.
3. Identify key transitions.
4. What effect did these transitions have on your motivation and perceptions at work at the time?

Step 3: Discussion. In small groups or with the entire class, answer the following questions:

Description

1. What elements do the lifelines share?
2. How do the lifelines differ?

Diagnosis

3. Can you delineate common phases or stages in your careers? in your lives?
4. For each stage identified, specify the key issues members of the group had to confront.
5. Identify the times of greatest stress.
6. What factors contributed to stress at these times?

Prescription

7. For each stage, specify ways stress at that time could be reduced.

Activity 3–3: THE CASE OF THE UNDECIDED ACCOUNTANT

Step 1: Read the Case of the Undecided Accountant.

INTRODUCTION

Bill Hunter looked at his clock and sighed. It was 11:00 P.M. and there were still four unfinished projects that were sitting on his desk that would have to wait until another day. As he was walking out of the office, he noticed that the light was on in the office of Dave Landis.

Bill: "What are you doing up here this time of night, Dave?"

Dave: "I suppose that I am in the same situation that you are. There are a number of things that just don't seem to get out. I'm trying to clean up some projects so I can see my desk again."

Bill mumbled goodbye and decided to head home. Bill's mind was recalling the events of the past few weeks. He had been promoted by the partnership group of Fitch, Olson & Company to a management position within the firm. He had perceived his promotion to be an important milestone in his accounting career. This was a promotion that had to be approved by the partner group. Secondly, the criteria established to meet the requirements of a manager were quite detailed. However, he was quickly becoming disillusioned with the lack of direction supplied by the partners for the office and the absence of a clearly defined set of objectives for the future. Bill had originally felt that the recent promotion would give him the opportunity to share his concerns and ideas to improve the undesired situations occurring in the office that seemed to be ignored instead of being addressed.

COMPANY BACKGROUND AND ORGANIZATION

Fitch, Olson & Company was a professional partnership of certified public accountants based in Billings, Montana. The company was started by Jim Fitch and Harold Olson in 1962 when they decided to leave the Big-Eight accounting firm of Arthur Anderson to form their own office. Their objective was to remain a smaller accounting firm which could provide personalized, yet high-quality, accounting services for its clientele. The company expanded to start an office in Great Falls, Montana in 1969 and Casper, Wyoming in 1976. The expansion to Wyoming had proved to be quite profitable because of the energy-related boom that occurred in Wyoming during the late 1970s. In 1979, Steve Martin replaced Harold Olson as the managing partner of the accounting firm. Martin had been primarily responsible for exploring the possibilities of expanding into Wyoming and for finalizing the merger with another accounting firm in Casper. Even though Martin was the third youngest partner at 37, his foresight of the profit potential of an expansion into Wyoming had given him a quick ticket to the top of the company. In 1980, the firm approved an aggressive expansion policy for the next ten years. There were mergers with other accounting firms in 1981, 1982 and 1983 that increased the geographical market of Fitch, Olson & Company to Bismarck, North Dakota, Boise, Idaho and Denver, Colorado. (See Table 3–11.) Once again the expansion to Bismarck, North Dakota, was influenced by the energy-related boom that was occurring in Western North Dakota. The firm decided in 1982 to establish its expansion plans for larger market areas. The long-term objectives became geared toward making Fitch, Olson & Company

Table 3–11 GROWTH OF FITCH, OLSON & COMPANY

	Offices	Partners	Employees	Gross Fees
1960	1	2	10	$ 350,000
1970	2	7	40	1,500,000
1980	3	14	85	3,250,000
1983	6	26	150	6,500,000

a large, widely-known regional accounting firm in the upper northwest.

The management of Fitch, Olson & Company was based on a one-man, one-vote partnership. This meant that all partners had equal representation within the partnership while discounting such variables as seniority and location. The power structure for the firm was centered around the managing partner and the executive committee. The executive committee consisted of the managing partner, from the Billings office, and the administrative partner from each of the other offices. (See Figure 3–5.)

The power structure has been centered in Billings since the company was founded. The managing partner has always been from the Billings office. In addition, the Billings office has more partners, professional staff and gross fees than any other office.

GREAT FALLS

The Great Falls office has the image of being the "dark horse" of the firm. The office experienced a strong period of growth from its inception in 1969 until 1975. Since 1975, the office has experienced little or no growth. (See Figure 3–6.) There has not been an additional partner admitted into the Great Falls office since 1973. The staff size is smaller than in 1975, and growth in gross fees have decreased when considering the inflation factor. This lack of growth was gaining attention and generating more concern from the other offices in the firm. The firm had made it clear that improvement would be expected.

CPA PROFESSION

The CPA profession is based on providing accounting services for individuals and businesses. The profession had its roots in bookkeeping services and tax return preparation. With the beginning of the Securities Exchange Commission in 1934, there was a new need for independent audits of financial information. There was also an increased awareness by third-party users of financial information, such as financial institutions and governmental agencies, for the need for independent

Figure 3–5 ORGANIZATION CHART, FITCH, OLSON & COMPANY, OCTOBER 31, 1983

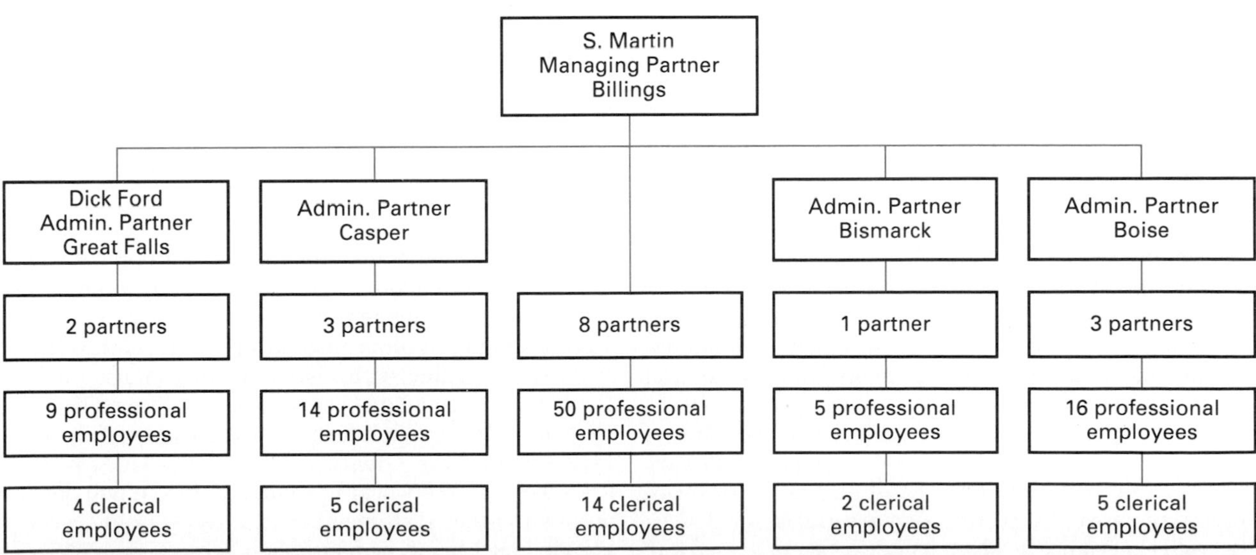

Figure 3–6 ORGANIZATION CHART, GREAT FALLS OFFICE, OCTOBER 1, 1983

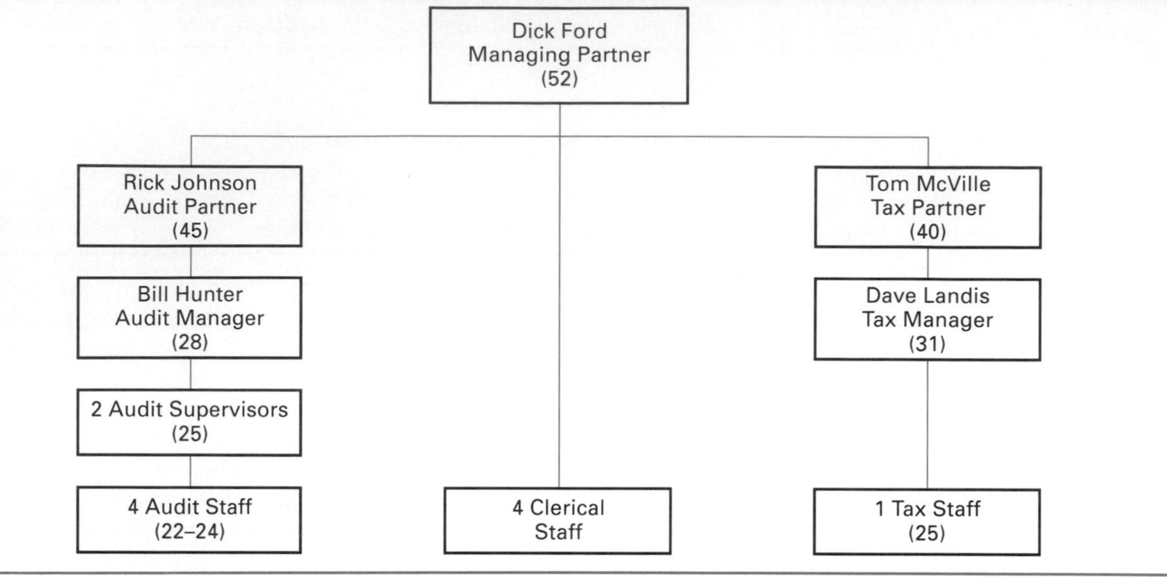

audits. There was a significant increase during the 1970s of people entering the public accounting profession. The following schedule shows the dramatic increase in the number of members of the American Institute of Certified Public Accountants.

Year	*Members*
1973	95,414
1975	112,494
1977	131,300
1979	149,314
1981	173,900
1983	201,764

Even with the influx of young members into the accounting profession, the main image of the accounting profession is one of conservatism. The conservatism projected was due to the profession's concern about overstating the company's financial position and earnings power in the audit area or, in the tax area, understating the company's tax liability.

There are three main fields within the accounting profession; audit, tax and management advisory services (MAS). The first two areas are self-explanatory. Management advisory services involves a wide range of services. This can include accounting system reviews, computer system reviews, preparation of accounting manuals, assistance with analysis of computer software and feasibility studies. Staff titles and responsibilities within the accounting profession are consistent. The titles and experience levels that are consistently used are:

Partner	+ 10 years
Manager	5–10 years
Supervisor	3–7 years
Senior Staff	1–3 years
Junior Staff	0–2 years

BILL HUNTER

Bill Hunter grew up in a small community in northern Idaho. He selected accounting as his undergraduate area of study mainly because of his interest in working with numbers. He began his career with a small, local accounting firm in Idaho. His work entailed both tax and accounting work mainly for small businesses. He accepted a position with the Great Falls office of Fitch, Olson & Company in 1980. He had become dissatisfied with his present situation and felt that the move to Fitch, Olson & Company would be an excellent move for his career. He would start at the supervisory level in the Great Falls office. He would be the highest audit staff member under the partner due to three individuals leaving the Great Falls office in 1978 and 1979. This move would promote his career by two to three years and would also provide him the opportunity to provide a large amount of input into the operation of the office.

He was satisfied with his work performance during the three years he had been working at Fitch, Olson & Company. He was comfortable with the trust he had received from the Great Falls partners. He was also satisfied with the working relationships he had developed with other staff members. He felt that his performance had been rewarded when he was promoted to the manager position after only two and one-half years with Fitch, Olson & Company:

> I was pleased when I received the announcement that I had been promoted to manager. It was a feeling of satisfaction to know that the partners felt that I should be rewarded with the promotion. However, the feeling becomes confused when I look at what is going on around me. I become frustrated whenever I look around; I'm better off when I just close my eyes.
>
> I know that there are a number of problems in the Great Falls office. That's clear when you see the amount of turnover that has occurred in the office. I've also heard there is increasing pressure to turn around the no-growth situation that has occurred with the management group. I am concerned about the direction, or I should say the lack of direction, that this office is taking. This office is a perfect example of management by crisis. It becomes frustrating to feel like we are floundering around.
>
> I find myself in an interesting, yet sensitive situation. I feel that I have a fair amount of influence in the management group. Because of that, I hear a lot of information from the partners that no other staff person does. Yet, because I'm in a supervisory position, I hear a lot of concerns and complaints from the staff. There have been a number of instances where I've been in the position of knowing what is happening on both sides of a conflict. The confidence both sides show when speaking with me is very satisfying.
>
> Staff motivation seems to be almost non-existent in the office. Maybe my view that motivated staff would help improve the current situation is too simplistic. The partnership group have goals for the entire firm and there seems to be motivation at the partner level. However, the motivation is not trickling down through the staff. The staff members that do well in the firm do so only because they are high achievers. There is so little interaction between the partners and the staff that even the best people become frustrated with the lack of direction that exists.
>
> The reward system here is interesting in that there seems to be no reward system. The promotions through the firm seem to be delegated on a time table rather than being given because they are earned. The compensation package meets industry averages when coming out of college. However, the raises for the first four or five years within the firm seem to be structured within very tight guidelines. The differentiation between raises given to the highest producers compared to average employees is very small during this period. Also, because the firm does not pay overtime, the hardest working staff members become frustrated at annual reviews when they see the little difference that their efforts have made. In one instance, five people at the same level in one office received exactly the same annual pay increase. I find that incredible and it seems clear to me that this type of system can only be a dissatisfaction to the best staff members. The long-term effect of this policy seems to be that the best people are leaving the firm.
>
> In an optimistic light, I see these problems as a challenge and an opportunity. The promotion to manager is considered a move into the lower rung of the management career ladder of the firm. Managers become more involved with the partners in firm objectives such as marketing efforts. Also, the various offices have monthly partner–manager meetings to discuss what is happening within the office and what should be done to improve the office. This could be an excellent opportunity for me to present various concerns and ideas that I have. I wouldn't feel that this could be an opportunity unless I felt confident about my position in the Great Falls partnership group.
>
> My future with this firm will involve increasing time spent on management responsibilities and assignments. Because of this, I have enrolled in a MBA program. We are currently studying organization theory and behavior. It would be nice if I could find the time to apply what I have learned into what could be done to understand and improve the current situation in this office. . . .

Step 2: Prepare the case for class discussion.

Step 3: Answer the following questions, individually or in small groups:

Description

1. Trace Bill Hunter's career so far.
2. What are Bill's concerns about his recent promotion?
3. What are Bill's concerns about Fitch, Olson & Company?

Diagnosis

4. What problems exist in the Great Falls office?
5. Using your knowledge of career development, evaluate the situation.
6. Using your knowledge of adult development, evaluate the situation.
7. Using your knowledge of personality or personal style, evaluate the situation.
8. Using your knowledge of attribution, evaluate the situation.
9. Using your knowledge of perception, evaluate the situation.
10. What possible stressors are inherent in the situation?

Prescription

11. What should Bill do next?

Step 4: Discussion. In small groups, with the entire class, or in written form, as directed by your instructor, share your answers to the questions in Step 3. Then answer the following questions:

1. What symptoms suggest a problem exists?
2. What problems exist in the case?
3. What theories and concepts help explain the problems?
4. How can the problems be corrected?
5. Are the actions likely to be effective?
6. What should be done now?

Reprinted by permission of the author, M. Tom Basuray, Professor of Management, Towson State University.

Activity 3–4: DIAGNOSIS OF ROLE PRESSURES

Step 1: Think about a situation in which you have experienced role conflict, role overload, or role ambiguity.

1. Describe the situation.
2. What role pressures did you experience at the time?
3. What caused them?
4. How did you deal with them?

Step 2: In groups of four to six, compare your answers to Questions 1–4 above.

Description

1. Identify common elements in the situations.

Diagnosis

2. List the types of role pressures experienced.
3. Specify the causes of them.

Prescription

4. Describe the different processes used to reduce them.
5. Suggest additional ways of reducing them.

Step 3: Discuss your group's answers with the entire class.

1. What are the most common types of role pressures?
2. What are the most common causes?
3. What means of reducing them are effective?

Activity 3–5: SOCIALIZATION EXERCISE

Step 1: Description. Think of two experiences: (1) where you socialized another person; and (2) where you were socialized. Describe each of these experiences in a paragraph.

Step 2: Diagnosis. Identify the socialization strategies used in each. Then, with a partner, reach consensus about the socialization strategies used in your scenarios.

Step 3: With the entire class, or in small groups, compare the strategies used in these situations.

1. What strategies did the participants experience when they were being socialized? (Your instructor may tally these on the blackboard.) What patterns do you see?
2. What strategies did the participants experience when they were socializing others? (Your instructor may tally these on the blackboard.) What patterns do you see?
3. For each strategy, consider the experiences you had when it was used, especially your feelings. (The instructor may list the outcomes of the various strategies.)
4. In which situations did you experience role conflict? role ambiguity?
5. In which situations did you experience stress?
6. Which strategies were effective? Why?
7. Which strategies are most linked to role conflict? role ambiguity? stress?

Activity 3–6: THE COROMED CORPORATION CASE

Step 1: Read the Coromed Corporation case.

At the March, 1983 national sales meeting Gary McDowan was having a conversation with Paul Anthony. Both men are sales representatives for Coromed's angiographic division. Gary was expressing his concern about John Peters' upcoming retirement. Peters is the angiographic division's national sales manager. Of major concern to Gary is John Peters' potential successor. Presently, the successor appears to be Jim Jacobs, the recently appointed western regional manager.

COMPANY BACKGROUND

Coromed Corporation of Dallas, Texas is a developer and manufacturer of advanced-technology medical devices with total sales of $133 million in fiscal year 1982. There are three divisions. The pacemaker division accounts for 61% of sales, the angiographic division accounts for 26%, and the remaining 13% is made up of a variety of smaller businesses. Although the pacemaker division accounts for the majority of sales, it is the angiographic division that contributes the most profit to the company (see Table 3–12).

In August 1979 top management decided to hire a separate sales force to handle the angiography line; prior to that time the pacemaker sales force handled all angiographic sales.

The angiographic product line is defined as those products that are used for diagnostic studies of and therapeutic treatments for the cardiovascular system. Long, thin, disposable catheters (plastic tubes) for injection of dye are the major strength of the line. The average price of these catheters is approximately $13 each. An average size hospital would purchase anywhere from 3,000–5,000 catheters per year. Coromed Corp. manufactures 150,000 catheters each month.

Due to strong increases in sales the angiographic sales force grew and was subsequently divided into an eastern and western region in December 1982. Up to that time Van Vincent was the acting sales manager. Van performed his duties from his home in the New York–Boston area. Corporate headquarters is 1500 miles away in Dallas, Texas. Van has been with Coromed for 18 years and is 63 years old. He has been a pacemaker divisional manager prior to his assignment in angiography. When the sales force was divided into two regions, Van was offered the job of national sales manager. Realizing that he would have had to relocate to corporate headquarters, Van declined the position and is presently the eastern regional manager. John Peters, who has been with Coromed for 18 years also and has worked at headquarters in various positions for most of the time, was appointed national sales manager (see Figure 3–7).

JIM JACOBS, WESTERN REGIONAL MANAGER

Jim Jacobs was appointed western regional manager in December 1982. Jim had worked for Coromed as a pacemaker sales representative for 3 years before quitting and trying his hand at other occupations. Two years later Jim was hired back by Coromed as an angiographic representative. During this most recent employment with Coromed, Jim befriended Stu Frost, the Vice President of Sales and Marketing at that time. Stu himself decided to split the sales force into two regions with Jim as the manager in the west, Van as the manager in the east, with both managers reporting to John Peters.

In January 1983 Stu Frost's responsibilities changed. However, the change was not related to the angiographic realignment. Stu's new position as Vice President of Marketing Planning has taken him out of any future sales management decision making.

Jim Jacobs is 38 years old with a B.A. in Business Administration. He has 1 year prior management experience with several years of sales experience behind him. Jim has acquired all his angiographic experience in his most recent activity with Coromed. He is very energetic and results-oriented and now manages seven people. He also has a very good rapport with his boss, John Peters. However, there have been complaints among some of Jacobs' salesmen. At the March '83 Sales Meeting a conversation between two salesmen on the topic went as follows:

Salesman 1: "Do you believe that guy Jacobs requesting us to submit an itinerary 10 weeks in advance? How am I supposed to know who the heck I'll be seeing and what I'll be saying to them 10 weeks from now?"

Table 3–12 SUMMARY OF OPERATIONS AND FINANCIAL INFORMATION, 1982 (IN $000'S)

	Pacing Systems	Angiographic	Other	Total
Sales	81,584	34,457	16,973	133,014
Operating costs				
Including:	75,029	21,733	20,973	117,735
Costs of Goods Sold				
Research & Devel.				
Selling				
General & Admin.				
Operating profit:	6,555 (34%)	12,724 (66%)	(4,000)	15,279

Figure 3–7 COROMED CORPORATION MARKETING ORGANIZATIONAL CHART

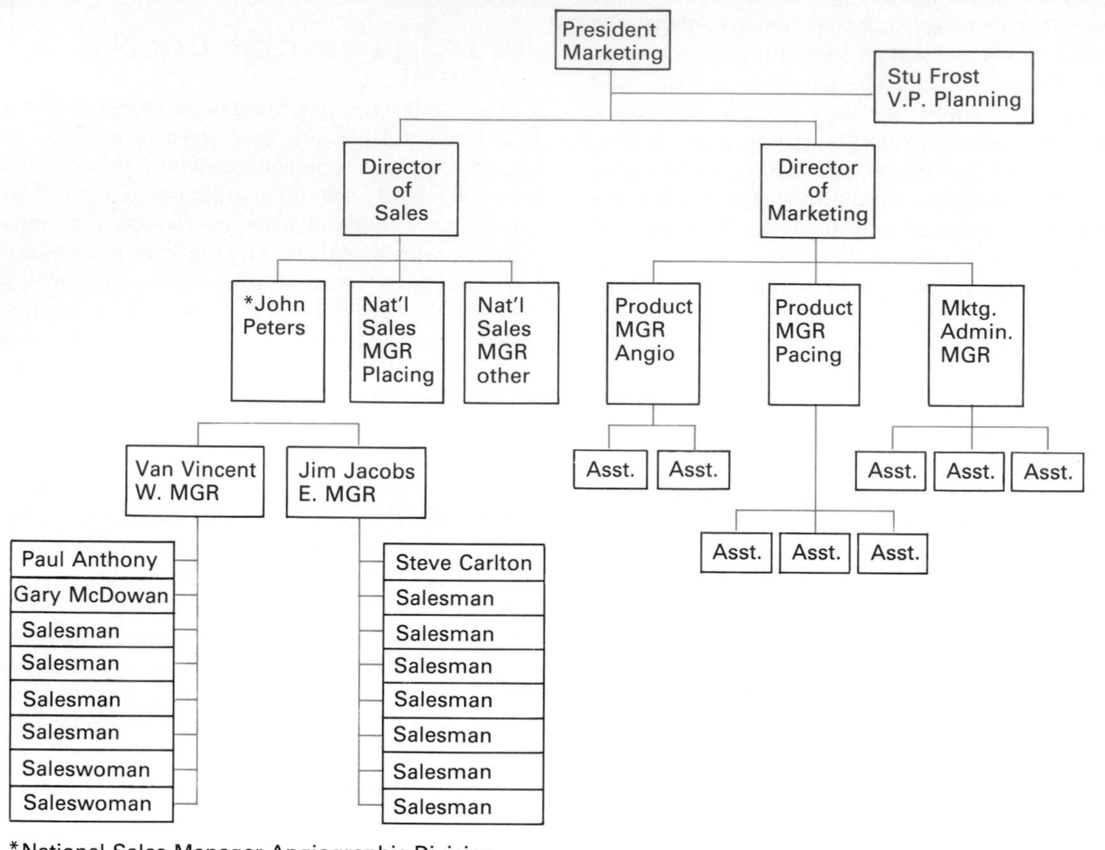

Salesman 2: "That stuff irks me too! The guy comes on like gangbusters. He has this incredible dictatorial style that just rubs me the wrong way. He had better be careful in the way he handles us. Ya know, most of us weren't born yesterday."

Salesman 1: "It just all boils down to the fact that Jacobs just does not know how to handle people. He's just not people oriented, it's as plain as that."

Within Jim's first 6 months as an angiographic sales representative there was a national sales meeting (Oct. '82). It was at this meeting that Jim had the following conversation with several of the other representatives:

> I'm having a great time working for Coromed. In my first 6 months with the company I have just about doubled my sales. I have gone from $1.3 million worth of business to $2 million already. Stu was thinking of cutting my territory but recently told me he wasn't going to afterall. He feels it would be real difficult for someone to replace me in that area and do as good a job as I have done.

At this point Paul Anthony asked how is Jim able to cover such a large territory (Georgia, South Carolina, Eastern Tennessee, Northern Florida) so well. Jim responded by saying he is into most of his accounts every 6–7 weeks. Paul found this a little hard to believe. In fact it was much later (after Jim's promotion), while Paul was training the new salesman who replaced Jim, that many of the accounts in the territory reported they had never heard of Jim Jacobs nor had they seen any Coromed representative in months.

PAUL ANTHONY, SENIOR ANGIOGRAPHIC SALES REPRESENTATIVE

Paul Anthony was hired as Coromed's first angiographic salesman four years ago. Paul came to Coromed with 2 years sales and marketing experience from a company that is also in the angiographic industry. He has a B.A. in management and will soon have an MBA. Paul is 31 years old, energetic, knowledgeable, and popular among the sales force. As a senior sales representative he has more responsibility than most of the other sales people. Because of additional responsibilities such as training new representatives and his tenure with the company he has assisted in training over half of the current angiographic sales force. Aside from his normal sales duties, Paul has special sales and marketing assignments asked of him from time to time from the Director of Sales and the Director of Marketing. Because of these special assignments which include giving instruction to new recruits at corporate headquarters, he has had much exposure to top management over the past four years. Various members of the sales force across the country contact him on a semi-monthly basis to share information with him and to sound out ideas on him. Paul reports directly to Van Vincent and has built up an excellent rapport with him and he is also one of a small handful of salesmen that John Peters calls from time to time when he is trying to feel out the sales force on new policies. At the recent national sales meeting, Peters and Paul spent an afternoon together playing golf.

GARY McDOWAN, ANGIOGRAPHIC SALES REPRESENTATIVE

Although Gary McDowan has been with Coromed longer than Paul, he has only been an angiographic sales representative for two years. Gary was a pacemaker salesman for 3 years before he decided he had a better future in the angiographic division. Gary has not had nearly as much exposure as Paul to top management but is well known nonetheless within the organization. At the recent national sales meeting, Gary won the Eastern Salesman of the Year award. Gary is 46 years old, has a B.A. in English and has just recently been asked to start training new representatives every so often. Gary reports to Van Vincent.

It was at the March 1983 national sales meeting that Gary expressed his concern about John Peters' upcoming retirement to Paul Anthony. The conversation went as follows:

Gary: "Paul, you know that Jim Jacobs appears as the likely successor to Peters don't you?"

Paul: "Unfortunately Gary I think you may be right."

Gary: "I really can't stand that guy Jacobs, Paul. Do you realize that he has alienated himself from many of the other sales reps because of his lack of maturity and understanding of others? All he wants to do is get to the top! Paul, my overwhelming concern with this issue expresses the concern of 10–12 of the other sales reps."[1]

Paul: "Every time I've ever talked to Jacobs all he has talked about is how great he is. I do realize a lot of the other guys are not fond of him either. Most of us know that Jim is somewhat of a fake; all he wants is to build an empire for himself."

Gary then appeared to have changed the subject abruptly and made the following statement:

Gary: "Paul, I'm very interested in becoming a regional manager as soon as possible. It's obvious with your seniority in the sales force and your popularity with top management that you're in line for Van's position when he retires in 2 years. I concede that position to you; however, I'll need all the help you can give me in obtaining the new and upcoming central region manager's position."

Paul: "You're right Gary. I look forward to the eastern regional manager's position in a few more years but what are you driving at?"

Gary: "The central region manager's slot will probably not be available for another 18 months. By that time Jim Jacobs will have had just about 2 years as a regional manager. Those two years will be two more years in management than anybody else will have at the time and it's evident that Jacobs wants to go to the top. Hopefully, Jim's unpopular reputation will be a factor in the future national sales management promotion. Nonetheless Paul, one of us will have to leapfrog over Jacobs to national sales manager in order to prevent the possibility of him getting the job."

Paul: "That's all well and good Gary but your strategy is based on you getting the central region. What about your competitor, Steve Carlton?"

STEVE CARLTON, ANGIOGRAPHIC SALES REPRESENTATIVE

Steve has been with Coromed Corp. for two years. He is extremely well liked by Peters, Vincent, Jacobs and the rest of the salesforce. Steve came to Coromed after two years of selling pharmaceuticals. He is 29 years old with a B.A. in political science and a Masters in Education. John Peters mentioned to Paul Anthony on the golf course that Steve was management material. Steve was asked by Peters to develop an ongoing sales training course for Coromed angiographic representatives which was first presented at the recent national sales meeting.

Steve had overheard Gary grumbling about Jim Jacobs at the national sales meeting and decided he should say something in Jim's defense:

Steve: "I have been reporting to Jim for close to five months now and I happen to think he's a great guy. I enjoy him and respect his knowledge very much."

Paul Anthony later mentioned to Gary that Peters told him on the golf course that Steve is in the running for the central regional manager's position.

GARY McDOWAN'S DILEMMA

Gary McDowan has several objectives that he would like met. He would like first of all to be promoted to a regional manager's position as soon as possible. Realizing that Paul Anthony seems to have the eastern regional manager's slot locked up when Van Vincent retires, he needs to work on obtaining the central regional manager's position when it becomes available. This is not going to be easy now that Steve Carlton is in the running. Gary's other objective is to somehow help prevent Jim Jacobs from being promoted to National Sales Manager when John Peters retires in two years. Many of the other representatives, including Paul Anthony, would like to have that promotion prevented as well. Gary feels that if he can find the right strategies and use them effectively he could very possibly meet both his objectives in the next 18–24 months.

NOTE

[1]Coromed Corp. has 15 angiographic sales reps nationwide.

Step 2: Prepare the case for class discussion.

Step 3: Answer each of the following questions, individually or in small groups, as directed by your instructor:

Description

1. Trace each salesperson's career.

Diagnosis

2. What problems exist at Coromed?
3. Using your knowledge of career development, evaluate the situation.
4. Using your knowledge of adult development, evaluate the situation.
5. Using your knowledge of personality and personal style, evaluate the situation.
6. Using your knowledge of role pressures, evaluate the situation.
7. What perceptual and attributional distortions exist?

Prescription

8. What should Gary do?

Step 4: Discussion. In small groups or with the entire class, or in written form, share your answers to the questions above. Then answer the following questions:

1. What symptoms suggest a problem exists?
2. What problems exist in the case?
3. What theories and concepts help explain those problems?
4. How can the problems be corrected?
5. Are the actions likely to be effective?

This case was prepared by Ron Metro, MBA candidate, under the supervision of Assistant Professor Alberto Zanzi.

CONCLUDING COMMENTS

In this chapter we examined the role personality and personal style play in organizational performance. Together with perception, attribution, and learning, personality exerts a core influence on individual behavior and attitudes. We also traced the impact of personal development—biosocial, family, and career—on individuals and organizations. At different life stages individuals differ in the major tasks they confront and their ability to tolerate the ambiguity, anxiety, and stress that results. The capacity of an individual to tolerate stress depends on his or her skills, values, expectations, and personality, as well as interactions with a potentially stressful environment. It also may depend on an individual's stage of personal development, as well as the interactions between biological, family, and career cycles.

We have seen the impact of developmental transitions on performance. You traced your own lifeline and identified times of crisis. You also noted experiences in which you felt role conflict, role overload, and role ambiguity. You identified experiences you had in being socialized and in socializing others.

In each case, you used a variety of theoretical perspectives, including personality, adult and career development, role conflict, overload, and ambiguity, as well as perceptual, communication, and motivation theories to enhance your understanding of the situation. In the Case of the Undecided Accountant and the Coromed Corporation case, you translated this understanding into prescriptions for change, for dealing with the problems you diagnosed. You also offered a prescription for dealing with role pressures you have experienced.

ENDNOTES

[1]This case is based on one prepared by Michael T. Sullivan.

[2]J.B. Rotter, Generalized expectancies for internal versus external control of reinforcement, *Psychological Monographs* 1, no. 609 (1966): 80.

[3]J.B. Rotter, External control and internal control, *Psychology Today* (June 1971): 37.

[4]*Ibid.*

[5]R. Christie and F.L. Geis (eds.), *Studies in Machiavellianism* (New York: Academic Press, 1970).

[6]*Ibid.*

[7]M. Friedman and R. Roseman, *Type A Behavior and Your Heart* (New York: Knopf, 1974).

[8]*Ibid.;* M.T. Matteson and C. Preston, Occupational stress, Type A behavior and physical well-being, *Academy of Management Journal* 25 (1982): 373–391.

[9]C.G. Jung, *Collected Works,* ed. H. Read, M. Fordham, and G. Adler (Princeton, N.J.: Princeton University Press, 1953).

[10]D.B. Myers and K.C. Briggs, *Myers–Briggs Type Indicator* (Princeton, N.J.: Educational Testing Service, 1962).

[11]A. Anastasi, *Psychological Testing* (New York: Macmillan, 1976).

[12]M.F.R. Kets de Vries and D. Miller, Personality, culture, and organization, *Academy of Management Review* 11 (1986): 262–279.

[13]See R. Gould, Adult life states: Growth toward self-tolerance, *Psychology Today* (February, 1975); H. Levinson, *The Seasons of a Man's Life* (New York: Knopf, 1978); G. Sheehy, *Passages* (New York: Dutton, 1976).

[14]E.G.C. Collins and P. Scott, Everyone who makes it has a mentor, *Harvard Business Review* 56 (1978): 9–18.

[15]See K.E. Kram, *Mentoring at Work: Developmental Relationships in Organizational Life* (Glenview, Ill.: Scott, Foresman, 1985).

[16]S.C. Bushardt, R.N. Moore, and S.C. Debnath, Picking the right person for your mentor, *SAM Advanced Management Journal* 47 (Summer 1982): 40–54.

[17]K.E. Kram and L.A. Isabella, Mentoring alternatives: The role of peer relationships in career development, *Academy of Management Journal* 28 (1985): 110–132.

[18]G.R. Roche, Much ado about mentors, *Harvard Business Review* 57 (January-February 1979): 17–28.

[19]D.M. Hunt and C. Michael, Mentorship: A career training and development tool, *Academy of Management Review* 8 (1983): 475–485; K.E. Kram, Phases of the mentor relationship, *Academy of Management Journal* 26 (1983): 608–625.

[20]K.E. Kram, Mentoring in the workplace. In D.T. Hall and Associates (eds.), *Career Development in Organizations* (San Francisco: Jossey-Bass, 1986).

[21]R.A. Webber, Career problems of young managers, *California Management Review* 18 (1976): 19–33.

[22]See S.S. Dubin, *Professional Obsolescence* (New York: English University Press, 1972).

[23]See T.P. Ference, The career plateau: Facing up to life at the middle, *MBA* 12 (1978); E.K. Warren, T.P. Ference, and J.A.C. Stoner, The case of the plateaued performer, *Harvard Business Review* 53 (1975): 30–38, 146–148.

[24]J.T. Carnazza et al., Plateaued and nonplateaued managers: Factors in job performance, *Journal of Management* 7(2) (1981): 7–25.

[25]D.T. Hall, Breaking career routines: Midcareer choice and identity development. In Hall and Associates, *op. cit.,* p. 133.

[26]*Ibid.,* p. 127.

[27]D.J. Levinson, The mid-life transition: A period in adult psychological development, *Psychiatry* 40 (1977): 99–112.

[28]D.T. Hall, Project work as an antidote to career plateauing in a declining engineering organization, *Human Resource Development* 24 (1985): 271–292.

[29]Levinson, *op. cit.*

[30]Gould, *op. cit.*

[31]F.W. Dalton, P.H. Thompson, and R.L. Price, The four stages of professional careers: A new look at performance by professionals, *Organizational Dynamics* 6 (1977): 19–42.

[32]*Ibid.*

[33]Ference, *op. cit.;* Warren et al., *op. cit.*

[34]L. Larwood and B.A. Gutek, Working toward a theory of women's career development. In B.A. Gutek and L. Larwood (eds.), *Women's Career Development* (Newbury Park, Cal.: Sage, 1987), pp. 170–183.

[35]*Ibid.*

[36]J.A. Raelin, An anatomy of autonomy: Managing professionals, *Academy of Management Executive* 3 (August 1989): 216–228; J.A. Raelin, C.K. Sholl, and D. Leonard, Why professionals turn sour and what to do, *Personnel* 62 (October 1985): 28–41.

[37]See J. Raelin, *Professional Careers* (New York: Praeger, 1983).

[38]J. Raelin, Examination of deviant/adaptive behaviors in the organizational careers of professionals, *Academy of Management Review* 9 (1984): 413–427.

[39]B. Leibowitz, C. Farren, and B.L. Kaye, *Designing Career Development Systems* (San Francisco: Jossey-Bass, 1986).

[40]The discussion of roles is based in large part on R.L. Kahn, D.M. Wolfe, R.P. Quinn, and J.D. Snoek, *Organizational Stress: Studies in Role Conflict and Ambiguity* (New York: John Wiley, 1964).

[41]C.D. Fisher and R. Gitelson, A meta-analysis of the correlates of role conflict and ambiguity, *Journal of Applied Psychology* 68 (1983): 320–333; A.G. Bedeian and A.A. Armenakis, A path-analytic study of the consequences of role conflict and ambiguity, *Academy of Management Journal* 24 (1981): 417–424; M. Van Sell, A.P. Brief, and R.S. Schuler, Role conflict and role ambiguity: Integration of the literature and directions for future research, *Human Relations* 34 (1981): 43–71.

[42]J.H. Greenhaus and N.J. Beutell, Sources of conflict between work and family roles, *Academy of Management Review* 10 (1985): 76–88, p. 77.

[43]*Ibid.*

[44]R.L. Valdez and B.A. Gutek, Family roles—a help or a hindrance for working women. In B.A. Gutek and L. Larwood, *op. cit.*

[45]See also F.S. Hall and D.T. Hall, *Dual Career Couples* (Reading, Mass.: Addison-Wesley, 1979) for a discussion of dual-career families.

[46]D.T. Hall and J. Richter, Balancing work life and home life: What can organizations do to help? *Academy of Management Executive* 2(3) (1988): 213–223; F.S. Hall and D.T. Hall, Dual careers—how do couples and companies cope with the problems? *Organizational Dynamics* 6 (1978): 57–77.

[47]J.C. Latack, Career transitions within organizations: An exploratory study of work, nonwork, and coping strategies, *Organizational Behavior and Human Performance* 34 (1984): 296–322.

[48]E.H. Schein, Organizational socialization and the profession of management, *Sloan Management Review* 9 (1968): 1–16.

[49]*Ibid.;* R.R. Ritti and G.R. Funkhouser, *The Ropes to Skip and the Ropes to Know,* 3d ed. New York: Wiley, 1987.

[50]J. Van Maanen, People processing: Strategies of organizational socialization, *Organizational Dynamics* 7 (1978): 19–36.

[51]*Ibid.*

[52]G.R. Jones, Psychological orientation and the process of organizational socialization: An interactionist perspective, *Academy of Management Review* 8 (1983): 464–474.

[53]Kahn et al., *op. cit.*

RECOMMENDED READINGS

Feldman, D. *Career Development.* Lake Forest, Ill.: Brace-Park, 1987.

Gutek, B.A., and Larwood, L. (eds.) *Women's Career Development.* Newbury Park, Cal.: Sage, 1987.

Hall, D.T., and Associates. *Career Development in Organizations.* San Francisco: Jossey-Bass, 1986.

Leibowitz, B., Farren, C., and Kaye, B.L. *Designing Career Development Systems.* San Francisco: Jossey-Bass, 1986.

Levinson, H. (ed.) *Designing and Analyzing Your Career.* Boston: Harvard Business School, 1989.

London, M. *Career Management and Survival in the Workplace.* San Francisco: Jossey-Bass, 1986.

Rose, S., and Larwood, L. (eds.) *Women's Careers: Pathways and Pitfalls.* New York: Praeger, 1988.

4

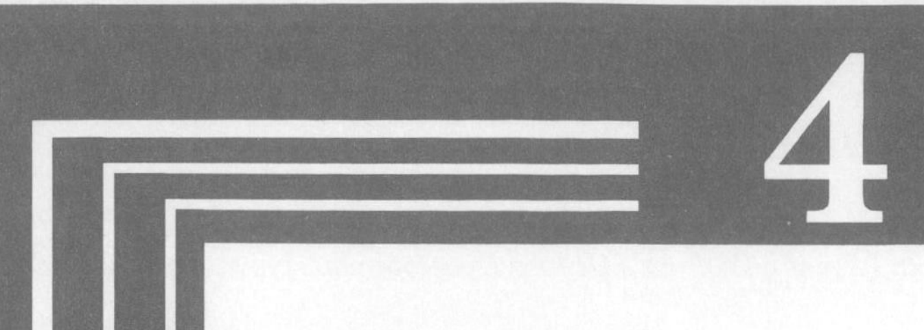

Motivating and Rewarding Individuals

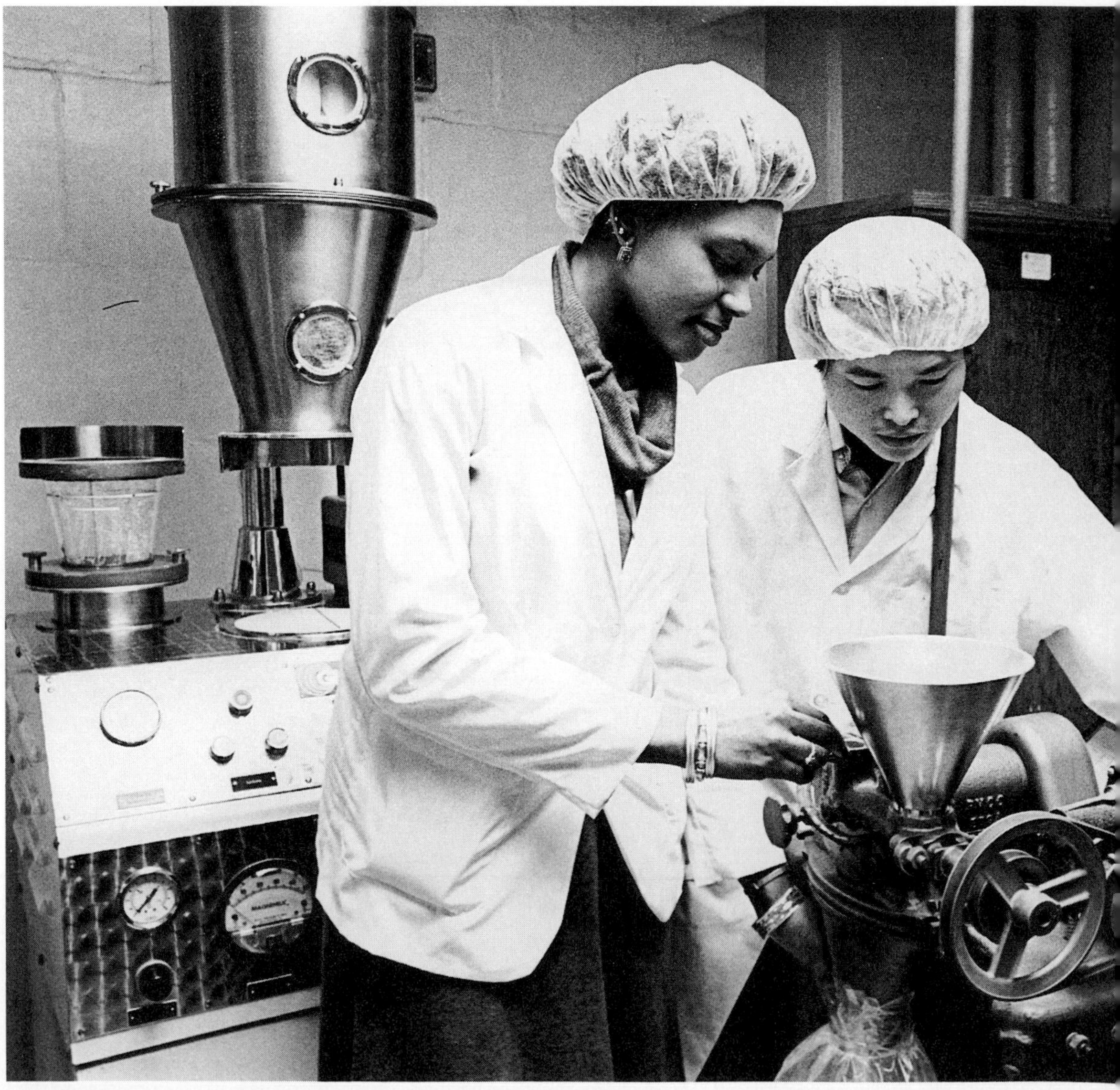

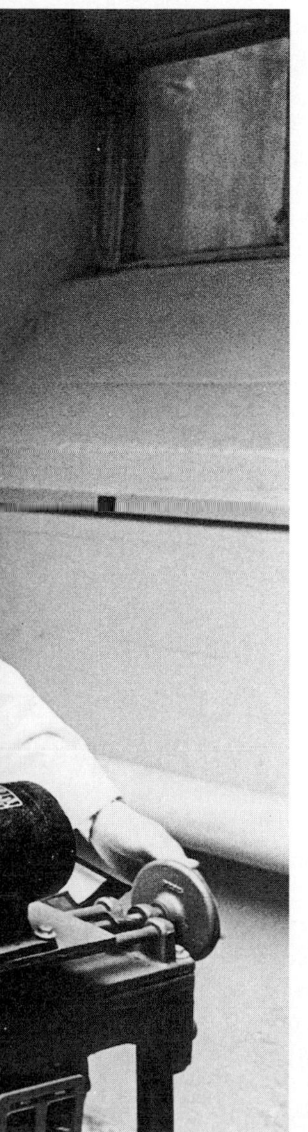

CHAPTER OUTLINE

LEARNING OBJECTIVES

After completing the reading and activities in Chapter 4, students will be able to

- identify, compare, and contrast the major motivation perspectives and theories;
- show how expectancy theory and goal-setting theory are integrating theories;
- apply the motivation theories, one at a time and together, to diagnosing a motivational situation;
- offer prescriptions for motivating employees;
- identify the major components of a reward system;
- comment on the use of wages and benefits in a reward system;
- describe and design an incentive system;
- discuss the role of employee ownership in the reward system; and
- specify the characteristics of an effective reward system.

Motivation Problem at Interval Corporation

When Benjamin Kane joined Interval Corporation he began working for Dr. Jeffrey Hoffman as a research technician. Dr. Hoffman had just been promoted from a research scientist to a principal investigator, the top scientific position in the Research and Development Division. He had been assigned to head the research for a new personal-care product funded by a large manufacturer of such projects. Ben Kane worked alone with Jeff Hoffman on this project from its inception. The small size of the team was unusual at Interval since most other projects had technicians working under research associates, or research scientists working for principal investigators; on no other project did a technician work directly for a principal investigator.

Hoffman was busy with several other projects so he gave Ben the freedom and responsibility to work as he wished toward accomplishing the research goals. Ben said he liked the responsibility and carried out the tasks with minimal supervision. Ben soon began to determine his own goals, write reports, and give presentations at research meetings. He and Jeff Hoffman interacted infrequently but had an excellent working relationship. Ben enjoyed his work so much that he often worked more than fifty hours a week without requesting overtime pay.

Because the research was successful funding was increased after a year to accommodate an additional researcher. Ben viewed the expansion of the team with mixed emotions. He knew that the new hire would have more knowledge and experience and a higher position than he did. Ben was eager for someone to participate more actively in the research but did not want to lose any of his responsibility.

Bob Rowen was hired as a research associate. His resume included a two-page list of publications and suggested that he had a knowledge of many techniques that would be helpful in the research. Within the first few weeks it became apparent that Bob did not have the skills or knowledge that his resume suggested. Hoffman and Kane discussed the problem and decided that perhaps Bob just needed time to adjust to the research project. After another month had passed Hoffman and Kane agreed that Bob lacked the skills needed for basic scientific research. Ben in particular began to feel frustrated that much of his time was spent helping Bob and not doing his own work.

Jeff Hoffman began to get angry about the low productivity of the group. During group meetings he would often yell at Bob or not speak to him at all. He often acted sarcastically and very directive; each day he spelled out in detail what Ben and Bob should do. Ben found this approach insulting and spoke to Hoffman about it. He told Hoffman that he knew his capabilities and should not compromise them because of Bob. Hoffman apologized and returned some of the responsibility to Ben Kane. Although Hoffman knew that Bob needed more direction, he supervised him only occasionally. Ben could still talk with Hoffman but began to dislike the cruel way he treated Bob. Ben was particularly annoyed that Bob's salary was at least one-third more than his. Ben found the situation so unpleasant that he began to work only eight hours a day; his productivity declined.

Hoffman realized that something had to be done with Bob so he spoke with his boss about him. His boss told Hoffman that he should decide what to do. Hoffman then spoke with Ben, who suggested that Jeff fire Bob since he was detracting from rather than contributing to the group. Hoffman met

with Bob; he told him that he would not fire him but thought that he should voluntarily quit. Bob chose to stay. Hoffman resented this so much that he made life as miserable as possible for Bob. Ben soon began looking for another job and two months later left the company.[1]

What caused the decline in Ben Kane's productivity, involvement, and satisfaction? Why did Ben seek a new job and leave Interval? We can attribute Ben's behaviors and attitudes in part to a decline in his work motivation. Communication and leadership dysfunctions (described in Chapters 7 and 8) also likely contributed to the problems.

This situation presents typical motivational concerns, including how to keep a high performer challenged and productive, making unproductive workers perform, and challenging workers to use their capabilities fully. More generally, motivation concerns include how to get desired outcomes from employees. Motivation influences and in turn can be affected by performance. What motivates individuals to behave, think, or feel in certain ways? What factors make you and others willing to work, be creative, achieve, produce?

Theory and research in the area of motivation provide a systematic way of diagnosing the degree of motivation and prescribing ways to increase it. Understanding theories of motivation broadens the diagnostic framework that can be applied to organizational situations.

In this chapter, we first examine five motivation perspectives: (1) needs theories, (2) equity theory, (3) reinforcement theory, (4) expectancy theory, and (5) goal setting. We describe each theory, show how it can be used to diagnose motivation in a given situation, and then comment on the prescriptions that follow from the diagnosis. We conclude the chapter with a consideration of the nature of reward systems in organizations.

NEEDS THEORIES

Think again about the situation experienced by Ben Kane. What could have caused the motivation problems he experienced? Why did his effort and productivity decrease, and why did he seek another position? Early motivation theorists would explain such a situation by saying that Interval Corporation failed to meet Ben's needs—his basic requirements for living and working productively. These theorists assumed that all people have needs, expectations, and desires. They further assumed that, to be successful, organizations must meet their employees' needs.

Can you identify Ben Kane's needs? To do a good job of identifying them, we probably would need to spend a great deal of time talking with Ben and observing his behavior, both in and out of the work situation. But, based on the information presented in the introduction, we might conjecture that he has a high need for autonomy since removing it seems to have contributed to his dissatisfaction and declining performance. Or he might have a high need for achievement; his high energy level during the first year of employment, when he assumed responsibility for the design and implementation of the research project, may reflect this need. Or he might have high esteem needs; he felt insulted in a variety of ways. Or he might have more basic physiological needs. Interval's failure to meet Ben's needs likely contributes to his decreased effort and subsequent job change.

In this section we present four of the most popular needs theories: (1) Maslow's hierarchy of needs theory; (2) McClelland's need for achievement theory; (3) Alderfer's ERG theory; and (4) Herzberg's two-factor theory. Each of these theories describes a specific set of needs the researchers believe individuals have, and each differs somewhat in the number and kinds of needs identified. Table 4–1 shows the different needs. The theories also differ as to how unfulfilled needs influence motivation, as discussed in the following sections.

Maslow's Hierarchy of Needs

Beginning in 1935, Abraham Maslow developed the first and one of the most popular and well-known motivation theories.[2] Maslow stated that individuals have five types of needs, arranged in a hierarchy from the most basic to the highest level (see Figure 4–1): (1) physiological, (2) safety, (3) belongingness and love, (4) esteem, and (5) self-actualization.[3]

Physiological needs are the most basic needs an individual has. These include, at a minimum, a person's requirement for food, water, shelter, and sex. Today we can think of such needs more broadly. For some workers, we might include the ability to care for their children among these basic physiological needs. We might also include medical or dental coverage among them. The wages individuals receive for working, as well as any supplementary benefits, often address these most basic needs. Some companies have also provided employees with subsidized lunch programs or company housing. Increasing numbers of organizations are providing workers with child care facilities or subsidized child care. Individuals with unsatisfied physiological needs are motivated to perform in order to continue to be employed and thus continue to have their basic needs satisfied.

Safety needs include a person's desire for security or protection. This translates most directly into concerns for short-term and long-term job security. Contracts signed between labor and management in the automobile industry, for example, have emphasized meeting workers' needs for security by guaranteeing their employment.[4] Other employers have tried to motivate workers

Table 4–1 COMPARISON OF NEEDS IN FOUR THEORIES

Maslow	Alderfer	McClelland	Herzberg
Physiological Safety and Security	Existence		Hygiene
Belongingness and Love	Relatedness	Need for affiliation	
Self-esteem Self-actualization	Growth	Need for achievement Need for power	Motivators

Figure 4–1 MASLOW'S HIERARCHY OF NEEDS

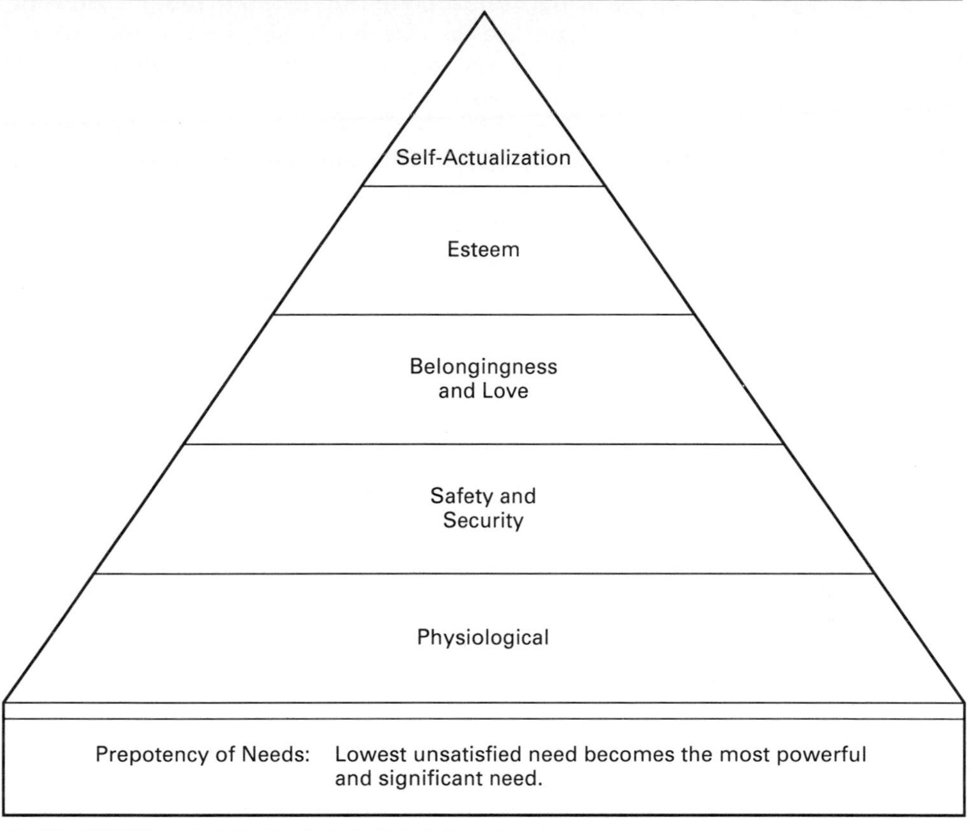

to produce and to remain with their organizations by offering pension benefits. More recently, organizations have attempted to protect the physical safety of their workers; for example, some offer an escort service at the end of the work day for those who park their cars in distant or dark parking lots and many have increased building security.

Belongingness and love needs focus on the social aspects of work and nonwork situations. Virtually all individuals desire affectionate relationships or regular interaction with others. Organizations meet these social needs by providing opportunities for social interactions such as regular coffee breaks, organized sports, and other recreational opportunities. Increasingly, organizations encourage workers to perform their jobs as members of work teams; these teams provide work-related opportunities for meeting social needs.

Esteem needs relate to a person's desire to master his or her work; demonstrate competence and accomplishments; build a reputation as an outstanding performer; hold a position of prestige; and feel self-esteem. If Ben Kane has esteem needs, Interval's top executives could motivate him by finding ways to give him respect or boost his self-worth; they might show they value his competence by offering a larger and more plush office or assigning a new title to his position. Some employers meet esteem needs by giving public recognition for good performance through Employee of the Month awards, promoting workers, giving more prestigious job titles, or offering increased responsibility.

Self-actualization needs reflect an individual's desire to grow and develop to his or her fullest potential. An individual often wants the opportunity to be creative on the job. Or he or she may want autonomy and responsibility. Organizations try to motivate these individuals by offering them challenging positions as well as the opportunity to advance in the organization. Did Ben Kane exhibit his self-actualization needs? Certainly Ben's willingness to assume more responsibility and perform tasks requiring advanced skills reflect his growth and learning needs. While his employment at Interval originally seemed to meet these needs, as reflected in his satisfaction and effort, what evidence suggests that his situation changed? His search for a new job and declining effort indicates some deficiency in having his needs met.

Prepotency of Needs Maslow ordered the needs in his hierarchy, beginning with the basic physiological needs and continuing through safety, belonging and love, esteem, and self-actualization. In his scheme, the lowest unsatisfied need becomes the *prepotent,* or most powerful and significant, need. The prepotent need motivates an individual to act to fulfill it; satisfied needs *do not motivate.* If, for example, a person lacks sufficient food and clothing, he or she acts to satisfy these basic physiological needs; hence, this person would most likely work to receive pay or other benefits to satisfy them. On the other hand, a person whose physiological, safety, and belongingness needs are satisfied is motivated to satisfy needs at the next level—the esteem needs. For this person, pay does not motivate performance unless it increases esteem, but a promotion or other changes in a job's title or status, which satisfy esteem needs, are likely to motivate.

Maslow recognized that the hierarchy of needs could, under certain circumstances, vary in order. He noted, for example, that for some people self-esteem must be satisfied before love, autonomy before other needs, or higher-order needs (esteem, self-actualization) before any lower-order ones (physiological, safety, social).[5] He also suggested that higher needs can differ from lower ones in their motivating value[6]: higher needs develop later; they can be less powerful because they influence an individual for a shorter period of time; responding to them can be delayed; meeting them may not be essential; they are less tangible and less observable; and they may be harder to satisfy.

Consider again the case of Ben Kane. To use Maslow's theory to diagnose the situation, we can ask three questions: (1) Which needs have been satisfied? (2) Which unsatisfied need is lowest in the hierarchy? (3) How can those needs be satisfied?

We can assume that Ben has satisfied his physiological, security, and belongingness needs; then, according to Maslow, esteem needs become prepotent. During his first year at Interval, the increasing opportunity to work directly for a principal investigator satisfied his esteem needs, and the chance to work independently motivated him because these work conditions satisfied his need for esteem and then his need for self-actualization. When the new organizational arrangements were introduced, however, Ben lost both his status and his autonomy. We can hypothesize that he was less motivated to work because he saw no way of satisfying his self-actualization and esteem needs. Determining whether this is actually true, however, would depend on information beyond that provided.

Research Support The popularity of this theory of motivation stems primarily from its simplicity and logic. One study found that the autonomy, esteem, and security needs of lower management were satisfied less than those of middle management; higher-order needs were the least satisfied for both groups.[7] Yet research conducted to test the theory generally does not support it. In general, research indicates that two or three categories of needs, rather than five, exist,[8] and that the relationships, relative importance, and sequences are not consistent from one individual to another. In addition, the ordering of needs may vary in different countries, and thus Maslow's theory may not be universal. For example, workers in countries characterized as high on uncertainty avoidance (e.g., Japan) value security over self-actualization.[9] A study of Liberian managers showed that they had higher self-esteem and security needs than Americans.[10] Different cultures may also place relatively more value on lower rather than higher needs or vice versa.

Finally, the research suggests that one need is not necessarily prepotent at a time[11]; that is, Ben Kane may not be motivated to satisfy, first, his need for esteem and then his need for self-actualization. Rather, several needs are often present simultaneously to varying extents; Ben may be motivated to satisfy both esteem and self-actualization needs simultaneously.

Alderfer's ERG Theory

Clayton Alderfer reorganized Maslow's need hierarchy in another way, into three types of needs: (1) existence, (2) relatedness, and (3) growth[12] (see Figure 4–2). Existence needs include both physiological and safety needs; they correspond to the lower-order needs described in the research related to Maslow's theory. *Relatedness* comprises both love and belongingness needs. *Growth* incorporates both esteem and self-actualization needs. Together with relatedness needs, growth needs comprise the higher-order needs in this model.

The Mechanism of Needs Satisfaction Alderfer, based on his findings, agreed with Maslow that unsatisfied needs motivate individuals. For example, individuals with unsatisfied relatedness needs (love and belongingness) would be motivated to produce if their performance resulted in satisfying these needs. Alderfer also agreed that individuals generally move up the hierarchy in satisfying their needs; that is, they satisfy lower-order before higher-order needs. He agreed with Maslow that as lower-order needs are satisfied they become less important, but Alderfer also felt that as higher-order needs are satisfied they become more important. For example, the more opportunity for autonomy an individual has in his or her job, the more his or her need for self-actualization is satisfied, and the more autonomy is required to continue to satisfy that need. Alderfer also indicated, however, that under some circumstances an individual might return to a lower need. If an employee is frustrated in satisfying growth needs, for example, he or she might be motivated to satisfy the lower-level relatedness needs instead. In this case, the individual might seek work situations that provide opportunities for social interaction rather than autonomy or responsibility.

Consider, for example, the employee who earns a good salary, has a reasonably high standard of living, and has made many friends at work. According to Maslow and Alderfer this person probably would be motivated to satisfy his

Figure 4–2 ALDERFER'S HIERARCHY OF NEEDS

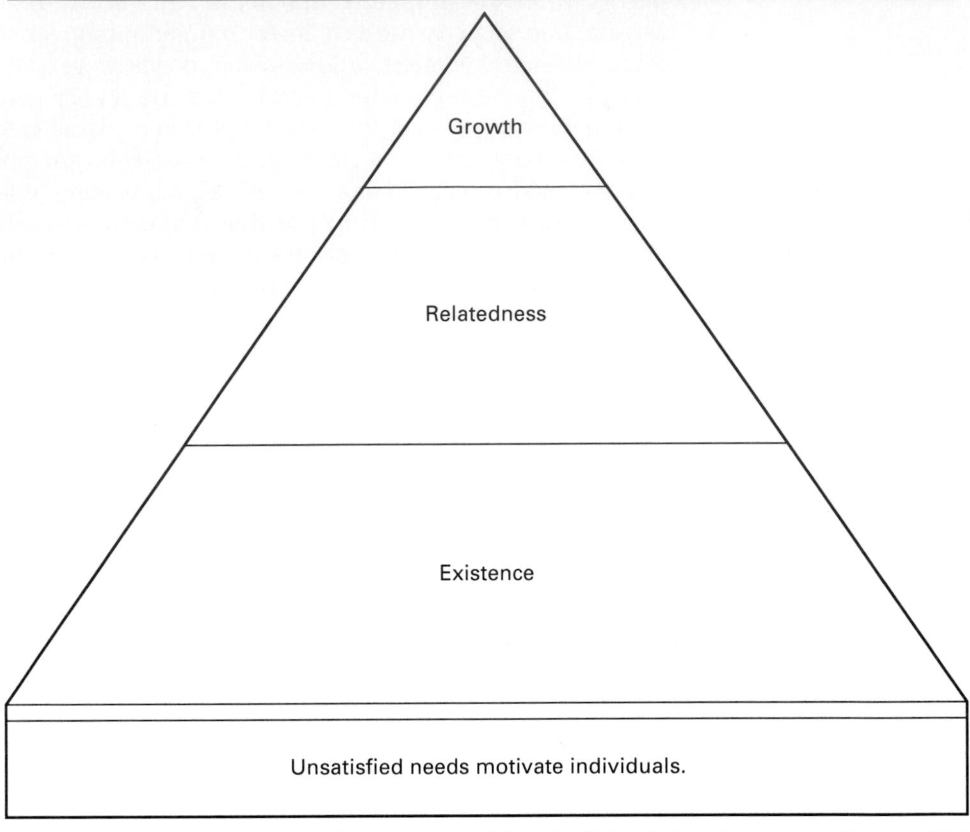

or her growth needs. What if, in trying to satisfy these needs, the individual finds that he or she is continually frustrated in attempts to get more autonomy and responsibility—features of a job that generally encourage individual growth? When asked, the employee now reports that having friends at work and getting together with them outside of work is most important. Frustration in satisfying a higher (growth) need has resulted in a regression to a lower level of (relatedness) needs.

Consider the case of Ben Kane. Is it possible that the frustration of Ben's higher-level needs has caused him to regress to a lower level of needs? Trying to satisfy relatedness needs rather than growth needs, as before, may have motivated him to leave the organization and take a new job. On the other hand need regression may not have occurred; Ben may feel that by joining another organization he can satisfy his growth needs.

In using Alderfer's theory to diagnose motivation situations such as those experienced at Interval we can ask questions similar to those we asked for Maslow, with the addition of three more. First, what needs are the individuals involved in the situation experiencing? Second, what needs have been satisfied and how have they been met? Third, which unsatisfied need is the lowest in the hierarchy? Fourth, have some higher-order needs been frustrated? Fifth, has the person refocused on a lower-level need? Sixth, how can the unsatisfied needs be satisfied? The case suggests that the addition of Bob Rowen to the team and Jeff Hoffman's inability to manage him are frustrating Ben's attempts to meet his growth needs.

Other Influences on Needs Alderfer attributes individual differences in various needs to differences in developmental level as well as experiences as a group member. For example, after Ben receives a B.S. his existence needs might predominate; as he attains financial security, his needs might shift to primary growth ones; later, when he has added financial responsibilities, such as a family or aged parents, satisfying his existence needs may again become important. Similarly, if Ben's experiences at Interval differ significantly from the experiences of other professionals there—for example, if he were the only employee given supervisory responsibility—then his needs might also differ significantly from the other professionals'. A careful analysis of individual development (described in Chapter 3) and the situation in group terms (described in Part Three) must accompany any diagnosis of motivation in organizational situations.

McClelland's Trichotomy of Needs

David McClelland and his associates, beginning in the 1950s, focused on needs similar to the higher-order needs identified by Maslow.[13] Specifically, these researchers said that each person has three types of needs. *Need for achievement* (Nach) is a need to accomplish and demonstrate competence or mastery; a person who continuously asks for and masters increasingly difficult tasks demonstrates a need for achievement. *Need for affiliation* (Naff) is a need for love, belonging, and relatedness; a person who seeks jobs high in social interaction shows this need. *Need for power* (Npow) is a need for control over one's own work or the work of others; a person who insists on autonomy in his or her work or who seeks supervisory responsibility likely has a need for power. A person may demonstrate each need overtly or covertly; thus Ben Kane may ask for more autonomy or work harder when given it. He may visibly delight in social activities or complain about always working alone. Although each person has all three needs to some extent, only one of them tends to motivate an individual at any given time. Ben Kane's need for achievement likely dominated his needs for affiliation and power when he first worked with Jeff Hoffman. Over time, and especially after Bob Rowen's hiring, his predominant need may have changed.

Identifying Needs Given the description of Ben Kane, which need do you think is dominant? Do you think his dominant need is the same as Jeff Hoffman's? Consider the people with whom you live or work. What is their predominant need? Which need motivates you now? Figure 4–3 helps you to identify your own or another's predominant need at any given time. Take a few moments and answer the questions posed here for yourself. Scoring your responses as indicated provides a rough estimate of your predominant need at this particular time. Note that occasionally an individual may experience more than one of these needs equally strongly. You might have equally positive responses to two or more sets of items.

McClelland and his colleagues devoted their initial attention and energy to studying the need for achievement, which they linked to effective managerial performance in the United States and abroad. Some of McClelland's earliest

Figure 4–3 IDENTIFICATION OF NEEDS ACCORDING TO MCCLELLAND'S TRICHOTOMY

1. Do you like situations where you personally must find solutions to problems?
2. Do you tend to set moderate goals and take moderate, thought-out risks?
3. Do you want specific feedback about how well you are doing?
4. Do you spend time considering how to advance your career, how to do your job better, or how to accomplish something important?

If you responded yes to questions 1–4, then you probably have a high need for achievement.

5. Do you look for jobs or seek situations that provide an opportunity for social relationships?
6. Do you often think about the personal relationships you have?
7. Do you consider the feelings of others to be very important?
8. Do you try to restore disrupted relationships when they occur?

If you responded yes to questions 5–8, then you probably have a high need for affiliation.

9. Do you try to influence and control others?
10. Do you seek leadership positions in groups?
11. Do you enjoy persuading others?
12. Are you perceived by others as outspoken, forceful, and demanding?

If you responded yes to questions 9–12, then you probably have a high need for power.

SOURCE: Based on R.M. Steers and L.W. Porter, *Motivation and Work Behavior* (New York: McGraw-Hill, 1979), pp. 57–64.

work involved measuring the extent of achievement motivation in different countries by analyzing and comparing the countries' folk tales.[14] He found a highly positive correlation between achievement themes in folk tales and the level of industrial development in that country. These researchers also proposed that those higher in need for achievement performed better than those with lower need for achievement. McClelland even stated that he could teach an individual the need for achievement. He has conducted training sessions that teach managers how to act like a person high in need for achievement. He claims the increased need for achievement in the participants results in higher performance.

More recently, McClelland, with David Burnham, has studied the need for power in individuals. In contrasting male managers in a sales organization with a high need for power to those with a high need for affiliation, for example, they found that managers with a need for power tended to run more productive departments than did managers with a high need for affiliation.[51] These results, which are examined in more detail in Chapter 9, suggest the importance of power to organizational performance.

Measuring Nach, Naff, and Npow Diagnosing the level of effort and performance possible in a country or an organization, then, involves determining its members' need for achievement. A variety of instruments can measure these three needs. McClelland used the projective Thematic Apperception Test (TAT) to measure need for achievement as well as need for affiliation and need for power. The TAT is a series of pictures of one or more people in various settings, similar to that shown in Figure 4–4. The respondent describes what he or she sees occurring in the picture. What do you see in Figure 4–4? Are these individuals holding a sales meeting to discuss problems related to the introduction of a new product? Are the people chatting during a coffee break? Or is the man in the back of the picture assigning projects to members of the group?

McClelland proposed that the respondent *projects* his or her needs into the

Figure 4–4 PICTURE SIMILAR TO THOSE USED IN PROJECTIVE TESTS SUCH AS THE TAT

description of the picture. For example, if you viewed the picture as a problem-solving meeting, then you would receive a positive score on need for achievement. If you viewed the picture as being a social gathering, then you would receive a positive score on need for affiliation. If you viewed the picture as being a situation dominated by a single person, then you would receive a positive score on need for power. Professional test administrators have detailed protocols for scoring the pictures in the TAT and similar tests. Because of the time and skill required in the administration and scoring of the test, its cost is relatively high and only a trained professional can administer and score it. For this reason others prefer the use of nonprojective tests such as the questionnaire shown in Figure 4–3.

Can McClelland's theory help diagnose the situation at Interval? To begin, we might assess Ben's, Jeff's, and even Bob's need for achievement, affiliation, and power. Then we can evaluate whether the nature and requirements of the situation fit with the type of people involved. We have conjectured that Ben has a high need for achievement. Would his job satisfy this need? At first, he certainly had the opportunity to set and meet challenging goals and take moderate risks. How does the introduction of Bob Rowen into the department help or hinder his meeting a need for achievement? This change seems to have reduced the extent to which Ben's job offers moderate challenges, opportunities for problem solving, and feedback about his performance. Are Ben's other needs being met? Clearly his relationship with Jeff Hoffman has become less collegial, perhaps adversely affecting his need for affiliation. And the importance of status and autonomy seemed to increase, making Ben's need for power more salient.

Acquisition of Motives McClelland, unlike other theorists, has emphasized the means to acquire various motives. He says, in particular, that training can increase an individual's need for achievement. He offers a prescription for individuals deficient in needs that might influence their effort and subsequent performance. He directs them to focus on *developing* certain needs; he teaches them to have a higher need for achievement.

In this way his theory differs from Maslow's and Alderfer's, which focus on satisfying existing needs rather than creating or developing new ones. Like the other needs theories, however, McClelland's approach suggests that increasing the environment's compatibility with individual needs should improve motivation and consequent performance. If, for example, Jeff Hoffman determines that Ben Kane has a high need for achievement, he should provide challenges for Ben rather than limiting his opportunities. If Jeff determines that Ben has a high need for affiliation, he should encourage more collaboration between them. If Jeff determines that Ben has a high need for power, he should increase Ben's autonomy and control over his work.

Herzberg's Two-Factor Theory

Frederick Herzberg and his associates' view of motivation complements that of the other needs theorists.[16] They suggest that *motivators*—features of a job's content, including responsibility, autonomy, self-esteem, and self-actualization opportunities—are factors that satisfy higher-order needs, motivate a person to exert more effort, and hence encourage the person to perform better. *Hygiene factors*—factors that can meet physiological, security, or social needs, including physical working conditions, salary, company policies and practices, benefits, or other features of a job's context—satisfy the lower-order needs and prevent dissatisfaction. This observation would separate workers into two groups: (1) those for whom *extrinsic* motivation—motivation from factors outside the job itself, such as pay, job title, or tenure—is most appropriate; and (2) those for whom *intrinsic* motivation—motivation from factors within the job, such as creativity, autonomy, and responsibility—is most appropriate. We contrast these two types of motivation later in this chapter.

For Herzberg there are two independent outcome dimensions (see Figure 4–5): (1) no satisfaction–satisfaction, which is addressed by motivators; and (2) dissatisfaction–no dissatisfaction, which is addressed by hygiene factors. A single dissatisfaction–satisfaction dimension does not exist. Unlike the other needs theories, the two-factor theory focuses on increasing overall *satisfaction* rather than relying on meeting individual needs. "It is primarily the 'motivators' that serve to bring about the kind of job satisfaction and . . . the kind

Figure 4–5 HERZBERG'S TWO-FACTOR THEORY

Hygiene Factors (Needs) *The Environment*	Motivators Factors (Needs) *The Job*
Job Dissatisfaction ⟷ No Job Dissatisfaction	No Job Satisfaction ⟷ Job Satisfaction
• Pay	• Meaningful and challenging work
• Status	• Recognition for accomplishment
• Security	• Feeling of achievement
• Working conditions	• Increased responsibility
• Fringe benefits	• Opportunities for growth and advancement
• Policies and administrative practices	• The job itself
• Interpersonal relations	

of improvement in performance that industry is seeking from its work force."[17] When Jeff Hoffman decreased Ben's autonomy, his satisfaction and ultimately his motivation decreased.

Hygiene factors do not encourage individuals to exert more effort, in part because they have been relatively available in organizations. But hygiene factors must be addressed first, to bring the individual to a point of no-dissatisfaction so that motivators can then increase satisfaction and ultimately motivate. For example, offering autonomy and responsibility when working conditions and other contextual factors are not resolved results in worker dissatisfaction and does not allow motivation to occur. Thus even when Jeff Hoffman returned some autonomy to Ben, his relatively low salary continued to result in dissatisfaction and restricted his motivation. In sum, making provision for hygiene factors causes workers to be in a neutral state in the job situation; only then can motivators be introduced, be expected to cause satisfaction, and ultimately lead to performance under this theory.

Research Support Herzberg's theory has been subjected to significant criticism. This criticism focuses on the research method used to collect data as well as the classification of some factors, especially pay, as both a motivator and a hygiene factor.[18] His theory also ignores individual differences and may overemphasize the importance of pleasure as a desired outcome. Still, this theory can offer significant insights into, if not definitive answers for, motivational problems.

For example, according to Herzberg, a manager's giving an individual a new job title without additional job responsibilities would not change performance because the manager is increasing a hygiene factor, which affects dissatisfaction and only allows motivation to occur. The new job title does not increase motivators, which affect satisfaction, effort, and performance. Similarly, if pay is considered a hygiene factor, merely giving pay increases without changing a job's content does not increase performance. These results form the basis of early attempts to enrich jobs, which involved increasing motivation rather than merely adding more of the same tasks to jobs (described in greater detail in Chapter 13).

Organizational Responses to Needs

Organizations can attempt to meet individuals' needs through good leadership (see Chapter 8), the introduction of special programs such as food or housing plans, the organization of individuals into work teams (see Chapter 5), the design of the reward system (see later sections of this chapter), and the design of jobs (see Chapter 13). Table 4–2 summarizes the ways in which organizations can satisfy different kinds of needs.

Changes in a job's content through increasing challenge, autonomy, and responsibility address the higher-order needs of esteem, achievement, and growth. Changes in the reward system, such as introducing pensions and new benefits, influence the lower-level physiological and security needs. The introduction of work teams focuses on social needs. Note that pay is a particularly powerful organizational change: it can meet both lower-order and higher-order needs.

Evaluation of Needs Theories

The extent to which current needs theories explain motivation in organizations has been questioned by some researchers. They maintain that the concept of needs is popular in psychology but is difficult to prove or disprove, for several reasons.[19] First, needs are difficult to specify and measure. Often, for example,

Table 4–2 WAYS OF SATISFYING INDIVIDUAL NEEDS IN THE WORK SITUATION

Need	Organizational Conditions
Physiological	pay mandatory breakfast or lunch programs company housing
Safety *Security*	company benefits plans pensions seniority pay
Love *Belongingness* *Relatedness* *Affiliation*	coffee breaks sports teams company picnics and social events work teams pay
Esteem	autonomy responsibility pay (as symbol of status) prestige office location and furnishings
Achievement *Competence*	job challenge pay
Power	leadership positions authority
Self-Actualization *Growth*	challenge autonomy

managers must assume what needs their subordinates have. Few instruments exist that can reliably or validly measure worker needs.[20] When possible, managers must discuss subordinates' needs with them, as well as request suggestions about ways organizations can better meet them.

Second, relating needs to various job characteristics can be problematic. We cannot be completely certain that a new company benefits plan better meets an individual's security needs, or that increasing autonomy responds to self-actualization needs. The complexity of human behavior and organizational life make drawing direct cause-and-effect relationships difficult. Often organizations must experiment with different responses and attempt to determine their impact through less than fully scientific studies.

Third, need-satisfaction models fail to account for variances in behaviors and attitudes. The needs theories would label Ben's declining performance solely a function of the failure of Interval Corporation's top management to meet his needs. Again, this limited analysis oversimplifies the situation and possible causes of the problems. Ben's low performance may instead be a function of ineffective leadership or dysfunctional organization design.

Fourth, attributing needs to individuals may stem from a lack of awareness of external forces that influence behavior, rather than to a certainty that the needs exist. In Ben Kane's case, for example, his declining performance may result from changes in the technology required to do his job or the scientific breakthroughs made by competitors, rather than from a failure of Interval Corporation to meet his needs.

Finally, care must be taken to avoid stereotyping individuals by applying a single, one-time categorization of their needs. Ben Kane's needs, for example, may change over time as a function of the situation in which he is employed.

There are significant cross-cultural differences in predominant needs. In France, belongingness heavily influences motivation, whereas in Holland fairness, and in the United States recognition, are the most influential.[21] Analysis of a questionnaire given to first-line supervisors in manufacturing organizations in these three countries indicated that United States managers were more individually (versus socially) motivated than their Dutch counterparts. Thus assessment of individual needs must be an on-going process, and strategies for meeting needs must be tailored to individual countries. Rewards for individual job accomplishment may work in the United States but could be perceived as unfair to the Dutch and decrease feelings of organizational belongingness in France.[22]

EQUITY THEORY

The second major type of motivation theory evolved from social comparison theory. Its basic premise is that individuals must assess and recognize their own level of performance and the "correctness" of their attitudes in a situation. But because they lack objective measures of performance or appropriate attitudes, they compare their performance and attitudes to others'. *Equity theory* uses social comparison theory in determining the motivational level of individuals. It assumes that people assess their job performance and attitudes by comparing both their contribution to work and the benefits they derive from it to the contributions and benefits of a "comparison other," an individual the person selects who in reality may be like or unlike the person. Ben Kane, for example, might compare his effort and rewards to those of Bob Rowen, other professionals in the company, friends or associates in other firms, or even the CEO of the organization.

Determination of Equity

Equity theory further posits that a person is motivated in proportion to the perceived fairness of the rewards received for a certain amount of effort.[23] You may have heard your colleague James say, "I'm going to stop working so hard—I work harder than Susan and she gets all the bonuses," or your classmate Sarah say, "Why should I bother studying? Alan never studies and still gets As. He's no smarter than I am." James and Sarah have compared their effort and the rewards they received to the effort and rewards of Susan and Alan. James and Sarah have *perceived* an inequity in a work and school situation. In fact, no actual inequity may exist, but the perception of inequity influences James's and Sarah's subsequent actions.

Specifically, James and Sarah compare their perceptions of two ratios: (1) the ratio of their outcomes to their inputs, to (2) the ratio of another's outcomes to inputs, as shown in Figure 4–6. *Outcomes* include pay, status, and job complexity; *inputs* include effort, productivity, age, sex, and experience. Thus they may compare their pay-to-experience ratio to another's ratio, or their status-to-age ratio to another's. For example, James may believe he receives $20 for each hour of effort he contributes to the job; in contrast, he may assess that Susan receives $40 for each hour of effort she contributes to the job. James perceives that his ratio of outcomes to inputs (20 to 1) is less than Susan's (40 to 1). In fact, Susan may only receive $10 for each hour of effort she contributes to the job. But according to equity theory facts do not influence motivation; *perceptions* of the situation do. Thus some workers may

Figure 4–6 EQUITY THEORY

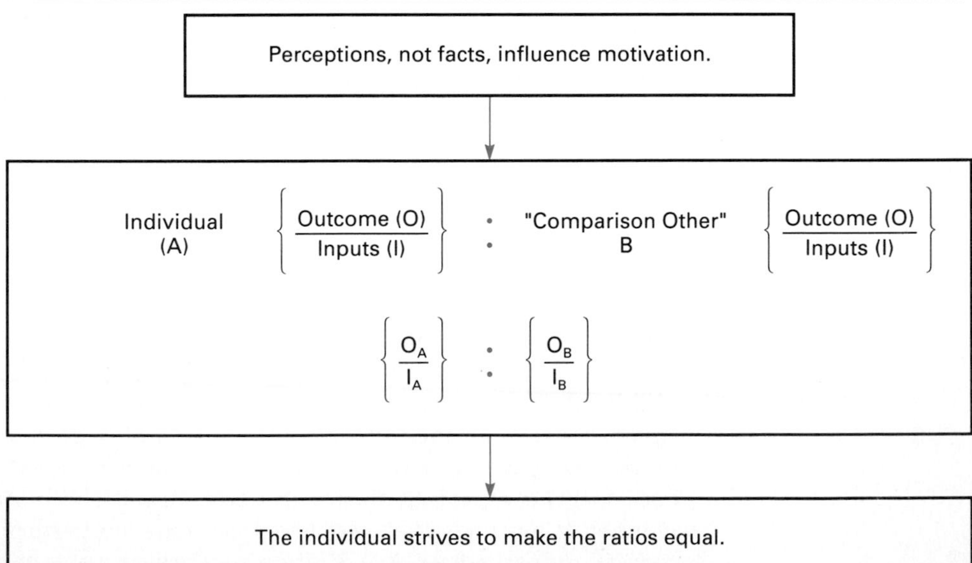

feel that they have more experience than a comparison other—a worker to whom they compare themselves—but receive less complex jobs to perform; and again perceived inequity exists.

Reduction of Inequity

According to equity theory, individuals are motivated to reduce any perceived inequity. They strive to make the ratios of outcomes to inputs, O/I, equal.[24] James, for example, wants both his and Susan's ratio to be 40/1. Sarah wants to perceive that her and Alan's ratios are equal as well. When inequity exists, the person making the comparison strives to make these ratios equal by changing either the outcomes or the inputs. James, for example, might reduce his inputs (his effort) to make the ratio the same as Susan's: he might spend ½ hour of effort for every $20 of outcome he receives, which would change his ratio to 20/.5 or 40/1, which equals Susan's. Or he might ask for a pay raise, so that he earns $40 per hour of effort.

If he cannot change his own inputs or outcomes, he might adjust either his *perception* of Susan's outcomes or inputs or his attitude toward the situation. He might reevaluate her effort, changing his perception of her ratio to 40/2, which then equals his of 20/1, so that the ratio of outcomes to inputs matches his. Or he might obtain more accurate information about her pay and adjust the ratio accordingly: he might learn that her pay is actually $20 and her ratio 20/1.

The Overjustification Effect

Theoretically, the same adjustment process occurs when a person perceives he or she receives too great a reward for the input or has too complex a job in comparison to others.[25] For example, the person who feels he or she has received undeserved time off, according to equity theory, would increase his or her inputs, perhaps by working longer hours, so that the perceived ratios are equal. If Ben Kane felt that he were being overpaid relative to his coworkers, would he complain to his bosses? Although early studies suggested that he would, recent research has questioned whether this *overjustification effect* really occurs.[26] However, many still believe that overpaying improves performance because it causes people to modify their inputs favorably.[27]

Empirical Evidence

While equity theory basically makes strong intuitive sense, empirical evidence has been mixed. One study showed that individuals exert an amount of effort that leads to the greatest payoff for the lowest expenditure of effort.[28] Another showed that employees' perceptions of the fairness of their pay relative to their coworkers' and to others' outside the organization, as well as the fairness and administration of rules for pay increases and promotion, were related most significantly to absenteeism; only their perceptions of the fairness of their pay to that of others' outside the organization were significantly related to turnover.[29] Recent research suggests that a time lag may exist in some individuals' reactions to inequity.[30] Further, individual characteristics such as sex, intelligence, social values, and locus of control may affect an individual's perception of inequity.[31]

The concept of *equity sensitivity* reflects these findings by suggesting that individuals have different preferences for equity that cause them to react consistently but differently to perceived equity and inequity.[32] Some people may actually prefer their ratios to be lower than their comparison others'; some prefer equal ratios; and others prefer their ratios to exceed the comparison others'. These preferences result from internal standards of the relation of their own inputs to their own outputs.

In a sense, equity theory may oversimplify motivational issues by not explicitly considering individual needs, values, or personalities. Thus we should supplement equity theory with other theoretical approaches to motivation. We might consider the joint influence of needs and perceptions of equity, for example. We must apply diverse perspectives in order to understand complex organizational behavior completely. Nevertheless, ensuring equity in orga-

Table 4–3 SAMPLE ITEMS FROM THE ORGANIZATIONAL FAIRNESS QUESTIONNAIRE

Dimension	Sample Items
Payrules	• The rules for giving pay raises are not fair to some employees. • The rules for giving pay raises to all employees are fair.
Pay Administration	• My supervisor knows who should be promoted and sees that they are promoted if he (or she) can. • My supervisor rates people fairly in giving raises.
Work Pace	• People are expected to do a fair day's work in my company. • Some employees can get away with working at a slow speed if they want to in my company.
Paylevel	• Persons who have the same education as I have are paid more than I am being paid. • When I compare my pay with the pay of working classmates, my pay is higher than theirs.
Rule Administration	• My supervisor will get after workers if they are late to work, play around in the office, or behave badly in other ways. • My supervisor allows workers to tease other employees, be late to their work stations, and to act improperly in other ways.
Distribution of Jobs	• My supervisor tends to assign unpleasant jobs to those he (or she) doesn't like. • My supervisor sees that everybody in my department does their share of the more unpleasant jobs.
Latitude	• In my department, as people learn their jobs, the supervisor lets them make more and more decisions on their own. • In working with me, my supervisor is fair in letting me decide how to do my work.

SOURCE: Reprinted with permission from The Organizational Fairness Questionnaire, by John E. Dittrich.

nizational policies and practices, specifically in the operation of reward systems, is essential to motivation.

Determining Equity in the Workplace

To determine whether equity exists in a workplace, we can use a questionnaire such as the Organizational Fairness Questionnaire. Table 4–3 shows some sample items from this instrument. How would Ben Kane respond to these questions? Certainly deficiencies seem to exist in pay rules, work pace, and rule administration. More detailed investigation of the situation at Interval Corporation might reveal additional inequities.

When inequity exists in an organization, individuals react in a variety of ways. As already mentioned,[33] some people adjust their inputs; for example, by exerting less effort or spending more time at work. Others change the outcomes; they request pay increases or more vacation time. Still others adjust their perception of their own or others' inputs and outcomes; they might revalue their own or others' effort, experience, or education; they might also rationalize the differences. Some workers leave the situation entirely, as Ben did. The remaining people may choose a different comparison person. Table 4–4 illustrates the conditions under which these alternatives occur and can be used to diagnose situations, such as that faced by Ben Kane, and the likely consequences.

Thus when high absenteeism, low productivity, high turnover, or other such symptoms exist, we should test whether inequity exists in the situation. More specifically we should assess the following:

1. What contributions or inputs does the person make to the situation? What is his or her level of education, effort, or experience?
2. What benefits or outcomes does the person receive? What is the level of job complexity, pay, or status of that person?
3. What is the ratio of the inputs to outcomes? Some quantification of both inputs and outcomes should occur. These can then be compared in ratio form. If the inputs or outcomes cannot be quantified, qualitative determination of the ratio must occur.

Table 4–4 CONDITIONS OF INEQUITY

Condition	Responses
$\frac{O_A}{I_A} > \frac{O_B}{I_B}$	A increases inputs A asks for reduced outputs B reduces inputs B asks for increased outputs A or B changes comparison person A or B rationalizes that equity exists A or B leaves the situation
$\frac{O_A}{I_A} < \frac{O_B}{I_B}$	B increases inputs B asks for reduced outputs A reduces inputs A asks for increased outputs A or B changes comparison person A or B rationalizes that equity exists A or B leaves the situation

4. Is the ratio the same, greater than, or less than the ratio of comparison others?

Answers to the first three questions must also be obtained for relevant others. The resulting ratios can then be compared. As noted earlier, Ben likely perceives that his ratio of outcomes to inputs is less than Bob Rowen's.

Equity theory does not negate needs theory. Rather it provides another perspective for analyzing motivation and predicting individuals' behaviors and attitudes. Consider again the situation experienced by Ben Kane. Not only does he seem to have unmet needs, but he perceives that inequity exists when he assesses the ratio of his pay to his knowledge and responsibility and compares it to the ratio of Bob Rowen's pay to his knowledge and responsibility. Thus we can use both needs theories and equity theory together in diagnosis.

REINFORCEMENT THEORY

Reinforcement theory applies behaviorist learning theories (described in Chapter 2) to motivation. Prompted by E.L. Thorndike's and B.F. Skinner's research conclusions that satisfying consequences strengthen stimulus–response connections and annoying consequences weaken them, reinforcement theory emphasizes the importance of feedback and rewards in motivating behavior. It uses four reinforcement techniques[34]: positive reinforcement, punishment, negative reinforcement, and extinction. These techniques differ along two dimensions (as shown in Table 4–5): first, whether they encourage or eliminate desired behavior; and second, whether reinforcement is used actively or passively.

Positive Reinforcement

Positive reinforcement involves *actively encouraging* a desired behavior, by repeatedly pairing desired behaviors or outcomes with rewards or feedback. An example is a person who packs tea sets and receives ten cents for each one packed. The desired behavior—packing the tea sets—is paired with the financial rewards. Likewise a person who completes a project in a way desired by his or her superiors may receive praise for the project. Verbal feedback accompanying good performance encourages repetition of the desired behavior.

Table 4–5 REINFORCEMENT OPTIONS

	Target Behavior	
Use of Reinforcement	To Encourage Desired Behavior	To Eliminate Desired Behavior
Active	Positive reinforcement	Punishment
Passive	Negative reinforcement (withhold punishment)	Extinction (withhold positive reinforcement)

According to reinforcement theory, this praise, or reinforcement of the behavior, stimulates its recurrence.

Feedback *shapes* behavior by encouraging the reinforced or rewarded behavior to recur. If a particular behavior is not precisely what is desired by a superior or client, repeated reinforcements of progressive approximations of the desired behavior can move the actual behavior closer to the desired behavior. For example, if an individual habitually comes to work late, his or her superior might make a positive comment when the person comes to work *less* late than usual. Additional praise might follow if the person comes more and more promptly, and praise would continue until the desired behavior occurred. This behavior would then be reinforced with praise (or even financial incentives) until it became more or less permanent, but praise would be discontinued if any reversion to previous behaviors occurred.

Punishment

Punishment *actively eliminates* undesirable behaviors. A superior officer uses punishment when giving kitchen patrol to a newly recruited army private who questions a directive about the employment of computers in his or her job.

Punishment often creates secondary consequences, tension and stress. In addition, the results of punishment tend to be less predictable and less permanent than those of other forms of operant conditioning. Thus punishment generally should be used only as a last-resort motivator.

Punishment refers to the application of an undesirable reinforcer to an undesirable behavior. In this way it differs from negative reinforcement, which refers to rewarding the withdrawal of an undesirable behavior. How will the private react to punishment? Most likely the recruit will feel bitterness or anger toward the superior; this attitude may have long-term negative consequences for the private's performance. Or the private may develop a negative attitude toward the activity—the use of computers—that the superior was conducting. Negative attitudes toward the administrator of the punishment often accompany negative attitudes toward the activity that inspired the punishment.

Punishment may also suppress behavior but not permanently eliminate it; this results because punishment does not offer an alternative to the undesirable behavior. If a worker repeatedly misuses a piece of equipment and receives punishment each time he or she does so, the behavior may not change because no correct way of using the equipment (an alternative to the undesirable behavior) has been presented.

Punishment of undesired behavior also may be offset by positive reinforcement for the same behavior from another source, such as peers.[35] The newly recruited army private's "speaking back" to a superior may be applauded by the other recruits. Or a worker's coworkers may encourage misuse of equipment, particularly if the worker is otherwise perceived to violate the group's standards for expected and acceptable production. (See Chapter 5 for further discussion of group behavior.)

Negative Reinforcement

In negative reinforcement, an individual *passively encourages* a desired behavior by withholding punishment. The term *negative* refers to the removal of the individual from a punitive (negative) situation when the desired behavior occurs. The reporter who refuses to name a source of information for a story is sent to jail (punished) and is then released (removing the punishment) on naming the source. Releasing (removing) the reporter from his or her punishment (jail) encourages or reinforces the desired behavior (naming the source). A clerk-typist who is always tardy is assigned the department's least desirable work (punishment); but when the clerk-typist arrives on time for a month he or she is given interesting and desired work (negative reinforcement).

Extinction

Extinction *passively eliminates* an undesired behavior by withholding positive reinforcement. Typically, the failure to apply positive reinforcements causes desired behaviors to cease. Consider the case at Interval Corporation. What effect did the absence of attention from Jeff Hoffman have when Bob Rowen was hired? How did Jeff Hoffman's behavior and attitudes toward Ben Kane change after Bob Rowen was hired? Jeff decreased Ben's status and responsibilities, which previously served as reinforcers of Ben's good performance. Reinforcers of pay, responsibility, and autonomy likely contributed to Ben's high-level performance; withholding these rewards resulted in extinction of his high-level performance behavior.

Removing positive reinforcements contributes to a change in performance. The withholding of reinforcement, in Ben's case, caused him to discontinue his productive behavior. Likewise, a person who repeatedly works overtime but receives neither compensation, status, nor praise for this added effort likely will stop the overtime hours, depending on other motivating forces at work. By withholding reinforcement, a supervisor often causes desired behaviors—productivity, creativity, attendance—to stop or be extinguished.

Reinforcement Schedules

The timing and frequency of reinforcement significantly influence its impact. Reinforcement schedules differ along two dimensions: (1) fixed-variable and (2) interval-ratio.

Fixed and variable schedules reflect the extent to which reinforcement is regular and known in advance. A paycheck is officially administered according to a fixed schedule; the employee receives a paycheck after completing his or her last desired behavior in that time period. Often this type of reinforcer loses the power to motivate good performance because it is received regardless of the individual's behavior. For example, in some situations a worker may produce shoddy goods or have a high absence record and still receive a weekly paycheck. In contrast, praise is typically given according to a variable schedule. The person giving praise does not determine in advance precisely when he or she will comment about an employee's behavior. Rather, a unique behavior may promote this type of reinforcement. Merit increases or bonuses may also be given on a variable schedule, as when a manager spontaneously decides to reward employee performance.

Interval and ratio schedules describe the extent to which reinforcement corresponds with a specific time interval (a week, month, or year) or a given number of responses or outputs, such as fifty units of a particular product. Christmas bonuses illustrate reinforcements given according to an interval schedule: they are given once a year, at a predetermined time. Piece-work rates illustrate reinforcement according to a ratio schedule: piece-work pay is given after a specific number of articles (or responses) are produced.

Table 4–6 illustrates the four schedules that result when these two dimensions are combined and suggests some applications of them. These schedules differ in their ability to encourage desired behavior in the short term and long run. In general, continuous reinforcement on fixed and interval schedules more effectively encourages desired behaviors in the short term; a weekly paycheck motivates workers to immediately perform as desired. Intermittent reinforcement according to variable and ratio schedules more effectively sustains desired behaviors over the long run; not knowing when (or if) a merit increase in pay will be given tends to motivate workers to continue performing at a high level in hopes such reinforcement will occur. Ensuring performance in the medium run might require adding a fixed-ratio component, such as an incentive program. The manager must select the reinforcement schedule that best fits with his or her goals. Getting workers "up to speed" quickly might call for using a fixed-interval reinforcement schedule. Making sure high quality performance continues would require supplementing it with a variable-interval or variable-ratio schedule, using praise and possibly offering special performance bonuses.

Most frequently a diversity of rewards should be applied, each according to different but complementary schedules. For example, a manager might use the weekly paycheck to encourage attendance, a merit bonus to motivate exceptional behavior, and periodic praise to stimulate day-to-day and longer term productivity. Adding to reinforcements on a fixed-interval or fixed-ratio schedule by using either a variable-interval or variable-ratio schedule, or both, should sustain any already-established desired behaviors. In trying to motivate an employee to show initiative, for example, a manager should begin praising the worker each time he or she demonstrates initiative, then gradually decrease the use of praise until only exceptional behavior receives comments. This movement from a fixed-ratio schedule to a variable-ratio schedule will

Table 4–6 SCHEDULES OF REINFORCEMENT

	Fixed	Variable
Interval	Reinforcement or reward given after the first proper response following a specified period of time	Reinforcement or reward given after a certain amount of time with that amount changing before the next reinforcement
	Weekly or monthly paycheck	Supervisor who visits shop floor on different unannounced days each week Unexpected merit bonuses
Ratio	Reinforcement or reward given after a specified number of proper responses	Reinforcement or reward given after a number of responses with that number changing before the next reinforcement
	Pay for piecework	Praise

sustain behavior over the long term. Or the manager might rely on weekly paychecks to reward a mechanic's productivity, then later add bonuses, with the time of awarding the bonus unannounced. This addition of reinforcements on a variable-interval schedule to those on a fixed-interval schedule also will help to sustain productivity.

Operant Conditioning Programs

Operant conditioning is widespread in work settings, but some firms have used more extensive behavior modification programs to increase performance levels.[36] In one of the earliest operant conditioning experiments in the workplace, Emery Air Freight applied a combination of positive incentives, goal setting, and praise to increase the utilization of containers for packing shipments. In one program, the freight packers set capacity goals for the shipping crates then compared their packing record to the goals set. Meeting their goals provided feedback about the quality of their behavior and reinforced the behavior that led to goal accomplishment. (We consider goal setting as a specific motivational technique in more detail later in this chapter.) Often, praise from supervisors accompanied the goal accomplishment. Praise acted as further reinforcement of the behaviors that led to the goal accomplishment and helped shape the desired behaviors as well. This program increased container utilization from approximately 40 percent to over 85 percent and eventually saved Emery more than $2 million.

At Michigan Bell, a program combining goal setting and positive reinforcement for telephone operators increased performance, in such areas as service promptness and average time per call, from the fiftieth percentile to the ninetieth percentile. Garbage collectors in Detroit, in another behavior modification program, saved the city over $1½ million in 1974—and each worker received a $350 bonus. Examples of organizational behavior management programs have become more common. They have been implemented in a wide range of settings (from insurance companies to private hospitals to furniture manufacturing plants) and have addressed diverse outcomes (from attendance to preventing hazardous conditions to earplug usage).[37]

Additional applications of reinforcement theory have received public attention.[38] Programmed instruction, for example, combines motivation theory and learning theory. Have you ever used a programmed text or computer application? Students have learned such subjects as algebra, accounting, and typing in this way. Programmed instruction typically has been used for teaching relatively simple subject matter. The learner responds to a series of questions about a given subject, either in a written text or on a computer terminal. After each correct answer, the learner moves to another question, which helps refine his or her knowledge of the subject by asking about a slightly different aspect of it. Thus correct answers are reinforced by the learner's having the opportunity to move forward in the instructional program. After an incorrect answer, the learner moves to a series of questions that provide additional information about the current, unmastered subject. Thus many questions are available to reinforce the learning of a particular subject. In this approach the learner gets immediate feedback about the accuracy of a response. Examples are Zenith Corporation, which has used programmed instruction to teach the features of their color televisions to wholesale sales representatives; and IBM, which has used it to train computer programmers.

Fitting Reinforcers to Behavior

At the same time that the popularity of positive reinforcement has increased, the assignment of reinforcers has become more complicated. What, for example, does the weekly paycheck or the annual Christmas bonus actually reinforce? Do supervisors praise their subordinates enough or at the best times? In universities, "society hopes that teachers will not neglect their teaching responsibilities, but *rewards* them almost entirely for research and publications."[39] In business, the organization "often is in a position where it *hopes* for employee effort in the areas of team building, interpersonal relations, creativity, etc., but it formally *rewards* none of these."[40]

These misguided reward systems, where undesired behaviors are reinforced or perceived to be reinforced, occur for four reasons.[41] First, organizational members may substitute measurable outcomes for true organizational goals. For example, organizations may reward the quantity of work produced by computer programmers and overlook the quality or efficiency of the programs written. They may rely on measuring tardiness or absenteeism of school teachers, both of which are easily observable and quantifiable, rather than evaluating teacher performance, which is more difficult to assess.

Second, managers may overemphasize the visible parts of a task. They may reward machine operators who have few breakdowns rather than those who look for more efficient ways of producing. They may reward a secretary's typing speed, rather than his or her initiative or interpersonal skills.

Third, organizational leaders may demonstrate hypocrisy about desired outcomes. The top managers at Interval Corporation, for example, might tell their employees they value initiative when in fact they seek an employee who quietly implements a superior's requests. Or they might state that innovation is their foremost goal, whereas in fact profit is the sole driving force.

Fourth, managers may feel societal or other pressures to reinforce behaviors they really do not desire. Emphasis on social consciousness, for example, may lead them to reward employees who perform public service, even hold political office, even though such activities may interfere with employees' efficiency or effectiveness on the job.

Note too that different reinforcers may be useful in different cultures. Praise may be valued over pay increases; job flexibility and autonomy over job titles.

Rules for Effective Operant Conditioning

What principles guide the effective use of reinforcement theory? How can "the folly of rewarding A, while hoping for B" be avoided? And how can individuals' perceptions of the use of reinforcement theory match its actual implementation? Managers can begin by determining the behaviors that are currently rewarded: they can administer a questionnaire to organizational members or interview them to obtain this information, and review actual rewards given and their circumstances for the previous year or two. If the reward system is incongruent with the organization's goals, then management can change it. This approach eliminates the almost impossible task of hiring only employees whose goals and motivations match top management's, or trying to train employees so they match.

Clay Hamner offers six rules for using operant conditioning techniques[42]:

1. *Do not reward all people the same.* Ben Kane's having the same level of responsibility and autonomy as Bob Rowen, even though their outcomes differed, was demotivating. Pay, praise, responsibility, and other reinforcements should be distributed fairly to all employees, according to relevant performance criteria (not sex or marital status, e.g.).
2. *Realize that failure to respond has reinforcing consequences.* Withdrawing reinforcement causes a behavior to cease; so does not applying reinforcement in the first place. Jeff Hoffman's failure to reinforce Ben's performance caused it to decline.
3. *Tell people what they can do to receive reinforcement.* Should they concentrate, for example, on quality, quantity, or both in their work? Should they emphasize reliable attendance, working overtime when needed, or both? This type of communication increases the similarity between perceptions and reality. If Ben Kane knows that his firm values a team effort over individual initiative, he can adjust his actions to resemble the desired behaviors.
4. *Tell a person what he or she is doing wrong* and find out why it is happening. Often, in universities, good teachers do not receive tenure because they have not done sufficient research or published enough. Department chairpersons, senior faculty, or other personnel with knowledge of tenure standards fail to regularly (at least yearly) evaluate their colleagues' performance on all dimensions and communicate the results to the nontenured faculty members. Organizations should institute performance evaluation systems that include regular and comprehensive feedback.
5. *Do not punish in front of others.* In using punishment, individuals should attempt to reduce the dysfunctional, secondary consequences associated with it. By keeping punishment private, the need for workers to "save face" with their coworkers or subordinates, which may cause them to act in ways detrimental to the organization's goals, is reduced.
6. *Make the consequences appropriate for the behavior.* Reinforcements, such as praise, bonuses, promotions, or demotions, should fit the type of behavior being reinforced. Giving a 20 percent pay increase to an employee to reinforce perfect attendance for one month in the year will confuse the employee about the importance of other work behaviors. Similarly, giving an employee who makes a breakthrough in the technology required for a new product only a pat on the back undervalues the significance of this contribution.

How, then, can reinforcement theory help diagnose the motivation of workers at Interval? We can ask the following questions:

1. What behaviors are desired? Does Jeff Hoffman want Ben Kane to demonstrate initiative and assume responsibility or be concerned only with conforming to his directives? Did he merely value Ben's reliability and not his effort or performance?
2. Are the behaviors observable and measurable? Certainly initiative and project performance are more difficult to measure than whether a directive is followed. If Hoffman wanted to use reinforcement theory

to help him identify ways of motivating Ben, we would encourage him to identify desired behaviors that can be observed and measured. These might include presenting all interim reports, establishing and meeting agreed-on deadlines, or suggesting at least two new research tasks for inclusion in the project.

3. What reinforces these behaviors? with what consequences? With the exception of his paycheck, Ben receives few positive reinforcements for his behavior after Bob Rowen joins the team. This causes the cessation of the behaviors—working overtime and assuming responsibility, e.g.—that previously were reinforced.
4. When are the reinforcements applied and with what consequences? Jeff Hoffman used limited positive reinforcers after hiring Bob Rowen. He withdrew his support of Ben and punished both Ben and Bob with verbal abuse. This caused Ben to reduce his effort and decrease his performance behaviors, which were previously reinforced by his receiving greater responsibility and more interesting tasks.
5. How can the reinforcement pattern be improved? Jeff Hoffman must reinforce the behaviors that result in the accomplishment of organizational goals. He can use praise, compensation, job redesign, goal setting, or other means to reinforce the desired behaviors.

Note that reinforcement theory should not be applied in isolation; it should be applied in conjunction with the principles of social learning presented in Chapter 2. Rewards or reinforcements must meet an employee's specific needs. They must be applied equitably. Managers must be clear about the behaviors they want to encourage and consistent in reinforcing them. They must also apply appropriate rewards according to an effective schedule.

EXPECTANCY THEORY

Expectancy theory, perhaps more than the preceding theories, offers a comprehensive view of motivation that integrates many of the elements of the needs, equity, and reinforcement theories. It considers the interface of the individual with both the situation and the environment.

The Earliest Formulation

Victor Vroom popularized this theory in the 1960s. His model stated that motivation was a function of expectancy, valence, and instrumentality[43]:

Motivation = E × V × I (Expectancy × Valence × Instrumentality).

This simple formulation identifies the three basic components of expectancy theory.

E, or expectancy, refers to a person's perception of the probability that effort will lead to performance. For example, a person who perceives that, if he or she works harder then he or she will produce more, has a high expectancy. A person who perceives that, if he or she works harder then he or she will be ostracized by other workers and will not receive the cooperation necessary for performing, has a lower expectancy. A person who sees no link between effort and performance will have zero expectancy. If expectancy is zero, then motivation will be lower than if expectancy is a positive number.

I, or instrumentality, refers to a person's perception of the probability that certain outcomes, positive or negative, will be attached to performance. For example, a person who perceives that he or she will receive greater pay or benefits if he or she produces has high instrumentality. A person who sees no link between performance and pay will have zero instrumentality. Motivation is a function of the degree of instrumentality in addition to expectancy and valence.

V, or valence, refers to a person's perception of the value of specific outcomes; that is, how much the person likes or dislikes receiving these outcomes. An individual with high esteem needs generally attaches a high valence to a new job title or a promotion. An individual with strong security needs values pension and retirement programs or the award of tenure. An individual with growth or self-actualization needs views challenging jobs or increased responsibility as motivating because of their high valence. Most individuals also value higher compensation. The value of specific outcomes also varies for different cultures. For example, in one study workers in English-speaking countries more often valued individual achievement over seniority; workers in Northern European countries more often valued job accomplishment over advancement.[44] When valence is high, motivation is likely to be higher than when valence is lower or negative.

The Multiple-Outcome Formulation

Vroom's simplified introduction of expectancy theory was followed in the 1970s by a more complex formulation[45]:

$$\textbf{Motivation} = [E \rightarrow P] \times \Sigma\, [(P \rightarrow O)(V)]$$

Here, $E \rightarrow P$ refers to the employee's perception of whether effort leads to performance; this is analogous to expectancy. $P \rightarrow O$ refers to the employee's perception of whether performance leads to outcomes, including fatigue, pay, benefits, and job challenge, among others. V refers to the valence, or value attached to the outcome.

To translate the case of Ben Kane into this formulation of motivation, if Ben perceives that devoting more hours to work will result in his performing challenging assignments, then $E \rightarrow P$ will be positive. If he perceives that he receives pay, praise, and more responsibility if he completes his tasks, then $P \rightarrow O$ will be positive. If Ben likes receiving money, praise, and responsibility, then V will be positive. If we arbitrarily assign values to $E \rightarrow P$ between 0 and 1, to $P \rightarrow O$ between 0 and 1, and to V between -1 and $+1$ (since individuals can attach a negative value to certain reinforcers), then we might assume in this case $E \rightarrow P$, $P \rightarrow O$, and V all receive highly positive values of 1, 1, and 1. Multiplying them (motivation $= 1$) represents the situation with a very high motivation potential. If, on the other hand, $E \rightarrow P$ and $P \rightarrow O$ remain 1 but the worker wins the $1 million lottery and no longer values the money earned on the job so much, V will drop; then the motivating value of the situation for the worker would be reduced. Alternatively, if $E \rightarrow P$ and V remain positive, but the worker perceives that performance is not rewarded equitably or at all (P → O approaches zero) then the motivating value of the situation would drop, and ultimately be zero. Similarly, if P → O and V remain positive, but E → P drops to zero, perhaps because the worker does not feel that hard work pays off in higher performance, then motivation will become zero because of the multiplicative formula.

Because performance can lead to multiple outcomes, each with different valences or values, each performance-to-outcome expectancy is multiplied by the corresponding valence. For example, Ben knows that if he produces he will receive pay, resulting in one positive performance-to-outcome expectancy. But Ben may also know that if he produces too much, he will be ostracized by other technicians for being a "rate-buster." This performance-to-outcome expectancy is much less positive and probably approaches zero. These products are then summed before being multiplied by the effort-to-performance expectancy. Thus, if we arbitrarily represent the first performance-to-outcome expectancy (P → O) as 1 and the second (P → O) as 0, the sum of the two is 1, which is less than if both expectancies were 1.

Again, we can assign values to E → P between 0 and 1, to each P → O expectancy between 0 and 1, and to each V between −1 and +1. Considering the case of Ben Kane again, if all parts of the equation receive highly positive values, then

$$\begin{aligned}\textbf{Motivation} &= [E \rightarrow P] \times \Sigma\,[(P \rightarrow O)(V)]\\ &= [1] \times [(1)(1) + (1)(1)]\\ &= (1) \times (1 + 1)\\ &= 2.\end{aligned}$$

If, on the other hand, all performance-to-outcome expectancies have a value of 0, then

$$\begin{aligned}\textbf{Motivation} &= [1] \times [(0)(1) + (1)]\\ &= (1) \times (0 + 0)\\ &= 0.\end{aligned}$$

The Intrinsic–Extrinsic Motivation Formulation

Barry Staw, among others, introduced a revised expectancy theory in the late 1970s.[46] According to this theory, performing a task has both intrinsic and extrinsic outcomes, which may differ in valence and which must be included in the calculation of motivation.[47] In this model, motivation is reduced if an individual does not value either intrinsic or extrinsic outcomes, or if the person perceives that either the intrinsic or extrinsic performance-to-outcome expectancies are low. For example, Bob Kane's motivation will be reduced if he does not like doing his tasks, or if he does not receive rewards he desires for performing them.

Empirical Support Evidence for the validity of the expectancy model is mixed.[48] Conceptual and methodological problems have been emphasized, with critics stating that (1) the model is too complex to measure; (2) the key variables of performance, effort, and valence lack consistent definition and operationalization; (3) repeated measures of the model's validity over time do not exist; and (4) no support exists for the multiplicative calculations of the model.[49] Other research suggests that factors other than personal expectancies, such as social norms, which play a significant role in behavior, are excluded from the expectancy model altogether.[50] Still, expectancy theory has dominated research on motivation since the early 1970s, principally because it has been supported empirically, incorporates other perspectives on motivation, and provides factors (expectancy, instrumentality, and valence) that managers can affect as means to increase employee motivation. In addition, its emphasis on the individual, with its ability to highlight individual differences, can also be of assistance to the practicing manager.

Does expectancy theory explain the motivational problems at Interval Corporation? To diagnose motivational problems using expectancy theory we must first answer the following questions:

1. *Does the individual perceive that effort will lead to performance?* Does Bob Kane perceive, for example, that if he works hard then he will produce? Not really: he may feel frustrated because his overtime hours seemed to result in increased supervision after Bob Rowen was hired.
2. *Does the individual perceive that certain behaviors will lead to specified outcomes?* Does Ben feel his performance will lead to rewards such as praise or more pay? Before Bob Rowen's arrival, Ben's performance seemed to result in more job responsibility. But his (perceived) above-average performance did not lead to pay increases.
3. *What values do individuals attach to these outcomes?* Ben seems to positively value both pay and autonomy—extrinsic and intrinsic outcomes.

A manager or worker could use the questionnaire in Activity 4–3 to address these questions and measure the level of individual motivation in a situation. Assume you are Ben Kane or his boss, Jeff Hoffman. How would you answer each of the questions? Use your answers to determine the level of Ben's work motivation. Then use your answers to identify any deficiencies in his job situation. Having identified deficiencies in the situation, a person who desires to improve Ben's motivation should ensure that the links between outcomes and desired performance are positive, that the rewards for Ben's performance are sufficiently large for him to notice and value them, and that any conflicting expectancies are eliminated.

The expectancy perspective implies the value of equity in the work situation as well as the importance of consistent rewards. In fact, both equity theory and reinforcement theory have been viewed as special cases of expectancy theory.[51] Although expectancy theory does not explicitly address individual needs, valences and instrumentalities may be a function of individual needs. Expectancy theory also addresses the issue of individual differences to a much greater extent than do needs theories. In addition, it offers the opportunity for quantification of the various facets of motivation. Hence expectancy theory, more than any other presented so far, offers a comprehensive diagnostic tool.

GOAL-SETTING THEORY

Just as expectancy theory can serve as an integrative view of motivation, so can goal setting. Setting goals can help individuals identify ways to meet their needs. Also, accomplishing goals can be reinforcing, as in the Emery Air Freight program described earlier. In these ways goal setting encourages individuals to exert effort and perform better.

Goals, which any member of an organization can set, describe a desired future state. Once established, goals can focus behavior and motivate individuals to achieve the desired end-state. Examples of goals are cutting costs, reducing absenteeism, increasing employee satisfaction, or changing the work climate. In 90 percent of the reported studies, goal setting has had a positive effect on performance.[52]

Goals can vary in three ways: (1) specificity, (2) difficulty, and (3) acceptance. The *specificity,* or clarity, of goals refers to the extent to which their accomplishment is observable and measurable. "Reducing absenteeism by 20 percent" is a highly specific goal for a manager; "developing subordinates" is a much less specific one. Goal *difficulty,* or the level of performance desired, can also vary significantly. A salesperson might set a goal to open ten new accounts per month, or one hundred new accounts; the first goal might be easy, the second extremely difficult. Third, individuals' *acceptance* of stated goals, or their commitment to accomplishing the goals, may vary. In general, a subordinate is less likely to accept a goal as his or her own or try to accomplish it if a manager assigns the goal, rather than *jointly* sets it with the subordinate.[53] Commitment is influenced by not only participation in goal setting, but the authority who sets the goals unilaterally or collaboratively; the existence of peer pressure to accomplish the goals; the values, incentives, and rewards associated with goal performance; the person's expectancy of success; and the existence of any self-administered rewards for goal accomplishment.[54]

Research has suggested that goals that are specific, moderately difficult, and yet accepted by a worker are more likely to be motivating than those that are not. A study of goal setting by truck drivers in a logging operation illustrates the motivational value of these combined factors.[55] The drivers loaded logs and drove them to the mill for processing. When their supervisors instructed them to "do their best," they underloaded their trucks, filling them to only 58–63 percent of their capacity. The researchers then assigned the drivers a goal of 94 percent of capacity but promised them no disciplinary action if they did not meet the goal. In the first three months they loaded to 80 percent, 70 percent, and 90 percent of truck capacity, respectively. In the second month the loggers tested the promise of no discipline, causing the drop in loading, but evidently fully accepted the goal thereafter. Further research recognized the role of feedback as a necessary condition for goal setting[56]: individuals required information about their effectiveness in meeting their goals as part of continuing to work toward them. In this case, performance was a function of employees' ability, acceptance of goals, level of the goals, and the interaction of the goals with their ability.[57]

Characteristics of the participants in goal setting, such as their authoritarianism or education, may have an impact on its effectiveness.[58] Note, too, that acceptance of goals has consequences for how difficult goals can be made: workers are likely to perform a task if the goals are difficult and accepted, but not if difficult and rejected.[59]

Research has indicated that goal-setting programs improve performance at both managerial and nonmanagerial levels over an extended period of time in a variety of organizations.[60] Management by objectives, known as MBO, is a formal evaluation program used in many organizations that emphasizes the formal setting of goals as a way of assessing and ultimately improving worker performance.

When joined with attempts to raise expectancies that effort leads to performance, setting difficult goals can boost productivity.[61] In very complex jobs, however, goal setting may not be feasible; it may lead only to bureaucratic behavior where setting the goals becomes an end in itself.

Looking again at the scenario in the introduction to this chapter, we can diagnose motivation by examining the goal-setting behavior in terms of the research just described. First, we ask whether Ben Kane and Bob Rowen (and even Jeff Hoffman) have goals. Next, we determine if the individuals accept their goals, which depends on whether the individuals perceive the goals as reasonable, are themselves self-assured, and have previous successes in accomplishing goals. Finally, we assess whether feedback has been provided en route to goal accomplishment. Has Jeff Hoffman discussed with Ben and Bob whether he perceives they are accomplishing their goals?

THE REWARD SYSTEM: APPLYING MOTIVATION THEORIES TO PRACTICE

An organization's reward system incorporates the motivational principles described so far into formal mechanisms for improving or reinforcing quality performance. Research has suggested that rewards now cause performance later, and rewards now cause satisfaction later.[62] Edward Lawler concluded that five factors influence satisfaction with a reward.[63] First, satisfaction with a reward depends on the amount received versus the amount the individual feels he or she should receive. Typically, the larger the reward individuals receive, whether extrinsic such as pay, or intrinsic such as job challenge, the more satisfied they feel. However, this feeling is moderated somewhat by their perception of whether the reward is justified. Assuming the overjustification effect exists in some cases, some individuals may feel uneasy if they receive a disproportionately large reward, particularly for the amount of effort they exert or in comparison to coworkers whom they perceive as similar. Second, comparison with what happens to others influences people's feelings of satisfaction. For example, if Ben Kane feels that he is being over- or under-rewarded in comparison to other employees whom he views as similar to himself, he may feel less satisfied than if he feels he is being treated equitably. Third, employees' satisfaction with both the intrinsic and extrinsic rewards received from their jobs affects overall job satisfaction: individuals who are dissatisfied with the reward system are likely to express dissatisfaction with their job overall. Fourth, people differ widely in the rewards they desire and in the value they attach to these rewards. Effective reward systems should meet workers' needs. Some individuals are willing to trade off flexible working hours for increased compensation; others choose increased benefits (sick leave, medical insurance, pension contributions) over salary increments. Fifth, many extrinsic rewards satisfy workers only because they lead to other rewards. For example, increased pay may satisfy workers because it results in more recreational opportunities or increased status for the employee. Certain other benefits may satisfy employees because they allow the worker to pursue educational and training opportunities and hence to grow.

These observations suggest the need for a diversified reward system. They also suggest that a comprehensive reward system demands a complete analysis of the organizational members and their work situations before choosing and allocating rewards. They emphasize the nature and consistency of rewards while not ignoring the individual members and their needs. An effective reward system must create a high quality of work life by offering sufficiently high and equitable rewards that meet individuals' needs. It must also encourage organizational effectiveness by rewarding better performance and attendance at work and by offering rewards that are congruent with management's style and the organization's structure. It must also avoid creating ethical dilemmas for those individuals it affects.[64]

Characteristics of the Reward System

Design of a reward system includes the two major types of rewards mentioned earlier: intrinsic and extrinsic. People who work because they find the work itself rewarding are intrinsically motivated; thus an appropriate reward system may offer increasing opportunities for challenge, responsibility, and growth as performance increases. Those who work because they receive such rewards as pay, promotions, or benefits are extrinsically motivated. Most researchers and practitioners agree that motivation in a work setting can occur because of the availability of both intrinsic and extrinsic rewards, the value attached to them, and the quality of their distribution in the organization.

Various characteristics of a reward system respond to an organization's environment, help accomplish the organization's goals, and contribute to (or occasionally contradict) the organization's culture, or the pattern of basic assumptions about the way employees adapt externally and integrate internally (see Chapter 14). Top management must determine, for example, whether it will assign pay on the basis of the jobs held by the workers or the skills and competencies workers have. Job-based pay rewards people for performing specific jobs and moving up the hierarchy, whereas skill-based programs reward people for building more competencies and increasing their skills. Job-based pay reinforces the link between an individual's job and organizational outcomes. It supports a culture that emphasizes bottom-line performance. Skill-based programs can be used independently or in conjunction with a job-based system. They support a culture that reflects a concern for individual development and learning and an environment that requires greater flexibility from a relatively permanent work force.[65]

Reward systems must also consider the market position of the pay levels, benefits, and other rewards offered. If, for example, Interval Corporation pays, on average, higher wages than its competitors, and learns that a major competitor pays, on average, lower wages, would Interval's management continue to offer high pay levels? Some companies prefer to take a leadership position in compensation: management of these organizations assumes that paying well will result in attracting the best people. Others are willing to risk attracting somewhat less qualified workers by offering lower financial rewards. The chosen market position certainly influences an organization's ability to cope with its environment: when a tight labor market exists organizations with an aggressive, "leader" strategy typically fare best in securing the workers they need. When, on the other hand, labor is very available, these compensation leaders may unnecessarily spend a premium.

Top management must also determine which organizational members are to make pay decisions. Responsibility can be decentralized throughout the organization to supervisors or can be centralized and systematized in a corporate compensation system. The decision-making process chosen frequently complements the organization's structure and reinforces its culture. Communication of compensation decisions varies among organizations from very secretive to very open. The communication policy chosen is frequently compatible with the extent of employee involvement in decision making in general.

Most reward systems include at least three components of compensation: (1) pay, (2) benefits, and (3) incentives. Yet organizations differ considerably in the relative amount of resources they devote to each. Some emphasize pay over benefits; others rely exclusively on incentives.[66]

The Wage Issue

The chief component of a typical organizational reward system is pay. According to the motivation theories, pay acts as a powerful reward. It can meet diverse needs and reinforce desired behaviors. However, because of the complexity and difficulty in applying pay correctly, organizations frequently misuse it as a reward. They may, for example, give all employees the same pay increase regardless of their performance. Organizations may not satisfy the needs they intend to meet with pay: individuals may be paid too much, and the high pay may outweigh an otherwise poor fit between an employee and his or her job. Many organizations use systematic wage and salary structures to ensure the equitable and effective distribution of pay. They assign each job to a wage category with an associated pay range; job holders receive wages within that range. Pay increases also occur in a prescribed fashion as the employee's longevity of employment increases and performance improves.

Distributing Benefits

Most organizations use benefits to supplement wages. Management uses benefits to motivate employees, improve morale, reward loyalty, increase job satisfaction, attract good employees, reduce turnover, prevent unionization, enhance employee security, maintain a favorable competitive position, and enhance the organization's image among employees.

A range of benefits exists, as shown in Figure 4–7. Managers must assess how well each benefit accomplishes the objectives of the reward system, responds to workers' needs, and is cost-effective. Some organizations offer flexible benefits plans—where individuals can select from an array of benefits—to prevent duplication of benefits and ensure that they respond to workers' needs. The use of benefits as part of the reward system is somewhat controversial.[67] While profit sharing and bonuses can be directly tied to performance, sick days and some health protectors are increasingly viewed as essential and separate from the reward system.

Using Incentives

Incentive programs are formalized reward programs that pay an individual or group of individuals for what they produce. They incorporate the motivational principles described earlier in the section on reinforcement theory. If a worker

Figure 4–7 EXAMPLES OF BENEFITS

Health Protectors	Income Supplements
Medical insurance	Bonuses
Dental insurance	Profit-sharing plans
	Stock bonus plans
Income Protectors	Stock options
Accidental death insurance	
Disability insurance	**Other Benefits**
Life insurance	Business and professional memberships
Pension	Club memberships
Retirement benefits	Company automobile
Supplementary unemployment benefits	Credit union
Workers' compensation	Day care
	Education costs
Time off with Pay	Flexible work arrangements
Holidays	Recreational facilities
Personal days	Subsidized housing
Maternity or paternity leave	Subsidized meals
Sabbaticals	
Sick leave	
Vacations	

packs shipping containers, then he or she receives a certain amount of money for each container filled; often, the more containers filled, the more pay the worker receives. Or a salesperson receives a fee for each container sold. Piecework systems, commission plans, and merit bonuses are the most common incentive systems; they directly link pay to performance.

Piecework systems tie compensation to individual performance by paying for each item produced. Commissions link pay to sales levels rather than production rates. Individuals may receive a certain percentage of total sales, new sales, or they may receive compensation for reaching a sales quota. Bonuses are one-time, lump-sum payments that are tied to exceptional performance. Organizations increasingly use these instead of merit increases because their cost in the long run is lower. By contrast merit increases reward past performance but become a cost of future performance regardless of its quality. A 6 percent merit increase, for example, applies for the rest of an employee's work life at the organization, even if his or her subsequent performance does not merit such a pay level.[68] Merit bonuses reward performance only once, for the period under consideration.

In designing incentive systems, and particularly those that tie a tangible reward to a measurable improvement in performance (also known as gain-sharing programs), organizational leaders frequently reduce the effectiveness of the reward system by committing one of a dozen errors. Reading 4–1, "Designing Effective Reward Systems," discusses these in greater detail. Incentives can reinforce organizational goals, and their use supports an emphasis on bottom-line performance. Although they can increase productivity and lower production costs, they can also adversely affect the quality of the product, cause workers to trade off long-term for short-term gains, and ignore the means by which individuals attain results.[69] The incentive systems of one group of high-performing banks and savings-and-loan organizations emphasized pay for performance and made incentives a large part of the total cash compensation.[70] Participation in the incentive program extended through much of the organization. To participate individuals were required to identify performance yardsticks that reflected top management's priorities. They used forecasts, goals, and budgets to judge whether progress was on target, and performance periods coincided with tasks to be done and goals to be reached.

Employee Ownership

Perhaps the ultimate reward for workers is to own part of the organization. In several European countries managers have become involved in the ownership of their organizations. Worker-owned cooperatives, such as the Mondragon Cooperatives in Spain, have increasingly served as a model for employee ownership of companies in the United States and elsewhere abroad.[71] In these organizations workers can exert control over the organization's direction and operation and avoid permanently closing plants. While these efforts have been well received by union leaders and workers in Europe, reaction by labor leaders in the United States has been less positive. Fear of the unknown, risks to workers, and attachment to the traditional adversarial relationship between union and management have contributed to this negative reaction.[72]

Worker representation on boards of directors has been viewed as a lesser form of worker ownership. Known as codetermination, this structure also gives workers a direct voice in the operation of their companies. Other worker participation ideas, such as work councils, have been incorporated into quality of working life programs (described in Chapter 13).

Criteria of an Effective Reward System

An effective reward system ties rewards to performance. Individuals who work harder, produce more, or produce better quality outputs should receive more rewards than poorer performers. Reward systems should also offer a sufficient number and diversity of rewards. Some organizations lack the resources to offer sufficient extrinsic rewards to motivate employees to perform or to encourage their satisfaction; in these cases, organizations must consider job enrichment or quality of working life programs (see Chapter 13) as ways of increasing possible intrinsic rewards instead.

The criteria for the allocation of rewards must be clear and complete. Individual organizational members should know whether they receive rewards for level or quality of performance, attendance, innovativeness, or effort, for example. The criteria for receipt of specific wages, benefits, or incentives must be clearly defined. In addition, different individuals should be treated differently when appropriate. Workers who perform at different levels or who have different needs often should not receive the same rewards. At the same time, management must ensure that workers perceive that an equitable distribution of rewards occurs. Finally, organizational rewards should compare favorably with rewards in similar organizations. For organizations to attract and retain qualified and competent employees they must offer rewards comparable to their competitors.

SUMMARY

Interval Corporation has at least one subordinate with a motivational problem. Ben Kane, once an outstanding performer with great enthusiasm for his job, has experienced declining performance and increasing dissatisfaction. We have examined this situation by applying diverse motivation theories to help us understand the events.

Using needs theories, such as Maslow's, Alderfer's, McClelland's, and Herzberg's, we hypothesized that Ben might have unsatisfied physiological, safety, social, esteem, or self-actualization needs (also called existence, relatedness, or growth needs). We considered whether he had a high need for achievement, affiliation, or power. We examined the motivators and hygiene factors in the situation.

Next we considered the ways in which equity theory provided insights into the situation. We noted that Ben perceived an inequity in the treatment he received when compared to that of Bob Rowen. Rather than adjusting his inputs or outputs, or changing his perceptions of his peer's inputs or outputs, Ben reduced the inequity by resigning.

Reinforcement theory focused our attention on the feedback Ben received about his performance. To encourage the type of performance that helps accomplish organizational goals, Ben must receive reinforcers that he values when he behaves in appropriate ways. For example, when he performs well, Jeff Hoffman could praise him or give him a pay increase. Analysis of the schedule of reinforcements must also occur.

As an integrating perspective, we used expectancy theory to diagnose the situation at Interval.[73] We assessed whether Ben Kane perceived that his effort led to performance; whether his performance led to certain outcomes; and whether he valued these outcomes. We also differentiated between the intrinsic and extrinsic components of his task and their relationships to motivation.

We examined the role of goal setting as a technique that assists workers in meeting their needs, encouraging equity in the workplace, reinforcing desired behaviors, and ensuring that expectancy, instrumentality, and valence are positive. Goals that are specific, moderately difficult, and accepted by the workers tend to be most motivating.

Finally, we considered the nature of reward systems in organizations. We looked at the factors that determine satisfaction with a reward and the characteristics of a reward system. We also considered the use of wages, benefits, and incentives in an organization. We concluded by identifying the principles that describe an effective and motivating reward system. A reward system should stimulate and support motivation by meeting workers' needs, ensuring equity, reinforcing desirable behaviors, and prompting the establishment of specific, moderately difficult, and accepted goals. To diagnose quality of motivation and the effectiveness of a reward system we can consider the questions in Figure 4–8.

Figure 4–8 DIAGNOSTIC QUESTIONS FOR MOTIVATION AND DESIGN OF REWARD SYSTEMS

- Do rewards satisfy individuals' needs?
- Are rewards applied equitably and consistently after desired behaviors?
- Do individuals value the rewards they receive?
- Are rewards consistently applied in proportion to performance?
- Do individuals perceive that their efforts correlate with performance?
- Do individuals set goals that are specific and moderately difficult, yet accepted?
- Do individuals receive feedback about their goal accomplishment as part of the organization's reward system?
- What type of reward system exists?
- Does it encourage desired outcomes such as innovation, productivity, or attendance?
- Are benefits and incentive systems effective in motivating desired outcomes?

READING

Reading 4–1: DESIGNING EFFECTIVE REWARD SYSTEMS

Michael J. Cissell

Reward systems are here to stay. Several leading corporations (for example, General Motors, American Airlines, General Electric, Xerox, TRW, Dana, NUCOR Steel, HUMANA) have been providing tangible rewards to employees in return for measurable improvements in productivity, quality, or cost reduction. The increased popularity of reward systems can be attributed to their compatibility with the following challenges facing U.S. management today:

- Encouraging the entrepreneurial and innovative spirit of employees.
- Meeting the ever-growing need of employees to be "in the know" and to participate in the decision-making process.
- Motivating employees to take control over their work to accomplish organizational objectives.
- Providing higher income for employees that is tied directly to their corresponding and quantifiable increases in productivity, quality, or cost reduction.
- Remaining competitive in a world market.
- Adhering to the U.S. capitalistic philosophy by meeting the "What's in it for me?" demand.

REWARD SYSTEMS

A reward system ties a tangible award directly to measurable performance improvement. In its pure sense, a reward system is "pay for performance." Traditional approaches to reward systems include such gainsharing plans as the Scanlon, Rucker, and Improshare plans. Reward systems, however, need not be as rigid as these traditional approaches. The most effective plans are custom designed to fit the organization's objectives and culture.

Profit sharing, while similar in approach and philosophy to customized reward systems, takes a different approach. Profit-sharing plans set aside a portion of the total company profits for a predetermined employee group or groups. A reward system, on the other hand, is tied directly to areas of impact in which a given employee or group of employees has directly improved performance. For example, an individual may receive a profit-sharing bonus at the end of the business year even if his or her own performance or the performance of his or her department/plant/operating group was significantly below expectations. Therefore, profit sharing does not provide a direct performance-to-reward link.

IMPLEMENTATION CONSIDERATIONS

Custom reward systems may be designed to meet a variety of organizational objectives—from increasing the rate of production to cutting the number of defects in the final product to improving customer service. Any reward system, however, should be considered a major intervention that could create problems unless it is designed or implemented with care. In this article I plan to brief you on some common recurring errors in reward system design and implementation and to describe how you can make sure your system avoids these pitfalls. This list of errors can be used as a checklist to ensure that your reward system will meet its objectives.

Error 1: Failure to Consider State of the Industry

The potential impact of a reward system depends to a degree on the current business stage of the company. Industries at both ends of the business cycle may have problems realizing the positive impact of a reward system. When a company is in a survival or turnaround mode, management doesn't have the time or the interest to focus on individual reward. A successful system requires the attention and support of top and middle management, but management's energy is focused elsewhere when a company is experiencing severe financial difficulty or being threatened by takeover.

At the other end of the spectrum, small companies that are experiencing rapid growth usually prefer a profit-sharing system over a reward system to motivate employees. The management of such companies apparently feels that profit sharing is easier to implement, and employees feel a more direct effect on the final product than they would in a large company. Managers of such companies hope that rapid growth and consequent profits will ensure positive results, even if the employee's share is not specifically tied to his or her effort.

During the last recession, many companies who had sustained significant losses or had negotiated wage concessions considered rigid gainsharing plans as a way to tie employees' pay increases to their productivity because gainsharing rewards are paid only after employees achieve measurable performance improvement. Contracted or regular wage increases, on the other hand, must be paid regardless of unit/company performance and typically represent a "forever" decision. Gainsharing may help companies to achieve their performance and compensation objectives in such situations, provided the employees perceive that they have a real opportunity to earn rewards. If performance standards and reward opportunities are unrealistically set, morale, quality, and productivity will be undermined.

Number of employees should also be considered when setting up a reward system. Small companies with 100 employees or less may be better suited for profit sharing, as mentioned above, because employees in a small firm feel that they have a significant role in the overall profitability of the company. The larger the organization, the more difficult it is to isolate the impact individuals or departments have on the overall profitability of the firm. As an example, what impact does one employee assembling power steering pumps feel he or she has on the profitability of a fully integrated automobile manufacturer? The employee will see little, if any, relationship between the improved quantity or quality of the power steering pumps he or she produces and the company's bottom-line profits. When employees are rewarded for their department's contribution to better and more power steering pumps, however, the motivation to excel is real and direct.

Error 2: Confusing Productivity and Quality Measures with Financial Performance

Operating managers rather than financial managers should be responsible and accountable for reward systems. Too often, financial managers equate productivity with profitability; although these terms are compatible, they are not synonymous. Although it can be defined in many ways, productivity really relates to the efficient and the effective use of labor, materials, energy, and capital. Productivity is controllable. Profitability may not be controllable because of market influences, product life cycles, management decisions, or government directives.

A reward system should, for purposes of equity, clearly relate to a performance measure or measures. To develop a financial rationale to back up the performance measures, companies should be able to determine what incremental improvements in efficiency are worth to the firm. These improvements are usually reflected in quantity, quality, scrap or rework, schedule attainment, cost reduction, or other factors that have an established output/input relationship or a one-time measurable cost takeout. As efficiencies are realized, the company gains additional funds or "savings" as compared with previous outlays. Under a performance reward system, a percentage of those savings are returned to the employees. The remainder of the generated savings are retained by the company for continued improvements to plant, equipment, or new technology or shareholders' dividends.

Error 3: Locking the Firm into a Rigid Sharing Formula

Traditional gainsharing formulas are usually "forever" plans. Rigid programs are dangerous because they limit management's flexibility. Neither gainsharing nor gainsharing formulas should last forever. Too often, companies lock themselves into a formula that cannot be modified as technology advances or the product mix changes. Leaving a formula "as is" will, with the passage of time, inaccurately compensate employees.

While formulas must be modified or changed for a system to be successful, these changes should be kept to a minimum and carefully communicated. Everyone must know the purpose and importance of the changes and believe the revisions are fair and equitable.

Management should also consider that a reward system can be used as a temporary rather than long-term organizational intervention. For example, several hospitals have installed special programs to dramatically curtail costs and enhance revenue. These programs make a "one time" reward to employee teams based on a percentage of the first-year savings from their approved ideas.

Error 4: Making Rewards Contingent on a Single Performance Measure

Companies sometimes reward improvements in individual or work group productivity while ignoring the total performance of the department or plant. Other firms have taken the equally dangerous approach of rewarding on a macro level and disregarding small group performance.

The use of small unit measures maximizes employee motivation to improve performance. Micro measures typically have a high degree of employee impact and control built in. On the down side, depending completely on unit measures gives the organization the least financial security. Some units may improve and earn rewards while the overall facility performance declines. Therefore, some type of unit measure coupled with an overall department measure is a positive compromise to motivate employees while assuring real gains. For example, in a steel mill, the quality control staff should be rewarded for the timely and accurate completion of their tests as well as improvement in the total mill yield or material utilization.

Error 5: Failure to Include All Employees in the Reward Opportunity

Most managers are willing to share the rewards of improved productivity with employees who are directly involved with producing the product, but they frequently ignore indirect and support personnel. Thus they overlook an important economic fact: The number of indirect and support personnel has been growing in recent years in comparison with the number of direct employees in most organizations. Thus it is increasingly important to motivate indirect and support personnel to improve their productivity. Management must recognize that such people are essential and contribute to the organization's profitability.

One rationalization that managers use to escape the

task of measuring the productivity of support and indirect personnel is the argument that it is "too difficult" to measure these functions. Each support function, however, includes at least one key result area that can be quantified and measured. For example, by recruiting qualified people and handling employees' grievances expeditiously, the human resources department helps operating managers meet their goals. These and other human resources functions are easily measured. By excluding indirect and support employees from sharing in performance rewards, management minimizes potential improvement and may create a counterproductive "have/have not" environment.

Error 6: Failure to Obtain Middle Management Commitment

Productivity improvement programs are usually mandated by senior management, but the actual responsibility for improving performance rests on the shoulders of middle management. Such managers may look on reward systems as an added burden while their employees receive the "reward." To win middle management support, such managers should be rewarded for improvements in their department's performance. Thus those at all levels will benefit and feel they are part of the process.

Error 7: Failure to Build Necessary Management Supervisory Skills

A reward system should not be dropped into an organization without preparation. Senior management needs to assess the current skill level required to support the intervention. Often, performance-contingent rewards will have to be coupled with a "new way of managing." Employees must learn to communicate with one another, problem solve, and take action to improve productivity. Managers must be prepared to listen and seek ideas from subordinates and effectively coach and reinforce behaviors that will lead to gains. In some companies needed skills will already be in place, and an orientation may be all that is needed. Too many companies, however, ignore essential skills and let the system run itself. The most successful reward systems require management attention, direction, and corrective action planning.

Error 8: Absence of Organization Input in System Design

A reward system demands a participative process. Many organizations mandate the plan from the top using only outside consultants in the design stage. Consultants should be facilitators—not "controllers." Each company has unique characteristics that, when assessed properly, will maximize the plan structure for both the company and the employees. An internal design team may be designated to work with an outside consultant to understand the corporate culture. If employees at a particular location are represented by a union, it is also wise to involve the union leaders in the process and keep them informed on a timely basis. The design team should consist of key people taken from a vertical slice of the company. Because this team will help achieve employee buy-in and minimize design and implementation errors, credible representatives from all parts of the organization are essential. The design team should explore factors that will work effectively within a given department or facility, or on a companywide basis. Design team employees should become proactive sponsors of the reward system.

Error 9: Failure to Convince Employees that Opportunity to Earn Rewards is Real

To establish a reward system, management must agree to share a portion of the savings that result from employee contributions to improved productivity. It is important that the potential reward be consistent with the additional effort called for. Furthermore, the reward must be perceived as "achievable" by employees. In many companies, the reward plan breaks down at this point. Some senior managers believe that hourly employees and support employees get intrinsic satisfaction from involvement in their jobs; and in the final analysis, senior managers resent "sharing" gains with the employees. One school of management believes that satisfaction and rewards are derived from the nature of the work and the improvement of the work process itself. This philosophy is not adhered to by most executive compensation plans: Senior executives often receive over half of their compensation from bonuses tied to performance. Employees recognize the paradox here: Reinforcers do not differ dramatically whether they are applied in the executive tower or on the plant floor.

To develop a sound reward system for those "on the plant floor," several variables must be taken into consideration. Some of these include the following:

- The performance factors the system is attempting to affect—productivity and quality. Because these factors require a high level of overall effort, they should receive higher rewards than such individual performance factors as safe work habits and good attendance.
- The time span of the system.
- The labor/management history of the company or location.
- The results of past productivity improvement systems.
- The potential financial return to the company from improvements in the performance measure.
- The current compensation of employees who will participate in the system. This is relevant because, for example, an additional $50 per month may be very significant to an employee earning minimum wage

but may be insignificant and thus not motivating to those earning $50,000 annually.

Error 10: Lack of Performance Feedback

Employees need accurate feedback about their performance. A good reward system must spell out "Here's what you need to do. Here is how you do it. This is what you get." The "how to" is transmitted by providing accurate performance feedback.

There are several principles of effective feedback. Specifically, effective feedback should

- Be expressed objectively rather than subjectively.
- Be expressed in terms of measured goals.
- Be expressed positively.
- Be expressed as soon after the desired performance as possible.
- Be easy to administer.
- Offer suggestions for improvement, if appropriate.

Supervisors and employees must master the skill of providing constructive feedback. The power of several individuals working toward a common goal is evident in the most successful reward systems. It is in the company's best interest to do everything possible to capitalize on team involvement. Feedback, coupled with tangible rewards, is a very powerful tool in making the involvement process successful.

Error 11: Cash Awards as the Only Option

Everyone knows that cash motivates. Cash is universally accepted as the medium of compensation. The inherent flaw in using cash is the fact that cash is the accepted medium of compensation. Cash pays the mortgage. Cash pays for the kids' braces. Cash pays the electric bill. Reward with cash, and it will be gone quickly—in mind and matter. While people value cash in the short term, another type of reward may be more effective in the long run.

Because enthusiastic and motivated employees are your ultimate objective, I believe that reward systems should be distinctive, even fun. The reward should be memorable and different from regular compensation to reinforce "pay for performance."

In many instances, merchandise has proven to be a viable alternative to cash. Merchandise is a proven performer and reinforcer in a reward system. It is easier to promote than cash and lasts as a motivator because whenever employees use the earned reward they experience a positive image of the company and their past performance. Merchandise gives participants the opportunity to receive some "luxury" guilt-free, rather than feeling the need to apply cash toward some family obligation. Travel is also a distinctive and well-received reward.

It is important to remember that what motivates one person may not motivate the next person. The world isn't all vanilla. Baskin Robbins built a business on supplying a wide variety of flavors. Variety in rewards will improve your results.

Error 12: Failure to Grant Rewards on a Timely Basis

Rewards have the greatest impact if they are perceived as positive, certain, and immediate. Thus rewards must be valuable enough to inspire extra effort, specific enough for employees to know what to expect for various levels of performance, and awarded close enough to the time that performance is measured to be a direct link to the level of performance. Thus good reward system design must include three factors: value, certainty, and immediacy.

SUMMARY

If designed properly, reward systems can be powerful tools. They can deliver significant bottom-line results while raising employees' morale and encouraging their participation. Well-designed and well-implemented systems are achieving measurable benefits for many successful U.S. corporations. Companies, employees, and customers ultimately win from a higher level of productivity and quality

Use this article as a checklist to ensure a high level of success with reward systems.

DISCUSSION QUESTIONS

1. What errors can occur in the design of a reward system?
2. What effect do these errors have on motivation in organizations?
3. How can these errors be avoided?

ACTIVITIES

Activity 4–1: NEEDS ASSESSMENT QUESTIONNAIRE

Step 1: Complete the following questionnaire.

Given below are several characteristics or qualities connected with your job. (You may use your job as student.) For each such characteristic, you will be asked to rate: *How important is this characteristic to you?* Each rating will be on a five-point scale, from 1 (very unimportant) to 5 (very important). Circle the number on the scale that represents your rating of the characteristic.

1. The feeling of self-esteem a person gets from being in that job.	1 2 3 4 5
2. The opportunity for personal growth and development in that job.	1 2 3 4 5
3. The prestige of the job inside the company (that is, regard received from others in the company).	1 2 3 4 5
4. The opportunity for independent thought and action in that job.	1 2 3 4 5
5. The feeling of security in that job.	1 2 3 4 5
6. The feeling of self-fulfillment a person gets from being in that position (that is, the feeling of being able to use one's own unique capabilities, realizing one's potential).	1 2 3 4 5
7. The prestige in my job position outside the company (that is, the regard received from others not in the company).	1 2 3 4 5
8. The feeling of worthwhile accomplishments in that job.	1 2 3 4 5
9. The opportunity in that job to give help to other people.	1 2 3 4 5
10. The opportunity in that job for participation in the setting of goals.	1 2 3 4 5
11. The opportunity in that job for participation in the determination of methods and procedures.	1 2 3 4 5
12. The authority connected with the job.	1 2 3 4 5
13. The opportunity to develop close friendships in the job.	1 2 3 4 5

Step 2: Score the questionnaire by completing the following equations.

Ratings for question 5	= ________	Divide by 1 = ________	Security
Ratings for questions 9 and 13	= ________	Divide by 2 = ________	Social
Ratings for questions 1, 3, and 7	= ________	Divide by 3 = ________	Esteem
Ratings for questions 4, 10, 11, and 12	= ________	Divide by 4 = ________	Autonomy
Ratings for questions 2, 6, and 8	= ________	Divide by 3 = ________	Self-Realization

Step 3: Complete the questionnaire again. This time rate *how much your job (or your job as student) provides this characteristic.* Put an X over the appropriate rating number for each question.

Step 4: Score the questionnaire as in step 2, using those ratings covered by an X.

Step 5: Discussion. In small groups or with the class as a whole, answer the following questions:

Description

1. Which is your highest score in step 2? your lowest?
2. How does this compare to scores of others in the class?
3. Which is your highest score in step 4? your lowest?
4. How does this compare to scores of others in the class?
5. How do the two sets of scores you obtain compare?

Diagnosis

6. How well does your job help satisfy your highest scoring need? your next highest scoring need?
7. Compare your answers to question 3 to the answers of others with the same score pattern and to the answers of others with different score patterns. Discuss your observations.

Adapted from Lyman W. Porter, ORGANIZATIONAL PATTERNS OF MANAGERIAL JOB ATTITUDES (New York: American Foundation for Management Research, 1964), pp. 17, 19.

Activity 4–2: EQUITY QUESTIONNAIRE

Step 1: Complete the following questionnaire.

Imagine that there are two people, yourself and a coworker. Even though this is a fictitious situation, imagine how you would actually feel if you were in it. Create your own description of the coworker, and imagine that he or she is very similar to you. Specifically, assume that the coworker (1) is the same sex you are, (2) is the same age, (3) has the same amount of education you do, (4) is interested in the same things you are, (5) has a similar background to yours, and (6) was hired at the same time as you. The only differences between you are that the coworker has heavier family responsibilities than you do and works more slowly than you do.

Below are three potential work situations you and your coworker might be in. *Circle* the letter of the situation (A, B, or C) in which you would feel most comfortable. *Check* the letter of the situation in which you would feel least comfortable.

A. You and a coworker are each paid $2.56 per hour for attending and tape recording various lectures for a current affairs analyst.

B. You are paid $1.28 per hour to attend and tape record various lectures for a current affairs analyst. A coworker receives $3.84 per hour to perform the same duties.

C. You are paid $3.84 per hour to attend and tape record various lectures for a current affairs analyst. A coworker receives $1.28 per hour to perform the same duties.

Step 2: Now consider the situation you indicated as being the least preferred.

Below are ten changes that could be made in the least preferred situation to make it more comfortable. Check which *one* of the changes you would be *most likely* to make in order to make the least preferred situation more comfortable.

1. Work faster or harder.
2. Work slower or less energetically.
3. Request lower wages for yourself.
4. Request higher wages for yourself.
5. Persuade coworker to work harder.
6. Persuade coworker to work less energetically.
7. Request higher wages for coworker.
8. Request lower wages for coworker.
9. Seek a new coworker.
10. Quit the job.

Step 3: Discussion. Answer the following questions in small groups or with the entire class:

Description

1. Which of the three situations did you prefer most? least?

Diagnosis

2. How does equity theory explain your choice?
3. What effect does the change have on the least-preferred situation?
4. Does it make it more or less equitable? Use equity theory to explain the change.
5. Can needs theories explain your choice or the impact of the change on the least-preferred situation?

Adapted from Weick, K.E. and Nesset, B. Preferences among forms of equity. *Organizational Behavior and Human Performance* 3 (1968): 400–416. Reprinted by permission of authors and publisher.

Activity 4–3: EXPECTANCY QUESTIONNAIRE

Step 1: Answer questions 1, 2, and 3 by circling the answer that best describes your feelings.

Question 1: Here are some things that could happen to people if they do their jobs *especially well*. How likely is it that each of these things would happen if you performed your job *especially well?* (You may use your job as student.)

	Not at All Likely		*Somewhat Likely*		*Quite Likely*		*Extremely Likely*
a You will get a bonus or pay increase	(1)	(2)	(3)	(4)	(5)	(6)	(7)
b You will feel better about yourself as a person	(1)	(2)	(3)	(4)	(5)	(6)	(7)
c You will have an opportunity to develop your skills and abilities	(1)	(2)	(3)	(4)	(5)	(6)	(7)
d You will have better job security	(1)	(2)	(3)	(4)	(5)	(6)	(7)

	Not at All Likely		Somewhat Likely		Quite Likely		Extremely Likely
e You will be given chances to learn new things	(1)	(2)	(3)	(4)	(5)	(6)	(7)
f You will be promoted or get a better job	(1)	(2)	(3)	(4)	(5)	(6)	(7)
g You will get a feeling that you've accomplished something worthwhile	(1)	(2)	(3)	(4)	(5)	(6)	(7)
h You will have more freedom on your job	(1)	(2)	(3)	(4)	(5)	(6)	(7)
i You will be respected by the people you work with	(1)	(2)	(3)	(4)	(5)	(6)	(7)
j Your supervisor will praise you	(1)	(2)	(3)	(4)	(5)	(6)	(7)
k The people you work with will be friendly with you	(1)	(2)	(3)	(4)	(5)	(6)	(7)

Question 2: Different people want different things from their work. Here is a list of things a person could have on his or her job. How *important* is each of the following to you? (You may use your job as student.)

	Moderately Important or Less			Quite Important			Extremely Important
How Important Is . . . ?							
a The amount of pay you get	(1)	(2)	(3)	(4)	(5)	(6)	(7)
b The chances you have to do something that makes you feel good about yourself as a person	(1)	(2)	(3)	(4)	(5)	(6)	(7)
c The opportunity to develop your skills and abilities	(1)	(2)	(3)	(4)	(5)	(6)	(7)
d The amount of job security you have	(1)	(2)	(3)	(4)	(5)	(6)	(7)
How Important Is . . . ?							
e The chances you have to learn new things	(1)	(2)	(3)	(4)	(5)	(6)	(7)
f Your chances for getting a promotion or getting a better job	(1)	(2)	(3)	(4)	(5)	(6)	(7)
g The chances you have to accomplish something worthwhile	(1)	(2)	(3)	(4)	(5)	(6)	(7)
h The amount of freedom you have on your job	(1)	(2)	(3)	(4)	(5)	(6)	(7)
How Important Is . . . ?							
i The respect you receive from the people you work with	(1)	(2)	(3)	(4)	(5)	(6)	(7)
j The praise you get from your supervisor	(1)	(2)	(3)	(4)	(5)	(6)	(7)
k The friendliness of the people you work with	(1)	(2)	(3)	(4)	(5)	(6)	(7)

Question 3: Below you will see a number of pairs of factors that look like this:

Warm weather → sweating (1) (2) (3) (4) (5) (6) (7)

You are to indicate by checking the appropriate number to the right of each pair how often it is true for you personally that the first factor leads to the second on your job (or your job as student). Remember, for each pair, indicate how often it is true by checking the box under the response which seems most accurate.

	Never		*Sometimes*		*Often*		*Almost Always*
a Working hard → high productivity	(1)	(2)	(3)	(4)	(5)	(6)	(7)
b Working hard → doing my job well	(1)	(2)	(3)	(4)	(5)	(6)	(7)
c Working hard → good job performance	(1)	(2)	(3)	(4)	(5)	(6)	(7)

Step 2: Using the questionnaire results.

The results from this questionnaire can be used to calculate a work-motivation score. A score can be calculated for each individual and scores can be combined for groups of individuals. The procedure for obtaining a work-motivation score is as follows:

a. For each of the possible positive outcomes listed in questions 1 and 2, multiply the score for the outcome on question 1 (P → O expectancies) by the corresponding score on question 2 (valences of outcomes). Thus, score 1a would be multiplied by score 2a, score 1b by score 2b, and so forth.
b. All of the 1-times-2 products would be added together to get a total of all expectancies-times-valences.
c. The total should be divided by the number of pairs (in this case, eleven) to get an average expectancy-times-valence score.
d. The scores from question 3 (E → P expectancies) should be added together and then divided by three to get an average effort-to-performance expectancy score.
e. Multiply the score obtained in Step c (the average expectancy-times-valence) by the score obtained in Step d (the average E → P expectancy score) to obtain a total work-motivation score.

Step 3: Discussion. Answer the following questions in small groups or with the entire class:

Description

1. What score did you receive? Compare it to the scores of other class members.

Diagnosis

2. How motivating is your job?
3. What factors influence your score?
4. How does the content of your job relate to your score?
5. Can you explain the score using expectancy theory?
6. Can you explain the motivation potential of your job using—
   a. reinforcement theory?
   b. equity theory?
   c. needs theories?

Prescription

7. How would you improve the motivating potential of your job?

Reprinted by permission from Nadler, D.A., and Lawler, E.E., III, "Motivation: A Diagnostic Approach." In *Perspectives on Behavior in Organizations,* edited by J.R. Hackman, E.E. Lawler, III, and L.W. Porter. New York: McGraw-Hill, 1977.

Activity 4–4: GOAL-SETTING EXERCISE

Step 1: Think about a job you now hold or a job you have held in the past. If you have never been employed think about an "ideal" middle-management job.

Step 2: Answer the following questions about that job:

1. How effective were (are) the methods used by your manager in generating maximum employee work performance? (Circle one)
   A. Highly effective
   B. Moderately effective
   C. Ineffective
2. How satisfied were (are) you with this job?
   A. Highly satisfied
   B. Moderately satisfied
   C. Unsatisfied

Step 3: Complete the job objectives questionnaire.

As employees, each of us has certain objectives that are part of our work. Sometimes, these objectives are spelled out in detail; other times, the objectives are simply intuitively "understood." The following statements refer to your job, and to the objectives that are associated with your job. Read each statement, then circle the number indicating *how untrue* or *how true* you believe each statement to be. (If you prefer, you can think about a job you've had with some organization in the past.)

	Definitely Not True	Not True	Slightly Not True	Uncertain	Slightly True	True	Definitely True
1. Management encourages employees to define job objectives.	−3	−2	−1	0	1	2	3
2. If I achieve my objectives, I receive adequate recognition from my supervisor.	−3	−2	−1	0	1	2	3
3. My objectives are clearly stated with respect to the results expected.	−3	−2	−1	0	1	2	3
4. I have the support I need to accomplish my objectives.	−3	−2	−1	0	1	2	3
5. Achieving my objectives increases my chances for promotion.	−3	−2	−1	0	1	2	3
6. My supervisor dictates my job objectives to me.	−3	−2	−1	0	1	2	3
7. I need more feedback on whether I'm achieving my objectives or not.	−3	−2	−1	0	1	2	3
8. My supervisor will "get on my back" if I fail to achieve my objectives.	−3	−2	−1	0	1	2	3
9. My job objectives are very challenging.	−3	−2	−1	0	1	2	3
10. Management wants to know whether I set objectives for my job or not.	−3	−2	−1	0	1	2	3
11. My supervisor will compliment me if I achieve my job objectives.	−3	−2	−1	0	1	2	3
12. My objectives are very ambiguous and unclear.	−3	−2	−1	0	1	2	3
13. I lack the authority to accomplish my objectives.	−3	−2	−1	0	1	2	3
14. Achievement of objectives is rewarded with higher pay here.	−3	−2	−1	0	1	2	3
15. My supervisor encourages me to establish my own objectives.	−3	−2	−1	0	1	2	3
16. I always have knowledge of my progress toward my objectives.	−3	−2	−1	0	1	2	3
17. My supervisor will reprimand me if I'm not making progress toward my objectives.	−3	−2	−1	0	1	2	3
18. My objectives seldom require my full interest and effort.	−3	−2	−1	0	1	2	3
19. Management makes it clear that defining job objectives is favorably regarded.	−3	−2	−1	0	1	2	3
20. My supervisor gives me more recognition when I achieve my objectives.	−3	−2	−1	0	1	2	3
21. My objectives are very concrete.	−3	−2	−1	0	1	2	3
22. I have sufficient resources to achieve my objectives.	−3	−2	−1	0	1	2	3
23. My pay is more likely to be increased if I achieve my objectives.	−3	−2	−1	0	1	2	3
24. My supervisor has more influence than I do in setting my objectives.	−3	−2	−1	0	1	2	3
25. I wish I had better knowledge of whether I'm achieving my objectives.	−3	−2	−1	0	1	2	3
26. If I fail to meet my objectives, my supervisor will reprimand me.	−3	−2	−1	0	1	2	3
27. Attaining my objectives requires all my skill and know-how.	−3	−2	−1	0	1	2	3

Step 4: For each of the nine "scales" (A through I), compute a TOTAL SCORE by summing the answers to the appropriate questions. Be sure to subtract "minus" scores.

Question Number	Question Number	Question Number	Question Number
1. + ( )	3. + ( )	6. + ( )	4. + ( )
10. + ( )	12. + ( )	15. + ( )	13. + ( )
19. + ( )	21. + ( )	24. + ( )	22. + ( )
Total Score	Total Score	Total Score	Total Score
A	B	C	D

Question Number	Question Number	Question Number	Question Number	Question Number
7. + ( )	9. + ( )	5. + ( )	2. + ( )	8. + ( )
16. + ( )	18. + ( )	14. + ( )	11. + ( )	17. + ( )
25. + ( )	27. + ( )	23. + ( )	20. + ( )	26. + ( )
Total Score	Total Score	Total Score	Total Score	Total Score
E	F	G	H	I

Step 5: Next, on the following graphs, write in a large "X" to indicate the TOTAL SCORE for each scale.

A	−9	−7	−5	−3	−1	1	3	5	7	9
B	−9	−7	−5	−3	−1	1	3	5	7	9
C	−9	−7	−5	−3	−1	1	3	5	7	9
D	−9	−7	−5	−3	−1	1	3	5	7	9
E	−9	−7	−5	−3	−1	1	3	5	7	9
F	−9	−7	−5	−3	−1	1	3	5	7	9
G	−9	−7	−5	−3	−1	1	3	5	7	9
H	−9	−7	−5	−3	−1	1	3	5	7	9
I	−9	−7	−5	−3	−1	1	3	5	7	9

Step 6: In small groups answer the following:

1. What common patterns exist in your questionnaire responses and graph?
2. Do the patterns that are highly effective, moderately effective, and ineffective differ? In what ways?
3. Do the patterns differ for jobs that are highly satisfying, moderately satisfying, and unsatisfying?

Step 7: Discussion. In small groups, with the entire class, or in written form, as directed by your instructor, answer the following:

1. What characteristics of goals and goal setting contribute to effective organizational behavior and satisfying organizational experiences?
2. What characteristics contribute to ineffective behavior and unsatisfying experiences?

Based on Peter Lorenzi, Henry P. Sims, Jr., and E. Allen Slusher, Goal setting, performance and satisfaction: A behavioral demonstration. *Exchange: The Organizational Behavior Teaching Journal* 7 (1982): 38–42.

Activity 4–5: MARIE NICOLE THOMPSON CASE

Step 1: Read the case of Marie Nicole Thompson.

Marie was feeling terrific as she walked to her 9:00 A.M. staff meeting on that crisp November morning. She had been working as Southport's assistant planning director for about five months and in the past three weeks the city had been awarded three major grants totalling more than two million dollars. Marie had played a major role in coordinating staff input, writing and editing the final versions of the applications, negotiating local support with neighborhood groups and elected officials, and even making an eleventh hour trip to Washington to rescue an important Urban Development Action Grant to revitalize the central business district. As she approached city hall, she began to reflect on the events of the past few months.

MARIE'S BACKGROUND

Marie considered herself a "child of the sixties" and was a bit surprised to feel settled in a small city like Southport. She was, however, just 45 minutes from a major metropolitan area and frequently took advantage of her location to make excursions to the city for concerts, plays, and shopping.

From the time she knew there was an outside world, Marie had wanted to escape her rural southern hometown—and she had. College in Chicago was followed by two years in the Peace Corps and then Washington, D.C. with several legislative positions on Capitol Hill. She left Washington after experiencing Potomac burnout, and took a professional job in her boss' congressional district office. The new environment and new people rekindled her enthusiasm. She particularly enjoyed being the congressman's liaison to local communities.

> When I moved to the district, I didn't have friends outside the congressman's office. The job required travel throughout the state meeting local business and government officials. The first friends I made were people who worked in the Southport Planning Department. I initially moved to Southport as a result of those friendships. Chuck Manning, the city planning director and Rich Gibson, who headed the Redevelopment Authority encouraged me to move there. It was Rich's wife who actually found my apartment.
>
> Later, when I came to work for the planning department, these two top-level people were already good friends of mine. In fact, Rich was instrumental in my getting this job. He had called to invite me to a going-away luncheon for Jane Allen, Chuck's assistant. I mentioned that I expected to be leaving my job soon, as well. After five years with the congressman, I was ready for a change. He suggested Jane's job, but quickly added, "Of course, you wouldn't want that! She sits in the office all day reading the Federal Register and crunching numbers!" I immediately thought, "Maybe it would be good for me to try something like that—not the detail work but to get a better grasp of how things work at the local level."
>
> By the time I slept on it and got around to calling Rich to say, "forget the whole thing," he had mentioned it to Chuck. A few days later I found myself meeting with Chuck (who was also the mayor's top assistant and confidant), to discuss the job. My first concern was with the salary, which was quite low, but he informed me there were ways to augment the base salary through the administrative portion of grants. I was also concerned about the detail work, number crunching and technical reading that occupied so much of Jane's time. Chuck felt that there was already enough technical expertise on the staff and indicated that he really wanted to utilize my Capitol Hill experience to bring in grants. He wanted someone to work with on a peer level. By the end of the meeting we both felt it could be made into a job I'd really like. Later, he often corrected me when I introduced him as my boss. "We're colleagues," he would say.
>
> I felt competent to do the task but a little apprehensive. During the past five years, my job never had me sitting in an office all day, and I didn't want to get trapped in that way. In my previous work I was always in meetings or on the phone interacting with constituents, government officials and lobbyists. I didn't do much sitting still, reading or typing. In congressional offices people are a lot more independent of one another. There's less of a hierarchical structure and each person sees him- or herself as directly connected to the senator or congressman. There isn't the whole bureaucracy to go through.

THE MOVE TO LOCAL GOVERNMENT

Chuck wanted Marie to start right away, since a grant deadline was approaching and Jane had already left. He was able to rush her on board by hiring her as a consultant. This approach would give her a chance to see if she liked the job, and him the time to complete formal hiring procedures. Both the planning director and assistant planning director were appointees of the mayor and required city council approval. They were funded by the city, while the other 13 planning department positions were funded by the various grant programs.

Once on the job, Marie discovered that the planning department stood out as the most professional of Southport's local agencies. The employees were hired on merit, not political connections—and they worked as professionals. In many ways the planning department received preferential treatment.

> Other city departments punched a central time clock, but the planning department kept its own records. The mayor would often raise the issue. He would joke about it and say, "I'm always explaining to my other department heads that you people have inspections and meetings and things like that." He always held it out that this was a special thing he was doing for the professional environment in our department.

Within the department were two senior secretaries who had been with the office 15 and 18 years and were widely respected.

> When I first started the job I had a hard time telling them apart. They were both in their early sixties and wore similar hairstyles. They were traditional in other

ways as well. They believed, for instance, that secretaries make coffee for the boss. One of them, Theresa, would always say: "If my boss wants a button sewn on, I'll sew on the button. I don't do well with these young women who come out of secretarial school and think that those aren't the jobs they're supposed to do." The two had been working side by side for the last four or five years. When one was out of the office, the other would pick up her work . . . and they knew the people who worked in city government as well as they knew projects.

My relations with them were cordial but strained. We never established closeness. We exchanged recipes, and I once asked Theresa to help me with some knitting. I was trying to say to her, "Yes, I'm a manager, but I have a life outside the office like everyone else." I think this has always been a problem for me—this balancing act. I don't know whether this is part of being a woman.

From the time that Marie began her job she had known that her predecessor, Jane Allen, had been greatly loved by the staff. Jane was about ten years younger than Marie and had just received her master's degree in city and regional planning from Harvard when she started as assistant to Chuck. Theresa liked to tell the story of the time rumors began circulating that Chuck might leave for an important position in the new governor's administration. Chuck was acting more tight-lipped than normal, and Theresa (given her long association with him) was feeling very left out. Her work showed it. Jane, who was in on the decision, sensed the unrest and arranged for Theresa to know long before others in the department that Chuck had declined the job. A bond was established between them.

Jane's influence was so strong that after a few weeks we actually had an exorcism. Things had gotten to . . . "Jane never did it this way." There were tears and accusations against me. Chuck told me that when Jane started working they had to have an exorcism of her predecessor. Now, three years later, people didn't seem to have a memory of that having occurred.

But Marie's difficulties with the staff did not end with the exorcism. She had frequently visited the planning office when she worked for the congressman, but her principal contacts had been Chuck, Rich, and Jane. The others had been a sea of faces without names—and even after coming to work for the department she spent most of her time with Chuck and Rich.

Chuck was always in meetings with the mayor. He was out of the office more than he was in. During Jane's last year there she was included in some of this. Immediately when I came in, I attended these meetings and regularly was out of the office. A lot of things would be decided by Chuck and me, and then just sort of done. We would often meet in the late afternoon after the rest of the staff left. Rich would sometimes join us, but he would also go for drinks with other staff people, something I rarely did. He had moved up through the ranks, starting as a CETA employee. He interacted well with almost everyone.

There were other friction points as well. There was some confusion between "Maria," the housing coordinator, and "Marie," the consultant to the planning director. Phone calls were often misdirected. Because Maria had been there longer, Chuck asked Marie if they could use her middle name, Nicole. Her full name was printed on her business cards, but she had never been called that.

There was this aura with Nicole. Chuck, Rich and the mayor immediately picked up on it. On the other hand, the rest of the office would speak *of* me as Nicole, but not *to* me as Nicole.

SETTLING IN

Marie enjoyed the work during the trial period as consultant and applied for the full-time position. In June she was interviewed and formally offered the job of assistant planning director. The mayor was to send a letter to the city council seeking approval for her appointment.

The day after I accepted the job, I walked into the office and Theresa said, with obvious pride, "Do you want to see the letter that makes you official?" It said, "Marie has a master's degree in planning from George Washington University." I had done relevant graduate work at George Washington in urban planning, but I did not complete the requirements for a degree. I am very sensitive about misrepresenting my credentials. Chuck had dictated this letter. It was incorrect. So I took the letter and said, "This has to be changed." I didn't think much about it . . . it was just something that had to be corrected before the letter went over to the city council. A few months later I learned that Theresa had gotten very upset that I would change something that Chuck had dictated. Here she was trying to build a bridge between us, and my response almost destroyed our relationship.

Once Marie was on permanent staff, she tried to emulate Jane's vaunted work habits. She agonized over deciphering a bureaucratic criticism of an environmental statement submitted by the city prior to her arrival. Surrounded by the Code of Federal Regulations (CFR), updates, and the letter which was leading her on a seemingly endless chase through the CFR, Marie began to feel Rich's warning about the job had been right. After two days and no progress, she decided to do what she had always done in Washington, D.C.: call the person who had written the letter and ask for an explanation of what he wanted in plain English. The call proved a great success; the bureaucrat explained what he wanted—a process that would take less than two hours and could be accomplished by filling out a chart and adding footnotes. And Marie had a good contact person to add to her Rolodex. When she took the new form to Theresa for typing, Marie informed her that she could throw away the 12 page blank form that Jane had drawn up since the streamlined version was all that was necessary.

> I also suggested that the office save money by stopping its subscription to the Federal Register and rely on other summary publications instead. With all the meetings Chuck and the mayor asked me to attend outside of the office, there really wasn't time to plow through that voluminous document.

As a result, Marie soon had a run-in with Maria over a missed deadline which had been announced in the Federal Register. Marie accepted the blame and made a new effort to keep up with these documents. She was upset, however, that Maria had complained to Chuck. He had sympathized with both and later commented to Marie, "You know the staff apparently thinks that you should remain in the office reading and writing all day instead of being on the phone and attending meetings. But I want you to know that the mayor and I really rely on your contributions to our meetings. I'm glad we could fit this job to your special talents. Perhaps we should talk about getting an assistant for you."

As time went on Marie became increasingly frustrated with schisms that existed within the department. For example, Maria, the housing coordinator, and Tom, the housing inspector, were constantly bickering. They were the most junior staff in the department. When the housing director left, Marie had recommended moving Maria up into that position.

There were also more fundamental divisions, the worst of which existed between the COG staff and others in the department. The Community Opportunity Grant (COG) was a $1 million grant the city had received to renovate low income housing in the Hispanic section of Southport. A fire had recently destroyed the COG office, forcing the COG staff to share space with the planning department.

> In a city which hadn't hired many minorities, suddenly there was Spanish being spoken over the phones. Theresa once remarked, "Why do they always speak that funny language?" The rest of the staff began to use "COG" in a very pejorative way . . . and it wasn't pejorative about the program; it was another way of demeaning Hispanics. When the COG staff moved into the planning office, our message slots, which had been in alphabetical order on a wallboard, were changed. The planning names were put on one board; the COG names on another. There was always this split. One of the first things I said to Chuck was, "We've got to integrate this office. COG has become a racial thing, although people have a convenient way not to make it racial by just saying 'COG.' "

LOOKING TOWARD THE FUTURE

As she walked up the steps to city hall, Marie realized that integrating the COG staff into the department would take some time—it was not something to be raised at today's staff meeting. She was eager to meet with the staff, feeling that they must have new respect for her. She had shown that all those meetings and phone calls were important, since they had resulted in grants that would help the city and keep their programs operating. During the grant-writing process, she had relied heavily on others to do the number crunching—so much so that her fear of numbers had become something of a joke. "But the coordination and strategy were mine," she thought. "And I knew the right people to go to for the help I needed."

At 8:45 A.M., when Marie reached her office she found a sealed envelope on her desk with "Marie" handwritten on it. Inside was a copy of a handwritten letter. She read:

> Chuck,
>
> It came to my attention last week that after telling me in July that you could not pay me my requested and, I thought, approved [salary] increase on the grounds that 1) we did not have the money and 2) you wanted to bring the staff up to an equal pay basis, you then granted Marie Thompson a $7000 per year increase with less than 6 months' service. This strikes me as contradictory and unfair. I feel a bit the fool for agreeing to work on the special project for a $300/yr increase. When we were all doing more for less I felt it was a worthwhile compromise. I now feel I was tricked.
>
> Rumor has it you are now planning to hire an assistant for Ms. Thompson. This will mean spending approximately $40,000 between Ms. Thompson and an assistant to do a job Jane Allen did very well for $19,000/yr. I feel you should know the staff's morale is low and these decisions have brought much discontent to some employees. The people who left and

many who are looking elsewhere for jobs have cited this issue as a major complaint within our Department.

I would also like you to know that your decision to fund the new assistant with C.D.B.G. [Community Development Block Grant] funds *without* consulting Maria first has diminished her desire to work with the team. I'm sure you can understand why, as Program Coordinator, she *should* have been included in the planning and decision making process.

My final point is my concern that this additional drain on administration funds means we in Housing will not be able to hire an assistant, *suitable* to our needs, and the promise of renegotiating the pay scale for Maria and yours truly in December will be no more than token consideration.

I hope that communication and genuine interest can reverse what I see as a serious deterioration of office morale. Although I now must question your interest in these matters, I want you to know that I, for one, am most willing to work for improvement in these areas.

Yours very truly,

Tom

As she finished reading, Chuck arrived at the office, and stopped, as he always did, to say good morning. "You must be feeling pretty good after your great successes," he said. "Are you ready for the staff meeting?"

Step 2: Prepare the case for class discussion.

Step 3: Individually, in small groups, or with the entire class, as directed by your instructor, answer the following questions:

Description

1. Describe the actions and attitudes of the members of the Planning Department.
2. What concerns does Marie Thompson express about her job and her relations with her coworkers?

Diagnosis

3. What problems exist in the Planning Department?
4. How do the following theories of motivation explain the problems in the case?
   a. needs theories
   b. equity theory
   c. reinforcement theory
   d. expectancy theory
   e. goal-setting theory
5. Evaluate the effectiveness of perception, attribution, and learning in this case.

Prescription

6. How could the situation be improved?

Step 4: Discussion. In small groups, with the entire class, or in written form, share your answers to the questions above. Then answer the following questions:

1. What symptoms suggest a problem exists?
2. What problems exist in the case?
3. What theories and concepts help explain the problems?
4. How can the problems be corrected?
5. Are the actions likely to be effective?

This case was written by Salvano Briceno, Susan Broh, Alan Caron, Margaret Dolpe, and Dorothy Renaghan under the supervision of Professor Walter Broadnax, Lecturer in Public Policy, for use at the John F. Kennedy School of Government, Harvard University.

Activity 4–6: MOTIVATIONAL PLAN

Step 1: Your objective is to select a behavior and get it to recur. Briefly describe a behavior you want another person to perform repeatedly.

1. How much is that person performing the behavior now?
2. What is your goal with respect to how often the person performs the behavior?
3. What reinforcement will get that behavior to recur? Describe it.
4. How often should you apply the reinforcement? Why?

Step 2: Implement your plan. Briefly describe what happened.

Step 3: Discussion. Share your experiences in small groups or with the class as a whole. Answer the following questions:

Description

1. Did the behavior recur? How often?

Diagnosis

2. Can you explain what happened using reinforcement theory?

Prescription

3. Offer an alternate motivational plan based on the following:
   a. needs theories
   b. equity theory
   c. expectancy theory
   d. goal-setting theory

Activity 4–7: SUPER SOAP, INC., (A) AND (B) CASE

Step 1: Read the Super Soap, Inc., (A) and (B) cases.

SUPER SOAP, INC. (A)

Robert Rose lit another cigarette and pondered his options. He had given up smoking years ago, but now the pressures of business were starting to affect him. In the morning, he would have to make a recommendation to the Board of Directors which would have profound impact on the whole company. That in itself did not bother him. He had made important decisions before. What bothered him was the personal animosity surrounding the issue. It threatened to destroy the enthusiasm of the founders. It might result in him losing one of his best friends.

History

Rose had been a student at Babson College. In one of his classes, the Professor had students create their own product and market it. It had seemed to Rose at the time that there were many women who enjoyed gambling, yet did not want to think of themselves as gamblers. These were the same women who would secretly purchase lottery tickets, attend bingo games, and yet condemn others who gamble. To appeal to this market, Rose created a product called Super Soap.

Super Soap was ordinary soap bars purchased from a local manufacturing company, but repackaged to include coupons in the package itself. These coupons could be redeemed for cash varying from 25¢ to $2.00. As part of Rose's class assignment, he created Super Soap and actually sold it on a limited basis. Results were far beyond expectation in terms of retail acceptance and customer enthusiasm.

After graduation, Rose's classmates went off to become line managers for large companies. But the Super Soap experience intrigued Rose, and he thought it could become a successful venture.

Rose attracted Mike Moore and Mary Brent to invest in the Super Soap venture and to actively work in the business. Rose was the President, Moore was Vice President of Marketing, and Brent was Vice President of Finance. Together, they constituted the Board of Directors and chief stockholders. They agreed to retain equity of the company among themselves and not to dilute the stock. Super Soap was incorporated as a business in 1977.

John Anderson joined the company shortly after incorporation to become Director of Operations. In order to minimize capital expenses, vendors supplied the soap, coupons, and the packing. A small hourly workforce of 10 assembled the materials and boxed them. These boxes would then be picked up by the three Account Representatives for delivery to stores in the Boston area. Other boxes would be shipped by UPS to Account Representatives located in New York City and Hartford.

Initial sales had been greater than expected. While Super Soap had not been able to crack the major retail outlets yet, independent grocery stores and drug stores in low socioeconomic sections of urban areas were enthusiastic about it.

In 1979, Super Soap reduced the size of the soap bar yet charged the highest price in the industry. Sales continued to expand beyond the one million dollar level. The reason for this was that the value of the coupons had gone up. The present redeemable range was from 0 to $50.00 and the odds of winning some money had been increased. The move attracted attention from the press and *Business Week* ran a small feature article on Super Soap. In the article, Rose made his now famous statement: "In the factory, we package bars of soap. In the store, we sell dreams."

Expansion of Operations

By the end of 1980, it was time for a major expansion of operations. In order to be attractive to discount chains, Super Soap would have to have internal capability to manufacture large quantities. Zayre expressed interest in ordering 50,000 cases. On the strength of past sales and the Zayre overture, Mary Brent reported that they could probably raise the necessary capital to expand manufacturing facilities through bank loans.

Moore, Brent, and Rose wanted to quickly develop full in-house production capabilities. In-house soap production and packaging would be conducted in Waltham, Mass., and Brooklyn, New York. They would buy out a printing operation so as to maintain tighter security over coupons. By 1984, Super Soap would manufacture two hundred thousand cases per year, and would double capacity in 1986.

Super Soap Recruits Buzz Swanson

In order to achieve this manufacturing goal, it would be necessary to hire a seasoned pro to become Vice President of Manufacturing. John Anderson reluctantly agreed with the necessity of this move and would become Plant Manager of the Brooklyn facility reporting to the new Vice President. An executive search firm located Buzz Swanson as a likely candidate for this new position.

Swanson was a 53 year old Assistant Plant Manager at the Procter & Gamble facility which manufactured Safeguard. His experience was perfect for the job, but he was asking for a salary of $60,000. This salary might be reasonable for Procter & Gamble, but Super Soap could hardly afford such an expense. A counteroffer was made of $30,000 plus bonus plus equity in Super Soap. Swanson replied that at his age, cash in hand was more important than the promise of money in the vague future.

Moore had told Robert that if Buzz received $60,000 he expected to receive the same amount. After all, Super Soap was marketing-oriented and his job had expanded considerably as new Account Representatives had been added. He was currently earning a base salary of $30,000; he would resign unless the salaries of the two positions were made comparable.

The Dilemma for Rose

There was no question in Rose's mind that Super Soap needed someone with Swanson's experience to develop an efficient full-scale operation. Sixty thousand dollars was probably what Procter & Gamble was paying for Plant Managers, but he wasn't sure.

If Super Soap could not attract someone with Swanson's qualifications, he wasn't confident that it could develop the type of high volume operation which would make them attractive to discount chains.

On the other hand, Rose knew that bringing in Swanson at $60,000 would trigger a demand to increase all executive salaries by at least 50%. Rose himself was only making a base salary of $40,000; he could not allow a subordinate to have a higher level of compensation. Current base salaries for himself, Brent, Moore, and Anderson totaled $110,000. In order to maintain their equity with Swanson, he could raise all management salaries by 50%. If he made that decision, he could well see that his five Account Representatives would demand an equivalent increase in compensation. The nonexempt employees would also begin to demand more money. Up to this point, everyone who joined Super Soap had done so knowing that the company could not afford to pay well. The payoff would be in the financial rewards which would come from being on the ground floor of an expanding company. This move could change that orientation.

On a worst-case basis, his budget for base salaries of all employees could jump from $345,000 to $517,500 in one year. Projected profits before taxes were expected to be only $150,000 next year and the additional expense would be devastating. Rose prided himself on his fiscal conservatism.

SUPER SOAP, INC. (B)
Determining Compensation Mix

Determine where you would put the emphasis. Place "=" if you think Super Soap should be average relative to its major competitors, a "+" if you think it should be more competitive than average, and a "−" if it should be less than average.

Situation #1

Super Soap is a young, dynamic and struggling company. There is no way it can compete with Lever Brothers or Procter & Gamble. Yet it must attract a manufacturing manager with some high level industry experience. Where would you place the emphasis?

Base	Bonus	Benefits

Situation #2

As it matures, Super Soap finds itself competing in a highly volatile market. Some years are excellent in terms of sales. Other years are terrible. The strategic plan is to maintain a highly aggressive marketing stance and retain competent staff. Where would you place a salesman?

Base	Bonus	Benefits

Step 2: Prepare the case for class discussion.

Step 3: Individually, in small groups, or with the entire class, as directed by your instructor, answer the following questions:

Description

1. Describe the situation at Super Soap.
2. What compensation options have been considered?

Diagnosis

3. What problem exists at Super Soap?
4. How do the following theories of motivation explain the problems in the case?
   a. needs theories
   b. equity theory
   c. reinforcement theory
   d. expectancy theory
   e. goal-setting theory
5. Evaluate the effectiveness of perception, attribution, and learning in this case.

Prescription

6. How should the situation be handled?

7. What base, bonus, and benefits should be offered? Why?

Step 4: Discussion. In small groups, with the entire class, or in written form, share your answers to the questions above. Then answer the following questions:

1. What symptoms suggest a problem exists?
2. What problems exist in the case?
3. What theories and concepts help explain the problems?
4. How can the problems be corrected?
5. Are the actions likely to be effective?

This case was prepared by Laurance J. Stybel. Available in looseleaf form from Lord Publishing, Inc., One Apple Hill, Natick, Mass. 01760

Activity 4–8: EDUCATIONAL TOYS, INC.

Step 1: Read the following description of Educational Toys, Inc.

Educational Toys is a large toy distributor that relies on "Educational Toy Account Representatives" who sell the products door-to-door or during neighborhood parties rather than through retail outlets. Each account representative has a supervisor who oversees his or her performance. Regional managers supervise from ten to fifteen supervisors each.

To date, the only information used in assessing a regional manager's performance has been the percentage of goods sold by the salespeople in the region. Regional managers receive 5 percent of the worth of the goods the account representatives in their region sell. Recently many managers have complained that they are not rewarded on many of the important parts of their job, such as training and development of account representatives, supervision of the supervisors, identification of the most appropriate products for their region, among other activities. The supervisors also receive rewards in the form of a 5 percent share of the worth of the goods sold by the account representatives.

Top management of Educational Toys, Inc., has agreed to revise the company's reward system for supervisors and regional managers. They want a system that is relatively easy to administer and consistent across the thirty sales regions of the country.

Step 2: In groups of four to six, design a reward system for the regional managers and supervisors.

Step 3: Discussion. In small groups or with the entire class, share your systems. Then answer the following questions:

1. What do these systems have in common?
2. How do they differ?
3. What are the strengths and weaknesses of each system?
4. What changes would you recommend?
5. What role do the regional managers and supervisors play in the determination of rewards?

Activity 4–9: COMPENSATION RATINGS

Step 1: You are the director of engineering at a rapidly growing firm in a fast-moving industry. Many of your engineers move into supervisory positions in your firm very quickly. Others, after two or three years, move into better positions in your competitors' companies. You want to be sure to keep those who work hard and make significant contributions to your firm. You must determine pay increases for the engineers described below. Beside each name, write the percentage increase you would give that person. Each currently earns between $25,000 and $43,000.

Herb Holliday. Herb has been with your firm over 3 years. While his work was quite good during his first year on the job, it has gotten progressively worse, even though he works quite hard at it. His coworkers have complained to you that he doesn't do his share—that he tries to get by on his old accomplishments and by his occasional brilliant insights. Others say his rich bride takes all his time and attention.

Eliza Everready. Eliza's rich husband can't understand why she works so hard. She's always the first in the office and the last to leave. During her three years with the firm she has become a leader among her peers because of her hard work. And you couldn't ask for better work from an employee. She uses her excellent skills to produce highly creative work in great quantities.

Stanley Snorr. Everyone thinks Stanley is a goof-off—except you. He certainly leads the irresponsible bachelor's life off the job, or so you've heard. His work is some of the best in his department, which surprises you since he never seems to work hard and you hired him a year ago, not for his skills, but because he was the boss's son.

Henry Hustle. Henry always looks as if he is working so hard he'll drop. Even though his coworkers praise his work, when you review it, the quantity does not seem up to par. Maybe he hasn't had a chance to make up the deficiencies in his skills you knew he had when you hired him a year ago. Still, he really needed a job then, and still does because of his mother's huge medical bills.

Carla Camphor. Carla has worked for you for five years, the longest of any engineer. Recently, you have noticed that the quality of her work has declined significantly. She just doesn't seem to be trying. Her coworkers have started to refuse to work with her—they say she isn't up to date and doesn't try to improve her skills. You know she isn't desperate for money since she has no dependents and already earns a nice salary.

Hermione Higglebottom. Hermione and her three fatherless children are struggling to make ends meet. She always works extra hours, generally taking piles of work home with her. She joined your firm a year ago; her strong recommendation as a hard worker from her previous employer got your attention even though you felt her academic background was outdated. You were right—the quality of her work has been below average. Even her coworkers have commented about it.

Michael Makeshift. Mike is a hot-shot engineer who has been with your firm for two years. His impressive academic credentials called him to your attention originally—and he hasn't disappointed you yet. His work is high quality, but he puts in a lot of overtime to make sure it's perfect. Everyone else says he does terrific work too. Mike married when he was in college; his salary barely makes ends meet for his wife and two children.

June James. Even though June is easily distracted by her family's financial and health problems, her work is of high quality. Her coworkers don't seem to think too much of her, though, perhaps because she doesn't seem to work too hard—she's often late for work and leaves early. You're a bit surprised by the high quality of her work since she was not one of the stronger applicants when you hired her a year ago.

Step 2: Now, in groups of four to six, reach consensus about the percentage increase each person should receive. Be prepared to justify the increases.

Step 3: Discussion. In small groups, or with the entire class, answer the following:

1. Explain your reasons for each increase.
2. Use any relevant theory of motivation to justify your compensation plan.
3. Which factors influence pay decisions? Should these factors be influential?

This exercise is based on one written by Edward E. Lawler, III, and is adapted with his permission.

Activity 4-10: DESIGNING AN INCENTIVE PROGRAM FOR SOFTSERVE ICE CREAM, INC.

Step 1: Read the following scenario:

Softserve Ice Cream, Inc., distributes ice cream novelties in supermarkets, drug stores, discount stores, cafeterias, and other miscellaneous retail outlets. They have a national sales force of 200 men and women who are assigned to various geographical areas across the United States.

Basically, the country is divided into 200 equal geographical areas, and each salesperson is assigned to one area. Some areas include one or more metropolitan areas; others include only small, suburban towns; still others are primarily rural in nature. Some salespeople service many large stores; others have primarily small stores and diners in their territories. Salespeople receive a flat 5 percent of all sales. Occasionally they receive a special prize for selling a specified amount of a new product.

When a vacancy arises in a sales territory, the most senior salesperson has the first choice of moving into that territory. New employees are hired for vacant territories into which no existing employee wants to move.

Turnover at Softserve Ice Cream ranges from 10 to 25 percent a year, depending on the general economic conditions. Recently, the company has had to hire more part-time employees to service the less desirable regions. The top executives feel that this turnover plus the lack of a permanent work force is becoming very costly for them. They also feel that their sales force could be much more productive.

Step 2: Individually or in small groups, design an incentive program for the sales force at Softserve Ice Cream.

Step 3: Discussion. In small groups or with the entire class, share the plans you developed. Then answer the following questions:

1. What elements do these plans have in common?
2. Will the employees be motivated to perform better? To remain in the organization? Why?
3. What options are available at a reasonable cost to organizations that want to pay for performance?
4. What problems are there with the use of incentive plans at Softserve Ice Cream?

CONCLUDING COMMENTS

In this chapter we developed a mutlifaceted view of motivation. This comprehensive perspective considers the major motivation theories of this century. For each case presented, diagnosis included an assessment of—

1. each individual's needs (needs theories);
2. the way the organization met or attempted to meet these needs (needs theories);
3. the assignment of rewards in terms of comparability among organizational members (equity theory);
4. the relationship of inputs to outcomes as perceived by various organizational members (equity theory);
5. the timing of reinforcement (reinforcement theory);
6. the nature of the rewards themselves (reinforcement theory);
7. the expectancy, instrumentality, and valence of various situations (expectancy theory);
8. the nature of intrinsic and extrinsic task motivation (expectancy theory); and
9. the type of goals set (goal-setting theory).

The first activities in this chapter offered tools and techniques for diagnosing motivational level. The cases of Marie Nicole Thompson and Super Soap, Inc., offered the opportunity for diagnosing motivational issues using a comprehensive perspective. Preparing a motivational plan, developing an incentive system, and designing a more comprehensive reward system were activities that integrated the diverse motivation theories.

ENDNOTES

[1]This case is based on one prepared by Deirdre Ann Dimancesco, MBA candidate 1990, Boston College.

[2]A.H. Maslow, *Motivation and Personality* (New York: Harper & Row, 1954), p. ix.

[3]*Ibid.*, pp. 80–92.

[4]See "Agreements between Ford Motor Company and the UAW," February, 1982, for an example of such an agreement.

[5]Maslow, *op. cit.*, pp. 98–99.

[6]Maslow, *op. cit.*, pp. 147–150.

[7]L.W. Porter, A study of perceived need satisfactions in bottom and middle management jobs, *Journal of Applied Psychology* 45 (1961): 1–10.

[8]See M.A. Wahba and L.G. Bridwell, Maslow reconsidered: A review of research on the need hierarchy theory, *Organizational Behavior and Human Performance* 15 (1976): 212–240; V.F. Mitchell and P. Moudgill, Measurement of Maslow's need hierarchy, *Organizational Behavior and Human Performance* 16 (1976): 334–349; E.E. Lawler III, *Motivation in Work Organizations* (Monterey, Cal.: Brooks/Cole, 1973).

[9]G. Hofstede, Motivation, leadership, and organization: Do American theories apply abroad?, *Organizational Dynamics* (Summer, 1980): 42–63.

[10]P. Howell, J. Strauss, and P.F. Sorensen, Research note: Cultural and situational determinants of job satisfaction among management in Liberia, *Journal of Management Studies* (May 1975): 225–227.

[11]Wahba and Bridwell, *op. cit.;* Mitchell and Moudgill, *op. cit.;* Lawler, *op. cit.*

[12]C.P. Alderfer, *Existence, Relatedness, and Growth: Human Needs in Organizational Settings* (New York: Free Press, 1972).

[13]D. McClelland, *The Achieving Society* (Princeton, N.J.: D. Van Nostrand, 1961).

[14]*Ibid.*

[15]D. McClelland and D.H. Burnham, Power driven managers: Good guys make bum bosses, *Psychology Today* (7) (1975): 69–71.

[16]F. Herzberg, B. Mausner, and B.B. Snyderman, *The Motivation to Work* (New York: Wiley, 1959).

[17]*Ibid.*

[18]See B.L. Hinton, An empirical investigation of the Herzberg methodology and two-factor theory, *Organizational Behavior and Human Performance* 3 (1968): 286–309, for a discussion of methodological problems; see M.D. Dunnette, D. Campbell, and M. Hakel, Factors contributing to job satisfaction and dissatisfaction in six occupational groups, *Organizational Behavior and Human Performance* 2 (1967): 143–174; R. House and L. Wigdor, Herzberg's dual-factor theory of job satisfaction and motivation: A review of the evidence and criticism, *Personnel Psychology* 20 (1968): 369–389; J. Schneider and E. Locke, A critique of Herzberg's classification system and a suggested revision, *Organizational Behavior and Human Performance* 14 (1971): 441–458; and P. Smith, L. Kendall, and C. Hulin, *The Measurement of Satisfaction in Work and Retirement* (Chicago: Rand McNally, 1969), for a discussion of evidence that shows a factor causing satisfaction for one person may cause dissatisfaction for another. Studies outside the United States also question the theory's validity: see R.A. Crabbs, Work motivation in the culturally complex Panama Canal Company, *Academy of Management Proceedings* (1973): 119–126; and G.H. Hines, Achievement motivation, occupations, and labor turnover in New Zealand, *Journal of Applied Psychology* 58(3) (1973): 313–317.

[19]G.R. Salancik and J. Pfeffer, An examination of need-satisfaction models of job attitudes, *Administrative Science Quarterly* 22 (1977): 427–456.

[20]Activity 4–1 shows one instrument for measuring needs.

[21]G.G. Alpander, A comparative study of the motivational environment surrounding first-line supervisors in three countries, *Columbia Journal of World Business* 19(3) (1984): 95–104.

[22]*Ibid.*

[23]J.S. Adams, Inequity in social exchange. In *Advances in Experimental and Social Psychology*, ed. L. Berkowitz, 2 (1965): 267–300. See also E. Walster, W. Walster, and E. Berscheid, *Equity: Theory and Research* (Boston: Allyn and Bacon, 1978).

[24]R.P. Vecchio, Predicting worker performance in inequitable settings, *Academy of Management Review* 7 (1982): 103–110, presents four mathematical models of equity theory.

[25]G.R. Oldham and H.E. Miller, The effect of significant other's job complexity on employee reactions to work, *Human Relations* 32 (1979): 247–260.

[26]D. Schwab, Construct validity in organizational behavior. In *Research in Organizational Behavior* vol. 2, ed. B. Staw (Greenwich, Conn.: JAI Press, 1980); M.R. Carrell and J.E. Dittrick, Equity theory: The recent literature, methodological considerations, and new directions, *Academy of Management Review* 3 (1978): 202–210; Walster et al., *op. cit.,* p. 128.

[27]J. Greenbert and G.S. Leventhal, Equity and the use of overreward to motivate performance, *Journal of Personality and Social Psychology* 34 (1976): 179–190.

[28]R.E. Kopelman, Psychological stages of careers in engineering: An expectancy theory taxonomy, *Journal of Vocational Behavior* 10 (1977): 270–286.

[29]M.R. Carrell and J.E. Dittrich, Employee perceptions of fair treatment, *Personnel Journal* 55 (1976): 523–524.

[30]R.A. Cosier and D.R. Dalton, Equity theory and time: A reformulation, *Academy of Management Review* 8 (1983): 311–319.

[31]M.R. Carrell and J.E. Dittrich, Equity theory, *op. cit.*

[32]R.C. Huseman, J.D. Hatfield, and E.W. Miles, A new perspective on equity theory: The equity sensitivity construct, *Academy of Management Review* 12 (1987): 232–234.

[33]Adams, *op. cit.;* Walster et al., *op. cit.,* pp. 131–141.

[34]E.L. Thorndike, *Behaviorism* (New York: Norton, 1924); B.F. Skinner, *The Behavior of Organisms: An Experimental Approach* (New York: Appleton-Century, 1938).

[35]S.F. Jablonsky and D.L. DeVries, Operant conditioning principles extrapolated to the theory of management, *Organizational Behavior and Human Performance* 7 (1972): 340–358.

[36]H.W. Babb and D.G. Kopp, Applications of behavior modification in organizations: A review and critique, *Academy of Management Review* 3 (1978): 281–292; W.C. Hamner and E.P. Hamner, Behavior modification on the bottom line, *Organizational Dynamics* 4 (1976): 8–21.

[37]K. O'Hara, C.M. Johnson, and T.A. Beehr, Organizational behavior management in the private sector: A review of empirical research and recommendations for further investigations, *Academy of Management Review* 10 (1985): 848–864.

[38]Note that the radical behaviorists do not support goal setting and accomplishment as legitimate reinforcers.

[39]S. Kerr, On the folly of rewarding A, while hoping for B, *Academy of Management Journal* 18 (1975): 773.

[40]*Ibid.*

[41]*Ibid.*

[42]W.C. Hamner, Reinforcement theory and contingency management in organizational settings. In *Organizational Behavior and Management,* ed. H.L. Tosi and W.C. Hamner (Chicago: St. Clair, 1974).

[43]V.H. Vroom, *Work and Motivation* (New York: Wiley, 1964).

[44]D. Sirota and M.J. Greenwood, Understand your overseas workforce, *Harvard Business Review* 14 (January-February 1971): 53–60.

[45]D.A. Nadler and E.E. Lawler III, Motivation: A diagnostic approach. In *Perspectives on Behavior in Organizations,* ed. J.R. Hackman, E.E. Lawler III, and L.W. Porter (New York: McGraw-Hill, 1977), pp. 26–38.

[46]B.M. Staw, *Intrinsic and Extrinsic Motivation* (Morristown, N.J.: General Learning Press, 1976).

[47]See W.E. Scott Jr., J. Farh, and P.M. Podsakoff, The effects of "intrinsic" and "extrinsic" reinforcement contingencies on task behavior, *Organizational Behavior and Human Decision Processes* 41 (1988): 405–425; and P.C. Jordan, Effects of an extrinsic reward on intrinsic motivation: A field experiment, *Academy of Management Journal* 29 (1986): 405–412, for examples of the two positions.

[48]R.J. House, H.J. Shapiro, and M.A. Wahba, Expectancy theory as a predictor of work behavior and attitudes: A reevaluation of empirical evidence, *Decision Sciences* 5 (1974): 481–506.

[49]See T. Connolly, Some conceptual and methodological issues in expectancy models of work performance, *Academy of Management Review* 1 (1976): 37–47; H.G. Heneman and D.P. Schwab, Evaluation of research on expectancy theory and predictions of employee performance, *Psychological Bulletin* 78 (1972): 1–9; and M.A. Wahba and R.J. House, Expectancy theory in work and motivation: Some logical and methodological issues, *Human Relations* 27 (1974): 121–147.

[50]L.E. Miller and J.E. Grush, Improving predictions in expectancy theory research: Effects of personality, expectancies, and norms, *Academy of Management Journal* 31 (1988): 107–122; T.R. Mitchell, Expectancy-value models in organizational psychology. In N.T. Feather, ed., *Expectation and Actions: Expectancy-Value Models in Psychology* (Hillsdale, N.J.: Lawrence Erlbaum Associates, 1982), pp. 293–312.

[51]See J.P. Campbell and R.D. Pritchard, Motivation theory in industrial and organizational psychology. In *Handbook of Industrial and Organizational Psychology,* ed. M.D. Dunnette (Chicago: Rand McNally, 1976); and E.E. Lawler III, *Motivation in Work Organizations* (Belmont, Cal.: Brooks/Cole, 1973).

[52]E.A. Locke, K.N. Shaw, L.M. Saari, and G.P. Latham, Goal setting and task performance, *Psychological Bulletin* 90 (1981): 125–152.

[53]E.A. Locke, G.P. Latham, and M. Erez, The determinants of goal commitment, *Academy of Management Review* 13 (1988): 23–39.

[54]*Ibid.*

[55]G. Latham and J.J. Baldes, The practical significance of Locke's theory of goal setting, *Journal of Applied Psychology* 59 (1975): 122–124.

[56]M. Erez, Feedback, a necessary condition for the goal setting–performance relation, *Journal of Applied Psychology* 62 (1977): 624–627.

[57]E.A. Locke, E. Frederick, E. Buckner, and P. Bobko, Effect of previously assigned goals on self-set goals and performance, *Journal of Applied Psychology* 69 (1984): 694–699.

[58]M. Erez, P.C. Earley, and C.L. Hulin, The impact of participation on goal acceptance and performance: A two-step model, *Academy of Management Journal* 28 (1985): 50–66.

[59]M. Erez and I. Zidon, Effect of goal acceptance on the relationship of goal difficulty to performance, *Journal of Applied Psychology* 69 (1984): 69–78.

[60]G.P. Latham and G.A. Yukl, A review of research on the application of goal setting in organizations, *Academy of Management Journal* 18 (1975): 824–845.

[61]D. Eden, Pygmalion, goal setting, and expectancy: Compatible ways to boost productivity, *Academy of Management Review* 13(4) (1988): 639–652.

[62]C.N. Greene and R.E. Craft Jr., The satisfaction–performance controversy, *Business Horizons* 15 (1972): 31–41.

[63]E.E. Lawler III, Reward systems. In *Improving Life at Work,* ed. J.R. Hackman and J.L. Suttle (Santa Monica, Cal.; Goodyear, 1977).

[64]See E. Jansen and M. Von Glinow, Ethical ambivalence and organizational reward systems, *Academy of Management Review* 19 (1985): 814–822, for a discussion of possible misfits between individual ethical positions and those maintained by the organizational reward system.

[65]See E.E. Lawler III, Reward systems in organizations. In J. Lorsch, ed., *Handbook of Organizational Behavior* (Englewood Cliffs, N.J.: Prentice-Hall, 1983).

[66]The Lincoln Electric Company in Cleveland, Ohio, illustrates this approach to compensation.

[67]D.E. Bowen and C.A. Wadley, Designing a strategic benefits program, *Compensation and Benefits Review* 21(5) (1989): 44–56.

[68]J.S. Overstreet, The case for merit bonuses, *Business Horizons* 28 (May-June, 1985): 53–58.

[69]T. Rollins, Productivity-based group incentive plans: Powerful, but use with caution, *Compensation and Benefits Review* 21(3) (1989): 39–50.

[70]J.R. Schuster and P.K. Zingheim, Designing incentives for top financial performance, *Compensation and Benefits Review* 18(3) (1986): 39–48.

[71]C. Rosen, Employee stock ownership plans: A new way to look at work, *Business Horizons* 26 (September–October, 1983): 48–56, describes a variety of these plans.

[72]R.N. Stern, W.F. Whyte, T. Hammer, and C.B. Meek, The union and the transition to employee ownership. In W.F. Whyte, T.H. Hammer, C.B. Meek, R. Nelson, and R.N. Stern, eds., *Worker Participation and Ownership* (Ithaca, N.Y.: ILR Press, 1983).

[73]T.R. Mitchell, Motivation: New directions for theory, research, and practice, *Academy of Management Review* 7 (1982): 80–88, argues that even greater integration is needed.

RECOMMENDED READINGS

Henderson, R.F. *Compensation Management: Rewarding Performance.* Reston, Va.: Reston, 1985.

Hills, F.S. *Compensation Decision Making.* Chicago: Dryden, 1987.

Luthans, F., and Kreitner, R. *Organizational Behavior Modification.* Glenview, Ill.: Scott, Foresman, 1975.

Maehr, M.L., and Kleiber, D.A. *Enhancing Motivation.* Greenwich, Conn.: JAI Press, 1987.

Nash, M.N. *Making People Productive.* San Francisco: Jossey-Bass, 1985.

Pinder, C.C. *Work Motivation: Theory, Issues, and Applications.* Glenview, Ill.: Scott, Foresman, 1984.

Steers, R.M., and Porter, T.W. *Motivation and Work Behavior* 3d ed. New York: McGraw-Hill, 1983.

5 Describing Group Performance

CHAPTER OUTLINE

Group Dynamics in the Oil Exploration Team
Formation
- Reasons for Group Formation
- Attractiveness of Group Membership
- The Impact of Cultural Diversity

Development
- Orientation
- Redefinition
- Coordination
- Formalization
- Termination
- Moving through the Stages
- Alternate Views of Group Development

Goals
Norms
- Classification Schemes
- Compliance with Norms

Roles
- Norm-Related Types
- Functional Types

Structural Configuration
Improving Work Team Effectiveness
- Characteristics of Effective Teams
- Formation and Development of Effective Teams
- Strategies for Team Building

Increasing Group Effectiveness
SUMMARY
READING
ACTIVITIES
CONCLUDING COMMENTS
ENDNOTES
RECOMMENDED READINGS

LEARNING OBJECTIVES

After completing the reading and activities in Chapter 5, students will be able to

- define a group;
- describe and explain a group's formation and development;
- identify the factors that contribute to group performance;
- describe the contribution of group goals to group effectiveness;
- outline the different roles individuals can play in organizations;
- discuss the ways norms influence group behavior and attitudes;
- compare and contrast five communication networks;
- diagnose the effectiveness of a work team; and
- prescribe ways for increasing group effectiveness.

Group Dynamics in the Oil Exploration Team

The four-person Oil Exploration Team was formed at the Far West Prospecting Company to develop oil projects in an undrilled area of Wyoming. Bill Jessup, the team leader, had more than fifteen years of prospecting experience, five of them in team leadership roles. Phil Johnson, an engineer, had ten years of experience. Jake Coleman and Brad Murray were the two geophysicists on the team; each had five years of experience on similar projects. With the exception of Jake, the team members had worked together on previous projects.

Top management of the company was excited about exploring for oil in this area, and this enthusiasm set a positive tone for the initial planning meetings of the Oil Exploration group. During the first month, each team member discussed a plan of attack from his vantage point. Bill, the team leader, discussed leasing opportunities. Phil, the engineer, discussed drilling and other costs involved in exploring the area. Jake raised questions about obtaining high-quality seismic data. Brad recognized that certain sands had oil reservoir potential in the subsurface. To have a series of high-quality prospects ready for presentation to upper management within four months, the group established a timetable of planning activities.

As the two geophysicists on the team, Jake and Brad had to work more closely with each other than with the rest of the team. In essence, they built on each other's knowledge—if Jake liked a particular area, Brad would interpret seismic data and make an independent assessment of its oil potential and vice versa. Brad complained that, although he was working hard to keep up with the timetable, Jake was not. Jake and Brad began to argue continuously.

As the deadlines set by the team came due, Jake consistently failed to meet them. When he did present something in team meetings, the group agreed that it was incomplete and inconsistent. Bill said that the team would often "joke about which stock excuse Jake would use when he didn't meet a deadline."

Finally, Brad decided to talk to Walt Bannister, the division Exploration Manager. Brad expected Walt to sympathize with the problems the team was having with Jake. Walt did not immediately support Brad's complaints, but immediately called Jake into his office for a closed-door discussion:

Walt: "Jake, what's the problem? Brad says you're not meeting the team's deadlines."

Jake: "Well, how can I? He's unclear about what he needs me to do. No sooner do I start working on one area, than he tells me to drop everything and . . ."

Brad: "C'mon Jake, the whole team agrees that I'm pulling my weight and that you're . . ."

Jake: "Nobody's ever said I haven't been meeting my . . ."

Brad: "You knew that the North Buck Draw prospect was supposed to . . ."

Walt: "Listen you guys. I want you to start working together. If there's a personality conflict here, then just put it aside and get some work done."

Brad: "But . . ."
Walt: "Do it!"

A few months later, the team presented its work to upper management. Management expressed their disappointment with the team's presentation. Soon after that, the team was disbanded.

About one year later, Jake's employment was terminated. The company cited lack of productivity as the reason for his termination. His performance on this team was cited as an example.[1]

Do the members of the Oil Exploration Team constitute a group? Do individuals sharing the same office constitute a group? Are a boss and his or her single subordinate a group? Is a Safety Razor Division a group? Is a Research and Development Department a group?

A group is viewed as two or more individuals who perceive of themselves as interdependent and act as a single unit, typically with a common goal.[2] The group's identity is recognized by nonmembers. Both members and nonmembers have expectations of group members, based on their training, past experiences, and past performance influencing their role.[3]

From the information in the introductory case, the Oil Exploration Team is a group. They view themselves as a unit since they jointly set the goal of identifying a series of high-quality prospects for top management to review within four months; they have a common timetable; and they collaboratively perform a variety of planning activities. Certainly the four individuals are interdependent, and their success in developing a series of high-quality prospects relies on their working together. The four members have been labeled a group—the Oil Exploration Team—by nonmembers of the group. These outsiders, including Walt Bannister and other top executives of Far West Prospecting, as well as the group members themselves, have expectations of Bill, Phil, Jake, and Brad that further delineate their roles.

Is the Oil Exploration Team an effective group? Clearly the team is not functioning as effectively as possible. Jake and Brad's arguing, Jake's missing deadlines, Brad's complaints to his boss Walt Bannister, management's dissatisfaction with the quality of the presentation, and Jake's eventual firing suggest problems at Far West Prospecting and, more specifically, with the Oil Exploration Team.

In this chapter we consider the group dynamics perspective by viewing a variety of factors that contribute to group performance and effectiveness. We begin by examining group formation and its influence on performance. Then we trace the steps in group development and use them as ways of delineating the breakdown of group productivity. We follow this with discussions of group goals, norms, roles, and structural configuration—aspects of group process that influence group performance. In the next section we offer a framework for diagnosing the effectiveness of and managing work teams. We conclude by discussing ways to improve group effectiveness. In the remaining chapters of Part Three we examine in more detail additional aspects of group functioning: decision making, communication, leadership, power, and conflict.

FORMATION

Why do people join groups and how do their reasons for joining affect group performance? How can managers constitute groups for maximum effectiveness? Consider the reasons you have joined groups in the past. Perhaps you liked the group members, you lived or worked near them, or you valued the goals they accomplished. Individuals may join *formal* groups—those officially sanctioned and organized by managerial or other authorities to accomplish organizational goals, such as departments or task forces. Managers can also organize such groups to perform specific work tasks. Or individuals may form *informal* groups—those that arise spontaneously in the organization or within formal groups, such as a clique or a network of professionals. Managers must recognize when such groups exist and encourage their performance.

Reasons for Group Formation

Groups form when individuals exhibit one or more of the following.[4] First, they may have *common needs* for food, security, esteem, autonomy, creativity, or challenge, among others. Food cooperatives form because individuals want to satisfy their basic needs for food at a low cost. Honorary societies form to meet the esteem needs of students or professionals. Flight clubs form so pilots can meet the need for challenge through competitive club activities.

Second, individuals may form groups because of their *common interests*. Engineers employed by different companies often join the same professional group. Faculty members may form a research group because of interest in the same or a related area of study. A manager may organize coworkers responsible for the same job into a group.

Third, groups may form because individuals have *common goals*. A board of directors of a company forms to help the company reach its profitability objectives. A marketing department forms to increase sales of a company's product. An executive forms a task force of individuals with a common goal such as improving customer service or reducing labor costs.

Fourth, the *physical proximity* of individuals may cause them to form a group. Employees in the same work area join together as a social group. Engineers with offices on the same floor more often become part of project teams than do engineers located in different buildings or cities.

Finally, groups may form because of *cultural similarity*. Expatriates frequently develop professional and social groups in their country of residence. New immigrants seek employment in organizations or departments where large numbers of culturally similar workers are employed.

The reason a group forms influences the nature and quality of the group's functioning. The nature of formation contributes to group cohesion—the forces that bind group members together—which in turn facilitates productivity.[5] In the introductory case, for example, the professionals at Far West Prospecting formed the Oil Exploration Team at the direction of the company's top management. We would expect them to have common goals but different needs and interests because of differences in their training, experience, and career stage. We would hypothesize that because of their common goal the members would have similar enthusiasm for the group's work. Their diverse needs and interests, however, may exert a different and even greater influence on the group's performance. If physical proximity were their only bond, we might predict different behavior. Diagnosing the causes of group formation, then, helps us predict and anticipate the ways a group is likely to act. When forming work teams, managers should be aware of potential members' similarities and dissimilarities in needs, interests, goals, location, and culture and their likely consequences.

Attractiveness of Group Membership

The attractiveness of group membership increases the more the group is viewed as cooperative, the greater the prestige experienced by the group, the more interaction among its members, the smaller the group's size, and the more others perceive the group as successful.[6] While the Oil Exploration Team is relatively small and initially viewed as cooperative, collaborative, and prestigious, we have little indication that the group is viewed in the same way at the end of the planning period. Its attractiveness likely diminishes: the group is disbanded.

Group membership, as in the Oil Exploration Team, can lose its attractiveness for a variety of reasons.[7] Jake may feel that the group makes unreasonable demands on individuals, or that some members dominate the group too often. Brad may feel that too much self-oriented behavior occurs: he may view Jake as reducing the attractiveness of group membership. Disagreement can occur during problem solving: certainly Jake and Brad argue about Jake's, and hence the team's, failure to meet deadlines. Competition might even exist between them, creating a less than desirable atmosphere in the group and reducing its attractiveness to all the members. Membership in a group may limit an individual's satisfaction by no longer meeting his or her needs. Consider, for example, the ways the group no longer meets Brad's needs. Individuals who are blamed for negative events in a group also begin to perceive of themselves as outsiders; these "scapegoats," who receive blame inappropriately, reduce their identification with a group. Finally, outsiders, in this case the top executives, may hold a negative view of the group and dissolve it altogether. The Oil Exploration Team seems to have members who show self-oriented behavior; in addition there are disagreements and competition among the members. The lack of attractiveness of membership on the team likely inhibits member efforts to perform well and reach the group's goals.

The Impact of Cultural Diversity

As noted earlier, differences in group members' needs, interests, and goals affect group performance. Diversity of group members with regard to age, sex, race, or ethnic origin can also have consequences for group performance. Specifically, diverse members may have different needs, interests, and goals; they may also bring significantly different experiences and frames of reference to a situation. Groups composed of individuals with diverse cultural backgrounds can have special difficulties in functioning.

Table 5–1 summarizes the advantages and disadvantages of cultural diversity in groups.[8] Multiculturalism brings diverse perspectives to the organization, resulting in multiple interpretations, greater openness to new ideas, increased flexibility, increased creativity, and improved problem-solving skills. Cultural diversity also facilitates dealing with a particular country or culture

Table 5–1 ADVANTAGES AND DISADVANTAGES OF CULTURAL DIVERSITY IN GROUPS

Advantages	Disadvantages
Culturally Synergistic Advantages: Organizational Benefits from Multiculturalism	Disadvantages Due to Cultural Diversity: Organizational Costs Due to Multiculturalism
Expanding Meanings	Diversity increases
Multiple perspectives	Ambiguity
Greater openness to new ideas	Complexity
Multiple interpretations	Confusion
Expanding alternatives	Difficulty converging meanings
Increasing creativity	Miscommunication
Increasing flexibility	Hard to reach a single agreement
Increasing problem-solving skills	Difficulty converging actions
	Hard to agree on specific actions
Culture-Specific Advantages: Benefits in Working with a Particular Country or Culture	Culture-Specific Disadvantages: Costs in Working with a Particular Country or Culture
Better understanding of foreign employees	Overgeneralizing
	Organization policies
Ability to work more effectively with particular foreign clients	Organization practices
	Organization procedures
Ability to market more effectively to specific foreign customers	Ethnocentrism
Increased understanding of political, social, legal, economic, and cultural environment of foreign countries.	

From Nancy J. Adler, *International Dimensions of Organizational Behavior* (Boston: PWS-Kent, 1986), p. 80. © by Wadsworth, Inc. Reprinted by permission of PWS-Kent Publishing Company, a division of Wadsworth, Inc.

because the group likely has someone who understands its environment and workers. At the same time, the diverse perspectives in a multicultural group may increase the ambiguity, complexity, or confusion in situations, if the group cannot reconcile different perspectives and use them constructively. Miscommunication and difficulty in reaching agreement may result. Cultural diversity can also result in assuming organizational practices in one country apply equally well to those in another when they in fact do not. Cultural diversity allows increased creativity and demands greater focus to understand other group members. Often this can result in better decisions and ultimately improved group effectiveness. But diversity can also cause decreased group cohesion, resulting from mistrust, miscommunication, and stress, which results in the inability to reach decisions and hence decreased effectiveness.

DEVELOPMENT

Once a group forms, it must resolve a variety of issues before it functions effectively. Tracing the development of groups provides one perspective for assessing a group's performance. Managers can also use their understanding of group development to identify and then remove obstacles to effective group performance.

Development occurs along two dimensions of group behavior: (1) task activity and (2) group process.[9] *Task activity* refers to the steps used to perform a task.[10] In the introductory case the task activities revolve around the identification of a series of high-quality prospects for oil drilling, including the specification of leasing opportunities and costs, obtaining and sharing seismic information, formulation of program options, and finalization of plans that will result in profitable new sites. *Group process* refers to the interpersonal interactions needed to accompany and accomplish task activities.[11] In the case of the Oil Exploration Team, group process describes the interactions among the four team members, including the group's goals, expectations of behavior, roles that guide and limit behavior, and patterned ways of interacting (described later in this chapter).

Figure 5–1 diagrams the stages of development described in the next sections. The solid arrows represent the typical development progression from one stage to the next and within stages. Creating an effective group requires a successful resolution of each task activity and group process stage. The following discussion traces the development of the Oil Exploration Team. It emphasizes the juxtaposition of task and process concerns at each stage and introduces the group processes in each domain.

Orientation

During the first or *forming* stage the group views the task and determines acceptable interpersonal behaviors.

Task: Orientation to Task The group members gather information about the nature of the group's task. At the first meeting of the Oil Exploration Team, the group members likely listen to Bill Jessup describe his perceptions of the group's goal. Other members might contribute their views. Each member then probably shares his perspective on the required activities.

Process: Testing and Dependence Group members discover acceptable interpersonal behaviors. Ideally these behaviors facilitate task accomplishment. Members of the Oil Exploration Team, for example, might experiment with leadership or followership behaviors, try out the roles of agenda setter, encourager, or summarizer, and in general learn the extent to which their efforts can focus on interpersonal interactions as opposed to task issues. We might assume, for example, that the tentative interaction pattern established in the previous stage does not work when tested, since arguments and criticisms ensue. This failure probably expedites their proceeding to the redefinition stage.

This stage can be particularly difficult for multicultural groups. Consider a group composed of members from the United States and Japan. While United States members may wish to focus immediately on task issues, the Japanese might emphasize the rituals for a new venture. Recognizing and managing these differences is essential to resolving the issues of this stage.

Figure 5–1 STAGES OF DEVELOPMENT OF GROUPS

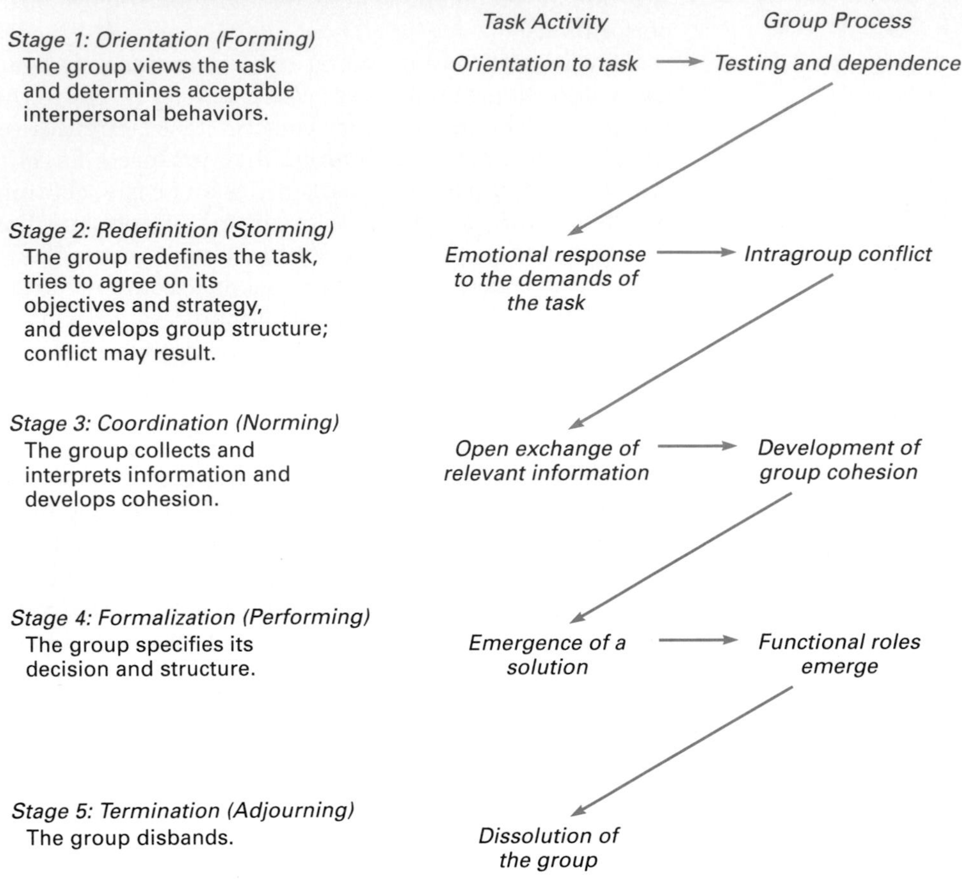

SOURCES: Based on A.C. Kowitz and T.J. Knutson, *Decision-Making in Small Groups: The Search for Alternatives* (Boston: Allyn and Bacon, 1980); B.W. Tuchman, Developmental sequences in small groups, *Psychological Bulletin* 63(1965): 384–399; B.W. Tuchman and M.C. Jensen, Stages of small group development revisited, *Group and Organization Studies* 2(1977): 419–427.

Redefinition

During the second or *storming* stage the group redefines the task, tries to agree on its objectives and strategy, and develops group structure; conflict may result.

Task: Emotional Response to the Demands of the Task Group members determine whether they like the task as well as their degree of commitment to it. At Far West Prospecting, the Oil Exploration Team must specify their commitment to the goals of this group. The lack of progress in meeting agreed-on deadlines is a symptom that not all team members have accepted the goal of preparing a series of high-quality prospects within four months. In real life we could verify this observation by polling group members regarding their attitudes about the task.

Process: Intragroup Conflict Disagreements by members of a group in their reactions to task demands often lead to conflict. Members may differ in the amount of time they will devote to a particular task, the priority they assign to the task, or the means they feel will best accomplish it. The sharper these differences, the greater the intragroup conflict that results. In the Oil Exploration Team, differences among members in their perceptions of the level of contributions made by each member help create such conflict. A manager who recognizes these differences may be able to reduce the conflict or make it functional for the group.

Coordination

During this stage, also called the *norming* stage, the group collects information and interprets it. Often the longest stage because of the time required for data collection and interpretation, arguments over interpretation frequently occur. Their resolution ultimately results in the development of group cohesion.

Task: Open Exchange of Relevant Interpretation and Opinions Here discussions about the nature of the task, alternatives, and possible action occur. Also group members should acknowledge that different emotional responses to the task are legitimate. A group's discussion about the types and quality of existing programs, as well as its members' participation in the process of developing a new program, illustrate the activities of this stage. The Oil Exploration Team's successful implementation of planning activities according to the timetable specified by the group members would indicate the successful performance of this stage. However, the disagreements that continue to occur among team members suggest that a successful exchange of relevant information does not occur. The manager of the team fails to employ successful mechanisms for examining and resolving differences.

Process: Development of Group Cohesion The members resolve their differences after an open exchange of relevant interpretations and opinion, and begin to act as a cohesive group. Often groups do not reach this stage and the group disintegrates. The Oil Exploration Team, for example, fails to develop cohesion with regard to either its task or social activities.

Formalization

The group specifies the final version of a decision. During the *performing* stage a solution or resolution of the task occurs and functional roles emerge.

Task: Emergence of a Solution At this stage the final choice of task activities and their implementation occur. The Oil Exploration Team tries to move to this stage: they submit their drilling proposal to top management. But management's negative reaction to its quality suggests that the team does not effectively resolve issues arising at previous stages of group development. They fail to resolve divergent emotional responses to the task and to exchange relevant information and opinions.

Process: Functional Roles Emerge as a Way of Problem Solving At this time, the assignment of roles that match a group's needs for leadership and expertise, as well as members' abilities and attitudes, occurs. Although each of the four members of the Oil Exploration Team has functional roles based on their expertise, they do not perform them effectively, as suggested by the unsatisfactory product, disbanding of the team, and eventual firing of Jake.

Termination

Some researchers have proposed a fifth stage of group development during which *adjourning* occurs. This refers to the dissolution of a group.[12] An obvious example is the Oil Exploration Team's disbanding one year later.

Moving through the Stages

A group may recycle through the stages of development, particularly if changes in the group's membership, task, or environment occur. For example, if a new member is added to the Oil Exploration Team, the group would begin its development anew. As it was, Bill, Phil, and Brad may have functioned effectively prior to Jake's joining the group.

Of course movement through stages that a group has already resolved may occur more rapidly the second time. For example, orientation of a new member may require ten minutes rather than the two hours it required to orient the entire group the first time. Or a group may use techniques they previously perfected to exchange relevant information and opinions effectively and efficiently.

A change in goals may also cause a group to return to a previous stage. When Walt Bannister sees that the Oil Exploration Team is experiencing difficulty in meeting its deadlines he may alter the group's task. Changes in the company's environment may alter the value of seeking new drilling sites. The extent and uniqueness of any environmental changes influence the speed with which the group moves through stages it has already resolved.

Some groups stick at one stage; that is, they fail to resolve the issues associated with that stage. Managers often must find ways to remove obstacles to advancement. In normally functioning groups, the orientation stage is shortest, followed in length by the redefinition and formalization stages; the coordination stage is longest. Groups experiencing difficulties tend to have an elongated formation stage.[13] Similarly, failure to move beyond redefinition signals a group's lack of conflict-resolution mechanisms (see Chapter 10). Occasionally groups remain at other stages as well. Arresting at the orientation stage suggests that the group lacks the skill to screen out irrelevant information and behavior. Inability to move beyond coordination often reflects a group with poor information, which hinders effective interpretation. Frequently dilemmas at various stages of development can remain unresolved when a group lacks clear goals, individual members have incompatible goals, or group management is dysfunctional.

Through what stages has the Oil Exploration Team moved? We have a sense that the group completed their orientation to task and identified basic behaviors acceptable to both the task and other group members; and they developed a set of tasks and timetable that would result in a quality proposal for new sites. But conflict surfaces during the exchanges between Jake and

Brad, and the group as a whole lacks mechanisms for effectively resolving differences and building a common view of the tasks. The group lacks functional norms for performing task activities and group process. Thus the team remains at stage 3: they spend most of their time arguing over their relative contributions to the tasks, not resolving the conflict created in the previous stage. The group does not exchange interpretations and opinions in a significant way, nor do its members develop group cohesion. Neither the team leader, Bill Jessup, nor his boss, Walt Bannister, finds ways to move the group successfully into the fourth stage; the team submits an unsatisfactory report to top management. In this case, adjournment occurs: top management disbands the group.

Alternate Views of Group Development

More recent research describes a model of group development called *punctuated equilibrium*. In this model a group spends the first half of its time working toward the direction set by the group at the end of its first meeting. Half-way through the time period the group experiences a transition, in which it uses the learning it has gained in the first phase to change its direction and generate the work for the second phase of its performance.[14]

Other recent analyses suggest a similarity between group development and organizational socialization (discussed in Chapter 3).[15] These processes occur simultaneously for groups and help us diagnose their developmental progress. Like group development, organizational socialization has been described as a four-step model.[16] Newcomers first confront and accept organizational reality by checking their own expectations and learning behaviors that are rewarded or punished; this corresponds to orientation to task and testing roles. Second they attempt to clarify their roles and learn ways to deal with change and ambiguity; this corresponds to an emotional response and accompanying intragroup conflict. Third they achieve role clarity in the socialization process; they exchange relevant information in the group development process. Finally, they experience satisfaction and commitment to the organization; the group reaches a solution and develops functional role-related behavior. Group development and organizational socialization thus show both temporal and conceptual parallels,[17] as illustrated in Table 5–2. Thus, to diagnose a situation completely and precisely, we should use these frameworks both separately and in concert to identify which processes are dysfunctional.

In the rest of this chapter we examine group process in greater detail. We look at the nature of group goals, norms, roles, and structural configurations. (In Chapter 6 we examine task activity in our discussion of group decision making.)

GOALS

What are the goals of the Oil Exploration Team? Top management's goal of exploring for oil in Wyoming might be the group's goal. Identifying high-quality prospects quickly might be its goal. Specifying the best possible sites, regardless of the time and cost to identify them, might be the team's goal. Or the group might lack an agreed-on goal.

Table 5–2 COMPARISON OF STAGES OF GROUP DEVELOPMENT TO STAGES OF SOCIALIZATION

	Group Development[a]	Organizational Socialization[b]
Stage 1: Orientation	1. Forming Establish interpersonal relationships Conform to organizational traditions and standards Boundary testing in relationships and task behaviors	1. Getting In (Anticipatory socialization) Setting of realistic expectations Determining match with the newcomer
Stage 2: Redefinition	2. Storming Conflict arising because of interpersonal behaviors Resistance to group influence and task requirements	2. Breaking In (Accommodation) Initiation on the job Establishing interpersonal relationships Congruence between self and organizational performance appraisal
Stage 3: Coordination	3. Norming Single leader emerges Group cohesion established New group standards and roles formed for members	3. Settling In (Role management) The degree of fit between one's life interests outside of work and the demands of the organization Resolution of conflicts at the workplace itself
Stage 4: Formalization	4. Performing Members perform tasks together Establishing role clarity Teamwork is the norm	

[a]Based on B. Tuchman, Developmental sequence in small groups, *Psychological Bulletin* 63 (1965): 384–399.
[b]Based on D.C. Feldman, A contingency theory of socialization, *Administrative Science Quarterly* 21 (1976): 433–454; D.C. Feldman, A practical program for employee socialization, *Organizational Dynamics* 7 (1976): 64–80.

SOURCE: Adapted from J. P. Wanous, A. E. Reichers, and S. D. Malik, Organizational socialization and group development: Toward an integrative perspective, *Academy of Management Review* 9 (1984): 670–683.

Rather than having a *group goal,* the goals of the individuals taken together might constitute the group's goal. Each member's desire to demonstrate his own expertise might constitute the team's goal. And what if one group member wants to use his performance on the project as a springboard to a job in another company? What would happen if one of the team members wants to sabotage the project?

Goals can be formal (specifically stated orally or in writing) or informal (implied in the actions of group members). A formal goal of the Oil Exploration Team is to develop a series of high-quality prospects. An informal goal might be to ensure the input of all group members. As noted in Chapter 4, the most effective goals are moderately difficult, specific, yet accepted by group members. For example, "identifying four possible sites by January 13" is a more specific objective than "planning for drilling." The specific objective must be sufficiently difficult and accepted by group members to be useful as a focus of group activity. Numerous specific objectives should comprise the group's goal.

Agreement about group goals increases the cohesiveness experienced by the group. In the case of the Oil Exploration Team, the four members ostensibly agree on the major goal: to develop a series of high-quality prospects within four months. But the group members may not agree about other group goals. Jake may be willing to sacrifice timeliness for higher quality data collection, while Brad may view the deadlines as unchangeable. These differences may explain the apparent lack of cohesion we observe.

Sometimes the goals of individual members may conflict with the group goals. In such situations, individuals may develop hidden agendas, or goals hidden from the group. For example, Jake may want to experiment with new data-analysis techniques even if they require more time than is available. Or Bill may prefer specific leasing opportunities that color his development of the timetable of activities. These hidden agendas likely hinder the group's performance. Thus diagnosis of group structure must include a search for and recognition of hidden agendas. In most cases individuals should be encouraged to surface them—the well-developed group has mechanisms for resolving them. Managers must be particularly attuned to the existence of hidden agendas and help surface them when appropriate. Handling hidden agendas should allow the development of clear, effective group goals.

NORMS

Underlying group development and implicit in group functioning are expectations that guide behavior. A student, for example, is expected to attend classes, prepare homework, and take examinations. A worker is expected to be at work on time, miss work only in case of illness, put in a "good day's work for a good day's pay." When these expectations are unwritten and informal they are called *norms*. Norms develop through the interaction of group members and reinforcement of behaviors by the group. Generally these expectations are in line with group goals and so are helpful in accomplishing organizational goals. In some cases, however, these expectations do not fit with the organization's goals. Some work groups, for example, insist that their members maintain a certain, often suboptimal, production level. In other organizations, arriving late is the norm for certain management-level employees.

Group members may act to encourage certain behaviors; for example, by reinforcing a specific level of production. Members may also discourage certain behaviors by responding negatively to their occurrence, such as by rejecting very high or very low performance. Suppose, for example, that one of the Oil Exploration Team members comes to the second planning meeting with a completed timetable of activities, whereas the remainder of the group comes unprepared. If the other group members ignore all suggestions made by the well-prepared member they may be signaling that such preparation is unexpected and unacceptable.

Norms generally develop for behaviors that group members view as important, such as performance, effort, attendance, and even work breaks. Most norms develop in one of four ways.[18] Supervisors or coworkers may at one time but not repeatedly *explicitly state* certain expectations. Bill Jessup, for example, might state at the first task force meeting that attendance is required; expected attendance at all subsequent meetings may become a norm. *Critical events* in a group's history may also establish norms. If a member of the team comes to the first meeting with a detailed timetable for developing the proposal but the group refuses to consider it, not preparing for meetings may become a norm. Third, the *initial pattern of behavior* may become a norm. If Bill dominates the first team meeting and the rest of the group says little, this pattern may persist at subsequent meetings. Finally, group members may *transfer behavior* from other situations to the group. The relative aggressiveness of some team members and the silence of others may reflect expected behaviors in previous work assignments, which are then brought to other group tasks.

There may be norms about attendance, performance, interpersonal interactions, and dress, but not all norms apply to everyone.[19] Different norms exist for managers and nonmanagerial employees, for professionals and nonprofessionals, for men and women. Leaders also play a role in enforcing and breaking norms. At Far West Prospecting, how might the norms for Walt Bannister differ from those for Jake and Brad? How might they differ for a bank vice president and a teller? How might they differ for the owner of a company and his or her employees? They might differ in the extent to which holders are expected to be innovative on the job, follow organizational rules and regulations, or demonstrate loyalty to a specific department or supervisor. How might these differences affect the performance of employees in a group such as the Oil Exploration Team? A member who is expected to demonstrate loyalty to his or her professional discipline might try to provide a larger role for that discipline in the drilling project than would an individual with more group loyalty.

Norms are established and enforced only about selected behaviors.[20] A group enforces norms that facilitate its survival, help predict the behavior of group members, prevent embarrassing interpersonal problems, express the group's central values, and clarify the group's identity.[21] *Sanctions* can be used to encourage norm compliance. Individuals who do not follow group norms may receive verbal reprimands or ridicule, formal punishments such as fines or firings, or informal actions such as isolation from the group. Individuals who follow group norms may receive positive reinforcements as well (see Chapter 4).[22] In the Oil Exploration Team norms should arise and be enforced that facilitate meeting the deadlines set by the group and help group members work cooperatively toward task accomplishment. Unfortunately, the group does not successfully enforce norms of collaboration and group performance, contributing to its inadequate product and ultimate dissolution.

Classification Schemes

Norms differ in their centrality to the organizational functioning of the behavior they govern. *Pivotal norms* guide behavior essential to the core mission of the organization. Expectations about the level of production or innovation required of workers fall into this category. *Peripheral norms* guide behaviors that are important, but not essential, to the performance of the organization's goals or mission. A dress code is an example.[23] The worker who violates pivotal norms often impedes the accomplishment of organizational goals; therefore he or she may receive chastisement from superiors, ostracism by coworkers, or lack of loyalty from subordinates. Violation of peripheral norms by employees typically has fewer negative consequences for the worker and the organization.

Another classification scheme describes a norm in one of three ways, according to whether the behavior is acceptable to or approved by group members.[24] Managers can apply this classification to identifying the norms that exist in their work group and understanding the consequences of them. First, the *unattainable-ideal norm* describes behavior where "more is better." For example, among a group of policemen, the more criminals arrested the better; among salespeople, the more sales the better; at Far West, the more prospects identified the better. Second, the *preferred-value norm* describes behavior where either too much or too little of a behavior receives disapproval from group members. For example, work groups often approve only a small range of output. Assembly-line workers who work too fast or too slow may violate this norm; Jake may violate it by missing deadlines. Third, the *attainable-ideal norm* describes behavior where approval occurs for increasing amounts of behavior until an attainable goal is reached; then, further goal-oriented behavior lacks value. For example, a physician receives approval for each new child he or she vaccinates against measles until the disease is erased, requiring no further vaccinations. An advertising executive receives approval for each new campaign idea he or she generates until the client chooses one of the ideas. The geophysicists may receive approval for each new site they identify until drilling begins at one of them.

Compliance with Norms

In any group, we can diagnose which type of norm is in operation, and whether violation of it contributes to low group performance or dysfunctional member attitudes. Can you think of some norms in groups to which you belong? How would you classify these norms? Has any group member violated the norm? What were the consequences of this violation? What norms operate among the professionals of the Oil Exploration Team? Which norms fit with the organization's goals? Which norms are not congruent with goals?

Workers in some countries, such as Japan and China, define themselves more in terms of the groups to which they belong than do workers in the United States. In these more group-oriented countries compliance with norms is more valued than in the United States because workers fear the ostracism that results from deviance.[25]

Diagnosing norms and compliance with them in a group or organization should precede any action since this may help explain group performance. Compliance with norms tends to increase as the group's size decreases, or as its homogeneity, visibility, or stability increases: members of small, homogeneous groups that are visible and stable experience greater norm compliance than large, heterogeneous groups that lack visibility and stability.[26]

Given the characteristics of the Oil Exploration Team, what would you predict about members' compliance with norms? Although the group is relatively small and visible, the four members have sufficiently diverse backgrounds and have come together recently enough to have relatively low norm compliance. The more the group's members are committed to the group's task, the more the group generates its own rules. Finally, the more a group controls information about its members the greater the compliance with norms. The members of the Oil Exploration Team may decide to keep their seismic findings secret until they submit their report, to prevent other exploration teams from benefitting prematurely from their findings. The members also try to reinforce the norms of meeting deadlines, although they experience some failure with regard to Jake's behavior in this regard. They try to develop and enforce norms of sharing and collaboration, and even using Walt Bannister as a third party to eliminate the dissension between Jake and Brad. Finally, they emphasize the value of each member's technical expertise as a way of portraying the strength of the group.

As the team's managers, Bill Jessup and Walt Bannister should diagnose what norms exist and whether norm violation in the Oil Exploration Team is responsible for the group's lack of performance. In addition, they should analyze the type of norms in operation so that they can prescribe and implement appropriate corrective action. This might mean changing their own or others' roles in the team, as described in the next section.

ROLES

In our discussion of role conflict and role ambiguity in Chapter 3, we noted that people have various roles—a prescribed set and pattern of activities, expectations, or potential behaviors—that may conflict with each other and are more or less clear. We pursue the idea of work roles further here by examining two classifications of roles. We first examine a scheme that relates to compliance with (or violation of) group norms. Then we look at a functional classification of roles.

Norm-Related Types

The extent to which group members comply with norms delineates one set of roles in a group.[27] The *leader* adheres to group norms and generally makes a special contribution to their identification and enforcement. In the Oil Exploration Team Bill Jessup has the position of leadership and thus can directly affect the group's norms. We can question whether he successfully sets effectiveness norms, given the dysfunctional group behavior that occurs.

The *regular* follows most, if not all, group norms; he or she contributes as a "good member." Two members of the team try to act as regulars. Phil Johnson and Brad Murray perform the tasks required by the leader, attend meetings regularly, and contribute to the discussion based on their expertise.

The *deviant* falls still lower in the hierarchy. This member deviates from the norms but is often tolerated by others in the group. The very high producer—for example, the team member who finishes each task several days before its deadline—may fall into the deviant category. Although this deviant breaks the production norms, the group still values the high level of performance. Is there a deviant on the Oil Exploration Team? Jake Coleman might view Brad Murray as one, although we lack data to verify this conclusion.

Finally, the *isolate* falls at the lowest level of the role hierarchy. The isolate does not meet group norms; therefore, the group rejects and does not value this member. Clearly, Brad Murray views Jake Coleman as an isolate. The member who continually argues against other members' ideas without offering constructive ideas of his or her own may also be viewed as an isolate.

By diagnosing roles in this way, we can anticipate to some degree the extent and quality of interaction among particular group members and the group's effectiveness. If Bill Jessup or Walt Bannister performs such an analysis he can develop strategies for altering members' roles (and norms) to better fit with the group's goals and increase its effectiveness.

Functional Types

Another widely used classification of roles describes the actual behaviors of various group members.[28] *Task roles* focus on task or goal accomplishment. The two geophysicists on the Oil Exploration Team should act as information givers, sharing their knowledge of various sands and earth formations so the group can draw conclusions about the likelihood the oil drilling will succeed. Phil Johnson might act as an evaluator, assessing the quality of suggestions in terms of their cost. As the formal leader of the group Bill Jessup acts as a coordinator when he combines the suggestions of group members.

Maintenance or *group building roles* direct the group toward positive member interaction and interpersonal behavior. Any of the Oil Exploration Team members may act as an encourager, by praising the ideas of other group members, or a gatekeeper, by encouraging others' participation.

Individual or *self-oriented roles* focus on satisfying an individual's needs. Such role behaviors frequently distract a group from effective functioning through individual dominance. Two group members who repeatedly argue with each other likely take blocker (stubbornly resisting or reacting negatively) or recognition-seeker (calling attention to oneself by bragging or boasting) roles, by stubbornly resisting others' ideas or calling attention to themselves by acting superior. Some group members may scapegoat others as a way of meeting their personal needs.

Table 5–3 lists examples of these three role types. Note that a group member may perform more than one role, and several members may perform the same role. Frequently a pattern of roles emerges for each group member. By tallying the nature and frequency of role behaviors and individuals' interactions in a group, an observer can identify the roles played by group members. This diagnosis is prerequisite to the evaluation of group functioning and effectiveness. It can also identify task and maintenance roles not played by any group members but important for group functioning. We can use the first two sets of roles listed in Table 5–3 as a basic checklist of roles that should be performed in

Table 5–3 CLASSIFICATION OF GROUP ROLES

Task-oriented roles	Initiator	Offers new ideas or suggests solutions to problems
	Information seeker	Seeks pertinent facts or clarification of information
	Information giver	Describes own experience or offers facts and information
	Coordinator	Coordinates activities, combines ideas or suggestions
	Evaluator	Assesses the quality of suggestions, solutions, or norms
Maintenance roles	Encourager	Encourages cohesiveness and warmth, praises and accepts others' ideas
	Harmonizer	Alleviates tension; resolves intragroup disagreements
	Gatekeeper	Encourages participation by others and sharing of ideas
	Standard setter	Raises questions about group goals; helps set goals and standards
	Follower	Agrees and pursues others' activities
	Group observer	Monitors group operations; provides feedback to group
Individual roles	Blocker	Resists stubbornly; negative; returns to rejected issues
	Recognition-seeker	Calls attention to self by boasting, bragging, acting superior
	Dominator	Manipulates group; interrupts others; gains attention
	Avoider	Remains apart from others; resists passively

SOURCE: K. Benne and P. Sheats, Functional roles of group members, *Journal of Social Issues* 2 (1948): 42–47.

groups such as the Oil Exploration Team. Which roles are not performed by any group members? Which roles are performed ineffectively by group members?

Think for a moment of a group to which you belong. Which roles did individuals perform at the group's most recent meeting or gathering? What types of behaviors occurred most frequently? Did the extent of task or maintenance role performance fit with the group's purpose and needs? Did a large number of self-oriented behaviors occur?

Now let us answer these questions with regard to the Oil Exploration Team. For a group that should be task-oriented, we have an indication that a reasonable number of individual roles occur; specifically, two members seem to act as blockers, recognition-seekers, and dominators. Some of the rest seem to act as avoiders, staying out of the discussion and apart from others. This analysis identifies dysfunctional roles in this group and lets us predict its poor performance. An effective group typically displays both task and maintenance roles in varying amounts, depending on the group's needs. It shows few, if any, individual roles since these tend to detract from effective group functioning.

Sometimes, however, even if individuals wish to play more functional roles, other group members may lock them into deviant or isolate roles. Scapegoating and projection by other group members can prevent an individual from adapting to the group's requirements. In addition, some members become dependent on other group members for approval or direction, causing dysfunctional behavior.

Effective managers can diagnose roles needed and played within a group. They can then act to reduce dysfunctional and increase functional role performance. Changing the roles of group members might require a structured intervention, such as training or formal analysis of their role performance.

If Bill Jenkins or Walt Bannister performed such a diagnosis of roles, he could devise and implement strategies for changing the types of roles performed. Sometimes individuals become stuck in roles that are not functional to the group. Applying the *role analysis technique* allows group members to share their expectations about role performance.[29] An individual lists his or her roles, and other group members, often with the help of a facilitator, revise the list by agreeing or disagreeing with the individual's perceptions. Eventually they achieve consensus about the team member's role performance.

STRUCTURAL CONFIGURATION

A group's structural configuration in part describes the relatively permanent role arrangements in groups. These arrangements reflect the nature of communication among role holders and can contribute to a group's cohesiveness. Figure 5–2 illustrates five such communication patterns or networks. The wheel network has a single person who alone communicates with all others in the work group. The Oil Exploration Team would have this structural configuration if only Bill Jessup communicated with the rest of the team members without their holding discussions among themselves. The Y (if we invert it) and the chain networks resemble the chain of command in a group. Communication flows up and down a hierarchy, with little skipping of levels or communication outside the hierarchy. The circle resembles the chain except that the communication loop is closed; for example, the lowest-level member of a group may have a top manager as a mentor and communicate with him or her directly. In the completely connected network, all group members regularly communicate with all other members. Most likely the Oil Exploration Team operates in this configuration. Additional configurations, such as a star or a barred circle, where two additional points are connected across the circle, represent variations of these.[30]

Of course a single network does not precisely describe communication in a group. Rather, communication in a group may be typified by one network, or the group may use variants of one or more networks. Identifying the predominant structural configuration, however, helps us explain or predict the performance and satisfaction of the group and its members.

Networks differ in a variety of ways. First, the way information is exchanged—the speed, accuracy, and saturation of the network—differentiate

Figure 5–2 COMMUNICATION NETWORKS AND THEIR CHARACTERISTICS

Network:

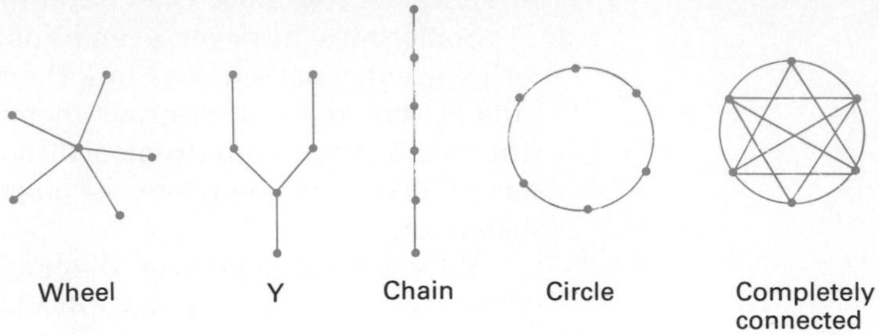

	Wheel	Y	Chain	Circle	Completely connected
Characteristics of Information Exchange:					
Speed	Fast	Slow	Slow	Slow	Fast-Slow
Accuracy*	Good	Fair	Fair	Poor	Good
Saturation	Low	Low	Moderate	High	High
Characteristics of Members					
Overall satisfaction	Low	Low	Low	High	High
Leadership emergence	Yes	Yes	Yes	No	No
Centralization	Yes	Yes	Moderate	No	No

*These accuracy estimates may change according to the nature and complexity of the task.

SOURCE: Based on A. Bavelas, Communication patterns in task-oriented groups, *Journal of Accoustical Society of America* 22 (1950): 725–730.

the five structural configurations. Second, the characteristics of network members, their overall satisfaction, whether leadership emerges, and the extent of centralization in the network, differs for the five configurations. Figure 5–2 summarizes the performance of various networks along these dimensions.

The *speed* of information exchange and ultimately of problem solving tends to be slowest in the Y, chain, and circle networks; somewhat faster in the completely connected; and fastest in the wheel. In the wheel configuration, for example, information exchange occurs relatively quickly between the center position and peripheral ones, flowing somewhat more slowly among the spoke positions because the center acts as an intermediary.

The *accuracy* of problem solving by the group; that is, the extent, frequency, and type of mistakes made, depends in part on the nature of the task. While accuracy of a very complicated task may be greater in a completely connected than in a wheel network, the reverse may be true for a very simple task, where too great an exchange of information in the completely connected network may distort the information disseminated.

The *saturation* of the network, or the amount of information passed along the network's segments, ranges from lowest in the wheel or Y, to highest in the circle and completely connected networks. Networks with low saturation tend to have a single, relatively central node that acts as a focus of information and limits the amount of information passed along the rest of the segments. In the highly saturated networks, in contrast, information passes relatively equally through all segments.

Member *satisfaction overall* seems to be higher in the circle and completely connected networks than in the other three. This satisfaction may also be associated with the sharing of leadership responsibility and the decentralized decision making in groups with those structural configurations, as well as the difficulty in isolating group members.

Leadership emerges most naturally in central positions of the wheel, Y, and chain networks. Here individuals who hold positions that link to at least two other positions tend to collect more information and hence can exert greater influence over other group members. The existence of *centralization of decision making* in the group; that is, whether a single person has primary responsibility for decision making or whether it is decentralized to many members of the group, resembles the emergence of leadership in the networks.

Think of a group to which you belong. Which network best describes the communication in the group? Is this network the most effective for the performance of the group? Which network best describes the Oil Exploration Team? Is the network the most effective for the performance of that group?

The most effective structural configuration varies among groups and within the same group at different times. Effective managers can help structure the best configuration for the group. In the Oil Exploration Team, for example, a wheel configuration may be best when the group is first formed, so that Bill Jessup can convey a large quantity of information to team members as rapidly as possible. But when the group must identify and evaluate alternatives for the program, more discussion is essential and a completely connected network would be more appropriate. Effectiveness occurs when a *fit* exists between the network, group members, and task characteristics.

IMPROVING WORK TEAM EFFECTIVENESS

Teams are "collections of people who must rely on group collaboration if each member is to experience the optimum of success and goal achievement."[31] They generally have specific projects with specified short- or long-term duration. Management groups, committees, task forces, and other work units strive to act as teams. Increasingly they recognize the importance of concerted effort to accomplish their goals.

Characteristics of Effective Teams

Figure 5–3 summarizes one view of the characteristics of an effective work team. Note that an effective work team has clear, shared goals; strong member participation; good diagnostic skills; the ability to meet leadership needs from within the group; consensus-seeking and -reaching mechanisms; member trust; and opportunities for member growth and creativity. For subgroups, task and process behaviors are equally important.

How many of these characteristics does the Oil Exploration Team have? While it appears that group goals are initially clear to and shared by all members, Jake's failure to meet deadlines indicates a decline in team effectiveness. Although all members participate in team activities and seem to freely express themselves, their empathy declines as deadlines are missed. They increasingly distrust each other. In part, the increasing dysfunctions of the group may occur because of insufficient leadership within the group: Bill Jessup seems unable to reduce dysfunctional disharmonies on the team. The

Figure 5–3 SOME CHARACTERISTICS OF AN EFFECTIVE WORK TEAM

Goals are clear to all, shared by all, and all care about and feel involved in the goals.

All members participate and are listened to.

When problems arise, the situation is carefully diagnosed before action is proposed; remedies attack basic causes.

As needs for leadership arise, various members meet them; anyone feels free to volunteer as he or she sees a group need.

Consensus is sought and tested; deviates are appropriated and used to improve the decision; decisions, when made, are fully supported.

Members trust one another; they reveal to the group what they would be reluctant to expose to others; they respect and use the responses they get; they can freely express negative reactions without fearing reprisal.

The group is flexible and seeks new and better ways of acting; individuals change and grow; they are creative.

The group produces the desired results; it must do what it exists to do and do it well enough to be considered effective.

Members freely express themselves and receive empathic responses.

Based in part on E.H. Schein, *Process Consultation* © 1969, Addison-Wesley Publishing Company, Reading, Mass. Pages 42–43. Reprinted with permission.

group also lacks effective consensus-reaching techniques and procedures for accurately diagnosing the causes of their failure to meet deadlines and secure acceptable performance from all team members.

Formation and Development of Effective Teams

A team-building program can begin when a new team is formed or when an existing team stops functioning effectively. In forming a new team, members should ideally follow four steps.[32] First, each member must determine the priority he or she attaches to participating in the team's activities and assess the personal importance of these activities. We might hypothesize, for example, that members of the Oil Exploration Team value group participation differently, reducing the team's effectiveness. Second, the members must share their expectations about working on the team. As discussed earlier, this orientation step is essential to effective group development. While the Oil Exploration Team aired some of their expectations during the first month, they subsequently discontinued the sharing, and team performance declined. Third, members must clarify the team's goals and objectives; they must agree to a core mission for the team. Finally, the team must formulate operating guidelines about the process of decision making, basic work methods, the extent and nature of member participation in discussion, ways of resolving differences, ways of ensuring that work is completed, and how to change nonproductive activities. Clearly the Oil Exploration Team did not satisfactorily formulate such guidelines. They lacked mechanisms for dealing with a member's failure to meet deadlines and for resolving the arguments between Jake and Brad.

To ensure the effectiveness and productivity of a task force, its leader must carefully constitute the task force, define and allocate resources, and manage day-to-day activities.[33] The individual who forms a task force must select members who have a vested interest in its mission, will be challenged by its task, and have complementary skills. The person who organizes a task force generally selects a leader or requests that the members participate in this selection. Once the leader has been selected, he or she should set agendas for group meetings, help reduce hidden agendas of the members, and build commitment to the task and to other task force members.

Consider how well top management of the Far West Prospecting Company formed the Oil Exploration Team and allocated resources to it. Now consider how well Bill Jessup managed the day-to-day activities. Diagnosis of the performance of the team suggests that the members had different priorities about team participation, failed to share their expectations, lacked agreed on goals, and had insufficient operating guidelines.

We can make a similar diagnosis for other existing teams. We can assess which steps a team has not handled well. We can also assess whether any team needs to demonstrate greater imagination and creativity. Figure 5–4 provides a checklist for scoring work-team creativity. Lower scores suggest a need for additional team-building activities.

Figure 5–4 DIAGNOSING WORK TEAM CREATIVITY

This scale will help you see to what extent the type of management and the organizational conditions support and encourage creative effort.

1. My ideas or suggestions never get a fair hearing.	1 2 3 4 5 6 7	My ideas or suggestions get a fair hearing.
2. I feel like my boss is not interested in my ideas.	1 2 3 4 5 6 7	I feel like my boss is very interested in my ideas.
3. I receive no encouragement to innovate on my job.	1 2 3 4 5 6 7	I am encouraged to innovate on my job.
4. There is no reward for innovating or improving things on my job.	1 2 3 4 5 6 7	I am rewarded for innovating and improving on my job.
5. There is no encouragement for diverse opinions among subordinates.	1 2 3 4 5 6 7	There is encouragement of diversity of opinion among subordinates.
6. I'm very reluctant to tell the boss about mistakes I make.	1 2 3 4 5 6 7	I feel comfortable enough with my boss to tell about mistakes I make.
7. I'm not given enough responsibility to do my job right.	1 2 3 4 5 6 7	I am given enough responsibility to do my job right.
8. To really succeed in this organization, one needs to be a friend or a relative of the boss.	1 2 3 4 5 6 7	There is no favoritism in the organization.
9. There are other jobs in this organization that I would prefer to have.	1 2 3 4 5 6 7	I have the job in this organization that I think I do best.
10. They keep close watch over me too much of the time.	1 2 3 4 5 6 7	They trust me to do my job without always checking on me.
11. They would not let me try other jobs in the organization.	1 2 3 4 5 6 7	I could try other kinds of jobs in the organization if I wanted to.
12. The management is made very uptight by confusion, disorder, and chaos.	1 2 3 4 5 6 7	The management deals easily with confusion, disorder, and chaos.
13. There is a low standard of excellence on the job.	1 2 3 4 5 6 7	There is a high standard of excellence on the job.
14. My boss is not open to receive my opinion of how he/she might improve his/her own performance on the job.	1 2 3 4 5 6 7	My boss is very open to suggestions on how he/she might improve his/her own performance.
15. My boss has a very low standard for judging his/her own performance.	1 2 3 4 5 6 7	My boss has a very high standard of excellence for judging his/her own performance.
16. I am not asked for suggestions on how to improve service to the customers.	1 2 3 4 5 6 7	The management actively solicits my suggestions and ideas on how to improve service to the customers.
17. My boss shows no enthusiasm for the work we are engaged in.	1 2 3 4 5 6 7	My boss exhibits lots of enthusiasm for the work we are engaged in.
18. Mistakes get you in trouble; they aren't to learn from.	1 2 3 4 5 6 7	Around here mistakes are to learn from and not to penalize you.
19. Someone else dictates how much I should accomplish on my job.	1 2 3 4 5 6 7	I'm allowed to set my own goals for my job.
20. The organization has too many rules and regulations for me.	1 2 3 4 5 6 7	The organization has adequate rules and regulations for me.

William Dyer, *Team Building*, © 1977, Addison-Wesley, Reading, Massachusetts. Pages 123–125. Reprinted with permission of the publisher.

Strategies for Team Building

To improve the performance of work teams, managers or outside consultants may prescribe a variety of team-building activities. Data collection is an essential activity. Managers, group members, or outside parties may use process observation as one means of data collection.[34] The process observer collects data about communication, decision making, and leadership in a team. He or she records information about group norms and roles by tabulating who talks to whom, how frequently, and about what topics. Other data collection activities include problem sensing with groups, individual interviews and group feedback, use of questionnaires and feedback, and assessment of total organizational functioning.[35]

Problem-solving activities have group members identify problems they experience with group behavior and task performance. They might specify, for example, uneven participation by various group members or lack of appropriate skills for task performance as group problems. The administration of interviews and questionnaires to group members also provides information about the effectiveness of team performance. Combinations of these data collection techniques, together with other data collection methods such as review of company documents or objective indices of performance, can provide a comprehensive set of information to use in team building.

The observer, interviewer, or other data collector then feeds this information back to team members. The process consultant may also help set agendas, coach the group or its members in effective interpersonal processes, and offer recommendations for more effective performance. The emphasis of such feedback and discussion of results is to help the team face their problems, evaluate their behaviors, and identify their challenges for future performance. To do so, team members address questions such as the following:

- What is it like to work here?
- What helps or hinders working together?
- What are our jobs and our responsibilities?
- What are our expectations of our team and each other?
- What changes could be made to improve performance?
- What does each group member need to do differently?
- What can this unit do to work more cooperatively?
- How do other teams or work units perceive us and vice versa?
- What commitment is each member willing to make to increase our effectiveness?[36]

Following data collection and feedback, team-building interventions provide opportunities for individuals to practice acting collaboratively and creatively. The team may use special techniques for improving group decision making and creative problem solving (see Chapter 6). Or they may use techniques designed to increase trust, improve communication, and encourage confrontation of conflict.[37] These include checking perceptual differences, practicing active listening, and giving better feedback (see Chapters 2 and 7), third-party interventions (see Chapter 10), and redesigning jobs (see Chapter 13).

For effective team building to occur, four conditions must exist.[38] First, the primary goal of a team development meeting must be explicit and well articulated. Second, this primary goal must be *owned* by the leader of the group and at least understood (preferably agreed to) by the work group members. Third, the leader's goal should be the condition within which third parties (consultants) work; that is, the primary purpose is defined by the leader, who sets the agenda and activities of the development meeting. Fourth, a consultant working with a team should help the leader to be explicit in *defining* and sharing the primary purpose. Such team-building activities would have been appropriate for the Oil Exploration Team. Periodic meetings to ensure a common purpose and ownership of goals would have facilitated their functioning as a team and probably increased their performance.

The protocol for building an effective multicultural team does not differ significantly from the general guidelines for team development. Managers can use diversity to enhance productivity and reduce dysfunctions in six ways.[39] First, selection of team members should emphasize their task-related skills, not their ethnic characteristics. Second, groups must acknowledge cultural differences and strive to overcome any barriers these create, early in the teams' existence. Third, the group leader must identify a superordinate goal as soon as possible. Fourth, power differences based on cultural background should be neutralized. Fifth, mutual respect must be developed, by selecting members based on their skills and experience and by minimizing cultural stereotypes. Finally, managers should use quality feedback to reinforce desired group behaviors and extinguish undesirable behaviors and attitudes. An exception to these goals is in countries in which an autocratic leadership style is expected, where team building may be inappropriate.

INCREASING GROUP EFFECTIVENESS

How can team members improve their group's performance? Clearly, changes can occur in a group's task activity and process. Group members can contribute to better group performance by increasing or improving the following three variables: (1) level of effort, (2) task performance strategies, and (3) member knowledge and skills.[40] Of course, changing these aspects of group functioning does not guarantee improved outcomes but should increase their likelihood. The following applies these variables to the Oil Exploration Team:

1. The level of effort a group applies to carrying out its task: the Oil Exploration Team may spend too little time on outside preparation or conduct too few or too short meetings.
2. The adequacy of the task performance strategies used by the group carrying out the task: Bill Jessup's agenda of activities may result in too much time spent on discussing and not enough on completing the components of the proposal.
3. The level and appropriateness of the knowledge and skills brought to bear on the task by group members: perhaps the Oil Exploration Team lacks members who have sufficiently diverse experience and expertise in developing drilling proposals.

Organizational members can then manipulate (1) behavioral norms, (2) task design, or (3) group composition as ways of potentially increasing these three variables.[41] Changing existing norms is most promising for increasing the effort of group members. The group or its leader can require regular attendance at meetings, extension of the time spent preparing for them, or extension of the length of meetings until a particular goal is reached.

Second, members of the group can redesign the task; this is most promising for improving task performance strategies. The group might, on the one hand, introduce greater specialization of responsibilities, or on the other, increase the amount of job enrichment (see Chapter 13). In other words, each team member could be given responsibility for a single, integral part of the task that best fits his or her expertise and experience.

Third, changing the composition of the group by adding new members or replacing existing members with individuals having different expertise would affect the knowledge and skills brought to bear on the task. Walt Bannister could reconstitute the Oil Exploration Team to include more geophysicists, for example, who have experience in developing similar proposals.

SUMMARY

Individuals belong to many groups, both inside and outside the workplace. Within organizations they may be part of permanent departments or less permanent task forces or committees. Characteristics of effective groups include the following:

- Members trust others or express their lack of trust.
- The group has clear and specific goals, jointly determined by the members and the leader.
- Most members feel a sense of inclusion.
- Participants talk directly to one another about what they are experiencing.
- Group members share leadership functions.
- Members risk disclosing threatening material.
- The group has high cohesion.
- Members identify with one another.
- Members recognize, discuss, and often resolve conflict.
- Feedback is given freely and accepted without defensiveness.
- Members feel that constructive change is possible.
- Group norms are developed cooperatively by the members and the leader.
- Group members use out-of-group time to work on problems raised in the group.[42]

In this chapter we first discussed the formation and development of groups. Next we considered four aspects of group process: goals, norms, roles, and configuration. With regard to goals we compared and contrasted individual goals with group goals and showed how group goals influence group performance and effectiveness. Then we examined several classifications of norms. These expectations of behavior in a group can affect the roles group members hold. Depending on their adherence to group norms, members can act in leader, regular, deviant, or isolate roles. They can also assume roles based on the functions they perform in a group: task, maintenance, or self-oriented. These

Figure 5–5 QUESTIONS FOR DIAGNOSING GROUP DYNAMICS

- Did the group form effectively?
- Did it effectively deal with all stages of development?
- What are the group's norms and are they functional?
- Does the group perform appropriate task and maintenance roles and avoid individual roles?
- Are individual and group goals appropriate and congruent?
- Is the group's structural configuration appropriate to the task, the people, and the information-processing tasks?
- Does the group have the characteristics of an effective work team?
- Does the group practice strategies for team building?

roles, in turn, influence the structural configuration in which interaction occurs in groups.

The chapter concluded with a summary of issues that must be considered in building effective teams and improving overall group effectiveness. Figure 5–5 lists the diagnostic questions that help assess group dynamics and group performance.

READING

Reading 5–1: PROFESSIONAL SUPPORT TEAMS

Mary Lou Davis-Sacks, Daniel R. Denison, and Russell A. Eisenstat

Although the three teams in this section [material not included with this reading—ed.] differed in many respects, they shared certain characteristics that distinguish them as professional support teams. Each team operated as a pool of experts waiting for a need to arise—a need to which it could apply its knowledge and skill. In so doing, it facilitated the work of those who performed the primary task of the organization. The tracking team generated reports on congressional deliberations for senior political officials in the executive branch of the federal government; the Fairfield systems team was responsible for its manufacturing plant for creating and maintaining the plant's computerized information system; and the maintenance and control team coordinated aircraft maintenance activities for its company.

SPECIAL SKILLS

Each team was composed of people who had specialized skills and knowledge not widely shared in their organizations. This expertise was critical in making it possible for members to respond to special organizational needs. It also created problems for the teams because it differentiated them from the rest of their organizations. This differentiation sometimes created tensions, especially when team members and their clients disagreed about what the organization needed to succeed.

The expertise the teams needed could not be simply bought off the street because some was organization specific and some required constant updating. Moreover, the teams often dealt with new and sometimes unexpected organizational problems, which sometimes made it impossible for managers to create clear performance guidelines for team behavior or to specify clearly what training members should obtain.

Thus, keeping member knowledge and skills current was a constant challenge that consumed considerable member time and energy. Partly because of the investment they made in skill development activities, team members sought and highly valued opportunities to exercise those skills. Showing what they could do was a major psychological payoff for the teams and their members. And they often became frustrated and listless when things were going so smoothly in the organization that there was little need for their expertise.

DISTINCTIVE RHYTHMS

The support teams we studied had a pulse or rhythm that clearly differentiated them from other types of work teams. Generally, members had little to do until others explicitly requested their services, or until some organizational triggering event occurred. In reflecting on life in these groups, we found ourselves using metaphors that suggested pent-up energy seeking release—such as "gathering storm clouds" or an "unmilked cow." Sometimes the tension of inactivity became so high that a team would create a crisis when none actually existed just so members could swing into action. Whenever an alarm actually did sound, the teams lept to the challenge like fire fighters dashing for their engine. Little was more satisfying to team members than using their expertise to bring an interesting problem under control.

Despite the considerable differences in the work the three teams did, a generic work cycle characterized all of them—a cycle that differentiates professional support teams from others described in this book. This cycle has four stages: scanning, diagnosing, proposing, and handing off.

Scanning. At this stage, the professional support team lies in wait, antennae extended, for a problem to emerge. Eventually, the team's client within the larger organization identifies the problem. The team may be either actively scanning the organization or passively waiting for the phone to ring. In either case, the dynamic is the same: waiting for a client to come up with a problem that requires the team's special expertise.

Diagnosing. Even though the client has presented the problem, the support team must reformulate it in members' own terms and technical language. Like a physician, the team often works with a set of symptoms from which members must develop an understanding of the underlying problem.

Proposing. In most cases, the team must produce a concrete proposal for action that the client can implement. This process involves considering various solutions and then agreeing on one that will be acceptable both to the team, because it is *right,* and to the client, because it looks as if it will *work.* The team must then translate the proposal back into a language and format that the client can understand and present it to the client for approval.

Handing off. One irony of professional support work is that someone else usually does final decision making about the teams' recommendations and the actual execution of the teams' ideas. Members often are not able to see the results of their work or learn why their proposals have been modified or rejected. Sometimes, a team must stand by and watch while its proposal is implemented differently than members ever imagined it would be—or, worst of all, set aside and never seriously considered.

Even though each of the teams we studied went through a cycle roughly like the one described above, the length of these cycles varied tremendously. The maintenance control team sometimes started a new cycle every fifteen minutes or so and often had multiple cycles going at the same time. These short cycles made up the bulk of the team's activity, even though the team also undertook long-cycle engineering projects on occasion. The Fairfield systems team was well along with work on a long-cycle project when its task changed radically. The plant manager who initially had given the team its mandate was replaced by someone who had a different view of what was needed. The team had to reframe its work in midcycle, which created considerable upheaval within the team and strained relations between the team and the new plant manager.

The federal agency tracking team also did not complete an entire cycle because what the team was supposed to monitor and report upon never happened. This team also differed from the others in that it was not charged with producing actual action plans; instead, it was to provide data and reports to those who would frame such plans. Despite the tracking team's being one step further removed from the action than were the maintenance control and systems teams, members of this team were equally committed to producing quality professional work, and they were dismayed when that work was prematurely terminated. Because professional support teams often wait eagerly for opportunities to bring their expertise to bear on organizational problems, they can become frustrated indeed when the work is terminated, interrupted, or redirected after it has finally gotten under way.

It is not unusual for professional support teams to carry on multiple cycles of varying lengths at the same time. All three of the teams we studied did so at one time or another, mixing long-term projects with immediate fire fighting. Although this mix can disrupt the normal rhythm of the teams' work, both long- and short-cycle projects do follow the basic four-stage process. Perhaps most significant, however, is that every cycle, whether long or short, ends with a hand-off to someone else. Whether the team's product is a repaired airplane, a report summarizing economic analyses, or a computer system, the team submits it to line managers for use at their discretion. If everything has gone well, no one even needs to be aware of the team's existence. This, obviously, can significantly limit the extent to which members are able to experience that special pride that comes from having seen an important piece of work all the way through to a successful conclusion.

CULTURAL CONFLICT

The professional support teams we studied were created specifically to serve as repositories of specialized knowledge and skills not otherwise available in their organizations. Members had both expertise and strong views about how it should be used: the tracking team knew just what kind of analyses it should do and what kinds of reports it should write; members of the maintenance control team had their own ideas about the decisions pilots should make in emergencies; and the systems team had clear opinions about the computer systems the Fairfield plant needed.

Yet members' expertise and the uniqueness of their professional skills also tended to create cultural conflict between team members and other organizational actors. When the professionals tried to explain their perspectives, they often seemed to others in their organizations to be speaking a foreign language. In the federal agency, for example, the technology and language of sophisticated economic analysis that were the stock and trade of the tracking team were less familiar to their political appointee clients. Moreover, the clients had little interest in the niceties of economic analysis. Instead, they sought concrete information that would help them achieve political objectives—aspirations with which the civil servants on the tracking team sometimes personally disagreed.

The systems and maintenance control teams experienced similar conflicts with their clients. Indeed, conflicts were exacerbated for these teams because both operated in organizations that sought, to the greatest extent possible, to use line personnel to perform tasks traditionally done by professionals. To team members, this practice seemed to devalue both their expertise and the importance of the team to the organization—a perception that occasionally prompted some defensiveness in their interactions with line personnel.

Cultural conflicts between the professional support teams and their clients were expressed in a variety of ways, ranging from merely symbolic disputes over how neat systems group members' desks needed to be to disagreement about major policy questions such as the role of advanced technology in a plant start-up. Team members took the conflicts seriously—whether over small or large issues—because they knew that having influence on their organizations required accommodation to line managers' needs and wishes. All three groups had to struggle constantly with an ongoing disparity between their considerable expertise and their limited authority.

More generally, all of the professional support teams we studied had to manage extremely complex relations with various other groups, both within and outside the organization. For example, the work of the maintenance control team involved coordinating relations between groups of maintenance workers employed by another company and the crews who worked for the team's own organization. Similarly, the systems team often had to arbitrate between the demands of corporate systems personnel and those of the local plant management team. And the role of the tracking team was quite literally to report the actions of one group (Congress) to another (a unit within the executive branch of government).

These activities require ongoing management of intergroup relations, and that, too, requires professional skill. Support teams typically are not trained in intergroup skills and, indeed, they may view such activities as outside the domain of their "real" work. That view is, perhaps, one reason why cultural conflicts between professional support teams and their clients sometimes get out of hand and can significantly impede accomplishment of the organization's work.

CONCLUSION: SEEKING BALANCE

The three teams we studied were constantly adjusting the balance between their two competing identities: that of skilled professionals and that of organizational members. Both identities are necessary for team effectiveness since the tasks of professional support teams typically require both high professional expertise and good relationships with line organizational personnel. As we have seen, however, these two identities also sometimes pull professional support teams in opposite directions. Support staff gain and maintain their professional expertise through cross-training by their fellow group members and through their involvement with extraorganizational professional groups. These activities were especially appealing to members of the teams we studied because they provided a level of intellectual stimulation that often was missing from their day-to-day organizational activities. Yet such activities also risked further increasing the cultural barrier between team members and their organizational colleagues.

Maintaining an appropriate balance between the need for professionalism and the need for organizational integration requires cooperation between those who manage the support teams and those who manage the line organization. The contributions needed from line and staff managers are complementary. Because the path of least resistance for support teams often involves engaging in professional development activities at the cost of members' involvement in the organization, it is important for the managers of such teams to push members toward organizational engagement. Strategies for accomplishing this include rotating line personnel through the support team, rotating support personnel through line operations, physically locating the team so it is close to line activities, developing "cousin" relationships between support teams and line teams, and so on.

There also are things that line managers can do to increase the chances that the organization will reap full benefit from its investment in professional support teams. Probably the most important and the most difficult is for line managers to understand that such teams are valuable precisely *because* they have an approach that differs from the rest of the organization. Once that is accepted, managers can engage in a variety of activities to validate and constructively exploit those differences—activities such as including the support team in policy-making deliberations, contributing resources for the further development of team members' professional skills, and inviting support teams to take initiative when the managers discover unmet organizational needs for which the team's professional expertise is relevant.

DISCUSSION QUESTIONS

1. What characteristics distinguish professional support teams?
2. Describe the work cycle of professional support teams.
3. Offer a protocol for professional support teams to perform effectively.

Davis-Sacks, M.L.; Denison, D. R.; and Eisenstadt, R.A., "Summary: Professional Support Teams." In J.R. Hackman (ed.), *Groups That Work (and Those That Don't)*. San Francisco: Jossey-Bass, 1990. Used with permission.

ACTIVITIES

Activity 5–1: THE PHARMACEUTICAL GROUP CASE

Step 1: Read the case of The Pharmaceutical Group.

"They refused to help us!" said John Gordon, a former lawyer from New Zealand enrolled in the MBA (Master of Business Administration) program of a European business school. He was describing his experience in a consulting project that he had just completed with five other MBA students.

"It was when Antonio, Anne and myself were preparing the slides for the presentation to the client about the results of Phase 1 of the project. The preparation of the slides was our part of the job. The others, Paul, Jan and Peter, were out of town interviewing industry executives for the next phase of the project. This is how the work had been divided. But when we started working on the slides we did not know how much it would take. We had made presentations before, but we had never had to prepare so many slides and with so much accuracy. So, we worked for several days until 01:00 A.M. until we realized that there were only two days left to the presentation to the client and we would never make it. This is when we asked Paul, Jan and Peter to help us. But they refused!"

"John, why worry? The project is finished and the client was very pleased," the case writer observed.

"I know, but I may face a similar situation soon in the real world, when I join a company, and I want to do better or at least work more efficiently!"

At the time of this discussion John was about to graduate. For the last five months, he had been working with five other students at a consulting project for a large European pharmaceutical company. The project was part of the MBA program. It involved the reorganization of the personnel department of the company. Now, at the end of the school year, he was reviewing the major events in the life of the project.

"Why were Paul, Jan and Peter unwilling to help?" asked the case writer.

"Well, because we told them that the slides would be done. Also, I think, they felt some antagonism toward us".

"Antagonism? Why?"

"Because there had been a tremendous number of arguments over how the presentation should be structured, arguments which basically opposed Paul, Jan and Peter against Anne, Antonio and myself. And this created a lot of tension. Part of the blame must go to me because I lost my temper on a couple of occasions".

"Why did you lose your temper?"

"Because I felt that Anne and I suggested good ideas during the discussions that were not accepted, not even adequately discussed, and there were decisions made by the whole group on the structure of the presentation to the client that were changed around constantly".

"By whom?"

"By Paul, Jan and Peter. First we would make a decision as a whole group. Then they would go away and work by themselves. When they came back the structure of the presentation looked entirely different. And that was it. We had to accept it".

"Were you the only one to complain about this?"

"No, also Anne".

"What about Antonio?"

"At that stage, Antonio was very quiet. He had been sick and had just come out of the hospital".

"Did Anne and you form a kind of alliance?"

"Uhm . . . probably, yah . . .".

"Why?"

"Well . . ., necessity . . .".

"What do you mean, necessity?"

"Well, that was the only way of having any kind of input in the discussions with the rest of the group".

"What do you mean?"

"Uhm . . . I suppose we had a common feeling of frustration about how things were done in our project group".

"Did you discuss these problems with the professor who was in charge of the project?"

"Certainly not".

"Why?"

"Well . . . the problem is that you don't feel comfortable talking to the professors until later in the year".

"Why?"

"I think for two reasons. First, you get to know them better, on a personal basis. Second, you understand the school's "system", which is certainly not the case in the first part of the year, particularly at the beginning".

"Why not?"

"Well . . . I think that at the beginning people feel intimidated, unsure, uncertain, for example, about how they are evaluated[1]. It is only toward the end, when they understand these things, that they feel comfortable to talk personally to the professors".

CONSULTING PROJECTS IN THE BUSINESS SCHOOL

This was not John's first experience with group works in the MBA program. The program lasted one year and was divided in modules of three to six weeks. In every module each student was assigned to different study groups of six to seven people that were expected to meet regularly to prepare the various school assignments. By the time the projects started, each student had already worked with five different groups, one for each of the five modules preceding the month of July, which was vacation time.[2]

Beginning in August, permanent student groups were formed to work until the end of the year on consulting projects for a variety of clients, from small local firms to large multinationals. The projects were intended to provide a realistic educational experience for the students. The school made always clear to the client companies that the purpose of the projects was two-fold: education and the provision of consulting services. But the experience was quite realistic and was taken very seriously by most of the students for at least two reasons. First, it was a part of the MBA program to which the faculty gave considerable importance. Second, the top management of the client companies was usually involved in the projects. The client companies also paid an administrative fee to the school and reimbursed all the expenses related to the projects. In addition, they granted a bonus of 10,000 Swiss Francs to the school if, in the end, they were particularly satisfied with the work of the students.

The students were responsible for planning, coordinating and executing all the activities related to the projects, although the faculty retained at all times some degree of control over the contacts with the client. In addition, the students were responsible for appointing a coordinator/leader, for accounting for all the project expenses and for maintaining documentation files.

The projects usually involved the research and analysis of published data, interviews with executives of the client company and other companies in the same and related industries, the analysis of all the information collected and the development of recommendations.

The parts of the work that most of the students seemed to like best included interviewing executives, making formal presentations to the client and generally having contacts with the business community. Asked about the reasons why the students liked especially these types of activities, one of them replied: "It is simple. It is a matter of both power and prestige. It is a matter of power because the students who have interviewed industry executives on project related issues are considered more knowledgeable about these issues so that the other members of the group have to defer to them in any discussion on such issues. It is a matter of prestige because contacts with the client and other executives give visibility to the students in the eyes of the faculty and the other group members".

The projects were conducted in parallel with the regular class sessions for the last five months of the MBA program. The last three or four months were also the time when most of the students were busy looking for jobs.

The projects were structured in four phases. The first involved an analysis of the industry in which the client company operated. The second involved an analysis of the client's company itself, its organization, its financial performance, etc. In the third phase, specific problems were identified and appropriate solutions were recommended. Suggestions on the implementation of these recommendations were developed in the fourth phase.

The end product of each of the first three phases was presented to the faculty for its review and criticism 7–10 days before it was actually presented to the client. The faculty was, usually, quite thorough in its review and sometimes demanded extensive revisions that required a substantial amount of additional work from the students. A key element of these presentations was a series of slides, to be projected on a screen, that contained a summary of the conclusions to be discussed during the presentation. The importance of preparing high quality presentations was underscored by the fact that usually they were attended by the top management of the client company. The quality of the presentations was obviously, also, a key factor in the awarding of the bonuses.

THE MEMBERS OF THE PHARMACEUTICAL GROUP

John was a twenty-seven-year-old New Zealander with a Masters degree from Harvard Law School. He had won a Fullbright Scholarship to study in the United States and, before enrolling in the MBA program, had worked in New Zealand and U.S. law firms specializing in Corporate Law. While he was in the business school, he often went to see his girlfriend who lived in a town fifty miles away. But he also liked to go out drinking with three other MBA students, an Englishman, an Australian and an American who were not members of his project group.

The other members of John's group were Anne, a French Canadian, Peter, an American, Antonio, a Filipino, Jan, a Dane and Paul who was also Canadian. Some of them had been together in formal study groups before. For example, Anne and John had been in the same study group in the second module of the program in February, and Paul, Jan and Peter had been together in the third module in March.

Anne was thirty-four years old. She had an undergraduate degree in Pharmacy and had worked as a product manager for a well-known Canadian pharmaceutical company. She was single. Talking of her social life in the first half of the program, she indicated that generally she was not interested in going out for drinks with other MBA students. Every once in a while, she liked to have dinner with her best friend in the school, who was a woman student from Canada, of about her age.

Antonio was twenty-six years old. He was the son of the owner of a large company in Manila. He had gone to Europe to obtain a business education, but was interested in going back to the Philippines to work for his father. In the business school he socialized with other Filipino students.

Peter was a former U.S. Marine officer. He was thirty-four years old and married. He had been quite successful in his military career, ending with the rank of Major and the position of military assistant at the White House.

Paul was a thirty-two-year-old Canadian with a Bachelor degree in Social Psychology and a postgraduate degree in Education. He had worked for several years conducting personnel training programs for Canadian Government agencies. Two years before going to Europe to get an MBA he had started his own consulting firm in the field of executive development and human relations. Soon after the beginning of the MBA program, he was joined by his Canadian wife and their two children.

Jan was a sailing buff. He was twenty-eight, had a Bachelor degree in business administration and had worked in sales management for Danish companies for four years before returning to school for an MBA.

Paul had considerable experience in team management and a good understanding of human relations problems because of his education and his prior consulting experience. The case writer asked him to describe what, in his view, were the main motivations of the members of his group.

"What did the various members of your group look for, in the project, if anything?"

Paul hesitated a lot before giving his views, saying that it was difficult to analyze the complexities of people's motivations. In the end, he said:

"In the case of Jan I think that he had developed, earlier in the school year, a reputation for being a difficult person to work with and his central motivation in the project was to try and change that, to experiment with being more of a team player in a situation of rotating leadership.

Anne saw the project as a chance to know more about an industry where she wanted to get a job after graduating. But she did not believe in group work. I think she felt superior to some of the members of the group. She often made fun of what they were saying during the discussions on the project. She also missed some important meetings. For example, before the beginning of the project, we had a meeting with the client to get his approval of the project. It was obviously a very important meeting and she said she would come. But she never came.

As far as Peter is concerned, his main interest was to see that the group would be the most organized and effective of the project groups at the business school . . . to see that everybody lived up to the expectations of the group.

Antonio is the person whose motivations I least understand. I am not sure what he thought that he got out of it, besides meeting the course requirements.

John saw the project as an opportunity to apply some of his skills in consulting. But he was not very committed. He had a problem in accepting the authority of the group, to subordinate himself to it. The first meeting of the group . . . he showed up three hours late!"

"What about yourself? We had to come to yourself".

"Yes, I wondered about myself all along. One of the things I liked was that it was work with our stamp of ownership on it. We as a group identified with this project. We were known as the Pharmaceutical Group. We identified together, fairly strongly at the beginning. We negotiated with the client, with the faculty and with other people as the Pharmaceutical Group, an identifiable work unit with common stakes in the work".

"It sounds like you enjoyed the life of the group".

"Yes, I am a conflict avoider. I like groups that work smoothly. I spent a good deal of energy in maintaining the group together, to talk to people who had problems, to make sure they would get what they needed out of the process. For example, I made an effort to keep Antonio informed about the work of the group when he was sick.

It was also my coordinator role, to communicate the group's position to the professor who was the project director and to handle the relationships of the group with outsiders".

PETER'S VIEW OF THE GROUP

Several members of the Pharmaceutical Group expressed their views of group work in the MBA program. One of them was Peter. During the work on the project, Peter sometimes kept a log recording the activities of the members of his group, their attendance to the meetings and their contribution.

"You have had a lot of experience in the Marines", said the case writer. "In your opinion, what is the difference between team work in this school and team work in the Marines?"

Peter replied in a sarcastic way. "There are terrific differences. The most striking one is the lack of commitment of many team members and the minimal amount of cooperation. This year, by the second module people would walk into the study room and say, "I am not a group person and I will not come to any group meeting unless there is a group project". In module three my study group was three people, Jan, Paul and I.

This is how the group of Jan, Paul and myself got started, in module three. In the third module the three of us got together to prepare for the basic exam[1]. After a while Gerard[2] joined us and he also brought Juan. Then Hans[3] came. He and I became fairly good friends. So we ended up with a group of six. We met together in room 35 every day after class to work on the basic exam. Sometimes other people came in. At one point, we were fourteen people in room 35, all from different study groups.

After the basic exam the original group of six continued to meet, every Sunday in one of our homes, until the last week of classes. We discussed cases and talked about particular subjects during the module that were difficult for the group as a whole. We met regularly even when we were all busy working in different projects. We would talk of finance, accounting and our career plans. After the discussion, but only then, we always had some food and drinks".

Asked why people from other study groups joined his group, Peter said: "Because their study groups were not meeting regularly and they felt the need to participate with somebody who was attempting to do something".

JAN'S VIEW OF GROUP WORK

In discussing with Jan the effectiveness of group work, the case writer asked him whether he thought that incidents such as the one of the preparation of the slides could be avoided by intervention of the project director or by assigning to a project a mix of students so that conflicts were less likely to arise.

"Oh, I have some doubts about this", said Jan, "because the professors make assumptions about the students that are often incorrect".

"What kind of assumptions?"

"Well. . . . let's see. . . . assumptions about the level of assertiveness of an individual, his or her desire to dominate, or not to dominate, matters of temper and in general, of personality".

"Why do you think the professors make mistakes about the personality of the students?"

"Because of isolation of the students from the professors".

"What do you mean?"

"Well, you see, at the beginning of the program there is little guidance given to the students. They feel like they are being dropped in a pool and being left alone to swim. This generates a lot of frustration. It creates a situation of opposition between professors and students and for all practical purposes it insures that there will be no disclosure to the faculty, by the students, of what is going on in the game".

"But even in a relationship of opposition, it is still possible to communicate".

"No! It has been a guiding principle in each of the groups that you can do almost anything but going to the faculty and let them know the internal problems of your group. You can talk to the faculty of your own problems. But talking about other people is very bad. Those who have done so have been exposed to severe internal sanctions".

"In the Pharmaceutical Group?"

"Not only in our group. It is a principle that works for all the groups".

"What kind of sanctions?"

"Well, you know. In a subtle way, a certain kind of isolation. It has to be subtle since we are among peers. It is also a matter of certain comments, dropped during the discussion, that are a kind of indirect criticism. But isolating from the rest of the group the one who talks to the professors is the worst sanction".

JOHN'S VIEW OF GROUP WORK

In discussing with John the incident regarding the preparation of the slides, the case writer asked why there were big arguments on the structure of the group presentation to the client, prior to the incident.

"Well," John said, "in most problems there are a number of ways in which you can approach them. And you have your way and I have my way. Unless we compromise we get nowhere!"

"You say that there are different approaches to the problem, but if you have to calculate a break-even point, isn't there only one way to go about it?"

"Oh, but that is not a problem".

"Well, then, what is a problem?"

"A problem is when we have to decide whether a firm has a market niche, or whether it has the capacity to pursue a given strategy, or how to structure a presentation".

"To structure a presentation?"

"Yes".

"Well, let's see. This is your presentation", said the case writer picking up from his desk a copy of John's group presentation. "What is there to be discussed about its structure? It seems well organized".

John laughed. "You are looking at the final product! It shows the characteristics of the pharmaceutical industry, the key developments in its business environment, the key aspects of the internal culture of our client company and how all these factors affect the organization of the personnel department. This is how our presentation was structured. But the linkage between industry and environmental factors and their effects on the organization of the personnel department are subject to a great deal of discussion. A single slide showing this linkage was discussed for an entire day. We were not sure that we could indeed reach any conclusion on the organizational requirements of the personnel department based on the little information that we did have. In other words, the judgment had to be made as to whether that was a valid conclusion to come to. There was a tremendous amount of discussion as to whether we could really do that. In all honesty, I think that the industry and environmental factors had no effect on the personnel department. This was what the arguments preceding the incident of the slides were all about".

John continued: "Let me give you another example. The case when we had to suggest specific improvements in the organizational structure of the Personnel Department of our client's company. We decided to develop a list of criteria to evaluate alternative structures such as cost efficiency or speed of delivery of personnel services. But we went through a lot of discussion as to whether we could really develop such criteria. And, assuming we could develop them, were they the best criteria to design an organization structure or were we picking them out of the air? I mean, at one stage there were thirty-three criteria that were being considered before they boiled down to the five we finally used. Some people felt that one criterion, say, cost efficiency, was more important than, say, speed of service delivery. So we had huge discussions about whether that was true or not and why, or whether two other criteria were actually the same and so on".

"What would be the considerations that were used to reduce the list of thirty-three criteria to the final five?", the case writer asked.

John smiled. "Well,. . . . they can be technical or nontechnical. Technical arguments are easily accepted by the group. But if you have only "gut" feeling that a criterion is not important, then you have to use other methods to get your point across".

"Like what?"

"Well, you try to find out who in the group is more receptive to your ideas. Or you argue long enough until they finally give in, since they may think it is a minor point anyway and they can live with it. Or you can try to isolate the opponents to form a coalition".

"Is there any other factor which determines whether you win an argument or not?"

"Oh, yes, there are considerations of individual personalities. For example, sometimes you will find the opinions of a given member of the group are not respected by the rest of the group, for one reason or another. Then, he or she will have a great deal of difficulty seeing his or her arguments accepted. Usually, people have a given perception of an individual's competence, of his or her strengths and weaknesses. It is interesting, however, that in the project groups, which last for several months, you may discover strengths in an individual which at first were not apparent. This explains why there is a consistent flux in the power structure of a project group".

"What do you mean with 'the power structure'?"

"Well, I mean the leadership. Different problems call for different types of competence, from quantitative to judgmental. So, when the problems under discussion change, different people with different types of competence become more influential. This is why there is a constant change in the dynamics of who is leading and who is not leading".

"This means that the leadership changes with the nature of the task?"

"Not only that. It changes with the nature of the person, the mood of an individual in a given day, whether he feels like pushing for some job to be done. It is also a matter of ability to get along with people so that I would think that there are very competent people who find it difficult to work with others. And then, there is the situation in which you can influence a group because you are friendly with other members of the group. You know each other well, talk the same language and generally agree with each other".

"So, the leadership tends to change with time within a group. How was it in your group? Who was the leader at the beginning?"

"I think my group was an unusual group. The initial appointed leader was Paul. But. . . . there was no real leader. It was a group of six strong-willed individuals without anyone attempting to become the leader of the group. It was very egalitarian".

THE REUNION AFTER GRADUATION

One month after graduating Peter, Jan and Paul had a small reunion at the business school. Peter had visited for some time his relatives in the United States and was on his way to start in his new job for a construction company in the Middle East. Jan had started to work for a Danish multinational company in the field of hospital services and was doing work for his company in the town where the business school was located. Paul had remained at the business school to work as a research assistant.

The three of them met with the case writer for an informal conversation and very quickly started talking of their experience with the Pharmaceutical Group.

From the tone of the conversation, it was easy to conclude that they were all quite pleased with the experience. At one point Peter said:

"I know what was good about our group. It had integrity".

"What do you mean?" asked the case writer.

"It is simple. We all respected each other. We listened to each other. We never dismissed out of hand any idea from anyone".

"Also," added Paul, "we made commitments and we stuck to them. It was a matter of reliability. If we said we would be at a meeting or do a specific piece of work, we would be at the meeting, do the work. If we could not, then we would let the rest of the group know it well in advance. It was a must. We would talk to the group, explain our problems, negotiate with them".

"It was not only a question of commitment," said Jan. "There was also the fact that for us group work was good in and of itself. Each one of us subordinated himself to the group. This is why we accepted people like Hans. He accepted the rules of the group. He subordinated himself to the group".

"Hans?" asked the case writer. "He was not a member of your group, the PG group".

"Oh, but I was not talking of the PG group. I was talking of our group".

"Your group? Which group?"

"Well, the group of Peter, Hans, Paul, and myself, Gerard and Juan who met every Sunday from the time of the basic exam until the end of the year, to discuss school problems".

NOTES

[1]In the first part of the year, the evaluation of the students focused in particular on how they contributed to class discussions. Specifically, they were evaluated on three dimensions: "Analytical Qualities", "Relevance" and "Effectiveness of Communication".

[2]The composition of the study groups changed every module.

[3]The basic exam, administered at the end of the fourth module, covered all major subjects taught in the business school. Students failing this exam were required to take a second exam. Failure in this second exam was a serious ground for dismissal.

[4]Gerard was a Swiss student who had been in Peter's study group in the first module.

[5]Hans was a Swiss student and Juan was a student from Columbia. Neither of the two was a member of Peter's study group in the third module.

Step 2: Prepare the case for class discussion.

Step 3: Answer the following questions individually, in small groups, or with the class as a whole, as directed by your instructor:

Description

1. Describe the situation experienced by the Pharmaceutical Group.
2. Describe the major individuals involved.

Diagnosis

3. How did the participants interact?
4. Evaluate the group dynamics. Apply the following conceptual frameworks in your analysis: (a) group formation; (b) group development; (c) goals; (d) norms; (e) roles; (f) structural configuration.
5. Did the group experience perceptual or attributional problems?

6. How did differences in personal and career development influence the participants' performance?
7. Did the group experience problems in motivation? Explain.

Prescription

8. What changes should have been made?

Action

9. What issues should be considered in implementing the prescription?

Step 4: Discussion. In small groups, with the entire class, or in written form, share your answers to the questions above. Then answer the following questions:

1. What symptoms suggest a problem exists?
2. What problems exist in the case?
3. What theories and concepts help explain the problems?
4. How can the problems be corrected?
5. Are the actions likely to be effective?

Activity 5–2: GROUP MEETING AT THE COMMUNITY AGENCY

ADVANCE PREPARATION

Gather role sheets for each character and instructions for observers.

Set up a table in front of the room with five chairs around it, arranged in such a way that participants can talk comfortably and have their faces visible to observers.

Read the following introduction and cast of characters:

INTRODUCTION

The Community Agency is a role-play exercise of a meeting between the chairman of the board of a social service agency and four of his subordinates. Each character's role is designed to recreate the reality of a business meeting. Each character comes to the meeting with a unique perspective on a major problem facing the agency as well as some personal impressions of the other characters developed over several years of business and social associations.

THE CAST OF CHARACTERS

John Cabot, the Chairman, was the principal force behind the formulation of the Community Agency, a multiservice agency. The agency employs 50 people, and during its nineteen years of operations has enjoyed better client relations, a better service record, and a better reputation than other local agencies because of a reputation for high-quality service at a moderate cost to funding agencies. Recently, however, competitors have begun to overtake the Community Agency, resulting in declining contracts. John Cabot is expanding every possible effort to keep his agency comfortably at the top.

Ron Smith, Director of the Agency, reports directly to Cabot. He has held this position since he helped Cabot establish the agency nineteen years ago.

Joan Sweet, Head of Client Services, reports to Smith. She has been with the Agency twelve years, having worked before that for HEW as a contracting officer.

Tom Lynch, Head Community Liaison, reports to Joan Sweet. He came to the Community Agency at Sweet's request, having worked with Sweet previously at HEW.

Jane Cox, Head Case Worker, also works for Joan Sweet. Cox was promoted to this position two years ago. Prior to that time, Jane had gone through a year's training program after receiving an MSW from a large urban university.

TODAY'S MEETING

John Cabot has called the meeting with these four managers in order to solve some problems that have developed in meeting service schedules and contract requirements. Cabot must catch a plane to Washington in half an hour; he has an appointment to negotiate a key contract which means a great deal to the future of the Community Agency. He has only 20 minutes to meet with his managers and still catch the plane. Cabot feels that getting the Washington contract is absolutely crucial to the future of the agency.

Step 1:

1. Five members from the class are selected to roleplay one of the five characters.
2. All other members act as observers.
3. All participants read the introduction and cast of characters.
4. The participants study the roles. All should play their roles without referring to the role sheets.
5. The observers read the instructions for observers.

Step 2:

1. When everyone is ready, John Cabot enters his office, joins the others at the table, and the scene begins.

2. Allow twenty minutes to complete the meeting. The meeting is carried to the point of completion unless an argument develops and no progress is evident after ten or fifteen minutes of conflict.

Step 3: Discussion. In small groups or with the class as a whole answer the following questions:

Description

1. Describe the group's behavior. What did each member say? do?

Diagnosis

2. Evaluate the effectiveness of the group's performance.
3. What effects did such characteristics as group development, goals, roles, norms, and structural configuration have on its effectiveness?
4. Did any problems exist in leadership, power, motivation, communication, or perception?

Prescription

5. How could the group's effectiveness be increased?

Activity 5–3: ACTON-BURNETT, INC., CASE

Step 1: Read the Acton-Burnett, Inc., case.

Bringing Acton-Burnett's June 12 executive committee meeting to a close, Hale Acton, III, chief executive officer and chairman of the board, asked Casey Ryan, vice president of marketing, and John Keene, vice president of corporate planning, to seriously reexamine the company's procedures for forecasting sales. Acton hoped that improved product demand projections would lead to better inventory control, financial planning and factory scheduling. Acton-Burnett had suffered significant losses in the first quarter of 1975 and expected even greater losses in the second quarter (the first losses the company had experienced since 1936). Acton felt that poor forecasting was one of several underlying factors contributing to the firm's current, poor performance.

Ryan and Keene met subsequently with Robert Herd, president and chief operating officer, to briefly discuss his ideas on the subject. The two men then decided to form a task force to investigate the forecasting problem. Ryan and Keene agreed to put David Baker, a recent graduate of Stanford's Graduate School of Business, in charge of the task force. Baker had been with Acton-Burnett for two years and was currently a special assistant to John Keene. Prior to his present assignment, Baker had worked as a financial analyst in Keene's financial planning group, and was now assigned to Keene's market planning group. The assistant to market planning was an intentional move on Keene's part to broaden Baker's exposure to different aspects of Acton-Burnett's business. Baker was regarded by both Keene and Ryan as an especially promising and capable individual.

COMPANY BACKGROUND

Acton-Burnett was the third largest U.S. producer of precious metal alloys and other specialized alloys for commercial and industrial use; its 1974 sales exceeded $400 million. The company was headquartered in Chicago and had four major sales offices and five plants dispersed throughout the United States. Its products included alloys of silver, gold, platinum, and other precious or rare metals. The company sold its alloys in the form of ingots, bars, coil, strip and wire. Most of its raw material was purchased from abroad. Acton-Burnett sold its products to a wide range of customers, including dealers in precious metals, jewelry manufacturers, scientific firms, and industrial companies which used precious metals or special alloys in the manufacture of instruments and other devices.

The company's present difficulties were precipitated by two sets of related events. The first was the 1974–1975 recession which had affected the company's sales to both industrial customers and jewelry manufacturers. The second factor was the rapid escalation which had occurred in the price of gold during the last six months of 1974. During 1974, the U.S. Congress had enacted legislation making it legal for private individuals and institutions to own and sell gold after January 1, 1975. Many industry sources felt that international gold speculators had intentionally driven up the price of gold during late 1974 in anticipation of a rush on gold by private U.S. investors. However, when the "public market" for gold opened in January, the expected demand did not materialize and the price of gold fell rapidly. The combination of the declining price of gold in early 1975 and Acton-Burnett's overly optimistic sales forecasts for the first two quarters of 1975 had resulted in excessive inventories of overvalued gold and sizable losses.

Acton-Burnett's current problems stood in dramatic contrast with the company's recent record of outstanding growth and profitability. The company had been founded by Acton's great-grandfather in 1881 and had always enjoyed a reputation for being a quality supplier of precious metals. However, during Hale Acton, III's ten-year stewardship as chief executive officer, the firm had quadrupled in size and had become the most profitable firm in the industry. Acton attributed this recent success to the company's aggressive marketing efforts and to an infusion of "professionally" trained managers into the company's organization. Under Acton and Herd's direction, the company was the first firm in the precious metals industry to develop a marketing organization in which market managers and product managers were responsible for focusing on specific market segments and applications. (Herd had been vice president of marketing prior to his promotion to president in 1973.)

Despite his family's obvious influence in the company, Acton had "come up through the ranks" and had a solid grounding in the business. Prior to becoming president of the company in 1965, Acton had attended the Advanced Management Program of the Harvard Business School. This experience had convinced him that several ideas he had developed over the years about marketing alloys were feasible, and he returned to Acton-Burnett determined to create a marketing organization and to hire business school–trained managers. In the ten years that followed, Hale Acton had hired a number of MBAs from Harvard, Stanford, Wharton, Columbia, and Dartmouth. It was generally acknowledged that many of these MBAs were received with some resistance from the "old-timers;" although several of them had gained considerable influence and success within the company, including Ryan (a Harvard MBA) and Keene (a Dartmouth MBA), both of whom were now vice presidents.

FORMATION OF THE TASK FORCE

After some discussion, Keene and Ryan concluded that the major area for the task force to study should be the marketing division, because it was the four market managers who made the final forecasts for product demand. The market managers based their forecasts on information they received from their product managers, the vice president of Sales, the vice president of Manufacturing, and the macroeconomic forecasts made by the vice president of Economic Analysis and Forecasting. (See Figure 5–6 for an organization chart of Acton-Burnett.)

Having decided on the task force's mandate, Ryan and Keene met with Baker and described the problem as they saw it. Ryan said that he would appoint three product managers to the task force to represent the marketing division. He suggested that it would not be necessary to involve the market managers (to whom the product managers reported) because they were currently very busy and had been resistant to similar changes in the procedures in the past. Keene, in turn, said that he would ask Vincent Ernst, vice president of Sales, to appoint a representative from Sales to the task force. He also suggested that two others, in addition to Baker, be assigned from Corporate Planning. The first was Cynthia Schrafft, a young Harvard MBA, who Keene felt would add analytic strength to the group; and the second was Jason Cassis, a man in his mid-fifties, who Keene thought would add "balance" because he was an "old-timer" and would be able to relate well to the product managers. Keene also added that he would ask Dr. Walter Hunneuus, vice president of Economic Analysis, to also appoint a representative from his group.

The three men then agreed that the task force would report back to Keene, Ryan and the market managers on August 4. After the August 4 presentation, Keene would arrange for a subsequent presentation to the president and chairman of the board later in the month.

INITIAL MEETING OF THE TASK FORCE

A week after his discussion with Keene and Ryan, Baker had his first meeting with the newly appointed task force. Its members included (in addition to himself, Cynthia Schrafft and Jason Cassis) the three product managers from the marketing division, Steve Eldredge, an economic analyst from Dr. Hunneuus's group, and Ezra Bowe, a special assistant to the vice president of Sales. (Please see Figure 5–7 for the names and positions of the task force members.)

The three product managers were all men in their middle to late forties and were obviously uneasy at the beginning of the meeting. Baker had had few prior contacts with them and did not know them well. By contrast, he knew Cynthia Schrafft and Jason Cassis fairly well because they also worked for Keene in Corporate Planning. Baker had previously worked with Schrafft and had come to admire her analytic ability, quickness, and perceptiveness. Although he had never worked directly with Cassis, he knew that Cassis was widely respected within the company for his competence, knowledge, and thoughtfulness.

Steve Eldredge, the representative from the Economic Analysis and Forecasting Group, was a Wharton MBA and a contemporary of Baker and Schrafft. Baker had once worked with Eldredge on a project before Eldredge had been transferred from Corporate Planning to Dr. Hunneuus's group. Baker had found this experience to be less than satisfying, with he and Eldredge disagreeing over several issues while working together.

Ezra Bowe, the representative from the Sales Division, was in his late fifties and had spent all of his career in sales. His last five years had been as a "trouble shooter," and special assistant to the vice president of Sales. Bowe, like Cassis, was well-liked and widely respected within the company.

The meeting had a slow and awkward beginning, with Ezra Bowe, Cynthia Schrafft, and the three product managers saying almost nothing. In contrast, Steve

Figure 5–6 ACTON-BURNETT, INC., SIMPLIFIED ORGANIZATION CHART

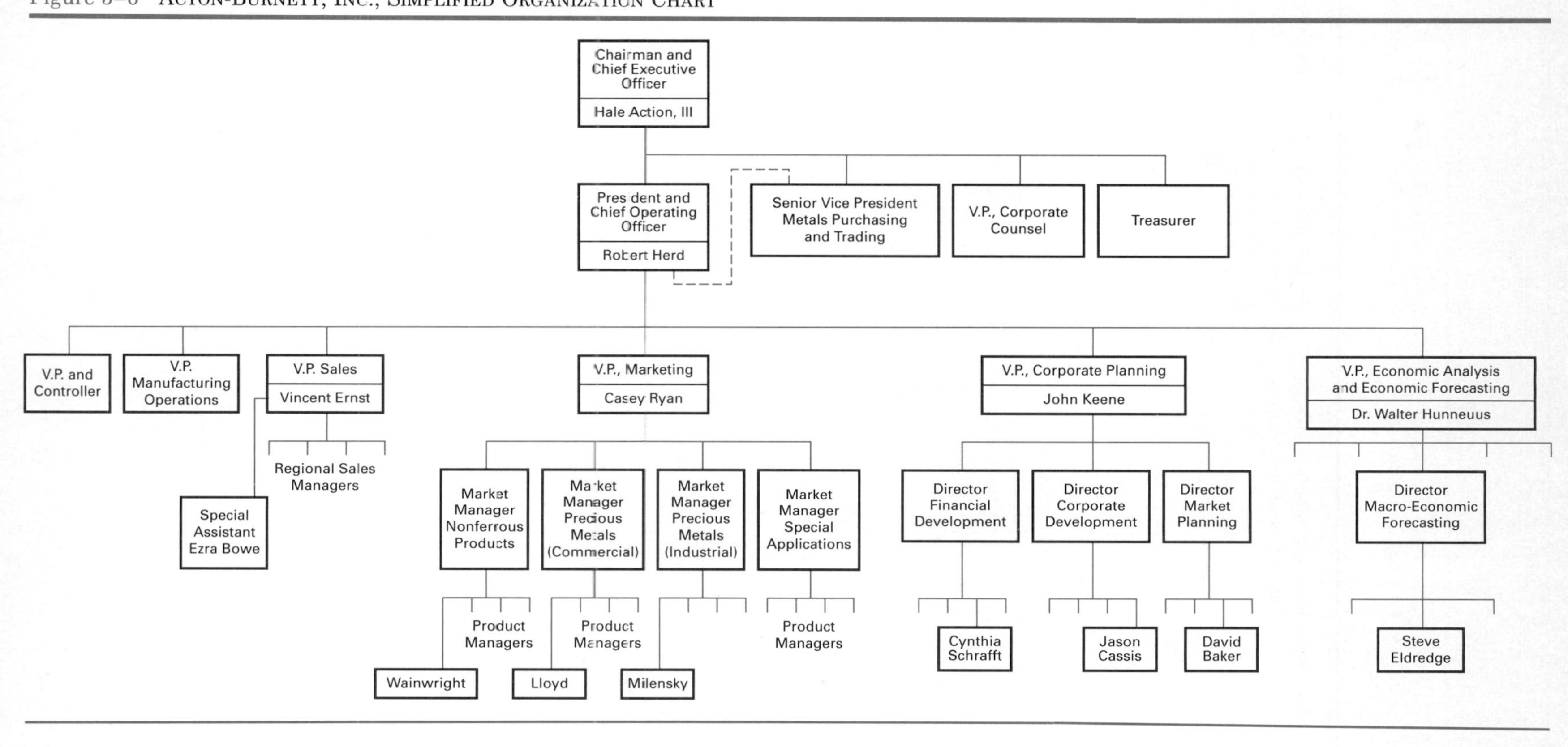

Figure 5–7 ACTON-BURNETT, INC., FORECASTING TASK FORCE

David Baker, 28, Chairman: Marketing Planning Analyst and Assistant to the Vice President of Corporate Planning. (Stanford MBA)

Cynthia Schrafft, 27: Financial Planning Analyst. Representative of Corporate Planning. (Harvard MBA)

Jason Cassis, 54: Corporate Development Specialist. Representative of Corporate Planning. (B.S., Missouri School of Mines, Rolla)

Peter Wainwright, 47: Product manager (Nonferrous Products Market Group). Representative of Marketing Division. (B.S., Wayne State)

Charles Lloyd, 43: Product manager (Precious Metals, Commercial Applications Market Group). Representative of Marketing Division. (B.S., Illinois Institute of Technology)

Charles Milensky, 48: Product manager (Precious Metals, Industrial Applications Market Group). Representative of Marketing Division. (Bronx High School of Science)

Ezra Bowe, 58: Special Assistant to the Vice President of Sales. Representative of the Sales Division. (B.M.S., Massachusetts Maritime Academy)

Stephen Eldredge, 29: Economic analyst. Representative of the Economic Analysis and Economic Forecasting Group. (MBA, Wharton)

Eldredge was quite vocal and emphatic about the need to develop a model for the internal forecasting process. Eldredge argued that it was essential for the task force to identify the basic underlying assumptions upon which the present product demand forecasts were based, and then to make a model of the entire process. Schrafft finally interrupted Eldredge to say that although she agreed a forecasting model might be useful in the future, she thought the creation of such a model should not be the task force's purpose. Rather, it should be one of the recommendations that the task force might make based on what they found. She also added that it was much more difficult to develop a single-firm forecasting model than it was to develop the macroeconomic models which Dr. Hunneuus and his group worked with.

After a long pause, Jason Cassis suggested that the task force divide up its work so that he and the three product managers could concentrate on the Marketing Division and Eldredge could concentrate on gathering whatever "hard data" he felt were necessary for a model. Baker thought that this was a good idea. He then asked Cynthia Schrafft and Ezra Bowe if they would be willing to concentrate on the Sales Division's inputs into the forecast. Schrafft and Bowe exchanged ideas briefly and then agreed to take responsibility for this part of the project. Shortly thereafter, the meeting adjourned, the consensus being that individual subgroups would stay in contact with Baker.

PREPARATION OF THE TASK FORCE REPORT

In the following five weeks, Baker spent much of his time working with Cassis and the three product managers on the Marketing Division's part of the study and with Schrafft and Ezra Bowe on the Sales Division's part. Cassis and the product managers worked well together and Baker found his meetings with them to be enjoyable and, at times, exciting. He also found that he, Schrafft and Bowe enjoyed working together and that the three of them were making considerable progress in identifying how the regional sales managers prepared the sales estimates which they gave to the vice president of Sales (which, in turn, constituted the Sales Division's inputs to the market managers). Eldredge, on the other hand, spent most of his time traveling to the various sales offices gathering data on historic sales trends as well as interviewing all of the product managers in the company headquarters. Baker's exchanges with Eldredge were brief and infrequent and occasionally, strained. Baker suspected that Eldredge resented Baker's more rapid progress within the company. He had also heard through the grapevine that Eldredge's boss, Dr. Hunneuus, was disturbed that he had not been asked by Acton to look at the forecasting problem, or by Keene and Ryan to head the task force. Several of Eldredge's comments reinforced Baker's suspicions, since Eldredge made it clear that the internal product demand forecasting should be done by Hunneuus's group instead of the market managers.

By July 23, Baker felt that the group had made enough progress to report back to Keene, Ryan and the market managers. The next day, he called the task force together to exchange their findings and to discuss a strategy for presenting their recommendations to Ryan and Keene on August 4. All of the task force members attended except Eldredge who was in New York City gathering sales data and could not make the meeting. Cassis and the three product managers were quite enthusiastic about several recommendations that they were sure would improve the quality of the product demand forecasts. Bowe and Schrafft also reported that they had found what they described as "some systematic biases" in the Sales Division's inputs into the forecast. However, they felt that they needed more time before they could make any specific recommendations. They did not think that they could make some "recommendations of a general nature" at the August 4 presentation.

After the meeting ended, Ezra Bowe took Baker aside and explained that the information he had on how the regional managers made their sales estimates was quite sensitive, and that he needed to discuss it with Vincent Ernst, the vice president of Sales, before proceeding further. Bowe said that he would first prepare a report of his findings for only Baker and Schrafft to look at; then, after the three had discussed it, he would take the report to Ernst. He said that he did not yet have all the information necessary and that the report would probably not be ready before the August 4 presentation. He also added that it would take several discussions with Ernst before his findings could be presented to the rest of the task force because he thought his report would place the Sales Division in an embarrassing situation. He expected, however, that once Ernst understood the report and its implications, some significant changes could be made to improve the Sales Division's inputs into the market manager's forecasts. He also felt that Ernst would support these recommendations. Schrafft joined Bowe and Baker partway through their conversation, and she concurred that all of this work could not possibly be completed by August 4. She suggested that their general recommendations be followed up at a later date with more specific recommendations after Bowe had discussed his report with Ernst.

During the following week, Jason Cassis and the product managers spent most of their time preparing for the presentation, while Ezra Bowe worked as rapidly as he could on his report. Cynthia Schrafft, in addition to consulting with Bowe on the report, concentrated on preparing some general recommendations about the Sales Division's input into the forecast.

Baker had spoken with Eldredge as soon as he returned from New York and briefed him on the results of the earlier meeting. Eldredge agreed to outline a proposal for the development of an internal planning model as his part of the August 4 presentation. Eldredge added that gathering his data had been a frustrating experience and that he suspected that the regional sales managers were hiding information from him.

THE AUGUST 4 REPORT OF THE TASK FORCE

Prior to the task force's oral presentation on August 4, Baker, Cassis and the three product managers agreed that Cassis should be the one to report his subgroup's findings and recommendations. The three product managers felt that if they made the presentation it would put them in an awkward position with their bosses, the market managers, because several of their conclusions were critical in nature. Baker agreed with this strategy. He also decided (with the approval of the other members of the task force) on a tentative agenda. The plan was for Baker to begin the oral report with a fifteen-minute summary of the group's purpose, what they saw as the general problems, and their major recommendations. He was to be followed by Eldredge, who would recommend that an internal forecasting model be developed to assist the market managers in making their individual product demand forecasts. Eldredge would also report on the historic sales data and on what he thought were the critical underlying assumptions which would have to be clarified in developing an internal forecasting model. Then, Cassis would report his subgroup's findings on how the Marketing Division should restructure its procedures for making future product demand forecasts. After Cassis's report was completed, Schrafft would present her general recommendations concerning the Sales Division's inputs into the product demand forecasts.

The presentation was scheduled to last from 10:00 A.M. to 1:00 P.M. in Casey Ryan's office. Baker had arrived at his own office at 8:00 A.M. to go over his notes and flip charts. Shortly after 9:00, Ezra Bowe came into Baker's office with a copy of the report he had been working on all week. Bowe had stayed up most of the night typing it himself so that Baker could see it before going into the meeting. Baker skimmed the six summary statements on the first page and was indeed surprised by what they said. It was clear that the regional sales managers were consistently overstating their sales estimates in order to ensure adequate inventory and rapid delivery. He called Schrafft on the telephone and the three decided to discuss Bowe's report the next day, but not to report any of its findings at the presentation.

The presentation began promptly at 10:00 A.M. Everyone seemed very much at ease except for the three product managers. The meeting went smoothly until Eldredge finished his portion of the presentation. Eldredge asked if there were any questions and one of the market managers said he hoped that what the others had to say would be more relevant than Eldredge's recommendations. He added, "You guys in Hunneuus's group can't even forecast what the economy is going to do; how the hell are you going to tell me what our customers are going to do with your models?" The other market managers laughed at this remark, and to save Eldredge further embarrassment, Baker said that Eldredge's recommendations would make more sense after the market managers heard the other reports.

Cassis then presented the report on the Marketing Division's procedures for forecasting product demand and the task force's recommendations on how they should be changed. During Cassis's presentation, the product managers asked him several questions of a clarifying nature which Baker felt were useful in getting certain points across to the market managers. At the conclusion of Cassis's presentation, Lloyd, one of the product managers, said that all three of them felt that the conclusions and recommendations were sound and that they were prepared as individuals to "stand solidly behind them" and take "personal responsibility" for their consequences.

Following this remark, Ryan, the vice president of Marketing, asked his market managers what they thought of Cassis's report. One of them said he thought the recommendations might improve the forecasts, while the other three said that the recommendations could not possibly work. Their comments included such arguments as the recommendations would not allow enough room for necessary subjective factors, and that the new procedures would involve too much red tape. The discussion became quite heated, with most of the questions being addressed to Cassis. Several times, the product managers were cut off by their bosses in their attempts to answer questions or clarify certain points. Finally, one of the market managers said to Cassis, "Jason, frankly, I'm amazed that this kind of nonsense could come from you. I would expect it from a tenderfoot like Baker or Schrafft or Eldredge, but from you? You've been around here long enough to know our business better than to come up with this nonsense." A second market manager added, "Look, I'm just getting things under control again so we won't lose money next quarter. The last thing I need is this garbage." He then turned to Ryan and said, "In no way am I going to swallow this stuff." Ryan began to respond, when Keene interrupted to say that he thought tempers were hot and that the recommendations were not as controversial as they might first appear to be. He suggested that the meeting be adjourned until 3:00 to give everyone a chance to cool off and think things over. Ryan agreed that the suggestion was a good one and the meeting ended at 11:30.

Keene asked Baker to remain after everyone else had left. Keene then closed the door and said to Baker, "We've got one hell of a mess here, and you better figure out what you're going to do at 3:00. In the meantime, Ryan and I will put our heads together and see what we can come up with." Baker picked up his notes and left.

When Baker returned to his own office, he found Eldredge sitting at his desk thumbing through the report that Ezra Bowe had left for him earlier in the morning. Baker explained that the report had been loaned confidentially to Baker for study purposes only, and that Bowe had told him that he had to discuss the report with his boss before presenting it to the full task force. Baker added that none of the report's data would be presented in the afternoon meeting, except in the most general terms. Baker continued by saying that it was important to respect Bowe's wishes and that the report would be shared with the task force when the time was right. Eldredge responded by saying that Bowe's data would certainly have made his own task much easier. He said he had suspected all along that the regional sales managers had been withholding information from him. Eldredge added that he had come by to say that he was angry that he had not received more support from Baker and Schrafft when the market managers had attacked him during the morning meeting. Baker explained his rationale for wanting to move the discussion on to another topic, and that one of his reasons for doing this was to get Eldredge out of the tough spot that he was in. He said he was sorry that Eldredge had interpreted it was a lack of support. Eldredge accepted his apology and left.

A few moments later, Schrafft came in to ask Baker to join her for lunch. The two spent most of their lunch discussing what Baker should do when the meeting reconvened at 3:00. After lunch, Schrafft accompanied Baker back to his office where they found Dr. Hunneuus waiting at Baker's door. Hunneuus said that he wanted some information on two of the points that Bowe had made on the first page of his report. Baker noticed that Hunneuus was holding a piece of yellow-lined paper with Bowe's six major points written on it. Hunneuus stated that he needed this information for a meeting that he had scheduled for 4:00 with Vincent Ernst, the sales vice president (and Bowe's boss), to get "some real progress going on the forecasting problem." Baker replied that it was impossible to give him that data, and that the report was considered confidential. Hunneuus smiled and asked how company information could be thought of as confidential when it was a corporate vice president who was asking for it. Hunneuus left by saying that he would get the information he needed from Ernst himself when they met at 4:00.

Schrafft, who had overheard Baker's exchange with Hunneuus, seemed incredulous at what had transpired. Baker explained that Eldredge had seen the report before lunch and that he had explained its confidentiality to him. Eldredge had presumably understood the situation, although he had not actually said that he would keep it confidential. Schrafft was by now quite angry, and said that if Ezra Bowe was in any way hurt or compromised by this turn of events, that it would be Baker's responsibility. She said that Bowe had taken a personal risk in sharing the information with them and that if Bowe ended up in trouble because of it, Baker's word would not "be worth a plugged nickel" in the future. Baker attempted to again explain what had happened, but Schrafft cut him off by saying, "You've got a problem, man, which you'd better fix in a hurry."

Step 2: Prepare the case for class discussion.

Step 3: Answer the following questions individually, in small groups, or with the class as a whole, as directed by your instructor:

Description

1. Describe the interactions among members of the task force.
2. What occurred at the initial meeting of the task force?
3. How were responsibilities for preparing the task force's report allocated?
4. Why did Schrafft give Baker an ultimatum?

Diagnosis

5. Do members of the task force function as a group?
6. Are they an effective group?
7. Evaluate the group dynamics in the task force. Apply the following conceptual frameworks in your analysis: (a) group formation; (b) group development; (c) goals; (d) norms; (e) roles; (f) structural configuration.
8. Did the task force members experience perceptual or attributional problems?
9. Did the task force members experience problems in motivation? Explain.
10. Did the task force function as a team?

Prescription

11. What changes should be made at Acton-Burnett?

Action

12. What problems will probably result from the implementation of the prescription?

Step 4: Discussion. In small groups, with the entire class, or in written form, share your answers to the questions above. Then answer the following questions:

1. What symptoms suggest a problem exists?
2. What problems exist in the case?
3. What theories and concepts help explain the problems?
4. How can the problems be corrected?
5. Are the actions likely to be effective?

Activity 5–4: PAPER TOWER EXERCISE

Step 1: Your instructor will organize the class into groups of five to eight people.

Step 2: Each group will receive one twelve-inch stack of newspapers and one roll of masking tape. The groups have twenty minutes to plan a paper tower that will be judged on the basis of three criteria: height, stability, and beauty. No physical work is allowed during the planning period.

Step 3: Each group has thirty minutes for the actual construction of the paper tower.

Step 4: Each group should sit near its tower. Your instructor will then direct you to individually examine all the paper towers. Your group must then come to a consensus as to which tower is the winner. A spokesperson from your group should report its decision and the criteria the group used in reaching it.

Step 5: Discussion. In your small groups, answer the following questions:

1. What percent of the plan did each member of your group contribute?
2. Did your group have a leader? Who? How was he or she chosen?
3. Which of the following best describes your role in the planning session: dominator, facilitator, inventor, design engineer, questioner, clarifier, negativist, humorist, artist? Which describes your role in the building session?
4. How did the group generally respond to the ideas that were expressed?
5. List specific behaviors exhibited during the planning and building session that you felt were helpful to the group.
6. List specific behaviors exhibited during the planning and building session that you felt were dysfunctional to the group.

Step 6: Discussion. With the entire class, answer the following questions:

1. How did the groups' behavior differ?
2. What characterized effective groups?
3. How does your knowledge of group dynamics, specifically norms, roles, goals, structure, and decision making, explain your own and other groups' behavior?
4. How could the behavior of the groups be improved?

This exercise is based on "The Paper Tower Exercise: Experiencing Leadership and Group Dynamics" by Phillip L. Hunsaker and Johanna S. Hunsaker, unpublished manuscript. A brief description is included in *Exchange: The Organizational Behavior Teaching Journal* 4(2) (1979): 49.

Activity 5–5: OBSERVATION AND ANALYSIS OF A GROUP'S BEHAVIOR

Step 1: Select a group to observe. Justify that it qualifies as a group.

Step 2: Spend at least five hours observing the group.

Step 3: Describe the group's behavior. Keep a log of your observations.

Step 4: Diagnose the group's behavior.

1. Trace its formation and development.
2. Describe its decision-making processes; evaluate them.
3. Identify its goals, norms, roles, and structural configuration; evaluate them.
4. Diagnose any communication problems.
5. Diagnose any motivation problems.
6. Is leadership effective? Diagnose leadership and power in the group.
7. Diagnose the group's overall effectiveness.

Step 5: Prescribe a plan for improving the group's effectiveness.

Step 6: Discussion. In small groups or with the class as a whole, or in writing, share your observations and analyses. Then consider the following questions:

1. What similarities are there among the groups? what differences? Can you develop profiles of types of groups?
2. What do effective groups look like? What do ineffective groups look like?
3. Trace the formation, development, decision making, and group structure of effective and ineffective groups. Compare and contrast the features of such groups.
4. Identify key elements in plans for increasing group effectiveness.

Activity 5–6: SUPER ED AND THE FOUR HORSEMEN

Step 1: Read the following scenario:

Michelle Gray had been working with Ed, a structural engineer, on a graphics application project which involved both the Computer Department in the Information Technology Division (which she represented) and the Infrastructure Department in the Multi-Cad Division (represented by Ed and his four managers) of a large engineering firm whose fame had been built in the glory days of nuclear power. Although Michelle actually worked for the Information Technology Division, she was temporarily assigned to the Multi-Cad Division. Multi-Cad was a new venture, and one which in her view seemed to have no clear goals, nor development plan. Ed and the four managers (known affectionately as "the Four Horsemen" or "the traveling team") spent more time attending conferences and trolling for new accounts than they did in the office.

Michelle had been frustrated by the lack of effective project management for quite some time, and Ed's decision that she should begin a translation task which she had specifically stated that she was not qualified for nor interested in was her breaking point.

"No!" she raged, "I will not work on that just because you say it is necessary. If you want the task to be a priority, you'll have to make that request through Vic" (her supervisor).

"But you are assigned to support this group, and this is something we need done. Besides, if we have this translator, we'll bring in twice the business, so I don't understand what the problem is," came Ed's somewhat puzzled reply.

Twice nothing is still nothing, Michelle thought to herself. The truth was that she did not want to work on this project at all. She was tired of working on a project that had only sporadic attention paid to it, and even less attention in terms of planning and management. Ed (known as Super-Ed to those in the department because of his somewhat irritating tendency to overuse one particular adjective!) seemed to think that if the team paid attention to this project once a month, an incredible (or to use Ed's word—super!) project would result. Michelle, on the other hand, felt that they should not continue to drag this project out. It was at the point where they should either commit themselves totally, or abandon the project entirely. Either way, an objective look at the entire project was necessary.

Part of the problem with this particular project was that it was done as a joint study with IBM, so the team was dealing primarily with "funny money" which had few limits placed on it. Whenever Ed's group needed a budget to charge time to, this particular project received some attention. A meeting would be called, tasks assigned, and a timetable drawn up. Two weeks later, as Michelle diligently worked on her tasks, everyone else would have flitted off to the latest "hot project." This left her incredibly frustrated since many of her tasks depended upon the completion of other tasks. Her own manager was in a different location, and she often did not see him for days at a time.

In the absence of official management, Ed decided that it was his duty to take charge. The classic "yes man," he constantly assured the team that they would "do well in spite of ourselves," an idea first presented by the first of the four horsemen. Michelle was tired of hearing this phrase, since she believed that they would not do well in spite of themselves, but only because of themselves. She was frustrated not only by this particular project, but by all of her projects with Multi-Cad. The story was always the same—a hit-and-run approach to project management. She was left with a list of tasks to complete and a disappearing project manager to help her complete them. To have Ed come in and drop more tasks on her because "they would bring in all kinds of business" frustrated her even more.

Step 2: Diagnose the situation.

1. What symptoms exist?
2. What problems exist?
3. Is this an effective team?

Step 3: Individually or in small groups, offer a strategy for building this work group into an effective team.

Step 4: Discussion. Share your or your group's plan with the entire class. Decide which approach would be most effective and which would be least effective.

This situation is based on a case prepared by Teresa Marzolf and is used with her permission.

CONCLUDING COMMENTS

Organizational members spend a great deal of time in groups: work teams perform many organizational activities. We can identify three aspects of group process:

1. Informational—giving, analyzing, and integrating information
2. Procedural—giving directions, coordinating activities, and maintaining goal direction
3. Interpersonal—inter-member attraction and attributing personal characteristics.[43]

These features permeate any discussion of group formation and development, norms, roles, goals, and structural configuration.

Observation of groups in the Community Agency and the Paper Tower exercises, and analysis of group behavior in the Pharmaccutical Group and Acton-Burnett, Inc., provide data for describing, diagnosing, and evaluating these and other features of the group process.

Strategies for improving group process and performance are either social, technical, or structural.[44] In Super Ed and the Four Horsemen you proposed such strategies for building an effective team. You may have offered social approaches, which influence the interpersonal processes and encourage new group social norms. Instead you may have proposed technical and procedural interventions, which primarily seek to alter technical skill levels and task-related norms. Finally, you may have offered structural changes, which focus on changing the environment in which groups function.[45] Chapters 12, 13, and 14 detail examples of these approaches.

ENDNOTES

[1]This case was based on one prepared by Barry Borak at the Boston College School of Management.

[2]M.E. Shaw, *Group Dynamics: The Psychology of Small Groups* (New York: McGraw-Hill, 1976), p. 6; C.P. Alderfer, Group and intergroup relations. In J.R. Hackman and J.L. Suttle (eds.), *Improving Life at Work* (Santa Monica, Cal.: Goodyear, 1977).

[3]Alderfer, *op. cit.*

[4]R.W. Napier and M.K. Gershenfeld, *Groups: Theory and Experience* 4th ed. (Boston: Houghton Mifflin, 1989).

[5]R.S. Ross, *Small Groups in Organizations* (Englewood Cliffs, N.J.: Prentice-Hall, 1989).

[6]Napier and Gershenfeld, *op. cit.*

[7]Napier and Gershenfeld, *op. cit.*

[8]N.J. Adler, *International Dimensions of Organizational Behavior* (Boston: Kent, 1986).

[9]B.W. Tuchman, Developmental sequences in small groups, *Psychological Bulletin* 63 (1965): 384–399; N.R.F. Maier, *Problem Solving and Creativity in Individuals and Groups* (Belmont, Cal.: Brooks/Cole, 1970); R.F. Bales and F.L. Strodtbeck, Phases in group problem solving, *Journal of Abnormal and Social Psychology* 46 (1951): 485–495.

[10]Tuchman, *op. cit.;* Maier, *op. cit.;* Bales and Strodtbeck, *op. cit.*

[11]A.C. Kowitz and T.J. Knutson, *Decision Making in Small Groups: The Search for Alternatives* (Boston: Allyn and Bacon, 1980); Tuchman, *op. cit.*

[12]B.W. Tuchman and M.C. Jensen, Stages of small group development revisited, *Group and Organization Studies* 2 (1977): 419–427.

[13]*Ibid.*

[14]C.J.G. Gersick, Time and transition in work teams: Toward a new model of group development, *Academy of Management Journal* 31 (1988): 9–41.

[15]J.P. Wanous, A.E. Reichers, and S.D. Malik, Organizational socialization and group development: Toward an integrative perspective, *Academy of Management Review* 9 (1984): 670–683.

[16]J.P. Wanous, *Organizational Entry: Recruitment, Selection, and Socialization of Newcomers* (Reading, Mass.: Addison-Wesley, 1980).

[17]*Ibid.*

[18]D.C. Feldman, The development and enforcement of group norms, *Academy of Management Review* 9 (1984): 47–53.

[19]J.W. Thibaut and H.H. Kelley, *The Social Psychology of Groups* (New York: Wiley, 1959).

[20]M.E. Shaw, *Group Dynamics* 3d ed. (New York: Harper, 1980).

[21]Feldman, *op. cit.*

[22]Napier and Gershenfeld, *op. cit.*

[23]E.F. Huse, and J.L. Bowditch, *Behavior in Organizations: A Systems Approach* 2d ed. (Reading, Mass.: Addison-Wesley, 1977).

[24]J. Jackson, A conceptual and measurement model for norms and values, *Pacific Sociological Review* 9 (1966): 35–47.

[25]Adler, *op. cit.*

[26]Napier and Gershenfeld, *op. cit.*

[27]A. Zaleznik, C.R. Christensen, and F.J. Roethlisberger, *The Motivation, Productivity, and Satisfaction of Workers* (Boston: Harvard Business School Division of Research, 1958).

[28]K.D. Benne and P. Sheats, Functional roles of group members, *Journal of Social Issues* 4 (1948): 41–49.

[29]I. Dayal and J. Tomas, Operation KPR: Developing a new organization, *Journal of Applied Behavioral Sciences* 4 (1968): 473–506.

[30]See Ross, *op. cit.;* R.R. Ross and M.G. Ross, *Relating and Interacting* (Englewood Cliffs, N.J.: Prentice-Hall, 1982); M.E. Shaw, Communication networks fourteen years later. In *Group Processes,* ed. L. Berkowitz (New York: Academic Press, 1978).

[31]W.G. Dyer, *Team Building: Issues and Alternatives* (Reading, Mass.: Addison-Wesley, 1979).

[32]*Ibid.*

[33]S.D. Van Raalte, Preparing the task force to get good results, *Advanced Management Journal* 47 (Winter 1982): 11–19.

[34]E.H. Schein, *Process Consultation* (Reading, Mass.: Addison-Wesley, 1969).

[35]U. Merry and M.E. Allerhand, *Developing Teams and Organizations: A Practical Handbook for Managers and Consultants* (Reading, Mass.: Addison-Wesley, 1977).

[36]P.R. Harris and R.T. Morgan, *Managing Cultural Differences* (Houston: Gulf, 1987), pp. 174–175.

[37]Merry and Allerhand, *op. cit.*

[38]R. Beckhard, Optimizing team-building effort, *Journal of Contemporary Business* (Summer 1972): 23–32.

[39]Adler, *op. cit.*

[40]J.R. Hackman and C.G. Morris, Improving group performance effectiveness. In *Advances in Experimental Social Psychology* vol. 8, ed. L. Berkowitz (New York: Academic Press, 1975), p. 345.

[41]*Ibid.,* p. 350

[42]G. Corey and M.S. Corey, *Groups: Process and Practice* (Monterey, Cal.: Brooks/Cole, 1979).

[43]Kowitz and Knutsen, *op. cit.*

[44]D.M. Herold, The effectiveness of work groups. In *Organizational Behavior,* ed. S. Kerr (Columbus, Ohio: Grid, 1979).

[45]*Ibid.*

RECOMMENDED READINGS

Barker, L.L., Wahlers, K.J., Watson, K., and Kibler, R.J. *Groups in Process*. Englewood Cliffs, N.J.: Prentice-Hall, 1987.

Forsyth, D.R. *An Introduction to Group Dynamics*. Monterey, Cal.: Brooks/Cole, 1983.

Hackman, J.R. (Ed.) *Groups That Work (And Those That Don't)*. San Francisco: Jossey-Bass, 1989.

Hendrick, C. (Ed.) *Group Processes and Intergroup Relations*. Newbury Park, Cal.: Sage, 1987.

Napier, R.W., and Gershenfeld, M.K. *Groups: Theory and Experience* 4th ed. Boston: Houghton Mifflin, 1989.

Ross, R.S. *Small Groups in Organizational Settings*. Englewood Cliffs, N.J.: Prentice-Hall, 1989.

Varney, G.T. *Building Productive Teams*. San Francisco: Jossey-Bass, 1989.

6

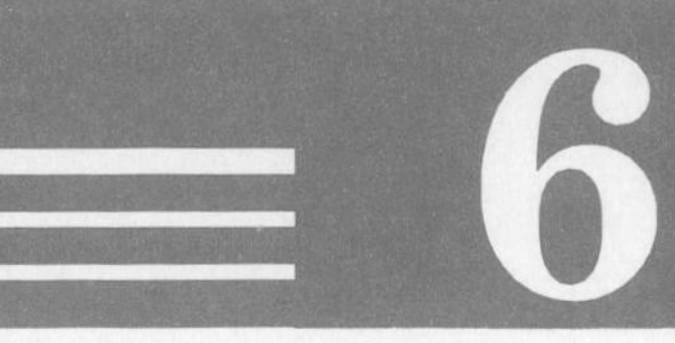

Analyzing and Improving Decision Making

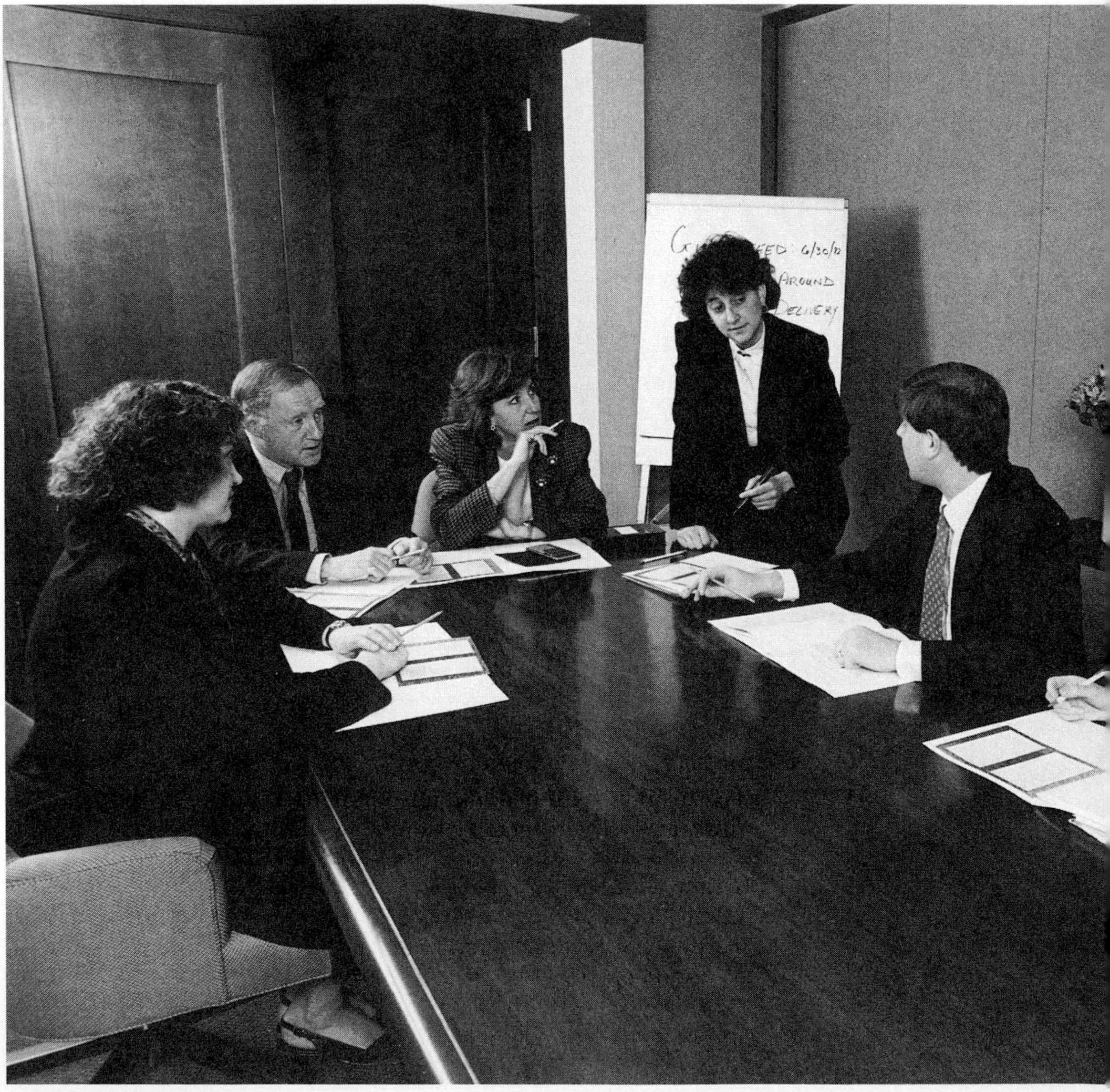

CHAPTER OUTLINE

Deciding Whether to Offer a Concentration in Entrepreneurship

Decisions and the Use of Information
- Programmed and Nonprogrammed Decisions
- Information and Decision Making

Characteristics of Effective Decisions
- Quality of the Decision
- Acceptance of the Decision
- Ethical Decision Making

The Decision-Making Process
- Situational Analysis
- Objective Setting
- Search for Alternatives
- Evaluation of Alternatives
- Making the Decision
- Evaluation of the Decision

Limitations of the Rational Decision-Making Process
- Simon's Bounded Rationality
- "Garbage Can" Model

Individual versus Group Decision Making
- Advantages and Disadvantages of Group Decision Making
- Factors that Affect Selection

Barriers to Decision-Making Effectiveness
- Biases in Selecting Alternatives

Ways to Improve Decision Making
- Brainstorming
- Nominal Group Technique
- Delphi Technique
- Consensus Mapping
- Creative Thinking

SUMMARY
READING
ACTIVITIES
CONCLUDING COMMENTS
ENDNOTES
RECOMMENDED READINGS

LEARNING OBJECTIVES

After completing the reading and activities in Chapter 6, students will be able to

- compare and contrast two types of decisions;
- offer two approaches each for making routine and nonroutine decisions;
- identify and describe the three characteristics of effective decision making and show how a decision meets these characteristics;
- discuss the influence of cultural differences on various steps in the rational process;
- comment on the characteristics of an ethical decision;
- trace the steps in the rational decision-making process;
- contrast the rational process to three alternate decision-making processes;
- assess the merits of individual versus group decision making; and
- offer three strategies for improving individual decision making.

Diane Sanger's first task as the new chairperson of the management department at Wildwood University was to lead her department in determining whether it should offer a concentration in entrepreneurship. While the fifteen faculty members in her department had gathered some information relevant to the decision and had conducted several discussions about the possible new concentration, they had been unable to focus the discussions and thus were unable to make a decision about the direction to take regarding the teaching of entrepreneurship. Diane decided that her priority was to make sure the department reached a good decision—positive or negative—about the introduction of the entrepreneurship major within the next three months. In this way she felt that the department could begin concrete planning for its introduction or turn its attention to other issues.

How should Sanger manage the decision-making process? What steps should she take? What additional information is required? Should she strive for consensus among department members—or should she make the best decision she can, given the available information? What techniques might help her identify and overcome obstacles to decision making?

In this chapter we begin by looking at the types of decisions managers and other organizational members make and the information they use to make them. Next we identify the characteristics of effective decisions and propose a series of steps for making high quality decisions. We then offer several alternate ways of thinking about the decision-making process. In the next section we compare and contrast individual and group decision making, and look at obstacles to decision making in both situations, proposing techniques for overcoming them and making more effective decisions.

DECISIONS AND THE USE OF INFORMATION

Consider the types of decisions made consciously (or unconsciously) by the administrators and faculty at Wildwood University. Diane Sanger, for example, schedules courses, prepares and implements the department budget, finalizes pay raises for the faculty, outlines ways to develop faculty members into better researchers and teachers, initiates new course and program ideas, and oversees hiring and other personnel decisions. Other faculty, as well as Diane Sanger, make course- and research-related decisions: what to cover in a course, how to measure student achievement, which research opportunities to pursue, and how to present research findings, for example. Such decisions can be classified in a variety of ways: managerial–nonmanagerial, work–nonwork, organization–group/individual, policy–one-time, formal–informal, routine–nonroutine, or programmed–nonprogrammed, for example.

Programmed and Nonprogrammed Decisions

In making programmed decisions, individuals devise specific solutions to problems that are substantially structured. Sometimes decisions are programmed because they have been repeatedly tested through past experience; other times they are programmed because the problem and its parameters are clearly defined.

Nonprogrammed decisions are unstructured, sometimes new or unique, and require special treatment. They are often problematic for managers and other organizational members. Such decisions become more common as individuals move up the organization's hierarchy. Because there may be no precedent for making this type of decision, a quality decision-making process (described later in this chapter) is very important.

Decision makers must seek creative ways of making nonprogrammed decisions since they cannot rely on either their own or others' experiences or standard solutions. Making a nonprogrammed decision often requires time, expertise, and creativity since the decision maker is breaking new ground. Sanger and her colleagues' decision about whether to offer a concentration in entrepreneurship is likely a nonroutine and nonprogrammed decision. She and her colleagues may not ever have been involved in deciding whether to offer a new concentration, and there may be no established policies or precedents to guide her thinking. Or the context in which the decision is being made may differ greatly from a situation in which similar decisions were made. Thus managers should recognize when the nature of a decision calls for a more creative decision-making process than they usually use.

Information and Decision Making

Effective decision making requires an individual to secure and use high quality and complete information. Too often, however, individuals tend to use accessible information rather than to continue seeking quality information.[1] Sanger might mistakenly use her subjective impressions of student interest in the major rather than polling students to obtain a more accurate count of potential majors. While using only readily accessible information can save time, it can also contribute to faulty decision making. Thus it is imperative that managers recognize that the quality of information they can readily acquire, such as reports from coworkers, off-hand comments by other employees, or one-time observations of behavior, may be inferior to the information potentially available and actually may not be adequate for the situation.

One way of describing information is to categorize it as basic, elaborating, or performance data,[2] as shown in Figure 6–1. *Basic* data include the list of alternatives from which choices are made and the criteria used to evaluate each alternative. Sanger, for example, must gather information about the department's options for the new concentration, describe several possible future scenarios given the decision, and decide how to assess the quality of each scenario. *Elaborating* data provide more insight into future conditions and criteria for evaluating them. *Performance* data include the likely consequences of various alternatives as well as the constraints that affect them. Sanger, for example, must assess the economic ramifications of offering the concentration versus not offering it, as well as any constraints that affect this action.

If managers and organizational members behaved rationally they would collect sufficient information to allow them to discriminate among alternate choices. Diane Sanger, for example, would collect sufficient information about faculty and student preferences, costs and benefits of new courses, and likely

Figure 6–1 TYPES OF INFORMATION

Basic Data
1. What are the alternatives?
2. What are the future conditions that might be encountered?
3. What are the criteria to be used in evaluating alternatives?

Elaborating Data
1. What are the probabilities of the future conditions?
2. What is the relative importance of the various criteria?

Performance Data
1. What are the payoffs (or costs) associated with various outcomes?
2. What are the constraints on the payoffs or costs?

SOURCE: G. Huber, *Managerial Decision Making* (Glenview, Ill.: Scott, Foresman, 1980), pp. 257–258.

future demand to make an informed decision about whether or not to offer the entrepreneurship concentration. But do individuals actually behave in this way? In fact, individuals vary in their access to information: they draw more easily on information that has caused an emotional reaction, is specific to the given situation, has been received most recently, and is most accessible to them.[3] Even when decision makers gather information they may not use it in decision making. Managers must ensure that they collect reliable and relevant information and allow sufficient time to use the information once they collect it. Recognizing constraints imposed by the nature of the decision and collecting and using quality information contribute to effective decision making.

CHARACTERISTICS OF EFFECTIVE DECISIONS

Effective decisions generally combine high quality decision making with acceptance by the decision makers involved.[4] The ethical appropriateness of a decision also contributes to its effectiveness.

Quality of the Decision

A good quality decision brings about the desired result while meeting relevant criteria and constraints. What would constitute a good-quality decision about the entrepreneurship concentration? Certainly a decision that met the needs of those affected by the decision, such as the faculty or students described in the introductory scenario, would qualify. So too would a decision that meets the financial, human, time, and other constraints existing in the situation. The quality of any decision depends on the level of the decision maker's task-related, interpersonal, and decision-making skills.[5] But a good decision-making *process,* described later in this chapter, also tends to lead to high-quality decisions.

Task-related skills are an individual's knowledge of the particular area in which the decision is being made—the technical aspects of the work operations. In the decision Sanger and her colleagues must make about the entrepreneurship concentration, for example, task skills refer to a knowledge of student demand for the major, faculty preferences and qualifications for staffing the required courses, and the cost of offering the new courses. With regard to other decisions Sanger makes, she must have task skills related to the scheduling process, course assignment procedure, budget specifications, and curriculum. These are her job concerns and her responsibility as a chairperson.

Interpersonal skills relate to the way individuals communicate and exert influence in their relations with others, for both work and nonwork purposes. Diane Sanger, for example, must be able to get her faculty to accept the decision for which she is responsible. Effective communication (described in Chapter 7) should facilitate understanding and acceptance of a decision. The effectiveness of interpersonal skills, and consequently of decision making and communication, depends to some extent on the quality of an individual's perception, attribution, and learning (described in Chapter 2) and on an individual's personality and personal development (discussed in Chapter 3). In addition, the motivational forces at work in a situation (presented in Chapter 4) also play a role.

Decision-making skills are the basic abilities to perform the components of the decision-making process, including situational analysis, objective setting, and generation, evaluation, and selection of alternatives (described later in this chapter).

Acceptance of the Decision

The Management Department must produce a decision that they and the rest of the University can accept, one they are willing to "live with" and use as the basis of further action. For example, approving the new concentration may be a high-quality decision, but the faculty may refuse to teach the new courses that compose it. Alternatively, not offering the concentration may be a high-quality decision, but students may protest the lack of entrepreneurship courses to the dean, or applications to the Management Department by students interested in entrepreneurship may remain low. Lack of acceptance by faculty may have such significant consequences for the organization that a decision to add the concentration may not be viewed as feasible. Or, not offering the concentration may make sense from the viewpoint of the department's task accomplishment, but may reduce the student pool and therefore be unacceptable to the top administration at the university.

Ethical Decision Making

In addition to evaluating a decision in terms of its quality and acceptance, we can also assess how well it meets the criterion of ethical justness. "Ethical issues are ever present in uncertain conditions where multiple stakeholders, interests, and values are in conflict and laws are unclear."[6]

Consider, for example, the situation faced by the senior executive at Beech-nut who learned that a component of the company's apple juice did not meet the standards stated on the label.[7] He was faced with the decision of whether to pull millions of dollars of inventory from store shelves, at a major financial loss to the company, or to ignore the situation. What decision do you think the executive made? Some of his bosses insisted that he neither notify the public about the falsity of the claims of purity nor remove the product from the shelves. The executive reportedly disagreed vehemently with them, telling them their decision was unethical and that he could not support it. Ultimately, the juice was reconstituted.

In a 1976 survey of *Harvard Business Review* readers, almost one-half of the respondents said that managers do not live up to high ethical standards.[8] Similarly, in a 1983 *Wall Street Journal* survey, 225 executives responded that they had been asked to behave unethically.[9]

Managers must recognize, however, that ethical decisions may be dependent on cultural context; whether a decision is ethical may be culturally relevant. What is viewed as unethical behavior—taking bribes, say—in one country may be viewed as ethical in another. How would you act if you believed taking bribes was unethical, but it was common practice in the country where you worked? A decision maker may resolve this dilemma by invoking his or her personal beliefs, or the decision maker may follow the norms of the culture in which the company is located.

A variety of models exist that can help assess what to do in such situations. In any case managers should assess whether their own and others' decisions meet ethical standards before implementing them.

THE DECISION-MAKING PROCESS

The steps in making a decision are key to its effectiveness. A variety of models exist for describing these steps.[10] In this chapter we describe the process as a systematic one, having six steps, as shown in Figure 6–2 and described in Table 6–1: (1) situational analysis, (2) objective and criteria setting, (3) search for alternatives, (4) evaluation of alternatives, (5) making the decision, and (6) evaluation of the decision.[11] Consider the decision that Diane Sanger and her colleagues must make about the new concentration. To ensure the most effective decision, she must systematically perform each of these steps, which are described in the next sections.

Situational Analysis

Decision making first requires asking such questions as, What are the key elements of the situation? What constraints affect the decision? And what resources are available?

In the situation faced by Diane Sanger, what are the key elements, constraints, and resources? The key elements include the performance history of the management department, students' requests for the concentration, and the increased national interest in entrepreneurship. Sanger and her colleagues must also consider previous attempts departments have made to introduce new concentrations. They must also consider their personal feelings and opinions

Figure 6–2 THE BASIC DECISION-MAKING PROCESS

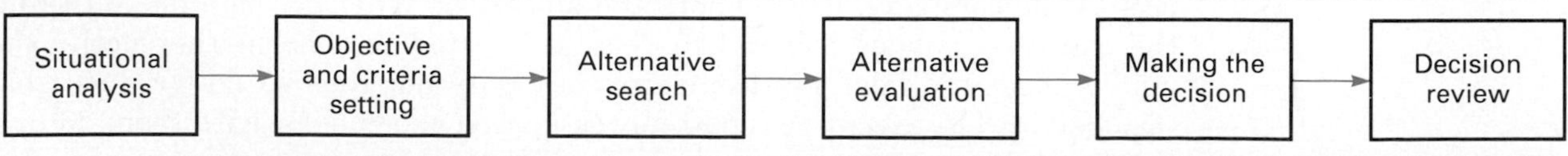

Table 6–1 SAMPLE DIAGNOSTIC QUESTIONS FOR THE SIX-STEP DECISION-MAKING PROCESS

Phase I	Situational Analysis	What are the key elements of the situation? What constraints affect the decision? What resources are available?
Phase II	Objective Setting	Is the problem stated clearly? Do group members understand what they will work on? By what criteria will decision making be judged?
Phase III	Search for Alternatives	Are those individuals most involved in the problem also involved in the decision making? Has complete information been sought? Are information holders involved in the decision making? Is a diversity of means used to generate ideas? Are all ideas encouraged, regardless of their content?
Phase IV	Evaluation of Alternatives	Do participants recognize that the process has switched to evaluation? Are criteria for assessment clearly specified and understood by group members? Are differences of opinion included in the evaluation? Are some alternatives pilot-tested?
Phase V	Making the Decision	Are group members clear that selection is occurring? Are they aware if they are satisficing or optimizing? Are action plans made to fit with the decision? Are group members committed to the decision?
Phase VI	Evaluation of the Decision	Are responsibilities for data collection, analysis, and reporting clearly assigned? Does a comprehensive evaluation plan exist? Does an evaluation schedule exist?

about the concentration. Constraints on the decision include the availability of faculty to teach new courses, the willingness of top administration to increase the department's budget for hiring new faculty and supporting more students, and the likely systemwide effects of introducing a new concentration.

While a lack of resources can act as a constraint on decisions made in this situation, the nature of financial, personnel, and time resources should also act as criteria for selecting among alternatives. If Sanger and her colleagues feel that student demand makes a quick solution to the situation compelling, then a phased introduction of the new concentration over a long period of time is not a feasible solution. Or if the department lacks faculty to staff the concentration and the university has limited funds for hiring more faculty, the financial resources may determine the decision. Or resources such as endowed chairs or special funds may exist that can be transferred to the management department. Consultants may be able to suggest ways around a staffing problem and thus provide assistance in analyzing and acting in this situation.

From this kind of situational analysis, the decision maker begins to formulate the issues to be addressed. Clearly, in the situation at Wildwood University, the issues focus on dealing with student demand for entrepreneurship studies.

Objective Setting

In this step, the decision maker identifies the goals and objectives that the decision must accomplish and specifies the criteria that are to be used to assess its quality, acceptance, and ethicality. For example, Sanger might focus on the objective of getting faculty approval for the new concentration, first in her department and then in the university. Or she might set a goal of offering one new entrepreneurship course during each of the next five years. A corporate president might set a goal of increasing overall program enrollment by 10 percent. A marketing specialist might set a goal of reducing advertising costs by $10,000 without decreasing its effectiveness. The accomplishment of these and similarly-set goals serves as one measure of the effectiveness of the decision and the decision process.

Often decision makers err at this step by confusing action plans with objectives. Decision makers must first set their goals and then determine ways of accomplishing them. For example, hiring new faculty is a way of accomplishing the goal of one new entrepreneurship course per year. Such hiring is not a goal itself but a means to a goal.

Whenever possible, decision makers should establish objectives that specify observable and measurable results.[12] Certainly reducing turnover, absenteeism, and costs, or increasing profits or productivity, by specified percentages or amounts, are objectives that are observable and measurable. Introducing new courses or securing faculty approval for a new concentration are also observable and measurable. However, objectives related to employee attitudes such as satisfaction, commitment, or involvement may be more difficult to measure and observe. Similarly, expressing objectives related to the effectiveness of work processes, employee performance, or personnel practices in observable and measurable ways may require skillful crafting by the decision maker, consistent with scientific standards of validity.

Criteria for assessing the decision about the new concentration might be its cost, ease of implementation, degree of acceptance by faculty, impact on enrollments, and so on. Criteria should also be measurable.

Search for Alternatives

In this step the decision maker specifies many realistic and potentially acceptable alternate solutions to the problem, or ways of meeting the objectives specified earlier. What alternatives are available to Diane Sanger and her department? They can approve the immediate introduction of the new concentration, support a phased-in introduction, sanction one or two new courses, or reject the new concentration completely. This step requires creativity and perseverance by the decision maker to develop a complete set of possibilities. Techniques for improving the generation of alternatives are described later in this chapter.

Managers and other organizational members must recognize that decision makers may not be able to generate a good set of alternatives.[13] Researchers on the subject have found that decision makers consider new alternatives only if they improve on, even to a small or marginal degree, known alternatives.

A culture's underlying values may also affect the type of alternatives they select. We might hypothesize, for example, that European countries may rely on historical patterns as the source of alternatives while more future-oriented cultures, such as Israel, may generate more new, untested alternatives.[14]

Evaluation of Alternatives

Here the decision maker appraises each alternative generated. Criteria for evaluation include such considerations as feasibility, cost, and reliability. In addition, the decision maker must assess the risk—or the likelihood of certain outcomes—involved in each alternative. These represent, however, only a subset of the criteria that can be used in evaluating the alternatives Sanger and her colleagues face. Are there other criteria that might be relevant in this situation? In Table 6–2 we see an evaluation of four alternatives Sanger and her colleagues might select to deal with the requests for more entrepreneurship courses. We can see that they likely differ in cost, feasibility, possible adverse consequences, and probability of success in resolving the issue.

Quantifying the alternatives can systematize their evaluation and dramatize differences among them, and may improve the quality of decision making. For example, we might score each of these four alternatives on their feasibility, cost, potentially adverse consequences, and probability of success. Summing the scores for each alternative then would allow us to rank-order them and ultimately select the highest ranked one. This process assumes that the criteria are equally weighted, that the numerical values are exact, and that ranks alone are sufficient to determine the best choice. More sophisticated statistical techniques can also be used for such an evaluation. In the situation faced by

Table 6–2 EVALUATION OF FOUR ALTERNATIVES OPEN TO DIANE SANGER

	Selected Decision Criteria			
Alternative	Cost (in $)	Feasibility	Likelihood of Adverse Consequences	Relative Probability of Success in Solving Problem
Offer the new concentration immediately	High	Moderate	Moderate	High
Phase in the new concentration over 5 years	Moderate	Moderate	Low	High
Offer two new entrepreneurship courses	Moderate	High	Low	Moderate
Change nothing	Low	Moderate	High	Low

Sanger, what alternative would you give the highest (most favorable) score? the lowest (least favorable) score? Obviously this approach to quantifying the evaluation of alternatives is highly subjective because the decision maker's rating of each criterion is incorporated into the overall evaluation.

Making the Decision

Ideally a decision maker should select the optimal or best alternative. Is there an optimal alternative for dealing with the situation at Wildwood University? Each of the alternatives listed in Table 6–2 has disadvantages as well as advantages, suggesting that no single decision is free from negative consequences. If the cost criterion outweighs all others, then "change nothing" would be the best decision. If a moderate cost is acceptable and low likelihood of adverse consequences is important, then phasing in the new concentration over five years or offering two new entrepreneurship courses would be the best decision. Offering the new concentration immediately offers no advantage over the phasing-in alternative.

Note that speed of and responsibility for decision making are also culturally based.[15] The United States tends to be characterized by relatively rapid decision making, whereas many Middle Eastern cultures, such as Egypt, downplay time urgency. Responsibility for decisions may rest on the individual, as in the United States, or with a group, as in Japan. Factors considered irrelevant in the United States, such as face saving, can be crucial in the decision processes of Oriental groups. Decision making also varies among cultures in the level of the hierarchy at which decisions are typically made. For example, Swedish workers are more comfortable with decentralized decision making than are Indian or French employees; and in Africa, middle managers rarely delegate authority.[16]

Evaluation of the Decision

Review of any decision is an essential step in effective decision making. Too often selecting an alternative and reaching a decision comprise the final step. Individuals must pause and recheck their decisions and the process that led to them as a way of increasing their decision-making effectiveness. In other words, once Sanger determines how to handle the situation she faces, she must review the steps that led to her decision. Where possible, she might check her thinking with another person. Together, they should also evaluate the implementation of the decision by assessing its outcomes. They can then compare the outcomes to the objectives set earlier, to see if they are met. Evaluation done prior to implementation is part of decision making. Evaluation performed after implementation is part of management control and may call for corrective action and follow-up.

In reviewing the quality of the decision-making process, decision makers and other organizational members should check that the key elements of the situation, as well as the constraints on and resources for the decision making, are specified. Objective setting should occur next, and it should result in a clearly stated problem and criteria for success, clearly communicated. An active search for alternatives, often using diverse idea-generation techniques, should follow. Evaluation of the alternatives means assuring that criteria for assessing them have been formulated and are systematically applied. Making the decision should include securing commitment to it and formulating an action plan.

LIMITATIONS OF THE RATIONAL DECISION-MAKING PROCESS

Some researchers have argued that the decision-making process described above does not adequately consider the complexity and ambiguity of organizational life. In this section we present some alternate models from the array available, each highlighting specific difficulties with the process presented. Managers and other organizational members might choose to modify some aspects of their decision-making process based on these alternate models.

Simon's Bounded Rationality

Herbert Simon, a Nobel prize winner, describes a three-step decision process.[17] In the first step, the decision maker searches the environment for conditions that call for a decision. Sanger operates at this *intelligence* stage when she listens to reports from faculty colleagues, analyzes her department's course offerings, and generally monitors the workplace. In the second step, the decision maker *designs* possible solutions to the problem. Thus Sanger and her colleagues must develop and analyze possible courses of action. Finally, the decision maker must make a *choice* among the available alternatives. Here Simon believes the decision maker will *satisfice,* or sacrifice the optimal solution for one that is satisfactory or "good enough." In selecting a site for a new manufacturing plant, for example, a corporate executive may determine that no perfect site exists, in which case he or she would choose a site that is satisfactory or "good enough."

This model directs the manager or other decision maker to regularly scan the environment for information, creatively formulate alternatives, and recognize that in some cases a less-than-optimal decision may be required. This approach places greater emphasis on the creative generation of reasonable alternatives, and less on the evaluation of alternatives to identify an optimal one, than the basic decision-making model. It also emphasizes the limitations of the basic model. In particular, finding the best alternative may be unrealistic, due to conflicting aspects of a situation such as constituencies with opposing objectives or the time and cost required to identify it. Increasingly, satisficing is an appropriate and effective decision-making strategy.

In a related model, called Decision Making by Objection, decision makers do not seek an optimal solution to a problem, but a course of action that has a low probability of making matters worse.[18] The decision makers first produce a rough description of an acceptable resolution of the situation. Then they propose a course of action, accompanied by a description of the positive outcomes of the action. When there is an objection to the alternative, more constraints are identified that further delimit the problem and more sharply define an acceptable resolution. A different course of action is then proposed.

This approach creates a series of courses of action, each one creating fewer objections than the previous one. Managers or decision makers can use this approach particularly to expedite the standard decision-making process. Thus Diane Sanger might choose to focus on a single course of action, such as getting a concentration in entrepreneurship approved, and decide whether it is acceptable rather than trying to identify the best of the alternatives for meeting student needs. However, while this approach may expedite decision making, it may also prevent a complete examination of feasible alternatives and result in premature selection of a marginally acceptable one.

"Garbage Can" Model

In contrast to the basic decision-making process discussed earlier, this model emphasizes the unsystematic quality of much real decision making in organizations.[19] In an organization with unclear goals, uncertain means of achieving them, and changing participants in decision making, a diverse set of problems, solutions, and participants are all present simultaneously. Sometimes decisions fit an available solution to an available problem in a way that resolves the problem, removing both the problem and solution from further consideration. The researchers note that this matching often occurs somewhat at random and use the image of a garbage can to reflect how problems and solutions may be mixed together. For example, if the university administration receives a special endowment to fund an entrepreneurship concentration, it resolves Sanger's problem about the new major immediately.

More commonly, individuals make decisions by oversight or flight. When participants focus their attention on significant problems, they often find that they can make a decision about a new, less significant problem quickly, without having to consider its appropriateness in depth. Similarly, solving the new problem may unintentionally result in a solution to the original problem. In trying to decide how to handle the problem of the new concentration, Sanger may be faced with a problem of meeting new university staffing guidelines that increase the number of courses some of her department's faculty must teach. She may decide to have faculty with low student credit-hours teach one additional course in entrepreneurship to resolve the deficiency, thus resolving the decision about the new concentration simultaneously.

This model suggests that decision makers should not overlook the potential value of serendipitous decisions even while applying the basic decision-making process described above. Reading 6–1, "Making Management Decisions: The Role of Emotion and Intuition," considers additional approaches to decision making.

INDIVIDUAL VERSUS GROUP DECISION MAKING

The decision-making process described so far can apply to decisions made by either individuals or groups. But group decision making brings different resources to a situation than does individual decision making, so wherever possible managers and others should choose the most appropriate forum for decision making.

Advantages and Disadvantages of Group Decision Making

When a group makes a decision, the involvement of more than one individual brings additional knowledge and skills to the decision; this tends to result in higher quality decisions.[20] A synergy occurs that causes the group decision to be better than the sum of the individual decisions. As any group becomes more diverse, attitudinally, behaviorally, and culturally, this advantage increases. "Cultural diversity provides the biggest asset for teams with difficult, discretionary tasks requiring innovation. Diversity becomes least helpful when working on simple tasks involving repetitive and routine procedures."[21] In addition, when individuals are involved in making a decision they generally become committed to it; consequently use of group decision making expedites its acceptance on both an individual and group basis. Thus involving the Management Department in the decision about the new concentration should increase its acceptance and hence members' commitment to the project. This in turn should help gain its acceptance throughout the university.

Time Required Group decision making generally takes more time than decision making by individuals. The exchange of information among many individuals, as well as the effort spent on obtaining consensus, is time consuming. Sometimes, to reach a decision more quickly or to reach a decision all group members can accept, groups satisfice rather than optimize, that is, they select a satisfactory but not the best solution. How would a satisfactory decision differ from an optimal one made by the Management faculty? A satisfactory decision might resolve the most important issues related to introducing the new concentration, while an optimal decision would resolve all the problems associated with its introduction.

Riskiness of Decisions Early research suggested that groups tend to make riskier decisions.[22] More recent research suggests that this *risky-shift* phenomenon is actually a *polarization* phenomenon: groups become more extreme in the direction of the initial predominant view.[23] Because no single person shoulders the consequences of a decision made by a group, individuals may feel less accountable and therefore accept more risky or extreme solutions.

Recognizing Expertise Groups may ignore individual expertise, opting instead for group consensus. Particularly as a member of a group of peers, an individual may be reluctant to discriminate among individuals on the basis of their expertise. Strong personality types and high-status members may dominate the discussion, causing less assertive and lower-status group members to go along with them.[24] Groups then may develop *groupthink*, a mode of thinking with a norm of concurrence-seeking behavior[25] (described in the next section). But when group members choose a colleague's solution that they consider to be good, the resulting decision equals the quality of a decision obtained by group decision making and is no riskier than a group decision.[26] The effectiveness of such a best-member strategy depends on the probability of the group's selecting the real best member and the potential for subjectivity in the solution.[27]

Groupthink Irving Janis first identified groupthink as a factor that influenced the misguided Bay of Pigs invasion in 1962.[28] The symptoms of groupthink arise when members of decision-making groups try to avoid being too critical in their judgments of other members' ideas and focus too heavily on developing concurrence. It occurs most frequently in highly cohesive groups, particularly in stressful situations. It is less common in multicultural groups because of the inherently different perspectives. Janis identifies eight symptoms of groupthink, as listed in Table 6–3.

Group members experiencing groupthink may feel invulnerable to criticism and hence believe that any action they take or decision they make will be positively received. They may also ignore external criticism, choosing instead to rationalize their actions or decisions as optimum. Some group members may also pressure other group members to agree with the group's decision; deviant opinions are either ignored or not tolerated, and members can neither question views nor offer disconfirming information. Recent research posits, however, that groupthink alone does not explain decision fiascoes. It does not incorporate the tendency of groups to exaggerate the value, relevance, and perceived quality of members' initial decision,[29] which underlies the tendency of groups to make riskier decisions. Still, when faced with pressure, groups of executives likely procrastinate, "pass the buck," or support other members' rationalizations about an appropriate decision.[30] How likely is the Management Department faculty to experience groupthink? Although we do not have sufficient data to make such a determination, critical evaluation of various options is essential to avoiding it.

Table 6–4 is a summary of the advantages and disadvantages of group decision making. By making a decision as a group, the Management Department faculty brings diverse knowledge and skills to the decision and should reach a higher quality and accepted decision.

Table 6–3 SYMPTOMS OF GROUPTHINK

Invulnerability	Members feel they are safe and protected from dangers, ostracism, or ineffective action.
Rationale	Members ignore warnings by rationalizing their own or others' behavior.
Morality	Members believe their actions are inherently moral and ethical.
Stereotypes	Members view opponents as truly evil or stupid and thus unworthy of or incompetent at negotiations around differences in beliefs or positions.
Pressure	Members pressure all individuals in the group to conform to the group's decision; they allow no questioning or arguing of alternatives.
Self-censorship	Members do not express any questions about the group's decision.
Unanimity	Members perceive that everyone in the group has the same view.
Mindguards	Members may keep adverse information from other members that might ruin their perceptions of consensus and the effective decision.

Based on I. Janis, Groupthink, *Psychology Today*, June, 1971.

Table 6–4 ADVANTAGES AND DISADVANTAGES OF GROUP DECISION MAKING

Advantages	Disadvantages
Brings multiple knowledge and skills to the decision	Requires more time
Expedites acceptance by the group	Ignores individual expertise, at times
Generally results in higher quality decisions	Satisfices even when better decision is possible
Increases commitment to decisions	Encourages riskier decisions
	Creates possibility of groupthink

Factors That Affect Selection

Six factors affect whether an individual or group decision-making process should be used (see Table 6–5). They are:

1. The *type of problem or task* to be solved. Individual decision making results in greater creativity, as well as efficiency, if policy dictates the correct solution; group decision making is superior when a task or problem requires a variety of expertise. Groups frequently produce better decisions if problems have multiple parts that can be addressed by a division of labor. Groups also tend to perform better than the average performance of individual members on problems that require estimates to be made. Such problems draw on diverse expertise to more precisely pinpoint the estimates. In contrast, individual decision making tends to lead to more effective decisions for problems that require completion of a series of complex stages, so long as the individual receives input from many sources.[31] Individual decision making here allows a better coordination of the phases in solving a problem.

Table 6–5 COMPARISON OF INDIVIDUAL AND GROUP DECISION MAKING

Factor	Individual	Group
Type of problem or task	when creativity or efficiency is desired	when diverse knowledge and skills are required
Acceptance of decision	when acceptance is not important	when acceptance by group members is valued
Quality of the solution	when "best member" can be identified	when several group members can improve the solution
Characteristics of individuals	when individuals cannot collaborate	when group members have experience working together
Climate of the decision making	when the climate is competitive	when the climate is supportive of group problem solving
Amount of time available	when relatively little time is available	when relatively more time is available

2. The necessity of *acceptance* of the decision for its implementation. Group decision making more often leads to acceptance than does decision making by individuals.
3. The importance of the *quality of the solution*. Group decision making generally leads to higher quality solutions, unless an individual has expertise in the decision area and this is identified in advance of the process.
4. The *personalities and capabilities* of the people involved in the decision. Some individuals have difficulty collaborating in a group setting; also, groups can ignore individual expertise.
5. The *climate* and *culture* of the decision making. Supportive climates (see Chapter 7) encourage group problem solving; competitive climates stimulate individual responses. In countries other than the United States, where group-oriented behavior is more valued and rewarded, group decision making occurs more frequently than decision making by individuals.[32]
6. The amount of *time available*. Group decision making takes much more time than individual decision making.

Consider again the Management faculty at Wildwood University. Should they make the decision about the entrepreneurship concentration by consensus? Using the six points described above, we can evaluate the decision process as follows:

1. The main decision the team members must make is to determine whether and how to introduce a new concentration. This type of problem requires some efficiency, diverse knowledge and skills, and perhaps a little creativity. For this reason, group decision making, with direction by a leader, would be appropriate.
2. Acceptance of the decision about the new concentration is moderately important since acceptance by the group can influence its acceptance by the rest of the organization, which can facilitate or hinder its implementation. Therefore, decision making by the group should prevail.
3. The quality of the solution is important, and the diverse expertise of team members should maximize it. Thus all should participate.
4. The case provides little information about the personalities and capabilities of the team members. We have no reason to assume that department members could not collaborate or would ignore individual expertise.
5. Likewise the case provides little information about the climate and culture in Wildwood University. In general, academicians are comfortable with group problem solving.
6. The department has no specified deadline by which they must decide on introducing the new concentration. The time frame seems appropriate for group decision making.

In conclusion, we would predict that group decision making by the Management faculty would be most appropriate. Group participation may also help reduce any stress related to the decision.[33]

BARRIERS TO DECISION-MAKING EFFECTIVENESS

Blocks to decision-making effectiveness include lack of clarity in stating the problem; not getting the needed information; premature testing of alternate strategies; premature choice of a particular alternative; a critical, evaluative, competitive decision-making climate that precludes systematic, well-reasoned decisions; pressures for conformity; lack of inquiry and problem-solving skills; and inadequate personal motivation to reach a quality and accepted decision.[34] Which of these exists in the management department?

Sanger, for example, may not recognize that inadequate faculty workload is a problem; she may instead limit her attention to the merits of the new concentration. Sanger's information may also be limited: she may rely too much on information from subordinates. If she uses this limited information, she may restrict her alternatives to two: supporting or rejecting the entrepreneurship concentration, excluding from consideration any alternatives related to the introduction of courses not configured into a major. Sanger and her colleagues should analyze her environment to determine the pressures and constraints it places on decision making. They should also evaluate their own motivation to reach a quality decision, risk-proneness, and problem-solving skills. This assessment may suggest the need for others outside the department to become involved in the decision making.

Biases in Selecting Alternatives

The variety of backgrounds and experiences of individuals and groups are both resources in decision making and sources of bias. Individuals frequently estimate probabilities incorrectly when making decisions. Such misestimations occur as a result of perceptual distortions, misattributions, and faulty learning, as described in Chapter 2. Research by Daniel Kahneman and Amos Tversky has highlighted why individuals make such mistakes.[35] Individuals overestimate the likelihood of an event if they can easily recall instances of it; such easy availability of "information" results in systematic bias in estimating overall frequencies. Thus a manager may overestimate the likelihood of a staff cutback rather than an expansion if he or she has only experienced the former. Individuals also tend to overestimate the likelihood of disasters and underestimate the probability of more common events.[36]

Individuals also incorrectly value the size of a sample of observations: they give as much or more credence to small samples as to larger, more representative ones. They might consider the rate of performance problems in a group of ten bookkeepers more representative of the organization than that in a group of fifty-five data entry clerks, when in fact the reverse is true.

Still others ignore the base rate, or the historical rate at which certain events occur. They assume, for example, that if no manager has been promoted in the last year, but five have been promoted for each of the previous ten years, that management promotions are very rare.

The same problem framed in different ways can result in different conclusions. Individuals are more risk averse when seeking gains, but risk prone when avoiding losses, even if the probability of both is identical. We also assume that we know more about uncertain events than we do, further biasing our evaluation of alternatives.

WAYS TO IMPROVE DECISION MAKING

How can barriers be overcome and decision making be more effective? Five techniques can improve the quality of information exchanged by group members in decision making and facilitate effective interpersonal interactions. In this section we examine brainstorming, the nominal group technique, the delphi technique, consensus mapping, and creative thinking.

Brainstorming

Groups use this technique when creativity is needed to generate many alternatives for consideration in decision making. In using brainstorming, individuals or group members list as many alternatives as possible without simultaneously evaluating the feasibility of any alternative. One person typically records all the ideas on a large, visible board or a piece of newsprint. For example, the Management faculty might use brainstorming to list all the ways of meeting the demand for entrepreneurship education. The absence of evaluation encourages group members to generate rather than defend ideas. Then, after ideas have been generated, they are evaluated and decisions are made.

Although brainstorming is useful for many types of decisions, it is most effective for simple, well-defined problems.[37] It encourages enthusiasm and a competitive spirit among group members in generating ideas; it prevents group members from feeling hopeless regarding the range of possibilities in a given situation.[38] While brainstorming can result in many shallow and useless ideas, it can push members to offer novel ideas as well.

Nominal Group Technique

This structured group meeting, often referred to as NGT, helps resolve differences in group opinion by having individuals generate and then rank order a series of ideas in the problem-exploration, alternative-generation, or choice-making stages of group decision making,[39] as described in Figure 6–3. Its advantage is that it allows individuals an equal opportunity to contribute to the decision making. First a group of individuals is presented with a stated problem. Each person individually offers several solutions in writing. The group then shares the solutions and lists them on a blackboard or large piece of paper, as in brainstorming. Next the group discusses and clarifies the ideas. They then rank and vote their preference for the various ideas. If the group does not reach agreement at this point, they repeat the ranking and voting procedures until they gain some consensus.[40]

The Management faculty might use this technique. The size of the group and the diverse expertise of its members might maximize its usefulness—it would encourage each member to individually think about and offer ideas on the content of the proposal. This technique would also direct group discussion and move the group toward resolution of the problem by systematically focusing on top-ranked ideas and eliminating less valued ones. It should encourage creativity by allowing extensive individual input into the process. Strong personality types less often dominate a group because of the opportunity for systematic input by all group members. NGT also encourages extensive exploration of the issues, builds in a forum for the expression of minority

Figure 6–3 STEPS IN NOMINAL GROUPING

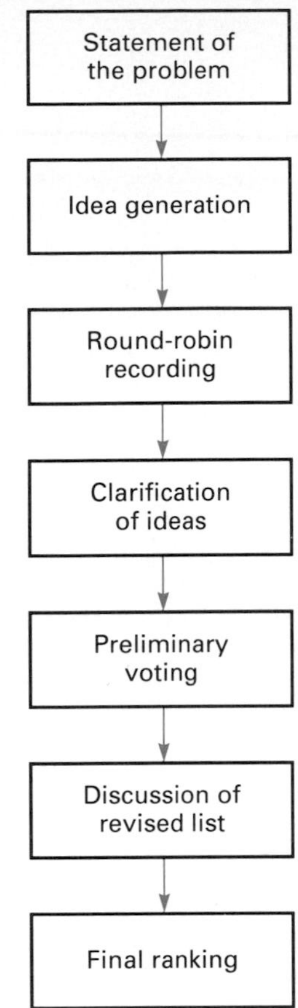

viewpoints, gives individuals some time to think about the issues before offering solutions, and provides a mechanism for reaching a decision expediently through the ranking–voting procedure.[41]

Delphi Technique

"Delphi may be characterized as a method for structuring a group communication process so that the process is effective in allowing a group of individuals, as a whole, to deal with a complex problem."[42] In the conventional delphi, shown in Figure 6–4, a small group designs a questionnaire that is completed by a larger respondent group. The results are then tabulated and used in developing a revised questionnaire which is again completed by the larger group. Thus the results of the original polling are fed back to the respondent group to use in subsequent responses. This procedure is repeated until the issues are narrowed, responses are focused, or consensus is reached. In another format, a computer summarizes the results and thus replaces the small group. Basically, the delphi has four phases: (1) exploration of the subject by individuals; (2) reaching understanding of the group's view of the issues; (3) sharing and evaluation of any reasons for differences; and (4) final evaluation of all information.[43]

Figure 6–4 STEPS IN THE DELPHI TECHNIQUE

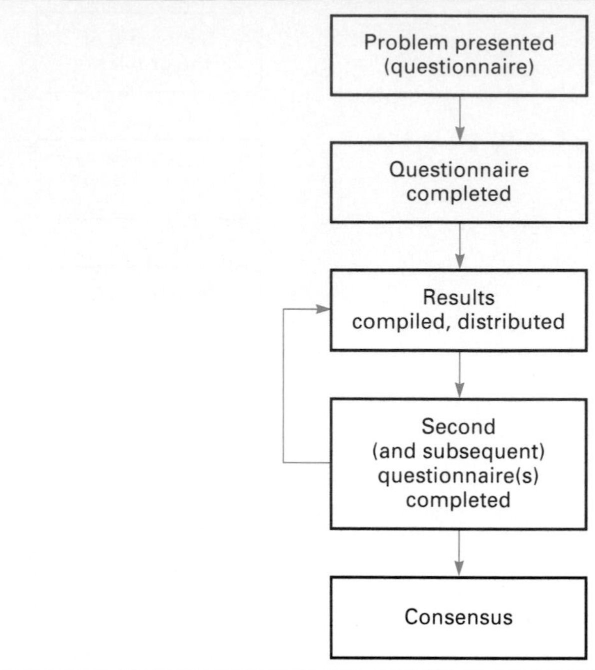

Delphi is very useful in a variety of circumstances.[44] First, if decision makers cannot apply precise analytical techniques to solving a problem but prefer to use subjective judgments on a collective basis, delphi can provide input from a large number of respondents. Second, if the individuals involved have failed to communicate effectively in the past, the delphi procedures offer a systematic method for ensuring that their opinions are presented. Third, the delphi does not require face-to-face interaction and thus succeeds when the group is too large for such a direct exchange. Fourth, when time and cost prevent frequent group meetings or when extensive premeeting communication between group members increases the efficiency of those meetings held, the delphi technique offers significant value for decision making. Fifth, the delphi can overcome hurdles where individuals disagree significantly or where the anonymity of views must be maintained to protect group members. Finally, the delphi technique reduces the likelihood of groupthink: it prevents one or more members from dominating by numbers or strength of personality.

Consensus Mapping

This technique begins after a task group has developed, clarified, and evaluated a list of ideas. It includes the following steps.[45] First, a person acting as a facilitator encourages participants to search for clusters and categories of listed ideas. This search for structure includes the listing and discussion of alternative clusters and categories by the entire group or subgroups and then production of a single classification scheme by group members working as a group, or in pairs or trios. Then the facilitator consolidates the different schemes developed by subgroups into a representative scheme which acts as a "strawman map" for the entire group. Group members next work to revise the strawman into a mutually acceptable solution. When there is more than one task group, a representative from each presents its revised map to other task groups' members. Finally, representatives from each of the task groups work to produce a single, consolidated map or solution.

Since this technique works best for consolidating results from several task forces or project groups, its use by the Management faculty probably would be limited. The top administration of Wildwood University could use the technique if they assigned several groups the task of developing a way of meeting the interest in entrepreneurship education. In general, this technique works best with complex problems that are multidimensional and have interconnected elements and many sequential steps.[46]

Creative Thinking

Creativity in decision making is concerned with changing usual patterns of thinking. In creative thinking, also called lateral thinking, individuals try to restructure a pattern to reassemble it in a new way and thus view a problem differently.[47] New patterns should be sought when old patterns are outdated or need improvement. Such thinking should avoid evaluation of alternatives and focus instead on their generation.

Creative thinking requires the suspension of judgment about the correctness of an alternative.[48] Individuals can delay judgment about the relevance of information to the decision being considered or the validity of an idea. Doing this allows ideas to survive longer and spawn other ideas. It also motivates other people to offer ideas they normally would reject and again stimulates new ideas. It may also result in the development of a new, more useful frame of reference for assessing the ideas.

Individuals can use a variety of techniques to encourage their creative thinking. First, they can use alternate thinking languages, such as by expressing a problem in mathematical terms rather than verbal language, or by using visual models rather than verbal expressions. We might suggest that Sanger express her alternatives graphically, in the form of a decision tree, for example. Second, decision makers can develop a questioning attitude as a way of gaining additional information. Third, they can also make lists as a way of increasing their ability to process the information gained.

Fourth, as suggested in Chapter 2, creative decision makers repeatedly challenge their assumptions. For example, Sanger or any of her colleagues might repeatedly ask the question "Why?" about each bit of information she gathers. Or other individuals or group members might take a devil's-advocate approach to the evaluation of alternatives and final choice of solutions to a problem. Creating analogies, reversing situations, and breaking down alternatives into their component parts also foster more creative decision making. These techniques and those described above reduce the perceptual, emotional, cultural, environmental, intellectual, and expressive blocks that hinder effective decision making.[49]

SUMMARY

Decision making is a basic process in organizational behavior. In this chapter we described the nature of the decision to be made and the information used to make it by faculty in the Management Department at Wildwood University.

Figure 6–5 DIAGNOSTIC DECISION-MAKING QUESTIONS

- What type of decision is being made?
- What types of information have been collected for making the decision?
- Do organizational members make high quality, accepted, ethical decisions?
- Do the decision makers follow the basic process of decision making?
- Do ways of dealing with the limitations of the process exist?
- Is the group appropriately involved in decision making?
- What barriers are there to effective decision making?
- What techniques can be used to overcome these barriers?

We noted that to make such decisions effectively individuals must have task skills, interpersonal skills, and decision-making skills. We outlined a basic decision-making process that helps improve the quality of decisions and encourages their acceptance by others. Decision makers must systematically analyze the situation, set objectives, generate, evaluate, and select alternatives, make the decision, and then evaluate the decision made. We also identified some alternatives to this rational process: Simon's concept of bounded rationality and the "garbage can" model of decision making.

The chapter next compared decision making by individuals and groups. The advantages and disadvantages of group decision making were presented, followed by factors that should affect the extent of involvement. We next identified some barriers to effective decision making and concluded by offering ways to overcome these barriers. Answering the questions in Figure 6–5 for each problem that arises should help increase the effectiveness of decision making by managers and other organizational members.

READING

Reading 6–1: MAKING MANAGEMENT DECISIONS: THE ROLE OF INTUITION AND EMOTION

Herbert A. Simon

The work of a manager includes making decisions (or participating in their making), communicating them to others, and monitoring how they are carried out. Managers must know a great deal about the industry and social environment in which they work and the decision-making process itself to make decisions well. Over the past 40 years, the technique of decision making has been greatly advanced by the development of a wide range of tools—in particular, the tools of operations research and management science, and the technology of expert systems.

But these advances have not applied to the entire domain of decision making. They have had their greatest impact on decision making that is well-structured, deliberative, and quantitative; they have had less impact on decision making that is loosely structured, intuitive, and qualitative; and they have had the least impact on face-to-face interactions between a manager and his or her coworkers—the give and take of everyday work.

In this article, I will discuss these two relatively neglected types of decision making: "intuitive" decision making and decision making that involves interpersonal interaction. What, if anything, do we know about how judgmental and intuitive processes work and how they can be made to work better? And why do managers often fail to do what they know they should do—even what they have decided to do? What can be done to bring action into closer accord with intention?

My article will therefore have the form of a diptych, with one half devoted to each of these topics. First, I will discuss judgmental and intuitive decision making; then I will turn to the subject of the manager's behavior and the influence of emotions on that behavior.

Sometimes the term rational (or logical) is applied to decision making that is consciously analytic, the term nonrational to decision making that is intuitive and judgmental, and the term irrational to decision making and behavior that responds to the emotions or that deviates from action chosen "rationally." We will be concerned, then, with the nonrational and the irrational components of managerial decision making and behavior. Our task, you might say, is to discover the reason that underlies unreason.

INTUITION AND JUDGMENT

As an appendix to the *Functions of the Executive* (Harvard University Press, 1938), Chester I. Barnard published an essay, based on a talk he had given in 1936 at Princeton, entitled "Mind in Everyday Affairs."[1] The central motif of that essay was a contrast between what Barnard called "logical" and "nonlogical" processes for making decisions. He speaks of "the wide divergence of opinion . . . as to what constitutes a proper intellectual basis for opinion or deliberate action." And he continues:

> By "logical processes" I mean conscious thinking which could be expressed in words or by other symbols, that is, reasoning. By "non-logical processes" I mean those not capable of being expressed in words or as reasoning, which are only made known by a judgment, decision or action.

Barnard's thesis was that executives, as contrasted, say, with scientists, do not often enjoy the luxury of making their decisions on the basis of orderly rational analysis, but depend largely on intuitive or judgmental responses to decision-demanding situations.

Although Barnard did not provide a set of formal criteria for distinguishing between logical and judgmental decision making, he did provide a phenomenological characterization of the two styles that make them easily recognizable, at least in their more extreme forms. In logical decision making, goals and alternatives are made explicit, the consequences of pursuing different alternatives are calculated, and these consequences are evaluated in terms of how close they are to the goals.

In judgmental decision making, the response to the need for a decision is usually rapid, too rapid to allow for an orderly sequential analysis of the situation, and the decision maker cannot usually give a veridical account of either the process by which the decision was reached or the grounds for judging it correct. Nevertheless, decision makers may have great confidence in the correctness of their intuitive decisions and are likely to attribute their ability to make them rapidly to their experience.

Most executives probably find Barnard's account of their decision processes persuasive; it captures their own feelings of how processes work. On the other hand, some students of management, especially those whose goal is to improve management-decision processes, have felt less comfortable with it. It appears to vindicate snap judgments and to cast doubt on the relevance of management-science tools, which almost all involve deliberation and calculation in decision making.

Barnard did not regard the nonlogical processes of decision as magical in any sense. On the contrary, he felt they were grounded in knowledge and experience:

> The sources of these non-logical processes lie in physiological conditions or factors, or in the physical and social environment, mostly impressed upon us unconsciously or without conscious effort on our part. They also consist of the mass of facts, patterns, concepts, techniques, abstractions, and generally what we call formal knowledge or beliefs, which are impressed upon our minds more or less by conscious effort and study. This second source of non-logical mental processes greatly increase with directed experience, study and education. (p. 302)

At the time I wrote *Administrative Behavior* (1941–42), I was troubled by Barnard's account of intuitive judgment (see the footnote on p. 51 of *AB*), largely, I think, because he left no clues as to what subconscious processes go on while judgments are being made.[2] I was wholly persuaded, however, that a theory of decision making had to give an account of both conscious and subconscious processes (see the end of p. 75 to the top of p. 76). I finessed the issue by assuming that both the conscious and the unconscious parts of the process were the same, that they involve drawing on factual premises and value premises, and operating on them to form conclusions that became the decisions.

Because I used logic (drawing conclusions from premises) as a central metaphor to describe the decision-making process, many readers of *Administrative Behavior* have concluded that the theory advanced there applies only to "logical" decision making, not to decisions that involve intuition and judgment. That was certainly not my intent. But now, after nearly 50 years, the ambiguity can be resolved because we have acquired a solid understanding of what the judgmental and intuitive processes are. I will take up the new evidence in a moment; but first, a word must be said about the "two brains" hypothesis, which argues that rational and intuitive processes are so different that they are carried out in different parts of the brain.

Split Brains and Forms of Thought

Physiological research on "split brains"—brains in which the corpus callosum, which connects the two hemispheres of the cerebrum, has been severed—has provided encouragement to the idea of two qualitatively different kinds of decision making—the analytical, corresponding to Barnard's "logical," and the intuitive or creative, corresponding to his "non-logical." The primary evidence behind this dichotomy is that the two hemispheres exhibit a division of labor: in right-handed people, the right hemisphere plays a special role in the recognition of visual patterns, and the left hemisphere in analytical processes and the use of language.

Other evidence in addition to the split-brain research suggests some measure of hemispheric specialization. Electrical activity in the intact brain can be measured by EEG techniques. Activity in a brain hemisphere is generally associated with partial or total suppression in the hemisphere of the alpha system, a salient brain wave with a frequency of about ten vibrations per second. When a hemisphere is inactive, the alpha rhythm in that hemisphere becomes strong. For most right-handed subjects, when the brain is engaged in a task involving recognition of visual pattern, the alpha rhythm is relatively stronger in the left than in the right hemisphere; with more analytical tasks, the alpha rhythm is relatively stronger in the right hemisphere. (See Doktor and Hamilton, 1973, and Doktor, 1975, for some experiments and a review of the evidence.[3])

The more romantic versions of the split-brain doctrine extrapolate this evidence into the two polar forms of thought labeled above as analytical and creative. As an easy next step, evaluative nuances creep into the discussion. The opposite of "creative," after all, is "pedestrian." The analytical left hemisphere, so this story goes, carries on the humdrum, practical, everyday work of the brain, while the creative right hemisphere is responsible for those flights of imagination that produce great music, great literature, great art, great science, and great management. The evidence for this romantic extrapolation does not derive from the physiological research. As I indicated above, that research has provided evidence only for some measure of specialization between the hemispheres. It does not in any way imply that either hemisphere (especially the right hemisphere) is capable of problem solving, decision making, or discovery independent of the other. The real evidence for two different forms of thought is essentially that on which Barnard relied: the observation that, in everyday affairs, men and women often make competent judgments or reach reasonable decisions rapidly—without evidence indicating that they have engaged in systematic reasoning, and without their being able to report the thought processes that took them to their conclusion.

There is also some evidence for the very plausible hypothesis that some people, confronted with a particular problem, make more use of intuitive processes in solving it, while other people make relatively more use of analytical processes (Doktor, 1978).[3]

For our purposes, it is the differences in behavior, and not the differences in the hemispheres, that are important. Reference to the two hemispheres is a red herring that can only impede our understanding of intuitive, "non-logical" thought. The important questions for us are "What is intuition?" and "How is it accomplished?" not "In which cubic centimeters of the brain tissue does it take place?"

New Evidence on the Processes of Intuition

In the 50 years since Barnard talked about the mind in everyday affairs, we have learned a great deal about the processes human beings use to solve problems, to make decisions, and even to create works of art and science. Some of this new knowledge has been gained in the psychological laboratory; some has been gained through observation of the behavior of people who are demonstrably creative in some realm of human endeavor; and a great deal has been gained through the use of the modern digital computer to model human thought processes and perform problem-solving and decision-making functions at expert levels.

I should like to examine this body of research, which falls under the labels of "cognitive science" and "artificial intelligence," to see what light it casts on intuitive, judgmental decision making in management. We will see that a rather detailed account can be given of the processes that underlie judgment, even though most of these processes are not within the conscious awareness of the actor using them.

THE EXPERT'S INTUITION

In recent years, the disciplines of cognitive science and artificial intelligence have devoted a great deal of attention to the nature of expert problem solving and decision making in professional-level tasks. The goal of the cognitive science research has been to gain an understanding of the differences between the behavior of experts and motives, and possibly to learn more about how novices can become experts. The goal of the artificial intelligence research has been to build computer systems that can perform professional tasks as competently as human experts can. Both lines of research have greatly deepened our understanding of expertise.[4]

Intuition in Chessplaying

One much studied class of experts is the grandmasters in the game of chess. Chess is usually believed to require a high level of intellect, and grandmasters are normally full-time professionals who have devoted many years to acquiring their mastery of the game. From a research standpoint, the advantage of the game is that the level of skill of players can be calibrated accurately from their official ratings, based on their tournament success.

From the standpoint of studying intuitive thinking, chess might seem (at least to outsiders) an unpromising research domain. Chessplaying is thought to involve a highly analytical approach, with players working out systematically the consequences of moves and counter-moves, so that a single move may take as much as a half hour's thought, or more. On the other hand, chess professionals can play simultaneous games, sometimes against as many as 50 opponents, and exhibit only a moderately lower level of skill than in games playing under tournament conditions. In simultaneous play, the professional takes much less than a minute, often only a few seconds, for each move. There is no time for careful analysis.

When we ask the grandmaster or master how he or she is able to find good moves under these circumstances, we get the same answer that we get from other professionals who are questioned about rapid decisions: It is done by "intuition," by applying one's professional "judgment" to the situation. A few seconds' glance at the position suggests a good move, although the player has no awareness of how the judgment was evoked.

Even under tournament conditions, good moves usually come to a player's mind after only a few seconds' consideration of the board. The remainder of the analysis time is generally spent verifying that a move appearing plausible does not have a hidden weakness. We encounter this same kind of behavior in other professional domains where intuitive judgments are usually subjected to tests of various kinds before they are actually implemented. The main exceptions are situations where the decision has to be made before a deadline or almost instantly. Of course we know that under these circumstances (as in professional chess when the allowed time is nearly exhausted), mistakes are sometimes made.

How do we account for the judgment or intuition that allows the chess grandmaster usually to find good moves in a few seconds? A good deal of the answer can be derived from an experiment that is easily repeated. First, present a grandmaster and a novice with a position from an actual, but unfamiliar, chess game (with about 25 pieces on the board). After five or ten seconds, remove the board and pieces and ask the subjects to reproduce it. The grandmaster will usually reconstruct the whole position correctly, and on average will place 23 or 24 pieces on their correct squares. The novice will only be able to replace, on average, about 6 pieces.

It might seem that we are witnessing remarkable skill in visual imagery and visual memory, but we can easily dismiss that possibility by carrying out a second experiment. The conditions are exactly the same as in the first experiment, except that now the 25 pieces are placed on the board at random. The novice can still replace about 6 pieces and the grandmaster—about 6! The difference between them in the first experiment does not lie in the grandmaster's eyes or imagery, but in his knowledge, acquired by long experience, of the kinds of patterns and clusters of pieces that occur on chessboards in the course of games. For the expert, such a chess board is not an arrangement of 25 pieces but an arrangement of a half dozen familiar patterns, recognizable old friends. On the random board there are no such patterns, only the 25 individual pieces in an unfamiliar arrangement.

The grandmaster's memory holds more than a set of patterns. Associated with each pattern in his or her memory is information about the significance of that pattern—what dangers it holds, and what offensive or defensive moves it suggests. Recognizing the pattern brings to the grandmaster's mind at once moves that may be appropriate to the situation. It is this recognition that enables the professional to play very strong chess at a rapid rate. Previous learning that has stored the patterns and the information associated with them in memory makes this performance possible. This, then, is the secret of the grandmaster's intuition or judgment.

Estimates have been made, in a variety of ways, of the number of familiar patterns (which psychologists now call chunks) that the master or grandmaster must be able to recognize. These estimates fall in the neighborhood of 50,000, give or take a factor of two. Is this a large number? Perhaps not. The natural language vocabularies of college graduates have been estimated to be in the range of 50,000 to 200,000 words, nearly the same range as the chess expert's vocabularies of patterns of pieces. Moreover, when we recognize a word, we also get access to information in our memories about the meaning of the word and to other information associated with it as well. So our ability to speak and understand language has the same intuitive or judgmental flavor as the grandmaster's ability to play chess rapidly.

Intuition in Computerized Expert Systems

A growing body of evidence from artificial intelligence research indicates that expert computer systems, capable of matching human performance in some limited domain, can be built by storing in computer memory tens of thousands of *productions*. Productions are computer instructions that take the form of "if-then" pairs. The "if" is a set of conditions or patterns to be recognized; the "then" is a body of information associated with the "if" and evoked from memory whenever the pattern is recognized in the current situation.

Some of our best data about this organization of expert knowledge come from the areas of medical diagnosis. Systems like CADUCEUS and MYCIN consist of a large number of such if-then pairs, together with an inference machine of modest powers. These systems are capable of medical diagnosis at a competent clinical level within their respective limited domains. Their recognition capabilities, the if-then pairs, represent their intuitive or judgmental ability; their inferencing powers represent their analytical ability.

Medical diagnosis is just one of a number of domains for which expert systems have been built. For many years, electric motors, generators, and transformers have been designed by expert systems developed by large electrical manufacturers. These computer programs have taken over from professional engineers many standards and relatively routine design tasks. They imitate fairly closely the rule-of-thumb procedures that human designers have used, the result of a large stock of theoretical and practical information about electrical machinery. Recognition also plays a large role in these systems. For example, examination of the customer's specifications "reminds" the program of a particular class of devices, which is then used as the basis for the design. Parameters for the design are then selected to meet the performance requirements of the device.

In chemistry, reaction paths for synthesizing organic molecules can be designed by expert systems. In these systems, the process appears relatively analytic, for it is guided by reasoning in the form of means-ends analyses, which work backward from the desired molecule, via a sequence of reactions, to available raw materials. But the reasoning scheme depends on a large store of knowledge of chemical reactions and the ability of the system to recognize rapidly that a particular substance can be obtained as the output of one or more familiar reactions. Thus, these chemical synthesis programs employ the same kind of mixture of intuition and analysis that is used in the other expert systems, and by human experts as well.

Other examples of expert systems can be cited, and all of them exhibit reasoning or analytic processes combined with processes for accessing knowledge banks with the help of recognition cues. This appears to be a universal scheme for the organization of expert systems—and of expert human problem solving as well.

Notice that there is nothing "irrational" about intuitive or judgmental reasoning based on productions. The conditions in a production constitute a set of premises. Whenever these conditions are satisfied, the production draws the appropriate conclusion—it evokes from memory information implied by these conditions or even initiates motor responses. A person learning to drive a car may notice a red light, be aware that a red light calls for a stop, and be aware that stopping requires applying the brakes. For an experienced driver, the sight of the red light simply evokes the application of brakes. How conscious the actor is of the process inversely, how automatic the response is, may differ, but there is no difference in the logic being applied.

Intuition in Management

Some direct evidence also suggests that the intuitive skills of managers depend on the same kinds of mechanisms as the intuitive skills of chessmasters or physicians. It would be surprising if it were otherwise. The experienced manager, too, has in his or her memory a large amount of knowledge, gained from training and experience and organized in terms of recognizable chunks and associated information.

Marius J. Bouwman has constructed a computer program capable of detecting company problems from an examination of accounting statements.[5] The program was modeled on detailed thinking-aloud protocols of experienced financial analysts interpreting such statements, and it captures the knowledge that enables analysts to spot problems intuitively, usually at a very rapid rate. When a comparison is made between the responses of the program and the responses of an expert human financial analyst, a close match is usually found.

In another study, R. Bhaskar gathered thinking-aloud protocols from business school students and experienced businessmen, who were all asked to analyze a business policy case.[6] The final analyses produced by the students and the businessmen were quite similar. What most sharply discriminated between the novices and the experts was the time required to identify the key features of the case. This was done very rapidly, with the usual appearances of intuition, by the experts; it was done slowly, with much conscious and explicit analysis, by the novices.

These two pieces of research are just drops of water in a large bucket that needs filling. The description, in detail, of the use of judgmental and analytical processes in expert problem solving and decision making deserves a high priority in the agenda of management research.

Can Judgment Be Improved?

From this and other research on expert problem solving and decision making, we can draw two main conclusions. *First,* experts often arrive at problem diagnoses and solutions rapidly and intuitively without being able to report how they attained the result. *Second,* this ability is best explained by postulating a recognition and retrieval process that employs a large number—generally tens of thousands or even hundreds of thousands—of chunks or patterns stored in long term memory.

When the problems to be solved are more than trivial, the recognition processes have to be organized in a coherent way and they must be supplied with reasoning capabilities that allow inferences to be drawn from the information retrieved, and numerous chunks of information to be combined. Hence intuition is not a process that operates independently of analysis; rather, the two processes are essential complementary components of effective decision-making systems. When the expert is solving a difficult problem or making a complex decision, much conscious deliberation may be involved. But each conscious step may itself constitute a considerable leap, with a whole sequence of automated productions building the bridge from the premises to the conclusions. Hence the expert appears to take giant intuitive steps in reasoning, as compared with the tiny steps of the novice.

It is doubtful that we will find two types of managers (at least, of good managers), one of whom relies almost exclusively on intuition, the other on analytic techniques. More likely, we will find a continuum of decision-making styles involving an intimate combination of the two kinds of skill. We will likely also find that the nature of the problem to be solved will be a principal determinant of the mix.

With our growing understanding of the organization of judgmental and intuitive processes, of the specific knowledge that is required to perform particular judgmental tasks, and of the cues that evoke such knowledge in situations in which it is relevant, we have a powerful new tool for improving expert judgment. We can specify the knowledge and the recognition capabilities that experts in a domain need to acquire as a basis for designing appropriate learning procedures.

We can also, in more and more situations, design expert systems capable of automating the expertise, or alternatively, of providing the human decision maker with an expert consultant. Increasingly, we will see decision aids for managers that will be highly interactive, with both knowledge and intelligence being shared between the human and the automated components of the system.

A vast research and development task of extracting and cataloging the knowledge and cues used by experts in different kinds of managerial tasks lies ahead. Much has been learned in the past few years about how to do this. More needs to be learned about how to update and improve the knowledge sources of expert systems as new knowledge becomes available.

Progress will be most rapid with expert systems that have a substantial technical component. It is no accident that the earliest expert systems were built for such tasks as designing motors, making medical diagnoses, playing chess, and finding chemical synthesis paths. In the area of management, the analysis of company financial statements is a domain where some progress has been made in constructing expert systems. The areas of corporate policy and strategy are excellent candidates for early development of such systems.

What about the aspects of executive work that involve the managing of people? What help can we expect in improving this crucial component of the management task?

KNOWLEDGE AND BEHAVIOR

What managers know they should do—whether by analysis or intuitively—is very often different from what they actually do. A common failure of managers, which all of us have observed, is the postponement of difficult decisions. What is it that makes decisions difficult and hence tends to cause postponement? Often, the problem is that all of the alternatives have undesired consequences. When people have to choose the lesser of two evils, they do not simply behave like Bayesian statisticians, weighing the bad against the worse in the light of their respective possibilities. Instead, they avoid the decision, searching for alternatives that do not have negative outcomes. If such alternatives are not available, they are likely to continue to postpone making a choice. A choice between undesirables is a dilemma, something to be avoided or evaded.

Often, uncertainty is the source of the difficulty. Each choice may have a good outcome under one set of environmental contingencies, but a bad outcome under another. When this occurs, we also do not usually observe Bayesian behavior; the situation is again treated as a dilemma.

The bad consequences of a manager's decision are often bad for other people. Managers sometimes have to dismiss employees or, even more frequently, have to speak to them about unsatisfactory work. Dealing with such matters face to face is stressful to many, perhaps most, executives. The stress is magnified if the employee is a close associate or friend. If the unpleasant task cannot be delegated, it may be postponed.

The manager who has made a mistake (that is to say, all of us at one time or another) also finds himself or herself in a stressful situation. The matter must be dealt with sooner or later, but why not later instead of sooner? Moreover, when it is addressed, it can be approached in different ways. A manager may try to avoid blame—"It wasn't my fault!" A different way is to propose a remedy to the situation. I know of no systematic data on how often the one or the other course is taken, but most of us could probably agree that blame-avoiding behavior is far more common than problem-solving behavior after a serious error has been made.

The Consequences of Stress

What all of these decision-making situations have in common is stress, a powerful force that can divert behavior from the urgings of reason. They are examples of a much broader class of situations in which managers frequently behave in clearly nonproductive ways. Nonproductive responses are especially common when actions have to be made under time pressure. The need to allay feelings of guilt, anxiety, and embarrassment may lead to behavior that produces temporary personal comfort at the expense of bad long-run consequences for the organization.

Behavior of this kind is "intuitive" in the sense that it represents response without careful analysis and calculation. Lying, for example, is much more often the result of panic than of Machiavellian scheming. The intuition of the emotion-driven manager is very different from the intuition of the expert whom we discussed earlier. The latter's behavior is the product of learning and experience, and is largely adaptive; the former's behavior is a response to more primitive urges, and is more often than not inappropriate. We must not confuse the "nonrational" decisions of the experts—the decisions that derive from expert intuition and judgment—with the irrational decisions that stressful emotions may produce.

I have made no attempt here to produce a comprehensive taxonomy of the pathologies of organizational decision making, but simply have given some examples of the ways that stress interacts with cognition to elicit counterproductive behavior. Such responses can become so habitual for individuals or even for organizations that they represent a recognizable managerial "style."

Organizational psychologists have a great deal to say about ways of motivating workers and executives to direct their efforts toward organizational goals. They have said less about ways of molding habits so that executives can handle situations in a goal-directed manner. When it comes to handling situations, two dimensions of behavior deserve particular attention: the response to problems that arise, and the initiation of activity that looks to the future.

Responding to Problems

The response of an organization to a problem or difficulty, whether it results from a mistake or some other cause, is generally one that looks both backward and forward. It looks backward to establish responsibility for the difficulty and to diagnose it, and forward to find a course of action to deal with it.

The backward look is an essential part of the organization's reward system. The actions that have led to difficulties, and the people responsible for those actions, need to be identified. But the backward look can also be a source of serious pathologies. Anticipation of it—particularly anticipation that it will be acted on in a punitive way—is a major cause for the concealment of problems until they can no longer be hidden. It can also be highly divisive, as individuals point fingers to transfer blame to others. Such outcomes can hardly be eliminated, but an organization's internal reputation for fairness and objectivity can mitigate them. So can a practice of subordinating the blame finding to a diagnosis of causes as a first step toward remedial action.

Most important of all, however, is the forward look: the process of defining the problem and identifying courses of action that may solve it. Here also the reward system is critically important. Readiness to search for problem situations and effectiveness in finding them need to be recognized and rewarded.

Perhaps the greatest influence a manager can have on the problem-solving style of the organization as a role model is making the best responses to problems. The style the manager should aim for rests on the following principles:

1. Solving the problem takes priority over looking backward to its causes. Initially, backward looks should be limited to diagnosing causes; fixing responsibility for mistakes should be postponed until a solution is being implemented.
2. The manager accepts personal responsibility for finding and proposing solutions instead of seeking to shift that responsibility either to superiors or to subordinates, although the search for solutions may, of course, be a collaborative effort involving many people.
3. The manager accepts personal responsibility for implementing action solutions, including securing the necessary authority from above if required.
4. When it is time to look backward, fixing blame may be an essential part of the process, but the primary focus of attention should be on what can be learned to prevent similar problems from arising in the future.

These principles are as obvious as the Ten Commandments and perhaps not quite as difficult to obey. Earlier, I indicated that stress might cause departures from them, but failure to respond effectively to problems probably derives more from a lack of attention and an earlier failure to cultivate the appropriate habits. The military makes much use of a procedure called "Estimate of the Situation." Its value is not that it teaches anything esoteric, but that through continual training in its use, commanders become habituated to approaching situations in orderly ways, using the checklists provided by the formal procedure.

Habits of response to problems are taught and learned both in the manager's one-on-one conversations with subordinates and in staff meetings. Is attention brought back repeatedly to defining the problems until everyone is agreed on just what the problem is? Is attention then directed toward generating possible solutions and evaluating their consequences? The least often challenged and most reliable base of managerial influence is the power to set the agenda, to focus attention. It is one of the most effective tools the manager has for training organization members to approach problems constructively by shaping their own habits of attention.

The perceptive reader will have discerned that "shaping habits of attention" is identical to "acquiring intuitions." The habit of responding to problems by looking for solutions can and must become intuitive—cued by the presence of the problem itself. A problem-solving style is a component of the set of intuitions that the manager acquires, one of the key components of effective managerial behavior.

Looking to the Future

With respect to the initiation of activity, the organizational habit we would like to instill is responsiveness to cues that signal future difficulties as well as to those that call attention to the problems of the moment. Failure to give sufficient attention to the future most often stems from two causes. The first is interruption by current problems that have more proximate deadlines and hence seem more urgent; the second is the absence of sufficient "scanning" activity that can pick up cues from the environment that long-run forces not impinging immediately on the organization have importance for it in the future.

In neither case is the need for sensitivity to the future likely to be met simply by strengthening intuitions. Rather, what is called for is deliberate and systematic allocation of organizational resources to deal with long-range problems, access for these resources to appropriate input from the environment that will attract their attention to new prospects, and protection of these planning resources from absorption in current problems, however urgent they may be. Attention to the future must be institutionalized; there is no simpler way to incorporate it into managerial "style" or habit.

It is a fallacy to contrast "analytic" and "intuitive" styles of management. Intuition and judgment—at least good judgment—are simply analyses frozen into habit and into the capacity for rapid response through recognition. Every manager needs to be able to analyze problems systematically (and with the aid of the modern arsenal of analytical tools provided by management science and operations research). Every manager needs also to be able to respond to situations rapidly, a skill that requires the cultivation of intuition and judgment over many years of experience and training. The effective manager does not have the luxury of choosing between "analytic" and "intuitive" approaches to problems. Behaving like a manager means having command of the whole range of management skills and applying them as they become appropriate.

ENDNOTES

1. Chester I. Barnard's (1938) *The Functions of the Executive* (Cambridge, Mass.: Harvard University Press), contains the essay on the contrast between logical and nonlogical processes as bases for decision making.
2. Simon, H. A. (1978) *Administrative Behavior,* 2nd ed. New York: Free Press. For a review of the artificial intelligence research on expert systems, see A. Barr and E. A. Figenbaum's (eds.) *The Handbook of Artificial Intelligence,* Vol. 2, Los Alamos, Cal.: William Kaufmann, 1982, pp. 77–294.
3. Two works that examine the split brain theory and forms of thought are R. H. Doktor's "Problem Solving Styles of Executives and Management Scientists," in A. Charnes, W. W. Cooper, and R. J. Niehaus's (eds.) *Management Science Approaches to Manpower Planning and Organization Design* (Amsterdam: North-Holland, 1978); and R. H. Doktor and W. F. Hamilton's "Cognitive Style and the Acceptance of Management Science Recommendations" (*Management Science,* 19:884–894, 1973).
4. For a survey of cognitive science research on problem solving and decision making, see Simon, H. A. (1979) *The Sciences of the Artificial,* 2nd ed., Cambridge, Mass.: The MIT Press, Chapters 3 and 4.
5. Marius J. Bouwman's doctoral dissertation, *Financial Diagnosis* (Graduate School of Industrial Administration, Carnegie-Mellon University, 1978).
6. R. Bhaskar's doctoral dissertation, *Problem Solving in Semantically Rich Domains* (Graduate School of Industrial Administration, Carnegie-Mellon University, 1978).

DISCUSSION QUESTIONS

1. Describe intuitive and judgmental decision-making processes.
2. Compare and contrast intuitive and judgmental decision making to the basic, rational process.
3. Cite three examples of intuition in managerial decision making.
4. Cite three examples of judgment in managerial decision making.
5. How can intuition and judgment improve managerial practice?

From *Academy of Management Executive,* February 1987.

ACTIVITIES

Activity 6–1: THE NASA EXERCISE

Step 1: Read the following instructions.

You are a member of a space crew originally scheduled to rendezvous with a mother ship on the lighted surface of the moon. Due to mechanical difficulties, however, your ship was forced to land at a spot some 200 miles from the rendezvous point. During landing, much of the equipment aboard was damaged, and, since survival depends on reaching the mother ship, the most critical items available must be chosen for the 200-mile trip. The 15 items left intact and undamaged after the landing include a box of matches, food concentrate, 50 feet of nylon rope, parachute silk, a portable heating unit, two .45 calibre pistols, one case of dehydrated Pet milk, two 100-lb. tanks of oxygen, stellar map (of the moon's constellations), life raft, magnetic compass, 5 gallons

Table 6–6 Scoring Sheet

Items	Indiv. Ranking	Group Ranking	Survival Expert's Ranking	Influence	Indiv. Accuracy	Group Accuracy
	Column 1	Column 2	Column 3	Column 4	Column 5	Column 6
Box of matches						
Food concentrate						
50 feet of nylon rope						
Parachute silk						
Portable heating unit						
Two .45 calibre pistols						
One case dehydrated milk						
Two 100-lb. tanks of oxygen						
Stellar map (of the moon's constellations)						
Life raft						
Magnetic compass						
5 gallons of water						
Signal flares						
First aid kit containing injection needles						
Solar-powered FM receiver-transmitter						
				Individual Influence Score	Individual Accuracy Score	Group Accuracy Score

of water, signal flares, first aid kit containing injection needles, and a solar-powered FM receiver-transmitter.

Your task is to rank order them in terms of their importance to your crew in reaching the rendezvous point. Using a scoring sheet like the one in Table 6–6, place the number 1 by the most important item, the number 2 by the second most important, and so on, through number 15, the least important. You have 15 minutes to complete this phase of the exercise.

Step 2: After the individual rankings are completed, your instructor will direct you to form groups of four to seven members. Each group should then rank order the fifteen items as a group. This group ranking should be a general consensus following a discussion of the issues, not just an averaging of each individual ranking. While it is unlikely that everyone will agree exactly on the group ranking, an effort should be made to at least reach a decision that everyone can live with. It is important to treat differences of opinion as a means of gathering more information, clarifying issues, and as an incentive to force the group to seek better alternatives. The group ranking should be listed in column 2.

Step 3: The instructor will provide the expert's rankings. Enter them in column 3.

Step 4: Each participant should compute the absolute difference between the individual ranking and the group ranking, and place the numbers in column 4; between the individual ranking and the expert's ranking and place the numbers in column 5; and between the group ranking and the expert's ranking and place the numbers in column 6. Then total the scores for columns 4, 5, and 6.

Step 5: Discussion. In small groups or with the entire class, answer the following questions:

Description

1. Describe your group's operation.
2. Describe the decision-making process used by your group.

Diagnosis

3. Which steps occurred in decision making? Which steps did you skip? Evaluate the effectiveness of the decision making.

Prescription

4. How could your group have made a more effective decision?

Activity 6–2: CREATIVE THINKING

Step 1: Complete the following problems:

1. How would you divide a square into four equal pieces?
2. How would you divide a square of cardboard to give an L shape with the same area as the square?
3. How would you describe "a one-pint milk bottle with half a pint of water in it?"
4. Design
   (a) an apple picking machine;
   (b) a cup that cannot spill;
   (c) a device to help cars to park.
5. Divide the following L shape into four pieces of exactly the same size:

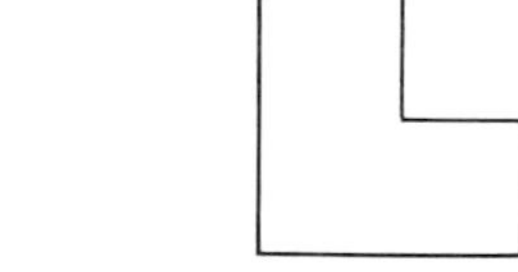

6. Offer several analogies to "finding your way in the fog."

Step 2: Discussion. Share your solutions with the class. Then think of additional possible solutions.

Activity 6–3: DIAGNOSING DECISION MAKING

Step 1: Think about a decision you recently made.

Step 2: Complete the following ratings about each step in the decision-making process by circling the number that best reflects your position on the continuum.

In making this decision, I

considered the key elements of the situation	7 6 5 4 3 2 1	ignored the key elements of the situation

considered the constraints that affected the decision	7	6	5	4	3	2	1	ignored the constraints that affected the decision
evaluated the resources that were available	7	6	5	4	3	2	1	did not consider the resources that were available
stated the problem clearly	7	6	5	4	3	2	1	did not state the problem clearly
involved individuals in decision making who were affected by the problem	7	6	5	4	3	2	1	did not involve relevant individuals in decision making
sought complete information	7	6	5	4	3	2	1	overlooked important information
involved information holders in the decision making	7	6	5	4	3	2	1	excluded information holders from the decision making
used a diversity of means to generate ideas	7	6	5	4	3	2	1	used only a single means to generate ideas
encouraged all ideas, regardless of their content	7	6	5	4	3	2	1	restricted ideas presented
identified when the process switched to evaluation	7	6	5	4	3	2	1	did not signal when process switched to evaluation
clearly specified criteria for assessing the decision	7	6	5	4	3	2	1	specified no criteria for assessing the decision
included differences of opinion in the evaluation	7	6	5	4	3	2	1	refused to allow differences of opinion to surface
pilot-tested some alternatives	7	6	5	4	3	2	1	conducted no pilot-testing
clearly indicated that selection was occurring	7	6	5	4	3	2	1	did not signal when process switched to selection
was aware whether I was satisficing or optimizing	7	6	5	4	3	2	1	did not specify whether I was satisficing or optimizing
made action plans to fit with the decision	7	6	5	4	3	2	1	offered no or inappropriate action plans
developed a comprehensive evaluation plan	7	6	5	4	3	2	1	omitted an evaluation plan

Step 3: Score each question by adding the numbers for the responses you gave. If your total score is 17–34 you have analyzed yourself as a very ineffective decision maker; if your score is 35–67, you have analyzed yourself as an ineffective decision maker; if your score is 68–85, you have analyzed yourself as an effective decision maker; if your score is 86 or above, you have analyzed yourself as a very effective decision maker.

Step 4: Now repeat Steps 1 to 3 for another decision.

Step 5: Discussion. In small groups, with the entire class, or in written form, as directed by your instructor, answer the following questions:

Description

1. How did your two decisions differ?

Diagnosis

2. What are your deficiencies as a decision maker?

Prescription

3. How could you improve your decision making?

Activity 6–4: ARCO COMPANY CASE

Step 1: Read the Arco Company case.

In early February, 1981, for reasons of declining profitability, the management of Arco Company, a Toronto-based producer of pumps and electrical controls, focussed their attention on the pumps division and the potential opportunities in the pumps market. Mounting problems in the division, opinions about which were numerous and various, prompted Max Chambers, Vice-President of manufacturing, to call a special meeting of key management personnel to discuss possible action. Five men from pumps and eight men from other areas attended. Figure 6–6 shows the meeting's attendants. Figure 6–7 is a partial organization chart of Arco.

Max began with a long, rambling talk in which he mentioned the main concerns in the pumps division:

Figure 6–6 Seating Arrangement for Special Meeting, Arco Company

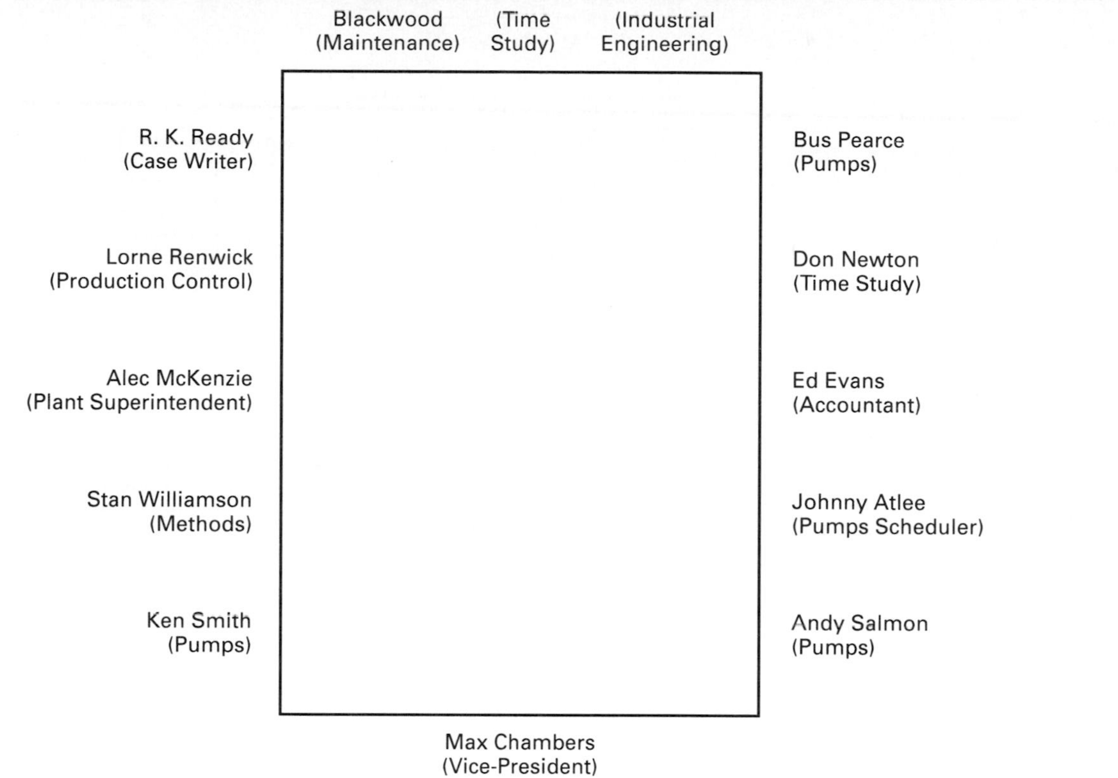

layout problems exacerbated by lack of floor space, and the high price of the pumps, which were manufactured in a job-shop format. The discussion, he said, should focus on "what changes, if any, we want to make in this pumps division." One change Max wanted discussed was the introduction of a mass-produced pump. To this end he introduced the name of a consultant, Jim Henderson, as someone who could assist in designing a new standard line. Or, he added, the pumps people could design the new line themselves. He closed his remarks by saying, "One thing I want is that you all contribute to the ultimate decision. I also want a full endorsement of whatever is decided."

The resulting discussion, in which everyone readily agreed that something had to be done about the pumps division, began with a discussion of Max's major proposal: having two lines, one to be streamlined, producing a standard pump, and one to continue the job-shop pump. Max elaborated on his concerns by saying that he wanted a new, cheaper pump to act as a catalyst to the sales people. He wanted the Sales department to develop a marketing plan to sell the new product.

Most of the discussion was among the electrical controls people, particularly Alec and Lorne. The pumps people, when pressed to contribute, indicated that they felt there were more urgent, immediate problems than developing a new pump. Max, Alec, and Lorne disregarded these remarks and continued to discuss the introduction of a new pump line. A few pointed and somewhat aggressive remarks were exchanged between Lorne and the pumps group. Further discussion centred on whether to hire Jim Henderson, the consultant, or do the survey themselves.

As the meeting closed, Max said, "I know that the President is ready to push the pumps business. If he is in this frame of mind, I think we should be prepared to assume the responsibility for organizing the manufacturing end of things. I shall be out of town until next Thursday. When I return, I would like your group decision about what to do in the pumps division. I shall go along with anything you decide."

BACKGROUND

The Arco Company, situated in a suburb of Toronto, was originally a producer of electrical controls. In 1976, the Company acquired the Delta Pump Company. Since that time, the ratio of electrical controls' sales to pumps' sales had increased from 2:1 to 4:1, while at the same

Figure 6–7 ARCO COMPANY, PARTIAL ORGANIZATION CHART, MANUFACTURING DIVISION

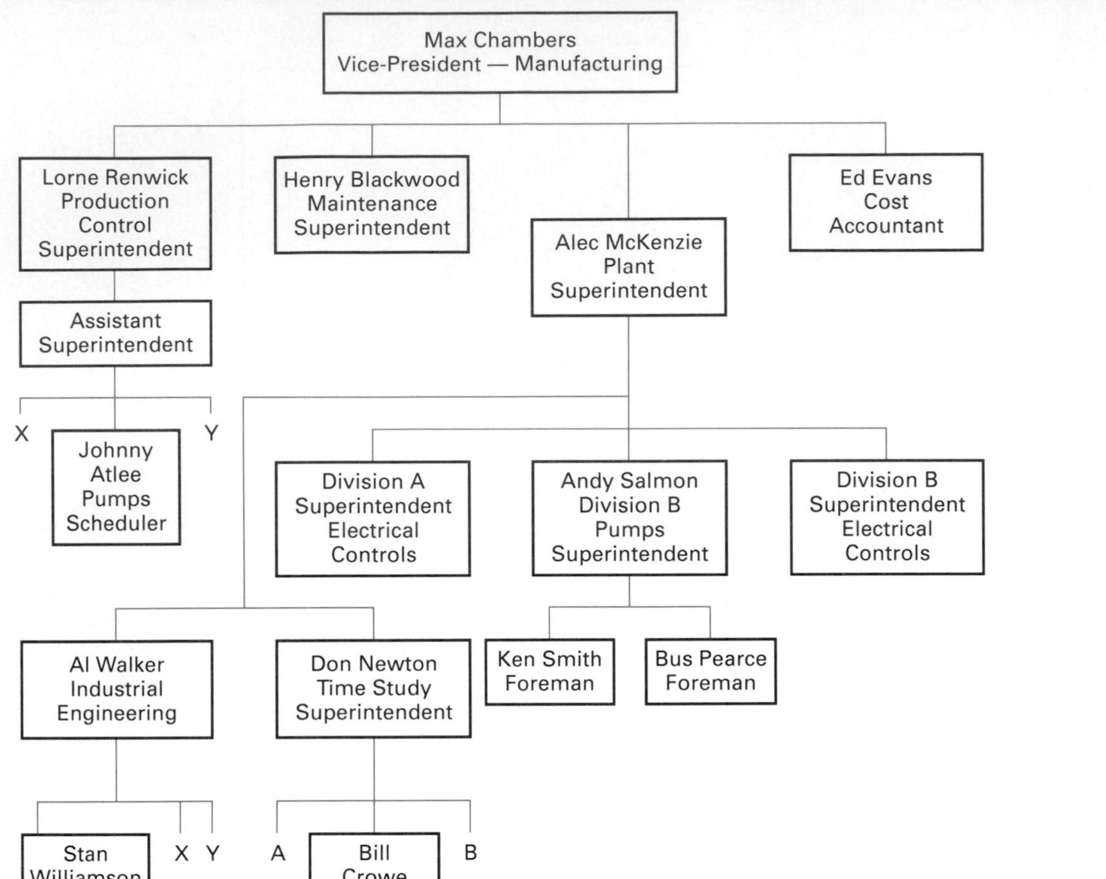

time, the Company's profitability had been decreasing. Management felt that the high market share they enjoyed in electrical controls was as much as they would be able to get.

The pumps division currently had a book loss; however, the Company cost accountant attributed that to the unrealistically high overhead allocated to the pumps division. He believed that if Arco had discontinued producing and selling pumps without another product line, its profitability would have been lower.

PUMPS DIVISION

The pumps division operated independently of the other divisions, but it utilized common service facilities such as production control, accounting, maintenance, industrial engineering, and industrial relations. Three management people from Delta Pumps joined Arco after the merger: Ed Evans, Cost Accountant, Andy Salmon, Pumps Superintendent, and Stan Williamson, Methods Supervisor. In addition, the two foremen, Bus Pearce and Ken Smith, had come to Arco from Delta.

Two years after the merger, in an effort to centralize industrial engineering, the Company abolished the Pumps' Department of Time Study and Methods and moved Stan Williamson to the Industrial Engineering Department, reporting to Al Walker. The time study responsibilities were assumed by Don Newton's time study department. Both Newton and Walker had been brought into Arco by Alec McKenzie. Figure 6–8 indicates the office lay-out plan. Figure 6–9 shows both the on- and off-the-job interactions of these people.

PROFILES AND OPINIONS

(Table 6–7 gives more detailed background on some of the participants.)

Max Chambers, Vice-President of Manufacturing

Max had a degree in engineering, with some work towards a Master's degree at M.I.T. While there, he studied under Douglas McGregor, the author of "The Human Side of Enterprise". He believed that if Arco

Figure 6–8 OFFICE LAYOUT, ARCO COMPANY

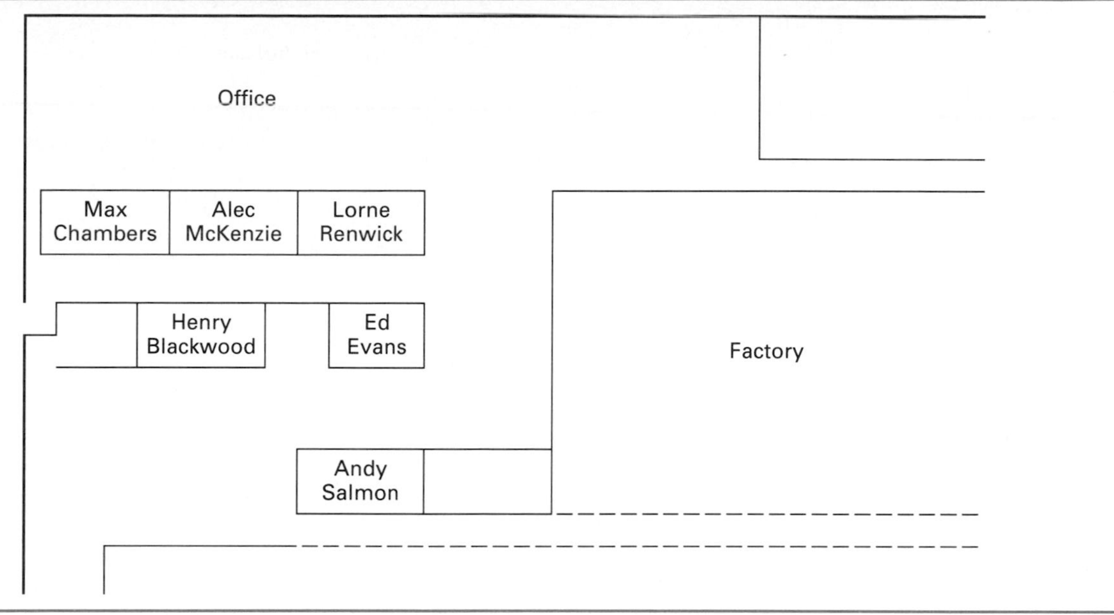

were to grow, it would have to be in the pumps division. To this end, he wanted to introduce a major change from job-shop pumps to mass-produced pumps. He had the agreement of the President of Arco to proceed in this direction, along with a promise of some financing to make the change. Regarding the issue of hiring a consultant to design the new layout, Max had hoped that the pumps division people would do the job themselves.

Lorne Renwick, Production Control Superintendent

Due to his long years of service with Arco, Lorne had a long-standing relationship with both the President of Arco and the President of the parent company. Most of the people in Arco felt that Lorne had a great deal of power. As Andy Salmon put it, "Lorne is the person you have to watch out for. Any time people do something different from the way he wants things done in his area, he stops you cold. There's no point in arguing with him once you find out that he is against you."

Lorne thought that having a new pump line was a good idea even though he disagreed with the idea of bringing in a consultant to design the layout. He had told Max so before the meeting. In Lorne's opinion, Max's idea was to increase pumps sales by introducing a new, profitable pump line, and the main purpose in calling the meeting was to get approval of the idea. He believed that Max wanted to use an outside consultant to design the new layout.

Lorne felt that the key men in the pumps division formed a "pumps clique" and he believed that the time had come to break it up. He felt the pumps people never shared their ideas with others and consciously tried to exclude others.

Lorne classified the executives in the Company into two classes: one group that thought up ideas and one group that got them through. He considered himself as part of the latter group.

Alec McKenzie, Plant Superintendent

Alec's father-in-law was the President of the parent company, and his position in the Company was seen by many as being a result of that relationship. He had very little management experience. He was an electrical engineer and taught an evening course in engineering. Alec had high aspirations for the Company.

He was strongly in favour of the consultant, although "at first I was opposed to the idea because I thought we could do it ourselves. As I thought about it, I began changing my mind."

Alec could not foresee pump sales increasing to the point where they could equal sales of electrical controls. He believed that the re-organization of the pumps division was a big job rather than a big decision, but that whatever was done would have to have the approval of Andy Salmon because Andy had the ideas; it would be

Figure 6–9 Established Patterns of Interaction, Arco Company

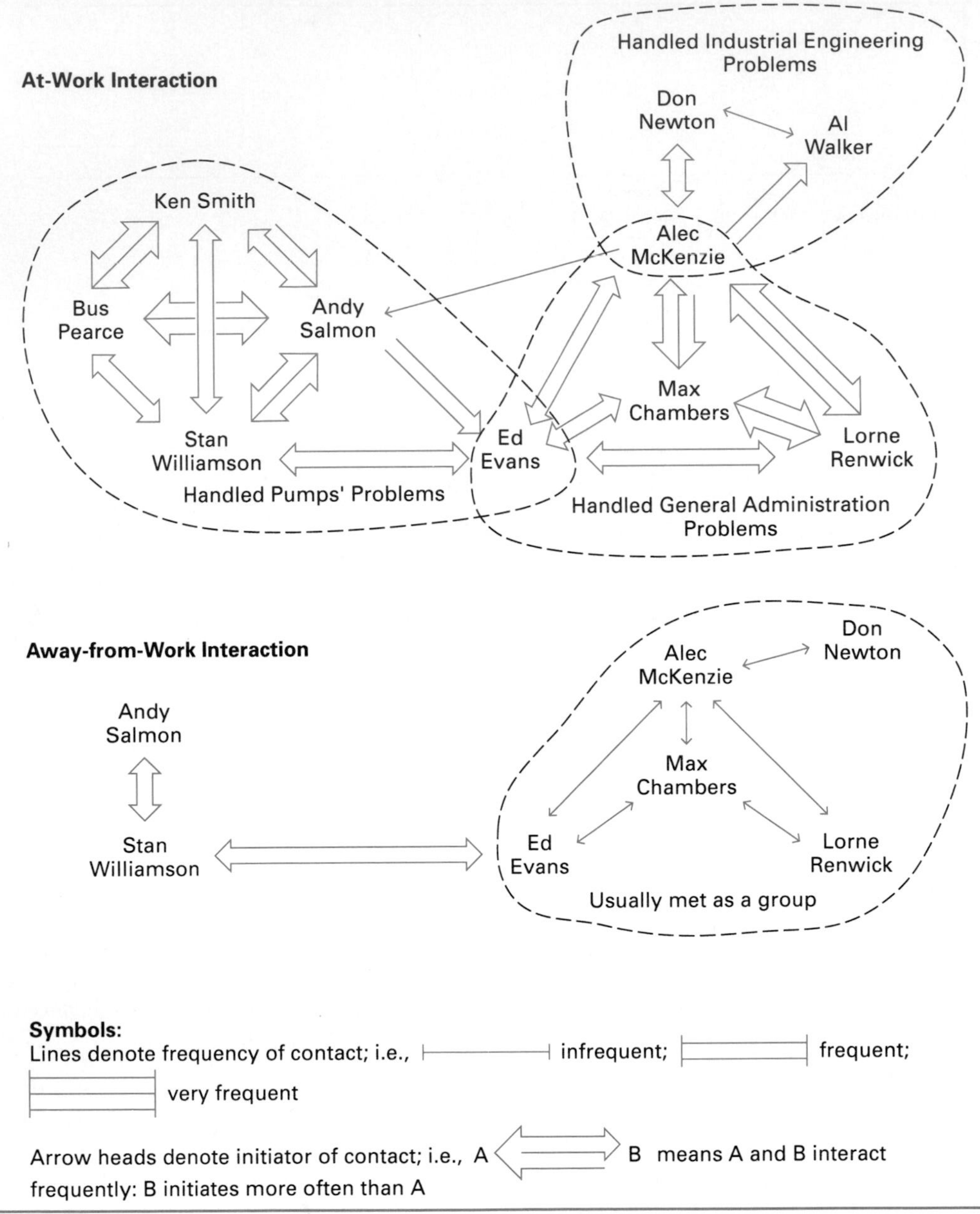

the consultant's job to pull the ideas together in report form.

Andy Salmon, Pumps Superintendent

Andy and Stan Williamson were probably the most knowledgeable pumps people in Canada. Andy did not feel that the electrical people at Arco knew much about the pumps area. He felt that the pumps people were dominated by the electrical group through Lorne's scheduling. "There is a problem of electrical storage moving into the pumps area. If we had someone who could stand up to Lorne, then possibly, this problem could be solved internally. I guess that's one of our major problems: not having someone who can referee a battle between, let's say, Lorne and Pumps."

Andy was confused by the meeting, as he was not sure whether Max had wanted the group's opinions or had just wanted support for his idea of a new pumps line. Usually these decisions were made by top management and passed on, so Andy's expectations were

Table 6–7 PERSONAL INFORMATION, MANUFACTURING PERSONNEL, ARCO COMPANY

	Position	Age	Service	Education	Marital Status	Outside Interest
Max Chambers	V.P. Manufacturing	48	19	Electrical Eng. U. of T. 1 yr. Post Grad. Bus. and Eng. Admin. at MIT	Married: one son	United Church—an executive President M.I.T. Club, Toronto
Stan Williamson	Methods Supervisor	59	31	2 yrs. Tech. School 4 yrs. Electrical course at night	Married: two sons and two daughters	Electronics and woodwork shop in basement—hobby
Bus Pearce	Foreman	49	32	2 yrs. Tech. School 3 yrs. night School: Mgmt. Training	Married: two daughters	
Lorne Renwick	Production Control Superintendent	59	42	1st yr. H.S.	Married: two sons	
Ken Smith	Foreman	47	23	Grade School	Married: one son and two daughters	Deacon, Baptist Church Treasurer, Leaside Foremen's Club Member, Chess Club President, Christian Men of Industry Bowling League
Andy Salmon	Pumps Division Superintendent	52	33	H.S. grad 1 yr. night classes: electricity	Married	
Alec McKenzie	Plant Superintendent	32	8	U. of T. Electrical Engineer	Married: one son and one daughter	Leaside Foreman's Club Member Professional Engineers Society Teaches course at U. of T. evening school, Gen. Mgmt.
Don Newton	Time Study Superintendent	34	1	H.S. Grad Night School, Ind. Supervisor	Married: one son and one daughter	Treasurer, Presbyterian Church Night Course at U. of T. in Administration Member, Ind. Engineering Assoc.
Ed Evans	Cost Accountant	53	25	U. of T. Comm. and Finance	Married	Member, Cost Accounting Group

unclear. In Andy's opinion, Max probably wanted to bring in an outsider to avoid the back-biting that would occur if the job were done internally.

Andy was in favour of expanding the pumps division, but would have preferred that he and Stan take on the responsibility for this expansion. He felt that he could make time to do the job and, if the consultant was only going to put ideas together, he and Stan could do it as well as the consultant. Andy and Alec McKenzie had discussed this idea, but Alec felt that the consultant would be the best alternative because the job could be done more quickly. Consequently, Andy agreed: "If that's the way they want it, that's the way we'll do it."

Stan Williamson, Methods Supervisor

Stan thought the meeting was a mess with no definite purpose. Max had just sat back and tried to get people to do what he wanted them to do, but in this case, it was not clear what that was. Stan had talked to Max later and tried to pin him down, but with no results.

"The thing that really disturbs me is that Andy feels that the pressure is getting too great. On top of all his problems, he has to deal with untrained people such as Alec McKenzie and Don Newton who have no experience in the pumps field at all. In the last 18 months or so, the carpet has really been pulled out from under the pumps people."

Ed Evans, Manufacturing Division Accountant

Ed felt that Max held the meeting to inform everyone at the same time about his plans for the pumps division. He believed that Max wanted to hire the consultant and that he would certainly be hired. He did not think the Sales department would change their approach to increase sales. In mentioning Lorne's contribution to the meeting, he said, "Lorne is a big talker. You can't believe much of anything he says. Anyway, he doesn't know anything about pumps—he is an electrical controls man."

Ken Smith, Pumps Assembly Foreman

Ken was disappointed that Max had been so indefinite about what should be done. He thought Max had been insincere in asking for opinions from the pumps people, since he had never done so before. Lorne had opposed pumps and blocked them at every turn in the past, so Ken did not believe that anything had changed. He also questioned the presence of such people as Henry, Lorne, John, Al Walker and others at a meeting which was supposed to deal with a pumps problem.

THE GROUP'S DECISION

When Max returned the following week, reports from the men ranged from Lorne Renwick's disapproval of hiring any consultant, to Stan Williamson's skepticism but willingness to cooperate, to the more widely held approval for hiring Jim Henderson. Max agreed to the decision. The consultant began work the following week.

THE CONSULTANT'S EFFORTS

A committee of six was formed to work with Jim Henderson, consisting of Andy Salmon (Co-Chairman) and Stan Williamson from pumps, and Don Newton, Bill Crowe and Alec McKenzie (Chairman) from other areas. The consultant was introduced only to members of the committee.

During the next two months, opinions about Jim and the project polarized. Except for formal meetings, Jim had little contact with pumps people, and all reported information to Max came from non-pumps committee members. Pumps personnel complained to each other that Jim would not take suggestions or ask questions, and were suspicious of the speediness and lack of consultation in arranging for the consultant.

Jim recommended an assembly line layout which utilized a conveyer. Only the non-pumps people were enthusiastic about the recommendation or project. Outwardly, Max Chambers remained neutral. Objecting to Jim and his proposal became the regular topic of discussion at the afternoon pumps division coffee break meetings.

ALEC'S BLOW-UP

On a Wednesday afternoon in April, 1981, Alec McKenzie was in a rage. He had just come from a pumps division coffee break meeting with Andy, Stan, and the two foremen. He had heard nothing but objections and criticisms about the consultant and the proposed conveyor set-up for the pumps area. Alex was still enthusiastic about the plan, but very discouraged by the meeting's outcome. Figure 6–10 shows some of the objections that had been raised by the pumps people.

Alec discussed his feelings with the case writer who happened to see him just as he left the pumps meeting. Alec was "so god-damned mad" he could "hardly talk at all" as he discussed his feelings. The meeting was the first time he had heard Andy's views. He explained that he was not "getting any suggestions; not a bit of constructive criticism at all . . . nothing but opposition and objections." Alec continually returned to those phrases. He was enthusiastic about the plan and had "hoped other people wanted things to improve . . . wanted things done in a way that would be a credit to themselves and the organization." His anger turned to the pumps people: "They don't want anything—all they want is to have things stay as they are."

Alec's explanations of the suggested line flow and equipment usage revealed four possible benefits for pumps: direct and indirect labour savings; reduced process time (from seven weeks to one week); doubled production capacity in two-thirds of the present space; and a clean, organized shop. In Alec's opinion, a short delivery time was a necessity in the market.

Walking through the pumps plant area, Alec explained the plans he had for the available space. In reviewing the existing layout, he pointed out messy, untidy spots in the production, assembly, and test areas where materials and work in process lay on the floor,

Figure 6–10 PUMPS GROUP OBJECTIONS TO PROPOSED ASSEMBLY LINE, ARCO COMPANY

1. What will happen if there is a breakdown? Will the workers just stand around or will they be sent home?
2. What happens if you have trouble on a machine and need a new tool? A man would have to go to the tool shop and then run three quarters of the way through the plant to get the end plate he was working on.
3. There is not supposed to be any material or inventory on the floor, so if there is a material shortage, there is nothing to do but shut down the line.
4. It will have to be a standardized product—no changes can be made in a pump.*
5. Jim Henderson will not listen to suggestions, and will not ask questions.

*Stan did not think they should worry about the design because he believed that the plan would never get into operation.

all the time referring to his embarrassment. "It's a discouraging, disgusting sight. You don't find this in other companies. It's an embarrassing, shameful, mess."

He spoke of the potential labour saving which could be realized with the new system, and of his own shame "to be associated with a company that looked like this." All he wanted, he emphasized, was "good, solid, constructive criticism, not just opposition and objections."

Although Alec recognized Arco's significant business opportunities, particularly in the pumps market, he was greatly distressed by the difficulty of getting ahead within the Company: "There's just no place to go, the Company's not providing anything."

Alec finally confided that until that afternoon's meeting, he had thought "sailing was clear." Now it appeared to him that everyone was sold on the plan except the four people who would have to make it work.

"We have the opportunity to do something really well, to do something we can be proud of, and all they want to do, as far as I can see, is just stay the same. I don't know what I'm going to do about it, but I've got to do something by tomorrow."

Step 2: Prepare the case for class discussion.

Step 3: Answer each of the following questions, individually or in small groups, as directed by your instructor:

Description

1. Briefly describe the decision to be made at Arco.
2. Describe the major individuals involved in the decision making.

Diagnosis

3. What situation did the pumps division face?
4. What was Chambers's objective?
5. What alternatives were considered? Were the alternatives feasible?
6. How completely were the alternatives evaluated?
7. Was a quality decision reached?

Prescription

8. How could more effective decisions be made?
9. What techniques could be used to improve decision making?

Step 4: Discussion. In small groups, with the entire class, or in written form, share your answers to the questions above. Then answer the following questions:

1. What symptoms suggest a problem exists?
2. What problems exist in the case?
3. What theories and concepts help explain those problems?
4. How can the problems be corrected?
5. Are the actions likely to be effective?

Activity 6–5: HOW BIASED IS YOUR DECISION MAKING?

Step 1: Answer each of the problems below.

1. A certain town is served by two hospitals. In the larger hospital about 45 babies are born each day, and in the smaller hospital about 15 babies are born each day. Although the overall proportion of boys is about 50 per cent, the actual proportion at either hospital may be greater or less than 50 per cent on any day. At the end of a year, which hospital will have the greater number of days on which more than 60 per cent of the babies born were boys?
   a. The large hospital
   b. the small hospital
   c. neither—the number of days will be about the same (within five per cent of each other)
2. Linda is 31, single, outspoken, and very bright. She majored in philosophy in college. As a student, she was deeply concerned with discrimination and other social issues, and participated in anti-nuclear demonstrations. Which statement is more likely:
   a. Linda is a bank teller
   b. Linda is a bank teller and active in the feminist movement
3. A cab was involved in a hit-and-run accident. Two

cab companies serve the city: the Green, which operates 85 per cent of the cabs, and the Blue, which operates the remaining 15 per cent. A witness identifies the hit-and-run cab as Blue. When the court tests the reliability of the witness under circumstances similar to those on the night of the accident, he correctly identifies the color of a cab 80 per cent of the time and misidentifies it the other 20 per cent. What's the probability that the cab involved in the accident was Blue, as the witness stated?

4. Imagine that you face this pair of concurrent decisions. Examine these decisions, then indicate which choices you prefer:

Decision I.

Choose between:

a. a sure gain of $240
b. a 25 per cent chance of winning $1,000 and a 75 per cent chance of winning nothing

Decision II.

Choose between:

c. a sure loss of $750
d. A 75 per cent chance of losing $1,000 and a 25 per cent chance of losing nothing

Decision III.

Choose between:

e. a sure loss of $3,000
f. an 80 per cent chance of losing $4,000 and a 20 percent chance of losing nothing

5. You've decided to see a Broadway play and have bought a $40 ticket. As you enter the theater, you realize you've lost your ticket. You can't remember the seat number, so you can't prove to the management that you bought a ticket. Would you spend $40 for a new ticket?

   You've reserved a seat for a Broadway play for which the ticket price is $40. As you enter the theater to buy your ticket, you discover you've lost $40 from your pocket. Would you still buy the ticket? (Assume you have enough cash left to do so.)

6. Imagine you have operable lung cancer and must choose between two treatments—surgery and radiation therapy. Of 100 people having surgery, 10 die during the operation, 32 (including those original 10) are dead after one year, and 66 after five years. Of 100 people having radiation therapy, none dies during treatment, 23 are dead after one year and 78 after five years. Which treatment would you prefer?

Step 2: Your instructor will give you the correct answer to each problem.

Step 3: Discussion. In small groups, with the entire class, or in written form, as directed by your instructor, answer the following questions:

Description

1. How accurate were the decisions you reached?

Diagnosis

2. What biases were evident in the decisions you reached?

Prescription

3. How could you improve your decision making to make it more accurate?

From D. Kahnemann and A. Tversky, Rational choice and the forming of decisions, *Journal of Business* 59 (4) (1986): 5251–5278; A. Tversky and D. Kahnemann, The framing of decisions and the psychology of choice, *Science* 211 (1981): 453–458; D. Kahnemann and A. Tversky, Extension needs intuitive reasoning, *Psychological Review* 90 (1983): 293–315; K. McKean, Decisions, decisions, *Discover Magazine,* June 1985.

Activity 6–6: DECISION MAKING IN GROUPS

Step 1: Your instructor will organize the class into nominal groups of five to eight people and present the task to you.

Step 2: Write your own ideas about the problem on a piece of paper.

Step 3: In the small groups, each person should contribute one idea and list it on a flip chart. This type of sharing should continue until all ideas are publicly recorded.

Step 4: Where necessary, briefly clarify each idea by means of examples and explanations, but do not debate for relative merits. Eliminate duplicate ideas and refine global ideas into two or more specific items.

Step 5: As individuals, rank or classify all ideas in writing according to criteria specified by the instructor.

Step 6: Tabulate and summarize all individual evaluations to produce a group decision.

Step 7: With the entire class, share the decisions you reached.

Step 8. The instructor will select a panel of experts (usually the entire class) who are informed about the task.

Step 9. You will receive a question or questionnaire to complete in writing.

Step 10: Your instructor or appointed members of the class will tabulate and summarize the data.

Step 11: The instructor will feed back and discuss the summarized data with the class.

Step 12: The instructor may repeat steps 9, 10, and 11 until some consensus is reached about the task or problem.

Step 13: With the entire class, share the decisions you reached.

Step 14: Your instructor will organize you into small groups of five to eight individuals.

Step 15: Each group will receive a problem or task.

Step 16: As a group, you are to brainstorm possible solutions to the problem; list all ideas without discussion on a large piece of newsprint.

Step 17: Using these ideas, reach consensus about a decision.

Step 18: With the entire class, share the ideas you generated.

Step 19: Discussion. In small groups, with the entire class, or in written form, compare and contrast the three approaches to decision making.

1. How did the approaches differ? How were they similar?
2. Which approach resulted in the most effective decisions?
3. Under what circumstances would each approach be effective? ineffective?
4. Offer ways of improving the effectiveness of the decision-making processes you used.

Based on Curtis W. Cook, Nominal group methods enrich classroom learning. *Exchange: The Organizational Behavior Teaching Journal* 5 (1980): 33–36.

Activity 6–7: CONGESTED TRAFFIC CASE

Step 1: Read the Congested Traffic case.

Al Mond was a good company man—at least Mr. Beech, the President of Terminal Distributors, Inc., thought so. Al joined Terminal, a food wholesaler located in a large metropolitan urban area, eight years ago, having previously worked as a warehouse foreman and then truck dispatcher for a competing firm.

Al liked working for Mr. Beech and was unusually conscientious in the performance of his duties, frequently voluntarily putting in extra hours, and initiating all sorts of ideas from insisting that all lights be turned off when not in use, to suggesting preventative maintenance for building, trucks and other equipment. Single, and without any apparent outside interests or hobbies, Al centered all his attention and concern on Terminal's operation.

As a result of his strong continuing commitment to the firm, Mr. Beech gradually increased Al's responsibilities, giving him carte blanche authority to make many important decisions. Al never abused this privilege, and using good judgment, enhanced his image with the boss. So great was Al's loyalty that some newer employees wondered if Al was a member of Mr. Beech's family.

Al's main job was to supervise the use of the firm's five trucks in picking up merchandise from other warehouses and making deliveries to retail customers. Each morning Al selected and grouped the accumulated customer orders. The goods were picked by warehousemen and placed on individual skids or flat trucks and then moved into a staging or loading area. Early the following morning Al arranged the pickup and delivery sequence for each truck, and once this was accomplished, the merchandise was simply loaded onto the trucks and the drivers made their stops in accordance with Al's routing.

From time to time the drivers became disagreeable and complained about having to criss-cross back and forth over the same territory. Some days extensive delays occurred because of detours around construction sites, and many new one-way streets posed another problem. Occasionally, and too often to suit the drivers, just one delivery was included to an outlying suburban location, necessitating long driving time between stops. Not only were the drivers unhappy, but frequently customers became angry because merchandise was delivered in a disgruntled manner, later than expected, and at a time that was just not convenient. Recently deliveries were being refused with greater frequency, which added to costs, and was a further complication and burden on the warehousemen who had to return the goods to inventory.

Besides, some drivers were starting to object to working overtime.

Each summer Al elected to take his annual vacation

during three successive weeks, and when this happened, Joe Peekan, Al's assistant and warehouse supervisor, took over Al's job.

What can you suggest to Joe to help overcome or at least reduce customer and driver complaints?

Step 2: Prepare the case for class discussion.

Step 3: Answer each of the following questions, individually or in small groups, as directed by your instructor:

Description

1. Describe the situation at Terminal Distributors.

Diagnosis

2. What decisions have to be made at Terminal Distributors?
3. What information is available for use in the decision making?
4. What process is used in making the decisions?
5. How effective is the decision making?

Prescription

7. How could more effective decisions be made?
8. What techniques could be used to improve decision making?

Step 4: Discussion. In small groups, with the entire class, or in written form, share your answers to the questions above. Then answer the following questions:

1. What symptoms suggest a problem exists?
2. What problems exist in the case?
3. What theories and concepts help explain those problems?
4. How can the problems be corrected?
5. Are the actions likely to be effective?

This case was prepared by Professor Walter F. Rohrs, Wagner College. Used with permission.

Activity 6–8: ETHICAL DECISION MAKING

Step 1: Read Cases 1–4. For each case, first decide what you would do and why. In doing this, consider what information you would use to investigate the question, what alternatives you would consider, and what criteria you would use in making your decision.

CASE 1: SALES REPRESENTATIVE IN THE MIDDLE EAST

You are the sales representative for your construction company in the Middle East. Your company has bid on a substantial project which it wants *very much* to get. Yesterday, the cousin of the minister who will award the contract suggested that he might be of help. You are reasonably sure that with his help the chances of getting the contract would increase. For his assistance, the minister expects $20,000. You would have to pay this in addition to the standard fees to your agent. If you do not make this payment to the minister, you are certain that he will go to your competition (who have won the last three contracts), and they *will* make the payment (and probably get this contract, too).

Your company has no code of conduct yet, although a committee was formed some time ago to consider one. The government of your country recently passed a Business Practices Act. The pertinent paragraph is somewhat vague, but implies that this kind of payment would probably be a violation of the act. The person to whom you report, and those above him, do not want to become involved. The decision is yours to make.

CASE 2: HAZARDOUS MATERIALS IN WEST AFRICA

For one year now, you have been international vice president of a multinational firm that produces and markets chemicals. The minister of agriculture in a small developing country in West Africa has requested a series of large shipments over the next five years of a special insecticide that only your firm prepares. The minister believes that this chemical is the only one that will rid one of his crops of a new infestation that threatens to destroy it. You know, however, that one other insecticide would probably be equally effective; it is produced in another country and has never been allowed in your own country.

Your insecticide, MIM, is highly toxic. After years of debate, your government has just passed a law forbidding its use in your country. There is evidence that dangerous amounts are easily ingested by humans through residue on vegetables, through animals that eat the crops, and through the water supply. After careful thought, you tell the minister about this evidence. He still insists on using it, arguing that it is necessary and it will be used "intelligently." You are quite sure that, ten years from now, it will begin to damage the health of some of his people.

Both the president and the executive vice president of your firm feel strongly that the order should be filled. They question the government's position, and they are very concerned about the large inventory of MIM on hand and the serious financial setback its prohibition will cause the company. They have made it clear, however, that the decision is up to you.

Note: While the company has a code of conduct and your government has a Business Practices Act, neither covers hazardous materials.

CASE 3: THE SOUTHEAST ASIAN ADVERTISING CAMPAIGN

You are the new marketing manager for a very large, profitable international firm that manufactures automobile tires. Your advertising agency has just presented for your approval elaborate plans for introducing a new tire into the Southeast Asian market. The promotional material clearly implies that your product is better than all local products. In fact it is better than some, but not as good as others. This material tries to attract potential buyers by explaining that for six months your product will be sold at a "reduced price." Actually, the price is reduced from a hypothetical amount that was established only so it could be "reduced." The ad claims that the tire has been tested under the "most adverse" conditions. In fact it has not been tested in the prolonged heat and humidity of the tropics. Finally, your company assures potential buyers that, riding on your tires, they will be safer in their car than ever before. The truth is, however, that they could have been equally safe on a competitor's tire that has been available for two years.

You know your product is good. You also know the proposed advertising is deceptive. Your superiors have never been concerned about such practices, believing they must present your products as distinctive in order to achieve and maintain a competitive edge. They are counting on a very favorable reception for this tire in Southeast Asia. They are counting on you to see that it gets this reception.

Whether you go with the proposed advertising or not is up to you. Your company has a code of conduct and your government has a Business Practices Act, but neither covers advertising practices.

CASE 4: CULTURAL CONFLICT IN THE MIDDLE EAST

You were quite upset last week when you read a strong editorial in the *New York Times,* written by a prominent journalist, that was highly critical of your company, especially its major project in a conservative Moslem country.

As the international vice president, you are responsible for this project, which is the building and running of large steel plant. Based on the figures, this plant makes a lot of sense, both for your company and for the government of the country that approved the project. But as the journalist pointed out, it is to be built in a rural area and will have a very disruptive effect upon the values and customs of the people in the whole region. There will be many consequences. The young people from the other towns will move to work at the plant, thereby breaking up families and eliminating their primary source of financial and personal security. Working the second or third shift will further interfere with family responsibilities, as well as religious observances. Working year round will certainly mean that many people will be unable to return home to help with the harvest. As the young people will be paid more and more, they will gain more influence, thereby overturning century old patterns of authority. And, of course, the Westerners who will be brought in will probably not live up to the local moral standards and will not show due respect for local women.

The journalist ended by charging your company with "cultural imperialism" and claiming that your plant, if actually built and put into operation, would contribute to the disruption of the traditional values and relationships that have provided stability for the country through many generations.

You had known there would be some social changes, but you did not realize how profound they could be. You have now examined other evidence and discovered that a factory built several years ago by another foreign firm in a similar location is causing exactly these problems—and more. Widespread concern in the country over these problems is one reason for the increasing influence of traditionalists and nationalists in the country, who argue for getting rid of all foreign firms and their disruptive priorities and practices.

Your company has a code of conduct and your government has a Business Practices Act, but neither deals with the destruction of traditional values and relationships. You are on your own here. A lot is at stake for the company, and for the people of the region into which you had planned to move. The decision is yours.

Step 2: In groups of four to six students, reach consensus about how to handle each situation.

Step 3: Discussion. In small groups, with the entire class, or in written form, as directed by your instructor, answer the following questions:

Description

1. What decisions did each group reach?

Diagnosis

2. How ethical were the decisions reached?
3. What criteria did you use to evaluate the decisions?

Prescription

4. How could you improve your decision making to make it more ethical?

From Nancy J. Adler, *International Dimensions of Organizational Behavior* (Boston: PWS-Kent Publishing Company, 1986) pp. 141–144.

CONCLUDING COMMENTS

The quality of information is a key ingredient in effective decision making. Information is used for analyzing a situation, setting objectives, and choosing an appropriate alternative to comprise the decision. The quality of information used can be raised through improved data collection, objectifying perceptions, and reducing misattributions. In the NASA Exercise you saw how using the rational decision-making process affects the quality of decisions and compared individual and group decision making. In the creative-thinking activity you had the opportunity to practice ways of increasing your decision-making effectiveness. You also analyzed the application of the decision-making process in two decisions you recently made.

People's perceptions of and attributions for particular events and people affect the way they make decisions. You considered the types of biases that affect decision making. In Ethical Decision Making you examined the ethical consequences of decisions. You also considered the quality of decision making at Arco and offered a way of making decisions effectively in the Congested Traffic case.

ENDNOTES

[1]C.A. O'Reilly III, Variations in decision makers' use of information sources: The impact of quality and accessibility of information, *Academy of Management Journal* 25 (1982): 756–771.

[2]G.P. Huber, *Managerial Decision Making* (Glenview, Ill.: Scott, Foresman, 1980); G.P. Huber, Decision support systems: Their present and future applications. In G.R. Ungson and D.N. Braunstein (eds.), *Decision-Making: An Interdisciplinary Inquiry* (Boston: Kent, 1982).

[3]A. Tversky and D. Kahneman, Availability: A heuristic for judging frequency and probability, *Cognitive Psychology* 4 (1973): 207–232; H.J. Einhorn and R.M. Hogarth, Behavioral decision theory: Processes of judgment and choice, *Annual Review of Psychology* 32 (1981): 53–88.

[4]N.R.F. Maier, *Problem Solving and Creativity in Individuals and Groups* (Belmont, Cal.: Brooks/Cole, 1970).

[5]The Subarctic Survival Problem, © 1974 Experiential Learning Methods, Plymouth, Michigan.

[6]L.K. Trevino, Ethical decision making in organizations: A person–situation interactionist model, *Academy of Management Review* 11 (1986): 601–617.

[7]Bilking babies and women, *Washington Post,* 19 February 1988; Nestle quietly seeks to sell Beechnut, dogged by scandal of bogus apple juice, *Wall Street Journal,* 6 July 1989, pp. A-4, B-4.

[8]S.N. Brenner and E.A. Molander, Is the ethics of business changing?, *Harvard Business Review* 55(1) (1977): 57–71.

[9]R. Ricklees, Ethics in America, *Wall Street Journal,* 31 October–3 November, 1983), p. 33.

[10]See J. Bulhart, *Effective Group Discussion* (Dubuque, Ia.: William C. Brown, 1986); J.T. Wood, G.M. Phillips, and D.J. Pedersen, *Group Discussion: A Practical Guide to Participation and Leadership* (New York: Harper & Row, 1986) for examples.

[11]W.C. Morris and H. Sashkin, *Organizational Behavior in Action* (St. Paul, Minn: West, 1976).

[12]L.S. Baird, R.W. Beatty, and C.E. Schneier, *The Performance Appraisal Sourcebook* (Amherst, Mass.: Human Resource Development Press, 1982).

[13]D. Braybrooke and C. Lindblom, *A Strategy of Decision* (Glencoe, Ill.: The Free Press, 1963).

[14]N. Alder, *International Dimensions of Organizational Behavior* (Boston: Kent, 1986).

[15]*Ibid.*

[16]P.R. Harris and G.T. Moran, *Managing Cultural Differences* (Houston: Gulf, 1987).

[17]H.A. Simon, *The New Science of Management Decision* (New York: Harper, 1960).

[18]P.A. Anderson, Decision making by objection and the Cuban Missile Crisis, *Administrative Science Quarterly* 28 (1983): 201–222.

[19]For a discussion of this model see M.D. Cohen, J.G. March, and J.P. Olsen, A garbage-can model of organizational choice, *Administrative Science Quarterly* 17 (1972): 1–25; J.G. March and J. Olsen, *Ambiguity and Choice in Organizations* (Bergin, Norway: Universiletsforlaget, 1976); M.K. Moch and L.R. Pondy, The structure of chaos: Organized anarchies as a response to ambiguity, *Administrative Science Quarterly* 22 (1977): 351–361.

[20]Recent research continues to confirm this observation. See, for example, J.P. Wanous and M.A. Youtz, Solution diversity and the quality of group decisions, *Academy of Management Journal* 29 (1986): 149–159; and P.C. Bottinger and P.W. Yetton, An integration of process and decision scheme explanations of group problem-solving performance, *Organizational Behavior and Human Decision Processes* 42 (1988): 234–249.

[21]Adler, *op. cit.,* p. 113.

[22]K. Dion, R. Baron, and N. Miller, Why do groups make riskier decisions than individuals?, In *Advances in Experimental Social Psychology* vol. 5, ed. L. Berkowitz (New York: Academic, 1970).

[23]H. Lamm and D.G. Myers, Group-induced polarization of attitudes and behaviors. In *Advances in Experimental Social Psychology* vol. 11, ed. L. Berkowitz (New York: Academic, 1978).

[24]A. Van de Ven and A. Delbecq, Nominal versus interacting group processes for committee decision-making effectiveness, *Academy of Management Journal* 14 (1971): 203–212.

[25]I. Janis, Groupthink, *Psychology Today,* June, 1971.

[26]P.W. Yetton and P.C. Bottinger, Individual versus group problem solving: An empirical test of a best-member strategy, *Organizational Behavior and Human Performance* 29 (1982): 307–321.

[27]H.J. Einhorn, R.M. Hogarth, and E. Klempner, Quality of group judgment, *Psychological Bulletin* 84 (1977): 158–172.

[28]Janis, *op. cit.*

[29]G. Whyte, Groupthink reconsidered, *Academy of Management Review* 14 (1989): 40–56; H. Lamm and D.G. Myers, Group-induced polarization of attitudes and behaviors. In *Advances in Experimental Social Psychology* vol. 11, ed. L. Berkowitz (New York: Academic Press, 1978).

[30]I.L. Janis and L. Mann, *Decision Making* (New York: Free Press, 1977).

[31]L.N. Jewell and H.J. Reitz, *Group Effectiveness in Organizations* (Glenview, Ill.: Scott, Foresman, 1981).

[32]See, for example, R.T. Pascale, Communication and decision making across cultures: Japanese and American comparisons, *Administrative Science Quarterly* 23 (1978): 91–110.

[33]S.E. Jackson, Participation in decision making as a strategy for reducing job-related stress, *Journal of Applied Psychology* 68 (1983): 3–19.

[34]D.W. Johnson and F.P. Johnson, *Joining Together: Group Theory and Group Skills* (Englewood Cliffs, N.J.: Prentice-Hall, 1975), pp. 269–270.

[35]See A. Tversky and D. Kahneman, *op. cit.;* A. Tversky and D. Kahneman, Judgment under uncertainty: Heuristics and biases, *Science* 185 (1974): 1121–1131; D. Kahneman and A. Tversky, On the psychology of prediction, *Psychological Review* 80 (1973): 251–273.

[36]P. Slovic, B. Fischhoff, and S. Lichtenstein, Behavioral decision theory, *Annual Review of Psychology* 28 (1977): 1–39.

[37]J.L. Adams, *Conceptual Blockbusting: A Guide to Better Ideas* 2d ed. (New York: W.W. Norton, 1979).

[38]*Ibid.*

[39]G.P. Huber, *Managerial Decision Making* (Glenview, Ill.: Scott, Foresman, 1980).

[40]A. Delbecq, A. Van de Ven, and D. Gustafson, *Group Techniques for Program Planning* (Glenview, Ill.: Scott, Foresman, 1975); Huber, *op. cit.*

[41]Van de Ven and Delbecq, *op. cit.*

[42]H.A. Linstone and M. Turoff (eds.), *The Delphi Method: Techniques and Applications* (Reading, Mass.: Addison-Wesley, 1975).

[43]*Ibid.*

[44]*Ibid.*

[45]S. Hart, M. Boroush, G. Enk, and W. Hornick, Managing complexity through consensus mapping: Technology for the structuring of group decisions, *Academy of Management Review* 10 (1985): 587–600.

[46]*Ibid.*

[47]These techniques are drawn from L. Adams, *op. cit.;* and E. De Bono, *Lateral Thinking: Creativity Step by Step* (New York: Harper & Row, 1970).

[48]De Bono, *op. cit.*

[49]Adams, *op. cit.*

RECOMMENDED READINGS

Arkes, H.R., and Hammond, K.R. *Judgment and Decision Making: An Interdisciplinary Reader*. New York: Cambridge University Press, 1986.

Bazerman, M. *Judgment in Managerial Decision Making*. New York: Wiley, 1986.

Fox, W.M. *Effective Group Problem Solving*. San Francisco: Jossey-Bass, 1987.

Harrison, E.F. *The Managerial Decision-Making Process* 3d ed. Boston: Houghton Mifflin, 1987.

Moore, C.M. *Group Techniques for Idea Building*. Beverly Hills, Cal.: Sage, 1987.

Nutt, P.C. *Making Tough Decisions*. San Francisco: Jossey-Bass, 1989.

Pennings, J.M. (ed.). *Decision Making: An Organizational Behavior Approach*. New York: M. Wiener, 1986.

Rowe, A.J. *Managing with Style: A Guide to Understanding, Assessing, and Improving Decision Making*. San Francisco: Jossey-Bass, 1987.

Rubenstein, M.F. *Tools for Thinking and Problem Solving*. Englewood Cliffs, N.J.: Prentice-Hall, 1986.

7

Developing Effective Communication

CHAPTER OUTLINE

LEARNING OBJECTIVES

After completing the reading and activities in Chapter 7, students will be able to

- describe, illustrate, and identify the steps in the communication process;
- compare and contrast communication that occurs upward, downward, and laterally, and offer strategies for communicating effectively in each direction;
- discuss how organizational structure and interpersonal relationships affect the accuracy of communication;
- specify the barriers to effective communication and propose strategies for reducing them;
- offer guidelines for increasing the effectiveness of interviews in organizations;
- specify and illustrate the dimensions of a supportive communication climate;
- compare an assertive style to aggressive and passive styles and illustrate its use; and
- show how active listening contributes to effective communication.

Communication Breakdown at King Publishing Company

Raymond Jain, Marketing Vice President of King Publishing Company, wondered whether the only solution to the problem he was encountering with his boss might have to be his own resignation.

Jain had come to King after completing an undergraduate degree in business and had risen over a fifteen-year period through staff and managerial jobs to his new executive position. He had never worked closely with Edward Vance, King's president, but was told he had been selected because of his strong performance over the past five years. The two men had shared little in managerial philosophy, but shared a mutual respect. Now, working closely with Vance, Jain's impression changed. Jain also sensed that Vance may have come to regret choosing him for the marketing position.

The sales projections had started the rift. Vance strongly supported the use of acquisitions to maintain the company's position. Jain was convinced that by allocating resources to the development of existing and related magazines, books, and software, and upgrading the company's technology to support their publication, King Publishing could beat the competition. He believed that if King Publishing executives understood the needs of the markets it could serve, could deliver the products in a timely fashion, and could continually upgrade them, it could retain its position of leadership. Vance's response to this view astonished Jain. Vance contended that Jain's ideas were impractical, that Jain was naive in proposing them, and that matters of policy were properly the province of the President.

Jain decided, based on the vehemence of Vance's response, to avoid further discussion where their opinions differed significantly. With Vance absorbed by other things, which typically took him out of town, Jain took steps to reshape the organization to fit his thinking. He modified the organization structure by eliminating some positions and changing others. He also changed the aims of the sales staff, from an emphasis on products to a focus on the customer's needs. Periodically Vance questioned Jain about these changes. Jain felt they remained in basic disagreement because on the rare occasions when they talked Vance could not "hear" his opposition to the acquisition strategy and see the advantages of Jain's approach.

Jain decided that the philosophical differences between himself and Vance were too deep to remain concealed. He was distressed that he could not speak freely to Vance and that communication had virtually ceased between them. Jain felt that he needed clarification of his area of authority. Although he anticipated that such a discussion might lead to more friction, he made the suggestion to Vance that they sit down and discuss their respective responsibilities. Vance agreed, promising a thorough review as soon as time permitted. However, Jain had yet to hear anything more on the subject.

From his point of view, Edward Vance was troubled by Jain's behavior since his appointment as Marketing Vice President. Early signs of trouble came when Jain wanted the company to invest vast sums in new and unproven equipment. To Vance, it was the more difficult way to expand sales. Vance also was disturbed by changes Jain had made in the organization. Jain's request for a meeting to discuss authority was troublesome to Vance, since his recent doubts about Jain's judgment left him wondering just how much authority this marketing vice president should have.

Especially annoying were Jain's tactics of gaining support for an idea

among other executives of the firm and carrying out irreversible changes without coming first to Vance with a specific proposal. Why couldn't his own directness be matched by a similar willingness on the part of his subordinate? Vance preferred directness; he felt that Jain was too smooth and subtle, and seemed unwilling to stand up for his beliefs in public. Vance wondered if they could continue to work together.[1]

What has been happening between Vance and Jain? What factors contribute to the present impasse? Why do Vance and Jain seem to communicate ineffectively? What would improve their communication?

In this chapter we examine the nature of effective communication. Defined as "the exchange of information between a sender and a receiver and the inference of meaning,"[2] communication is a central organizational process. The exchange of information between different organizational participants links the different subsystems of an organization. As a linking mechanism, communication is a central feature of the *structure* of groups and organizations (as discussed in Chapters 5 and 11): it builds and reinforces interdependence between various parts of the organization. The inference of meaning occurs as a function of a variety of personal and situational factors (described in Chapters 2, 3, and 5).

This chapter first describes the components of communication. Then it looks at the directions communication can take. Next it lists a variety of factors that affect quality communication. The chapter then discusses issues related to a special type of communication in organizations—interviewing. It concludes with strategies for improving communication accuracy.

COMPONENTS OF COMMUNICATION

Perception, attribution, motivation, personality, and personal development all affect the way a person transmits information and receives information transmitted by another. A simple example illustrates the communication process. One of my students recently asked me how long an upcoming examination would be. I answered by stating, "One hundred questions." When the student asked that simple question and I responded, we both participated in a complex communication process. In communication, an *input* is *transformed* by *encoding* and *decoding*, resulting in another meaning, or *output*, which is *fed back* to the sender.[3] Figure 7–1 illustrates the steps of the process.

Encoding

Once a person has a meaning to convey, he or she needs to determine the means to convey that meaning—the way to *encode* it. The sender uses his or her own *frame of reference* as the background for encoding information. It includes the individual's view of an organization or situation, as a function of

Figure 7–1 THE COMMUNICATION PROCESS

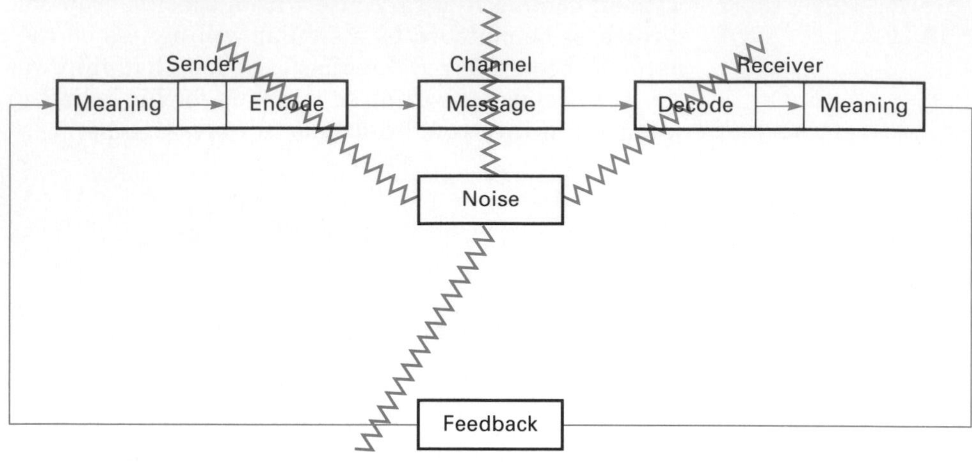

personal education, interpersonal relationships, attitudes, knowledge, and experience.

Going back to my simple example, first, my student had a meaning she wished to convey. I later learned that she wanted to determine the comprehensiveness of the examination—she did not want to know the exact number of questions, but rather what material would be covered. Notice that this meaning differs from the question she asked. She really wanted to know whether the test would cover the material presented in class, readings and text assignments, and the optional videos shown. Next, she had to decide how to encode this meaning. She had to decide, for example, an efficient way of getting the needed information. She considered, probably unconsciously, whom she should ask: a classmate? a teaching assistant? the professor? Should she ask the question by phone, in a letter, or directly? What specific question should she ask so that she would be understood? What nonverbal messages (e.g., an attitude of pleading? of arrogance? of total ignorance?) should accompany her question? How else might my student have encoded this message? She might have asked what topics would be covered on the examination; or requested me to list all the textbook chapters that would be included; or inquired if class lectures would be covered. In encoding a message, a sender must consider what is the most effective way to convey the desire for certain information.

Transmission

The actual transmission of a message follows encoding: the sender must convey the message to the receiver. Here, my student came to my office with her textbook and class notebook. She walked in and asked how long the examination would be. Thus the transmission of her message took place primarily by verbal channels. Because she showed me the text for the course, I knew which class's examination she was referring to (she was in two of my courses). But other methods of transmission are available, as summarized in Table 7–1. Why did my student choose face-to-face communication? She probably felt that I could more easily show and explain the examination's content to her, and she could receive immediate feedback to her question.

Table 7–1 COMMUNICATION METHODS

Method	Advantages	Disadvantages
Telephone	Verbal Permits questions and answers Convenient Two-way flow Immediate feedback	Less personal No record of conversation Message might be misunderstood Timing may be inconvenient May be impossible to terminate
Face-to-face	Visual Personal contact Can "show" and "explain" Can set the mood Immediate feedback	Timing may be inconvenient Requires spontaneous thinking May not be easy to terminate Power or status of one person may cause pressure
Meetings	Can use visuals Involves several minds at once Two-way flow	Time-consuming Time may be inconvenient One person may dominate the group
Memorandum	Brief Provides a record Can prethink the message Can disseminate widely	No control over receiver Less personal One-way flow Delayed feedback
Formal Report	Complete; comprehensive Can organize material at writer's leisure Can disseminate widely	Less personal May require considerable time in reading Language may not be understandable Expensive One-way flow Delayed feedback
Teleconference	Saves time for travel Visual Lessens impact of power/status Makes users be better prepared	Miss interpersonal contact Not good for initial brainstorming sessions Expensive

Reprinted with permission from P.V. Lewis, *Organizational Communication: The Essence of Effective Management* 3d ed. (New York: Wiley, 1987), p. 9. Reprinted by permission of the publisher.

Decoding

I performed the next step of the communication process. I needed to decode the message I had received, to attach some meaning to it. An individual's decoding of a message, like encoding, depends on his or her frame of reference. I might have interpreted my student's question in several different ways, based on frame of reference. I might, for example, have viewed her question as a plea for an easy exam; or I might have felt that she literally wanted the information she requested—the number of questions. If there had been conflict between the student and me, I might have interpreted the question as something meant to annoy me or distract me from my work. If my usual perception is that the student is a hard worker, then I might have interpreted the question as another indication of her industriousness. If I were dealing with a student who was taking the course on a pass–fail basis, I might have interpreted the question to mean "How many questions must the student answer correctly to pass the examination?" As it turned out, I did not at first understand the question accurately, as a request for information about the comprehensiveness as opposed to the length of the examination, with no particular feelings involved.

Noise

Many decodings reflect some noise in the communication system, or distortions of the message sent and received. Distortions suggest that some factors, such as conflict between myself and the student or my attribution of industriousness, affected my understanding of the message in such a way that I did not "hear" what my student intended. Noise can mean literal physical noise that interferes with transmission, such as static on a telephone line or the noise created by office or plant machinery. But noise can also include characteristics of the sender or receiver, such as their socioeconomic background, experience, education, or value system. We examine noise again later in this chapter.

Feedback

My feedback to my student, in which I provided only the length of the examination, indicated inaccurate understanding. If I had told the sender (my student), "Don't be so lazy; study all the material," I would also have been conveying a different, inaccurate understanding, one colored by my own perceptual processes, by the means the sender chose to encode and transmit the message, or by some noise that interfered with accurate reception.

Several slips can occur in communication. Senders may transmit messages other than the ones they intend. Receivers may decode messages in ways that differ from the senders' intentions. Lines of transmission may be blocked. Feedback may not occur. And noise may infringe on the process.

Now consider the situation at King Publishing. What messages do you think Vance sent to Jain? Assuming he definitely wanted to change the status quo at King, did he encode this message accurately? How might he encode the message so that Jain fulfilled his wishes? What channels should he use to convey this message? In the case, he failed to use any channel. He could instead talk to Jain face-to-face. Sending him a memorandum might be more powerful, yet more alienating. And how did Jain decode the messages? He allowed the lack of direct communication to justify using his own discretion in reshaping the organization.

Consider now what Jain might say to Vance about the future of the company. Once he decides how to handle the situation he communicates his intentions to Vance. How does he encode his message? What medium does he use to convey the message? The case implies that on the rare occasion they meet, Vance uses face-to-face communication, although not very persuasively or effectively. What noise likely is present in the communication? Clearly differences in their views of the basis for organizational effectiveness create noise; so does Vance's absence from the company. Their different styles of communication and preference for confrontation may also contribute to the noise. But the feedback Vance gives to Jain—his being disturbed and troubled—reflects the communication dysfunctions at King Publishing. Vance and Jain must try to communicate as accurately as possible the messages they intend to send and are intended to receive.

THE DIRECTION OF COMMUNICATION

Subtle differences exist in the nature of communication between Vance and Jain because of the direction of the communication.

Downward Communication

Managers use this type of communication to disseminate information and give orders and directives to subordinates. Top management must find ways to honestly share both good news and bad news with employees. They should also provide for feedback and recognition that a message received by the subordinate may differ significantly from that sent by the boss. Encouraging face-to-face communication between all levels of managers and employees, through plant visits, management–employee discussion groups, company newsletters, or even a communication hot-line in the organization, can facilitate accurate downward communication.

Too often, however, downward communication is one-way, with no provision for feedback. Although most managers may intend to communicate accurately to their subordinates, some may consciously or unconsciously distort downward communication. Power differences (discussed in Chapter 9) affect and can distort downward communication. Managers can also withhold, screen, or manipulate information.[4] What results from this type of communication? Subordinates can become very distrustful of their managers and circumvent them to obtain accurate information. They may rely more on rumors, often obtaining equally distorted information. In some organizations, downward communication between bosses and subordinates is relatively accurate, but information from top management often fails to reach lower level employees accurately; managers may adjust or delay it along the way so it better fits their objectives. Such distortions in downward communication occur, for example, when a company experiences a financial crisis, which often precipitates significant layoffs.

Although open communication has been considered a panacea for many organizational problems, some researchers have argued that characteristics of the individuals involved, their relationships, and the organization and environment in which they function should influence how open communication should be.[5] Reading 7–1, "Reconsidering Openness in Organizational Communication," discusses this issue in greater detail. Disclosure and directness can backfire if, for example, subordinates are not prepared to receive the information being sent. Can you think of a situation where this might occur? Also, cultural differences can exist in the meaning and value attached to downward communication. Relatively authoritarian societies emphasize this direction over others, while more egalitarian societies encourage and better support upward and lateral communication.

Upward Communication

Primarily a feedback vehicle, upward communication refers to messages sent from subordinates to their bosses. Bosses must create a climate that promotes honest upward communications as a way of counteracting employees' tendencies to hide potentially damaging information. Such a climate encourages employee participation in decision making, rewards openness, and limits inflexible policies and arbitrary procedures. Acting constructively on information communicated upward reinforces its future occurrence and limits executive isolation.

How would you describe and evaluate upward communication from Jain to Vance? Does Jain accurately communicate his ideas about the future direction of King Publishing to his boss? Does Jain provide feedback to Vance about his views of Vance's ideas? Although Jain initially seems to try to share his views with Vance, he soon stops communicating upward when he perceives Vance's opposition to his ideas. Jain then limits upward communication, seemingly as a way of protecting his actions from his boss's scrutiny.

Managers such as Jain need to be encouraged to share information about their attitudes, work developments, and even mistakes with their bosses since this type of communication can increase personal and organizational effectiveness. Overemphasizing downward communication, remaining office-bound, and improperly delegating responsibilities can increase executive isolation.[6] Vance's frequent absences, failure to listen to Jain, and laissez-faire attitude toward Jain's changes have surely contributed to their dysfunctional communication.

Lateral Communication

Organizational members frequently share information, engage in problem solving, and coordinate work flow with employees at their same level in the organization. While some messages need to go through formal channels, many can be handled through informal channels, or laterally. Workers assembling different parts of a product may coordinate the use of inventories by lateral (or horizontal) communication; sales representatives may discuss field problems with technical services personnel; the Marketing Vice President may resolve sales problems by gathering information from other marketing vice presidents. Although subordinates in different or distant departments may have problems communicating directly and may rely on the hierarchy for an exchange of information (e.g., passing it from subordinate to manager to top manager to second manager to second subordinate), direct communication between subordinates typically has greater speed and accuracy. Distortions in lateral communication can occur at any place in the two-way model: encoding, transmission, decoding, noise, or feedback.

Gatekeepers and Boundary Spanners Special roles in the organization can facilitate accurate lateral communication. *Gatekeepers* screen information and access to a group or individual.[7] Situated at a crossroads of communication channels, these positions act as nerve centers, where they switch information among people and groups.[8] Gatekeepers can also communicate extensively internally and externally with professionals outside the organization; in this case they act as boundary spanners.[9] Staff specialists, such as human resources professionals, who interact with line management groups, fill such roles. Technical gatekeepers in a research laboratory bring supplier information to their own and other groups in the organization.[10] Managers also act as gatekeepers, sharing information with subordinates, superiors, and peers.

Boundary spanners exist where two groups or units interact. Product managers, department representatives to a task force, or individuals holding other liaison positions between two groups or units, such as the research and development and marketing departments, act as boundary spanners. They serve the roles of information processor and representative for an organization or its subunits to others outside the unit's boundary.[11] They differ from gatekeepers in their emphasis on facilitating the exchange of information rather than acting primarily as a screening device. A purchasing agent, sales representative, or public relations director, for example, can act as a communication link between a department's or organization's internal and external environments.

In R&D laboratories, individuals in boundary-spanning roles perform significant communication activities.[12] These individuals gather information from other groups and external sources as a way of remaining current technologically and coordinating with other work groups.[13] One study of an engineering laboratory demonstrated that such roles stem from the perceived competence of the individual and the extent of colleague consultation in which that person engages.[14] Acting as an internal spanner or liaison between the laboratory and the rest of the organization frequently served as a prerequisite for the role of external liaison between the laboratory or larger organization and an outside organization.

FACTORS THAT AFFECT THE QUALITY OF COMMUNICATION

The quality of communication results from a number of factors. It might, as indicated earlier, be due to the receiver's perceptions, attributions, learning, personality, or role set, as discussed in Chapters 2 and 3. In this section we discuss the following factors: (1) the structure of the organization, (2) the interpersonal relationship between the sender and the receiver, (3) the nature of feedback, (4) noise, (5) the use of language, (6) listening skills, (7) the attitudes of the parties, (8) nonverbal communication, and (9) the extent of cross-cultural sensitivity.

Organizational Structure

Almost all organizations are hierarchies: they include both superiors and subordinates. Although structural factors facilitate and direct communication to a high degree in most organizations, according to several studies, these same hierarchical arrangements contribute to communication difficulties in organizations as well. As noted earlier, lower-level organizational members, such as Jain, tend to suppress unfavorable information and to communicate irrelevant information upward to bosses such as Vance.[15] As also discussed earlier, this occurs because people feel that their superiors may regard them unfavorably if they pass along negative information.

In addition, organizations have various degrees of centralization (see Chapter 11). Centralization of authority at the higher levels of the organization restricts the dissemination of information. Some organizational members may have access to more information than others; some subunits may have different information from other subunits. Since some people know much more or different information, centralization, which discourages shared information, increases the potential for misunderstandings among various subunits.

The extent to which organizations have specialized work groups also influences the quality of communication. Where differences exist between departments in their goals and expertise, communication among peers may be limited. Mechanisms to link different departments should be sought. In addition, encouraging full expression, confrontation, and working through of disagreements is important.[16] When possible, power differences between departments should also be recognized and reduced. And, as described in Chapter 4, reward systems that encourage lateral communication should be instituted.

Interpersonal Relationships

The relationship between the two people (or two groups) communicating, as well as the type of climate they create during their communication, also affects the accuracy with which messages are given and received. Four aspects of interpersonal relationships influence communication in organizations: (1) the sender's and receiver's *trust* of each other; (2) the sender's and receiver's *influence* over each other; (3) the sender's *mobility aspirations;* and (4) the *norms and sanctions* of the group(s) to which the sender and receiver belong.[17]

When people trust each other, their communication tends to be more accurate and open; when they distrust each other, they are more likely to be secretive or hesitant to talk openly. If Vance trusts Jain, for example, he is more likely to present the problem and alternatives to him than to give Jain his decision about the future of the company as a fait accompli. When the receiver has considerable influence over the sender, the sender's communications are likely to be somewhat guarded, often because the sender distrusts the receiver. This may explain the unwillingness by Jain to share with Vance his plans for restructuring. This effect is similar to the hierarchical effect examined above. Likewise upwardly mobile senders are likely to alter communication in a way that helps their personal advancement. That is, Jain may underestimate the importance of and even ignore the comments made by his subordinates if they do not fit with his plans. Finally, group norms (or expected standards of behavior) and sanctions (expressions of approval or disapproval by the group) may limit the amount or type of information people feel they can legitimately discuss. In many work groups, for example, it is unacceptable to talk about failure in the group.

The informal organization also creates a communication pattern, commonly known as the *grapevine.* Carrying information outside official channels, the grapevine can either supplement or replace the organizational hierarchy as a communication conduit. While the grapevine can provide information about employee attitudes, serve as an emotional outlet for workers, and even spread true information, it can also disseminate rumors and false information.[18] Fig-

Figure 7–2 Observations about the Grapevine

1. The grapevine is a significant part of an organizational communication system with regard to (a) quantity of information communicated and (b) quality of information, such as its importance and its effects on people and performance.
2. The quality of management decisions depends on quality of information inputs that management has, and one useful input is information from the grapevine.
3. Successful communication with employees depends on (a) understanding their problems, (b) understanding their attitudes, and (c) determining gaps in employee information (the grapevine is a valuable source of these kinds of inputs).
4. The quality of management decisions is significantly affected by management's success in listening to and interpreting the grapevine.
5. The quality of management communication programs is significantly affected by management's capacity to understand and to relate to the grapevine.
6. The grapevine cannot be suppressed or directly controlled, although it may be influenced by the way management relates to it.
7. The grapevine has both negative and positive influences in an organization.
8. The grapevine can provide useful inputs even when information it carries is known to be incorrect.
9. In normal organizational situations, excluding situations such as strikes and disasters, the grapevine on the average carries more correct information than inaccurate information.
10. The grapevine carries an incomplete story.
11. Compared with most formal communications, the grapevine tends to speed faster through an organization, so it can affect people very quickly.
12. Grapevine communications are *caused.*
13. Men and women are approximately equally active on the grapevine.
14. Nonverbal communication is significant in interpreting verbal grapevine communication.
15. Informal leaders often serve as message centers for receiving, interpreting, and distributing grapevine information to others.
16. Typical grapevine activity usually is not a sign of organizational sickness or health; that is, grapevine activity is a normal response to group work.

From P.V. Lewis, *Organizational Communication: The Essence of Effective Management* 3d ed. (New York: Wiley, 1987), pp. 47–48. Reprinted by permission of the publisher.

ure 7–2 lists a series of observations about the grapevine. Managers and other organizational members must recognize that the grapevine is alive and functioning in all organizations.

Nature of Feedback

Compare the diagram of the communication process shown in Figure 7–3 to that shown in Figure 7–1. How do they differ? The two-way communication shown in Figure 7–1 emphasizes the role of feedback in the process. *Feedback* refers to an acknowledgement by the receiver that the message has been received; it provides the sender with information about the receiver's understanding of the message being sent. For example, if I nod my head and say "Yes" in response to my student's question about the length of an upcoming examination, I am acknowledging that I heard her question, but I may be suggesting that it is a question I do not want to answer or do not feel I should

Figure 7–3 One-Way Communication

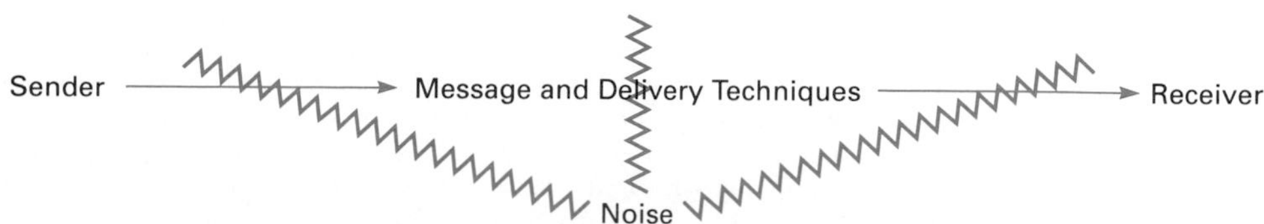

answer. If I instead tell her about the courses she can take next semester, I am providing feedback that either I did not hear or did not understand her question. If, on the other hand, I answer her by stating "50 questions" or "100 questions" then I am indicating that I have taken her question literally and am responding to it; my answers show whether I understood her question.

However, often one-way communication occurs between managers and their subordinates. Because of inherent power differences in their positions (see Chapter 9) managers may give large quantities of information and directions to their subordinates without providing the opportunity for the subordinates to show their understanding or receipt of the information. These managers often experience conflict between their role as authorities and a desire to be liked by subordinates. Other managers have relied on the use of written memoranda as a way of communicating with subordinates. In addition to the inherent lack of feedback involved in this format, the use of a single channel of communication also limits the effectiveness of downward communication.

Why do some managers not involve their subordinates in two-way communication? In some situations, managers do not trust their subordinates to contribute effectively. In other situations, lack of self-confidence by the manager makes him or her appear disinterested in or unconcerned about subordinates' opinions. Or superiors assume that subordinates have the same goals as their bosses, and thus feel that input from the subordinates is not required. What is your attitude toward feedback? You can assess it by completing the questionnaire shown in Figure 7–4. (The higher your score, the more discomfort you feel in giving feedback.) Recognizing discomfort in giving or receiving feedback is a key step in eliminating this barrier and improving the quality of managerial communication.

Encouraging feedback from subordinates helps to show them that you are concerned about them as individuals, in ways that go beyond merely ensuring that they produce. For example, I might view my student's question about the

Figure 7–4 FEEDBACK QUESTIONNAIRE

Indicate the degree of discomfort you would feel in each situation given below, by circling the appropriate number: 1—high discomfort; 2—some discomfort; 3—undecided; 4—very little discomfort; 5—no discomfort.

1 2 3 4 5 1. Telling an employee who is also a friend that he or she must stop coming to work late.
1 2 3 4 5 2. Talking to an employee about his or her performance on the job.
1 2 3 4 5 3. Asking an employee if he or she has any comments about your rating of his or her performance.
1 2 3 4 5 4. Telling an employee who has problems in dealing with other employees that he or she should do something about it.
1 2 3 4 5 5. Responding to an employee who is upset over your rating of his or her performance.
1 2 3 4 5 6. An employee's becoming emotional and defensive when you tell him or her about mistakes in the job.
1 2 3 4 5 7. Giving a rating that indicates improvement is needed to an employee who has failed to meet minimum requirements of the job.
1 2 3 4 5 8. Letting a subordinate talk during an appraisal interview.
1 2 3 4 5 9. An employee's challenging you to justify your evaluation in the middle of an appraisal interview.
1 2 3 4 5 10. Recommending that an employee be discharged.
1 2 3 4 5 11. Telling an employee that you are uncomfortable in the role of having to judge his or her performance.
1 2 3 4 5 12. Telling an employee that his or her performance can be improved.
1 2 3 4 5 13. Telling an employee that you will not tolerate his or her taking extended coffee breaks.
1 2 3 4 5 14. Telling an employee that you will not tolerate his or her making personal telephone calls on company time.

examination as her way of approaching me about other, more significant personal problems. The way I respond to her question, such as by asking her if there is any other way I can help her or if she has any other questions, may encourage this sharing.

Subordinates also have responsibility for encouraging two-way communication. While superiors may attempt to protect their power positions, subordinates attempt to protect the image their boss holds of them. Frequently, for example, subordinates withhold negative information about themselves or their activities. Or they may fail to inform their superior about their needs and values. Other subordinates mistrust their superiors and so withhold any information from them.

Why do these situations arise? Some subordinates may assume that they and their bosses have different goals. Others mistrust their bosses. Still others lack persistence in seeking responses from their supervisors. Finally, subordinates must show that they, too, are willing to build relationships with their superiors. For example, if my student feels that my response is inadequate, she has the responsibility to provide some feedback that reflects this perception. She might state, "I didn't really want to know the exact number of questions but rather what material would be covered." Or she might nod, suggesting that the information I provided was sufficient.

Consider the situation at King Publishing. Does quality feedback facilitate communication? Although the case implies that both Vance and Jain know how their messages about the direction of the company have been received, no explicit feedback occurs. Jain heard Vance's response to technical innovation, but did not counter it with feedback about his disagreement. Rather he acted surreptitiously to implement his own agenda. Similarly, Vance did not confront Jain or provide concrete feedback about his opposition to Jain's approach. Silence occurred instead.

Noise

Interference that occurs during the communication process is called *noise*. If you try to hold a conversation with another person while walking near a building under construction, you have experienced the effect of physical or audible noise on communication. But noise may also be inaudible. The presence of a silent third party during a conversation may act as noise that distracts the receiver from hearing what the speaker said. Or the frame of reference of the receiver may cause that person to hear the message in a way other than the one in which it was intended.

What types of noise likely exist in communications between Vance and Jain? What types might exist between Jain and his subordinates? Differences in their roles in the organization may create noise. Biases in their attributions for poor performance may create noise. So too may various perceptual predispositions, such as different personal and organizational goals, attitudes, and orientations. Vance's and Jain's previous experience in dealing with similar situations may also create noise.

Use of Language

The choice of words or language in which a sender encodes a message influences the quality of communication. Because language is a symbolic representation of a phenomenon, there is room for interpretation and distortion of meaning. Consider an instructor who decides to present an entire class in a foreign language that few or none of the students understand. Consider a salesperson who describes a product using so many technical specifications that his or her client cannot easily determine the product's characteristics. Think about a manager whose directions are so ambiguous that his or her subordinate cannot determine the most appropriate way of acting. In each of these cases, the inappropriate use of language limits the quality of effective communication.

A sender can create misunderstandings by using language in a number of ways.[19] The sender may use words that are too abstract and have many mental images associated with them. Or the sender may overgeneralize messages and fail to recognize subtleties. As noted earlier, the use of jargon frequently creates misunderstandings, as does the use of slang or colloquialisms. Some senders consciously use messages to confuse the issue. Others leave information out of messages. Both Vance and Jain may create misunderstandings in each of these ways: Vance may not encode his disapproval of Jain's actions clearly; and Jain may not justify expenditures for technical innovation sufficiently.

As for feedback, misuses of language are especially common between superiors and their subordinates. For example, a subordinate can create misunderstandings by distorting information upwards: telling the boss only good news, paying the boss compliments whenever possible, always agreeing with the boss, avoiding offering personal opinions different from the boss's, insulating the boss from information detrimental to him or her, covering up information potentially damaging to oneself, and selecting words that project only favorable impressions.[20] Likewise, the boss can create misunderstandings by withholding information or omitting the emotional content of a message.

Listening Skills

Not only does the sender influence the effectiveness of communication, but the listening by the receiver helps determine communication quality. A supervisor or executive "must have, among other abilities, the ability to listen intelligently and carefully to those with whom he (or she) works."[21] This calls for *active listening* by individuals. In active listening, the receiver "does not passively absorb the words which are spoken to him. He (or she) actively tries to grasp the facts and the feelings in what he (or she) hears, and tries, by listening, to help the speaker work out his (or her) own problems."[22] In his or her part of the conversation, the active listener reflects the feelings heard to test perceptual accuracy. The listener also shares ownership of any problem identified with the speaker.

Active listening requires determining what the speaker is trying to say from his or her own viewpoint.[23] Active listening therefore requires the receiver to listen for the total meaning the other person conveys. The receiver must try to determine both the content of a message and the feelings underlying it. Consider a subordinate who asks to leave work an hour early. Active listening would require the manager to determine the feelings—worry, fatigue, or frustration, for example—underlying the question. The listener must next acknowledge these feelings: the manager must respond to both the question and the feelings expressed. Finally, active listening calls for noting all the cues, both verbal and nonverbal, in communication. Other guidelines for listening are shown in Figure 7–5.

Figure 7–5 GUIDELINES FOR LISTENING

1. Listen patiently to what the other person has to say, even though you may believe it is wrong or irrelevant. Indicate simple acceptance (not necessarily agreement) by nodding or injecting an occasional "um-hm" or "I see."
2. Try to understand the feeling the person is expressing, as well as the intellectual content. Most of us have difficulty talking clearly about our feelings, so careful attention is required.
3. Restate the person's feeling, briefly but accurately. At this stage, simply serve as a mirror and encourage the other person to continue talking. Occasionally make summary responses such as "you think you're in a dead-end job," or "you feel the manager is playing favorites"; but in doing so, keep your tone neutral and try not to lead the person to your pet conclusions.
4. Allow time for the discussion to continue without interruption and try to separate the conversation from more official communication of company plans. That is, do not make the conversation any more "authoritative" than it already is by virtue of your position in the organization.
5. Avoid direct questions and arguments about facts; refrain from saying "that's just not so," "hold on a minute, let's look at the facts," or "prove it." You may want to review evidence later, but a review is irrelevant to how a person feels now.
6. When the other person does touch on a point you do want to know more about, simply repeat his or her statement as a question. For instance, if the person remarks "nobody can break even on his expense account," you can probe by replying, "you say no one breaks even on expenses?" With this encouragement he or she will probably expand on the previous statement.
7. Listen for what isn't said—evasions of pertinent points or perhaps too-ready agreement with common cliches. Such omissions may be clues to a bothersome fact the person wishes were not true.
8. If the other person appears genuinely to want your viewpoint, be honest in your reply. But in the listening stage, try to limit the expression of your views since these may condition or suppress what the other person says.
9. Focus on the content of the message; try not to think about your next statement until the person is finished talking.
10. Don't make judgments until all information has been conveyed.

Attitudes of the Parties

Attitudes of each person or group toward collaboration and competition can also affect the quality of communication. Parties with competitive attitudes

- define conflict as win–lose,
- pursue only their own goals,
- understand their own needs, but publicly disguise them,
- aggrandize their power
- use threats to get submission,
- overemphasize their own needs, goals, and position,
- adopt an attitude of exploiting the other party whenever possible,
- emphasize only differences in positions and the superiority of their own position, and
- isolate the other person or group.[24]

Particularly when one or both individuals or groups takes a competitive attitude, communication between them can project this we–they or win–lose perspective. A we–they attitude can polarize the interacting groups and thus establishes a communication barrier between them.

Nonverbal Communication

The use of gestures, movements, material things, time, and space can clarify or confuse the meaning of verbal communication.[25] For example, the kind of facial expressions that accompany a request for time off may indicate its importance or frivolity. If an interviewer arrives at an interview late, the interviewee may interpret any comments as less sincere than if the interviewer is prompt. A salesperson may use props to illustrate aspects of a sales pitch.

Nonverbal cues serve five functions. They *repeat* the message the individual is making verbally: an individual who nods after he or she answers affirmatively confirms the verbal message with the nonverbal gesture. They can *contradict* a message the individual is trying to convey. An individual who pounds the table while stating that he or she does not care about the situation being discussed uses verbal and nonverbal communication that disagree. The nonverbal communication may in some cases be more powerful or accurate than the verbal communication. Nonverbal cues may also *substitute* for a verbal message: an individual with "fire in his eyes" conveys information without using verbal messages. Nonverbal cues may add to or *complement* a verbal message: a supervisor who beams while giving praise increases the impact of the compliment on the subordinate. Or nonverbal communication may *accent* or underline a verbal message; for example, speaking very softly or stamping your feet shows the importance you attach to a message.[26]

Senders must recognize the significance of nonverbal communication and use it to increase the impact of their verbal communication. They must also recognize that nonverbal signals may give a different message than they intend. English-speaking managers who supervise non-English-speaking workers often experience this problem.[27] A gesture, for example, may have different meaning in different cultures: "the A-OK gesture (the thumb and forefinger circled), as used in the United States, means that things are fine, great, or that something has been understood perfectly. But Brazilians interpret it as an obscene gesture, and to the Japanese it means money."[28] Receivers must also acknowledge the importance of nonverbal communication and look for nonverbal cues that support or contradict verbal information.

Extent of Cross-Cultural Sensitivity

Cross-cultural issues may affect the quality of communication. For example, differences in norms for the appropriate amount of interpersonal space exist in different cultures. Effective communication requires deciphering the basic values, motives, aspirations, and assumptions across geographical, occupational, functional, or social class lines.[29] It also means seeing our own culture as different but not necessarily better.[30] Cross-cultural miscommunication occurs when a receiver misunderstands the message transmitted by a sender of another culture. Consider the following example:

> An American company eager to do business in Saudi Arabia sent over a sales manager to "get something going." . . . The salesman learned that he had repeatedly insulted his contacts by his impatience, refusal of coffee, the "all business talk" attitude and aggressive selling. Even incidental acts such as handing people paper with his left hand, and exposing the side of his shoe while sitting on the floor were improper Saudi customs.[31]

What types of miscommunication occurred here because of cultural differences? Now consider a study of 436 People's Republic of China managers which found that formality dominated their daily exchanges.[32] What communication dysfunctions might result in their interactions with managers from the United

States, who are often comfortable using first names and more informal interactions?

To ensure quality communication, communicators should first assume that cultural differences exist, and they should then try to view the situation from the perspective of their foreign colleagues.[33] They can then adjust their encoding or decoding to respond to likely differences. Knowledge of the characteristics of diverse cultures facilitates such an adjustment. A cultural integrator—a person who understands the differences between another society and the home country and the ways the organization can adapt to them—can also reduce the barrier of inadequate cross-cultural sensitivity.[34] Companies can select a cultural integrator from among home-country nationals familiar with the host country or host-country nationals familiar with home-country culture and the firm's operations. How might a cultural integrator help the salesman trying to do business in Saudi Arabia described above?

INTERVIEWS

Communication problems are most acute when organizational members conduct some type of employee evaluation, such as an employment interview or performance appraisal. In employment interviews communicators transmit information that allows them to make decisions about the fit between a job applicant and an available position. In performance appraisal, supervisor and subordinate share information about the subordinate's performance to date and future development.

Types of Questions

The interviewer can ask open-ended questions or closed-ended questions. *Open-ended* questions, such as "Tell me about your experience in financial analysis," or "What do you consider your weaknesses as an employee?," allow the interviewee to structure the response to the question and present information that he or she feels is important. *Closed-ended* questions, such as "Tell me the first thing you would say to a potential customer," or "How many employees have you supervised during the past year?," allow the interviewer to focus a response more precisely. Some combination of the two approaches is most effective. The interview can move from open-ended questions to closed-ended questions, alternate the two types of questions, or begin with closed-ended questions and end with open-ended ones. Figure 7–6 is an example of one possible structure of an interview.

The types of questions asked must also be geared to the nature of the position to be filled. For example, in interviewing supervisory candidates a manager might ask the following questions:

1. Why do you want to be a supervisor?
2. What are the functions and duties of a supervisor as you see them?
3. What personal characteristics and other qualifications do you have that would help you to become a good supervisor?
4. How do you feel about taking on the added responsibilities and demands that come with a supervisory job?

Figure 7–6 SAMPLE INTERVIEW GUIDELINES FOR A SELECTION INTERVIEW

Opening

- Give a warm, friendly greeting—smile.
- Names are important—yours and the applicant's. Pronounce it correctly and use first and last names consistently. Tell the applicant what to call you and then ask the applicant for his or her preferred form of address.
- Talk briefly about yourself (your position in the company and then your personal background, hobbies, interests, etc.) to put the applicant at ease so that she or he might reciprocate with personal information.
- Ask the applicant about hobbies, activities, or some other topic that you believe will be of interest to "break the ice."

Structure the Interview

- State the purpose of interview: "The purpose of this interview is to discuss your qualifications and to see whether they match the skills needed to work as a selection interviewer. First, let's talk about your work experience and next your education and training. Then I will give you a preview of what the interviewer's job is really like. Finally, there will be a chance to ask about anything you want. How's that?"
- Since you plan to take notes, mention this to the applicant: "By the way, I will be taking some notes during the interview so that I don't miss any pertinent information that may come from our discussion. Okay?"

Work Experience: Most Relevant Job

- Use this comprehensive opening question: 'Let's talk about your work experience. How about starting with the job that you feel gave you the best preparation for working as a selection interviewer. Tell me all about the job: how you got it, why you chose it, your actual job duties, what you learned on the job, the hours and your attendance record, the pay, why you left (or are leaving), and things like that."
- Probe and follow up to cover each of these items thoroughly: how the applicant got the job, reasons for choosing it, job duties, etc.
- Summarize the major facts and findings from the applicant's most relevant job. For example: "Let me summarize what we have covered to make sure that I've got it right. You worked as a ________ where most of your time was spent doing ________ and ________, and you used these skills, ________ and ________. You chose the job because of ________ and your reasons for leaving it are ________ and ________. Anything else to add?"

Other Work Experience

- If time is available, discuss other jobs the applicant has held that might be pertinent. Get a brief overview of each job the applicant has held. Emphasize jobs held in the last five years or less, since older experience is less likely to be relevant for your decision.
- Ask the work experience questions you specifically prepared for this applicant when you planned the interview.
- Summarize your major findings about all jobs. When the summary is satisfactory to the applicant, go on to discuss education and training.

After the Interview

- Take time to write summary notes immediately. Describe the applicant's behavior and the impressions he or she created. Cite facts and specific incidents from the interview or from the person's work or educational history.
- Wait a day and then complete the Evaluation Form.

5. Do you think you could be a supervisor in any department other than your own? Where?
6. If you were a supervisor, could you motivate subordinates and take disciplinary action against employees, including former coworkers, if necessary? How would you handle, say, a worker with a high rate of absence?[35]

Questions that you might ask in interviewing a candidate for an executive position include the following:

1. What criteria would you (a) use in measuring your own performance over the next year and the following years, (b) like your performance measured by, and (c) use in measuring your superior's performance and your relation to him or her?

2. Assume we faced a significant cut in expenditures;—for example, 10 to 20 percent within a year or two. How would you go about planning and implementing such a cut in the areas of your responsibility?[36]

In most interviews the interviewer tries to make the interviewee feel at ease by beginning with questions that are relatively easy to answer and then moving on to questions that the interviewee may find more difficult.

Collecting Performance Data

Increasing the effectiveness of communication and the reliability of appraisals requires supervisors to obtain complete descriptions of subordinate behavior. When organizational members rely on a single source of information, persistent biases occur. Research studies suggest, for example, that employees' self-ratings tend to be considerably higher than either their peers' or their supervisor's.[37] In addition, different raters notice different aspects of employees' performance; nurses who rated themselves or their peers focused on such factors as dependability, availability in emergencies, and personal appearance, whereas their supervisors attended more to the amount of effort they exerted on the job.[38] Another study indicated that raters who had a positive affect toward ratees were most lenient and those with a negative affect were least lenient.[39] Finally, all raters demonstrated halo effects in their ratings: if the raters thought the nurses did well in one area, such as dependability, they tended to think the employee did well in several areas.[40] Here again we see the influence of perceptual distortions on communications about performance.

Guidelines for Effective Interviewing

Conducting interviews effectively requires the manager to share facts about actual performance as they occur rather than from memory. In a selection interview both parties might focus on information presented in the resume or in work samples provided by the applicant. At King Publishing Edward Vance might meet with Raymond Jain more frequently to share his observations of Jain's performance.

Such meetings should focus only on job-related behavior. They should emphasize direct observational data, rather than rely on hearsay reports from others, and describe specific behavior rather than make evaluative statements or describe an individual's personality. Vance, for example, might describe the structural changes Jain has made and offer a viable alternative to each one. Jain could communicate in the same specific way, carefully delineating the benefit of each change he has made. In performance evaluations supervisors should express both positive and negative behaviors and use the same basic form and level of detail for each subordinate.

With regard to performance, research suggests that individuals prefer specific to general feedback.[41] They also prefer feedback that suggests an external or situational cause of poor performance to feedback that suggests an internal or personal cause (see Chapter 2).[42] In all types of interviewing, managers should periodically review the communication procedures to ensure consistency.

IMPROVING COMMUNICATION ACCURACY

What can individuals do to improve their communication in both formal and informal settings? In this section we examine three ways of increasing communication effectiveness: (1) creating a supportive communication climate; (2) using an assertive communication style; and (3) using active listening techniques.

Creating a Supportive Climate

In communicating with Raymond Jain, Edward Vance should create a trusting and supportive environment. Creating such a climate has the objective of shifting from *evaluation* to *problem solving* in communication. He should avoid making Jain feel defensive—that is, threatened—by the communication. Superiors, subordinates, and other communicators can create such an atmosphere in six ways[43] (summarized in Table 7–2):

1. They use descriptive, as opposed to evaluative, speech. They present feelings or perceptions that do not imply that the receiver needs to change. Vance might describe which of Jain's actions he opposes, rather than evaluating them as bad.
2. They take a problem orientation, rather than trying to control the listener. A problem orientation implies a desire to collaborate in exploring a mutual problem rather than trying to alter the listener. Together Vance and Jain might discuss the future direction of King Publishing as a problem to be mutually solved, rather than one trying to dominate the other executive.

Table 7–2 CLIMATE DIMENSIONS

Dimensions of Supportive Climate	Dimensions of Defensive Climate
Description—giving and asking for information	Evaluation—praising, blaming, passing judgment, calling for different behavior
Problem Orientation—jointly collaborating in defining problems and seeking solutions	Control—attempting to persuade others by imposing your personal attitudes on them
Spontaneity—dealing with others honestly and without deception	Strategy—manipulating others
Empathy—identifying with others' positions or problems	Neutrality—showing lack of concern for others
Equality—deemphasizing status and power differences, respecting others	Superiority—reflecting dominance over others
Provisionalism—postponing taking sides and being open to new information and interpretations	Certainty—being dogmatic, wanting to win rather than solve a problem

Based on J.R. Gibb, Defensive communication, *ETC: A Review of General Semantics* 22 (1965).

3. They are spontaneous and honest rather than appearing to use "strategy," which involves ambiguous and multiple motivations. They do not appear to be concealing their true aims. For instance, Jain would openly discuss his restructuring efforts rather than implement them surreptitiously.
4. They convey empathy for the feelings of their listener rather than appearing unconcerned or neutral about his or her welfare. They give reassurance that they are identifying with the listener's problems rather than denying their legitimacy. Thus both Vance and Jain need to demonstrate a clearer understanding of the other's perspective in addressing the future of King Publishing.
5. They indicate that they feel equal rather than superior to the listener. They suggest that they will enter a shared relationship, not simply dominate the interaction.
6. Finally, they communicate that they will experiment with their own behavior and ideas rather than be dogmatic about them. They do not give the impression that they know all the answers and need help from no one. Both Vance and Jain seem to operate in isolation; they need to collaborate to reach the best solution to King Publishing's future.

In addition, supportive communication emphasizes a congruence between thoughts and feelings and communication.[44] An individual who feels unappreciated by a supervisor, for example, must communicate that to the supervisor rather than deny it or communicate the feeling inaccurately. Communication must also validate an individual's importance, uniqueness, and worth. Nondefensive communication "recognizes the other person's existence; recognizes the person's uniqueness as an individual, rather than treating him or her as a role or a job; acknowledges the worth of the other person; acknowledges the validity of the other person's perception of the world; expresses willingness to be involved with the other person, at least during the communication."[45]

The Johari Window Model In addition, interpersonal communication can be improved by encouraging individuals to communicate using as complete knowledge of themselves and others as possible. The *Johari Window* provides an analytical tool individuals can use to identify information that is available for use in communication.[46] Table 7–3 illustrates this model of interpersonal knowledge. Note that information about an individual is represented along two dimensions: (1) information known and unknown by the self and (2) information known and unknown by others.

Table 7–3 JOHARI WINDOW

	Known by Self	Unknown by Self
Known by Others	Open Self	Blind Self
Unknown by Others	Concealed Self	Unknown Self

Based on a model developed by Drs. Joseph Luft and Harry Ingham and described in *The Personnel Relations Survey* by Jay Hall and Martha S. Williams, Teleometrics International, The Woodlands, Texas.

Together these dimensions form a four-category representation of the individual. The *open* self is information known by the self and known by others. Both Jain and Vance provide their view of the significance (or insignificance) of technical innovation for King Publishing. The *blind* self is information unknown by the self and known by others, such as others' perceptions of your behavior or attitudes. Vance's vehemence about the company's future may be part of his blind self. The *concealed* self is information known by you and unknown by others; secrets we keep from others about ourselves fall into this category. Jain's opinions about company policy became part of his concealed self. What did Vance conceal from Jain and other employees? Finally, the *unconscious* self is information that is unknown to the self and unknown to others. To ensure quality communication, where possible an individual should communicate from his or her open self to another person's open self. The amount of information concealed or in the blind spot should be limited.

Using an Assertive Style

An *assertive* style refers to communicating in a way that stands up for personal rights, without violating another person's, and expressing personal needs, opinions, and feelings in honest and direct ways. Assertive behavior is "self-expressive; honest; direct and firm."[47] It is reflected in both the content and the nonverbal style of the message. The assertive delegator, for example, "is clear and direct when explaining work to subordinates, doesn't hover, (and) . . . criticizes fairly, objectively, and constructively."[48]

Consider the situation of a boss whose subordinate has missed two important deadlines in the last month. How would the boss respond assertively? The boss might say to the worker, "I know you missed the last two deadlines. Is there an explanation I should know? You must meet the next deadlines. You should have let me know the problems you were facing and explained the situation to me rather than saying nothing." Note that an assertive response can include the expression of anger, frustration, or disappointment.

We can contrast this to *nonassertive* and *aggressive* styles, as summarized in Table 7–4. Nonassertive communication describes behavior where the sender does not stand up for personal rights and thus indicates that his or her feelings are unimportant; the person may be hesitant, apologetic, or fearful. Consider again the situation of the missed deadlines. Nonassertive behavior might involve saying nothing to your worker, hoping the situation will not recur. Individuals act nonassertively because they may mistake assertion for aggression, mistake nonassertion for politeness or being helpful, refuse to accept their personal rights, experience anxiety about the negative consequences of assertiveness, or lack assertiveness skills.[49]

Aggressive communication stands up for an individual's rights without respecting the rights of the other person. Aggressive behavior attempts to dominate and control others by sounding accusing or superior. In the situation of the missed deadlines, an aggressive response might be, "You always miss deadlines. You're taking advantage of me and the situation. If you miss another deadline, you're fired." While such a response may result in the desired behavior in the short run, its long-term consequences are likely to be dysfunctional, resulting in distrust between boss and subordinate, uncontrollable anger, and even sabotage by the worker. Individuals may act aggressively because they are compensating for previous nonassertive behavior, feel vulnerable or

Table 7–4 A COMPARISON OF NONASSERTIVE, ASSERTIVE, AND AGGRESSIVE COMMUNICATION

	Nonassertive (No Influence)	Assertive (Positive Influence)	Aggressive (Negative Influence)
Verbal	Apologetic words. Veiled meanings. Hedging; failure to come to the point. Rambling; disconnected. At a loss for words. Failure to say what you really mean. Qualifying statements with "I mean," "you know."	Statement of wants. Honest statement of feelings. Objective words. Direct statements, which say what you mean. "I" messages.	"Loaded" words. Accusations. Descriptive, subjective terms. Imperious, superior words. "You" messages that blame or label.
Nonverbal			
General demeanor	Actions instead of words, hoping someone will guess what you want. Looking as if you don't mean what you say.	Attentive listening behavior. Generally assured manner, communicating caring and strength.	Exaggerated show of strength. Flippant, sarcastic style. Air of superiority.
Voice	Weak, hesitant, soft, sometimes wavering.	Firm, warm, well modulated, relaxed.	Tense, shrill, loud, shaky; cold, "deadly quiet," demanding; superior, authoritarian.
Eyes	Averted, downcast, teary, pleading	Open, frank, direct. Eye contact, but not staring.	Expressionless, narrowed, cold, staring; not really "seeing" others.
Stance and posture	Leaning for support, stooped, excessive head nodding.	Well balanced, straight on, erect, relaxed.	Hands on hips, feet apart. Stiff and rigid. Rude, imperious.
Hands	Fidgety, fluttery, clammy	Relaxed motions	Clenched. Abrupt gestures, fingerpointing, fist pounding.

powerless, overreact because of past emotional experience, believe aggression is the only approach, or have received praise in the past for aggressiveness.[50]

Using Active Listening Techniques

As discussed earlier, active listening requires receiving both the content and the intent of a message. A variety of techniques facilitate the checking and clarifying of messages by the receiver.

Paraphrasing The receiver can *paraphrase* the message conveyed by the sender. Using this technique, the receiver states in his or her own way what the other person's remarks convey. For example, if the sender states, "I don't like the work you have been doing," the receiver might paraphrase it as "You are saying that you are dissatisfied with my performance"; or the receiver might paraphrase it as "You are saying that you want to assign me different types of work to do." Note that these ways of paraphrasing the original message suggest very different understandings of the original statement. The sender, on receiving this feedback from the receiver, can then clarify his or her meaning.

Perception Checking Alternatively, the receiver may *perception-check;* that is, describe what he or she perceives is the sender's inner state at the time of communication, to check his or her understanding of the message. For example, if the sender states, "I don't like the work you have been doing," the receiver might check his or her perception of the statement by asking, "Are you dissatisfied with me as an employee?" or "Are you not satisfied with the quantity of my output?" Note that answers to these two questions identify different feelings.

Behavior Description A third way of checking and clarifying is through *behavior description.* Here the individual reports specific, observable actions of others without making accusations or generalizations about their motives, personality, or characteristics. Similarly, *description of feelings,* where the individual specifies or identifies feelings by name, analogy, or some other verbal representation, can increase active listening. For example, to help others understand you as a person, you should describe what others have done that affects you personally or as a group member. Then you can let others know as clearly and unambiguously as possible what you are feeling.

SUMMARY

In this chapter we examined the basic communication process: a sender encodes a message and transmits it through channels to a receiver, who decodes the message. Feedback from the receiver to the sender indicates whether any message and what message was received. Noise often distorts communication. Upward, downward, and lateral communication have unique characteristics that influence their effectiveness.

A variety of factors can affect the quality of communication. In this chapter we discussed organizational structure, interpersonal processes, the nature of feedback, noise, the use of language, listening skills, attitudes of the communicators, nonverbal communication, and extent of cross-cultural sensitivity. We also described interviews as a special but common form of communication in organizations. We concluded by offering three strategies for more effective communication, including creating a supportive climate, using an assertive style, and practicing active listening techniques. Figure 7–7 offers a series of

Figure 7–7 DIAGNOSTIC QUESTIONS ABOUT COMMUNICATION

- What encoding and decoding errors occur in communication?
- How effective are downward, upward, and lateral communication?
- What special roles exist to facilitate communication?
- What factors affect the accuracy of communication?
- What barriers to communication exist?
- Does communication include feedback?
- What noise affects communication?
- Are the attitudes of the communicating parties compatible?
- How effective is nonverbal communication?
- Does communication lack cross-cultural sensitivity?
- Are interviews conducted effectively?
- Is the climate supportive or defensive?
- Do individuals use assertive, nonassertive, or aggressive communication?
- Do individuals use active listening techniques?

diagnostic questions to use in assessing communication effectiveness. Managers can use the answers to plan ways for ensuring quality communication.

READING

Reading 7–1: RECONSIDERING OPENNESS IN ORGANIZATIONAL COMMUNICATION

Eric M. Eisenberg and Marsha G. Witten

Many organizational theoreticians and researchers uncritically accept the efficacy of open communication. Recently, however, some writers (Eisenberg, 1984; March & Olsen, 1970; McCaskey, 1982; Pascale & Athos, 1981; Pfeffer, 1977) have argued that organizational participants are strategists oriented toward multiple goals who communicate in ways that may not be completely open, but nevertheless may be effective. This agrees with recent work that rejects simple models of communication in favor of a more complex view of managers and employees as strategic, symbolic actors (Pfeffer, 1981; Pondy, 1978; Putnam & Pacanowsky, 1983; Weick, 1979, 1980).

This essay extends these lines of argument by examining the key assumptions that underlie the idea that opening up lines of communication is a panacea for organizational ills. It traces the development of the ideology of openness in organizational communication from its origins in the human relations movement, describes its use in contemporary organizational research, and proposes an alternative, contingency model of communication in organizations.

THE LEGACY OF HUMAN RELATIONS

Early Human Relations

The emphasis of the early human relations movement on open superior–subordinate communication stemmed from an assumption about the need for uniform goals among organizational members. Viewing workers as latent cooperators (Bendix, 1974), Harvard researchers saw open communication between manager and employee as an integrating mechanism (Mayo, 1945; Roethlisberger & Dickson, 1947). First, by persuading employees to disclose their feelings about their jobs and superiors, this talking would simultaneously relieve worker stress and allow management to discover untapped sources of worker motivation (Perrow, 1986). Second, by increasing frequency of contact between workers and management, the employee would identify with the goals of the company. Morale and productivity would improve.

To achieve these ends, early human relations practitioners stressed frequent downward communication from superiors to increase integration and show a sincere interest in the employee (Bendix, 1974) and disclosive communication upward on the part of the employee. The former could be achieved by developing a managerial elite trained to communicate lucidly and unemotionally with workers. The latter was facilitated by nondirective personnel interviews. In these interviews, employees were encouraged to achieve emotional relief by airing grievances and frustration to counselors, even though the counselors were powerless to change the employees' circumstances (Wilensky & Wilensky, 1951). Employees were encouraged specifically to discuss personal problems with interviewers, under the assumption that useless emotional complications and obsessive thinking that could interfere with work performance might be reduced (Mayo, 1945).

Reexaminations of early human relations research reveal that economic rewards, better discipline, and the anxieties caused by the national depression contributed more to improved performance than did improved communication (Carey, 1967; Conrad, 1985; Franke & Kaul, 1978). Peter Drucker (1974) spoke for many in management when he referred to early human relations as a kind of psychological manipulation in which the exploitation of "individual fears, anxieties, and personality needs replaces the old fear of being punished or of losing one's job" in controlling employees (p. 243).

Later Human Relations

The early human relations school has been criticized by those who view its goals and techniques as serving managerial interests over those of workers (Bendix, 1974; Edwards, 1979; Perrow, 1986). Later advocates of human relations emphasized the *mutual* responsibility of managers and employees to create "supportive relationships" through open communication (Likert, 1967).

Likert's concern for supportive relationships inspired much of the research on openness conducted in the communication field. Notable within this tradition is work by Redding (1972) and Jablin (1985), who defined an open communication relationship as one in which both parties perceive the other to be a willing and receptive listener, and refrain from responses which might be seen as negative or nonaccepting. From this perspective, the ideal managerial climate is characterized by supportiveness, empathy, participation, and trust, achieved in part by the "candid disclosure of feelings" (Redding, 1972, p. 330).

When subjected to empirical tests, these later conceptions have fared only slightly better than the earlier human relations theories. Numerous contingencies moderate the relationship between openness and employee attitudes and behaviors. For example, Miner's (1982) review of research on Likert's System-4 model and other related theories found only mixed support for the importance of supportive relationships. He further concluded that their impact varied across hierarchical levels. While some studies indicate a linkage between supervisor openness and subordinate satisfaction (cf., Jablin, 1985), others indicate negative findings (e.g., Rabinowitz, Falkenbach, Travers, Valentine, & Weener, 1983). In one study, Wiio (cited in Goldhaber, 1983) found that open communication was associated with greater *dissatisfaction* with the job and the organization. Dissatisfaction is not necessarily a reason to be less open, since conflict can engender compromise and positive change, but it does indicate the relationship between open communication and employee attitudes is not as simple as is sometimes presumed. Instead, the effect of openness on attitudes is moderated by the nature of the information that is shared and the extent to which revelations expose points of significant disagreement.

Finally, subordinates' preferences for open communication vary depending upon characteristics of their superiors. While subordinates generally prefer open communication, they are less at ease disclosing information to superiors who they perceive as "highly involved in political activities" (Jablin, 1981, p. 273). McGregor (1967) correctly anticipated the need for a contingency approach to communication: "virtually every variable associated with human interaction may be 'dysfunctional' at both extremes. Like other variables, the openness of communication is relative for all practical purposes, not absolute. . . . Even in the most intimate personal relationships—marriage, for example—absolutely open communication could destroy the relationship" (pp. 162–163).

RECONSIDERING OPENNESS

Openness has been identified three different ways in the literature. First, openness has been treated as the *disclosure of personal information.* This is due to an emphasis from the early human relations movement, in which the disclosure of employees' feelings and the resultant emotional relief were important for effective superior-subordinate relationships. Secondly, openness involves *disclosure of nonpersonal information* (such as work plans or objectives). This is reflected in later work by Likert, Redding, and Jablin, in which openness is defined as supportiveness rather than unrestricted candor. A third view of openness overlaps the first two and addresses the linguistic choices associated with being more or less open; that is, how *clear or ambiguous* disclosure may be. This is most apparent in work on language and symbolism in organizations (cf., Eisenberg & Riley, in press; Pondy, Frost, Morgan, & Dandridge, 1983).

Openness as Personal Disclosure

In advice that recalls Mayo's (1945) notion of nondirective interviewing, Imberman (1979) argued that frequent listening sessions that encourage employees to share their feelings lead to better labor-management relations and a decreased likelihood of strikes. Closer in spirit to the later human relations theorists, Stagnaro (1982) contended that managers should conduct leveling sessions in which they communicate openly with employees about their performance, skills, ability, and feelings. He believed that honesty would not backfire as long as managers listened carefully, avoided emotionalism, and viewed employees who left the organization as a result of leveling sessions as the "removal of stress from the organization" (p. 19).

Sessions of this kind can backfire for both managers and employees. While disclosure and directness are appropriate under certain circumstances, this approach can cause serious discomfort, confusion, emotional demands, and more stress than is alleviated. Those who prescribe disclosive communication assume that by understanding the other person better, one will be better able to get along with him or her. However, this assumption is counter to common sense and empirical evidence. Most work relationships are *non*interpersonal, because participants are low in "intrinsic commitment" and, subsequently, little private psychological-level information is exchanged (Conrad, 1985; Parks, 1982). Furthermore, close relationships that result from mutual disclosure can complicate rather than simplify employees' work lives (Conrad, 1985). While it is possible that increased knowledge of another person may lead to an improved work relationship, it is also possible that knowing someone better may increase the probability of serious disagreement that could jeopardize the future of the relationship (Bochner, 1984).

The idea that open communication may not always be good is resisted by many because it contradicts deeply held beliefs about human relationships. When asked to describe their *ideal* superior-subordinate relationship, most people respond that it should be trusting, open, and honest (Jablin, 1985). Often, however, these beliefs about communication differ from actual behavior in organizations (Steele, 1975). Managers frequently use "manipulative persuasion" to disguise self-interest, to distort information, and to overwhelm others (Allen, Madison, Porter, Renwick, & Mayes, 1979). Although most managers believe they are supportive when dealing with poor performers, in actuality, their behavior may contradict this belief (Fairhurst, Green, & Snavely, 1984). Research about subordinates reveals a similar pattern. When communicating with superiors, subordinates deviate from openness to protect self-interests; messages directed upward in organizations are "largely edited, cautious, and inaccurate" (Krone, 1985, p. 9).

Openness as Disclosure of Nonpersonal Information

The assertion that the free flow of task-related, nonpersonal information increases organizational effectiveness is true only under certain conditions. Between superiors and subordinates, labor and management, and the organization and its publics, both individual and group goals can be promoted through the cautious disclosure of information.

In collective bargaining, seasoned negotiators use ambiguity and concealment as a matter of course—research shows that open disclosure does not lead to better settlements and may reduce the likelihood of satisfactory agreements (Putnam & Jones, 1982). At times, norms against openness are a matter of convention. For example, in many organizations there are strict informal rules against the discussion of controversial topics at meetings; real differences are hammered out backstage (Steele, 1975). In organizations that depend on public perceptions of legitimacy for survival, communication about technical activities may be restricted to prevent internal conflicts that could damage the organization's image (Meyer & Rowan, 1977). Finally, openness must be restricted in the treatment of confidential or proprietary information (Steele, 1975).

Overly disclosive communication may be harmful to organizations during a crisis. Kleinfield (1985) explored the public disclosures of wrongdoing in corporations such as E. F. Hutton and General Electric. In such situations, employees must be reassured that the organization will not repeat its mistakes and that the company is worthy of their continued commitment. Simple prescriptions of openness do little to help managers cope with such complex problems.

Perhaps the most publicized claim made about openness in organizations is that the free exchange of information equalizes power relationships and reduces the likelihood of political behavior. For example, Naisbitt (1982) argued that the open communication characteristic of his ideal network structures would help members to treat each other as peers, regardless of formal status. Similarly, Peters and Waterman (1982) contended that the informal, free-wheeling communication that characterizes their excellent organizations reduces political maneuvering.

Increased exchange of information alone may not be sufficient to equalize power relationships. Power is derived from information only when the individual is able to make sense out of the raw data and has the opportunity and is willing to act on it (Blackburn, 1981; Mechanic, 1962). Members who have superior abilities and are in better positions to translate information into action will dominate those who lack this ability. Even in organizations where there is free exchange of information, power is manifested in the dynamics of ordinary interaction through who initiates, terminates, and sets the agenda for what gets talked about (Conrad & Ryan, 1985; Eisenberg, Monge, & Farace, 1984). Similarly, people have varying abilities based on position and credibility to make information salient for others (Weick, 1979). For these reasons, more disclosive communication alone cannot make people equal or remove the politics from organizational behavior.

Disclosure of technical information is especially risky for lower-level employees. Lower-level participants have few means of building power bases other than from the highly specialized information uniquely in their possession (Hickson, Hinings, Lee, Schneck, & Pennings, 1971). As a result, the sharing of technical information can reduce lower-level employees' access to informal power within the organization (Mechanic, 1962). In contrast, managers and executives can rely on legitimate authority (position power) if their technical knowledge becomes widely shared.

Upward communication in organizations presents a more fundamental dilemma for employees. Although the interests of the organization often are best served when employees reveal all they know about problems and opportunities, revealing such information can be damaging to the individual's job security and career aspirations. The disincentives to reveal negative information are well-documented (e.g., the space shuttle tragedy) and less dramatically shown in research on the "mum effect" and on upward distortion in organizational hierarchies (cf., Jablin, 1979). Individuals may feel trapped between conflicting motivations, that is, to reveal what they know for the good of the company, but to do so at their own peril. Openness often involves risks people are unwilling to take, and they will resist strongly if openness is imposed (Zalzenik, 1971). While it is admirable to strive for an organizational climate in which people feel comfortable speaking openly with one another, such a goal is unreasonable unless we are realistic about the good reasons people have for concealment. According to Conrad (1985), "the norms and political realities of organizations thus reward people for closed, not open communication" (p. 104).

Openness as Clear, Unambiguous Communication

Many managers place excessive "trust in increasing the clarity of communication between people, especially when disagreements are substantive. Getting a currently hopeless impasse clear is often unwise and likely to make things worse" (Pascale & Athos, 1981, p. 94). At all levels, members of organizations stand to gain from the strategic use of ambiguity (Eisenberg, 1984). In this way, organizational participants can express their feelings ("I have some reservations about giving this assignment to Joe") and can deny specific interpretations, should they arise ("You mean, you don't think he's bright enough to do the job?").

It can be especially useful to use strategic ambiguity when coping with the multiple interactional goals associated with supervisory positions. The ability of a manager conducting a performance appraisal "to use strategically ambiguous statements and comments may improve subordinate performance by allowing him or her the freedom and creativity to excel" (Goodall, Wilson, & Waagen, 1986, p. 77). Vague, metaphorical, and humorous suggestions are methods of communicating multiple messages which could not be expressed as easily in a literal fashion. While one risk of such strategies is that the subtlety will be lost on the audience, employees tend to be sensitive to this kind of communication. Usually, they can tell, for example, when the boss is at the same time conveying a more serious message (Ullian, 1976; Winick, 1976).

Researchers of organizational evaluation processes found that beliefs tend to be self-perpetuating, despite managers' efforts to overcome their biases. Once an initial assessment of another person has been made, there is a tendency mainly to attend to information that supports this first impression (Jones & Nisbet, 1972). For this reason, full disclosure is risky, but equivocation can serve as a kind of character insurance for people who are perceived as credible (Williams & Goss, 1975).

Overly explicit communication can affect task-related decisions and attributions about character. Indiscriminant explicitness limits options and can endanger plans (Bok, 1983). Often, sophisticated managers learn the hard way about the liabilities of speaking too soon (Pascale & Athos, 1981). Many managers who have been overly explicit in their policies have paid dearly later on, when a violation by a valued employee forces them to choose between making a good decision and remaining consistent with previous pronouncements.

The manager who is overly explicit in the statement of missions and goals also takes a risk. When missions are couched in unequivocal terms, conflict is unavoidable; when goals are stated concretely, they often are strikingly ineffective (Edelman, 1977). Ambiguous missions and goals allow divergent interpretations to coexist and are more effective in allowing diverse groups to work together. Further, ambiguous missions allow organizations greater freedom to respond to environmental changes (Keesing, 1974).

In public sector organizations, formal agreements often are constructed as purposefully ambiguous so that representatives of various constituencies can claim victory for their respective groups (Ring & Perry, 1985). Clear articulation of strategy may be inappropriate, since such disclosure provides a rallying point for the opposition, and over time leads executives to exercise inadequate caution. "Ambiguity in strategy, characteristic of many public organizations, therefore, may be an asset" (Ring & Perry, 1985, p. 279). The need for ambiguity in communication extends beyond formal organizations. All societies require a degree of value-consensus in order to survive; as a rule, this consensus is engendered through the creative use of communication. Political discourse is rarely literal, and usually a psychological sense of community (Sarason, 1974) or sense of oneness (Becher, 1981) is sufficient in modern social life (Hart, 1984). In communities whose members strive for extreme levels of communitas, ambiguity is absolutely essential for the maintenance of a sense of common understanding (Myerhoff, 1975).

TOWARD A CONTINGENCY PERSPECTIVE ON ORGANIZATIONAL COMMUNICATION

In this paper, an undifferentiated view of the benefits of open communication has been critiqued. This is not an objection to all suggestions regarding the beneficial effects of open communication or a suggestion that managers stop talking with their employees. Some organizational activities, particularly those having safety or legal implications, require clear, complete communication. Here, concealing information would lead to the worsening of some problems over time, making them less manageable if confronted in the future.

It is laudable to sensitize employees and managers to the benefits of empathic listening; to create an atmosphere of mutual respect and willingness to entertain new ideas; to share feelings and sentiments when individuals so desire; and to establish as much as possible in a context of unequal power a climate of trust and mutual concern. Endorsement of these goals does not equal supporting openness in all circumstances. Instead, the development of a contingency perspective in which communication strategies reflect individual goals and situational characteristics is proposed. Future research should move systematically toward identifying appropriateness norms for open communications (Derlega & Grzelak, 1979), that is, the conditions under which managers and employees choose to be more or less open.

The reasoning behind an individual's decision to be

more or less open can involve many different contingencies. Four types are suggested by this review: individual, relational, organizational, and environmental.

Individual contingencies are personal motives, preferences, and styles that affect communicative choices. If one knows that someone is highly ambitious in pursuing a career path or, alternatively, that one's primary concern is to keep his/her private life separate from his/her work life, his/her degree of openness can be explained regarding these desired ends. Similarly, it is expected that a communicator's personal style (e.g., loquacity or shyness) would affect the extent to which he or she communicates openly with others.

Relational contingencies refer to the closeness or shared history between organizational members. In part, choices to reveal or conceal information can be explained by an expediency model, since interactants in a relatively closed group with a long history can communicate less explicitly without compromising understanding (Bernstein, 1964). Attention to relational contingencies also may indicate tact, politeness, and the preservation of intimacy as possible explanations for one's degree of openness. For example, usually the decision to reveal highly personal information to another employee depends on the degree of trust and respect in the relationship.

Organizational contingencies are constraints on communication related to the job, the tasks at hand, or the interests of the organization as a whole. For example, a decision not to reveal company secrets or a decision to hold back information from employees about a tentative plan may be justified because it furthers or protects organizational interests. Alternatively, a decision to share information about the big picture with employees can be viewed as one way of promoting more participative, democratic decision making.

Lastly, *environmental* contingencies may constrain an organization's internal and external communication. Particularly in organizations that are highly regulated or those in the public eye, communicative choices must be considered in light of how they will be interpreted by various publics. For example, managers and CEOs monitor their degree of openness with the public as a way of protecting their organizations from possible threats to legitimacy or survival.

Often, the development of theories of human communication parallels the dominant values of society. Definitions of what constitutes *effective* communication have evolved from a concern with serving societal ends, to a focus on individual goal attainment, and most recently to a combined concern with personal goals and situational adaptation (Rawlins, 1985). The perspective presented here is consistent with this latter view. A contingent, differentiated view of organizational communication, one that eschews indiscriminant calls for openness in favor of a more subtle characterization of organizational life, is desirable.

REFERENCES

Allen, R. W., Madison, D. L., Porter, L. W., Renwick, P. A., & Mayes, B. T. (1979) Organizational politics: Tactics and characteristics of its actors. *California Management Review,* 22(1), 77–83.

Becher, T. (1981) Towards a definition of disciplinary cultures. *Studies in Higher Education,* 6, 109–122.

Bendix, R. (1974) *Work and authority in industry.* Berkeley, CA: University of California Press.

Bernstein, B. (1964) Elaborated and restricted codes. *American Anthropologist,* 66(6), 55–69.

Blackburn, R. S. (1981) Lower participant power: Toward a conceptual integration. *Academy of Management Review,* 6, 127–131.

Bochner, A. P. (1984) The functions of human communication in interpersonal bonding. In C. Arnold & J. Bowers (Eds.), *Handbook of rhetorical and communications theory* (pp. 544–621). Boston: Allyn and Bacon.

Bok, S. (1983) *Secrets: On the ethics of concealment and revelation.* New York: Pantheon Books.

Carey, A. (1967) The Hawthorne studies: A radical criticism. *American Political Science Review,* 32, 403–416.

Conrad, C. (1985) *Strategic organizational communication.* New York: Holt, Rinehart, & Winston.

Conrad, C., & Ryan, M. (1985) Power, praxis, and self in organizational communication theory, In R. McPhee & P. Tompkins (Eds.), *Organizational communication* (pp. 235–258). Beverly Hills, CA: Sage.

Derlega, V., & Grzelak, J. (1979) Appropriateness of self-disclosure. In G. J. Chelune (Ed.), *Self-disclosure* (pp. 151–176). San Francisco: Jossey-Bass.

Drucker, P. (1974) *Management: Tasks, responsibilities, practices.* New York: Harper & Row.

Edelman, M. (1977) *Political language: Words that succeed and policies that fail.* New York: Academic Press.

Eisenberg, E. M. (1984) Ambiguity as strategy in organizational communication. *Communication Monographs,* 51, 227–242.

Eisenberg, E. M., Monge, P. R., & Farace, R. V. (1984) Coorientation on communication rules in managerial dyads. *Human Communication Research,* 11, 261–271.

Eisenberg, E. M., & Riley, P. R. (in press) Symbols and sense-making in organizations. In G. Goldhaber (Ed.), *Handbook of organizational communication.* Norwood, NJ: Ablex.

Fairhurst, G. T., Green, S. G., & Snavely, B. K. (1984) Face support in controlling poor performance. *Human Communication Research,* 11, 272–295.

Franke, R., & Kaul, J. (1978) The Hawthorne experiments: First statistical interpretation. *American Sociological Review,* 43, 623–643.

Goldhaber, G. (1983) *Organizational communication* (3rd ed.). Dubuque, IA: Brown.

Goodall, H. L., Jr., Wilson, G. L., & Waagen, C. L. (1986) The performance appraisal interview: An interpretive reassessment. *Quarterly Journal of Speech,* 72, 74–87.

Hart, R. P. (1984) The functions of human communication in the maintenance of public values. In C. Arnold & J. Bowers (Eds.), *Handbook of rhetorical and communication theory* (pp. 749–791). Boston: Allyn and Bacon.

Hickson, D., Hinings, C., Lee, C., Schneck, R., & Pennings, J. (1971) A strategic contingencies theory of intraorganizational power. *Administrative Science Quarterly,* 16, 216–229.

Imberman, W. (1979) Strikes cost more than you think. *Harvard Business Review,* 57(3), 133–142.

Jablin, F. M. (1979) Superior-subordinate communication: The state of the art. *Psychological Bulletin,* 86, 1201–1222.

Jablin, F. M. (1981) An exploratory study of subordinates' perceptions of supervisory politics. *Communication Quarterly,* 29, 269–275.

Jablin, F. M. (1985) Task/work relationships: A lifespan perspective. In M. L. Knapp & G. R. Miller (Eds.), *Handbook of interpersonal communication* (pp. 615–654). Beverly Hills, CA: Sage.

Jones, E., & Nisbet, R. (1972) The actor and the observer: Divergent perceptions of the causes of behavior. In E. Jones, D. Kanouse, H. Kelly, R. Nisbett, S. Valins, & B. Weiner (Eds.), *Attribution: Perceiving the causes of behavior* (pp. 78–94). Morristown, NJ: General Learning Press.

Keesing, R. M. (1974) Theories of culture. In B. Siegel, A. Beals, & S. Tyler (Eds.), *Annual review of anthropology* (Vol. 3, pp. 73–91). Palo Alto, CA: Annual Reviews.

Kleinfield, N. R. (1985, July) When scandal haunts the corridors. *New York Times,* pp. 1, 7.

Krone, K. (1985) *Subordinate influence in organizations: The differential use of upward influence messages in decision making contexts.* Unpublished doctoral dissertation, University of Texas, Austin.

Likert, R. (1967) *The human organization.* New York: McGraw-Hill.

March, J. G., & Olsen, J. (1970) *Ambiguity and choice in organizations.* Bergen. Norway: Universitetsforlaget.

Mayo, E. (1945) *The social problems of an industrial civilization.* Cambridge, MA: Harvard University Press.

McCaskey, M. B. (1982) *The executive challenge: Managing change and ambiguity.* Boston: Pitman.

McGregor, D. (1967) *The professional manager.* New York: McGraw-Hill.

Mechanic, D. (1962) Sources of power of lower participants in complex organizations. *Administrative Science Quarterly,* 7, 249–264.

Meyer, J., & Rowan, B. (1977) Institutionalized organizations: Formal structure as myth and ceremony. *American Journal of Sociology,* 83, 340–363.

Miner, J. (1982). *Theories of organizational structure and process.* Chicago: Dryden Press.

Myerhoff, B. (1975) Organization and ecstasy: Deliberate and accidental communitas among Huichol Indians and American youth. In S. Moore & B. Myerhoff (Eds.), *Symbol and politics in communal ideology* (pp. 33–67). Ithaca, NY: Cornell University Press.

Naisbitt, J. (1982) *Megatrends.* New York: Warner Books.

Parks, M. P. (1982) Ideology in interpersonal communication: Off the couch and into the world. In M. Burgoon (Ed.), *Communication yearbook* 5 (pp. 79–108). New Brunswick, NJ: Transaction Books.

Pascale, R. T., & Athos, A. G. (1981) *The art of Japanese management.* New York: Simon & Schuster.

Perrow, C. (1986) *Complex organizations* (3rd ed.). New York: Random House.

Peters, T. J., & Waterman, R. H. (1982) *In search of excellence.* New York: Harper & Row.

Pfeffer, J. (1977) The ambiguity of leadership. *Academy of Management Review,* 2, 104–112.

Pfeffer, J. (1981) Management as symbolic action: The creation and maintenance of organizational paradigms. In B. Staw & L. L. Cummings (Eds.), *Research in organizational behavior* (Vol. 3, pp. 1–52). Greenwich, CT: JAI Press.

Pondy, L. R. (1978) Leadership is a language game. In M. Lombardo & M. McCall (Eds.), *Leadership: Where else can we go?* (pp. 87–99). Durham, NC: Duke University Press.

Pondy, L. R., Frost, P., Morgan, G., & Dandridge, T. (1983) *Organizational symbolism.* Greenwich, CT: JAI Press.

Putnam, L., & Jones, T. (1982) The role of communication in bargaining. *Human Communication Research,* 8, 262–280.

Putnam, L., & Pacanowsky, M. (1983) *Communication and organizations: An interpretive approach.* Beverly Hills, CA: Sage.

Rabinowitz, W., Falkenbach, K., Travers, J., Valentine, C., & Weener, P. (1983) Worker motivation: Unsolved problem or untapped resource? *California Management Review,* 25(2), 43–56.

Rawlins, W. K. (1985) Stalking interpersonal communication effectiveness: Social, individual, or situational integration? In T. Benson (Ed.), *Speech communication in the 20th century* (pp. 109–129). Carbondale, IL: Southern Illinois University Press.

Redding, W. C. (1972) *Communication in the organization: An interpretive review of the research.* New York: Industrial Communication Council.

Ring, P. S., & Perry, J. L. (1985) Strategic management in public and private organizations: Implications of distinctive contexts and constraints. *Academy of Management Review,* 10, 276–287.

Roethlisberger, F., & Dickson, W. (1947) *Management and the worker.* Cambridge, MA: Harvard University Press.

Sarason, S. (1974) *The psychological sense of community: Prospects for a community psychology.* San Francisco, CA: Jossey-Bass.

Stagnaro, F. (1982) The benefits of leveling with employees: ROLM's experience. *Management Review,* 71(7), 16–20.

Steele, F. (1975) *The open organization: The impact of secrecy and disclosure on people and organizations.* Reading, MA: Addison-Wesley.

Ullian, J. A. (1976) Joking at work. *Journal of Communication,* 26(3), 129–133.

Weick, K. (1979) *The social psychology of organizing* (2nd ed.). Reading, MA: Addison-Wesley.

Weick, K. (1980) The management of eloquence. *Executive,* 6(3), 18–21.

Weick, K. (1984) Organizational communication: Toward a research agenda. In L. Putnam & M. Pacanowsky (Eds.), *Communication and organizations: An interpretive approach* (pp. 13–29). Beverly Hills, CA: Sage.

Wilensky, J., & Wilensky, H. (1951) Personnel counseling: The Hawthorne case. *American Journal of Sociology,* 57, 265–280.

Williams, M. L., & Goss, B. (1975) Equivocation: Character insurance. *Human Communication Research,* 1, 265–270.

Winick, C. (1976) The social context of humor. *Journal of Communication,* 26(3), 124–128.

Zalzenik, A. (1971) Power and politics in organizational life. *Harvard Business Review,* 49(2), 51–59.

DISCUSSION QUESTIONS

1. Evaluate the assumption that opening lines of communication solves organizational problems.
2. Under what circumstances is open communication effective?
3. What contingencies affect the nature of effective communication?

From E.M. Eisenberg and M.G. Witten, Reconsidering openness in organizational communication, *Academy of Management Review* 12 (3)(1987): 418–426. Reprinted by permission.

ACTIVITIES

Activity 7–1: DIAGNOSING COMMUNICATION

Step 1: Think about a work situation in which you have been or are currently involved.

Step 2: Complete the following questions about that situation:

1. I Think My Communication With My Subordinates:

	7	6	5	4	3	2	1	
Increases my credibility								Decreases my credibility
Is precise								Is imprecise
Is clear								Is unclear
Answers more questions than it raises								Raises more questions than it answers
Is effective								Is ineffective
Is competent								Is incompetent
Is productive								Is unproductive
Gets the results I want								Does not get the results I want
Is impressive								Is unimpressive
Creates a positive image of me								Creates a negative image of me
Is good								Is bad
Is skillful								Is unskillful

Is relaxed	|__|__|__|__|__|__|	Is strained
Is self-rewarding	|__|__|__|__|__|__|	Is not self-rewarding
Does not embarrass me	|__|__|__|__|__|__|	Does embarrass me

Total Score ______

2. *I Think My Communication With My Supervisor:*

	7 6 5 4 3 2 1	
Increases my credibility	|__|__|__|__|__|__|	Decreases my credibility
Is precise	|__|__|__|__|__|__|	Is imprecise
Is clear	|__|__|__|__|__|__|	Is unclear
Answers more questions than it raises	|__|__|__|__|__|__|	Raises more questions than it answers
Is effective	|__|__|__|__|__|__|	Is ineffective
Is competent	|__|__|__|__|__|__|	Is incompetent
Is productive	|__|__|__|__|__|__|	Is unproductive
Gets the results I want	|__|__|__|__|__|__|	Does not get the results I want
Is impressive	|__|__|__|__|__|__|	Is unimpressive
Creates a positive image of me	|__|__|__|__|__|__|	Creates a negative image of me
Is good	|__|__|__|__|__|__|	Is bad
Is skillful	|__|__|__|__|__|__|	Is unskillful
Is relaxed	|__|__|__|__|__|__|	Is strained
Is self-rewarding	|__|__|__|__|__|__|	Is not self-rewarding
Does not embarrass me	|__|__|__|__|__|__|	Does embarrass me

Total Score ______

3. *I Think My Communication With My Peers:*

	7 6 5 4 3 2 1	
Increases my credibility	|__|__|__|__|__|__|	Decreases my credibility
Is precise	|__|__|__|__|__|__|	Is imprecise
Is clear	|__|__|__|__|__|__|	Is unclear
Answers more questions than it raises	|__|__|__|__|__|__|	Raises more questions than it answers
Is effective	|__|__|__|__|__|__|	Is ineffective
Is competent	|__|__|__|__|__|__|	Is incompetent
Is productive	|__|__|__|__|__|__|	Is unproductive
Gets the results I want	|__|__|__|__|__|__|	Does not get the results I want
Is impressive	|__|__|__|__|__|__|	Is unimpressive
Creates a positive image of me	|__|__|__|__|__|__|	Creates a negative image of me
Is good	|__|__|__|__|__|__|	Is bad
Is skillful	|__|__|__|__|__|__|	Is unskillful
Is relaxed	|__|__|__|__|__|__|	Is strained
Is self-rewarding	|__|__|__|__|__|__|	Is not self-rewarding
Does not embarrass me	|__|__|__|__|__|__|	Does embarrass me

Total Score ______

Step 3: Score each question by adding the numbers for the responses you gave. If your total score for a question is 15–36 you have analyzed yourself as a very ineffective communicator; if your score is 37–58, you have analyzed yourself as an ineffective communicator; if your score is 59–80, you have analyzed yourself as an effective communicator; if your score is 81 or above, you have analyzed yourself as a very effective communicator.

Step 4: Discussion. In small groups, with the entire class, or in written form, as directed by your instructor, answer the following questions:

Description

1. In which type of communication are you most effective? least effective?

Diagnosis

2. What are your deficiencies as a communicator?

Prescription

3. How could you improve your communication?

Reprinted with permission from L. Sussman and P.D. Krivonos, *Communication for Supervisors and Managers*. Sherman Oaks, Calif.: Alfred Publishing, 1979.

Activity 7–2: CHERIE COSMETICS, LIMITED, ELEGANTE DIVISION CASE

Step 1: Read the Cherie Cosmetics, Limited, case.

Heather King, General Manager of the Elegante Division of Cherie Cosmetics Limited, had written a memo to Bob Shaw, Vice-President of Operations, over three weeks ago, on August 11, 1983. Her objective was to elicit some response from operations that would lead to better communications between Marketing and Operations. Bob Shaw had always been responsive and Heather was unable to explain the three weeks of silence. It was now only three days until the next meeting with Operations and Heather felt she had not made any progress towards improving the communications process.

CHERIE CANADA LTD.

Cherie Canada Ltd., a wholly-owned subsidiary of the International Cherie Company of New York, was directed by Ralph Nolk, Executive Vice-President and Managing Director. The company marketed from the Toronto head office both men's and women's fragrance and cosmetic products in four distinctive product lines. Each division was headed by a General Manager who, along with the Vice-president of Operations, Bob Shaw, reported to Ralph Nolk (see Figure 7–8).

Heather King had joined Cherie Canada Ltd. nine years ago when she made a career change from teaching school. She was proud of the progress that she had made from her early start as an inexperienced, young sales representative for the Mystique division to General Manager of the new Elegante division.

ELEGANTE DIVISION

The international Cherie Company already had a high quality image world wide when it launched the Ele-

Figure 7–8 CHERIE COSMETICS, LIMITED, ORGANIZATION CHART

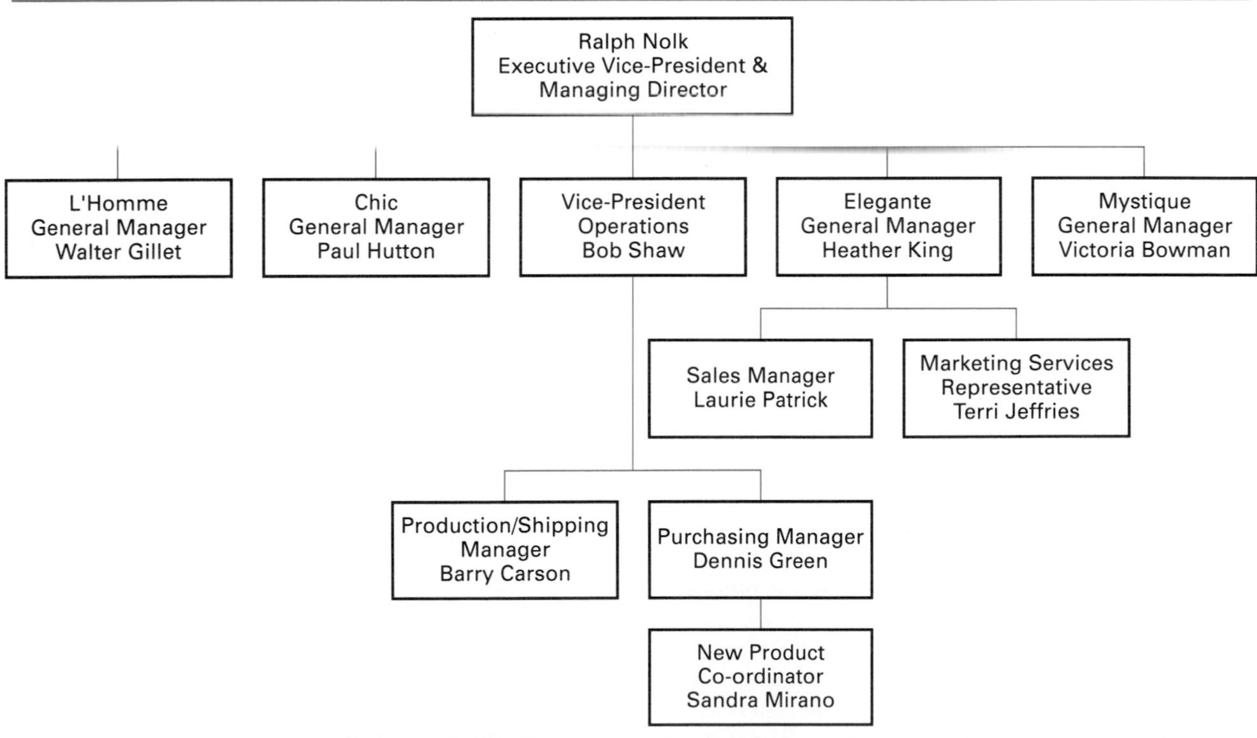

gante line in February of 1979 in New York. The Elegante product line was the most exclusive cosmetic line of the prestigious company. Distribution was expanded from the United States market to include the United Kingdom in 1980 and Italy, Austria and Canada in 1981. Canada, with only ten retail outlets in 1983 permitted to carry the product, represented 35% of Elegante's international business but only 1.5% of Cherie Canada Ltd.'s total sales in all product lines.

Elegante was the first new product line that Cherie Company had announced in twelve years; therefore, Heather wanted to insure a smooth introduction of the new line. Heather knew that there would be difficulties in introducing a new product with new formulae, new packaging and new containers. In preparation for the product launch, Heather had prepared and presented a demonstration and slide presentation of the product to the operations group in November of 1980 before the Canadian Elegante launch in February of 1981. She included operation managers, support staff and the assembly line workers involved in preparing the product. The presentation was enthusiastically received by all participants and Heather felt confident about the product launch.

NEW PRODUCT CHALLENGES

From the first days of production, however, Heather felt that the Operations group did not understand the product line. Although Heather had attempted to prepare them with the demonstration and slide presentation, Operations personnel did not appear to be fully aware of the complexities of the product and seemed unable to deal with resulting difficulties.

Heather's main contact with Operations was Dennis Green, the Purchasing Manager. Although Dennis had been a Purchasing Agent with Cherie for twelve years, Heather was concerned that he may lack the flexibility and sense of urgency necessary to understand the marketing of a fledgling product in the 1980's.

While production for all of Cherie's products was driven by sales forecasting, forecasting in the volatile cosmetic industry was, at the best of times, a shot in the dark. A lack of sales history, and the dynamics of a new product line made forecasting for the Elegante line even more difficult.

Operations needed to be responsive to marketing changes in advertising and distribution as well as general marketing strategy. Production runs for Elegante products were only 200 units compared to 5,000 units per run for other Cherie products. Elegante was, therefore, most vulnerable to errors in shipping, warehousing, purchasing, production or planning. Any errors would be highly visible and costly in the restricted Elegante market.

From the beginning, errors in shipping and warehousing had resulted in short shipments to stores; errors in production had resulted in Elegante's exclusive distributors receiving products with loose caps or missing components; and errors in purchasing had at times delayed product availability. These costly errors had not only affected sales, but had also dampened employee morale within the division. Members of the Elegante division felt that it was necessary to double and triple check everything that they requested from operations.

In January of 1982, Bob Shaw hired Sandra Mirano to fill a new position within the Operations Group, that of New Product Co-ordinator reporting to Dennis Green. Bob hoped that the new position would improve communication between Marketing and Operations not only for the Elegante line but also for all Cherie product lines.

After Sandra's appointment, however, the communication process continued to deteriorate. The tester unit difficulties finally broke the already strained relationship between Sandra and Heather.

THE TESTER UNITS SITUATION

Tester units for potential Elegante consumers were used by each retail outlet across Canada. These tester units were vital to the success of the high priced Elegante line, for they allowed trial of the product by consumers prior to purchase. The tester units had, however, been delayed for several months and Heather was unable to determine the cause of the delay.

The basic makeup tester units had arrived from Italy in January, 1983. In April, they were still not ready for distribution because the screening and filling necessary for their use had not been completed by Elegante's supplier. Five phone calls and three memos over the next month to Sandra Mirano requesting the reasons for the delay were ignored.

On May 25, 1983, Heather bypassed Sandra and wrote to Dennis Green requesting the status of the tester units. Heather did not receive any reply from Dennis and her many subsequent phone calls to him were ignored. Finally, on August 1, Heather bypassed Dennis and called the supplier, Ryan Casey, directly, to request a status report on the tester units. Ryan Casey said that he had not received a direction from Dennis to finish the tester units. He said Dennis sometimes "dragged his heels" but reminded Heather that her direct request would annoy Dennis. Heather said that she would accept full responsibility for any problems. Ryan Casey was instantly responsive and said that he would begin the screening immediately.

COMMUNICATION BREAKDOWN

At the Marketing and Operations (MOPS) meeting of August 10, 1983, Dennis verbally attacked Heather for her breach of procedure by calling Ryan Casey di-

Figure 7–9 CHERIE COSMETICS, LIMITED, INTER OFFICE MEMO

DATE: August 11, 1983
TO: Bob Shaw
FROM: Heather King
RE: Operations and Sales/Marketing Relations—Elegante Canada

Dear Bob:

Success in business depends upon various functions of an organization working harmoniously toward the same goal. I feel that success, therefore, will continue to elude Elegante in Canada unless both the Operations and Sales/Marketing groups get back on track leading to the same end . . . to make Elegante a profitable business!!

In recent months, Bob, I've felt that relations between our two groups have been strained. Serious problems have covered the gamut of shipping, warehousing, purchasing, production, planning—and you know that we could both produce files of correspondence to show that the brand has suffered the impact of these problems. For example:

a) *Shipping* —gift with purchase items for Holt Renfrew shipped to The Bay, Vancouver.
—short-shipments of items in stock, both saleable and collateral.
—errors in picking (French collaterals sent when English is requested by code).

b) *Warehousing*—misplacement of Cosmetic Zipper Bags, Lip and Eye Pencils, Makeup Brush collection, all resulting in lost sales.
—confusion of old formula with new formula, lotions and creams.

c) *Production* —loose caps.
—poor glueing
—empty lipstick in Elegante carton.
—missing items in gift items and saleable items (puffs, components, etc.).

d) *Planning* —lack of response for several months to requests for balance-out sheets on phase-outs and discontinuations.

e) *Purchasing* —three months to reservice vital tester units, collaterals, etc.
—misplacement of original carton artboards.
—inaccessibility of key staff.

All of the above have had a negative impact on Elegante SALES, not to mention our credibility and morale.

Relations continue to deteriorate. . . . Yesterday's incident with Dennis Green—indignant that I had "breached procedures" by calling Ryan Casey directly—serves to underscore the fact that we do not "have our eyes on the same target". Dennis was concerned more about procedures than results, even after his department had failed to respond to a memo dating back to May 25 and several phone calls later, pertaining to the tester units in question. I was more concerned with meeting commitments to open a new door on schedule with all the necessary selling tools.

Procedures notwithstanding, we need and want *results* on the Elegante brand. The tester units are a vital element in a successful launch; without them, our corporate investment of newspaper advertising, direct mail, training, demonstration, construction, etc. is jeopardized. If Dennis Green is prepared to accept responsibility for this huge investment, then I suggest he take up the matter with Mr. Nolk.

Lest the intention of this memo be misunderstood, let me clearly state that some progress has been made on the Elegante brand in the Operations area in the past year. That success is due, in large part, to your personal involvement and you know that I appreciate that very much. I would like to believe that everyone in the Operations area shares your commitment to our success. I would like to believe that everyone in Operations is as concerned with *results* as they are with procedures.

Bob, I fully appreciate the workload of your people. However, I can't understand, nor can I accept, the lack of attention to the recent "Tester" situation and others of its ilk. Elegante may not be the top priority brand in the eyes of many departments—but if people continue to ignore it and continue to look upon it as a "step-sister brand", then we shall never make it the success it has the potential to be. This "second class" attitude will only lead to further erosion of profits which will ultimately have to be absorbed by the corporation in one way or another. The ramifications of that on future growth and progress of our company are, needless to say, very many indeed!

In the interest of promoting a better understanding of each other's day-to-day pressures and responsibilities, I would like to propose an exchange; an invitation for Sandra Mirano (and anyone else you wish) to spend one or two days with us at the Bloor Street office and, in return, the opportunity for Terri and Laurie to take time at the plant with various departments. In this way, perhaps we will be able to recognize our objectives as mutual ones. . . .

I am looking to discussing the above or any other positive *action* to get Elegante back into a profitable, success-oriented position.

Regards,

Heather

HK/sd
encl.

P.S. Hope I do not have to wait until our next MOPS meeting for an apology from Dennis.

rectly. Dennis stated that he was "not going to be run by Marketing" and that "Casey is my supplier and I alone will deal with him". He finished by noting "I don't only work for Elegante. I have other brands and other priorities to worry about".

This outburst by Dennis took place just as the meeting was breaking up and Heather was stunned by Dennis's verbal abuse. Heather's feelings were highly charged; she felt it was time to lay her case before Bob Shaw, Dennis's boss. If she didn't find a solution to the current difficulties she faced another quarter of missed sales opportunities.

Heather expected that her memo to Bob Shaw (Figure 7–9) would produce some immediate response. Bob was proactive; he was accessible to Heather and never made her feel that Marketing was an interruption. Bob had been only two years with the Canadian operation but he had worked for Cherie's Australian operation for several years where he developed a reputation for being a top operations manager with an appreciation for marketing dynamics. He showed his understanding of marketing as soon as he assumed his Canadian position in 1981 by making marketing a working part of the operations meetings. He changed the monthly operations (OPS) meeting to the MOPS meeting. Bob attended all MOPS meetings and he was aware of how upset Heather was after the August 10 meeting.

Although Heather had talked to Bob on several occasions during the three weeks since she had written the memo, he had never mentioned the memo to her. She was unable to explain his lack of responsiveness. Heather wondered if she should raise the issue with Bob Shaw before the September 8 MOPS meeting or discuss the situation and a solution at the meeting.

Step 2: Prepare the case for class discussion.

Step 3: Answer each of the following questions, individually or in small groups, as directed by your instructor:

Description

1. Briefly describe the Tester Units situation.
2. How would you describe the relationship between Heather King, Bob Shaw, Dennis Green, and Sandra Mirano?

Diagnosis

3. What type of communication breakdown occurred in the Elegante Division?
4. Did two-way communication occur?
5. What factors affected communication accuracy?
6. What barriers to communication existed?

Prescription

7. What techniques could be used to improve communication?

Step 4: Discussion. In small groups, with the entire class, or in written form, share your answers to the questions above. Then answer the following questions:

1. What symptoms suggest a problem exists?
2. What problems exist in the case?
3. What theories and concepts help explain those problems?
4. How can the problems be corrected?
5. Are the actions likely to be effective?

Activity 7–3: ONE-WAY VERSUS TWO-WAY COMMUNICATION

Step 1: Your instructor will select one student to act as the communicator. He or she will be given two pictures to describe to you.

Step 2: The communicator will describe a picture to you. You are to reproduce the picture he or she is describing. The communicator may neither ask if you have questions, request information from you, nor speak with you nonverbally. You may not communicate with the communicator either verbally or nonverbally.

Step 3: The communicator will describe a second picture to you. Again, you are to reproduce the picture he or she is describing. This time you may ask the communicator any questions you wish, about his or her directions or anything else.

Step 4: Your instructor will direct you to score the pictures.

Step 5: Discussion. With the entire class, answer the following questions:

1. Which trial was more satisfying? Why?
2. Which trial yielded more accurate results? Why?
3. How can we translate our experience here into improving communication in organizational situations?

Activity 7–4: BILL CREIGHTON CASE

Step 1: Read the Bill Creighton case.

On the evening of November 12, 1986 Bill Creighton, Senior Associate and Mark Finney, Administrative Associate at Sterling Bank vented their frustrations in Finney's Wall Street office. Finney had been avoiding Bill for several days until Creighton finally caught up with him at 8:00 pm just as Finney was leaving for home. Creighton was frustrated because Finney was not giving him any meaningful assignments. Finney was tired of taking heat for "the unknown Canadian". After a relatively charged but short exchange, Finney told Creighton that he should do something for himself because Finney could not help him.

The temporary transfer Bill had pushed so hard for in Toronto was quickly blowing up into a nightmare. He knew that he would have to straighten things out in a hurry or waste six months in New York and put a black mark on his otherwise unblemished record.

INVESTMENT BANKING

By the 1980's, several hundred banking organizations around the world were providing an increased array of investment banking products and services. Some organizations were exclusively investment banks (such as New York based Salomon Brothers) while others provided both investment banking and commercial banking products and services. The Sterling Bank was a British commercial bank whose main thrust in recent years had been investment banking. Sterling operated a Schedule B bank in Canada and a commercial bank in the U.S. The Canadian operations were headquartered in Toronto while the U.S. operations were headquartered in New York. In Canada, Sterling competed primarily with the investment bank oriented Schedule B banks as well as the Canadian investment dealers. In the U.S., Sterling competed primarily with the large U.S. commercial banks (such as Citicorp, Bankers Trust and Morgan Guaranty) and the large U.S. investment banks (such as Salomon Brothers and First Boston Corporation).

Investment banking was an intermediary role that involved selling debt and equity securities to retail clients and institutions, raising debt and equity capital for companies that required financing, advising client organizations on financial transactions such as mergers & acquisitions and providing general financial advice on how firms should manage their balance sheets. Investment banks and the investment banking divisions of the commercial banks were typically divided into the following major areas: (1) Corporate Finance involved developing and marketing financial products that allowed firms to raise debt and equity capital. The corporate finance group acted as underwriters and assumed the risk of issuing new capital. This function typically had the highest profit margins because the compensation reflected the underwriting risk. Corporate Finance also included the highly profitable mergers & acquisitions function which acted on behalf of clients who were interested in making acquisitions or who were the targets of takeover bids. (2) Trading and Sales distributed the new issues generated by Corporate Finance and responded to clients' needs to purchase securities. Trading and Sales included debt and equity transactions that were executed in institutional and retail markets. (3) Research conducted research on a wide range of financial securities. Research findings were made available to clients and were used to support decisions in the Corporate Finance and Sales and Trading functions.

By 1986, the investment banking industry was undergoing several fundamental changes. Firms were becoming larger and more international. The industry was being deregulated and competition was increasing. As a result, risk and returns were at all time highs and MBA's were being lured with incredibly lucrative salaries and bonuses. In addition, the industry was under close scrutiny because of some high profile insider trading scandals, in which some very senior Wall Street bankers were found guilty of illegally earning astronomical profits. Because the industry was driven by huge profits, many observers concluded that investment bankers were driven by greed. It was not unheard of for young investment bankers to earn hundreds of thousands of dollars per year. The most successful investment bankers earned millions of dollars per year. Most of that income was earned through annual bonuses. Bonus formulae varied from firm to firm, but most depended on the firm's profitability, the department's profitability and the individual's contribution. Some firms encouraged team work by weighting bonuses for team results. Other firms fostered "star systems" where individuals were rewarded primarily for individual effort. Because every investment banking deal demanded highly specialized skills from several areas, cooperation among colleagues was key to succeeding and earning the really big money. Investment bankers were bright (usually graduating from the top of their class), aggressive and focussed; most bankers logged more than 60 hours per week and 100 hours per week was not uncommon, particularly for the younger bankers.

BILL CREIGHTON

Bill started his investment banking career in the summer of 1983 when he joined Anderson Clarke Limited, a major Canadian investment dealer. Previously, he had earned a commerce degree from a small U.S. college, spent a year in the finance department of a large Canadian packaged goods company. He earned his MBA from The University of Western Ontario in 1982 and was a research assistant for a senior faculty member in finance for one year. Bill was Canadian but had been exposed to many cities in North America because of the extensive traveling his father had done when Bill was growing up. Bill joined Anderson Clarke at age 25 and spent just over two years in the Corporate Finance department working on a variety of investment banking deals. During that time, Bill established himself as bright, keen and ambitious. He saw himself as a "mad professor: I was fun and unconventional. I was the only one who could walk into a senior executive's office and baffle him because I treated him like one of the guys instead of some demi-god." The combination of Bill's likable manner and his outstanding work earned him considerable respect in Anderson Clarke. In particular, Brian Nelson, the firm's most senior investment banker, became Bill's mentor.

The Sterling Bank made a strong push in Canada in the spring of 1984. They brought in a new senior management team and lured Nelson away from Anderson Clarke to become their new Canadian President and spearhead their investment banking thrust. Bill remembered being shocked by Nelson's decision to leave Anderson Clarke: "He didn't say a word to any of us about it and then boom, he's gone. I feel as though he betrayed our team and he betrayed me." Bill did not hear from Nelson until the spring of 1985 when Nelson offered Bill a job with Sterling in Toronto. Bill was happy with Anderson Clarke and rejected Nelson's initial offer. But Nelson persisted for several months and eventually got Bill's interest by adding a sweetener: if he came to Sterling, Bill could spend six months to a year in Sterling's New York or London office. Bill knew that some experience in New York would really round out his development so he joined Sterling in August 1985.

ADJUSTING TO STERLING

Bill and Nelson agreed that it would be appropriate for Bill to spend two or three months with Sterling in Toronto and then transfer to New York in December or January. That would allow Bill to get to know Sterling and vice versa. Other than Nelson, Bill did not know anyone else in Sterling. Unlike at Anderson Clarke, Nelson did not work closely at all with Bill. In fact, Bill and Nelson did not work on any deals together. Bill's new boss was Howard MacIntosh, an Executive Vice President. MacIntosh was also a relatively new member of Sterling's senior management team. Although MacIntosh and Nelson got along, they had very different operating styles. Nelson was a consummate investment banker: he understood the technical aspects of all of his deals and was smooth as silk in managing his clients. He was the perfect senior statesman for Sterling. MacIntosh was different. He had been with a large, established Canadian investment dealer for his entire career and had distinguished himself as a strong marketing person. Whereas Nelson was calm and cool, MacIntosh was emotional and sometimes brash. Bill described MacIntosh as "a bull in a china shop. At times, he had very little tact. But if he liked you, he could be just like a teddy bear."

Initially, MacIntosh saw Bill as Nelson's boy and rode Bill very hard for the first couple of months. It was not uncommon for MacIntosh to raise his voice or yell at someone to make a point. Bill recalled doing his first financial analysis for MacIntosh and MacIntosh screaming: "What the hell is this garbage? That's not the way we do it around here. Who taught you this crap anyway?" Even though his analysis was sound, Bill realized that he had to prove himself all over again in Sterling and especially to MacIntosh. Within a few months, Bill had earned MacIntosh's respect. In fact, MacIntosh eventually told Bill that he was "the best Associate that I have and you're the easiest to get along with . . . as long as you think you are being treated fairly".

NEGOTIATING FOR NEW YORK

By the end of November, Bill had the impression that the "powers" at Sterling were not keen on sending him to New York. As Nelson once told Bill: "We're not in the habit of hiring people for New York. We don't want them to think that we'll pick the plums off the tree and send them down." Nelson had not told MacIntosh about the New York deal he had struck with Bill until late in October. Moments after MacIntosh had learned of the deal, he called Bill into his office. He told Bill flat out: "Listen, you work for me now so your deal with Nelson is off. If you want to go to New York, you and I have to re-negotiate". As far as Bill was concerned, the deal he had cut with Nelson should be honoured. Over the next several weeks, Bill pressed MacIntosh on the issue and MacIntosh hinted that he *might* get to New York in a year. If he did get there, it would be for no more than three months. In Bill's mind, that would be reneging on the deal. Bill made it clear, without ever explicitly saying it, that if he was not assured of going to New York for 6–12 months he would leave Sterling.

When Bill returned from a week's vacation in late March, MacIntosh told him about his annual performance bonus. Sterling had made its bonus decisions while Bill was on vacation. Bill was not happy with the bonus; in fact, he was extremely disappointed. Before

Bill had joined Sterling, Nelson had led him to believe that his total compensation package at Sterling would be considerably higher than his Anderson Clarke package. However, based on the bonus MacIntosh had just given to Bill, the Sterling package was marginally below what the Anderson Clarke package would likely have been. Bill was angry and let MacIntosh know it. In a move to apparently appease Bill, MacIntosh told him that he had changed his mind and would send Bill to New York for six months starting in September. Bill remembered MacIntosh saying: "I don't give anything easily to anyone. You know that's just the way I am." However, MacIntosh's concession on New York didn't entirely satisfy Bill. He was still really steamed about the compensation issue.

Later that same day, Bill got a call from Nelson. Because they no longer worked together, Bill hadn't talked with Nelson for some time. However, Nelson had heard from the grapevine that Bill was really upset and he wanted to find out why. Bill told him that it had been over six months since he joined Sterling, that he hadn't been transferred to New York yet and finally, that his bonus was ridiculous. Bill told Nelson he was really tired of being "jerked around" and he thought that Sterling was not honouring the deal that had brought Bill from Anderson Clarke. Nelson, in his customary unemotional manner, assured Bill that things would work out. After his meeting with Nelson, Bill reasoned that Nelson had called MacIntosh later that day because Nelson was worried about Bill quitting Sterling. In an effort to cool Bill down, Nelson overruled MacIntosh's agreement with Bill and moved the transfer date to May. When Nelson told Bill about the change, Bill told him that he didn't want to leave in May because he was busy on several large Toronto deals, he wouldn't be very busy in New York (investment banking is very slow over the summer months) and a very close friend was transferring to New York in September. Finally after a joint meeting in April, the three of them agreed that Bill would go to New York in September for at least six months.

ARRANGING THE TRANSFER

There were several groups in corporate finance that Bill considered transferring to in New York. He eventually decided that he would learn the most in the High Yield Group and he spoke to MacIntosh about his preference. The High Yield Group was a small, highly focused group that worked exclusively on "junk bonds", which were specialized debt securities that were frequently used to finance leveraged buyouts.[1] MacIntosh had indicated to Bill that he knew someone in the High Yield Group in New York. In fact, MacIntosh had briefly met Nick Mantia, Executive Vice President in charge of the U.S. High Yield Group, at a recent meeting of Sterling's executive vice presidents. MacIntosh agreed to arrange things with Mantia. Bill found out later that MacIntosh made a short call to Mantia. Bill guessed that the call went something like the following: "Nick, it's Howard MacIntosh from Toronto. How are you doing? Yeah, we met at the EVP's meeting in Florida last month. Listen, I've got a good young Senior Associate named Creighton who wants to spend six months with your group. Have you got room for him in September? Great. Why don't you have your Administrative Associate call him and take care of the details? Thanks a million."

Bill called Mantia several times in August to ask a few questions about the High Yield Group. Mantia was never available and he didn't return any of Bill's calls. Bill did get two phone calls from Mike Finney, the Administrative Associate, and they briefly discussed the kind of deals Bill might work on. They also agreed that Bill would attend the High Yield Group weekly meeting on September 16. He could meet the 20-person team, be briefed on the current deals and then move to New York. Bill attended the 8:00 am meeting on September 16—but arrived 10 minutes late. Nick Mantia was chairing the session and did not stop when Bill arrived. After about an hour Mantia said: "By the way, there's a new guy here. Who is he? (Bill was the *only* "new guy" in the room; he waved his hand.) Oh yeah, you're the guy down from Canada aren't you? Tell us something about yourself." Before Bill had finished introducing himself, Mantia rushed out of the boardroom to another meeting. Bill never had the chance to shake his hand. After the two hour meeting ended, Bill met two people he was going to work with on a deal: Tom Soward, Vice President and Ken Conrad, Senior Associate. Bill also met Mark Finney. Finney showed Bill his office and asked him to get started right away on the deal with Soward and Conrad. Bill was confused; he was only in New York for the day. He wasn't moving to New York for two more weeks. There had been a misunderstanding. Finney was annoyed; he had rushed around the day before to arrange things for Bill.

ARRIVING IN NEW YORK

Bill finally arrived in New York in the last week of September. It was an intimidating experience. Bill had worked on some New York deals from Canada but he had always been on a team with people he knew. He went into the U.S. High Yield Group as an unknown. He had worked on some leveraged buyout deals in Canada but none that had relied on junk bonds very much. He wondered if he would be up to speed technically in the High Yield Group. He also wondered what barriers might exist because he wasn't part of a "class." During the strong bull markets of the mid-1980's, the large investment banks on Wall Street had hired as many as

100 new Associates each year. The incoming "classes" spent their initial training together, helped each other on deals and developed very strong social ties. By working and socializing together, investment banking "classmates" developed a strong sense of professional trust in each other. As an outsider, Bill did not have any such ties and had not yet earned the trust of his High Yield colleagues. Bill spent the first week getting adjusted and trying to meet the rest of his new colleagues. He never did manage to meet Mantia. The High Yield Group was relatively small by Wall Street standards with only 20 professionals, including two Executive Vice Presidents.

Mantia had recently brought in a huge leveraged buyout deal from Hoyle Inc., a major international containerized shipping company. It was the biggest and potentially the most profitable deal that the High Yield Group had seen all year. The Hoyle deal was initially staffed by Soward, Conrad and some analysts (generally, analysts were undergraduate students who worked on Wall Street for two years before returning to graduate school). The Hoyle deal was referred to as a "black hole" deal. It was so big and so complex that it could totally consume as many Associates as were thrown into it. In contrast, a normal deal was staffed by a Senior or Executive Vice President, a Vice President and one or two Associates. Soward needed some extra bodies for Hoyle and was willing to let Bill assume some relatively small, safe tasks. Even though he was a fourth-year Associate and he was more than capable to assume more responsibility on the Hoyle deal, Bill was still an unknown quantity in New York. Bill participated in several team meetings on the Hoyle deal through October and early November. Bill, Soward and Conrad updated each other during those meetings in Soward's office.

On two occasions, Nick Mantia popped into the meetings and inquired about the progress of the deal. Mantia specifically addressed his questions to either Soward or Conrad even though some of the questions could only be answered by Bill. For those questions, Soward acted like an interpreter, repeating Bill's answer to Mantia. Bill was livid. Mantia was treating him like a total rookie. To make matters worse, Mike Finney, who was responsible for farming out work from the Senior and Executive Vice Presidents, was not giving any work to Bill because none of them had asked for him to be on their deals. Bill dropped into Finney's office almost every day to ask about any new work that could be assigned to him. Finney never had anything for him. Bill was frustrated because he was stuck with only a small number of simple tasks and he was being treated like a ghost by the senior people in High Yield, especially Mantia. He had called Howie MacIntosh twice in October and asked him to speak to Mantia. Since Mantia was not speaking to Bill, he never knew if MacIntosh had spoken to Mantia. Bill figured that MacIntosh wasn't anxious to make things easy for Bill in New York. MacIntosh was concerned about losing Bill. In one of their phone calls, MacIntosh had said: "If you try to end-run me and stay in New York, I'll yank you out of there faster than you can say Sterling Bank."

In their late night meeting on November 12, Bill's frustration came to the surface. Bill was not known for his diplomacy or for flowery language and he always called a spade a spade:

Bill: "Look Mark, I'm tired of sitting around here doing nothing. What the hell is going on? I've been twiddling my thumbs for over a month, I still don't have a secretary and Nick hasn't said boo to me since I've been here."

Mark: "So what do you want me to do? You came down here without any credibility—you're not even a Vice President. No one from Toronto called to even see if you'd arrived and Mantia's riding my butt because you're not doing anything. You're a bloody thorn in Nick's side and he's taking it out on me. And no one else is asking for you on their deals. Let's fact it Bill—you're a big question mark down here. Why don't you get some back-up from your senior guy in Toronto?"

Bill: "Wait a minute, I just missed making VP for three reasons: I am relatively new to Sterling, they considered it a real perk that I was sent to New York and, because I am only 28, they didn't want to put any noses out of joint. They told me I am VP quality, but politics got in the way. So I don't think that my capabilities should be an issue.

Mark: "Yeah, I agree—your capabilities shouldn't be an issue. In fact Tom (Soward) and Ken (Conrad) are real impressed with your work. But nobody else down here *who counts* knows that."

Bill: "I've already spoken to MacIntosh and nothing has changed. I can't get an appointment with Mantia to talk to him. Sonya (Mantia's secretary) treats me like her son, but the bastard doesn't even say hello to me. I've thought about going into his office and talking to him about it."

Mark: "Listen cowboy, this is New York. You don't walk into an EVP's office without his invitation or without an appointment. Those guys are working on billion dollar deals. They've been known to fire wise-ass Associates who have interrupted them."

Bill: "I've also talked to Paul Harper (the other Executive Vice President of the U.S. High Yield Group) about my situation. He said he would speak to you about getting me some more work."

Mark: "Harper hasn't said squat to me about you."

Bill: "C'mon Mark, I busted my tail to get this transfer to New York. I don't care if I have to call Toronto and have work sent to me; there's no way I'm going to sit on my hands for the next four months. I'm tired of being treated like a first-year Associate. And there's no way I'm going back to Toronto before my time is up."

Mark: "Suit yourself, Bill. I feel for you but there is nothing I can do. I think you had better do something for yourself. If I were you, I'd work through your senior guy in Toronto. Frankly, it sounds like you've been hung out to dry and he's not doing anything to help you. But you better do something. Listen, I've got to leave now or my wife will kill me. Let me know how things go."

Bill spent the balance of that evening reflecting on his situation. He wondered if he was responsible for the mess he was in—had he mismanaged his bosses? Or had he been mismanaged by them—first Nelson, then MacIntosh and finally Mantia? Although he was unsure about why certain things had happened, he focused on what he should do the next day. He had already called his parents and some friends in Toronto to talk about the options that were available to him. But he had no idea which option to choose or how *exactly* to exercise the option he chose.

NOTE

[1]Leveraged buyouts were acquisitions that were paid for with the unused debt capacity of the *acquired* company. The acquiring company issued bonds with higher than normal yields ("junk bonds") to attract investors and to secure financing for the acquisition. Originally, junk bonds were used by smaller, riskier companies. By 1986, the junk bond market in the U.S. had taken off and major corporations such as B.F. Goodrich and Texaco had issued junk bonds. Junk bonds were not very prevalent in Canada in 1986.

Step 2: Prepare the case for class discussion.

Step 3: Answer each of the following questions, individually or in small groups, as directed by your instructor:

Description

1. What communication occurred in the case?

Diagnosis

2. Where did the communication process break down?
3. In what direction did communication occur?
4. How did the organizational arrangements influence communication?
5. How did interpersonal relations influence communication?
6. What other factors affected communication?

Prescription

7. What techniques could be used to improve communication?

Step 4: Discussion. In small groups, with the entire class, or in written form, share your answers to the questions above. Then answer the following questions:

1. What symptoms suggest a problem exists?
2. What problems exist in the case?
3. What theories and concepts help explain those problems?
4. How can the problems be corrected?
5. Are the actions likely to be effective?

Activity 7–5: NONVERBAL COMMUNICATION

Step 1: Your instructor will organize you into groups of five or six people. Two groups will work together; one will act as a decision-making group and the other as observers.

Step 2: The decision-making group should rank-order the importance of the eight leadership characteristics listed below. You have approximately ten minutes to complete the task. During the ranking procedure the decision-making group may communicate only verbally. You may not use gestures, facial movements, body movements, or any other nonverbal communication.

List of Leadership Traits

_______ extroverted personality
_______ sensitivity to others
_______ technical expertise
_______ strong ethical values
_______ task orientation or concern for production
_______ charisma
_______ internal locus of control
_______ power

Step 3: After watching the decision making, observers should answer the following questions:

1. How effective was communication?
2. What barriers to communication existed?
3. What purpose does nonverbal communication serve?

Step 4: Discussion. With the two groups (decision makers and observers) together or with the entire class, answer the following questions:

1. How effective was communication?
2. What happens when nonverbal communication is absent?
3. What purposes does nonverbal communication serve?

Based on "The Blind Decision-Makers" by Jeffrey Powers, *Exchange: The Organizational Behavior Teaching Journal* 1 (January 1975): 32–33.

Activity 7–6: IMPROVING LISTENING EFFECTIVENESS

Step 1: Your instructor will organize you into groups of five or six people.

Step 2: You are to discuss the topic "Communication Problems I Have Encountered," or another topic provided by your instructor, for approximately five to ten minutes.

Step 3: After five to ten minutes, your instructor will impose the "listening rule." This rule states that in order for a person to enter the conversation he or she must paraphrase the previous speaker's comments to that person's satisfaction. Once the new speaker has successfully paraphrased the comments, he or she may make any comments. Before the next person enters the conversation, he or she must paraphrase the previous comments, and so on. You should continue the discussion until your instructor tells you to stop.

Step 4: Discussion. In small groups or with the entire class, answer the following questions:

1. Describe your feelings during the discussion.
2. How well do people listen?
3. How can listening be improved?

Activity 7–7: ARE YOU REALLY LISTENING?

Step 1: Below are some statements that were made by employees to their manager. Read each statement and select the response that best represents active listening by placing an X next to it.

1. Each day brings new problems. You solve one and here comes another. . . . What's the use?
   ______ a. I'm surprised to hear you say that.
   ______ b. That's the way it is. There's no use getting upset over it.
   ______ c. I know it's frustrating and sometimes discouraging to run into problem after problem.
   ______ d. Give me an example so I know what you're referring to.
2. At our meeting yesterday, I was counting on you for some support. All you did was sit there and you never said anything!
   ______ a. I was expecting you to ask for my opinion.
   ______ b. You're evidently upset with the way I handled things at the meeting.
   ______ c. Hey, I said some things on your behalf. You must not have heard me.
   ______ d. I had my reasons for being quiet.
3. I don't know when I'm going to get that report done. I'm already swamped with work.
   ______ a. See if you can get someone to help you.
   ______ b. All of us have been in that situation, believe me.
   ______ c. What do you mean swamped?
   ______ d. You sound concerned about your workload.
4. I've been scheduled to be out of town again on Friday. This is the third weekend in a row that's been messed up!
   ______ a. Why don't you talk with someone higher up and get it changed?
   ______ b. Going on the road must be a burden to you.
   ______ c. Everyone has to be on the road—it's part of the job.
   ______ d. I'm sure this is the last trip you'll have to make for a while.
5. It seems like other people are always getting the easy jobs. How come I always get the hard ones?
   ______ a. You feel I'm picking on you and that I'm being unfair in assigning work.
   ______ b. What evidence do you have for saying that?
   ______ c. If you'd look at the work schedule, you'd see that everyone has hard and easy jobs.

_______ d. What about that job I gave you yesterday?

6. When I first joined this company, I thought there would be plenty of chances to move up. Here I am, four years later, still doing the same thing.
   _______ a. Let's talk about some of the things you could do to be promoted.
   _______ b. Maybe you just haven't worked hard enough.
   _______ c. Don't worry, I'm sure your chance will come soon.
   _______ d. Getting ahead must be important to you. You sound disappointed.
7. Performance evaluations are here again. I wish I could just give all my people good ratings—it sure would be easier.
   _______ a. I know, but that's not possible.
   _______ b. We all feel that way; don't get upset over it.
   _______ c. Performance evaluations seem to bother you.
   _______ d. Just do the best you can.
8. It's the same old thing day in and day out. Any child could do this job!
   _______ a. Your work is evidently getting you down and making you feel useless.
   _______ b. I always thought you liked your job.
   _______ c. What good is complaining going to do?
   _______ d. If you've got some ideas on improving your job, I'll be happy to listen.
9. I really appreciate getting the promotion. I just hope I can do the job.
   _______ a. Don't worry. I'm sure you'll get better as you get more experience.
   _______ b. What makes you think you can't do the job?
   _______ c. Don't worry. Most people have those same feelings.
   _______ d. I'm sure you can do it, or you wouldn't have been promoted.
10. I'm tired. That last sale really wore me out. I don't think I can handle another customer.
   _______ a. Sure you can. Just rest a few minutes and you'll be fine.
   _______ b. What have you been doing that's gotten you so tired?
   _______ c. You sound like you're exhausted.
   _______ d. We all get feeling that way; don't worry about it.

Step 2: Your instructor has information about the appropriate responses. You can verify your answers with these data.

Step 3: Two volunteers are to be selected. These volunteers will be asked to role-play a common communications encounter. Everyone else is to act as observers.

Step 4: As observers, be prepared to discuss the following issues:

1. Did the situation seem to be satisfactorily resolved?
2. How did active listening help resolve it? Why?
3. What barriers, if any, emerged during this activity?
4. How might you make use of this technique in interpersonal communication?

Activity 7–8: COMMUNICATING ASSERTIVELY

Step 1: The following questions will be helpful in assessing your assertiveness.* Be honest in your responses. All you have to do is draw a circle around the number that describes you best. For some questions the assertive end of the scale is at 0, for others at 4. Key: 0 means no or never; 1 means somewhat or sometimes; 2 means average; 3 means usually or a good deal; and 4 means practically always or entirely.

1.	When a person is highly unfair, do you call it to attention?	0	1	2	3	4
2.	Do you find it difficult to make decisions?	0	1	2	3	4
3.	Are you openly critical of others' ideas, opinions, behavior?	0	1	2	3	4
4.	Do you speak out in protest when someone takes your place in line?	0	1	2	3	4
5.	Do you often avoid people or situations for fear of embarrassment?	0	1	2	3	4
6.	Do you usually have confidence in your own judgment?	0	1	2	3	4
7.	Do you insist that your spouse or roommate take on a fair share of household chores?	0	1	2	3	4
8.	Are you prone to "fly off the handle"?	0	1	2	3	4
9.	When a salesman makes an effort, do you find it hard to say "No" even though the merchandise is not really what you want?	0	1	2	3	4

10. When a latecomer is waited on before you are, do you call attention to the situation?	0	1	2	3	4
11. Are you reluctant to speak up in a discussion or debate?	0	1	2	3	4
12. If a person has borrowed money (or a book, garment, thing of value) and is overdue in returning it, do you mention it?	0	1	2	3	4
13. Do you continue to pursue an argument after the other person has had enough?	0	1	2	3	4
14. Do you generally express what you feel?	0	1	2	3	4
15. Are you disturbed if someone watches you at work?	0	1	2	3	4
16. If someone keeps kicking or bumping your chair in a movie or a lecture, do you ask the person to stop?	0	1	2	3	4
17. Do you find it difficult to keep eye contact when talking to another person?	0	1	2	3	4
18. In a good restaurant, when your meal is improperly prepared or served, do you ask the waiter/waitress to correct the situation?	0	1	2	3	4
19. When you discover merchandise is faulty, do you return it for an adjustment?	0	1	2	3	4
20. Do you show your anger by name-calling or obscenities?	0	1	2	3	4
21. Do you try to be a wallflower or a piece of the furniture in social situations?	0	1	2	3	4
22. Do you insist that your property manager (mechanic, repairman, etc.) make repairs, adjustments or replacements which are his/her responsibility?	0	1	2	3	4
23. Do you often step in and make decisions for others?	0	1	2	3	4
24. Are you able openly to express love and affection?	0	1	2	3	4
25. Are you able to ask your friends for small favors or help?	0	1	2	3	4
26. Do you think you always have the right answer?	0	1	2	3	4
27. When you differ with a person you respect, are you able to speak up for your own viewpoint?	0	1	2	3	4
28. Are you able to refuse unreasonable requests made by friends?	0	1	2	3	4
29. Do you have difficulty complimenting or praising others?	0	1	2	3	4
30. If you are disturbed by someone smoking near you, can you say so?	0	1	2	3	4
31. Do you shout or use bullying tactics to get others to do as you wish?	0	1	2	3	4
32. Do you finish other people's sentences for them?	0	1	2	3	4
33. Do you get into physical fights with others, especially with strangers?	0	1	2	3	4
34. At family meals, do you control the conversation?	0	1	2	3	4
35. When you meet a stranger, are you the first to introduce yourself and begin a conversation?	0	1	2	3	4

Step 2: Scoring. Look at your responses to questions 1, 2, 4, 5, 6, 7, 9, 10, 11, 12, 14, 15, 16, 17, 18, 19, 21, 22, 24, 25, 27, 28, 30, and 35. These questions are oriented toward *nonassertive* behavior. Do your answers to many of these items tell you that you are rarely speaking up for yourself? Or are there perhaps some specific situations which give you trouble?

Look at your responses to questions 3, 8, 13, 20, 23, 26, 29, 31, 32, 33, and 34. These questions are oriented toward *aggressive* behavior. Do your answers to many of these questions suggest you are pushing others around more than you realized?

You may examine your *assertive* responses by noting how often you answered 3 or 4 to the questions in the first paragraph and 0 or 1 to the questions in the second paragraph. In short, it is assertive to "usually" take the action described in the first group of items, and to rarely do those things described in the second set of items.

Step 3: Check the statement indicating your most likely response to each situation below.†

1. When there's an unpleasant job that has to be done, I . . .
   a. do it myself.
   b. give it as punishment to someone who's been goofing off.
   c. hesitate to ask a subordinate to do it.
   d. ask someone to do it just the same.
2. When the boss criticizes me, I . . .
   a. feel bad.
   b. show her where she's wrong.
   c. try to learn from it.
   d. apologize for being stupid.
3. When an employee isn't working out, I . . .
   a. give him rope to hang himself.
   b. do everything I can to help him work out before I have to fire him.
   c. put off firing him as long as possible.
   d. get rid of him as quickly as possible if the guy is no good.
4. When my salary increase isn't as large as I think it should be, I . . .

a. tell the boss in no uncertain terms what to do with it.
b. keep quiet about it.
c. say nothing, but take it out on the boss in other ways.
d. feel bad.

5. When a subordinate continues to ignore instructions after I've explained something for the third time, I . . .
   a. try to give her something else to do.
   b. keep telling her until she does it.
   c. tell her that if she doesn't do it right this time, she's out the door.
   d. try to explain it in a different way.
6. When the boss rejects a good idea of mine, I . . .
   a. ask why.
   b. walk away and feel bad.
   c. try it again later.
   d. think about joining the competition.
7. When a co-worker criticizes me, I . . .
   a. give her back twice the dose she gave me.
   b. avoid her in the future.
   c. feel bad.
   d. worry that she doesn't like me.
8. When someone tells a joke I don't get, I . . .
   a. laugh with the rest of the group.
   b. say it was a lousy joke.
   c. say I didn't get it.
   d. feel stupid.
9. When someone points out a mistake I've made, I . . .
   a. sometimes deny it.
   b. feel guilty as hell.
   c. figure it's only human to make mistakes now and then.
   d. dislike the person.
10. When a subordinate fouls up a job, I . . .
    a. blow up.
    b. hate to tell him about it.
    c. hope that he'll do it right the next time.
    d. don't give him that job to do again.
11. When I have to talk to a top executive, I . . .
    a. can't look the person in the eye.
    b. feel uncomfortable.
    c. get a little nervous.
    d. enjoy the interchange.
12. When a subordinate asks me for a favor, I . . .
    a. sometimes grant it, sometimes not.
    b. feel uncomfortable if I don't grant it.
    c. never grant any favors if I can help it. It sets a bad precedent.
    d. always give in.

Step 4: Scoring.

1. Nonassertive managers hate to ask people to do unpleasant work, and they often wind up doing it themselves (answers *a* and *c*). The aggressive manager might give such odious tasks as punishments (answer *b*). The assertive manager might hesitate to ask the subordinate, but would ask just the same (answer *d*).
2. The aggressive manager argues with the boss when criticized (answer *b*). Feeling bad or guilty, though a common reaction, is a nonassertive response (answer *a*). But apologizing for being stupid is the limit (answer *d*). The assertive response, assuming the criticism is valid, is to try to learn from the remark (answer *c*).
3. The hard-nosed, authoritarian manager would get rid of a "bad" employee as quickly as possible (answer *d*). The nice-guy manager would put if off—forever, if possible (answer *c*)—and would give the poor performer rope to hang himself so the manager would feel justified in firing him (answer a). The assertive manager would try hard to help the employee work out, but would fire him in the end if necessary (answer *b*).
4. When people don't like a situation, but they say nothing about it, resentment builds up in them. This resentment often leads to forms of passive aggression; they "get back" in other, devious ways. Answers *b, c* and *d* are compliant reactions. Choice *a* is an aggressive reaction. No assertive choice was given here.
5. Choices *b* and *d* are both assertive ones. Choice *a*—giving the employee something else to do—is evading responsibility and a compliant reaction. Threatening is the hard-guy approach (answer *c*).
6. Planning to join the competition is passive aggression: "I'll get even; they'll be sorry!" Choices *a* and *c* are assertive responses.
7. Choice *a*—"giving her back twice the dose she gave me"—is the aggressive response. Choices *b, c,* and *d* are all nonassertive. No assertive choice was given here.
8. Choices *a* and *d* are nonassertive responses. Assertive people are not afraid to say they didn't get the joke (answer *c*). The aggressive person blames the guy for telling a lousy joke (answer *b*).
9. A common reaction when someone points out a mistake we have made is to feel guilty, to dislike the person for telling us about it, and perhaps even to deny we did it. But assertive people know they have the right to make mistakes.
10. Blowing up at an employee is a tough-guy approach, showing no respect for the employee's rights and feelings (answer *a*). Choices *b, c,* and *d* are all nonassertive responses to this problem. No assertive response was given.
11. It's normal to be a little nervous when you have to

talk to an executive, but feeling so uncomfortable that you can't even look the person in the eye is extreme nonassertiveness. If you enjoy the interchange, that's assertive (answer *d*). And that's great.

12. Managers who don't feel comfortable negotiating with subordinates sometimes make a policy of not granting any favors. Nice-guy managers just about always grant favors and feel uncomfortable if they don't. The assertive manager feels free to say yes or no, depending on the circumstances (answer *a*).

Step 5: Discussion. Compare your responses to the questions in steps 1 and 3. How assertive are you? In what situations do you act assertively? nonassertively? aggressively? How can you act more assertively? Individually, in small groups, or with the entire class, offer three to five strategies for acting more assertively.

Step 6: The instructor will divide the class into groups of three and assign each group one of the following communication styles: assertive, nonassertive, or aggressive. Your group should prepare a short role play that illustrates how you would respond to the following situation in your assigned style. (The instructor or another member of the class will assume the role of your boss during the role play.)

> Your boss has recently given you an assignment that you neither like nor feel you have the qualifications to perform. You will be meeting with the boss on another matter in ten minutes and must decide whether and how to express your reaction to the assignment.

Step 7: Discussion. Compare the role plays. How was the communication the same? different? Which role plays illustrated effective communication? ineffective communication? Why?

*From *Your Perfect Right: A Guide to Assertive Living* (Fifth Edition) © 1986 by Robert E. Alberti and Michael L. Emmons. Reproduced by permission of Impact Publishers, Inc., P.O. Box 1094, San Luis Obispo, CA 93406. Further reproduction prohibited.

†Reprinted with permission of the publisher from *Mastering Assertiveness Skills* pp. 74–77 © 1984 Elaine Zuker. Published by AMACOM, a division of American Management Association, New York. All rights reserved.

Activity 7–9: THE APPRAISAL INTERVIEW

Advance Preparation: Gather the following materials:

1. General instructions
2. Role sheets for George Stanley and Tom Burke
3. Instructions for observers

Set up the following: A table in front of the room to represent the interviewer's desk, and two chairs arranged by the desk in such a way that the participants can talk comfortably and have their faces visible to the observers.

Step 1:

1. Two members from the class are selected, one to role-play the supervisor who conducts the appraisal interview and the other to role-play the employee interviewed.
2. All other members act as observers.
3. All participants read the general instructions.
4. The participant who will conduct the interview studies the role of George Stanley while the participant who is to be interviewed studies the role of Tom Burke. Both should play their role parts without referring to their role sheets.
5. The observers read the instructions for observers.

General Instructions for Appraisal Interview

George Stanley is the head of the electrical section of the engineering department at the American Construction Company. The responsibilities of the department include designing, drafting, making cost estimates, keeping maps up to date, checking standards and building codes, doing field inspections and follow up, and the like. Eight first-line supervisors report to George Stanley. Their duties are partly technical and partly supervisory. The organizational chart for Stanley's section is shown in Figure 7–10.

Company policy requires that each section head interview each of his or her supervisors once a year. The purpose is to: (1) evaluate the supervisor's performance during the year; (2) give recognition for jobs well done; and (3) correct weaknesses.

The evaluation interviews were introduced because the company believes that employees should know how they stand and that everything should be done to develop management personnel. Today Stanley will conduct an evaluation interview with Tom Burke, one of the supervisors reporting to him.

Tom Burke has a college degree in electrical engineering; in addition to his technical duties—which often take him to the field—he supervises the work of one junior designer, six draftsmen, and two clerks. He is

Figure 7–10 ORGANIZATIONAL CHART FOR THE ELECTRICAL SECTION

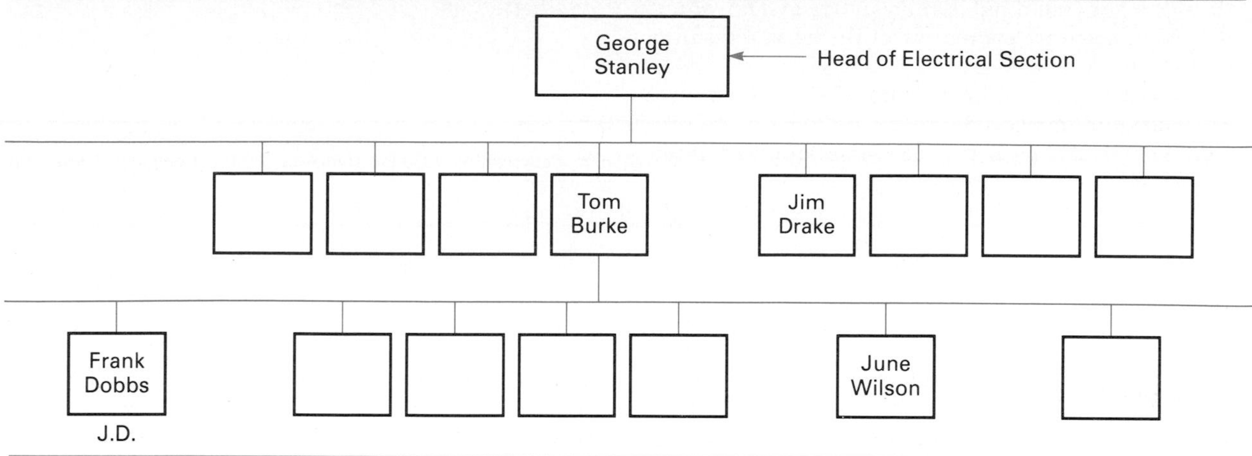

highly paid, as are all the supervisors in this department, because of the job's high requirements in technical knowledge. Burke has been with the company for twelve years and has been a supervisor for two years. He is married and has two children. He owns his home and is active in the civic affairs of his community.

Step 2:

1. When everyone is ready, George Stanley enters his office and sits at his desk. A moment later, Tom Burke enters the office and the scene begins.
2. The amount of time needed to complete the interview will vary, but twenty to thirty minutes is usually adequate. The interview is carried to the point of completion unless an argument develops and no progress is evident after ten or fifteen minutes of conflict.

Step 3: Discussion. In small groups or with the entire class, answer the following questions:

Description

1. Briefly summarize the main events of the meeting.
2. Describe the perceptions and attributions Stanley and Burke appear to have about each other. What effects do these have?

Diagnosis

3. Evaluate the communication process during the interview.
4. Were perceptions and attributions accurate?
5. Which distortions occurred?

Prescription

6. Is it possible for most interviewers to avoid the pitfalls in this type of situation? How?
7. How can performance-appraisal interviews be improved?

Variations:

1. One or two new pairs of participants may role-play in order to permit comparison of different interview styles and their outcomes.
2. A Stanley and a Burke exchange roles and role-play the case again. Observers read the role instructions for both players.
3. The class is divided into small groups; each prepares the role of either Burke or Stanley, and then representatives are chosen to role-play in front of the class.

Instructions for Observers

1. Observe the manner in which Stanley began the meeting.
   a. What did the interviewer do, if anything, to create a permissive atmosphere?
   b. Did the interviewer state the purpose of the interview early in the session?
   c. Was the purpose stated clearly and concisely?
2. Observe how the interview was conducted.
   a. To what extent did the interviewer learn how Burke felt about the job in general?
   b. Did the interviewer use broad, general questions at the outset?
   c. Did Stanley criticize Burke?
   d. Did Stanley praise Burke?
   e. Did he accept Burke's feelings and ideas?
   f. Which one talked the most?
   g. What things did the interviewer learn?

3. Evaluate the outcome of the interview.
   a. To what extent did Stanley arrive at a fairer and more accurate evaluation of Burke as a result of the interview?
   b. What things did Stanley do, if any, to motivate Burke to improve?
   c. Were relations better or worse after the interview? If worse, why?
   d. In what ways might the interviewer have done a better job?

CONCLUDING COMMENTS

Ineffective communication may be the biggest problem facing organizations. People's perceptions of and attributions for particular events and people affect the way they communicate with each other—the way they send messages and receive them. When different people have different perceptions, slip-ups and misunderstandings often occur in their communication. An individual's position in the organization's structure also influences the nature of communication.

In this chapter you had the opportunity to diagnose communication in a work situation in which you have been involved yourself, as well as in the Cherie Cosmetics, Limited, and Bill Creighton cases. A variety of exercises also offered the chance to see demonstrations of various aspects of the communication process and to practice ways of improving communication skills. The One-way versus Two-way communication Exercise illustrated the role of feedback in organizations. Nonverbal Communication showed the power of gestures, facial expressions, and body movements in communication. In Improving Listening Effectiveness, Are You Really Listening?, Communicating Assertively, and the Performance-Appraisal Role Play, you practiced strategies for increasing communication effectiveness.

ENDNOTES

[1]This case was based on one prepared by Blair Hawley, Phillips Exeter Academy.

[2]C.A. O'Reilly III and L.R. Pondy, Organizational communication. In *Organizational Behavior,* ed. S. Kerr (Columbus, Oh.: Grid, 1979), p. 121.

[3]W.V. Haney, *Communication and Interpersonal Relations: Text and Cases* (Homewood, Ill.: Irwin, 1979).

[4]P.V. Lewis, *Organizational Communication: The Essence of Effective Management* 3d ed. (New York: Wiley, 1987).

[5]E.M. Eisenberg and M.G. Witten, Reconsidering openness in organizational communication, *Academy of Management Review* 12 (1987): 418–426.

[6]Lewis, *op. cit.*

[7]J.P. Barnard, The principal players in your organization's information system, *Supervisory Management* 28 (1978): 65–90.

[8]H. Mintzberg, *The Structuring of Organizations* (Englewood Cliffs, N.J.: Prentice-Hall, 1978).

[9]R. Katz and M.L. Tushman, A longitudinal study of the effects of boundary-spanning supervision on turnover and promotion in research and development, *Academy of Management Journal* 26 (1983): 437–456.

[10]T.J. Allen and S.I. Cohen, Information flow in research and development laboratories, *Administrative Science Quarterly* 14 (1969): 12–19.

[11]H. Aldrich and D. Herker, Boundary-spanning roles and organization structure, *Academy of Management Review* 2 (1977): 217–230.

[12]M. Tushman and D. Nadler, Communication and technical roles in R&D laboratories. In B. Dean and J. Goldhar, eds., *Management of Research and Innovation* (New York: TIMS, North Holland, 1980), pp. 91–111; D.G. Ancona and D.F. Caldwell, Beyond task and maintenance: Defining external functions in groups, *Group and Organization Studies,* 13 (1988): 468–494.

[13]E.B. Roberts and A.R. Fusfeld, Critical functions: Needed roles in the innovation process. In R. Katz, ed., *Career Issues in Human Resource Management* (Englewood Cliffs, N.J.: Prentice-Hall, 1982), pp. 182–207.

[14]M.L. Tushman and T.J. Scanlan, Characteristics and external orientations of boundary-spanning individuals, *Academy of Management Journal* 24 (1981): 83–98.

[15]C.A. O'Reilly and K.H. Roberts, Information filtration in organizations: Three experiments, *Organizational Behavior and Human Performance* 11 (1974): 253–265.

[16]D. Fisher, *Communication in Organizations* (St. Paul, Minn.: West, 1981).

[17]O'Reilly and Pondy, *op. cit.*

[18]Lewis, *op. cit.*

[19]W.V. Haney, *Communication and Organizational Behavior* (Homewood, Ill.: Irwin, 1979).

[20]Fisher, *op. cit.*

[21]C.B. Rogers and R.E. Farson, Active listening. In D. Kolb, I. Rubin, and J. McIntire (eds.), *Organizational Psychology: Readings on Human Behavior in Organizations* (Englewood Cliffs, N.J.: Prentice-Hall, 1984), pp. 255–267.

[22]*Ibid.,* p. 1.

[23]*Ibid.*

[24]D.W. Johnson and F.P. Johnson, *Joining Together: Group Theory and Group Skills* (Englewood Cliffs, N.J.: Prentice-Hall, 1975).

[25]For other categorizations, see J. Ruesch and W. Kees, *Notes on the Visual Perception of Human Relations* (Los Angeles: University of California Press, 1956); S. Duncan, Nonverbal communication, *Psychological Bulletin* 72 (1969): 65–68; R.P. Harrison and M.L. Knapp, Toward an understanding of nonverbal communication systems, *Journal of Communication* 22 (1972): 399–352; G.M. Goldhaber, *Organizational Communication* (Dubuque, Ia.: William C. Brown, 1979).

[26]See M.L. Knapp, *Nonverbal Communication in Human Interaction* (New York: Holt, Rinehart & Winston, 1972); P. Ekman, Communication through nonverbal behavior. In S.S. Tomkins and C.E. Izard, eds., *Affect, Cognition, and Personality* (New York: Springer, 1965).

[27]C.L. McKenzie and C.J. Qazi, Communication barriers in the workplace, *Business Horizons* 26 (March–April 1983): 70–72.

[28]P.R. Harris and R.T. Moran, *Managing Cultural Differences* 2d ed. (Houston: Gulf, 1987), p. 43.

[29]E.H. Schein, Improving face-to-face relationships, *Sloan Management Review* (Winter 1981): 43–52.

[30]*Ibid.*

[31]L. Copeland, Making costs count in international travel, *Personnel Administrator* (July 1984): 47.

[32]W.W. Hildebrandt, A Chinese managerial view of business communication, *Management Communication Quarterly* 2 (November 1988): 217–234.

[33]N.J. Adler, *International Dimensions of Organizational Behavior* (Boston: Kent, 1986).

[34]R.C. Maddox and D. Short, The cultural integrator, *Business Horizons* 31 (November–December 1988): 57–59.

[35]W.T. Woltz, How to interview supervisory candidates from the ranks, *Personnel* 57 (September–October 1980): 31–48.

[36]S.G. Ginsburg, Preparing for executive position interviews—Questions the interviewer might ask or be asked, *Personnel* 57 (July–August 1980): 31–44.

[37]R.J. Klimoski and M. London, Role of the rater in performance appraisal, *Journal of Applied Psychology* 59 (1974): 445–451; R.L. Holzback, Rater bias in performance ratings: Superior, self-, and peer ratings, *Journal of Applied Psychology* 63 (1978): 579–588.

[38]Holzbach, *op. cit.*

[39]A.S. Tsui and B. Barry, Interpersonal affect and rating errors, *Academy of Management Journal* 29 (1986): 586–599.

[40]See, for example, R. Jacobs and S.W.J. Kozlowski, A closer look at halo error in performance ratings, *Academy of Management Journal* 28 (1985): 201–212.

[41]D.R. Ilgen, T.R. Mitchell, and J.W. Frederickson, Poor performers: Supervisors' and subordinates' responses, *Organizational Behavior and Human Performance* 27 (1981): 386–410; R.C. Lider and T.R. Mitchell, Reactions to feedback: The role of attributions, *Academy of Management Journal* 28 (1985): 291–308.

[42]Lider and Mitchell, *op. cit.*

[43]J.R. Gibb, Defensive communication, *ETC: A Review of General Semantics* 22 (1965).

[44]W.G. Dyer, *The Sensitive Manipulator* (Provo, Utah: Brigham Young University Press, 1980).

[45]D.A. Whetton and K.S. Cameron, *Developing Management Skills* (Glenview, Ill.: Scott, Foresman, 1984), p. 209.

[46]J. Hall, Communication revised, *California Management Review* 15 (1973); J. Luft, *Group Processes: An Introduction to Group Dynamics* (Palo Alto, Cal.: Mayfield Publishing, 1970).

[47]R.E. Alberti and M.L. Emmons, *Your Perfect Right* (San Luis Obispo, Cal.: Impact, 1982), p. 19.

[48]E. Zuker, *Mastering Assertiveness Skills* (New York: AMACOM, 1983), p. 79.

[49]A.J. Lange and P. Jakubowski, *Responsible Assertive Behavior* (Champaign, Ill.: Research Press, 1976).

[50]*Ibid.*

RECOMMENDED READINGS

Barnlund, C.D. *Communicative Styles of Japanese and Americans*. Belmont, Cal.: Wadsworth, 1989.

Goldhaber, G. *Organizational Communication* 5th ed. Dubuque, Ia.: William C. Brown, 1990.

Goldhaber, G., and Barnett, G. (eds.) *Handbook of Organizational Communication*. Norwood, N.J.: Ablex, 1988.

Gudykunst, W.B. *Culture and Interpersonal Communication*. Newbury Park, Cal.: Sage, 1988.

Jablin, F., Putnam, L., Roberts, K., and Porter, L. (eds.) *Handbook of Organizational Communication: An Interdisciplinary Perspective*. Newbury Park, Cal.: Sage, 1987.

Kreps, G.L. *Organizational Communication*. New York: Ungman, 1986.

Lewis, P.V. *Organizational Communication: The Essence of Effective Management* 3d ed. New York: Wiley, 1987.

Zuker, E. *Mastering Assertiveness Skills*. New York: AMACOM, 1983.

Evaluating Leadership and Leading Effectively

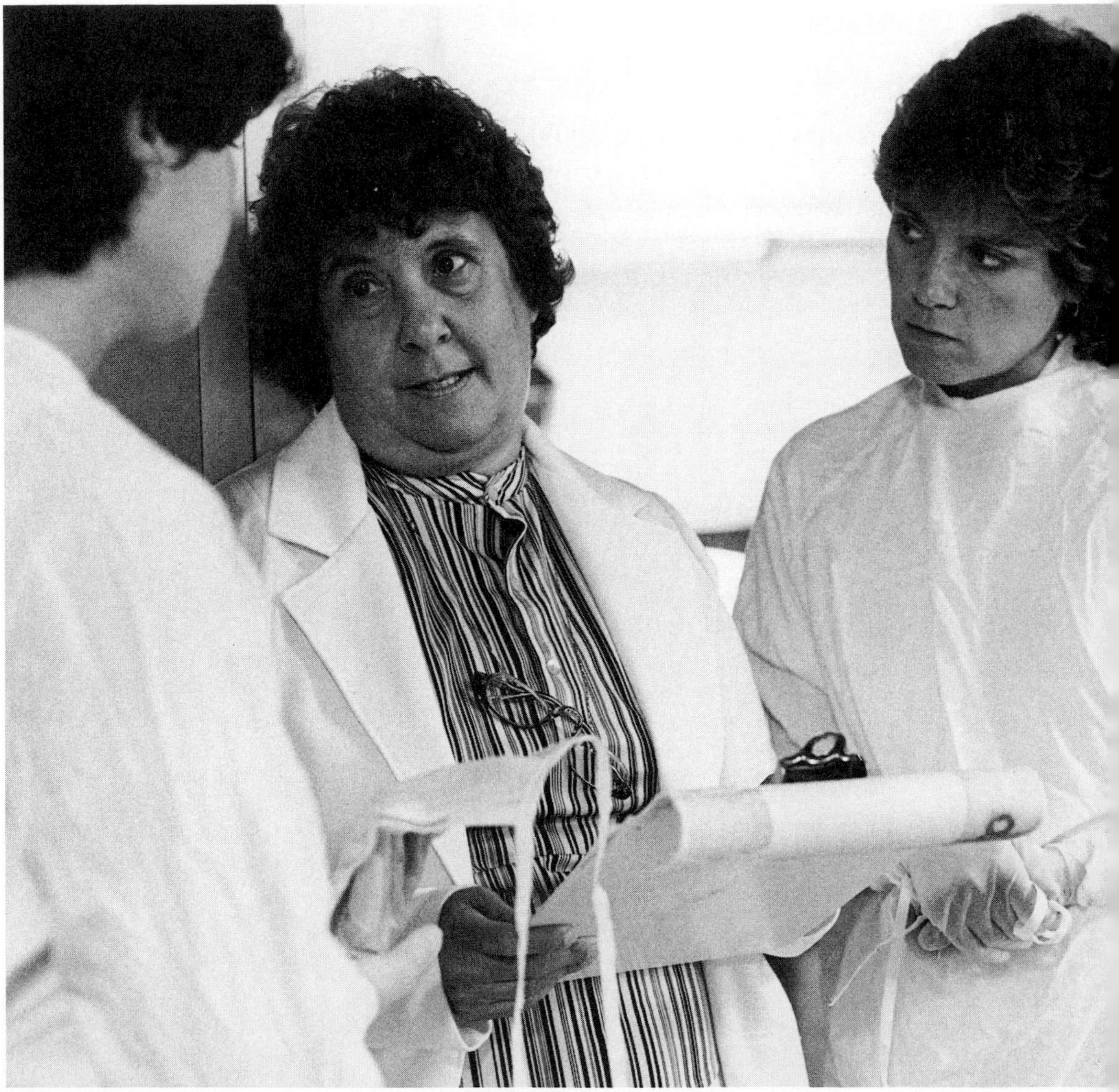

CHAPTER OUTLINE

LEARNING OBJECTIVES

After completing the reading and activities in Chapter 8, students will be able to

- show how trait theories contributed to our understanding of effective leadership;
- specify the behavioral dimensions of leadership and diagnose their existence;
- identify the roles of managerial work and discuss their use in effective management;
- list the situational contingencies that influence leadership and their implications for choosing a leadership style;
- show how follower attributions influence leadership;
- show what substitutes for leadership might exist in a given situation and how a manager might use them;
- offer a prescription for becoming a transformational leader; and
- offer a strategy for effective leadership.

Leading a Glaucoma Project Team

After receiving her medical degree in 1979 and her doctorate in epidemiology in 1983, Dr. Karen Kornet gained international notoriety for her research work. In 1985, she was named the Director of the Epidemiology Center at a major medical center. Two years later, Kornet organized a group of two ophthalmologists, two nutritionists, an epidemiologist, and a data analyst under her supervision to perform an epidemiological study aimed at identifying factors associated with juvenile glaucoma. Although these professionals were aware of Kornet's reputed style—she had been called the Female Dictator—they were enthusiastic about working with her on the project since they were committed to eradicating glaucoma.

During the start-up phase of the study, the group members met and got acquainted, received an orientation to the research design, and accepted the study's main objective as described by Dr. Kornet. Little discussion occurred. The second meeting followed a similar pattern: Karen Kornet elaborated on the study protocol. During the third meeting, Dr. Kornet gave the nutritionists and ophthalmologists a five-hour food-frequency questionnaire for them to administer as a pretest. The epidemiologist and data analyst had previously reviewed the questionnaire.

Following the pretesting, the group met to discuss the questionnaire. The nutritionists and ophthalmologists felt the questionnaire was too long: they questioned Dr. Kornet about the viability of sustaining patient interest and ensuring quality patient care for a five-hour period, and they complained that they could not maintain the pretest schedule. She retorted, "It's got to be done this way. Don't be so lazy!" The epidemiologist and data analyst supported Dr. Kornet. They agreed that shortening the questionnaire was inappropriate and criticized their colleagues' negative attitudes toward it. Dr. Kornet instructed the nutritionists and ophthalmologists to pretest the questionnaire once again before attending the next scheduled meeting. She gave them some specific directions about the pretest schedule and procedures, but provided no suggestions about ways to sustain patient interest and ensure patient care for five hours. She also adjourned the meeting before they could discuss their objective further. Instead she attacked the four professionals for their unwillingness and inability to administer the questionnaire during the five-hour time period.

When the group reconvened, one nutritionist and one ophthalmologist were absent from the meeting. The remaining nutritionist and ophthalmologist said nothing about the questionnaire. Dr. Kornet also did not discuss the questionnaire. Pretesting continued for several more days. Then the group met again. They learned that the nutritionist and ophthalmologist who had missed the previous meeting had resigned from the study. The remaining nutritionist and ophthalmologist continued to complain about the questionnaire and the study procedures.[1]

Why was the morale of the nutritionists and ophthalmologists low? Why was their turnover high? Why did they complain about their supervision by Dr. Kornet? How did their supervision affect their performance? Symptoms of low morale, dissatisfaction, and turnover can signal motivation, communication, personal development, role conflict, and group dynamics problems. To diagnose the problems that the glaucoma study group faces, we can ask, for example: On the basis of what perceptions does Dr. Kornet act? Does she attribute the causes of her colleagues' behavior correctly? Do they attribute her behavior correctly? Are the study group members' needs met? Does the leader recognize differences in their personal development? Does she define their roles clearly? Does she use two-way communication with the rest of the team and attempt to encourage quality communication?

Answering these questions probably will not explain completely Dr. Kornet's failure to build high morale, a positive team attitude, and effective performance among her subordinates. So we can analyze the situation from another perspective: the nature and effectiveness of the leadership exhibited by Dr. Karen Kornet. Low productivity, high absenteeism and turnover, low satisfaction, and low morale are also symptoms of ineffective leadership. Dr. Kornet and group leaders like her must choose an appropriate leadership style to encourage employee performance.

We can define a *leader* as an individual who influences others to act toward a particular goal or end-state. Since Karen Kornet influences her subordinates to act toward completing the glaucoma study, then she is in this sense a leader. But does she demonstrate effective leadership?

In this chapter we examine the nature of effective leadership. We look at five major perspectives: (1) trait, (2) behavioral, (3) managerial roles, (4) situational, and (5) transformational, in order of their predominance in management thought, to help us offer strategies for effective leadership. After describing theories representative of each perspective, we explore their applications to managerial effectiveness.

THE TRAIT PERSPECTIVE

Trait theory suggests that we can evaluate leadership and propose ways of leading effectively by considering whether an individual possesses certain personality traits, social traits, and physical characteristics.[2] Popular in the 1940s and 1950s, trait theory attempted to predict which individuals successfully become leaders and then whether they are effective. Leaders' traits included intelligence, personal adjustment, originality, enthusiasm, and persistence. Does Dr. Karen Kornet have these traits? Does she interact often and well with others? Does she show patience, tact, and sympathy? Is she tall, neither too heavy nor too thin, and physically attractive? Does she demonstrate social maturity?

Research has suggested that having these characteristics should facilitate effective leadership.[3] Can you think of any individuals whom you consider effective leaders but who lack these characteristics? A major limitation of trait theory is that traits that might be associated with leadership in one situation do not predict leadership in another.[4] In addition, the traits required for leadership attainment differ from those necessary for effective leadership performance. Although one researcher suggested that four traits predominate in the research—(1) intelligence, (2) social maturity and breadth, (3) inner motivation and achievement drive, and (4) human relations attitudes[5]—no clear pattern of which traits make an effective leader has emerged.

The use of the trait approach now has more historical than practical interest to managers. But some view the transformational perspective, described later in the chapter, as a natural evolution of the trait perspective.

THE BEHAVIORAL VIEW

Limitations in the ability to predict effective leadership through traits caused researchers during the 1950s to examine a person's *behavior* as a way of increasing leadership effectiveness. The behaviors studied were important to, but not sufficient for, effective management.

Behavioral Dimensions

Some of the earliest research, in the 1930s, by Kurt Lewin, Ralph White, and Ronald Lippitt, set the stage for the behavioral perspective. They had evaluated the impact of authoritarian, democratic, and laissez-faire adult leaders on the performance and satisfaction of members of boys' clubs.[6] They concluded that laissez-faire leadership was less efficient and less satisfying to members than was democracy. Under democratic leadership the boys showed the most work interest, originality, and creative thinking. Autocracy resulted in more dependence and less individuality than did democracy.

In later studies, the types of leadership behaviors investigated typically fell into two categories: (1) production-oriented and (2) employee-oriented. *Production-oriented leadership,* also called concern for production, initiating structure, or task-focused leadership, involves acting primarily to get the task done. A supervisor who tells his or her subordinates that they should do "everything they can to get the job done on time" demonstrates production-oriented leadership. So does a manager who uses an autocratic style or fails to involve workers in any aspect of decision making. Karen Kornet could be considered a production-oriented leader.

Employee-oriented leadership, also called concern for people or consideration, focuses on supporting individual workers in their activities and involving workers in decisions. A boss who demonstrates great concern for his or her workers' satisfaction with their jobs and commitment to their work has an employee-oriented leadership style. Such a superior often involves workers in departmental decisions.

Ohio State University Studies Studies in leadership at Ohio State University classified individuals on two dimensions: (1) initiating structure, which resembles production-oriented leadership; and (2) consideration, which resembles employee-oriented leadership.[7] *Initiating structure* reflects the degree to which the leader structures his or her own role and subordinates' roles toward accomplishing the group's goal. Such structuring can occur through scheduling of work, assigning employees to tasks, and maintaining standards of performance. *Consideration* refers to the degree to which the leader emphasizes individuals' needs through two-way communication, respect for subordinates' ideas, mutual trust between leader and subordinates, and consideration of subordinates' feelings.

As shown in Table 8–1, these studies found that managers high in initiating structure and consideration had departments with the highest performance, lowest grievance rate, and lowest turnover. Managers low in these behaviors had departments with the lowest performance, highest grievance rate, and highest turnover. Managers high on one dimension and low on the other had mixed outcomes. According to this research, managers should strive to demonstrate both initiating structure and consideration.

Which of these dimensions did Karen Kornet demonstrate? She seemed to be high in initiating structure and low in consideration. Not surprisingly, then, we see low performance, a high grievance rate, and high turnover from the study group members. Dr. Kornet must be high in *both* initiating structure *and* consideration. In this case she would need to provide more opportunities for the open exchange of ideas and greater consideration of her colleagues' views and feelings.

University of Michigan Studies A series of leadership studies at the University of Michigan, which looked at managers with an employee orientation and a production orientation, yielded similar results.[8] In these studies, which related differences in high-productivity and low-productivity work groups to differences in supervisors, highly productive supervisors spent more time in planning departmental work and in supervising their employees; and less time in working alongside and performing the same tasks as subordinates. They accorded their subordinates more freedom in specific task performance and tended to be employee-oriented.[9] Does this research explain the productivity of the glaucoma study group? Although Karen Kornet spent a reasonable amount of time in planning and supervising, she also limited the team's input into and freedom in specific task performance; she was production-oriented but not employee-oriented, resulting in deteriorating performance.

The Japanese Study A thirty-year research study in Japan examined *performance* and *maintenance* leadership behaviors.[10] While these behaviors resemble the dimensions specified in the Ohio State and University of Michigan

Table 8–1 OUTCOMES OF THE OHIO STATE LEADERSHIP STUDIES' BEHAVIORAL MODEL

		Manager's Initiating Structure	
		High	Low
Manager's Consideration	High	High performance Low grievance rate Low turnover	Low performance Low grievance rate Low turnover
	Low	High performance High grievance rate High turnover	Low performance High grievance rate High turnover

studies, performance differs somewhat from production-oriented or initiating structure leadership. It specifically refers to forming and reaching group goals through fast work speed; high quality, accuracy, and quantity outcomes; and observation of rules. Maintenance behaviors preserve the group's social stability by dealing with subordinates' feelings, reducing stress, providing comfort, and showing appreciation. The results suggested that there are more circumstances in the United States where performance-type leadership alone is associated with high productivity and satisfaction. The Japanese, according to this study, prefer leadership high on both dimensions over performance-dominated behavior, except when work is done in short-term project groups, when subordinates are prone to anxiety, or when effective performance calls for very low effort.

The Managerial Grid The behavioral perspective on the ideal management style has been incorporated into leadership training programs known as Grid Organization Development.[11] Robert Blake and Jane Mouton call for so-called 9,9 management—high concern for people *and* high concern for production—which results in "team management," or making contributions that make a difference. In team management the manager shares participation in goal setting, problem solving, and decision making. Rather than ignoring different points of view, it encourages open confrontation and resolution of differences as well as open critique and feedback. The effective leader demonstrates initiative, inquires fully into the background and status of problems and projects, advocates for his or her ideas, engages in constructive conflict-solving behavior, makes decisions, and engages in the evaluation of work. By participating in such a training program, Karen Kornet could become a more effective leader: she would be able to draw quality performance from her group of highly committed individuals who share a common purpose and use mutual respect and trust among work group members to accomplish the individuals', group's, and organization's goals.

Subsequent research has suggested, however, that the appropriate behaviors for effective leadership are contingent on various aspects of the situation, as described later in this chapter.

MANAGERIAL ROLES

Henry Mintzberg's study of chief executive officers suggested a different way of looking at leadership.[12] He observed that managerial work encompasses ten roles: three that focus on *interpersonal* contact—(1) figurehead, (2) leader, and (3) liaison; three that involve mainly *information processing*—(4) monitor, (5) disseminator, and (6) spokesman; and four related to *decision making*—(7) entrepreneur, (8) disturbance handler, (9) resource allocator, and (10) negotiator. Note that almost all roles include activities that could be construed as leadership—influencing others toward a particular goal. In addition, most of these roles can apply to nonmanagerial positions as well as managerial ones. The role approach resembles the behavioral and trait perspectives because all three call for specific types of behavior independent of the situation; however, the role approach is more compatible with the situation approach and has been shown to be more valid than either the behavioral or trait perspective.

Figurehead. The manager, acting as a symbol or representative of the organization, performs diverse ceremonial duties. By attending Chamber of Commerce meetings, heading the local United Way drive, or representing the president of the firm at an awards banquet, a manager performs the figurehead role.

Leader. The manager, interacting with subordinates, motivates and develops them. The supervisor who conducts quarterly performance interviews or selects training opportunities for his or her subordinates performs this role. This role emphasizes the socioemotional and people-oriented side of leadership. Although it may include some task activities, these are more often incorporated into the decisional roles, described below.

Liaison. The manager establishes a network of contacts to gather information for the organization. Belonging to professional associations or meeting over lunch with peers in other organizations helps the manager perform the liaison role. Additional aspects of this role are discussed in Chapter 10.

Monitor. The manager gathers information from the environment inside and outside the organization. The manager may attend meetings with his or her subordinates, scan company publications, or participate in company-wide committees as a way of performing this role.

Disseminator. The manager transmits both factual and value information to subordinates. Managers may conduct staff meetings, send memoranda to their staff, or meet informally with them on a one-to-one basis to discuss current and future projects.

Spokesperson. The manager gives information to people outside the organization about its performance and policies. The manager who oversees preparation of the annual report, prepares advertising copy, or speaks at community and professional meetings fulfills this role.

Entrepreneur. The manager designs and initiates change in the organization. The supervisor who redesigns the job of subordinates, introduces flexible working hours, or brings new technology to the job performs this role.

Disturbance handler. The manager deals with problems that arise when organizational operations break down. A person who finds a new supplier for an out-of-stock part on short notice, who replaces unexpectedly absent employees, or who deals with machine breakdowns performs this role.

Resource allocator. The manager controls the allocation of people, money, materials, and time by scheduling his or her own time, programming subordinates' work efforts, and authorizing all significant decisions. Preparation of the budget is a major aspect of this role.

Negotiator. The manager participates in negotiation activities. A manager who hires a new employee may negotiate work assignments or compensation with that person.

While not all managers perform every role, some diversity of role performance must occur. Managers can diagnose their own and others' role performance and then offer strategies for altering it if necessary. Table 8–2 shows the most frequent roles played by a variety of managers. The choice of roles depends to some extent on the manager's specific job description and the sit-

Table 8–2 EIGHT MANAGERIAL JOB TYPES

Managerial Job Type	Key Roles	Examples
Contact person	Liaison, Figurehead	Sales Manager Chief Executives in service industries
Political manager	Spokesperson, Negotiator	Top government, hospital, university managers
Entrepreneur	Entrepreneur, Negotiator	Owner of small, young business CEO of rapidly changing, large organization
Insider	Resource allocator	Middle or senior production or operations manager Manager rebuilding after crisis
Real-time manager	Disturbance handler	Foreman Head of organization in crisis Head of small, one-manager business
Team manager	Leader	Hockey coach Head of R&D group
Expert manager	Monitor, Spokesperson	Head of specialist group
New manager	Liaison, Monitor	Manager in a new job

Adapted from H. Mintzberg, *The Nature of Managerial Work* (Englewood Cliffs, N.J.: Prentice-Hall, 1973).

uation in question, although most managers should perform all of these roles during the work week. Reading 8–1, "The Role of the Manager: What's Really Important in Different Management Jobs," elucidates some of these differences.

Consider some managers you have observed. Now consider your own performance in managerial roles. Finally, consider Karen Kornet's performance. What roles did a manager perform in each of these situations? Did the managers limit themselves to one or two roles, or perform a range of roles? Should they have performed some roles more frequently? Should they have performed some less frequently? Mintzberg's view of managerial behavior offers a diagnostic perspective that complements those of perception, attribution, motivation, communication, personal development, group dynamics, and leadership. Besides leadership, the roles he identifies emphasize motivation (interpersonal roles), communication (informational roles), and decision making (decisional roles). Effective managers—and leaders—can develop a protocol for action based on the role analysis. Introducing the leadership style that fits best with the situation, as described in the next sections, strengthens this protocol.

SITUATIONAL LEADERSHIP

Contingency or situational models assert that no single way of behaving works in *all* situations. Rather, appropriate behavior depends on the circumstances at a given time. The development of situational models was a response to the failure of earlier, more universalist theories to explain or predict effective behavior. Effective managers diagnose the situation, identify the leadership style that will be most effective, and then determine if they can implement the required style.

Situational Influences

Subordinate, supervisor, and task considerations have been hypothesized to influence whether consideration and initiating-structure leadership behaviors correlate with subordinate or follower satisfaction, performance, and morale.[13] *Subordinate considerations* refer to expertise, experience, competence, knowledge of a job, hierarchical level of occupied position, expectations concerning leader behavior, perceived organizational independence, and other psychological aspects. *Supervisor considerations* refer to the similarity of attitudes and behavior to those of higher management and the degree of upward influence. *Task considerations* describe the degree of time urgency, amount of physical danger, permissible error rate, presence of external stress, degree of autonomy, degree of job scope, importance and meaningfulness of work, and degree of ambiguity. Some researchers have suggested that leadership strategies in any sociocultural setting, such as an occupational or organizational group, have strong underlying similarities but must change as the setting changes over time.[14] Other research suggests that the effect of leader behaviors on unit performance is altered by such intervening variables as the effort of subordinates, their ability to perform their jobs, the clarity of their job responsibilities, the organization of the work, the cooperation and cohesiveness of the work group, the sufficiency of resources and support provided to the group, and the coordination of work group activities with those of other subunits.[15] Thus leaders must respond to these and broader cultural differences in choosing an appropriate leadership style.

If, for example, subordinates have the expertise and competence needed to accomplish an organizational goal, then an employee-oriented leadership style is more effective than if followers lack the required expertise and competence. If superiors and subordinates have the same attitudes, then subordinates may be more willing to accept production-oriented leadership. If time urgency and physical danger accompany a task, then production-oriented leadership behavior may be more effective. Researchers would hypothesize, therefore, that the appropriateness of Dr. Kornet's leadership style would depend on such conditions as her subordinates' expertise, experience, and knowledge of the job; her own attitudes and influence; and certain characteristics of the task. Consideration of these three dimensions leads us toward a situational theory of leadership.

A leader or manager operating on a global scale must also integrate traits and behaviors that make him or her effective in diverse cultures. A global manager is a sensitive, innovative, and participative leader who can communicate interculturally, builds on cultural differences through international collaboration, and leads change in the organization to improve intercultural performance.[16] Such a manager must continuously acquire current information about the culture and adapt his or her leadership style to the culture in which he or she is functioning.

McGregor's Theory X and Theory Y

Douglas McGregor's theory of leadership has often been misinterpreted as a one-best-way prescription for managerial behavior.[17] Rather it calls for a leadership style based on individuals' assumptions about other individuals, together with characteristics of the individual, the task, the organization, and the environment. McGregor posited that managers have so-called Theory X or Theory Y assumptions (among other types) about their employees. *Theory X* managers assume that people are lazy, extrinsically motivated, incapable of self-discipline or self-control, and want security and no responsibility in their jobs. *Theory Y* managers assume people do not inherently dislike work, are intrinsically motivated, exert self-control, and seek responsibility.

Historically, Theory Y has been viewed solely as a call for participative management. Instead, a Theory Y manager, after assessing his or her preferred managerial style, motives and limitations, past experiences, as well as characteristics of the task, its organizational context, and the environment, chooses a leadership style. He or she may act paternalistically, consultatively, or autocratically, for example. A Theory X manager, because of his or her limited view of the world, has only one leadership style: autocratic. Figure 8–1 summarizes this contingency perspective. It illustrates the way assumptions influence action tendencies, which together with internal and external modifiers should prescribe effective leadership behavior.

Consider the glaucoma study group from McGregor's perspective. Can we pinpoint why morale dropped, complaints increased, and productivity declined? First we must assess Karen Kornet's assumptions about individuals. Because she chastises her colleagues for being lazy, we can infer that she has Theory X assumptions about her subordinates. Her autocratic managerial style fits with Theory X assumptions. However, this style does not seem to fit with the task, organizational norms, history of the organization, and experience of the subordinates. These factors seem to call for greater consultation with and participation by the professional study group members. Even if Dr. Kornet has Theory Y rather than Theory X assumptions, her autocratic style does not fit with external conditions. This misfit explains the negative outcomes in the introductory case.

How can a manager such as Karen Kornet use McGregor's theory for ensuring leadership effectiveness? What prescription would McGregor offer for improving the situation? If Dr. Kornet has Theory X assumptions, he would probably advise her to review them and, if possible, adopt Theory Y assumptions. Such a change might call for management training and development or merely self-reflection by Karen. If Dr. Kornet has Theory Y assumptions, he would advise her to alter her leadership style. In any case she must diagnose the situation and then fit her style to it.

Exchange Theory

Dansereau and his associates challenged the notion of a single leadership style. In their vertical dyad-linkage model of leadership they emphasized the inter-

Figure 8–1 HOW THEORY Y RELATES TO MANAGERIAL STYLE AND BEHAVIOR

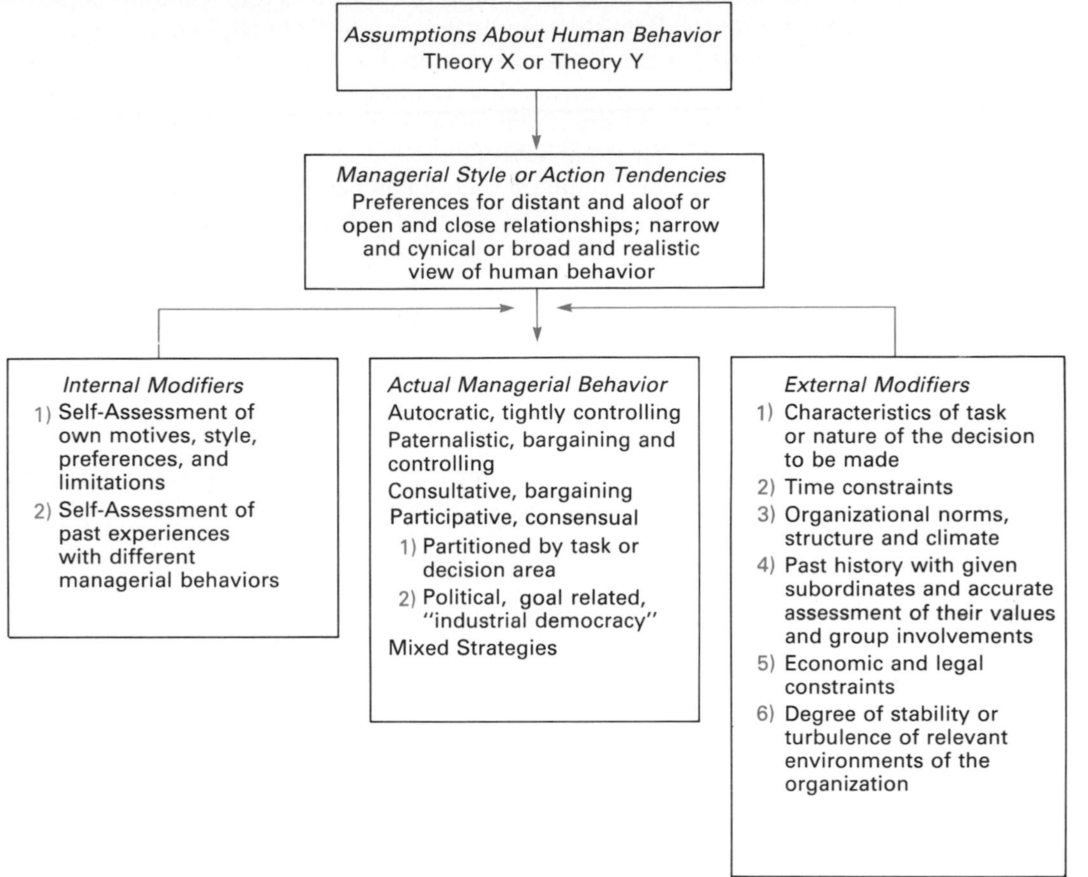

E.H. Schein, The Hawthorne studies revisited: A defense of Theory Y, Sloan School of Management Working Paper #756–74. Cambridge: Massachusetts Institute of Technology, December, 1974, p. 3.

action of the leader with the group he or she supervises.[18] The leader exchanges resources, such as increased job latitude, influence on decision making, and open communication, for members' commitment to higher involvement in organizational functioning.[19] By behaving to increase the exchange of resources between leaders and members, a leader can increase follower productivity, job satisfaction, and satisfaction with supervision; and gains are greater for those with low exchange relations than those with high relations.[20] (Exchanging resources also accompanies the power behavior of leaders, described in Chapter 9.)

According to this research, leaders behave differently toward two types of followers.[21] The *cadre,* or in-group, includes those employees whom the leader allows a great deal of latitude. They experienced higher performance ratings, lower propensity to quit, greater satisfaction with supervision, and greater actual job performance. The *hired hands,* or out-group, includes those workers whom the leader allows little latitude; this resulted in poor outcomes. Supervisors made internal attributions about their followers consistent with the perceived status of the subordinates as in-group or out-group members, suggesting a relationship between exchange theory and attribution theory[22] (described later in this chapter). Karen Kornet seemed to treat all her subordinates as hired hands, allowing them little latitude. This might explain their negative responses to her leadership. In related research, leaders who reported to a hired hand claimed they had less competent, less attentive, and less sensitive bosses, encountered greater resistance to change, and had less valuable rewards available for themselves.[23]

The research on exchange theory has been criticized because it relies on a narrow data base, does not sufficiently study the organizational outcomes associated with the exchange relationship, and operationalizes exchanges in diverse and inconsistent ways.[24] Yet it encourages managers and other organizational members to diagnose the status of followers vis-à-vis leaders in choosing a leadership style.

Fiedler's Theory

Fred Fiedler developed and tested the first leadership theory explicitly called a contingency model. He stated that the most effective leadership style depended on the nature of the given situation.[25] Fiedler argues that changing an individual's leadership style is quite difficult. He proposes instead that organizations should "engineer the job to fit the manager,"[26] or put individuals in situations that fit with their style. He specifically identified three features of any situation where task-oriented, as opposed to relationship-oriented leadership, is more likely to be effective: (1) leader–member relations, (2) task structure, and (3) position power of the leader.[27]

Leader–member relations refers to the extent to which the group trusts and respects the leader and is willing to follow his or her directions. A leader who has subordinates who readily follow instructions, set and accept goals, or take initiative has good leader–member relations. A leader who has difficulty getting cooperation from workers does not.

Task structure describes the degree to which the task is clearly specified and defined or structured, as opposed to ambiguous or unstructured. Putting a wheel assembly on an automobile or disbursing cash in a bank are structured tasks. Determining the contents of an investment portfolio, selecting a new chief operating officer, or designing a research protocol are unstructured tasks.

Position power means the extent to which the leader has official power; that is, the potential or actual ability to influence others in a desired direction due to the position he or she holds in the organization. (See Chapter 9 for further discussion.) A manager, chief executive officer, or other supervisor has position power. A staff member or nonmanagerial employee does not.

Fiedler considers leader–member relations, followed by task structure, and then position power, to have the greatest weight in determining effective leadership style. Table 8–3 shows the style recommended as most effective for each combination of these three situational factors. The recommendations are based on the degree of control or influence the leader can exert in his or her leadership position. Where leader–member relations are good, the task is structured, and the leader has position power, as in Situation I, the leader can exert a great deal of control and influence on subordinates. Even as position power weakens or the task becomes less structured, the ability to exert control does not immediately disappear because of the strong relationship between leader and followers.

In general, high control situations (I, II, and III) call for task-oriented

Table 8–3 FIEDLER'S MODEL OF EFFECTIVE LEADERSHIP

	Description of the Situation				
	Leader–Member Relations	Task Structure	Power Position	Example	Effective Leadership Style
I	Good	Structured	Strong	Bomber crew	Task-oriented
II	Good	Structured	Weak	Basketball team	Task-oriented
III	Good	Unstructured	Strong	ROTC	Task-oriented
IV	Good	Unstructured	Weak	Board of directors of cooperative	Relations-oriented
V	Poor	Structured	Strong	Antiaircraft artillery crew	Relations-oriented
VI	Poor	Structured	Weak	Surveying team	Relations-oriented
VII	Poor	Unstructured	Strong	ROTC	Either
VIII	Poor	Unstructured	Weak	Management teams	Task-oriented

SOURCE: Adapted from F.E. Fiedler, *A Theory of Leadership Effectiveness* (New York: McGraw-Hill, 1967), p. 37. Reprinted with permission.

leadership because they allow the leader to take charge. The low control situation (VIII) also calls for task-oriented leadership because it *requires* rather than *allows* the leader to take charge. Where leader–member relations are poor, the task is unstructured, and the leader lacks position power, the leader must exert a great deal of influence to prevent the group from acting aimlessly, making little progress toward their goals. Moderate control situations (IV, V, and VI), in contrast, call for relationship-oriented leadership because the situations challenge leaders to get the cooperation of their subordinates.[28] (Situation VII calls for either type.) One research study has suggested that leaders receiving scores in the middle 25 percent of the distribution may be more effective in all leadership situations because of their greater flexibility.[29]

In spite of extensive research to support the theory, critics question the reliability of the measurement of leadership style and the range and appropriateness of the three situational components.[30] However, managers can use this model to diagnose the nature of several contingencies that affect leadership style and begin to identify the appropriate style for a given context.

Path–Goal Theory

Path–goal theory represents a more successful attempt to reconcile the previous contradictory and diffuse research findings in the area of leadership. Its name derives from leaders' attempts to influence subordinates' perceptions of goals and the paths to achieve them.[31]

Links to Motivation Theory This theory links effective leadership to effective motivation, particularly when expectancy theory is used to explain motivation. (See Chapter 4 for discussion of expectancy theory.) The leader acts to strengthen the expectancy, instrumentality, and valence of a situation. The effective leader ensures that more effort leads to greater performance. He or she increases expectancy in a subordinate's job, for example, by providing better machinery or training for workers so that if they put in effort on the job they will perform better. The leader also ensures that performance leads to outcomes: he or she reinforces desired behaviors with pay, praise, or promotion. The leader can increase the valence in a situation by ensuring that workers value the rewards they receive or that the rewards offered are valued by the workers. The leader can make sure that rewards, such as compensation, praise, or promotion, meet subordinates' or coworkers' needs.

Characteristics of an Effective Style An effective leadership style involves the following[32]:

First, the leader must recognize and arouse subordinates' needs for outcomes over which the leader has some control. The leader must identify, for example, promotion opportunities or work assignments that he or she controls and subordinates desire.

Second, the leader must increase personal payoffs to subordinates for work-goal attainment. Workers who produce as expected must receive rewards for their outputs. High producers, for example, should receive greater rewards in pay, status, or praise than low producers.

Third, the leader must facilitate the path to these payoffs by coaching and directing. Subordinates must see which goal accomplishment results in desired outcomes. The leader must show a subordinate who desires a promotion or a change in job responsibilities how he or she can achieve it.

Fourth, the leader should help subordinates clarify expectancies by demonstrating what types of effort lead to high performance, and then what outcomes result from that performance. If, for example, working overtime is desired, the leader must show the worker how this type of effort results in better job performance. He or she must also show workers how advancement or good work assignments will be given to those who perform well. Leaders may also jointly set goals with workers as a way of motivating them to perform. (See Chapter 4 for discussion of goal setting as a motivational technique.)

Fifth, the leader must reduce frustrating barriers to attaining outcomes and rewards. He or she must make sure that subordinates have the equipment, training, and knowledge to perform required tasks.

Sixth and finally, the leader must increase the opportunities for personal satisfaction that result from effective performance. Leaders must encourage performance based on both intrinsic and extrinsic motivation of workers (see Chapter 4). Where possible, for example, workers must be given tasks that they find interesting and challenging, as well as tasks to which rewards such as pay and status are attached.

Styles of Leadership Leaders can choose among four styles of leadership: (1) directive, (2) supportive, (3) participative, and (4) achievement-oriented.[33] A leader with a *directive* style informs subordinates what is expected of them, gives specific guidance as to what should be done, and shows how to do it. A manager demonstrates directive leadership if he or she provides subordinates with a plan of activities, as well as a complete set of written instructions for implementing them.

A leader with a *supportive* style is friendly and approachable and shows concern for the status, well-being, and needs of subordinates. A supervisor with an "open door policy," who encourages subordinates to come to him or her with any and all problems, has this style.

A leader with a *participative* style consults with subordinates, solicits their suggestions, and takes suggestions into consideration before making a decision. Any boss who makes decisions by group consensus uses this style.

A leader with an *achievement-oriented* style sets challenging goals, expects subordinates to perform at their highest level, continuously seeks improvement in performance, and shows a high degree of confidence that subordinates will assume responsibility, put forth effort, and accomplish challenging goals. The manager who relies on the goal-setting technique described in Chapter 4 to motivate employees has an achievement-oriented style.

Which style does Karen Kornet demonstrate? She informs her subordinates about her expectations and gives them very explicit guidance about how to perform their jobs; she has a directive style. But is this an effective one?

Choosing a Style Choosing a leadership style first requires a good quality diagnosis of the situation. The manager or nonmanagerial leader must decide what behavior would be most effective. The manager or leader must then determine whether he or she can supply the behavior. The appropriate leadership style is influenced first by *subordinates' characteristics,* particularly subordinates' abilities and the likelihood that the leader's behavior will cause subordinates satisfaction now or in the future. Second, style is dependent on the *environment,* or the subordinates' tasks, the formal authority system, and the primary work group. The appropriate style for Dr. Kornet, for example, depends on her subordinates' skills, knowledge, and abilities, as well as their attitudes toward her. It also depends on the nature of their activities, the lines of authority in the organization, and the integrity of their work group. The most desirable leadership style helps the individual achieve satisfaction and accomplish goals while complementing the subordinates' abilities and the characteristics of the situation. "The nature of (group) goals, the task technology involved in achieving the goals, and the culture or broader organization in which the groups exist" influence the relationship between leaders and followers.[34]

> When task demands are clear to subordinates, leader directiveness is seen more as a hindrance. . . . Supportive leadership will have its most positive effect on subordinate satisfaction for subordinates who work on stressful, frustrating, or dissatisfying tasks. . . . Achievement-oriented leadership will cause subordinates to strive for higher standards of performance and to have more confidence in their ability to meet challenging goals. . . . Where participative leadership is positively related to satisfaction, regardless of the predispositions of subordinates, the tasks of the subjects appear to be ambiguous and ego-involving.[35]

Table 8–4 offers a sample of situations in which each type of leadership style is likely to result in positive, desirable outcomes. The right-hand columns indicate whether each of the four prototype leadership styles fits with the feature of the situation listed in the left-hand column, when considered independently of other situational characteristics. For example, only directive

Table 8–4 EFFECTIVE LEADERSHIP STYLES UNDER DIFFERENT CONDITIONS

Sample Situational Characteristics	Leadership Styles			
	Directive	Supportive	Achievement	Participative
Task				
Structured	No	Yes	Yes	Yes
Unstructured	Yes	No	Yes	No
Clear goals	No	Yes	No	Yes
Ambiguous goals	Yes	No	Yes	No
Subordinates				
Skilled in task	No	Yes	Yes	Yes
Unskilled in task	Yes	No	Yes	No
High achievement needs	No	No	Yes	No
High social needs	No	Yes	No	Yes
Formal authority				
Extensive	No	Yes	Yes	Yes
Limited	Yes	Yes	Yes	Yes
Work group				
Strong social network	Yes	No	Yes	Yes
Experienced in collaboration	No	No	No	Yes
Organizational culture				
Supports participation	No	No	No	Yes
Achievement-oriented	No	No	Yes	No

leadership is inappropriate when the task is structured, since directive leadership is redundant. For subordinates with high achievement needs, in contrast, only an achievement style will satisfy their needs. In general, a leader-environment-follower interaction theory of leadership notes that effective leaders first analyze the deficiencies in a follower's ability, motivation, role perception, and work environment that inhibit performance, then act to eliminate these deficiencies.[36]

In the case of Karen Kornet and the glaucoma project, members of the study group were professionals who perceived that they had the ability to contribute meaningfully to the design of the study. Thus Karen's directive leadership behavior did not meet their needs. In addition, her use of a directive style in the implementation of a clearly specified protocol for the pretest was redundant. Most likely another leadership style would have been more effective. Participative leadership, for example, could have expedited individual satisfaction and complemented the individual's abilities and the stable environment. Dr. Kornet could also have used an achievement-oriented style and continued to remain actively involved in the study by setting goals jointly with team members. She might also have considered relinquishing task control completely, providing only socioemotional support with a supportive style. Selection of a particular style depends both on her diagnosis of group members' needs and the nature of the task. If the professionals had a strong need for esteem or achievement, then an achievement-oriented or participative style would have been preferable to a supportive one. If instead they had a high need for affiliation or belongingness, the supportive style would be better.

Diagnosis Using the Path–Goal Theory As a contingency theory, application of the path–goal theory as part of a diagnostic framework first requires an assessment of the situation, particularly its participants and environment, and then a determination of the most congruent leadership style. Pertinent questions include the following:

1. *What is the nature of the environment, the subordinates' tasks, the formal authority system, and the primary work group?* In the case of the glaucoma study group, the environment is a fairly stable and nonintrusive one in which the researchers can perform their tasks without interference. Their tasks are clear and they have performed them numerous times before. Team leadership is clearly delegated to Dr. Kornet. The study group has limited experience working together.
2. *What are the subordinates' abilities and leadership preferences?* We can infer from the case description that the study team members are professionals with sufficient training to perform the tasks assigned to them. They prefer less control and direction from their leader.
3. *Which style responds to the environmental contingencies?* Any nondirective style fits best with the environment, although the researchers' lack of experience as a work team may limit the value of a participative style.
4. *Which style enhances the subordinates' characteristics?* As suggested earlier, an achievement-oriented or participative style best fits the subordinates' needs, abilities, and experiences.
5. *Does the leader use the style called for by various contingencies? If not, how can the leader resolve the difference?* If there is a mismatch, then either the situation or the leader must change. A comparison of the styles that respond to the environment and enhance the subordinates' characteristics suggest that participative and achievement-oriented styles meet both criteria. Either style could fit, although the achievement-oriented style may be more appropriate for Dr. Kornet.

Empirical Support Although some research has supported path–goal theory, especially as it predicts subordinate satisfaction, overall research has yielded mixed results.[37] Some research has suggested that this theory is robust and has wide applicability,[38] but the theory does not consider all aspects of leader behavior.[39] Additional validation of the impact of the four leadership styles,[40] and specific criteria to be used in choosing a particular leadership style in various situations, are still needed.

Vroom–Yetton Model

Victor Vroom and Philip Yetton introduced a theory of leadership that focuses on decision making by managers with a defined group of subordinates or a single subordinate.[41] It consists of a procedure for determining the extent to which leaders should involve subordinates in the decision-making process. According to this theory, the manager can choose one of the five basic processes for involving subordinates in decision making, listed in Table 8–5. For problems where one subordinate could participate in making the decision, the leader or manager chooses from solving the problem himself or herself with available information (AI or AII), solving the problem himself or herself with information or ideas from the subordinate (CI), jointly solving the problem

Table 8–5 DECISION-MAKING PROCESSES

For Individual Problems	For Group Problems
AI You solve the problem or make the decision yourself, using information available to you at that time.	AI You solve the problem or make the decision yourself, using information available to you at that time.
AII You obtain any necessary information from the subordinate, then decide on the solution to the problem yourself. You may or may not tell the subordinate what the problem is, in getting the information from him. The role played by your subordinate in making the decision is clearly one of providing specific information which you request, rather than generating or evaluating alternative solutions.	AII You obtain any necessary information from subordinates, then decide on the solution to the problem yourself. You may or may not tell subordinates what the problem is, in getting the information from them. The role played by your subordinates in making the decision is clearly one of providing specific information which you request, rather than generating or evaluating solutions.
CI You share the problem with the relevant subordinate, getting his ideas and suggestions. They *you* make the decision. This decision may or may not reflect your subordinate's influence.	CI You share the problem with the relevant subordinates individually, getting their ideas and suggestions without bringing them together as a group. Then *you* make the decision. This decision may or may not reflect your subordinates' influence.
GI You share the problem with one of your subordinates and together you analyze the problem and arrive at a mutually satisfactory solution in an atmosphere of free and open exchange of information and ideas. You both contribute to the resolution of the problem with the relative contribution of each being dependent on knowledge rather than formal authority.	CII You share the problem with your subordinates in a group meeting. In this meeting you obtain their ideas and suggestions. Then, *you* make the decision which may or may not reflect your subordinates' influence.
DI You delegate the problem to one of your subordinates, providing him with any relevant information that you possess, but giving him responsibility for solving the problem by himself. Any solution which the person reaches will receive your support.	GII You share the problem with your subordinates as a group. Together you generate and evaluate alternatives and attempt to reach agreement (consensus) on a solution. Your role is much like that of chairman, coordinating the discussion, keeping it focused on the problem, and making sure that the critical issues are discussed. You do not try to influence the group to adopt "your" solution and are willing to accept and implement any solution which has the support of the entire group.

SOURCE: Reprinted by permission from V.H. Vroom, and A.G. Jago, Decision-making as a social process: Normative and descriptive models of leader behavior, *Decision Sciences* 5 (1974): 745.

with the subordinate (GI), or delegating problem-solving responsibility (DI). For problems where a group of subordinates could participate in the decision making, the manager or leader chooses from making the decision himself or herself with available information (AI or AII), solving the problem himself or herself with information or ideas from subordinates (CI or CII), or solving the problem with subordinates as a group (GII).

The Original Model for Choosing a Problem-Solving Approach Selection of the appropriate decision process involves assessing the characteristics of any particular problem. The actual decision style chosen depends on the amount of time available to make the decision and the decision maker's preference for involving subordinates in the process as a way of training and developing them. A manager who has to decide in the next week which of three subordinates to promote must choose a process that ensures a high quality decision and a decision that the subordinates will accept and be committed to executing. The manager must recognize time constraints on the decision and the extent to which subordinates should be given experience in making decisions.

Figure 8–2 illustrates the original normative model, expressed as a decision tree. To make a decision, the leader asks each question, A through H, corresponding to each box encountered, from left to right, unless questions may be skipped because the response to the previous question leads to a later one. For example, a "No" response to question A allows questions B and C to be skipped; a "Yes" response to question B after a "Yes" response to question A allows question C to be skipped. When the set of feasible processes for group problems includes more than one process (e.g., a "No" response to each question results in problem type 1, for which every decision style is feasible), final selection of the single approach can use either minimum number of hours (AI, AII, CI, CII, and GII preferred, in that order), or maximum subordinate involvement (GII, CII, CI, AII, and AI preferred, in that order), as secondary criteria. A manager who wishes to make the decision in the shortest time possible, and for whom all processes are appropriate, should choose AI (solving the problem himself or herself using available information) over any other process. A manager who wishes to maximize subordinate involvement in the decision making, for example as a training and development tool, should choose DI or GII (delegating the problem to the subordinate, or reaching a decision together with subordinates) if all processes are feasible and time is not limited. A process using the former criterion is called Model A behavior; the latter, Model B,[42] and similar choices can be made by analyzing individual problems in the same way. Research has shown that decisions made using processes from the feasible set result in more effective outcomes than those using other processes.[43]

According to the normative model, how should Dr. Kornet have made decisions about the questionnaire and pretest procedures? Figure 8–3 presents the analysis. Applying the normative model results in the decision style GII: the leader should share the problem with the subordinates as a group, then generate and evaluate alternatives together and attempt to reach consensus on the solution. This analysis also suggests that the feasible set does not include the process used by Dr. Kornet—AI, the manager or leader solves the problem or makes the decision himself or herself, using information available at that time. This process is inappropriate for the particular characteristics of the situation. In particular, it fails to obtain the acceptance of the subordinates for the activities they must implement.

Figure 8–2 DECISION PROCESS FLOW CHART FOR BOTH INDIVIDUAL AND GROUP PROBLEMS

A. Is there a quality requirement such that one solution is likely to be more rational than another?
B. Do I have sufficient info to make a high quality decision?
C. Is the problem structured?
D. Is acceptance of decision by subordinates critical to effective implementation?
E. If I were to make the decision by myself, is it reasonably certain that it would be accepted by my subordinates?
F. Do subordinates share the organizational goals to be attained in solving this problem?
G. Is conflict among subordinates likely in preferred solutions? (This question is irrelevant to individual problems.)
H. Do subordinates have sufficient info to make a high quality decision?

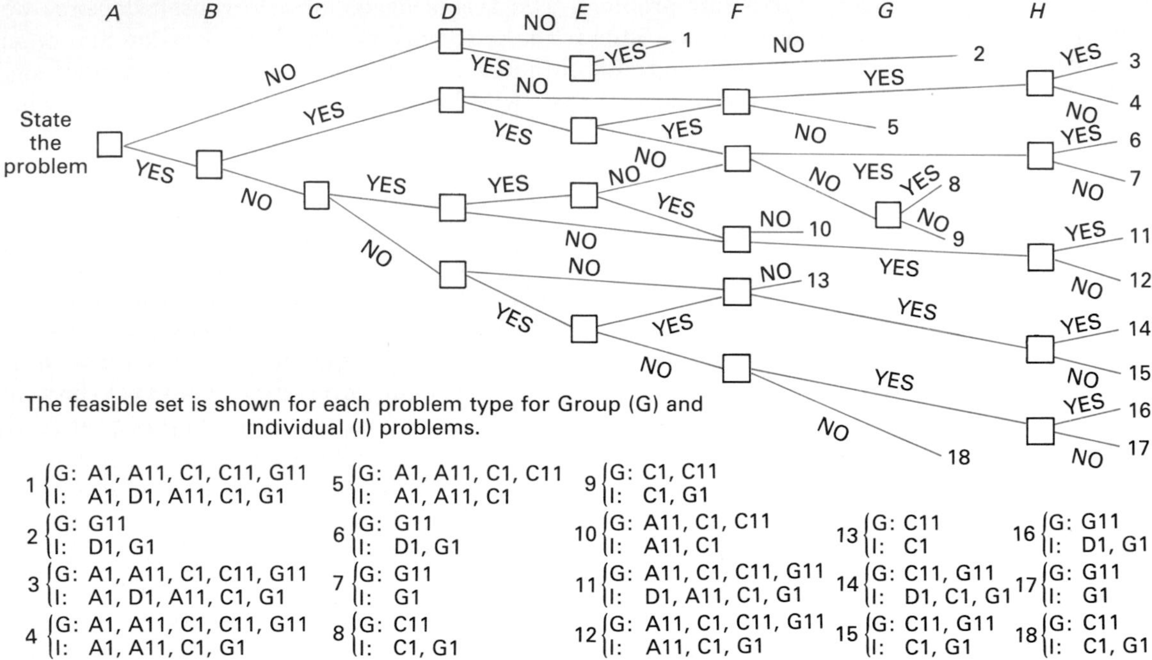

SOURCE: Reprinted from V.H. Vroom and A.G. Jago, Decision making as a social process: Normative and descriptive models of leader behavior, *Decision Sciences* 5(1974): 748.

Limitations of the Original Model The normative model provides a set of diagnostic questions for analyzing a problem, yet it likely oversimplifies the process. Its narrow focus on the extent of subordinate involvement in decision making, for example, probably limits its usefulness.

Recent Reformulation A newer model uses the same decision processes—AI, AII, CI, CII, GII, GI, DI—and employs the criteria of decision quality, decision commitment, time, and subordinate development as well. It also fails to capture a range of probability in responses, since it calls for only a "Yes" or "No" response to each diagnostic question. Finally, it does not explicitly consider significant aspects of the situation, such as the amount of information available to subordinates, time constraints, and geographical constraints on the decision making. In addition, because of its complexity, a computer is required to process the data.[44]

Although this model focuses on specific aspects of behavior and identifies key aspects of the situation, it has several drawbacks.[45] It focuses on only a

Figure 8–3 SOLUTION TO DR. KAREN KORNET'S PROBLEM USING THE NORMATIVE MODEL

Analysis:

A. Is there a quality requirement such that one solution is likely to be more rational than another? Yes. Some study protocols will be more effective than others.
B. Do I have sufficient information to make a high-quality decision? No. Dr. Kornet does not have a complete knowledge of all options and their implications.
C. Is the problem structured? No. The determination of the best protocol is not clear cut and cannot be made according to a formula.
D. Is acceptance of the decision by subordinates critical to effective implementation? Yes. Effective job performance depends, in part, on staff members performing activities they want to do and taking responsibility for determining and accomplishing a series of tasks.
E. If I were to make the decision by myself, is it reasonably certain that it would be accepted by my subordinates? No. As suggested by the resignations of the two team members, not all study group members will accept their superior's decision.
F. Do subordinates share the organizational goals to be attained in solving this problem? Yes. They are committed to eradicating juvenile glaucoma.
G. Is conflict among subordinates likely in the preferred solutions? (This question is skipped in moving through the decision tree.)
H. Do subordinates have sufficient information to make a high-quality decision? Yes. The study group members have participated in similar studies and also have the technical knowledge to make a high-quality decision.

Synthesis Using Original Model:

Problem Type: 16
Feasible Set: GII
Model A Behavior: GII
Model B Behavior: GII

small part of leadership. It also treats decision processes as discrete episodes, at one point in time, and does not recognize that some decisions extend over a period of time and involve a variety of participants. Finally, it excludes a "trial balloon" type of process, where a leader tests a tentative autocratic decision with subordinates before finalizing it. Managers can use either the original or revised versions to help select one aspect of leadership style: the nature and extent of follower involvement in decision making. While it addresses only one aspect of leadership, choice of a process can complement responses to other aspects of the situation described in this chapter.

Situational Leadership Model

In an attempt to integrate previous knowledge about leadership into a prescriptive model of leadership style, Paul Hersey and Kenneth Blanchard developed a situational model of leadership that specified the readiness of followers, defined as the ability and willingness to accomplish a specific task, as the major contingency that influences appropriate leadership style.[46] Follower readiness incorporates the follower's level of achievement motivation (see Chapter 4), ability, and willingness to assume responsibility for his or her own behavior in accomplishing specific tasks, and education and experience relevant to the task.

This situational model incorporates two dimensions of leadership style. First, *task behavior* is "the extent to which the leader engages in spelling out the duties and responsibilities of an individual or group. These behaviors include telling people what to do, how to do it, when to do it, where to do it, and who is to do it."[47] Second, *relationship behavior* is "the extent to which a leader engages in two-way or multi-way communication. The behaviors include listening, facilitating, and supportive behaviors."[48] Combining these dimensions results in four styles (see Figure 8–4):

Figure 8–4 MODEL OF SITUATIONAL LEADERSHIP

Task Behavior
The extent to which the leader engages in defining roles telling what, how, when, where, and if more than one person, who is to do what in
- Goal-setting
- Organizing
- Establishing time lines
- Directing
- Controlling

Relationship Behavior
The extent to which a leader engages in two-way (multi-way) communication, listening, facilitating behaviors, socioemotional support
- Giving support
- Communicating
- Facilitating interactions
- Active listening
- Providing feedback

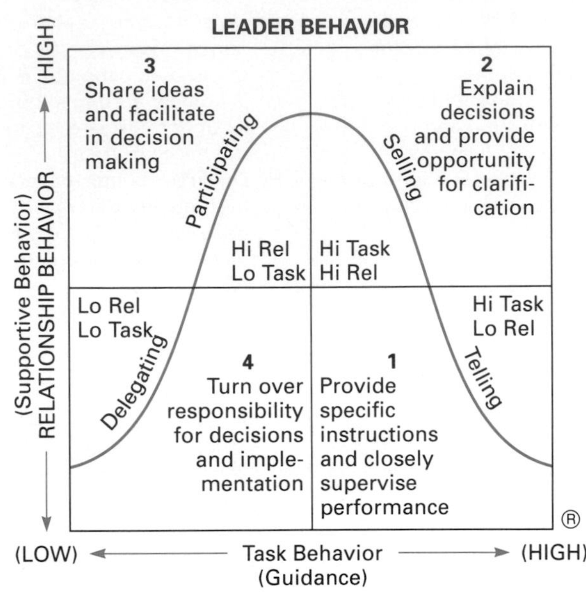

Decision Styles

1
Leader-made decision

2
Leader-made decision with dialogue and/or explanation

3
Leader/follower-made decision or follower-made decision with encouragement from leader

4
Follower-made decision

FOLLOWER READINESS

High	Moderate		Low
R4	R3	R2	R1
Able and willing or confident	Able but unwilling or insecure	Unable but willing or confident	Unable and unwilling or insecure

FOLLOWER DIRECTED — LEADER DIRECTED

Ability has the necessary knowledge, experience and skill

Willingness has the necessary confidence, commitment, motivation

When a Leader Behavior is used appropriately with its corresponding level of readiness, it is termed a High Probability Match. The following are descriptors that can be useful when using Situational Leadership for specific applications:

S1	**S2**	**S3**	**S4**
Telling	Selling	Participating	Delegating
Guiding	Explaining	Encouraging	Observing
Directing	Clarifying	Collaborating	Monitoring
Establishing	Persuading	Committing	Fulfilling

SOURCE: P.H. Hersey and K.H. Blanchard, *Utilizing Human Resources* 5th ed. Copyrighted material from Leadership Studies, Inc. All rights reserved. Used by permission.

1. Using a *Telling, Guiding, Directing,* or *Establishing* style, the leader provides specific instructions and closely supervises performance. This style combines below average amounts of relationship-oriented behavior with above average amounts of task-oriented behavior, to result in leader-made decisions. Leaders should use this style when followers have low readiness—are unable and unwilling or insecure.
2. Using a *Selling, Explaining, Clarifying,* or *Persuading* style, the leader explains decisions and provides opportunity for clarification. This style combines above average amounts of relationship-oriented be-

havior with above average amounts of task-oriented behavior, to result in leader-made decisions with clarification. Leaders should use this style when followers have moderate to low readiness—are unable but willing or confident.

3. Using a *Participating, Encouraging, Collaborating,* or *Committing* style, the leader shares ideas and helps facilitate decision making. This style combines above average amounts of relationship-oriented behavior with below average amounts of task-oriented behavior, to result in jointly made decisions or follower-made decisions with encouragement from the leader. The leader should use this style when followers have moderate to high readiness—are able but unwilling or insecure.
4. Using a *Delegating, Observing, Monitoring,* or *Fulfilling* style, the leader turns over responsibility for decisions and implementation to followers. This style combines below average amounts of relationship-oriented behavior with below average amounts of task-oriented behavior, to result in follower-made decisions. The leader should use this style when followers have high readiness—are able, willing, and confident.

While some researchers have questioned the conceptual clarity, validity, robustness, and utility of the model, and the instruments used to measure leadership style, others have supported the utility of the theory.[49] The Leadership Effectiveness and Description (LEAD) scale and related instruments are widely used in industrial training programs. Managers can use the situational model analytically, to understand leadership deficiencies, and together with the path–goal model, prescriptively, to delineate the appropriate style for dealing with a diversity of subordinates and situations. Karen Kornet, for example, could assess the readiness of the members of the project team and choose the appropriate style. Most likely she would learn they have high readiness, calling for a delegating style. Her selection of a directing style is a misfit and helps explain the group performance problems.

Attributional Model

Attribution theory suggests that a leader's judgment about his or her followers is influenced by the leader's attribution of the causes of the followers' behaviors.[50] Recall that attributions are influenced by an individual's viewpoint and involvement in the situation—whether the person is an actor in or observer of the event, whether an action or event succeeds or fails, and whether the action is intentional (see Chapter 2). Effective leaders identify the correct cause and then act accordingly.

Leaders often link themselves with successes in a group and remove themselves from failures by manipulating their attributions of subordinates' behavior in the desired direction.[51] They might, for example, suggest to subordinates that the group's success was due to the interpersonal support or skills of the leader, and that the group's failure was due to time constraints, lack of resources, or absence of member skills. Leaders also more often attribute poor performance to a subordinate when that person has a poor work history than when the subordinate has a good one.[52] Recent research suggests that after a leader acts in accordance with his or her attributions of followers' behavior, followers may adjust their attributions of leader behavior in terms of their view of the appropriateness of his or her responses.[53]

Leaders' Attributional Processes As part of diagnosing the situation, as a prelude to effective leadership, leaders must determine whether personal or situational factors cause a subordinate's behavior. To do this, a leader processes three types of information about a subordinate's actions.[54] First, the leader considers whether the behavior is distinctive or unique to a particular task. If Dr. Kornet has never received questions about her proposed research methodology from a nutritionist on her team, she might view the nutritionist's behavior as unique or distinctive. Second, the leader assesses the consistency or frequency of the behavior. The repeated complaints by one ophthalmologist and one nutritionist and their subsequent resignation from the project reflect consistent behavior. Third, the leader assesses the extent to which other followers demonstrate the same behavior. If the entire team complains about the study methodology, consensus exists. In sum, behavior viewed as distinctive, inconsistent, and of high consensus is more likely to be attributed to characteristics of the situation than of the person.

A leader is more likely to attribute subordinate behavior to the situation when "(1) the subordinate has no prior history of poor performance on similar tasks, (2) the subordinate performs other tasks effectively, (3) the subordinate is doing as well as other people who are in a similar situation, (4) the effects of failures or mistakes are not serious or harmful, (5) the manager is dependent upon the subordinate for his or her own success, (6) the subordinate is perceived to have other redeeming qualities (popularity, leadership skills), (7) the subordinate has offered excuses or an apology, or (8) there is evidence indicating external causes."[55] Leaders thus make attributions about the cause of performance before deciding what action to take.[56] Managers must be able to diagnose their own and others' attributional processes as part of leading effectively.

If Karen Kornet perceives her subordinates' situations, rather than them personally, as responsible for their actions, she is more likely to redesign the job, provide more resources, or change the situation in some other way, than she is to reprimand them or offer training or coaching as a way of altering their personal skills, effort, or motives. Figure 8–5 summarizes this attributional model of leadership. Understanding the correct attributions should result in implementation of more appropriate actions.

Followers' Attributional Processes Followers, too, attribute certain causality to leaders' behavior. "Whether or not leader behavior actually influences performance or effectiveness, it is important because people believe it does."[57] Thus subordinates tend to view leaders as the cause of group behavior and, depending on members' attitudes toward a group's behavior, they develop either positive or negative attitudes about and reactions to the leader. In addition, a group's previous performance affects members' ratings of its leader: in a laboratory study, when individuals were told that a group had performed well in the past, they rated the leader as behaving fairly consistently and providing somewhat more task structure.[58] Thus Karen Kornet's subordinates perceive her as ineffective because they attribute the group's performance problems to her efforts rather than to their own. In other words, as actors in the situation their attributional bias is to attribute failure to the situation (in

Figure 8–5 AN ATTRIBUTIONAL LEADERSHIP MODEL

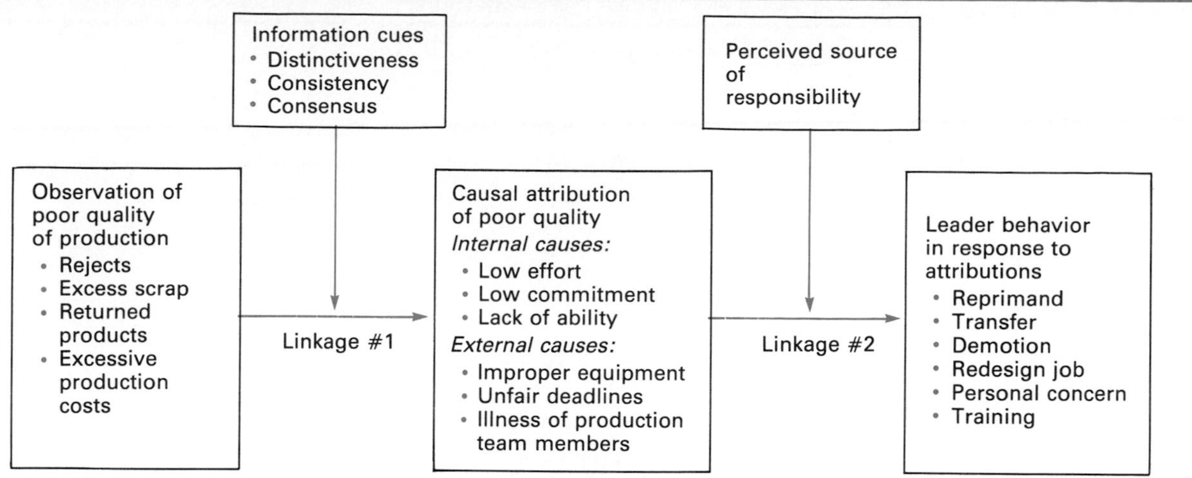

Adapted from Terence R. Mitchell and Robert E. Wood, An empirical test of an attributional model of leader's responses to poor performance. In *Academy of Management Proceedings,* ed. Richard C. Huseman, 1979, p. 94.

this case, their supervisor) rather than to their personal characteristics. Perception is reality for the manager, and attribution processes influence it.

Operant Conditioning Model

Positive reinforcement (described in Chapters 2 and 4) explains leadership differently and is represented in Figure 8–6. Applying this model provides another way for managers to understand and increase the impact of their leadership behaviors.

According to the conditioning model, (1) the leader's behavior prompts behavior by subordinates; (2) the subordinates' responses then either reinforce, extinguish, or punish the leader's behavior. At the same time, it is a reciprocal process: (3) subordinates' behavior also causes responses in other parts of the organization; (4) these responses in turn reinforce, extinguish, or punish the subordinates' behavior. For example, a manager may engage in joint goal setting with his or her subordinates; the subordinates respond by accomplishing the goals. This response reinforces the leader's behavior because of its desirable consequences, causing the leader to repeat the joint goal setting. If instead the subordinates fail to meet the goals set, this response would likely extinguish their boss's attempts to set goals with them jointly. The subordinates' performance in the first situation results in the organizational consequences of top management's rewarding their effective performance. In the second case, the organizational consequences might be management's provision of training, job redesign, or transfers for leader or followers.

This simple version of the model can be expanded into a more dynamic one that explicitly considers exchanges among individuals or with the environment. In this case both leaders and followers repeatedly interact in a series of independent events, thus repeatedly reinforcing, punishing, or extinguishing given behavior.[59] For example, the repeated goal accomplishment of the work-

Figure 8–6 Operant Conditioning Model of Leadership: The Behavioral Contingencies for Leadership

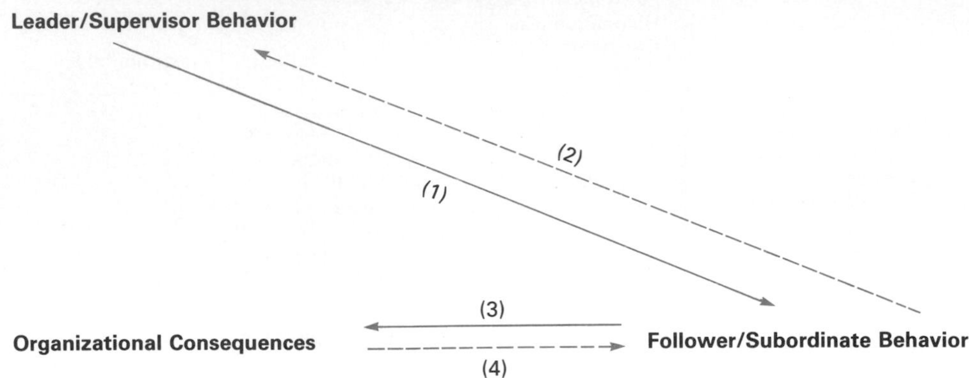

Source: Adapted from T.R.V. Davis and F. Luthans, Leadership reexamined: A behavioral approach, *Academy of Management Review* 4 (1979): 240. Reprinted with permission.

ers we have just described would cause their supervisor to continue his or her present leadership style.

Using this model diagnostically, we can ask:

1. What behavior does the leader prompt in his or her subordinates?
2. How do the subordinates respond?
3. Do their responses reinforce, punish, or extinguish leader behavior?
4. Have the leader and subordinates identified the influences on the subordinates' behavior?
5. Is the individual behavior produced by subordinates reinforcing to the leader's behavior and vice versa?
6. Are the organizational consequences of subordinates' behavior reinforcing for their behavior?

Consider the behavior of Dr. Kornet. She begins by giving glaucoma team members very explicit directions about how to perform their work. If they perform their work according to her requirements, their performance reinforces her leadership style, in this case an autocratic one. If they disobey, resist, or ignore her instructions, they begin to extinguish her behavior, and ultimately she may change the way she interacts with them. We might predict that over time the subordinates' failure to perform according to Dr. Kornet's specifications will cause her and her bosses to examine her leadership behavior. If top management supports Dr. Kornet, we would predict that the subordinates would no longer act independently of their superior's instructions; if top management reprimands Dr. Kornet, the autonomy of research team members is likely to persist.

Substitutes for Leadership

While previous theories assume that some leadership style will be effective in each situation, Steven Kerr and John Jermier argue that certain individual, task, and organizational variables prevent leaders from influencing subordinate attitudes and behaviors in an effective manner.[60] *Substitutes for lead-*

ership, or characteristics that negate leadership influence, are those that structure the task for the followers or give them positive strokes or support for their actions.

The following features of leadership situations may provide structuring or stroking behavior that makes actual leadership unnecessary or undesirable[61] (see Table 8–6):

1. Characteristics of subordinates: (a) ability, knowledge, training, experience; (b) need for independence; (c) professional orientation; (d) indifference toward organizational rewards

Table 8–6 SUBSTITUTES FOR LEADERSHIP

	Will Tend to Neutralize	
Characteristic	Relationship-Oriented, Supportive, People-Centered Leadership: Consideration, Support, and Interaction Facilitation	Task-Oriented, Instrumental, Job-Centered Leadership: Initiating Structure, Goal Emphasis, and Work Facilitation
of the subordinate		
1. ability, experience, training, knowledge		X
2. need for independence	X	X
3. "professional" orientation	X	X
4. indifference toward organizational rewards	X	X
of the task		
5. unambiguous and routine		X
6. methodologically invariant		X
7. provides its own feedback concerning accomplishment		X
8. intrinsically satisfying	X	
of the organization		
9. formalization (explicit plans, goals, and areas of responsibility)		X
10. inflexibility (rigid, unbending rules and procedures)		X
11. highly-specified and active advisory and staff functions		X
12. closely-knit, cohesive work groups	X	X
13. organizational rewards not within the leader's control	X	X
14. spatial distance between superior and subordinates	X	X

From S. Kerr and J.M. Jermier, Substitutes for leadership: Their meaning and measurement, *Organizational Behavior and Human Performance* 26 (December 1978): 375–403.

2. Characteristics of the task: (a) unambiguous and routine; (b) methodologically invariant; (c) providing its own feedback concerning accomplishment; (d) intrinsically satisfying
3. Characteristics of the organization: (a) formalization (explicit plans, goals, and areas of responsibility); (b) inflexibility (rigid, unbending rules and procedures); (c) highly specified and active advisory and staff functions; (d) closely knit, cohesive work groups; (e) organizational rewards not within the leader's control; (f) spatial distance between superior and subordinates.

One study of nursing work indicated that the staff nurses' education, cohesion of the nurses, and work technology substituted for the head nurse's leadership behaviors in determining staff nurses' performance. More educated nurses, for example, could work autonomously, without leadership by the head nurse.[62] This study also suggested that the leader's behavior, in this case assertiveness by the head nurse, interacts with characteristics of the organization, such as links between rewards and performance, to alter performance. Other research provides some preliminary support for the validity of the model.[63]

Consider once more the opening scenario. Where the task is clear and staff members have extensive professional training, the need for a hierarchical superior to play a dominant role may be minimized, since the group members and the task can be sources of structuring and stroking behavior in themselves. The effectiveness of these substitutes helps explain the problems encountered by Dr. Kornet: she only supplements already strong structuring and stroking behaviors.

TRANSFORMATIONAL LEADERSHIP

Recent thinking about effective leadership has supplemented the situational approach with a revival of trait theory that emphasizes the importance of a leader's charisma. Robert House has proposed a theory of leadership which suggests that effective leaders use dominance, self-confidence, a need for influence, and conviction of moral righteousness to increase their charisma and consequently their leadership effectiveness.[64] A laboratory study of charismatic leadership that used college students as subjects compared subordinates of charismatic leaders to subordinates of noncharismatic leaders (see Table 8–7). Subordinates of charismatic leaders had higher performance and satisfaction and less role conflict than subordinates of noncharismatic leaders high on either concern for task or concern for people.[65] Charismatic leadership has been criticized, as a concept, because of the difficulty in defining and operationalizing it.[66]

Using charisma to inspire his or her followers, a transformational leader talks to followers about how essential their performance is, how confident he or she is in the followers, how exceptional the followers are, and how he or she expects the group's performance to break records.[67] A transformational leader changes an organization by developing a vision for it, communicating that vision to organizational members, mobilizing them to accept and help achieve it, and then institutionalizing the new changes, as shown in Figure 8–7.[68]

Table 8–7 BEHAVIORAL COMPONENTS OF CHARISMATIC AND NONCHARISMATIC LEADERS

	Noncharismatic Leader	Charismatic Leader
Relation to Status quo	Essentially agrees with status quo and strives to maintain it	Essentially opposed to status quo and strives to change it
Future Goal	Goal not too discrepant from status quo	Idealized vision which is highly discrepant from status quo
Likableness	Shared perspective makes him/her likable	Shared perspective and idealized vision makes him/her a likable and honorable hero worthy of identification and imitation
Trustworthiness	Disinterested advocacy in persuasion attempts	Disinterested advocacy by incurring great personal risk and cost
Expertise	Expert in using available means to achieve goals within the framework of the existing order	Expert in using unconventional means to transcend the existing order
Behavior	Conventional, conforming to existing norms	Unconventional or counternormative
Environmental Sensitivity	Low need for environmental sensitivity to maintain status quo	High need for environmental sensitivity for changing the status quo
Articulation	Weak articulation of goals and motivation to lead	Strong articulation of future vision and motivation to lead
Power Base	Position power and personal power (based on reward, expertise, and liking for a friend who is a similiar other)	Personal power (based on expertise, respect, and admiration for a unique hero)
Leader-Follower Relationship	Egalitarian, consensus seeking, or directive	Elitist, entrepreneur, and exemplary
	Nudges or orders people to share his/her views	Transforms people to share the radical changes advocated

Reprinted with permission from A. Conger and R.N. Kanungo, Toward a behavioral theory of charismatic leadership in organizational settings, *Academy of Management Review* 12 (1987): 641.

More specifically, first the leader helps subordinates recognize the need for revitalizing the organization by developing a felt need for change, overcoming resistance to change (see Chapter 14), and avoiding quick-fix solutions to problems. Encouraging subordinates to act as devil's advocates with regard to the leader, building networks outside the organization, visiting other organizations, and changing management processes to reward progress against competition also helps them recognize a need for revitalization. Individuals must disengage from and disidentify with the past as well as view change as a way of dealing with their disenchantments with the past or the status quo.

Second, the transformational leader creates a new vision and mobilizes

Figure 8–7 TRANSFORMATIONAL LEADERSHIP: A THREE-ACT DRAMA

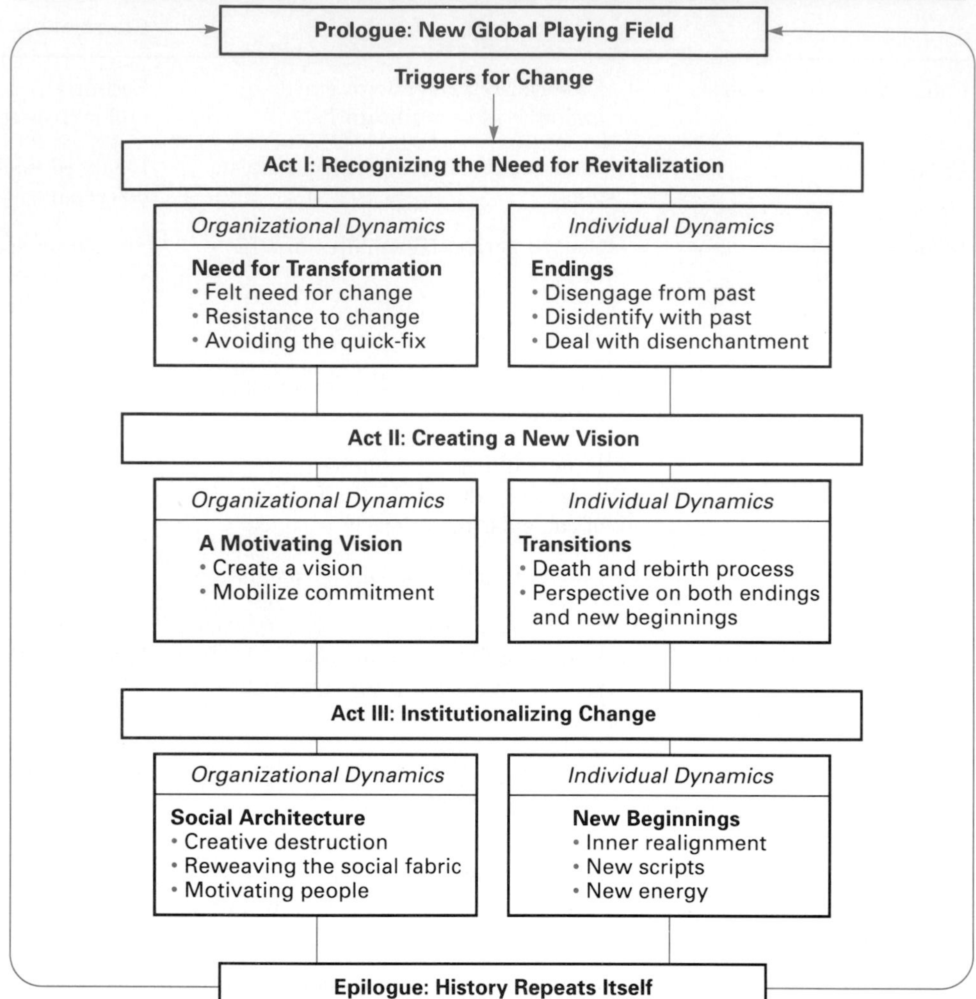

Reprinted with permission from N.M. Tichy and M.A. Devanna, *The Transformational Leader* (New York: Wiley, 1986), p. 29. © 1986, reprinted by permission of John Wiley & Sons, Inc.

commitment to it. He or she can use planning or education as ways of generating commitment. Alternate options include changing the composition of the team, altering management processes, and helping organizational members reframe the way they think about the business.

Finally, the transformational leader institutionalizes change by replacing old technical, political, cultural, and social networks with new ones. For example, the leader can identify key individuals and groups, develop a plan for obtaining their commitment, and institute a monitoring system for following the changes. Or he or she can specify cultural values to change and the main holders of those values, and then design and implement a plan for making the cultural change.

A transformational leader motivates subordinates to achieve beyond their original expectations in one of three ways: "1. By raising our level of awareness, our level of consciousness about the importance and value of designated outcomes, and ways of reaching them. 2. By getting us to transcend our own self-interest for the sake of the team, organization, or larger society. 3. By altering our need level on Maslow's (or Alderfer's) hierarchy or expanding our portfolio of needs and wants."[69] But there may be a "dark side" to charismatic leadership—if the leader overemphasizes devotion to himself or herself.[70]

The charisma of a leader also "cascades" to his or her followers, according to a study of management in a New Zealand government agency.[71] The amount of transformational leadership observed at one management level was also noted at the next lower level. The reverse was not necessarily true however: more charismatic followers did not necessarily have more charismatic leaders. Thus training higher level managers in transformational skills should have a more widespread impact in an organization than training only lower level managers.

Basically, this type of leader attempts to motivate followers (primarily subordinates or peers) to perform better. Lee Iacocca has been called a transformational leader because he moved Chrysler from the edge of bankruptcy to profitability by altering the political structure, reward system, union–management relations, and cultural system there.[72]

Transformational leaders "attempt and succeed in raising colleagues, subordinates, followers, clients, or constituencies to a greater awareness about issues of consequence. This heightening of awareness requires a leader with vision, self-confidence, and inner strength to argue successfully for what he [or she] sees is right or good, not for what is popular or is acceptable according to established wisdom of the time."[73] Transformational leaders consider themselves to be change agents; are courageous risk takers; believe in people and try to empower others; act according to a well-articulated set of core values; are continuous learners who learn from their mistakes; can deal with complex, ambiguous, and uncertain problems and situations; and can dream and share these dreams with others in the organization.[74] These leaders also focus on gaining knowledge from both successes and failures; monitor the environment and use networks for security information; and also experiment to facilitate innovation.[75]

Recall our discussion of motivation in Chapter 4. We noted that individuals worked to satisfy certain needs and achieve desired outcomes. A boss who is a transformational leader motivates subordinates to do better than they expected, in three ways.[76] First, the leader raises their consciousness about the importance of certain outcomes, such as high productivity or efficiency. Second, he or she shows the value of workers' concentrating on their work team's good rather than personal interest. Third, the leader raises workers' need levels so that they value challenges, responsibility, and growth. Managers identified as top performers rated higher on transformational leadership than a group of ordinary managers.[77] Likewise CEOs of major business divisions of corporations who succeeded in developing new businesses differed from those who attempted new business development and failed.[78] They inspired pervasive commitment throughout the division by insisting that the entire division pursue new business development; making new business development part of the job and not the object of special rewards; demonstrating intense, undistracted, and long-term personal commitment to new business development; and assigning the best people to new business development. They built confidence among their subordinates by helping them increase their competence and giving them the freedom to take initiative. They applied appropriate discipline to the process by carefully selecting the new venture, using the appropriate strategy, and managing failures. Union leadership has also used transformational behaviors, with varying success.[79]

Does Dr. Kornet demonstrate this type of leadership? Certainly she has self-confidence and a conviction of moral righteousness. She dominates her subordinates and seems to demonstrate a need for influence. If we use the perspective of transformational leadership, however, these characteristics are important but not sufficient for effective leadership. To be effective, she must take a developmental orientation toward her followers, by elevating their potential, setting examples, assigning tasks on an individual basis, increasing subordinate responsibilities, delegating challenging work, serving as a role model, keeping subordinates informed, providing intellectual stimulation, seeking ways of acting, and being more proactive.[80]

SUMMARY

Environmental and organizational changes have contributed significantly to the importance of adequate leadership, yet few comprehensive prescriptions for effective leadership exist. Figure 8–8 shows the approaches discussed in this chapter. Historically, research first linked effective leadership to the traits of individuals. Next leadership was associated with two types of behavior: initiating structure (production orientation) and consideration (employee orientation). Then situational approaches to leadership, which report that the nature of effective leadership depends on particular features of a situation, such as leader–member relations, the structure of the situation, the needs of subordinates, and the readiness of followers, predominated. Today the situational approach remains viable, although the call for the transformational

Figure 8–8 PERSPECTIVES FOR DEFINING EFFECTIVE LEADERSHIP

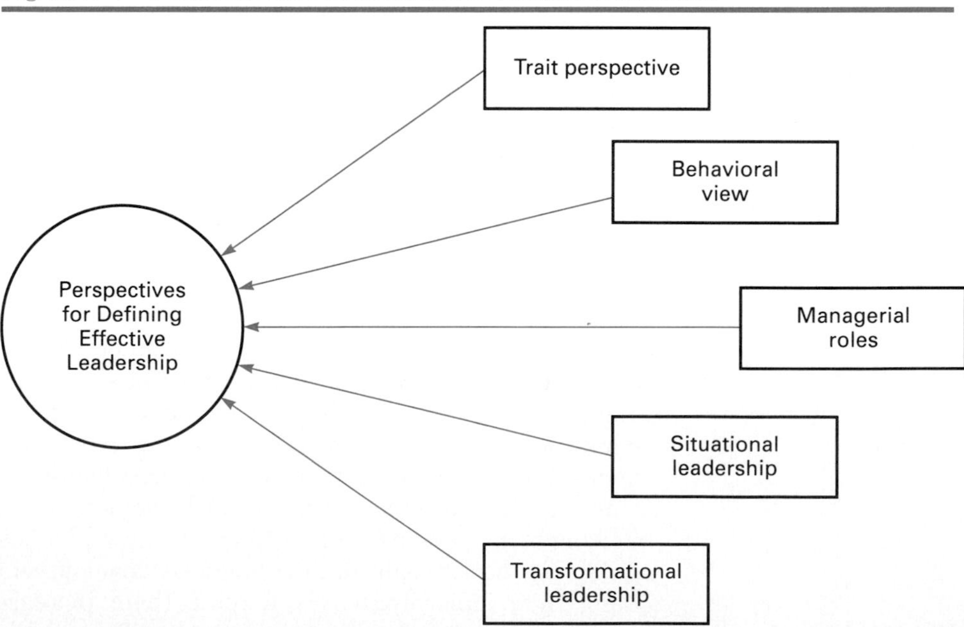

Figure 8–9 DIAGNOSTIC QUESTIONS FOR EVALUATING LEADERSHIP EFFECTIVENESS

- Do the managers have the traits necessary for effective leadership?
- Do the managers display the behaviors required for effective leadership?
- Do managers exhibit balanced managerial roles?
- Do the leaders encourage the appropriate amount of participation in decision making?
- Does the leadership style fit with the nature of the task, leader–member relations, and the position power of the leader?
- Is leadership superfluous to the situational features and the followers' needs?
- Does it meet their needs?
- Does the leadership style fit with the maturity of the followers?
- Do followers attribute attitudes to the leaders accurately?
- Are effective leader and subordinate behaviors reinforced?
- Do transformational leaders exist?

leader is loud. Some have even tied leadership effectiveness once again to leader traits. John Kotter proposes, for example, that effective leadership in senior management jobs requires a broad knowledge of and solid relations within the industry and the company, an excellent reputation, a strong track record, a keen mind, strong interpersonal skills, high integrity, high energy, and a strong drive to lead.[81] The new leader also needs to be able to anticipate future conditions, create images of desired future states, establish shared values in the organization, empower workers, and demonstrate self-understanding.[82]

In this chapter we have examined each of these perspectives in turn. We have shown the way trait, behavioral, situational, and transformational theories, separately and together, explain the situation experienced by the glaucoma research team. To diagnose leadership effectiveness in general, we can ask questions such as those shown in Figure 8–9.

READING

Reading 8–1: THE ROLE OF THE MANAGER: WHAT'S REALLY IMPORTANT IN DIFFERENT MANAGEMENT JOBS

Allen I. Kraut, Patricia R. Pedigo, D. Douglas McKenna, and Marvin D. Dunnette

Can we safely assume (to paraphrase Gertrude Stein) that "a manager is a manager is a manager"? Should we expect the jobs of all managers to be pretty much the same? And should managers expect their colleagues' jobs to be like their own? Well, "yes" and "no," according to the research described below. An analogy to team sports may help illustrate this answer, and suggest implications for organizational performance.

One of the signs of a successful athletic team is its almost uncanny ability to perform as a single unit, with the efforts of individual members blending seamlessly together. When this level of teamwork exists, unusual things happen. Quarterbacks complete blind passes, throwing the ball to spots on the field where they "know" their favorite receiver will be. The point guard playing basketball lobs a pass high above the basket, which enables a leaping teammate to catch it in midair and make a spectacular slam dunk. This level of teamwork requires a great deal of practice and natural ability, but members of the team must also have a clear understanding of their own roles, the roles of their teammates, and the way they must work together to be successful.

In addition to understanding specialized roles and assignments, players must also recognize the things that everyone, regardless of his or her position, must be ready and willing to do if the team is to win. When necessary, the quarterback must block like a lineman to allow the halfback to break free of the defense; diminutive kickers must tackle kick return specialists twice their size to stop a touchdown. The point is that the demands of a team sport call for each participant to be both a specialist and a generalist.

Management, we believe, is a team sport that makes similar demands of its players. Unfortunately, many executives (the "team captains") and managers do not recognize how managerial jobs are similar and yet different across organizational levels and functions. This lack of mutual understanding among management players can make it very difficult for them to appreciate one another's work and coordinate their work activities. It can make winning that much harder.

In addition to being able to coordinate work more effectively, executives who understand similarities and differences in managerial jobs gain other advantages. For example, they are better able to:

- Communicate performance expectations and feedback to subordinate managers.
- Prepare others and themselves for transitions to higher organizational levels or different functions.
- Forecast how different managers would perform if promoted or moved into a new function.
- Ensure that management training and development programs are targeted to fit the needs of managers as they change positions.
- Diagnose and resolve confusion regarding managerial roles, responsibilities, and priorities.

For the most part, research on managerial work has focused on the *common* denominators of management jobs. Indeed, a considerable amount of research has been published on this subject.[1] We, however, have recently completed a study designed to shed light on the *differences in management roles and activities across different levels and functions.* We started with a sample of 1,412 managers[2] and asked them to rate the relative importance of 57 managerial tasks to their jobs. Their choices included "Of utmost importance," "Of considerable importance," "Of moderate importance," "Of little importance," "Of no importance," and "I do not perform this task." Almost all tasks were rated "Of moderate importance" or higher.

Using these importance ratings, we statistically identified seven major factors or groups of management tasks:[3]

- Managing individual performance,
- Instructing subordinates,
- Planning and allocating resources,
- Coordinating interdependent groups,
- Managing group performance,
- Monitoring the business environment, and
- Representing one's staff.

We then studied how important these seven factors and their component tasks were to managers at different levels and functions.

FIRST-LEVEL MANAGERS: ONE-TO-ONE WITH SUBORDINATES

The first two factors involve supervising others. These activities are most important to first-level managers and decline in importance as one rises in management. (See Figure 8–10.)

"Managing individual performance" was rated the single most important set of activities by first-level management. Such tasks include motivating and disciplining subordinates, keeping track of performance and providing feedback, and improving communications and individual productivity. These tasks are traditionally associated with lower-level management. Although Figure 8–10 shows that many executives continue to see these tasks as very important, it is clear that their importance drops off as one moves up the management hierarchy.

The tasks in the "managing individual performance" set are listed in order of the percentage of the total sample who rated each as of "utmost" or "considerable importance."

76% Motivate subordinates to change or improve their performance.

76% Provide ongoing performance feedback to subordinates.

69% Take action to resolve performance problems in your work group

69% Blend subordinates' goals (e.g., career goals, work performances) with company's work requirements.

63% Identify ways of improving communications among subordinates.

50% Keep track of subordinates' training and special skills as they relate to job assignments to aid their growth and development.

Figure 8–10 SUPERVISING INDIVIDUALS

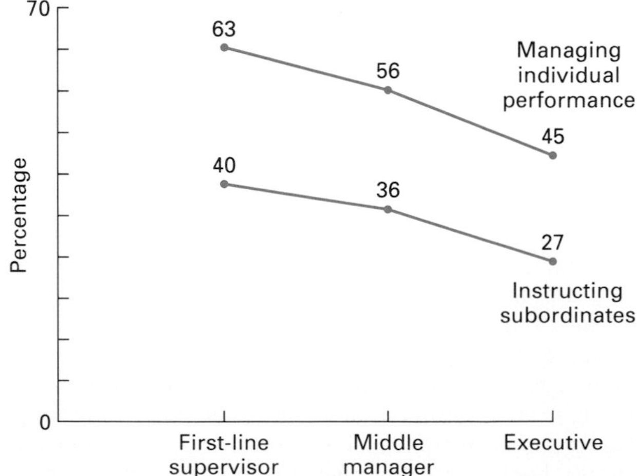

Numbers refer to the percentage of managers who said the task was of "the utmost" or "considerable" importance.

48% Resolve conflicts among subordinates.
40% Discipline and/or terminate personnel.
37% Review subordinates' work methods to identify ways to increase productivity.

The cluster *"instructing subordinates"* includes training, coaching, and instructing employees in how to do their job. Of moderate importance to most first-level managers, this cluster is considerably less important to executives.

For the "instructing subordinates" set the items are listed below:

52% Inform subordinates about procedures and work assignments.
46% Explain work assignments to subordinates.
44% Provide technical expertise to help subordinates resolve work problems or questions.
43% Train subordinates in new techniques or procedures.
6% Schedule daily activities of subordinates.

MIDDLE MANAGERS: LINKING GROUPS

The concept of linking groups seems to drive the middle manager's work. Three task factors involve linking groups. The importance of these tasks jumps sharply (an average of 19 points) from first- to middle-level management. Thus, managers going from the lowest level of supervision to middle management need to develop skills in several new areas if they are to link groups successfully. The importance of these tasks drops slightly for executives (see Figure 8–11).

The most important tasks for middle management involve *"planning and allocating resources"* among different groups. Examples include estimating group resource requirements and making decisions about how resources should be distributed. One part of this cluster includes translating general directives into specific plans and communicating their benefits. Middle managers and executives see these tasks as crucial to their jobs.

The relative importance of the "planning and allocating resources" tasks is shown below:

72% Establish target dates for work products or services.
70% Estimate resource requirements for operational needs.
67% Develop evaluation criteria to measure progress and performance of operations.
65% Decide which programs should be provided with resources (e.g., manpower, materials, funds, etc.).
63% Translate general directives (e.g., strategic plans) from superiors into specific operational plans/schedules/procedures, etc.
58% Communicate the benefits or opportunities posed by a new idea, proposal, project, or program.
40% Distribute budgeted resources.

Figure 8–11 LINKING GROUPS

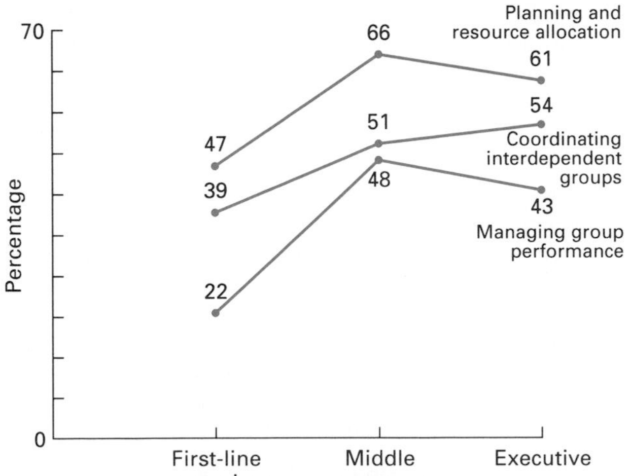

Numbers refer to the percentage of managers who said the task was of "the utmost" or "considerable" importance.

Both middle managers and executives also rate *"coordinating interdependent groups"* as highly important to their jobs. This cluster includes reviewing the work and plans of various groups and helping them set priorities as well as negotiating and integrating various group plans and activities. This cluster—which involves bringing several efforts together to create a final product—jumps sharply in importance when a supervisor moves into higher management.

The tasks in "coordinating interdependent groups" were rated in this way:

70% Stay informed of the goals, actions, and agendas of top management.
60% Persuade other organizational groups to provide the information/products/resources needed by your work group.
58% Monitor events, circumstances, or conditions outside your work group that may affect its goals and/or performance.
53% Persuade other managers to provide support and/or resources for a new project or program.
51% Set priorities for responding to other groups.
50% Determine the possible effects of changes in the activities or outputs of your work group on other organizational groups.
45% Maintain awareness of the goals and plans of other groups within the organization.
44% Negotiate working agreements with other groups for the exchange of information, products, and/or services.
43% Ensure coordination of the activities and outputs of interdependent groups.
42% Integrate the plans of related organizational groups.
42% Provide advice or assistance to managers of other organizational groups.

39% Disseminate information about the activities of your work group to other groups.
27% Gather information on the needs/capabilities/resources (e.g., information, services) of other groups in the company.

Of the three factors most important to middle management, the biggest shift in importance occurs for the factor *"managing group performance."* This includes managing the performance of various work groups and working with subordinate managers on this performance.

Rated low in importance by first-level managers, "managing group performance" increases sharply (by 26 percentage points) in importance for those in middle management. It is the hallmark change for those going into middle management. While the middle manager must still monitor the performance of individual supervisors, measuring and managing group-level performance indicators becomes a significantly more important part of his or her responsibilities.

The items in "managing group performance," and their level of importance are as follows:

57% Define areas of responsibility for managerial personnel.
50% Inform managers when performance in their groups does not meet established goals or standards.
48% Meet with managers to discuss the likely effects of changes on their groups.
44% Monitor your work group's performance by reading reports, information system outputs, or other documents.
25% Prepare production and productivity reports.
23% Gather or review information on the activities and progress of several different work groups.

Figure 8–12 MONITORING THE BUSINESS ENVIRONMENT

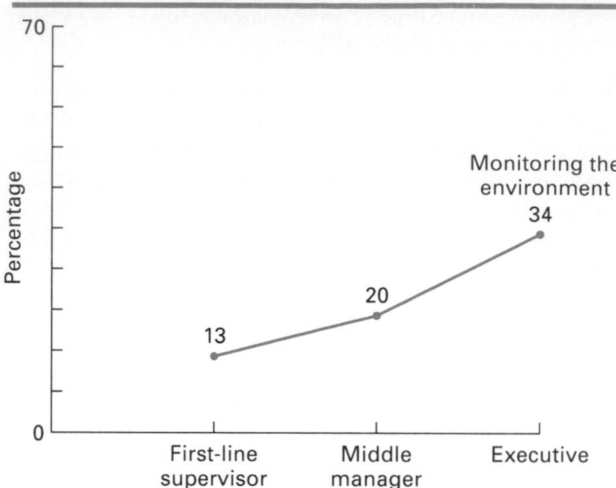

Numbers refer to the percentage of managers who said the task was of "the utmost" or "considerable" importance.

EXECUTIVES: AN EYE ON THE OUTSIDE

The activities encompassed in *"monitoring the business environment"* are a sharp shift in emphasis for managers reaching the executive ranks (see Figure 8–12). These activities require the executive to have an increased awareness of sales, business, economic, and social trends.

For managers below the executive ranks, these tasks rate the lowest in importance. At what point do managers need to become aware of and proficient in adopting new viewpoints for their high-level jobs? Clearly, executives find that this expanded perspective is a key requirement of their position.

The tasks involved in "monitoring the business environment" and their importance ratings are as follows:

47% Develop/maintain relationships with management-level customers or clients from the outside business community.
38% Participate in task forces to identify new business opportunities.
37% Monitor sales performance and promotional activities.
36% Gather information about trends outside your organization.
35% Identify developing market trends.
32% Develop/maintain relationships with management-level vendors or consultants in the business community.
31% Consult on companywide problems.
26% Attend outside meetings as a company representative.
20% Monitor multinational business and economic trends.
15% Release company information to the public (e.g., the news media).

MANAGERS AT ALL LEVELS: THE AMBASSADOR

Unlike the factors discussed earlier, which rise or drop in importance as the manager moves up the corporate ladder, *"representing your staff"* is ranked equally high by all levels of management (see Figure 8–13). This is the spokesperson role, noted in earlier studies by Henry Mintzberg. It involves representing one's work group to others and includes communicating the needs of one's work group to others, helping subordinates interact with other groups, and acting as the work group's representative.

The importance ratings of tasks involved in "representing your staff" are as follows:

Figure 8–13 REPRESENTING PEOPLE

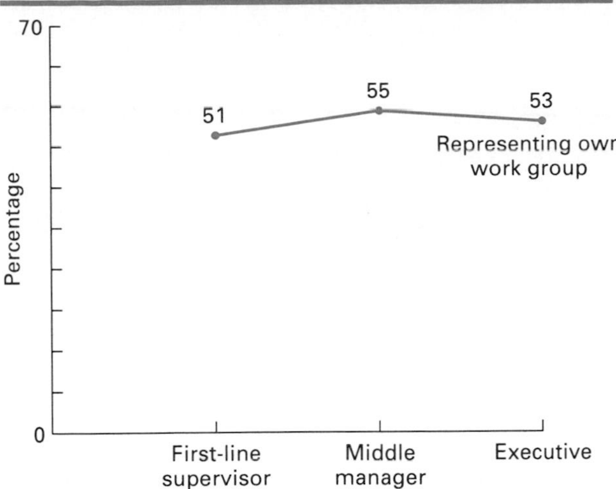

Numbers refer to the percentage of managers who said the task was of "the utmost" or "considerable" importance.

68% Develop relationships with managers of other organizational groups that may be able to provide your work group with information/products/services/resources.

59% Communicate the needs or requirements of your work group to managers of other organizational groups.

58% Provide information on the status of work in your work group to managers of groups that depend on you for information/products/services/resources.

57% Determine the appropriate response(s) to managers demanding information/products/services/other resources from your work group.

48% Provide information or assistance to subordinates interacting with other organizational groups.

46% Communicate capabilities and resources of your work group to other managers in the organization.

39% Serve as an intermediary between your subordinates and managers of other organizational groups.

One might speculate that a big transition regarding such activities takes place when one is initially promoted into management. Until then individuals may have spoken only for themselves; thus, some adjustment is required before the manager will recognize and take on the role of group ambassador.

DIFFERENCES ACROSS ORGANIZATIONAL FUNCTIONS

Most managers would argue that different functions present significantly different management challenges. Our data permit some tests of this hypothesis.

We examined the importance of management tasks across three functions: (1) *marketing,* which includes managers in the sales and related support organization, (2) *manufacturing,* which includes managers in all phases of the manufacturing process, and (3) *administration,* which includes managers in finance, planning, and related staffs such as personnel.

As Figure 8–14 shows, the importance levels of managerial task factors are remarkably similar across functions, although some noteworthy differences exist. (The three levels of management are weighted equally in each function so that no one level has undue influence.) Marketing and administration appear to differ most in their rating of factors, with manufacturing falling in between.

"Instructing subordinates" is least important among marketing managers (27% said it was of "the utmost" or "considerable importance"), perhaps because so much of the training of marketing employees is done in corporate-sponsored programs. In administration, however, where many highly specific staff jobs and relatively little formal corporate training exists (at least in this company), "instructing subordinates" is a relatively more important management activity.

On the other hand, we suspect that a high level of professionalism among most administrative staff reduces the emphasis that their managers place on "managing individual performance" (50%). This factor, by contrast, is considerably more important in marketing (59%).

"Representation" is rated highest in importance by managers in marketing (59%). Obviously, these managers represent the company's products to others, mainly customers. By contrast, the demand for representing one's staff is 11 points lower among managers in administration. These relative differences apply also for "planning and allocating resources," which is rated highest by marketing (63%) and manufacturing (59%), and lowest by administration (52%). The activities involved in coordinating interdependent work groups is equally important for all three functions (47%).

"Managing group performance" is of somewhat higher importance to the managers in manufacturing (43%) and somewhat lower to managers in administration (32%). Presumably the administration function is made up of more specialists and professionals who work alone.

The activities involved in "monitoring the outside business environment" take on the highest importance for managers in marketing (32%). This external orientation, which results from their interaction with customers and need to remain current on competitors' products and marketing strategies, should not be too surprising.

Overall, our data suggest there are indeed differences in the importance of various managerial tasks across functions. Nevertheless, the similarities across the entire spectrum of functions are clearly more striking.

Figure 8–14 THE IMPORTANCE OF MANAGERIAL ACTIVITIES

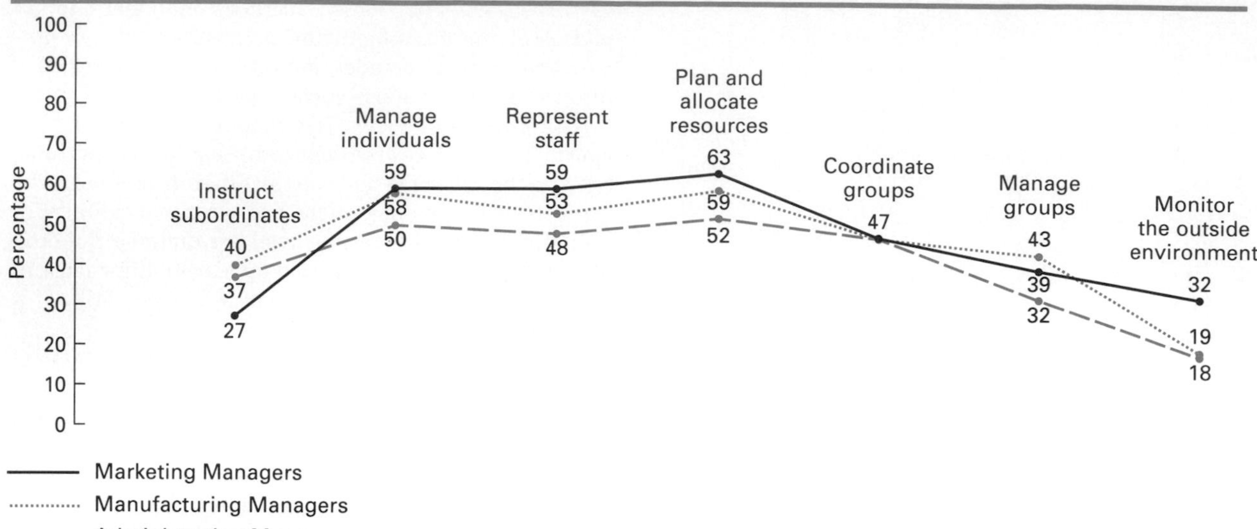

Numbers refer to the percentage of managers in each function who said the task was of "the utmost" or "considerable" importance.

(Such conclusions are also suggested in the findings of Cynthia M. Pavett and Alan W. Lau in their extension of Mintzberg's work.[4]) This suggests that a common approach to selecting, training, and developing managers may be both feasible and desirable for many functions in an organization.

Where significant differences do exist across functions, a common management development program or cross-functional work assignments may make managers more aware of different functions' perspectives, and help them avoid seeing all managers' jobs as either the same or unique. As John Kotter has noted in his work on executive behavior, people with narrow functional backgrounds who are promoted into general management positions may face a very difficult transition.[5]

Appropriate preparation may minimize such hardships.

THEORETICAL IMPLICATIONS

While we think this study has a number of practical implications that can help organizations make more effective use of their managerial resources, it is important to consider its limitations as well. First, the data are based on managers' own perceptions of the importance of various tasks. Certainly their bosses, peers, and subordinates may have a different view of things.[6] Second, because we took a "snapshot" of managers at different levels, rather than following a group of managers over time, we cannot be certain that managers will experience the differences we describe as they move to higher-level management jobs; however, because the company whose managers we surveyed strictly follows a "promote from within" policy, it seems likely that the differences we note are indeed changes accompanying upward moves.

Despite these limitations, the study provides a carefully gathered record of the role and task perceptions of a large sample of real managers working in a diverse array of positions. As we noted at the beginning of this article, the results can be interpreted as supportive of Mintzberg's view that managerial jobs involve essentially the same managerial roles[7] as well as Katz and Kahn's argument that managers do different things at different levels.[8]

In support of Mintzberg, we found that managers at all levels rated most of the tasks on the questionnaire of some importance. The differences we observed were typically differences in the degree of importance of the tasks, not differences in whether the tasks were important at all. Yet, as Katz and Kahn would maintain, these differences are significant. Considering the costs of a manager's time, the difference between outstanding and average performance may well depend on the priority he or she assigns to each of the many tasks that are basically important.[9]

PRACTICAL IMPLICATIONS

How should we prepare our managers to meet the various demands that different managerial roles place on them? Who should we select to move up the management hierarchy? What training can we provide? How can we develop the skills essential for the manager's and team's success? The findings of this study provide some clues as to how a winning team can be fostered by training, development, and selection.

Training

Typically, management training has emphasized the basics of management: individually focused supervision, motivation, career planning, and performance feedback. All of these aspects should clearly be a central focus in the training of first-level managers. Given that managers continue to use these skills as they move up the hierarchy, periodic reinforcement also seems appropriate. Our study, however, indicates that training for managers above the first level must cover more than these one-to-one skills.

To help middle managers deal successfully with their responsibilities for managing and linking groups, training at this level should focus on skills needed for designing and implementing effective group and intergroup work and information systems; defining and monitoring group-level performance indicators; diagnosing and resolving problems within and among work groups; negotiating with peers and superiors; and designing and implementing reward systems that support cooperative behavior. As these topics suggest, the psychology of the individual, so important to the first-level manager, gives way to social psychology and sociology when one reaches middle management. Since the latter topics are generally less well known and more abstract than the former, it is not surprising that the transition to middle management can be very confusing and disorienting.

The executive's need to emphasize the external environment can also be partially addressed through training. The curriculum should focus on broadening the executive's understanding of the organization's competition, world economies, politics, and social trends. A number of executive training institutes and university-based programs are geared toward providing these broadening experiences; however, we think it is a serious mistake to wait until a person becomes an executive before teaching him or her to recognize the importance of attending to the relationship between the business and its environment. Consider the potential advantages of having middle and lower-level managers who understand the nature and strategic direction of their organization's business and are constantly on the lookout for opportunities and threats in the environment. We think this perspective should receive continuous attention in management training and development efforts at all levels.

Development

Planned development programs can also contribute to expanding the skill base of managers. At the first level, experiences such as filling in for the middle manager during vacation times, acting as a liaison between linked functions, or representing the entire function at important meetings can build group management and coordination skills.

For the middle manager, increased customer contact, visits to other organizations, and subscriptions to important business and trade publications can help impart the skills necessary for the executive ranks.

Selection

The results of this study also have implications for the selection of managers. Given our findings, it should not be surprising that executives are often chosen from the marketing function; these people have had their eyes on the outside environment for the majority of their careers. Yet through planned development, employees and managers from other functions can also acquire the skills required in executive management, and their contribution to overall decision making can be significant.

A WINNING TEAM

The results of this study clearly identify the different roles that managers play and can provide organizations with the framework for building management training and development programs. By understanding the common and different roles played by managers as they move up the management hierarchy, we can develop programs that ensure that these managers have the skills needed to put together a winning team.

ENDNOTES

1. The questionnaire used in this study was based on an extensive review of research on managerial activities. A classic work in this area is *Management Behavior, Performance, and Effectiveness,* by J. P. Campbell, M. D. Dunnette, E. E. Lawler, and K. Weick, New York: McGraw-Hill, 1970. Another work that strongly influenced the questionnaire because of its depiction of the dynamic quality of managerial work, is L. Sayles's *Leadership,* New York: McGraw-Hill, 1979, aptly subtitled "What Effective Managers Really Do and How They Do It."
2. This study was conducted by the authors in a large U.S. business enterprise. A random sample, designed to overrepresent higher-strata managers, resulted in 1,412 respondents: 658 first-line managers, 553 middle managers, and 201 executives. After extensive pretesting, a list of 65 activities was used on the final survey questionnaire. Through statistical analyses, these activities were "factored," or grouped, into seven sets, which comprised 57 activities. (Eight activities fit poorly into the seven sets and were dropped.)

   Despite, or perhaps because, we used a literature search as the basis for our list of activities, some activities valued in this and other organizations may not have appeared in our survey. In passing we might mention that the importance placed on various activities is not necessarily related to "good" performance. The correlation between importance and effectiveness has simply not been examined in this study. By the same token, these activities are not necessarily the "correct" or "best" ones for any particular position. It remains to be determined which activities are desirable or appropriate, especially for the future.

3. Other investigators have studied patterns of management tasks. For example, James MacDonald and his colleagues (Charles Youngblood and Kerry Glum) report their comprehensive effort to determine training needs of first- and second-level supervisors working at AT&T in their book *Performance Based Supervisory Development,* Amherst, MA: Human Resource Development Press, 1982. Since they were concerned specifically with developing training guidelines, their categories of management (listed below) are much more focused on knowledge and skill development than are the seven behavioral factors developed in our investigation. Their categories of supervision include the following:

   Planning the job
   Controlling the job
   Providing performance feedback
   Managing time
   Decision making
   Problem solving
   Maintaining upward communications
   Maintaining downward communications
   Maintaining peer communications
   Creating a motivating atmosphere
   Developing subordinates
   Self-development
   Providing written communications
   Involvement with meetings
   Community relations

   Of more direct relevance to our work is the recent work reported by Fred Luthans, Stuart Rosenkrantz, and Harry Hennessey in "What Do Successful Managers Really Do? An Observation Study of Managerial Activities," *The Journal of Applied Behavioral Science,* 21(2), 1985, 255–270. See also Fred Luthans, "Successful vs. Effective Real Managers," *The Academy of Management Executive,* May 1988, 127–132. Luthans and his colleagues observed and recorded the actual activities of managers at all management levels and in many types of organizations. Observations were recorded according to four categories: *communication,* consisting of exchanging information and processing paperwork; *traditional management,* consisting of planning, decision making, and controlling; *human resource management,* consisting of motivating, disciplining, managing conflict, staffing, and training/developing; and *networking,* consisting of socializing, politicking, and interacting with outsiders.

   It should be noted that the seven factors developed from our investigation encompass all the categories studied by MacDonald and Luthans in their earlier investigations.

4. See C. M. Pavett and A. W. Lau, "Managerial Work: The influence of Hierarchical Level and Functional Speciality," *Academy of Management Journal,* 26(1), 1983, 170–177.
5. See J. P. Kotter, *The General Managers,* New York: Free Press, 1982.
6. An excellent review of the pro's and con's of various means to study managerial work is the report "Studies of Managerial Work: Results and Methods," by M. W. McCall, A. M. Morrison, and R. L. Kaplan, Greensboro, NC: Center for Creative Leadership, 1975.
7. A well-known book on this subject, Henry Mintzberg's *The Nature of Managerial Work,* New York, Harper, 1973, is based on observations of a dozen chief executive officers. His work has been replicated by others, such as L. B. Kurke and H. E. Aldrich, "Mintzberg Was Right!: A Replication and Extension of the Nature of Managerial Work," *Management Science,* 29, 8, 1983, 975–984.
8. D. Katz and R. L. Kahn's *Social Psychology of Organizations* (2nd Ed.), New York: Wiley, 1978, presents a view of very different demands, cognitive and emotional, on managers at various levels in an organization.
9. Finally, some further support for the argument that managers do some things differently at various levels was shown in one of Luthans' earlier investigations based on observations of some 53 managers (see Endnote 3). Comparisons between top executives and front-line supervisors revealed that executives engaged in much more networking, considerably more planning and decision making, and less staffing than front-line supervisors. These results are certainly compatible with ours.

DISCUSSION QUESTIONS

1. Describe seven major factors or groups of management tasks.
2. Compare and contrast first-level managers, middle managers, and executives on the management tasks they perform.
3. Offer strategies for developing a winning managerial team.

From *Academy of Management Executive,* 1989, vol. 3, No. 4, pp. 286–293. Reprinted by permission.

ACTIVITIES

Activity 8–1: LEADERSHIP STYLE INVENTORY

Step 1: Complete the following questionnaire:

This inventory is designed to provide you with personal data about the frequency with which you tend to select particular leadership behaviors. As you fill out the inventory, give a high rank to those words which best describe the way you most often behave as a leader and a low rank to the words which describe the way you least often behave as a leader.

You may find it hard to choose the words that best describe your leadership behavior because there are no right or wrong answers. Different behaviors described in the inventory are equally good.

There are nine sets of four words listed below. *Rank order* the four words in each set across the pag · assigning a 4 to the word which best describes your leadership behavior, a 3 to the next best, a 2 to the next best, and a 1 to the word which is least descriptive of your behavior as a leader. *Be sure to assign a different rank number to each of the four words in each set.* Do not make ties.

	A	*B*	*C*	*D*
1.)	_____ Forceful	_____ Negotiating	_____ Testing	_____ Sharing
2.)	_____ Decisive	_____ Teaching	_____ Probing	_____ Unifying
3.)	_____ Expert	_____ Convincing	_____ Inquiring	_____ Cooperative
4.)	_____ Resolute	_____ Inspirational	_____ Questioning	_____ Giving
5.)	_____ Authoritative	_____ Compelling	_____ Participative	_____ Approving
6.)	_____ Commanding	_____ Influential	_____ Searching	_____ Collaborating
7.)	_____ Direct	_____ Persuasive	_____ Verifying	_____ Impartial
8.)	_____ Showing	_____ Maneuvering	_____ Analytical	_____ Supportive
9.)	_____ Prescriptive	_____ Strategical	_____ Exploring	_____ Compromising
	Words Numbered:	*Words Numbered:*	*Words Numbered:*	*Words Numbered:*
	2 3 4 5 7 8 = _____	1 3 6 7 8 9 = _____	2 3 4 5 8 9 = _____	1 3 6 7 8 9 – _____
	_____ Column A (Tell Score)	_____ Column B (Sell Score)	_____ Column C (Consult Score)	_____ Column D (Join Score)

Scoring. Each column corresponds to a different leadership behavior: Column A—Tell; Column B—Sell; Column C—Consult; Column D—Join. To determine how frequently you use each of these behaviors, insert on the lines directly below each column how you ranked the designated words. For example, in Column A (the "Tell" column), words numbered 2, 3, 4, 5, 7, 8 are designated. Now do the same for the other three columns. After you have completed this, add up the numbers on each line to get column scores.

Step 2: Complete the Leadership Scoring and Profile Sheet as directed.

Your Present Leadership Repertoire. The chart on the next page can be developed into a graphic profile of your present repertoire of leadership behavior. Shade in the area which corresponds to each of your scores from the inventory above. For example, if you scored 15 on *TELL* behavior, then shade the area up to the 15 on the chart under *TELL*. The ruled-in percentile provides you a way of comparing yourself to other managers who have taken the inventory. The percentiles are keyed to indicate the number of managers who scored *below* a particular score. For example, a score of 17 on *TELL* means over 80% of the managers tested use a *TELL* behavior less frequently than you do.

Your Leadership Inclinations. Two additional scores may be obtained from the inventory: Manipulativeness and Emphasis on Human Resources. To obtain these, complete the following calculations by first inserting

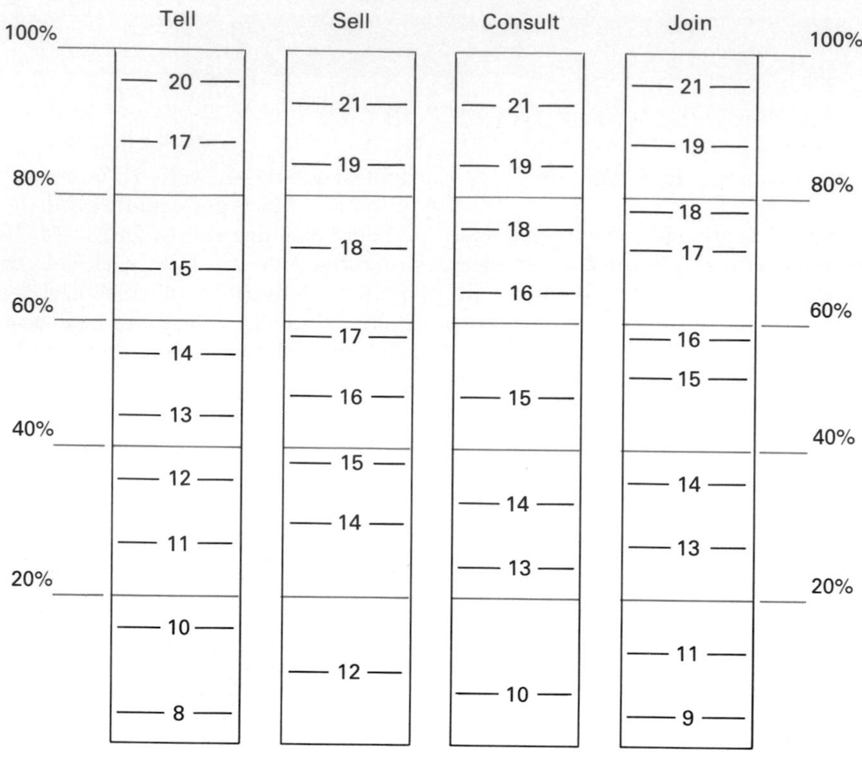

your Tell, Sell, Consult and Join scores on the lines below.

Manipulativeness = *Sell* + *Consult* − *Tell* − *Join*
= ______ (Preserve minus sign if any)

Human Resources = *Join* + *Consult* − *Tell* − *Sell*
= ______ (Preserve minus sign if any)

These scores may now be charted below. (Note that it is possible to chart a negative score.)

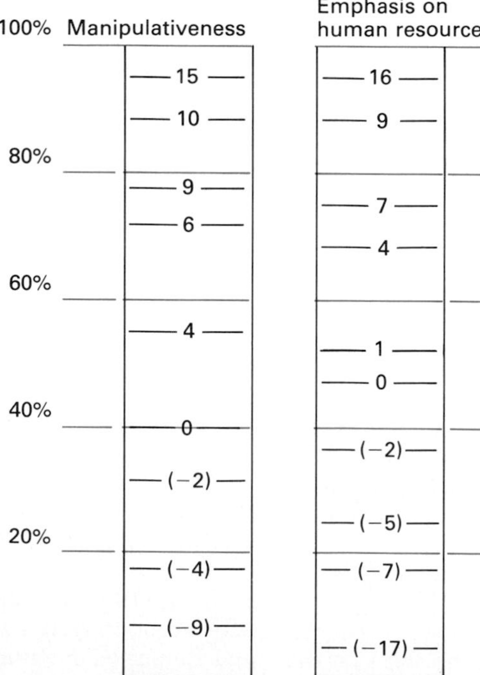

Step 3: Interpret the scores.

Figure 8–15 depicts four primary ways a leader may choose to behave in a given situation. The rectangle represents the amount of authority a leader has in a particular situation so that "Tell" represents a point on the continuum where maximal use of authority is made by the leader and minimal freedom is given to subordinates in the decision-making process. Each of these primary leadership behaviors is more fully explained in Table 8–8.

WHAT THE TELL, SELL, CONSULT AND JOIN SCORES MEAN

Your Tell, Sell, Consult and Join scores indicate the frequency with which you use each of the primary leadership behaviors. In part, your use of these behaviors reflects how you see yourself, your subordinates and your current work situation. For example, if you work in an environment where subordinates are perceived as mature and experienced, then chances are you are going to use more frequently Consult and Join behaviors. On the other hand, if you have little tolerance for ambiguity, then you may tend to frequently use Tell and Sell behaviors. Your scores are also a reflection, in part, of your leadership inclinations. Generally, people tend to emphasize leadership behaviors which fit their personality or which they have learned work for them or with which they feel comfortable. Some managers, by their very nature, find it very hard to be assertive and use a tell approach, while others are very comfortable behaving that way. The point to remember is that your present repertoire of leadership behavior is *not* an unchangeable part of your personality but rather represents how you presently choose to behave on the job. Hence, it is more important to begin to explore why you emphasize the behaviors you do and whether or not such behaviors are the most effective than to conclude "that's just the way I am." In addition, you will want to explore why you tend to use less frequently some of the leadership behaviors. On page 383, there is a place set aside for you to consider which forces tend to shape your leadership inclinations.

WHAT THE MANIPULATIVENESS AND HUMAN RESOURCES SCORES MEAN

The manipulativeness score measures the degree to which the leader attempts to gain subordinate's acceptance of his or her decisions. Manipulation, as defined by the dictionary, is "artful management of control." It is in this context that manipulativeness is used here and not in the context of unfair or dishonest acts. If we examine the beliefs underlying the Tell and Sell behavior in Table 8–8, we find the primary difference between Tell and Sell is that in Sell the leader also "seeks to reduce any resistance through persuasion"—hence, a manipulative act is added to Sell. Similarly, the difference between Consult and Join is the leader's belief that consulting subordinates is useful in order "to increase subordinate's ownership and commitment"—hence, Consult also involves a manipulative act. If you score high on manipulativeness, it may be

Figure 8–15 CONTINUUM OF LEADER BEHAVIOR

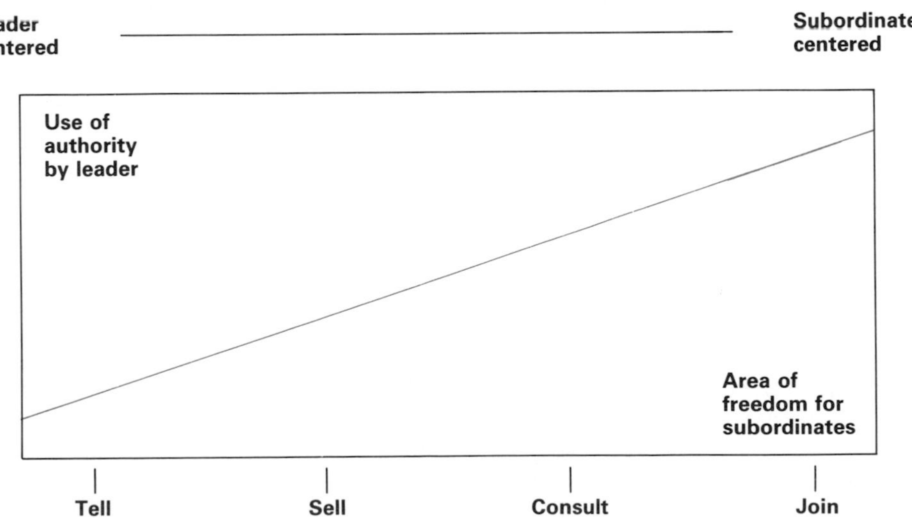

Based largely on R. Tannenbaum and W.H. Schmidt, How to choose a leadership pattern, *Harvard Business Review* (March-April 1958): 95–101. In the original article, Tell was represented by position 1; Sell by position 2; Consult by positions 3, 4, and 5; and Join by positions 6 and 7.

Table 8–8 A DESCRIPTION OF LEADER BEHAVIORS

Leadership Behavior	Action Taken	Underlying Beliefs
Tell	Leader identifies the problem, considers alternative solutions and announces the final decision to subordinates for implementation.	Leader feels subordinate participation in the decision is unnecessary, unwarranted or not feasible. Hence, no opportunity to participate is provided.
Sell	Leader takes responsibility for identifying the problem and determining the final decision. But rather than simply announcing the decision the leader takes the added step of trying to persuade subordinates to accept the decision.	Leader recognizes the potential for subordinate resistance from merely announcing the final decision and therefore *seeks to reduce any resistance through persuasion.*
Consult	Leader identifies the problem, consults subordinates for possible solutions and then announces the final decision.	Leader recognizes the potential value of *effectively culling ideas* from subordinates and believes such action will *increase subordinate's ownership and commitment* to the final solution.
Join	Leader defines the problem and then joins subordinates in making the final decision. The leader fully shares decision-making authority with subordinates.	Leader believes subordinates are capable of making high quality decisions and that subordinates want to do the right thing. The leader believes human resources are best utilized when decision-making authority is fully shared.

because you have experienced a strong need to insure subordinate acceptance of your decisions or because you perceive your subordinates or work setting necessitate such behavior. While some managers tend to employ manipulative behavior, even when such behavior is really unnecessary, whether or not you tend to do so depends upon a careful diagnosis of the forces in your work setting. Do you tend to frequently Sell or Consult even when Telling is all that is necessary? Do you tend to avoid Join situations because you don't want to give up control even though Joining is called for? Do you use manipulative behaviors because you are comfortable doing so or because your situation or subordinates necessitate such action?

The human resources score measures the tendency of the leader to use behaviors which reflect confidence in his or her subordinates' ability to make decisions. As one moves to the right on the leadership continuum, in Figure 8–15, there is an increasing emphasis placed on the use of subordinates as resources. Hence, the leader who relies more on Consult and Join rather than Tell and Sell tends to utilize subordinates more often in joint decision-making situations. Again, to what extent you rely on these behaviors because of your own tendencies or out of real necessity should be carefully evaluated by you.

WHICH BEHAVIORS ARE BEST?

By now it should be clear that one leadership behavior is no better than any other—to be effective the leader must be able to choose correctly the behavior that a particular work situation calls for *and* be effective in the use of that behavior. While this instrument cannot help you decide how to behave, it can help you examine more carefully your present leadership inclinations and help you begin to explore whether or not it might be useful to begin developing other behaviors. For example, if you frequently use Tell and Sell behaviors, you might want to think about why you tend to favor these over Consult and Join. Are you uncomfortable with less directive behaviors? Do your subordinates have difficulty working independently? Or does the nature of the job require acting this way? In general, the more you understand why you choose the leadership behaviors you do, the more potentially effective you can be as a leader. And, much like the golfer, the more you are comfortable and skilled using the various clubs available to you, the greater your potential versatility in selecting a behavior that is likely to be effective. Below, space is provided for some personal reflection and analysis of your present work situation.

Personal Analysis

A. I tend to frequently use (____ Tell; ____ Sell; ____ Consult; ____ Join) behaviors because of:

1st, the way I see myself ____________________

____

____

2nd, the way I see my subordinates ____________

____

____

3rd, the way I see my work situation ___________

____

____

B. I tend to less frequently use (____ Tell; ____ Sell; ____ Consult; ____ Join) behaviors because of:

1st, the way I see myself ____________________

____

____

2nd, the way I see my subordinates ____________

____

____

3rd, the way I see my work situation ___________

____

____

Step 4: Discussion. In small groups or with the class as a whole, answer the following questions:

Description

1. What does your profile look like?
2. Does your profile surprise you?

Diagnosis

3. How would you act if you were Karen Kornet, described in the introduction to the chapter?
4. Compare the profiles of people with the same action plans. Do they have the same leadership style?
5. Compare the profiles of people with different action plans. Do they have the same leadership style?
6. How well does your profile predict the nature of your actions?
7. Think of two situations you have faced. What leadership style fits best with those situations?

Reprinted with permission by John F. Voigo, Leadership Development Group, 101 Timber Dr., Storrs, CT. 06268.

Activity 8–2: WHITBREAD MERSEYSIDE CASE

Step 1: Read the Whitbread Merseyside case.

In December 1981 Mr. Bernard King, Managing Director of Whitbread West Pennines, met with Len Oliver, the newly appointed general manager of Whitbread Merseyside, to discuss the troubled state of affairs in the company's Merseyside operations. Plagued by strikes, a history of poor brewery management and a recent rapid decline in sales volume and market share, the Merseyside company was considered to be one of Whitbread's most serious problem areas. Mr. King presented his view of the situation to Len Oliver.

> We can't just throw up our hands and say 'Liverpool is unmanageable'. We earn a lot of money there and we could be earning a lot more. What you've got to do, Len, is break the mold. Business as usual is not good enough. I'll support you—but how you do it is up to you.

THE COMPANY

Whitbread and Company was established in 1742 when Samuel Whitbread founded a brewery bearing his name in London. The company gradually expanded to become a national brewer, and by the 1980's it operated twenty breweries and forty-one distribution depots in the United Kingdom as well as 7000 pubs and more than 100 Beefeater steak houses. The company also played a role in the wine, spirits and soft drinks industries in the U.K. Sales in the year ending February 28, 1981 were £782 million and net profits were £60 million. Since 1978, growth in sales had been approximately 11% per year while profits had increased an average of 16% per annum.

Whitbread's operations were managed as nine regional companies, listed in Figure 8–16. The West Pennines company consisted of three sites, Liverpool, Salford and Blackburn (Shadsworth), which combined distribution and production operations, and five separate distribution depots. Whitbread Merseyside (Liverpool based) was a sub unit of Whitbread West Pennines, comprising Whitbread's Liverpool operation and depots in Birkenhead (across the Mersey River from the Liverpool brewery) and in Llandudno, North Wales.

Bernard King became Managing Director of Whitbread West Pennines in June 1981, having spent the previous six years running the company's soft drink operations. He inherited a situation which was considered by many observers to be an industrial relations nightmare, with profit performance significantly below standard. Peter Watkins, the general manager of Whitbread Merseyside when Bernard arrived, explained some of the origins of the company's industrial relations problems to his new boss:

> When you realize that not so long ago Liverpool dock workers were kept in cages, with a chosen few allowed out to unload ships for the day, you begin to understand why the Liverpool workers and their unions are so militant. They are tough, smart (often smarter than the managers who are trying to control them), and a number of them are waging an ideological war to overthrow the capitalist system. The result of this has been that many major British Union disputes, particularly dock and transport disputes, have begun in Liverpool and then spread to the rest of the country.
>
> Whitbread's history of labour problems here is a long one. Our employees belong to the Merseyside branch of the Transport and General Worker's Union (the 'T and G'), which is reputed to be the toughest branch of a tough union. The full time union official who runs Merseyside is a strong character who more than once has forced a firm out of business. In the late 1960's we went through a major struggle with him and the T and G to have the third man eliminated from our delivery fleet. In the early 1970's the issue was our use of hired transport. We wanted to maintain a fleet of trucks and employees capable of meeting our base monthly load, and use hired transport to meet our seasonal peaks. The union felt we should staff to meet our peak loads on a year round basis. These are just two of the struggles we've had over the years, and both were long acrimonious disputes involving intermittent work stoppages and slow downs, and demanding a huge amount of management time.
>
> We have also added to our own problems. In 1972, for instance, senior Whitbread management announced that over the next several years a number of regional breweries, including Liverpool, would be closed. The result was that many of our older, stable employees left the company and were replaced by younger, more transient people. However, one year later the order was rescinded. The growth of lager beer had significantly exceeded market projections, which meant that the breweries would stay open after all. Then, in quick succession in 1973 and 1974, it was again announced that the breweries would be closed, and then that they would stay open.
>
> This vacillation was the result of differences of opinion concerning the appropriate size of a new brewery which the company was planning to build at Samlesbury, near Blackburn. Production planners wanted this to be a very large, efficient brewery, which would absorb the capacity of small local breweries like Liverpool, Blackburn and Salford, and it was their intentions which led to the second closure announcement. However, the marketers in Whitbread believed that the existence of these local breweries was very important to British beer drinkers who didn't want to drink a standardized product, but something which had been brewed locally to local tastes. In the end it appears to have been a draw, as the Blackburn brewery was closed in 1978 after Samlesbury opened, but Liverpool and Salford are still in operation. The uncertainty generated by the whole exercise definitely hurt our relationship with the unions.
>
> More recently, Bernard, we have tried to put in place wealth creation schemes which would result in profit sharing for hourly paid workers. Unfortunately, your predecessor put a plan in place in 1978, the region's peak year, and most workers gained nothing because profits have never recovered to 1978 levels. The unions wasted no time in convincing them that it was just another management ploy to get more work for no extra pay. To make matters worse, the workers in the Samlesbury plant, which exports 50% of its volume to healthier regions, have benefitted, so now the workers we were most interested in, like those in Liverpool, have an extra grudge against us.

After his first six months as Managing Director (which included two major strikes in Liverpool and a temporary brewery closure because of quality problems), Bernard King concluded that management changes were needed if the region were to progress. He decided to place Peter Watkins in charge of the Blackburn operations, where he had spent much of his early career, and to look for a new man to run Whitbread Merseyside. What he wanted, he said, was someone "big, strong, and dumb enough to accept the job".

Figure 8–16 Map Illustrating the Locations of Distribution Depots and Production Sites Within the UK, Whitbread & Company PLC as at 1st March 1981

Depot	Vehicles
Scotland	11
1. Rutherglen	
2. Aberdeen	
3. Elgin	
East Pennines	102
4. Castle Eden	
5. Woodlesford	
6. Loughborough	
7. Tinsley	
8. Grimsby	
West Pennines	123
9. Shadsworth	
10. Penrith	
11. Salford	
12. Birkenhead	
13. Liverpool	
14. Llandudno	
Wales	36
15. Cardiff	
16. Rhymney	
17. Carmarthan	
Flowers	80
18. Mailsea	
19. Gloucester	
20. Stratford	
21. Wednesbury	
22. Plymouth	
23. Tiverton	
24. Truro	
Wessex	55
25. Romsey	
26. Newport (IDW)	
27. Lancing	
28. Stonehenge	
29. Upton	
30. Portsmouth	
Wethereds	20
31. Marlow	
London	92
32. Lewisham	
33. Manor Park	
34. Chiswick	
35. Yarmouth	
36. Dunstable	
37. Hornsey	
38. Hoddesdon	
39. Waterdon Rd	
Fremlins	35
40. Maidstone	
41. Faversham	
TOTAL	554

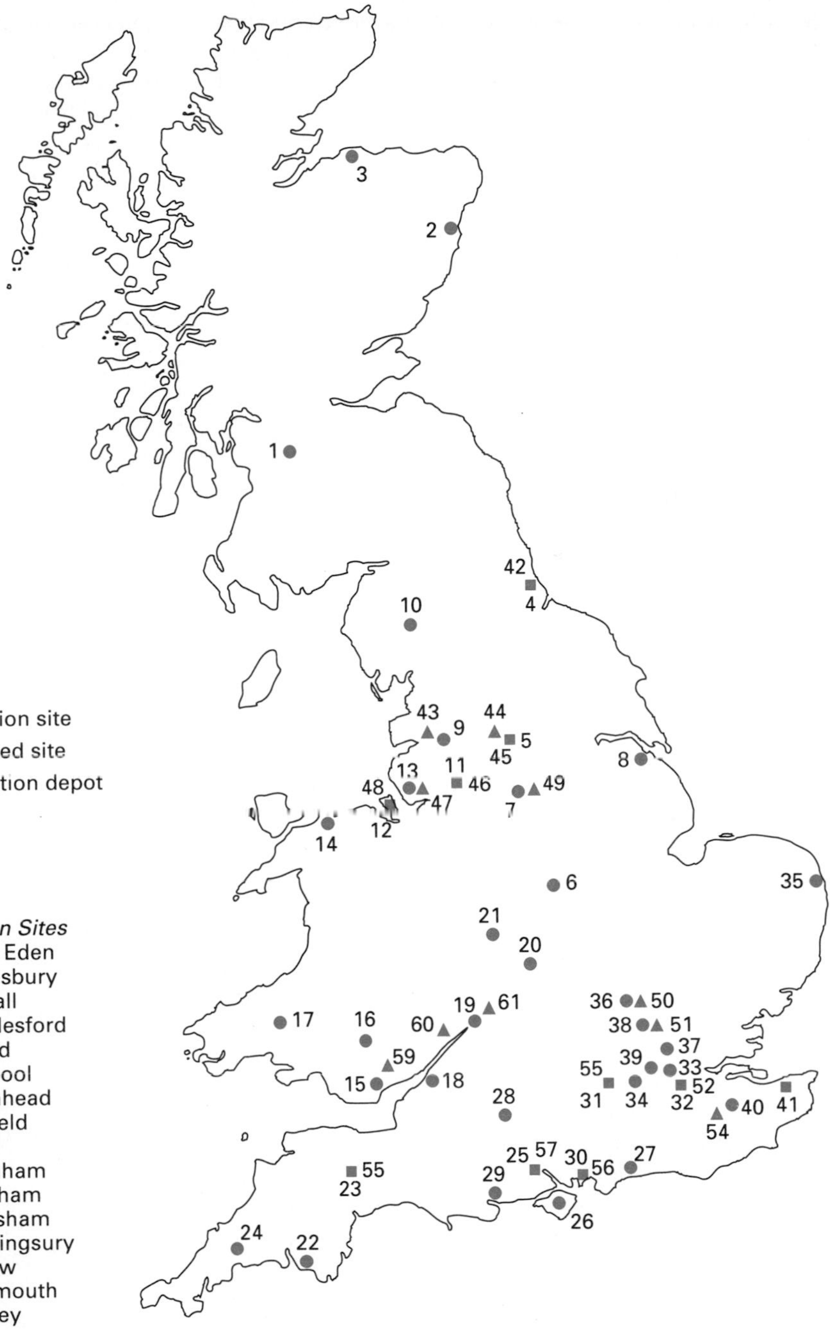

▲ Production site
■ Combined site
● Distribution depot

Production Sites
42. Castle Eden
43. Samiesbury
44. Kirkstall
45. Woodlesford
46. Salford
47. Liverpool
48. Birkenhead
49. Sheffield
50. Luton
51. Tottenham
52. Lewisham
53. Faversham
54. Wateringsury
55. Marlow
56. Portsmouth
57. Romsey
58. Tiverton
59. Cardiff
60. Magor
61. Cheltenham

LEN OLIVER

Len Oliver was recommended to Bernard King by a Whitbread manager who knew Len and thought he could do the job in Liverpool. Len had joined Whitbread in 1976 in a senior distribution post after spending 17 years with a major British food products company where he was primarily involved in distribution and industrial relations issues. After a few years as Distribution Manager, a job which involved solving a number of serious industrial relations issues, Len had been appointed general manager of Whitbread's Sheffield operations. He commented:

> When I arrived in Sheffield in 1978, the business had been growing nicely and a new management structure had just been put into place. I was told not to make any major changes for 12 months, to let everyone get used to the new structure and to me. Unfortunately, volumes started to fall in 1979—it wasn't just our problem, it was the whole industry—and I couldn't just sit still. I started cutting people, and in the end I reduced the original level of 400 employees to approximately 300.

Before taking over Whitbread Merseyside, Len Oliver met separately with Bernard King to learn more about the recent industrial relations situation in Liverpool. Bernard described the situation as follows:

> I had not been in my job two days when the Shadsworth brewery went on strike. I did not get good advice from my local managers on this issue, but in the end, after a two week walk out, the T and G came back to work without gaining anything. I learned a lot about the union from that strike, and they learned that I don't back down. Then there was the Liverpool strike. Although the brewery has only 20 employees, the strike spread to the 40 workers in the packaging operation, and they jointly picketed our distribution centres, effectively shutting down all of Whitbread Merseyside. At one point, it appeared that our Samlesbury plant would also be picketed, which would have been a disaster of major proportions.
>
> This strike, and the second one which followed it (a total of six weeks), were a major test of will between ourselves, the union, and Whitbread senior management in London. They were precipitated by two new managers that Peter Watkins had hired to try to restore order and supervisory morale in the brewery. We suspended five hard core troublemakers whom the new managers had seen, in spite of repeated warnings, in a pub during working hours. The suspension was followed by an investigation, that ultimately led to their dismissal. During the investigation the union officials said to us 'are you really sure you want to go through with this?' We could have backed down, as we had so many times before, but we decided that the time had come to take a stand, to support our first line managers.
>
> At one point during the second strike, I was called to London to meet senior Whitbread managers, who told me that I should give the union officials whatever they wanted, so the strike could be ended. I replied that, if they forced me to do that, I would have to resign. It was a rather tense meeting, but I did not concede. As the strike dragged into November, however, we decided that perhaps we should permanently close the brewery. When I announced this to Merseyside management, they objected and said that they felt the union would yield, as they now finally understood that we were serious. They were right and two days later the workers returned to work, minus the infamous five.

LEN OLIVER'S FIRST WEEK

Len Oliver began his new job in Liverpool on January 5, 1982. From the first day, he made a point of being very visible and accessible, talking formally and informally to his managers, union officials and hourly paid workers. He explained to everyone that he came with no preconceived notions about what should be done at Liverpool, but when he did decide, they would be told openly and clearly. This message was received with skepticism by the union leaders, who were convinced that Oliver had been sent to Merseyside to close the brewery, and intended to give both him and Whitbread a very hard time if he tried to do so.

During the first week, Len's focus was twofold; to gain an understanding of the business situation facing Whitbread Merseyside, and to make an assessment of the individuals he would be working with. (An organization chart is presented in Figure 8–17.) A recently completed report (see Appendix) suggested that the company's market share decline was the result of high prices, underinvestment in pubs, not taking advantage of a trend to cask beer[1], and stiff competition from local brewers. The market share decline was apparent in both the free trade business (sales to pubs not allied to any brewer) and the tied trade business (pubs owned by Whitbread). In spite of the fact that he had no personal experience at developing or managing pubs, Len was somewhat disturbed after discussing the report with the free trade and tied trade managers. He commented:

> The free trade manager does not believe that we have a problem. He seems to think that we have a God given right to survive. Unfortunately, he's been here a long time and his attitudes will be difficult to change. I think he sees himself as the number two manager

Figure 8–17 WHITBREAD MERSEYSIDE ORGANIZATION CHART

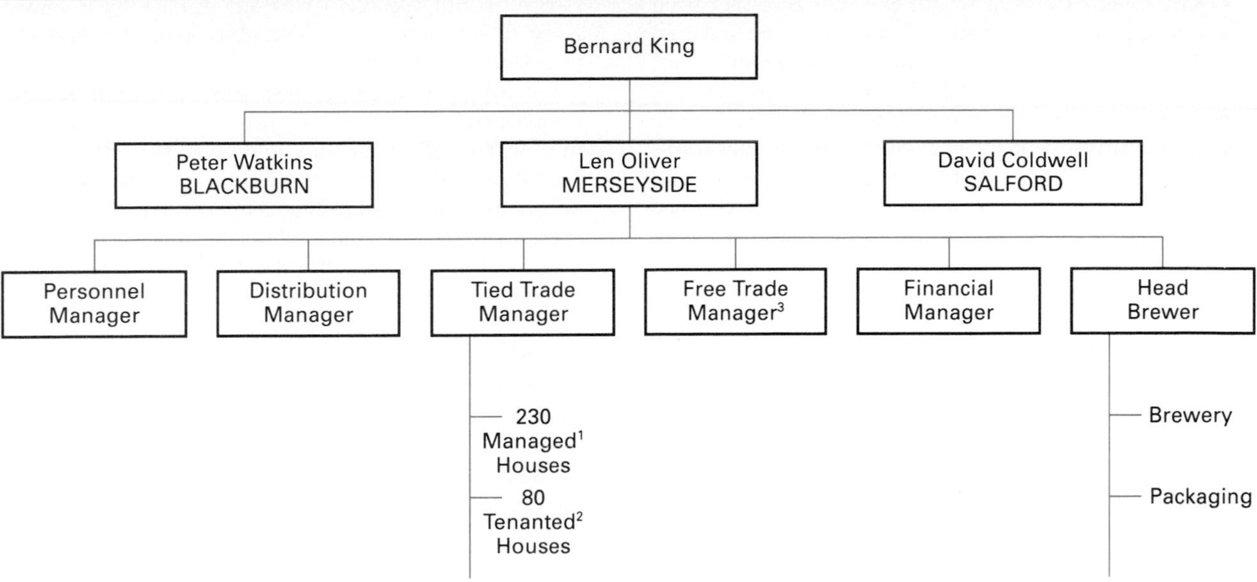

[1]Managed Houses were owned by Whitbread and managed by Whitbread employees.
[2]Tenanted Houses were owned by Whitbread and managed by entrepreneurs who leased the pubs from the company.
[3]Free Houses were pubs not owned by a brewer, and free to buy from whatever supplier they wished.

in Merseyside, but he does not appear to me to be a good manager of people.

The tied trade manager, on the other hand, has only been here about eight months and is new to the brewing business. In spite of this, he's a very independent character and his position seems to be 'I've got pubs to run and I know what I'm doing' However, I hear that the pub managers dislike and distrust him as he is very aggressive, openly runs checks on their honesty, and insists they are in their pubs virtually all the time. His drive is to reduce costs in general and overheads in particular.

Len also examined volume and profit figures during his first week in Liverpool and these confirmed his belief that the Merseyside operation was earning approximately 50% less than it should have been. As shown in Table 8–9, volume sold in the Merseyside region had fallen from 356,000 barrels to approximately 250,000 barrels in a 2 year period. Part of this decline was due to a transfer of business to Whitbread's take home division, but most of it was due to declining trading conditions and the 1981 strikes. The Liverpool brewery was operating at approximately 60% of its 300,000 barrel per year capacity, and beers which it could not produce were shipped in from other Whitbread breweries.

After examining these figures, Len commented:

In spite of the fact that they have laid off 157 people here since the volume decline began in 1979, there

Table 8–9 WHITBREAD MERSEYSIDE PERFORMANCE (FEBRUARY 28 YEAR END)

	Volume (barrels)	Profit (£)
1977–78	365	N
1978–79	355	4,824
1979–80	356	5,524
1980–81	308	6,000
1981–82 (est.)	250	4,800

Further probing revealed the employment figures presented in Table 8–10.

are still far too many (see Table 8–10). Based on my Sheffield experience, I would say that this operation should be run with about 300 people. I am not just talking about a reduction in weekly paid employees; there are about 70 middle level managers in this operation, and that's about 30 too many! One of the most blatant offenders is the distribution operation.

We initially grew into this area by acquisition, and we still have too many depots, too many trucks, too many people. Naturally, I have talked with the distribution manager. He is very apprehensive; he knows he has problems. He strikes me as an honest man; he's genuinely concerned about Whitbread Merseyside and Liverpool's severe problems, but he's not getting the job done. I was told before I came here that I'd probably have to replace him, but I'm not sure if that's the best move. The problem is complex because we can't simply combine our various depots. The union has negotiated different restrictive practices in each location, which means such things as manning levels, overtime rules, and the organization of work are different in Birkenhead than they are in Liverpool, even though one is just across the river from the other.

The one area that clearly is not overstaffed is the brewery. It was reduced from 30 to 20 hourly employees in the last round of cuts, and that is the minimum they can get by with. Due to a quality problem prior to my arrival, the brewery was shut for a time, and a new head brewer and number two brewer were brought in. Although new to the job, the head brewer has worked in this brewery before and appears competent. He reports to Samlesbury in terms of the quality of product he makes, cleanliness standards, and so on, but to me with respect to issues relating to his workforce.

The problem with the brewery is the incredible resentment that resides there. They hate every manager up to and including Bernard King for firing their five ringleaders, and they hate me because I'm the new boss and because I was put in here by Bernard King. They could start another strike at any time on the slightest pretext.

I should also mention that when quality problems temporarily closed the Liverpool brewery, we shipped in beer from other Whitbread breweries and our local customers didn't notice the difference. Another marketing myth destroyed! And there is certainly enough excess capacity at Samlesbury to absorb the total Liverpool production. We don't need this Liverpool brewery!

At the end of his first week in Liverpool, Len took a few minutes to talk about his personal situation and the need for change at Merseyside.

It's a good thing I'm here without my family, because I'm spending 15 hours a day on the job, and it looks as if it will continue that way for some time. I am eating with managers every night, and then we usually go out for a few drinks. Although the managers are being quite protective of one another, I don't detect any jealousy of me—I don't think any of them wanted this job! In fact the personnel manager, who appears competent, had already arranged a transfer to Samlesbury before my arrival. It takes effect in about a month's time, but I could probably stop it if I wanted to. . . .

I have talked directly with the union leaders. There are two key guys. The full time union official is the incredibly tough character that Bernard first met in the Shadsworth dispute and then again in the Liverpool battles. He is 62 years old and has lost his last two fights with Bernard—I wonder if he's getting tired. It could be expensive to find out, of course. The other man is the full time union convenor, a company employee, who is 57. He is reputed to have been a firebrand in his youth, but has settled a little now.

Table 8–10 1981 YEAR END EMPLOYMENT

	Weekly Paid	Monthly Paid	Total
Production[1]	68	20	88
Cellar Service	—	36	36
Tied Trade	19	38	57
Free Trade	—	16	16
Distribution	161	62	223
Administration	9	18	27
	257	190	447

[1]Brewery and packaging

Of course the young shop stewards below him are as tough and militant now as he was in earlier years.

My style is not to sit around. Bernard is expecting me to create changes, so is the union, so are my managers. I don't think next week is too early to begin.

APPENDIX

Analysis of Market Share Loss

Between 1978 and 1981 our share in the North West has declined from 18.26% to 16.36%, representing a 21% volume decline.

3. *Pricing* Whitbread has been one of the price leaders in the North West for 1½–2 years. At retail prices, we have been up to 8p per pint more expensive than the local brewers. For example, in 1979 the difference between Whitbread and Boddingtons was 1p/pint. In the two years of recession since then, the difference has been 5p/pint. Combined with the under-investment, the Whitbread pub will be perceived as offering a lower value for money package.

Whitbread Market Share—North West

	1978	1979*	1980	1981
Total beer	18.26%	19.08%	17.86%	16.36%
Tied trade	20.36%	21.48%	19.94%	18.60%
Free trade	14.71%	16.19%	15.29%	13.73%

*Increased share due to Tetley strike.

The decline is due to a number of factors working together rather than any single factor.

A. Tied Trade

1. *House Location* In West Pennines, 41% of the volume loss is accounted for by the Liverpool Managed Houses. Sixty-six of these houses (¼ of the Estate) represented 50% of the managed loss. The principal reasons for the decline in these houses were: thirty-two due to non-trading factors such as urban redevelopment, recession, and industrial decline; eighteen due to high prices; and sixteen due to miscellaneous factors. In addition, the recent growth of unemployment in Merseyside is concentrated in areas of Whitbread strengths (e.g. Ellesmere Port where we have 44% share). Whitbread also has above average presence in the inner city area (19% of the total), which has experienced above average growth in unemployment.

2. *Investment* Compared with our major competitors, Whitbread has under-invested in the tied estate. For example, between 1976 and 1980 Allied spent 64% more on its pubs. Bass 48% more on its. As a consequence, a large proportion of our estate is untidy and unattractive.

Tied Trade Investment 1986–1980

	Per Tied House (£)	Gross Spending (£)
Allied	3,500	127M
Courage	2,300	60M
Bass	2,200	89M
Whitbread	1,300	46M

4. *Cask Beer* Between 1969 and 1979, the cask beer market grew by 26%. By 1980 cask beer has grown to 20.7% of the market at a time when the total beer market was declining. Whitbread West Pennines' share of the draught market in 1979/80 was 13.4%, but our share of cask beer was estimated at only 1.3% (representing 1.7% of our draught volume). Cask beer represented about 75% of the local brewer volumes and, amongst the nationals, Bass had 25% of its volume in cask, Allied 15% of its volume in cask.

5. *Local Brewer's Performance* We estimate that our share loss has been gained by the local brewers in the North West. (e.g. Local 1.4% down, Nationals 5.6% down 1980 v. 1981). The major reasons why the locals have performed better are covered previously, but in addition we feel that the locals have achieved a better image partly as a result of price, signage, etc., and also because the consumer has developed a 'small and local is best' philosophy. Local brewery brands consistently outperform national brands in terms of product preference.

B. Free Trade

1. *Small Accounts* In order to improve our Free Trade profitability, we have closed our 0–20 barrel per year accounts. As a result we have shed 12,000 barrels from the business, most of which we planned to transfer to wholesalers. However, we would estimate that more than 50% of the transferred volume has been lost from the business. Our current intention is to evaluate the closure of 20–50 barrel accounts, which would put at risk a further 22,000 barrels. There is evidence that

other brewers, notably Bass, are accepting small accounts closed by Whitbread.

2. *Price* Price is playing an increasing part in consumer choice. Up to 1980, Free Trade accounts would equalise their retail prices regardless of the wholesale price. More recently, however, the retail prices now reflect the wholesale price and consequently, as Whitbread has been a price leader, the consumer has decided on the lower priced alternative on the same bar. The wholesale price differences, especially against the local brewers, have been significant.

NOTE

[1]Cask beer was made the "old fashioned way", which meant that it was conditioned in the cask rather than the brewery, and dispensed in the pub with a hand pump.

Step 2: Prepare the case for class discussion.

Step 3: Answer the questions below, individually, in small groups, or with the class as a whole, as directed by your instructor.

Description

1. How did Len Oliver interact with his subordinates and with the union?
2. How would you describe Oliver's leadership style?

Diagnosis

3. Was Oliver an effective leader? Justify your answer by applying each of the following theories: (a) trait, (b) behavioral, (c) roles (d) situational and (e) transformational.
4. Was Oliver an effective manager?
5. Did Oliver experience problems in managing groups? of motivation? communication? issues of personal development? perception or attribution?

Prescription

6. What should Oliver do now?
7. Offer a plan for effective leadership and management at Whitbread Merseyside.

Action

8. What issues will arise in implementing this plan?

Step 4: Discussion. In small groups, with the entire class, or in written form, share your answers to the questions above. Then answer the following questions:

1. What symptoms suggest a problem exists?
2. What problems exist in the case?
3. What theories and concepts help explain the problems?
4. How can the problems be corrected?
5. Are the actions likely to be effective?

Activity 8–3: LEADERSHIP ROLE PLAY

Step 1: Divide the class into groups of seven people. Read the general description of the situation below. The instructor will distribute seven roles to each group. Each person in the group should then prepare one role. In preparing for the role play, try to put yourself in the position of the person whose role you are playing.

GENERAL DESCRIPTION OF THE SITUATION

It is August 1st, and you are about to have a meeting with the six people you are living with during the summer in an old Victorian house in the city of Medropolis. This city has exciting cultural and educational possibilities, a lovely beach area nearby, a large depressed inner-city area, and a rather conservative political atmosphere.

You are a national group who has come here this summer for various reasons:

Lee West is here for a summer rest after a very demanding work year.

Sandy Brown is a community organizer in the inner city.

Fran Miller is a counselor at an inner city mental health center.

Cam Jones is summer director of curriculum at School District 3 in Medropolis' inner city.

Jan Johnson is teaching summer courses at the medical school.

Brooks Baines is studying philosophy by taking summer courses at the university.

Sam Smith is a secretary in School District 3 for the summer.

You must all return to your homes by August 15th. Sandy, Cam, and Fran lived here last year and will continue to live here next year.

You have an important decision to make at this meeting. Mr. Robert Stodge, the superintendent of School District 3, has asked a close friend of yours, Jane Goodenough, for seven people to help him with a census on the weekend of August 12–13. Mr. Stodge is an organization man who cares much about doing what the State Education Director asks of his superintendents. His assistant, David Guitar, loves his work with the people of the district, which he feels is slowly developing a community sense; he is responsible for the organization of the census. It is rumored that several inner-city schools may be consolidated within the next two years, and that School District 3's continued existence may be in question. Your friend has asked you to decide whether or not you will accept this two-day assignment *as a group*. You do not know whether your collection of data will be used responsibly or be a waste of time.

You are to call your friend in a half hour and report your decision. You all agreed when you set the meeting time that you could make your decision in half an hour. (If you don't call Jane within that time, she will call you).

Step 2: Each group of seven participants should convene the group meeting in part of the room. You have one-half hour to make a decision about whether to conduct the census.

Step 3: Report your group's decision to your instructor.

Step 4: Discussion. Answer the following questions, in small groups or with the entire class:

Description

1. Characterize each participant. How are they similar? different?

Diagnosis

2. What problems did you encounter in reaching agreement? Why?
3. Did a leader emerge?
4. Was the leader effective?
5. Using your knowledge of leadership theories, analyze the leadership you experienced.
6. Did you experience stress?
7. Did you experience issues of adult development?
8. Using motivation, communication, and perceptual theories, explain the outcomes of the meeting.

Reprinted by permission of Sara Ann Rude, St. Louis, Missouri.

Activity 8–4: DECISION-MAKING CASES

Step 1: Read each case below.

Step 2: For each case, apply the Vroom and Yetton model and indicate the most appropriate decision-making process. Be sure to list your answers to each diagnostic question and the resulting problem style.

CASE I

You are president of a small but growing Midwestern bank, with its head office in the state's capital and branches in several nearby market towns. The location and type of business are factors which contribute to the emphasis on traditional and conservative banking practices at all levels.

When you bought the bank five years ago, it was in poor financial shape. Under your leadership, much progress has been made. This progress has been achieved while the economy has moved into a mild recession, and, as a result, your prestige among your bank managers is very high. Your success, which you are inclined to attribute principally to good luck and to a few timely decisions on your part, has, in your judgment, one unfortunate by-product. It has caused your subordinates to look to you for leadership and guidance in decision-making beyond what you consider necessary. You have no doubts about the fundamental capabilities of these men but wish that they were not quite so willing to accede to your judgment.

You have recently acquired funds to permit opening a new branch. Your problem is to decide on a suitable location. You believe that there is no "magic formula" by which it is possible to select an optimal site. The choice will be made by a combination of some simple common sense criteria and "what feels right." You have asked your managers to keep their eyes open for commercial real estate sites that might be suitable. Their knowledge about the communities in which they operate should be extremely useful in making a wise choice.

Their support is important because the success of the new branch will be highly dependent on your managers' willingness to supply staff and technical assistance during its early days. Your bank is small enough for everyone to feel like part of a team, and you feel that this has and will be critical to the bank's prosperity.

The success of this project will benefit everybody. Directly, they will benefit from the increased base of operations, and, indirectly, they will reap the personal and business advantages of being part of a successful and expanding business.

CASE II

You are regional manager of an international management consulting company. You have a staff of six consultants reporting to you, each of whom enjoys a considerable amount of autonomy with clients in the field.

Yesterday you received a complaint from one of your major clients to the effect that the consultant whom you assigned to work on the contract with them was not doing his job effectively. They were not very explicit as to the nature of the problem, but it was clear that they were dissatisfied and that something would have to be done if you were to restore the client's faith in your company.

The consultant assigned to work on that contract has been with the company for six years. He is a systems analyst and is one of the best in that profession. For the first four or five years his performance was superb, and he was a model for the other more junior consultants. However, recently he has seemed to have a "chip on his shoulder," and his previous identification with the company and its objectives has been replaced with indifference. His negative attitude has been noticed by other consultants, as well as by clients. This is not the first such complaint that you have had from a client this year about his performance. A previous client even reported to you that the consultant reported to work several times obviously suffering from a hangover and that he had been seen around town in the company of "fast" women.

It is important to get to the root of this problem quickly if that client is to be retained. The consultant obviously has the skill necessary to work with the clients effectively. If only he were willing to use it!

CASE III

You have recently been appointed manager of a new plant which is presently under construction. Your team of five department heads has been selected, and they are now working with you in selecting their own staffs, purchasing equipment, and generally anticipating the problems that are likely to arise when you move into the plant in three months.

Yesterday, you received from the architect a final set of plans for the building, and, for the first time, you examined the parking facilities that are available. There is a large lot across the road from the plant intended primarily for hourly workers and lower level supervisory personnel. In addition, there are seven spaces immediately adjacent to the administrative offices, intended for visitor and reserved parking. Company policy requires that a minimum of three spaces be made available for visitor parking, leaving you only four spaces to allocate among yourself and your five department heads. There is no way of increasing the total number of such spaces without changing the structure of the building.

Up to now, there have been no obvious status differences among your team, who have worked together very well in the planning phase of the operation. To be sure, there are salary differences, with your Administrative, Manufacturing, and Engineering Managers receiving slightly more than the Quality Control and Industrial Relations Managers. Each has recently been promoted to his new position, and expects reserved parking privileges as a consequence of his new status. From past experience, you know that people feel strongly about things which would be indicative of their status. So you and your subordinates have been working together as a team, and you are reluctant to do anything which might jeopardize the team relationship.

CASE IV

You are executive vice president for a small pharmaceutical manufacturer. You have the opportunity to bid on a contract for the Defense Department pertaining to biological warfare. The contract is outside the mainstream of your business; however, it could make economic sense since you do have unused capacity in one of your plants, and the manufacturing processes are not dissimilar.

You have written the document to accompany the bid and now have the problem of determining the dollar value of the quotation which you think will win the job for your company. If the bid is too high, you will undoubtedly lose to one of your competitors; if it is too low, you would stand to lose money on the program.

There are many factors to be considered in making this decision, including the cost of the new raw materials and the additional administrative burden of relationships with a new client, not to speak of factors which are likely to influence the bids of your competitors, such as how much they *need* this particular contract. You have been busy assembling the necessary data to make this decision but there remain several "unknowns," one of which involves the manager of the plant in which the new products will be manufactured. Of all your subordinates, only he is in the position to estimate the costs of adapting the present equipment to their new purpose, and his cooperation and support will be necessary in ensuring that the specifications of the contract will be met. However, in an initial discussion with him when you first learned of the possibility of the contract, he seemed adamantly opposed to the idea. His previous experience has not particularly equipped him with the ability to evaluate projects like this one, so that you were not overly influenced by his opinions. From the nature of his arguments, you inferred that his opposition was ideological rather than economic. You recall that he was actively involved in a local "peace organization" and, within the company, was one of the most vocal opponents to the war in Vietnam.

Step 3: Compare your responses to those given by Vroom and Yetton. Your instructor will distribute these.

Step 4: Discussion. In small groups or with the class as a whole, answer the following questions:

1. In what situations would using the Vroom and Yetton model improve your decision making?
2. In what situations would the model be of little value?

Reprinted with permission from V.H. Vroom and A.G. Jago, "Decision making as a Social Process: Normative & Descriptive Models of Leader Behavior," *Decision Sciences 5* (1974): 750–753.

Activity 8–5: MAYOR EVAN SWEENEY CASE

Step 1: Read the Mayor Evan Sweeney case.

Late one January evening, Evan Sweeney slumped into the easy chair in his living room, wearily rubbing his eyes. It was 11:30 PM, and he had just returned home from a school committee meeting at the Dykins School to find his wife and three children already asleep. For the first time since before a breakfast meeting long ago that morning, Sweeney was alone, not on stage. Too many days had been like this, he thought, since he had taken office as mayor of Centralville, Massachusetts—a city of 53,000—just three weeks earlier. Four years on the city council had given him more than an inkling of how government could challenge the mind and invade his private life, but nothing had prepared him for the pressures of the mayor's office.

THE NEW MAYOR

Born and raised in Centralville, Evan Sweeney had left town for college at the University of Massachusetts, Amherst, and then served four years in the Navy during the Vietnam era. Subsequently, he returned to Centralville to enter the family printing business with his father and brother, married his high school sweetheart, bought a house in a comfortable residential neighborhood, and became active in several civic and church organizations. Sweeney's wife was a homemaker, and their three young children attended public schools.

At age 40, Sweeney was a seasoned local politician. Always fascinated by the swirling events of politics, he had worked in several gubernatorial and congressional campaigns before taking on the job of managing his best friend's campaign for the state senate. They lost, but Sweeney decided to launch his own political career. He ran for city council the following year and won, was re-elected two years later with the highest margin in the city, and then decided on unseating the incumbent mayor, who was serving his second term. He campaigned for mayor energetically but fell short—losing with just 48 percent of the votes. Two years later, he tried again. In the general election just past, he swept to victory, defeating the six-year incumbent decisively.

In the last two months, he had disentangled himself from the printing business—with the understanding that he could come back when his political career was over—and prepared to take office as Centralville's full-time mayor at an annual salary of $33,000.

CAMPAIGN ISSUES

Sweeney's campaign for mayor had raised several key issues. Some of the communities in the outlying areas of greater Boston near Centralville were benefitting from development in the form of suburban shopping centers and industrial parks. Although Centralville had several large tracts of vacant land, its share of this development did not match in either quantity or quality what some of its neighbors were securing. Denouncing this "differential development," Sweeney had pledged to use the mayor's powers to the utmost to build up Centralville's tax base.

Sweeney had also promised to improve the quality of the city's schools, citing declining reading and mathematics scores and a decrease in the percentage of the town's high school graduates going on to college. His call for excellence in education had won him support from the teachers' organization as well as several parent groups. As mayor, he now chaired the school committee.

Sweeney had trumpeted his slogan, "Centralville stands for excellence and pride," throughout the campaign as a way of reflecting his concern that the city was falling behind the rest of the state economically and educationally. The slogan was also a short-hand way of raising the subtler issue: that the incumbent mayor dressed and talked like a small-town salesman (which he was), relied on a "kitchen cabinet" of old cronies for advice, and seemed hopelessly out of date to many of the younger citizens of the city.

Sweeney emphasized his managerial experience during the campaign, stressing that he would more effectively deliver city services than his opponent. He pointedly compared his private sector responsibilities to the incumbent's and promised to bring more private sector know-how to the mayor's office—for example, in managing contracts for snow removal and garbage collection.

Beyond these issues, Sweeney had made very few specific promises about what he would do in office. He had, however, pledged many times to be a "responsive mayor" and to maintain an "open door" for all citizens and civic groups that wanted to express their concerns about city government.

CITY GOVERNMENT

Centralville's government was organized into 14 departments that operated under the mayor's authority, including police, fire, public works, planning and community development, health, inspectional services, assessing, and water and sewers. It also had a quasi-independent housing authority, whose members (save one) were appointed by the mayor for staggered terms.

Four of the nine city councillors had been elected for the first time in the recent election but only one of these individuals was aligned with Sweeney. He barely knew the other three. Of the remaining five councillors, three were people with whom he had clashed during his two terms on the council; they had resented his political ambition.

The school committee was elected independently, but the mayor served as its ex officio chairman. Ironically, given the voters' apparent response to Sweeney's campaign position on schools, five of the other six school committee members had been re-elected. The one other new member was a close family friend of Sweeney's and seemed receptive to his feelings about the need for educational improvements.

As the new mayor, Sweeney had only two jobs to fill in his own office—his secretary and an aide who could be paid $19,000.

All of his department heads had originally been appointed by a previous mayor but had then secured civil service status after one year on the job. Therefore, Sweeney had not had the chance to put his own people into place when he took office. Some turnover was imminent, though. The public works director had publicly announced his intention to retire in the spring; the planning director had left as of January 1 to take a higher paying job in a neighboring community; and the police chief had told Sweeney in private—but pledged him to secrecy—that he would announce in June that he would retire in September.

PENDING BUSINESS

During three weeks in office, Sweeney had begun to penetrate the "mysteries" of the city budget to which he had paid minimal attention when he served on the city council. The city had finished the past two fiscal years with a razor-thin surplus and, according to the former mayor, was going to finish the current year in the black, too. Sweeney had learned to his dismay, though, that this forecast was probably over-optimistic. Particularly troubling were unsettled labor contracts with the police and fire unions and public works department employees, which could well lead to retroactive wage and benefit payments back to the previous July.

It was hard to tell exactly where the city stood financially, though, since the most recent expense reports available were for October. The antiquated computer system ran months behind in recording revenues and expenditures. Moreover, the city operated on a cash basis, with no encumbrance system for purchasing. A major snowstorm in December had apparently "busted" the budget for snow removal, with more than six weeks of winter remaining. The city's private auditing firm had recommended a complete revamping of the financial management system.

These facts were closely connected with problems that the city was having with the federal Department of Housing and Urban Development. HUD charged that Centralville had made undocumented expenditures with its CDBG allocation; it therefore had declared more than $200,000 in audit exceptions for which it demanded reimbursement.

As for the coming budget, several school committee members were beginning to say in public that a 15 percent increase in the school department's funds was necessary to implement needed reforms. Requests from his department heads were rolling in, too. Each seemed to have some critical project that required buying new equipment or adding personnel to the city payroll.

The city's current tax revenues were inadequate to finance more than inflation increases in the city's budget, and an effort to override Proposition 2½ the previous year had been voted down decisively by the voters. As part of a search for other revenue sources, a consultant hired by the previous administration had reported—in a study received but never publicized by the former mayor—that the city's water and sewer fees covered less than 50 percent of the costs providing those services and had recommended that user fees be raised accordingly to make the department self-sufficient.

Complicating the tax issue was the fact that the electric utility serving the city had just won a property tax abatement case in the courts, and this would subject the city to a one-time only retroactive payment of $2.5 million.

The city was experiencing some housing problems that had attracted recent attention in its weekly newspaper. Centralville's housing stock was aging—but not gracefully. Nonetheless, development pressures in neighboring communities were forcing property values up rapidly in the West End of the city. With property revaluation pending in the coming year, it did not escape long-time residents of that area that their assessments might rise substantially. Some people were worrying that they might be forced to sell if their property taxes rose precipitously. Conditions in the city's rental housing market were also unfavorable for long-time residents. Many of the multi-family dwelling units, including two-family houses as well as apartment buildings, were being purchased by out-of-towners as speculative investments. There were growing fears that condominium conversion might increase dramatically in the coming years, forcing current renters to move.

SWEENEY'S DAY

The work day just past had been like too many others in the three weeks of his mayoralty.

It began with breakfast with the executive committee of the Centralville Chamber of Commerce, which was seeking his support for a program to improve the city's business climate by promoting facade renovation on the buildings along Main Street in the main shopping district.

Arriving at the office at 9:15, he encountered a steady stream of visitors, including (1) the officers of the local VFW post who wanted him to pose for photos while purchasing the first ticket for their annual raffle, (2) a delegation from his old Boy Scout troop which presented him with a plaque honoring his election, (3) a retired city employee with complaints about his treatment by the city's retirement board, (4) a citizen disturbed about proposed changes in an MBTA bus route, (5) another citizen disgruntled about his water bill, (6) and another concerned about his property tax assessment.

The day's mail brought four invitations to speak at dinners or meetings of various local civic associations. It also brought an invitation to attend a three-day conference at Harvard's Kennedy School of Government in late February.

Among this correspondence was a petition from 35 residents of the Arborton neighborhood demanding city intervention to deal with late night noise from a nearby bar recently taken over by new owners. The mail also contained a letter written by the president of the Bonton Corporation, which employed 175 workers, who informed the mayor of a pending sale of his firm to a larger, out-of-town corporation that would expand operations if alterations in sewer hookups could be arranged at city expense.

With the mail was a folder containing 18 resumes from candidates for the planning director's job. Three new applications had arrived that day. Sweeney glanced through them, wondering when and how he would decide on a few candidates to interview.

At lunchtime, Sweeney left the office to attend a senior citizens group meeting at a nearby church. Munching a sandwich and circulating at the informal gathering, the mayor heard many complaints about crime on the streets of the city and about the need for better transportation services for elderly citizens needing to shop, get to the doctor, or take advantage of recreation opportunities. At 2 PM, Sweeney swung by police headquarters to inspect the department's cruisers. His police chief had insisted he look personally at their dilapidated condition so he would understand why it was essential for the new city budget to include funds for a dozen new vehicles.

Back in his office at 4 PM, Sweeney held a scheduled meeting with Arthur Johnson, the private attorney who represented the city in its labor relations. A native of Centralville, Johnson had a general law practice, mixing real estate work and corporate clients. He had handled Centralville's collective bargaining for the past six years, but he had no other experience in labor law and no other municipal clients. Sweeney was uncomfortable about the delay in negotiating arrangements with city unions, cautious about the potential for political trouble, and skeptical about whether Johnson had the expertise necessary to represent the city effectively. But he himself had little experience in labor relations and only casually knew Johnson from his civic activities. Sweeney hoped he could get the measure of the man through this meeting but was uncertain what exactly he should try to learn.

At 5:30 PM, Sweeney called home to say hello to his wife and chat with his children. Then, spooning out a large bowl of soup, he sat down with Christopher Demarest, the city auditor, to discuss the latest forecasts of the city's budgetary position. Demarest had been auditor for 12 years and had civil service tenure in the job. His new projections were different in several important respects from his previous estimates; and the overall financial picture seemed worse than Sweeney had expected. The mayor found Demarest's explanations unconvincing. He couldn't help wondering whether they were correct yet, and he began to have grave doubts about whether this man would be able to manage the essential changes in the city's financial systems.

After a sometimes heated discussion with Demarest, Sweeney had just enough time to drive over to the Dykins School to chair the school committee meeting at 7:30 PM. Routine business was completed quickly, but three groups of parents prolonged the meeting for hours. The first group was concerned that the series of textbooks used in American history courses was too watered down to give students a real sense of how American government and the national economy had evolved over the years. Another group of parents urged creation of an expanded after-school care program to reduce the number of "latchkey" kids left unsupervised by working parents. The third parent group was disturbed that school bus drivers did not insure that their charges were using seat belts.

HOME AT LAST

Back home, unwinding before bed, Sweeney struggled to recall just what he had been doing that morning. He felt both exhilarated and deeply disturbed. Being mayor meant dealing with so many challenging issues; he felt that he really had the chance to contribute to the welfare of the city. He had big dreams—about the city's future and his own chances for advancing to higher office. It was a much different feeling than he had as a city councillor.

But Sweeney also felt worried that he would not be able to deal effectively with the steady stream of issues that often threatened to engulf him. Too many of these matters involved complicated situations about which his previous experience had given him no preparation. Moreover, he knew that he couldn't keep up his current pace of work—he would become exhausted and his family would be neglected. But it was difficult to see how he could cut back significantly. The demands of the job were extraordinary. As it was, he had too little time to read documents and reports related to city problems. And some issues that he knew would later be important—most notably, the city's growing housing problems—were getting no attention at all.

It would certainly help if he had a few trusted assistants who could handle some of the work. But he often felt alone. His one aide was a young man who had worked faithfully in the campaign, but it wasn't clear what skills he had that would help with the mayor's current tasks. Sweeney's department heads, in theory, should be a major asset; but he didn't know the members of his administration well enough to judge whom he could trust and who could do what well. Even the opportunity to name a few of his own people to key jobs was a problem. He knew that he should be thinking ahead to the appointments he would be making in the next few months, but there never seemed to be time.

If his days continued to be like this one, he wasn't sure that he would ever find the time to focus on these longer-term concerns.

Step 2: Prepare the case for class discussion.

Step 3: Individually, in small groups, or with the entire class, as directed by your instructor, answer the following questions:

Description

1. Describe Evan Sweeney's day.
2. What leadership and management responsibilities does Evan have?

Diagnosis

3. Is Evan an effective leader?
4. Is Evan an effective manager?
5. Using Mintzberg's roles, how would you evaluate Evan's managerial behavior?
6. How do leadership theories help us evaluate Evan's leadership?
7. Does Evan motivate his employees effectively? Explain your answer using theories of motivation.
8. Describe the nature of perception and communication in the case.
9. Evaluate the group dynamics in this case.

Prescription

10. What should Evan do differently? Why?
11. Offer Evan a plan for acting effectively as a leader and manager.

Action

12. What impact will this plan likely have?

Step 4: Discussion. In small groups, with the entire class, or in written form, share your answers to the questions above. Then answer the following questions:

1. What symptoms suggest a problem exists?
2. What problems exist in the case?
3. What theories and concepts help explain the problems?
4. How can the problems be corrected?
5. Are the actions likely to be effective?

Activity 8–6: MANAGERIAL DIARY

Step 1: Select a manager to observe.

Step 2: Keep a diary of the manager's activities for as long as one day. Observe him or her as much as possible during that time.

Step 3: For each activity list the work role performed, as follows:

Activity	Duration	Role

Step 4: Discussion. Answer the following questions, in small groups or with the entire class:

Description

1. Which activities did the manager perform?

Diagnosis

2. Which roles did the manager perform? Which roles did the manager omit?
3. Was the manager effective? Why or why not?
4. Was the manager an effective leader? Use appropriate leadership theories to explain your answer.

Activity 8–7: PLANNING FOR EFFECTIVE LEADERSHIP

Step 1: Using your knowledge of leadership theory, formulate a ten-point plan for effective leadership.

Step 2: In groups of four or five, compare your plans and draw up a master plan.

Step 3: Compare the plans of different groups. Consider their similarities and differences. Which theories were most useful in formulating such a plan?

CONCLUDING COMMENTS

Although theories of leadership have become fairly sophisticated, they still cannot completely prescribe effective leadership or account for the complexity and dynamism of most organizational situations. In the ideal situation, the prescriptions derived for the leadership effectiveness from the various theories were congruent; in some situations, however, different theories offer different analyses of and solutions to leadership problems, making the choice of appropriate action more difficult.

Although leadership is a very complex phenomenon, we can use leadership theories to help us evaluate it and offer ways of encouraging its effectiveness. Activities in this chapter allowed the identification of leadership style, a consideration of its implication for organizational performance, as well as practice in implementing various styles. The decision-making cases illustrated the selection of a process most likely to result in an effective decision. Analysis of the cases of Whitbread Merseyside and Evan Sweeney, as well as planning for effective leadership, allowed the application of diverse perspectives on leadership and management.

Effective leadership is an elusive concept. It influences the effectiveness of individuals and groups in organizations, as well as organizational performance as a whole.[83] Characteristics of an effective leader include a heightened sense of social responsibility, the willingness to relinquish some authority, and the assumption of responsibility for the career development of subordinates.[84] But the relationship between leaders and followers has lately been changing: together they must maintain quality with reduced resources, deal with expectations of shared power and responsibility, deal with their interdependence through collaboration and communication, involve more people in decision making, integrate technical and human resources, and develop new competencies in organizational behavior.[85]

ENDNOTES

[1]This case is based on one prepared by Deborah A. Decker at the Boston College School of Management.

[2]J.C. Barrow, The variables of leadership: A review and conceptual framework, *Academy of Management Review* 2 (1977): 231–235.

[3]R.M. Stogdill, *Handbook of Leadership: A Survey of Theory and Research* (New York: Free Press, 1974).

[4]R.M. Stogdill, Personal factors associated with leadership: A survey of the literature, *Journal of Psychology* 25 (1948): 35–71.

[5]E. Ghiselli, *Explorations in Managerial Talent* (Pacific Palisades, Cal.: Goodyear, 1971).

[6]R. White and R. Lippitt, Leader behavior and member reactions in three "social climates." In *Group Dynamics: Research and Theory* 3d ed., ed. D. Cartwright and A. Zander (New York: Harper & Row, 1968).

[7]R.M. Stogdill and A.E. Coons (eds.), *Leader Behavior: Its Description and Measurement* (Columbus: Ohio State University Bureau of Business Research, 1957).

[8]E. Fleishman, E.F. Harris, and R.D. Burtt, *Leadership and Supervision in Industry* (Colum-

bus: Ohio State University Press, 1955); E. Fleishman and E.F. Harris, Patterns of leadership behavior related to employee grievances and turnover, *Personnel Psychology* 1 (1959): 45–53.

[9]R.L. Kahn and D. Katz, Leadership practices in relation to productivity and morale. In *Group Dynamics,* ed. D. Cartwright and A. Zander (Evanston, Ill.: Row, Peterson, 1953), pp. 585–611.

[10]J. Misumi and M.F. Peterson, The performance-maintenance (PM) theory of leadership: Review of a Japanese research program, *Administrative Science Quarterly* 30 (1985): 198–223.

[11]See R.R. Blake and J.S. Mouton, *Executive Achievement: Making It at the Top* (New York: McGraw-Hill, 1986); R.R. Blake and J.S. Mouton, A comparative analysis of situationalism and 9,9 management by principle, *Organizational Dynamics* 10 (Spring 1982): 20–43; R.R. Blake and J.S. Mouton, Theory and research for developing a science of leadership, *Journal of Applied Behavioral Science* 18 (1982): 275–291.

[12]H. Mintzberg, *The Nature of Managerial Work* 2d ed. (Englewood Cliffs, N.J.: Prentice-Hall, 1979).

[13]S. Kerr, C.A. Schriesheim, C.J. Murphy, and R.M. Stogdill, Toward a contingency theory of leadership based on consideration and initiating structure literature, *Organizational Behavior and Human Performance* 12 (1974): 73.

[14]N.W. Biggart and G.G. Hamilton, An institutional theory of leadership, *Journal of Applied Behavioral Sciences* 234 (1987): 429–441.

[15]See G.A. Yukl, *Leadership in Organizations* 2d ed. (Englewood Cliffs, N.J.: Prentice-Hall, 1989).

[16]P.R. Harris and R.T. Moran, *Managing Cultural Differences* 2d ed. (Houston: Gulf, 1987).

[17]D. McGregor, *The Human Side of Enterprise* (New York: McGraw-Hill, 1961); E.H. Schein, The Hawthorne studies revisited: A defense of Theory Y, Sloan School of Management Working Paper #756-74 (Cambridge: Massachusetts Institute of Technology, 1974), p. 3.

[18]F. Dansereau, G. Graen, and W.J. Haga, A vertical dyad-linkage approach to leadership within formal organizations: A longitudinal investigation of the role-making process, *Organizational Behavior and Human Performance* 23 (1975): 46–78.

[19]T.B. Scandura and G.B. Graen, Moderating effects of initial leader–member exchange status on the effects of a leadership intervention, *Journal of Applied Psychology* 69 (1984): 428–436.

[20]*Ibid.*

[21]D. Duchon, S.G. Graen, T.D. Table, Vertical dyad linkage: A longitudinal assessment of antecedents, measures, and consequences, *Journal of Applied Psychology* 71 (1986): 56–60.

[22]R.L. Heneman, D.B. Greenberger, and C. Anonyuo, Attributions and exchanges: The effects of interpersonal factors in the diagnosis of employee performance, *Academy of Management Journal* 32 (1989): 466–476.

[23]J. Cashman, F. Dansereau, G. Graen, and W. Haga, Organizational understructure and leadership: A longitudinal investigation of the role-making process, *Organizational Behavior and Human Performance* 15 (1976): 278–296.

[24]R.M. Dienesch and R.C. Liden, Leader–member exchange model of leadership: A critique and future development, *Academy of Management Review* 11 (1986): 618–634.

[25]F.E. Fiedler, *A Theory of Leadership Effectiveness* (New York: McGraw-Hill, 1967), pp. 45–46.

[26]*Ibid.;* R.W. Rice, Construct validity of the least preferred coworker score, *Psychological Bulletin* 85 (1978): 1199–1237; F.E. Fiedler, Engineer the job to fit the manager, *Harvard Business Review* 43 (1965): 115–122.

[27]*Ibid.*

[28]F.E. Fiedler and M.M. Chemers, *Leadership and Effective Management* (Glenview, Ill.: Scott, Foresman, 1974), pp. 78–87.

[29]J.A. Kennedy Jr., Middle LPC leaders and the contingency model of leader effectiveness, *Organizational Behavior and Human Performance* 30 (1982): 1–14.

[30]R. Singh, Leadership style and reward allocation: Does least preferred coworker scale measure task and relationship orientation?, *Organizational Behavior and Human Performance* 32 (1983): 178–197.

[31]R.J. House, A path–goal theory of leader effectiveness, *Administrative Science Quarterly* 16 (1971): 321–338; and R.J. House and T.R. Mitchell, Path–goal theory of leadership, *Journal of Contemporary Business* (Autumn 1974): 81–97.

[32]House and Mitchell, *op. cit.*

[33]House and Mitchell, *op. cit.*

[34]R.J. House and M.L. Baetz, Leadership: Some empirical generalizations and new research directions. In B.M. Staw (ed.), *Research in Organizational Behavior* (Greenwich, Conn.: JAI Press, 1979), pp. 341–423.

[35]House and Mitchell, *op. cit.*

[36]J.C. Wofford and T.N. Srinivasan, Experimental tests of the leader-environment-follower interaction theory of leadership, *Organizational Behavior and Human Performance* 32 (1983): 35–54.

[37]J. Indvik, Path–goal theory of leadership: A meta-analysis, *Proceedings of the Academy of Management Meetings* (1986): 189–192.

[38]J. Fulk and E.R. Wendler, Dimensionality of leader–subordinate interactions: A path–goal investigation, *Organizational Behavior and Human Performance* 30 (1983): 241–264.

[39]G.A. Yukl and J. Clemence, A test of path–goal theory of leadership using questionnaire and diary measures of behavior, *Proceedings of the Twenty-First Annual Meeting of the Eastern Academy of Management* (1984): 174–177.

[40]C. Schriesheim and S. Kerr, *op. cit.;* Barrow, *op. cit.,* p. 325; House and Mitchell, *op. cit.*

[41]V.H. Vroom and P.W. Yetton, *Leadership and Decision Making* (Pittsburgh: University of Pittsburgh Press, 1973); V.H. Vroom and A.G. Jago, *The New Leadership: Managing Participation in Organizations* (Englewood Cliffs, N.J.: Prentice-Hall, 1988).

[42]Vroom and Jago, *op. cit.*

[43]R.H.G. Field, A test of the Vroom–Yetton normative model of leadership, *Journal of Applied Psychology* 67 (1982): 523–532.

[44]Vroom and Jago, *op. cit.*

[45]Yukl, *op. cit.*

[46]P. Hersey and K.H. Blanchard, *Management of Organizational Behavior* 4th ed. (Englewood Cliffs, N.J.: Prentice-Hall, 1982).

[47]*Ibid.,* p. 172.

[48]*Ibid.*

[49]R.P. Vecchio, Situational leadership theory: An examination of a prescriptive theory, *Journal of Applied Psychology* 72 (1987): 444–451; C.L. Graeff, The situational leadership theory: A critical view, *Academy of Management Review* 8 (1983): 285–291; D.C. Lueder, Don't be mislead by LEAD, *Journal of Applied Behavioral Science* 21 (1985): 143–151; D.C. Lueder, A rejoinder to Dr. Hersey, *Journal of Applied Behavioral Science* 21 (1985): 154; P. Hersey, A letter to the author of "Don't be misled by LEAD," *Journal of Applied Behavioral Science* 21 (1985): 152–153.

[50]J. Bartunek, Attribution theory: Some implications for organizations, *Business Horizons* 24 (1981): 66–71.

[51]B. Calder, An attribution theory of leadership. In *New Directions in Organizational Behavior,* ed. B.H. Staw and G.R. Salancik (Chicago: St. Clair Press, 1977).

[52]T. Mitchell and R. Wood, Supervisor responses to subordinates' poor performance: A test of the attributional model, *Organizational Behavior and Human Performance* 25 (1980): 123–138.

[53]M. Martinko and W.L. Gardner, The leader/member attribution process, *Academy of Management Review* 12 (1987): 235–249.

[54]See H.H. Kelley, Attribution theory in social psychology. In D. Levine (ed.), *Nebraska Symposium on Motivation* (Lincoln: University of Nebraska Press, 1967); Green and Mitchell, *op. cit.;* T.R. Mitchell and R.E. Wood, An empirical test of an attributional model of leaders' responses to poor performance, *Academy of Management Proceedings* (1979): 94.

[55]Yukl, *Leadership in Organizations, op. cit.,* p. 168.

[56]S.G. Green and T.R. Mitchell, Attributional processes of leaders in leader–member interactions, *Organizational Behavior and Human Performance* 23 (1979): 429–458; G.H. Dobbins, Effects of gender on leaders' responses to poor performers: An attributional interpretation, *Academy of Management Journal* 28 (1985): 587–598.

[57]J. Pfeffer, The ambiguity of leadership, *Academy of Management Review* 2 (1977): 104.

[58]J.R. Larson Jr., J.H. Lingle, and M.M. Scerbo, The impact of performance cues on leader-behavior ratings: The role of selective information availability and probabalistic response bias, *Organizational Behavior and Human Performance* 33 (1984): 323–349.

[59]T.R.V. Davis and F. Luthans, Leadership reexamined: A behavioral approach, *Academy of Management Review* 4 (1979): 237–248.

[60]S. Kerr and J.M. Jermier, Substitutes for leadership: Their meaning and measurement, *Organizational Behavior and Human Performance* 22 (1978): 375–403.

[61]*Ibid.*

[62]J.E. Sheridan, D.J. Vredenburgh, and M.A. Abelson, Contextual model of leadership influence in hospital units, *Academy of Management Journal* 27 (1984): 57–78.

[63]See, for example, J.D. Ford, Departmental context and formal structure as constraints on leader behavior, *Academy of Management Journal* 24 (1981): 274–288; J.P. Howell and P.W. Dorfman, Substitutes for leadership: Test of a construct, *Academy of Management Journal* 24 (1981): 714–728; and J.P. Howell and P.W. Dorfman, Leadership and substitutes for leadership among professional and nonprofessional workers, *Journal of Applied Behavioral Sciences* 22 (1986): 29–46.

[64]R.J. House, A 1976 theory of charismatic leadership. In *Leadership: The Cutting Edge,* ed. Hunt and Larson, *op. cit.*

[65]J.M. Howell and P. Frost, A laboratory study of charismatic leadership, *Organizational Behavior and Human Decision Processes* 43 (1989): 243–269.

[66]A.R. Willner, *The Spellbinders: Charismatic Political Leadership* (New Haven, Conn.: Yale University Press, 1984); A. Conger and R.N. Kanungo, Toward a behavioral theory of charismatic leadership in organizational settings, *Academy of Management Review* 12 (1987): 637–647.

[67]B.M. Bass, Leadership: Good, better, best, *Organizational Dynamics* 13 (Winter 1985): 26–40.

[68]N.M. Tichy and D.O. Ulrich, The leadership challenge: A call for the transformational leader, *Sloan Management Review* 26 (1984): 59–68; N.M. Tichy and M.A. Devanna, *The Transformational Leader* (New York: Wiley, 1986).

[69]B.M. Bass, *Leadership and Performance Beyond Expectations* (New York: Free Press, 1985), p. 20.

[70]S.J. Musser, The determinants of positive and negative charismatic leadership (Grantham, Pa.: Messiah College, 1987). Cited in Yukl, *Leadership in Organizations, op. cit.*

[71]B.M. Bass, D.A. Waldman, B.J. Avolio, and M. Bebb, Transformational leadership and the falling dominoes effect, *Group and Organization Studies* 12 (March 1987): 73–87.

[72]Tichy and Ulrich, *op. cit.*

[73]Bass, *Leadership Beyond Expectations, op. cit.,* p. 17.

[74]Tichy and Devanna, *op. cit.*

[75]W.G. Bennis and B. Nanus, *Leaders: The Strategies for Taking Charge* (New York: Harper & Row, 1985).

[76]Bass, Leadership: Good, better, best, *op. cit.*

[77]J.J. Hater and B.M. Bass, Superiors' evaluations and subordinates' perceptions of transformational and transactional leadership, *Journal of Applied Psychology* 73 (1988): 695–702.

[78]I.C. MacMillan, New business development: A challenge to transformational leadership, *Human Resource Management* 26 (1987): 439–454.

[79]B. Spector, Transformational leadership: The new challenge for U.S. unions, *Human Resource Management* 26 (1987): 3–16.

[80]Bass, Leadership: Good, better, best, *op. cit.*

[81]J.P. Kotter, *The Leadership Factor* (New York: Free Press, 1988), p. 30.

[82]R.E. Byrd, Corporate leadership skills: A new synthesis, *Organizational Dynamics* 16 (Summer 1987): 34–43.

[83]J.E. Smith, K.P. Carson, and R.A. Alexander, Leadership: It can make a difference, *Academy of Management Journal* 27 (1984): 765–776.

[84]M. Bisesi, Strategies for successful leadership in changing times, *Sloan Management Review* 25 (Fall 1983): 61–64.

[85]R. Lippitt, The changing leader–follower relationships of the 1980s, *Journal of Applied Behavioral Science* 18 (1982): 395–403.

RECOMMENDED READINGS

Bass, B.M. *Leadership and Performance Beyond Expectations*. New York: Free Press, 1985.

Bryman, A. *Leadership and Organizations*. London: Routledge and Kegan Paul, 1986.

Conger, J.A. *The Charismatic Leader*. San Francisco: Jossey-Bass, 1989.

Kotter, J.P. *The Leadership Factor*. New York: Free Press, 1988.

Mintzberg, H. *The Nature of Managerial Work* 2d. ed. Englewood Cliffs, N.J.: Prentice-Hall, 1979.

Tichy, N.M., and Devanna, M.A. *The Transformational Leader*. New York: Wiley, 1986.

Vroom, V.H., and Jago, A.G. *The New Leadership: Managing Participation in Organizations*. Englewood Cliffs, N.J.: Prentice-Hall, 1988.

Yukl, G.A. *Leadership in Organizations* 2d ed. Englewood Cliffs, N.J.: Prentice-Hall, 1989.

9

Using Power and Negotiating

CHAPTER OUTLINE

LEARNING OBJECTIVES

After completing the reading and activities in Chapter 9, students will be able to

- show the relationship between power and dependence;
- diagnose the extent, location, and types of power in an organization;
- cite causes of powerlessness and strategies for empowering others;
- discuss the role of informal networks, alliances, and trade relations in securing power;
- offer ways of securing more power and discuss the ethical issues involved;
- compare and contrast the distributive and integrative bargaining paradigms;
- outline the negotiating process; and
- specify the major issues for effective cross-cultural negotiation.

Using Power in Negotiations at Eastern Airlines

The strike by Eastern Airlines employees in March, 1989, drew national attention, and was blamed for the demise of a major airline. Eastern's machinists voted to strike and were joined on the picket lines by the airline's pilots and flight attendants, who also walked off the job. These employees were willing to send the airline into bankruptcy and lose their jobs rather than continue to work for Frank Lorenzo: "We're just not going to live under the continued pressure of Mr. Lorenzo," stated one of the pilots.[1] The airline pilots were viewed as key to the ability of Eastern to weather the strike and hence to the strike's effectiveness. " 'I would say, if the pilots support the strike in a hardcore way, the assets of Eastern Airlines will change hands fast and at distressed prices,' said one New York analyst who follows the airline and its parent, Texas Air Corp."[2]

A request by the employees for President Bush to intervene by ordering a special emergency board to halt the strike was denied. As of June 15, 1989, the Eastern Shuttle had been sold to Donald Trump, and Frank Lorenzo was attempting to operate a substantially smaller Eastern Airlines.

Why did the machinists strike? Why was Eastern Airlines unable to continue operating when they did strike? Who controlled the future of the airline? Why? Who had the most influence over these decisions? Did the machinists? the pilots? Frank Lorenzo? President Bush?

Power is the potential or actual ability to influence others in a desired direction; it is "the ability to get things done the way one wants them to be done."[3] Did the machinists' union have the power to shut down Eastern? Did the pilots or flight attendants have power? Did Frank Lorenzo? Did President Bush? Did the flying public?

The process of negotiation has also received significant attention from researchers and practitioners. *Negotiation* is a process for reconciling different, often incompatible, interests of interdependent parties. While union and management typically engage in formal negotiations, managers and employees often negotiate more informally—about work assignments, salary, schedules, and budgets, for example. Implicit in successful negotiations is the ability to recognize, use, and deal with power differences. Were the machinists, pilots, Frank Lorenzo, or President Bush involved in negotiations? How did they use the negotiating process to deal with the attempts of the individuals and groups to influence Eastern's operations?

In this chapter we examine power and negotiations. We begin by considering the reasons individuals or groups exert power. We then examine the sources from which they derive power. Next we examine the use of negotiation. We describe two bargaining paradigms, the negotiation process, and strategies and tactics of negotiations. We conclude with cross-cultural issues in negotiation in organizations.

POWER IN THE ORGANIZATION

Organizational researchers have increasingly cited the value of identifying and using power behavior to improve individual and organizational performance.[4] Theorists and practitioners have translated an early view of power, which considered it evil and mainly stemming from coercion,[5] into a model of viable political action in organizations. Yet, while functional and advantageous in many situations, power behavior can also create conflict, which frequently is dysfunctional for the organization, as in the introductory case.

Different individuals and groups within and outside the organization can exert power. Individual employees, including top and middle management, technical analysts and specialists, support staff, and other nonmanagerial workers can influence the actions an organization takes to reach its goals. Formal groups of employees, such as various departments, work teams, management councils, task forces, or employee unions; as well as informal groups, such as workers with offices near each other or those who see each other socially, can similarly exercise power. In addition to individuals or groups within the organization, nonemployees may try to influence the behavior of an organization and its members. Owners, suppliers, clients, competitors, employee associations (e.g., unions and professional associations), the general public, and the board of directors may exert power that affects the organization.[6]

Individuals can exert influence in a variety of ways.[7] They may exert regular, ongoing influence, such as when managers demonstrate authority over subordinates. Or they can attempt to influence periodically, when unique circumstances occur, such as at the expiration of a labor contract or a change in the economic or technological environment. Influence can focus on specific individuals, groups, or even events, or occur more generally, with the entire work situation as a target. Some individuals use charisma or a network of contacts to create personal influence, while others try to influence rules, regulations, policies, and procedures rather than individuals. Influence attempts also vary in their formality: calling a meeting to discuss and resolve a major organizational problem differs from trying to handle it informally over coffee, in the hallways, or otherwise without systematic planning and implementation. Finally, influence attempts can be constructive or destructive. How would you characterize the situation at Eastern?

Society as a whole and individuals outside the organization attempt to influence organizational behavior by using existing or developing social norms, imposing formal constraints, conducting pressure campaigns, instituting direct controls on the organization, or obtaining membership on a board of directors.[8]

Who exerts power in the situation described in the opening scenario? Does the head of the machinists' union? Does the head of the pilots' union? Does the head of the flight attendants' union? Does Frank Lorenzo? Does the Federal Mediation Board? We can begin our diagnosis of power by identifying those exerting influence.

POWER AND DEPENDENCE

How can power be assessed? One way is by measuring the extent or force of the dependence that flows in the opposite direction from power in a relationship. In other words, the power that A has over B is determined by the degree of dependence that B has on A. Why do individuals initiate an act of power? Their job-related dependence may cause individuals to do so.

Nature of Dependence

Dependence arises in part because a person, group, or organization relies on another person, group, or organization to accomplish his, her, or its tasks. It may also arise for other reasons, such as a previous history of assistance by one person, or a psychological reliance by one person on another. A subordinate depends on his or her boss for directions and resources. A supervisor in turn depends on his or her subordinates for assistance in accomplishing tasks and identifying obstacles to achieving a work group's goal. The person being relied or depended on automatically has some power—potential or actual ability to influence the other. Individuals who are dependent attempt to secure power to neutralize their dependence on others.

What types of dependence does Frank Lorenzo have? Among others, he relies on the machinists and pilots for the functioning of Eastern and hence in part for his compensation. He also depends on the flying public to continue to purchase tickets on Eastern. What dependences does the machinists' union show? Its leaders depend on the support of the machinists in agreeing to their strike strategy and for continuing to vote them into office. They also rely on the pilots' union to support any walkout by the machinists. The machinists themselves depend on their union leadership for high quality decisions and negotiations with management. They also depend on the support of the pilots for their jobs. Each of these groups, then, has some degree of power over the others. And each group attempts to secure more power for itself to neutralize the power of others that accompanies their dependence.

Now consider a job you have held. On whom did you depend in performing your work? Did you depend on your boss, your coworkers, customers, or maybe the owner of the company?

A job holder's dependence depends on characteristics of the organization and its environment.[9] Dependence increases as an organization becomes larger and causes greater reliance on specialization resulting from division of labor. As the uncertainty of the environment increases or an organization's dependence on it grows, managers also become more dependent on others to facilitate environmental interactions, thus reducing their relative power compared to others. As an organization's goals become more ambitious, managers become more dependent on others involved in coordinating their actions to accomplish these goals, and need to find ways to increase their power. Technology also contributes to dependence by increasing specialization and hence managers' dependence on specialists. Finally, dependence is a function of the formal structure, measurement systems, and reward systems in organizations. For example, diffusing authority throughout an organization, to individuals other than the managers, creates greater managerial dependencies and calls for power behavior by the managers.

Dealing with Dependence

Individuals engage in power-oriented behavior to reduce their dependence on others, as mentioned above. (They also try to increase the dependence of others on them, thus increasing their own relative power.[10]) A technician who must rely on his or her boss for pay raises may reduce this dependence by developing power as a result of becoming indispensable, perhaps by acquiring unique expertise or knowledge. Similarly, a director of purchasing may attempt to reduce his or her dependence on a supplier by finding alternate sources of goods or services. The divisional sales manager may reduce his or her dependence on a single salesperson by ensuring that another salesperson knows the products and territory sufficiently well to act as a replacement if necessary.

As the number of job-related dependencies increases, a manager (or other employee) increases the time and energy he or she devotes to power-oriented behavior.[11] To cope with dependence, managers draw from one or more bases of power and establish trade relations and alliances, described later in this chapter. A technician, for example, may attempt to acquire unique knowledge, charisma, or special information as bases of power; a director of research may collect, analyze, and control information about product trends or technological innovations. A manager may generate power over others by creating a sense of obligation in them, building their belief in his or her expertise, encouraging them to identify with the manager, or making others feel or be dependent on the manager for resources.[12]

Diagnosing dependence is a key step in understanding and using power. A power-dependence analysis involves asking the following questions:

1. Whom do you really depend on? How important is each dependency? What is the basis of each dependency?
2. Are any of these dependencies obviously inappropriate or dysfunctional? If so, what has created that pattern of dependence?
3. How much effective power-oriented behavior do you engage in? Is it enough to cope well with the dependencies in the job?
4. Does the manner in which you generate or use power have any negative consequences for the organization? If so, exactly what are they?[13]

Consider once more the introductory scenario. Can you do a power-dependence analysis for this situation? Although the data presented in the introductory scenario are limited, a manager's information at hand is also incomplete and imperfect. Figure 9–1 offers two examples of possible dependence diagrams. They show dependence in only a single direction, although obviously some degree of mutual dependence exists. According to these diagrams, who has the greatest need to exert power on an ongoing basis? Frank Lorenzo, as shown here, relies on the most constituencies. He typically uses many sources of power to reduce his dependence. But the dependence of the machinists increased recently. In normal circumstances they have less dependence on union leaders and pilots—and even on Frank Lorenzo. Because they have increased their dependence, they have also increased their need to exert power. Threatening and then conducting a strike, as well as building alliances with pilots, are two ways of increasing power and reducing dependence.

Now consider other people to whom we typically attribute power: the President of the United States, or the head of a large corporation. What would their dependence diagrams look like? What would their power-dependence analyses reveal?

Figure 9–1 DEPENDENCE DIAGRAMS FOR EASTERN AIRLINES

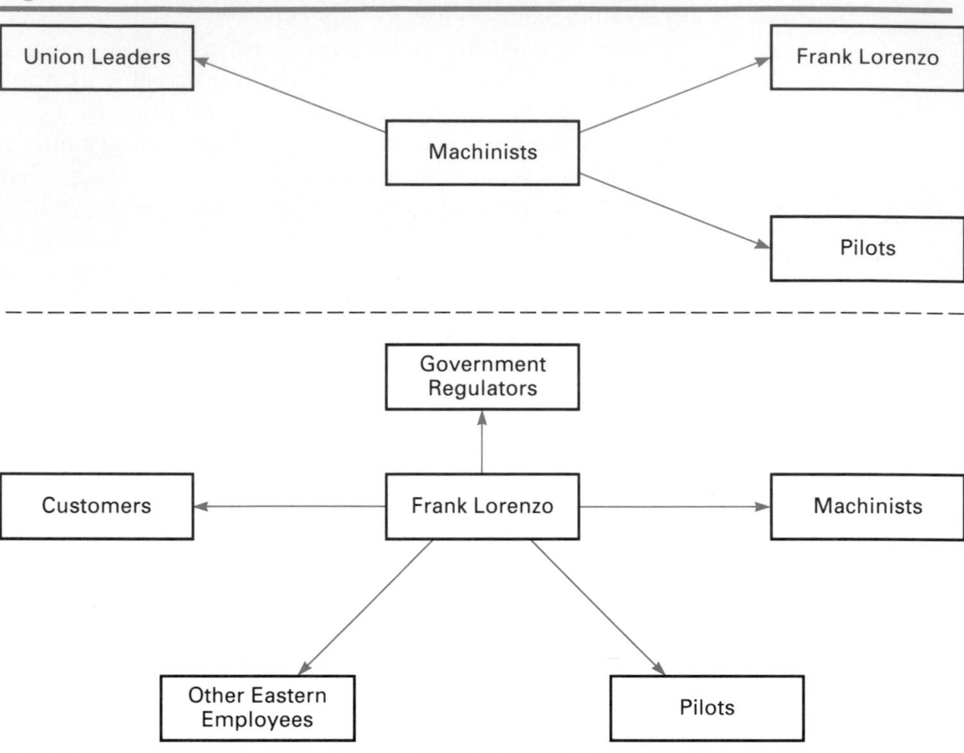

POWER AS EXCHANGE

Recent definitions of power have described it as a property of a social relationship. Historically power has been defined in terms of exchange processes[14]: one person, who commands services needed by others, exchanges them for compliance with his or her requests. For example, a supervisor exchanges time off for high quality performance by workers. Or management concedes to union demands to avoid a strike. Note that viewing power as a function of ties of dependence or interdependence is describing an exchange relationship in another way.[15] For example, a supervisor often has power because subordinates depend on him or her for rewards—the supervisor exchanges rewards for good performance. In the exchange relationship, each party exercises a kind of power by providing something of value to the other.

A social exchange network exists when an individual or group negotiates with another over the allocation of valued resources.[16] Consider the resources top management at Eastern has available to exchange with the mechanics for their services. Now consider the resources the mechanics have available to exchange with the pilots for their support in the negotiations. (We discuss the control of resources as a source of power in greater detail later in this chapter.)

INDIVIDUAL NEEDS FOR POWER

A third way of viewing power looks at individual needs for power (described in Chapter 4). The *need for power* is an individual motivator that causes a person to seek and build power.[17] You may recall that individuals with a high need for power try to influence and control others, seek leadership positions in groups, enjoy persuading others, and are perceived by others as outspoken, forceful, and demanding.[18] Often politicians, top managers, or informal leaders are perceived as having a high need for power. Do any individuals in the opening case have a high need for power? While the case does not provide sufficient data for us to answer this question, we may conjecture that some union leaders and some members of Eastern management have, among other needs, a need for power. We must gather additional data to verify their needs, as well as those of the machinists, pilots, flight attendants, and even members of the regulatory agencies.

Two types of men demonstrate a need for power. (Although the research did not include women, realistically either sex could be either type.) The first type has a *personal* and *individualistic* emphasis in his need for power. He "strives for dominance. He is the impulsive tough guy. He may be rude, fight with others, boast of sexual conquest and try to exploit women. Such men tend to reject institutional responsibility and hate to join organizations."[19] These individuals influence subordinates to be responsible to them personally rather than organizational relationships as a whole.

The second type, in contrast, has a need for power with a strong *social* and *institutional* theme. He focuses on organizational commitment for himself and subordinates by trying to create "a good climate for regular work. His subordinates have both a sense of responsibility and a clear knowledge of the organization." Loyal to the organization, "they are less defensive and more willing, when they need it, to seek expert advice in personal matters. They collect fewer status symbols."[20] This kind of loyalty improves their performance, from the organization's viewpoint.

Diagnosis of the two specific types of individuals in an organization may allow us to predict their power behavior and its consequences for organizational performance. We would predict, for example, that individuals high in need for power would more likely look for opportunities to exert power than individuals high in other needs. Similarly, the machinists' union and Eastern's management might both work more effectively if they include primarily social or institutional-power types (the second type above) rather than personal-power types (the first type above).

Note that power is not limited to individuals. Subunits such as organizational departments and work teams can also exercise power; and we can diagnose the power of subunits just as we do for individuals.

POWER RELATIONS

Most of the influence attempts described so far are directed downward in the organization. Managers, for example, can give direct orders to subordinates, establish guidelines for their decision making, approve or reject their decisions, or allocate resources to them.

But lateral influence can also occur: peers can offer advice or provide service. Peers may also use influence to control others: to audit or determine the acceptability of others' work; or to stabilize or specify what is permitted from others.[21]

Individuals can also exert upward influence, typically to promote or protect their self-interest.[22] They can control the type of information passed to superiors; and may consciously withhold information they feel is detrimental to themselves. Occasionally workers punish or reward their superiors, by either withholding or providing a quality work effort, for example. Managing the boss effectively requires understanding and responding to his or her needs.[23]

Influence attempts between entities at the same level, such as functional departments, line and staff groups, or labor and management, often result in competition.[24] The parties often resort to power struggles, which result from the tendency to try to strengthen one's own power vis-à-vis the other party's. As two parties' interdependence increases, they can afford conflict less and less. Thus they may come to rely on negotiation and cooperation, rather than a power struggle, to resolve their differences.

Powerlessness

Powerlessness in organizations can occur as a result of various organizational factors, such as characteristics of the reward system, aspects of job design, and the style of a supervisor.[25] Significant organizational changes, excessive competition, an impersonal bureaucratic climate, or poor communications can contribute to a member's powerlessness. Lack of either competence-based or innovation-based rewards, or unappealing rewards, can also inspire such feelings. Jobs with low task variety, unrealistic goals, too many rules, few opportunities for advancement, or lack of appropriate resources breed powerlessness. Finally, an authoritarian supervisor who emphasizes failure or lacks reasons for his or her actions exacerbates such a situation.

Rosabeth Moss Kanter argues that women in management have experienced powerlessness because of a combination of formal and informal practices that put them into low-power positions.[26] (These same practices extend to men.) Symptoms of powerlessness include a job holder receiving overly close supervision, being rules-minded and overly concerned with routines, and doing all the work him- or herself.[27]

Managers can contribute to the powerlessness of a job holder, particularly when it is a woman, in five ways.[28] First, they may patronizingly overprotect her; by failing to suggest her for high-risk, visible assignments, for example. Men are given the opportunity to turn around failing ventures; women are not. Second, managers may fail to provide signs of managerial support. They may listen only to negative comments about a female employee and thus invite others to look for her failings. Third, they may assume that a woman does not know the ropes. Fourth, they may ignore women in informal socializing. Finally, they may fail to provide organizational supports by not sharing power with women. As a result of these tendencies, the training of women has focused on overcoming power deficits and equalizing their influence in the workplace.

There are national differences in the extent to which less powerful members of organizations accept the unequal distribution of power.[29] In the higher power-distance countries, where employees accept that their boss has more power than they (Venezuela, Colombia, and the Philippines, e.g.), bypassing superiors is considered insubordination. In low power-distance countries (e.g., New Zealand, Norway, and Austria) bypassing one's boss is acceptable.

Acquiescence is a response frequently used by individuals in powerless jobs, and women use it more often than men.[30] Acquiescers fail to realize that they can use the more powerful strategies of negotiation, coalition formation, and persuasion in these situations.

Empowering Others

Recent research suggests that individuals often can increase their own power by sharing it with others.[31] Managers can facilitate this sharing by helping subordinates, in particular, to tap into the sources of power described in this chapter. Managers can also give empowering information, such as by providing emotional support, offering words of encouragement and facilitating successful mastery of a task; and serve as role models.[32] Other strategies for a manager include providing a positive emotional atmosphere, rewarding staff achievements in visible and personal ways, expressing confidence in subordinates' abilities, fostering initiative and responsibility, and building on success.[33] Reading 9–1, "Leadership: The Art of Empowering Others," discusses these strategies in more detail.

What gives the people at Eastern Airlines the ability to influence others in the direction they desire? They derive their power from the following sources (see Figure 9–2): (1) the position they hold, (2) their personal characteristics, (3) the resources or information they can access and control, and (4) any informal networks, trade relations, or alliances they form.

Ethical Issues

How legitimate is the use of power in organizations? Certainly the Machiavellian view of power, with its manipulative and autocratic connotations, raises questions about the ethics of power. Likewise the abuse of power, a favorite

Figure 9–2 SOURCES OF POWER

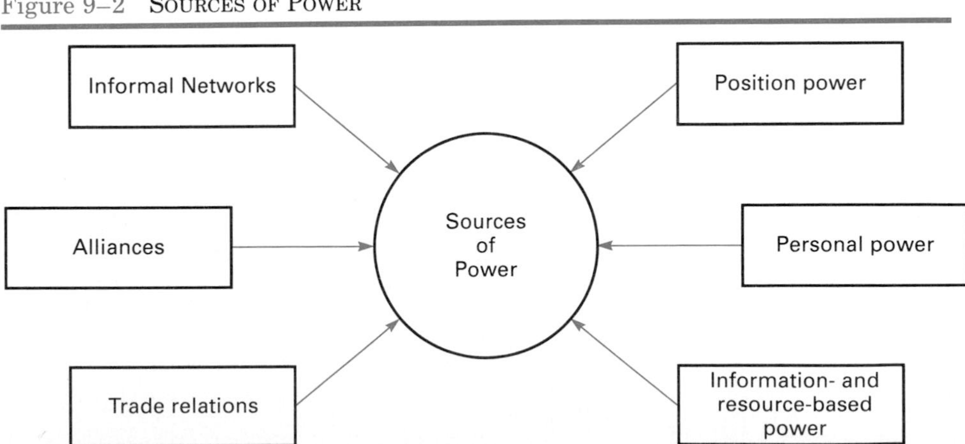

in political arenas, raises ethical issues. Remember Richard Nixon's Watergate scandal or the earlier Teapot Dome scandal in Warren Harding's administration?

But the use of power has been encouraged in organizations, so long as it does not abuse the rights of others. It helps managers attain organizational goals, facilitate their own and others' accomplishments, and expedites effective competition in the workplace. Power, when viewed as potential or actual influence, is an essential part of effective leadership and management.

Managers must establish guidelines for the ethical use of power in their organizations. They and other organizational members must emphasize its contribution to organizational effectiveness and control its abuses. Ensuring that the rights of all organizational members are guaranteed is one criterion for its ethical use.

POSITION POWER

Individuals frequently derive power from the position or job they hold in an organization (see Figure 9–3).

Authority

Possessing *legitimate* power, managers can exert influence over others simply because of the authority associated with their jobs. Frank Lorenzo had such power. It resulted in his subordinates obeying rules or orders he gave them because they viewed them as legitimate due to the position he held. Lower level supervisors can also have authority that gives them power. Such job

Figure 9–3 POSITION POWER

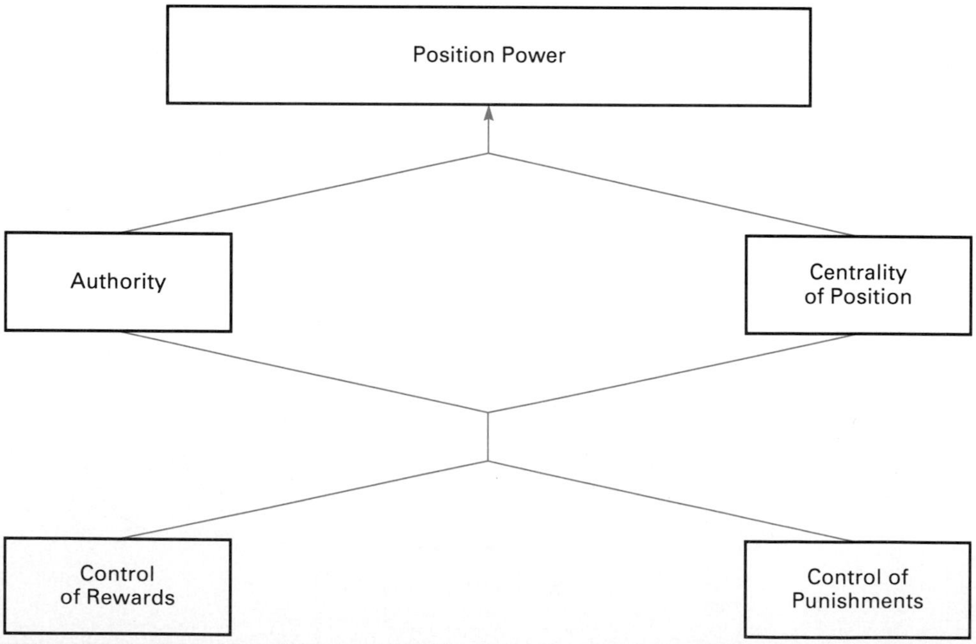

holders provide direction for and control over the work done by their subordinates simply because of their relative position in the hierarchy. Who at Eastern does not have power due to their position? Clearly the machinists cannot use the authority of their position as a source of power.

Centrality

Other positions accrue power because of their *centrality*. The more the activities of a position are linked and important to those of other individuals or subunits, the greater their centrality.[34] A superintendent of schools, for example, has greater centrality than the school committee, because the activities of more jobs are linked to him or her than to the elected officials. Sometimes a job that lacks official authority can develop position power because it becomes central to other positions. The administrative assistant to the chief executive officer of a company can develop such centrality. Consider too the position power of the Chief of Staff to the President of the United States. While he (or she, in the future) has some power because of his place in the hierarchy, he also becomes the gatekeeper (see Chapter 7) to the President and accrues power because of his centrality.

Control of Rewards and Punishments

Individuals with position power frequently add to their authority because they control the delivery of rewards in an organization. An individual who has control over organizational *rewards,* including pay raises, status, and desirable work assignments as well as praise, recognition, or group sanctions, may use them to encourage compliance to desired behaviors or goals by others.

A manager might also force individuals to behave in certain ways by punishing them. He or she might demote or dismiss them, increase the directions provided to them, or withhold compensation or promotions. A manager uses this power effectively if his or her subordinates believe that obeying the manager will result in the receipt of extrinsic or intrinsic rewards. Frank Lorenzo and the other managers at Eastern Airlines have some reward and punishment power, since they influence the hiring, promotion, and compensation of various employees. The machinists and pilots have control over neither.

PERSONAL POWER

Personal power is based on the knowledge or personality of an individual that allows him or her to influence the behavior of others (see Figure 9–4).

Expertise

An individual who has unique or special knowledge, skills, and experience may use this expertise as a source of influence and as a way of building personal power. A physician can influence patients to act in certain ways because he or she exerts expert power when giving advice based on medical knowledge. A computer specialist can influence nontechnical staff to act in ways he or she desires because of the special knowledge he or she has that may be critical to

Figure 9–4 PERSONAL POWER

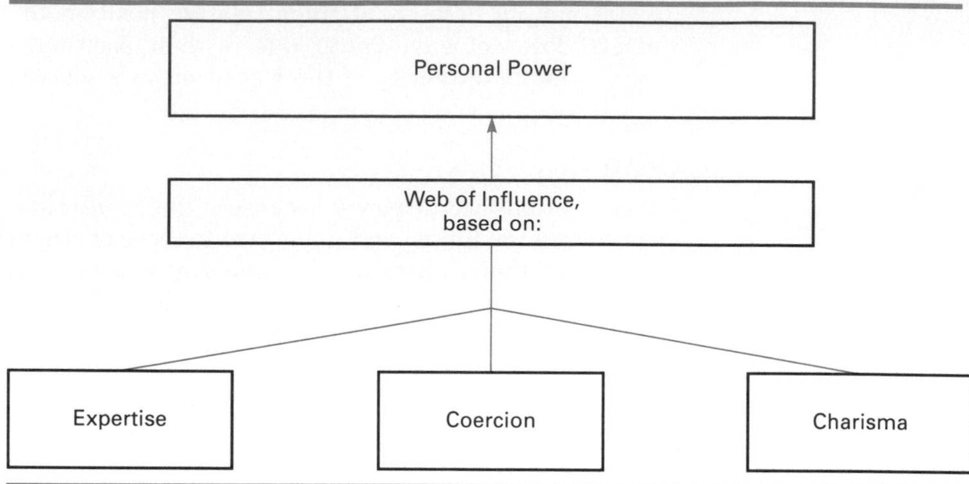

the rest of the staff. As organizations have become increasingly technology-oriented, computer specialists and other technical workers have acquired greater power. Likewise, the director of research in a public school system may use his or her unique knowledge about enrollment trends to influence staffing patterns or the allocation of other resources.

Charisma

Some individuals influence others because they have charisma or others identify with them. An individual with charisma often exerts power because he or she attracts others to follow. A movie star, politician, or any organizational member with a charismatic personality may use this base of power. A person who identifies with another person can be influenced by that individual; and the person being identified with exerts power.

Does anyone in the introductory scenario have charismatic power? To precisely assess use of this source, we would have to observe the individuals in person or otherwise gather more data about their personalities and behaviors.

Coercion

A manager who exerts power over someone because that person fears him or her uses *coercive power*. Frank Lorenzo could threaten to replace any striking workers, take the airline into bankruptcy, or sell the components of the airline, and thus had coercive power. Can you think of other individuals you know who exert such power? How effectively do they influence behavior in a direction they desire?

The use of coercive power often has secondary, dysfunctional consequences. It can create ongoing stress and anxiety for workers. In extreme cases it can encourage them to increase absenteeism, rate of turnover, and even sabotage in the workplace. Job holders who use other sources of power often wield greater influence than those who rely solely on coercive power.

RESOURCE- AND INFORMATION-BASED POWER

Access to resources or information provides a source of influence. This differs from expert power in its greater transience: expertise is more permanent than information-based power. However, the first individuals to learn to use a new computer system, for example, may provide rapid assistance to other organizational members and thus secure both resource- and information-based power.

Control of Resources and Information

Power may also come from the control of scarce resources, such as the allocation of money, materials, staff, or information. Individuals who formulate rules to regulate the possession of resources, as well as those who actually possess, allocate, and use the resources, acquire power.[35] A person who determines or administers a budget controls resources and secures power. Workers who control the scheduling of prized machinery or allocation of computer equipment can also acquire resource-based power. The power of organizational subunits, such as individual managers, union leaders, or the executive committee, is a function of their ability to cope with uncertainty and their unsubstitutability, among other things. In addition, a unit's centrality may interact with its power and its ability to acquire internal resources in an organization.[36]

Individuals also implement power by making choices in the identification and use of resources, along three dimensions: (1) internal-external, (2) vertical-lateral, and (3) legitimate-illegitimate.[37] Along the internal-external dimension, people may rely on resources internal to the organization, such as exchanging favors or forming networks with other employees. When these sources fail or become inadequate, individuals may turn outside the organization for resources, such as by joining professional organizations or forming alliances outside the organization.

The vertical-lateral dimension refers to individuals exerting influence through relating to superiors or subordinates, as opposed to peers. Mentor-protege activities occur vertically; coalition formation occurs laterally.

The third dimension contrasts normal and extreme behavior. For example, most organizational members view forming coalitions as legitimate and sabotaging production as illegitimate. Which strategies do individuals and groups at Eastern Airlines use? Are they effective?

Coping with Uncertainty

Some organizational members help others reduce uncertainty in the workplace caused by unclear task demands, a rapidly changing environment, introduction of new technology, or an ambiguous organizational structure. Managers or nonmanagerial employees who can reduce the ambiguity in these and other uncertain situations may acquire power. Employees in a chemical plant who know the relevant regulations of the Environmental Protection Agency may secure information-based power. So may managers who acquire information about pending layoffs, introduction of new technology, or budget shortfalls. Consider an agency in state government that experiences a 15 percent budget cutback. The manager who knows which, if any, workers will lose their jobs because of the deficit and arranges for transfers or retraining for them helps them cope with uncertainty. Or consider the role a research and development department can play in bringing a new technology "on-line" in a company. The department's members can not only educate workers to its use but modify it to meet product demands and organizational needs. This department would gain power, not only from their expertise but from their ability to use it to help other members clarify the significance of, and respond effectively to, environmental and organizational changes. In general, the more an individual or group copes with uncertainty, the more power it has.

Boundary-spanner roles (see Chapters 7 and 11 for further discussion) have significant power potential. Individuals in such roles as public relations director or purchasing agent deal with the outside environment for the benefit of the organization's members. Their ability to cope with uncertainty for others is one source of power; the ability to channel or control information going to the organization's members is another. Identification of boundary spanners and diagnosis of their effectiveness in this role, then, are important means of assessing power in organizations.

Who copes with uncertainty in the Eastern Airlines situation? The union leaders try to reduce uncertainty for their members by presenting the options clearly and completely. The union can also pass rules and regulations, allocate its funds, and clarify its procedures for such decisions as employee strikes. Frank Lorenzo could also reduce uncertainty, by meeting the union's demands or consistently maintaining his stance. President Bush also had the potential for exerting power by reducing uncertainty: he could have invoked emergency provisions that would have halted the strike (at least temporarily).

Unsubstitutability

In general, the less substitutable the activities of an individual or group in an organization, the more power it has. Consider an organization in which you have worked. Who or which group performed activities that no one else could readily perform? The president was probably less substitutable than a clerical worker. The chief financial officer may have been more substitutable than the director of product development. The MIS or EDP departments might also have been unsubstitutable because of their unique knowledge. A unit that can bring resources into the organization from the outside may also have low substitutability.

Who in the Eastern situation has power because of their lack of substitutability? The pilots likely have this power: they are difficult to replace. The machinists might also derive some power from this source. How substitutable is Frank Lorenzo? Of course, unsubstitutability as a source of power interacts with other sources, affecting the relative power of each person or group involved in the Eastern situation.

The use of power can have positive consequences when the person who controls information or resources gives related job holders open access to them. Political alliances with sponsors, peers, and subordinates (described later in this chapter) can also facilitate the effective sharing of power.

In the introductory case, which job holders have access to resources? Certainly Frank Lorenzo has information about the actual financial situation at Eastern, some of which is also known by the union. The union leaders have information about the employees' willingness to strike and the national union's willingness and ability to pay strike benefits.

INFORMAL NETWORKS, TRADE RELATIONS, AND ALLIANCES

Individuals and groups can acquire power by increasing their contacts with others. They can build informal networks, create trade relations, and foster alliances.

Informal Networks

Informal networks play a significant role in the exercise of power. The operation of the informal network may result in transfer of legitimate authority from a supervisor to an influential subordinate. To identify an informal network, we can ask the following questions:

1. Who has relevant information?
2. To whom does that person communicate the information?
3. How many others have access to it?
4. What potential sources of power exist in the team?

Trade Relations

Reciprocity and lateral exchange form trade relationships that contribute to the accrual and exercise of power. Managers typically participate in trade relationships with lateral network members to get their jobs done.[38] Consider the head of the machinists' union at Eastern. What peers are indispensable to his influence attempts? Certainly he (or she, in the future) must engage the support of the head of the pilots' union if negotiations are to succeed. The head of the machinists' union must provide services to the pilots in exchange for services the pilots will provide. Managers can further enhance their power, compared to the others', in the trade relationship in four ways.[39] First, their reputation for making things happen increases support. Second, alliances add to their power to attain results. Third, the position a manager holds can further empower him or her. Fourth, a manager can develop a favored standing vis-à-vis other peers and thus increase his or her power. Can the head of the machinists' union gain more power in any of these ways? Certainly these leaders should have developed networks of peers that can now be called on to help attain their purpose.

Alliances

Forming alliances addresses the issue of finding a way to create influence without having or using formal authority.[40] Such alliances can be organized as a *coalition,* "an interacting group of individuals, deliberately constructed, independent of formal structure, lacking its own internal formal structure, consisting of mutually perceived membership, issue oriented, focused on a goal or goals external to the coalition, and requiring concerted member action."[41] At Eastern Airlines a coalition of machinists and pilots formed to strengthen their influence on Frank Lorenzo. These individuals created their own structure of striking workers. Together they focused on goals of improving pay and working conditions for the machinists and took the concerted action of a strike. Coalitions such as these interact around issues and respond with joint action.

But alliances between two or more individuals also form when they have resources or favors to exchange. Such reciprocity can occur among peers, between supervisors and subordinates, or among members of different organizations. They might exchange any of the currencies shown in Table 9–1. In making any exchange, a person using influence needs to view the other as a potential ally and understand his or her world; the influencer must also know how to use exchange, focus on effectiveness, and use a repertoire of influence approaches.[42]

Allies frequently join into a coalition to support a mutual interest, as described previously. They bring their larger pool of resources to the situations, including greater expertise and commitment. They often act politically to support or oppose an organizational program, policy, or change.[43] Negotiations play a major role in their actions.

Table 9–1 COMMONLY TRADED ORGANIZATIONAL CURRENCIES

Inspiration-Related Currencies	
Vision	Being involved in a task that has larger significance for the unit, organization, customers, or society.
Excellence	Having a chance to do important things really well.
Moral/Ethical Correctness	Doing what is "right" by a higher standard than efficiency.
Task-Related Currencies	
Resources	Lending or giving money, budget increases, personnel, space, and so forth.
Assistance	Helping with existing projects or undertaking unwanted tasks.
Cooperation	Giving task support, providing quicker response time, approving a project, or aiding implementation.
Information	Providing organizational as well as technical knowledge.
Position-Related Currencies	
Advancement	Giving a task or assignment that can aid in promotion.
Recognition	Acknowledging effort, accomplishment, or abilities.
Visibility	Providing chance to be known by higher-ups or significant others in the organization.
Reputation	Enhancing the way a person is seen.
Importance/Insiderness	Offering a sense of importance, of "belonging."
Network/Contacts	Providing opportunities for linking with others.

Table 9–1 CONTINUED

Relationship-Related Currencies	
Acceptance/Inclusion	Providing closeness and friendship.
Personal Support	Giving personal and emotional backing.
Understanding	Listening to others' concerns and issues.
Personal-Related Currencies	
Self-Concept	Affirming one's values, self-esteem, and identity.
Challenge/Learning	Sharing tasks that increase skills and abilities.
Ownership/Involvement	Letting others have ownership and influence.
Gratitude	Expressing appreciation or indebtedness.

Reprinted, by permission of publisher, from A.R. Cohen and D.L. Bradford, Influence without authority: The use of alliances, reciprocity, and exchange to accomplish work, *Organizational Dynamics* (1988): 11. © 1988. American Management Association, New York.

Let us look at the introductory scenario again. What types of power do the people have? Figure 9–5 summarizes the sources of power each person or group probably uses. Note that the individuals and groups use multiple sources of power. Generally, however, some sources are viewed as having a greater effect than others. Typically the more bases of power an individual can draw on, the more powerful that person is.

Figure 9–5 SOURCES OF POWER AT EASTERN AIRLINES

Union Leaders

Authority
Centrality
Expertise
Charisma
Control of information

Frank Lorenzo

Authority
Centrality
Control of rewards and punishments
Expertise
Coercion
Access to resources
Coping with uncertainty

Machinists

Expertise

Pilots

Expertise
Coping with uncertainty
Unsubstitutability

President Bush

Authority
Centrality
Control of rewards and punishments
Expertise
Charisma
Coercion
Access to resources
Coping with uncertainty

As part of our assessment of power in any situation, then, we can check, for each source of power, the following:

1. For whom does that source provide power?
2. Do the sources used fit with features of the organizational situation?
3. What changes should be made to increase the fit?

An observer must recognize that characteristics of the manager, his or her subordinates, and the organization may influence the appropriate source from which to draw power.

USE OF NEGOTIATION

"Negotiation is a process in which two or more parties, who have both common interests and conflicting interests, put forth and discuss explicit proposals concerning specific terms of a possible agreement."[44] The two or more parties attempt to reach an agreement that is acceptable to both (or all).

Negotiations typically have four key elements.[45] First, the parties involved in negotiating demonstrate some degree of *interdependence*. At Eastern, Lorenzo relied on the machinists to keep the airline functioning; the machinists depended on Lorenzo for their employment with acceptable wages and benefits. Power, as discussed earlier in this chapter, influences the nature of interdependence and the relative ability of each party to exercise its preferences. Second, *some perceived conflict* exists between the parties involved in the negotiations. The machinists and Frank Lorenzo differed in their view of the way Eastern's financial resources should be allocated; they also differed in their perspective about where decision-making authority should reside. Third, the parties have the potential to participate in *opportunistic interaction*. In other words, each party tries to influence the other through various negotiating actions. Each party cares about and pursues its own interests by trying to influence decisions to its advantage. Finally, the *possibility of agreement* exists.

In what types of negotiations have you participated? You may have negotiated an increase in salary from your employer. You may have negotiated a different grade from a professor. You may have read about negotiations between union and management, as in the introduction to this chapter.

In the political arena, as in the introductory scenario, bargaining and negotiations are particularly important. Interest groups and political parties use power to influence authorities to give them what they want.[46] How often do we think that political figures concern themselves more with power development than with their management responsibilities?[47]

In negotiating, managers or other organizational members choose a strategy that reflects their level of concern for their own and the other party's outcomes. Research suggests that a party with high concern about both parties' outcomes will take a problem-solving approach. A party with low concern about its own outcomes and high concern about the other party's will yield to the other. A party with high concern about its own outcomes and low concern about the other party's will contend for its own preferences. And a party with low concern about its own and the other's outcomes will not act at all.[48] Thus managers and other parties should recognize the range of negotiating styles available to them and the situations in which each style is likely to be used and appropriate.

BARGAINING PARADIGMS

The negotiating process demonstrates a fundamental tension between the *claiming* and *creating* of value.[49] Value claimers view negotiations purely as an adversarial process. Each side tries to *claim* as much of a limited "pie" as possible, by giving the other side as little as possible. Each party claims value through the use of manipulative tactics, forcible arguments, limited concessions, and hard bargaining.

In contrast, value creators call for a process that results in joint gains to each party. They try to *create* additional benefits for each side in the negotiations. They emphasize shared interests, developing a collaborative relationship, and negotiating in a pleasant, cooperative manner.

A negotiator incorporates these strategies, singly or in combination, in one of two basic paradigms. *Distributive bargaining* takes an adversarial or win-lose approach. *Integrative bargaining* takes a problem-solving or win-win approach.

Distributive Bargaining

The classical view of negotiation considers bargaining as a win-lose situation: one party's gain is the other party's loss. Known also as a zero-sum type of negotiation, because the gain for one party equals a loss for the other and hence adds up to zero, this approach characterizes the purchase of used cars, property, and various material goods in organizations. It has also been applied to salary negotiations and labor–management negotiations.

Distributive bargaining emphasizes the claiming of value. The choice of opening offers, the ability to influence the opponent to view the situation in a way favorable to the negotiator, and the careful planning of offers and counteroffers can influence the ability to claim value and win the negotiation. Power plays a key role in success in distributive bargaining, because it increases a party's leverage and ability to shape perceptions.

Integrative Bargaining

Recent research encourages negotiators to transform bargaining into a win-win situation.[50] Here both parties gain as a result of negotiations. Known also as a positive-sum type of negotiation, because the gains of each party yield a positive sum, this approach has recently characterized international negotiations, labor–management negotiations, and specific job-related bargaining. Integrative bargaining might have occurred at Eastern if the union were willing to give management more rights in whom to hire, fire, or assign to jobs, in exchange for higher pay. In other negotiations, management has been willing to give workers job security but smaller wage increments, resulting in gains to both management (lower wage costs) and workers (increased job security).

THE NEGOTIATION PROCESS

We can identify four basic steps in effective negotiation using either distributive or integrative bargaining. First, the parties *prepare* for the negotiations. Second, they determine their *best alternative* to a negotiated settlement. Third, they identify their own and the other party's *interests*. Fourth, they make *tradeoffs,* and in integrative bargaining attempt to create joint *gains* for the parties involved.

Preparation

Eastern's union and management began their preparation long before the time described in the introduction. Each gathered information about the other side—its history, members of the negotiating team and their likely behavior, previous settlements made by the parties. The union also likely gathered data about Eastern's financial situation, the options available to Frank Lorenzo, and the likelihood of the pilots' and flight attendants' joining them in the event of a strike. The management team probably tried to ascertain the union's likely demands, their ability to withstand a strike, and areas in which they might make concessions.

Top management should play a key role in planning for negotiations, particularly those with other companies. As summarized in Figure 9–6, top managers begin by identifying a negotiating goal and rallying the company behind it. They continue by building the negotiating team and preparing it for negotiations. This step includes collecting information, setting targets, and defining a framework for analyzing issues. Finally, top management may participate in or oversee the negotiation talks and announcement of the agreement. Assessing results ends the role of top management as shown in Figure 9–6; however, they are frequently responsible for or involved in implementation of the agreement afterward.

Evaluation of Alternatives

Each party must determine the range of acceptable agreements. The two sides attempt to identify the *bargaining range* and reach an agreement within it. Consider the issue of wages at Eastern Airlines. Assume the machinists want a \$4.-per-hour wage increase but will settle for \$3. Figure 9–7(A) illustrates their target price (\$4.) and resistance price (\$3.). Now assume Frank Lorenzo wants to pay \$1. more per hour, but is willing to pay \$2. more. (B) illustrates his target price (\$1.) and resistance price (\$2.). The *bargaining range* is the prices where both sides can satisfy their wishes; it is the overlap between the parties' resistance points. Figure (C) shows that no bargaining range exists for the machinists and Frank Lorenzo, given these resistance points. If, however, the union convinces Frank Lorenzo that their services are more valuable than he originally thought, he may raise his resistance point to \$3.50, as shown in (D). Then a bargaining range exists between \$3. and \$3.50.

Bargainers also determine the other options acceptable to them and identify their best alternative if a negotiated settlement is not reached. The machinists, for example, determined that striking was their best alternative, and they eventually resorted to it.

Figure 9–6 THE ROLE OF TOP MANAGEMENT IN NEGOTIATIONS

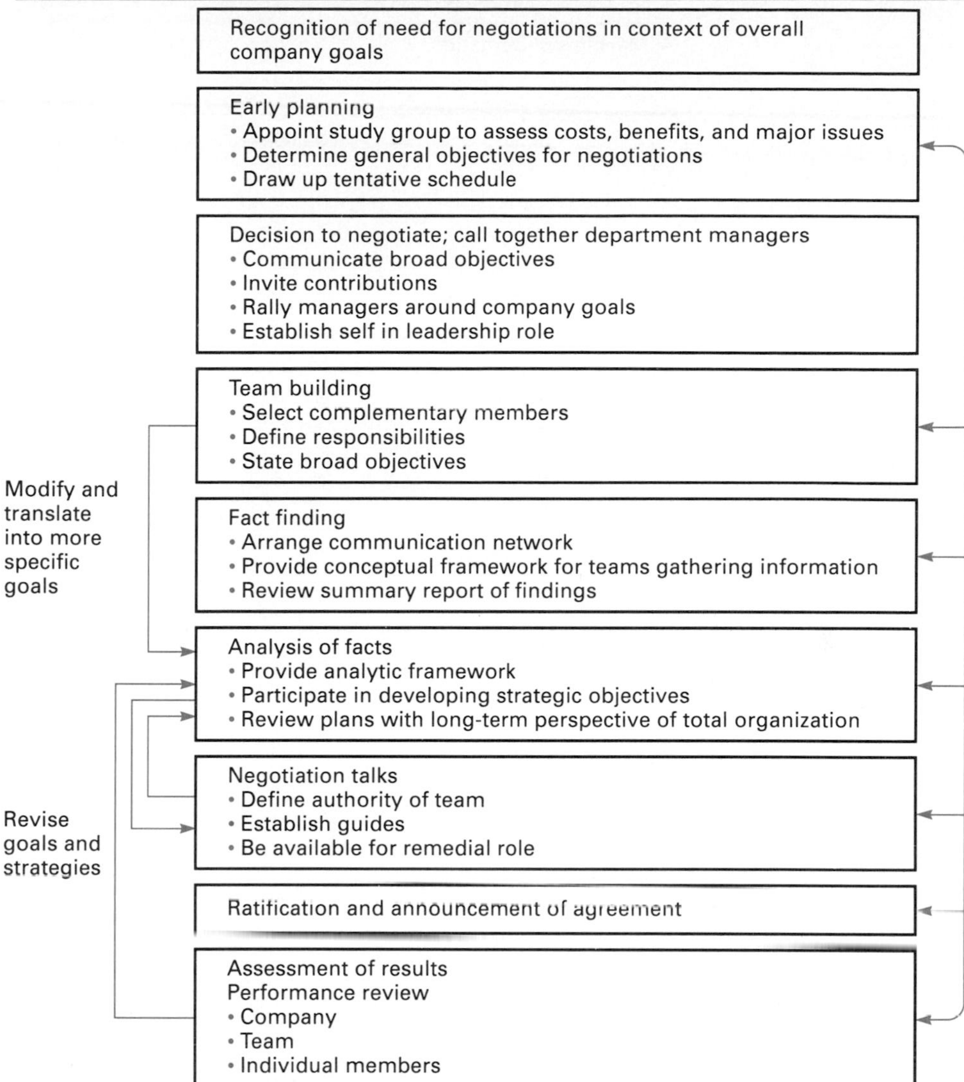

Reprinted with permission from J. Brooks and E. Brooks, The role of top management in negotiations, *MSU Business Topics* (Summer 1979): 81.

Identifying Interests

Negotiators act to satisfy their own interests. Often in doing so they ignore or simplify the views of their opponents, especially when forced to consider uncertain future events.[51] They must also assess the other party's interests and then decide how they will respond to them in their offers. Accurately assessing one's own and another party's interests is essential in effective negotiations.

Even though negotiators try to reach agreements on a specific position on a specific issue, more than one position may actually respond to their interests. Underlying interests are generally broader and may be satisfied with different positions. The machinists may argue for a specific wage increase, but their underlying aim may really be the removal of Frank Lorenzo as the owner of

Figure 9–7 HYPOTHETICAL BARGAINING RANGES FOR WAGE DEMANDS AT EASTERN AIRLINES

Eastern Airlines. Managers' interests can include their reputation, relationship with other parties, long-term organizational goals, various precedents, or even the bottom line. Effective negotiations call for satisfying interests by identifying and exploring a range of positions held on specific issues.

In assessing what interests are at stake, managers can use the following advice.[52] First, they should consider both tangible interests and subtler interests, such as reputation, fairness, and precedent. Second, they should separate interests from issues and positions. Third, they must recognize that interests may have either intrinsic or instrumental value. Fourth, they must understand that interests depend on perceptions, which are subjective. Fifth, they should note that interests and issues can change, intentionally or accidentally.

Making Tradeoffs and Creating Joint Gains

Bargainers use tradeoffs to satisfy their own and others' interests. Recent labor–management negotiations have traded wage increases for job security provisions. Either position would meet the interests of maintaining a certain standard of living. One way to assess tradeoffs is to begin by identifying the best and worst possible outcomes, to then specify possible increments that tradeoffs can reflect, and then to consider how the increments relate to the key issues.

In addition to making tradeoffs as a way of reaching a satisfactory negotiating outcome, integrative bargaining attempts to create gains for both parties. One party may offer something relatively less valuable to it but more valuable to the other party. The parties may build on shared interests. They may also use economies of scale to create joint gains.

In particular, both parties gain as a result of the following actions:

- Differences in *relative valuation* can lead to exchanges, directly or by "unbundling"—considering separately—differently valued interests.
- Differences in *forecasts* can lead to contingent agreements when (1) the items under negotiation are uncertain and themselves subject to different probability estimates, or (2) each party feels that it will fare well under and perhaps can influence a proposed contingent resolution procedure.
- Differences in *risk aversion* suggest insurancelike risk-sharing arrangements.
- Differences in *time preference* can lead to altered patterns of payments or actions over time.
- Different *capabilities* can be combined.
- Other differences (evaluation criteria, precedence and substance, constituencies, organizational situation, conceptions of fairness, etc.) can be fashioned into joint gains.
- *Mutually preferred positions* on single issues can create common value.
- *Shared interests* on a range of settlements can be made salient or linked to create common value.
- *Economies of scale* can lead to the creation of private and common value.[53]

NEGOTIATION STRATEGIES AND TACTICS

There are three common negotiation strategies: (1) competition, (2) collaboration, and (3) subordination, described in detail in Table 9–2. A party that uses the competitive strategy focuses on its own goals at the expense of the other party's. The individual or group may use secrecy, threats, or bluffs as a way of hiding its own goals and uncovering the other party's. This type of strategy frequently accompanies distributive bargaining.

The collaborative strategy emphasizes pursuing common goals held by the two parties. Typically used with integrative bargaining, this strategy calls for each party to accurately communicate its needs to the other. Both parties take a problem-solving approach and look for solutions that satisfy both parties.

The third strategy describes one party's subordinating its goals, or putting them after the other party's, to avoid conflict. This individual or group becomes overly concerned with the other's goals, rather than its own or both parties'.

Choice of a negotiating strategy may depend on (1) the desired relationship

Table 9–2 CHARACTERISTICS OF NEGOTIATION STRATEGIES

Competitive	Collaborative	Subordinative
1. Behavior is purposeful in pursuing own goals at the expense of the other party.	Behavior is purposeful in pursuing goals held in common with others.	One party consciously subordinates own goals to avoid conflict with other party.
2. Strategy involves secrecy and keeping one's cards close to the vest. It is characterized by high trust in one's self and low trust in the other party.	Strategy calls for trust and openness in expressing one's thoughts and feelings, actively listening to others, and actively exploring alternatives together.	Strategy means that one party is totally open to the extreme of exposing his or her vulnerabilities and weaknesses to the other.
3. Parties have accurate personal understanding of own needs, but publicly disguise or misrepresent them. Neither party lets the other know what it really wants most, so that the other won't know how much it is really willing to give up to attain the goal.	Parties have accurate personal understanding of own needs, and represent them accurately to the other party. Each party has empathy and cares about the needs of the other party.	One party is so concerned with the other's needs that his or her needs are buried or repressed.
4. Parties use unpredictable, mixed strategies and the element of surprise to outfox the other party.	Parties' actions are predictable. While flexible behavior is appropriate, it is not designed to take the other party by surprise.	One party's actions are totally predictable; his or her position is always one that caters to the other party.
5. Parties use threats and bluffs and put each other on the defensive. Each always tries to keep the upper hand.	Parties share information and are honest with each other. They treat each other with mutual understanding and integrity.	One party gives up own position to mollify the other.
6. Search behavior is devoted to finding ways of appearing committed to a position; logical and irrational arguments alike may serve this purpose. Each party engages in destructive manipulation of the other's position.	Search behavior is devoted to finding mutually satisfying solutions to problems; utilizing logical, creative and innovative processes; and developing constructive relationships with each other.	Search behavior is devoted to finding ways to accommodate to position of other party.
7. Success is often enhanced (when teams or organizations are involved on each side) by creating a bad image or stereotype of the other, by ignoring the other's logic, and by increasing the level of hostility. These tend to strengthen ingroup loyalty and convince competitors that one means business.	Success demands that bad stereotypes be dropped, that ideas be given consideration on their merit (regardless of sources), and that hostility not be induced deliberately. In fact, healthy, positive feelings about others are both a cause and an effect of other aspects of collaborative negotiations.	Success is determined by minimizing or avoiding all conflict and soothing any hostility. Own feelings are ignored in the interest of harmony.

Table 9–2 CONTINUED

Competitive	Collaborative	Subordinative
8. Unhealthy extreme is reached when one party assumes that everything that prevents the other from attaining its goal facilitates movement toward one's own goal; thus each party feels that an integral part of its goal is to stop the other from attaining its goal.	Unhealthy extreme is reached when one party assumes that whatever is good for others and the group is necessarily good for one's own self, when one cannot distinguish one's identity from that of the group or the other party, or when one party will not take responsibility for itself.	Unhealthy extreme is characterized by complete acquiescence to the other's goal at the expense of personal or organizational goals. Concern with harmony results in total avoidance of conflict; the subordinate party becomes a doormat for the other party.
9. Key attitude/behavior is "I win, you lose."	Key attitude/behavior is "What is the best way to meet the goals of both parties?"	Key attitude/behavior is "You win, I lose."
10. If impasse occurs, a mediator or arbitrator may be required.	If difficulties arise, a facilitator skilled in group dynamics may be used.	If behavior becomes chronic, assertiveness training or a psychotherapist may be used.

Reprinted, by permission of publisher, from R.W. Johnston, Negotiating strategies: Different strokes for different folks, *Personnel* (March-April 1982)

between the negotiating parties, and (2) the importance of substantive (content) outcomes.[54] Figure 9–8 illustrates the way the importance of these two types of outcomes can influence the strategy chosen by one of the parties. In Situation 1 both the relationship outcome and substantive outcome are important to the manager; this calls for *trusting collaboration,* where both parties demonstrate openness and seek win-win outcomes. Situation 2 calls for *open*

Figure 9–8 CONSIDERING A UNILATERAL NEGOTIATION STRATEGY

Is the Relationship Outcome Very Important to the Manager?	Is the Substantive Outcome Very Important to the Manager? Yes	No
Yes	*Strategy C1* **Trustingly Collaborate** when both types of outcomes are very important *Situation 1*	*Strategy S1* **Openly Subordinate** when the priority is on relationship outcomes *Situation 2*
No	*Strategy P1* **Firmly Compete** when the priority is on substantive outcomes *Situation 3*	*Strategy A1* **Actively Avoid Negotiating** when neither type of outcome is very important *Situation 4*

Reprinted with permission from G.T. Savage, J.D. Blair, and R.L. Sorenson, Consider both relationships and substance when negotiating strategically, *Academy of Management Executive* 3(1) (1989): 40.

subordination, since establishing a relationship overshadows the substantive outcome. Situation 3 demands *firm competition* to attain the desired substantive results at the expense of the relationship. Situation 4 calls for *active avoidance* of negotiation since the negotiator values neither outcome.

Figure 9–9 is a decision tree for incorporating the other party's priorities into the strategy selection diagrammed in Figure 9–8. The manager asks the following questions, in order (from left to right in the figure): (1) Is the substantive outcome very important to the manager? (2) Is the relationship outcome very important to the manager? (3) Is the substantive outcome very important to the other party? (4) Is the relationship outcome very important to the other party? Responses to the questions indicate the type of negotiation strategy that best fits with the desired outcomes.

Additional negotiation strategies include (1) *principled collaboration,* where negotiations are based on a set of mutually agreed-on principles, (2) *focused subordination,* where acquiescence occurs only to key needs, (3) *soft competition,* which avoids aggressive tactics and dirty tricks, (4) *passive avoidance,* which involves delegating the negotiations, and (5) *responsive avoidance,* by applying standard operating procedures or developing policies to address the other party's concerns.[55]

Tactics that accompany these strategies can include waiting out the other party, suddenly shifting methods, approach, or argument, taking a unilateral action and thus treating the negotiation outcome as a *fait accompli,* bland

Figure 9–9 SELECTING AN INTERACTIVE STRATEGY

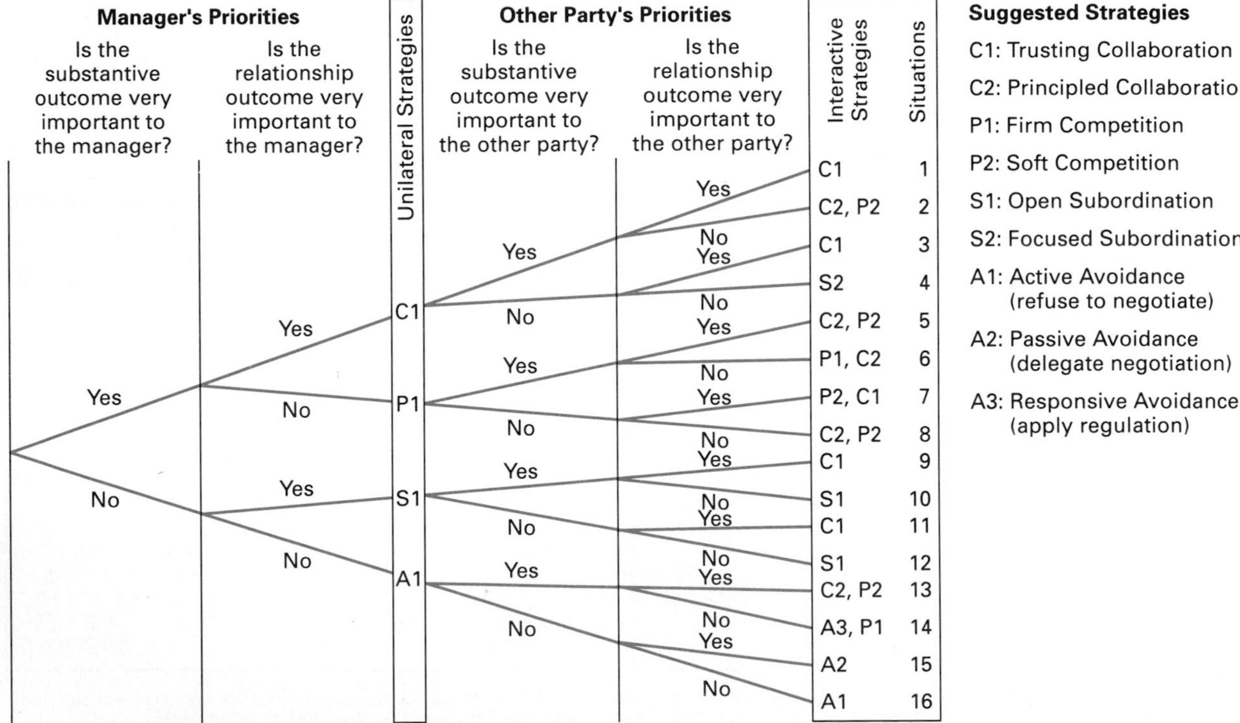

Reprinted with permission from G.T. Savage, J.D. Blair, and R.L. Sorenson, Consider both relationships and substance when negotiating strategically, *Academy of Management Executive* 3(1) (1989): 42.

withdrawal, apparent withdrawal, doing the reverse of what is expected, imposing time, dollar, or deadline limits, appearing to move toward one goal when actually moving toward another, carefully granting or withholding favors, and showing anger or intimidating the other party.[56] We can assess the ethical appropriateness of the tactics chosen by the answer to two questions: "Are the 'rules' known and accepted?" and "Can the situation be freely entered and left?"[57] More basic questions illuminate the second: Will your self-image remain positive if you use a given tactic? How would you feel if someone did it to you? Would you be comfortable advising others to use it? What would happen if everyone who bargained used it? Are there alternate tactics available?

CROSS-CULTURAL ISSUES IN NEGOTIATIONS

The assumptions that underlie effective negotiations differ significantly in various parts of the world. The Eastern Airline negotiations, for example, would not look the same in Japan or China as they do in the United States.

The general approach to negotiations in Asia focuses on saving face for the Asians and the other party.[58] Being too frank, critical, insincere, impatient, and unadaptable results in ineffective negotiations. In Asia questions are asked indirectly, not directly: "I've developed a short-cut for manufacturing these garments at a lower cost but ensuring higher quality, and would appreciate any suggestions you have for improving it." Not "Can you make this garment cheaper but improve its quality?"

Negotiating with Soviets, in contrast, has historically posed different dilemmas. Soviets emphasize building arguments on asserted ideals and deemphasize relationship building. They appeal to ideals and make few concessions. An opponent's concessions are viewed as weaknesses and are almost never reciprocated. They have been described as not trying to build a continuing relationship, often offering an extreme initial position, and ignoring any deadlines.[59]

Arabs, on the other hand, use primarily an affective rather than an ideological or factual negotiating style. They request and make concessions throughout the negotiating process, and almost always reciprocate an opponent's concessions. Initial positions are extreme, but deadlines are casual. They focus on building a long-term relationship.[60]

North Americans appeal to logic and counter opponents' arguments with objective facts rather than subjective feelings or asserted ideals. They may make small concessions early and then usually reciprocate an opponent's concessions. But they take a moderate initial position, build only a short-term relationship, and value deadlines greatly.[61]

In Japan, the negotiating protocol reflects the Japanese tendency to personalize business relations: they prefer to conduct many preliminary get-togethers so they can know the businesspeople with whom they deal.[62] Their negotiations are characterized by politeness, a nonrevealing manner, a nonconfrontational manner, and persistence.[63]

Table 9–3 compares the negotiating styles of the Japanese, North Americans, and Latin Americans. Negotiators must respond to cultural idiosyncracies about the choice of location, physical arrangements, participants, time

Table 9–3 A CROSS-CULTURAL PERSPECTIVE OF NEGOTIATION STYLES

Japanese	North American	Latin American
Emotional sensitivity highly valued.	Emotional sensitivity not highly valued.	Emotional sensitivity valued.
Hiding of emotions.	Dealing straightforwardly or impersonally.	Emotionally passionate.
Subtle power plays; conciliation.	Litigation not as much as conciliation.	Great power plays: use of weakness.
Loyalty to employer. Employer takes care of its employees.	Lack of commitment to employer. Breaking of ties by either if necessary.	Loyalty to employer (who is often family).
Group decision-making consensus.	Teamwork provides input to a decision maker.	Decisions come down from one individual.
Face-saving crucial. Decisions often made on basis of saving someone from embarrassment.	Decisions made on a cost benefit basis. Face-saving does not always matter.	Face-saving crucial in decision making to preserve honor, dignity.
Decision makers openly influenced by special interests.	Decision makers influenced by special interests but often not considered ethical.	Execution of special interests of decision maker expected, condoned.
Not argumentative. Quiet when right.	Argumentative when right or wrong, but impersonal.	Argumentative when right or wrong; passionate.
What is down in writing must be accurate, valid.	Great importance given to documentation as evidential proof.	Impatient with documentation as obstacle to understanding general principles.
Step-by-step approach to decision making.	Methodically organized decision making.	Impulsive, spontaneous decision making.
Good of group is the ultimate aim.	Profit motive or good of individual ultimate aim.	What is good for group is good for the individual.
Cultivate a good emotional social setting for decision making. Get to know decision makers.	Decision making impersonal. Avoid involvements, conflict of interest.	Personalism necessary for good decision making.

Reprinted with permission from P. Casse, *Training for the Multicultural Manager: A Practical and Cross-Cultural Approach to the Management of People* (Washington, D.C.: Society of Intercultural Education, Training, and Research 1982).

limits, and status differences in the bargaining process.[64] They must also recognize the value attached to various tactics. For example, different cultures may differ in their initial offers, relative use of verbal and nonverbal tactics, and willingness to employ dirty tricks. In one study, negotiators in Japan and the United States used promises more often and "No's" less often than Brazilian negotiators.[65]

Chinese norms are similar to Japanese ones and are based on the influence of Confucius, which emphasizes harmony, position in the social system, morality, and reliance on kinship.[66] Figure 9–10 presents recommendations for North Americans who negotiate with the Chinese.

In sum, American negotiators involved in cross-cultural negotiations should be aware of the way negotiators view the process itself, be careful of the use of a "middle man," make the assumption the other party can be trusted, consider the process as a problem-solving exercise, recognize the importance of protocol, carefully select the negotiating team, and understand the nature of decision making.[67] Negotiators should note that they may face serious ethical dilemmas, since conflicts often exist between the laws of the home and host countries as well as with the negotiator's own moral standards.

SUMMARY

Power may be one of the least understood but most important areas of organizational behavior. Individuals exert power to overcome job-related dependencies; or social exchanges may create power; or individuals may have a need for power.

This chapter described the sources and uses of power in organizations. We identified position, personal, and resource- and information-based power. We analyzed the use of informal networks, alliances, and trade relations in securing power.

We continued the chapter by looking at negotiation as the ritualized use of power in organizations. Two bargaining paradigms, distributive and integrative, were described and compared. Then the process of negotiation was outlined. We also examined a set of negotiation strategies and tactics. We concluded the chapter by considering the cross-cultural issues in negotiation. Figure 9–11 is a list of diagnostic questions for assessing the effective use of power and negotiations in organizations.

Figure 9–10 Advice for Americans Who Negotiate with Chinese

Preparation

Choose interpreters familiar with both cultures.
Include negotiating style in the training agenda.
Enter negotiations even when no immediate benefit is apparent.
Select negotiators with a more restrained style.

Carrying out the Negotiation

Emphasize the similarities rather than the differences in positions.
Emphasize the strategic, long-range process of negotiation and the gradual accumulation of mutual trust.
Plan for long negotiation sessions.
Allow frequent recesses for private consultations by the teams.
Avoid aggressive behavior, and practice patience.
Be politely formal, and minimize expressions of emotions.
Remember that behavior outside negotiations is as important as behavior during the negotiating sessions.
Assess nonverbal responses, and do not interpret silence as an expression of either approval or disapproval.
Address the group as a whole rather than individuals.

Concluding

Weigh the short-term benefits versus long-term costs of possible concessions.
Be willing to exchange some advantages for a lasting mutual attraction.
Allow for a short delay in the final stages before concluding the negotiations.
Thank the Chinese team for concluding the negotiations to the satisfaction of both sides.

Based on D. Shenkar and S. Ronan, The cultural context of negotiations: The implications of Chinese interpersonal norms, *Journal of Applied Behavioral Science* 23 (1987): 272–273.

Figure 9–11 DIAGNOSTIC QUESTIONS FOR POWER AND NEGOTIATION

- Who has power in the organization?
- From what sources does this power stem?
- Is power properly placed?
- Are alliances, informal networks, or trade relations used to develop power?
- How is powerlessness overcome in the organization?
- What types of negotiations occur in the organization?
- Do the negotiations tend to be distributive or integrative?
- What types of preparations for negotiations occur?
- Are interests identified, the best alternative to a negotiated agreement determined, and bargaining range identified?
- How effective are intercultural negotiations?

READING

Reading 9–1: LEADERSHIP: THE ART OF EMPOWERING OTHERS

Jay A. Conger

> One ought to be both feared and loved, but as it is difficult for the two to go together, it is much safer to be feared than loved . . . for love is held by a chain of obligation which, men being selfish, is broken whenever it serves their purpose; but fear is maintained by a dread of punishment which never fails.
>
> *The Prince,* Niccolo Machiavelli

In his handbook, *The Prince,* Machiavelli assures his readers—some being aspiring leaders, no doubt—that only by carefully amassing power and building a fearsome respect could one become a great leader. While the shadowy court life of 16th-century Italy demanded such treachery to ensure one's power, it seems hard to imagine Machiavelli's advice today as anything but a historical curiosity. Yet, interestingly, much of the management literature has focused on the strategies and tactics that managers can use to increase their own power and influence.[1] As such, a Machiavellian quality often pervades the literature, encouraging managers to ensure that their power base is strong and growing. At the same time a small but increasing number of management theorists have begun to explore the idea that organizational effectiveness also depends on the sharing of power—that the distribution of power is more important than the hoarding of power.[2]

While the idea of making others feel more powerful contradicts the stereotype of the all-powerful executive, research suggests that the traditional ways of explaining a leader's influence may not be entirely correct. For example, recent leadership studies argue that the practice of empowering—or instilling a sense of power—is at the root of organizational effectiveness, especially during times of transition and transformation.[3] In addition, studies of power and control within organizations indicate that the more productive forms of organizational power increase with superiors' sharing of power and responsibility with subordinates.[4] And while there is an increasing awareness of this need for more empowering leadership, we have only recently started to see documentation about the actual practices that leaders employ to effectively build a sense of power among organizational members as well as the contexts most suited for empowerment practices.[5]

In this article, I will explore these practices further by drawing upon a recent study of senior executives who proved themselves highly effective leaders. They were selected by a panel of professors at the Harvard Business School and management consultants who were well acquainted with them and their companies. The study included eight chief executive officers and executive vice-presidents of *Fortune* 500 companies and successful entrepreneurial firms, representing industries as diverse as telecommunications, office automation, retail banking, beverages, packaged foods, and management consulting. In each case, these individuals were responsible for either the creation of highly successful companies or for performing what were described as remarkable turnarounds. During my study of these executives, I conducted extensive interviews, observed them on the job, read company and other documents, and talked with their colleagues and subordinates. While the study focused on the broader issue of leadership styles, intensive interviews with these executives and their subordinates revealed that many were characterized as empowering leaders. Their actions were perceived as building confidence during difficult organizational transitions. From this study, I identified certain organizational contexts of powerlessness and management practices derived to remedy them.

In this article I will also illustrate several of these practices through a series of vignettes. While the reader may recognize some of the basic ideas behind these practices (such as providing greater opportunities for initiative), it is often the creative manner in which the leader deploys the particular practice that distinguishes them. The reader will discover how they have been carefully tailored to fit the context at hand. I might add, however, that these practices represent just a few of the broad repertoire of actions that leaders can take to make an empowering difference in their organizations.

A WORD ABOUT EMPOWERMENT

We can think of empowerment as the act of strengthening an individual's beliefs in his or her sense of effectiveness. In essence, then, empowerment is not simply a set of external actions; it is a process of changing the internal beliefs of people.[6] We know from psychology that individuals believe themselves powerful when they feel they can adequately cope with environmental demands—that is, situations, events, and people they confront. They feel powerless when they are unable to cope with these demands. Any management practice that increases an individual's sense of self-determination will tend to make that individual feel more powerful. The theory behind these ideas can be traced to the work of Alfred Bandura, who conceptualized the notion of self-efficacy beliefs and their role in an individual's sense of personal power in the world.[7]

From his research in psychology, Bandura identified four means of providing empowering information to others: (1) through positive emotional support during experiences associated with stress and anxiety, (2) through words of encouragement and positive persuasion, (3) by observing others' effectiveness—in other words, having models of success with whom people identified—and (4) by actually experiencing the mastering of a task with success (the most effective source). Each of these sources of empowerment was used by the study executives and will be identified in the practice examples, as will other sources identified by organizational researchers.

Several Empowering Management Practices

Before describing the actual practices, it is important to first draw attention to an underlying attitude of the study participants. These empowering leaders shared a strong underlying belief in their subordinates' abilities. It is essentially the Theory Y argument;[8] if you believe in people's abilities, they will come to believe in them. All the executives in the study believed that their subordinates were capable of managing their current situations. They did not employ wholesale firings as a means of transforming their organizations. Rather, they retained the majority of their staff and moved those who could not perform up to standard to positions where they could. The essential lesson is that an assessment of staff skills is imperative before embarking on a program of empowerment. This basic belief in employees' abilities underlies the following examples of management practices designed to empower. We will begin with the practice of providing positive emotional support.

1. *The Squirt-gun Shootouts: Providing a Positive Emotional Atmosphere.* An empowering practice that emerged from the study was that of providing positive emotional support, especially through play or drama. For example, every few months, several executives would stage dramatic "up sessions" to sustain the motivation and excitement of their staff. They would host an afternoon-long, or a one- or two-day event devoted solely to confidence building. The event would open with an uplifting speech about the future, followed by a special, inspirational speaker. At these events there would often be films meant to build excitement or confidence—for example, a film depicting a mountain climber ascending a difficult peak. The message being conveyed is that this person is finding satisfaction in the work he or she does at an extraordinary level of competence. There would also be rewards for exceptional achievements. These sessions acted as ceremonies to enhance the personal status and identity of employees and revive the common feelings that bound them together.[9]

An element of play appears to be especially liberating in situations of great stress and demoralization. In the study's examples, play allowed for the venting of frustrations and in turn permitted individuals to regain a sense of control by stepping back from their pressures for a moment. As Bandura suggests, the positive emotional support provided by something like play alleviates, to some extent, concerns about personal efficacy.[10]

For example, one of the subjects of the study, Bill Jackson, was appointed the head of a troubled division. Demand has outstripped the division's ability to maintain adequate inventories, and product quality had slipped. Jackson's predecessors were authoritarian managers, and subordinates were demoralized as well as paranoid about keeping their jobs. As one told me, "You never knew who would be shot next." Jackson felt that he had to break the tension in a way that would allow his staff to regain their sense of control and power. He wanted to remove the stiffness and paranoia and turn what subordinates perceived as an impossible task into something more fun and manageable.

So, I was told, at the end of his first staff meeting, Jackson quietly pulled out a squirt-gun and blasted one of his managers with water. At first, there was a moment of stunned silence, and then suddenly the room was flooded with laughter. He remarked with a smile, "You gotta have fun in this business. It's not worth having your stomach in ulcers." This began a month of squirt-gun fights between Jackson and his managers.

The end result? A senior manager's comment is representative: "He wanted people to feel comfortable, to feel in control. He used waterguns to do that. It was a game. It took the stiffness out of the business, allowed people to play in a safe environment—as the boss says, 'to have fun.' " This play restored rapport and morale. But Jackson also knew when to stop. A senior manager told me, "We haven't used waterguns in nine months. It has served its purpose. . . . The waterfights were like being accepted into a club. Once it achieved its purpose, it would have been overdone."

Interview after interview with subordinates confirmed the effectiveness of the squirt-gun incident. It had been experienced as an empowering ritual. In most contexts, this behavior would have been abusive. Why did it work? Because it is a management practice that fit the needs of subordinates at the appropriate time.

The executive's staff consisted largely of young men, "rough and ready" individuals who could be described as fun-loving and playful. They were accustomed to an informal atmosphere and operated in a very down-to-earth style. Jackson's predecessor, on the other hand, had been stiff and formal.

Jackson preferred to manage more informally. He wanted to convey, quickly and powerfully, his intentions of managing in a style distinct from his predecessor's. He was concerned, however, that his size—he is a very tall, energetic, barrel-chested man—as well as his extensive background in manufacturing would be perceived as intimidating by his young staff and increase their reluctance to assume initiative and control. Through the squirt-gun fights, however, he was able to (1) relieve a high level of tension and restore some sense of control, (2) emphasize the importance of having fun in an otherwise trying work environment, and (3) direct subordinates' concerns away from his skills and other qualities that intimidated them. It was an effective management practice because he understood the context. In another setting, it might have been counter-productive.

2. *The "I Make a Difference" Club: Rewarding and Encouraging in Visible and Personal Ways.* The majority of executives in the study rewarded the achievements of their staffs by expressing personal praise and rewarding in highly visible and confidence-building ways. They believed that people appreciated recognition of their hard work and success. Rewards of high incentive value were particularly important, especially those of personal recognition from the leader. As Rosabeth Kanter notes, a sense of power comes " . . . when one has relatively close contact with sponsors (higher level people who confer approval, prestige, or backing.)"[11] Combined with words of praise and positive encouragement, such experiences become important sources of empowerment.

The executives in the study took several approaches to rewards. To reward exceptional performance, one executive established the "I Make a Difference Club." Each year, he selects two or three staff members to be recognized for their excellence on the job. It is a very exclusive club, and only the executive knows the eligibility rules, which are based on outstanding performance. Inductees are invited to dinner in New York City but are not told beforehand that they are about to join the "I Make a Difference Club." They arrive and meet with other staff members whom they believe are there for a staff dinner. During dinner, everyone is asked to speak about what is going on in his or her part of the company. The old-timers speak first, followed by the inductees (who are still unaware of their coming induction). Only after they have given their speeches are they informed that they have just joined the club. As one manager said, "It's one of the most wonderful moments in life."

This executive and others also make extensive use of personal letters to individuals thanking them for their efforts and projects. A typical letter might read, "Fred, I would personally like to thank you for your contribution to ———, and I want you to know that I appreciate it." Lunches and dinners are hosted for special task accomplishments.

Public recognition is also employed as a means of rewarding. As one subordinate commented about his boss,

> He will make sure that people know that so and so did an excellent job on something. He's superb on giving people credit. If the person has done an exceptional job on a task or project, he will be given the opportunity to present his or her findings all the way to the board. Six months later, you'll get a call from a friend and learn that he has dropped your name in a speech that you did well. It makes you want to do it again.

I found that the investment in rewards and recognition made by many of these executives is unusually high, consuming a significant portion of their otherwise busy day. Yet the payoff appeared high. In interviews, subordinates described these rewards as having an empowering impact on them.

To understand why some of these rewards proved to be so successful, one must understand their organizational contexts. In some cases, the organizations studied were quite large, if not enormous. The size of these organizations did little to develop in employees a sense of an "I"—let alone an "I" that makes a difference. It was easy for organization members to feel lost in the hierarchy and for their achievements to be invisible, for recognition not to be received for personal contributions. The study's executives countered this tendency by institutionalizing a reward system that provided visibility and recognition—for example, the "I Make a Difference Club," presentations to the Board, and names dropped in speeches. Suddenly, you as a member of a large organization stood out—you were special.

Outstanding performances from each of the executives' perspectives was also something of a necessity. All the executives had demanding goals to achieve. As such, they had to tend to subordinates' sense of importance and contribution. They had to structure reward systems that would keep people "pumped up"—that would ensure that their confidence and commitment would not be eroded by the pressures placed on them.

3. *"Praising the Troops": Expressing Confidence.* The empowering leaders in the study spent significant amounts of time expressing their confidence in subordinates' abilities. Moreover, they expressed their confidence throughout each day—in speeches, in meetings, and casually in office hallways. Bandura comments that "people who are persuaded verbally that they possess the capabilities to master given tasks are likely to mobilize greater sustained effort than if they harbor self-doubts and dwell on personal deficiencies when difficulties arise."[12]

A quote from Irwin Federman, CEO of Monolithic Memories, a highly successful high-tech company, captures the essence and power of a management that builds on this process:

> If you think about it, we love others not for who they are, but for how they make us feel. In order to willingly accept the direction of another individual, it must make you feel good to do so. . . . If you believe what I'm saying, you cannot help but come to the conclusion that those you have followed passionately, gladly, zealously—have made you feel like somebody. . . . This business of making another person feel good in the unspectacular course of his daily comings and goings is, in my view, the very essence of leadership.[13]

This proactive attitude is exemplified by Bob Jensen. Bob assumed control of his bank's retail operations after a reorganization that transferred away the division's responsibility for large corporate clients. Demoralized by a perceived loss in status and responsibility, branch managers were soon asking, "Where's our recognition?" Bob, however, developed an inspiring strategic vision to transform the operation. He then spent much of his time championing his strategy and expressing his confidence in employees' ability to carry it out. Most impressive was his personal canvass of some 175 retail branches.

As he explained,

> I saw that the branch system was very down, morale was low. They felt like they'd lost a lot of their power. There were serious problems and a lot of staff were just hiding. What I saw was that we really wanted to create a small community for each branch where customers would feel known. To do that, I needed to create an attitude change. I saw that the attitudes of the branch staff were a reflection of the branch manager. The approach then was a manageable job—now I had to focus on only 250 people, the branch managers, rather than the 3,000 staff employees out there. I knew I had to change their mentality from being lost in a bureaucracy to feeling like the president of their own bank. I had to convince them they were special—that they had the power to transform the organization. . . . All I did was talk it up. I was up every night. In one morning, I hit 17 branches. My goal was to sell a new attitude. To encourage people to "pump iron." I'd say, "Hi, how's business?", encourage them. I'd arrange tours of the branches for the chairman on down. I just spent a lot of time talking to these people—explaining that they were the ones who could transform the organization.

It was an important tactic—one that made the branch managers feel special and important. It was also countercultural. As one executive told me, "Bob would go out into the field to visit the operations, which was very unusual for senior people in the industry." His visits heightened the specialness that branch managers felt. In addition, Bob modeled self-confidence and personal success—an important tactic to build a sense of personal effectiveness among subordinates.[14]

I also watched Jack Eaton, president of a regional telephone company, praise his employees in large corporate gatherings, in executive council meetings, and in casual encounters. He explained his philosophy:

> I have a fundamental belief and trust in the ability and conscientiousness of others. I have a lot of good people. You can turn them loose, let them feel good about their accomplishments. . . . You ought to recognize accomplishment as well as build confidence. I generally do it in small ways. If someone is doing well, it's important to express your confidence to that person—especially among his peers. I tend to do it personally. I try to be genuine. I don't throw around a lot of b.s.

This practice proved especially important during the transition of the regional phone companies away from the parent organization.

4. *"President of My Own Bank": Fostering Initiative and Responsibility.* Discretion is a critical power component of any job.[15] By simply fostering greater initiative and responsibility in subordinates' tasks, a leader can empower organizational members. Bob Jensen, the bank executive, is an excellent example of how one leader created opportunities for greater initiative despite the confines of his subordinates' positions. He transformed what had been a highly constricted branch

manager's job into a branch "president" concept. The idea was simple—every manager was made to feel like the president of his own community bank, and not just in title. Goals, compensation, and responsibilities were all changed to foster this attitude. Existing measurement systems were completely restructured. The value-of-funds-generated had been the principal yardstick—something over which branch managers had only very limited control because of interest rate fluctuations. Managers were now evaluated on what they could control—that is, deposits. Before, branch managers had rotated every couple of years. Now they stayed put. "If I'm moving around, then I'm not the president of my own bank, so we didn't move them anymore," Jensen explained. He also decentralized responsibilities that had resided higher in the hierarchy—allowing the branch manager to hire, give money to charities, and so on. In addition, a new ad agency was hired to mark the occasion, and TV ads were made showing the branch managers being in charge, rendering personal services themselves. The branch managers even thought up the ad lines.

What Jensen did so skillfully was recognize that his existing managers had the talent and energy to turn their operations around successfully, but that their sense of power was missing. He recognized their pride had been hurt and that he needed to restore a sense of ownership and self-importance. He had to convince his managers through increased authority that they were no longer "pawns" of the system—that they were indeed "presidents" of their own banks.

Another example—this one demonstrating a more informal delegation of initiative—was quite surprising. The setting was a highly successful and rapidly growing computer firm, and the study participant was the vice-president of manufacturing. The vice-president had recently been hired away from another firm and was in the process of revamping manufacturing. During the process, he discovered that his company's costs on its terminal video monitors were quite high. However, he wanted his staff to discover the problem for themselves and to "own" the solution. So one day, he placed behind his desk a black-and-white Sony TV with a placard on top saying $69.95. Next to it he placed a stripped-down version of the company's monitor with a placard of $125.95. Both placards reflected the actual costs of the two products. He never said a word. But during the day as staff and department managers entered their boss's office, they couldn't help but notice the two sets. They quickly got the message that their monitor was costing twice as much as a finished TV set. Within a month, the manufacturing team had lowered the monitor's costs by 40%.

My first impression on hearing this story was that, as a subordinate, I would be hard pressed not to get the point and, more important, I would wonder why the boss was not more direct. Ironically, the boss appears to be hitting subordinates over the head with the problem. Out of context, then, this example hardly seems to make others feel more competent and powerful. Yet staff described themselves as "turned on" and motivated by this behavior. Why, I wondered? A little history will illustrate the effectiveness of this action.

The vice-president's predecessor had been a highly dictatorial individual. He tightly controlled his staff's actions and stifled any sense of discretion. Implicitly, his behavior said to subordinates, "You have no ideas of your own." He fired freely, leaving staff to feel that they had little choice in whether to accept his orders or not. By his actions, he essentially transformed his managers into powerless order-takers.

When the new vice-president arrived, he found a group of demoralized subordinates whom he felt were nonetheless quite talented. To restore initiative, he began to demonstrate the seriousness of his intentions in highly visible and symbolic ways. For example, rather than tell his subordinates what to do, he started by seeding ideas and suggestions in humorous and indirect ways. The TV monitor is only one of many examples. Through these actions, he was able eventually to restore a sense of initiative and personal competence to his staff. While these examples are illustrative of effective changes in job design, managers contemplating job enrichment would be well advised to consult the existing literature and research before undertaking major projects.[16]

5. *Early Victories: Building on Success.* Many of the executives in the study reported that they often introduced organizational change through pilot or otherwise small and manageable projects. They designed these projects to ensure early success for their organizations. For example, instead of introducing a new sales structure nationwide, they would institute the change in one region; a new technology would have a pilot introduction at a single plant rather than systemwide. Subordinates described these early success experiences as strongly reinforcing their sense of power and efficacy. As Mike Beer argues:

> In order for change to spread throughout an organization and become a permanent fixture, it appears that early successes are needed. . . . When individuals, groups, and whole organizations feel more competent than they did before the change, this increased sense of competence reinforces the new behavior and solidifies learning associated with change.[17]

An individual's sense of mastery through actual experience is the most effective means of increasing self-efficacy.[18] When subordinates are given more complex and difficult tasks, they are presented with opportunities to test their competence. Initial success experiences will make them feel more capable and, in turn, empowered. Structuring organizational changes to ensure initial successes builds on this principle.

CONTEXTS OF POWERLESSNESS

The need to empower organizational members becomes more important in certain contexts. Thus, it is important to identify conditions within organizations that might foster a sense of powerlessness. Certain circumstances, for instance, appear to lower feelings of self-efficacy. In these cases, subordinates typically perceive themselves as lacking control over their immediate situation (e.g., a major reorganization threatens to displace responsibility and involves limited or no subordinate participation),[19] or lacking the required capability, resources, or discretion needed to accomplish a task (e.g., the development of new and difficult-to-learn skills for the introduction of a new technological process).[20] In either case, these experiences maximize feelings of inadequacy and lower self-confidence. They, in turn, appear to lessen motivation and effectiveness.

Figure 9–12 identifies the more common organizational factors that affect these self-efficacy or personal power beliefs and contribute to feelings of powerlessness. They include organizational factors, supervisory styles, reward systems, and job design.

For example, during a major organizational change, goals may change—often dramatically—to respond to the organization's new direction. Rules may no longer be clearly defined as the firm seeks new guidelines for action. Responsibilities may be dramatically altered. Power alliances may shift, leaving parts of the organization with a perceived loss of power or increasing political activity. Certain functional areas, divisions, or acquired companies may experience disenfranchisement as their responsibilities are felt to be diminished or made subordinate to others. As a result, employees' sense of competence may be seriously challenged as they face having to accept and acquire new responsibilities, skills, and management practices as well as deal with the uncertainty of their future.

In new venture situations, uncertainty often appears around the ultimate success of the company's strategy. A major role for leaders is to build an inspiring picture of the firm's future and convince organizational members of their ability to achieve that future. Yet, market lead times are often long, and tangible results may be slow in coming. Long work hours with few immediate rewards can diminish confidence. Frustration can build, and questions about the organization's future can arise. In addition, the start-up's success and responses to growth can mean constant change in responsibility, pushing managers into responsibilities where they have had little prior experience; thus, failure may be experienced initially as new responsibilities are learned. Entrepreneurial executives may be reluctant to relinquish their control as expansion continues.

Bureaucratic environments are especially conducive to creating conditions of powerlessness. As Peter Block points out, bureaucracy encourages dependency and submission because of its top-down contract between the organization and employees.[21] Rules, routines, and traditions define what can and cannot be done, allowing little room for initiative and discretion to develop. Employees' behavior is often guided by rules over which

Figure 9–12 CONTEXT FACTORS LEADING TO POTENTIAL STATE OF POWERLESSNESS

Organizational Factors

Significant organizational changes/transitions
Start-up ventures
Excessive, competitive pressures
Impersonal bureaucratic climate
Poor communications and limited network-forming systems
Highly centralized organizational resources

Supervisory Style

Authoritarian (high control)
Negativism (emphasis on failures)
Lack of reason for actions/consequences

Reward Systems

Noncontingency (arbitrary reward allocations)
Low incentive value of rewards
Lack of competence-based rewards
Lack of innovation-based rewards

Job Design

Lack of role clarity
Lack of training and technical support
Unrealistic goals
Lack of appropriate authority/discretion
Low task variety
Limited participation in programs, meetings, and decisions that have a direct impact on job performance
Lack of appropriate/necessary resources
Lack of network-forming opportunities
Highly established work routines
Too many rules and guidelines
Low advancement opportunities
Lack of meaningful goals/tasks
Limited contact with senior management

Source: Adapted from J. A. Conger and R. N. Kanungo, The empowerment process: Integrating theory and practice, *Academy of Management Review* (July 1988).

they have no say and which may no longer be effective, given the present-day context.

From the standpoint of supervision, authoritarian management styles can strip away subordinates' discretion and, in turn, a sense of power. Under an authoritarian manager, subordinates inevitably come to believe that they have little control—that they and their careers are subject to the whims or demands of their boss. The problem becomes acute when capable subordinates begin to attribute their powerlessness to internal factors, such as their own personal competence, rather than to external factors, such as the nature of the boss's temperament.

Rewards are another critical area for empowerment. Organizations that do not provide valued rewards or simply do not reward employees for initiative, competence, and innovation are creating conditions of powerlessness. Finally, jobs with little meaningful challenge, or jobs where the task is unclear, conflicting, or excessively demanding can lower employees' sense of self-efficacy.

IMPLICATIONS FOR MANAGERS

Managers can think of the empowerment process as involving several stages.[22] Managers might want to begin by identifying for themselves whether any of the organizational problems and characteristics described in this article are present in their own firms. In addition, managers assuming new responsibilities should conduct an organizational diagnosis that clearly identifies their current situation, and possible problems and their causes. Attention should be aimed at understanding the recent history of the organization. Important questions to ask would be: What was my predecessor's supervisory role? Has there been a recent organizational change that negatively affected my subordinates? How is my operation perceived by the rest of the corporation? Is there a sense of disenfranchisement? Am I planning to change significantly the outlook of this operation that would challenge traditional ways of doing things? How are people rewarded? Are jobs designed to be motivating?

Once conditions contributing to feelings of powerlessness are identified, the managerial practices identified in this article and in the management literature can be used to provide self-efficacy information to subordinates. This information can result in an empowering experience for subordinates and may ultimately lead to greater initiative, motivation, and persistence.

However, in applying these practices, it is imperative that managers tailor their actions to fit the context at hand. For example, in the case of an authoritarian predecessor, you are more likely to need praise and confidence-building measures and greater opportunities for job discretion. With demanding organizational goals and tasks, the practices of confidence building and active rewarding, an element of play, and a supportive environment are perhaps most appropriate. The specific character of each practice must necessarily vary somewhat to fit your particular situation. For instance, what makes many of the previous examples so important is that the executives responded with practices that organizational members could relate to or that fit their character—for instance, the television and squirt-gun examples. Unfortunately, much of today's popular management literature provides managers with tools to manage their subordinates, yet few highlight the importance of matching the practice to the appropriate context. Empowering is not a pill; it is not simply a technique, as many workshops and articles would lead us to believe. Rather, to be truly effective it requires an understanding of subordinates and one's organizational context.

Finally, although it is not as apparent in the examples themselves, each of the study executives set challenging and appealing goals for their organizations. This is a necessary component of effective and empowering leadership. If goals are not perceived as appealing, it is difficult to empower managers in a larger sense. As Warren Bennis and Burt Nanus argue: "Great leaders often inspire their followers to high levels of achievement by showing them how their work contributes to worthwhile ends. It is an emotional appeal to some of the most fundamental needs—the need to be important, to make a difference, to feel useful, to be part of a successful and worthwhile enterprise."[23] Such goals go hand in hand with empowering management practices. They were and are an integral part of the empowerment process I observed in the companies I studied.

A WORD OF CAUTION

In closing, it is important to add a note of caution. First of all, empowerment is not the complete or always the appropriate answer to building the confidence of managers. It can lead to overconfidence. A false sense of confidence in positive outcomes may lead employees and organizations to persist in what may, in actuality, prove to be tactical errors. Thus, a system of checks and balances is needed. Managers must constantly test reality and be alert to signs of "groupthink."

Some managers may be incapable of empowering others. Their own insecurities may prevent them from instilling a sense of power in subordinates. This is ironic, since often these are the individuals who need to develop such skills. Yet, as Kanter argues, "Only those leaders who feel secure about their own power outward . . . can see empowering subordinates as a gain rather than a loss."[24]

Certain situations may not warrant empowerment. For example, there are contexts where opportunities

Figure 9–13 STAGES OF THE EMPOWERMENT PROCESS

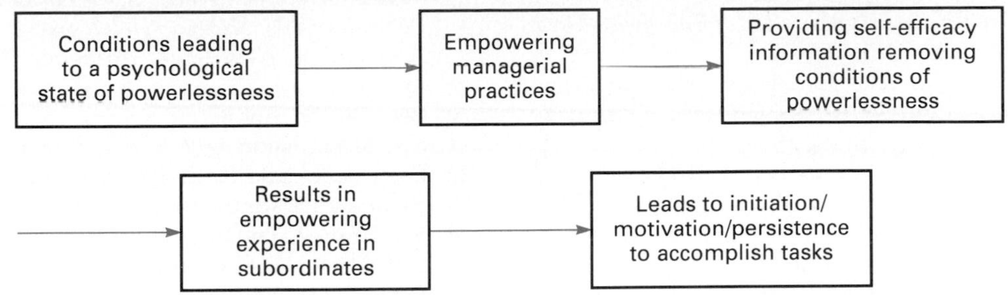

SOURCE: Adapted from J.A. Conger and R.N. Kanungo, The empowerment process: Integrating theory and practice, *Academy of Management Review* (July 1988).

for greater initiative or responsibility simply do not exist and, in some cases, subordinates may be unwilling or unable to assume greater ownership or responsibility. As Lyman Porter, Edward Lawler, and Richard Hackman point out, research "strongly suggests that only workers with reasonably high strength of desire for higher-order need satisfaction . . . will respond positively and productively to the opportunities present in jobs which are high in meaning, autonomy, complexity, and feedback."[25] Others may not have the requisite experience or knowledge to succeed. And those given more than they are capable of handling may fail. The end result will be the opposite of what you are seeking—a sense of powerlessness. It is imperative that managers assess as accurately as possible their subordinates' capabilities before undertaking difficult goals and empowering them to achieve.

Second, certain of the empowerment practices described in this article are not appropriate for all situations. For example, managers of subordinates who require structure and direction are likely to find the example of the manager "seeding" ideas with the television set an ineffective practice. In the case of a pressing deadline or crisis, such seeding is inappropriate, given its longer time horizons.

When staging playful or unconventional events, the context must be considered quite carefully. What signals are you sending about yourself and your management philosophy? Like rewards, these events can be used to excess and lose their meaning. It is imperative to determine the appropriateness and receptivity of such practices. You may inadvertently mock or insult subordinates, peers, or superiors.

In terms of expressing confidence and rewarding, both must be done sincerely and not to excess. Praising for nonaccomplishments can make rewards meaningless. Subordinates may suspect that the boss is simply flattering them into working harder.

In general, however, empowerment practices are an important tool for leaders in setting and achieving higher goals and in moving an organization past difficult transitions.[26] But remember that they do demand time, confidence, an element of creativity, and a sensitivity to one's context to be effective.

ENDNOTES

1. See, for example, J.P. Kotter, *Power in Management,* New York: AMACOM, 1979, and J. Pfeffer, *Power in Organizations,* Marshfield, MA: Pitman, 1981.
2. See P. Block, *The Empowered Manager,* San Francisco: Jossey-Bass, 1987; W.W. Burke, "Leadership as Empowering Others," In S. Srivastva (Ed.), *Executive Power,* San Francisco: Jossey-Bass, 1986, pp. 51–77; and R.M. Kanter, *The Change Masters,* New York: Simon & Schuster, 1983.
3. W. Bennis and B. Nanus, *Leaders,* New York: Harper & Row, 1985; and R.M. Kanter, "Power Failure in Management Circuits," *Harvard Business Review,* July–August 1979, pp. 65–75.
4. See Kanter, Endnote 3; and A. S. Tannenbaum, *Control in Organizations,* New York: McGraw-Hill, 1968.
5. See J.A Conger and R.N. Kanungo, "The Empowerment Process: Integrating Theory and Practice," *Academy of Management Review,* July 1988; and R.J. House, "Power and Personality in Complex Organizations, in L.L. Cummings and B.M. Staw (Eds.), *Research in Organizational Behavior: An Annual Review of Critical Essays and Reviews,* Vol. 10, Greenwich, CT: JAI Press, 1988. The author is grateful to Rabindra N. Kanungo for his insights and help in conceptualizing the empowerment process.
6. See Conger and Kanungo, Endnote 5.
7. A. Bandura, "Self-Efficiency: Toward a Unifying

Theory of Behavioral Change," *Psychological Review,* 1977, 84(2), pp. 191–215.
8. D. McGregor, *The Human Side of Enterprise,* New York: McGraw-Hill, 1960.
9. See J.M. Beyer and H.M. Trice, "How an Organization's Rites Reveal Its Culture," *Organizational Dynamics,* Spring 1987, pp. 4–25.
10. A. Bandura, *Social Foundations of Thought and Action: A Social Cognitive View,* Englewood Cliffs, NJ: Prentice-Hall, 1986.
11. See Kanter, Endnote 3, p. 66.
12. See Bandura, Endnote 10, p. 400.
13. W. Bennis and B. Nanus, *Leaders,* New York: Harper & Row, 1985, pp. 64–65.
14. See Bandura, Endnote 10.
15. See Kanter, Endnote 3.
16. See J.R. Hackman, "The Design of Work in the 1980s," *Organizational Dynamics,* Summer 1978, pp. 3–17.
17. M. Beer, *Organizational Change and Development,* Santa Monica, CA; Goodyear, 1980, p. 64.
18. See Bandura, Endnote 10.
19. F.M. Rothbaum, J.R. Weisz, and S.S. Snyder, "Changing the World and Changing Self: A Two Process Model of Perceived Control," *Journal of Personality and Social Psychology,* 1982, 42, pp. 5–37; and L.Y. Abramson, J. Garber, and M.E.P. Seligman, "Learned Helplessness in Humans: An Attributional Analysis," in J. Garber and M.E.P. Seligman (Eds.), *Human Helplessness: Theory and Application,* New York: Academic Press, 1980, pp. 3–34.
20. See Kanter, Endnote 2.
21. See Block, Endnote 2.
22. See Conger and Kanungo, Endnote 5.
23. Bennis and Nanus, Endnote 13, p. 93.
24. See Kanter, Endnote 3, p. 73.
25. L.W. Porter, E.E. Lawler, and J.R. Hackman, *Behaviors in Organizations,* New York: McGraw-Hill, 1975, p. 306.
26. See N.M. Tichy and M.A. Devanna, *The Transformational Leader,* New York: John Wiley, 1986.

DISCUSSION QUESTIONS

1. Under what circumstances are organizational members likely to experience powerlessness?
2. In what ways can a leader provide empowering information to others?
3. Describe four empowering leadership practices. In what situations would each be appropriate?

Reprinted from *Academy of Management Executive,* 1989, 3(1), pp. 17–24.

ACTIVITIES

Activity 9–1: DIAGNOSIS OF SOURCES OF POWER

Step 1: Think of the three people who had the most influence over you in the last year. Choose one experience where each person influenced you. Describe each of these experiences in one paragraph.

Step 2: In dyads, identify the sources of power used in each experience. Reach consensus with your partner.

Step 3: With the class as a whole, the instructor will tally the frequency of each source of power used. Then the instructor will ask you to describe the outcomes or consequences (behaviors and attitudes) of each influence experience.

Step 4: Discussion. In small groups or with the entire class, answer the following questions:

Description

1. Which sources of power were used most frequently? least frequently?

Diagnosis

2. Under what circumstances was each type of power used? Does a pattern emerge?
3. Which types were most effective? least effective?

Prescription

4. How could these people tap into additional sources of power?

Activity 9–2: EMPOWERMENT PROFILE

Step 1: Complete the following questionnaire.*

For each of the following items, select the alternative with which you feel more comfortable. While for some items you may feel that both a and b describe you or neither is ever applicable you should select the alternative that better describes you most of the time.

1. When I have to give a talk or write a paper, I . . .
   _____ a. Base the content of my talk or paper on my own ideas.
   _____ b. Do a lot of research, and present the findings of others in my paper or talk.
2. When I read something I disagree with, I . . .
   _____ a. Assume my position is correct.
   _____ b. Assume what's presented in the written word is correct.
3. When someone makes me extremely angry, I . . .
   _____ a. Ask the other person to stop the behavior that is offensive to me.
   _____ b. Say little, not quite knowing how to state my position.
4. When I do a good job, it is important to me that . . .
   _____ a. The job represents the best I can do.
   _____ b. Others take notice of the job I've done.
5. When I buy new clothes, I . . .
   _____ a. Buy what looks best on me.
   _____ b. Try to dress in accordance with the latest fashion.
6. When something goes wrong, I . . .
   _____ a. Try to solve the problem.
   _____ b. Try to find out who's at fault.
7. As I anticipate my future, I . . .
   _____ a. Am confident I will be able to lead the kind of life I want to lead.
   _____ b. Worry about being able to live up to my obligations.
8. When examining my own resources and capacities, I . . .
   _____ a. Like what I find.
   _____ b. Find all kinds of things I wish were different.
9. When someone treats me unfairly, I . . .
   _____ a. Put my energies into getting what I want.
   _____ b. Tell others about the injustice.
10. When someone criticizes my efforts, I . . .
    _____ a. Ask questions in order to understand the basis for the criticism.
    _____ b. Defend my actions or decisions, trying to make my critic understand why I did what I did.
11. When I engage in an activity, it is very important to me that . . .
    _____ a. I live up to my own expectations.
    _____ b. I live up to the expectations of others.
12. When I let someone else down or disappoint them, I . . .
    _____ a. Resolve to do things differently next time.
    _____ b. Feel guilty, and wish I had done things differently.
13. I try to surround myself with people . . .
    _____ a. Whom I respect.
    _____ b. Who respect me.
14. I try to develop friendships with people who . . .
    _____ a. Are challenging and exciting.
    _____ b. Can make me feel a little safer and a little more secure.
15. I make my best efforts when . . .
    _____ a. I do something I want to do when I want to do it.
    _____ b. Someone else gives me an assignment, a deadline, and a reward for performing.
16. When I love a person, I . . .
    _____ a. Encourage him or her to be free and choose for himself or herself.
    _____ b. Encourage him or her to do the same thing I do and to make choices similar to mine.
17. When I play a competitive game, it is important to me that I . . .
    _____ a. Do the best I can.
    _____ b. Win.
18. I really like being around people who . . .
    _____ a. Can broaden my horizons and teach me something.
    _____ b. Can and want to learn from me.
19. My best days are those that . . .
    _____ a. Present unexpected opportunities.
    _____ b. Go according to plan.
20. When I get behind in my work, I . . .
    _____ a. Do the best I can and don't worry.
    _____ b. Worry or push myself harder than I should.

Step 2: Score your responses as follows:

Total your a responses:_____
Total your b responses:_____

(Your instructor will help you interpret these scores.)

Step 3: Discussion. In small groups or with the entire class, answer the following questions:

Description

1. Look at the two totals. Which score is highest? Which is lowest?
2. Do your scores describe you well? Why or why not?

Diagnosis

3. Think of some experiences you have had that confirm your score.
4. Think of some experiences you have had that disconfirm your score.
5. How does this information help you to act more effectively in organizations?

"The Empowerment Profile" from *The Power Handbook* by Pamela Cuming. Copyright © 1980 by CBI Publishing. Reprinted by permission of Van Nostrand Reinhold Co., Inc.

Activity 9–3: SOCIAL POWER EXERCISE

Step 1: Your instructor will divide the class into six groups of equal size. Each group will be assigned one of the following bases of power: (1) punishment; (2) reward; (3) referent; (4) legitimate; (5) expert; (6) information:

Step 2: Read the following scenario:

You are an instructor in a college class and have become aware that a potentially good student is repeatedly absent from class and sometimes unprepared when present. The student seems to be satisfied with the grade you have given, but you would like to see the student attend regularly, be better prepared, and thus do better in class. You even feel that the student might get really turned on to pursuing a career in this field, which is an exciting one for you. You are respected and liked by your students, and it irritates you that this person treats your teaching with such a cavalier attitude. You want to influence the student to start attending class regularly.

Step 3: You have fifteen minutes to prepare an influence plan.

Step 4: Each group should select one person to play the instructor. Each group should then pick, from their own or another group, a student who is to be the recipient of the instructor's attempt.

Step 5: Each group in turn should conduct their role play. During the role play, members of other groups should think of themselves as the student being influenced. After the presentation, record your reaction to the influence by completing the questionnaire below as if you were the student being addressed by the teacher.

REACTION TO INFLUENCE QUESTIONNAIRE

Circle the number of each of the scales below which indicates the best statement completion for you as the student in the role play. That is, think of yourself on the receiving end of the influence attempt described and record your own reaction.

I. Type of power used ____________________

A. As a result of the influence attempt I will . . .
definitely not comply 1 2 3 4 5 *definitely comply*

B. Any change that does come about will be . . .
temporary 1 2 3 4 5 *long lasting*

C. My own personal reaction is . . .
resistant 1 2 3 4 5 *acceptant*

D. As a result of this influence attempt my relationship with the professor will probably be . . .
worse 1 2 3 4 5 *better*

II. Type of power used ____________________

A. As a result of influence attempt I will . . .
definitely not comply 1 2 3 4 5 *definitely comply*

B. Any change that does come about will be . . .
temporary 1 2 3 4 5 *long lasting*

C. My own personal reaction is . . .
resistant 1 2 3 4 5 *acceptant*

D. As a result of this influence attempt my relationship with the professor will probably be . . .
worse 1 2 3 4 5 *better*

III. Type of power used ____________

A. As a result of influence attempt I will . . .
definitely not comply 1 2 3 4 5 *definitely comply*

B. Any change that does come about will be . . .
temporary 1 2 3 4 5 *long lasting*

C. My own personal reaction is . . .
resistant 1 2 3 4 5 *acceptant*

D. As a result of this influence attempt my relationship with the professor will probably be . . .
worse 1 2 3 4 5 *better*

IV. Type of power used ____________

A. As a result of influence attempt I will . . .
definitely not comply 1 2 3 4 5 *definitely comply*

B. Any change that does come about will be . . .
temporary 1 2 3 4 5 *long lasting*

C. My own personal reaction is . . .
resistant 1 2 3 4 5 *acceptant*

D. As a result of this influence attempt my relationship with the professor will probably be . . .
worse 1 2 3 4 5 *better*

V. Type of power used ____________

A. As a result of influence attempt I will . . .
definitely not comply 1 2 3 4 5 *definitely comply*

B. Any change that does come about will be . . .
temporary 1 2 3 4 5 *long lasting*

C. My own personal reaction is . . .
resistant 1 2 3 4 5 *acceptant*

D. As a result of this influence attempt my relationship with the professor will probably be . . .
worse 1 2 3 4 5 *better*

VI. Type of power used ____________

A. As a result of influence attempt I will . . .
definitely not comply 1 2 3 4 5 *definitely comply*

B. Any change that does come about will be . . .
temporary 1 2 3 4 5 *long lasting*

C. My own personal reaction is . . .
resistant 1 2 3 4 5 *acceptant*

D. As a result of this influence attempt my relationship with the professor will probably be . . .
worse 1 2 3 4 5 *better*

Step 6: The instructor will then tabulate the results to each question by influence type.

Step 7: Discussion. Individually in writing, in small groups, or with the entire class, answer the following questions:

1. Which kind of influence is most likely to immediately result in the desired behavior?
2. Which will have the most long-lasting effects?
3. What effect will using a particular base of power have on the on-going relationship?
4. Which form of power will others find most acceptable? least acceptable?
5. In which kinds of situations is each kind of power most effective and useful? least effective and useful? Build a contingency framework for the use of different kinds of power.

Based on G. Aiken, An exercise in social power, *Exchange: The Organization Behavior Teaching Journal 3* (1978): 38–39.

Activity 9–4: ROBIN CARTER AND THE BOSTON MUSEUM OF SCIENCE CASE

Step 1: Read the case of Robin Carter and the Boston Museum of Science, Parts (A) and (B)

ROBIN CARTER AND THE BOSTON MUSEUM OF SCIENCE (A)

Robin Carter joined the staff of Boston's Museum of Science in 1986, one year after receiving her MBA from the Simmons College Graduate School of Management. Although she had applied for a job managing all of the museum's revenue-generating activities, Carter was offered a newly-created position as head of exhibitions and special events. This opportunity had materialized during the course of her interviews with the director of the museum, Roger Nichols.

Dr. Nichols viewed Robin Carter as one who could use project management principles to coordinate and produce the elaborate special exhibitions with which the museum was increasingly involved. He was highly enthusiastic about adding a professional manager to his staff. Once at the museum, however, Robin found that the professional staff was highly resistant to working with someone who had neither a science nor a museum background. Further, she had been hired without the knowledge and in the absence of the man who would be her immediate superior, and his behavior toward her was openly hostile.

Robin considered offering her resignation to the director, but by December felt that she had developed an acceptable working relationship with her boss, and that she was building considerable credibility with the other four associate directors. Her staff was increased and she was given major budget responsibility. In addition Robin received a promotion from unit to section manager.

In the following paragraphs Robin Carter describes how she established herself and a new department within the Museum of Science organization.

Personal Background

Robin Carter had been one of the older students in her MBA class at the Simmons College Graduate School of Management, starting the program full-time when she was 43.

She described the events leading to her entering Simmons as follows:

> My first job was with the Peace Corps in Nepal in 1962, after graduating from Katherine Gibbs. I was married overseas and worked for the UN for a while. Then I had my first child and worked for five years while my husband went through the seminary. I had two additional children and was at home for nine years.

When her youngest child started school Robin was asked to manage a fabric business, which she was able to reorganize and make profitable. She later took a full-time job with a company which was starting up a program to teach English in Saudi Arabia; Robin successfully managed the project, including the hiring of overseas personnel. The president of the company subsequently offered to assist her if she decided to return to school.

As an entering MBA student, Robin was concerned about her age, her lack of an undergraduate degree, and about having been out of school for twenty-five years. Although the course work was difficult and the hour-long commute exhausting, she managed, and as she says now, "In a large class you build on each other's strengths."

During the time she was at Simmons the health of her former boss began to deteriorate, and when she graduated Robin was asked to take on a major role in the firm's management. Six months later a decision was made to cease operations.

The Museum of Science

In early 1986 Robin Carter began an intense job-search process, using all the resources of the Simmons Placement Office, as well as all the leads and contacts she had made elsewhere. "I approached it very much as they tell you to," she recalls. "Send out resumes, call people you know, follow every lead and talk to every human being you possibly can."

An executive recruiter sent Robin to the Museum of Science, where she was interviewed by the director, Roger Nichols. Dr. Nichols was known in museum circles as the man who had developed a relatively small and conservatively-run science museum into the foremost institution of its kind in the world. As Robin described it, Boston's Museum of Science was "a sleepy, non-profit institution that was being cranked into the 20th century with a speed that would make most non-profit institutions look like they were standing still."

Located within walking distance of M.I.T., and serving a metropolitan area with a density of universities, hospitals, and "hi tech" firms unlike any other in the U.S., the Museum of Science was able to draw on an extensive array of resources for its programs, exhibits, and professional staff. During Dr. Nichol's tenure the museum's Board of Trustees had grown in stature; among Boston's business and professional leaders the Museum of Science ranked with the Boston Symphony and the Museum of Fine Arts as a desirable philanthropic affiliation. In 1987 the trustees included chief executives from Boston's largest banks, insurance companies, and technology firms, as well as prominent doctors, lawyers and educators. Between 1982 and 1987 the operating budget increased from $2 million to $16 million, and the staff grew to 400 from less than one-hundred. Figure 9–14 is taken from a letter from Nichols included in the 1985–86 annual report which describes the nature of the changes occuring during this period.

Initially Robin Carter was interviewed for a job overseeing revenue areas, such as the shop and parking garage, but as they talked Nichols became extremely enthusiastic about using her to direct special exhibits, as well as all of the special events that went on within the museum. Large-scale "theme" exhibitions, which drew upon the professional resources of a number of museum departments, were an area of increasing interest for Nichols, and he perceived a need to have a permanent staff member who would coordinate and monitor the production of these exhibitions.

As a minister's wife Robin was not enthusiastic about working for a non-profit institution; nonetheless the job had several advantages. Although the proposed salary was barely adequate, she would have 23 vacation days annually—in addition to holidays—and the museum was prepared to send her to several museum management programs. Then there was the institution itself: "For me there were ethical considerations," Robin said. "The Museum of Science was a place I could stand behind 100%."

Robin acknowledged that the prospect of working for Roger Nichols was also very appealing:

> What I learned at my first interview was that the director had come in after a man who had been there forty years. Roger Nichols is a creative, innovative force. He is not a manager. He is a ball of fire, he is driven, and he has more ideas than you can imagine. So what he knew he needed was people who can manage at a time of transition.

Figure 9–14 REPORT OF THE YEAR 1985–86 FROM THE PRESIDENT, ROGER L. NICHOLS

Undeniably, the last two years have been the busiest ever at this Museum. When we issued our last Annual Report to you, you may recall that it featured a beautiful color photograph of the *CHINA* exhibition on the front cover. The exhibition had just opened after 80 frantic days of preparation, and our entire staff had thrown itself full force into the fray, installing the exquisite components, arranging for myriad extra activities and demonstrations, recruiting volunteers and exhibit guides, and tending to the social needs and personal accommodations of our 20 visiting artisans, who soon became our friends.

It doesn't seem possible, but that was two years ago! Since then, we went on to complete the six-month stay of the *CHINA* exhibition—the most successful in our history; and entered into a new phase of Museum life, climaxed by the opening of our new wing and the Mugar Omni Theater. It is not an exaggeration to say that *CHINA* changed everything! This Museum is not the same place it was in 1985 when the gentle Chinese artisans said their final "dzai jin's" and returned to their home provinces half-way around the world.

What is different? For one thing, we introduced the concept of blockbuster exhibitions, and in these two years have opened such crowd pleasers as *Return of the Dinosaurs, Robots and Beyond,* and *India: A Festival of Science.* Other smaller but exciting exhibitions, like *The Mary Rose, Science of Sports,* and *Wolves and Humans,* have also kept the pace fast and upbeat. Even now, while *India* still lures enthralled audiences, a new extravaganza, *Ramesses the Great,* looms on the horizon.

In these intervening months, we also welcomed the largest crowds in our history—moving from an annual attendance of 800,000 to an attendance of 1.2 million per year, and an expectation of 1.5 million this year!

The new wing is a friendly meeting place with its new Café and greatly enlarged Shop, greeting visitors until well into the middle evening hours.

Without a doubt, the Mugar Omni Theater is an additional educational headline attraction here at Science Park. Its every showing is packed with children of all ages—6 to 60 and well beyond—sharing in the magic moments of outer space travel. The theater's current offerings—*The Dream Is Alive,* which recounts the adventure of the US space shuttle experiences; and *New England Time Capsule,* made for us especially and featuring original and highly acclaimed music created by John Williams—are still thrilling a full house with every showing.

To top off the successes of these two years, our Development Office raised more than 18 million dollars during this period—something never before accomplished in such a short time frame! We take it as a sign that we have earned your respect and your continuing and generous support, and we are truly grateful.

All of this activity means that we did not take time out to prepare a formal Annual Report documenting the year 1985–86. Instead, we are presenting here a summary of the Auditors Report for that period, together with the names of those persons responsible for our successes.

We are now preparing a two-year report that will chronicle the events we have briefly skimmed here and bring you up to date on the activities that will bring us to the brink of a new decade. I know you will understand the priority we placed on doing the job first . . . and writing about it later!

Until our next report, in a few months, thank you once again for your support of all we are doing at Science Park.

Roger Nichols

continued

Figure 9–14 CONTINUED

STATEMENT OF SUPPORT, REVENUE, EXPENSES, AND CHANGES IN FUND BALANCES FOR THE YEAR ENDED APRIL 30, 1986

	Operating Funds	Endowment Funds	Plant Funds	Combined Totals 1986	Combined Totals 1985
Support and revenue:					
Support:					
Unrestricted gifts and grants	$ 4,443,770			$ 4,443,770	$ 1,682,862
Restricted gifts and grants	507,633	$ 439,169	$ 263,275	1,210,077	692.541
Total support	4,951,403	439,169	263,275	5,653,847	2,375,403
Revenue:					
Admissions	3,355,504			3,355,504	1,663,164
Education Contracts and Courses	1,194,421			1,194,421	1,039,474
Memberships, including business	1,191,730			1,191,730	878,927
Investment income and gains, net	858,686	554,557	4,008	1,417,251	665,591
Ancillary Services	3,229,519			3,229,519	1,890,783
Miscellaneous	99,273			99,273	73,632
Total revenue	9,929,133	554,557	4,008	10,487,698	6,211,571
Total support and revenue	14,880,536	993,726	267,283	16,141,545	8,586,974
Expenses:					
Program services:					
Education	1,729,643			1,729,643	1,271,421
Exhibits maintenance and development	1,569,373			1,569,373	792,991
Planetarium and OMNIMAX Theaters	451,231			451,231	303,705
Other	95,091			95,091	213,485
Total program services	3,845,338			3,845,338	2,581,602
Support services:					
Development, campaign and memberships	806,995			806,995	694,997
Marketing and Publications	1,100,022			1,100,022	609,675
Administration and general	1,257,145			1,257,145	995,335
Building maintenance and utilities	1,578,532			1,578,532	1,503,766
Visitor and Volunteer services	2,296,869			2,296,869	1,371,905
Total support services	7,039,563			7,039,563	5,175,678
Total expenses	10,884,901			10,884,901	7,757,280
Excess of support and revenue over expenses	3,995,635	993,726	267,283	5,256,644	829,694
Transfers:					
Exhibits construction and building renovations	(1,656,372)		1,656,372		
Other transfers, net	106,330		(106,330)		
Total transfers	(1,550,042)		1,550,042		
Net increase in fund balances	2,445,593	993,726	1,817,325	5,256,644	829,694
Fund balances, beginning of year, as previously reported					40,109,577
Cumulative effect of accounting change for restricted gifts and grants					(957,242)
Fund balances, beginning of year, as restated	2,301,838	8,117,411	29,562,780	39,982,029	39,152,335
Fund balances, end of year	$ 4,747,431	$9,111,137	$31,380,105	$45,238,673	$39,982,029

Robin described her job description as it developed:

> What Roger needed was someone to manage the big theme exhibitions, which come to us from other countries, other institutions, and so require extensive transport and installation arrangements, but which also require a unified marketing and promotional effort. An example would be the "India" exhibit which was here during the summer of 1987. Like the earlier China exhibit, this kind of project is different in both size and scope. Not only are there the artifacts which must be catalogued and displayed, but there are special events, educational programs, tie-ins with other areas of the museum. These are expensive exhibits to mount, and so we must have sufficient publicity to ensure that the admissions meet expectations. The museum is 80% self-supporting, which means that most of our operating funds come from admissions, the store, the restaurants, and parking. And corporate donations are based on traffic, because they want the visibility. So it is essential that the museum both attract visitors and provide them with a pleasant experience.
>
> What I was hired to do is project management. I was to bring the efforts of all the different departments into a cohesive whole, so that from the visitor's point of view an exhibition could come across as a total picture. Marketing would not outsell a modest exhibit; or, if an exhibit was to be spectacular, we would have proportional education programs. The reality would meet the visitors' expectations.

The Boston Museum of Science, which also housed the Hayden Planetarium, was located on the Charles River between Boston and Cambridge, almost equidistant from M.I.T. and the Massachusetts General Hospital. Physical facilities included a parking garage which could accommodate 1000 cars, three restaurants, and a substantial gift shop. The Omni Theater, opened in March, 1987, featured the world's largest film format projection and sound system, housed in a domed structure four stories high.

The Museum of Science was organized into five divisions, each under the aegis of an associate director. (See Figure 9–15 for an outline of organization.) The divisions were further divided into sections and units.

Figure 9–15 ADMINISTRATIVE STAFF

President and Director
Roger L. Nichols
Assistant to the President: Amelia Brock
Executive Secretary: Jean Buitekan
Deputy Director: Sally A. Zinno
Special Assistant to the President: Bradford I. Towle

Administration and Finance Division
Associate Director and Division Head: Arthur J. Keeley
Museum Purchasing: Stephen Martinson, Head

Other Administrative Services
Employee Services: Marilyn K. Valvo, Head
Data Processing: Anne Pfohl, Head
Physical Plant and Technical Services Section: Lawrence J. Ralph, Head
Electronics and Technical Services: Kevin Pearson, Head
Garage and Security: Keith James, Head

Operations Section
Assistant Division Director and Section Head: William Murphy
Museum Store: Margaret Dasha, Head
Group Sales and Telemarketing: Sarah J. Gindel, Head
Function Sales: Jonnet Holladay, Head

Education and Visitor Services Division
Associate Director and Division Head: Peter J. Ames
Education Section: A. William Kochanczyk, Head
Discovery Spaces: Carol B. Barleon, Head
Library: Edward D. Pearce, Head
Public Services Section: Phyllis Dohanian, Head
Admissions: Kori Scarborough, Head
Volunteer Services: Pamela Phillips Swain, Head
Interpretation and Training: Paul Fontaine, Head
Special Events and Exhibitions Coordination: Robin Bullard Carter, Head
Educational Technology Section: Inabeth Miller, Head
ComputerPlace: Virginia Woolley, Head
Science Resource Center: Henry Robinson, Head
Special Program Services: Brent R. Jackson, Head

Exhibits Division
Associate Director and Division Head: Lawrence Bell
Traveling Exhibits: Janice Crocker, Head

Theaters and Marketing Division
Associate Director and Division Head: John W. Jacobsen
Omni Theater: Mary Jane Dodge, Head
Planetarium Section: John M. Carr, Head
Marketing Section: Dana L.B. Wilson, Head
Publications: Lorraine T. Welsh, Head

Resources Division
Associate Director and Division Head: Dominic C. Varisco
Development Section: Barry A. Burlingham, Head
Development: Linda Tober, Unit Head
Corporate Membership: Lynn Porter, Head
Membership: Linda Wolf, Head

Other Development Services
Governmental Grants and Support: P. Cardie Texter, Head
Special Events and Traveling Exhibitions Support Coordinator: Stephanie Beidler

There had been a good deal of re-structuring and turnover at the associate director level prior to Robin's joining the Museum; as of early 1988 only two associate directors had been at the museum longer than Robin had.

Existing Policies and Practices

Despite the enthusiastic sponsorship of Roger Nichols, Robin Carter experienced a period of extreme difficulty in forging a working relationship with the museum's associate directors, including her own boss, a man she did not meet until she had been at the museum for six weeks. Robin described the beginning of her career at the museum as follows:

> The museum of was not ready for me. It is a very complex institution that found itself stretched in many ways, with systems not able to handle all of the demands. I was thrust into the middle of a difficult transition, and I had no idea what the politics were and what the hidden agenda might be.

Robin also discovered that, as inspiring and energizing as he was, Roger Nichols proved to be something of a problem as a manager. Dr. Nichols had a habit of acting on his ideas without consulting others. This often meant that he hired people and inserted them into the organization regardless of qualifications. He also recruited staff members to work on new projects without consulting their superiors. Robin explained how this impulsiveness with respect to hiring had affected her own situation:

> The director had a tendency to hire people because he liked something about them. Sometimes he was right and sometimes he was wrong. I had an MBA but no museum experience, and the first reaction of the museum body was, why was she hired? I knew that right away. I knew that I had to prove myself to the other 300 or 400 people here.

Robin described Nichols' mode of operating as follows:

> He was an M.D. who had a tenured seat at Harvard, and he had come to the museum five years earlier. He had wonderful vision, tremendous dynamism. He was the kind of person you are willing to give so much for. But I could see that there were drawbacks. He pulled people out of departments and gave them authority that they shouldn't have had. He created tensions between people.
>
> My own boss had no idea I had been hired and was very upset. Why was an MBA hired, for a job that didn't exist, and he was stuck with me? I had been hired for a job Roger developed in his imagination. Every time something new came up, he'd say, "Why don't we let Robin do that?" Within a month of my being here his five associate directors were off the wall. They didn't know what my job was, and neither did I.

Robin explained her initial perception of the working environment as follows:

> People were very territorial. They very much owned their jobs. They take great personal and professional pride in what they do. So putting a non-museum person in charge of major projects was not well-received.
>
> What I had to do, because my job was so undefined, was to find out who in the museum would play with me at all. There were a few that saw that maybe I could lighten their load, but the majority saw me as a pain in the neck. Project management had never existed in the museum before, and it is an approach that requires the support of everybody.
>
> The director *told* people about the change to project management, but that didn't mean anything because they had no experience with it. They were sure that it would be more trouble than it was worth. What I had to do was teach people how budgeting was done, how my job worked, that I wasn't making decisions for them but needed *their* decisions to do my job. I continually reinforced that they were the ones that had the responsibility.

She described how she approached her job initially:

> There was one exhibit on the floor and one in planning, and those people began to report to me. I decided I would listen to them and learn from them, rather than assume I had anything to offer at this point. My management style is very hands-off. I tried to be extremely supportive of the two people who were doing the project, letting them make the decisions and tell me what they were doing. I put in my time on that exhibit, making very sure that I knew what was happening so I could learn how these things worked, but not interfering.
>
> In the meantime we were developing a number of exhibits, including one on Robotics, and I had to start working on it because it was my project. I had hired a staff member to work on it. When I hired people I told them, "One of the most important jobs you have here is diplomacy. We're a new department and no one quite trusts us yet." We set up meetings of the teams on each project and we sent people notes and follow-up notes. People began to see that if they needed to know something about a project we were the people to ask.
>
> I also was fighting a battle in the budget area.

People would decide whether or not they would contribute anything out of their department budget, and I wanted the budgets viewed as total project budgets. Then, if a cut has to be made it is made on the total project, instead of cutting a whole piece of it out. There had been a lot of turnover in the finance area—there have been four people since I have been here, and I have had to sell the concept to each one.

As her role developed Robin was charged with managing the opening festivities for all major exhibitions. She devised a system for classifying exhibitions according to scope and type and set up a committee of top-level managers to oversee planning of large-scale exhibitions, thus ensuring that the associate directors were involved in all major projects.

The Associate Director of Education and Visitor Services

The most difficult problem for Robin proved to be her relationship with her immediate supervisor, Peter Ames. Ames had been hired as director of her department in April of 1986 but was not to begin work at the museum until mid-July. When he arrived to find Robin, an MBA without any science background, he was furious; he proceeded to treat her in a manner which prompted her to think about leaving. Robin described this period as follows:

In mid-summer I started reporting to a new associate director who, had he been there when I was interviewed, never would have hired me. He was a lawyer by training, and he was difficult—at best—to deal with. He was all over my case about everything. The first couple of meetings with him unnerved me. Every time I tried to talk with him he would cut me off and tell me what was on his mind. It was impossible to get through to him. After six weeks I was ready to hand in my resignation.

I knew we were having trouble communicating but I also knew that he wasn't going to do anything about it. I finally decided that I would try asking him to tell me about himself.

He handed me his resume. I said, "No, Peter, I want to know what you do in your spare time. What you like to eat. Where do you go on the weekends?" It seemed to break the ice. He began to open up, although he still didn't care who *I* was. He was convinced that I was a misfit, so I had to find a way to show him that I was going to be an asset to him. I had to figure out what he wanted to prove, because he was so argumentative about everything. He was so defensive and anxious he couldn't deal with the rest of us. But then he had just arrived, too.

Robin soon realized that she was at a disadvantage with Ames because she had a direct line to the top:

Of course Roger and I had already developed a strong rapport, and now Peter, my new boss, had to deal with this triangular relationship. But I had to be able to work with Peter in such a way that he wasn't going to mess me up. I had to develop a relationship with him in order to make him feel that I supported and worked for him, when at the same time I was constantly being called into the director's office. When he first saw me coming out of the director's office he snapped at me. "What were you in there for? Never go in there without telling me!" He was very threatened by my direct contact with the director. So I was careful to keep him informed about everything I did. I kept him in touch on what I was doing, where I was going, and what projects I was working on. But it was very difficult. Who was I really reporting to?

Despite her difficulty with Ames, Robin learned that at least one associate director had discovered that her "interference" had resulted in several well-executed projects, which had reflected well on the professional staff without costing them an undue amount of effort. As Robin explained later, "What he said was that I had taken on many things which other people weren't prepared to do, and as a result I had justifiably acquired a lot of power and influence at the museum. It frequently happens here that people are willing to take on a project but not really the responsibility for executing it."

As an example Robin cited the previous year's Washburn Awards Dinner, the first major project to be her total responsibility:

This was an important assignment. It was the first project I did as an employee here and it is also their largest fund-raising dinner. The dinner was scheduled for October.

I hired an assistant and the two of us worked on this project all by ourselves. I had told her, "This project must be flawless." Roger Nichols is the kind of person who can always find something that isn't quite right. He is wonderful at congratulating you, but he will always add, "Next time let us make sure that we do the following."

I interviewed the woman who had done it the year before. I got to know a woman who worked here who had done a lot of these kinds of projects. I had to be sure that everything that could possibly go wrong was addressed beforehand.

The food, the audio-visual presentation, hosting special guests, the written materials—everyone on the Board of Trustees has an idea of how these things should be done. Who sits at what table, what happens when—these events only work if they are good from the point of view of the people who pay for them. So I listened a lot and figured out what was important to each and every one of them. I would say, "Alright, and what else is on your mind?"

One of the concerns was the upstairs bathroom, which would be used extensively by people before going into dinner. It had to be kept clean. The handling of people—this building is not set up for functions, and we had to figure out the easiest way to get people from one floor to another. We had to be able to get a feeling for what the event would be like from the point of view of the guests. This is what I harp on with my staff: how do you make a visit here a pleasant experience for a *visitor?* Our viewpoint here can become very inverted.

At the end of the evening Roger Nichols came to me and said, "This is the first event that we have done at the museum that has been perfect."

Robin added that her success in managing the Awards Dinner did not further her credibility with anyone but Nichols. In order to gain the trust and cooperation of the other professionals, Robin spent much of her time visiting the departments, asking questions, and reassuring people that she was there to work with them. In Robin's words,

I knew that I couldn't get raises or promotions or anything if I didn't get the associate directors' support. I need the other five people to view me as credible and as a person worth working with. I knew that it would be very, very dangerous to just hook my star to the director.

I got acquainted with people, learned what they did, and was very up front about my lack of a science background. I would say, what I am good at is management. What you are good at is the content of this exhibit. I'm good at making sure it works and you know what it needs to have value. I tried to get them to view my department's contribution as another layer, and not to take away from what they were contributing.

The Process of Developing an Exhibition

The 1988 Ramesses II exhibition would be representative of the new "blockbuster" approach favored by Nichols. The project would engage the resources of the entire museum and would be promoted on a scale to entice the interest, and hopefully attendance, of a large segment of the northeastern population. A promotional brochure published by the museum communicated the importance of the exhibit as follows:

Since much of our knowledge of Ramesses II and his time comes to us through the science of archaeology, the Boston Museum of Science is honored to host the only Northeast United States appearance of the Ramesses the Great exhibition.

This largest and most varied assembling of treasures from Egypt's Golden Age ever brought to the United States offers a dual opportunity that may come only once in a lifetime. First, a journey back over 3000 years to the time of Ramesses the Great and the New Kingdom to examine the priceless evidences and artifacts of Egyptian accomplishments. And second, the chance to explore the methods and analyses that led archeologists to their discoveries.

The exhibition's opening in late April was preceded by a massive publicity effort, including numerous articles and advertisements in Boston-area publications and billboards featuring the Ramesses coffin with the slogan, "Grand opening April 30." An article in the May 14 *Boston Ledger* described the week of special events leading up to the opening of the exhibit, which included a champagne and caviar reception for Queen Farida, the former queen of Egypt:

A full week of festivities royally welcomed Egypt's most famous pharaoh Ramesses the Great to the bank of Boston's Nile—the Charles River. Before the show's public unveiling, Museum of Science volunteers and staffers braced themselves for a series of private receptions, dinners and exhibit tours to fete Fidelity and Sheraton corporate sponsors, museum trustees and VIPs and an unexpectedly huge press contingent. To top off the excitement, the museum even planned one big final fundraising bash of their own.

Numerous additional exhibits within the museum were planned to support and expand on the Ramesses material. There were to be lectures and a film series, as well as several museum-sponsored trips to Egypt scheduled to coincide with the exhibition.

Robin explained that the current Rameses II exhibition was not typical, in that most projects were not as elaborate and did not require so much involvement from senior management. She described the usual process as follows:

In many cases ideas originate with Roger. He will hear about something marvelous and go after it. There is a process whereby exhibit proposals go to the exhibit department, then to a committee, and then up to Roger. But often Roger will say, "I want this exhibit," and whether or not everyone agrees, it comes here.

With Rameses I felt that I needed control of the budget. Each department had a part of a $6 million budget and they were unwilling to let it be seen as part of a whole. There was a lot of in-fighting. It was finally decided that Roger would head up the project and that I would work with him directly on it. But without control of their budget, I could not make any of the other department directors do anything.

Robin described the usual process of developing an exhibition as follows:

1. Brainstorming—Robin and all involved department heads would talk about what the exhibit as visualized would need in terms of total programming, what Robin called "a pool of intentions."
2. All costs of the exhibit would be determined.
3. Robin's department would develop a budget and make a recommendation based on what the departments each projected as their part of the exhibit.
4. A project budget was developed and Robin communicated to each of the departments what their budget was, in return for what they were expected to contribute to that particular exhibit.
5. Robin would periodically report back to individual departments on their performance with respect to the budget.

Robin added that because she did not have the "final clout," departments could spend their allotment for the Ramesses exhibition however they wished. "If the associate director didn't back me up there would be nothing I could do about it," she explained. "I didn't have that final control, and no one wanted to relinquish that much power—the budget for Ramesses was $6 million."

For the Ramesses exhibit Robin and the project managers met with the associate directors every week. But even on smaller projects she made it a point to involve management from other departments as soon and as often as possible. She explained that this was necessary in order to ensure that the promotion and educational programs all were directed at the same target audience:

One of the ways we get people to buy into a unified concept is to bring all of the departments together at the very early stages and say, "This is kind of what the exhibit is going to look like and this the kind of scope we are planning. The marketing effort will be pretty extensive. We may need to add some programming. So you come back and tell us what you think."

When I actually go into a department to get something, it may be because that department is out of sync with the others. For example, marketing uses numbers in ways that can be very deceptive. The Kenya exhibit has 250 artifacts and the Ramesses exhibit 72, but Kenya is taking 400 square feet and the Rameses II exhibit is being housed in the entire museum. So using the number in promotion pieces is very deceptive, because with Kenya there are a lot of little things, like combs and pieces of paper. Finally we were able to get them to see that it was not good to oversell.

The Situation in January, 1988

After eighteen months at the Museum of Science Robin Carter felt that she had achieved a measure of acceptance. She had increased her own staff to thirteen people. She was currently managing $8.5 million worth of projects. She had been promoted from unit to section head, and, since there were few other women managers at her level, she found that other women in the museum had begun to come to her for counseling.

There continued to be a good deal of turnover among associate directors. Robin rationalized the stability of her own department as follows:

My department was created by a man who understood the need for it. He understood that to make the museum a world-class one they would have to do more theme exhibitions and that they would have to be managed well to achieve maximum effect. He has an awareness of what is happening in the museum industry, that we are competing with other "leisure" activities, and that we have to be very effective in competing for that time. My department was his solution to how to manage a continual flow of new things, to keep the audience enticed and coming back.

Robin believed that she and Peter Ames had finally developed a good working relationship, as she realized when he told her one day that, "It's amazing that we think so much alike!" Robin commented, "Part of it was his own anxiety about adapting to a new environment. He is very outspoken and he was having problems with almost everyone." Further,

He is very clear-thinking, but he takes in information in certain ways and he shuts down very quickly if he isn't getting it that way.

Over time he built a bit better relationship with the director himself, and as our own relationship became stronger he became more comfortable. I was always on budget, always kept him informed, always produced the visual aids he needed, gave him graphs and support material that made him feel he had a grasp on what I was doing. I gave him things that he would then take to Roger. Now he very rarely interferes with what I do.

We work extremely well together now. I don't think

it's because he likes me any better. It's because I have proven to be his most valuable staff member. He knows he can depend on me. But it took a long time.

ROBIN CARTER AND THE MUSEUM OF SCIENCE (B)

On December 10, 1987, Roger Nichols, director of the Boston Museum of Science, died unexpectedly. As his brilliant leadership of one of Boston's major institutions came to an abrupt end, Robin Carter and the rest of the Museum of Science staff were left both saddened and disoriented. In late January 1988, Robin described how the death of the director had affected her own position at the museum:

> The evening before he died, I had met with him unexpectedly. I was working late, we had a meeting scheduled the next day, and he called me into his office and told me that he was going to make me an acting associate director. I was going to be put in charge of a new, branch museum in another city, a project in which he was extremely interested. He told me, "You have remarkable talents in administration and management, and although you are weak in science and education, you are the best person I have to send on this project."
>
> The next morning he was dead. I was no longer an acting associate director. The project was going to be put on hold. I was devastated—at my loss of a friend and of a person with whom I had worked closely. Then, the interim director and the board chairman became very, very anxious about the Ramesses exhibit. It was the biggest thing on our plate for the year, and the man who was responsible for it was gone.

Robin was able to manage the Ramesses exhibit, although, in her words, "The board put me through hoops doing presentations. They were scared. I knew we could do the job, but *they* needed to know that we could do the job."

A larger question for Robin was whether or not her position, and her future, would be assured at the museum. She felt that she "got along well" with the interim director, but that as a 32-year veteran of IBM, he was not a risk-taker. Robin assessed her situation as follows:

> I am not concerned about keeping this job. I believe that three of the associate directors completely support this department. It takes a load off of them and brings a consistent level of professionalism to every exhibit.
>
> The issue for me is whether I can go from here to somewhere else. This museum is on the cutting edge of science museums all over the world, and it takes a kind of energy and entrepreneurial disposition to run it. I came here because I believed in the vision of the director, and because it was not your typical staid, non-profit institution. I'll only stay if it remains that kind of dynamic place.

During the following months Robin began interviewing for positions outside the museum. Events had developed which convinced her of the need to change jobs. The interim director appeared to be permanent. More to the point, her relationship with her boss, Peter Ames, had deteriorated to an alarming state. According to Robin, resentment built up over her closeness with Nichols had manifested itself in his treating her in an authoritarian, dictatorial manner:

> After Roger died I began to find out how angry Peter had been about my relationship with the director. He turned on me. He thought I had been given too much freedom. Everything I do now has to have his approval. I write everything for him, and he presents it. I no longer speak for myself.

Although the Ramesses exhibit had been extremely successful, and Robin recently had been offered a new job at the museum, she did not feel that there was sufficient support for her efforts to make it worth her while to continue. She summarized her reasons for deciding to leave as follows:

> The current acting director is likely to be here much longer than I thought. I was told directly that he does not believe that women belong in senior management.
>
> The Ramesses exhibit was budgeted to make $ .5 million based on 600,000 attendance. We had over 700,000 and made $3 million. I got no credit or recognition. The financial statements do not attribute the increase in revenue to the exhibition.
>
> I have been offered a new position, which is very subtle acknowledgment that I am valued as an employee. It is as section head for operations, which means I would manage admissions, group sales, the stores, telemarketing—all revenue-producing activities except the restaurants, which are subcontracted. What they call "ancillary services." I would have many more people reporting to me, but it is still a lateral move.
>
> I felt it was the interim director's way of saying that they want me and that there is a place for me. But there would be no growth. Within the context of the museum, I would be moving into an area which is regarded as a necessary evil. I would have to move to another museum to move up.
>
> I want the opportunity to help something grow. I want to be a member of senior management. And so,

> I believe that at age 47, I must work somewhere for five years and establish myself.

In August, Robin accepted a job offer managing the financial, development, and "business" operations of a four-year-old non-profit service and training organization. She would be working on an equal basis with the three founding directors. She described the rationale for this move as follows:

> My next job will be working as part of senior management with three people who know very little about finance or business. They view me as the business savior. This new situation appeals to me for the following reasons:
>
> I am supportive of their mission; there is potential for growth; there is the challenge of an entrepreneurial venture; I can develop credibility as a senior manager; I will have a voice in policy-making and a chance to speak on behalf of the firm.

Robin concluded by saying that she would have done better to have entered the museum as a specialist, since "manager" was still an unfamiliar, and unpalatable, term there, and as such she had been viewed with skepticism:

> One of my main strengths is being able to see how all the pieces fit together. I have always thought of myself as a generalist. Being a general manager means that I know and understand finance, marketing communications. But if you tell someone you are a general manager, they say, what's that? Is it that you're not good at anything, or that you are sort of good at everything?
>
> The understanding of what goes on between people is far more important than understanding basic things which are easy to learn. You can learn accounting. It is harder to learn effective communications, how to listen, to hear what people are saying, to negotiate. It requires being able to step out of yourself, not to be threatened, to realize that it might not work out the way you wanted it. It is so much easier to make a decision and do something than it is to get other people to work together.

Step 2: Prepare the case for class discussion.

Step 3: Answer the following questions, individually, in small groups, or with the entire class, as directed by your instructor:

Description

1. Briefly list the key events and identify the main actors in the case.
2. Describe Robin Carter's job responsibilities at the Museum of Science.

Diagnosis

3. What problems existed in this organization?
4. What influenced Robin's actions?
5. What sources of power did she develop and use?
6. Did she use power effectively?
7. Did she develop alliances, informal networks, or trade relations?
8. Did she exert political influence in the organization? If so, what type?
9. Was she an effective leader?
10. Was Robin an effective negotiator?
11. What strategies and tactics did she use?
12. How effectively did she motivate and communicate with her coworkers? her boss?
13. How do theories of personal and career development explain the problems she encountered?

Prescription

14. Looking back at the entire case, what advice would you have given Robin?
15. How could she have used power better?
16. How could she have negotiated more effectively?

Action

17. What costs and benefits would be associated with this plan of action?

Step 4: Discussion. In small groups, with the entire class, or in written form, share your answers to the questions above. Then answer the following questions:

1. What symptoms suggested a problem existed?
2. What problems existed in the case?
3. What theories and concepts help explain the problems?
4. How were the problems corrected?
5. Was the action effective?
6. What problems remain to be corrected?
7. How would you correct them?

This case was prepared by Jeanne Stanton for the Institute for Case Development and Research, Graduate School of Management, Simmons College,

Activity 9–5: THE USED CAR ROLE PLAY

Step 1: Read the following background information:

You are about to negotiate the purchase/sale of an automobile. The seller advertised the car in the local newspaper. (Note: Both role-players should interpret "local" as the town in which the role play is occurring.) Before advertising it, the seller took the car to the local Volkswagen dealer, who has provided the following information:

1986 VW Jetta diesel, standard shift.
White with red upholstery, tinted glass.
AM/FM radio.
30,450 miles; steel belted radial tires expected to last 65,000.
45 miles per gallon on diesel fuel at current prices (usually about 10 percent less than regular gasoline).
No rust; dent on passenger door barely noticeable.
Mechanically perfect except exhaust system, which may or may not last another 10,000 miles (costs $300 to replace.)
"Blue book" retail value, $5,000; wholesale, $4,400 (local 1988 prices).
Car has spent its entire life in the local area; it is the only used diesel Jetta within a 60-mile radius.

Step 2: Your instructor will divide the class into groups of two—the buyer and the seller of the used car. Your instructor will then distribute the roles to each group. After assigning one role to each group member, read the role description. Then spend five minutes "getting into your role." As part of your preparation, answer the three questions at the end of your role description.

Step 3: After you have read about and prepared your roles, negotiate with the other party. Spend about fifteen to twenty-five minutes meeting with the other person and decide on a course of action. When you have reached an agreement complete the following information:

Price:
Manner of Payment:
Special Terms and Conditions:
Signed by:
Seller: ______________________
Buyer: ______________________

Step 4: The instructor will ask each pair to report its agreement. Then describe the process used in your negotiation.

Step 5: Answer the following questions with the entire class:

Description
1. What solution did each group reach?

Diagnosis
2. What are some key features of the bargaining situation?
3. What influenced the effectiveness of negotiations?
4. What effect did the bargaining range have on the negotiations?
5. What effect did each party's interests and best alternative to a negotiated agreement (BATNA) have on the negotiations?

Prescription
6. How could the effectiveness of the negotiations be improved?

Based on the role play developed by Professor Leonard Greenhalgh of Dartmouth College and used with his permission.

Activity 9–6: UGLI ORANGE ROLE PLAY

Step 1: The instructor will divide the class into groups of three—in each group one person will play Dr. Roland, one will play Dr. Jones, and one will be an observer. The instructor will then distribute the roles to each group. After assigning one role for each group member, read the role descriptions. Then spend five minutes "getting into your role."

Step 2: The group leader will read—

> I am Mr(s). Cardoza, the owner of the remaining Ugli oranges. My fruit-exporting firm is based in South America. My country does not have diplomatic relations with your country, although we do have strong trade relations.

After you have read about your roles, you may negotiate with the other firm's representative. Spend about ten minutes meeting with the other firm's representative and decide on a course of action. Be prepared to answer the following questions:

1. What do you plan to do?
2. If you want to buy the oranges, what price will you offer?
3. To whom and how will the oranges be delivered?

Step 3: The observers will report the solutions reached. Then they will describe the process used in their negotiating team.

Step 4: Discussion. Answer the following questions with the entire class:

Description

1. What solution did each group reach?

Diagnosis

2. What are some key features of a bargaining situation?
3. What influences the effectiveness of negotiations?

Prescription

4. How can the effectiveness of negotiations be improved?

Reprinted by permission of the author, Robert J. House, University of Toronto.

Activity 9–7: SALARY NEGOTIATIONS

INTRODUCTION

In this simulation, you will play the role of either a manager or subordinate in a negotiation over salary. Both in securing employment as well as promotions, we frequently are in a position to negotiate with our superiors over salary; and, once we achieve managerial rank, we do the same with subordinates. This is one of the most common and, at the same time, most personal forms of negotiation; for many people, it is also the most difficult. Since salary can be a means of satisfying many needs—economic, recognition, status, or competitive success measure—it leads to complex negotiations.

PROCEDURE

Step 1: (5 Minutes) The class will be divided into groups of three; two will be assigned the roles of manager and subordinate, the other as an observer. Role-players will be assigned either an "A" or a "B" role in one of the Salary Simulations. Assemble with your trio in the place specified by the instructor.

Step 2: (5 Minutes) Read your assigned role and prepare a strategy. If you are an observer, review the Observer Reporting Sheet and make sure you understand what to look for.

Step 3: (10 Minutes) Carry out your discussion with your counterpart. If you finish before the allotted time is up, review the sequence of events with the other party and tell the other what he or she did that was productive or unproductive to the negotiations.

If you are an observer, make brief notes during the role-play on your Observer Reporting Sheet. When the role-play is over, review the sheet and add further details where necessary.

Step 4: (10 Minutes) In your trio, discuss the outcome of the negotiation. The observer should report what he or she saw each party doing. Review what steps or positions seemed most and least useful.

At the end of the time for Step 4, the observer should hand his Observer Reporting Sheet to the instructor.

Step 5: (5 Minutes) In your trio, change role assignments so that the person filling an A role now fills a B role, the person filling the B role now becomes observer, and the previous observer now fills an A role.

Step 6: (5 Minutes) Repeat step 2.

Step 7: (10 Minutes) Repeat step 3.

Step 8: (10 Minutes) Repeat step 4.

Steps 9, 10, 11, 12: (30 Minutes) Repeat steps 5, 6, 7, 8.

Observer Reporting Sheet

Round ________.

How did A open the meeting? ____

____

____

How did B respond to the way A opened the meeting? ______________________________

____

____

Was an agreement reached? Yes ________, no ________.

What was the salary agreed to, if there was an agreement? ____________________

Were there any other added features in the settlement achieved? ____________________

____

Will future relations between A and B be better (+), worse (−), or the same (=) as a result of this meeting? List the opinions of A, B, and the observer.

A ________, B ________, Observer ________.

Step 13: (30 Minutes) The instructor will post the results from the three sets of role-plays. Examine the different outcomes and explore reasons why they occurred and their consequences.

Step 14: Discussion Questions

1. Were there any differences in the way negotiations were handled when:
   a. Both parties in a role-play were satisfied?
   b. One was satisfied?
   c. Both were dissatisfied?
2. Were some people playing the same role dissatisfied with an outcome that others in the same role found satisfying? Why? How do you account for this?
3. Poll quickly those who were satisfied with the outcome. Ask why they were satisfied.
4. Poll quickly those who were dissatisfied with the outcome. Ask why they were dissatisfied.
5. What was the effect of observing another's negotiation on how you negotiated? Did what you see as an observer affect how satisfied you felt with your own outcome?

Developed by Roy J. Lewicki and published in Lewicki and Litterer, *Negotiations: Readings, Exercises, and Cases,* Richard D. Irwin, 1985. Used with permission.

Activity 9–8: PETER CLAUSEN CASE

Step 1: Read the case of Peter Clausen.

THE ADVERTISING AGENCY

It was 8:30 on a Monday morning and Peter Clausen was going through his mail in his office located in a modern building in Bigtown in Indolandia. He had just returned from a lovely weekend spent with his wife and two children on a beach not too far from the city.

Peter was the managing director of McKintosh, the leading advertising agency in Indolandia, which was set up 10 years ago as a joint-venture between a small local agency and McKintosh, New York. McKintosh had 70 subsidiaries and affiliated agencies in 56 countries and prided itself on being amongst the top 10 advertising agencies in the world.

Peter, who was born in Denmark, joined McKintosh in Copenhagen 11 years ago as an account executive in the client service department. On his own initiative he was transferred to New York from where he was sent to Indolandia two and a half years ago. At the age of 36 he was in charge of 55 members of staff, one being his British creative director, Dick White.

As the workload increased, he tried to have another expatriate brought in to act as head of the client service department. However, his request for a work permit from the government had been turned down. Since most of McKintosh's clients were multinational firms with expatriate directors or marketing managers, they expected an expatriate on the agency side to be their main contact. It was for this reason that Peter had to spend a substantial amount of his time in meetings with clients, a task he felt was rather superfluous since he had full trust in his local client service staff. Instead of discussing the conceptual and main creative work with the agency's team before it was presented to the client, he often found himself seeing the material at the same time as the clients and then selling it to them regardless of whether he liked the output or not. To overcome this problem he brought in additional expatriates on tourist visas from offices in the neighbouring countries for short periods whenever major advertising campaigns had to be developed.

BUSINESS PRINCIPLES OF McKINTOSH

McKintosh's reputation in the market was that of an agency with good creative work, coupled with the best quality final products locally available such as artwork, photography, typesetting, films. The latter was due to the fact that the majority of the advertising material was brought in from the US or Europe only to be adopted locally. McKintosh also had the image of a reliable and trustworthy partner—highly appreciated in a country like Indolandia where media rates (prices for space in print media or time on air on radio and television) were practically never fixed and where it was possible to obtain agency commissions from so-called "official" rates of up to 70%. Most agencies in town charged their clients the full "official" rates or offered them a small discount, pocketing the rest for themselves. As this business was very profitable and the purchase of space and time in the media made up the bulk of advertising budgets of almost all clients, agencies were able to offer development work on advertising campaigns either very cheaply or free of charge.

Peter Clausen's predecessor had decided to implement a different system. He had asked his media buyers to bargain very hard to obtain the lowest rates of all agencies in the country, based on the fact that they placed more orders than anyone else. On the obtained rate he then slapped a standard agency commission of 20% and charged the total to the customers. As a result McKintosh could claim and prove that in terms of media buying they were the cheapest agency in Indolandia. To make up for the lost revenue, however, McKintosh's fees for creative services and artwork were higher than those of most of their competitors. Most of McKintosh's clients not only accepted, but appreciated, this more open pricing policy.

CONTROL MECHANISM

Peter Clausen happily went along with this system which had even enabled him to attract new clients into the agency. He did this by comparing the amount of money clients of other agencies spent for a given media plan with the proposal his own media buyers would give him. Peter also considered this a useful control mechanism for his own staff in the media department which under the given rate system could find it rather easy to divert funds into their own pockets in the form of kick-backs from the media owners.

Another substantial part of McKintosh's business was the printing of advertising material such as brochures, labels, cartons, point-of-sale material, posters, etc. Almost each job was somewhat unique. Differences in paper quality, size, quantities, colour scheme, delivery schedule and so on made it necessary to request quotations from printers for each new job. These differed substantially, even for similar work to be done, due to a variety of factors, one of them probably being the lack of knowledge on the printer's side of their own costs.

This situation necessitated quotations from at least three printers for each job, a time consuming, but, as Peter felt, worthwhile effort. It forced printers who knew that their prices would be compared with their competitors to quote realistically. Peter also assumed that it would reduce the opportunities for the print buyers to give out favours to certain suppliers, since all quotations had to be delivered to the office in closed envelopes and would be opened only in the presence of himself or his financial director. Over time Peter Clausen had visited the most important printers in Bigtown to look at their facilities and at the same time to explain to them their purchasing procedures. He also got personally involved in negotiations with both printers and media from time to time. During those meetings, Peter tried to demonstrate to suppliers as well as to his own print and media buyers that it was he and not his staff who took the final decision. He hoped that this would reduce the temptation of suppliers to offer special incentives to his buyers in exchange for attractive orders.

AN UNEXPECTED VISITOR

Peter Clausen had gone through all of his mail and had just stepped out of his office when he met Mr. Chan, the representative of one of Indolandia's biggest printers, in the corridor. He knew him quite well and somehow liked him—probably because his company had always delivered on time and also produced good quality material. Mr. Chan was Chinese and probably part of the family who owned the company. He was a tough negotiator, knowledgeable and self-confident and his relationship with the buying department was apparently good.

That morning Mr. Chan seemed to be quite irritated. When Peter invited him into his office for a chat he gladly accepted, especially since the chief buyer he wanted to see was not around. Mr. Chan immediately started to talk about his business relationship with McKintosh. He stated that over time the volume of jobs he received from the agency had steadily diminished, despite the fact that he had never let his customers down and delivered the best quality in town. Peter admitted that he had been unaware of this and promised to look into the matter. Mr. Chan further explained that it was McKintosh's chief buyer who was pushing him out of business and who might gradually squeeze the whole agency out of business by making it uncompetitive.

It was at that moment that Peter realized that the discussion involved him in much more than exchanging pleasantries. Mr. Chan continued to accuse his chief buyer of having forced him not only to include in his quotations, "the usual 10%", but then 15% and even 25% lately, to be paid to him as soon as the agency had paid the printer. Mr. Chan felt that the chief buyer had not asked the other printers to increase their percentages. As a result his quotations had probably become so high they were no longer considered.

After listening attentively to Mr. Chan's accusations, Peter Clausen asked Mr. Chan how to solve the problem. Mr. Chan shrugged his shoulders and advised him to get rid of his chief buyer. Then asked whether he would repeat his accusation in front of the chief buyer and other witnesses Mr. Chan smiled and said, "Do you think I want to kill my business? Do you think I want to kill myself? Even if you repeat what I have told you I shall always deny having made those statements. It is your problem, and my problem, but I can try to get orders from other sources while you might price yourself out of the market." With those last words he stood up and walked out of the door.

MR. TANI'S COMMENT

The nice weekend was soon forgotten. Peter realized that he had to do something. Probably the whole agency knew about "the usual 10%." His staff might even laugh about his control procedures, his closed envelopes and visits to suppliers.

Would there by any way to confront his chief buyer with some hard facts? Was there any way of firing him? Peter suddenly remembered that his secretary had once told him that the chief buyer was closely related to somebody in the immigration department of the government and had even helped Peter to obtain the first extension of his work permit, which was very difficult to obtain without special connections, or a substantial amount of money.

Peter called in his financial director, Mr. Tani, a man who had worked for over 30 years for a European multinational, had an impeccable track record and had joined the agency six years ago after he had reached the retirement age in his former firm.

To Peter this man was the only person in the agency he could trust and whose advice he highly appreciated, mainly because of Mr. Tani's maturity and fatherly attitude towards him and everybody else in the agency.

After having recounted the discussion with Mr. Chan, Peter asked him how the agency could stop fraudulent activities in the agency and how to get rid of the chief buyer and anybody else involved in "illegally taking money which did not belong to the company". The more Peter actually talked about it the more desperate, frustrated and at the same time, aggressive he became towards Mr. Tani who patiently sat listening to him. When Peter finally stopped talking and invited Mr. Tani to comment, he replied with a question. "Peter", he said, "How long have you been in this country?" And before Peter could react, he added, "Have you never realized that you work in Indolandia?"

Step 2: Prepare the case for class discussion.

Step 3: Individually, in small groups, or with the entire class, as directed by your instructor, answer the following questions:

Description

1. Describe the situation Peter Clausen faces.

Diagnosis

2. In what types of negotiations was he involved?
3. Did he use power effectively? How could he have used it better?
4. Did he build informal networks, alliances, or trade relations?
5. How effectively did he conduct negotiations inside and outside the organization?
6. What problems arose?

Prescription

8. How should he handle the 10-percent dilemma?
9. How might he ensure that negotiations meet his ethical standards?

Action

10. What likely would have been the consequences?

Step 4: Discussion. In small groups, with the entire class, or in written form, share your answers to the questions above. Then answer the following questions:

1. What symptoms suggest a problem exists?
2. What problems exist in the case?
3. What theories and concepts help explain the problems?
4. How were the problems corrected?
5. Was the action effective?
6. What problems remain to be corrected?
7. How would you correct them?

This case was prepared by Hellmut Schütte, Affiliate Professor at INSEAD.

CONCLUDING COMMENTS

Effective power holders—

1. are sensitive to what others consider to be legitimate behavior in acquiring and using power;
2. have good intuitive understanding of the various types of power and methods of influence;
3. tend to develop all types of power to some degree, and they use all influence methods;
4. establish career goals and seek out managerial positions that allow them to successfully develop and use power;
5. use all their resources, formal authority, and power to develop still more power;
6. engage in power-oriented behavior in ways that are tempered by maturity and self-control;
7. recognize and accept as legitimate that, in using these methods, they clearly influence other people's behavior and lives.[68]

In this chapter, the Sources of Power diagnosis and the Empowerment Profile provided data about personal power experiences. In the cases of Robin Carter and Peter Clausen you saw how individuals drew on diverse sources of power and used negotiations in their organizations. The Used Car, Ugli Orange, and Salary Negotiation role-plays gave you the opportunity to practice your negotiating skills.

ENDNOTES

[1]B. Butterfield, Looming Eastern strike could doom the airline, *Boston Sunday Globe,* 19 February 1989, p. A-1.

[2]*Ibid.*

[3]G.R. Salancik and J. Pfeffer, Who gets power—and how they hold on to it: A strategic-contingency model of power, *Organizational Dynamics* (Winter, 1977): 3–21.

[4]R.M. Kanter, Power failures in management circuits, *Harvard Business Review* 57 (1979): 65–75.

[5]A. Kaplan, Power in perspective. In *Power and Conflict in Organizations,* ed. R.L. Kahn and E. Boulding (London: Tavistock, 1964); M. Weber, *The Theory of Social and Economic Organization* (Glencoe, Ill.: Free Press, 1947).

[6]H. Mintzberg, *Power in and around Organizations* (Englewood Cliffs, N.J.: Prentice-Hall, 1983).

[7]*Ibid.*

[8]*Ibid.*

[9]J.P. Kotter, Power, dependence, and effective management, *Harvard Business Review* 55 (1977): 125–136.

[10]*Ibid.*

[11]*Ibid.*

[12]J.P. Kotter, Power, success, and organizational effectiveness, *Organizational Dynamics* 6 (1978): 27–40.

[13]*Ibid.*

[14]P.M. Blau, *Exchange and Power in Social Life* (New York: John Wiley & Sons, 1964).

[15]R.M. Emerson, Power-dependence relations, *American Sociological Review* 27 (1962): 31–41.

[16]B. Markovsky, D. Weller, and T. Patton, Power relations in exchange networks, *American Sociological Review* 53 (1988): 220–236.

[17]D. McClelland and D.H. Burnham, Power driven managers: Good guys make bum bosses, *Psychology Today* (December 1975): 69–71.

[18]R.M. Steers and L.W. Porter, *Motivation and Work Behavior* (New York: McGraw-Hill, 1979).

[19]McClelland and Burnham, *op. cit.*

[20]McClelland and Burnham, *op. cit.*

[21]L. Sayles, *Leadership: What Effective Managers Really Do and How They Do It* (New York: McGraw-Hill, 1979).

[22]R. Allen, D. Madison, L. Porter, P. Renwick, and B. Mayes, Organizational politics: Tactics and characteristics of its actors, *California Management Review* 22 (1979): 77–83.

[23]J. Gabarro and J. Kotter, Managing your boss, *Harvard Business Review* 58 (1980): 92–100.

[24]W.F.G. Mastenbroek, *Conflict Management and Organization Development* (Chichester, England: Wiley, 1987).

[25]J.A. Conger and R.N. Kanungo, The empowerment process: Integrating theory and practice, *Academy of Management Review* 13 (1988): 471–482.

[26]Kanter, *op.cit.*

[27]Kanter, *op. cit.*

[28]R.E. Spekman, Influence and information: An exploratory investigation of the boundary person's bases of power, *Academy of Management Journal* 22 (1979): 104–117.

[29]G. Hofstede, Motivation, leadership, and organization: Do American theories apply abroad?, *Organizational Dynamics* (Summer 1980); G. Hofstede, *Culture's Consequences: International Differences in Work-Related Values* (Beverly Hills, Cal.: Sage, 1980).

[30]L.A. Mainiero, Coping with powerlessness: The relationship of gender and job dependency to empowerment-strategy usage, *Administrative Science Quarterly* 31 (1986): 633–653.

[31]P. Block, *The Empowered Manager* (San Francisco: Jossey-Bass, 1977); and R.M. Kanter, *The Change Masters* (New York: Simon and Schuster, 1983).

[32]A. Bandura, Self-efficacy: Toward a unifying theory of behavioral change, *Psychological Review* 84 (1977): 191–215.

[33]J.A. Conger, Leadership: The art of empowering others, *Academy of Management Executive* 3(1) (1989): 17–24.

[34]D.J. Hickson, C.R. Hinings, C.A. Lee, R.E. Schneck, and J.M. Pennings, A strategic contingencies theory of intraorganizational power, *Administrative Science Quarterly* 16 (1971): 216–227; note that resource control and network centrality interact with hierarchial authority to create structural sources of power, as described by W.G. Astley and P.S. Sachdeva, Structural sources of intraorganizational power: A theoretical synthesis, *Academy of Management Review* 9 (1984): 104–113.

[35]J. Pfeffer and G.R. Salancik, *The External Control of Organizations* (New York: Harper & Row, 1978).

[36]J.D. Hackman, Power and centrality in the allocation of resources in colleges and universities, *Administrative Science Quarterly* 30 (1985): 61–77.

[37]D. Farrell and J.C. Petersen, Patterns of political behavior in organizations, *Academy of Management Review* 7 (1982): 403–412.

[38]R.E. Kaplan, Trade routes: The manager's network of relationships, *Organizational Dynamics* (Spring, 1984).

[39]*Ibid.*

[40]A.R. Cohen and D.L. Bradford, Influence without authority: The use of alliances, reciprocity, and exchange to accomplish work, *Organizational Dynamics* (1988): 5–16.

[41]W.B. Stevenson, J.L. Pearce, and L.W. Porter, The concept of "coalition" in organization theory and research, *Academy of Management Review* 10 (1985): 256–268.

[42]*Ibid.*

[43]*Ibid.*

[44]M. Ways, The virtues, dangers, and limits of negotiation, *Fortune* (15 January 1979).

[45]D.A. Lax and J.K. Sebenius, *The Manager as Negotiator* (New York: Free Press, 1986).

[46]W.A. Gamson, *Power and Discontent* (Homewood, Ill.: Dorsey Press, 1968).

[47]D.H. Fenn Jr., Finding where the power lies in government, *Harvard Business Review* 57 (1979): 144–153.

[48]D.G. Pruitt, Strategic choice in negotiation, *American Behavioral Scientist* 27 (November-December 1983): 167–194.

[49]Lax and Sebenius, *op. cit.*

[50]R. Fisher and W. Uri, *Getting to Yes: Negotiating Agreement without Giving in* (Boston: Houghton Mifflin, 1981).

[51]J.S. Carroll and M.H. Bazerman, Negotiator cognitions: A descriptive approach to negotiators' understanding of their opponents, *Organizational Behavior and Human Decision Processes* 41 (1988): 352–370.

[52]Lax and Sebenius, *op. cit.*

[53]Lax and Sebenius, *op. cit.*

[54]G.T. Savage, J.D. Blair, and R.L. Sorenson, Consider both relationships and substance when negotiating strategically, *Academy of Management Executive* 3(1) (1989): 37–48.

[55]*Ibid.*

[56]J. Nierenberg and I.S. Ross, *Women and the Art of Negotiating* (New York: Simon and Schuster, 1985).

[57]Lax and Sebenius, *op. cit.*

[58]J.A. Reeder, When West meets East: Cultural aspects of doing business in Asia, *Business Horizons* 30(1) (1987): 263–275.

[59]N.J. Adler, *International Dimensions of Organizational Behavior* (Boston: Kent, 1986).

[60]E.S. Glenn, D. Witmeyer, and K.A. Stevenson, Cultural styles of persuasion, *International Journal of Intercultural Relations* vol. 1 (New York: Pergamom, 1984).

[61]*Ibid.*

[62]M. Kublin, The Japanese negotiating style: Cultural and historical roots, *Industrial Management* 29 (May-June 1987): 18–23.

[63]O. Shenkar and S. Ronen, The cultural context of negotiations: The implications of Chinese interpersonal norms, *Journal of Applied Behavioral Science* 23 (1987): 263–275.

[64]Adler, *op. cit.*

[65]J. Graham, The influence of culture on business negotiations, *Journal of International Business Studies* 16 (Spring 1985): 81–96.

[66]Shenkar and Ronen, *op. cit.*

[67]P.R. Harris and R.T. Moran, *Managing Cultural Differences* 2d ed. (Houston: Gulf, 1987).

[68]Kotter, Power, dependence, *op. cit.*

RECOMMENDED READINGS

Baldwin, D.A. *Paradoxes of Power*. Oxford: Basil Blackwell, 1989.

Fisher, R., and Brown, S. *Getting Together*. Boston: Houghton Mifflin, 1988.

Greiner, L. *Power and Organization Development: Mobilizing Power to Implement Change*. Reading, Mass.: Addison-Wesley, 1988.

Lax, D.A., and Sebenius, J.K. *The Manager as Negotiator*. New York: Free Press, 1986.

Lewicki, R.J., and Litterer, J.A. (eds.) *Negotiation: Readings, Exercises, and Cases*. Homewood, Ill.: Irwin, 1985.

Mintzberg, H. *Power in and around Organizations*. Englewood Cliffs, N.J.: Prentice-Hall, 1983.

Nierenberg, J., and Ross, I.S. *Women and the Art of Negotiating*. New York: Simon and Schuster, 1985.

Srivastava, S. *Executive Power*. San Francisco: Jossey-Bass, 1986.

10

Delineating Conflict and Intergroup Behavior

CHAPTER OUTLINE

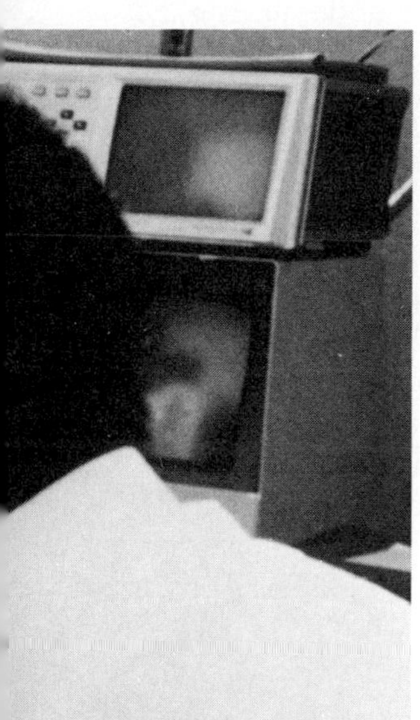

LEARNING OBJECTIVES

After completing the reading and activities in Chapter 10, students will be able to

- diagnose the existence, level, and stage of conflict in an organization;
- predict the outcomes of conflict in an organization;
- describe four types of intergroup relations and their behavioral and attitudinal consequences;
- diagnose the causes of stress and offer ways of managing it;
- diagnose examples of perceptual differences, task relations, and power differences among groups and their influence on intergroup relations; and
- describe a range of strategies for dealing with conflict and interactions between groups.

One week before a computer trade show, the marketing department of a leading software company, International Software, Ltd. (ISL), directed their technical services department to prepare a system for publicly demonstrating the company's new software. The manager of the support group immediately assigned the most experienced consultant to lead the assignment team.

Mark, the expert consultant, outlined a game plan for the week. He organized the project into a checklist of tasks. Various marketing representatives were contacted to verify that their requirements were listed on the checklist. On Friday morning the computer system was shipped to New York. With a sigh of relief Mark told his manager, "Even though we accomplished our mission, this project was a nightmare and I'm afraid it's not over yet."

Mark and his manager discussed the various problems related to the task. "Marketing should be more concerned about this type of demo. It's their baby. They should be in charge," noted Mark. Mark went on to describe the major problems he encountered: incorrect installation procedures, inaccurate documentation, marketing's unwillingness to test the installation, and Mark's inexperience with this type of task. Mark's manager suggested that they jointly submit a status report documenting their effort as a way of justifying any shortcomings on their part.

During the trade show the marketing representatives reported that not all the demos were functioning correctly. Mark and his manager both agreed that, "It was marketing's problem. They had ample time to test and correct any problems while Mark was installing the software last week." Two days after the trade show, the technical services group received three similar requests for computing systems with demo installations. After hearing the news Mark exclaimed, "There is no way I will put in any more seventeen-hour days!!! Something has to be done about marketing!!!"[1]

The complaints by Mark and the failure of the demos to function correctly are symptoms of organizational problems at ISL. We might attribute these symptoms to problems of individuals, such as those discussed in Part Two of this book: lack of appropriate skills, inaccurate perceptions and attributions, negative expectancies about effort and performance outcomes, dilemmas in personal development, or role conflict. We might also view the symptoms as the result of problems in group performance, decision making, communication, or leadership, as described in the earlier chapters of Part Three. However, in the case of the marketing and technical services staff of ISL, our diagnosis must also examine the conflict that exists in and between these professional groups as well as the nature of their interactions in general.

Did the marketing representatives and technical services staff at ISL cooperate or compete? Did they communicate effectively? What were the consequences? What contributed to or caused these dysfunctional interactions? How would you describe the relationship between the marketing representatives and the technical services staff at ISL?

In this chapter we answer these questions by first using a perspective of conflict and then introducing special issues associated with intergroup relations. We begin by considering the nature of conflict in organizations: its levels, stages, and consequences. We also look at the stress that frequently accompanies conflict. We then describe the typical ways groups interact as well as the behavioral and attitudinal consequences of these interactions. We examine three influences on group interactions: perceptual differences, task issues, and power differences between groups. We conclude the chapter by examining prescriptions for dealing with conflict, managing stress, and improving the relations between groups, discussing both interpersonal process and structural strategies.

THE NATURE OF CONFLICT

"Conflict is the result of incongruent or incompatible potential influence relationships."[2] It starts when one party perceives that another party has impeded or will frustrate one or more of its concerns.[3] It can occur between and within individuals, groups, and organizations as a whole.

Conflict most commonly occurs in four circumstances.[4] First, when mutually exclusive goals or values actually or are perceived to exist by the groups involved, conflict can occur. In the opening scenario, for example, marketing and technical services may not have compatible values. Marketing may settle for a less-than-satisfactory demo, whereas technical services may accept only a technically perfect solution; these differences result in disagreement and some degree of conflict. Second, behavior designed to defeat, reduce, or suppress an opponent may cause conflict. Union and management have historically experienced conflict for this reason. Similarly, if marketing created unattainable demands, they would reduce the status of technical services and contribute to conflict. Third, groups that face each other with mutually opposing actions and counteractions cause conflict. Finally, if each group attempts to create a relatively favored position vis-à-vis the other, conflict may ensue. If both marketing and technical services attempt to show top management they are superior to the other group by demonstrating the other's ineptness, conflict occurs.

OUTCOMES OF CONFLICT

Conflict can have either functional or dysfunctional—positive or negative—outcomes. Effective managers learn how to create functional conflict and manage dysfunctional conflict. They develop and practice techniques for diagnosing the causes and nature of conflict and transforming it into a productive force in the organization. At International Software, for example, Mark and his manager should use the disagreement between marketing and technical services as a springboard for improving their interactions in the future and building a stronger product and customer-oriented team.

Functional Consequences

Some conflict is beneficial. It can encourage organizational innovation, creativity, and adaptation. The failures of organizations such as the Penn Central Railroad and Studebacker, for instance, have been traced to too much harmony: the lack of conflict caused a failure to adapt to a changing environment.[5] Conflict also can result in more worker enthusiasm or better decisions. Can you think of a situation where such positive outcomes occurred? Perhaps during a disagreement with a friend or coworker you came to hold a different perspective on an issue or learned that your own perceptions or information had been inaccurate. Or perhaps a group to which you belonged formed a new partnership as a way of handling competition for limited resources.

Improved ideas through the exchange and clarification of individual thoughts can also result. Sometimes conflict leads to a search for new approaches as a way of resolving disagreements or long-standing problems. It can also simply energize participants and result in greater productivity.

Dysfunctional Consequences

But conflict can also be viewed as dysfunctional for organizations, although this should not be the only view of conflict. It can reduce productivity, lower morale, cause overwhelming dissatisfaction, and increase tension and stress in the organization. It can arouse anxiety in individuals, increase the tension in an organizational system and its subsystems, lower satisfaction, and decrease productivity. In addition, some people, often the losers in a competitive situation, feel defeated and demeaned. In this case the distance between people increases, and a climate of mistrust and suspicion may arise. Individuals or groups may focus narrowly on their own interests, preventing the development of teamwork. Production and satisfaction may decline; turnover and absenteeism may increase. Diagnosing the location and type of conflict, described in the next sections, is the first step in managing conflict so that it results in functional outcomes.

LEVELS OF CONFLICT

To manage conflict effectively, managers must pinpoint precisely where it exists so they can choose appropriate management strategies. We can describe six levels of conflict: (1) intrapersonal, (2) interpersonal, (3) intragroup, (4) intergroup, (5) intraorganizational, and (6) interorganizational, as shown in Figure 10–1.[6]

Intrapersonal Conflict

An individual may experience internal conflict in choosing between incompatible goals, or he or she may experience role conflict (described in Chapter 3). Mark, the expert consultant at ISL, may want to produce the best demonstration possible, but he may also have to meet a tight deadline. Or the goal of producing a high quality product may compete with the goal of showing the marketing department's inadequacies. In making such choices, Mark may experience affective or cognitive conflict.

Figure 10–1 LEVELS OF CONFLICT

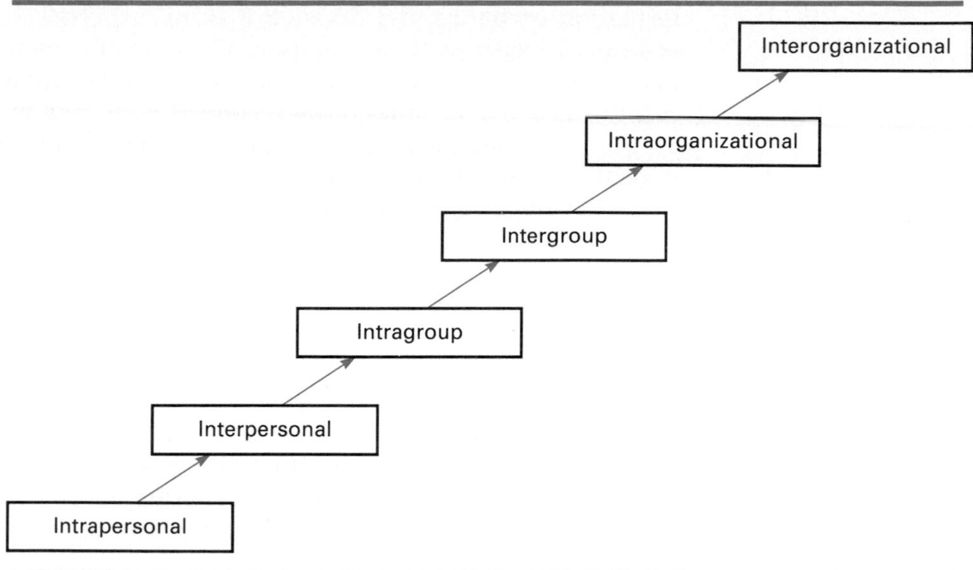

Affective conflict occurs when competing *emotions* accompany the incompatible goals and result in increased stress, decreased productivity, or decreased satisfaction for the individual. Thus Mark may experience both frustration and excitement in preparing the demo.

Cognitive conflict describes the *intellectual discomfort* created by incompatible goals. Mark may know the best way to prepare the demonstration system but sacrifice its quality to meet the imposed deadline. Such conflict may have productive consequences: the person involved may secure more and better information before acting. Alternatively such conflict may paralyze the individual's ability to act. Thus Mark may be so torn between desiring to produce an optimal demonstration system and being required to develop a suboptimal one within the time limits that he fails to do either.

Interpersonal Conflict

When two individuals disagree about issues, actions, or goals, and when this occurs where joint outcomes are important, there is interpersonal conflict. A disagreement between the director of marketing and Mark about responsibility for the demonstration system may result in this level of conflict. So may a disagreement between Mark and his manager about the best way to handle the situation. Interpersonal conflict often arises from differences in individuals' perceptions, orientations, or status. It may motivate individuals to surface additional relevant issues, or it may shut down any further communication.

Intragroup Conflict

A group may also experience either substantive or affective conflict. *Substantive* conflict is similar to cognitive conflict; it is based on intellectual disagreement. For example, when various members of the technical services staff at ISL draw different conclusions about the nature of the demonstration, they may experience substantive conflict. Such conflict often results in better information exchange and decision making. *Affective* conflict is based on the emotional responses to a situation. For example, members of the marketing department may feel passionate (and even irrational) about the importance of some products over others; the technical staff may experience different and conflicting emotions about the same products or situation. Affective conflict may also result when interacting individuals have incompatible styles or personalities (described in Chapter 3).

Intergroup Conflict

Intergroup conflict exists between or among groups, such as the marketing department and the technical services department at ISL. It also can exist between groups primarily responsible for planning versus those responsible for operations, or between line and staff groups.

Union workers and their nonunion managers, or union leadership and top management, can also be viewed as separate but interacting groups, although some view union–management interactions as examples of interorganizational rather than intergroup conflict. Union and management groups may have different interests that affect their interactions. Workers join unions to obtain greater compensation, achieve more rights on the job, as well as meet social or self-esteem needs. The backdrop for their interaction in the United States is mandated by the formal labor contract, or *collective bargaining agreement.* This specifies the rules of the workplace, amounts of compensation, and methods for settling disputes between labor and management. Representatives of union and management negotiate a contract acceptable to both sides. The ease or rancor involved in reaching and then implementing this agreement often determines whether labor–management relations are congenial or hostile. The existence of conflict between union and management varies in different countries: in Sweden and Germany little manifest conflict exists; in Italy and Canada manifest conflict is more common.

Managers should diagnose when intergroup conflict potentially or actually exists. In such situations they should emphasize problem-solving approaches to group interactions rather than competitive, win–lose behavior.

Intraorganizational Conflict

While in one sense encompassing all of the previous levels of conflict, intraorganizational conflict is diagnosed when conflict characterizes overall organizational functioning. *Vertical conflict* is that between supervisor and subordinates. Managers and subordinates, for example, may disagree about the best ways to accomplish their tasks or the organizational goals; union representatives and plan managers may argue about work rules throughout the organization. *Horizontal conflict* exists between employees or departments at the same level. At ISL the marketing, technical services, and manufacturing departments may repeatedly experience conflict over the manufacturing, installation, testing, and selling of software. *Diagonal* or *line–staff conflict* often occurs over the allocation of resources throughout the organization—to product development or product sales, for example—or over the involvement of staff people in line decisions. Finally, *role conflict* (described in Chapter 3) can be pervasive in an organization. Such conflict throughout an organization can energize workers and inspire innovation, but, uncontrolled and unmanaged, it can also demoralize workers and cause performance to deteriorate.

Interorganizational Conflict

Conflict can also exist between organizations. The amount of conflict may depend on the extent to which two or more organizations create uncertain conditions for competitors, suppliers, or customers, attempt to access or control the same resources, encourage communication, attempt to balance power in the marketplace, and develop procedures for resolving existing conflict.[7] Recent attempts to manage such conflict and ensure that it has a positive impact on organizational performance has emphasized the formation of strategic alliances and partnerships, as described in Chapter 9. Identifying the level of conflict is a prerequisite to selecting appropriate strategies for managing it. Accurate diagnosis also involves specifying the stage of conflict, described in the next section, since not all conflict is overt warfare.

STAGES OF CONFLICT

The nature of conflict changes over time. When a group cannot accomplish a goal or complete a task, they experience frustration. Then those involved may perceive that conflict exists and formulate ideas about the conflict issue. They gather information and consider multiple points of view to gain a better understanding of the conflict issue. Those affected respond, resolving the conflict or igniting more conflict.[8]

Diagnosing the nature of conflict is aided by considering it as a sequence of conflict episodes. Regardless of the level of conflict, each episode proceeds through one or more of five possible stages (shown in Figure 10–2): (1) latent, (2) perceived, (3) felt, (4) manifest, and (5) conflict aftermath.[9] By specifying the stage of conflict a manager can determine its intensity and select the best strategies for managing it. In the next sections we examine these stages in turn.

Latent Conflict

Conflict begins when the conditions for conflict exist. Individuals or groups may have power differences, compete for scarce resources, strive for autonomy,

Figure 10–2 STAGES OF CONFLICT

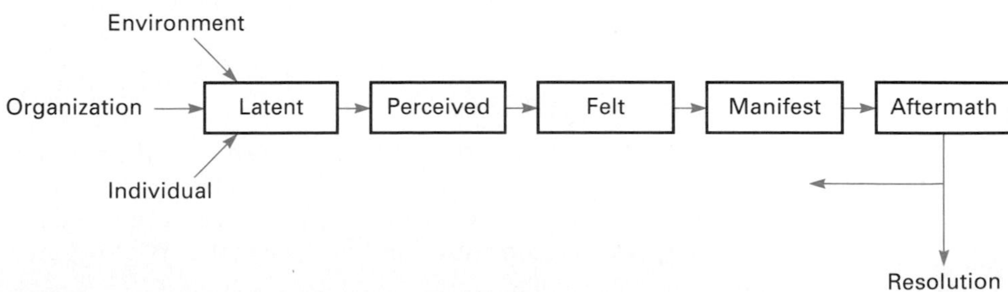

have different goals, or experience diverse role pressures. These differences provide the foundation for disagreement and ultimately conflict. Departments such as marketing and technical services at ISL frequently experience latent conflict. Inherent differences in perceptions and attitudes contribute to their relationship. Can you think of other situations where latent conflict exists, or where you have experienced latent conflict yourself?

Perceived Conflict

In the next stage individuals or group members know that conflict exists. They recognize differences of opinion, incompatible goals or values, efforts to demean the other party, or the implementation of opposing actions. At ISL, if Mark misunderstands or disagrees with the marketing department's requirements or its position on the quality of the demo required, perceived conflict may exist. If the marketing department questions the amount of time technical support gives to finishing the demonstration system, then perceived conflict may exist.

Felt Conflict

When one or more parties feels tense or anxious as a result of such disagreements or misunderstandings, conflict has moved beyond the perceived stage to the felt stage. Typically there is a time lag between intellectually perceiving conflict and feeling it "in the pit of your stomach." Here the conflict becomes personalized to the individuals or groups involved. Have you experienced felt conflict? Do you think Mark experiences felt conflict? His refusing to work any more seventeen-hour days suggests that he feels tense—a sign of felt conflict.

Manifest Conflict

Observable behavior designed to frustrate another's attempts to pursue his or her goals is the most overt form of conflict. Both open aggression and withdrawal of support illustrate manifest conflict. At this stage conflict must be used constructively or resolved for effective organizational performance to occur. If Mark confronts the marketing department about his frustration and dissatisfaction with their interactions, manifest conflict may ensue. Demonstrated anger and refusal to support marketing's demands would further reflect this stage of conflict; so would a high level of creative tension or more positive verbalizations.

Conflict Aftermath

A conflict episode ends with its aftermath, after the conflict has been managed and the resulting energy heightened, resolved, or suppressed. Unresolved conflict, which exists everywhere, simply sows the seeds for manifest conflict later. The *process* continues and is a normal part of organizational life.

STRESS IN ORGANIZATIONS

Hans Selye first used the term *stress* to apply to humans (rather than animals) in the 1930s.[10] Stress often accompanies or results from both positive and negative conflict. It refers to a psychological and physiological state that results when certain features of an individual's environment, including noise, pressures, job promotions, monotony, or the general climate, attack or impinge on that person. Both positive and negative events can give rise to stress, and stress in turn can have positive and negative consequences.

In stress situations individuals experience (1) alarm, (2) resistance, and (3) exhaustion, as shown in Figure 10–3.[11] In the *alarm* stage individuals face a *stressor*—an aspect of a situation that causes a rise in adrenaline or anxiety. Stressors include role conflict, role overload, task ambiguity, uncertainty, competition, and other aspects of a work or nonwork situation. If the stressor persists, individuals respond to it during the *resistance* stage. They may deal with the stressor directly or use it to stimulate creative behaviors. In dysfunctional situations, they may adopt a previously successful coping behavior, deny the stressor, withdraw physically or psychologically from the situation, or persist in responding whether or not the response is effective.[12] When stressors persist and either result in positive outcomes or create physiological or psychological damage, *exhaustion* has occurred.

Think about a situation in which you experienced stress. How did you feel? What contributed to the stress? What alleviated it? How did you perform when you experienced stress? You may have felt stress when you have had too many tasks to complete in too short a time. Or you may have felt stress when you failed to advance in an organization because of poor supervision, lack of a mentor or sponsor, or the inability to become autonomous in your work. Or you may have experienced stress when you received a promotion and questioned your ability to fulfill the new responsibilities.

Some people respond to stress by becoming more productive and creative. Have you ever heard a friend or coworker say, "I work best when I have a deadline in sight; I can't do anything productive unless I feel some pressure"? This person likely uses the stress resulting from time pressure constructively—to increase his or her productivity. However, others experience gastrointestinal, glandular, and cardiovascular disorders or respond to stress by overeating, drinking excessively, or taking tranquilizers.[13] Others become impatient, detached, or filled with despair. Such physiological and psychological reactions can decrease a person's satisfaction, creativity, and productivity, which in turn

Figure 10–3 STAGES OF STRESS

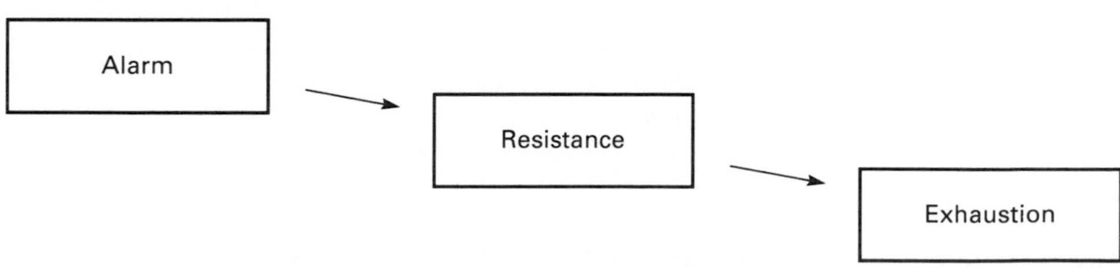

often increases a person's level of stress, in turn causing a further decrease in effectiveness.

Causes of Stress

Stress has become increasingly common in organizations, largely because of increased job complexity and increased economic pressures on individuals. Individual career characteristics, such as occupational level, career stage, and stage of adult development (described in Chapter 3) may cause stress. Individuals at the beginning of their career, who are trying to establish themselves, often experience stress; "midcareer crisis" is virtually synonymous with stress; and facing the changes of retirement creates significant stress for individuals. Table 10–1 lists the major life-stress events for individuals in the United

Table 10–1 LIFE-STRESS EVENTS

Complete the scale by circling the mean value figure to the right of each item if it has occurred to you during the past year. To figure your total score, add all the mean values circled (if an event occurred more than once, increase the value by the number of times). Life event stress totals of 150 or less indicate generally good health, scores of 150 to 300 indicate a 35–50 percent probability of stress-related illness, and scores of 300 + indicate an 80 percent probability.

Life Event	Mean Value
1. Death of spouse	100
2. Divorce	73
3. Marital separation from mate	65
4. Detention in jail or other institution	63
5. Death of a close family member	63
6. Major personal injury or illness	53
7. Marriage	50
8. Being fired at work	47
9. Marital reconciliation with mate	45
10. Retirement from work	45
11. Major change in the health or behavior of a family member	44
12. Pregnancy	40
13. Sexual difficulties	39
14. Gaining a new family member	39
15. Major business readjustment	39
16. Major change in financial state	38
17. Death of a close friend	37
18. Changing to a different line of work	36
19. Major change in the number of arguments with spouse	35
20. Taking out a mortgage or loan for a major purchase	31
21. Foreclosure on a mortgage or loan	30
22. Major change in responsibilities at work	29
23. Son or daughter leaving home	29
24. In-law troubles	29
25. Outstanding personal achievement	28
26. Wife beginning or ceasing work outside the home	26
27. Beginning or ceasing formal schooling	26

Table 10–1 CONTINUED

Life Event	Mean Value
28. Major change in living conditions	25
29. Revision of personal habits	24
30. Troubles with the boss	23
31. Major change in working hours or conditions	20
32. Change in residence	20
33. Changing to a new school	20
34. Major change in usual type and/or amount of recreation	19
35. Major change in church activities	19
36. Major change in social activities	18
37. Taking out a mortgage or loan for a lesser purchase	17
38. Major change in sleeping habits	16
39. Major change in number of family get-togethers	15
40. Major change in eating habits	15
41. Vacation	13
42. Christmas	12
43. Minor violations of the law	11

States, and provides a way of calculating the probability an individual will experience stress-related illness. Note that the significance of specific events may vary in different cultures.

Interpersonal variables, such as leadership style (see Chapter 8) and extent of group cohesion and participation (see Chapter 5), also contribute to stress experienced by individuals, in and out of the workplace. Where the personalities of leaders and followers conflict, such as when an extroverted employee is supervised by an introverted manager or when an individual with a thinking decision-making orientation clashes with an individual with a feeling decision-making orientation, stress often occurs. Again, this stress may result in improved decision making or deteriorating performance.

The relationship between stressors and stress may be affected by an individual's personality, culture, or nonwork environment. In addition, professional women experience unique stressors: discrimination, stereotyping, conflicting demands of work and family, and feelings of isolation.[14]

The Stress Audit

In many organizations today, managers find that they must be more sensitive than in the past to potential stressors in their organizations, to maintain productive, involved employees. They must recognize that employees may try to minimize stress, even at the expense of promotions or significant pay increases. Managers and employees must be aware that a certain amount of stress may be necessary for creative and productive work. The total absence of stress in the workplace may result in complacency.

Yet predicting the level of stress in situations can be difficult, largely because stress is often person-specific. Often times features of jobs we intuitively rate as stressful, such as the mental demands and responsibilities of an air traffic controller or the life-and-death situations of a police officer, are neither disliked nor experienced as stressful by the job holders themselves.[15] Alternatively, simple requests for overtime or revisions of completed work may cause stress in some people. Managers must be sensitive to the implications of various actions for creating stress—and encourage actions where stress has positive consequences.

Let us consider again the situation at International Software, Ltd., described in the introduction to this chapter. We can evaluate the extent of dysfunctional stress in the situation by performing a *stress audit,* which helps identify the symptoms and causes of stress.[16] In such an audit, we might ask the following questions:

1. Do any individuals demonstrate physiological symptoms?
2. Is job satisfaction low, or are job tension, turnover, absenteeism, strikes, or accident proneness high?
3. Does the organization's design contribute to the symptoms described?
4. Do interpersonal relations contribute to the symptoms described?
5. Do career-development variables contribute to the symptoms described?
6. What effects do personality, sociocultural influences, and the nonwork environment have on the relationship between the stressors—individual careers, interpersonal relations, and organizational design—and stress?

To answer questions 1 and 2 completely and accurately requires a more thorough description of the situation. Yet even the brief introductory scenario offers some evidence of individual frustration, declining satisfaction, and performance problems—all possible indicators of stress. To answer questions 3 through 6 requires an understanding of issues discussed in other chapters and an application of the diagnostic questions offered there.

Stress can also result from dysfunctional relations between groups. Such intergroup interactions are discussed in the next part of this chapter.

INTERACTING GROUPS

Because an organization is a system (see Chapter 1), no two groups in it can exist truly independently. Rather, one group may depend on another for raw materials, other resources, information, or assistance in performing a task. We can describe this interdependence, in transactional terms, as the exchange of resources, such as budgeted funds, support services, products, and information, between two work units.[17] Work units become increasingly interdependent in several circumstances: as more resources are exchanged in a given amount of time, or more exchanges occur in a given amount of time, interdependence increases. As a greater variety of resources are exchanged, interdependence increases. The extent to which resources flow both ways between the units also increases interdependence. In ISL, the marketing representatives and technical services staff exchange services and information; because the transactions between them are relatively frequent and important, these groups have a relatively high degree of interdependence.

Such interdependence can be described as one of four types: (1) pooled, (2) sequential, (3) reciprocal, and (4) team, as shown in Figure 10–4.[18] The letters A through D in the figure refer to four separate groups; the arrows show whether the groups interact directly and the direction of the interaction. In pooled interdependence, for example, groups A, B, C, and D have no direct interactions. In team interdependence the groups all interact in both directions with every other group. Although any group may demonstrate any of these types of interdependence at specific times, one type predominates in a group's relationship with other groups. At different times, for example, the marketing department and the technical services department at ISL may demonstrate pooled, sequential, or team interdependence, although reciprocal interdependence characterizes their relationship the majority of the time. In the next sections we examine each of these types.

Managers should assess the nature and extent of interdependence in an organization so that they understand the potential for conflict and the impact of one part of the organization on another part. This assessment occurs through interviewing and observing key organizational members such as top and middle managers. Data about the nature of the work flow, the people with whom group and organizational members interact most frequently, and the types of decisions made by various individuals or groups illuminate the nature of interdependence experienced by various groups in an organization.

Figure 10–4 TYPES OF INTERDEPENDENCE

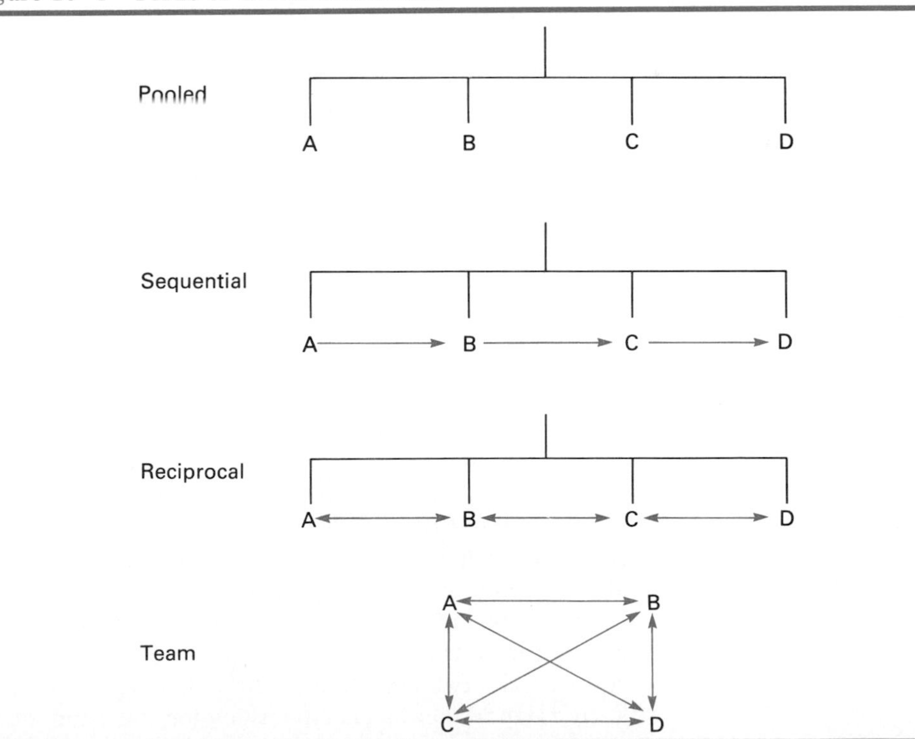

Pooled Interdependence

Groups that rely on each other only because they belong to the same parent organization show pooled interdependence. Two restaurants in a fast-food chain show pooled interdependence because their reputations depend on their identification with the parent organization. Two subsidiaries in a conglomerate, such as two department stores in a national chain, may show pooled interdependence because they share a common advertising agency or benefit from mass buying power. The maintenance workers and the cafeteria workers in a single organization are two departments that, for the most part, demonstrate pooled interdependence. Groups with pooled interdependence may obtain their reputation, staff resources, financing, or other services from corporate headquarters; basically, however, they operate as separate groups or organizations.

Because these groups have limited interactions, pooled interdependence has few potentially dysfunctional consequences for groups until their representatives need to work together. Such groups may be required to compete for resources, but such interactions are limited. The marketing department and the technical services department at ISL demonstrate more than pooled interdependence. They share more than common resources, reputation, or services.

Sequential Interdependence

Sequential interdependence occurs when one group's operations precede and act as prerequisites for a second group's. In a manufacturing plant, the assembly group and the packing group exhibit sequential interdependence. In the post office, workers at the central post office demonstrate sequential interdependence with the letter carriers in local post offices: postal workers in the central office must sort the mail before the local letter carriers can sort and deliver it. In a hospital, nurses have sequential interdependence with the purchasing department: the purchasing department buys supplies, which the nurses then use. But the nurses have more than sequential interdependence with the physicians, since the interaction does not end when nurses receive directions from physicians; they also provide input into the physicians' decisions about patient care.

At ISL, the technical services department demonstrates sequential interdependence with the comptroller's office, which determines the budget for the department. Technical services should have more than sequential interdependence with the marketing department, since they should work collaboratively to ensure that demos run smoothly and customers receive promised services. Although technical services staff often receive directions from marketing, they should also provide input into the feasibility of marketing's claims and requirements.

The second group in the sequence may experience difficulty in accomplishing its tasks if its members do not interact effectively with its predecessor. If the first group does not complete its job on time, for example, the performance of the second group is jeopardized. This may cause the members of the second group to resent the first group and limit their interactions with it. Where collaborative relations do not exist between these groups, even sabotage may occur at the extreme. The technical services department may alter the marketing department's specifications for the demo or fail to meet the deadline.

Reciprocal Interdependence

Two groups whose operations precede and act as prerequisites to the other's have reciprocal interdependence. Sales and support staff typically have this type of interdependence. A salesperson selling computer hardware relies on technical support staff to handle installation problems; the support staff requires the sales staff's input in identifying customer problems. At ISL, the marketing representatives demonstrate reciprocal interdependence with the technical services staff. The two groups must repeatedly interact to perform their jobs effectively.

As the extent of group interdependence increases, the potential for conflict and dysfunctional behavior increases correspondingly. Reciprocal interdependence easily results in dysfunctional behaviors and attitudes. Because each group relies on the other to perform its own job effectively, any problems between them may result in reduced productivity or decreased worker satisfaction. Conflict is common when there is reciprocal interdependence.

Team Interdependence

Where multiple groups interact, reciprocal interdependences may be multiplied. In such cases we can characterize the interdependence as parallel to the completely connected communication network (described in Chapter 7).[19] In this case, each group's operations precede and act as prerequisites for every other group's operations, when their functioning is considered over time. For example, the various departments supervised by a vice president of marketing—sales, support, advertising, and research—may exhibit this type of interdependence. We might characterize the overall interdependence of nurses, physicians, and hospital administration in this way. Groups with team interdependence have the greatest potential for conflict and the highest requirements for effective communication. Table 10–2 summarizes the types of interdependence and their potential for conflict.

Intergroup relations have significant consequences for individual behavior.

Table 10–2 TYPES OF INTERDEPENDENCE AND THEIR POTENTIAL FOR CONFLICT

Type of Interdependence	Definition	Potential for Conflict
Pooled	Two groups that have the same parent organization	Low
Sequential	Two groups where one group's operations precede and act as prerequisites for the second group's	Moderate
Reciprocal	Two groups whose operations precede and act as prerequisites to the other's	High
Team	Multiple groups, all of whose operations precede and act as prerequisites to the others'	High

The interplay of groups affects the way a person constructs his or her reality. For example, the relative position of an individual as upper, middle, or lower in the organizational structure of which he or she is a part determines that person's perception of events.[20] Intergroup issues, described in the next section, are part of the relationship between subgroups of a larger group, and between groups themselves.

PERCEPTUAL DIFFERENCES AMONG GROUPS

We noted earlier in this book that the perception of events and the attributions of their causes are subjective. Perceptual differences influence group and intergroup interactions. The particular role an individual holds or the group to which he or she belongs influences these perceptions. One study of unionized manufacturing workers over a three-year period traced the changes in attitudes associated with changes in roles.[21] Workers who were promoted to foreman demonstrated significant promanagement and anti-union attitudes; those who later returned to worker roles reverted to their previous pro-union and antimanagement attitudes. This adjustment occurs primarily because of the strong group identity that occurs for most members (see Chapter 5). In contrast, those workers who became union stewards became only slightly more pro-union and antimanagement, probably because of the greater similarity between their old and new roles.

In another study, managers in a large organization received detailed descriptions about a company and were then asked to describe its biggest problem.[22] The majority of the managers identified the major problem as being in their own functional area. Sales managers cited sales problems as most important; production managers identified production problems. These differences in personal concerns also may influence the way each group views the other's actions. The marketing department's and technical services department's perceptions of the tasks and collaboration needed to prepare the demo may differ; each department's perceptions of its own and the other's expertise and time constraints may differ too. These perceptual differences between groups can create role conflict (discussed in Chapter 3).

Orientations

All groups evaluate events in terms of their own orientations, and their goal, time, and social orientations may differ. Managers should understand the differences in groups' orientations to help them predict and handle issues that might arise in the groups' interactions.

Goal Orientation Differences in personal concerns and orientations often accompany differences in goals. Marketing departments typically concern themselves with the attractiveness of a product to consumers. Research and development groups focus on the product's innovative characteristics and its value to the advancement of scientific knowledge. Production departments emphasize a product's ease of production and susceptibility to cost controls. How might goal differences between the marketing department and the technical services department at ISL create perceptual differences? These groups may differ in their attitudes toward introducing new products, promising immediate service, or accomplishing other goals; and these differences affect their perceptions of requests by customers or the marketing department itself.

Time Orientation Groups also differ in the extent to which they focus on events now and in the future. A research and development department, for example, has a long-term orientation, since new product formulation takes long periods of time. In contrast, a production department has a short-term orientation, since its goals emphasize meeting immediate inventory needs. The marketing department may reflect a short-term orientation in its concern for selling the product now, whereas the technical services staff may have a different time orientation in its concern for keeping the product functional over the medium or long term.

Social Orientation The social or extrawork orientations of groups might also differ. Consider a group of unionized nurses and the nonunionized physicians. The nurses would be more involved with union activities and would probably choose their friends from other nurses or union members. The physicians would be oriented toward their professional group—other physicians. What are the implications of these different orientations?

Although neither the marketing department nor the technical services department in the introductory case likely has union members, their professional allegiances and consequent social interactions probably differ. The marketing representatives and technical services staff may also differ in their stages of personal or career development (see Chapter 3) and their professional training; thus their social orientations and consequently their perceptions might differ. Can you think of a scenario where two groups might experience problems because of such social differences?

Attitudinal Sets

Attitudinal sets also contribute to the perceptual differences evidenced by interacting groups. Diagnosing differences in attitudinal sets among groups can help managers and other group members plan for possible conflicts. One such set reflects the extent to which a group has a competitive or cooperative attitude.[23] A group with a competitive attitude toward other groups may encourage its members to have negative attitudes toward the task, distrust other group members, dislike other group members, and act without considering others. A group with a cooperative attitude toward other groups, in contrast, may encourage trust, mutual influence, coordination of effort, and acceptance of differences within the group itself and between its members and the other group's members.

A second attitudinal set is the extent to which a group, because of the individuals in it, has a *cosmopolitan* versus *local* orientation. Cosmopolitans are "those low on loyalty to the employing organization, high on commitment to specialized role skills, and likely to use an outer (professional) reference group orientation." Locals are "those high on loyalty to the employing organization, low on commitment to specialized role skills, and likely to use an inner (organizational) reference group orientation."[24] We might hypothesize that the marketing representatives have a local orientation, whereas the technical services staff has a cosmopolitan one. If this is true, their perceptions would differ and such differences might result in the symptoms we observed in the introductory scenario.

Status Differences

Individuals' perceptions frequently influence their view of their own roles and status—rank and standing relative to others—in an organization.[25] Often these perceptions lack clarity and validity. A group of nurses may perceive they have relatively low status, compared to a group of physicians, and hence make few demands on the physicians, allowing them to direct and organize the nursing staff's work. For effective performance, however, each interacting group must understand clearly what the organization and other groups expect of it. Each group must also assess whether these expectations fit with its own perceptions of its members' jobs and positions in the organization's hierarchy.

Differences in education, experience, or background may influence perceptions of status. Such differences may be reinforced by the rewards assigned in the organization. Real or perceived differences about the relative status of two groups influence their interactions. Differences in identity due to race, gender, ethnicity, and religion unfortunately also affect perceptions of status. Managers must ensure that distinctions based on these factors do not play a dysfunctional role in intergroup interactions. At ISL, for example, the marketing department acts as if it has greater status than the technical services department. Their different perceptions about status reduce the effectiveness of the interactions between these groups.

THE NATURE OF TASK RELATIONS

The activities or processes that interdependent groups perform and the way these activities interrelate play a significant role in intergroup relations. Both the sequencing of task activities and the clarity and certainty of the task itself have consequences for intergroup relations.

Task Interaction

Tasks performed by group members can be independent, dependent, or interdependent of tasks performed by members of the same or different groups. Where one group's task can be done without any relationship to another group's, the task relations are *independent.* A machine operator and an accountant can each perform his or her task without any assistance from the other. Where one group's task follows and has another's as a prerequisite, the second group has tasks *dependent* on the first group's. Company recruiters depend on line managers to identify the types of personnel required. Where each group's task follows and is prerequisite, at some time, to the other's, their tasks are *interdependent.* The copy editor of a publishing firm works on a manuscript provided by an author, who then checks the changes made by the editor.

The nature of task relations generally resembles the nature of interdependence among groups described earlier. Groups showing pooled interdependence most often have independent task relations; groups showing sequential interdependence most often have dependent task relations; groups showing reciprocal or team interdependence most frequently have interdependent task relations.

Groups with independent tasks have much less potential for problematic relations with other groups than those with dependent or interdependent task relations because the independent task groups have less interaction. Interdependent tasks most frequently contribute to problematic relations between interacting groups. What are the consequences of the task relations between the marketing representatives and technical services staff? Their high interdependence creates a potential for conflict, which is realized by their competitive, rather than collaborative, behavior.

Task Ambiguity

The ambiguity or certainty of task relationships describes whether interactive groups have clear, predetermined processes of activity. Ambiguity in a task often contributes to difficulty in two or more groups' interactions. The technical services staff, for example, should have some tasks clearly delineated in the specifications for the demonstration system written by the marketing department. Other tasks may be less clearly specified and rely on the technical staff's assessment of particular situations. In the case of the marketing staff, however, new technology, new research findings, and changing demands from the clients for new products often increase the uncertainty of their task.

Often, too, a particular group does not understand its responsibilities and the requirements of its task. This situation also results in more task uncertainty. Marketing, for example, might not understand its responsibility in developing the demonstration software. Consequently, conflict may arise and contribute to the dysfunctional interactions between marketing and technical services departments.

POWER DIFFERENCES

Interacting groups often experience performance difficulties when they differ in power, or the amount of influence and control they have over others. We discussed power in Chapter 9, but this section highlights three ways power differences affect intergroup relations.

Perceptions of Substitutability

If the activities of one group are viewed as replaceable, or if another group can perform the same work, the group is considered substitutable. If a manufacturing group, for example, is perceived to be able to perform development activities, then manufacturing considers the research and development group substitutable, diminishing its power. The less a group is perceived to perform substitutable tasks, the more power it possesses.

At ISL, which group is more substitutable—marketing or technical services? If we assume that the technical services staff have the unique technical knowledge required to sell and support the computer software, they would be less substitutable and therefore have more power from this source than the marketing department. Of course, without customers—who have even greater unsubstitutability and ultimate power—the technical services staff would not have jobs.

Ability to Cope with Uncertainty

How well a group can deal with and compensate for a rapidly changing environment also influences its power.[26] Typically, engineers can cope with uncertainty better than technicians because of their broader professional training and more diverse experiences; hence they have greater power from this source.

At ISL, which departments can cope with uncertainty most effectively? The technical services staff seem more able to cope with uncertainty than the marketing representatives. Any difference would contribute to power differences between the two groups and potentially to dysfunctional intergroup relations.

Control of or Access to Resources

The amount of money, people, and time a group controls also influences its power. The greater the amount of resources it controls, the more power the group has. Managers who control budgets often have greater power than those who do not. Further, when two groups must divide resources, disagreements often arise about their optimal allocation, creating conflict between them. In hospitals, physicians typically have greater access to resources and more influence over their allocation than do nurses, which may further contribute to differences in power between the two groups. Does either the marketing department or the technical services department have greater access to resources than the other? If so, they likely increase their power and may stimulate conflict because of it.

STRATEGIES FOR MANAGING CONFLICT AND INTERGROUP RELATIONS

When diagnosis indicates that a manager must deal with conflict or intergroup relations, he or she may want to encourage greater *integration,*[27] or collaboration among groups. "The three ongoing management tasks can be defined as (a) creating and maintaining shared appreciations of interdependencies, (b) reaching agreement about appropriate coordination and control strategies, and (c) implementing and maintaining these strategies."[28] In this section we look at conflict-handling behaviors and activities, stress-management approaches, and structural mechanisms for managing conflict. Reading 10–1, "Managing Conflict," offers a complementary perspective to the one presented here.

Conflict that is a matter of principle, has large stakes, and involves a single transaction tends to be more difficult to manage than conflict around divisible issues where neither side must completely give in to the other, has small stakes, and involves a long-term relationship.[29] If one party is viewed as gaining at the expense of the other, is incohesive, has weak leadership, feels harmed, and has no neutral third party available as an intermediary, conflict is difficult to manage productively or resolve.[30]

Intervention Styles

Individuals can use at least five behaviors for dealing with conflict: (1) avoidance, (2) accommodation, (3) compromise, (4) forcing, and (5) collaborating.[31] As shown in Figure 10–5, these differ in the extent to which they satisfy a party's own concerns and the other party's concerns. For example, a person or group that uses an *avoiding* mode is unassertive in satisfying its own concerns and uncooperative in satisfying others' concerns. In contrast, a person or group who uses a *collaborating* mode is both assertive and cooperative.

Each style is appropriate to different situations individuals or groups face in organizations. Table 10–3 summarizes the use of these five modes by a group of chief executives. The behavior an individual or group chooses depends on that party's experiences in dealing with conflict, his or her own dispositions in interpersonal relations, as well as the specific elements of a particular conflict episode.

Avoidance Individuals or groups may withdraw from the conflict situation. They act to satisfy neither their own nor the other party's concerns. If Mark or his manager refused to discuss the difficulties encountered in finishing the demonstration system, they would be avoiding the conflict. This mode works best when individuals or groups face trivial or tangential issues, when they have little chance of satisfying their personal concerns, when conflict resolution is likely to result in significant disruption, or when others can resolve conflict more effectively.

Accommodation Individuals or groups who use this behavior demonstrate a willingness to cooperate in satisfying others' concerns while at the same

Figure 10–5 MODEL OF CONFLICT-HANDLING MODES

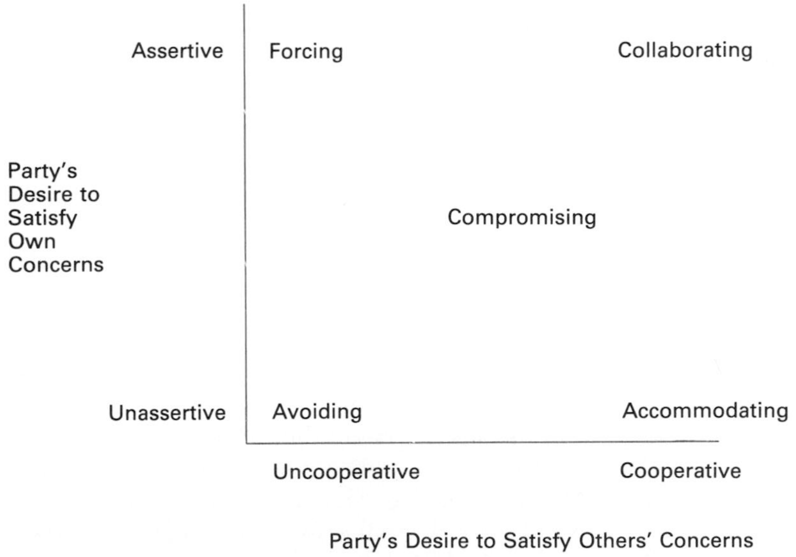

SOURCE: Adapted from K.W. Thomas, "Conflict and Conflict Management" in M.D. Dunnette (ed.), *Handbook of Industrial and Organizational Psychology,* Rand McNally, 1976. Used by permission of Houghton Mifflin Company.

Table 10–3 USES OF THE FIVE CONFLICT MODES, AS REPORTED BY A GROUP OF CHIEF EXECUTIVES

Conflict-Handling Modes	Appropriate Situations
Competing	1. When quick, decisive action is vital—e.g., emergencies. 2. On important issues where unpopular actions need implementing—e.g., cost cutting, enforcing unpopular rules, discipline. 3. On issues vital to company welfare when you know you're right. 4. Against people who take advantage of noncompetitive behavior.
Collaborating	1. To find an integrative solution when both sets of concerns are too important to be compromised. 2. When your objective is to learn. 3. To merge insights from people with different perspectives. 4. To gain commitment by incorporating concerns into a consensus. 5. To work through feelings which have interfered with a relationship.
Compromising	1. When goals are important, but not worth the effort or potential disruption of more assertive modes. 2. When opponents with equal power are committed to mutually exclusive goals. 3. To achieve temporary settlements to complex issues. 4. To arrive at expedient solutions under time pressure. 5. As a backup when collaboration or competition is unsuccessful.
Avoiding	1. When an issue is trivial, or more important issues are pressing. 2. When you perceive no chance of satisfying your concerns. 3. When potential disruption outweighs the benefits of resolution. 4. To let people cool down and regain perspective. 5. When gathering information supersedes immediate decision. 6. When others can resolve the conflict more effectively. 7. When issues seem tangential or symptomatic of other issues.
Accommodating	1. When you find you are wrong—to allow a better position to be heard, to learn, and to show your reasonableness. 2. When issues are more important to others than yourself—to satisfy others and maintain cooperation. 3. To build social credits for later issues. 4. To minimize loss when you are outmatched and losing. 5. When harmony and stability are especially important. 6. To allow subordinates to develop by learning from mistakes.

SOURCE: Kenneth W. Thomas, Toward multi-dimensional values in teaching: The example of conflict behaviors, *Academy of Management Review,* 1977, 2, Table 1, p. 487. Reprinted by permission.

time acting unassertively in meeting their own. Accommodating individuals often smooth over conflict. If the marketing representatives respond to Mark's complaints by apologizing, promising to change in the future, or acceding to Mark's demands, they would be using accommodating behaviors. This mode builds social credits for later issues, results in harmony and stability, and satisfies others.

Compromise This mode represents an intermediate behavior on both the assertiveness and cooperation dimensions. It can include sharing of positions but not moving to the extremes of either assertiveness or cooperation. Hence it often does not maximize the satisfaction of both parties. In one study, compromisers had a communication style different from avoiders: they were more likely to focus on communicating information about the job product or plan than about rules, regulations, or policies.[32] Compromise works well when goals are important but not sufficiently important for the individual or group to be more assertive, when two parties have equal power, or when significant time pressure exists.

Forcing Using this mode, one party tries to satisfy its own concerns while showing an unwillingness to satisfy the other's concerns to even a minimal degree. Mark may refuse to work on any more demonstrations unless the marketing department totally changes its way of interacting with the technical services department. In competition, one party asserts its own concerns. This strategy works well in emergencies, on issues calling for unpopular actions, in cases where one party is correct in its position, or where one party has much greater power than another.

Collaborating This mode emphasizes problem solving, with the goal of maximizing satisfaction for both parties. Each party evinces both assertive and cooperative behavior. Collaborating means seeing conflict as natural, showing trust and honesty toward others, and encouraging the airing of every person's attitudes and feelings. Parties can use it when their objectives are to learn, use information from diverse sources, and find an integrative solution. If the marketing and technical services departments meet and seek a mutually satisfactory way of developing the demonstration software, they are taking a collaborative or problem-solving approach. (See Chapter 9 for further discussion.)

Conflict-Handling Activities

Certain types of conflict, such as disagreements about goals or values, may call for the parties to *control the differences* between them by acknowledging their existence and then acting without attempting to resolve them. Such differences may be so ingrained in the conflicting parties that effectively managing those involved may preclude resolution of the differences within any reasonable period of time or without changing underlying value systems.

Occasionally, in small group situations, individuals deliberately escalate conflict as a way of ultimately resolving it.[33] An outsider purposely seeks to increase the frustration of the parties, as a way of redirecting the conflict's course, increasing participants' understanding of the situation, or leading to a search for more constructive behaviors.

Three specific intervention techniques typify the strategies that focus on improving the process of interactions between two or more groups: (1) confrontation meeting, (2) organizational mirror, and (3) other third-party interventions.

Confrontation Meeting This technique addresses problems experienced by interacting groups that result in dysfunctional organizational performance. It is a one-day meeting where two interacting groups share the problems they face and offer solutions for resolving them.

The one-day meeting occurs as follows.[34] First a top manager introduces the issues and goals that are the focus of discussion during the day and on which the two groups experience problems. (The manager may have identified these issues through prior discussions with group members.) Then, in small subgroups of the various interacting groups, the participants gather more detailed information about the problems they face. Next representatives from each subgroup report to the entire group on their list of items. In natural work groups, participants set priorities for the problems and determine early action steps; they set a concrete agenda about the steps they will take to resolve their problems. Implementation of the plan follows. A top management team continues to meet to plan and monitor follow-up action. Four to six weeks later the group reconvenes to report its progress. The confrontation meeting is most effective in dealing with intergroup problems when there is a need for the whole management group to examine its own workings, when very limited time is available for the activity, when top management wishes to improve conditions quickly, when there is enough cohesion in the top team to ensure follow-up, when there is real commitment to resolving the issues on the part of top management, and when an organization is experiencing, or has recently experienced, some major change.[35]

Organizational Mirror This is "a set of activities in which a particular organizational group, the host group, gets feedback from representatives of several other organizational groups about how it is perceived and regarded."[36] A consultant begins by conducting preliminary interviews with all groups' members. Then he or she reports data from these interviews to the invited and host groups. The groups then discuss the data presented. Small, heterogeneous groups with representatives from the diverse groups meet, discuss the data further (if appropriate), and develop action plans for the identified problems. Implementation of the action plans follows. Like the confrontation meeting, the organizational mirror requires top management commitment and follow-up for effective action to result.

Third-Party Interventions This approach is frequently used in labor–management interactions to resolve intergroup conflict that occurs. The third party can act as mediator, arbitrator, or fact-finder. One study of sixty-nine situations suggested that third parties provided mediation, confrontational consultation, and procedural consultation, in that order of frequency.[37] Third parties must demonstrate professional expertise and control of the social processes used, control over the situation at hand, moderate knowledge of the principles, issues, and background factors, and neutrality or balance with respect to substantive outcomes, personal relationships, and conflict-resolution methodology.[38]

A third party may escalate conflict as a way of increasing creativity or surfacing the issues to ultimately defuse the conflict.[39] The third party may stimulate the conflict by changing its antecedent conditions, such as leadership style or organizational structure. He or she may extend the conflict issues, by stressing differences or introducing new facets of existing issues. Increasing the number of parties involved, possibly resulting in coalition formation, can also augment conflict. A third party can also stimulate escalative behaviors, such as by teaching the parties to fight fair or showing them ways to prove their points. Finally, he or she can identify consequences that encourage escalation, such as by convincing a party it will lose face if it does not fight for its beliefs. Because of the potential side effects and lack of qualified third-party change agents, few individuals or groups request escalative interventions. What might happen at ISL if such a strategy were used?

A third party can assume an active role of identifying areas of agreement and disagreement between the parties, as in the *interpersonal-facilitator approach.*[40] Or a third party can direct an *interface conflict-solving approach,* in which he or she leads key members of opposing groups through a series of meetings and activities that identify and resolve differences.[41] In the interpersonal facilitator model, contact between parties occurs primarily through the facilitator, who acts as a go-between, message carrier, spokesperson for one or both groups, or a solution proposer. The facilitator deals with the leaders or key members of the disputing parties, who meet to exchange positions and formulate proposals or counterproposals. This model works best when two people are involved and personal "chemistry" prevents constructive discussion.

In the interface conflict-solving model, the third party sets expectations, establishes group rules, determines the sequence of speaking, ensures candor, curbs expressions of hostility, avoids evaluations, introduces procedures to reduce disagreements, ensures understanding of positions or statements, and checks implementation of agreed-on changes.

Each group first meets separately to prepare a description of the ideal relationship between the groups. Each group then selects a spokesperson, who presents the conclusions at a general meeting of the groups. After the large group meeting, each participant identifies similarities and differences in the two descriptions, to develop an integrated model that can direct the functioning of both groups. Then each group characterizes the actual conditions at that time. The groups jointly formulate a statement of problems. Then together they propose steps for improving the situation. This approach works best when support of group members is key to change, when leaders do not know the entire problem, or when the problem is inherent to the culture of the groups involved.

Managing Stress

Effective organizational members must know how to manage stress—when to increase and decrease it. The key to constructively managing stress is to recognize both its energizing and destructive effects.[42] Managers can encourage productive stress; they can help employees build challenge into their work and assume incremental responsibility and autonomy over time.

Managers can also help individuals cope with dysfunctional stress.[43] First they can encourage individuals to secure treatment for the symptoms of stress. Many organizations now provide free employee health and counseling services, as well as stress-reduction workshops, to help individuals deal with and reduce stress. Second, they can organize stress-reduction activities such as yoga, exercise, diet, or psychological support that help change the people and improve their resistance to dysfunctional stress. Third, managers can help change or remove stressors. They can redesign jobs to reduce role overload, role ambiguity, or, conversely, boredom. They can also change organizational policies to give individuals more control over their work activities.

Managers therefore should be trained in stress-symptom identification and should ask questions such as the following[44]:

- What are the stress symptoms I observe? Have these symptoms been observed before? When and for how long have they been observed?
- What has happened at work that could trigger a severe stress reaction? Is this what the employee is stressed about? Have I been a stress carrier, contributing to the employee's problems?
- Is there a possible medical (mental or physical) problem?
- Does this employee have a long-standing personality problem that was noted long before these symptoms occurred?
- Has the employee effectively coped with stress in the past? In what way has the person coped?
- Are there resources available (work counseling, coworker support, managerial support) to help reduce the symptoms?

Fourth, managers can help individuals cope with stress by encouraging adaptive behaviors. They can delegate some of the work of overworked employees to others, encourage an employee who experiences a poor working relationship with a colleague to confront his or her coworker constructively, or clarify ambiguous roles.[45] Managers can simultaneously discourage maladaptive behaviors, by discouraging overworked employees from accepting additional work or encouraging workers to withdraw from ambiguous roles.

The costs of stress are high. One study of a hypothetical organization with 2000 employees and gross sales of $60 million per year estimated that stress-related factors cost the organization $1780 per employee each year.[46] Another study estimated the cost of executive stress at almost $10 billion per year.[47] Increasing numbers of employees are suing their employers as responsible for stress experienced on the job.[48] Clearly the diagnosis and reduction of stress can contribute significantly to increased individual and organizational effectiveness.

Structural Mechanisms

Redesigning formal reporting relationships, adding special managerial roles, or using standard operating procedures more extensively and effectively can improve the management of conflict and intergroup relations. Altering the nature of task relations between two groups may also improve intergroup behavior or reduce conflict. We examine job redesign strategies in detail in Chapter 13 but briefly outline pertinent structural mechanisms here.

Hierarchy A common superior is assigned to coordinate the work of two interacting groups. This position acts as a conduit for information, often setting priorities for interacting groups or individuals and resolving disputes between them. At ISL, for example, a senior vice president of marketing who supervises both marketing representatives and technical services staff might act as a common superior. Because neither the marketing department nor the technical services department has significant autonomy, this management strategy could be implemented successfully in this situation. In general, it works best when interacting groups are reasonably close in function or work on similar projects.

Plans and Goals Plans and goals direct the activities of interacting groups while minimizing their interaction. By using plans, even the integration of groups geographically distant can be effective. The use of common, or superordinate, goals can have an influence similar to plans: they can refocus the efforts of conflicting groups and rearrange group boundaries.[49] A specification of rules and regulations to govern the activities of the technical services department vis-à-vis marketing and vice versa might reduce existing conflict. At the same time, because of the complexity of their jobs, plans might limit the effectiveness of their role performance if they prevent either group from adapting to changes in the situation.

Linking Roles Individuals are temporarily placed in positions to act as conduits between interacting groups. They expedite communication by resolving issues through a person at the same level in the organization rather than by using a common supervisor to solve them.[50] A designated marketing representative serving as a liaison who facilitates communication between the marketing and technical services departments acts in a linking role, but a representative of the technical services staff may also fulfill this role. Sometimes linking roles can distort communication and even contribute to conflict if they inaccurately or inappropriately alter information passed between groups.

Task Forces Special groups of representatives from all parties can be convened to work on problems faced by the interacting groups. Task forces integrate by presenting the ideas of one group to the others' representatives. Task forces typically include one representative from each group affected by or involved in a particular problem or task. A task force of representatives from marketing, technical services, and even manufacturing and product development may be convened to deal with the problems experienced in setting up the computer demonstration.

Integrating Roles or Units Analogous to the typically informal linking roles, a permanent coordinating individual or group of people can be appointed to act as an interface between interacting groups. A project or product manager, for example, coordinates the decisions of such interdependent groups as sales representatives, R&D engineers, and the production line. A unit manager in a hospital, who may be either a medical or nonmedical person, may fulfill the role of coordinating all activities of a particular medical service, such as outpatient, emergency, or obstetrics.

Project or Product Structure This structure groups together individuals who work on the same product or project. In the case of a hospital, medical teams that include a nurse, physician, social worker, and other support personnel may service a small group of patients with similar illnesses, in the same ward, or with the same primary-care physician. In the case of ISL, a product team that includes marketing representatives, some technical services staff, and product development engineers, among others, would form a close working relationship and share a common focus on developing and marketing specific computer systems. (Chapter 11 describes this structure in greater detail.)

Matrix Organization This highly sophisticated organizational design integrates both functional departments and project groups through a dual authority and reporting system. In a matrix organization, each individual has two superiors. For example, Mark might report to the manager of technical services and the manager of the product being demonstrated. The marketing representatives would report to the vice president of marketing and the product manager. This structure itself is inherently conflict-ridden because of the duality of command. As discussed in Chapter 11, however, matrix structures have been used to help organizations cope effectively with very complex, uncertain, and dynamic environments.

What mechanisms can ISL use to improve the relationship between the marketing and technical services departments? Since the present hierarchy does not result in effective intergroup relations, top management should explore the use of other mechanisms, especially linking roles, task forces, or integrating roles. Reorganizing into a project structure may increase the collaboration by these two groups. A matrix organization, on the other hand, may offer flexibility at too high a cost; it may also increase rather than reduce dysfunctional conflict.

SUMMARY

Conflict frequently characterizes individuals and groups in organizations. It can exist at the intrapersonal, interpersonal, intragroup, intergroup, intraorganizational, and interorganizational levels. As a dynamic force, conflict progresses from the latent to perceived, felt, and manifest stages, and finally to a conflict aftermath. Its consequences can be functional—increased creativity and exchange of ideas, for example—or dysfunctional—increased stress, absenteeism, turnover, or decreased satisfaction and performance. Stress often accompanies conflict, which too can have functional or dysfunctional consequences for individuals and organizations.

Interacting groups are especially prone to conflict. Effective intergroup relations require managers and other organizational members to diagnose the extent and causes of their interdependence. Groups can demonstrate pooled, sequential, reciprocal, or team interdependence. Groups experiencing reciprocal or team interdependence more often experience dysfunctional conflict and other problems than those showing pooled or sequential interdependence.

Perceptual differences, including time, goal, and social orientations, attitudinal set, and status differences create differences between groups. Task relations reflect the nature of group interdependence and can reinforce problematic interactions. Power differences, including the extent of a group's substitutability, its ability to cope with uncertainty, and its access to resources, influence the effectiveness of its interactions with other individuals or groups.

Figure 10–6 is a list of questions for diagnosing conflict and intergroup relations in organizations. Prescriptions for managing conflict and improving

Figure 10–6 DIAGNOSTIC QUESTIONS FOR MANAGING CONFLICT AND INTERGROUP RELATIONS

- Is there conflict in the organization?
- What level of conflict exists?
- What stage of conflict exists?
- Is there evidence of stress in the situation?
- What causes and results from stress in the situation?
- What is the nature of the relationship between groups in the organization?
- What factors contribute to these relationships?
- How effective are intergroup relations?
- Are there mechanisms for effectively managing conflict, stress, and intergroup relations?

intergroup relations include the use of process strategies, management of stress, and introduction of structural mechanisms. Their effectiveness depends on the parties involved and the nature of the situation.

READING

Reading 10–1: MANAGING CONFLICT

Leonard Greenhalgh

Managers or change agents spend a substantial proportion of their time and energy dealing with conflict situations. Such efforts are necessary because any type of change in an organization tends to generate conflict. More specifically, conflict arises because change disrupts the existing balance of resources and power, thereby straining relations between the people involved. Since adversarial relations may impede the process of making adaptive changes in the organization, higher-level managers may have to intervene in order to implement important strategies. Their effectiveness in managing the conflict depends on how well they understand the underlying dynamics of the conflict—which may be very different from its expression—and whether they can identify the crucial tactical points for intervention.

CONFLICT MANAGEMENT

Conflict is managed when it does not substantially interfere with the ongoing functional (as opposed to personal) relationships between the parties involved. For instance, two executives may agree to disagree on a number of issues and yet be jointly committed to the course of action they have settled on. There may even be some residual hard feelings—perhaps it is too much to expect to manage feelings in addition to relationships—but as long as any resentment is at a fairly low level and does not substantially interfere with other aspects of their professional relationship, the conflict could be considered to have been managed successfully.

Conflict is not an objective, tangible phenomenon; rather, it exists in the minds of the people who are party to it. Only its manifestations, such as brooding, arguing, or fighting, are objectively real. To manage conflict, therefore, one needs to empathize, that is, to understand the situation as it is seen by the key actors involved. An important element of conflict management is persuasion, which may well involve getting participants to rethink their current views so their perspective on the situation will facilitate reconciliation rather than divisiveness.

Influencing key actors' conceptions of the conflict situation can be a powerful lever in making conflicts manageable. This approach can be used by a third party intervening in the conflict or, even more usefully, by the participants themselves. But using this perceptual lever alone will not always be sufficient. The context in which the conflict occurs, the history of the relationship between the parties, and the time available will have to be taken into account if such an approach is to be tailored to the situation. Furthermore, the conflict may prove to be simply unmanageable: one or both parties may wish to prolong the conflict or they may have reached emotional states that make constructive interaction impossible; or, perhaps the conflict is "the tip of the iceberg" and resolving it would have no significant impact on a deeply rooted antagonistic relationship.

Table 10–4 presents seven perceptual dimensions that form a useful diagnostic model that shows what to look for in a conflict situation and pinpoints the dimensions needing high-priority attention. The model can thus be used to illuminate a way to make the conflict more manageable. The point here is that conflict becomes more negotiable between parties when a minimum number of dimensions are perceived to be at the "difficult-to-resolve" pole and a maximum number to be at the "easy-to-resolve" pole. The objective is to shift a viewpoint from the difficult-to-resolve pole to the easy-to-resolve one. At times, antagonists will deliberately resist "being more reasonable" because they see tactical advantages in taking a hard line. Nevertheless, there are strong benefits for trying to shift perspectives; these benefits should become apparent as we consider each of the dimensions in the model.

Issues in Question

People view issues on a continuum from being a matter of principle to a question of division. For example, one organization needed to change its channel of distribution. The company had sold door-to-door since its founding, but the labor market was drying up and the sales force was becoming increasingly understaffed. Two factions of executive sprung up: the supporters were open to the needed change; the resisters argued that management made a commitment to the remaining sales

Table 10–4 CONFLICT DIAGNOSTIC MODEL

	Viewpoint Continuum	
Dimension	Difficult to Resolve	Easy to Resolve
Issue in question	Matter of principle	Divisible issue
Size of stakes	Large	Small
Interdependence of the parties	Zero sum	Positive sum
Continuity of interaction	Single transaction	Long-term relationship
Structure of the parties	Amorphous or fractionalized, with weak leadership	Cohesive, with strong leadership
Involvement of third parties	No neutral third party available	Trusted, powerful, prestigious, and neutral
Perceived progress of the conflict	Unbalanced: one party feeling the more harmed	Parties having done equal harm to each other

force and, as a matter of principle, could not violate the current sales representatives' right to be the exclusive channel of distribution.

Raising principles makes conflict difficult to resolve because by definition one cannot come to a reasonable compromise; one either upholds a principle or sacrifices one's integrity. For some issues, particularly those involving ethical imperatives, such a dichotomous view may be justified. Often, however, matters of principle are raised for the purpose of solidifying a bargaining stance. Yet, this tactic may work *against* the party using it since it tends to invite an impasse. Once matters of principle are raised, the parties try to argue convincingly that the other's point of view is wrong. At best, this approach wastes time and saps the energy of the parties involved. A useful intervention at this point may be to have the parties acknowledge that they *understand* each other's view but still believe in their own, equally legitimate point of view. This acknowledgment alone often makes the parties more ready to move ahead from arguing to problem solving.

At the other extreme are divisible issues where neither side has to give in completely; the outcome may more or less favor both parties. In the door-to-door selling example, a more constructive discussion would have ensued had the parties been able to focus on the *economic* commitment the company had to its sales force, rather than on the *moral* commitment. As it was, the factions remained deadlocked until the company had suffered irrevocable losses in market share, which served no one's interests. Divisible issues in this case might have involved how much of the product line would be sold through alternative channels of distribution, the extent of exclusive territory, or how much income protection the company was willing to offer its sales force.

Size of Stakes

The greater the perceived value of what may be lost, the harder it is to manage a conflict. This point is illustrated when managers fight against acquisition attempts. If managers think their jobs are in jeopardy, they subjectively perceive the stakes as being high and are likely to fight tooth and nail against the acquisition. Contracts providing for continued economic security, so-called golden parachutes, reduce the size of the stakes for those potentially affected. Putting aside the question of whether such contracts are justifiable when viewed from other perspectives, they do tend to make acquisition conflicts more manageable.

In many cases the perceived size of the stakes can be reduced by persuasion rather than by taking concrete action. People tend to become emotionally involved in conflicts and as a result magnify the importance of what is really at stake. Their "egos" get caught up in the winning/losing aspect of the conflict, and subjective values become inflated.

A good antidote is to postpone the settlement until the parties become less emotional. During this cooling-off period they can reevaluate the issues at stake, thereby restoring some objectivity to their assessments. If time does not permit a cooling off, an attempt to reassess the demands and reduce the other party's expectations may be possible: "There's no way we can give you 100 percent of what you want, so let's be realistic about what you can live with." This approach is really an attempt to induce an attitude change. In effect, the person is being persuaded to entertain the thought, "If I can get by with less than 100 percent of what I was asking for, then what is at stake must not be of paramount importance to me."

A special case of the high-stakes/low-stakes question is the issue of precedents. If a particular settlement sets a precedent, the stakes are seen as being higher because future conflicts will tend to be settled in terms of the current settlement. In other words, giving ground in the immediate situation is seen as giving ground for all time. This problem surfaces in settling grievances. Thus, an effective way to manage such a conflict is to emphasize the uniqueness of the situation to downplay possible precedents that could be set. Similarly, the perceived consequences of organizational changes for individuals can often be softened by explicitly downplaying the future consequences: employees are sometimes assured that the change is being made "on an experimental basis" and will later be reevaluated. The effect is to reduce the perceived risk in accepting the proposed change.

Interdependence of the Parties

The parties to a conflict can view themselves on a continuum from having "zero-sum" to "positive-sum" interdependence. Zero-sum interdependence is the perception that if one party gains in an interaction, it is at the expense of the other party. In the positive-sum case, both parties come out ahead by means of a settlement. A zero-sum relationship makes conflict difficult to resolve because it focuses attention narrowly on personal gain rather than on mutual gain through collaboration or problem solving.

Consider the example of conflict over the allocation of limited budget funds among sales and production when a new product line is introduced. The sales group fights for a large allocation to promote the product in order to build market share. The production group fights for a large allocation to provide the plant and equipment necessary to turn out high volume at high-quality levels. The funds available have a fixed ceiling, so that a gain for sales appears to be a loss for production and vice versa. From a zero-sum perspective, it makes sense to fight for the marginal dollar rather than agree on a compromise.

A positive-sum view of the same situation removes some of the urgency to win a larger share of the spoils at the outset. Attention is more usefully focused on how one party's allocation in fact helps the other. Early promotion allocations to achieve high sales volume, if successful, lead to high production volume. This, in turn, generates revenue that can be invested in the desired improvements to plant and equipment. Similarly, initial allocations to improve plant and equipment can make a high-quality product readily available to the sales group, and the demand for a high-quality product will foster sales.

The potential for mutual benefit is often overlooked in the scramble for scarce resources. However, if both parties can be persuaded to consider how they can both benefit from a situation, they are more likely to approach the conflict over scarce resources with more cooperative predispositions. The focus shifts from whether one party is getting a fair share of the available resources to what is the optimum initial allocation that will jointly serve the mutual long-run interests of both sales and production.

Continuity of Interaction

The continuity-of-interaction dimension concerns the time horizon over which the parties see themselves dealing with each other. If they visualize a long-term interaction—a *continuous* relationship—the present transaction takes on minor significance, and the conflict within that transaction tends to be easy to resolve. If, on the other hand, the transaction is viewed as a one-shot deal—an *episodic* relationship—the parties will have little incentive to accommodate each other, and the conflict will be difficult to resolve.

This difference in perspective is seen by contrasting how lawyers and managers approach a contract dispute. Lawyers are trained to perceive the situation as a single episode: the parties go to court, and the lawyers make the best possible case for their party in an attempt to achieve the best possible outcome. This is a "no-holds-barred" interaction in which the past and future interaction between the parties tends to be viewed as irrelevant. Thus the conflict between the parties is not really resolved; rather, an outcome is imposed by the judge.

In contrast, managers are likely to be more accommodating when the discussion of a contract is viewed as one interaction within a longer-term relationship that has both a history and a future. In such a situation, a manager is unlikely to resort to no-holds-barred tactics because he or she will have to face the other party again regarding future deals. Furthermore, a continuous relationship permits the bankrolling of favors: "We helped you out on that last problem; it's your turn to work with us on this one."

Here, it is easy, and even cordial, to remind the other party that a continuous relationship exists. This tactic works well because episodic situations are rare in real-world business transactions. For instance, people with substantial business experience know that a transaction is usually not completed when a contract is signed. No contract can be comprehensive enough to provide unambiguously for all possible contingencies. Thus trust and goodwill remain important long after the contract is signed. The street-fighting tactics that may seem advantageous in the context of an episodic orientation are likely to be very costly to the person who must later seek accommodation with the bruised and resentful other party.

Structure of the Parties

Conflict is easier to resolve when a party has a strong leader who can unify his or her constituency to accept and implement the agreement. If the leadership is weak, rebellious subgroups who may not feel obliged to go along with the overall agreement that has been reached are likely to rise up, thereby making conflict difficult to resolve.

For example, people who deal with unions know that a strong leadership tends to be better than a weak one, especially when organizational change needs to be accomplished. A strongly led union may drive a hard bargain, but once an agreement is reached the deal is honored by union members. If a weakly led union is involved, the agreement may be undermined by factions within the union who may not like some of the details. The result may well be chronic resistance to change or even wildcat strikes. To bring peace among such factions, management may have to make further concessions that may be costly. To avoid this, managers may find themselves in a paradoxical position of needing to boost the power of union leaders.

Similar actions may be warranted when there is no union. Groups of employees often band together as informal coalitions to protect their interests in times of change. Instead of fighting or alienating a group, managers who wish to bring about change may benefit from considering ways to formalize the coalition, such as by appointing its opinion leader to a task force or steering committee. This tactic may be equivalent to cooptation, yet there is likely to be a net benefit to both the coalition and management. The coalition benefits because it is given a formal channel in which the opinion leader's viewpoint is expressed; management benefits because the spokesperson presents the conflict in a manageable form, which is much better than passive resistance or subtle sabotage.

Involvement of Third Parties

People tend to become emotionally involved in conflicts. Such involvement can have several effects: perceptions may become distorted, nonrational thought processes and arguments may arise, and unreasonable stances, impaired communication, and personal attacks may result. These effects make the conflict difficult to resolve.

The presence of a third party, even if the third party is not actively involved in the dialogue, can constrain such effects. People usually feel obliged to appear reasonable and responsible because they care more about how the neutral party is evaluating them than by how the opponent is. The more prestigious, powerful, trusted, and neutral the third party, the greater is the desire to exercise emotional restraint.

While managers often have to mediate conflicts among lower-level employees, they are rarely seen as being neutral. Therefore, consultants and change agents often end up serving a mediator role, either by design or default. This role can take several forms, ranging from an umpire supervising communication to a messenger between parties for whom face-to-face communication has become too strained. Mediation essentially involves keeping the parties interacting in a reasonable and constructive manner. Typically, however, most managers are reluctant to enlist an outsider who is a professional mediator or arbitrator, for it is very hard for them to admit openly that they are entangled in a serious conflict, much less one they cannot handle themselves.

When managers remain involved in settling disputes, they usually take a stronger role than mediators: they become arbitrators rather than mediators. As arbitrators, they arrive at a conflict-resolving judgment after hearing each party's case. In most business conflicts, mediation is preferable because the parties are helped to come to an agreement in which they have some psychological investment. Arbitration tends to be more of a judicial process in which the parties make the best possible case to support their position: this tends to further polarize rather than reconcile differences.

Managers can benefit from a third-party presence, however, without involving dispute-resolution professionals per se. For example, they can introduce a consultant into the situation, with an *explicit* mission that is not conflict intervention. The mere presence of this neutral witness will likely constrain the disputants' use of destructive tactics.

Alternatively, if the managers find that they themselves are party to a conflict, they can make the conflict more public and produce the same constraining effect that a third party would. They also can arrange for the presence of relatively uninvolved individuals during interactions; even having a secretary keep minutes of such interactions encourages rational behavior. If the content of the discussion cannot be disclosed to lower-level employees, a higher-level manager can be invited to sit in on the discussion, thereby discouraging dysfunctional personal attacks and unreasonable stances. To the extent that managers can be trusted to be even-handed, a third-party approach can facilitate conflict management. Encouraging accommodation usually is preferable to imposing a solution that may only produce resentment of one of the parties.

Progress of the Conflict

It is difficult to manage conflict when the parties are not ready to achieve a reconciliation. Thus it is important to know whether the parties believe that the conflict is escalating. The following example illustrates this point.

During a product strategy meeting, a marketing vice-president carelessly implied that the R&D group tended to overdesign products. The remark was intended to be a humorous stereotyping of the R&D function, but it was interpreted by the R&D vice-president as an attempt to pass on to his group the blame for an uncompetitive product. Later in the meeting, the R&D vice-president took advantage of an opportunity to point out that the marketing vice-president lacked the technical expertise to understand a design limitation. The marketing vice-president perceived this rejoinder as ridicule and therefore as an act of hostility. The R&D vice-president, who believed he had evened the score, was quite surprised to be denounced subsequently by the marketing vice-president, who in turn thought he was evening the score for the uncalled-for barb. These events soon led to a memo war, backbiting, and then to pressure on various employees to take sides.

The important point here is that from the first rejoinder neither party wished to escalate the conflict; each wished merely to even the score. Nonetheless, conflict resolution would have been very difficult to accomplish during this escalation phase because people do not like to disengage when they think they still "owe one" to the other party. Since an even score is subjectively defined, however, the parties need to be convinced that the overall score is approximately equal and that everyone has already suffered enough.

DEVELOPING CONFLICT MANAGEMENT SKILLS

Strategic decision making usually is portrayed as a unilateral process. Decision makers have some vision of where the organization needs to be headed, and they decide on the nature and timing of specific actions to achieve tangible goals. This portrayal, however, does not take into account the conflict inherent in the decision-making process; most strategic decisions are negotiated solutions to conflicts among people whose interests are affected by such decisions. Even in the uncommon case of a unilateral decision, the decision maker has to deal with the conflict that arises when he or she moves to *implement* the decision.

In the presence of conflict at the decision-making or decision-implementing stage, managers must focus on generating an *agreement* rather than a decision. A decision without agreement makes the strategic direction difficult to implement. By contrast, an agreement on a strategic direction doesn't require an explicit decision. In this context, conflict management is the process of removing cognitive barriers to agreement. Note that agreement does not imply that the conflict has "gone away." The people involved still have interests that are somewhat incompatible. Agreement implies that these people have become committed to a course of action that serves some of their interests.

People make agreements that are less than ideal from the standpoint of serving their interests when they lack the *power* to force others to fully comply with their wishes. On the other hand, if a manager has total power over those whose interests are affected by the outcome of a strategic decision, the manager may not care whether or not others agree, because total power implies total compliance. There are few situations in real life in which managers have influence that even approaches total power, however, and power solutions are at best unstable since most people react negatively to powerlessness per se. Thus it makes more sense to seek agreements than to seek power. Furthermore, because conflict management involves weakening or removing barriers to agreements, managers must be able to diagnose successfully such barriers. The model summarized in Table 10–4 identifies the primary cognitive barriers to agreement.

Competence in understanding the barriers to an agreement can be easily honed by making a pastime of conflict diagnosis. The model helps to focus attention on specific aspects of the situation that may pose obstacles to successful conflict management. This pastime transforms accounts of conflicts—from sources ranging from a spouse's response to "how was your day?" to the evening news—into a challenge in which the objective is to try to pinpoint the obstacles to agreement and to predict the success of proposed interventions.

Focusing on the underlying dynamics of the conflict makes it more likely that conflict management will tend toward resolution rather than the more familiar response of suppression. Although the conflict itself—that is, the source—will remain alive, at best, its expression will be postponed until some later occasion; at worst, it will take a less obvious and usually less manageable form.

Knowledge of and practice in using the model is only a starting point for managers and change agents. Their development as professionals requires that conflict management become an integral part of their use of power. Power is a most basic facet of organizational life, yet inevitably it generates conflict because it constricts the autonomy of those who respond to it. Anticipating precisely how the use of power will create a conflict relationship provides an enormous advantage in the ability to achieve the desired levels of control with minimal dysfunctional side effects.

DISCUSSION QUESTIONS

1. How do you know when conflict is managed effectively?
2. What seven dimensions of a conflict situation require high-priority attention?
3. Under what circumstances are issues in each dimension easy to resolve?
4. Under what circumstances are issues in each dimension difficult to resolve?

Reprinted from "Managing Conflict" by Leonard Greenhalgh, *Sloan Management Review,* Summer 1986, pp. 45–51, by permission of the publisher.

ACTIVITIES

Activity 10–1: Health Manager in the Middle: The Case of Ms. X

Step 1: Read Health Manager in the Middle: The Case of Ms. X.

Traditionally health organizations lacked middle management as compared with industry; there were essentially top managers and supervisors. Most health organizations were not big enough to warrant skilled middle managers. With the increase in size of health organizations, and the increased importance of management, middle management responsibility for significant medical care operations, such as hospital departments or group practices, is now often given to well-trained skilled, capable lay managers. Many of these are women. Often they have many years of experience and an MBA or its equivalent. The enhanced career opportunities of well-paid and responsible middle management positions are however offset with significant problems. Too often the middle manager is responsible for the performance of a medical care unit controlled by physicians over whom the manager has relatively little power. This is the story of one such example, the case of Ms. X. She is the practice manager for a group practice in a teaching hospital. The problems, however, are not at all dissimilar to those of any middle manager in a health organization, whether it be a hospital, an HMO or a group practice.

ROLE AND RESPONSIBILITIES

As practice manager she reports to the hospital administration; the medical director of her unit reports to the Department of Medicine and she has a dotted-line relationship to him. She is responsible for the administrative staff of approximately twenty-five people, for monitoring the budget, and for reporting on her cost center. Her group practice has some 25,000 patient visits a year, and is staffed by fifty doctors all of whom are fulltime salaried employees of the hospital.

She is also responsible for interfacing with other hospital departments, such as medical records, and for developing new programs.

PROBLEMS FROM THE MEDICAL DIRECTOR'S POINT OF VIEW

Because of the wide variety of different skills and professionals, secretaries, nurses, nurse practitioners, doctors, social workers, psychologists, nutritionists, etc., there are major conflicts on a day-to-day basis which are seldom resolved.

Who answers the phone? Does the nurse pick it up if the secretary is busy? Who covers lunch? What does an aide or nurse practitioner do? The major conflicts are between secretaries and doctors. The secretaries see themselves as oriented to doctors, not the nurses or the unit. Some doctors work better with nurse practitioners than others. Who's in charge, the nurse or the doctor? They're supposed to be equal partners, but it does not always work out that way. He is supposed to be responsible for patient care and for efficiency. But that is a personal conflict since he is not only an administrator but a clinician and spends only a minor proportion of his time on administration.

The group of doctors is not homogeneous. While the young doctors have a positive orientation to primary health care, the old stagers see themselves as outcasts and somewhat resent their functions. All of the doctors, since this is a teaching hospital, are split between their clinical, research and educational responsibilities. But since there are not any incentives for productivity, it is difficult for him to exert any influence over the productivity of the physicians supposedly working in the group practice, since they respond to the traditional incentives of research publication.

He finds that he has conflicts within himself over his role and interests. The practice is supposed to provide an accurate data flow and to increase productivity as well as to reduce no shows, which create a loss to the practice. They are also supposed to emphasize patient education as a preventive measure. Yet there are no incentives to do this. Ms. X, his practice manager, is responsible also for productivity, for trouble shooting, for screwups in the appointment system, for scheduling and for routine lab slips. Yet she has to deal with doctors over these issues and is regarded by them as an outsider, so needs his help. She gets the flack and he is protected. He wonders what kinds of skills, experience, and background would best enable someone in Ms. X's positions to perform her varied responsibilities and tasks.

THE PROBLEMS AS MS. X SEES THEM

Ms. X feels herself to be very much in the middle; she is between the upper millstone of a group of independent physicians and the lower millstone of a bureaucratic administrative system. She has to be able to influence not only her physicians, and her nonphysicians, but the overall hospital structure and not least her medical director.

With regard to her physicians, it is difficult to get her doctors to agree together or to think of themselves as a group. They are reluctant to give up control over the schedule or the way they do things. How can she get them to start thinking as a group especially if her medical director is reluctant to exert himself? In other words, how can she influence her boss? This becomes a conflict in loyalties between her institution, her boss, and her staff. While she is willing to acknowledge and accept her own responsibility for solving these problems, she cannot help believing that matters would be improved if there were better selection of physicians working in this kind of environment, or if there were well-designed incentives that were appropriate to the goals of a group practice. Since here staff come from hospital and not practice backgrounds, perhaps also nurses and secretaries should better be selected for this new kind of endeavor.

Everybody has different agendas and different points of view. All are on straight salary without incentives or bonuses. She often wonders whether she has the right kinds of skills to perform this incredible balancing act. She has to promote an ambulatory care philosophy, to be a hospital politician, to supervise detail, and to be an effective manager. What kind of experience, background, or training would best fit someone to do this impossible task? Is it reasonable for her to be held responsible for the performance of so many diverse people without the authority to do it? Yet how could she be given the authority or even exert it?

The nurses do the day-to-day management, but are not responsible for the residents. Yet someone has to deal with them being late, or when they do not show up, or do not see patients. How can you motivate them when they do not demonstrate responsibility? Her medical director is not there all the time and does not want to be bothered about minor details. She is not responsible for the nurses, yet is responsible for the unit's performance. She is also responsible for developing long-range plans for her unit while her staff, whether doctors or not, are essentially short-run oriented.

In fact only the secretaries report to her because the nurses report to the nursing department and the doctors to her medical director. She is supposed to be responsible for costs, yet she has no influence over those that spend the money. She is supposed to be a politician, a negotiator, and a mediator yet has not had the training to do this.

BASIC ISSUES

As Ms. X reflected on the challenges and problems of her job, she wondered once again, what kinds of background skills and training the role required. How can she influence her boss? How can she integrate the diverse professionals and personalities she is responsible for? How can she influence the hospital system to create the necessary incentives that would enable her to do her job? And finally, how can she get her staff to be more oriented toward marketing and strategic management given that these are crucial elements that will help determine the future of the practice, and yet are foreign concepts?

As she reflected, she concluded that she had many more questions than answers.

Step 2: Prepare the case for class discussion.

Step 3: Answer the following questions, individually, in small groups, or with the entire class, as directed by your instructor:

Description

1. Describe the various groups with which Ms. X interacts.

Diagnosis

2. Is there functional or dysfunctional conflict?
3. What level of conflict exists?
4. At what stage is the conflict?
5. What causes the conflict?
6. How do intergroup relations contribute to the conflict?

Prescription

7. How would you improve the situation?

Action

8. What costs and benefits probably will result from implementing the prescription?

Step 4: Discussion. In small groups, with the entire class, or in written form, share your answers to the questions above. Then answer the following questions:

1. What symptoms suggest a problem exists?
2. What problems exist in the case?
3. What theories and concepts help explain the problems?
4. How can the problems be corrected?
5. Are the actions likely to be effective?

Case prepared by Alan Sheldon, Distributed by the Pew Curriculum Center for Health Policy and Management, Harvard School of Public Health, Boston, Massachusetts.

Activity 10–2: CONFLICT QUESTIONNAIRE

Step 1: Complete the following questionnaire:

Directions: Consider situations in which you find your wishes differing from those of another person. For each of the following statements, think about how likely you are to respond in that way to such a situation. Check the rating that best corresponds to your response.

	Very Unlikely	Unlikely	Likely	Very Likely
1. I am usually firm in pursuing my goals.	______	______	______	______
2. I try to win my position.	______	______	______	______
3. I give up some points in exchange for others.	______	______	______	______
4. I feel that differences are not always worth worrying about.	______	______	______	______
5. I try to find a position that is intermediate between his and mine.	______	______	______	______
6. In approaching negotiations, I try to be considerate of the other person's wishes.	______	______	______	______
7. I try to show the logic and benefits of my positions.	______	______	______	______
8. I always lean toward a direct discussion of the problem.	______	______	______	______
9. I try to find a fair combination of gains and losses for both of us.	______	______	______	______
10. I attempt to immediately work through our differences.	______	______	______	______
11. I try to avoid creating unpleasantness for myself.	______	______	______	______
12. I might try to soothe the other's feelings and preserve our relationships.	______	______	______	______
13. I attempt to get all concerns and issues immediately out in the open.	______	______	______	______
14. I sometimes avoid taking positions that would create controversy.	______	______	______	______
15. I try not to hurt others' feelings.	______	______	______	______

Step 2: Scoring. Assign points to each response as follows: very unlikely = 1, unlikely = 2, likely = 3, very likely = 4. For each mode listed below, write the scores under the item number. Then add the scores on the three items for each dimension.

Competing:	Item 1 ______	Item 2 ______	Item 7 ______	Total ______
Collaborating:	Item 8 ______	Item 10 ______	Item 13 ______	Total ______

Compromising:	Item 3 ______	Item 5 ______	Item 9 ______	Total ______
Avoiding:	Item 4 ______	Item 11 ______	Item 14 ______	Total ______
Accommodating:	Item 6 ______	Item 12 ______	Item 15 ______	Total ______

Step 3: Discussion. In small groups or with the class as a whole, answer the following questions:

1. What did your score pattern look like?
2. Do any patterns emerge among groups in the class?
3. Which modes have you found to be most commonly used? least commonly used?
4. Which modes have you found to be most effective? least effective?
5. In what situations has each mode been most effective?

Adapted from Thomas Kilmann Conflict Mode Instrument, copyright © 1974. Xicom, Inc., Tuxedo, NY 10987. Reprinted with permission of Xicom, Inc., Tuxedo, NY (914) 351–4735.

Activity 10–3: HOLLOW SQUARE: A COMMUNICATION EXPERIMENT

Step 1: Your instructor will organize you into teams of between seven and ten members. Then each team should divide itself into two or three groups: planners, operators, and observers (if your instructor so states).

Step 2: Each group will receive instructions that it should follow precisely.

Step 3: You should perform the Hollow Square exercise.

Step 4: Discussion. Evaluate your experience by answering the following questions:

Description
1. What did it feel like to be a planner?
2. What did it feel like to be an operator?
3. What did the observers see happening?

Diagnosis
4. What influenced the relationship between the groups?

Prescription
5. How could the interaction have been improved?

Reprinted from: J. William Pfeiffer and John E. Jones, (eds.), *A Handbook of Structured Experiences for Human Relations Training*, Vol. II. San Diego, CA: University Associates, Inc., 1974. Used with permission.

Activity 10–4: DIAGNOSIS OF CONFLICT AND ITS CAUSES

Step 1: Think about a conflict you have experienced.

1. Describe the situation.
2. What symptoms of conflict did you experience?
3. What level of conflict was it?
4. What stage of conflict was it?
5. What caused the conflict?
6. What outcomes resulted from the conflict?
7. How did you manage the conflict?

Step 2: In groups of four to six, compare your answers to questions 1–7 above.

Description
1. Identify common elements in the conflict situations.

Diagnosis
2. List the symptoms of conflict.
3. Specify the causes of conflict.

Prescription
4. Describe the different processes used to manage the conflict.
5. Suggest additional ways of managing the conflict.

Step 3: Discuss your group's answers with the rest of the class.

1. What are the most common symptoms of conflict?
2. What are the most common causes of conflict?
3. What are effective ways of managing conflict?

Activity 10–5: DIAGNOSIS OF STRESS

Step 1: Complete the following questionnaire by checking the appropriate column:

Do You Frequently	Yes	No
1. Neglect your diet?		
2. Try to do everything yourself?		
3. Blow up easily?		
4. Seek unrealistic goals?		
5. Fail to see the humor in situations others find funny?		
6. Act rude?		
7. Make a "big deal" of everything?		
8. Look to other people to make things happen?		
9. Have difficulty making decisions?		
10. Complain you are disorganized?		
11. Avoid people whose ideas are different from your own?		
12. Keep everything inside?		
13. Neglect exercise?		
14. Have few supportive relationships?		
15. Use psychoactive drugs, such as sleeping pills and tranquilizers, without physician approval?		
16. Get too little rest?		
17. Get angry when you are kept waiting?		
18. Ignore stress symptoms?		
19. Procrastinate?		
20. Think there is only one right way to do something?		
21. Fail to build in relaxation time?		
22. Gossip?		
23. Race through the day?		
24. Spend a lot of time lamenting the past?		
25. Fail to get a break from noise and crowds?		

Step 2: Score your responses by scoring 1 for each "Yes" answer and 0 for each "No" answer. Total your score.

1–6 There are few hassles in your life. Make sure, though, that you aren't trying so hard to avoid problems that you shy away from challenges.

7–13 You've got your life in pretty good control. Work on the choices and habits that could still be causing some unnecessary stress in your life.

14–20 You're approaching the danger zone. You may well be suffering stress-related symptoms and your relationships could be strained. Think carefully about choices you've made and take relaxation breaks every day.

Above 20 Emergency! You must stop now, rethink how you are living, change your attitudes, and pay scrupulous attention to your diet, exercise, and relaxation programs.

Step 3: Discussion. In small groups or with the class as a whole, answer the following questions:

Description

1. What was your score?
2. How much stress does this represent?
3. How does this compare to scores of others in the class?

Step 4: Think about a stressful situation you have experienced.

1. Describe the situation.
2. What symptoms of stress did you experience at the time?
3. What caused the stress?
4. How did you reduce the stress?

Step 5: Individually or in small groups, offer a plan for coping with or reducing stress.

Source: Adapted with permission from "Stress Index" by A.E. Slaby, M.D., Ph.D., M.P.H., *60 Ways to Make Stress Work for You* (Summit, N.J.: PIA Press, 1988).

Activity 10–6: WORLD BANK: AN INTERGROUP NEGOTIATION

Step 1: The class is divided into two groups. The size of each of the groups should be no more than ten. Those not in one of the two groups are designated as observers. However, groups should not have less than six members each. The instructor will play the role of the referee/banker for the World Bank.

Step 2: Read the World Bank Instruction Sheet below.

WORLD BANK GENERAL INSTRUCTION SHEET

This is an intergroup activity. You and your team are going to engage in a task in which money will be won or lost. *The objective is to win as much as you can.* There are two teams involved in this activity, and both teams receive identical instructions. After reading these instructions, your team has 15 minutes to organize itself and to plan its strategy.

Each team represents a country. Each country has financial dealings with the World Bank. Initially, each country contributed $100 million to the World Bank. Countries may have to pay further monies or may receive money from the World Bank in accordance with regulations and procedures described below under sections headed Finance and Payoffs.

Each team is given twenty cards. These are your *weapons*. Each card has a marked side *(X)* and an unmarked side. The marked side of the card signifies that the weapon is armed. Conversely, the blank side shows the weapon to be unarmed.

At the beginning, each team will place ten of its twenty weapons in their armed positions (marked side up) and the remaining ten in their unarmed positions (marked side down). These weapons will remain in your possession and out of sight of the other team at all times.

There will be *rounds* and *moves*. Each round consists of seven moves by each team. There will be two or more rounds in this simulation. The number of rounds depends on the time available. Payoffs are determined and recorded after each round.

1. A move consists of turning two, one, or none of the team's weapons from armed to unarmed status, or vice versa.
2. Each team has 2 minutes for each move. There are 30-second periods between moves. At the end of 2 minutes, the team must have turned two, one, or none of its weapons from armed to unarmed status, or from unarmed to armed status. If the team fails to move in the allotted time, no change can be made in weapon status until the next move.
3. The length of the 2½-minute periods between the beginning of one move and the beginning of the next is fixed and unalterable.

Each new round of the experiment begins with all weapons returned to their original positions, ten armed and ten unarmed.

Finances

The funds you have contributed to the World Bank are to be allocated in the following manner:

$60 million will be returned to each team to be used as your team's treasury during the course of the decision-making activities.

$80 million will be retained for the operation of the World Bank.

Payoffs

1. If there is an attack:
   a. Each team may announce an attack on the other team by notifying the referee/banker during the 30 seconds following *any* 2-minute period used to decide upon the move (including the seventh, or final, decision period in any round). The choice of each team during the decision period just ended counts as a move. An attack may not be made during negotiations.
   b. If there is an attack (by one or both teams), two things happen: (1) the round ends, and (2) the World Bank levies a penalty of $5 million for each team.
   c. The team with the greater number of armed weapons wins $3 million for each armed weapon it has over and above the number of armed weapons of the other team. These funds are paid directly from the treasury of the losing team to the treasury of the winning team. The referee/bankers will manage this transfer of funds.
2. If there is no attack:
   At the end of each round (seven moves), each team's treasury receives from the World Bank $2 million for each of its weapons that is at that point unarmed, and each team's treasury pays to the World Bank $2 million for each of its weapons remaining armed.

Negotiations

Between moves each team has the opportunity to communicate with the other team through its negotiators.

Either team may call for negotiations by notifying the referee/bankers during any of the 30-second periods between decisions. A team is free to accept or reject any invitations to negotiate.

Negotiators from both teams are *required* to meet after the third and sixth moves (after the 30-second period following that move, if there is no attack).

Negotiations can last no longer than 3 minutes. When the two negotiators return to their teams, the 2-minute decision period for the next move begins once again.

Negotiators are bound only by: (a) the 3-minute time limit for negotiations, and (b) their required appearance after the third and sixth moves. They are otherwise free to say whatever is necessary to benefit themselves or their teams. The teams similarly are not bound by agreements made by their negotiators, even when those agreements are made in good faith.

Special Roles

Each team has 15 minutes to organize itself to plan team strategy. During this period before the first round begins, each team must choose persons to fill the following roles. (Each team must have each of the following roles, which can be changed at any time by a decision of the team.)

- *Negotiators*—activities stated above.
- A *representative*—to communicate team decisions to the referee/bankers.

- A *recorder*—to record the moves of the team and to keep a running balance of the team's treasury.
- A *treasurer*—to execute all financial transactions with the referee/bankers.

Step 3: Each group or team will have 15 minutes to organize itself and plan strategy before beginning. Before the first round each team must choose (a) two negotiators, (b) a representative, (c) a team recorder, (d) a treasurer.

Step 4: The referee/banker will signal the beginning of round one and each following round and also end the exercise in about one hour.

Step 5: Discussion. In small groups or with the entire class, answer the following questions:

Description

1. What occurred during the exercise?

Diagnosis

2. Was there conflict? What type, level, or stage?
3. What contributed to the relationships among groups?
4. Evaluate the power, leadership, motivation, and communication among groups.

Prescription

5. How could the relationships have been more effective?

Adapted from: J. William Pfeiffer and John E. Jones, (Eds.), *The 1975 Annual Handbook for Group Facilitators*, San Diego, CA: University Associates, Inc., 1975. Used with permission.

Activity 10–7: THE BORDER DISPUTE

Step 1: Your instructor will divide the class into two groups or into several sets of two groups. One group will act as representatives who negotiate for Arak; the second for Barkan.

Step 2: Read the following information about the situation the two countries face.

SITUATION

There are two developing countries, Arak and Barkan, who have an unresolved border dispute. The result has been continuous squabbling over resource rights and political jurisdiction.

The two countries have come together for one last chance at solving the dispute through negotiation. A failure to resolve the border dispute at this last conference will result in war between the two countries. To prevent war, the conference must end with a treaty agreed upon and signed in its entirety.

BACKGROUND

You have been selected to represent your country at this conference because of your patriotism and grasp of the perilous situation which confronts your country. The future welfare of your country is at stake, and your countrymen are depending upon you to bring about a favorable and honorable solution to the dispute.

NEGOTIATION

The negotiation is scheduled to last thirty minutes. As each minute of the negotiation passes, both of the countries are involved in a costly defense buildup for the possibility of a war. If no agreement is reached after thirty minutes, then war will break out.

TREATY

A treaty form will be provided. (See Figure 10–7.) Complete all the necessary information. The negotiation is not over until the treaty is complete and signed by both negotiators. The treaty must include all details of the agreement.

THE DISPUTED REGION

The region is 50 miles wide and 180 miles long and divided into two areas of contention. The region is bounded on the north by Arak and on the south by Barkan. The Blue Ocean borders the region on the west and the country Cordan borders the region in the east. The two areas of dispute are:

Area I: Coastal Valley and Mountains

The history of Area I is tumultuous. Many small wars between Arak and Barkan have been waged over this area in the last 100 years because of its rich agricultural and natural resource potential. The area has been alternately owned by Arak and Barkan and as a result the area is populated by both Arakians and Barkanians. In addition to the valley near the coast, there is a mountainous region with peaks from 3000 to 6000 feet high which is heavily forested but sparsely inhabited.

The people who live in Area I have no particular allegiance to either Barkan or Arak, but they do have a strong allegiance to their own township. For this reason, the townships shown on the map cannot be sub-

Figure 10–7 Border Dispute Treaty Form

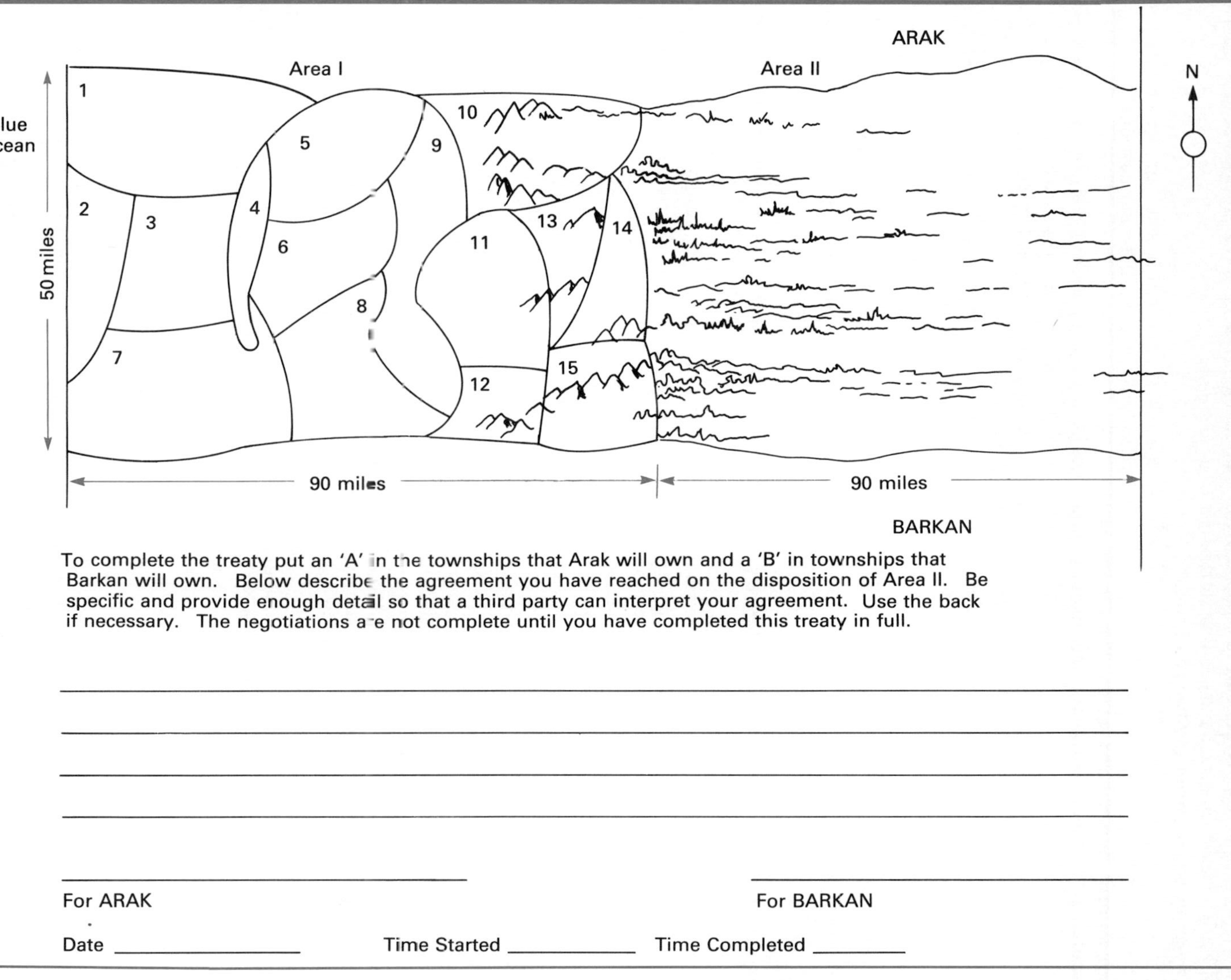

To complete the treaty put an 'A' in the townships that Arak will own and a 'B' in townships that Barkan will own. Below describe the agreement you have reached on the disposition of Area II. Be specific and provide enough detail so that a third party can interpret your agreement. Use the back if necessary. The negotiations are not complete until you have completed this treaty in full.

____

____

____

____

For ARAK　　　　　　　　For BARKAN

Date __________ Time Started __________ Time Completed __________ divided in any way. Presently, Area I is occupied by a United Nations peacekeeping force pending settlement of the negotiations between the two countries.

Area II: Desert Region

This is an arid, uninhabited region. The average annual rainfall is two inches and that comes in one or two storms in the winter.

Step 3: Your instructor will distribute roles to each group. You should then spend fifteen minutes (or the amount of time directed by your instructor) to prepare for negotiations.

Step 4: Your instructor will signal that the negotiation is to begin. You have thirty minutes to reach an agreement.

Step 5: Discussion. In small groups or with the entire class, answer the following questions:

Description
1. What solution did you reach?
2. What process did each group use?

Diagnosis

3. How would you describe the relationship between the groups?
4. Analyze the effectiveness of the negotiations.

Prescription

5. How could the negotiations have been improved?

CONCLUDING COMMENTS

Conflict by itself is neither good nor bad. It must be assessed within the context of the individuals, groups, and organizations involved. The effective organizational member may endure or consciously create conflict. Diagnosing its causes should aid in controlling its dysfunctions and encouraging functional ties. The Conflict Questionnaire, Diagnosis of Conflict, and Diagnosis of Stress exercises provided assessments of personal predispositions for experiencing and abilities for managing conflict in organizations. Ms. X experienced conflict due to her position as a health manager in the middle of interacting constituencies.

Conflict often arises because organizations comprise numerous sets of interacting individuals and groups. In this chapter we examined the special issues of interacting groups. Perceptual differences, the nature of task relations, and power differences influence both group interaction and effectiveness. "Differing perceptions of interdependence, lack of agreement about strategies, and conflict are promoted when (a) asymmetries exist in status and access to information, (b) different people and departments use different performance criteria and reward structures, (c) some people and departments are pursuing short-run objectives and others are pursuing long-run objectives, (d) job dissatisfaction and task ambiguities stimulate unilateral actions to change roles and reduce ambiguities, (e) some shared resources are scarce, and (f) different training and knowledge bases create semantic barriers and perceptual diversity."[51]

The World Bank and Border Dispute exercises further exemplified the impact of competitive behavior. The Hollow Square Planning Problem illustrated the special problems interacting groups of planners and implementers experience. Effective performance called for open and honest communication, shared perceptions of organizational situations, and identification with more than one group as means of improving the interaction. The nature of an organization's structure, discussed in the next part of the book, can facilitate such performance.

ENDNOTES

[1]This case is based on one prepared by John Brian Sutter at the Boston College School of Management.

[2]B. Kabanoff, Potential influence structures as sources of interpersonal conflict in groups and organizations, *Organizational Behavior and Human Decision Processes* 36 (1985): 115.

[3]K.W. Thomas, Conflict and conflict management. In *Handbook of Industrial and Organizational Psychology,* ed. M.D. Dunnette (Chicago: Rand McNally, 1976), pp. 889–935.

[4]A.C. Filley, *Interpersonal Conflict Resolution* (Glenview, Ill.: Scott, Foresman, 1975).

[5]S.P. Robbins, *Managing Organizational Conflict: A Nontraditional Approach* (Englewood Cliffs, N.J.: Prentice-Hall, 1974).

[6]C.H. Coombs, The structure of conflict, *American Psychologist* 42(4) (1987): 355–363, reduces these to three types for small groups.

[7]J. Pfeffer, Beyond management and the workers: The institutional function of management, *Academy of Management Review* 1 (1976): 36–46; H. Assael, Constructive roles of interorganizational conflict, *Administrative Science Quarterly* 14 (1968): 573–581.

[8]K.W. Thomas, Organizational conflict. In *Organizational Behavior,* ed. S. Kerr (Columbus, Ohio: Grid, 1979).

[9]L.R. Pondy, Organizational conflict: Concepts and models, *Administrative Science Quarterly* 12 (1967): 296–320.

[10]H. Selye, *The Stress of Life* (New York: McGraw Hill, 1956).

[11]H. Selye, *The Stress of Life* 2d ed. (New York: McGraw Hill, 1976).

[12]C.N. Cofer and M.H. Appley, *Motivation: Theory and Research* (New York: Wiley, 1964).

[13]D.R. Frew, *Management of Stress* (Chicago: Nelson Hall, 1977), p. xix; see also A.P. Brief, R.S. Schuler, and M. Van Sell, *Managing Job Stress* (Boston: Little Brown, 1981).

[14]D.L. Nelson and J.C. Quick, Professional women: Are distress and disease inevitable?, *Academy of Management Review* 10 (1985): 206–218; G.L. Cooper and M.J. Davidson, The high cost of stress on women managers, *Organizational Dynamics* 10 (Winter 1982): 44–53.

[15]S.V. Kasl, Epidemiological contributions to the study of work stress. In *Stress at Work,* ed. G.L. Cooper and R. Payne (New York: Wiley, 1978).

[16]M. Kets de Vries, Organizational stress: A call for management action, *Sloan Management Review* 21 (1979): 3–14.

[17]J.E. McCann and D.L. Ferry, An approach for assessing and managing interunit interdependence, *Academy of Management Review* 4 (1979): 113–119.

[18]J.D. Thompson, *Organizations in Action* (New York: McGraw Hill, 1967); A.H. Van de Ven, A.L. Delbecq, and R. Koenig Jr., Determinants of coordination modes within organizations, *American Sociological Review* 41 (1976): 322–338.

[19]Van de Ven et al., *op. cit.*

[20]K.K. Smith, An intergroup perspective on individual behavior. In H.J. Leavitt, L.R. Pondy, and D.M. Boje, eds., *Readings in Managerial Psychology* 4th ed. (Chicago: University of Chicago Press, 1989).

[21]S. Lieberman, The effects of changes in roles on the attitudes of role occupants, *Human Relations* 9 (1956): 385–417.

[22]D.C. Dearborn and H.A. Simon, Selective perception: A note on the departmental identifications of executives, *Sociometry* 21 (1958): 290.

[23]D.W. Johnson and F.P. Johnson, *Joining Together: Group Theory and Group Skills* (Englewood Cliffs, N.J.: Prentice-Hall, 1975).

[24]A.W. Gouldner, Cosmopolitans and locals: Toward an analysis of latent social roles, *Administrative Science Quarterly* 2 (1958): 290.

[25]R.L. Kahn, D.M. Wolfe, R.P. Quinn, and J.D. Snoek, *Organizational Stress: Studies in Role Conflict and Ambiguity* (New York: John Wiley, 1964).

[26]D. Hickson, C. Hinings, C. Lee, R. Schneck, and J.A. Pennings, A strategic contingencies theory of intraorganizational power, *Administrative Science Quarterly* 23 (1978): 65–90.

[27]P. Lawrence and J. Lorsch, *Organization and Environment: Managing Differentiation and Integration* (Homewood, Ill.: Irwin, 1969).

[28]J. McCann and J.R. Galbraith, Interdepartmental relations. In P.C. Nystrom and W.H.

Starbuck, eds., *Handbook of Organizational Design vol. 2* (New York: Oxford University Press, 1981), p. 68.

[29]L. Greenhalgh, Managing conflict, *Sloan Management Review* (Summer 1986): 45–51.

[30]*Ibid.*

[31]Thomas, Conflict and conflict management, *op. cit.*

[32]D.D. Morley and P. Shockley-Zalabak, Conflict avoiders and compromisers: Toward an understanding of their organizational communication style, *Group and Organization Studies* 11 (December 1986): 387–402.

[33]E. Van de Vliert, Escalative intervention in small-group conflicts, *Journal of Applied Behavioral Science* 21 (1985): 19–36.

[34]R. Beckhard, The confrontation meeting, *Harvard Business Review* 45 (1967): 154.

[35]*Ibid.*

[36]W.L. French and C.H. Bell Jr., *Organization Development: Behavioral Science Interventions for Organization Improvement* 2d ed. (Englewood Cliffs, N.J.: Prentice-Hall, 1978).

[37]H. Prien, Strategies for third-party intervention, *Human Relations* 40 (1987): 699–720.

[38]R.E. Walton, *Interpersonal Peacemaking: Confrontation and Third-Party Consultations* (Reading, Mass.: Addison-Wesley, 1969), p. 150.

[39]Van de Vliert, *op. cit.*

[40]R.R. Blake and J.S. Mouton, Overcoming group warfare, *Harvard Business Review* 62(6) (1984): 98–108.

[41]*Ibid.*

[42]B. Schneider, Organizational behavior, *Annual Review of Psychology* (Washington, D.C.: Annual Reviews, 1985).

[43]T.D. Jick and R. Payne, Stress at work, *Exchange: The Organizational Behavior Teaching Journal* 5 (1980): 50–56.

[44]J.M. Ivancevich and M.T. Matteson, Employee claims for damages add to the high cost of job stress, *Management Review* (November 1983).

[45]G.L. Cooper, *The Stress Check* (New York: Pitman, 1981).

[46]K. Albrecht, *Stress and the Manager: Making It Work for You* (Englewood Cliffs, N.J.: Prentice-Hall, 1979).

[47]J.W. Greenwood III and J.W. Greenwood Jr., *Managing Executive Stress: A Systems Approach* (New York: Wiley, 1979).

[48]Ivancevich and Matteson, *op. cit.*

[49]M. Sherif and C.W. Sherif, *Groups in Harmony and Tension* (New York: Harper & Row, 1953).

[50]R. Likert and J. Likert, *New Ways of Managing Conflict* (New York: McGraw Hill, 1976).

[51]McCann and Galbraith, *op. cit.*, p. 67, cites M. Dalton, *Men Who Manage* (New York: Wiley, 1959); J.M. Dutton and R.E. Walton, Interdepartmental conflict and cooperation: Two contrasting studies, *Human Organization* 25 (1966): 207–220; and W. Kornhauser, *Scientists in Industry* (Berkeley: University of California Press, 1962).

RECOMMENDED READINGS

Brown, R. *Group Processes: Dynamics within and between Groups*. Oxford: B. Blackwell, 1988.

Hocker, J.L., and Wilmot, W.W. *Interpersonal Conflict* 2d ed. Dubuque, Ia.: William C. Brown, 1985.

Mastenbroek, W.F.G. *Conflict Management and Organization Development*. Chichester, England: Wiley, 1987.

Rahim, M.A. *Managing Conflict in Organizations*. New York: Praeger, 1986.

Smith, K.K. *Groups in Conflict*. Dubuque, Ia.: Kendall/Hunt, 1982.

Stroebe, W., et al. (eds.) *The Social Psychology of Intergroup Conflict: Theory, Research, and Applications*. Berlin: Springer-Verlag, 1988.

Stulberb, J.B. *Taking Charge: Managing Conflict*. Lexington, Mass.: Lexington Books, 1987.

Taylor, D.M., and Moghaddam, F.M. *Theories of Intergroup Relations: International Social Psychological Perspectives*. New York: Praeger, 1987.

Ury, W.L., Brett, J.M., and Goldberg, S.B. *Getting Disputes Resolved: Designing Systems to Cut the Costs of Conflict*. San Francisco: Jossey-Bass, 1988.

11

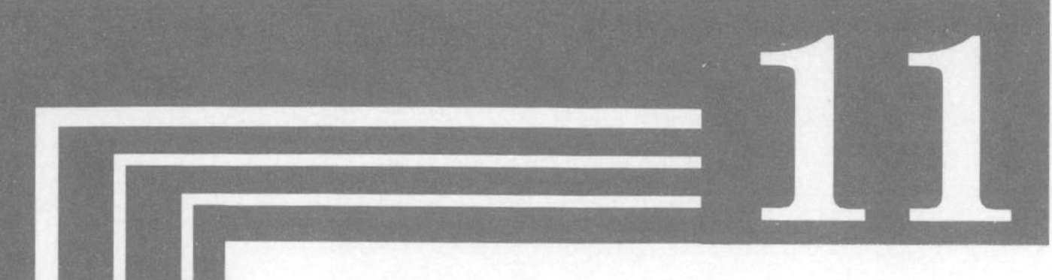

Evaluating and Selecting Organizational Structures

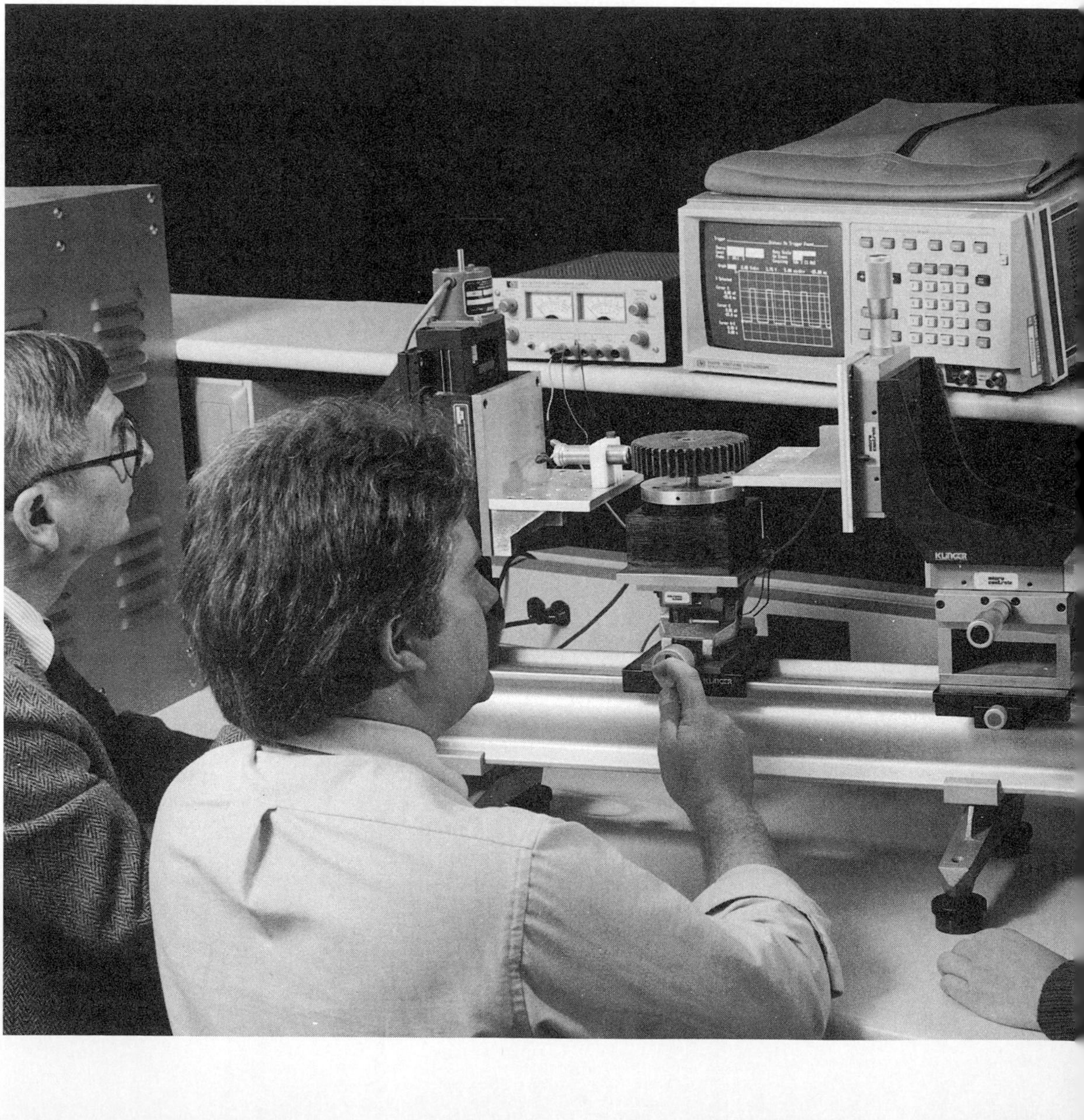

CHAPTER OUTLINE

The Organization Structure of Gateway, Inc.

Division of Labor
- Horizontal Differentiation
- Vertical Differentiation
- Personal Differentiation
- Spatial Differentiation

Coordination
- Mutual Adjustment
- Direct Supervision
- Standardization of Work Processes
- Standardization of Outputs
- Standardization of Skills

Bases of Departmentation
- Function
- Product or Project
- Customer or Client
- Geographical Location
- Multiple Bases

Configurations According to Means of Coordination
- Simple Structure
- Machine Bureaucracy
- Professional Bureaucracy
- Divisionalized Form
- Adhocracy

The Dynamic Network Model

Information-Processing Structures
- Mechanistic versus Organic Organizations
- Information-Processing Capability

The Multinational Corporation

The Informal Organization
- Comparison to the Formal Organization
- Functions of the Informal Organization

Impact of Organizational Structure on Employee Attitudes and Behaviors

SUMMARY
READING
ACTIVITIES
CONCLUDING COMMENTS
ENDNOTES
RECOMMENDED READINGS

LEARNING OBJECTIVES

After completing the reading and activities in Chapter 11, students will be able to:

- represent an organization's formal structure with an organizational chart;
- distinguish between various types of differentiation in an organization;
- assess the nature of coordination in an organization;
- compare and contrast various bases of departmentation;
- compare and contrast five structural configurations based on coordinating mechanisms;
- describe organic and mechanistic structures;
- show the differences between high and low information-processing capacity structures;
- discuss possible structural configurations for the multinational corporation and their implications for effectiveness; and
- discuss the ways the informal organization differs from the formal organization and the implications for effectiveness.

Gateway, Inc., produces an electronic component known as a *power supply,* which transforms an electrical input into an electrical output of a different, more useful type. It powers a variety of products, such as televisions, computers, and communication systems, that cannot operate directly from the electricity obtained from a typical wall outlet. Because of the almost unlimited applications that require a power supply, the power supply industry has more competitors worldwide than any other electronic component. Figure 11–1 shows the organization chart for Gateway, Inc.

The electronics industry today has emphasized fitting more power-handling capability into a small package size. As a result, power supplies have decreased in size while maintaining and even improving in reliability. A recent development, known as *hybrid technology,* reduces the physical size of complex, low power circuitry and has become an essential investment for companies that compete in the electronics industry.

Hybrid technology requires strict manufacturing process control and specialized personnel; it is also easily affected by variations in the environment. It requires an investment in expensive equipment, the operation of which requires substantial training and development. Constant interaction between personnel at all levels is required to ensure a smooth operation.[1]

The term *structure* refers to the delineation of jobs and reporting relationships in an organization. Its principal function is to influence and coordinate the work behavior of the organization's members in accomplishing the organization's goals. The structure shown in Figure 11–1 reflects the formal interactions at Gateway, Inc. It shows the grouping of individuals into departments, the formal reporting relationships, and the way the activities of various organizational members are coordinated. How do you think Gateway's structure facilitates or impedes communication, decision making, leadership, group and intergroup relations, employee motivation, and other aspects of organizational behavior?

In this chapter we examine several structural models and their implications for organizational performance. We begin by discussing division of labor and coordination of activities in organizations. We identify and discuss the major configurations for departmental structures. Next we introduce a complementary classification of structures according to the means of coordination in an organization. We examine the relatively new network model next. We also look at the information-processing capabilities of various structures. We discuss the structural issues faced by the multinational corporation. We conclude the chapter by considering the nature of the informal organization and then offering a general approach for building effective organizational structures.

DIVISION OF LABOR

Organizations differ in their job titles and the assignment of duties and responsibilities to the jobs they create. Review the organization chart of Gateway.

Figure 11–1 PARTIAL ORGANIZATION CHART FOR GATEWAY, INC.

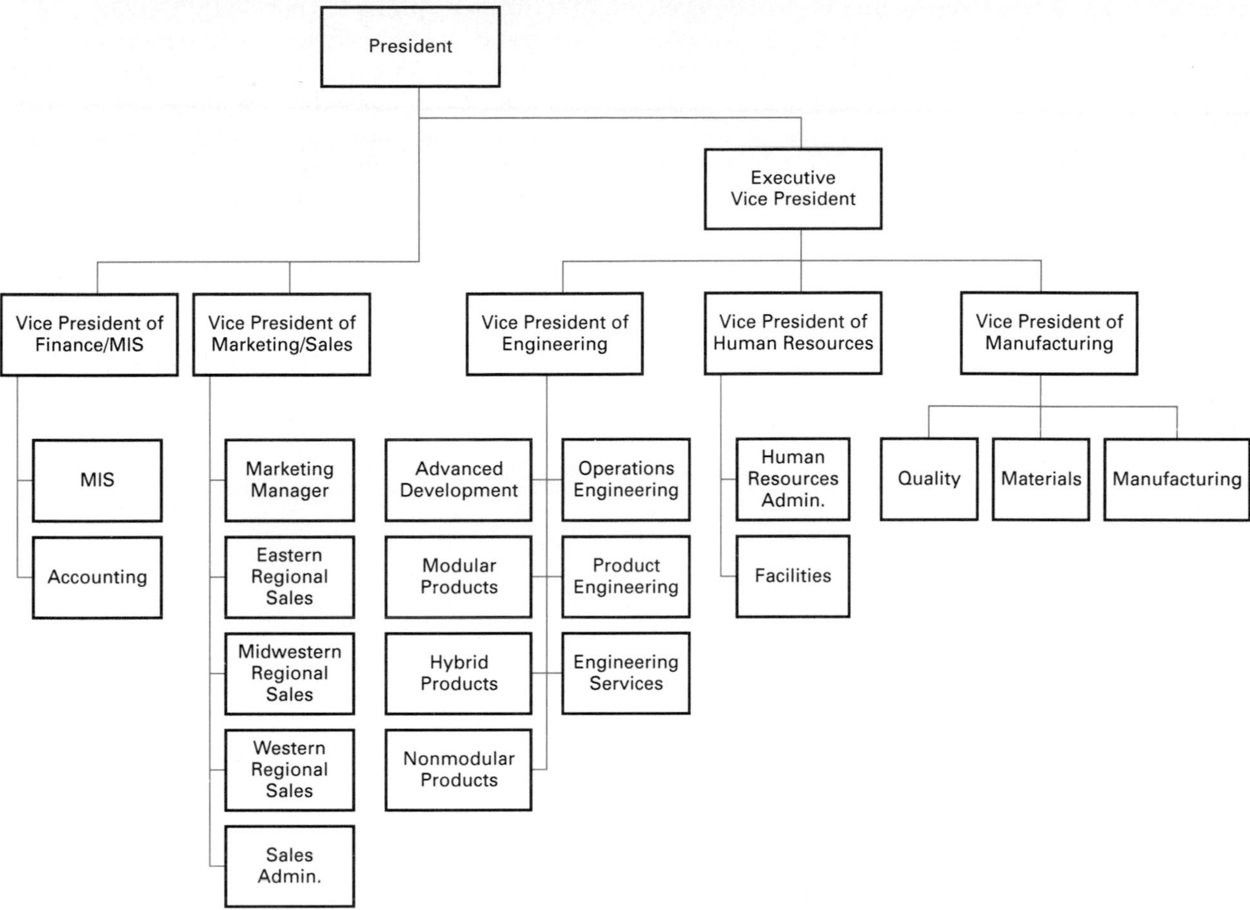

It is a pictorial representation of the formal lines of authority and communication in an organization. Each box represents either a particular department or job. The box labeled Western Regional Sales represents a sales staff based in San Francisco. It might include four district sales managers and their staffs, as well as an office support staff. The blocks labeled President, Executive Vice President, VP Finance/MIS, VP Marketing/Sales, VP Engineering, and VP Human Resources represent single jobs. The solid lines that connect a subunit to a position or department on a level above or below the subunit represent reporting relationships. For example, the executive vice president reports directly to the president; the vice president of manufacturing reports to the executive vice president.

Division of labor refers to the way organizations allocate work tasks and responsibilities along with the accompanying authority; it reflects the extent to which organizations have specialization of tasks and roles.[2] An accounts receivable clerk has a relatively specialized job: he or she repeatedly does a limited number of tasks and fulfills a single, formal role. The vice president for operations has a less specialized job. Two technical people might have equally specialized jobs, one employee performing cost analyses for new products, and a second developing recruitment plans for new employees.

Typically, the lower in the organizational chart we look, the more often we see positions with extensive specialization. The drafting and design staff performs more specialized activities than their boss; the assembly line workers have more specialized tasks than their supervisors or the plant foreman. Differentiation, which is in effect another name for division of labor, is of four different types (see Figure 11–2): (1) horizontal, (2) vertical, (3) personal, and (4) spatial.[3]

Horizontal Differentiation

The division of work at the same level in the hierarchy can occur by function, customer, product, process, or even geographical area. Gateway, for example,

Figure 11–2 TYPES AND DEGREES OF DIFFERENTIATION

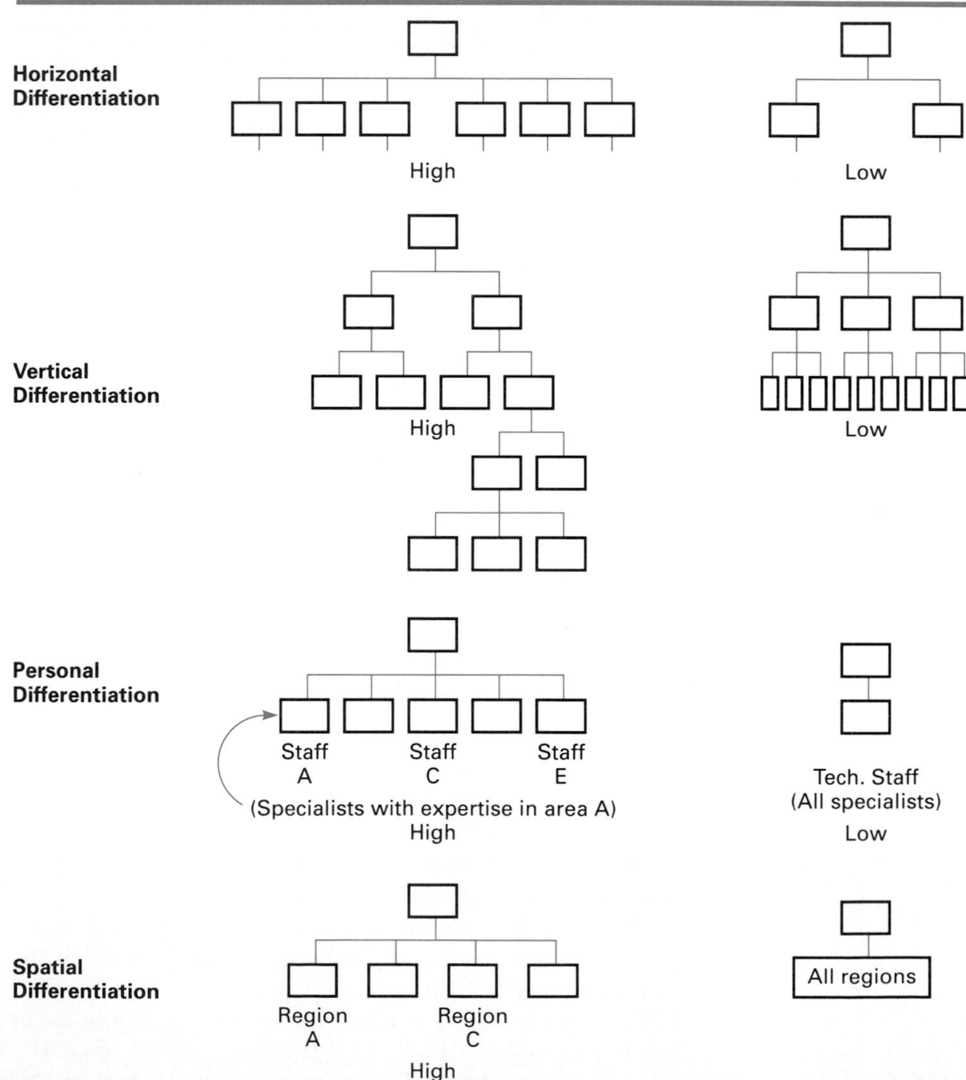

is horizontally divided into functional departments, such as finance/MIS, marketing/sales, engineering, and human resources. The Engineering Division is also horizontally differentiated, into seven departments: advanced development, modular products, hybrid products, nonmodular products, operations engineering, product engineering, and engineering services.

The extent of horizontal differentiation can vary extensively from one organization to another, depending on such factors as a manager's preference, and the size, age, goals, and product or service of the organization. As horizontal differentiation increases, potential barriers to communication (see Chapter 7) also increase. Because communication occurs more easily within a unit than across units, horizontal differentiation may limit the expertise used in making decisions, unless there is extensive coordination and communication between and among groups.

Vertical Differentiation

Specialization as a result of differences in levels in the organization's hierarchy creates this type of division of labor. *Tall* organizations, such as Citibank, AT&T, and Mobil Oil Company, have relatively high vertical differentiation. *Flat* organizations, such as professional organizations (e.g., law firms and consulting firms), many social service agencies, and scientific or technical organizations, have lower vertical differentiation.

Increasing vertical differentiation increases the checks and balances that limit the number of mistakes made in action. Where there is an extensive (taller) hierarchy, decisions made by lower level employees are more often checked by higher level employees than is the case in flatter organizations. Tall structures offer the second advantage of providing more avenues for advancement within the organization; the blocking of employees because of nonpromotability of others is less frequent (see Chapter 3). Also, closer fitting of individuals' personal needs and abilities with available jobs is possible because of the diversity of available jobs.

But tall structures often slow decision making if multiple levels of the hierarchy are involved in the process. If centralization of decision making accompanies vertical differentiation, workers low in the hierarchy may experience motivation problems as a result of lack of autonomy and involvement. Of course even in a tall structure, decentralization of decision making is possible.

How extensive is the vertical differentiation at Gateway? The hierarchy appears to consist of approximately six levels. Given the size of the organization—less than 200 employees—vertical differentiation is relatively high.

Personal Differentiation

Division of labor can also occur according to individual expertise or training. A medical outpatient clinic served by physicians with such specialties as gerontology, dermatology, and pediatric ophthalmology, has relatively high personal specialization. So does a research "think tank," where individual faculty members have subject-area expertise and more specialized knowledge in their area of research. Various departments within an organization can also vary in their degree of personal differentiation. Extensive personal differentiation takes advantage of unique capabilities in the work force.

Where at Gateway is personal differentiation likely to be highest? Where is it the lowest? Areas that require specialized training, such as research and development, likely have high personal differentiation. Jobs that require less unique knowledge or advanced training, such as manufacturing, typically have low personal differentiation.

Spatial Differentiation

Some organizations have division of labor by geographical location. Organizations with multiple operating sites illustrate spatial differentiation. A retail department store with numerous suburban stores, a fast-food chain such as McDonald's or Burger King, a bank, and a large accounting firm show this type of differentiation.

Look again at Gateway. Where does it have spatial differentiation? Its marketing division exemplifies this type of division of labor. Now think of an organization with which you are familiar. Draw its organization chart. What are some of the features of your organization's division of labor? How does it compare to the structure of Gateway shown in the figure?

COORDINATION

When an organization differentiates into positions and departments in a hierarchy, some mechanisms for ensuring communication and integrated decision making among these groups must be instituted for the organization to function effectively. These mechanisms must be introduced at all levels of the organization and may differ among the various subunits. Typically, the more differentiation exists in an organization, the more it requires coordination, or integration, for effective performance.

Coordination refers to the extent and means by which an organization integrates or holds together its various parts and facilitates their working together to accomplish a common goal or activity. It occurs through (1) mutual adjustment, (2) direct supervision, (3) standardization of work processes, (4) standardization of outputs, and (5) standardization of skills.[4]

Mutual Adjustment

The simplest form of coordination occurs through informal communication, where two or more people speak directly to one another as needed. When you speak with a coworker about scheduling your vacation, you are using mutual adjustment. When a salesperson checks with an inventory clerk by telephone about the availability of a certain product, he or she is coordinating by mutual adjustment. Very simple and very complex organizations generally must rely heavily on mutual adjustment. In the first situation, mutual adjustment sufficiently coordinates the work. In the second, mutual adjustment reduces ambiguity in communication and task performance. Using this type of coordination effectively requires high quality communication, as described in Chapter 7.

Direct Supervision

More formalized control exists where one individual takes responsibility for the work of others. As groups or organizations increase in size, mutual adjustment becomes insufficient as a coordinating mechanism; here management might add supervision as a means of coordination. The foreman of Gateway's manufacturing plant oversees the work of numerous supervisors, who in turn have responsibility for the work of numerous line workers. In addition to direct supervision, these supervisors may also use other means of coordination, such as mutual adjustment and standardization of work processes.

Direct supervision, as a means of coordination, has probably received the greatest attention in the organizational literature. It involves coordination through a *chain of command.* At Gateway, one chain includes the President, Executive Vice President, Vice President of Engineering, and his or her subordinates. At Gateway, the workers experience *unity of command;* that is, each employee has only one supervisor. In some integrated structures, discussed later in this chapter, unity of command does not always exist.

Span of Control Direct supervision also occurs over a certain number of employees, whose activities a manager directs and supervises. Known as *span of control,* the number of immediate subordinates varies extensively, from one to one hundred or more. For example, the president of Gateway has a span of control of three; the VP of Marketing/Sales has a span of five.

While research once specified an optimal span of control (five to ten people for middle management and slightly more for top management), a contingency approach now prevails.[5] The ability and expertise of a manager and his or her subordinates influences the effectiveness of span of control. The greater a manager's expertise, the broader an effective span of control can be. When a manager lacks ability, he or she must devote more time to supervising subordinates and thus can operate effectively only with a smaller span of control. Likewise subordinates with greater expertise require less supervisory time from their superiors. In these situations the span of control can be larger.

The nature of the tasks also influences effective supervision. The more interrelated the tasks that are performed in subordinate positions, or the greater the similarity of the tasks of subordinates, the more individuals a manager can supervise. Further, if a supervisor can duplicate instructions for more than one subordinate, the span of control can increase. The stability of the tasks performed by those in subordinate positions also is significant. If the tasks remain the same over time, subordinates require less supervision and hence the supervisor's span of control can increase.

The degree of geographic dispersion of those in subordinate positions is also associated with span of control. The closer subordinates are to each other and the supervisor, the less time a manager must spend in physically moving among them to give and receive information. The widespread availability of electronic communications has facilitated such communication, even at a geographical distance, and should allow larger spans of control.

Finally, the amount and type of interaction required between a superior and those in even higher positions affect span of control. A supervisor who must spend extensive time interacting with his or her supervisors has less time available for supervising others, which calls for a smaller span of control, or greater decentralization of decision making.

Standardization of Work Processes

A specification of the procedures or content of work also coordinates the activities of different job holders. In a restaurant chain, for example, the procedure for baking pizzas may be specified and even written down, or formalized, in a procedures manual. In a bank, the steps in reconciling cash at the end of the day may be specified for a teller. Lawyers may follow a specified set of procedures to file a brief. Standardization of work processes is typically useful for coordinating highly specialized or relatively unskilled jobs and repetitive tasks, or for simplifying parts of very complex jobs. Specifying the steps required to perform a job reduces the need for either mutual adjustment or direct supervision.

Standardization of Outputs

The specification of the results and outcomes of work, as well as standards of performance at the output stage, also provide direction and coordination for workers. Managers judged on the profit their groups make demonstrate coordination by this type of standardization. So do salespersons who must meet a certain quota. These employees have relatively great discretion in the processes they use to accomplish the outputs. Frequently they use additional coordinating mechanisms, specifically mutual adjustment, to facilitate meeting the performance standards.

Standardization of Skills

The final type of coordination specifies the training, expertise, or credentials required to perform the work. The work of medical practitioners, teachers, lawyers, and other professionals is coordinated in this way; they apply specialized knowledge and skills in approaching particular problems and tasks. Accounting and engineering departments often use mutual adjustment along with standardization of skills.

Which of these coordinating mechanisms does Gateway use? Gateway probably uses all five coordinating mechanisms. The primary mode of coordination differs in various parts of the organization: coordination of production line workers relies on standardization of work processes; middle managers in staff or support departments use direct supervision and mutual adjustment; engineers rely on standardization of skills; the marketing staff depends on standardization of outputs; and top management relies on mutual adjustment. Additional coordinating mechanisms include the use of plans, linking pins, and integrating roles (described in Chapter 10).

When looking at the organization at Gateway, we must evaluate whether these mechanisms coordinate adequately. Can you see parts of the chart where additional formal coordination should occur? Or would mechanisms different from those presently used coordinate more effectively? Diagnosis of an organization's structure requires a response to such questions.

BASES OF DEPARTMENTATION

So far we have identified division of labor and coordinating mechanisms as common structural elements of organizations. Now we consider some typical methods of organizing these elements into organizational configurations or structures at specific levels in the organization. Structuring occurs separately at each hierarchical level and in each subunit of the organization. The structural pattern for top management may differ from that of middle management; groupings of nonmanagerial employees may look very different as well. In this section we examine the following ways of grouping subunits: (1) by function, (2) by product or project, (3) by customer or client, (4) by geographical location, and (5) along multiple bases.

Function

Departmentation by function describes the structure of many manufacturing and service organizations. The concept refers to grouping employees according to the major category of work activity. For example, a manufacturing organization might have research and development, human resources, management, engineering, production, marketing, and finance divisions. Within the human resources management division, we might find a further functional grouping of work into training, recruitment, compensation, planning, and organization-development departments. Within the marketing division, we might find functional groups such as market research, advertising, sales, and sales support departments.

Consider the organization shown in Figure 11–3. This chart might represent a toy manufacturer, an advertising agency, or a paper mill. Different vice presidents supervise departments of finance, operations, research and development, and so on; each of these areas may have departments specialized further by function or on other bases. Look again at the organizational chart for Gateway in Figure 11–1. Is this a functional structure? The grouping of workers into finance/MIS, marketing/sales, engineering, and manufacturing suggests a functional arrangement at the top level.

What advantages does a functional structure offer? It reinforces professional identities, since it groups individuals according to their functional specialties and encourages them to work primarily with individuals with related training and expertise.[6] Now look at the Human Resources Department at Gateway. Here the human resources professionals work together, sharing ideas and collaborating on special projects. Promotions tend to occur within a functional area, enhancing professional development. The functional structures also minimize duplication of effort: there is only one MIS department and one account-

Figure 11–3 FUNCTIONAL STRUCTURE

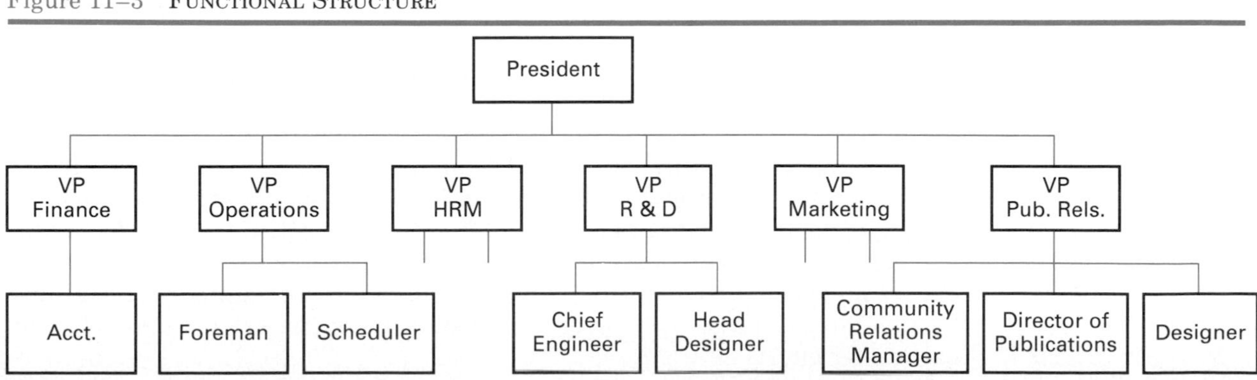

ing department. These serve the entire organization, not selected divisions or departments.

The functional structure has several limitations, however. First, it often suffers from coordination and control problems.[7] Barriers arise between departments because of basic differences in expertise, goals, and operating procedures of different functions. Because communication among departments may be limited, and since this structure emphasizes using the hierarchy to make decisions and handle exceptions, organizational problems may receive a slow response. In the functional structure, some individuals may become overly identified with their functional area and lose sight of overall organizational goals. Competition for resources may arise between departments, resulting in conflict in the organization. Two departments, for example, may argue over the adequacy of their staffing budget.

The functional structure works most effectively under four conditions. First, if an organization has a well-developed product or service, then procedures that are standardized, or at least well known and regularly implemented as part of the functional structure, act as coordinating mechanisms and reduce barriers between functions. Second, if an organization operates in a stable environment, then it has less need to respond quickly to environmental changes; the slower decision making that characterizes this structure is appropriate. Third, if the roles in an organization group easily into functional areas, then coordination is expedited by a structure that builds on these relationships. Finally, if an organization is small- to medium-sized, lateral communication throughout the organization is easier than if the organization is large. Does Gateway have these characteristics? We examine the characteristics calling for a functional structure in more detail in Chapter 12.

Product or Project

Grouping employees can be done according to the product or project on which they work rather than according to their functional area. In this case subunits with different functional expertise working on the same product or project are grouped together. NASA popularized project management in the 1960s by using it for managing its various space projects; and the Apollo, Saturn, and Space Shuttle projects have since become household words. More recently, some high technology firms have turned to project structures. Figure 11–4 and 11–5 show examples of this type of departmentation.

The organization (A) shown in the top of Figure 11–4 has project categories at the director level, but the directors supervise functional managers of marketing, manufacturing, and research and development. The organization (B) shown in the bottom of Figure 11–4 has project responsibility at two levels. Project responsibility can also occur only lower in an organization, as when a VP of Manufacturing supervises directors of various projects.

In a product structure, an organization is organized, at one or more levels of the hierarchy, by product. As shown in Figure 11–5, product managers can supervise various functional groups instead. In either product or project management, the structure lasts only for the life of the project. When the project ends, employees receive new assignments. Manufacturers such as Procter and Gamble and General Mills may use product management for most of their marketing efforts.

This structure encourages organizations to differentiate among products or

Figure 11–4 EXAMPLE OF PROJECT MANAGEMENT

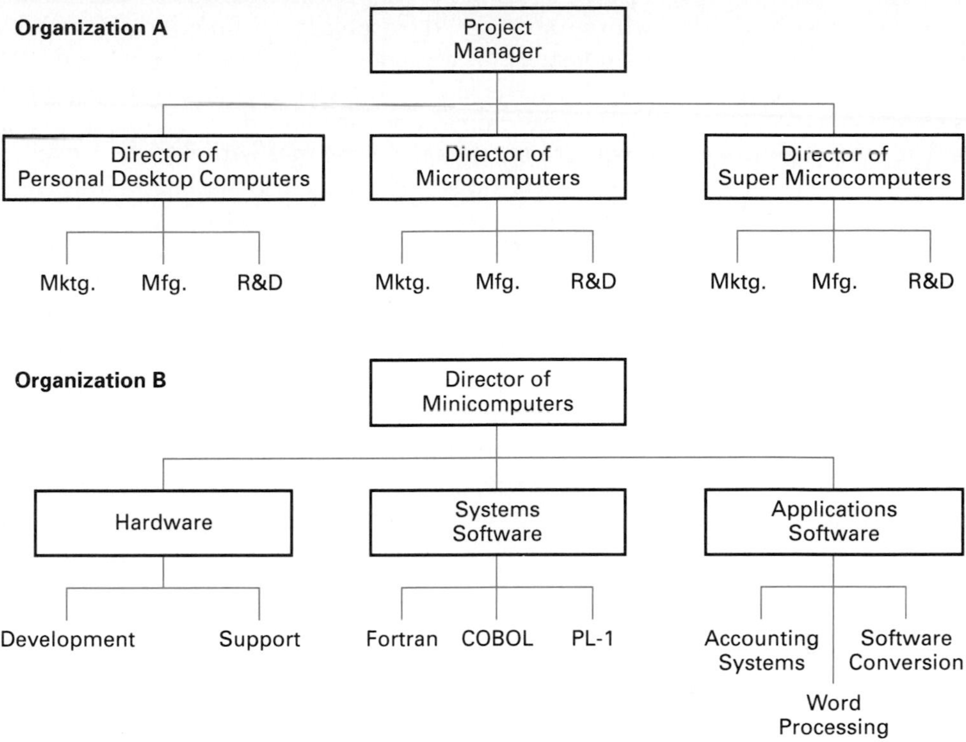

projects and focus on their unique assets and problems in production and sales. For example, the development, production, sales and distribution of a new cereal must face different issues than does the development of a new hair-care product. Similarly, introducing new scheduling software to the marketplace creates some similar, but many different, problems than introducing a new microcomputer. Thus project or product management allows organizations to focus on problems and opportunities unique to a particular product.

This organization structure also allows organizations to respond more quickly

Figure 11–5 EXAMPLE OF PRODUCT MANAGEMENT

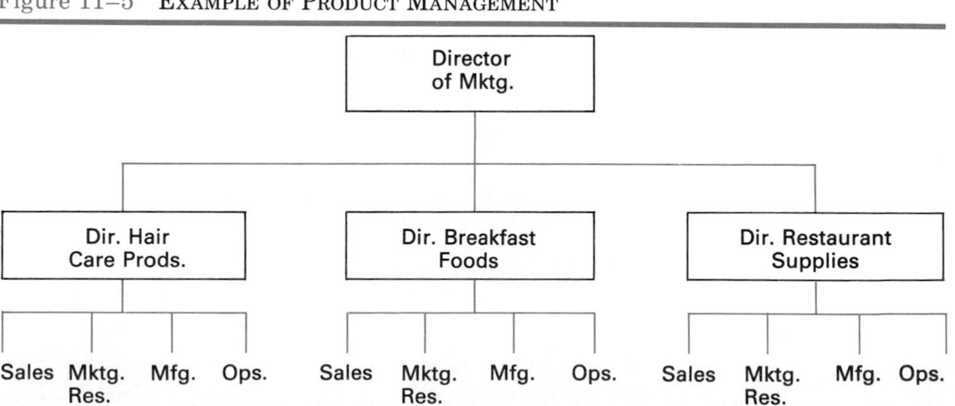

to changes affecting the project or product. Because work efforts are narrowly focused on product or project concerns, team members have common goals, which increases their ability to function effectively. Because of their close involvement in a product or project, they have a better understanding of the specific needs of the situation and can respond to new requirements imposed by the environment or customer more quickly and effectively. In addition, this structure encourages personnel with different expertise and professional loyalty to focus on a common goal. Bringing diverse expertise to a single problem also allows a speedier resolution of it.

Some duplication of expertise generally exists on different project teams; thus project or product management may cost more than functional departmentation. In addition, because of the consequent lack of identification with a profession as a whole, individuals may fail to keep pace with developments in their area of expertise, focusing instead on specific product or project developments. A human resources professional, for example, who provides training for a single product division may lose touch with more general advances in training.

Organizing into a product structure focuses employee efforts on dealing with the unique issues involved in developing and distributing a diverse product mix. Consequently it allows a relatively fast response to increased competition and other environmental changes.

Consider Gateway. What would its organizational chart look like if departmentation were by product? Figure 11–6 offers one possible chart. What advantages does this offer over the functional structure shown in Figure 11–1? What disadvantages does it have?

Customer or Client

This organization structure parallels departmentation by product or project because it addresses the unique needs of specific customer or client groups. Figure 11–7 is a prototype of such a structure, which groups employees according to the client they serve. Incorporating a client-oriented structure allows a company to structure product markets to match the needs of different clients—young urban professionals, senior citizens, or families with one or more school-age children, for instance.

This structure shares the advantages of a product or project structure. It

Figure 11–6 Gateway, Inc., as a Product Structure

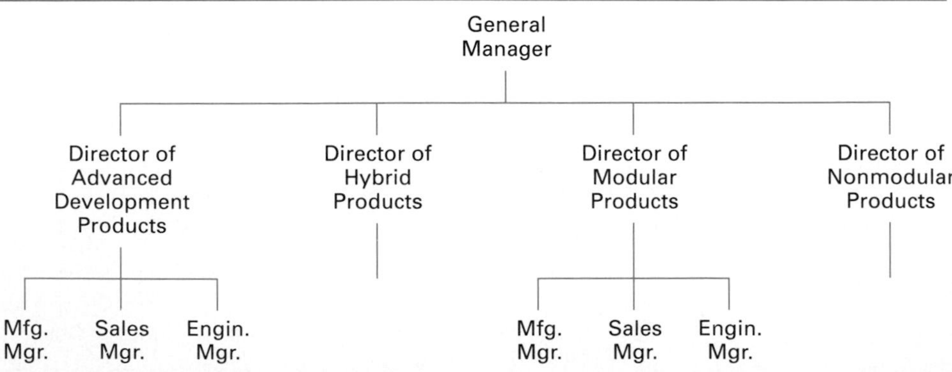

Figure 11–7 DEPARTMENTATION BY CLIENT

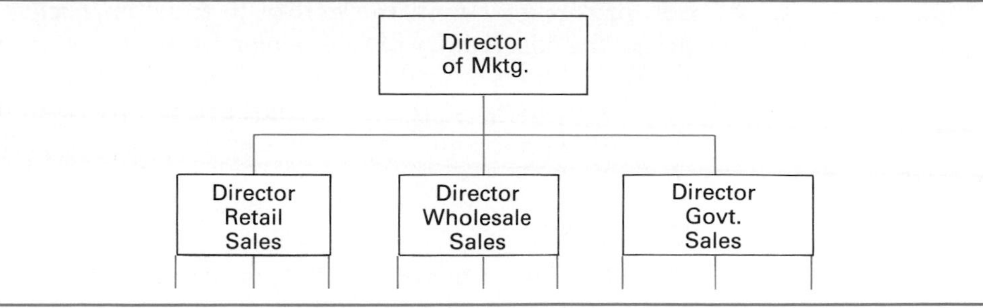

has the ability to differentiate among clients and focus on their unique concerns. It also allows a fast response to changes in client needs and brings diverse expertise to solving a single client's problems.

However, departmentation by client also suffers from the same disadvantages as the product or project structure. It can be costly because of the provision of redundant services. It can also distract individuals from maintaining state-of-the-art knowledge in their own fields if they pay more attention to client needs than their own professional development.

Geographical Location

Choosing a structure that includes geographical location lets an organization take advantage of regional differences in preferences and costs. Departmentation by geographical location, illustrated in Figure 11–8, describes this type of structure. Workers are grouped according to either their own geographical location or the geographical location of the clients they serve. Often the marketing division of a company uses this structure.

Look again at Figure 11–1. Gateway has three regional sales offices, and these reflect departmentation by geographical location to a limited extent.

Figure 11–8 DEPARTMENTATION BY GEOGRAPHICAL LOCATION

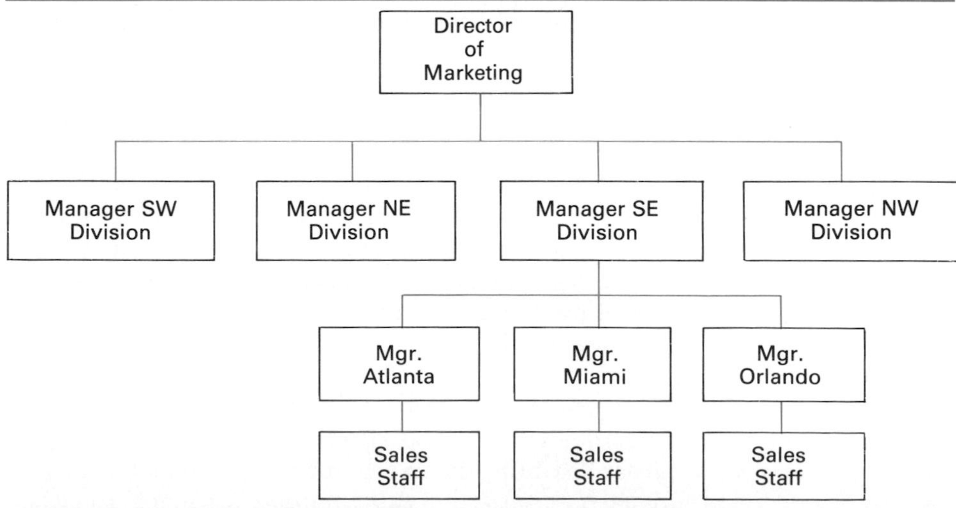

The advantages of this structure parallel those of departmentation by product, project, or client: the ability to focus on issues unique to geographical areas, the opportunity to focus expertise on special geographical problems, and the cost savings or profit opportunities associated with geographical diversity. The disadvantages are also similar: potentially redundant services and failure to develop professionally in areas of functional expertise.

Multiple Bases

The integrated structure is a hybrid structure that incorporates different bases of departmentation. It responds to the needs of a changing and complex environment. The specific integrated form chosen must help organizational members focus on both client needs and the marketing of the organization's product and services.

Characteristics of an Integrated Structure The integrated structure has four major characteristics. First, flexible groupings of individuals allow an organization to take a functional, product, project, geographical, or client orientation. These groupings change as organizational needs change. Thus task forces may be organized or disbanded as an organization introduces new products or withdraws obsolete ones. Or a project team may form, perform its assigned tasks, and then return its members to their original functional areas. Second, the grouping of individuals emphasizes a market focus. A bank may organize temporary or permanent work teams to service small business, institutional, or other special interest group accounts. In addition, the integrated structure also emphasizes the identification of the market for the organization's product or service. Third, the integrated structure calls for decentralized decision making; that is, the relative autonomy, responsibility, and accountability of middle managers and professional staff. Finally, the grouping of employees occurs across functional divisions, as in the project structure.

This structure encompasses a variety of organizational configurations. Top management may organize task forces composed of members of various departments. They might also create permanent committees. Or they may develop a matrix structure.

In one study of public accounting firms, four factors influenced the type and degree of integration in the structure.[8] The first was the firm's strategy in developing specializations in given industries, segmenting the market, or developing unique technical expertise. The greater the emphasis on specialization, segmentation, and expertise, the more prevalent the integrated structure as a way of providing services across divisions. The second factor was the partner-in-charge, or top management of the firm. The third was office or organizational size. The smaller the office or organization, the greater the need for the flexibility inherent in an integrated structure. Fourth, client requirements, particularly demands for a variety of services, mandated an integrated structure. Let us examine one prototype of an integrated structure, the matrix, in more detail.

Matrix—An Integrated Structure Departmentation along multiple dimensions describes the matrix organization,[9] which responds to needs for relatively great flexibility by an organization. The matrix structure most commonly uses departmentation by function *and* product/project, as shown in Figure 11–9.

Figure 11–9 MATRIX STRUCTURE

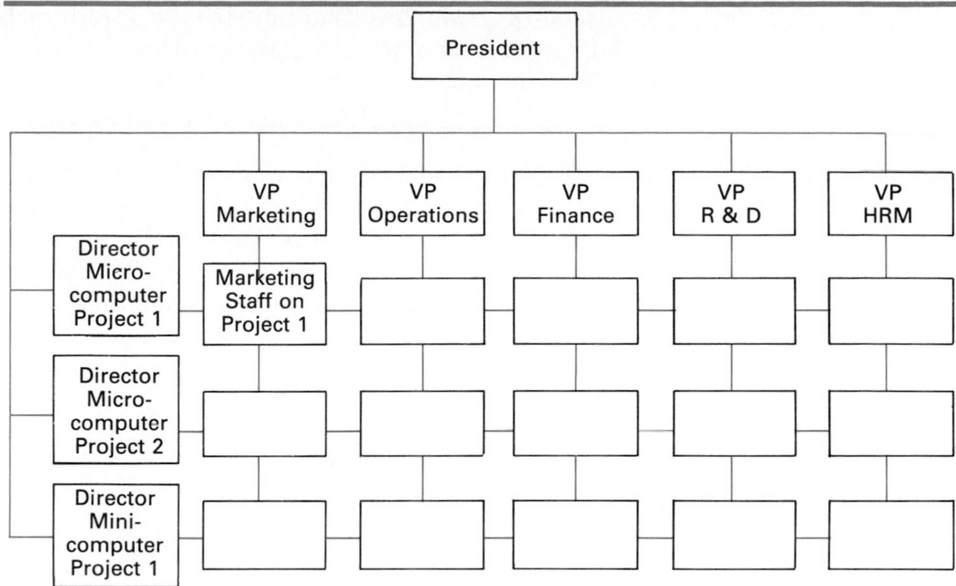

Each cell represents one or many employees who serve on the project listed for that row and are part of the staff listed in that column.

Such a structure can respond well to an organization's strategies of diversification and globalization, such as by adding worldwide product managers to geographical profit centers.

As high technology has forced organizations to deal with extreme ambiguity and volatility in the environment, many organizations have found that more traditional structures—departmentation by function, project/product, location, or clientele—are inadequate and ineffective. Such companies as Boeing, TRW, Texas Instruments, and Corning Glass instituted the matrix structure as a way of responding to their environments.[10]

The matrix structure violates the unity-of-command principle, since most employees have at least two superiors—one in the project or product line, the second in the functional domain. A member of the marketing staff on project 1 reports to both the vice president of marketing and the director of microcomputer-project 1. As in departmentation by function, the matrix reinforces professional identities and development.

The matrix structure poses three kinds of problems. First, extensive overhead costs are incurred due to the dual-authority systems, which require a larger number of managerial personnel than the traditional structures. Second, potential conflict exists when two managers have responsibility for the evaluation and allocation of time of the same employee. The product manager for partnership banking and the vice president of lending may perceive that they must compete for the time of a loan officer who works on the partnership banking project. One researcher has argued that for a matrix structure to be effective top management must clearly delegate authority to the project manager, and the functional manager must agree to accept a role subordinate to the project manager on the project team.[11] Finally, potential ambiguity exists in the reporting relationships. The loan officer in the example above may be confused about who has final authority when his or her two bosses disagree.

Making a matrix work requires ensuring that the roles of the project and functional managers are clear. There should be a policy and procedures for quickly surfacing problems, and the project manager should have enough power to negotiate with the functional manager.[12] Many organizations have determined that these costs do not outweigh the benefits offered by the increase in coordination provided by the matrix structure. Too, the matrix is an inherently unstable, process-intense form that must be well managed.[13] Reading 11–1, "Matrix Management: Contradictions and Insight," summarizes the tradeoffs. Many organizations have introduced combinations of the matrix and other structures described above, to take advantage of the assets of both matrix and departmentation by product, project, client, or geographical location.

How would a matrix structure change the organization of Gateway? Figure 11–10 offers a possible organization chart.

CONFIGURATIONS ACCORDING TO MEANS OF COORDINATION

A more comprehensive classification of organizational structures groups them according to their mechanisms of coordination.[14] Five structural paradigms result. Table 11–1 shows each type, its basic means of coordination, and the bases of departmentation it likely accompanies. A simple structure relies on mutual adjustment and direct supervision for coordination and often includes functional departmentation. The machine and professional bureaucracies also

Figure 11–10 PARTIAL ORGANIZATION CHART FOR GATEWAY, INC., USING A MATRIX STRUCTURE

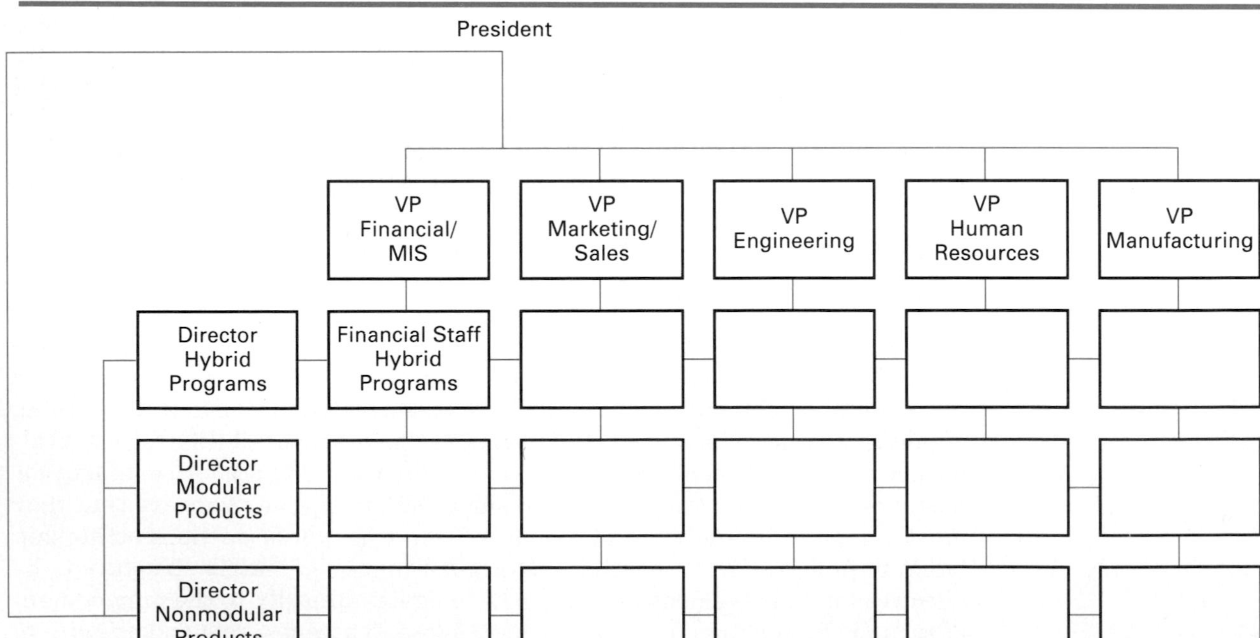

Table 11–1 TYPES OF STRUCTURE ACCORDING TO MEANS OF COORDINATION

Structure	Means of Coordination	Types of Departmentation Typically Included
Simple structure	Mutual adjustment, direct supervision	Functional
Machine bureaucracy	Direct supervision, standardization of work processes	Functional
Professional bureaucracy	Standardization of skills	Functional
Divisionalized form	Standardization of outputs	Product, project, clientele, geographical location
Adhocracy	Mutual adjustment	Integrated (matrix or other forms)

include functional departmentation but rely on standardization of processes and skills, respectively. The divisionalized form uses standardization of outputs and often incorporates departmentation by product, project, client, or geographical location. The adhocracy relies on mutual adjustment for coordination and often includes features of the integrated structure.

Simple Structure

This type of organization relies on mutual dependence and direct supervision as the major coordinating mechanisms. A men's clothing store, a family restaurant, and a small consulting firm probably have this structure. It often exists in relatively young and small organizations because they can tolerate the lack of sophistication inherent in this structure. We might also view such organizations as having a functional structure with few departments.

In the simple structure, the top manager has significant control. Thus entrepreneurs frequently organize their firms along these lines. As an organization grows, the simple structure frequently departmentalizes further by function. As it becomes larger still, it moves to a more complex structural form that relies on other means of coordination.

Gateway likely began as a simple structure, possibly as shown in Figure 11–11. A single product was developed and manufactured by the company, under the supervision of the owner and founder. There was relative flexibility and minimal departmentation. As the organization developed more products, however, it became too complex to remain a simple structure.

Machine Bureaucracy

As some organizations increase in size, horizontal and vertical differentiation—into departments and a hierarchy—increases. Frequently accompanied by standardization and formalization of behavior, specialization characterizes the machine bureaucracy. Direct supervision and standardization of work proc-

Figure 11–11 GATEWAY, INC., AS A SIMPLE STRUCTURE

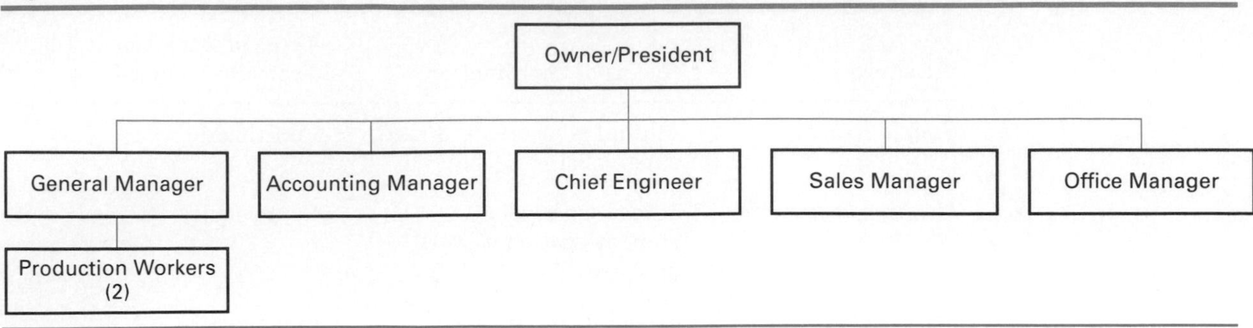

esses provide the key coordinating mechanisms. Relatively large operating units prevail in the machine bureaucracy. Large-scale manufacturing organizations, such as automobile, steel, equipment, and consumer goods manufacturers, typically organize in this way.

The structure of Gateway shown in Figure 11–1 could be a machine bureaucracy, especially its manufacturing operations. Note that with a machine bureaucracy different parts of an organization may have different structural configurations. These organizations increase their division of labor and introduce functional specialization as they grow, until a reasonably extensive hierarchy exists. Extensive written procedures and standardization of work processes, as well as direct supervision, coordinate the relatively differentiated work force.

Professional Bureaucracy

This structure shares some of the formalization inherent in the machine bureaucracy. Instead of standardization of work processes, however, it emphasizes standardization of skills for coordination. A professional bureaucracy typically has little vertical or horizontal differentiation but extensive personal differentiation. Look at the partial organization chart of a family services agency in Figure 11–12. The structure is relatively flat, but there is extensive differentiation according to specialty.

Figure 11–12 ORGANIZATION CHART OF A FAMILY SERVICES AGENCY

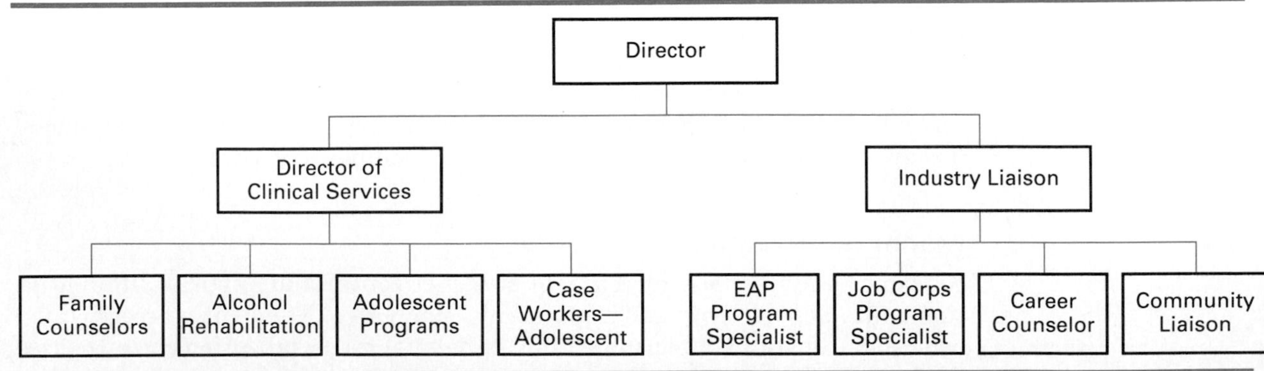

Organizations of this type generally have large numbers of professionals, such as engineers, teachers, physicians, or social workers. Schools, hospitals, and universities frequently take the form of the professional bureaucracy. Although parts of Gateway could be characterized as a professional bureaucracy, especially the Engineering Department, its overall manufacturing orientation requires a more heterogeneous structure.

Divisionalized Form

Think for a minute of IBM, Ford Motor Company, Exxon, General Foods, AT&T, or Shearson/American Express. Since these companies deal with diversified products, each creates units by market or product. The divisionalized structure may represent aspects of departmentation by project or product design (see Figure 11–13), or it may represent a conglomerate—a collection of relatively autonomous companies owned by a single parent organization.

Large banks frequently take a divisionalized structure, with separate lending, commercial, and international divisions. Divisions can also be regionally-based: some international firms have United States, United Kingdom, Far Eastern, and South American divisions. Each division generally has its own functional or project/product structure.

The divisionalized organization emphasizes standardization by outputs: each manager has bottom-line responsibility, and both the managers' and the organization's performance are judged by these outputs. Divisionalized structure allows organizations to respond to a heterogeneous environment, particularly diverse cultures. An organization can set up mini-organizations to meet the unique needs of various countries and cultures. This structure also allows increased control over large organizations. By breaking the organization into profit-oriented units, managers can be held more accountable. Finally, this structure takes advantage and reduces the liabilities of a diverse product mix by emphasizing rather than ignoring it.

Divisionalized organizations tend to be older and larger than other forms. Gateway might move into this structure as it expands its product lines, increases in size, and ages. At some time, it might divisionalize into product or market divisions.

Adhocracy

This form uses a variety of ad hoc or temporary liaison devices, such as task forces, integrating roles, project teams, or matrix structures, to encourage mutual adjustment among organizational members. Adhocracy calls for a flex-

Figure 11–13 A DIVISIONALIZED STRUCTURE

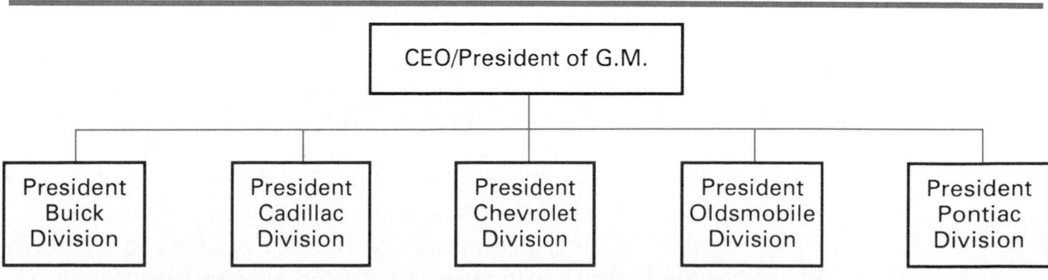

ible structure that can respond to a complex, changing environment. It tends to operate best in environments with sophisticated technologies. Information technologies, such as electronic mail and video conferencing, can facilitate the teamwork required in such structures. The matrix organization, described above, is a classic form of adhocracy.

Gateway does not fall into this category. Its structure is too functionally oriented; it includes only one project team. As this company expands and faces a more diverse and dynamic environment, and as its technologies become even more sophisticated, Gateway may move toward an adhocracy.

THE DYNAMIC NETWORK MODEL

A more recent model of organizational structure is the *dynamic network,* a form of structure or type of system extending beyond the boundaries of a single organization.[15] Responding to the competitive environment they face, organizations are increasingly relying on joint ventures, subcontracting, licensing activities, and new business ventures; the dynamic network can take a variety of forms.[16] For example, individual firms may join together into a partnership to work on international projects. In construction, the general contractor and its subcontractors form a stable and continuous network over time. In the German textile industry, associations of specialists form, each with unique expertise. Strategic partnering in high technology firms is another example. Network organizations have also been described as a matrix organization extended beyond traditional organizational boundaries. RCA and Sharpe, for example, formed a joint venture to supply both companies with semiconductors.[17]

Dynamic networks have four characteristics.[18] First, independent organizations within the network perform the business functions. Such *vertical disaggregation* occurs for product design, marketing, manufacturing, and other functions. Second, *brokers* assemble the business groups, by subcontracting for required services, creating linkages among partners, or locating such functions as design, supply, production, and distribution. Third, *market mechanisms,* such as contracts or payment for results, rather than plans, controls, or supervision, hold the functions together. Finally, *full-disclosure information systems* link the various components of the network.

The interdependence of firms that results from their being part of a network creates an *industry synergy.* Together, by pursuing different strategies yet complementing each other as part of a network, they meet the need for innovation and efficiency. The dynamic network model can also be applied within an organization, to foster innovation through a new organization structure that parallels the formal structure.

INFORMATION-PROCESSING STRUCTURES

Structures described by departmentation and coordination can also be categorized as either mechanistic or organic.[19] This classification originated in a study of Scottish electronics firms that linked structure to the nature of the technological environment.[20] The researchers found that as the environment became less stable and more dynamic, organizations tended to evolve from mechanistic to organic. We can also describe structures according to the extent to which they facilitate the collection and processing of information.[21] How do these types of organizations differ?

To select a structure, organizations identify the information-processing needs of the particular hierarchical level or subunit. The particular structure chosen then reflects the information-processing needs of that level or subunit: discrete subunits form to meet different needs and are then linked to one another. For example, we can hypothesize that top management, to select a structure for Gateway, has identified different information-processing needs for each functional area, formed subunits around these needs, and then linked the subunits with direct supervision, standardization of work processes, and standardization of skills.

Mechanistic versus Organic Organizations

Mechanistic Structure Functional and bureaucratic organizations typically have the stability and relative inflexibility of a *mechanistic* structure. Activities are specialized into clearly defined jobs and tasks. A manufacturing organization with a single assembly line divided into innumerable specialized activities is typically a mechanistic structure. So is a hospital with clearly established protocols for providing care.

In a mechanistic organization, persons of higher rank typically have greater knowledge of the problems facing the organization than those at lower levels. Unresolved problems are thus passed up the hierarchy.

Standardized policies, procedures, and rules guide much of the decision making in the mechanistic organization. Such organizations often have detailed manuals of organizational policies. Supervisors frequently answer questions or solve problems by referring the employee to the correct section of the procedures manual. When such organizations are unionized, the extent of standardization and formalization is typically even greater; the union contract often lists a majority of the organization's employment policies. Rewards are chiefly obtained through obedience to instructions from supervisors. Mechanistic organizations encourage conformity and discourage innovation, since innovation often necessitates disobedience of company regulations.

Organic Structure Characterized by flexible organizational designs and the ability to adjust rapidly to change, many of the structures described earlier are organic, including integrating and adhocratic structures.

In an organic structure, job descriptions and specialization are deemphasized. Persons become involved in problem solving whenever they have the knowledge or skills to help solve the problem. A marketing analyst, rather than the vice president of marketing, may be asked to contribute to the organization's strategic plan if he or she has the required knowledge. An engineer with unique expertise in the design of new product might join a marketing task force.

People holding higher positions are not necessarily assumed to be better informed than employees at lower levels. Organic organizations emphasize decentralization of decision making, where responsibility and accountability are pushed as low in the organization as is possible and effective. These organizations frequently include large numbers of professional employees, for whom involvement in decision making is natural. Structures such as project teams or a matrix, integrating or liaison roles, and task forces that bring together individuals with diverse functional expertise, are frequently introduced.

Organic organizations rely on ad hoc problem solving more than existing regulations, policies, and procedures to deal with problems. Supervisors might answer a question by referring an employee to a coworker with knowledge in the problem area. If a problem is sufficiently large or puzzling, the supervisor might convene a task force of workers to address the issues.

Organic organizations encourage innovation and problem-solving behavior. Management allocates rewards to individuals who demonstrate initiative and knowledge. Position in the hierarchy and seniority have relatively little importance unless they are associated with special expertise.

If Gateway is like other functionally departmentalized organizations or machine bureaucracies, it has a mechanistic structure. It has job activities specialized into clearly defined jobs and tasks. It uses the hierarchy to resolve problems. Standardized policies, procedures, and rules guide decision making. It rewards obedience to superiors.

Information-Processing Capability

Structures with a *low information-processing capacity* have mechanisms that process information relatively slowly. They include structures with departmentation by function and geographical location, machine bureaucracies, professional bureaucracies, and divisionalized structures. These structures have the characteristics of mechanistic organizations. In particular, they rely on the hierarchy for communication and problem solving. Significant barriers to lateral communication exist, thereby slowing the processing of information.

Structures with a *high information-processing capacity* have mechanisms that process information relatively quickly and accurately. High capacity organizations include departmentation by product, project, client, or along multiple bases, simple structures, or adhocracies. Top management of these organic organizations might regularly convene task forces to address special organizational problems. Liaison roles that facilitate lateral communication and break down barriers between departments are also common. Increasingly, electronic media such as FAX machines, BITNET, and electronic mail can enhance an organization's information-processing capacity.

THE MULTINATIONAL CORPORATION

Organizations that operate in more than one country face unique problems in developing an effective organization design. They may begin in the United States and then expand into Europe or Asia, as Exxon and Ford Motor Company did. They may begin in Japan and then add divisions in the United States, as did Honda and Nissan. Or they may begin in Europe and expand worldwide. Such companies may develop to take advantage of low-cost production opportunities in other countries or to diversify and expand their markets.

While many of the models described in this chapter can be applied to multinational corporations, these organizations have some unique characteristics. The structure of each must respond to variations in values and attitudes in

Table 11–2 DIFFERENCES BETWEEN AMERICAN AND JAPANESE FIRMS

American	Japanese
Short-term employment	Life-time employment
Individual decision making	Consensual decision making
Individual responsibility	Collective responsibility
Rapid evaluation and promotion	Slow evaluation and promotion
Explicit, formalized control	Implicit, informal control
Specialized career path	Nonspecialized career path
Segmented concern	Holistic concern

Based on W. Ouchi, *Theory Z* (Reading, Mass.: Addison-Wesley, 1978).

the different countries of its operation. It also must recognize variations in the importance of egalitarianism, individualism, and other cultural characteristics. Consider a multinational corporation with divisions in France, Italy, and Germany. French and Italian managers like highly centralized and formalized structures; Germans like decentralized structures with high formalization.[22] Or consider how Japanese and American firms differ, shown in Table 11–2. Japanese prefer less specialization, taller hierarchies, greater formal centralization but less operational centralization than United States firms.[23] The multinational firm that operates in both the United States and Japan must somehow reconcile these differences.

The impact of culture on structure is not clear. Multinational corporations may call for a more hybrid structure, or they may not. In studies of banks in Hong Kong, organizations in prerevolutionary Iran, and some Japanese organizations, multinational corporations had the structures of their home rather than host countries.[24] However, other studies suggest that organizational structures vary among different countries.[25]

THE INFORMAL ORGANIZATION

So far we have focused our discussion on the formal organization, which describes the prescribed lines of communication, authority, and reporting relationships. The *informal organization,* in contrast, describes the behavior that complies with and supports the formal structure of an organization. Sometimes these operating relationships and patterned interactions differ from those described in the organizational chart. For example, a quality-control manager may formally report to the chief engineer but informally interact almost exclusively with the plant general manager. Or a chief financial officer may officially report to a company's executive vice president but actually deal exclusively with the president of the firm.

Comparison to the Formal Organization

Let us compare a representation of the informal organization of Gateway, shown in Figure 11–14, to its formal chart, shown in Figure 11–1. Differences

Figure 11–14 PARTIAL INFORMAL ORGANIZATION OF GATEWAY, INC.

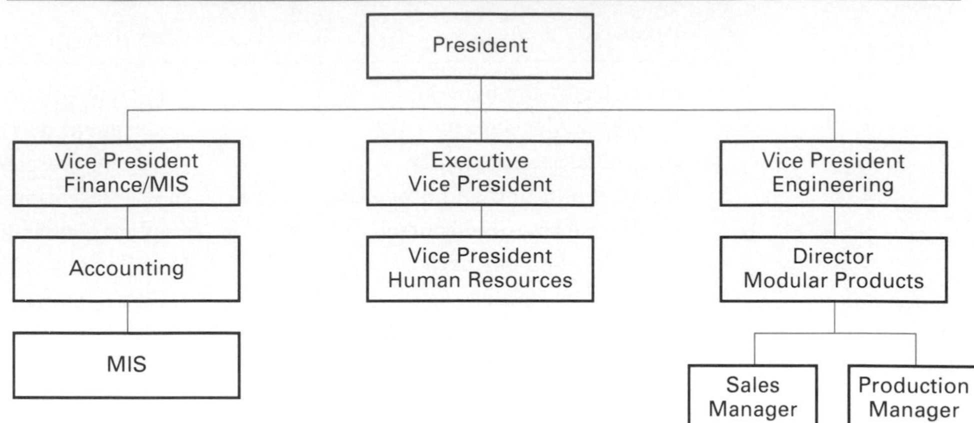

in these charts arise for four major reasons. First, employees may lack knowledge of official channels of communication and so use others. Some lower-level employees, for example, may rely on former supervisors for information rather than going to current superiors with questions and problems. Technical employees with a problem may go directly to the person they feel has greatest expertise in a particular area, rather than referring it to their boss.

Second, interpersonal obstacles may prevent workers from using the formal reporting channels. Some workers may experience personality clashes with their bosses and seek assistance from other managers. The head of MIS may work more effectively with the Executive VP than with the VP of Finance/MIS. Other workers may have difficulty communicating with managers because of different personal styles, experiences, or perceptions of job requirements.

Third, workers may be able to obtain a faster response if they bypass certain channels. If a worker has difficulty obtaining needed supplies, he or she may request them directly from the purchasing agent rather than relying on his or her boss to obtain them, or waiting for the required paperwork to go through channels. Going to the president of a company for an answer may speed a middle manager's ability to respond to a competitor's introduction of a new product.

Fourth and finally, in some organizations nonofficial relationships become legitimized and substitute for the formal ones. In this case top management may redesign the official reporting relationships to reflect the informal ones that facilitate employee performance and the accomplishment of organizational goals.

Functions of the Informal Organization

The informal organization meets employee needs by serving diverse functions.[26] It may provide employees with a sense of belonging, security, social interaction, self-respect, and recognition. (See Chapter 3 for a discussion of basic needs.) It also eases formal communication by offering informal communication links and a source of practical information for employee decision making. Some employees may also use the informal organization to express stress and tension. But the informal organization may also create conflicting loyalties, restrict productivity by creating dysfunctional group norms, create rumors that lead to false information, and resist organizational changes.[27]

Comparing the formal and informal organizations of Gateway suggests significant differences in the intended and actual operation of the company. In diagnosing the structure of an organization, the analyst must check for such discrepancies and attempt to assess the causes. Viewing the informal organization may provide the analyst with a partial prescription for an improved organizational design. The informal organization can either aid or hinder the work specified by the formal structure. Diagnosis of organizational structure should pinpoint dysfunctional differences.

IMPACT OF ORGANIZATIONAL STRUCTURE ON EMPLOYEE ATTITUDES AND BEHAVIORS

Organizations frequently evolve through several structures as they grow, change their product or market, or experience greater competition. They often evolve through function, product, product/matrix, and matrix stages, for example.[28] Effective organization design is dynamic.

Implementation of an organizational structure has an influence on employee behaviors and attitudes. Research has examined the relationship of seven organizational characteristics to the satisfaction and performance of organizational members: (1) hierarchical level; (2) type of position (such as line versus staff); (3) span of control; (4) subunit size; (5) organization size; (6) number of hierarchical levels relative to the organization's overall size (its tallness or flatness); and (7) centralization versus decentralization of decision making or control.[29] The results are as follows.[30] First, increased satisfaction generally accompanies movement up the organizational hierarchy. In other words, as the individual climbs the ladder, satisfaction from the job itself and the esteem associated with the job both increase. Second, the tallness or flatness of a structure shows some relationship to employee satisfaction: high level executives in tall organizations and low level executives in flat organizations experience the most satisfaction of all executives. Third, line and staff job holders do not differ consistently in their satisfaction. Fourth, job satisfaction seems to increase as span of control increases. Among engineers and scientists specifically, performance also seems to increase as span of control increases. Fifth, departmental, subunit, or organizational size alone is not correlated with employee behaviors or attitudes. Sixth, centralization or decentralization of an organization relates to the satisfaction only of low-level employees: the greater the decentralization, the greater their satisfaction. Finally, as an organization becomes more mechanistic, individuals perceive decreasing control over their own behavior and consequent decreases in their intrinsic motivation.

What would you predict about the attitudes and behaviors of employees at Gateway? According to the research, their attitudes would depend on their position in the hierarchy, the number of employees who report to each supervisor, the number of levels in the hierarchy, and the extent of decentralization of decision making in the organization.

Table 11–3 COMPARISON OF PARADIGMS OF ORGANIZATIONAL STRUCTURE

Organization by Departmentation	Classification by Means of Coordination	Mechanistic versus Organic	Information-Processing Capacity
Departmentation by function	Simple structure Machine bureaucracy Professional bureaucracy	Mechanistic	Low capacity
Departmentation by product or project	Adhocracy	Organic	High capacity
Departmentation by geography or client	Divisionalized structure	Mechanistic or organic	Moderate capacity
Departmentation along multiple dimensions	Adhocracy	Organic	High capacity

SUMMARY

This chapter described a variety of organizational structures and their components. It began by examining the division of labor and coordinating mechanisms. Then it considered the ways various types of differentiation and coordination determine paradigms of structure. Table 11–3 summarizes the basic paradigms of organizational structure in the four classification schemes discussed.

We first looked at structures where departmentation occurs according to function, product or project, client, geographical location, and along multiple dimensions. We compared and contrasted these structures and delineated the conditions under which each structure is most effective. Then we considered structures that differ in their primary coordinating mechanisms. We discussed the characteristics of the simple structure, machine bureaucracy, professional bureaucracy, divisionalized form and adhocracy. We then compared mechanistic and organic structures, followed by structures with low and high information-processing capacity. We also considered the special structural issues faced by the multinational corporation. The chapter then considered the informal organization vis-à-vis the formal structure. It concluded with a discussion of the impact of organizational structures on employee attitudes and behaviors. Figure 11–15 offers a list of questions for diagnosing organizational structures.

Figure 11–15 QUESTIONS FOR DIAGNOSING ORGANIZATIONAL STRUCTURE

- What division of labor is there?
- What coordinating mechanisms are there?
- What structural configuration would describe the organization?
- How would you describe information processing in the organization?
- Does the informal organization reinforce or contradict the formal organization structure?

READING

Reading 11–1: MATRIX MANAGEMENT: CONTRADICTIONS AND INSIGHTS

Erik W. Larson and David H. Gobeli

Matrix management has been championed by many as the best way to manage the development of new products and services.[1] Born out of the aerospace race, matrix management is a "mixed" organizational form in which normal hierarchy is "overlayed" by some form of lateral authority, influence, or communication. In a matrix, there are usually two chains of command, one along functional lines and the other along project lines. Perham published, during the early 1970s, a list of matrix users which included such prestigious companies as American Cyanamid, Avco, Carborundum, Caterpillar Tractor, General Telephone and Electronics, Hughes Aircraft, ITT, 3M, Monsanto Chemical, TRW, and Texas Instruments.[2]

While matrix enjoyed widespread popularity in the seventies, discord has begun to surface in the eighties. For example, Texas Instruments reportedly dumped its matrix system, citing it as one of the principle reasons for economic decline.[3] Medtronic, one of the leading producers of cardiac pacemakers, scrapped its formal matrix system after two years of frustration.[4] Similarly, Xerox recently abandoned matrix, claiming that it had created a stranglehold on product development.[5] Probably the most damning criticism can be found in the popular *In Search of Excellence,* in which Peters and Waterman assert that the tendency toward hopelessly complicated and ultimately unworkable structures "reaches its ultimate expression in the formal matrix organization structure [which] regularly degenerates into anarchy and rapidly becomes bureaucratic and noncreative."[6]

Is matrix management an unworkable system that eventually stifles the development of new products and services? Or is matrix management an effective mechanism for managing development projects in organizations? Hard evidence on the efficacy of matrix is virtually nonexistent. For the most part the literature consists of anecdotal success or failure stories. We believe that the issue has been obscured further by failing to recognize that there are different types of matrix. We further contend that the mixed reviews of matrix pertain more to different types of matrix rather than to matrix management in general.

While matrix has been applied to a number of different contexts (i.e., financial services, hospitals, construction), our focus is on its application to product development. To pursue this issue, we sampled over 500 managers, experienced in the development of new products and services, and collected data regarding both the usage and effectiveness of different matrix structures in their company. Before reporting the results, three different forms of matrix structures will be described and their relative advantages and disadvantages discussed.

THREE MATRIX STRUCTURES

Galbraith has distinguished different forms of matrix on a continuum which ranges from the functional organization to the pure project organization.[7] The functional organization is the traditional hierarchical structure in which the organization is usually broken down into different functional areas, such as engineering, research, accounting, and administration. When applied to a product development effort, the project is divided into segments and assigned to relevant functional groups with the heads of the functional groups responsible for their segments of the project. Coordination is provided by functional and upper levels of management.

At the other end of the spectrum is the project organization, in which all the resources necessary to complete a project are separated from the regular functional structure and set up as a self-contained team headed by a project manager. The project manager has direct authority over all the personnel on the project.

Matrix organizations lie between these two extremes by integrating the functional structure with a horizontal project structure. Instead of dividing a project into separate parts or creating an autonomous team, project participants report simultaneously to both project and functional managers. The open violation of the principle of unity of command is the trademark of a matrix management.

Companies apply this matrix arrangement in a variety of different ways. Some organizations set up temporary matrix systems to deal with specific projects while matrix may be a permanent fixture in other organizations. In addition, specialists may work full-time on one project or contribute to a variety of projects. One useful way to examine different forms of matrix management is in terms of the relative influence of project and functional managers; three different forms of matrix can be identified.

A *Functional Matrix* occurs when the project manager's role is limited to coordinating the efforts of the functional groups involved. Functional managers are responsible for the design and completion of technical requirements within their discipline. The project manager basically acts as a staff assistant with indirect authority to expedite and monitor the project. Conversely, *Project Matrix* refers to a situation in which the project manager has direct authority to make decisions about personnel and work flow activities. Functional managers' involvement is limited to providing services and advisory support. Finally, a *Balanced Matrix* is one in which the project manager is responsible for defining what needs to be accomplished while the functional managers are concerned with how it will be accomplished. More specifically, the project manager establishes the overall plan for completing the project, integrates the contributions of the different disciplines, sets schedules, and monitors progress. The functional managers are responsible for assigning personnel and executing their segment of the project according to the standards and schedules set by the project manager. The merger of "how and what" requires both parties to share responsibility and authority over work flow operations. Table 11–4 summarizes these descriptions as well as the functional and project organization for reference.[8]

Matrix is essentially a compromise between the traditional functional organization and a pure project organization. It is more flexible than a functional organization but not as flexible as a project team. At the same time, it is more efficient than a project team, but incurs administrative cost which is unnecessary in a functional organization. Table 11–5 summarizes the major advantages and disadvantages reported in the literature.

Many of the problems associated with matrix are in contradiction with its strengths. Critics have described matrix as being costly, cumbersome, and overburdening to manage, while proponents praise its efficiency and flexibility. Everyone agrees that matrix is a delicate system to manage, but few have discussed the relative efficacy of different types of matrix. With this in mind, the three types of matrix structures will be compared according to the advantages and disadvantages associated with matrix. Table 11–6 summarizes the tentative conclusions of this discussion.

Table 11–4 PROJECT MANAGEMENT STRUCTURES

Functional Organization	The project is divided into segments and assigned to relevant functional areas and/or groups within functional areas. The project is coordinated by functional and upper levels of management.
Functional Matrix	A person is formally designated to oversee the project across different functional areas. This person has limited authority over functional people involved and serves primarily to plan and coordinate the project. The functional managers retain primary responsibility for their specific segments of the project.
Balanced Matrix	A person is assigned to oversee the project and interacts on an equal basis with functional managers. This person and the functional managers jointly direct work flow segments and approve technical and operational decisions.
Project Matrix	A manager is assigned to oversee the project and is responsible for the completion of the project. Functional managers' involvement is limited to assigning personnel as needed and providing advisory expertise.
Project Team	A manager is put in charge of a project team composed of a core group of personnel from several functional areas and/or groups, assigned on a full-time basis. The functional managers have no formal involvement.

Advantages

- *Efficient Use of Resources*—All three forms of matrix allow specialists as well as equipment to be shared across multiple projects.
- *Project Integration*—Granting the project manager more control over work activities should increase project integration, but at the same time quality may suffer since input from functional areas is less concentrated.
- *Flexibility*—The multidisciplinary involvement inherent in all three kinds of matrix should enhance flexibility and adaptive reactions. This should be especially true for the Balanced Matrix in which consensus through give-and-take are necessary to win joint approval. The Functional Matrix and Project Matrix are likely to be less flexible since authority is more clearly defined, making decisions less negotiable.
- *Information Flow*—Vertical information flow should be enhanced under all forms of matrix, since one of the roles of the project manager is to be a central communication link with top management. Lateral communication, however, should be strongest in a Balanced Matrix. This is probably due more to necessity than design. Shared decision making places a premium on close communication through which agreements are eventually shaped. Conversely, lateral communication may suffer a bit under a project

Table 11–5 ADVANTAGES AND DISADVANTAGES OF A MATRIX ORGANIZATION

Advantages	Disadvantages
+ Efficient use of resources—Individual specialists as well as equipment can be shared across projects.	– Power struggles—Conflict occurs since boundaries of authority and responsibility deliberately overlap.
+ Project integration—There is a clear and workable mechanism for coordinating work across functional lines.	– Heightened conflict—Competition over scarce resources occurs especially when personnel is being shared across projects.
+ Improved information flow—Communication is enhanced both laterally and vertically.	– Slow reaction time—Heavy emphasis on consultation and shared decision making retards timely decision making.
+ Flexibility—Frequent contact between members from different departments expedites decision making and adaptive responses.	– Difficulty in monitoring and controlling—Multidiscipline involvement heightens information demands and makes it difficult to evaluate responsibility.
+ Discipline retention—Functional experts and specialists are kept together even though projects come and go.	– Excessive overhead—Double management by creating project managers.
+ Improved motivation and commitment—Involvement of members in decision making enhances commitment and motivation.	– Experienced stress—Dual reporting relations contribute to ambiguity and role conflict.

using Functional Matrix since the project manager and functional managers are not as dependent upon each other as in a Balanced Matrix.

- *Discipline Retention*—A key advantage that matrix has over the pure project team approach is that it allows participants to sustain their link with their functional area while working on multidisciplinary projects. This not only provides a home port for spe-

Table 11–6 COMPARATIVE ADVANTAGES AND DISADVANTAGES OF THREE TYPES OF MATRIX STRUCTURES

Advantages	Functional Matrix	Balanced Matrix	Project Matrix
+ Resource efficiency	High	High	High
+ Project integration	Weak	Moderate	Strong
+ Discipline retention	High	Moderate	Low
+ Flexibility	Moderate	High	Moderate
+ Improved information flow	Moderate	High	Moderate
+ Improved motivation and commitment	Uncertain	Uncertain	Uncertain
Disadvantages			
– Power struggles	Moderate	High	Moderate
– Heightened conflict	Low	Moderate	Moderate
– Reaction time	Moderate	Slow	Fast
– Difficulty in monitoring and controlling	Moderate	High	Low
– Excessive overhead	Moderate	High	High
– Experienced stress	Moderate	High	Moderate

cialists to return to once work on the project is completed but also helps participants to remain technically sharp in their discipline. Still, the ability of participants to maintain ties with their specialty area is likely to decline as their involvement becomes more and more under the jurisdiction of the project manager.

- *Motivation and Commitment*—Inherent in all types of matrix is a high degree of involvement in decision making, which should enhance personal commitment and motivation. Team spirit, however, is likely to be higher under a Project Matrix since participant involvement is more project focused. Still, many specialists find interacting with different types of people and performing a wide range of activities frustrating. It is difficult to conclude which structure will elicit the highest levels of commitment and motivation.

Disadvantages

- *Power Struggles*—Matrix is predicated on tension between functional managers and project managers who are in competition for control over the same set of resources. Such conflict is viewed as a necessary mechanism for achieving an appropriate balance between complex technical issues and unique project requirements. While the intent is noble, the effect is sometimes analogous to opening Pandora's box. Legitimate conflict spills over to a more personal level, resulting from conflicting objectives and accountabilities, disputes about credit and blame, and attempts to redress infringements on professional domains. The Balanced Matrix is more susceptible to these kinds of problems since power and authority are more negotiable under this system. Power struggles should be reduced under functional and project matrixes since the relative authority of each party is more clearly defined.
- *Heightened Conflict*—Any situation in which equipment and people are being shared across projects lends itself to conflict and competition for scarce resources. A Functional Matrix, however, should alleviate some of these problems since specialists can directly appeal to their functional superior to resolve conflicting demands on their time and energy.
- *Reaction Time*—While shared decision making enhances the flexibility of the Balanced Matrix, the drawback is the time necessary to reach agreement. The Project Matrix should produce faster results since the project manager is not necessarily bound to a consensus style of decision making, which is formalized in a Balanced Matrix. For the same reason, the Functional Matrix should be quicker than the Balanced Matrix, but not as fast as the Project Matrix since decision making has to be coordinated across functional lines.
- *Monitoring and Control*—Matrix is susceptible to passing the buck, abdication of responsibility, and cost accounting nightmares. This is particularly true for Balanced Matrix in which responsibility is explicitly shared across functional and project lines. While in principle each functional area is responsible for its particular segment of the project under a Functional Matrix, contributions naturally overlap, making it difficult to determine accountability. The Project Matrix centralizes control over the project, permitting more efficient cost-control and evaluation systems.
- *Excessive Overhead*—All three forms of matrix increase administrative overhead by instituting the role of project manager. Administrative costs, in the form of salaries, are likely to be higher for the Balanced and Project forms of matrix due to the greater roles of the project manager.
- *Experienced Stress*—The very nature of development projects tends to make it a very stressful experience for participants. Matrix management appears to exacerbate this problem. Multiple reporting relationships and divided commitment across projects heighten role conflict and ambiguity. Stress is likely to be a more serious problem where ambiguity is the greatest: the Balanced Matrix. Both the Functional Matrix and the Project Matrix are likely to reduce ambiguity and associated stress, since lines of authority and responsibility are more clearly defined.

Overall, these comparisons indicate that the advantages and disadvantages associated with matrix are not necessarily true for all three forms of matrix and that each type of matrix has its own unique set of strengths and weaknesses. The comparisons also suggest that the Project Matrix is superior in many ways to the other two forms of matrix. The Project Matrix is likely to enhance project integration, increase reaction time, diminish power struggles, and improve the control and monitoring of project activities and costs. On the down side, technically quality may suffer since functional areas have less control over their contributions.

The Functional Matrix is likely to improve technical quality as well as provide a better system for managing conflict across projects. The Achilles' heel is that functional control is maintained at the likely expense of poor project integration. The Balanced Matrix represents a compromise between the two extreme approaches and as such shares to a lesser degree several of the advantages of the two other approaches. At the same time, it is the most delicate system to manage and is more likely to succumb to many of the problems associated with matrix.

The questions that need to be addressed are: What has been the experience of actual companies with these different matrix structures? Which form of matrix is the most widely used? More to the point, does practice support theory? Do practitioners support our conclusion that the Project Matrix is the most effective form of matrix for developing new products and services?

THE STUDY

This study is part of a research program sponsored by the Project Management Institute (PMI). PMI is the professional association for practitioners of project management and has over 5,000 members worldwide. Data were collected by means of a mailed questionnaire which was sent to randomly selected PMI members in both Canada and the United States. Repeated mailings yielded a 64 percent response rate. This study is based on the 510 respondents who reported that they were primarily involved in development projects directed at creating new products, services, and/or processes.

Over thirty percent of the sample were either project managers or directors of project management programs within their firm. Sixteen percent were members of top management (i.e., president, vice-president, or division manager) while 26 percent were managers in functional areas such as marketing, operations, and accounting. Eighty percent share the common experience of having been a project manager at some time during their career.

The sample represents a wide variety of industries. For example, 14 percent were involved in developing pharmaceutical products, 10 percent were in aerospace, and 10 percent were involved in developing computer and data processing products. Among the other industries represented in lesser numbers are telecommunications, medical instruments, glass products, petrochemical products, software development, and housewares goods.

As we report our findings, we are keenly aware that individual perceptions do not provide the best basis for drawing inferences about effectiveness. Still, the breadth of the study provides a useful referent point for assessing the current status of matrix in North America.

Matrix: Usage

In order to ascertain experience with matrix, respondents were asked two questions: Has your organization ever used matrix management to develop new products or services? If so, what is the likelihood matrix will be used again? If they responded that it would not be used again, then they were asked to state the reasons why. Figure 11–16 represents the results for these two questions.

Over three-quarters of respondents reported that their company has used matrix. Of those who responded yes, 89 percent felt that matrix would probably or definitely continue to be used. Only 1 percent reported that matrix would definitely not be used again. Among the reasons given for dropping matrix were breakdowns in coordination between functional and project managers, a shift towards using project teams to complete projects, and the size of their organization was too small to take advantage of a matrix system. Still, the overwhelming opinion was that matrix is the dominant mode for managing development projects in the organizations sampled and will continue to be so.

These results address matrix in general. The usage of the three types of matrix was measured by having respondents indicate the number of current projects ("many," "few," or "none") in their organization that utilized each structure (see Figure 11–17). Respondents based their responses on a capsule description of each structure (as presented in Table 11–4).

All three forms of matrix were widely used. Project Matrix was the most popular, with over 78 percent of the respondents reporting that this form of matrix was being used to manage development projects in their company. Seventy-four percent reported that their firm used the Functional Matrix while 68 percent reported using the Balanced Matrix.

Since size affects economies of scale, availability of resources, and integration requirements, usage rates for the different structures were compared to the size of the firm. The only significant variation occurred in companies with less than 100 employees. Over 84 percent of respondents working in small firms reported using a Project Matrix while the usage levels were lower for both the Balanced Matrix (62 percent) and Func-

Figure 11–16

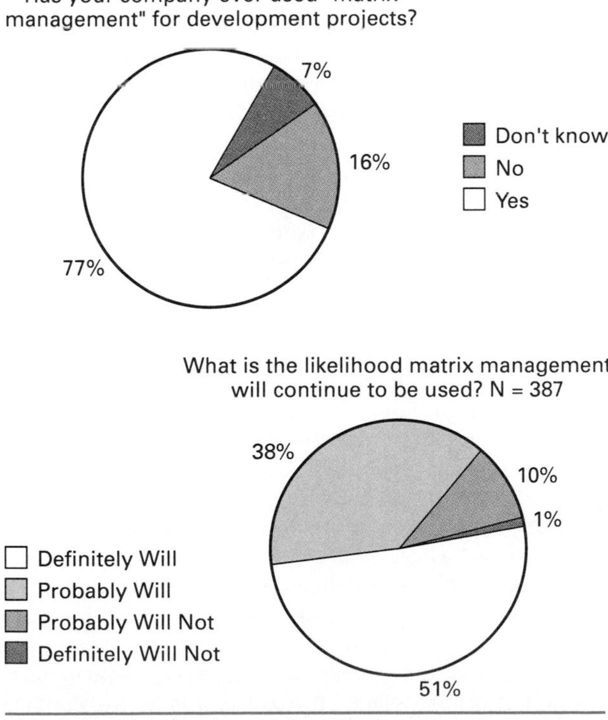

Figure 11–17 USAGE OF DIFFERENT MATRIX STRUCTURES

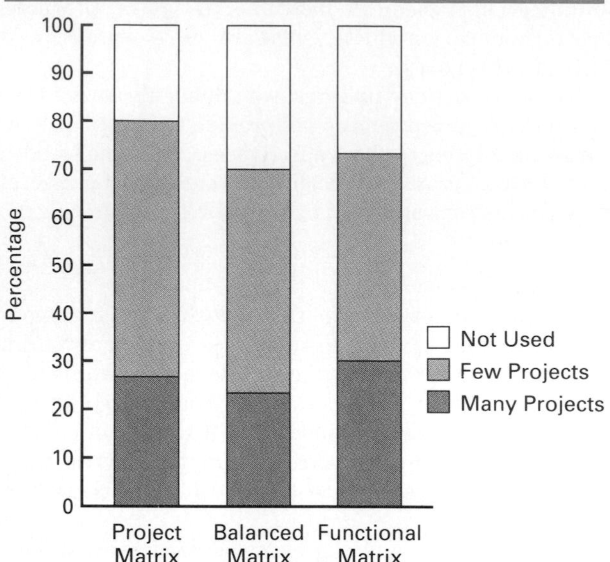

Figure 11–18 RATED EFFECTIVENESS OF DIFFERENT MATRIX STRUCTURES

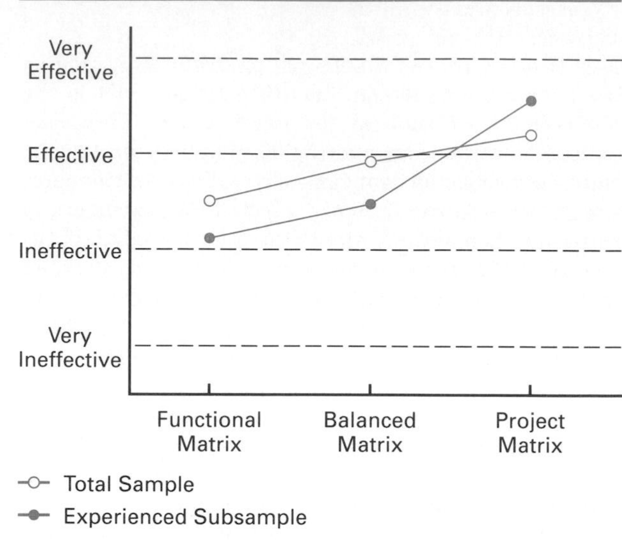

tional Matrix (56 percent). No differences were revealed in the usage patterns of large and medium-sized firms.

Matrix: Effectiveness

Respondents were asked to rate the effectiveness of each of the matrix structures they had experienced. Controlling cost, meeting schedule, and achieving technical performance parameters were among the factors considered in evaluating the different structures. The average rating for each form of matrix is reported in Figure 11–18. The results indicate a strong preference for the Project Matrix, which was rated above effective. The Balanced Matrix was considered effective, while the Functional Matrix was rated below effective.

The ratings for the total sample are somewhat clouded by the fact that not all the respondents had direct experience with each of the three matrix structures. A more valid reference point can be obtained from the 123 respondents who had direct experience with all three structures. Their ratings are also reported in Figure 11–18, and here the pattern is further reinforced. The Project Matrix received the highest rating while the Functional Matrix was rated as ineffective. The Balanced Matrix received only a marginal rating.

Potential variations in the above results were examined for the size of the firm. One of the reasons mentioned for dropping matrix was that the organization was too small to sustain a matrix structure. However, when effectiveness ratings were examined according to size of the firm, size had little impact on the ratings. For example, both respondents in firms of less than one hundred employees and respondents in firms of greater than 1,000 employees rated Project Matrix as the most effective.

The results indicate a strong preference for a Project Matrix in which the project manager has primary responsibility and control over development activities. These results may have been tempered by self-interest since a significant portion of the sample was project managers. To examine this potential bias, the ratings of project managers were compared with those of top management and managers in other functional areas. These results revealed only minor differences in the ratings of the three groups. Top management, project managers, and even functional managers were in agreement that the Project Matrix is the most effective form of matrix. The Functional Matrix was considered the least effective, even by the functional managers.

DISCUSSION AND CONCLUSIONS

While matrix might be viewed as being cumbersome, chaotic, and anarchical by critics, it is still widely used by North American businesses. Over three-fourths of the respondents reported that their organization has tried matrix and will continue to use it. These results contradict the notion that the popularity of matrix is waning, suggesting instead that matrix is the dominant mode for completing development projects. The support is strong, but not without reservations. The following comment from one respondent is typical of the feelings toward matrix management: "Matrix management works, but it sure seems difficult at times. All matrix managers must keep up their health and take stress tabs."

More specifically, all three forms of matrix were popular, with the Project Matrix having a slightly higher usage rate than either the Balanced Matrix or the Functional Matrix. Size of the firm affected usage patterns only with regard to small firms which were found to have a much stronger preference for the Project Matrix. The effectiveness data confirmed our prediction concerning the relative efficacy of the different matrix structures. The Project Matrix was consistently rated superior to the other two forms of matrix. The Balanced Matrix received a marginal rating, while the Functional Matrix was considered ineffective. These effectiveness ratings were not affected by the size of the firm.

The results of this study reveal an interesting contradiction. If the Project Matrix form is considered the most effective, why are the other two forms used nearly as often?

One explanation for this contradiction can be found in the work of Davis and Lawrence.[9] They argue that matrix systems tend to evolve over time, beginning first with a Functional Matrix, followed by a shift towards a Balanced Matrix, and ultimately maturing into a Project Matrix. The comparable usage patterns among the matrix structures suggests that the organizations sampled may be at different stages of matrix development.

A related factor is resistance to change. Matrix management, especially the Project Matrix form, represents a radical departure from the conventional functional approach to organizing. Such change is likely to evoke strong resistance. This is especially true among functional managers, who perceive their authority being usurped by the project manager. Since authority typically resides along functional lines before the introduction of matrix, it would seem only natural that vested interests play a role in choosing a weaker form of matrix. Several project managers commented that their company's reliance on a Functional Matrix was politically motivated and that their functional counterparts strongly opposed expanding the role of project managers over projects.

This condition also underscores once again the need to recognize that not all matrix structures are the same. Our position is that much of the recent criticism leveled at matrix is more relevant to the balanced and functional forms of matrix. Conversely, much of the support for matrix probably comes from those using the Project Matrix form. While more rigorous studies are needed to substantiate this claim, the responses from practitioners in this study support this argument. The final lesson to be learned is a relatively simple one: managers who are concerned with the development of new products and services should consider moving to a Project Matrix if they haven't already done so, especially if they see the disadvantages of a Functional Matrix and a Balanced Matrix occurring in their firm.

REFERENCES

1. See, for example, Leonard Sayles, "Matrix Management: The Structure with a Future," *Organizational Dynamics* (Autumn 1976), pp. 2–17; W.C. Goggin, "How the Multi-Dimensional Structure Works at Dow-Corning," *Harvard Business Review* (January/February 1974), pp. 54–65; Jay Galbraith, ed., *Matrix Organizations: Organization Design for High Technology* (Cambridge, MA: MIT Press, 1971).
2. H. Perham, "Matrix Management: A Tough Game to Play, *Dun's Review* (August 1970), pp. 31–34.
3. *Business Week,* "An About Face in TI's Culture," July 5, 1982, p. 77.
4. David H. Gobeli and W.R. Rudelius, "Managing Innovation: Lessons from the Cardiac Pacing Industry," *Sloan Management Review* (Summer 1985), pp. 29–43.
5. *Business Week,* "How Xerox Speeds Up the Birth of New Products," March 19, 1984, pp. 58–59.
6. Tom Peters and Robert Waterman, *In Search of Excellence* (New York, NY: Harper and Row, 1982), p. 49.
7. Jay Galbraith, "Matrix Organization Designs—How to Combine Functional and Project Forms," *Business Horizons* (February 1971), pp. 29–40.
8. For those readers interested in a more comprehensive description of matrix, we recommend: Stanley Davis and Paul Lawrence, *Matrix* (Reading, MA: Addison-Wesley Publishing Co., 1977); D.R. Kingdon, *Matrix Organization* (London: Tavistock, 1973); Lynn Stuckenbruck, "The Matrix Organization," *Project Management Quarterly* (1979), pp. 21–33.
9. Stanley Davis and Paul Lawrence, op. cit.

DISCUSSION QUESTIONS

1. In what forms does the matrix exist?
2. What are the advantages and disadvantages of the matrix?
3. To what extent is the matrix currently used in the United States?
4. Is the matrix a viable organizational structure?

ACTIVITIES

Activity 11–1: APEX COLLEGE

Step 1: Read the information about Apex College below.

Apex College clears its students for promotion or graduation each term. Currently it has the organizational structure shown in Figure 11–19. The student-record clerks record all grades received. The transcript-approval clerks compare student transcripts to course and credit requirements for each grade. Billing clerks check the arithmetic on the students' bills and enter correct charges and credits on the students' accounts. Loan clerks check to ensure that all loan requirements are met. Cashier clerks examine the students' financial status to authorize promotion.

Step 2: Answer the following questions, individually, in small groups, or with the entire class, as directed by your instructor:

Description

1. Describe the division of labor.
2. Describe the coordinating mechanisms used.
3. What method of organizing is used?

Diagnosis

4. What kinds of problems does this type of organization solve? create?
5. Is this the most effective kind of organization?

Prescription

6. What changes would you recommend?

Step 3: Discussion. In small groups or with the class as a whole, share your answers to the above questions. Then answer the following:

1. What symptoms suggest a problem exists?
2. What problems exist in the case?
3. What theories and concepts help explain the problems?
4. How can the problems be corrected?
5. Are the actions likely to be effective?

Figure 11–19 ORGANIZATION CHART FOR APEX COLLEGE

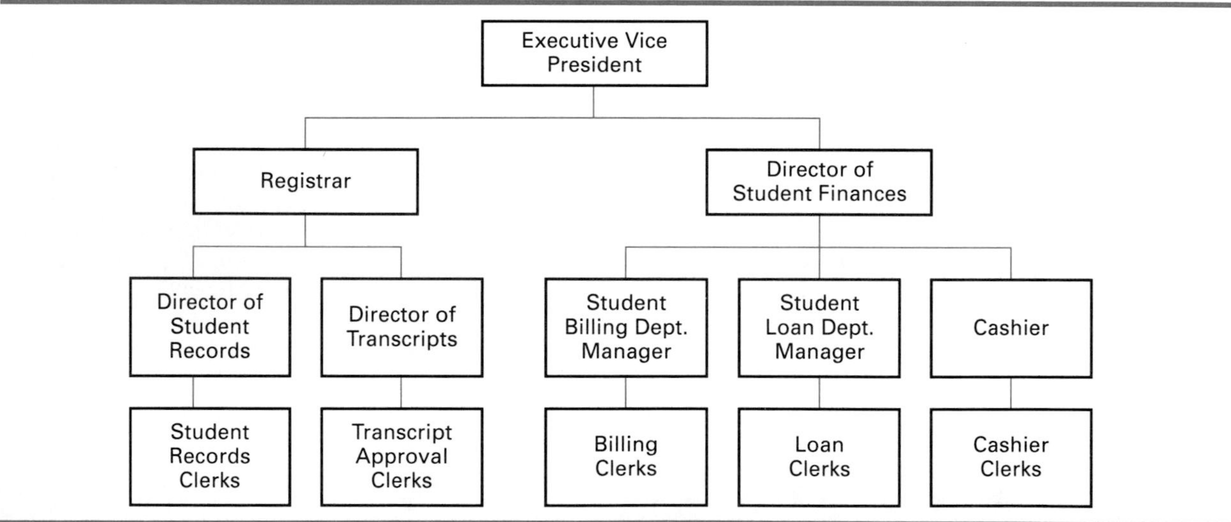

Activity 11–2: ANALYSIS OF ORGANIZATIONAL CHARTS

Step 1: Study the organization charts of three organizations presented in Figures 11–20 through 11–22. Compare and contrast them.

Step 2: Answer the following questions individually, in small groups, or with the entire class, as directed by your instructor:

Figure 11–20 ORGANIZATION CHART OF A LIBRARY

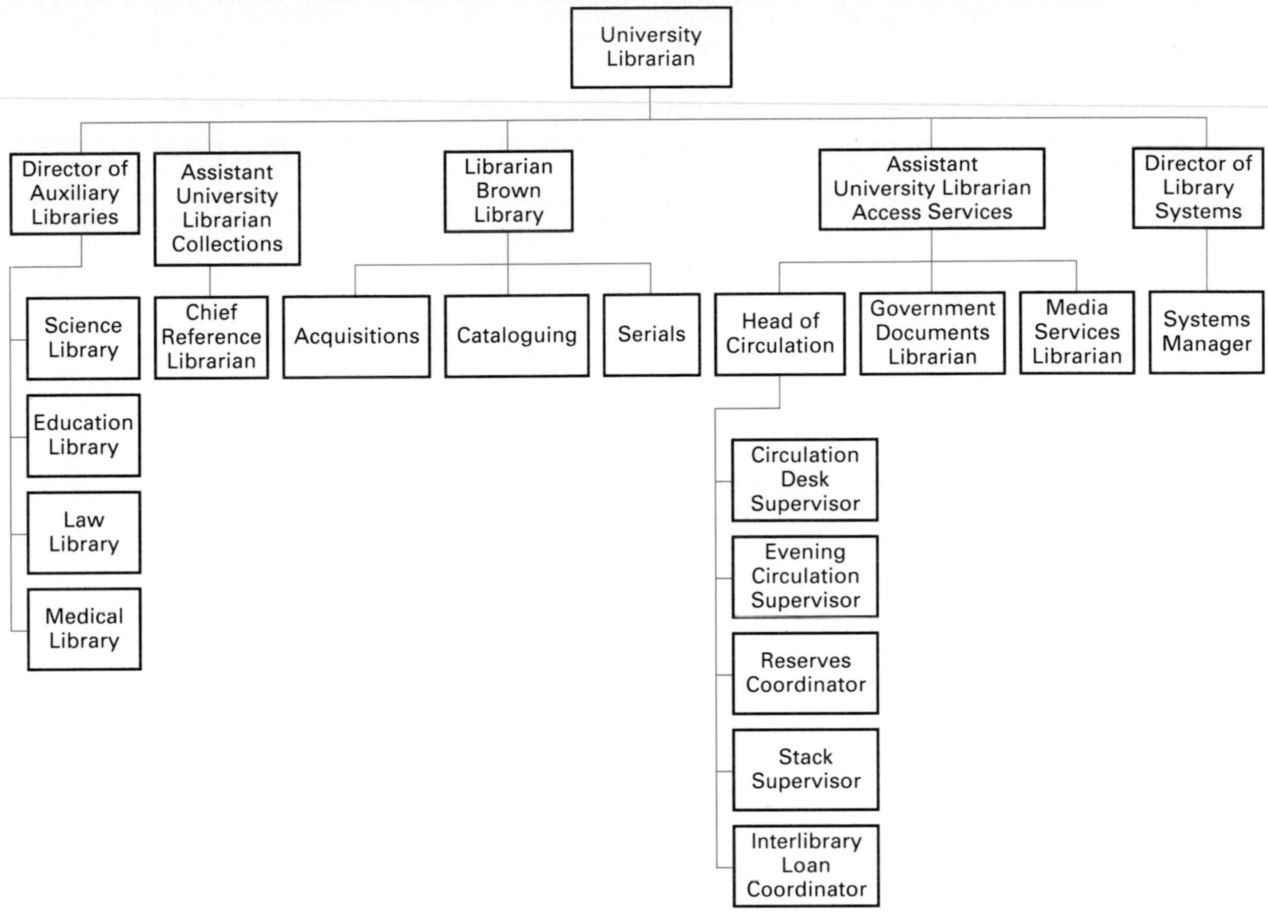

University Librarian
Director of Auxiliary Libraries
Assistant University Librarian Collections
Librarian Brown Library
Assistant University Librarian Access Services
Director of Library Systems
Science Library
Education Library
Law Library
Medical Library
Chief Reference Librarian
Acquisitions
Cataloguing
Serials
Head of Circulation
Government Documents Librarian
Media Services Librarian
Systems Manager
Circulation Desk Supervisor
Evening Circulation Supervisor
Reserves Coordinator
Stack Supervisor
Interlibrary Loan Coordinator

Figure 11–21 ORGANIZATION CHART OF A COMPUTER SOFTWARE COMPANY

President
12-Bit Product Group
18-Bit Product Group
36-Bit Product Group
16-Bit Product Group
Engineering
Marketing
Engineering
Marketing
Engineering
Marketing
Engineering
Marketing
Manufacturing
Sales
Finance & Administration

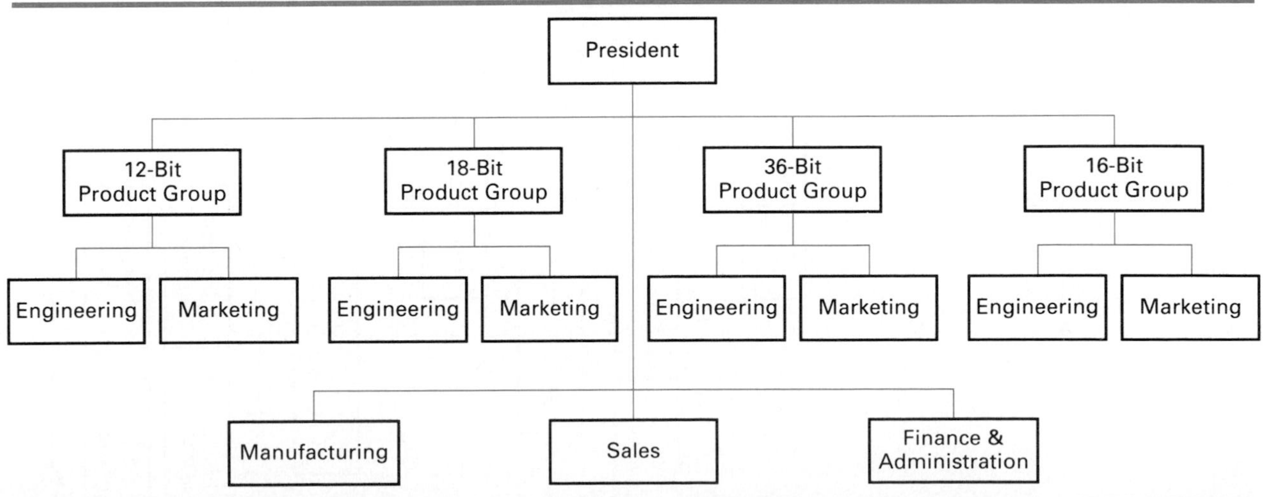

Figure 11–22 ORGANIZATION CHART OF A MEDICAL PRODUCTS COMPANY

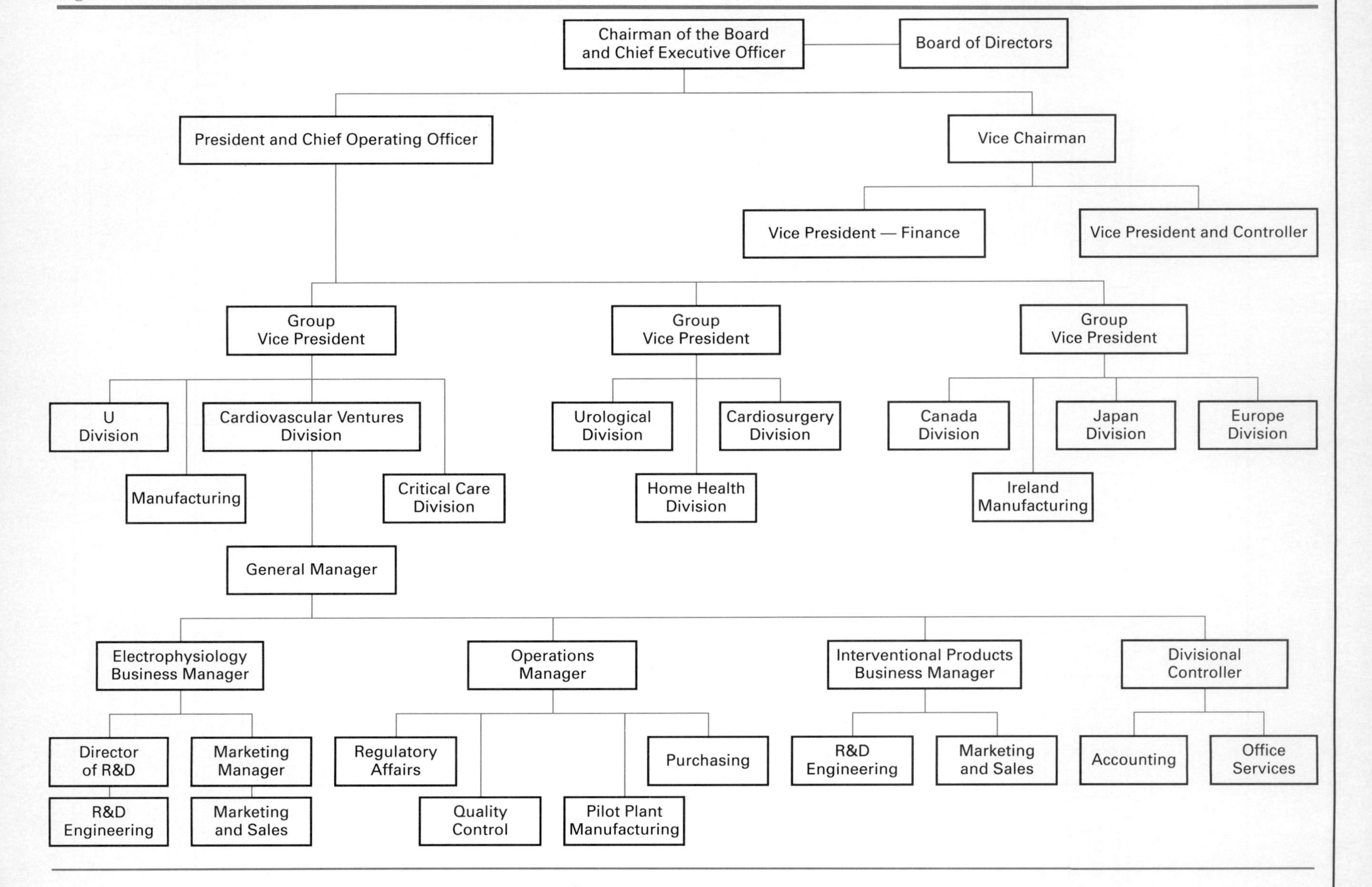

Description

1. Describe the division of labor and coordinating mechanisms for each.

Diagnosis

2. Analyze the method of organizing for each organization.
3. Compare and contrast these designs.
4. What kind of organization does each chart probably represent?
5. What employee attitudes and performance probably occur in each organization?

Prescription

6. What structural changes, if any, might benefit each organization?

Activity 11–3: REORGANIZATION AT JACKSON COMPANY CASE

Step 1: Read the Reorganization at Jackson Company case.

PART I

Jackson Company is a major snack foods and beverage manufacturing corporation formed by a merger between Snack Fo—a snack foods company—and Jackco Company—which manufactured a wide line of carbonated beverage flavors.

After the merger, Snack Fo became the snack foods division and continued to operate as an independent profit center. This division handled the Research and Development, Manufacturing and Marketing functions under a President who reported to the Chief Executive Officer (CEO) of Jackson Company. Snack Fo had one large technical facility which centralized all technical functions under a Vice President who reported to the President. Snack Fo was recognized as a leader and innovator in the snack foods business and top management felt the centralized technical function was a major contributor to their leadership position.

Jackco had three divisions prior to the merger: Bevman, Jackco Domestic and Jackco International. Bevman was the manufacturing division, and was organized as a cost center. Bevman transferred the products it manufactured to Jackco Domestic and Jackco International which were organized as profit centers and handled the marketing and sales of products. Bevman was handled by a Vice President, who reported to an Executive Vice President of Jackson Company. Jackco Domestic and Jackco International were headed by Presidents who reported to the CEO of Jackson Company. These three divisions covered the beverage business.

Prior to 1976 the technical functions—Research and Development, Quality Assurance,[1] and Quality Control[2]—for the beverage business were dispersed among all three divisions, but the major part of the effort was located within Bevman Division. A staff of thirty people reported to a Director of Research, and were physically located in the largest domestic manufacturing facility. The Director of Research reported to the Vice President of Bevman, and was responsible for New Product Development and Quality Assurance. Quality Control was handled by Plant Chemists assigned to each of the 15 plus separate manufacturing plants located at strategic locations around the world. The Plant Chemists reported to the plant managers of their respective plants. (See Figure 11–23.)

There was some degree of overlap between the central group and the Plant Chemists particularly in the area of ingredient approval. In their Quality Assurance role, the central group had overall responsibility for approving all ingredients and all finished products. A portion of this responsibility was delegated to the Plant Chemists who were responsible for approving certain locally available ingredients as well as all of the finished product prior to shipment. Copies of the analytical results plus samples of locally approved ingredients and finished products were sent to the Central Laboratory for recheck. Often the results of the Plant Chemist would not agree with the results of the Central Laboratory, thus necessitating decisions to either redo the product or leave it in the marketplace. This decision was made by the Vice President of Bevman with advice from the Director of Research.

PART II

In 1976 Jackson Company decided to centralize the technical functions for the beverage business. The centralization within Snack Fo served as a model for the new organization which would cover all of the technical service activities within Bevman and some of the activities within Jackco Domestic and Jackco International. Since this new function would consolidate some technical activities from all three beverage divisions, the management of Jackson Company decided to create a new position, Vice President of Technical Services (VP-TS) who would report directly to the Jackson Company CEO.

The management decided that no one within the present technical organization was capable of handling this new position, and that it would be filled from outside

Figure 11–23 ORGANIZATIONAL RELATIONSHIP BEFORE THE CHANGE, JACKSON CO.

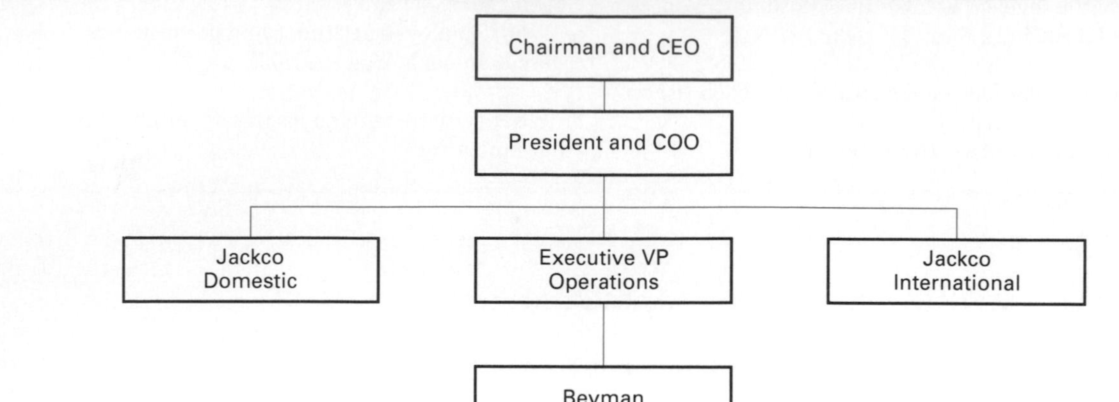

the company. No announcement of the position was made to the existing staff.

In the fall of 1976, an experienced manager from a food company was recruited and assigned the position of VP-TS. The new manager, Dr. Brower, was just finishing work toward his Ph.D. degree on a part-time basis. He had no previous experience on a top team. Dr. Brower was told that he would report to the CEO and that his broad assignment was to centralize the Research and Development, Quality Control, and Quality Assurance functions for the beverage business. He was in his new assignment for four weeks before any general announcement was made concerning his appointment. A copy of the announcement is shown below.

November 26, 1976

TO: All Vice Presidents, Department Heads & Managers

FROM: Vice President Personnel

It gives me great pleasure to announce the appointment of Dr. H.A. Brower to the position of Vice President of Research and Technical Services.

Dr. Brower has previous experience with Peptona, USA. In his new position he will report to the office of the CEO.

Please join me in welcoming Dr. Brower and his wife Sarah to the Jackson family.

Dr. Brower was told by the CEO that the people in the present organization were poorly organized and motivated. With respect to this problem, the CEO gave him the charge to develop the appropriate facilities and organization to handle the centralized technical service function. He was given the authority of a Division Vice President with the guidance that expenditures over $100,000 would require the CEO's approval.

Dr. Brower's first step was to recruit from his previous company several people whom he had recognized as quality performers. One of these people, Mr. French, was given the assignment of managing the Quality Control (QC) function. Mr. French had been responsible for the Quality Control Laboratory in one of the plants belonging to Dr. Brower's previous employer.

Dr. Brower and Mr. French had long discussions about methods to organize the Quality Control Department. A specific problem that concerned Dr. Brower was the present structure in which a Plant Chemist reported to each Plant Manager. He felt that the Plant Manager had too much vested interest in assuring that products from his plant were approved by the QC Laboratory, and thus might direct Plant Chemists to approve non-specification products. He also was concerned about the unclear authority in ingredient approval. Finally, Dr. Brower felt it was within his "centralization assignment" to have the Plant Chemists report to the new Technical Services Division.

In late 1977 Mr. French proposed a new organization structure in which the domestic plant chemists would report to him and the international plant chemists to a long-time company employee, Mr. Samson. (See Figure 11–24.) Mr. Samson was well respected for his knowledge of the ingredients and processes required to produce quality products. The proposed organization, particularly with respect to Mr. Samson, was discussed in detail by Dr. Brower and Mr. French.

Prior to Dr. Brower's arrival, Mr. Samson had responsibility for the total Quality Control program and had served as an advisor to the Plant Chemists. In that position he had supervised two chemists and two technicians in the Central Laboratory. The new position involved less overall responsibility but more supervisory responsibility.

Figure 11–24 PROPOSED CHANGES IN STRUCTURE AT JACKSON COMPANY

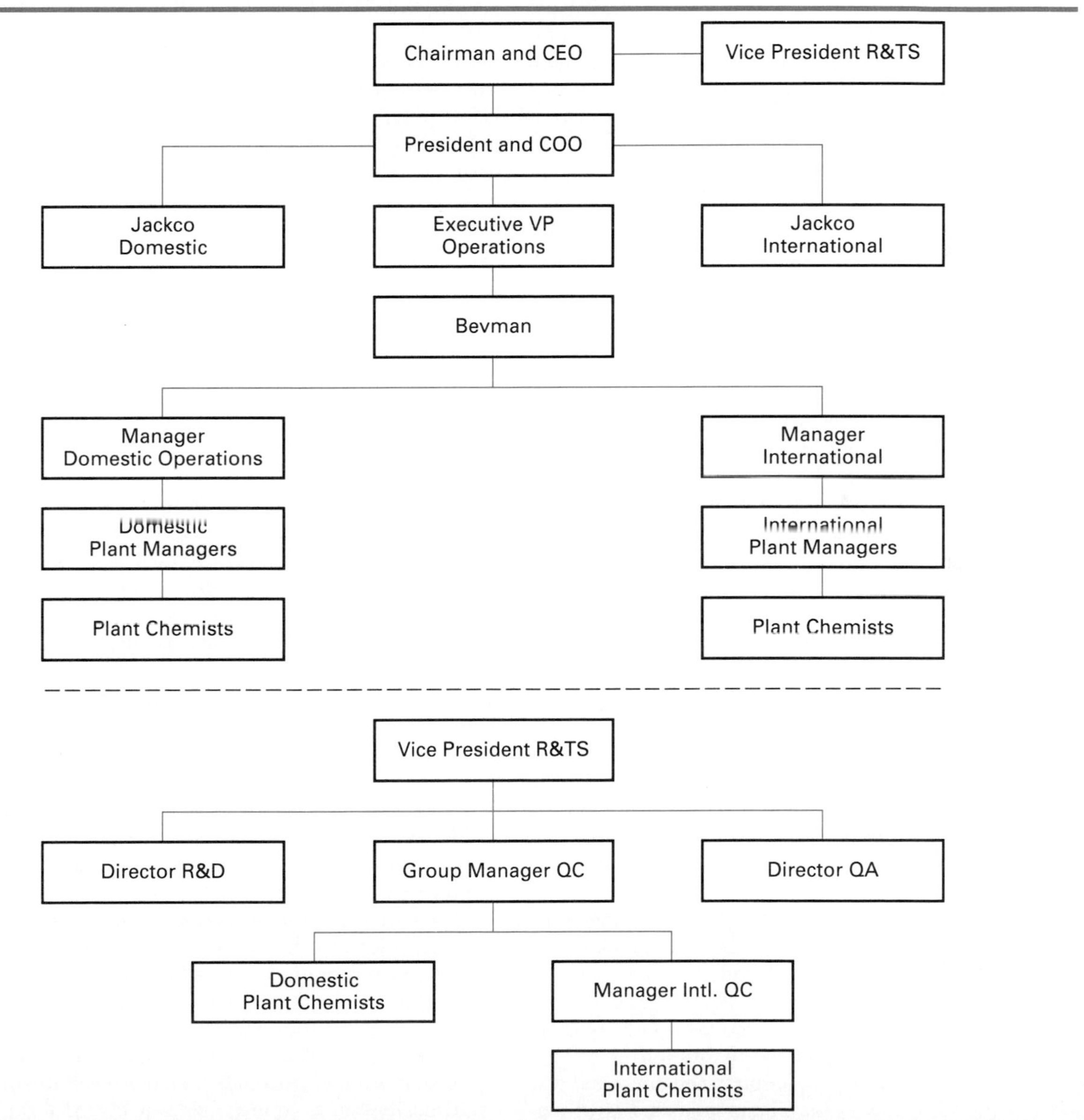

The discussion centered about how Mr. Samson would view this new position and whether he could handle the responsibility. Ultimately, the structure was approved; Mr. Samson agreed to the move, and a plan was developed to implement the structural change.

Prior to any further action, Dr. Brower met with the CEO and obtained his agreement with the changes. Dr. Brower then met with the Vice President of Bevman, Mr. Roberts, told him of the proposed change and stated that it had the approval of the CEO. Mr. Roberts pledged his full support to the change.

The action plan for the reorganization involved two steps. First, a letter describing the change was to be sent to each Plant Manager by Mr. Roberts. After this activity was completed, Mr. French and Mr. Samson were to personally take a second letter to each Plant Chemist. This second letter described the change and was signed by both Mr. Roberts and Dr. Brower. It was decided not to change the reporting relationships unilaterally, but to work on a plant-by-plant basis until the conversion was complete.

PART III

The program progressed slowly, because the international travel required significant time commitments from Mr. French and Mr. Samson. The program was also delayed by dissension within the Plant Manager group. The dissent primarily centered in the international area. Letters from Mr. Roberts were all mailed the same day, but problems in the international mail system caused the letters to reach the Plant Managers over a two-week period. Two Plant Managers, Mr. O'Leary in Ireland and Mr. Valdez in Uruguay, did not even receive their copies of the letter. Once the letters began arriving, the Plant Managers were rapidly in telephone communication with each other and with the International Operations Manager. The conversion program was placed on hold in the international area until Mr. Roberts was satisfied that communications were complete. The changeover was finally accomplished in June, 1978.

Certain Plant Managers were unhappy with the new organization. This was particularly noticeable in the Brazil and Ireland plants where the Plant Manager routinely told the Plant Chemist that the change was temporary and that things would revert back to "normal".

In August, 1978, the Argentina Plant Manager decided that the Plant Chemist assigned to his plant should be discharged, and he gave the Plant Chemist a written discharge letter. Upon review, Dr. Brower, Mr. French, and Mr. Samson concurred with the dismissal. Word of this incident spread to all of the plants but no official description of the situation leading to the dismissal was ever circulated. A few Plant Chemists asked Mr. Samson about the incident, and in each case he answered their questions fully, stating that the problem involved dishonesty on the part of the chemist. Although he upheld the decision, Dr. Brower felt that the Argentina Plant Manager had overstepped his authority and discussed this problem at length with Mr. Roberts. Ultimately, they decided that potential delays in international communication required delegation of certain authority over the Plant Chemists to the Plant Managers, but that discharge was outside that authority. Mr. Roberts communicated this decision by letter to the Argentina Plant Manager with copies to the International Operations Manager and Dr. Brower.

One major goal of Dr. Brower was to insure that no products contained unapproved ingredients. During the Fall of 1978 and the Winter and Spring of 1979, a number of times at various plants, products were manufactured with materials that had not been approved by the Central Laboratory. These situations were identified only when an ingredient was disapproved after the product had been shipped to customers. In each of these cases Mr. French wrote a letter to the Plant Chemist associated with the problem and reiterated the Division goal. Copies of the letter were sent to Mr. Samson and to the Plant Manager involved.

In early August, 1978, a large shipment of orange flavor was made from the Ireland Plant. One week after the shipment, the Central Laboratory sent a telex disapproving the Orange Oil used in the August orange flavor shipment.

NOTES

1. Quality Assurance is defined as overall responsibility for product quality.
2. Quality Control, in this firm, is defined as the day-to-day checking of product quality.

Step 2: Prepare the case for class discussion.

Step 3: Answer the following questions, individually, in small groups, or with the entire class, as directed by your instructor:

Description

1. Describe the original organization at Jackson Company in terms of division of labor and coordinating mechanisms.
2. Classify the organization using (a) form of departmentation, (b) means of coordination, (c) organic versus mechanistic classifications, and (d) information-processing capacity.
3. Describe the organization at Jackson after the reorganization plan was implemented in terms of division of labor and coordinating mechanisms.
4. Classify the new organization by (a) form of de-

partmentation, (b) means of coordination, (c) organic versus mechanistic classification, and (d) information-processing capacity.

Diagnosis

5. Evaluate the appropriateness of both the original and new structures.
6. How does the new structure respond to information-processing needs?
7. Do you think the reorganization was justified? Why or why not?
8. Given the reactions of some of the employees to the changes in organization, how much did the new structure consider worker needs?
9. Were the proposed changes communicated effectively?
10. What changes in the formal organization resulted in shifts in the informal organization?

Prescription

11. What additional changes are required?

Action

12. Was the process used to redesign the organization and then implement the changes effective? What costs and benefits resulted?

Step 4: Discussion. Answer the following questions, individually, in small groups, or with the entire class, as directed by your instructor:

1. Describe the changes instituted at the Jackson Company.
2. To what problems did the reorganization respond?
3. What other problems exist?
4. What theories and concepts help explain the problems?
5. Did the reorganization help? Why or why not?
6. What other changes are needed?

Activity 11–4: FERGUSONCHEMICAL EUROPE CASE

Step 1: Read the Fergusonchemical Europe case.

On a gray day in February 1985, Ian Robertson, Land Transportation Manager for Fergusonchemical Europe, sat in his office reviewing a recent organization survey. The results confirmed his worst fears. The survey, which had used scientific sampling procedures, showed that Fergusonchemical Europe's customers were receiving their products when promised only 75 percent of the time. Table 11–6 presents a summary of the survey findings.

These recent findings alone gave management adequate grounds for concern and, combined with information acquired from previous reports, it was clear that Fergusonchemical Europe's customer service was unsatisfactory. The earlier surveys, two in particular, had disturbed the regional distribution management team and had motivated Regional Distribution Manager Philippe Magistretti, Marine Manager Peter Gordon, and Ian Robertson to initiate the recently completed survey.

In 1983, a survey of sales personnel showed that the sales personnel of Fergusonchemical Europe did not consider their organization competitive in areas important to customers. In addition, a 1984 survey of plastics users in the United Kingdom found that Fergusonchemical was not viewed as competitive as British Petroleum, Shell, or DSM in significant areas of customer service. The same two issues were cited repeatedly by Fergusonchemical customers as sources of frustration. First, Fergusonchemical frequently did not deliver on time. Second, when deliveries were delayed, Fergusonchemical often failed to inform the customers. Given the environment facing the chemical industry in Europe in general, and strategic decisions recently made by Fergusonchemical Europe in particular, distribution management realized, as did senior management, that the existing level of customer service had to be considerably improved.

FERGUSONCHEMICAL EUROPE AND THE INDUSTRY

Fergusonchemical Europe, a wholly-owned subsidiary of Ferguson Corporation, was the ninth largest chemical company in Europe with revenues in 1984 of approximately 2.5 billion dollars. Fergusonchemical's products were classified into seven different chemical product lines. These product lines included: elastomers, plastics, solvents, plasticizers and intermediates, specialties, paramins, and olefins. Each product line was managed by a vice president based at company headquarters in Munich.

In addition to seven product segments, Fergusonchemical Europe was also divided into nine wholly-owned subsidiaries, each one serving one or more Western European countries: the United Kingdom, France, Belgium, West Germany, Netherlands, Italy, Spain, Portugal, and Sweden. Each affiliate had a managing director as well as a marketing manager who coordinated sales within each product line. Salespeople reported to their respective marketing managers who, in turn, reported to both the affiliate managing director and a product vice president located in Munich. Because of this dual reporting relationship, Fergusonchemical Europe had a matrix organization design. Figure 11–

Table 11–6 STATISTICAL CHECK, LAST WEEK OF JANUARY 1985, CUSTOMER DELIVERY RELIABILITY

	Sweden			U.K.			Netherlands		
	Before	Onday	After	Before	Onday	After	Before	Onday	After
P & I		3			8			1	
Specialties		2			2	3		2	
Elastomers		4		1	12	1		1	
Paramins		2		1	12	2		2	
Plastics		3			9	4		2	
Solvents		2	1		13			3	
Total		16	1	2	67	10		11	
*Total %**		94	6	2	85	13		100	

	Raw Data				Weighted Percentages		
	Total				Total %		
	Before	Onday	After	Total	Before	Onday	After
P & I	3	40	1	44	7	91	2
Specialties	3	22	11	36	8	61	31
Elastomers	4	33	12	49	8	67	25
Paramins	6	28	14	48	13	58	29
Plastics	2	30	18	50	4	60	36
Solvents	—	52	5	57	—	91	9
Total	18	205	61	284			
						Weighted	
Total %	6	72	22		5	75	20

*Raw data numbers of deliveries checked. Not statistically weighted.
Weather: The last week of January 1985 was affected by the thaw restrictions of truck movement in France. This particularly affected resins and elastomers.

25 presents an organization chart for Fergusonchemical Europe. Figure 11–26 presents a partial organization chart which includes regional distribution personnel.

During the 1980's, a number of factors contributed to an increasingly competitive environment for European chemical companies. A key development was the creation of overcapacity, especially in the area of commodity chemicals. In response to strong demand and high earnings during the 1970's, a number of chemical companies expanded their production facilities. Favorable market opportunities during the 1970's also attracted a number of new competitors, primarily from the Gulf oil countries. Their access to large inexpensive oil reserves and relatively low labor costs posed a significant challenge to existing European chemical companies. Projections indicated that chemical companies based in the Middle East would continue to offer increasing competition in the future.

In addition to excess capacity and growing competition, European chemical companies in 1985 were still recovering from the devastating effects of the economic recession of the early 1980's. A number of European chemical companies, including German-based BASF and Hoechst and Dutch-based DSM, initiated strategic diversification programs in response to an increasingly competitive business environment.

Fergusonchemical Europe, however, opted not to concentrate on diversification. Instead, the organization adopted what it termed a "value-added strategy", which influenced product decisions as well as customer relationships. With the existing industry overcapacity in commodity chemicals, Fergusonchemical Europe decided to focus on the production and sale of specialty chemicals. As specialty chemicals require a more lengthy complex production process, they can command higher prices and therefore offer greater profit potential. Fergusonchemical Europe believed that its technical expertise, production facilities, and resource base gave it a competitive advantage in this market segment.

In addition, the organization made a commitment to value-added customer service, using technical expertise, product knowledge, resource availability and dedicated effort. Fergusonchemical Europe promised to provide a level of customer service superior to that of-

Germany			France			Italy			Belgium		
Before	Onday	After	Before	Onday	After	Before	Onday	After	Before	Onday	After
2	13			12	1	No Deliveries			1	3	
1	5	3	1	8	1	1	3	3			1
3	4	3		5	5		2	3		4	
1	2	6		6	2	4	3	3		1	1
1	9	5		2	2	1	3	3		2	4
	10	1		6	1		6	2		2	
8	43	18	1	39	12	6	17	14	1	12	14
12	62	26	2	75	23	16	46	38	4	44	52

Weighing Calculation				
Region				
Weight	Before	Onday	After	
0.06	0.42	5.46	0.12	
0.07	0.56	4.27	2.17	
0.12	0.96	8.04	3.00	
0.15	1.95	8.70	4.35	
0.20	0.80	12.00	7.20	
0.40	—	36.40	3.60	
1	4.69	74.87	20.44	100

fered by the competition. Executives described this new strategy as a change from production orientation to market orientation. The need for increased sensitivity to customer requirements was stressed throughout the organization.

Paul Stinson, President of Fergusonchemical Europe, was responsible for the development, articulation and selling of the new value-added strategy to both internal and external constituencies. This strategy was summarized by Paul Stinson in a document entitled *Our Future Vision* which was published and widely distributed to company personnel.

SALES, DISTRIBUTION, AND CUSTOMER SERVICE OPERATIONS

In order to implement Fergusonchemical's goal of providing superior customer service, the existing structure needed reassessment. Each affiliate marketing manager served as the link between salespeople, the affiliate managing director and the relevant product vice-president at headquarters.

Affiliate marketing managers were assisted with their responsibilities by a secretary and a customer service coordinator. Customer service coordinators were responsible for ensuring that orders generated by sales personnel were smoothly executed. Activities frequently performed by customer service coordinators included processing orders, securing warehouse space, arranging for transportation needs, and answering customers' questions. Customer service coordinators usually reported to a single marketing manager and were considered members of the product team within each affiliate. In cases where product lines were small, a customer service coordinator would work with several marketing managers. In addition to expediting customers' orders, customer service coordinators occasionally assisted marketing managers with other administrative responsibilities. Fergusonchemical Europe employed approximately 120 customer service coordinators within their nine affiliate organizations. Figure 11–27 presents a demographic profile of customer service coordinators.

It was apparent from the findings of the recent corporate surveys that the existing organization of the

Figure 11–25 STRUCTURE OF FERGUSONCHEMICAL EUROPE

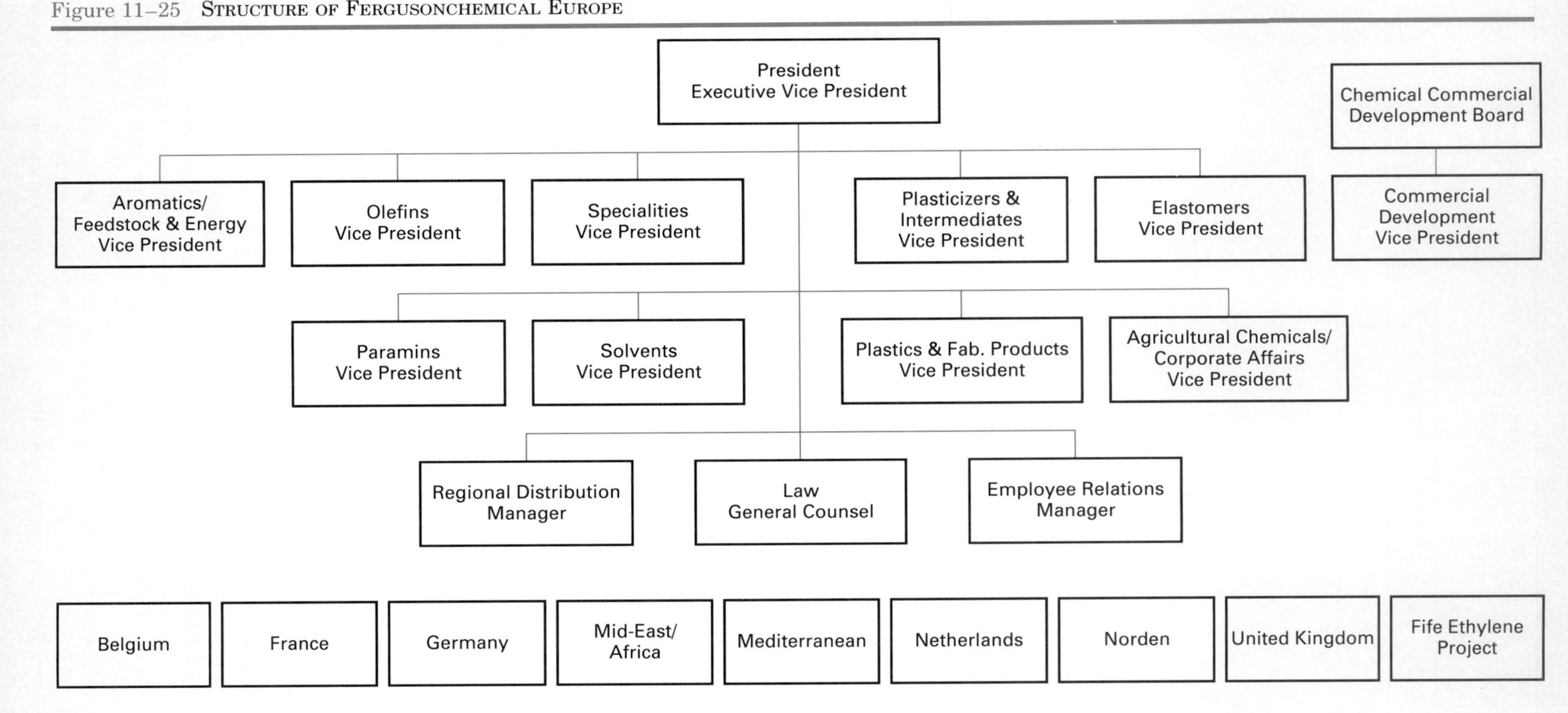

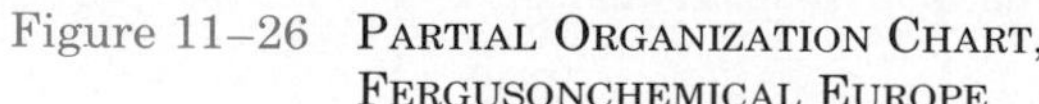
Figure 11–26 PARTIAL ORGANIZATION CHART, FERGUSONCHEMICAL EUROPE

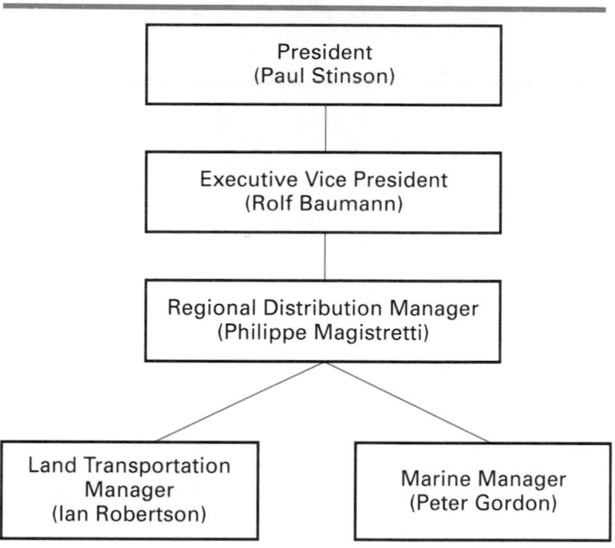

distribution function was unsatisfactory. The regional distribution team (Philippe Magistretti, Ian Robertson and Peter Gordon) was seriously concerned and began a reappraisal of Fergusonchemical Europe's distribution system.

The team felt strongly that distribution activities must be able to meet the dual objective of performing value-added customer service in a cost effective manner. In their discussions, regional distribution management personnel frequently referred to recent management books which stressed the importance of quality in all business activities.

Regional distribution management was particularly concerned about the assignment of customer service coordinators to individual product groups within affiliate organizations. The team was convinced that this structure was both inefficient and ineffective. In most cases, a single customer service coordinator worked within a product group. Therefore, when this person was unavailable because of illness, vacation, or other job responsibilities, customer inquiries frequently went unanswered. Philippe Magistretti and his colleagues maintained that the existing arrangement put customer service "at risk".

Although regional distribution management was willing to acknowledge differences amongst productive groups, there were many similarities in the activities performed by customer service coordinators. With the current structure, it was difficult for customer service coordinators to assist or learn from one another. Opportunities for career growth and advancement were also restricted because customer service coordinators were isolated within individual product groups. The regional distribution team realized that the present system was inhibiting economies of scale with respect to customer service operations.

Studies indicated that optimum economies of scale could be reached only if a minimum of five customer service coordinators were centrally situated. A recent phone survey supported the team's case for reorganization. The survey showed that customer service coordinators took an average of 70 seconds to answer an inquiry. Regional distribution management believed that all customer inquiries should be answered within 30 seconds. Figure 11–28 presents the results of the telephone survey.

PROPOSED REORGANIZATION

The recent survey on delivery time delays convinced the regional distribution management team that it must prepare and implement a reorganization plan. The proposed reorganization would remove customer service coordinators from the individual product groups and consolidate them in a central location within each affiliate organization. Instead of each customer service coordinator reporting to an individual affiliate marketing manager, all customer service coordinators would report to an affiliate distribution manager.

The regional distribution team realized that the reorganization plan alone could not rectify the problem of late deliveries. Recent studies had shown that delivery times being quoted to customers were clearly unrealistic for some products. In addition, certain job descriptions needed rewriting in order to give better customer service. However, their analysis showed that a majority of late deliveries were attributable to an inappropriately organized customer service function.

Philippe Magistretti, Ian Robertson, and Peter Gordon were aware that their proposed reorganization would encounter stiff opposition. Affiliate marketing managers in particular would strongly resist the proposed reorganization. On numerous occasions affiliate marketing managers had stressed that the customer service coordinator was the corner-stone of the product team, serving as a vital communications link to the market. Placing the customer service coordinators on the product teams also enhanced their accessibility and commitment to product team members. Marketing managers feared that these benefits would be lost after the reorganization. Finally, affiliate marketing managers questioned whether customer service coordinators were qualified to assume the new responsibilities which the proposed reorganization would entail.

Customer service coordinators also expressed concern regarding the reorganization. Fergusonchemical Europe was described by numerous customer service coordinators as a product driven company where the jobs

Figure 11–27 REGIONAL CUSTOMER SERVICE COORDINATOR PROFILES, FERGUSONCHEMICAL EUROPE

Previous job:
7% had Co. Marketing experience
Percentage
0
10
20
30
Higher Into Job
Secretary
Plant
Controllers
Distrib.
Marketing
Education:
70% have no technical training
Percentage
0
10
20
30
Ordinary
Secretarial
Comm.
Higher comm.
Higher techn.
University
Age at end 1984 (average 38)
80% above 30 years old
Percentage
0
10
20
30
20-24
25-29
30-34
35-39
40-44
45-49
50-54
55-59
Service with Co. to end 1984 (average 13)
60% more than 10 yrs with Co.
0
10
20
30
0-4
5-9
10-14
15-19
20-24
25-29
30-34
35-39
Years in customer service to end 1984 (average 7 years):
80% more than 5 yrs in C.S.
0
10
20
30
40
50
0-4
5-9
10-14
15-19
20+

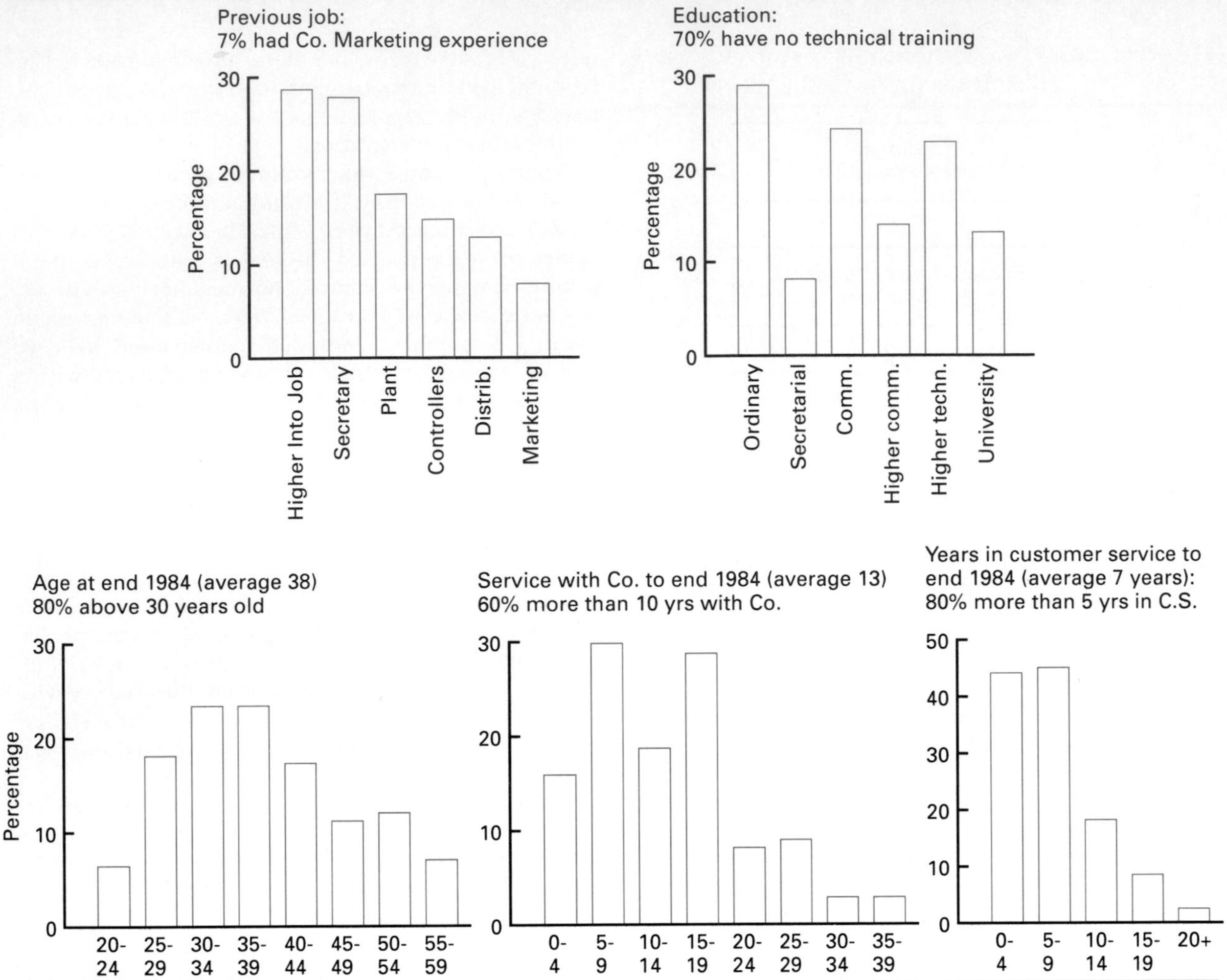

Figure 11–28 TELEPHONE SURVEY, FERGUSONCHEMICAL EUROPE (REGIONAL AVERAGE/HIGH/LOW VERSUS AFF'S)

Seconds
0
20
40
60
80
100
120
140
160
180
200
220
240
260
280
L
Avg
H
S
GB
NL
D
F
I
B

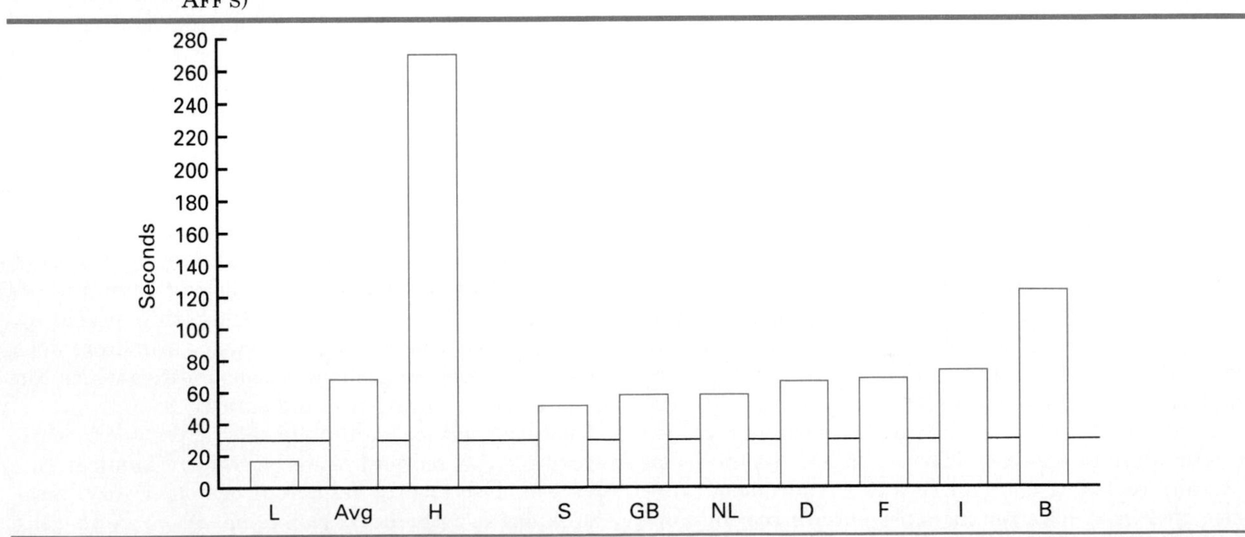

considered most attractive were associated with the product lines. Functional jobs, on the other hand, were viewed by many as "a necessary evil", a concept fostered by some affiliate marketing managers. Customer service coordinators therefore feared loss of both status and identification with a product team with the proposed reorganization.

Richard Elsner, customer service coordinator for the United Kingdom affiliate, voiced the concern of many customer service coordinators. "My biggest source of job satisfaction is helping the customer, particularly when it requires a little bit extra. To help your customers you need rapport and influence within the product team. My fear is that if I am isolated from my product team, I will lose the rapport and influence necessary to help my customers".

Customer service coordinators also worried about possible conflicts of interest between customer service and cost. As members of a product team, customer service coordinators generally tried to maximize customer service even if it meant costs would be higher. Would a central affiliate distribution center sacrifice customer service in order to reduce costs?

In addition to the above obstacles, the regional distribution management team realized that it operated within a matrix organization of product lines, affiliates, and functions. However, Philippe Magistretti, Ian Robertson and Peter Gordon felt no doubt that the reorganization was necessary. Furthermore, the Executive Vice President of Fergusonchemical Europe, Rolf Baumann, had publically stated that he supported the establishment of centralized customer service groups within the affiliate organizations. Failure to improve the current level of customer service might well endanger Fergusonchemical Europe's recently adopted business strategy. The question now facing regional distribution management was how to achieve acceptance and implement the proposed reorganization plan.

Step 2: Prepare the case for class discussion.

Step 3: Answer the following questions, individually, in small groups, or with the entire class, as directed by your instructor:

Description

1. Describe the original organization at Fergusonchemical Europe in terms of division of labor and coordinating mechanisms.
2. Classify the original organization using (a) form of departmentation, (b) means of coordination, (c) organic versus mechanistic classifications, and (d) information-processing capacity.
3. Describe the proposed reorganization in terms of division of labor and coordinating mechanisms.
4. Classify the proposed reorganization using (a) form of departmentation, (b) means of coordination, (c) organic versus mechanistic classifications, and (d) information-processing capacity.

Diagnosis

5. Compare and contrast the original and proposed organizations.
6. How do the structures respond to changing information-processing needs?
7. How do the structures respond to the employees' needs?
8. Comment on differences in communication, span of control, unity of command, and decentralization in the structures.
9. What problems does each structure solve? create?

Prescription

10. What changes were required in the original structure?
11. Does the reorganization provide the needed changes?

Action

12. Was the process used to redesign the organization and then implement the changes effective? What costs and benefits resulted?

Step 4: Discussion. In small groups or with the entire class, share your answers to the questions above. Then answer the following questions:

1. What symptoms suggested that problems existed?
2. What problems exist in the case?
3. What theories and concepts help explain the problems?
4. How were the problems corrected? How should they have been corrected?
5. Will the proposed changes likely be effective?

Activity 11–5: MAGNACOMP, INCORPORATED

Step 1: Read the description of Magnacomp Incorporated below.

In this exercise you are operating as members of a work team producing Magnaunits. These are assembled from subassemblies and these subassemblies have to be built from smaller units.

The job of your team is to work together to assemble the final product "Z" at the lowest cost and with acceptable quality. Product cost is measured by the total employee-minutes required to produce the product. The following labor cost schedule is the basis for computing the total cost for a team completing the exercise with an acceptable quality answer.

Number of Members	Cost in $/employee/minute
3	100
4	125
5	150
6	175
7	200
8	225
9	265
10	305

Thus a team completing the task successfully in 15 minutes with five members would have a total cost of $150 × 5 × 15 = $11,250.

Quality is determined by the accuracy of the answer. Deviations greater than ± 10 percent will not be acceptable, and a new answer must be computed.

The assembly process is straightforward and there are no tricks in the method.

A deck of cards corresponding to individual parts will be distributed to each company by the instructor. They are identical for each company. These cards, representing raw materials coming into the plant, are in a random order. Operation cards also accompany the individual parts cards. Each part is coded by a letter-number combination. Before the parts can be assembled, various indicated computations must be performed. The parts can then be assembled into subassemblies by performing the appropriate operations.

Work flow is indicated by flow charts, Figures 11–29 and 11–30, which show how assemblies are formed. They do not show the combining operations. The operations necessary to combine subassemblies are indicated on the operations cards included with the parts, and in the description of operations, Tables 11–7 and 11–8.

Figure 11–29 MAGNACOMP, INCORPORATED, PROJECT 1, FLOW CHART FOR MANUFACTURING

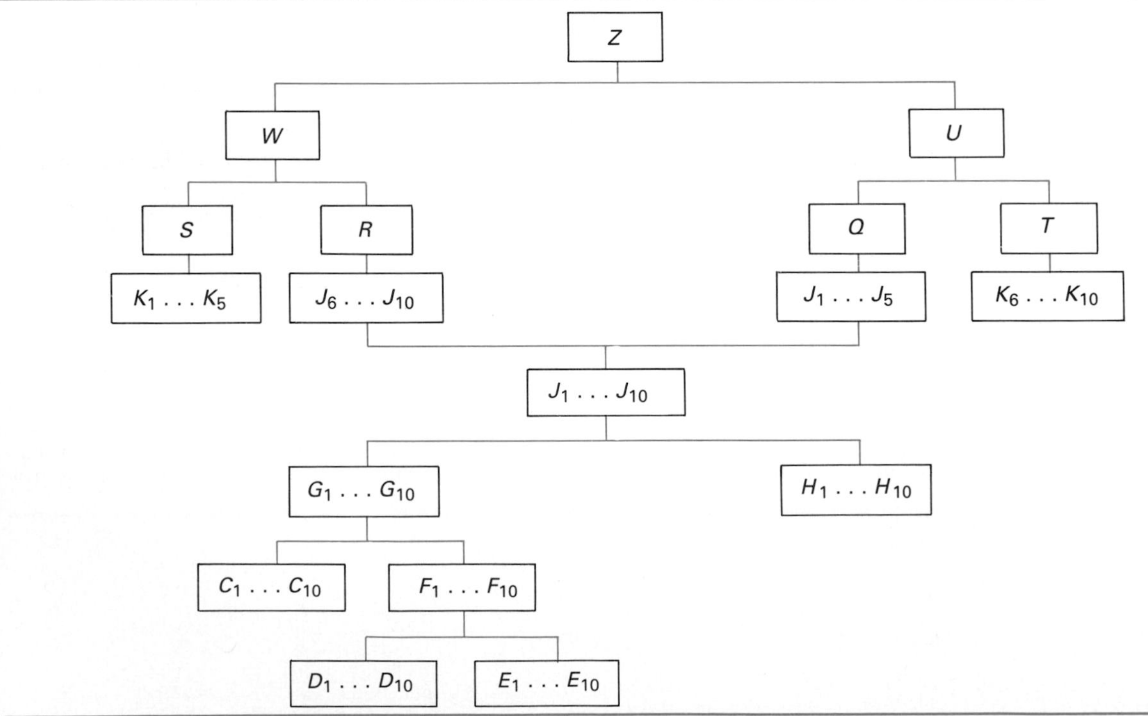

Figure 11–30 MAGNACOMP, INCORPORATED, PROJECT 2, FLOW CHART FOR MANUFACTURING

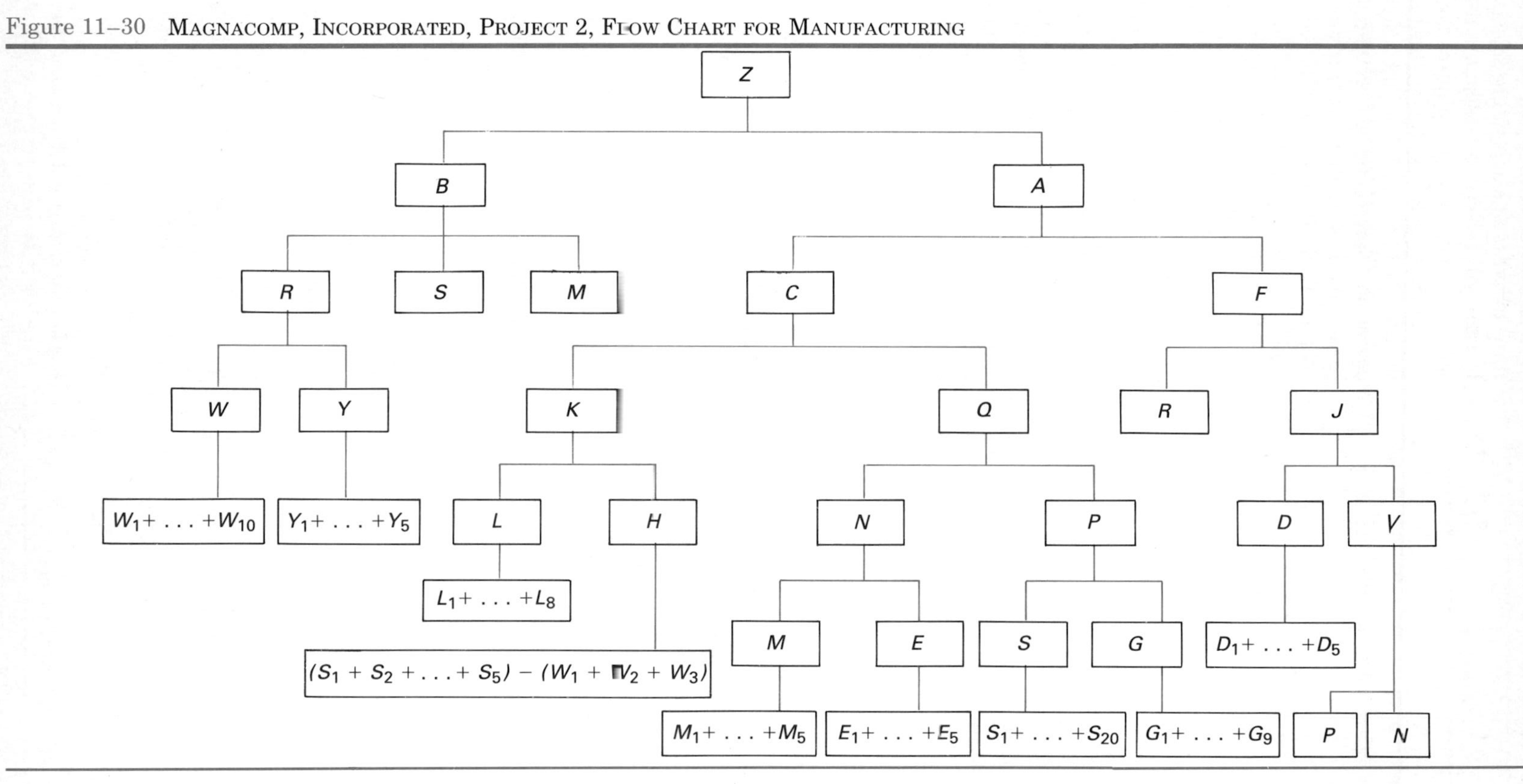

Table 11–7 MAGNACOMP, INCORPORATED, PROJECT 1

Operations
1. $Z = W + U$
2. $U = Q \div T$
3. $W = S \div R$
4. $S = K_1 + \ldots + K_5$
5. $R = J_6 + \ldots + J_{10}$
6. $Q = J_1 + \ldots + J_5$
7. $T = K_6 + \ldots + K_{10}$
8. $J_1 \ldots J_{10} = G_1 - H_1, G_2 - H_2, \ldots G_{10} - H_{10}$
9. $G_1 \ldots G_{10} = F_1 \times C_1, F_2 \times C_2, \ldots F_{10} \times C_{10}$
10. $F_1 \ldots F_{10} = D_1 - E_1, D_2 - E_2, \ldots D_{10} - E_{10}$
11. Where $C_1 \ldots C_{10}$; $E_1 \ldots E_{10}$, $D_1 \ldots D_{10}$; $H_1 \ldots H_{10}$ and $K_1 \ldots K_{10}$ are numerical values.

The team determining the value of "Z" within ± 10 percent at the lowest cost will be declared the winner. If ties in cost occur, the team with the most accurate answer will win.

Two trials will be run: Project 1 and Project 2.

Table 11–8 MAGNACOMP, INCORPORATED, PROJECT 2

Operations
1. $Z = A + B$
2. $B = R - S + M$
3. $R = W \times Y$
4. $W = W_1 + \ldots + W_{10}$
5. $Y = Y_1 + \ldots + Y_5$
6. $A = C \div F$
7. $C = Q \times K$
8. $K = L \div H$
9. $L = L_1 + \ldots + L_8$
10. $H = (S_1 + \ldots + S_5) - (W_1 + W_2 + W_3)$
11. $Q = P \div N$
12. $N = M - E$
13. $P = S + G$
14. $M = M_1 + \ldots + M_5$
15. $E = E_1 + \ldots + E_5$
16. $S = S_1 + \ldots + S_{20}$
17. $G = G_1 + \ldots + G_9$
18. $F = R \div J$
19. $J = D - V$
20. $D = D_1 + \ldots + D_5$
21. $V = P - N$
22. *Where* $G_1 \ldots G_9$; $S_1 \ldots S_{20}$; $M_1 \ldots M_5$; $E_1 \ldots E_5$; $L_1 \ldots L_8$; $W_1 \ldots W_{10}$; $Y_1 \ldots Y_5$; and $D_1 \ldots D_5$ are numerical values.

Step 2: Team leaders will be selected. There will be three to five teams depending on class size. Each leader in turn will select two assistants from the class. Each team will then have 10 minutes for a private preliminary planning session. During this time decisions should be made as to an initial organization structure, and an operations plan should be formulated. At this time each team should estimate its manpower needs for the simulation. Each team will be allowed to select additional persons for the simulation, and they will be selected at the end of this planning period. Care should be taken in selecting additional personnel since the evaluation of performance of the group will be affected by the size of the team. If the team is understaffed it may not be competitive with the other teams in the exercise, and if it is overstaffed the cost of additional personnel will reduce the efficiency measure of the team.

Step 3: The selection of additional team personnel will occur. Those class members not selected will act as observers and report to the class during the discussion period.

Step 4: A second planning session will now be conducted with the complete team. You will have ten minutes.

Step 5: Begin the exercise. Complete the Project 1 phase of the Magnacomp, Incorporated simulation. You will have twenty minutes.

Step 6: At the conclusion of Project 1 a ten-minute period will be provided to allow each team to analyze its mode of operations and make changes if necessary.

Step 7: Complete the Project 2 phase of the exercise. You will have twenty minutes.

Step 8: Discussion. After the exercise each team should analyze its mode of operation, its effectiveness, the organization structure developed, the communication channels, and the advantages and disadvantages of the system employed.

Description

1. Prepare an organization chart of your company.
2. Is this the initial form of organization you used? If you modified your initial structure, when, how, and why?
3. How did each member feel about his or her role in the simulation? Why?
4. Do differences exist between the various teams in the exercise with respect to these questions?

5. How was the team's performance? How does it compare with the other teams'?

Diagnosis

6. Can differences be explained in terms of organization structure?
7. How was the division of labor, coordination, and communication handled in the organization?

Prescription

8. What changes would have improved the organization's functioning?

Reprinted by permission from *Managing for Organizational Effectiveness: An Experiential Approach,* by F.E. Finch, H.R. Jones, and J.A. Letterer. New York: McGraw-Hill, 1976, pp. 82–84.

Activity 11–6: RESTRUCTURING AN ORGANIZATION

Step 1: Review the structure of the School of Management shown in Figure 11–31.

Step 2: Individually, in small groups, or with the entire class, as directed by your instructor, redesign the structure in two ways.

Step 3: Discussion. Share your designs with the entire class. Evaluate the advantages and disadvantages of the original and the new structures.

Activity 11–7: ANALYSIS OF ORGANIZATION STRUCTURE

Step 1: Select an organization and learn about its structure by reviewing its organization chart, interviewing key members, and observing activities.

Step 2: Answer the following questions, individually or in small groups, as directed by your instructor:

Description

1. Draw the organization's chart.

Diagnosis

2. Describe and evaluate the division of labor.
3. Describe and evaluate the coordinating mechanisms.
4. Describe and evaluate the methods of organizing.
5. Describe and evaluate information processing.
6. Describe and evaluate attitudes and behaviors of members.
7. Is the structure effective?

Prescription

8. What changes should be made to increase its effectiveness?

Figure 11–31 Structure of a School of Management

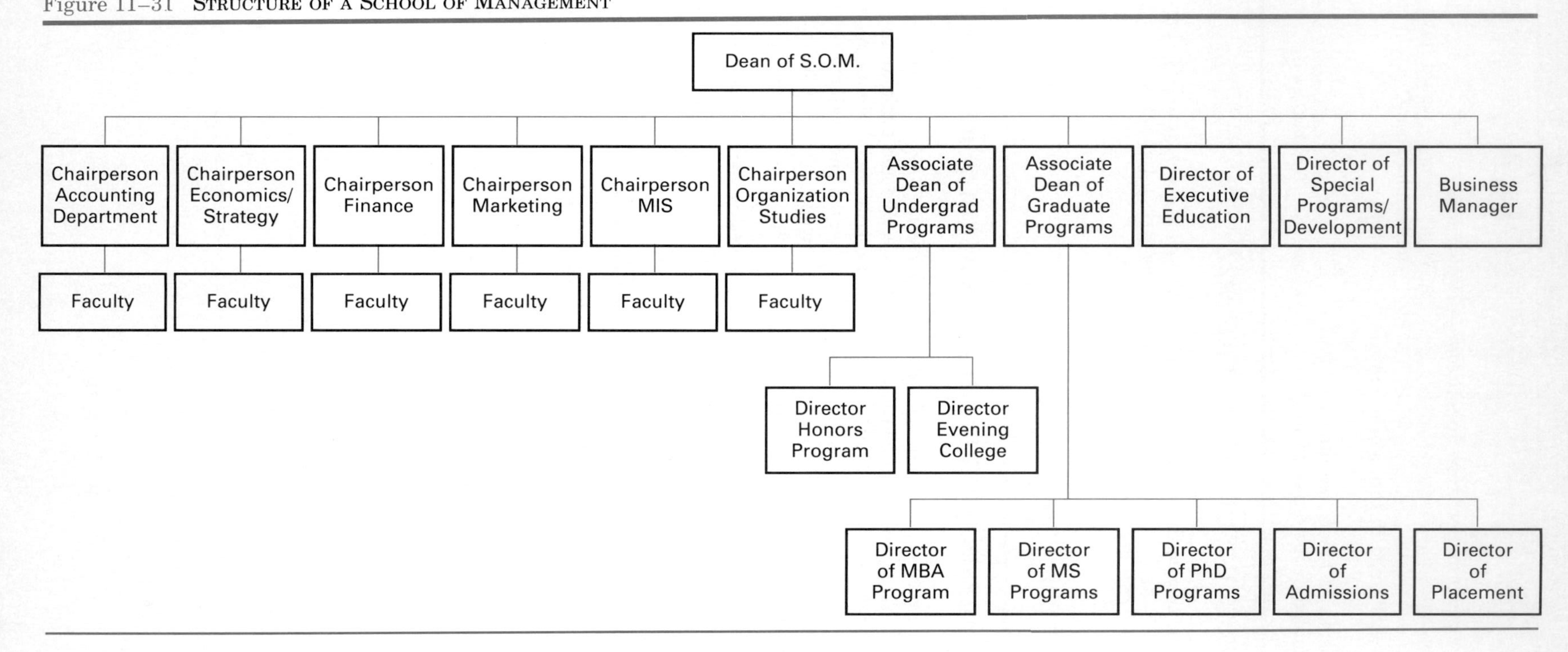

CONCLUDING COMMENTS

As organizations have come to face more complex problems, new structures have emerged to respond to the need to process more information, more quickly. First project/product management, later matrix organizations, and now what we call integrated structures have been developed as new structures. Organizations have moved from mechanistic structures—functional departmentation, simple structures, machine and professional bureaucracies—to more organic ones—adhocracies, product/project management, and integrated structures. They have moved from structures with low information-processing capacity to ones with a high capacity. In analyzing Apex College, a library, a medical products company, and a computer software developer, you identified various dimensions of organization structure and saw their place in organization design. Magnacomp, Inc., let you develop and experience additional organization structures. You practiced changing the structure of a school of management.

Analysis of the Jackson Company and Fergusonchemical Europe identified different structural configurations and their implications for effectiveness. Often the informal, rather than the formal, organization transacts much of the work of organizations.

Chapter 12 extends this analysis of organizational issues by providing a framework for predicting the effectiveness and efficiency of each organizational structure under various environmental and organizational conditions.

ENDNOTES

[1]This description was provided by Sean Dresel, Research and Development Engineer, a graduate student at the Carroll School of Management, Boston College.

[2]D.S. Pugh, D.J. Hickson, C.R. Hinings, K.M. MacDonald, C. Turner, and T. Lupton, A conceptual scheme for organizational analysis, *Administrative Science Quarterly* 8 (1953): 289–315.

[3]P.R. Lawrence and J.W. Lorsch, Differentiation and integration in complex organizations, *Administrative Science Quarterly* 12 (1967): 1–47, P.R. Lawrence and J.W. Lorsch, *Organization and Environment* (Boston: Harvard University Graduate School of Business, Division of Research, 1967).

[4]H. Mintzberg, *Structure in Fives: Designing Effective Organizations* (Englewood Cliffs, N.J.: Prentice-Hall, 1983).

[5]B.J. Hodge and W.P. Anthony, *Organization Theory: An Environmental Approach* (Boston: Allyn and Bacon, 1979), pp. 243–244.

[6]W.B. Brown and D.J. Mobey, *Organization Theory and Management: A Macro Approach* (New York: Wiley, 1980).

[7]A. Walker and J. Lorsch, Organizational choice: Product versus function, *Harvard Business Review* 46 (1968).

[8]J.R. Gordon, L.S. Corsini, and M.L. Fetters, Restructuring accounting firms for better client service, *Sloan Management Review* 26 (Spring 1985): 43–55.

[9]J.R. Galbraith, *Organization Design* (Reading, Mass.: Addison-Wesley, 1977); E.W. Larson and D.H. Gobeli, Matrix management: Contradictions and insight, *California Management Review* 29 (Summer 1987): 126–138; J.L. Brown and N.M. Agnew, The balance of power in a matrix structure, *Business Horizons* 25 (November-December 1982): 51–54.

[10]J.R. Galbraith and R.K. Kazanjian, Organizing to implement strategies of diversity and globalization: The role of matrix design, *Human Resource Management* 25 (Spring 1986): 37–54.

[11]J.M. Sinclair, Is the matrix really necessary?, *Project Management Journal* 15 (March 1984): 49–55.

[12]W.F. Joyce, Matrix organization: A social experiment, *Academy of Management Journal* 29 (1986): 536–561; D.H. Hamburger, Making matrix management work, *Project Management Journal* 16 (December 1985): 82–89.

[13]Galbraith and Kazanjian, *op. cit.*

[14]Mintzberg, *op. cit.*

[15]R.E. Miles and C.C. Snow, Organizations: New concepts for new forms, *California Management Review* 28 (Spring 1986): 62–73.

[16]W.W. Powell, Hybrid organizational arrangements: New form or transitional development?, *California Management Review* 30 (Fall 1987): 67–87.

[17]Galbraith and Kazanjian, *op. cit.*

[18]Miles and Snow, *op. cit.*

[19]C.R. Gullett, Mechanistic vs. organic organizations: What does the future hold?, *The Personnel Administrator* 20 (1975): 17.

[20]T. Burns and G.M. Stalker, *The Management of Innovation* (London: Tavistock, 1966).

[21]M.L. Tushman and D.A. Nadler, Information processing as an integrating concept in organizational design, *Academy of Management Review* 3 (1978): 613–625.

[22]G. Hofstede, Motivation, leadership and organization: Do American theories apply abroad?, *Organizational Dynamics* (Summer 1980): 42–63; Europe's new managers, *Business Week* (24 May 1982): 117.

[23]J.R. Lincoln, M. Harrada, and K. McBride, Organizational structures in Japanese and U.S. manufacturing, *Administrative Science Quarterly* 31 (1986): 338–364.

[24]See P.H. Birnbaum and G.Y.Y. Wong, Organizational structure of multinational banks from a culture-free perspective, *Administrative Science Quarterly* 30 (1985): 262–277; R.M. Marsh and H. Mannar, Technological implications theory: A Japanese test, *Organization Studies* 1(2) (1980): 161–183; J. Conaty, H. Mahmoude, and G.A. Miller, Social structure and hierarchy: A comparison of organizations in the U.S. and prerevolutionary Iran, *Organization Studies* 4(2) (1983): 105–128.

[25]M. Maurice, A. Soye, and M. Warner, Society differences in organizing manufacturing units: A comparison of France, West Germany, and Great Britain, *Organization Studies* 1 (1980): 59–86.

[26]P.E. Han, The informal organization you've got to live with, *Supervisory Management* 28 (October 1983): 25–28.

[27]*Ibid.*

[28]H.F. Kolodney, Evolution to a matrix organization, *Academy of Management Review* 4 (1979): 543–553.

[29]L.L. Cummings and C.J. Berger, Organization structure: How does it influence attitudes and performance?, *Organizational Dynamics* 5 (1976): 34–49; J.D. Sherman and H.L. Smith, The influence of organization structure on intrinsic versus extrinsic motivation, *Academy of Management Journal* 27 (1984): 877–884.

[30]*Ibid.*

RECOMMENDED READINGS

Hall, R.H. *Organizations, Structures, Processes, and Outcomes* 4th ed. Englewood Cliffs, N.J.: Prentice-Hall, 1987.

Jelinek, M., Litterer, J.A., and Miles, R.E. (eds.) *Organization by Design: Theory and Practice* 2d ed. Dallas: Business Publications, 1986.

Miller, D., and Friesen, P.H. *Organizations: A Quantum View*. Englewood Cliffs, N.J.: Prentice-Hall, 1984.

Mintzberg, H. *Structure in Fives: Designing Effective Organizations*. Englewood Cliffs, N.J.: Prentice-Hall, 1983.

Nystrom, P.C., and Starbuck, W.H. *Handbook of Organizational Design* vols. 1 and 2. New York: Oxford University Press, 1981.

Robbins, S.P. *Organization Theory: Structure, Design, and Applications* 2d ed. Englewood Cliffs, N.J.: Prentice-Hall, 1986.

12

Considering the Environment, Technology, and Other Influences on Organizational Design

CHAPTER OUTLINE

Restructuring at IBM
Components of the Environment
- Economic Environment
- Technological Environment
- Political/Legal Environment
- Sociocultural Environment

Environmental Dimensions
- Complexity
- Dynamism
- Hostility/Munificence

Typologies of Technology
- Definition of Technology
- Production Processes
- Task Performance
- Knowledge Technology

Technology's Impact on Organizational Design
- Regulation
- Sophistication

Organizational Goals
- Goal Formation
- Diversity of Goals
- Goal Incompatibility

Organizational Strategy
Characteristics of the Work Force
- Worker Characteristics
- Professional and Nonprofessional Employees

Size and Age of the Organization
- Size
- Age

Organizational Life Cycle
- Stages of Growth
- Decline
- Implications for Organizational Design

Redesigning the Organization
SUMMARY
READING
ACTIVITIES
CONCLUDING COMMENTS
ENDNOTES
RECOMMENDED READINGS

LEARNING OBJECTIVES

After completing the reading and activities in Chapter 12, students will be able to

- identify the components and dimensions of the environment and evaluate the appropriateness of an organization's structure for its environment;
- offer several typologies of technology and discuss their implications for organizational design;
- describe the nature, formation, and types of organizational goals and show ways in which organization design can consider these goals;
- discuss the relationship of an organization's strategy to its structure;
- describe an organization's work force and show its significance to the organization's structure;
- show how an organization's age and size influence its structure;
- trace the stages in an organization's development and show their relationship to the organization's structure; and
- design a structure that most effectively considers the organization's environment, technology, goals, strategy, work force, age, size, and stage of growth.

New York—International Business Machines Corp., frustrated by three years of disappointing results, unveiled a sweeping effort to decentralize decision-making at the world's largest computer company.

IBM Chairman John Akers described the changes as the company's biggest restructuring in at least six years and possibly its biggest in three decades. They shift broad responsibility from Mr. Aker's beleaguered management committee to IBM's six main product and marketing groups.

The high-technology giant also named one of its toughest troubleshooters, Terry Lautenbach, to a powerful new post overseeing all six groups.

IBM has long been criticized for being too unwieldy to spot market niches and develop new products quickly. Mr. Akers is known to have fretted in recent years that he was spending too much time resolving daily turf battles and logjams.

"This is a major delegation of authority," Mr. Akers said. "In many ways, we now have several IBM companies." Mr. Akers, who has shunned the press over the past year, spent an hour here yesterday explaining the restructuring to a group of reporters.

Personal Computer Division

IBM, based in Armonk, N.Y., also took steps to resolve some deep in-house marketing clashes that had pitted rival products in competition for the same customers. It moved its personal computer division into the same group as its older typewriter division, a sign that those two markets are converging. It also moved a slow-selling line of midrange computers into the same group as IBM's core business: the large mainframe computers that run most big companies' and governments' finances. . . .

Mr. Akers was clearly under heavy pressure to make changes at IBM, as the company's turnaround proved increasingly elusive. While its mainframe business is still the overwhelming market leader, it has seen market share erode badly in recent years in midrange products and in personal computers, its most visible market. Analysts said that last year, IBM's U.S. revenue fell slightly, while many other computer companies saw business surge.

Wall Street has been losing patience with the company. IBM's 1987 earnings would have fallen for the third year in a row without special items. Its stock lagged the Standard & Poor's 400 by nearly 40% in 1986 and by about 10% last year.

Initiated By Akers

Still, company insiders said, the restructuring was entirely Mr. Akers's plan, and wasn't forced on him by the IBM board. A director said the board learned of the plan at its meeting last Tuesday. "John found everything was coming onto his desk, and he had more than he could cope with," another director said, "He wanted an organization which resolved more problems before they got to him." . . .

In part, Mr. Akers's restructuring of IBM is simply an effort to reinvigorate his troops and shine up the company's tarnished image. He rechristened every one of IBM's blandly named product groups, giving them some

uncharacteristic new glitz. For example, the old Information Systems & Storage Group will become IBM Enterprise Systems.

"These kinds of changes are part of IBM's culture," said Bob Djurdjevic, an industry consultant and former IBM employee. "This recharges the top executives' batteries. It kicks the year off on a high note and starts them running in a new direction."

Whether the cosmetics and cheerleading will translate into more revenue isn't certain. IBM only last year finished a massive contraction that clearly didn't solve all of its problems. Tens of thousands of employees moved into sales jobs, and more than 13,000 others took early retirement. . . .

Mr. Akers emphasized that one of his most urgent objectives is to make IBM faster at bringing out new products. "Our development and manufacturing teams will frankly spend less time at corporate headquarters," he said. In addition, he said that over the next couple of years, "many thousands" of corporate staff members will be moved into posts that bring them into closer contact with customers.

One new product area the reorganization appeared to emphasize is a segment of IBM's midrange product line known as the 3X. Formerly in a division with IBM's other midrange computers, it now stands in a group by itself.

Some analysts suggested this separation could confuse midrange customers, or brand the 3X a "stepchild," as Mr. Djurdjevic, the consultant, put it. Other analysts said they believe Mr. Akers's assertion that the separation is a sign of IBM's high hopes for the 3X, which has more than 250,000 customers. One of IBM's biggest new products of 1988 will be the first major addition to the 3X line in years, a machine code-named "Silverlake."[1]

What factors influenced IBM's decision to decentralize decision making to its product and marketing groups? How effective is this new structure likely to be? In general, what contingencies should influence management's choice of the most appropriate and effective structure for an organization?

In this chapter we address these questions by providing a comprehensive framework for evaluating the contingencies that managers must consider in designing an organization's structure. We evaluate IBM's decision to change its structure. We *diagnose* the impact of an organization's (1) environment, (2) technology, (3) goals, (4) strategy, (5) work force, (6) age and size, and (7) life-cycle stage on its structure. Note that these contingencies influence the individual and group behavior discussed in earlier sections of this book, as well as the organization's structure as described in this chapter.

In this chapter we examine changes in these contingencies and organizational structures as organizations grow and change over time. We conclude the chapter by prescribing a methodology for redesigning organizational structures. Note that design is an ongoing process, and it should occur within and across the various hierarchical levels or subunits of an organization.

COMPONENTS OF THE ENVIRONMENT

Economic and market circumstances, technological innovations, federal, state, and local legislation, and political, social, and cultural conditions external to an organization comprise its environment and influence its functioning. Thus organizational management must select structures that most effectively respond to the environment they face. To do this managers must first diagnose the nature of the environment their organization faces.

Most organizations face a demanding, intrusive, and somewhat uncontrollable environment. Managers should use organization design as one way of interfacing effectively with the environment.

Economic Environment

Organizations typically confront an unpredictable economic environment. In a few years inflation moved from double digits to 4 percent, and now is higher again. The prime rate, which influences an organization's ability to borrow and hence to function in the marketplace, has similarly fluctuated. Organizations must be able to respond to the changing availability of money by reducing costs or using its increased availability as an opportunity for innovation or expansion.

National and international competitors, as well as suppliers and customers, comprise the market aspect of the economic environment. For example, the reorganization at IBM combined the personal computer and typewriter divisions in response to customers' signalling the convergence of the two markets. The accompanying decentralization was intended to allow IBM to identify potential markets and develop new products rapidly.

The internationalization of business has compounded the complexity and unpredictability of the environment. Organizations must learn to function in a world-wide economy, with diverse economic conditions in various locales. In many industries, competition has become more heated in the last five years, forcing organizations to restructure as one way of coping more effectively.

Technological Environment

IBM and other computer manufacturers face a constantly changing technological environment. Frequent advances in computer technology require continued emphasis on research and development. Product development must incorporate and "sell" the new technology. In addition, automation and computerization speed the dissemination of information and can increase competitors' productivity. Organization structure thus must facilitate the acquisition, development, and introduction of new technology.

Political/Legal Environment

Government regulations have increasingly constrained management's actions in its production and employment practices. Occupational safety and health guidelines, equal employment opportunity regulations, and foreign trade tariffs and policies influence the way IBM and other organizations can do business. In addition, the current political climate—either pro- or anti-business—influences IBM's and other companies' ability to compete in the United States and abroad.

Sociocultural Environment

Demographic changes have occurred as the population has shifted geographically, the relative age distribution of workers and customers has changed, and the educational level and expectations of organizational members have increased. Many workers have moved from the industrial northeast and midwest to the south and west, reducing the pool of skilled workers available to companies such as IBM in some of its locations. As the general population has aged and mandatory retirement has been eliminated, early retirement incentives have been used at companies such as Polaroid, Digital Equipment Corporation, and elsewhere to make way for young workers. Overall, organizational members are now better educated than their predecessors, and they have higher expectations about the kinds of jobs they want to hold.

Organizations seek creative ways of attracting new customers or clients and meeting workers' needs. Workers have demanded greater participation in decision making. Attempts to unionize white-collar workers and workers in high technology organizations have made top management more committed to managing workers effectively. Organizations have adopted flexible structures to respond to these aspects of the environment.

Consider an organization such as a discount supermarket, a large university, a chain of specialty stores, or an oil refinery. How would you describe its sociocultural environment? What impact might this environment have on the organization's structure? How would the multiple aspects interact to affect structure?

ENVIRONMENTAL DIMENSIONS

We can evaluate the components of the environment along three dimensions: (1) complexity, (2) dynamism, and (3) hostility/munificence.[2] Managers must fit the organization structures described in Chapter 11 to the aspects of the environment described in the next sections.

Complexity

The number and diversity of environmental elements that affect organizations vary considerably from one to another. A branch bank must deal with the four subenvironments described above, while a local pizza parlor must respond primarily to the economic environment and secondarily to the sociocultural environment. The branch bank has a more complex environment than does the pizza parlor.

A multinational firm, which must deal with the unique characteristics of the cultures and countries in which it operates, also experiences greater environmental complexity than does a similar organization that operates only in the United States. An organization that serves retail and wholesale markets faces a more complex environment than a comparable organization that only markets its product through retail outlets.

The greater the complexity of the environment faced by an organization, the greater the decentralization its decision making should be. This assumes, of course, that qualified and dedicated people exist in sufficient numbers at lower levels of the organization. Top management of the branch bank should decentralize decision making more than the owners of a pizza parlor; and the partners of a public accounting firm should encourage decentralization more than the director of a one-office accounting firm. Decentralization should also accompany the increased differentiation that occurs when divergent or heterogeneous expertise, goals, or personal orientations exist in an organization.[3]

What types of expertise exist at IBM? Certainly the various products and markets call for different expertise. Most likely the goals of these various groups also differ. While all groups want to increase revenues, some might emphasize servicing existing accounts, whereas others might encourage the development of new customers.

Decentralizing decision making places expertise and authority in direct contact with the essential information in the environment. It allows an organization to respond more quickly to changes in the environment. Moving IBM's decision making from the hands of a management committee to the product and marketing groups thus allows a faster response to new market trends and the demand for new products. IBM can meet the introduction of new products by competitors with a faster introduction of its own. But decentralization must be done only to the extent that adequate control can be maintained. The organization must be able to deal with new or sophisticated information more quickly, directly, and effectively than before. As the environment becomes increasingly complex, organizations may divisionalize as one way of dealing with diverse environmental elements. The divisionalized structure works best in larger, relatively older companies, with complex economic, technological, political/legal, and sociocultural environments.

Dynamism

The degree to which an organization's environmental elements change predictably over time also influences the most effective structure. Changes in the prime rate, for example, affect the availability of funds to organizations. Ongoing technological advancements demand reactions from organizations. New federal legislation may require policy changes in banks, hospitals, and other organizations in regulated industries.

Technological change occurs so rapidly and unpredictably that it may make products obsolete within six to twelve months of their introduction; manufacturers of computer chips, for example, face a highly uncertain environment for this reason. Passage of a law limiting condominium conversion in Boston in the mid-1980s created great uncertainty for developers and real estate agents; almost overnight, they could no longer market their product to certain types of customers.[4] The tightening of funds for mortgages further harmed the housing industry there.

The more frequently and unpredictably the environment changes, the more organic an organization's structure should be (see Chapter 11). (Again, this assumes certain intraorganizational conditions exist, including experienced people who want to and can function in an organic organization.) Recall that organic structures are relatively impermanent, emphasize lateral relationships, decentralize decision making, and deemphasize status and rank differences. Mechanistic structures, in contrast, use standardized policies and procedures to guide decision making, specialize activities into clearly defined tasks, use the hierarchy to resolve problems, and reward conformity.

Organizations can operate in relatively stable environments with a functional, mechanistic, and/or bureaucratic structure. In dynamic situations, however, organizations should move to the more organic project management, integrated, and/or adhocratic forms.[5] IBM faces a very dynamic environment. Its competition continuously introduces new products, and changes in technology are ongoing. Does its reorganization respond to the dynamic environment? Clearly the restructuring of product and market groups creates a more organic structure than existed before. But becoming more organic may also mean conversion to a simpler structure. Recent research has indicated that divisionalized firms facing instability reduced the uncertainty by divesting themselves of some of their businesses because they could better understand the remaining markets.[6]

Mechanisms to Alter Information Processing As its environment becomes more uncertain and unpredictable, an organization requires increased flexibility. Top management can respond to this need in two ways.[7] First, they can deal with the uncertainty by reducing the amount of information processed by a subunit. Creation of slack resources, such as lead time, overtime, extra machine capacity, and extra staff, reduces the amount of information processed by each department, work team, or division. Creation of self-contained tasks, whereby each group has all the resources needed to produce a given product or output, also limits the amount of information a unit must process, to that directly relevant to its task. Second, top management can deal with the uncertainty by helping subunits process information more quickly. The use of computer systems helps speed information processing. Creation of lateral relationships, such as liaison roles or task forces, which move the decision making down in the hierarchy to where the information exists, serves a similar purpose. Of course organizations do not adapt to a changing environment solely by making structural alterations. They may also change personnel, processes, or strategy.[8]

Which of these approaches does IBM use to deal with a dynamic environment? By focusing on product groups IBM provides to each group the resources it needs to produce its product and speed the flow of information laterally. The company certainly uses computer systems extensively. By combining divisions it may create slack resources, although the contraction in employment prior to the reorganization suggests a reduction in total resources rather than creation of slack resources.

Integrator Role Lateral linkages help organizations respond to environmental needs by increasing the flow of information within the organization or between the organization and its environment. Integration, like coordination, is "the quality of the state of collaboration that exists among departments that are required to achieve unity of effort by the demands of the environment."[9] *Integrators* hold a formal coordinating role between departments differentiated in social, time, or goal orientation. They should have four primary characteristics.[10] First, integrators should be seen as having the competence and knowledge to contribute to important decisions. They should not rely on the authority associated with the positions they hold as the basis for such contributions, but should use their expertise instead. Second, they must have balanced orientation and behavior patterns so they can communicate well with diverse types of employees; they must understand, respect, and help facilitate the goals and orientations of diverse groups in the organization. Third, integrators need to feel they are rewarded for total product responsibility—both process and outcomes—including the performance of their coworkers, not solely for their performance as individuals; this calls for a broad perspective. Fourth, integrators must have the capacity to resolve interdepartmental conflicts and disputes; they must be able to diagnose the causes and consequences of conflicts and offer constructive ways of resolving them (see Chapter 10).

Boundary-Spanner Holders of this role also improve organizational-environmental interaction, by reducing the ambiguity in information available to organizational members (described in Chapter 10). In contrast to integrators, who facilitate internal coordination, communication, and action, boundary-spanners process information and represent an organization or its subunits to others *outside* the organization's or unit's boundary.[11] An organization's ability to adapt to environmental contingencies depends in part on the expertise of boundary-role incumbents as information processors.

Hostility/Munificence

The degree to which the environment creates conflict, threat, or unexpected or overwhelming competition for an organization is described as its hostility or munificence. An organization that has limited competition in its service area may experience a relatively munificent environment. In contrast, if an organization's product is threatened with obsolescence because of a technological breakthrough in the marketplace, or if the organization experiences overwhelming and debilitating price competition or is the focus of governmental investigation or unexpected regulation, it faces a hostile environment. An organization that faces a takeover attempt or possible bankruptcy also experiences a hostile environment. So does an organization that experiences strong questions from the public about its failure to demonstrate social responsibility; those organizations that pollute the environment or ignore other community needs in the course of their operations may face this kind of pressure.

Organizations with highly hostile environments require equally high centralization of decision making. Centralization allows the fastest and most controlled means of responding to competition or other threatening events. Organizations typically use this design strategy in the short run, and it takes priority over other strategies. In contrast, organizations that experience environmental pressures in a generally munificent environment increase their specialization and the deployment of professionals to specialized areas.[12] Organizations have difficulty coping with a hostile environment over a prolonged period of time since it detracts from doing business effectively.

Would you describe the environment of IBM as hostile or munificent? While IBM clearly does not face a munificent environment, neither did it face an extremely hostile one at the time of the reorganization. No unexpected competition or takeover attempts threatened the company; thus the need to centralize decision making did not exist.

Table 12–1 shows one assessment of IBM's environment, along with those of a public accounting firm, a fast-food restaurant franchise, a university, and

Table 12–1 TYPICAL ENVIRONMENTS OF SELECTED ORGANIZATIONS

Environmental Dimension	IBM	Public Accounting Firm	Fast-Food Franchise	University	Steel Manufacturer
Complexity	High	High	Low	High	Moderate
Dynamism	High	Moderate	Low	Moderate	Moderate
Hostility	Moderate	Low	Low	Low	Moderate

a steel manufacturer. Note that differences in their environments call for different organization structures. An organization manages its interaction with the environment through the selection of base of departmentation—functional, project, or integrated, for example—and organizational configuration—simple structure, machine bureaucracy, professional bureaucracy, divisionalized structure, or adhocracy, as described in Chapter 11.

Selection of Organizational Configuration What types of structural configuration fit best with different environments? Table 12–2 summarizes the way an organization's structure relates to the three dimensions of environment.[13] Table 12–3 shows the design top management should select for the organizations shown in Table 12–1. Note, for example, that IBM should have an organic structure, with decentralized decision making and some top management control; a neighborhood restaurant, in contrast, should have a mechanistic structure, with centralized decision making.

Design Dilemmas Dilemmas arise when an organization's environment has competing forces, ones that call for opposite strategies. Top management of IBM, for example, may at times face an environment both complex and hostile. Should such an organization have centralized or decentralized decision making? The usual approach to resolve this type of dilemma is to create diverse structures within the same organization. Marketing and research and development departments may form project structures, whereas manufacturing uses functional ones. Alternatively, work units can change their structures as task and environmental demands change.[14] Again, management must view design

Table 12–2 DESIGN RESPONSES TO THE ENVIRONMENT

Dimension	Response
Complexity	As environmental complexity increases, decentralization of decision making should increase; ultimately divisionalization may be appropriate.
Dynamism	As the environment becomes more dynamic or unpredictable, organization structure should become more organic.
Hostility	When an organization faces a hostile environment, centralization of decision making must occur, at least temporarily.

Table 12–3 DESIGN RESPONSES TO THE ENVIRONMENT BY SELECTED ORGANIZATIONS

Environmental Dimension	IBM	Public Accounting Firm	Fast-Food Franchise	University	Steel Manufacturer
Complexity	Decentralized decision making	Decentralized decision making	Centralized decision making	Decentralized decision making	Moderately decentralized decision making
Dynamism	Organic	Hybrid	Mechanistic	Hybrid	Hybrid
Hostility/ Munificence	Some top management control	Little top management control	Little additional top management control	Little top management control	Some top management control

as an ongoing process in the organization and make adjustments whenever necessary.

Another approach calls for creating temporary structures used only in times of crisis. For example, an organization may have a management council that convenes only in response to hostile environmental events such as a takeover attempt or unexpected product introductions by a competitor. At all other times, a decentralized structure exists.

TYPOLOGIES OF TECHNOLOGY

At the same time as most organizations face an increasingly dynamic and unpredictable environment, they also must deal with changing and complicated technologies. Thus managers must select the appropriate structure for the technology used in each part of their organization. Some organizations use technology as a way of dealing with environmental uncertainty. By selecting nonroutine or innovative technologies, they can respond more effectively to the unique and unpredictable demands made by the environment.[15]

Definition of Technology

The technical system used by an organization in producing and delivering its product or service is likely, under certain conditions, to significantly influence the nature of effective organizational structures. Technology includes the processes that convert raw materials into finished products, as well as the delivery of services. Thus technology can refer to both production machinery and the intellectual or analytical processes used to transform information into a product idea. Three researchers, Joan Woodward, James Thompson, and Charles Perrow, laid the foundation for the diagnosis and analysis of technology and its impact on organizational structure.

Production Processes

Joan Woodward classifies technology in three ways. *Unit technology* describes craft processes that produce custom-made products such as housewares, clothing, or art work, and services such as legal and medical ones. *Mass production,* such as automobile or heavy-equipment manufacturing, refers to assembly-line operations to produce standardized consumer goods. *Continuous flow* technology, such as is used by chemical and oil refiners, describes an unsegmented, ongoing production process.[16]

How would you classify the manufacturing of personal computers? Is the technology the same as for their design and development? Manufacturing uses a mass-production technology, whereas design and development rely more on a unit process. A recent reformulation of this classification has proposed the addition of a fourth type of technology: technical batch (or unit) processing, which is used for aircraft production and check processing.[17] Like traditional unit processing, this technology has a small scale of operations. Unlike traditional batch processing, however, required knowledge complexity is high.

Task Performance

James Thompson describes technology in terms of the tasks performed by an organizational unit.[18] A *long-linked* technology involves the repetitive application of one technology to a standardized raw material. Mass-production assembly lines, such as those in the post office or steel manufacturing, use this technology. A *mediating* technology repeatedly applies a standardized method to unique raw materials. A social service agency employs standardized counseling techniques to diverse clients. *Intensive* technology applies diverse techniques and knowledge to various raw materials, the particular techniques used varying according to the given problem or situation. Thus hospital patients receive different treatments, depending on their symptoms and diagnosed problems.

Consider the technology used by IBM once again. Long-linked, mass-production, and intensive technologies are used by different units in the organization. Manufacturing uses a long-linked technology; human resources management uses a mediating one; and technical support uses an intensive one. Now consider an organization in which you have worked. What types of technology did you use?

Knowledge Technology

In a third classification scheme, Charles Perrow focuses specifically on knowledge technology.[19] *Task variability* refers to the number of exceptions that a job-holder encounters in the course of his or her work. An assembly-line worker encounters relatively low task variability, whereas a physician in family medicine encounters high task variability. *Problem analyzability* addresses the extent to which the technology is well understood by those who use it. A salesperson's job has relatively low problem analyzability, whereas a quality-control engineer's job is high on this dimension.

Combining these two dimensions results in four types of technology, shown in Table 12–4. *Routine* technology, such as that used by many government agencies and manufacturing companies, involves few exceptions and is well

Table 12–4 PERROW'S CLASSIFICATION OF TECHNOLOGY

		Task Variability	
		Routine with Few Exceptions	High Variety with Many Exceptions
Problem Analyzability	Well defined and analyzable	Routine	Engineering
	Ill defined and unanalyzable	Craft	Nonroutine

SOURCE: Based on C. Perrow, A framework for the comparative analysis of organizations, *American Sociological Review* 32 (April 1967): 194–208.

defined, understood, and analyzable. *Craft* technology, such as that used by a potter, also has few exceptions but is ill defined and unanalyzable. Organizations such as bridge-builders have an *engineering* technology, which has many exceptions but is well understood. *Nonroutine* technology, such as that used by a psychiatrist, has many exceptions and is not well understood.

TECHNOLOGY'S IMPACT ON ORGANIZATIONAL DESIGN

Henry Mintzberg distills the three typologies discussed above into two dimensions on which effective structure depends—regulation and sophistication.[20]

Regulation

Regulation refers to the extent to which machinery and equipment control an organization's worker. Regulating technology includes Woodward's mass-production and continuous-flow technologies, Thompson's long-linked and mediating technologies, and Perrow's routine and engineering technologies. Mintzberg suggests that a more regulating technology calls for a more bureaucratic structure. In other words, the more routine the technology, the less the need for flexibility, since responses to the technology can be predetermined and nonvariant. Nonregulating technology includes Woodward's unit technology, Thompson's intensive technology, and Perrow's craft and nonroutine technologies. Less regulating systems such as these call for an organic structure.[21] In other words, the less routine the technology, the greater the need for flexibility.

Sophistication

Sophistication describes the complexity or intricacy of the technology. As a technical system increases in sophistication, an organization requires increasingly elaborate administrative structure, more support staff who have decision-making responsibilities, and more integrating and linking devices.

Table 12–5 summarizes the types of technology and preferred design response for each type, under most situations. As noted earlier, technology varies among departments of an organization. Thus manufacturing has a regulating, sophisticated technology and therefore calls for a mechanistic structure with extensive support staff. Marketing has a nonregulating, sophisticated technology and therefore requires a more organic structure with extensive support staff. Once again think of a job you have held. How would you describe its technology? What structure would respond most effectively to this type of technology?

Effective organization structures buffer or protect the technology from environmental influences or disturbances.[22] The more specific the technology, such as that of a mechanized bottle-capper, the less tolerance the process has for disturbances, and the more the organization must elaborate its structure and administration to protect the operation from disturbances by the environment. IBM has a very elaborate structure, since it faces a highly turbulent environment and must protect the integrity of its technology. In general, as organizations become more automated they require increasing rules and regulations, centralized control, and support staff.

These factors suggest that IBM should have unique structures for the various parts of the organization. The specific structures should respond to the technology used by each part of the organization. As the technology changes, the structures may have to change as well. Note, however, that such change

Table 12–5 DESIGN RESPONSES TO VARIOUS TYPES OF TECHNOLOGY

Mintzberg's Classification	Woodward's Classification	Thompson's Classification	Perrow's Classification	Design Response
Regulating	Mass production Continuous flow	Long-linked Mediating	Routine Engineering	Bureaucratized (mechanistic) structure
Nonregulating	Unit	Intensive	Craft Nonroutine	Organic structure
Sophisticated				Extensive support staff Elaborate administrative structure Linking devices
Unsophisticated				Little support staff Simple administrative structure

may be unique to certain countries, such as the United States. In Japan, for example, the impact of technological change on design is less significant than are worker-centered contingencies such as career development and employee welfare.[23]

ORGANIZATIONAL GOALS

Organizations such as IBM, a large department-store chain, a law office, and a hospital, have diverse goals that might relate to market share, profitability, product innovation, or quality of working life. What other goals might these organizations have? Currently, at IBM, top management wants to make the company better able to spot market niches and develop new products quickly, as ways of reinvigorating workers and increasing revenues. Consider now other organizations you have observed—a small retail store, your local government, a library, an elementary school, or a brokerage house. Can you identify the goals of these organizations? How do they change over time? Managers must identify the goals of all parts of an organization first, and then choose the design most likely to facilitate their accomplishment.

Goal Formation

Goals are the desired results of organizational or individual activities.[24] They are "the objects toward which organizations direct their energies and concerns. . . . Goals are collective ends translated into socially meaningful terms."[25] They focus attention, provide a rationale for organizing activities, offer a standard of assessment of performance, legitimize individual and organizational behavior, and provide an identity for the individual.[26] They communicate higher management's philosophy and intentions, and motivate people to achieve.

Some theorists have described goal formation as a three-step process.[27] First, coalitions form and bargain over possible goals. Often competing coalitions provide others with inducements so that their own goals will predominate. Second, coalition leaders attempt to strengthen and clarify the goals by trying to satisfy, at least minimally, the goals of all coalition members. Third, group leaders and members adjust the goals to fit with their past experience with the same or similar goals.

Assume top management at IBM has the goal of increased revenue for the newly formed personal computer–typewriter group. Members of management and the product groups attempt to reach agreement about the specifics of this goal and how they will jointly attain it. Modifications in process and outcome occur that increase the compatibility of the group goal with those of the subgroups (personal computers and typewriters) and their members. Finally, participants adjust the desired level of revenue based on their past experiences.

Others view the process of goal formation as identifying constraints on an organization's operation[28] (e.g., by specifying the available resource pool or the extent of research expertise) and determining what the organization can and should accomplish given these limitations. The amount of revenues desired, for example, may evolve from the available human resource pool or current market share.

Neither goal formation process is straightforward. Organizations continually experience difficulty in specifying clear, responsive, and responsible goals.

Diversity of Goals

The nature of organizations' goals can vary significantly from one to another. One clothing manufacturer, for example, may focus on high output regardless of product quality; another may consider producing only high-quality clothing, even in small quantities, as its major goal. A public health agency may have frequency-of-service goals; and a volunteer organization, such as the P.T.A., may have a high rate of participation as one of its goals. Some organizations change their goals over time. Witness the case of IBM, described in the introduction: new product development became a high priority goal as market competition increased.

Table 12–6 reflects the diversity of goals organizations might have. It shows three typologies, each of which spans a range of possible goals. Not surprisingly, some similarities exist between them—output goals and management goals, for example. Together, these typologies list most of the types of goals organizations choose. Which types of goals is IBM or similar organizations likely to have? Can you give an example of each type of goal? Table 12–6 provides some examples in the right-hand column.

Goal Incompatibility

As indicated in Chapter 1 in discussing a systems view of organizational behavior, organizations frequently have multiple goals, and these may conflict with one another. For example, goals in the area of public responsibility may require costs that detract from profitability. The goal of providing the highest quality service may conflict with the goal of minimizing costs. These conflicts frequently arise from an incongruence between different goal types, such as innovation and productivity goals, or societal and output goals. In addition, a misfit between the goals of influential individuals, groups, or departments in

Table 12–6 THREE TYPOLOGIES OF ORGANIZATIONAL GOALS AND EXAMPLES

Type of Goal	Definition	Example
Perrow's Classification		
Societal	Creation and maintenance of cultural values through production of goods or services	To increase the number of managers on boards of charitable organizations
Output	Kinds and quantities of outputs produced	To increase production by 15%
System	The functioning of an organization's system independent of its production of goods or services	To introduce a project structure
Product	Specific characteristics of goods or services	To develop a line of men's cologne
Derived	Organization's use of power in areas apart from production of goods and services	To introduce a mentoring program

continued

Table 12–6 CONTINUED

Type of Goal	Definition	Example
Drucker's Classification		
Market standing	The organization's position in the market; quality and share of the market	To become the sales leader in portable typewriters
Innovation	The value of new product development	To develop two new products
Productivity	The level of output organization-wide	To increase production of shoes by 35%
Physical and financial resources	The nature and extent of resources used in product development and production	To reduce the cost of raw materials by 10%
Profitability	Profit and return on investment	To increase profit by 5%
Manager performance and development	Managerial output, growth, activities, and style	To send all managers to at least one training course
Worker performance and attitudes	Individual output, turnover, absenteeism, satisfaction, and morale	To reduce turnover to less than 10% a year
Public responsibility	The organization's use of natural resources and contribution to the public good	To seek alternate sources of raw materials
Gross's Classification		
Output	Kinds and levels of output	To add three products to the product line
Adaptation	Those that contribute to the ability to respond to environmental changes; emphasis on research and development, for example	To double the R&D staff
Management	Managerial output, activities, and style	To increase the amount of time managers spend in planning activities
Motivation	Encouraging employee motivation	To introduce an incentive program
Position	Those associated with each job in the organization	To increase the autonomy associated with each job

SOURCES: C. Perrow, *Organizational Analysis: A Sociological View* (Belmont, Cal.: Wadsworth, 1970); P. Drucker, *The Practice of Management* (New York: Harper, 1954); E. Gross, The definition of organizational goals, *British Journal of Sociology* 20 (1969): 277–294.

an organization may prevent diverse constituencies from agreeing on the organization's goals. At IBM, for example, the increased importance of product groups may have resulted from differences in John Akers's goals and those of other top managers. At other companies, return on investment for stockholders may seem to conflict with greater compensation and better quality of work life for employees. Thus, defining an organization's goal or goals requires significant and complex action to reconcile conflicting and incompatible goals. Dysfunctional goal displacement—where individuals or groups divert their energies from the organization's original goals to different ones—as the solution to resolving incompatible goals, must be avoided.

Organization structures should facilitate goal accomplishment. The restructuring at IBM, for example, was intended to refocus the product divisions. Institution of a product structure encourages development of new products and exploitation of market niches. Typically, the more extensive and heterogeneous the goals, the more complex the structure needed to respond to them.[29]

ORGANIZATIONAL STRATEGY

An organization's strategy, or its basic missions, purpose, or niche, also influences its structure. One schema classifies organizations into four strategic types.[30] *Defenders* are organizations that produce a small number of products for a small segment of the market. Cray Computer Company, which produces a high-speed, high-capacity, very expensive computer, likely has this strategy. They emphasize planning and cost control, rather than a search for new products. The resulting structure tends to be relatively bureaucratic, emphasizing high horizontal differentiation, centralized control, an elaborate hierarchy, and extensive formalization.

Prospectors, in contrast, find and develop new products and markets; they emphasize innovation and rapid introduction of new products. Minnesota Mining and Manufacturing Company (3M) likely has this strategy. These organizations call for a relatively organic structure, with less division of labor, greater flexibility, and more decentralized decision making and control. 3M frequently purchases small companies and adds them, intact, to their organization.

Analyzers combine characteristics of both defenders and prospectors. Many banks act as analyzers. They enter new markets or introduce new products after the prospectors. They also maintain efficiency, like defenders. This strategy calls for a hybrid structure, one that has moderately centralized control and encourages both flexibility and stability. Many banks combine elements of product and functional structures. The organization structure has some parts, such as operations, with bureaucratic characteristics, and other parts, such as R&D or marketing, with organic characteristics.

Finally, *reactors* design their strategies based on what others in the market have done, and they lack a structural imperative. They may pursue one of the other three strategies incidentally but often do so improperly and hence perform ineffectively.

How would you characterize IBM? It can be viewed as a prospector, since it wishes to emphasize innovation and new products. It can also be viewed as an analyzer, since it offers some of its products after competitors have introduced similar ones. Its adoption of a more organic structure with decentralized decision making fits with this strategy. Reading 12–1, "Network Organizations: New Concepts for New Forms," shows how the dynamic network structure responds to strategic considerations. In any case, managers must identify the organization's strategy and then select the design that best responds to this contingency.

CHARACTERISTICS OF THE WORK FORCE

What types of employees comprise the work force at IBM? The product groups described in the introductory scenario certainly include highly trained individuals with specialized knowledge. Although the manufacturing staff in each group likely includes different types of workers, overall we can characterize the employees as relatively professionalized.

Worker Characteristics

Organization structures typically depend to some extent on the professionalism, expertise, and group memberships (e.g., union affiliation) of employees. Other employee characteristics that can influence organization structure include education, work experience, and other demographic characteristics; work values and motivation; life and career stages; commitment and other attitudes; and personality variables.[31] These attributes in turn may affect the extent of involvement in decision making preferred by various organizational members. For example, we might hypothesize that individuals who value internal control and are beyond the entry stage of their careers may function more effectively in decentralized structures than those who value external control and lack work experience.

Professional and Nonprofessional Employees

Organizations might consider the work force in a particular department, division, or other unit when designing an organization's structure. Professionals generally prefer more decentralized, organic structures, although in some organizations the professional bureaucratic model (described in Chapter 11) is used. Less skilled workers seem better able to perform effectively with centralization of authority and more rules and procedures; increasingly, however, even many of these workers desire greater autonomy and involvement in decision making (discussed further in Chapter 13).

SIZE AND AGE OF THE ORGANIZATION

The growth and aging of an organization also determine the most effective structure.

Size

As organizations increase in size, they typically become more heterogeneous in their orientations as well as in the products and services they provide. This change necessitates increased differentiation. Depending on the environment and the technology faced by the organization, this differentiation may result in a move from a simpler functional structure to any of the more complex ones. Figure 12–1 illustrates a typical progression, showing a restaurant that increases in size. An increase in both the average size of departments and the formalization of organizational behaviors accompany an increase in size.[32]

A group of researchers in Aston, England, who studied organizations believe

Figure 12–1 CHANGES IN ORGANIZATION STRUCTURE WITH INCREASES IN SIZE

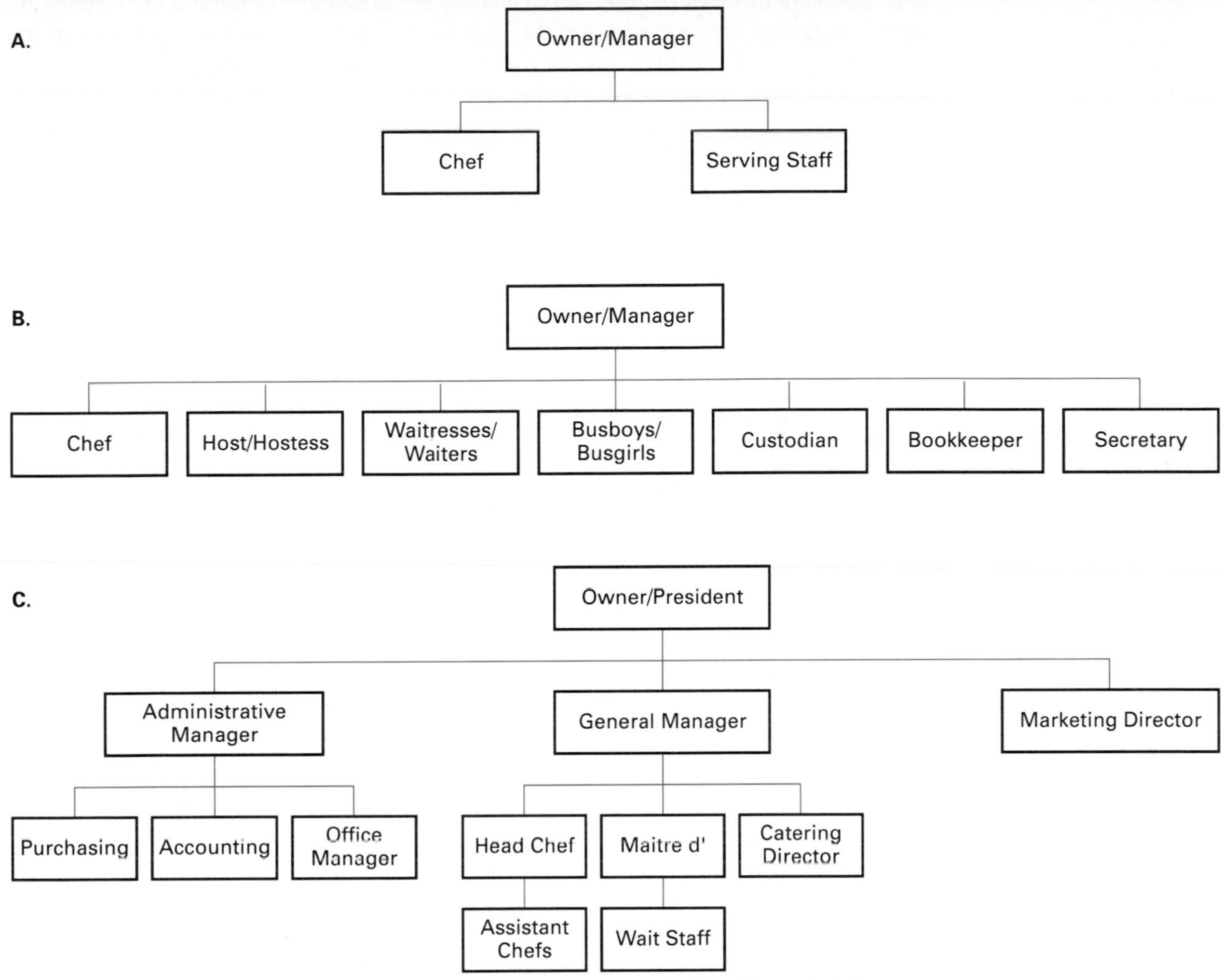

that size dictates certain structural dimensions, specifically the structuring of activities, specialization, standardization, formalization, span of control, and centralization.[33] Other researchers who studied the same organizations found that organizational size also modifies the influence of technology on structure.[34] While the results suggest the importance of knowing an organization's size in diagnosing the effectiveness of its structure, the impact of size should not preclude the consideration of other contingencies.

Age

The age of an organization, not surprisingly, often correlates with its size. As an organization ages, its behavior tends to become more standardized and formalized. The aging of the United States Government illustrates this relationship quite well. Early communication occurred primarily through mutual adjustment. As the Government got older, more procedures became standardized, and its structure became more mechanized and bureaucratic. Because age and size often correlate, separating the influences of each contingency on organizational structure poses difficulties for organizational analysts. In redesigning organizations, managers must consider the implications of both contingencies.

ORGANIZATIONAL LIFE CYCLE

As noted earlier, some organizations evolve through various organizational structures, such as from functional, to project, to matrix, to project again. At the same time, most organizations also evolve through a life cycle, or a series of developmental stages, akin to those described for individuals in Chapter 3. Researchers have noted that these stages occur in a predictable sequence that is not easily reversed.[35] Of course not every organization passes through every stage described.

Stages of Growth

Organizational growth can be described as movement through four stages (shown in Table 12–7): entrepreneur, collectivity, formalization, and elaboration.[36]

Entrepreneur Stage Organizational creation is "a network building enterprise that centers on the inception, diffusion, and adaptation of a set of ideas among a group of people"; they commit to these ideas and enact them.[37] They move from *first ideas* about the organization, to *commitments* and initial *planning,* and then to *implementation* to make the new organization operational.[38] This stage incorporates two stages of small-business growth: existence and survival.[39] *Existence* concerns development of a customer base, reliable delivery

Table 12–7 SUMMARY MODEL OF THE ORGANIZATIONAL LIFE CYCLE

Entrepreneurial Stage	Collectivity Stage	Formalization and Control Stage	Elaboration of Structure Stage
Marshalling of resources	Informal communication and structure	Formalization of rules	Elaboration of structure
Lots of ideas	Sense of collectivity	Stable structure	Decentralization
Entrepreneurial activities	Long hours spent	Emphasis on efficiency and maintenance	Domain expansion
Little planning and coordination	Sense of mission	Conservatism	Adaptation
Formation of a "niche"	Innovation continues	Institutional procedures	Renewal
"Prime mover" has power	High commitment		

Reprinted by permission of R.E. Quinn and K. Cameron, Organizational life cycles and shifting criteria of effectiveness: Some preliminary evidence, *Management Science* 29 (January 1983), Copyright 1983 The Institute of Management Sciences.

of a product, and building a sufficient cash flow to support a company's activities. Growth occurs through the creativity of the organization's leaders. In the *survival* stage, the company becomes concerned with generating a profit. There is little formal planning and few formal systems. Growth occurs through supervision provided by the leader to a growing number of employees.

Collectivity Stage Organizations typically experience rapid growth at this stage. While innovation and expansion continue, some attempts to stabilize and routinize the organization begin.[40] Also known as the *success* stage, the owner now must decide whether to stabilize the company at its present size or strive for more growth.[41] The owner can consolidate the company, professionalize its functional management, and remove himself or herself from an active management role; or the owner can reinvest the profits in growth. Although members remain committed to the organization at this stage, perhaps by continuing to work long hours, their involvement increasingly becomes a function of the incentives offered. Tasks must offer challenge and variety; the organization must provide growth opportunities; or employees ask for frequent, quality communication.[42]

Formalization Called "the transition [which] represents the most dramatic change in the early evolution of organizations,"[43] this maturation process signals the movement of an organization from entrepreneurial to professional.[44] Apple Computer's ouster of Steven Jobs illustrates this transition. In this stage, also called the *take-off* stage, the owner must address delegation of responsibility and sufficiency of cash to finance growth.[45] As a company matures, owner and management diverge, although the owner maintains stock control. The transition from an owner-manager to a hired manager frequently signals the beginning of this stage in small businesses. In larger organizations, emphasis on the structural elaboration through functional specialization, development of systematic reward and evaluation systems, and emphasis on formal planning and goal setting reflect this stage.[46] The change in focus at this point may motivate the more entrepreneurial, innovative workers to leave the organization to seek new outlets for their creativity. Individuals whose goals and orientations are more compatible with the stabilization and formalization processes replace them.

Elaboration The mature organization strives to adapt to changing conditions, renew itself, and find continued growth opportunities. Developing *resource maturity,* the company must consolidate its growth, expand its management staff and capabilities, elaborate into line and staff positions, and ensure a return on investment.[47] Some organizations diversify their product markets as a way of ensuring continued growth, others search for new products and growth opportunities.[48] Organizations often emphasize decentralization of decision making and team effort as ways of adapting[49]; alternatively, they may elaborate formal systems by institutionalizing adaptation systems.[50] If a mature organization fails to adapt, decline may result.[51]

The politics and power associated with each stage of development is likely to differ.[52] The early stage (entrepreneur or existence) is characterized by the entrepreneur's exercise of power to shape the organization in his or her image. He or she does this by making or controlling all decisions and creating meaning in the firm. Power in the later stages (formalization, collectivity, success, take-off, or resource maturity) involves developing policies and procedures that support the managers' self-interests and maintain their power. Acquiring political support for managerial decisions becomes increasingly important at this point.[53] In the decline or redevelopment stages, managers compete for scarce resources to maintain a stake in the organization.

Decline

Rather than growing and stabilizing, some organizations experience decline. Such organizations "fail to anticipate, recognize, avoid, neutralize, or adapt to external or internal pressures that threaten the organization's long-term survival."[54]

A declining organization generally passes through a series of stages too.[55] First, it is blind to early signs of its decline, which good information could halt. Next, management recognizes the need to change but takes no action; prompt action at this stage would stem the decline. In the third stage, the organization takes action but selects an inappropriate one; correct action here, determined by the particular situation, would reverse the decline. In the fourth stage, the organization reaches the point of crisis and faces its last chance for reversing the decline. In some cases an effective reorganization, often after declaring legal bankruptcy, can facilitate this reversal. If the organization reaches the fifth and final stage, it is forced to dissolve. The speed of its dissolution depends on how forgiving an environment it faces. Figure 12–2 shows organizational decline as a downward spiral.

Some organizations find that, rather than stabilizing at their present size or growing, they must reduce their work force as a way of responding to environmental or technological changes. IBM, for example, encouraged workers to take early retirement in response to competitive pressures, as a way of reducing salary costs. Declining economic conditions or shifts in demand for a product or service may mandate downsizing. Downsizing can also result from increasing automation if it reduces the total number of employees necessary to do the same job as previously. Restructuring to increase efficiencies or economies of scale often occurs at the same time.

In the initial crisis stage, management centralizes decision making temporarily and simplifies the organization structure. But to ensure that the best employees stay with the organization, management must share decision making and control. Thus the organization moves from centralization in the short-term to decentralization in the longer run.[56] In fact, as part of the decline, top management often witnesses a strong work effort by employees, due to ongoing role expectations, a lingering hope of saving the company, the availability of more motivating tasks, and the need to make positive impressions on future employers.[57]

Implications for Organizational Design

Diagnosing an organization's position in its life cycle should provide managers with additional data to use in designing an effective structure. They can also focus on finding solutions to the dominant problems associated with each stage of growth.[58] Young organizations require structures that can accommodate innovation and respond to uncertainty. As an organization moves into the collective or success stage, some formal procedures and policies can be intro-

Figure 12–2 ORGANIZATIONAL DECLINE AS A DOWNWARD SPIRAL

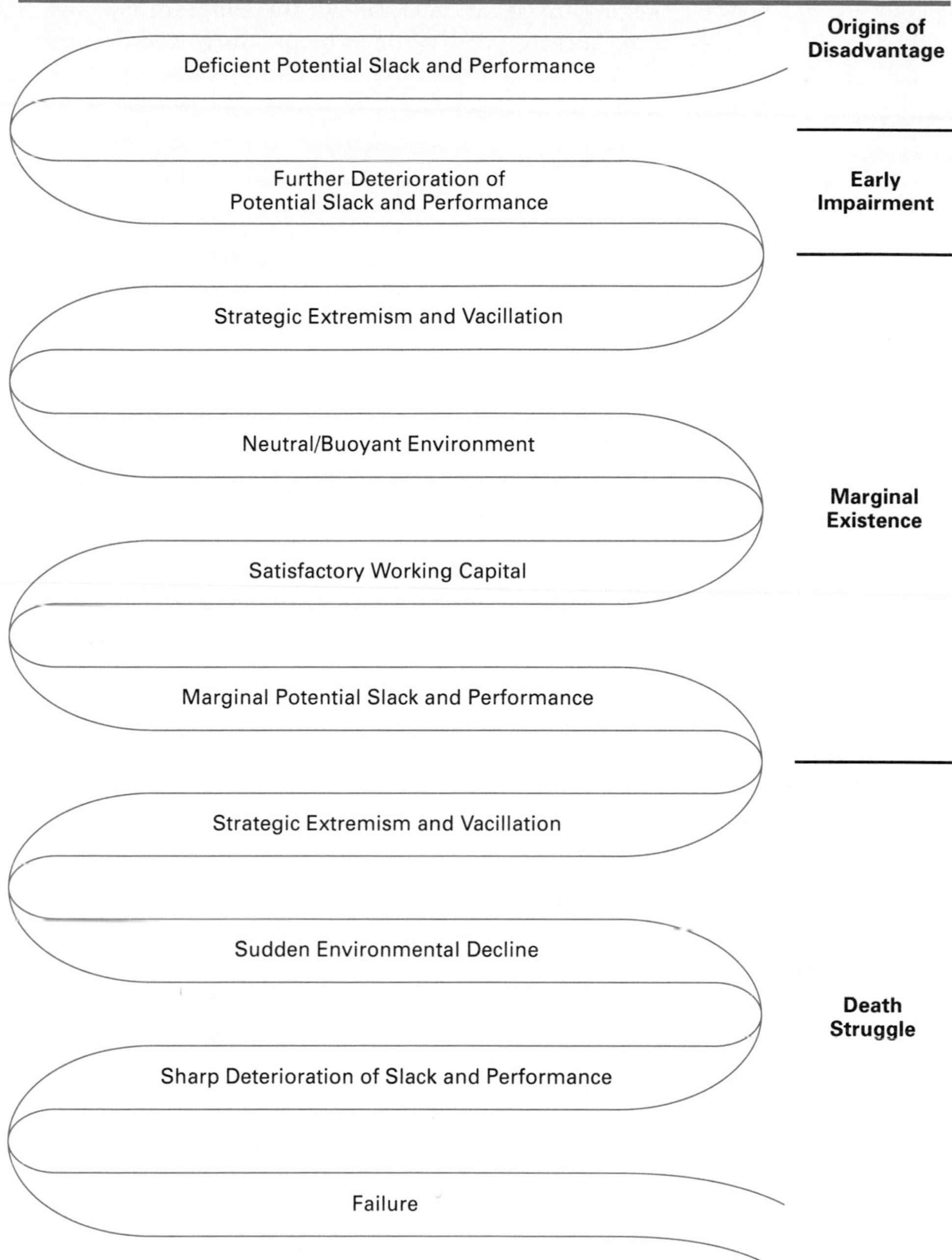

Reprinted with permission from Large corporate failures as downward spirals, by D.C. Hambrick and R.A. D'Aveni, published in *Administrative Science Quarterly* 33 (1) by permission of *Administrative Science Quarterly*.

duced, but overall the organization likely has relatively informal communication and structure. As an organization formalizes, top management typically introduces formal planning, evaluation, and reward systems. Functional structures with centralized decision making often fit with the control, specialization of tasks, and authority required at this stage. Such mechanistic structures facilitate stability in an organization. Ultimate survival, however, may require an organization to demonstrate adaptability and flexibility. More organic structures typically allow the decentralized decision making and team action that facilitate organizational effectiveness at this stage.

REDESIGNING THE ORGANIZATION

When an organization does not function effectively due to a misfit between these contingencies and its structure, the prescription for change should specify organizational redesign. In particular, organizational redesign is likely to improve such problems as failure to innovate, low productivity, redundant work efforts, ineffective communication, extensive red tape, failure to respond quickly enough to the environment, and inability to use the skills of workers effectively.

The process of redesigning an organization might look like the example shown in Figure 12–3. It always involves periodically and repeatedly fitting the pieces of the organizational chart together in a new way. This rearrangement must follow an assessment of the nature of the task, the people, and the existing organizational structure for compatibility and changeability. IBM made such a reassessment and decided to reorganize. The process of redesign must also take into account that change is more than a technical or analytical activity. The redesign must explicitly consider managers' and other employees' abilities to function effectively in the new structure, and deal with resistances they are likely to create (see Chapter 14).

Figure 12–3 AN ECLECTIC DESIGN PROCESS

Step 1. Preliminary Project Planning
- Determine client's hopes and goals for program.
- Establish program scope.
- Assess special needs of target population.
- Choose design model.
- Select top-down vs. bottom-up process.
- Determine appropriate depth of investigation.
- Consider resource/budget factors.

Step 2. Project Start-up
- Create parallel organization/steering committee/task force.
- Present leadership with rationale for program.
- Establish program parameters.
- Establish program goals, phases, time frames.
- Agree on steering-group processes.
- Decide on outward and upward communication channels during project.

Step 3. Project Study/Analysis
- Review/update general organization diagnosis.
- Scan and collect data in line with design model.
- Determine alternative tasks and task processes.
- Test task processes against company mission and operative goals.
- Involve affected employees in review of work context and task processes.
- Project outcomes.
- Critique optimal design using design-model principles, standards, project goals, and organization experience.

Step 4. Implementation Planning
- Develop and test prototypes.
- Determine implementation process.
- Match task processes and people.
- Create support systems.

Step 5. Implementation
- Foster climate conducive to change.
- Form work groups.
- Begin team building/training/management development.
- Institutionalize changes.

Step 6. Implementation Monitoring
- Hold status-review meetings, fine-tune design.
- Conduct independent program evaluation.
- Establish ongoing organization learning mechanism.

Reprinted by permission of publisher, from M.W. Stebbins and A.B. Shani, Organization design: Beyond the "Mafia" model, *Organizational Dynamics* 17(3) © 1989. American Management Association, New York.

Such an assessment should address a series of questions. What contingencies have changed? How should the organization's design respond to the changes? Do dysfunctions exist in the present structure? What are the dysfunctions? How can they be corrected? What impact will the changes have on other aspects of organizational functioning, such as motivation, communication, leadership, group dynamics, and individual development? IBM's top management decided that increased competitive pressures and a dynamic environment called for increased efficiencies. They restructured the organization to allow faster product development and identification of market niches.

SUMMARY

The redesign of organizations offers an additional framework for understanding organizational functioning and a different type of prescription for the many organizational problems discussed earlier. As either a complement or an alternative to interpersonal prescriptions, structural changes can profoundly affect organizational functioning.

In this chapter, we examined the influence of an array of contingencies on organizational structure, summarized in Table 12–8. We examined the significance of the environment, technology, goals, strategy, organizational demographics, and organizational life cycle on organizational structure and design. Using the case of IBM, we considered the implications of these contingencies for their restructuring.

Table 12–8 CONTINGENCIES AFFECTING ORGANIZATIONAL DESIGN

Contingency	Impact on Structure
Goals	Extent of specialization
Strategy	Organic vs. mechanistic structure
Environment	
complexity	Simple vs. bureaucratized structure
change	Organic vs. mechanistic structure
hostility	Centralization vs. decentralization
uncertainty	Nature of information-processing mechanisms
Technology	
regulation	Organic vs. mechanistic structure
sophistication	Extent of support staff development
Work Force	Extent of specialization
professionalism	
expertise	
group membership	
values	
Size	Simple vs. elaborated structures
Age	Simple vs. elaborated structures

Figure 12–4 DIAGNOSTIC QUESTIONS FOR REDESIGNING ORGANIZATIONS

- Are job groups relatively homogeneous and meaningful?
- Are unit groupings of manageable size?
- Is there sufficient coordination among the groupings?
- Have groupings considered the impact of the organization's environment?
- How complex is the environment—is decision making sufficiently decentralized?
- How unpredictable is the environment—is the structure sufficiently organic, and are the information-processing mechanisms sufficient?
- How hostile is the environment—is the structure temporarily centralized?
- Have groupings considered the impact of the organization's technology?
- How regulated is the technology—is the structure sufficiently organic?
- How sophisticated is the technology—is there sufficient support staff?
- Is the technology sufficiently buffered from the environment?
- Have groupings been designed to accomplish the organization's goals—is the division of labor sufficiently specialized?
- Are there linkages among groups that might have different goals?
- Have groupings been designed to meet the needs and abilities of the work force—is the structure sufficiently specialized to respond to differences in employee professionalism? expertise? group membership? values?
- Does the structure make sense for the organization's size—is the structure sufficiently elaborated?
- Does the structure make sense for the organization's age? How old is the organization—is the structure sufficiently elaborated?
- Does the structure make sense for the organization's stage of development?
- Do organizations at the entrepreneurial, collective, and elaborated stages have relatively organic designs?
- Do organizations at the formalization stage have more mechanistic structures?

Organizational design must include a regular, systematic diagnosis of current organizational structure, the contingencies affecting it, and the fit between the structure and these contingencies. Figure 12–4 is a set of diagnostic questions for redesigning organizations.

READING

Reading 12–1: NETWORK ORGANIZATIONS: NEW CONCEPTS FOR NEW FORMS

Raymond E. Miles and Charles C. Snow

These are turbulent times in the world of organizations. Following a decade of declining productivity and failed organizations, many U.S. companies in the eighties have been forced to rethink their competitive approaches. Rapid technological change, as well as shifting patterns of international trade and competition, have put intense strain on these organizations' ability to keep pace with a set of new and often unpredictable competitors. One prominent executive, describing the current business landscape, says, "Not only is it a competitive jungle out there, new beasts are roaming around that we can't even identify."

Two major outcomes of the search for new competitive approaches are already apparent:

- First, the search is producing a new organizational form—a unique combination of strategy, structure, and management processes that we refer to as the *dynamic network*. The new form is both a cause and a result of today's competitive environment: The same "competitive beast" that some companies do not understand has been the solution to other companies' competitive difficulties.
- Second, as is always the case, the new organizational form is forcing the development of new concepts and language to explain its features and functions and, in the process, is providing new insights into the workings of existing strategies and structures. In the future, many organizations will be designed using concepts such as vertical disaggregation, internal and external brokering, full-disclosure information systems, and market substitutes for administrative mechanisms.

In the following sections, we describe these new concepts and the dynamic network forms. We then examine their implications for management practice, organizational redesign, and government policy in trade and industry issues.

BUILDING BLOCKS OF CURRENT THEORY: STRATEGIC CHOICE AND FIT

Based on research conducted during the late sixties and seventies, there is now widespread agreement that most industries can contemporaneously support several different competitive strategies. Sociologists, for example, have described "generalist" organizations that are able to survive in a variety of environments alongside "specialist" organizations that thrive only in narrower segments or niches.[1] Economists have shown that in a given industry some firms compete primarily on the basis of cost leadership, some differentiate their product or service in the eyes of consumers, and others simply focus on a particular market segment.[2]

The most common competitive strategies, sometimes referred to as generic strategies, have been labeled Prospectors, Defenders, and Analyzers.[3] Prospectors are "first-to-the-market" with a new product or service and differentiate themselves from their competitors by using their ability to develop innovative technologies and products. Alternatively, Defenders offer a limited, stable product line and compete primarily on the basis of value and/or cost. Analyzers pursue a "second-in" strategy whereby they imitate and improve upon the product offerings of their competitors. Thus, they are frequently able to sell widely because of their ability to rationalize other firms' product designs and methods of production.

The Prospector-Defender-Analyzer typology, besides indicating overall strategic orientation, also specifies the major organizational and managerial features needed to support these competitive strategies. Defenders, for example, rely heavily on the functional organization structure developed around the turn of the century and its accompanying managerial characteristics of centralized decision making and control, vertical communications and integration, and high degrees of technical specialization.[4] Prospectors, on the other hand, use more flexible structures such as autonomous workgroups or product divisions in which planning and control are highly decentralized. These structures, pioneered in the twenties and thirties and refined in the fifties, facilitate market responsiveness but at the expense of overall specialization and efficiency. Finally, Analyzers often employ a "mixed" structure such as the matrix wherein project, program, or brand managers act as integrators between resource groups and program units. Matrix structures, which were widely adopted in the sixties, blend features of both the functional and divisional structures and thus are designed to be simultaneously efficient and flexible.[5]

Current theory in the area of strategy, structure, and process is founded largely on the twin concepts of strategic choice and fit. Managers make strategic choices based on their perceptions of the environment and of their organizations' capabilities. The success of these choices rests on how well competitive strategy matches environmental conditions and whether organization structure and management processes are properly fitted to strategy. Historically, strategy and structure have evolved together. Each advance in structural form was stimulated by the limitations of the previous form, and, because each new form built on the previous form, it helped to clarify the strengths and limitations of its predecessor. Also, each development in structure permitted new competitive strategies to be pursued. Saying all of this in different language, ways of doing business traditionally have been highly contingent on ways of organizing, and major competitive breakthroughs have been achieved by firms that invented, or were quick to apply, new forms of organization and management.[6]

BUILDING BLOCKS OF NEW THEORY: DYNAMIC NETWORKS AND INDUSTRY SYNERGY

New organizational forms arise to cope with new environmental conditions. However, no new means of organizing or managing arrives full-blown; usually it results from a variety of experimental actions taken by innovative companies. The competitive environment of the eighties is pushing many companies into this innovative mode, and the United States is on the verge of another breakthrough in organizational form. In order to describe this emerging form, illustrate its distinctive competence, and discuss the contributions it makes to the understanding of previous organizational forms, we must broaden the current theoretical framework summarized above to include new ways of looking at individual organizations and how they interact with each other in their respective industries.

Signs of the new organizational form—such as increased use of joint ventures, subcontracting and licensing activities occurring across international borders, and new business ventures spinning off of established companies—are already evident in several industries, so the realization of this new form simply awaits articulation and understanding. As noted, we have chosen to call this form the dynamic network to suggest that its major components can be assembled and reassembled in order to meet complex and changing competitive conditions.[7] Briefly, the characteristics of the dynamic network are as follows (see Figure 12–5):

- *Vertical Disaggregation*—Business functions such as product design and development, manufacturing, marketing, and distribution, typically conducted within a single organization, are performed by independent organizations within a network. Networks

Figure 12–5 A Dynamic Network

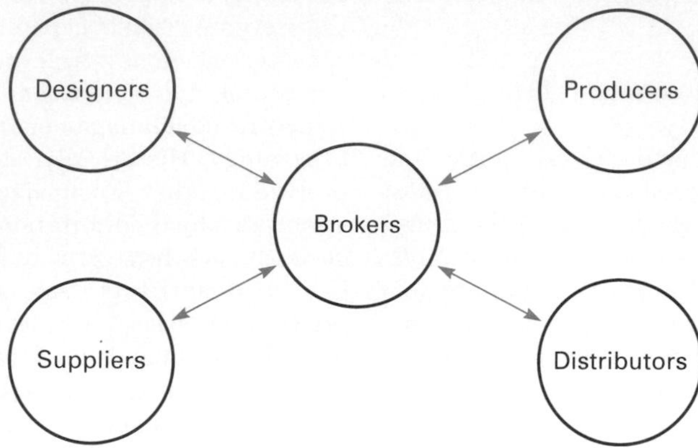

may be more or less complex and dynamic depending on competitive circumstances.

- *Brokers*—Because each function is not necessarily part of a single organization, business groups are assembled by or located through brokers. In some cases, a single broker plays a lead role and subcontracts for needed services. In other cases, linkages among equal partners are created by various brokers specializing in a particular service. In still others, one network component uses a broker to locate one or more other functions.
- *Market Mechanisms*—The major functions are held together in the main by market mechanisms rather than plans and controls. Contracts and payment for results are used more frequently than progress reports and personal supervision.
- *Full-Disclosure Information Systems*—Broad-access computerized information systems are used as substitutes for lengthy trust-building processes based on experience. Participants in the network agree on a general structure of payment for value added and then hook themselves together in a continuously updated information system so that contributions can be mutually and instantaneously verified.

In order to understand all of its ramifications, the dynamic network must be viewed simultaneously from the perspective of its individual components and from the network as a whole. For the individual firm (or component), the primary benefit of participation in the network is the opportunity to pursue its particular distinctive competence. A properly constructed network can display the technical specialization of the functional structure, the market responsiveness of the divisional structure, and the balanced orientation characteristic of the matrix. Therefore, each network component can be seen as complementing rather than competing with the other components. Complementarity permits the creation of elaborate networks designed to handle complex situations, such as international construction projects, which cannot be accomplished by a single organization. It also permits rapid adjustment to changing competitive conditions such as those found in many consumer goods industries (such as apparel or electronics).

Viewing the network as a whole, each firm's distinctive competence is not only enhanced by participation in the network, it is held in check by its fellow network members. That is, if a particular component performs its role poorly or somehow takes unfair advantage of another component, then it can be removed from the network (due to the independence that allows the network to reshape itself whenever necessary). However, removal of a component means that the initiating component and/or the responsible broker must find a replacement part or encourage one of the remaining components to perform the missing function. In either case, the network as a whole is likely to operate temporarily at undesirable levels. Thus, there is complementarity present in every well-conceived network that encourages each participant, singly and in combination, to perform capably and responsibly.

With this grasp of the means and motivation underlying the dynamic network form, it is possible to create a theoretical analog that enhances understanding of the role played by existing organizational forms within their own industries. We refer to this phenomenon as *industry synergy*. This concept comes from our belief that there is symmetry between the characteristics and operations of the dynamic network and the features and behavior of the firms within an industry (or major industry segment).

As noted earlier, most industries are able to support companies pursuing different competitive strategies.

Each strategy type both contributes to, and benefits from, the demand for goods and services in the industry, shaping its contribution around its own distinctive competence. Each firm, according to current theory, competes symbiotically with other firms in the industry for a share of the total market. However, when viewed from the industry perspective, each firm also has a synergistic role to play that might be described as *implicit interdependence* among competitors. For example, in order to maintain its long-run viability, the total industry must meet the dual objectives of innovation and strategies required by every healthy industry.[8] Using the language introduced earlier, every industry to some extent *requires* the presence of Prospectors, Defenders, and Analyzers. Prospectors generate the technological and product innovations that push the industry forward, Analyzers rationalize some of these innovations for marketability and ease of manufacture, and Defenders lower costs to the minimum in certain product areas to facilitate mass consumption. In a manner analogous to the complementarity of the network form, each of these strategy types requires the presence of the others in order to perform its own role to the fullest. In turn, the industry's long-run aggregate performance is better than it otherwise would be if any one of the generic competitive strategies was missing.

DYNAMIC SYNERGY

Although no definitive research can be cited as evidence, it appears from case studies and observation that the mix of strategic roles required for industry synergy changes as the industry evolves. Several different patterns can be ascertained. First, and perhaps most obviously, embryonic industries are heavily populated with firms pursuing the Prospector strategy. A current example is the bioengineering "industry," in which many relatively small firms are experimenting with different technologies and product-service configurations. Less obvious is the claim that such industries are likely to remain latent until firms begin playing Analyzer and Defender roles. In the early days of the automobile industry, growth was not especially dramatic as various companies experimented with steam, electric, and internal combustion technologies, as well as various distribution methods. Rapid growth occurred only after Henry Ford played a Defender role by installing an assembly-line for manufacturing a single type of car on a standardized basis and by forming a distribution network of franchise dealers that sold cars to the mass market. Similarly, one would predict that in today's bioengineering industry, growth gains will be greatest when some large established company acquires one or more small R&D firms and begins to produce standardized products in large volume.

A second pattern of strategic mix involves mature industries. Here one would expect fewer participants than in new industries and a much greater proportion of firms using the efficiency-oriented Defender strategy. However, in order to prevent the industry from heading into decline, a few firms must behave as Prospectors (probably in limited areas). An example is the major home appliance industry. Over the last 15 years, dramatic gains in market share have been made by White Consolidated Industries, a company that relies exclusively on the Defender approach. Although much of the industry appears to have the characteristics of a commodity business, with advanced automated production systems churning out standardized products on a cost-effective basis, portions of the industry deal with innovative products and technologies (e.g., the "smart" kitchen). In these innovative areas, the leadership role is played by companies such as General Electric. To maintain its health, a mature industry requires the successful performance of both kinds of strategic roles.

Finally, there are industries in transition, for which the desired mix of competitive strategies is more varied and changing. One example is the electronics industry (including computers and semiconductors). Neither a new nor a mature industry, electronics is in the growth stage, but its segments are growing at much different rates. Consequently, over the next several years, there is the potential for this industry to achieve great success if it develops a comprehensive mix of competitive strategies. However, there is also the possibility that this industry will not realize its potential if the strategic mix becomes too narrow.

Consider the following scenario. Hewlett-Packard, a company that has traditionally competed as a Prospector across most of the markets in which it operates recently has attempted to play an uncustomary role in its computer business. Within its Business Computers Group, Hewlett-Packard has tried to achieve the standardization, coordination, and integration most characteristic of the Analyzer, and it is having difficulty grafting this approach onto its present organization and management culture. If the approaches taken in the reorganization of its computer business are forced onto other HP businesses, then it is possible that across the entire company Hewlett-Packard will dilute its strength as *both* a Prospector and an Analyzer. Similarly, Intel, which has traditionally prided itself on its high-technology production competence, has recently begun to design, produce, and market business computer network systems. It, too, must be careful not to dilute its primary distinctive competence as it moves into new businesses requiring different technical and organizational abilities. If, as these examples suggest, certain companies do not maintain their primary distinctive competence, then the industry as a whole may not exhibit the comprehensive mix of competitive strategies needed to achieve long-term success.

In sum, a healthy industry's needs for innovation and efficiency are met through the complementary efforts of firms pursuing different strategies, each of which is based on a primary distinctive competence. By regularly being "first-to-the-market," Prospectors sustain technological innovation and are the principal contributors to the design of new products and services. By competing primarily as efficient producers, Defenders uphold quality levels while driving down the costs of standardized goods and services. The most important role played by Analyzers is that of transferring information throughout the industry, especially as it concerns the standardization of technology and product design. By sorting through the experiments conducted by Prospectors to determine those technologies, products, and services most amenable to rationalization, Analyzers establish a new plateau from which the next round of innovation can be launched. Subsequently, by developing successful approaches to mass production and marketing of new products, the Analyzer sets broad efficiency targets that Defenders try to surpass.

DIFFUSION OF THE DYNAMIC NETWORK FORM

Returning to the dynamic network shown in Figure 12–5 it can be argued that Prospectors essentially play the *designer* role within an industry, Analyzers play the *marketing/distribution* role (and also contribute as information brokers), and Defenders perform the *producer* role. By relating the components of the network form to the synergistic roles played by firms within an industry, it is possible to forecast where and how rapidly the network form may emerge.

Aspects of the new form can be identified even in capital-intensive industries where large investments, relatively indivisible production functions, and other factors make it difficult for companies to move toward the network structure. Often firms in these industries have a limited range of distinctive competence even though they may perform all of the activities associated with a given business. In the petroleum industry, for example, most of the major firms have sought vertical integration as a means of assuring an uninterrupted flow of operations, ranging from the acquisition of raw materials to the sale of consumer petroleum products. Yet, these companies are not all equally skilled at performing each step of the exploration (supply), refining (production), product development (design), and marketing/distribution process. Thus, even though vertical disaggregation may be feasible in this industry, it is unlikely to occur in the short run. Presumably, if vertical disaggregation were easier to implement, some of the major firms would divest their less central functions and focus only on those value-added activities most closely associated with their abilities. Our prediction is that Defender companies would choose to perform the producer role, Prospectors would select the designer role, and so on.

In labor-intensive industries, where vertical disaggregation is less costly and easier to administer, the network form is gaining in popularity much more rapidly. In fact, one of our studies uncovered the partial use of the network structure over twenty years ago.[9] During the sixties and seventies, developments in the college textbook publishing industry caused many of the major firms to reevaluate their publishing activities and to modify their organization structures. For example, virtually every publishing company got out of the printing and binding business and simply contracted for these services as needed. Also, several companies allowed key editors to form their own publishing firms which then became subsidiaries of the parent companies. These subsidiaries usually engaged in new publishing approaches, thereby developing an expertise that the parent company could tap into whenever appropriate. Lastly, some publishers drastically cut back their in-house operations in art, graphics, and design, choosing instead to subcontract this work to smaller, specialized groups that comprised a cottage industry around the major publishers. Thus, in the space of ten years or so, several of the major college textbook publishers in effect developed networks in which portions of the producer and designer roles were moved out of the original companies into smaller specialty firms. The major companies simply retained those functions that were closest to their traditional distinctive competence (such as McGraw-Hill in product development and Prentice-Hall in sales).

As the United States continues to become more of a service economy, the case of textbook publishing (and many other examples) may well suggest the pattern by which other labor-intensive industries move toward the dynamic network model. The rationale for "people" and service businesses to adopt this structure is clearcut. The dynamic network is a far more flexible structure than any of the previous forms, it can accommodate a vast amount of complexity while maximizing specialized competence, and it provides much more effective use of human resources that otherwise have to be accumulated, allocated, and maintained by a single organization. The practice of leasing entire workforces, already in use in construction, hotel management, and retail sales, is a network characteristic that will become even more prevalent in the future. As managers gain experience and confidence in these network designs and practices, the dynamic network form will spread accordingly.

IMPLICATIONS

A new organizational form is both a cause and a result of the changing nature of competition. As organizations formulate new strategies to meet new competitive conditions, they find that their structures and management systems also require modification. Simultaneously, as new organizational forms become better understood and more widely used, new competitive strategies are easier to implement. The dynamic network form, as indicated earlier, has appeared as a means of coping with the business environment of the seventies and eighties. Its arrival now has implications for the way managers view the future directions of their companies, for the approaches used to manage existing structures, and for the way in which public policy is used to restore competitive vigor.

Strategists

Strategic planners have a growing literature to call upon as they formulate objectives and strategies for their companies. Frameworks are available to help strategists determine their companies' distinctive competence, generate strategic options, analyze competitors' behavior, and so on. However, all of these frameworks ignore or underemphasize the concept of industry synergy and the key industry roles defined by the network model. From these concepts, several recommendations for the strategic decision maker can be derived. First, the strategist must examine the industry's current mix of competitive strategies as a means of forecasting the industry's prospects for long-term viability. A healthy industry must at a minimum have firms with the ability to perform the designer and producer roles. Next, the strategist must try to anticipate how the industry's strategic mix might change over time. All firms are generally aware that as an industry matures, the mix of competitive strategies is likely to shift from a high proportion of Prospectors to a high proportion of Defenders. Therefore, the astute strategist can develop moves within this overall scenario that are not obvious at first glance. For example, it might be advantageous to become the first Defender in an embryonic industry. Or it might be desirable to be the last Prospector in a mature industry. Basically, the strategist can be prepared to offer "nonobvious" strategies by thinking in terms of strategic roles and synergies at the industry level. Finally, the strategist must be ready to show the organization how it can change directions in order to take advantage of new opportunities or counter competitive threats. The logic of the dynamic network model indicates that this flexibility can be achieved largely through vertical disaggregation. Thus, an organization may be able to obtain competitive advantage by performing only those activities closest to its distinctive competence, contracting with other components of a network for goods or services on an ad hoc basis, and perhaps serving as a broker in yet other areas. IBM used this approach in developing its personal computer (the PC jr.). Initially lagging behind its competitors, IBM quickly assembled a network of designers, suppliers, producers, and marketers to put together its first product offering. Later, after it had established itself in the market, IBM reintegrated portions of the network into its primary operating system.

Policymakers

The concepts of industry synergy and dynamic network can be used to examine aspects of international competition and their implications for public policy. The U.S. economy is becoming increasingly connected to world markets, so dynamic networks in many industries now operate across national boundaries. This fact complicates the recommendations made above to strategists. For example, in the case of a purely domestic industry, long-term viability rests on member firms playing a heterogeneous set of roles such as designer, producer, and marketer/distributor. In the case of an international industry, however, one or more of these roles may be best suited to foreign firms. Presently, some large U.S. industries have the bulk of their manufacturing and assembly operations located overseas. The domestic portion of the industry is quite homogeneous, with a few firms performing the designer role and the remainder performing the marketing/distribution role. In these situations, long-term industry health is an international concern, and individual firm strategists must take this into account as they try to anticipate the industry's strategic mix over time. Further, calls for a national industrial policy to revitalize declining industries will fail, according to the logic of the dynamic network model, if they implicitly rely on an improper role for American firms. The realities of international competition indicate that many American "producers" should rethink their industry role and attempt to find a more valuable location in an international network. Apparently, this is happening in the steel industry. Several American firms have achieved recent success by reorienting their plants toward customized products and applications instead of commodity products.[10] These companies cannot compete well in most commodity steel markets, so it is to their advantage to play a designer role in the industry and leave the producer role to foreign competitors.

Managers and Organization Designers

The final set of implications applies to managers, especially those in a position to redesign their organizations. Executives who perceive the network form as a competitive advantage for their companies now have an explicit model to guide their redesign efforts. On the other hand, some companies cannot or will not vertically disaggregate and completely adopt the new form. Nevertheless, these companies desire the benefits of the network approach. Managers of these companies need ideas for, and the means of, altering their existing organizations so as to simulate desirable features of the dynamic network.

In companies whose distinctive competence is best served by traditional organization structures, there may still be pressure to demonstrate more flexible, innovative behavior. The network model suggests that these companies can be more innovative by setting up special units focused on innovation in which brokers bring resources together and later transfer results to the larger operating system. A number of mechanisms for supplementing existing structures are available, including internal venturing or "intrapreneurship," external coventuring, idea markets, and innovator roles such as idea champions, sponsors, and orchestrators. Taken together, these structures, processes, and interpersonal roles comprise an innovating organization that operates parallel to the main system.[11] Developed and used in companies such as IBM, Texas Instruments, Minnesota Mining and Manufacturing, and others, these innovating mechanisms can be employed by more traditional firms to keep pace with developments in their industries. Some companies may choose to internally generate more ideas and innovations, while others may rely on external coventuring schemes to create needed innovations. In either case, advances made by the innovating system are integrated into the larger organization only after their utility has been clearly demonstrated.

CONCLUSIONS

Current "merger mania" notwithstanding, it seems likely that the eighties and nineties will be known as decades of largescale disaggregation and redeployment of resources in the United States and of a reshaping of strategic roles across the world economy. By the turn of the century, we expect U.S. firms to be playing producer roles primarily in high-technology goods and service industries (agriculture may be regarded as a high-tech industry). These industries are characterized by sophisticated products and delivery systems for which the United States has a worldwide competitive advantage. In more mature industries, especially those containing a large proportion of commodity products or services, we would expect U.S. firms to play primarily designer and distributor roles, with production limited to special-needs products and prototype designs to be licensed for production abroad. Of course, the United States will play a major marketer/distributor role in most industries throughout this period.

These shifting alignments will create both competitive challenges and opportunities for managers and policymakers. The greatest barrier to success will be outmoded views of what an "organization" must look like and how it must be managed. Future forms will all feature some of the properties of the dynamic network form, particularly heavy reliance on self-managed workgroups and a greater willingness to view organizational boundaries and membership as highly flexible. We anticipate, ultimately, that key business units—such as a design engineering group or prototype-production team—will be autonomous building blocks to be assembled, reassembled, and redeployed within and across organizational and national boundaries as product or service life cycles demand.

REFERENCES

1. Michael T. Hannan and John H. Freeman, "The Population Ecology of Organizations," *American Journal of Sociology,* vol. 82 (March 1977): 929–964; and Howard E. Aldrich, *Organizations and Environments* (Englewood Cliffs, NJ: Prentice-Hall, 1979).
2. Michael E. Porter, *Competitive Strategy* (New York, NY: Free Press, 1980).
3. Raymond E. Miles and Charles C. Snow, *Organizational Strategy, Structure, and Process* (New York, NY: McGraw-Hill, 1978).
4. Alfred D. Chandler, Jr., *Strategy and Structure* (New York, NY: Doubleday, 1962).
5. Stanley M. Davis and Paul R. Lawrence, *Matrix* (Reading, MA: Addison-Wesley, 1977).
6. Raymond E. Miles and Charles C. Snow, "Fit, Failure, and the Hall of Fame," *California Management Review,* Vol. XXVI (Spring 1984): 10–28.
7. Ibid.
8. Economists do not agree on a single definition of industry health. Classical equilibrium theory states that firms in a competitive industry should not make profits in excess of the normal bank rate of return. Another economic theory, however, says that excess profits are required for industry innovation. Yet another theory maintains that excess profits may be rightfully earned by firms that minimize buyers' search and information-processing costs (by consistently offering high-quality products, etc.). Our criteria of long-run industry health are taken from Paul R. Lawrence and Davis Dyer, *Renewing American Industry* (New York, NY: Free Press, 1983).
9. Miles and Snow, *Organizational Strategy, Structure, and Process,* op. cit., Chapter 10.
10. Joel D. Goldhar and Mariann Jelinek, "Plan for Economies of Scope," *Harvard Business Review,* Vol. 61 (November/December 1983): 141–148.
11. See Jay R. Galbraith, "Designing the Innovating

Organization," *Organizational Dynamics* (Winter 1982), pp. 5–25; and Gifford Pinchot, III, *Intrapreneuring* (New York, NY: Harper and Row, 1985).

DISCUSSION QUESTIONS

1. What significance does the Prospector-Defender-Analyzer typology have for organization structures?
2. What are the characteristics of the dynamic network form?
3. How does the mix of strategic roles change over time? What is the significance of these changes for organizational structures?
4. What implications does the dynamic network form have for managers' views of management, the future directions of their organizations, and public policy?

ACTIVITIES

Activity 12–1: LUXOR S.A. CASE

Step 1: Read the Luxor S.A. case.

FROM PROFESSIONAL TO MANAGERIAL LEADERSHIP

"It is always painful to make a decision like this, but for the company's sake, we have no choice; we must find a solution to this problem and find it now!" These words, spoken by Mr. Johnson, Direct Sales Department Director, referred to the difficult task of making a decision about George Helmer, Area Sales Manager.

It was April 20, 1988 and Mr. Johnson had asked the Personnel Director, the Group Marketing Director, and a few other colleagues of Luxor S.A. to meet with him to discuss this case in particular as well as the issue in general.

COMPANY BACKGROUND

Luxor S.A., with administrative headquarters and research laboratories located in Luxembourg, had been established in 1973. It had been one of the first companies to manufacture and sell computers to retailers, using a network of subsidiaries and agents in over 80 countries. The company was organized around some key functions such as R&D, Production, Finance, Human Resources, and Sales. (See Figure 12–6 for the Overall Organization Chart.)

Figure 12–6 LUXOR S.A. OVERALL ORGANIZATION CHART (1975)

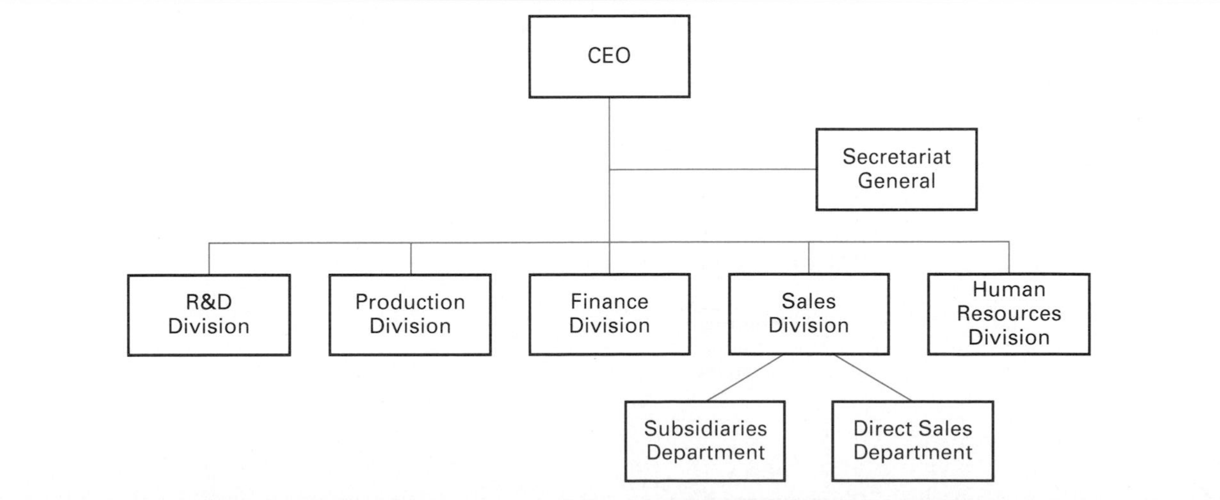

In this highly competitive business environment, growth depended on intensive, innovative research and development. Thus the company had always had a policy of investing a significant percentage of its revenue on modernizing its facilities, in research and development activities, and in expanding its worldwide network.

PROFILE OF A SALES PROFESSIONAL

George Helmer, 56 years old, had joined Luxor S.A. in 1975 as a sales representative in the District Sales Division of the company, i.e., the division in charge of all the countries where Luxor had no subsidiaries.

George had had the necessary characteristics to be an outstanding salesman—tenacity, persuasion and verbal skills, excellent contacts with clients. His sales technique was simple but highly efficient, "Meet the potential client, win his trust with informal conversation, let him talk about his business concerns, and then convince him you have the right product for him." Once the client had placed an order, George would keep in touch, become familiar with him through regular visits and small presents. This strategy, based on creating a friendship with the client, often would take a lot of George's time, but the results had been significant. Clients had become faithful and regular customers of the company and George had soon become one of the best salesmen in his sector, highly appreciated both by the clients and his superiors.

In 1980, he was promoted to Country Sales Manager, responsible for Holland. (See Figure 12–7 for the Direct Sales Division Organization Chart.) George had been pleased to accept this promotion, as it gave him the opportunity to enlarge his range of customers and improve his sales performance. And indeed, the Holland sector soon registered one of the best sales records in Europe.

Two years later in 1982, George Helmer was promoted again for good services to become Regional Sales Manager for the Western Europe region, in charge of the Benelux countries. George felt honored by this promotion, though sometimes he did miss his former position. Being responsible for three countries meant having to supervise a team of sales representatives and, therefore, fewer opportunities to be in direct contact with clients.

In 1985, George was made Area Sales Manager for Europe, when the position became available. He was then in charge of 12 countries, and George admitted that he had had some difficulties at first. He had sometimes felt snowed under with work but, all in all, considered that he had come through rather well.

He was perceived by his subordinates as an easy-going manager, as having a "laissez-faire" management style. Actually, his subordinates were often on their own, since George was still trying to work in the field visiting clients as much as possible. Concerned mainly

Figure 12–7 LUXOR S.A.—LUXEMBURG DIRECT SALES DEPARTMENT (1975)

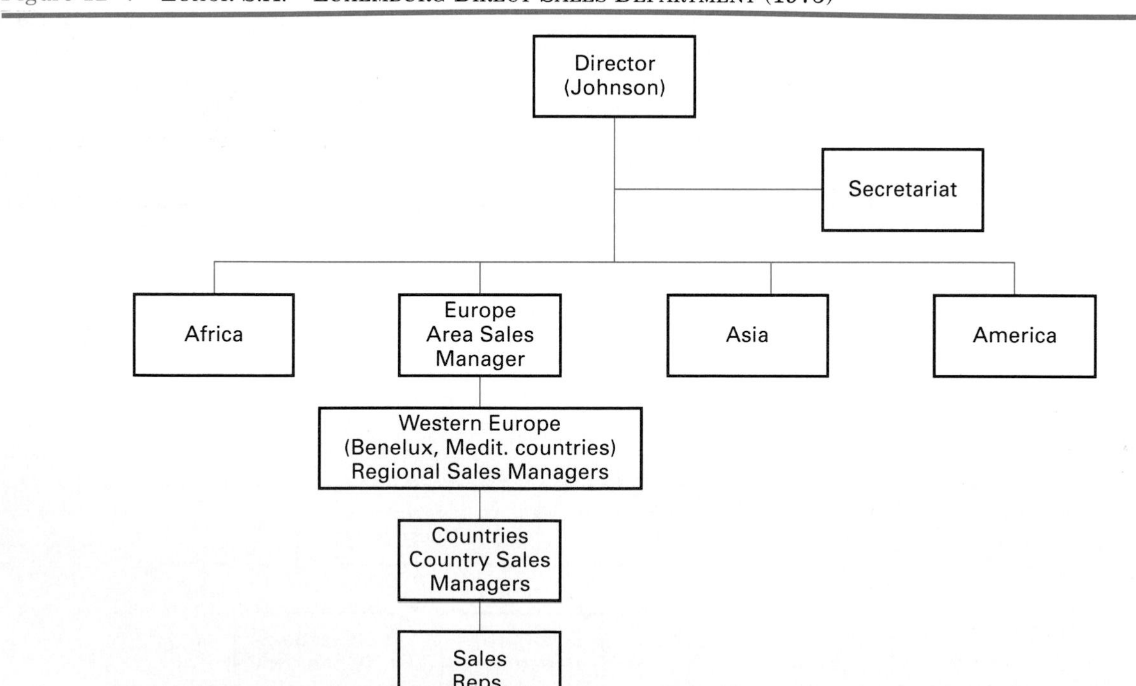

with clients and sales performance, he was pragmatic about operational matters. As long as sales records were good in his department, he considered that the other aspects of being a manager, i.e. regarding his team and the company, were minor.

On the whole, George was fully satisfied with his career development, especially as his education had been merely trade school and some crash courses in electronics and computer science. "I owe my position to hard work, loyalty and expertise in the sales field," he would often say to his children, proudly showing them the awards "for excellent sales performance" which he had received in 1979 and 1981.

Everything seemed to be going well until 1986. Then, George Helmer started to encounter some serious difficulties which Mr. Johnson felt were caused by the market and company changes made by Luxor S.A. at that time.

MARKET CHANGES

The company occupied a strong position in the international market and was justifiably proud of its development since the 1973 founding. However, during the late '70s, basic changes occurred in the international computer market which Luxor S.A. had to take into account. The major changes were:

- Competition had become tougher, especially from the U.S. and Japan which had attacked the European market in force.
- Computer retailers had also become more demanding regarding the product and its business potential. They were expecting original, highly professional customized products which would give them an edge in the market. They also wanted a comprehensive product line with a good range of software.
- Knowing the clients' markets and the latest concepts in marketing had become essential to establish successful business relations with clients and to penetrate new markets.

Increased market pressure and a more demanding clientele drastically changed the role of sales people; instead of selling ready-made products, they began working *with* the clients, identifying their specific product needs as well as advising them on appropriate market strategies. In other words, from purely sales people, they were becoming consultants, seeking solutions to specific problems relating to existing and future markets, providing clients with marketing support, i.e. doing research to develop the products required by the retailers' own customers (end users such as companies, schools, etc.). Salespeople had to have higher technical and scientific competence, financial and marketing knowledge, and negotiation skills. Handling clients and preparing projects had to be highly professional.

COMPANY CHANGES

In late 1986, the new CEO decided that Luxor S.A. needed a structural reorganization and policy revision to maintain a viable position in the global market. Keeping in mind the external changes in the business, the company intended to take the necessary steps to become an innovative, trend-setting, marketing-driven organization. Under the new philosophy, a company would need to work in close partnership with its retailers. Luxor S.A. also recruited a consultant, a management specialist to advise the CEO on reorganization and managerial issues. The new marketing orientation implied a different way of working, i.e.:

- Creating new functions (marketing)
- Redefining roles (managerial instead of professional)
- Introducing marketing people into the sales sector (combining both departments)
- Coordinating all the departments more efficiently (teamwork)
- Using new technology and equipment
- Using specialists in each position, i.e. MBAs, software specialists, etc. instead of generalists

At the beginning of 1987, the CEO sent the following memo along with the new decisions to all the company's executives:

> Luxor S.A. is a medium-sized company which, because of its geographical spread and the diversity of its markets, experiences all the logistic problems of a multinational. As a consequence, we must solve, with limited human resources and systems, complex problems due to ever increasing pressures from our environment. Clear and efficient structures, supported by good management of human resources, are the essential conditions for success and constitute the first priority. I rely on you all to help our Group with the progressive implementation of our new organization."

Business priorities were set on actions that would have a high impact on improving sales and financial results. In the first phase, the company especially wanted:

- to have better control of the Group's margin and pricing guidelines;
- to put all its efforts on the European and North American markets;
- to establish a detailed analysis of the customers' most important needs and Luxor's position vis-à-vis those needs;
- to prepare a detailed analysis of specific needs in each product segment;
- to design operating plans for all subsidiaries.

A new recruitment strategy was implemented and an international trainee program established to prepare new managers. Good professionals and managers were defined as follows:

- Professionals should be creative, relationship oriented, respected, have a strong personality and be known outside the company. They were also expected to have the latest technical expertise in hardware and software.
- Managers should have good planning capability, be able to lead a team, be fair and impartial, be problem-solvers, decision-makers and good coordinators.
- Luxor S.A. should encourage initiative, entrepreneurship and the delegation of responsibility.

THE NEW STRUCTURE

For the first time in the company's history, a Group Marketing structure was set up, combining four divisions: Research, Marketing Services, Product Management, and Sales. (See the New Overall Organization Chart in Figure 12–8 and the Group Marketing Division Organization Chart in Figure 12–9.) The new marketing policy was intended for direct sales as well as the subsidiaries. Thus, instead of functioning rather independently, sales became directly linked to the new Group Marketing structure.

In order to achieve better coordination amongst all the departments, National and International Project Handling procedures were established. Briefing sessions were held with the salesmen and retailers to identify their needs and prepare project checklists with all the necessary commercial and technical information details required by Product Management to handle a project more efficiently and professionally. They selected 11 clients as a sample to study and learn in more depth about their needs and their own clientele. With this reorganization, Luxor management switched from a 'family' and 'artisanal' orientation to a more sophisticated (high tech) professional management style. The new emphasis was on communication and coordination.

CAUGHT IN THE MIDDLE

The new strategy for the Direct Sales Division and the formerly neglected subsidiaries was to recruit bright young academics with a background in computers for key managerial positions. Traditional executives were not happy with this decision, preferring to hire people from apprenticeships or trade schools as the company had always done. But management continued this policy, convinced that the Direct Sales Division was providing a good preparation for other functions (marketing, subsidiaries, . . .) and was an ideal place to train newcomers and prepare them for playing key roles within the company.

All the executives of the Direct Sales Division were visited personally by the Group Marketing Director and asked to practice the new company strategy and structure. George Helmer, as Area Sales Manager of Europe, held a key position with regard to the function's responsibilities and tasks, e.g.:

- Organization of the department
- Planning
- Leadership and motivation of his team
- Preparation of sales budget
- Analysis of market potential

George, who had not been used to having so many different new tasks and responsibilities, felt a bit overloaded and bewildered. The sales planning and budget, which would have to be established on a much longer term, had to be submitted to Production, Marketing and Accounting before any action could take place. He had always found it easier just to do the work himself. He could not adjust to the new management approach which implied the staff's active participation in deci-

Figure 12–8 LUXOR S.A. NEW OVERALL ORGANIZATION CHART (1987)

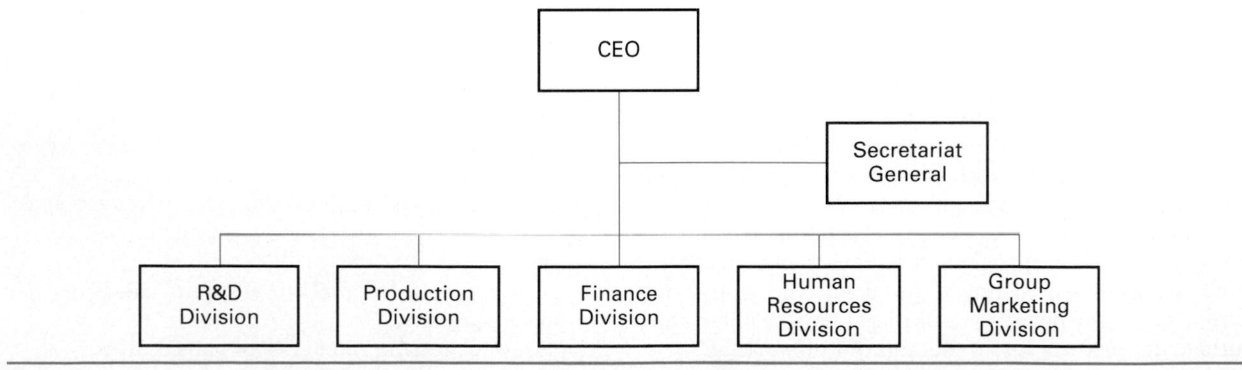

Figure 12–9 LUXOR S.A. GROUP MARKETING DIVISION ORGANIZATION CHART (1987)

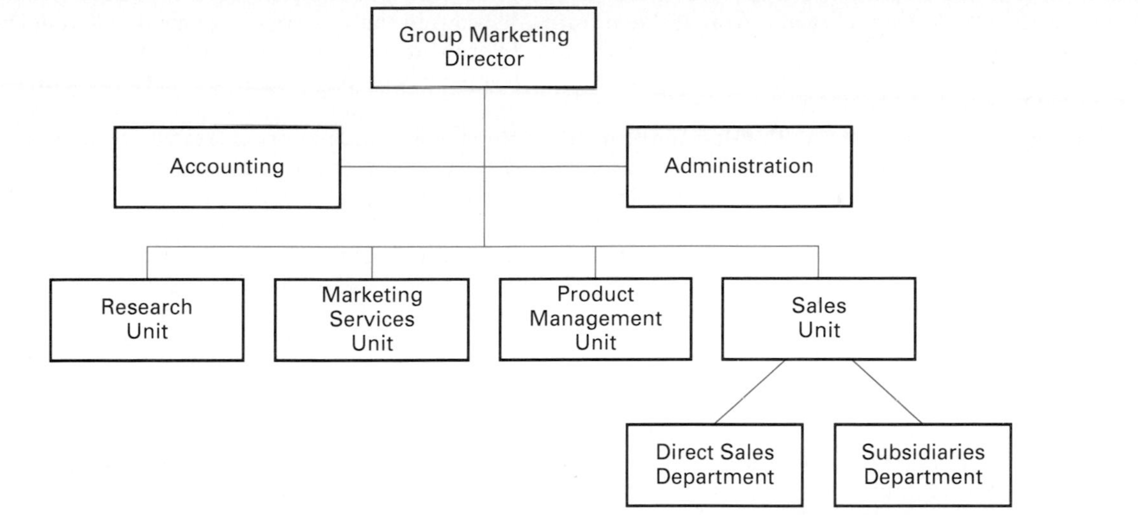

sion-making. "Motivation, delegation, entrepreneurship, communication", . . . were only buzzwords to him. He considered the old system to be most efficient, i.e. the manager makes the decisions and his subordinates implement them, and he felt it should so remain.

He had difficulty accepting the new marketing orientation. "My role has always been to sell products to the clients," he said, "clients are not markets. Markets do not concern salespeople. We have always done it well without market researchers, marketing analysis and the like. I don't see why the company tries to modify something that works well! Those sophisticated complications are not necessary."

Moreover, George Helmer now had highly qualified colleagues; they were bright, young and dynamic. He and they did not share many similar interests. Their language, attitudes and views of the work were also different from his. He did not really understand them and felt somewhat threatened by them. Almost immediately, the old executives and staff members in the department formed a sort of "club". Amongst this group, George was nearly the only one to believe that it was possible to collaborate with the new generation. Confident in his powers of persuasion, he intended to get on well with them, win their trust, and then give them his views on sales.

George had fairly positive results, until it came to discussing details. George was still describing his sales technique, his team, his department and its previous performances, whereas his young colleagues were talking about new approaches to sales, new computer technologies and software, market potentials, the Group's evolution and growth projections for the company.

While the newcomers were trying to carry George along with them in this new business world, his old colleagues were pulling him back to them. "You see!" they were telling him, "we don't share the views of these new recruits. They are nothing like the colleagues we had before. These young people are ambitious. They want to know about everything, to contribute and be involved in everything, even in business management issues and decisions. Our old colleagues were excellent salespeople, because sales were their only objective and preoccupation. We feel sure that they will soon be wanting us and the old system back, simply because the one important thing those technocrats don't have is experience! We are the ones who know what sales are about."

George, who did not want any conflict, decided to keep quiet, do his work and wait. He had always found that to be the best way to avoid making a blunder and running into trouble. One thing he was discovering was that the skills he had used as a salesman did not help him face his new responsibilities and he did not know how to cope with them.

George's passive behavior soon irritated his young subordinates and new colleagues; they reproached him for not being a decision-maker. The more they tried to carry him along, the more George withdrew inside himself. The atmosphere was becoming heavy and tensions increased. George was losing all credibility amongst his subordinates, who began to go directly to the Department Director, Mr. Johnson, each time there was an important issue to be discussed. "There's no use going to see Mr. Helmer," one of his young colleagues reported, "he won't make a decision. We don't receive any support from him."

Even his old colleagues and friends no longer came to tease him or ask for his personal advice as they used to do. George was feeling more and more isolated from the others.

ADAPTING OR REGRESSING

In October 1987, Mr. Johnson, the Division Director, invited George to his office to discuss his performance as a manager. He wondered why George was being so inactive; he was expecting George, as Area Sales Manager, to present proposals and decisions to change the atmosphere in his department. George said that he was reflecting on the problem and was trying to find a solution that would satisfy everybody.

So Mr. Johnson waited a few more weeks. When those decisions were still not received and George did not seem to be making any moves, Mr. Johnson began systematically discussing the business issues directly with the Regional and Country Sales Managers.

George felt rejected both by the hierarchy and by his subordinates. He was suffering but did not know how to handle it. He applied himself to keeping a friendly contact with his subordinates. Each time they came to present an idea or a decision, he showed interest in their work, encouraged them and told them he trusted their decisions. But deep inside, he was frustrated that the new colleagues were being given more importance than he was, and that he had lost his power and authority with his people. He felt that he deserved better after so many years of good and faithful service to the company.

The Country Sales Manager commented, "Although Mr. Helmer formally accepted the new organization, I think he is still refusing it, perhaps unconsciously, by behaving passively. He avoids meeting people and talking to anyone in the department, unless he is obliged to."

A few months later, George was still in a state of depression and began to "regress", as one of his colleagues put it. "Mr. Helmer is constantly talking about his 'glorious past', one of his subordinates reported, "he minimizes our capacities and criticizes the new marketing structure. He keeps giving us the details of his sales performance 10 years ago, telling us that his former colleagues were real sales experts, that we are inexperienced and still have to learn the job and prove ourselves as he did. As to the new marketing structure, he sees it as an obstacle, a useless burden on the system. For him, the client will always remain king, and he believes that all the other company departments should take their lead from and depend on the sales." In his work, George became inefficient, a matter of concern for his superiors. The Direct Sales Department needed efficiently performing people, especially in key managerial positions.

George's attitude towards the younger people and his glorification of the past were creating more and more tensions in the department. Some people could no longer tolerate it and either asked for a transfer or left the company. Rapid turnover amongst the administrative staff caused numerous administrative mistakes. George Helmer was unable to control what was happening in his department, so he retreated more and more into his ivory tower.

The situation had become so critical that management, concerned with the poor performance of this key department, again tried to discuss the matter with George and help him overcome his problems. Once again, the new structure and strategy and his own key managerial role in the new system were explained to him. George replied calmly, "I don't have any serious objections to the new marketing-oriented structure, but I want to see concrete evidence that it is really necessary, and that the business has improved since it was established."

In February 1988, Mr. Johnson proposed to transfer a Country Sales Manager from another regional department to help George with his job. George agreed to this idea.

Three months later, with the same problem still not solved, Mr. Johnson arranged a meeting with the Personnel Director, the Group Marketing Director and some other colleagues.

After his opening remark, Mr. Johnson stated, "I think you all know the situation; my first question is, 'What do we do about Mr. Helmer?' But, before you react to that question, I want to bring another matter of concern to your attention which is at least as important, if not more, than the first issue."

He then went on, "This is not the first time we have experienced such problems with our staff, and it is probably not the last case. There are other 'Helmers' around. What do we do about them? How can we solve this problem now? George's case is an important issue, but I believe that we should also consider the general problem of adapting to new functions and environments in the future. Keep in mind that the present sales representatives and managers could go through the same problems in 10 or 15 years from now. Things change rapidly in today's business world. The people who fit perfectly in the present environment and in their present functions will not necessarily fit in other future circumstances. If we do not design a program to prepare and help people progressively handle organization and market changes, we will inevitably experience other leadership shocks and conflicts. What we need is a management perspective that will help people change and adapt as circumstances demand. How do we do that? Where should we start?"

Step 2: Prepare the case for class discussion.

Step 3: Answer the following questions, individually, in small groups, or with the entire class, as directed by your instructor:

Description
1. Describe the 1975 organization of Luxor S.A.
2. Describe the reorganization of international operations.
3. Classify each organization using (a) base of departmentation, (b) means of coordination, and (c) information-processing capacity.

Diagnosis
4. What contingencies influence the reorganization?
5. What type of structure does each contingency call for?
6. How does this structure fit with the actual reorganization of Luxor S.A.?

Prescription
7. What changes are required now?

Action
8. How effective is the change process?

Step 4: Discussion. In small groups, with the entire class, or in written form, share your answers to the above questions. Then answer the following questions:

1. What symptoms suggest a problem exists at Luxor S.A.?
2. What problems exist in the case?
3. What theories and concepts help explain the problems?
4. How can the problems be corrected?
5. Are the actions likely to be effective?

Activity 12–2: WORDS-IN-SENTENCES COMPANY

Step 1: Form companies and assign workplaces. Each group should include between seven and twelve people and should consider itself a company. In this exercise you will form a "mini-organization" with several other people. You will be competing with other companies in your industry. The success of your company will depend on (a) your objectives, (b) planning, (c) organization structure, and (d) quality control. It is important, therefore, that you spend some time thinking about the best design for your organization.

Step 2: Read the directions below and ask your instructor about any points that need clarification.

DIRECTIONS

You are a small company that manufactures words and then packages them in meaningful English-language sentences. Market research has established that sentences of at least three words but not more than six words are in demand. Therefore, packaging, distribution, and sales should be set up for three- to six-word sentences.

The words-in-sentences industry is highly competitive; several new firms have recently entered what appears to be an expanding market. Since raw materials, technology, and pricing are all standard for the industry, your ability to compete depends on two factors: (1) volume and (2) quality.

GROUP TASK

Your group must design and participate in running a WIS company. You should design your organization to be as efficient as possible during each ten-minute production run. After the first production run, you will have an opportunity to reorganize your company if you want.

RAW MATERIALS

For each production run you will be given a "raw material word or phrase." The letters found in the word or phrase serve as the raw materials available to produce new words in sentences. For example, if the raw material word is "organization," you could produce the words and sentence: "Nat ran to a zoo."

PRODUCTION STANDARDS

There are several rules that have to be followed in producing "words-in-sentences." If these rules are not followed, your output will not meet production specifications and will not pass quality-control inspection.

1. The same letter may appear only as often in a manufactured word as it appears in the raw material word or phrase; for example, "organization" has two o's. Thus "zoo" is legitimate, but not "zoonosis." It has too many o's and s's.
2. Raw material letters can be used again in different manufactured words.
3. A manufactured word may be used only once in a sentence and in only one sentence during a production run; if a word—for example, "a"—is used once in a sentence, it is out of stock.
4. A new word may not be made by adding "s" to form the plural of an already used manufactured word.

5. A word is defined by its spelling, not its meaning.
6. Nonsense words or nonsense sentences are unacceptable.
7. All words must be in the English language.
8. Names and places are acceptable.
9. Slang is not acceptable.

MEASURING PERFORMANCE

The output of your WIS company is measured by the total number of acceptable words that are packaged in sentences. The sentences must be legible, listed on no more than two sheets of paper, and handed to the Quality Control Review Board at the completion of each production run.

DELIVERY

Delivery must be made to the Quality Control Review Board thirty seconds after the end of each production run.

QUALITY CONTROL

If any word in a sentence does not meet the standards set forth above, all the words in the sentence will be rejected. The Quality Control Review Board (composed of one member from each company) is the final arbiter of acceptability. In the event of a tie vote on the Review Board, a coin toss will determine the outcome.

Step 3: Design your organization using as many group members as you see fit to produce your words-in-sentences.

Step 4: Production Run 1. The group leader will hand each WIS company a sheet with a raw material word or phrase. When the instructor announces "Begin production," you are to manufacture as many words as possible and package them in sentences for delivery to the Quality Control Review Board. You will have ten minutes. When the instructor announces "Stop production," you will have thirty seconds to deliver your output to the Quality Control Review Board. Output received after thirty seconds does not meet the delivery schedule and will not be counted.

Step 5: While the output is being evaluated, you may reorganize for the second production run.

Step 6: Production Run 2.

Step 7: The results are presented.

Step 8: Discussion. In small groups, and then with the entire class, answer the following questions:

Description

1. Draw the organizational chart for your WIS company.

Diagnosis

2. Analyze its structure: describe (a) division of labor, (b) mechanisms of coordination, and (c) structural configurations.
3. Using your knowledge of organization design and the contingencies that influence it, evaluate your WIS company's structure.

Prescription

4. How could you have designed a more effective organizational structure?

The origin of this exercise is unknown.

Activity 12–3: FOODSPLUS CASE

Step 1: Read the FoodsPlus case.

Mr. Julius Mwanza, Managing Director of FoodsPlus, was considering a proposal to re-organize the company. FoodsPlus was an African holding company that managed investments in six operating companies. In its early history, it had been a centrally managed holding company. Three years ago FoodsPlus had decentralized much of the management responsibility and control to the operating companies in order to reduce the influence of headquarters executives and to develop the local managers in the operating companies.

Decentralization had served its purpose, but Mr. Mwanza now was not certain it still was appropriate. He felt that the operating companies were running away and that he no longer had sufficient control. Although his role now was more as a strategist, evaluator and coordinator, he did not seem to be getting the information he needed to accomplish these tasks.

There were no standardized operating reports coming to him but that bothered him less than the inter-company coordination situation. No one seemed to have information on, or to be in control of, the numerous inter-company transfers of raw materials, by-products or other transactions. All the operating companies wanted more capital, but he could not tell to where it should be allocated. Mr. Mwanza now wondered whether or not these companies were being managed effectively. Maybe it was time to re-centralize the whole corporation.

BACKGROUND

Prior to the creation of FoodsPlus, there had been one large company known as Premier Brands. Premier had been founded early in the colonial period by European and Indian businessmen to provide basic dietary foodstuffs: wheat and maize meal. Twenty years ago, Premier came to the financial aid of another company, Ace Bakeries Ltd., and shortly assumed control as majority owner. The acquisition was Premier's first major expansion. Several years later, because of the imminent retirement of some of the founders, controlling interest in Premier was sold to FoodsPlus which had been incorporated by local African businessmen.

FoodsPlus and Ace Bakeries both traded on the national stock exchange. However, effective majority control of all operating companies was held by FoodsPlus (see Figure 12–10). Each company was a separate legal entity with separate management teams, and separate (although with some overlap) boards of directors. The operating companies were all in the agro-processing and food industries.

The FoodsPlus group of companies faced numerous challenges inherent in African food and agro-processing industries. Many of the company's products were staple food items and subject to rigorous government price control laws. Price controls were established on the raw materials, often its by-products and the final product's selling price. These price control regulations affected the individual companies' costs and revenues, and were often cited by managers as the reasons for poor performance.

A continuing problem was shortages. Due to unpredictable weather, maize and wheat shortages occurred quite regularly. These commodities were controlled by the National Cereals Councils, which in turn sold them to processing companies. Many of FoodsPlus' products could become political in nature. When there were shortages, the politics became severe. Accusations of windfall profits and black marketing often were levelled at the companies. The government would step in with its own teams and closely supervise the allocation and distribution of cereals. One recent example highlights this problem. The government had purchased spoiled yellow maize. The maize contained a toxic fungus which if consumed could potentially harm humans. Very quickly, customers stopped buying maize as rumors circulated concerning its quality. One manager commented on the effect of shortages, "We lost good distributors. Some didn't come back to us." In times like these, Mr. Mwanza seemed to work continuously at managing relationships between FoodsPlus and organizations in its external environment—government, suppliers, and customers.

The Former System

Until recently FoodsPlus had expatriates in the top management positions and had operated with a centralized management system. FoodsPlus also had large investments in companies in neighboring countries but had lost most of these as a result of nationalization or during periods of social turmoil. Supervision of these companies across national borders had required the skills of an experienced executive group; and a centralized management system was needed to coordinate communication, co-operation, and resource sharing among the widely dispersed companies. The former Managing Director staffed the group office with other expatriates to oversee the operating companies. Mr. Mwanza commented:

> After independence most of the operating managers were new to their positions. Africans were finding their way into management jobs during the 1960s and 1970s, but because we lacked experience we required specialized assistance to perform effectively.

Figure 12–10 FoodsPlus Organization Chart

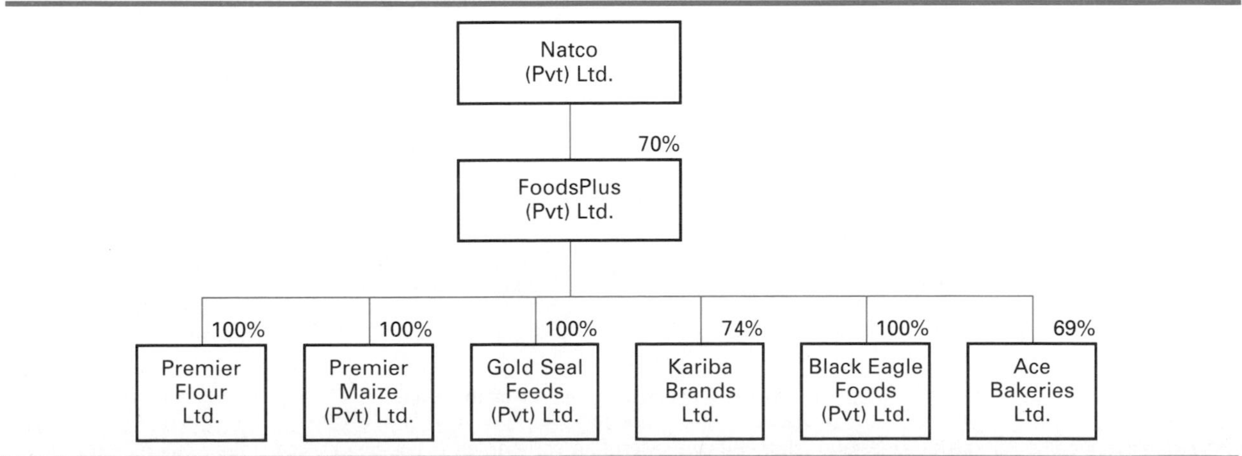

The experienced advisors provided guidance and advice.

The centralized structure is shown in Figure 12–11. It had been set up so that the Group Managing Director headed an office of 14 senior executives. These 14 executives had functional responsibility for the operating companies, but only in an advisory capacity. Direct line responsibility was between the Group Managing Director, and the various General Managers of the operating companies. The centralized structure was designed to render assistance services, and FoodsPlus executive advisors had no power to implement policies, only to offer advice. FoodsPlus operated with its subsidiaries under revolving 10 year management agreements, whereby it earned a management fee of ½% of gross sales to cover its overhead.

This system began to fall apart. The nationalization of assets in neighboring countries took away much of the responsibility and work from the expatriate advisors. Although they supposedly had no implementation power, some tried to impose their authority. The Group Managing Director attempted to police this behavior and to minimize its occurrence. However, some operating company General Managers felt their authority was usurped by the advisory group. On occasion, an advisor would tell his counterpart in an operating company what to do without ever telling the General Manager. Conflict was common. One of the original advisers still working with one of the operating companies recalled the old system:

We supervised the assets in four countries from headquarters. At times, it was frustrating. The turnover rate amongst government personnel in some of those countries was high—a Minister in the morning, a nobody after lunch. Also Group Advisors were expected to fill in for vacationing personnel at the subsidiary level in all the countries. There was frequent travel.

In theory, we were supposed to communicate with our counterpart executives in the operating companies through the respective General Manager. In practice, this was difficult. We had to talk directly since the talk was often too technically detailed for the General Manager to understand. I suppose that is how a communications problem started.

On routine technical and purchasing matters, our advice was usually taken. On controversial matters, that was another story. Controversy usually erupted over quality or pricing of by-products exchanged between the companies. In those days transfer prices were set at an agreed amount. Changes in these transfer prices were then related to the percentage change in the price of cereals. A 10% price increase in maize translated to a 10% increase in the maize by-product.

Under the centralized system, there was no formal performance evaluation system in place, at either the holding company or operating company level. Group Advisors and General Managers received their compensation increases from the Group Managing Director,

Figure 12–11 FOODSPLUS CENTRALIZED MANAGEMENT STRUCTURE, 1963–1983

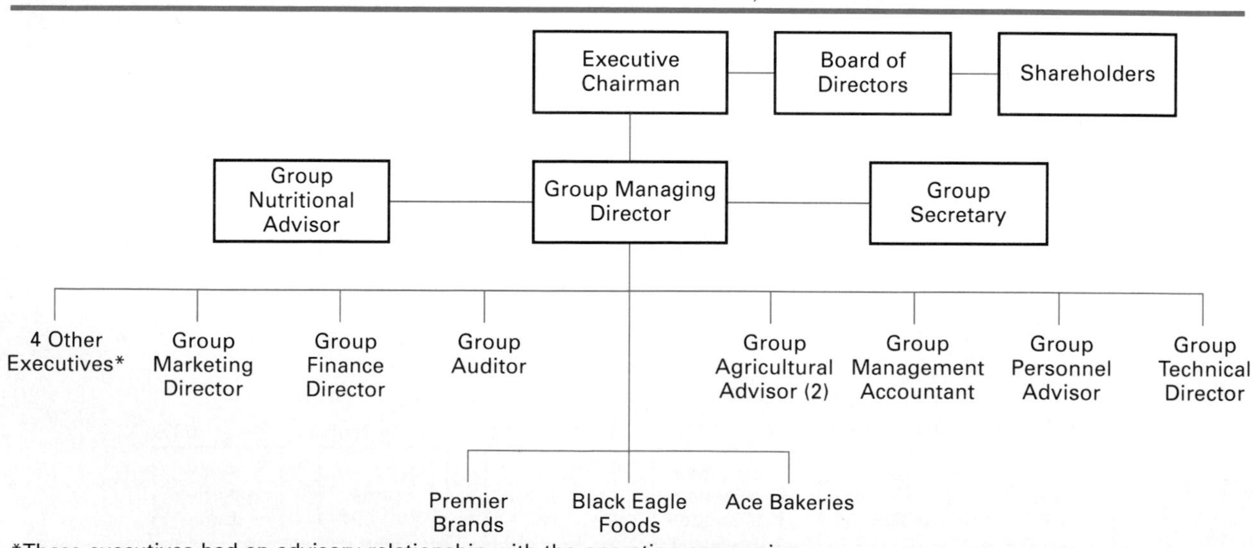

and General Managers awarded increases to executives and staff at the operating company level.

De-Centralization

Julius Mwanza began his career at Premier Brands and rose to the position of General Manager. He was the first Group Managing Director to be promoted to the holding company level from an operating company. Prior to his appointment, the group executives had been mostly expatriates. When Mr. Mwanza first took over, his impression was that there were roughly a dozen executives who did not have enough work and who occupied themselves criticizing the existing system in place and causing unnecessary conflict. Since he had been General Manager of Premier Brands, and had experienced the problem first hand, he felt strongly that the system had to be changed in order to improve organizational effectiveness.

The Structure

> Under the old system we were over-centralized: too many chiefs, and not enough tribesmen.
>
> (—operating company executive)

This feeling had been widely held at the operating company level. Julius Mwanza and the FoodsPlus Board decided that a change was necessary. They announced a policy of de-centralization, and disbanded the advisory group. All the advisory group executives were offered positions in the operating companies, and the practice of downward advice ended. They were promised that no one would lose their position or take a decrease in compensation as a result of the transition. Although some former group advisors earned more compensation than their respective General Managers, this situation was gradually corrected. All of the secretarial staff also were moved with their respective former group executive. The management agreements in place with the operating companies were nullified. All of the Boards of the subsidiaries had outside Directors removed, and the General Manager and Group Managing Director were installed together with an independent, outside Chairman. The operating companies were to be given independence and autonomy.

Prior to the de-centralization, Premier Brands had become very large and was profitable. However, management did not know which of the 4 business areas profits were coming from (flour, maize, animal feeds, or food products); and whose performance was responsible for the profit. The company had grown too large and people did not have the time to pay attention to detailed operations. The solution was to split the company into 4 separate entities: Premier Flour, Premier Maize, Gold Seal Feeds (animal feeds), and Kariba Brands (consumer foodstuffs). Senior department managers at Premier were chosen to take charge of the new companies. The idea was to give these managers more responsibility and the time to manage smaller pieces of the company. The General Managers would now have increased operating responsibility and decision-making would be located closer to the action in operations. One of these individuals spoke of the change:

> My mandate was to make my division a viable entity. If it made money, FoodsPlus would keep it. Otherwise, they might sell it off. I was told to go in there and if I made the company lose less money I would be doing a good job. If I got it to break-even, that would be really good. If it made money, that would be outstanding. I was given the privilege of picking the ten best people from Premier to join my company with me.

For budgets and investment decisions, new executive committees (in operations, personnel, finance and marketing) were formed, comprised of the functional executives from each of the companies. These committees were chaired by the Group Managing Director, and took over the functions formerly held by the advisory officers. Approval for capital decisions rested at the Board level of operating companies and then required ratification by the FoodsPlus Board. FoodsPlus' overhead was allocated approximately on the basis of company size and gross margins, not the amount of FoodsPlus time or effort spent with the company.

Each company was responsible for preparing its own budgets for approval by FoodsPlus. General Managers forecast revenue and expenses, and set their profit budgets which went to the company board for initial approval.

The new de-centralized organization was monitored through the following reporting systems:

1. All General Managers were required to submit a monthly written report to the Group Managing Director. This report presented an overall assessment on profitability, budget variances, and other company issues such as security. During the times of shortages, the General Managers reported once a week.
2. There was a monthly meeting of all General Managers with the Group Managing Director. The meeting discussed each of the subsidiaries and their current problems.
3. There was also a monthly meeting called the "finance and general purpose meeting". This was a meeting of the Group Managing Director and Group Financial Director with all of the senior executives of a subsidiary (General Manager, Production Manager, Finance Manager, Marketing Manager). These

meetings discussed management decisions specific to the subsidiary. Any capital asset that had to be bought, improved or demolished was discussed and decided upon and then referred to the Board of the subsidiary for approval.

Mr. Mwanza offered his views on the impact of change:

The change was necessary and possible at that point because the subsidiary General Managers were experienced enough to operate on their own and their management teams didn't need advisers.

However, 1983 was a very rough transitional year. The former group advisors still felt like group officers, and tried to behave the same way. They continued to take the major decisions to the Group Managing Director and 'go over the head' of their respective General Managers. Although there were no serious power struggles, I had to bridge a lot of meetings. Most of the 14 former group executives quit soon after the de-centralization was announced. As of now, only 4 former group executives remain within the organization, and all are at the operating company level. None have yet been promoted to the General Manager level.

On intra-company pricing, my role is to act as the arbitrator to make sure the boys are not killing each other. If there is a dispute over pricing, we will hold a special meeting.

One of the original group advisors, now an executive at one of the operating subsidiaries, talked about the new system:

When de-centralization occurred, I was asked what position and title I wanted. My salary remained the same, and my salary and benefits were still paid by FoodsPlus, although this amount is crosscharged to the subsidiary company. I am classified as executive level. This distinction includes General Managers, Financial Managers, and some Marketing Managers.

Now, in general terms, I report to the General Manager, since part of my function is to help the General Manager. I now have very limited contact with the Group Managing Director.

Performance Evaluation

There were two levels of management employees: the executive level and the graded management staff. Appraisals were only completed on a formal basis for the graded management staff in grades 4 (middle grade) through 8 (top grade). The appraisals were done by the Personnel Manager.

On the other hand, executive level employees (Production, Finance, Marketing, Personnel Managers) were responsible to the General Manager. One General Manager stated:

I cannot evaluate them. All I can do is 'devaluate' them. I can only say that a certain executive in the company is not doing his job. If I don't say anything, then they are assumed to be doing their job by the FoodsPlus Board.

Remuneration packages for executive level employees included a base salary, house, car, servants, security service, and substantial educational allowances for children.

Mr. Mwanza shared his perspective on performance evaluation in the new system:

At present, there is no system for assessing the General Managers at the subsidiary company level. Basically, to date we have been surviving. It's very unfair to grade executives on corporate performance when most of the companies were just arbitrarily spun off from Premier Brands. They have no control over their raw material prices from the Cereal Councils.

A senior executive in one of the companies talked about his perception of performance evaluation:

I am paid by FoodsPlus. The FoodsPlus Board determines my raises, but I have no idea how they are calculated. I don't even know that the increases have any relationship to performance. You just know if you are not performing—you'll be asked to leave.

The most rewarding thing I get is when the auditors have signed the accounts and I have shown a contribution to FoodsPlus and the Board says thanks to us for getting their books done on time and operating within budget.

One former group advisor had not noticed a change in performance evaluation with the new system. "I have no idea how performance is assessed. My budgets are always approved without change. My annual salary review is signed by Julius Mwanza. I guess that means I am doing good work."

THE OPERATING COMPANIES

A brief description of each of the operating subsidiary companies' activities follows.

Premier Flour

Premier was the country's largest wheat milling company and had a 74% market share. Although market demand was relatively stable, wheat supply was unstable because of unpredictable drought and pestilence problems. Since bread was one of the country's major staple foods, it was strictly price controlled. Decisions on flour pricing, quality and distribution were very sensitive. Premier had rebounded from recent losses in a year of drought, and exhibited minor liquidity problems. Premier sold 54% of its annual flour production to a sister company, Ace Bakeries, at a small discount from "market price"[1] for bulk purchases. It also sold its entire by-product supply of wheat bran to another sister company, Gold Seal Feeds.

Premier Maize

Premier Maize was newly created from the breakup of Premier Brands. Its primary business was production of another staple food—maize meal, and it held a 60% market share. The maize was milled to produce maize meal (83%), maize bran (7%) and maize germ (9%). Maize meal was price controlled. Its production and prices were scrutinized closely by politicians and the public, and this pressure had led to very small profit margins. Although profit margins were low, volumes were high. Premier Maize had just gone ten months without operating because of a drought and the resulting maize shortage, but still had managed to earn a profit. At full capacity, this company was expected to be very profitable. It sold maize bran to a sister company, Gold Seal Foods, at roughly 65% below its market price. Another by-product, maize germ, was sold to Black Eagle Foods, for extraction of refined cooking oil.

Gold Seal Feeds

Gold Seal, founded two years ago, was the largest animal feeds company in the country. Its final products were not price controlled. In addition, Gold Seal produced animal veterinary products and mineral supplements. Most of its raw materials were by-products from sister companies' processes. These by-products were not price controlled. It purchased 100% of its wheat bran from Premier Flour at prices 16–18% below market price, 100% of its maize bran from Premier Maize at prices 65% below market price, and 100% of its maize cake from Black Eagle Foods. Gold Seal had the greatest return on capital largely because it benefited most from low intra-group prices. It also had a low equity base (mostly loans from other companies with low payback terms). In the view of FoodsPlus management, Gold Seal had outstanding long term growth potential.

Kariba Brands

Kariba Brands started operations at the same time as Gold Seal, and was the smallest company in the group. It produced breakfast cereals, pet foods, animal feeds, sausage filler and other consumer food products. It also acted as distributor of Black Eagle oil, produced by its sister company. It purchased at a discount all of Ace Bakeries' stale bread for use in its animal feeds. It also was viewed as having very good potential for growth and increased profits.

Black Eagle Foods

Originally a joint venture with a European businessman, Black Eagle was one of the older companies in the group. It produced spaghetti and other pastas, and edible corn oil products. Corn oil products were especially sensitive to price control and increases required approval. A recent price increase application had taken 4 years to get approved. Black Eagle purchased 100% of its maize germ needs from Premier Maize at prices 45% of market price, and sold all of its maize cake to Gold Seal Feeds at prices 52% less than market price.

Ace Bakeries

Ace was a long established company, acquired by Premier in 1960. It was the country's largest bakery. Although its market share hovered around 50%, there had been a steady decline over the decade. Ace produced only one product—a 500 gram loaf of bread. It had very small margins, and was closely price controlled. Its performance was highly dependent on selling large volumes of bread and operating economies of scale. Ace bought 100% of its wheat requirement from Premier Flour at bulk discount rates, and sold all of its stale bread to Kariba at discounted rates. Ace's falling market share was a source of concern to the management of FoodsPlus.

Inter-Company Transfers

FoodsPlus operating companies sold numerous final products and by-products between themselves. A flow chart indicating the flow of products and by-products between subsidiary companies can be found in Figure 12–12, and a chart indicating which products were price controlled can be found in Table 12–9. A summary of each company's financial performance is listed in Table 12–10.

An important issue that FoodsPlus faced was intra-group pricing. The General Managers were responsible for setting the price of their by-products. The operating companies sold significant products and by-products amongst each other, at prices that ranged from market value (commercial prices) to as little as 35% of market value (preferential prices). Given that most sales were at preferential prices, it was difficult for FoodsPlus to accurately assess financial performance of the various group companies. Intra-group pricing methods were based on the two following methods:

1. The negotiation method normally produced a contract between two companies. Some of these contracts had been in place for long periods of time.

Figure 12–12 FOODSPLUS (PVT.) LTD. FLOW OF PRODUCTS AND BY-PRODUCTS

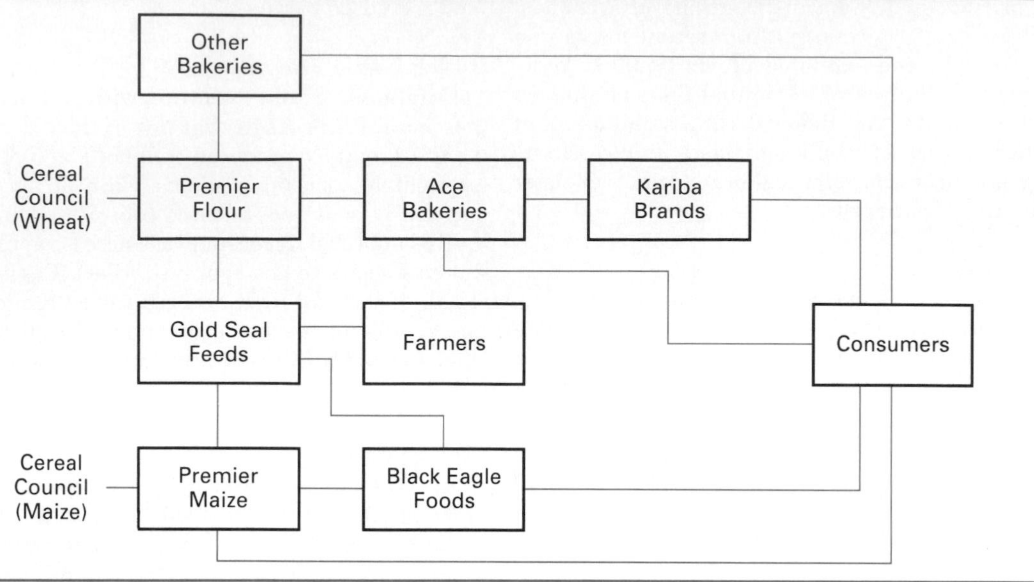

Table 12–9 FOODSPLUS SCOPE OF PRICE CONTROLS

	Price Controlled	Not Subject to Price Controls		
Company	Final Products	Final Products	By-Products Sold	By-Products Purchased
Premier Flour (PF)	Flour		Wheat bran to GSF	
Premier Maize (PM)	Maize meal		Maize bran to GSF Maize germ to BE	
Gold Seal Feeds (GSF)		Animal feeds Animal veterinary products Mineral supplements		Wheat bran from PF Maize bran from PM Maize cake from BE
Kariba Brands (KB)	Black Eagle corn oil (distribution)	Breakfast cereals Pet foods Animal feeds Sausage filler Other consumer food products		Stale bread from Ace
Black Eagle (BE)	Black Eagle corn oil	Spaghetti, pastas	Maize cake to GSF	Maize germ from PM
Ace Bakeries	Bread		Stale bread to KB	

Table 12–10 FOODSPLUS SUBSIDIARIES PERFORMANCE

	Return on Capital		Profits After Tax		Gross Margin	Current Ratio
	This Year	Year Ago	This Year	Year Ago	This Year	Year Ago
Premier Flour	11.53%	–1.24%*	25,372,440	(2,731,420)*	13.6%	0.73
Premier Maize	25.50%	N/A*	12,438,120	N/A*	8.9%	1.45
*Gold Seal Feeds***	71.28%	17.86%*	3,777,860	946,320*	13.1%	1.00
Kariba Brands	1.85%	–12.30%*	46,760	(309,840)*	16.6%	0.97
Black Eagle Foods	9.18%	11.90%	447,140	579,440	9.8%	1.32
Ace Bakeries	11.17%	45.30%	3,825,860	15,519,180	7.2%	1.00

*Figures are for seven month period only from the date of the breakup of Premier into the four separate entities.

**The capital invested in Gold Seal was low, and a long term loan, which was not being repaid, was regarded as quasi-equity. This inclusion would reduce the ROC figures.

Prices were below market prices and were now in need of revision. These supply contracts set forth prices, quantities, mode of transportation and costs of transportation. If agreement could not be achieved then the directive method had to be used.

2. The group directive method was used in cases where an operating company requested a raw material pricing assistance. For instance, in a case where Premier Flour applied for a price increase from FoodsPlus for by-products sold to Gold Seal Feeds, Gold Seal might be able to persuade FoodsPlus not to approve the increase.

A NEW ORGANIZATIONAL STRUCTURE?

In assessing the de-centralized system, Mr. Mwanza worried that the change had led to too much General Manager independence, and that maybe FoodsPlus was too removed from its investments. He was aware of the serious implications that yet another organizational change might have, but he wanted to come up with a structure that would operate smoothly, and yet still allow him to monitor the overall corporate performance on behalf of the FoodsPlus Board of Directors. He was having difficulty keeping track of all the company data that he was receiving and would probably need new staff to assist him. He wanted to improve communications and synergy across the various operating companies—in marketing, finance, production and planning. Mr. Mwanza did not want to return to the bygone days of advisors; instead, co-ordinators or administrators might be a better head office group. But, what would ensure that a repetition of the earlier dissatisfaction with a centralized system would not occur again?

Mr. Mwanza also wanted to formulate a policy on price control management, intra-group pricing, budgeting, capital investment and long-term planning. FoodsPlus had long desired to diversify into new business ventures, but lacked the organizational system to plan for them. A recent foray into real estate development had in Mr. Mwanza's words "taken a few years off my life". What industries should be investigated, and should the new business ventures be mergers, acquisitions, or new startups? Would it be better to shift emphasis out of price controlled foods, or was FoodsPlus management too specialized in food-related industries?

NOTE

[1]Market price was defined as the price that a FoodsPlus subsidiary would receive from another non-related company, for both final products and by-products.

Step 2: Prepare the case for class discussion.

Step 3: Answer the following questions, individually, in small groups, or with the entire class, as directed by your instructor:

Description

1. Describe the former, centralized structure of FoodsPlus.
2. Describe the current, decentralized structure.

Diagnosis

3. Describe the environment, technology, goals, strategy, work force, size, age, and life-cycle stage of the organization at each of these times.
4. What type of structure does each of these contingencies call for?
5. How well do the existing and proposed structures fit with the structure called for by the contingencies?

Prescription

6. What changes should be made in the current organization structure?

Action

7. What changes are likely to result from implementing these changes?

Step 4: Discussion. In small groups, with the entire class, or in written form, share your answers to the above questions. Then answer the following questions:

1. What symptoms suggest a problem exists at Foods-Plus?
2. What problems exist in the case?
3. What theories and concepts help explain the problems?
4. How can the problems be corrected?
5. Are the actions likely to be effective?

Activity 12–4: CITY OF BROOKSIDE REDESIGN

Step 1: Review the organization structure of the City of Brookside shown in Figure 12–13.

Step 2: Answer the following questions, individually, in small groups, or with the entire class:

Figure 12–13 CITY OF BROOKSIDE, EXISTING ORGANIZATION

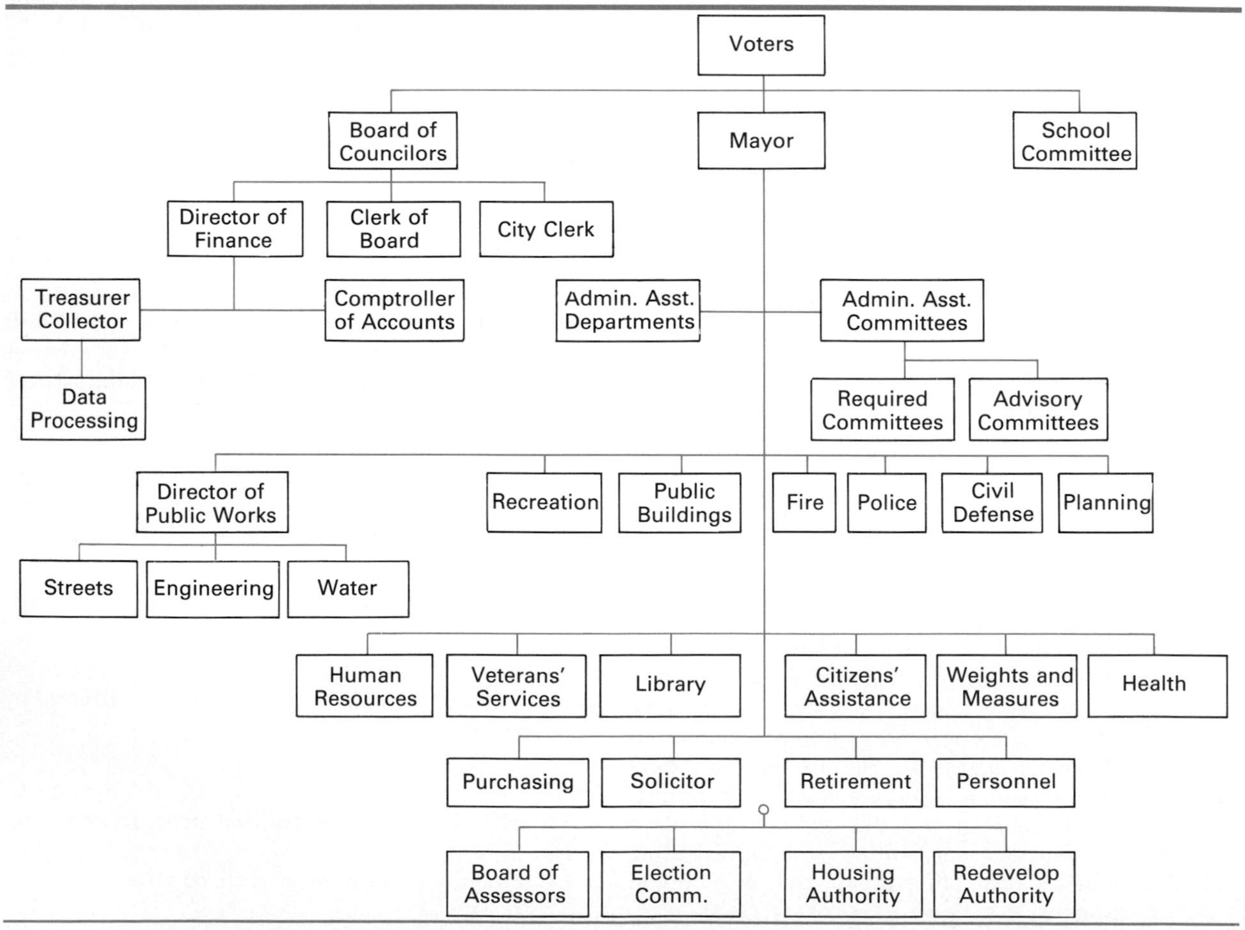

- Voters
  - Board of Councilors
    - Director of Finance
      - Treasurer Collector
        - Data Processing
      - Comptroller of Accounts
    - Clerk of Board
    - City Clerk
  - Mayor
    - Admin. Asst. Departments
    - Admin. Asst. Committees
      - Required Committees
      - Advisory Committees
    - Director of Public Works
      - Streets
      - Engineering
      - Water
    - Recreation
    - Public Buildings
    - Fire
    - Police
    - Civil Defense
    - Planning
    - Human Resources
    - Veterans' Services
    - Library
    - Citizens' Assistance
    - Weights and Measures
    - Health
    - Purchasing
    - Solicitor
    - Retirement
    - Personnel
    - Board of Assessors
    - Election Comm.
    - Housing Authority
    - Redevelop Authority
  - School Committee

Description

1. Describe the organization's structure: its division of labor and coordinating mechanisms.
2. What structural paradigms best describe the organization?

Diagnosis

3. Describe the nature of the following contingencies: (a) goals, (b) environment, (c) technology, (d) work force, (e) size, and (f) age.
4. How does the organization's structure fit with these contingencies?
5. Is the current design appropriate? effective?

Prescription

6. What changes should be made?

Activity 12–5: CENTURY SUPERMARKET REDESIGN

Step 1: Review the organizational structure of the regional operations and sales divisions of Century Supermarket shown in Figure 12–14.

Step 2: Answer the following questions, individually, in small groups, or with the entire class:

Description

1. Describe the organization's structure: its division of labor and coordinating mechanisms.
2. What structural paradigms best describe the organization?

Diagnosis

3. Describe the nature of the following contingencies: (a) goals, (b) strategy, (c) environment, (d) technology, (e) work force, (f) size, and (g) age.
4. How does the organization's structure fit with these contingencies?
5. Is the current design appropriate? effective?

Prescription

6. What changes should be made?

Activity 12–6: ORGANIZATIONAL LIFE CYCLES EXERCISE

Step 1: Choose two organizations.

Step 2: Collect written documents that trace the history of each organization. Interview organization members who are familiar with the development of the organization. Gather any additional data available about the organization's growth and development.

Step 3: In dyads or triads, share the data you have collected. Trace the stages in each organization's development. What issues did the organization face at each stage? What problems did the organization encounter in its development? Compare and contrast the development of the two organizations. How were they similar? different?

Step 4: Discussion. In small groups or with the entire class, identify the stages in development you have identified. Which stages do these organizations have in common? How did the development of these organizations differ? How do effective organizations differ from ineffective organizations in their development?

Activity 12–7: ORGANIZATION REDESIGN PROBLEM

Step 1: Choose an organization and become familiar with its structure and operation by reviewing organization documents, interviewing members, and observing operations.

Step 2: Describe the organization's operation.

Step 3: Diagnose the organization's structure. Consider division of labor, coordinating mechanisms, structural paradigms, and the contingencies that influence its structure. Evaluate its effectiveness.

Step 4: Prescribe a redesign of the organization based on your analysis in Step 2.

Figure 12–14 ORGANIZATIONAL CHART FOR THE REGIONAL OPERATIONS AND SALES DIVISIONS OF CENTURY SUPERMARKET

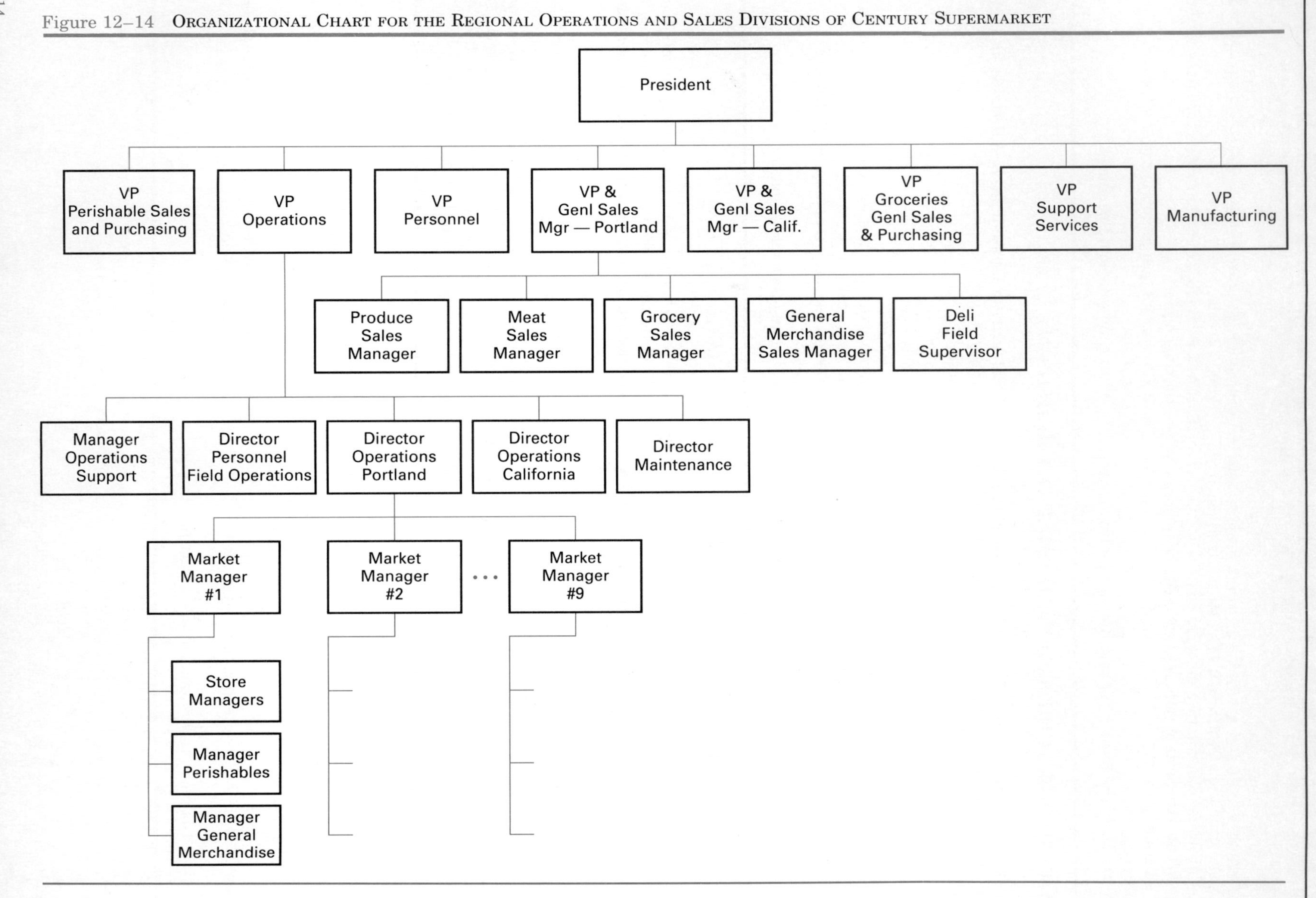

CONCLUDING COMMENTS

Organization design must include, first, a systematic diagnosis of the current organization structure. Next, managers or analysts must identify the nature of the contingencies that affect the structure. They must first specify the nature of the environment along the dimensions of complexity, change, and hostility. Second, they should consider the nature of technology—the extent to which it is regulated and sophisticated. Third, they should examine the nature of organizational goals and strategy. Fourth, they should investigate the nature of the organization's work force, its size, and its age. Finally, managers or analysts should trace the organization's growth and development, specifying its stage in its life cycle. Based on the nature of these contingencies, managers can improve the odds of having an effective structure through a scientific, well-informed approach.

The activities of this chapter provided practice in such diagnosis and prescription. They offered the opportunity to evaluate the current structure and redesign the structure of Luxor S.A., FoodsPlus, the City of Brookside, and Century Supermarket. They offered a chance to design a Words-in-Sentences-Company and to redesign another organization. The next chapter continues the discussion of organization structure by focusing on the design of jobs.

ENDNOTES

[1]Excerpted from M.W. Miller and P.B. Carroll, "IBM unveils a sweeping restructuring in bid to decentralize decision making." Reprinted by permission of *Wall Street Journal,* © Dow Jones & Company, Inc. 1988. All rights reserved worldwide.

[2]See G.G. Dess and D.W. Beard, Objective measurement of organizational environments, *Academy of Management Proceedings* (1982): 345–349; and D.D. Dess and D.W. Beard, Dimensions of organizational task environments, *Administrative Science Quarterly* 29 (1984): 52–73; also S.M. Shortell, The role of environment in a configurational theory of organizations, *Human Relations* 30 (1977): 275–302; and R.B. Duncan, Characteristics of organizational environments and perceived environmental uncertainty, *Administrative Science Quarterly* 17 (1972): 313–327. H. Mintzberg, *The Structuring of Organizations* (Englewood Cliffs, N.J.: Prentice-Hall, 1979); and H. Mintzberg, *Structure in Fives: Designing Effective Organizations* (Englewood Cliffs, N.J.: Prentice-Hall, 1983) specify five dimensions: complexity, diversity, change, hostility, and uncertainty.

[3]P.R. Lawrence and J.W. Lorsch, Differentiation and integration in complex organizations, *Administrative Science Quarterly* 12 (1967): 1–47.

[4]E. Quinn, Council OKs permit rule on some condo conversion, *The Boston Globe,* 19 December 1985.

[5]See also T. Burns and G.M. Stalker, *The Management of Innovation* (London: Tavistock, 1961); E. Harvey, Technology and the structure of organizations, *American Sociological Review* 33 (1968): 247–259.

[6]B.W. Keats and M.A. Hitt, A causal model of linkages among environmental dimensions, macro-organizational characteristics, and performance, *Academy of Management Journal* 31 (1988): 570–598.

[7]J.R. Galbraith, Organization design: An information-processing view, *Interfaces* 4 (1974): 28–36.

[8]C.S. Koberg, Resource scarcity, environmental uncertainty, and adaptive organizational behavior, *Academy of Management Journal* 30 (1987): 798–807.

[9]P.R. Lawrence and J.W Lorsch, *Organization and Environment* (Cambridge, Mass.: Harvard University Press, 1965), p. 11.

[10]P.R. Lawrence and J.W. Lorsch, New management job: The integrator, *Harvard Business Review* (November-December 1967).

[11]H. Aldrich and D. Herker, Boundary-spanning roles and organization structure, *Academy of Management Review* 2 (1977): 217–230.

[12]See the study by M. Yasai-Ardekani, Effects of environmental scarcity and munificence on the relationship of context to organizational structure, *Academy of Management Journal* 32 (1989): 131–156.

[13]Mintzberg, *op. cit.,* discusses these concepts in much greater detail.

[14]R.B. Duncan, Multiple decision-making structures in adapting to environmental uncertainty, *Human Relations* 26 (1973): 273–291; H.R. Johnson, Interactions between individual predispositions, environmental factors, and organizational design. In R.H. Kilmann, L.R. Pondy, and D.P. Slevin (eds.), *The Management of Organizational Design* vol. 2 (New York: North-Holland, 1976), pp. 31–58.

[15]J.R. Montanari, Managerial discretion: An expanded model of organization choices, *Academy of Management Review* 3 (1978): 231–241; W.A. Randolph and G.G. Dess, The congruence perspective of organization design: A conceptual model and multivariate research approach, *Academy of Management Review* 9 (1984): 114–127.

[16]J. Woodward, *Industrial Organizations: Theory and Practice* (London: Oxford University Press, 1965).

[17]F.M. Hull and P.D. Collins, High-technology batch production systems: Woodward's missing type, *Academy of Management Journal* 30 (1987): 786–797.

[18]J. Thompson, *Organizations in Action* (New York: McGraw-Hill, 1967).

[19]C. Perrow, A framework for comparative analysis of organizations, *American Sociological Review* 32 (April 1967): 196.

[20]Mintzberg, *Structuring of Organizations, op. cit.*

[21]J.D. Ford and J.W. Slocum Jr., Size, technology, environment, and the structure of organizations, *Academy of Management Review* 2 (1977): 561–575; L.W. Fry, Technology structure research: Three critical issues, *Academy of Management Journal* 25 (1982): 532–552.

[22]M. Jelinek, Technology, organizations, and contingency, *Academy of Management Review* 2 (1977): 17–26.

[23]J.R. Lincoln, M. Hanada, and K. McBride, Organizational structures in Japanese and United States manufacturing, *Administrative Science Quarterly* 31 (1986): 338–364.

[24]F. Kast, Organizational and individual objectives. In *Contemporary Management: Issues and Viewpoints,* ed. J.W. McGuire (Englewood Cliffs, N.J.: Prentice-Hall, 1974).

[25]W.J. Gore, *Administrative Decision Making* (New York: Wiley, 1964), pp. 184–185.

[26]R.M. Steers, *Organizational Effectiveness: A Behavioral View* (Santa Monica, Cal.: Goodyear, 1977), p. 21.

[27]R.M. Cyert and J.G. March, *A Behavioral Theory of the Firm* (Englewood Cliffs, N.J.: Prentice-Hall, 1963).

[28]H. Simon, *The New Science of Management Decision* (New York: Harper & Row, 1960).

[29]P.E. Connor, *Organizations: Theory and Design* (Chicago: Science Research Associates, 1980).

[30]R.E. Miles and C.C. Snow, *Organizational Strategy, Structure, and Process* (New York: McGraw-Hill, 1978).

[31]Connor, *op. cit.,* p. 227.

[32]Connor, *op. cit.,* p. 227.

[33]See J. Child, Organizational structure, environment, and performance: The role of strategic choice, *Sociology* 6 (1972): 1–22; D.S. Pugh, D.J. Hickson, C.R. Hinings, and C. Turner, The context of organizational structures, *Administrative Science Quarterly* 14 (1969): 91–114.

[34]D.J. Hickson, D.S. Pugh, and D. Pheysey, Operations technology and organization structure: An empirical reappraisal, *Administrative Science Quarterly* 14 (1969): 378–398.

[35]See, for example, D. Lavoie and S.A. Culbert, Stages in organization and development, *Human Relations* 31 (1978): 417–438; I. Adizes, Organizational passages: Diagnosing and treating life-cycle problems in organizations, *Organizational Dynamics* (Summer 1979): 3–24; L. Greiner, Evolution and revolution as organizations grow, *Harvard Business Review* (July-August 1972): 37–46.

[36]These steps parallel the four-stage business cycle: startup, growth, maturity, and decline.

[37]A.S. Van de Ven, Early planning, implementation, and performance in organizations. In J.R. Kimberly and R.H. Miles (eds.), *The Organizational Life Cycle* (San Francisco: Jossey-Bass, 1980), pp. 83–133.

[38]J.M. Bartunek and B.M. Betters-Reed, The stages of organizational creation, *Journal of Community Psychology* 15(3) (1987): 287–303.

[39]N.C. Churchill and V.L. Lewis, The five stages of small business growth, *Harvard Business Review* (May-June, 1983).

[40]Greiner, *op. cit.;* Adizes, *op. cit.*

[41]Churchill and Lewis, *op. cit.*

[42]R. Walton, Establishing and maintaining high commitment work systems. In Kimberly and Miles, *op. cit.,* pp. 208–291.

[43]J.R. Kimberly and R.E. Quinn, *Managing Organizational Transitions* (Homewood, Ill.: Irwin, 1984), p. 15.

[44]D. Miller and P. Friesen, Archetypes of organizational transition, *Administrative Science Quarterly* 25 (1980): 269–299; D. Miller and P. Friesen, The longitudinal analysis of organizations: A methodological perspective, *Management Science* 28 (1982): 1013–1034; E.H. Schein, The role of the founder in creating organizational culture, *Organizational Dynamics* 12 (1983): 1–12.

[45]Churchill and Lewis, *op. cit.*

[46]See G.L. Lippitt and W.H. Schmidt, Crisis in a developing organization, *Harvard Business Review* 45 (1967): 102–112; B.R. Scott, Stages of corporate development Part I, Case No. 9–371–294 (Boston: Intercollegiate Case Clearing House, 1971).

[47]Churchill and Lewis, *op. cit.*

[48]Scott, *op. cit.*

[49]Greiner, *op. cit.*

[50]D. Katz and R.L. Kahn, *The Social Psychology of Organizations* (New York: Wiley, 1978).

[51]See D.A. Whetten, Sources, responses, and effects of organizational decline. In Kimberly and Miles, *op. cit.,* pp. 342–372.

[52]B. Gray and S.S. Ariss, Politics and strategic change across organizational life cycles, *Academy of Management Review* 10 (1985): 707–723.

[53]K.G. Smith, T.R. Mitchell, and C.E. Summer, Top-level management priorities in different stages of the organization's life cycle, *Academy of Management Journal* 29 (1985): 799–820.

[54]W. Weitzel and E. Johnson, Decline in organizations: A literature integration and extension, *Administrative Science Quarterly* 34 (1989): 91–109.

[55]*Ibid.*

[56]S.P. Robbins, *Organization Theory: Structure, Design, and Applications* 2d ed. (Englewood Cliffs, N.J.: Prentice-Hall, 1987).

[57]R.I. Sutton, The process of organizational death: Disbanding and reconnecting, *Administrative Science Quarterly* 32 (1987): 542–569.

[58]See R.K. Kazanjian, Relation of dominant problems to stages of growth in technology-based new ventures, *Academy of Management Journal* 31 (1988): 257–279.

RECOMMENDED READINGS

Davis, S.M. *Future Perfect.* Reading, Mass.: Addison-Wesley, 1987.

Hanna, D.P. *Designing Organizations for High Performance.* Reading, Mass.: Addison-Wesley, 1988.

Kimberly, J.R., and Miles, R.H. (eds.) *The Organizational Life Cycle.* San Francisco: Jossey-Bass, 1980.

Kimberly, J.R., and Quinn, R.E. *Managing Organizational Transitions.* Homewood, Ill.: Irwin, 1984.

Meyer, M.W., and Zucker, L.G. *Permanently Failing Organizations.* San Francisco: Jossey-Bass, 1989.

Mintzberg, H. *Structure in Fives: Designing Effective Organizations.* Englewood Cliffs, N.J.: Prentice-Hall, 1983.

Morgan, G. *Creative Organization Theory: A Resourcebook.* Newbury Park, Cal.: Sage, 1989.

Pasmore, W.A. *Designing Effective Organizations: The Sociotechnical Systems Perspective.* New York: Wiley, 1988.

13

Reviewing Work Design and Encouraging Innovation

CHAPTER OUTLINE

LEARNING OBJECTIVES

After completing the reading and activities in Chapter 13, students will be able to

- discuss the impact of automation and computerization on work design;
- compare and contrast the major approaches to work design;
- redesign a job, first using work simplification and then a work enrichment approach;
- describe the varieties of sociotechnical redesign and their uses;
- discuss the purpose and effectiveness of quality-of-working-life programs and provide examples of them;
- discuss the process of innovation and its relationship to work redesign;
- offer strategies for increasing innovation in organizations;
- comment on the differences in work redesign between the United States and elsewhere; and
- indicate which work design approach would be most effective in a given situation.

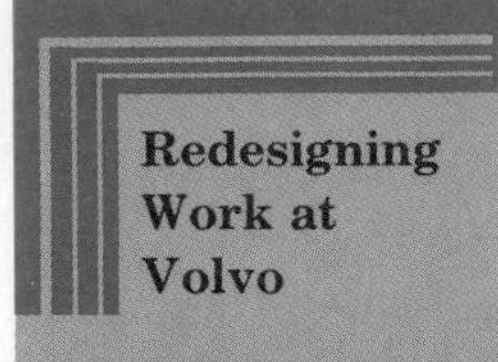

In a trial run, Roger Holtback, president of Volvo Car Corp., exchanged his usual Saville Row suit for coveralls and assembled a car all by himself at a new plant in Uddevalla, Sweden. Holtback managed to drive off in the finished Volvo 740, though it was by no means free of defects. "It started nicely, but it wouldn't have been delivered to a customer," Holtback says. "I felt like an apprentice." Still, this 1987 experiment reinforced Volvo's radical decision to mass-produce the midline 740 at Uddevalla without using assembly lines.

In full production since early this year, the plant employs teams of 7 to 10 hourly workers. Each team works in one area and assembles four cars per shift. Since members are trained to handle all assembly jobs, they work an average of three hours before repeating the same task. Uddevalla thus avoids the classic problems associated with work cycles of only one or two minutes on conventional assembly lines, where the mind-numbing routine leads to boredom, inattention, poor quality, and high absenteeism.

Human Concerns

Volvo's attempt to eliminate these problems and still operate efficiently is bringing worldwide attention to Uddevalla. Throngs of reporters, especially from Japan, were on hand when the plant recently opened its doors to visitors. It is stirring up interest in the U.S., where the United Auto Workers and American carmakers are searching for an assembly system that can compete in terms of productivity and quality with Japanese plants while making the work less onerous.

But Holtback insists that Uddevalla should not be viewed merely as an effort to make workers happy. "We're not doing this because we are nice guys," he says. "We are not doing this because we like experiments." Although Volvo refuses to release productivity figures, the company claims that Uddevalla already produces cars with fewer hours of labor and better quality than its three other Swedish plants.

It wasn't a lack of success in the car business that drove Volvo to design such a radically different system. Sales totaled $16.1 billion in 1988, a 50% increase since 1983. Last year, operating profits totaled $1.2 billion, and Volvo has no net debt. But it has a problem that haunts all Swedish manufacturers: The country's highly educated, well-trained labor force doesn't like to work in factories.

Volvo's Swedish plants suffer absenteeism of 20%, and almost one-third of its workers quit yearly. More pay does not motivate Swedes; taxes take up to 70% of any overtime pay. With unemployment at 1.6%, there is no lack of jobs. Says Per-Olov Bergstrom, a national bargainer for the Swedish Metal Workers' Union, "The main problem in the '90s simply will be to keep a work force."

So Volvo built the new, $220 million plant in Uddevalla, a North Sea port that once boasted a large shipbuilding industry. To bring jobs back to the area, the Swedish government aided Volvo with large tax write-offs. And the Metal Workers' Union, a staunch supporter of work reforms, cooperated with the company in planning the plant and training the work force.

Such labor–management cooperation is not unusual for Volvo. The company chairman and CEO, Pehr G. Gyllenhammar, put two union delegates on Volvo's board in 1971, before Swedish law required it.

Volvo has also been a leader in experimenting with new work systems. Its Kalmar plant, opened in 1974, grouped 15 to 20 employees in teams that also operated without a moving assembly line. Each team builds large sections of a car, and Kalmar now has an average work cycle of 30 minutes. The company says productivity is higher here than at its large, conventional assembly plant at Gothenburg, which has relatively few teams. But absenteeism at Kalmar remains at 17%, only a notch below Gothenburg's 19% to 20%.

Uddevalla goes much further than Kalmar. It is divided into six assembly plants, each of which has eight teams. The teams largely manage themselves, handling scheduling, quality control, hiring, and other duties normally performed by supervisors. Indeed, there are no first-line foremen and only two tiers of managers. Each team has a spokesperson/ombudsman, who reports to one of six plant managers, who in turn report to Leif Karlberg, president of the entire complex.

Morale seems high at Uddevalla. Absenteeism is only 8%. Workers have a spectacular view of a fjord. The plant is well lighted, and noise is subdued. "This factory is exceptional even for Sweden," says Mariane Apelman, a former shipyard welder and now a shop steward. "My children are 9, 10, and 11. They'll have a good work environment when they graduate. This is the right way." Volvo gives its workers 16 weeks' training before they are allowed near a car, and on-the-job orientation lasts 16 months more. Pay averages $10 an hour.

Volvo's goal is to produce 40,000 cars a year by 1991 in single-shift production. That's a relatively small volume compared with the average 120,000 production of most auto plants. Other Volvo plants produce all of the 740's components and perform the major operations of stamping, welding, and painting car bodies that are shipped to Uddevalla.

'Craftsmanship'

After entering the plant, the car bodies glide noiselessly on magnetic tracks to the assembly points, where Volvo-designed machines lift and tilt the body to any angle. More than 80% of the assembly can be done from a comfortable working position with no bending or stretching. Teams determine how long they'll work on a car and take responsibility for fixing defects. Boasts Volvo's Karlberg: "This isn't just new production technology. It is the death of the assembly line. We've brought back craftsmanship to auto making."

But skeptics question whether Volvo's approach will spread. "I don't think it will be any kind of industrial revolution," says John F. Krafcik, a consultant to the International Motor Vehicle Program at the Massachusetts Institute of Technology who has studied 80 auto plants. "Uddevalla can achieve a high level of quality," he adds, "but there is no way it can match the productivity of a reasonably efficient, mass-production system, Japanese or American."

Japanese auto makers, the most efficient in the world, show no indication of switching from the moving assembly line. U.S. companies have taken a few steps in that direction, and many in the UAW prefer a Volvo-style, autonomous group approach to the Japanese system of closely supervised teams. If the Volvo concept does indeed increase efficiency over the longer term, then pressures may mount in the U.S. to begin replacing the assembly line.[1]

How effective is the Uddevalla plant? How do turnover, absenteeism, performance, satisfaction, and involvement of workers here compare to those at other plants? What action has management taken to increase worker performance, decrease absenteeism and turnover, and encourage worker satisfaction?

As noted in Chapter 12, technological advances in automation and computerization are dramatically changing the workplace. In the automobile and other manufacturing industries, robotics have permeated the production process. Computer-integrated manufacturing (CIM), and computer-aided design and computer-aided manufacturing (CAD/CAM), have computerized production by automating specific operations and tying them together into large systems.[2] These changes have both prompted and responded to the selection of organizational structures discussed in Chapters 11 and 12 to improve product and service quality and increase worker productivity. Together, organizational design and work design address system-wide organizational issues as well as concerns about individual performance and satisfaction.

Consider, for example, the manufacturing of chocolate candy bars. Originally the process was manually performed and mechanically paced, with workers directly controlling the melting, molding, and wrapping processes. Automating the line and replacing workers with "intelligent" computers significantly streamlined the manufacturing process and increased productivity. Now consider the more complicated process of designing and manufacturing circuit boards for computers. How would computer-aided design and manufacturing affect their production? What role would CIM or CAD/CAM play at the Volvo plant in Uddevalla? How should the work be designed to respond to such automation? In this chapter we attempt to answer these questions by examining diverse ways of designing work in a variety of organizational settings. We suggest work design as a way of facilitating organization-wide performance in the workplace, as well as motivating individual workers to produce.

Work redesign is the alteration of the content or context of a job by altering its activities, adjusting the interaction between it and its holders, changing the conditions of work, modifying the nature and extent of supervisory relations, or changing the scope of individual responsibility. Such changes often motivate or respond to technological innovation such as increased automation, the introduction of CIM or CAD/CAM systems, or the advent of new technical systems. They are also introduced to increase employee motivation. At Volvo, for example, teams of workers assemble entire cars, rather than parts of cars, or individuals adding single components on an assembly line. These changes are directed toward improving individual and group performance and satisfaction.

Work redesign has its roots in the various historical perspectives introduced in Chapter 1: scientific management, classical theory, human relations, and systems theory. Redesigning work addresses issues such as the quantification and simplification of work, the ability to modify the supervisory hierarchy, the importance of humanizing work, and variations in job interdependence. It also has its roots in Herzberg's theory of motivation (see Chapter 4), which provided the foundation of job enrichment, discussed later in the chapter.

Appropriate work design helps incorporate technical advances into an organization in a way that results in better worker performance. It helps reinforce the benefits of particular organizational designs by emphasizing or de-emphasizing job specialization, introducing new ways of coordinating work, and modifying the chain of command within job sequences. Work redesign can increase worker satisfaction and affect both intrinsic and extrinsic motivation.

Inappropriate work design leads workers to complain that their jobs are boring and do not require their skills and knowledge, or alternatively, that their jobs are too complex and demanding. Either way, productivity may lag, quality may decrease, or schedules may slip. In contrast, Volvo's management claims that the design of work at Uddevalla significantly reduced absenteeism (to 8%) and turnover.

In this chapter we first examine the major approaches to work design: work simplification, work enrichment, and alternate work arrangements. Next we consider programs designed to improve the quality of work life in organizations, which may incorporate some or all of the approaches to redesign discussed in the first parts of the chapter. Then we look at innovation in organizations. We also investigate differences in work design among the United States and other countries. We conclude by offering prescriptions for improving the design of work.

WORK SIMPLIFICATION

How would you describe the jobs of traditional assembly line workers, cafeteria workers, or employees in a fast food restaurant? Work simplification characterizes these jobs. It emphasizes the reduction of a job to its component parts, then a reassembly of these parts into an optimally efficient work process. For example, a clerk in an accounts payable department might first open all incoming mail, then sort it by payment date, place the pile with the most recent date on the desk, write checks for each of these accounts, and enter the payments into the ledger. In the manufacture of lacquer bookcases and storage units, the process might be divided into many discrete tasks, each performed by a separate individual. One worker, for example, might cut the backs of the bookcases; another might insert the shelf pegs into the frames; still another might attach the doors for the storage units.

Characteristics

Work simplification emphasizes six features.[3] First, *mechanical pacing,* or the use of an automated assembly line, monitors the speed of production. Automobile manufacturing plants have historically had mile-long assembly lines from which individual workers take the incomplete product, perform their task, and then return the more-completed product to the assembly line. Second, individuals perform *repetitive* work. In furniture manufacturing, for example, one worker might assemble only shelves or attach doors, check for defects, or label packaged products. Third, each individual concentrates on only a *fraction* of the product. For example, a single worker inserts the pegs on which the shelves rest; another worker attaches door hinges. If Volvo were to use work simplification, one worker may attach the hub caps, another the doors. Fourth, the process specifies the *tools and techniques* used in production: workers have no discretion in the way they manufacture the product; the procedure for performing each task is predetermined. Fifth, *limited social interaction* occurs among workers. This results partly from the speed of the assembly line and partly from the emphasis on workers performing highly specified tasks. Finally, work simplification breaks a job down into specific and relatively simple tasks that require *minimal training*. Consequently some manufacturing workers complain about the low skill requirements of their jobs and lack of opportunity to use their craftsmanship.

The Implementation Process

Typically work simplification should occur when jobs have become overly complex or when greater precision in the design of tasks and their interrelationships facilitates productivity. Work simplification uses industrial engineering methods. To begin, industrial engineers study the exact series of motions in a job, using detailed observation records and drawing extensive diagrams of the work process. Next they monitor the time required for each part of the job. Then they identify and attempt to eliminate all false, slow, and useless movements. Finally they redesign the job, by collecting into one series the quickest and best movements. To accomplish the last step, work simplification typically involves extensive use of machines, optimum spacing of rest periods, great specialization of work activities, and matching of workers to jobs best suited to their abilities, experience, and aptitudes.

To be most effective, work simplification must incorporate some elements of human-factors engineering. Engineers must design equipment in accord with the mental and physical characteristics of the operators, for example. Human-factors engineers take a product of a design engineer and adjust it to the operators' biological and social characteristics.[4] They recognize that isolated work stations reduce personnel interaction and information sharing; thus, if management values interpersonal interaction, they might consider clustering work stations or opening up the physical work space to facilitate information exchange.

Work simplification, however, can create significant dysfunctions. Workers may become bored or have limited opportunities for individual growth. Simplified job design may not meet workers' higher-order needs (see Chapter 4) and thus reduce motivation. Top management may automate and mechanize production for its own sake, rather than for improving worker performance. An effective work simplification redesign must find ways of ensuring that the process operates smoothly and cost-effectively. Management must find ways of efficiently moving and repositioning items between operations, assembling separate tasks into a more efficient total process, balancing the line to reduce down-time in less time-consuming tasks and encourage effective work pacing, and providing sufficient external supervision.[5]

The introduction of a highly efficient, well-automated assembly line at the Lordstown assembly plant of General Motors in the early 1970s highlights many implementation issues.[6] The line used new engineering techniques, provided workers with easier access to the car bodies, and eliminated tedious tasks. But it was also the fastest moving assembly line in the industry. "Although management claimed that the changes in job sequence and method in some assembly work did not bring a substantial change in the overall speed or pace of the assembly line, the workers perceived the job change as 'tightening' the assembly line. The union charged that the GMAD (General Motors Assembly Division) brought a return of an old-fashioned line speedup and a 'sweatshop style' of management reminiscent of the 1930's, making the men do more work at the same pay."[7] Worker unrest was accompanied by sabotage and decreased product quality and suggested to some a need for management to respond to workers' dissatisfaction with the repetitive work.

Why did the Volvo plant not choose to use work simplification? At Uddevalla, as at an increasing number of manufacturing plants, automated processes reduce the need for work simplification. Those jobs that are the best candidates for simplification can be replaced with robotics or other forms of automation. Thus top management at Volvo chose to enrich, rather than simplify, jobs.

Do any jobs benefit from work simplification, given the potential negative consequences? Jobs that require limited amounts of information processing and decision making by workers and whose workers have low social and growth needs are candidates for work simplification.[8] So are jobs that have become overly complex or can benefit from more careful design. The number of such jobs and individuals is decreasing as workers become better educated and look for more challenge and autonomy in their jobs. Thus managers must choose situations in which to implement work simplification very carefully.

WORK ENRICHMENT

Top management of the Uddevalla facility decided to enrich jobs. They now use work teams who have the discretion to make job assignments, order supplies, determine schedules, and monitor business data. The teams essentially manage themselves; only two tiers of managers—and no first-line foremen—supervise them. Management who chooses to enrich jobs can incorporate one of three major approaches (described in the next section and summarized in Figure 13–1): (1) job enlargement, (2) job enrichment, and (3) sociotechnical redesign.

Job Enlargement

Job enlargement offers the opposite solution to work simplification for redesigning work, and it has historical significance in the evolution of work-design methods. It increases the scope of the job, modifying it horizontally, by increasing the number of activities or different processes a job involves. Rather than encouraging an individual to concentrate on a fraction of the product, job enlargement requires workers to perform numerous, often unrelated, tasks.

The earliest job enlargement programs involved *job extension,* in which the

Figure 13–1 THREE APPROACHES TO WORK ENRICHMENT

Job Enlargement

Horizontally increases the scope of a job, by either extending the number of activities performed by the job holder or rotating the job holder through a variety of unrelated activities.

Job Enrichment

Horizontally and vertically increases the scope of a job, by increasing the skill variety, task identity, task significance, autonomy, and feedback in the job.

Sociotechnical Redesign

Uses autonomous or self-regulating work groups in which teams of workers regulate and control their tasks as well as perform many roles traditionally assigned to management, such as making job assignments and determining work processes.

redesign extended work by combining several jobs.[9] For example, workers who formerly soldered only black wires to the panel of an electric calculator, and workers who soldered only yellow wires to the panel, subsequently attached all 2331 wires for each calculator.[10] Many workers view such programs as giving them "more of the same work" to do, rather than significantly improving their jobs. Early experiments with job enlargement seemed encouraging, but more recent research suggests less clear-cut results, and even serious flaws, in this method of redesign.[11]

Job rotation is a more common form of job enlargement. In this case, a worker performs two or more tasks but alternates among them in a predefined way over a period of time. For example, a worker might attach the wheel assembly one week, inspect it the next, and organize the parts for assembly during the third. Job rotation provides an organization with a hedge against absenteeism, since workers can perform more than a single function. It also can facilitate career advancement by cross-training workers. The Uddevalla plant likely incorporates formal or informal job rotation in the assignment of activities by its work teams. A more sophisticated variant of job rotation is often incorporated into training programs.

Job Enrichment

Instead of altering only the horizontal dimensions of a job, as with job enlargement, *job enrichment* involves changing a job both horizontally (adding tasks) and vertically (adding responsibility). Frederick Herzberg's motivation–hygiene model (see Chapter 4) provided the roots for job enrichment programs, calling for increasing motivators in jobs, which he labeled *enriching* them.[12]

This early job enrichment model evolved and was replaced by the *job characteristics model,* which traces motivation and satisfaction to psychological states experienced by individuals and then links these states to the characteristics of jobs. Five core characteristics of a job significantly influence the behaviors and attitudes of workers: (1) skill variety, (2) task identity, (3) task significance, (4) autonomy, and (5) feedback.[13]

Skill variety describes the degree to which a job requires the worker to perform activities that challenge his or her skills and use diverse abilities. A state police trooper's job requires more skill variety than a crossing guard's. A branch manager in a bank uses more diverse skills and abilities than a bank teller. Participating in the assembly of an entire car, as at Uddevalla, requires more skills than assembling a single part. As a practical matter, skill variety often equates with a variety of tasks.

Task identity refers to the degree to which a job requires completion of a whole and identifiable piece of work—doing a job from beginning to end, with a visible outcome. The work teams at Uddevalla assemble an entire car; as a group, their job has task identity. Depending on the allocation of responsibilities within the team, however, task identity for individuals may vary.

Task significance reflects the degree to which a job is perceived to have a substantial impact on the lives of other people. While task significance depends on individuals' perceptions, and may even vary for a specific job, some jobs inherently seem to have more task significance. Classroom teaching has greater task significance than lunchroom monitoring, for example. Likewise assembling an entire car has more significance than assembling only an engine.

Autonomy is the degree to which a job gives the worker freedom, independence, and discretion in scheduling work and determining how he or she will carry it out. Many salespeople have relative autonomy in their jobs; restaurant owners also have jobs with autonomy. The workers at Uddevalla became essentially self-managing and now perform scheduling, quality control, and hiring duties, among others, for the car assembly; they too have substantial autonomy.

Feedback refers to the degree to which a worker, in carrying out the work activities required by a job, gets information about the effectiveness of his or her efforts. A clerk who receives a list of transcription errors each day receives feedback. The workers at Uddevalla quickly learn whether their products meet quality standards. Feedback comes from both one's supervisor and the work itself, as well as from other sources such as customers and peers.

Skill variety, task identity, and task significance influence the extent to which an individual job holder experiences the job as meaningful. When workers use their diverse abilities, complete entire tasks, and view their work as having an impact on others' lives, they are more likely to experience their jobs as *meaningful*. Autonomy in a job influences the extent to which an individual believes he or she is *responsible for outcomes* of the job. Generally a manager is likely to feel more responsible for his or her job outcomes than is a person the manager supervises. Feedback in a job increases an individual's *knowledge of the actual results* of work activities. Increasing the amount of information available to a job holder increases the individual's ability to know and evaluate his or her effectiveness. These critical psychological states—experienced meaningfulness, experienced responsibility, and knowledge of results—in turn affect such personal and work outcomes as internal work motivation, "growth" satisfaction, general job satisfaction, and work effectiveness. Figure 13–2 summarizes these relationships.

An individual's knowledge and skill, strength of his or her growth needs (for learning, personal accomplishment, and development), and satisfaction with the work context moderate the links between the core job characteristics and critical psychological states, and between the critical psychological states

Figure 13–2 THE JOB CHARACTERISTICS MODEL

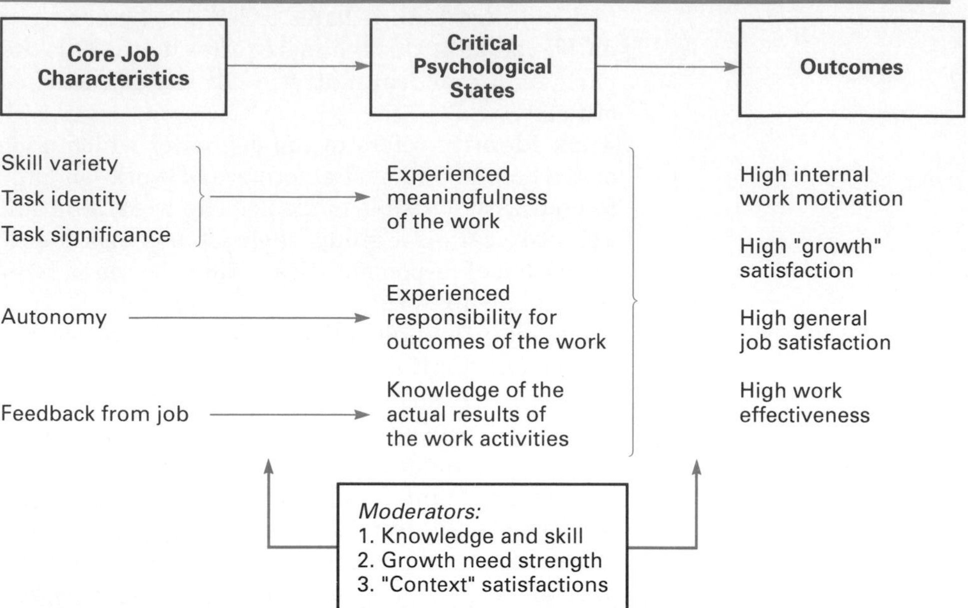

Source: J.R. Hackman/G.R. Oldham, *Work Redesign*, © 1980, Addison-Wesley Publishing Co., Inc., Reading, Massachusetts. Fig. 4.6. Reprinted with permission of the publisher.

and outcomes.[14] For example, individuals who have the skills and knowledge to perform enriched jobs are probably more satisfied than those who are less competent. Individuals with high growth needs typically respond more positively to enriched jobs than do those with low growth needs, because the latter may not value such opportunities or may be negatively stressed by them. Individuals satisfied with their work context may be more able to take advantage of the opportunities provided by enriched jobs than those dissatisfied with the work context, because the latter are too preoccupied with that aspect of the work.

The job characteristics approach calls for enriching a job by improving one or more of the core dimensions,[15] as shown in Table 13–1. *Combining tasks,* such as by having a typist proofread his or her own work, increases skill variety and task identity. *Forming natural work units,* such as by having a worker or small group of workers assemble an entire car, in order to distribute work in a natural and logical way, increases task identity and task significance. *Establishing client relationships,* such as by having bank loan officers always deal with the same clients, increases skill variety, autonomy, and feedback. *Loading a job vertically* to combine implementation and control, such as by giving production workers responsibility for quality control or meeting schedules, increases autonomy. *Opening feedback channels,* by letting the worker know about his or her performance while a job is being done, through setting goals and monitoring their accomplishment, increases knowledge of results.

Job enrichment is an appropriate response to declining motivation due to overly specialized jobs where workers lack control of the job process. Declining work motivation, dissatisfaction with growth opportunities and a job in general, and lack of work effectiveness all signal a need for job enrichment. In addition, today's changing work force, which includes more highly educated

Table 13–1 Ways to Improve Core Job Dimensions

Job Redesign Activity	Core Dimension Affected
Combine tasks	Skill variety Task identity
Form natural work units	Task identity Task significance
Establish client relationships	Skill variety Autonomy Feedback
Load a job vertically	Task identity Task significance Autonomy
Open feedback channels	Feedback

individuals, often requires job redesign. Enriching jobs helps meet the needs of such workers. Volvo management indicated that they instituted job enrichment in the manufacturing jobs at the Uddevalla plant for the last reason.

The redesign at Uddevalla follows the job characteristics model. The lack of a plant-wide assembly line and emphasis on performance and control of work by teams result in jobs that emphasize skill variety, task identity, task significance, autonomy, and feedback. How have top management and work teams ensured a positive loading of the jobs on the core dimensions? Top management has done this in several ways. They combined various tasks so that workers assemble most or all of a significant product component. They reduced the amount of prefabrication required and increased the amount of craftmanship in the jobs. They formed work groups to assemble entire cars, increasing skill variety, task identity, task significance, and autonomy. Management also increased worker involvement in production scheduling and reduced the number of supervisory levels to enhance autonomy. Finally, they increased feedback on the quality of the finished product, through goal-setting activities and worker involvement in some quality-control procedures.

Sociotechnical Redesign

Sociotechnical redesign addresses the particular problems in introducing new technology into a work system effectively. It incorporates some principles of job enrichment through its emphasis on using work teams, using the design to meet worker needs and increase motivation. Researchers at the Tavistock Institute in England were the first to note the negative impact of new technology on worker productivity and satisfaction.[16] In both the coal mining and textile weaving industries, the introduction of new technology conflicted with strong work cultures and social systems.[17] Automobile manufacturers in the United States experienced similar resistance to increasing automation of the assembly line, resulting in greater absenteeism, increased sabotage, and lowered productivity.[18]

To combat such problems, Scandinavian automobile manufacturers—Saab and Volvo—introduced the concept of *autonomous work groups* for meeting workers' social needs while introducing technological innovation into work.[19] These self-regulating groups, in which employees who perform interdependent tasks work in a common unit, controlled their own task assignments and division of labor. Volvo at Uddevalla relies on autonomous work groups to assemble entire cars, and the teams "largely manage themselves." Even before Uddevalla, the introduction of autonomous or self-regulating groups had a significant impact on workers. In 1975, for example, a specially built Volvo plant operated at 100 percent efficiency, compared to 80 percent in other Volvo plants.[20] In the mining industry, productivity in autonomous work groups rose from 78 to 95 percent; in the weaving industry, from 80 to 95 percent. Turnover dropped correspondingly.[21]

Table 13–2 summarizes the differences between old paradigms and the new, sociotechnical paradigm of work design. Clearly work design at Uddevalla uses the new paradigm: autonomous work groups integrate and optimize social and technical systems; related tasks are joined and performed by self-regulating groups; there are few layers of management, encouraging a collaborative relationship. Ideally employee commitment and performance increase, and

Table 13–2 CHARACTERISTICS OF OLD AND NEW PARADIGMS OF WORK DESIGN

Old Paradigm	New Paradigm
Technology comes first.	Social and technical systems are optimized together.
People are extensions of machines.	People complement machines.
People are expendable spare parts.	People are resources to be developed.
Tasks are narrow and individual; skills are simple.	Related tasks make an optimum grouping; skills are multiple and broad.
Controls—for example, supervisors, staff, procedures books—are external.	Individuals are self-controlled; work groups and departments are self-regulating.
Organization chart has many levels; management style is autocratic.	Organization chart is flat; management is participative.
Atmosphere is competitive and characterized by gamesmanship.	Atmosphere is collaborative and cooperative.
Only the organization's purposes are considered.	Individual and social purposes, as well as the organization's, are considered.
Employees are alienated: "It's only a job."	Employees are committed: "It's my job!"
Organization is characterized by low risk taking.	Organization is innovative: New ideas are encouraged.

SOURCE: M.R. Weisbord, Participative work design: A personal odyssey, *Organizational Dynamics* 13 (Spring 1985): 17. Used by permission. Adapted from E. Trist, The evolution of socio-technical systems—A conceptual framework and an action research program, research paper No. 2, June 1981 (Ontario Ministry of Labor, Ontario Quality of Working Life Center, Toronto).

Volvo's management expects these positive outcomes. The introduction of autonomous or self-regulating work groups alleviates the isolation and boredom traditionally felt by manufacturing workers. Sociotechnical redesign should also moderate the negative effects of increasing automation of the work processes.

Such new sociotechnical work design requires that workers have the ability to regulate and control their tasks, to influence their transactions with the environment and to differentiate themselves from other groups sufficiently. Self-regulating groups perform many roles traditionally assigned to management, such as making job assignments and determining work processes.

Limitations of Work Enrichment

Research has suggested that job enrichment improves productivity and satisfaction and decreases turnover and absenteeism.[22] Volvo certainly redesigned jobs to accomplish these objectives. Yet, one study of autonomous work groups suggests that their impact may be limited—and accompanied by dysfunctional consequences. Factors within a work place or the individuals involved may limit its application. A British confectionery company that introduced work groups found they improved intrinsic job satisfaction but not work performance, turnover, job motivation, organizational commitment, or mental health. Both managers and employees liked the system in spite of the personal stress that arose from managing it.[23]

Figure 13–3 is a checklist for evaluating the several factors that may affect job enrichment. Complete this checklist for a job you have held or have some familiarity with, then score your responses. The lower the total score (1 or 2), the more conducive the job is to being enriched; the higher the score (4 or 5), the less effective job enrichment efforts are likely to be. In general job enrich-

Figure 13–3 Job Enrichment Evaluation Form

The Job Itself		
1. Quality is important and attributable to the worker.	/1/2/3/4/5/	Quality is not too important and/or is not controllable by the worker.
2. Flexibility is a major contributor to job efficiency.	/1/2/3/4/5/	Flexibility is not a major consideration.
3. The job requires the coordination of tasks or activities among several workers.	/1/2/3/4/5/	The job is performed by one worker acting independently of others.
4. The benefits of job enrichment will compensate for the efficiencies of task specialization.	/1/2/3/4/5/	Job enrichment will eliminate substantial efficiencies realized from specialization.
5. The conversion and one-time set up costs involved in job enrichment can be recovered in a reasonable period of time.	/1/2/3/4/5/	Training and other costs associated with job enrichment are estimated to be much greater than expected results.
6. The wage payment plan is not based solely on output.	/1/2/3/4/5/	Workers are under a straight piece work wage plan.
7. Due to the workers' ability to affect output, an increase in job satisfaction can be expected to increase productivity.	/1/2/3/4/5/	Due to the dominance of technology, an increase in job satisfaction is unlikely to significantly affect productivity.

continued

Figure 13–3 CONTINUED

Technology		
8. Changes in job content would not necessitate a large investment in equipment and technology.	/1/2/3/4/5/	The huge investment in equipment and technology overrides all other considerations.
The Workers		
9. Employees are accustomed to change and respond favorably to it.	/1/2/3/4/5/	Employees are set in their ways and prefer the status quo.
10. Employees feel secure in their jobs; employment has been stable.	/1/2/3/4/5/	Layoffs are frequent; many employees are concerned about the permanency of employment.
11. Employees are dissatisfied with their jobs and would welcome changes in job content and work relationships.	/1/2/3/4/5/	Employees are satisfied with their present jobs and general work situation.
12. Employees are highly skilled blue- and white-collar workers, professionals, and supervisors.	/1/2/3/4/5/	Employees are semi- and unskilled blue- and white-collar workers.
13. Employees are well educated with most having college degrees.	/1/2/3/4/5/	The average employee has less than a high school education.
14. Employees are from a small town and rural environment.	/1/2/3/4/5/	The company is located in a large, highly industrialized metropolitan area.
15. The history of union-management (if no union, worker-management) relations has been one of cooperation and mutual support.	/1/2/3/4/5/	Union-management (worker-management) relations are strained and the two parties are antagonistic to one another.
Management		
16. Managers are committed to job enrichment and are anxious to participate in its implementation.	/1/2/3/4/5/	Managers show little interest in job enrichment and even less interest in having it implemented in their department.
17. Managers have attended seminars, workshops, and so forth, are quite knowledgeable of the concept, and have had experience in implementing it.	/1/2/3/4/5/	Managers lack the training and experience necessary to develop and implement job enrichment projects.
18. Management realizes that substantial pay offs from job enrichment usually take one to three years to materialize.	/1/2/3/4/5/	Management expects immediate results (within six months) from job enrichment projects.

Total Score _____ ÷ 18 = ____________

Job Enrichment Rating

Source: William E. Reif and Ronald C. Tinnell, "A Diagnostic Approach to Job Enrichment," pp. 29–37, *MSU Business Topics*, Autumn 1973. Reprinted by permission of the publisher, Division of Research, Graduate School of Business Administration, Michigan State University.

ment programs work better for less complex jobs than inherently richer ones. Managers can expect enrichment to succeed only if workers want and seek fulfillment in their work and value jobs requiring skill and effort. Thus managers must recognize that differences in employer and employee goals may hinder the effectiveness of work enrichment programs. Some managers may want their workers to demonstrate initiative and autonomy, but the workers want little involvement and learning; or the opposite may be true. Managers must diagnose the nature of a job itself, the technology involved, the workers involved, and management to predict the likely impact and appropriateness of work enrichment.[24]

ALTERNATE WORK ARRANGEMENTS

In contrast to the forms of work design discussed above, which focus primarily on the content of jobs, alternate work arrangements address the *context*. This approach to redesign can help meet worker needs and provide a context that supports better performance and increased satisfaction. Particularly as the composition of the work force changes, this redesign approach becomes an increasingly useful option. There are two ways of altering a job's context: (1) changing the work hours and (2) changing the work location.

Flexible Hours

In programs that offer workers flexible hours, also known as flextime programs, workers have some discretion in creating their work schedules. For example, one accounts receivable clerk in an insurance company might work from 7 A.M. to 3 P.M., whereas another might work from 10 A.M. to 6 P.M.

Basic Forms Alternate work schedules take three basic forms: (1) discretionary systems, where workers choose the precise days or hours worked; (2) the compressed work week, where the traditional number of hours in a five-day week are worked in four days; and (3) part-time employment.[25]

Discretionary systems include flexible working hours and staggered starts.[26] Flextime, probably the most common discretionary system, offers workers the choice of starting and ending times so long as they work certain specific hours daily (such as 10 to 3) and meet the hour requirements (usually thirty-five to forty) of a normal work week. In principle, flextime offers employees many options, but in fact, requiring certain core hours and total hours to be worked may limit the number of options significantly. Workers may be left only with the opportunity to work from 8 to 5 or 9 to 6, for example. Under a staggered system, an employee chooses what time to begin his or her working day, generally within a three- to four-hour span, and then works a fixed number of hours. In a staggered week, workers alternate between working a four-day, thirty-two-hour week and a six-day, forty-eight-hour week.

The *compressed work week* has arisen from attempts to shorten the work week in order to cut costs and increase worker satisfaction. *Compressing* means reducing the work week into fewer days. Four ten-hour work days is a common configuration. The four-day work week may result in greater employee satisfaction, but this improved attitude may occur at the expense of employee efficiency. Scheduling work in two-week rather than one-week blocks enhances the attractiveness of this option: the employee may work four days, have a four day break, then work four more days, followed by a normal two-day weekend break.

Part-time employment differs from discretionary systems and compressed work weeks in several ways. It includes jobs done by permanent employees who work less than whole days, and these jobs may have either predictable or unpredictable hours. But recently two new variations of part-time work have emerged: job sharing and job splitting. In job sharing, one whole job is divided into two parts according to time and day of the week. Together, the job holders are responsible for completing the work, and each typically performs all the tasks of the job. One might work mornings and the second afternoons; or one might work the first two-and-a-half days of a five-day week while the second works the last half of the week. In job splitting, jobs are divided according to tasks or skills rather than schedule. In splitting a secretarial job, for example, one person might take all dictation while the second does all the typing.

Contract employment can also be viewed as a variant of part-time employment. Here, workers are hired to perform specific projects or tasks, and they are paid for the completed task or product. Software development and distribution companies often hire this type of employee because it provides them with maximum flexibility—they pay only for completed work. Workers, too, retain flexibility and autonomy by having the discretion to develop their own work schedules so long as they complete the project by the specified deadline.

Program Features The major variables in flexible-hour programs are (1) band width, (2) core hours, (3) flexible hours, (4) length of the work week, (5) banking of time, (6) variability of schedule, and (7) supervisors' roles in the program.[27] The *band width,* or the total number of hours in the interval between the earliest possible starting time and the latest finishing time, typically ranges from nine to twelve hours, although some extensions beyond this width are possible. Typically the greater the band width, the more discretion individuals have in creating their own schedules. A band width of 7 A.M. to 8 P.M. obviously provides more flexibility than one of 8 A.M. to 6 P.M. The extent of a band width depends on the nature of the jobs involved, other jobs with which they interact, and even the time zone in which the organization is located.

Individuals' choices also depend on the number and specificity of the *core hours*—the hours employees must work—and the number of *flexible hours*—the hours within which employees can decide to stop or start work. As the number of core hours increases and is specified and the number of flexible hours decreases, workers lose discretion in devising their personal schedules.

The *length of the work week* is another variable in an alternate work schedule. Compressed schedules, for example, usually shorten the work week permanently. In truly flexible systems, workers can bank hours, or carry forward a surplus or deficit of hours worked. They can also *vary their schedules;* that is, change hours from day to day and week to week without prior supervisory approval. Note that a *supervisor's role*—the extent of his or her scheduling and monitoring of employee activities—influences the effective implementation of a flexible-hour program. Supervisor support for the system is essential.

Flexible Location

Workers are increasingly seeking and receiving the option of performing their jobs at a site or sites apart from the organization's physical plant. Computer programmers, in particular, can often perform their jobs remotely, typically at home. Eliminating commuting time can potentially increase productivity. However, since these workers may miss the social interaction that working at the office or plant provides, this arrangement does not work for everyone.[28]

Managing alternate work options requires managers to screen candidates carefully and develop a flexible training program. Managers must also establish a viable work plan by setting appropriate performance goals. They must find creative ways to monitor the number of hours worked and ensure that the organization's needs are met. They must maintain open communication, provide ongoing support, and remain flexible in dealing with employees who take advantage of the alternatives.[29]

Effectiveness of Alternate Schedules

A number of studies have documented the benefits of alternate work schedules, especially flextime.[30] In general, this redesign of job context increases productivity because of reduced use of sick leave; decreases turnover, absenteeism, and overtime; increases employee satisfaction and morale; and decreases transportation demand during peak hours. Most organizations that have installed flextime systems have maintained them.[31]

The major resistance to atypical work schedules stems from the perception that all work must be done at the same time by all workers because of the interdependence of the tasks. To overcome this constraint, scheduling tasks carefully and building a small inventory of different product components might be required. Flextime does not work at all when a company has multiple continuous shifts, machine-paced assembly work, few employees, or highly interdependent operations.[32]

Flextime has experienced continued success in Europe for some time. Several companies in West Germany and Austria have even considered introducing a *flexyear*.[33] In this arrangement, workers agree to a number of hours they intend to work in the following year but have the freedom to allocate them as they desire. They receive equal amounts of pay each month but may work two or three times as many hours in one month as in another.

Implementing alternate work schedules is a major challenge for management, but the savings can be dramatic. At Pacific Gas and Electric, after installation and administration of a flextime system costing $40,000 for a department of 575 draftsmen, first-year savings of $300,000, due to increased production, decreased overtime, decreased sick leave, and decreased absenteeism, more than equalled the expense.[34] Nevertheless managers should view implementation of alternate work schedules as a redesign option but not a panacea for motivational or performance problems.

QUALITY-OF-WORKING-LIFE PROGRAMS

Quality-of-working-life (QWL) programs incorporate many principles of job enrichment and sociotechnical redesign into comprehensive efforts to improve the quality of a working situation. Such programs have focused on ensuring adequate and fair compensation, a safe and healthy work environment, personal growth and development, satisfaction of social needs in the workplace, personal rights, compatibility between work and nonwork activities, and the social relevance of work life.[35] Quality-of-working-life programs typically include participative problem solving, job enrichment, innovative reward systems, and improvements to the work environment. Clearly managers can be instrumental in introducing such programs.

The 1970s witnessed a significant increase in concern about quality of working life. In 1974, for example, Congress established the National Center for Productivity and Quality of Working Life, an agency supporting studies directed at improving productivity and the growth of QWL activities.

Program Characteristics

QWL programs encourage workers to participate with management in decision making about problems and opportunities in the workplace. They are concerned with work's impact on people, organizational effectiveness, and worker participation in organizations.[36] Their activities include participative decision making and problem solving, restructuring the basic nature of jobs and work systems, fitting rewards to the desired work processes and outcomes, and improving the work environment.[37]

An early and well-known QWL program was initiated at the General Motors assembly plant in Tarrytown, New York, in 1970—a time when the plant had one of the poorest production and labor records at GM. The plant manager invited workers to participate in the planning and implementation of changes in plant operations, and many of the workers' suggestions were adopted. Plant management followed this by conducting voluntary, joint training of workers and supervisors in problem solving; 95 percent of the work force volunteered to participate in the three-day, paid training program. Subsequent evaluations showed that the quality of performance increased, absenteeism dropped, and the number of grievances fell from 2000 in 1972 to 32 in 1978.[38] Other early QWL experiments were conducted at the Rushton Mining Company in Pennsylvania, the Harmon Manufacturing Company plant in Bolivar, Tennessee, and the General Foods plant in Topeka, Kansas.[39] Similar early experiments with QWL in the automobile industry replaced the assembly line with work teams and improved communication between workers and supervisors. They were modeled after the sociotechnical redesign programs introduced in Sweden, described earlier in this chapter.

Since their first introduction, quality-of-working-life programs have become more comprehensive. In the automobile industry, Ford and General Motors have used QWL programs as ways to cut costs and improve productivity. Ford created employee involvement groups at selected plants, which offered suggestions on ways to improve performance, in exchange for information to their union leaders about business plans and upcoming business events such as layoffs.[40]

By the end of 1983, ten GM plants had introduced an operating team system in which teams of ten to fifteen workers received all work assignments and allocated them during regular team meetings. These teams often operated as quality circles or experiments with job enrichment.[41] The Saturn plant of General Motors, with its "$5 billion effort to build small cars in the U.S. at costs competitive with the Japanese,"[42] extended this concept further:

> Instead of cogs in a system, Saturn's workers will be full partners. Representatives of the United Auto Workers will sit in on all planning and operating committees. Work teams will operate without foremen. To emphasize the new equality, old job titles will be replaced with neutral ones, and blue-collar workers will earn a salary, just like managers. Both will earn bonuses based on performance. And al-

> though the UAW will keep the right to strike, it will try to agree on changes in pay by consensus with management instead of in formal bargaining. The union will have a say in managers' salaries, too. . . .
>
> The basic groups in Saturn plants will be work units of 6 to 15 UAW members who will elect a "counselor" from their own ranks. The team will decide who does which job. It will also maintain equipment, order supplies, and set the relief and vacation schedules of its members. Each group will have a personal computer for keeping tabs on business data, ranging from production schedules to freight pickups and deliveries.
>
> Like experimental teams already working in a few GM facilities, the Saturn units will be responsible for controlling variable costs and doing quality inspections. But they will have far more authority than that. If a team comes up with a better idea for a new piece of equipment, Saturn's finance and purchasing departments must respond. The experts can't shrug off suggestions, as they tended to before. They must reach a consensus with the team. Power, in a word, will rest with the workers.[43]

The Uddevalla plant, described in the introduction to this chapter, also incorporates characteristics of QWL programs. Its emphasis on teamwork and employee participation in significant decision making are intended to increase workers' satisfaction and productivity and decrease their absenteeism and turnover.

At Xerox, QWL teams of eight to ten volunteers met weekly to discuss production problems and the status of previously offered recommendations.[44] By 1983, sixty to sixty-five committees of hourly workers at Packard Electric dealt with health and safety problems, work-related issues, and control limits for defects; some also operated as semi-autonomous work groups.[45]

Some QWL projects have also included so-called *quality circles*—work teams of five to ten members who originally focused on enhancing the quality of production and now recommend all types of improvements to work processes.[46] In 1985, more than 90 percent of the Fortune 500 companies, including Westinghouse, Hewlett-Packard, Digital Equipment Corporation, Texas Instruments, Xerox, Eastman Kodak, Procter and Gamble, Polaroid, TRW Systems, General Motors, Ford, IBM, and American Airlines, had some form of quality circles.[47]

Other variables in QWL projects include union support and involvement in the process, voluntary participation by employees, guarantees of job security, training programs in team problem solving, initiation of job redesign efforts, availability of skill training, involvement of workers in planning and forecasting, periodic meetings between workers and management to discuss plant production and operations, and responsiveness to employee concerns.[48] Union–management cooperation is the key to many QWL efforts, and some organizations form joint union–management committees to solve problems.[49] Table 13–3 compares and contrasts three generations of QWL programs, indicating how programs have developed from the earliest experiments (as at Tarrytown); to the programs of the 1980s such as employee involvement groups at Ford and quality circles in many large companies; to the programs of the 1990s as illustrated by General Motors's Saturn plant.

Table 13–3 FIRST-, SECOND-, AND THIRD-GENERATION QWL PROGRAMS

	First Generation	Second Generation	Third Generation
Structure			
Integration	QWL outside of/parallel to regular organizational structure; perceived as a program	Some integration of QWL with regular organizational structure	QWL inseparable from regular organizational structure; organizational structure becomes flatter
Adaptation	QWL structure externally imposed by centralized experts/authority	QWL structure shows some adaptations and local variations	Each local QWL structure unique to the particular working environment
Centralization	QWL structure centralized	QWL structure partly centralized, partly decentralized	QWL structure decentralized
Involvement	QWL structure involves only selected employees	QWL structure involves many or most employees	QWL structure involves all employees
Process			
Decision Making	Decision making is management prerogative; QWL provides input to management decisions	Ranges from QWL responsibility for some decisions at discretion of managers to managers being removed from day-to-day work decisions	Roles of management, nonmanagement and union redefined; decisions now made by those closest to impact; organization managed jointly at all levels
Facilitation	Facilitation provided by centralized, external resources	Facilitation moved under decentralized, local control	Each employee acquires skills of facilitator; takes on role as needed
Training and Education	Need for training and education determined and provided by centralized, external sources; focus on orientation for all; skills for facilitators	Groups identify own training needs and arrange as needed; focus on skills needed for QWL process, for all participants	Training locally determined; expands to include any process or work-related skill needed; all acquire skills in QWL process and organization management including financial, etc.
Union-Management Relationship	Formal union-management relationship adversarial; much time spent building up informal communication, respect, trust	Union-management relationship takes on more collaborative, cooperative tone; both sides move back and forth between collaborative and adversarial roles as needed	Collaborative union-management relationship formalized, or roles redefined as traditional distinctions between management and nonmanagement become blurred

Table 13–3 Continued

	First Generation	Second Generation	Third Generation
Content			
Issues	Issues peripheral to the business; tend to focus on the environmental	Expanded range of issues moves beyond environmental to encompass employee, union, planning, policy, business, and day-to-day work issues; constraints are contract and company policy	No distinction between "QWL issues" and other issues; all ideas considered; contract and company policy built on QWL foundation

London, M. *Change Agents: New Roles and Innovation Strategies for Human Resources Professionals.* San Francisco: Jossey-Bass, 1988, pp. 142–143. Used with permission.

Effectiveness of QWL Programs

The intended results of QWL programs include reduced costs, rapid delivery and high quality of products, low turnover, and low absenteeism for the organization; as well as increased self-esteem, satisfaction, security, involvement, participation, and growth for the workers.[50] QWL programs should be considered as a redesign option whenever appropriate conditions exist. Overall they have resulted in increased productivity and improved worker well-being. A review of the empirical research provides substantial evidence of their effectiveness.[51]

Although there have been relatively few failures, the introduction of QWL programs has not been smooth.[52] Relative success may depend on whether a program creates permanent or temporary structures: one study of 415 middle managers in four manufacturing plants indicated that the managers had more positive attitudes if they participated in permanent rather than temporary problem-solving groups.[53] In a retail chain, by contrast, tough economic times and internal political changes led to the demise of QWL programs. Worker participation in QWL programs always affects industrial relations, often resulting in low grievance rates, low absentee rates, fewer disciplinary actions, more positive worker attitudes, and greater participation in suggestion programs.[54] But for these programs to be effective, the organization's culture must support them; too often companies try to just implement programs instead of changing the entire organization.

Employees in several companies that instituted quality circles experienced better health and greater safety on the job.[55] Other benefits included improved employee satisfaction, morale, job interest, commitment, and involvement; increased opportunity for individual growth; greater sense of ownership and control of the work environment; development of managerial ability for circle leaders; improved communication in the organization; and greater understanding and respect between management and workers.[56]

But quality circles also have many potential problems, such as emphasizing profit to the exclusion of employee growth, failing to keep management and members informed, perceptions of management manipulation of the circles, failure to incorporate circles' suggestions, selecting inappropriate problems for circles to address, and overestimating expected benefits.[57] The long-run impact of quality circles is also questionable. In one study, improvements in performance and attitudes occurred right away, lasted for about two years, but then returned to previous levels.[58] The universal impact of circles is also unproven. For example, the problem-solving and personality styles of managers (see Chapter 3) were shown to differentially influence the reaction to quality circles and the use of participative management.[59] Thus managers must adapt any redesign approach to the specific situations they face to maximize its effectiveness.

INNOVATION

Work design can either foster or hinder innovation in organizations. Conversely, technological innovation can motivate work redesign. Together, in partnership with organizational design, they affect organizational and individual performance. International competition has forced United States industry to adopt and implement innovations in the workplace, particularly updating manufacturing technology. Organizations can use or invent innovation; or serve as vehicles for innovation; or organizations themselves, such as business-education collaboratives, can be innovative combinations.[60]

How does innovation come about? It begins with the recognition that there is a demand for a new product or process and that it is technically feasible. Next, the basic idea is formulated, integrating the technical and market issues into a design concept. In the problem-solving stage, next, the design is elaborated, and resource and technical problems are addressed. A solution, often an invention, moves the design into a prototype of the new product or process. In the development stage, an innovator faces and attempts to solve problems associated with production. Finally, the solution is used and then diffused throughout the workplace.[61] Reading 13–1, "Innovation Processes in Multinational Corporations," discusses the innovation process in this particular type of organization.

Figure 13–4 offers a compatible view of a technical innovation project. The process, as represented here, has six stages: preproject, project possibilities, project initiation, project execution, project outcome evaluation, and project transfer.[62] Successful innovation calls for the functions shown in Table 13–4. Building flexibility into work through sociotechnical redesign or flexible arrangements can facilitate the performance of these functions.

The managerial challenges of dealing with innovation can be significant. Managers and employees must adopt a mind-set that encourages the development and presentation of new ideas. They also must willingly expend resources for innovative activities. Minnesota Mining and Manufacturing (3M) Company, for example, encourages managers to become idea champions, who push innovations through the organization's hierarchy.[63] The design of work at 3M must facilitate such innovation. Organic forms of organizational design (see Chapter 11) also aid the innovation process.

The factory of the twenty-first century will incorporate significant applications of computer technology. A redesign of work must accompany the more widespread use of CAD/CAM technology, greater office automation, and increased robotics. Uddevalla offers one response to this sophisticated technology.

Figure 13–4 A Multistage View of a Technical Innovation Project

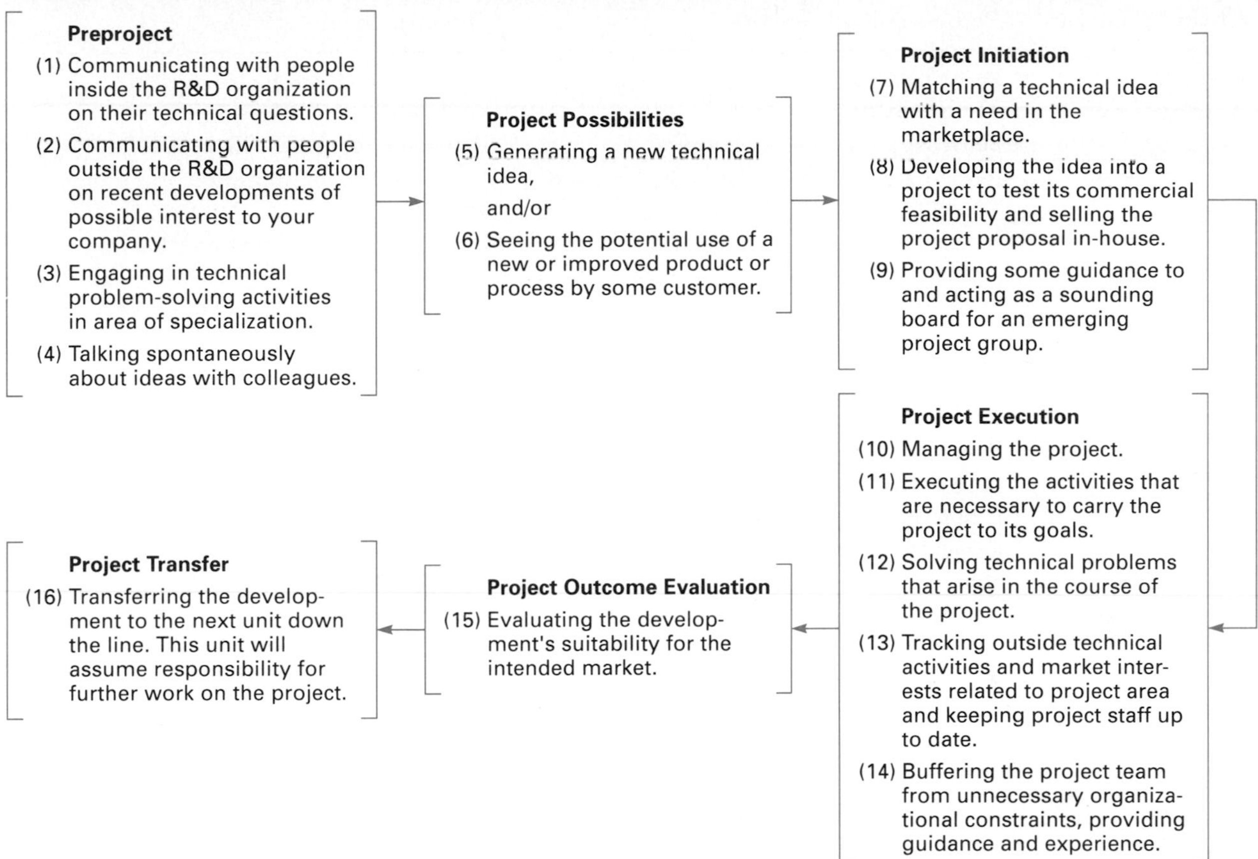

Reprinted from Staffing the innovative technology-based organization, by E.B. Roberts and A.R. Fusfeld, *Sloan Management Review*, Spring 1981, pp. 19–34, by permission of the publisher.

Table 13–4 Critical Functions in the Innovation Process

Critical Function	Personal Characteristics	Organizational Activities
Idea Generating	Expert in one or two fields. Enjoys conceptualization; comfortable with abstractions. Enjoys doing innovative work. Usually is an individual contributor. Often will work alone.	Generates new ideas and tests their feasibility. Good at problem solving. Sees new and different ways of doing things. Searches for the breakthroughs.
Entrepreneuring or Championing	Strong application interests. Possesses a wide range of interests. Less propensity to contribute to the basic knowledge of a field. Energetic and determined; puts self on the line.	Sells new ideas to others in the organization. Gets resources. Aggressive in championing his or her "cause." Takes risks.

continued

Table 13–4 CONTINUED

Critical Function	Personal Characteristics	Organizational Activities
Project Leading	Focus for decision making, information, and questions. Sensitive to the needs of others. Recognizes how to use the organizational structure to get things done. Interested in a broad range of disciplines and in how they fit together (e.g., marketing, finance).	Provides the team leadership and motivation. Plans and organizes the project. Insures that administrative requirements are met. Provides necessary coordination among team members. Sees that the project moves forward effectively. Balances the project goals with organizational needs.
Gatekeeping	Possesses a high level of technical competence. Is approachable and personable. Enjoys the face-to-face contact of helping others.	Keeps informed of related developments that occur outside the organization through journals, conferences, colleagues, other companies. Passes information on to others; finds it easy to talk to colleagues. Serves as an information resource for others in the organization (i.e., authority on who to see or on what has been done). Provides informal coordination among personnel.
Sponsoring or Coaching	Possesses experience in developing new ideas. Is a good listener and helper. Can be relatively objective. Often is a more senior person who knows the organizational ropes.	Helps develop people's talents. Provides encouragement, guidance, and acts as a sounding board for the project leader and others. Provides access to a power base within the organization—a senior person. Buffers the project team from unnecessary organizational constraints. Helps the project team to get what it needs from the other parts of the organization. Provides legitimacy and organizational confidence in the project.

Reprinted from Staffing the innovative technology-based organization, by E.B. Roberts and A.R. Fusfeld, *Sloan Management Review*, Spring 1981, pp. 19–34, by permission of the publisher.

WORK DESIGN OUTSIDE THE UNITED STATES

Many of the approaches to work design we have examined so far in this chapter have their roots outside the United States. West Germany and Japan have focused on continually improving product design and manufacturing, while simultaneously giving workers responsibility for contributing to these improvements. Work enrichment efforts have bloomed in Scandinavia. Volvo and Saab established precedents in the automobile industry with the introduction of autonomous work groups. The Uddevalla plant extends this work design one step farther. Worker ownership, a way of salvaging bankrupt companies or increasing employee motivation, has its model abroad in such cooperatives as Mondragon in Spain.

United States workers resemble the Scandinavian work force in one important respect: both include highly educated workers. In part because of this similarity, efforts to apply autonomous work groups in the United States have been relatively successful, as described earlier. The stronger role of unions in the United States, however, has affected their introduction; in the United States, union support has been a prerequisite for their successful implementation.

Japanese management practices also have had a major impact on work design in the United States. Conceived in the United States but developed in Japan to encourage quality control in production, quality circles were rediscovered and modified by companies in the United States in the 1980s, to address a range of productivity issues. The Japanese also use closely supervised teams in manufacturing and rely on careful control of inventory and production steps to ensure productivity. These design strategies fit with the Japanese emphasis on control, long-term planning and investment, and teamwork. Original attempts to import the Japanese approach intact to the United States led to some problems, but adjusting quality circles and Japanese team designs to U.S. culture has increased their effectiveness. Managers can borrow practices and approaches from other countries but must recognize that some translation and adaptation may be necessary for effective application elsewhere.

PRESCRIBING WORK REDESIGN

The choice of work design as a prescription for organizational problems depends on the nature of problems diagnosed. Redesign often offers a good solution to poor motivation, ineffective communication, stress, issues of individual development, and nonproductive group behavior. But it cannot overcome poor selection of personnel. Job redesign cannot be done apart from a consideration of job incumbents and their individual qualities. Similarly, future selection of employees must be done in a manner that is consistent with the work design the organization uses, to optimize the compatibility of worker and work situations.

We can redesign job content by simplifying or enriching the work. Work simplification corrects problems associated with overly complex jobs in which a job holder experiences role conflict, role ambiguity, or role overload.

The three approaches to job enrichment address different and, to some extent, opposite problems than does work simplification. Job enlargement responds to jobs that have become overly simplified, often because of the specialization of routine tasks. Job enrichment can correct problems of poor motivation resulting from work that has become meaningless, devoid of responsibility, or detached from its consequences. The sociotechnical approach deals with situations where introduction of a new technology infringes on, limits, or eliminates the social interactions of the individuals at different stages of development.

Redesigning the context of a job can accompany, or occur independently of, the redesign of a job's content. High absenteeism, difficulty in filling job positions, or simply management's desire to respond better to individual workers' needs for flexibility in scheduling and performing their work, may call for introducing flexible work hours or locations.

Organizations have used quality-of-working-life programs to increase productivity, cut costs, and improve worker well-being. We can use such programs to provide a comprehensive response to diverse symptoms, as well as to those problems calling for job enrichment or alternate work arrangements. Employee participation is a major component of QWL programs and of management in general in the United States. At best it may result in increased productivity and performance; at worst, it may be no less effective than nonparticipatory management.[64] Figure 13–5 lists a series of diagnostic questions that assess organizational readiness for participation in work redesign.

SUMMARY

In this chapter, we have examined the introduction of automation and technological innovation into the workplace and considered their significance for job design. We considered the use of the following approaches to redesign: work simplification, job enrichment, and alternate work arrangements. We also

Figure 13–5 QUESTIONS FOR ASSESSING ORGANIZATIONAL READINESS FOR PARTICIPATION IN WORK REDESIGN

1. To what extent is upper management willing to recognize and reward innovation?
2. To what extent do employees have influence over the physical work environment?
3. To what extent is bottom-up communication—especially of problems—encouraged?
4. To what extent does the prevailing organizational culture place a value on taking responsibility for problems rather than placing blame on others?
5. To what extent is management encouraged to make changes and take risks in striving to reach goals?
6. To what extent is the management philosophy of involving subordinates in problem solving consistent with the philosophy and behavior of top management?
7. To what extent has upper management in the past demonstrated support of projects and needs of middle managers and supervisors?
8. In unionized settings two additional factors deserve consideration: What is the history of union–management collaboration in joint projects? To what extent are the union and management willing to share in the success or failure of joint projects?
9. To what extent does the organization explicitly reward group success? Can this reward system overcome any cultural history of individualism?
10. To what extent do supervisors and managers use a team approach to achieve the work group's objectives?
11. To what extent do company information systems provide timely information on factors over which departments have control?
12. To what extent are the problems in the organization measurable, linear, consistent, and characterized by short time frames?
13. To what extent is the work process and technology such that people work on small, fragmented pieces and thus cannot solve problems in their department or are resisted by other departments when they propose solutions?
14. To what extent does the organization provide a stable working environment through long-term employment and work teams with stable membership?
15. To what extent do potential team leaders have the interpersonal and group skills needed to be effective leaders?
16. To what extent is there a willingness to reallocate resources (time, money, and people) to establish work teams?

Adapted from G.W. Meyer and R.G. Stott, Quality circles: Panacea or Pandora's box?, *Organizational Dynamics* 13 (Spring 1985): 47. Some questions were adapted by the authors from materials developed by the General Motors Education and Training and Organizational Research and Development Departments and the General Motors Department of the United Auto Workers, referenced in *Employee Participation Groups: Reference Manual* (Detroit: G.M. Corporation Managerial Educational Services, 1980).

Figure 13–6 DIAGNOSTIC QUESTIONS FOR WORK REDESIGN AND INNOVATION

- Are the jobs sufficiently specialized?
- Are the jobs sufficiently enriched?
- Do alternate work arrangements exist? Are they effective?
- Do quality-of-working-life projects exist? Are they effective?
- Do work redesign efforts match the workers' needs?
- Does innovation occur in the organization?
- Does a good quality innovation process exist?

reviewed a variety of quality-of-working-life programs, each designed to incorporate these and other redesign efforts into the work place. We described the process of innovation and discussed its links to work design. We also considered the nature of work redesign abroad.

Managers should view work redesign as an additional option for increasing organizational performance. Work redesign often accompanies organizational redesign, and together they can facilitate innovation in the work place. Figure 13–6 is a series of diagnostic questions for assessing work redesign. Note that ineffective work design can itself be an organizational problem, in addition to being a solution to other problems.

READING

Reading 13–1: INNOVATION PROCESSES IN MULTINATIONAL CORPORATIONS

Sumantra Ghoshal and Christopher A. Bartlett

INTRODUCTION

It was over twenty years ago that Vernon (1966) proposed the product cycle theory that identified the ability to innovate as the raison d'être for multinational corporations (MNCs). Over the last two decades, many new theories have been proposed to explain why MNCs exist, but innovations have continued to occupy the center stage in all the diverse and eclectic approaches (see Calvet 1981 for a brief review). The strength that allows a firm to invest and manage its affairs in many different countries is its ability to create new knowledge—to innovate—and to appropriate the benefits of such innovations in multiple locations through its own organization more effectively than through market-mediated mechanisms (Buckley and Casson 1976; Rugman 1982).

While theories of the multinational firm highlight the importance of innovations for the existence of such organizations, the emerging phenomenon of global competition (Hout, Porter, and Rudden 1982; Hamel and Prahalad 1985) has made innovations even more important for their survival. While traditionally many MNCs could compete successfully by exploiting scale economies or arbitraging imperfections in the world's goods, labor, and capital markets, such advantages have tended to erode over time. In many industries, MNCs no longer compete primarily with numerous national companies, but with a handful of other giants who tend to be comparable in terms of size, international resource access, and worldwide market position. Under the circumstances, the ability to innovate and to exploit those innovations globally in a rapid and efficient manner has become essential for survival and perhaps the most important source of a multinational's competitive advantage.

In sharp contrast to this practical importance, the topic of innovations in MNCs has received relatively little research attention. Not one of the over 4,000 studies on the topic of innovations (for references, see Gordon et al., 1975; Kelly and Kranzberg 1978; Mohr 1982) has focused specifically on the innovation process in the setting of a multinational corporation. Similarly, in the field of management of MNCs, past research has focussed overwhelmingly on strategy, defined implicitly as the way to enhance efficiency of current operations (see Ghoshal 1986b for a review), or structure, with most attention paid to the determinants of headquarters-subsidiary relations as opposed to their consequences. While some efforts have been made to investigate certain isolated aspects of distributed research and development in MNCs (Ronstadt 1977; Terpstra 1977), the issue of management of innovations has remained peripheral to research on the topic of management of multinational corporations.

THE STUDY

This paper is based on some of the findings of a recently concluded study of innovations in nine large MNCs, viz., Philips, GE, and Matsushita in the consumer electronics industry; L.M. Ericsson, ITT, and NEC in the telecommunications switching industry; and Unilever, Procter and Gamble, and Kao in the soaps and detergents industry. The choice of these industries and companies was based on the logic of maximum variety—the three industries represented very different requirements in terms of local responsiveness and global integration (Prahalad 1975; Porter 1986); within each industry, the selected firms were comparable in terms of size and strategic positions but, because of the differences in their national origins and administrative histories, had very significant differences in their organizational forms and processes (for descriptions and illustrations of these differences, see Bartlett and Ghoshal 1987).[1]

In each of these companies, we tried to identify as many specific cases of innovations as possible and to document their histories in the richest possible detail. To this end, 184 managers of these companies were interviewed, both at the corporate headquarters and also in their national subsidiaries in the United States, the United Kingdom, Germany, Italy, Japan, Singapore, Taiwan, Australia, and Brazil. None of the interviews lasted less than an hour and some took place during multiple meetings involving up to eight hours. We also collected and analyzed relevant internal documents relating to the histories of these innovations. This effort led to identification of thirty-eight cases of innovations for which we could reconstruct fairly extensive histories. While the descriptions possibly suffered from the well-known biases of historical reconstruction, we made all possible efforts to cross validate the stories through multiple sources and eliminated from the list those cases where different respondents differed significantly in their narration of the sequence of events that led to the innovations. These thirty-eight innovation cases constitute the primary data base for this report.

FOUR DIFFERENT INNOVATION PROCESSES

The innovation process[2] is one of the most complex of all organizational processes, and any stylized representation of this complexity cannot but be guilty of oversimplification. However, past research has suggested a generic stages model, shown in Figure 13–7, that views the innovation process as consisting of three sequential but also interacting sub-processes of sensing, response, and implementation.[3]

To innovate, a firm must sense changes that may demand adaptation or allow exploitation of any internal capability. The acquired stimuli must then be addressed through the firm's response mechanisms: technologies and products must be developed, processes must be improved or adapted, or an available capability must be converted into a functional form that satisfies a latent, emerging, or existing demand. Finally, the innovation must be exploited through efficient and effective implementation.

As suggested earlier, this is a highly simplified representation of a complex organizational process. In practice the different stages may be neither as discrete, nor as neatly sequential (Gross et al. 1971; Ginzberg and Reilly 1957). In any specific case, it may be extremely difficult to specify where the sensing process ends and the response process begins, or at what point the implementation phase may be said to have commenced. Similarly, the sequence suggested in the model, while logical, is not an invariant order of events. In reality, the process may be much more iterative, or even circular, with a high degree of interaction among all the three stages (Zaltman et al. 1973).

Despite its simplicity, the model provides a useful starting point for analyzing the administrative tasks of organizing for innovations. To innovate, a firm must develop appropriate capabilities to sense, respond, and implement. But just the capabilities are not enough; the firm must also create appropriate linkages to tie these capabilities together so that they function in an integrative manner. These two dimensions, viz., the configuration of organizational capabilities and the nature of their interlinkages provide, in Roethlisberger's (1977) terms, a "walking stick" for exploring the phenomenon of innovation-organization links.

Figure 13–7 A MODEL OF THE INNOVATION PROCESS

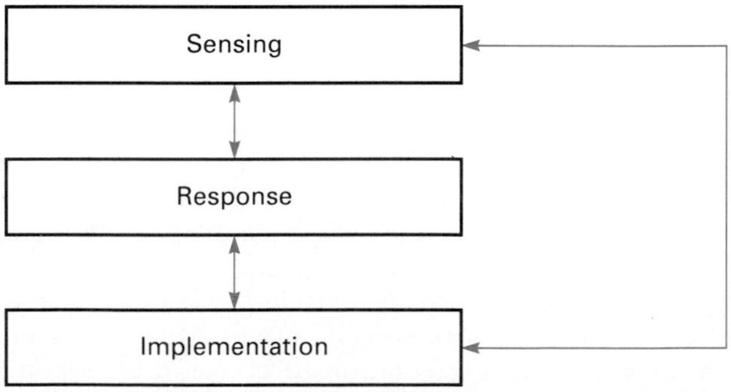

Table 13–5 summarizes our analysis of the thirty-eight innovation cases in terms of this process model.[4] For each case, we identified the administrative unit or units that carried out the sensing, response, and implementation tasks. This analysis revealed four different patterns in terms of the locations where the three tasks were carried out and, hence, in terms of the interlinkages among organizational units that were required to create and implement the innovation. Each of these patterns represents a different organizational process; collectively they suggest a scheme for classification of innovation processes in multinational corporations.[5] The table represents this classification scheme, and groups the thirty-eight innovation cases according to these categories, each of which is described and illustrated in the following pages.

The Center-for-Global Innovation Process

Center-for-global innovations are those where the center, i.e., the parent company or a central facility such as the corporate R&D laboratory, creates a new product, process, or system for worldwide use.[6] Most instances of center-for-global innovations that we came across in the course of our study were technological innovations but they were spread around a wide spectrum from minor modifications to substantial reorientations (Normann 1971). Most of the cases involved no participation of the national subsidiaries except for relatively routine tasks such as marketing support or nominal assembly at the implementation stage. In some others, one or more national organizations also contributed in relatively minor ways in the sensing process, while the response task, in all cases, was entirely carried out at the center. The process by which L.M. Ericsson, the Swedish manufacturer of telecommunications switching and terminal equipments, created the AXE digital switch is one example of this innovation process.

Impetus for the AXE came from early sensing of both shifting market needs and emerging technological changes. The loss of an expected order from the Australian Post Office, combined with the excitement generated by the new digital switch developed by CIT-Alcatel, a small French competitor virtually unknown outside its home country, set in motion a formal review process within Ericsson's headquarters. The review resulted in a proposal for developing a radically new switching system based on new concepts and a new technology. The potential for such a product was high, but the costs and risks were also enormous. The new product was estimated to require over $50 million and about 2,000 man-years of development effort and take at least 5 years before it could be offered in the market.

Table 13–5 INNOVATION PROCESSES IN MULTINATIONAL CORPORATIONS

Innovation Process	Description of Process (locations where different tasks are carried out) — Sensing	Response	Implementation	Number of Cases Observed
1. *Center-for-global*	At the center (occasionally, some input may be provided by a particular national subsidiary)	Always at the center	In a number of organizational units world-wide	13
2. *Local-for-local*	In a particular national unit	In the same national unit	In the same national unit	11
3. *Local-for-global*	In a particular national unit	In the same national unit (possibly with some minor help from the center)	Initially in the national unit, subsequently in many units in the world-wide organization of the company	8
4. *Global-for-global*	Many organizational units, including the center and a number of national subsidiaries	Many organizational units, including the center and a number of national subsidiaries	A number of organizational units worldwide	6

Even if the design turned out to be spectacular, diverting all available development resources during the intervening period could erode the company's competitive position beyond repair.

In sharp contrast to almost all the "principles of innovation" proposed by Drucker (1985), corporate managers of Ericsson decided to place their bet on the proposal for the AXE switch, as the new product came to be called. The process they adopted was not "incremental" (Quinn 1985), unless the term is so defined as to be all encompassing. A detailed, event-by-event documentation of the history of the switch by a key participant in the development process (Meurling 1985) shows little "controlled chaos" but rather the deliberateness and commitment of a programmed reorientation (Normann 1971). The company provided full authority and all resources so that Ellemtel, the R&D joint venture of Ericsson and the Swedish telecommunications administration, could develop the product as quickly as possible. For over four years, the technological resources of the company were devoted exclusively to this task. The development was carried out entirely in Sweden, and by 1976, the company had the first AXE switch in operation. By 1984 the system was installed in fifty-nine countries around the world.

Not all the cases of center-for-global innovations that we documented were equally effective. NEC, for example, designed the NEAC sixty-one as a global digital switch and developed it through its traditional centralized development process. However, while the Japanese engineers at the corporate headquarters had excellent technical skills, they were not familiar with the highly sophisticated and complex software requirements of the telephone operating companies in the United States, the principal market at which the product was aimed. As a result, while the switch was appreciated for its hardware capabilities, early sales suffered because the software did not meet some specific end user needs that were significantly different from those of Japanese customers.

The Local-for-Local Innovation Process

Local-for-local innovations are those that are created and implemented by a national subsidiary entirely at the local level. In other words, the sensing, response, and implementation tasks are all carried out within the subsidiary. Most cases of such innovations that we came across tended to be market led rather than technology driven and usually involved only minor modifications of an existing technology, product, or administrative system.

The ability of its local subsidiaries to sense and respond in innovative ways to local needs and opportunities has been an important corporate asset for Unilever. While advanced laundry detergents were not appropriate for markets like India, where much of the laundry was done in streams, a local development that allowed synthetic detergents to be compressed into solid tablet form gave the local subsidiary a product that could capture a significant share of the traditional bar soap market. Similarly, in Turkey, while the company's margarine products did not sell well, an innovative application of Unilever's expertise in edible fats allowed the company to develop a product from vegetable oils that competed with the traditional local clarified butter product, ghee.

As with center-for-global innovations, local-for-local innovations are not always as effective. In Philips, for example, the British subsidiary spent a large amount of resources to create a new TV chassis for its local market that turned out to be indistinguishable from the parent company's standard European model. As a consequence, for years Philips had to operate five instead of four television set factories in Europe.

The Local-for-Global Innovation Process

Local-for-global innovations are those which emerge as local-for-local innovations, are subsequently found to be applicable in multiple locations, and are then diffused to a number of organizational units. Thus, while the initial sensing, response, and implementation tasks are undertaken by a single subsidiary, other subsidiaries participate in the subsequent implementation process, as the innovation is diffused within the company.

Such was the case when Philips' British subsidiary reorganized the structure of its consumer electronics marketing division based on an analysis of changes in its product line and a growing concentration in its distribution channels. The traditional marketing organization which operated with a standard set of distribution, promotion, and sales policies applied uniformly to all product lines was proving to be increasingly ineffective in dealing with the large-volume chains that had come to dominate the retail market. Further, Philips' undifferentiated marketing strategies were constraining efforts in the differentiated and rapidly changing markets for its diverse products. To cope with this problem, the U.K. subsidiary abolished this uniform structure for each product line and organized the marketing department into three groups; an advanced system group for dealing with the technologically sophisticated, high-margin, and image-building products like Laservision and compact disc players; a mainstay group for marketing high-volume mature products such as color TV and VCR; and a mass group for mass merchandizing of the older, declining products like portable cassette players and black-and-white TV sets.

This new organization allowed the company to differentiate the nature and intensity of marketing support it provided to different products according to their stages in the product life cycle and to engage various elements of the marketing mix—including promotion, pricing, and distribution—in a more selective and differentiated manner. Within the first year of implementation, the new organization had helped reduce aggregate selling expenses from 18 to 12 percent. During the same period, while overall market demand for consumer electronics products in the United Kingdom had fallen by 5 percent, the subsidiary's sales in this business had risen by 49 percent, including a 400 percent rise in sales to Dixons, the largest reseller chain.

Meanwhile, increasing concentration in the distribution channels and growing necessity for differentiating marketing approaches for different products became manifest Europe-wide. The new model of the marketing organization developed by the British subsidiary was clearly appropriate for many other subsidiaries and, despite some initial resistance, the innovation was transferred to most other national organizations.

Resistance to such transfers, however, is both widespread and strong in MNCs, and it blocked several attempted local-for-global innovations we studied. For example, management of Unilever was unable to transfer a zero phosphate detergent developed by its German subsidiary to other European locations. Insisting that its market needs were different, the French subsidiary insisted on developing its own zero-P project.

The Global-for-Global Innovation Process

Global-for-global innovations are those that are created by pooling the resources and capabilities of many different organizational units of the MNC, including the headquarters and a number of different subsidiaries, so as to arrive at a jointly developed general solution to an emerging global opportunity, instead of finding different local solutions in each environment or a central solution that is imposed on all the units. As an ideal type, this category of innovations involves participation of multiple organizational units in each of the three stages of sensing, response, and implementation. However, the key feature that distinguishes it from the other categories is that the response task is shared, instead of being carried out by a single unit. One of the best examples we observed of this mode of innovation was the way in which Procter and Gamble developed its global liquid detergent.

Despite the success of liquid laundry detergents in the United States, all attempts to create a heavy-duty liquid detergent category in Europe failed due to different washing practices and superior performance of European powder detergents which contained levels of enzymes, bleach, and phosphates not permitted in the United States. But P&G's European scientists were convinced that they could enhance the performance of the liquid to match the local powders. After seven years of work they developed a bleach substitute, a fatty acid with water softening capabilities equivalent to phosphate, and a means to give enzymes stability in liquid form.

Meanwhile, researchers in the United States had been working on a new liquid better able to deal with the high-clay soil content in dirty clothes in the United States, and this group developed improvements in the builders, the ingredients that prevent redisposition of dirt in the wash. Also during this period, the company's International Technology Coordination Group was working with P&G scientists in Japan to develop a more robust surfactant (the ingredient that removes greasy stains), making the liquid more effective in the cold water washes that were common in Japan. Thus, the units in Europe, the United States, and Japan had each developed effective responses to its local needs, yet none of them had cooperated to share their breakthroughs.

When the company's head of R&D for Europe was promoted to the top corporate research job, one of his primary objectives was to create more coordination and cooperation among the diverse local-for-local development efforts, and the world liquid project became a test case. Plans to launch Omni, the new liquid the U.S. group had been working on, was shelved until the innovations from Europe and Japan could be incorporated. Similarly, the Japanese and the Europeans picked up on the new developments from the other laboratories. Joint effort on the part of all these groups ultimately led to the launch of Liquid Tide in the United States, Liquid Cheer in Japan, and Liquid Ariel in Europe. All these products incorporated the best of the developments created in response to European, American, and Japanese market needs.

ASSOCIATIONS BETWEEN INNOVATION PROCESSES AND ORGANIZATIONAL ATTRIBUTES

As we reviewed the key characteristics of the participating organizational components for each of the innovations listed in Table 13–5, four attributes, viz., (1) configuration of organizational assets and slack resources, (2) nature of inter-unit exchange relationships, (3) socialization processes, and (4) intensity of communication, appeared to have some systematic associations with the organization's ability to create innovations through the different processes we have described. These associations among the organizational factors and innovation processes are schematically represented in Figure 13–8, and are briefly described and illustrated in the following pages.

Configuration of Organizational Assets and Slack Resources

In some companies such as Matsushita, most key organizational assets and slack resources were centralized at the headquarters. Even though 40 percent of Matsushita's sales were made abroad, only 10 percent of its products were manufactured outside of Japan. The Japanese manufacturing facilities were also the most advanced and well-equipped plants of the company, producing almost all of its sophisticated products. R&D, similarly, was fully centralized in seven research laboratories in Japan. The center-for-global process appeared to contribute most of the significant innovations in companies with such a centralized configuration of organizational assets and resources. In Matsushita, for example, *all* new consumer electronics products introduced between 1983 and 1986 were developed by the parent company in Japan and were subsequently introduced in its different foreign markets.

In companies like Philips, ITT and Unilever, on the other hand, manufacturing, marketing, and even R&D facilities were widely dispersed throughout the organization. The local-for-local (and, to a lesser extent, local-for-global) process contributed a significant number of innovations in these companies. The dispersal of assets and resources was perhaps at its most extreme in the telecommunications business of ITT. The company had practically no central research of manufacturing activity, and each major national subsidiary was fully in-

Figure 13–8 Associations between Innovation Processes and Organizational Attributes

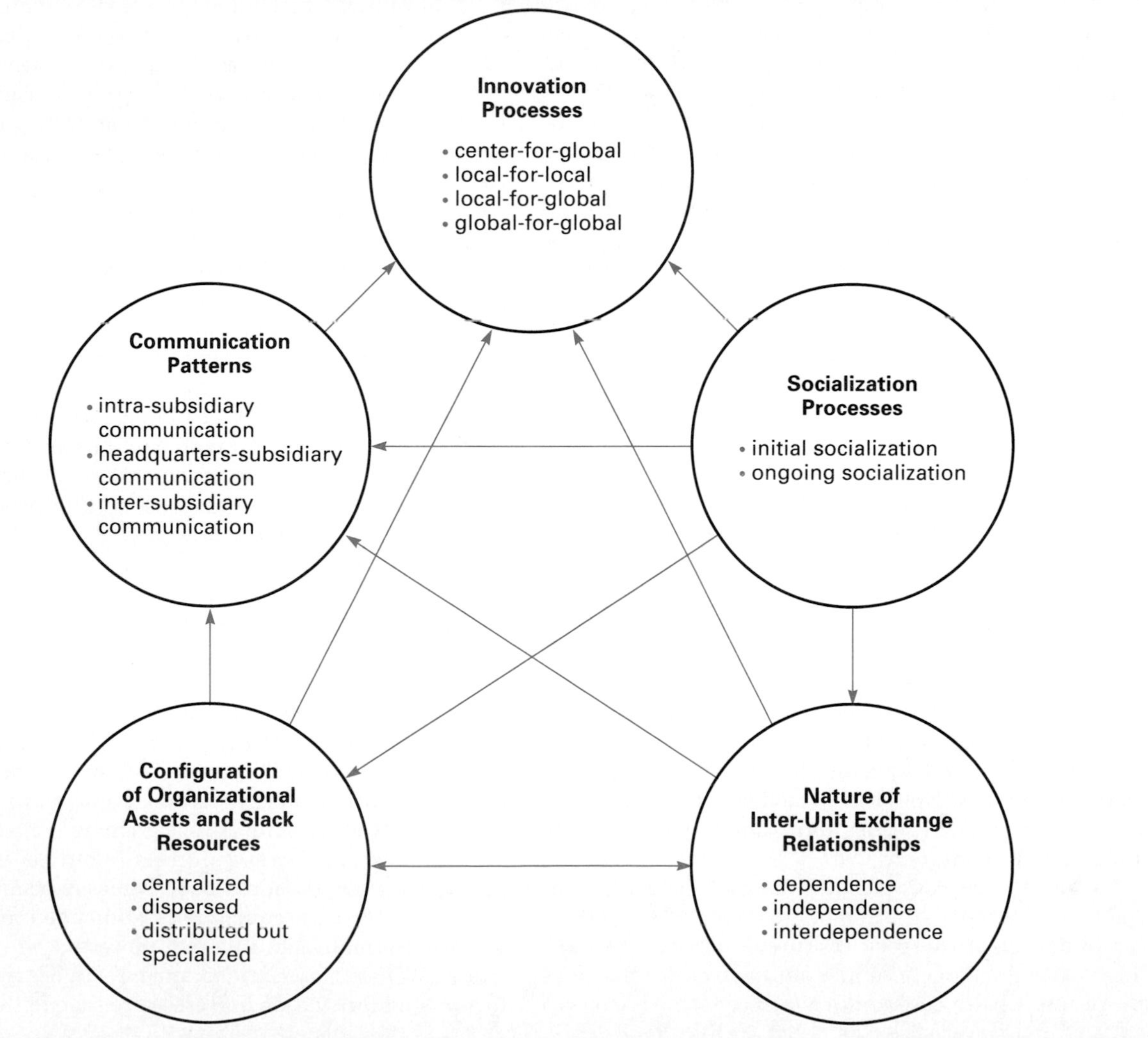

tegrated and self-sufficient in its ability to develop, manufacture, and market new products. Up until the advent of digital switching, all major products including the Metaconta and Pentaconta switches were initially developed in one or the other subsidiary and were subsequently "redeveloped" by other subsidiaries, resulting in many different varieties of the same product being sold in different markets. In Philips, similarly, the list of local-for-local innovations is endless—the first stereo color TV set was developed by the Australian subsidiary, teletext TV sets were created by the British subsidiary, "smart cards" by the French subsidiary, and the programmed word processing typewriter by North American Philips—to cite but a few examples.

Some of the companies we surveyed were gradually adopting a third system of asset and resource configuration. Instead of either centralization or decentralization, they were developing an interconnected network of specialized assets distributed around the world. Ericsson, NEC, and Procter and Gamble were the most advanced in building such a system, and it is only in these companies that we saw some cases of successful global-for-global innovations (even in these companies, however, most innovations came through the other processes).

In NEC, organizational assets were traditionally centralized and most innovations were created through the center-for-global process. The NEAC 61 digital switch, for example, was developed entirely in the company's central facilities in Japan, even though the product was principally aimed at the North American market. Subsequently, however, the company developed specialized software capabilities in the United States, while hardware expertise remained at the center. Such a distribution of resources allowed NEC to approximate the global-for-global process in developing the NEAC 61E auxiliary switch: the headquarters took the lead in building the hardware while the subsidiary participated significantly in designing the software. Similarly, the global liquid project of P&G that we have described earlier in the paper was made possible and necessary because three different research units responsible for product development in Japan, Europe, and the United States had each developed specialized capabilities that the others did not possess.

Several researchers have shown how resource configuration constrains all aspects of organizational actions and interactions (Emery and Trist 1965; Aldrich 1976). In the specific context of research on organizational innovations, a number of authors have highlighted the importance of distributed slack resources for creation and innovations (March and Simon 1958; Cyert and March 1963; Mohr 1969; Mansfield 1968; Kanter 1983). It has also been argued that local slack may have opposite effects on creation of innovations and adoption of innovations created elsewhere (Wilson 1966; Sapolsky 1967). Finally, the observation that interdependent, specialized resources might lead to joint innovations is also not new to the literature (Thompson 1967; Kanter 1983). Thus, the innovation process-resource configuration associations we observed are entirely consistent with what would be predicted by existing theory, if applied to the specific context of large, multi-unit organizations.

Nature of Interunit Exchange Relationships

In most of the countries in our sample, interactions among the national subsidiaries were extremely limited and dyadic relationships between the headquarters and each of the different subsidiaries were the dominant form of interunit exchanges. In some of these companies such as Kao, the large Japanese manufacturer of soaps and detergents, these dyadic exchange relationships were based primarily on subsidiary dependence on the headquarters. National subsidiaries of this company had neither the competence nor the legitimacy to initiate any new programs or even to modify any product or administrative system developed by the parent company. For example, a particular brand of liquid shampoo that was extremely successful in Japan failed to produce desired effects when introduced in Thailand. The product, aimed to suit the sophisticated needs of the Japanese market, could not compete effectively with simpler but less expensive local products and developed only a marginal 7 percent of market share despite considerable marketing investments. However, the nature of the problem could be identified and some remedial measures taken only after marketing experts from the headquarters visited the subsidiary along with executives from Dentsu, Kao's Japanese advertising agents. The local manager acknowledged that "Japan's expertise, knowledge, and resources made it appropriate for them to make such decisions." In companies where subsidiaries had developed such highly dependent relationships with the headquarters, the center-for-global process was often the exclusive source of innovations. For example, in Kao we did not come across a single case of any other innovation process.

In some other companies, such as ITT and Philips, the subsidiaries had considerable strategic and operational autonomy, though the headquarters exercised varying degrees of administrative control through the budgeting and financial reporting systems. In these companies, where subsidiaries were relatively independent of the headquarters, local-for-local innovations were far more prevalent.

The local-for-global and global-for-global processes essentially require the involvement of multiple organizational units, including a number of different national subsidiaries, and are realizable only when inter-subsidiary exchange relationships are prevalent in the company. However, in all the cases where these innovation processes were effective, such exchange relationships among organizational units appeared to be based on reciprocal interdependence (Thompson 1967), rather than on either dependence or independence.

In Procter and Gamble, for example, teams consisting of representatives from different national organizations in Europe (Euro-brand teams) coordinate regional strategies for different products of the company. For each product group, the team is headed by the general manager of a particular subsidiary and includes brand managers from other major subsidiaries. These teams provide one of the many mechanisms in the company that promote exchange relationships among the different national subsidiaries. Further, by ensuring that general managers from different subsidiaries head the different teams, the company creates reciprocal interdependencies in the relationships since each general manager recognizes that the level of cooperation he can expect from the brand managers or other subsidiaries in his team is dependent on the level of cooperation his brand managers extend to the other product teams that are headed by the general managers of other subsidiaries.

In contrast, ITT's attempt to develop the System 12 digital switch through a similar global-for-global process floundered because of the absence of such interdependencies. Recognizing that the technical resources required for developing the switch could not be assembled in any one location in its highly decentralized international organization, ITT management decided to adopt the global-for-global process of designing and building the switch through coordinated and joint action involving most of its major national operations. However, conditioned by a long history of local independence, the national subsidiaries resisted joint efforts and common standards leading to constant duplication of efforts, divergence of specifications, delays and an enormous budget overrun.

The effects of centralization and decentralization on innovation has been a topic of considerable debate in the literature. While most authors have argued in favor of a negative correlation between centralization and creation of innovations and a positive correlation between centralization and internal diffusion of innovations (for a review, see Zaltman et al. 1973), it has also been suggested that the relationships may be contingent on the type of innovation as well as the extent to which information and perspectives are shared among members of the organization (Downs and Mohr, 1979). Our findings support the general view that centralization of authority and the resulting dependency relationship between the headquarters and subsidiaries facilitate diffusion of center-for-global innovations but impede creation of local-for-local innovations, while decentralization of authority and the resulting independence of subsidiaries have precisely the opposite effects.

The facilitating influence of reciprocal interdependencies on local-for-global and global-for-global innovations observed by us also finds some support in exchange theory (Emerson 1972). Such interdependencies induce mutual cooperation (March and Simon 1958) and overcome both the bureaucratic and entrepreneurial traps described by Kanter (1983) as impediments to joint problem solving on the part of different organizational members.

Before concluding our discussion on inter-unit exchange relationships, we should note that the configuration of organizational resources tend to have considerable influence on the governance of such exchange, and vice versa. Theoretically, such associations are predicted by the resource dependency perspective (Pfeffer and Salancik 1978). When resources are centralized, as in Matsushita, Kao, and NEC, dyadic relationships of subsidiary dependence on the headquarters can be expected and are also observed. When resources are decentralized, as in Philips and Unilever, the subsidiaries exercise considerable independence and autonomy. Similarly, autonomous and resourceful subsidiaries are able to attract further resources for extension of current activities or creation of new ones, thereby establishing the reverse link between the nature of exchange relationships and the future flow of resources within the organization. Historically, location decisions for new manufacturing capacity in Philips were influenced by the relative power of different subsidiaries almost as much as by the dictates of production and distribution economies. On the other hand, Matsushita captured a very significant research facility in the United States when it acquired Motorola's TV business and senior corporate managers expected this research unit to play a major role in designing components and products for worldwide use. However, this role was inconsistent with the traditional basis of headquarters-subsidiary relationship in the company, and the capability was lost when most research engineers left in response to increasing functional control from the headquarters and the resulting loss of their local independence.

Organizational Socialization Processes

One interesting observation we made in the course of the study is that managers in both Philips and Matsushita were highly socialized into the very strong cultures of their respective organizations, though in very different ways. Further, while collectively, at the center, Matsushita managers continually sought change, individually, as expatriate managers in different national subsidiaries, they were relatively more likely to take a "custodial" stance, resisting change to centrally designed products, processes, and even routine administrative systems. Expatriate managers in Philips, in contrast, were generally more willing to champion local initiatives and thereby foster local-for-local innovations.

Van Maanen and Schein (1979) have argued that the nature of initial and ongoing socialization processes of organizations have some important influences on members' attitudes toward change. Certain socialization processes lead to custodial behavior and resistance to change, while others facilitate both content and role innovations on the part of socialized members. At least in the cases of Philips and Matsushita, the associations between socialization processes and attitude toward change proposed by these authors appear to explain the observed behavioral differences quite remarkably.

Initial post-recruitment training and subsequent career structures are two important constituents of the organizational socialization process, and are both quite different for managers in the two companies. In Matsushita, college graduates are recruited at the center in large batches and are collectively socialized through a common training program that continues for one year or more. Managerial recruits in Philips, on the other hand, are recruited from diverse locations in small numbers, and are quickly posted to different units so as to learn on the job. While cohorts meet infrequently for some classroom sessions, initial socialization tends to be relatively more individually oriented, dependent on the new member establishing personal relationships with existing members, often his or her senior colleagues, on a one-to-one basis.

Before being assigned overseas, Matsushita managers are exposed to another strong dose of formal training. The company's formidable Overseas Training Center (OTC) prepares managers for overseas tours of duty by ensuring that they thoroughly understand Matsushita's practices and values. Expatriate managers are usually posted to a foreign location for relatively long periods, usually five to eight years, after which they return to the headquarters. They may be posted abroad once more, later in their careers, and often to the same location where they had worked earlier, though at more senior levels. In Philips, given the relatively insignificant role of the home country operations in the worldwide business of the company, a large number of managers spend a significant part of their careers abroad continuously, spending between two and three years in a number of different subsidiaries. Many of these managers retire abroad, while some return to take up top level corporate positions toward the end of their careers.

As suggested by Van Maanen and Schein, collective socialization such as in Matsushita results in relatively stronger conformity to the values that the collectivity is socialized into. Thus, when change is proposed within that collectivity (such as in the headquarters which is seen as the repository of those values), it tends to be supported. However, local changes in national subsidiaries that attempt to modify values, systems, or processes designed by that collectivity tend to be resisted. In contrast, individual socialization, as in Philips, tends to produce less homogeneity of views and greater willingness to change at local levels.

Similarly, the differences in career systems can also be expected to result in very different attitudes to local innovations. In Philips, expatriate managers follow each other into key management and technical positions in the company's national organizations around the world, they perceive themselves as a distinct subgroup within the organization and come to develop and share a distinct subculture. In Matsushita, on the other hand, there is very little interaction among the expatriate managers in different subsidiaries, and they tend to view themselves as part of the parent company on temporary assignment to foreign locations. Consequently, Philips managers tend to identify strongly with the national organization's point of view and to serve as champions of local level changes, while Matsushita managers become more prone to implementing centrally designed products and policies.

Received theory, as well as our own observations in the nine companies, suggests that organizational socialization processes have significant influences on both the basis of internal exchange relations within organizations, and the configuration of assets and slack resources—the two other influencing variables in our model. Institutionalized processes of initial and ongoing socialization of new members lie at the core of organizational cultures and form the administrative routines that govern internal exchange behavior and exercise of choice (Ouchi 1980; Schein 1985; Nelson and Winter 1982). Shared goals and values lead to fluidity in the internal distribution of power, and to flexibility in its use (Pascale and Athos 1981; Kanter 1983). Configuration of organizational resources is a product of organizational goals and internal power structures (Pfeffer and Salancik 1978; Mintzberg 1983) and is thereby indirectly influenced by the socialization processes that affect both these determinants. Illustrations of these influences abound in the organizations we studied. The "ization" program of Unilever—a commitment to "localize" Unilever in each country as well as to "Unileverize" each local operation—is a case in point. This program—backed by extensive ongoing training activities, a planned company-wide transfer policy, and significant commitment of top management time devoted to ensure its reinforcement and salience—has led simultaneously to a gradual reconfiguration of the company's resources from being almost totally decentralized to becoming more specialized and interdependent, and the restructuring of inter-unit interactions from an internal norm of fiercely protected subsidiary autonomy to much greater sharing of influence in which subsidiary initiatives are circumscribed by a significant and substantive role of the center in setting and coordinating strategies, particularly with regard to development and introduction of new products.

Communication Patterns

Almost all studies on innovation-organization linkages have emphasized the central role of communication in facilitating organizational innovations (Allen 1977; Allen, Lee, and Tushman 1980; Burns and Stalker 1961; Kanter 1983; Rogers and Shoemaker 1971). Collectively, this body of theoretical and empirical literature has found consistent support for the proposition that communication is a prerequisite for innovations and, more specifically, that intra-organizational communication is perhaps the most important determinant of an organization's ability to create and institutionalize innovations.

Internal communication patterns in the nine companies we studied could be broadly categorized into three groups. In some companies such as ITT and Philips, internal communication within each subunit (the headquarters or individual national subsidiaries) was intense, but the level of communication among subunits (between the headquarters and each of the subsidiaries as well as among the subsidiaries themselves) was relatively low. In some others, such as Matsushita, communication links between the headquarters and most of the different subsidiaries were especially strong, but internal communication within the subsidiaries as well as communication among the subsidiaries tended to be limited. Finally, the third group consisted of companies like Procter and Gamble and L. M. Ericsson, where both internal communication within subunits and communication among subunits tended to be relatively rich and frequent. Local-for-local innovations were the most common in the first group of companies (although some of them, such as Philips, could also create innovations through the local-for-global process), center-for-global innovations were dominant in the second, and only the third group could create innovations through all the four processes we have described.

By examining internal communication patterns in Philips, one can see how they support local-for-local innovations. Historically, the top management in all national subsidiaries of Philips consisted not of an individual CEO but a committee made up of the heads of the technical, commercial, and finance functions. This system of three-headed management had a long history in Philips, stemming from the functional independence of the two founding Philips brothers, one an engineer and the other a salesman, and has endured as a tradition of intensive intra-unit cross-functional communication and joint decision making within each subsidiary.

In most subsidiaries, these integration mechanisms exist at three organizational levels. At the product management level, article teams prepare annual sales plans and budgets and develop product policies. A second tier of cross-functional coordination takes place through the group management team, which meets once a month to review results, suggest corrective actions, and resolve any inter-functional differences. The highest level cross-functional coordination and communication forum within the subsidiary is the senior management committee (SMC) consisting of the top commercial, technical, and financial managers of the subsidiary. Acting essentially as the local board, the SMC ensures overall unity of effort among the different functional groups within the local unit, and protects the legitimacy and effectiveness of the communication forums at lower levels of the organization. These multilevel cross-functional integrative mechanisms within each subsidiary lie at the heart of Philips' ability to create local innovations in its different operating environments.

If the challenge for improving the efficiency of local-for-local innovations lies in strengthening cross-functional communication within subsidiaries, the key task for enhancing the effectiveness of center-for-global innovations lies in building linkages between the headquarters and the different subsidiaries of the company. The main problem of centrally created innovations is that those developing new products or processes may not understand market needs, or that those required to implement the new product introduction are not committed to it. Matsushita overcomes these problems of center-for-global innovations by creating multilevel and multifunctional linkages between the headquarters and each of the different subsidiaries and these linkages facilitate both the communication of local market demands from the subsidiary to the center, and also central coordination and control over the subsidiary's implementation of the company's strategies and plans, including those of implementing innovations.

The communication links that connect different parts of the Matsushita organization in Japan with the video department of MESA, its U.S. subsidiary, are illustrative of headquarters-subsidiary communication systems in the company. The vice president in charge of this department of MESA has his roots in Matsushita Electric Trading Company (METC), the central organization that has overall responsibility for the company's overseas business. Although formally posted to the United States, he continues to be a member of the senior management committee of METC and spends about a third of his time in Japan. The general manager of this department had worked for fourteen years in the video product division of Matsushita Electric Industries (MEI), the central production and domestic marketing company in Japan. He maintains almost daily communication with the central product division in Japan and acts as its link to the local American market. The assistant manager in the department, the most junior expatriate in the organization, links the local unit to the central factory in Japan. Having spent five years in the factory, he is and acts as its local representative and handles all day-to-day communication with factory personnel.

None of these linkages is accidental. They are deliberately created and maintained and reflect the company's desire to preserve the different perspectives and priorities of its diverse groups worldwide, and ensure that they have linkages to those in the headquarters who can represent and defend their views. Unlike in companies that try to focus headquarters-subsidiary communication through a single channel for the sake of efficiency, Matsushita's multilevel and multifunctional linkages create a broad band of communication through which each central unit involved in creating center-for-global innovations have direct access to local market information, while each local unit involved in implementing those innovations also has the opportunity to influence the innovation process.

Finally, a few companies like P&G and Ericsson are able to create organizational mechanisms that facilitate simultaneously intense intra-unit communication, extensive headquarters-subsidiary communication, and also considerable flow of information among the different subsidiaries. As a result, these companies are able to create innovations through all the four processes.

In Ericsson, for example, intra-subsidiary communication is facilitated both by a culture and tradition of open communication and, more specifically, by extensive use of ad hoc teams and special liaison roles with the express mandate of facilitating intra-unit integration. Headquarters-subsidiary communication is strengthened by mechanisms such as deputing one or more senior corporate managers as members of subsidiary boards. Unlike many companies whose local boards are pro forma bodies aimed at satisfying national legal requirements, Ericsson uses its local boards as legitimate forums for communicating objectives, resolving differences, and making decisions. Intersubsidiary communication is facilitated by a number of processes such as allocating global roles to subsidiaries for specific tasks (for example, Italy is the center for transmission system development, Finland for mobile telephones, and Australia for rural switches) which require them to establish communication links worldwide. However, perhaps the single factor that has the strongest effect on facilitating communication in the dispersed Ericsson organization is its long-standing policy of transferring large numbers of people back and forth between headquarters and subsidiaries.

Executive transfers in Ericsson differ from the more common transfer patterns in multinational corporations in both direction and intensity, as a comparison with NEC's transfer processes will demonstrate. Where NEC may transfer a new technology through one or perhaps a few key managers, Ericsson will send a team of 50 or 100 engineers and managers for a year or two; while NEC's flows are primarily from headquarters to subsidiary, Ericsson's is a balanced, two-way flow with people coming to the parent not only to learn but also to bring their expertise; and while NEC's transfers are predominantly Japanese, Ericsson's multidirectional process involves all nationalities.

Australian technicians seconded to Stockholm in the mid-1970s to bring their experience with digital switching into the development of AXE developed enduring relationships that helped in the subsequent development of a rural switch in Australia through the global-for-global process. Confidences built when an Italian team of forty spent eighteen months in Sweden to learn about electronic switching provided the basis for greater decentralization of AXE software development and a delegated responsibility for developing the switch's central transmission system through a local-for-global process.

Communication may be the final cause (Mohr 1982) that influences innovation processes in organizations, but it is itself a product of different organizational attributes such as the configuration of resources (Pfeffer 1982), internal governance systems (Kaufman 1960), and culture (Schein 1985). Our descriptions of the mechanisms that facilitate communication in some of the companies we surveyed illustrate these linkages, which are part of the model represented in Figure 13–8.

CONCLUSION

In this paper we have identified four organizational attributes that influence the different multinational innovation processes: configuration of organizational assets and slack resources; basis for inter-unit exchange relationships that reflect the distribution of power within the company; training, transfer, and other processes of socializing members; and the nature of intra- and inter-unit communication. Each of these has been identified by earlier researchers as key factors that influence an organization's ability to innovate. Burns and Stalker (1961) emphasized the importance of decentralized authority and intra-unit communication for promoting "grass-roots" innovations (local-for-local, in our terms). Lorsch and Lawrence (1965) highlighted the relevance of cross-functional integration. Quinn (1985) and Peters and Waterman (1982) illustrated the need for fluid power structures and dispersal of organizational resources. And Kanter (1983), in her description of the "integrative organization," identified each of these elements as key requirements for promoting organizational innovations. Thus, our overall findings broadly confirm those of many others who have investigated the effects of different organizational attributes on innovative capability of firms.

At the same time, our findings provide a point of departure and an avenue for incremental extension of existing theory. The source of this extension lies in our explicit focus on multi-unit organizations which necessitates simultaneous consideration of organizational attributes both within individual units and across multiple units. In contrast, most of past research has been limited to organizational subcomponents as the level of analysis, even though conclusions have sometimes been generalized at the level of the total organization. In the case of Burns and Stalker, the level of analysis is stated quite explicitly: "The twenty concerns that were subject of these studies were not all separately constituted business companies. This is why we have used concern as a generic term. . . . [Some of them] were small parts of the parent organization." The other researchers have similarly observed a district sales office of General Electric or a department in the headquarters of 3M, or a divisional data processing office of Polaroid, but not the overall organizational configuration in any one of these physically and goal-dispersed organizations. Given the possibility that there may be trade-offs between integration and differentiation at different levels of the organization (Lawrence and Lorsch 1967), findings at the level of organizational subcomponents can serve as useful hypotheses but not as validated conclusions at the level of multi-unit, complex organizations.

By broadening the focus to include inter-unit interactions, we have identified four different organizational processes through which innovations may be created and institutionalized in multi-unit companies. It is also manifest that the different processes are facilitated by organizational attributes that are not only different but possibly also contradictory. Local-for-local innovations, for example, tend to be incremental (Quinn 1985) and unprogrammed (Drucker 1985) changes that are facilitated by distributed resources and decentralized authority—attributes of the organic concern described by Burns and Stalker. Some center-for-global innovations, on the other hand, can be reorientations (Normann 1971) that are highly programmed, and they may be facilitated by precisely the opposite characteristics of centralization of organizational resources and authority. Factors that facilitate innovativeness on the part of a subunit may not be those that facilitate their adoption of innovations created elsewhere in the company, nor their participation in joint efforts. By differentiating among the processes, we have taken a step, albeit small, in the direction of a more disaggregated analysis of innovation-organization links advocated by Downs and Mohr (1979).

Our findings of the organizational attributes that facilitate each of these different innovation processes are summarized in Table 13–6. Given the exploratory nature of the study, these findings are, at best, grounded hypotheses that clearly require more systematic and rigorous analysis. These hypothesis, however, have some significant consequences for theory and therefore appear to be deserving of the additional efforts that are necessary to test and validate them.[7]

At a more normative level, the complexity and diversity of technological, competitive, and market environments confronting most worldwide industries may require participating multinationals to create organizational mechanisms that would facilitate simultaneously all the innovation processes we have described. Although a few companies in our sample had begun to achieve this state on a partial and temporary basis, creating such a capability on a more general and permanent basis may be a challenge of considerable magnitude, given the potential contradictions in organizational attributes that facilitate each of these innovation processes. A more systematic study on the topic can lead to reliable suggestions on how these potential contradictions can be overcome. Based on our discussions with a number of MNC managers to whom we have presented our findings, we are convinced that such a study would be of great value to them.

NOTES

1. This study of innovations in MNCs was a part of a larger research project on management of multinational corporations which covered a number of issues other than management of innovations. The overall findings of the project are being reported in our forthcoming book, *Managing Across Borders: The Transnational Solution.*
2. The term *innovation* has been defined in many different ways. However, these definitions can be broadly classified into two categories: those that see innovation as the final event—"the idea, practice, or material artifact that has been invented or that is regarded as novel independent of its adoption or nonadoption" (Zaltman et al. 1973:7), and those who, like Myers and Marquis, see it as a process "which proceeds from the conceptualization of a new idea to a solution of the problem and then to the actual utilization of a new item of economic or social value" (1969:1). We adopt the latter definition and, throughout the paper, use the terms innovation and innovation process interchangeably.

Table 13–6 ASSOCIATIONS BETWEEN INNOVATION PROCESSES AND ORGANIZATIONAL FACTORS: A SUMMARY

Innovation Process	Configuration of Assets and Stock Resources	Socialization Processes	Nature of Inter-Unit Exchange Relationships	Communication Patterns
1. *Center-for-global*	Centralized at headquarters	Formal and collective initial training, transfers of few people from headquarters to subsidiaries, infrequently and for long terms	Subsidiaries dependent on headquarters	High density of communication between headquarters and subsidiaries
2. *Local-for-local*	Dispersed to subsidiaries	Informal and individual initial training; subsidiary-to-subsidiary transfers of an international cadre of managers	Subsidiaries independent of headquarters	High density of communication within subsidiaries
3. *Local-for-global*	Dispersed to subsidiaries	Informal but both collective and individual initial training; subsidiary-to-subsidiary transfers of an international cadre of managers	Subsidiaries independent of headquarters but mutually dependent on each other	High density of communication within and among subsidiaries.
4. *Global-for-global*	Distributed, specialized	Both collective and individual initial training, two-way transfers of large numbers of managers among headquarters and the different subsidiaries	Headquarters and subsidiaries mutually dependent on one another	High density of communication within subsidiaries, among subsidiaries, and between the headquarters and the subsidiaries

3. The sense-response-implement model has an extensive history in multiple fields. It is directly adopted from the unfreeze-change-refreeze framework in the field of organization development proposed by Lewis and subsequently enhanced by Bennis, Schein, Beckhard, and others. For a brief review of this literature, see Lorange et al. (1986). The same model, with different labels, has been adopted in the marketing field to describe the new product introduction process (see, for example, Urban and Hauser 1980), and by many scholars who have studied the organizational innovation process (see Zaltman et al. 1973 for a review).
4. To save space, we do not list the thirty-eight innovation cases, but interested readers can find such a list in Ghoshal (1986:a).
5. Both the spirit of this analysis and the actual methodology were inspired by the work of Bower (1980). However, given a relatively large number of cases, a more formal case clustering approach was adopted.
6. The terms global and worldwide have been used

somewhat loosely in the paper to imply many different national subsidiaries or environments.

7. We have since pursued this research direction and the results tend to support the hypotheses. These findings will be reported in a forthcoming paper.

BIBLIOGRAPHY

Aldrich, H.E. "Resource Dependency and Interorganizational Relations." *Administration and Society* 7 (1976): 419–54.

Allen, T.J. *Managing the Flow of Technology*. Cambridge, MA: MIT Press, 1977.

Allen, T.J., and S. Cohen. "Information Flow in R&D Laboratories." *Administrative Science Quarterly* 14 (1969): 12–19.

Allen, T.J.; D.M.S. Lee; and M.L. Tushman. "R&D performance as a Function of Internal Communication, Project Management, and the Nature of Work." *IEEE Transactions on Engineering Management* EM-27 (1980): 2–12.

Bartlett, C.A., and S. Ghoshal. "Managing Across Borders: New Strategic Requirements." *Sloan Management Review* (Summer 1987): 7–17.

———. *Managing Across Borders: The Transnational Solution*. Boston: Harvard Business School Press, forthcoming.

Bower, J.L. *Managing the Resource Allocation Process*. Boston: Harvard Business School Press, 1980.

Buckley, P.J., and M.C. Casson. *The Future of the Multinational Enterprise*. London: MacMillan Press, 1976.

Burns, T., and G.M. Stalker. *The Management of Innovation*. London: Tavistock, 1961.

Calvet, A.L. "A Synthesis of Foreign Direct Investment Theories and Theories of the Multinational Firm." *Journal of International Business Studies* (Spring-Summer 1981): 43–59.

Cyert, R.M., and J.G. March. *A Behavioral Theory of the Firm*. Englewood Cliffs, NJ: Prentice-Hall, 1963.

Downs, G.W., and L.B. Mohr. "Conceptual Issues in the Study of Innovation." *Administrative Science Quarterly* 21 (1976): 700–14.

———. "Toward a Theory of Innovation." *Administration and Society* 10, no. 4 (1979): 379–407.

Drucker, P.F. *Innovation and Entrepreneurship*. New York: Harper and Row, 1985.

Emerson, R.N. "Exchange Theory, Part II: Exchange Relations, Exchange Networks, and Groups as Exchange Systems." In J. Berger, M. Zelditch, and B. Anderson, (eds.), *Sociological Theories in Progress*, (vol. 2). Boston: Houghton Mifflin, 1972.

Emery, F.E., and F.L. Trist. "The Contextual Texture of Organizational Environments." *Human Relations* 18 (1965): 21–31.

Ghoshal, S. "The Innovative Multinational: A Differentiated Network of Organizational Roles and Management Processes." Ph.D. diss. Graduate School of Business Administration, Harvard University, 1986(a).

———. "Global Strategy: An Organizing Framework." Paper presented to the Annual Conference of the Academy of International Business, London, 1986(b), forthcoming in the *Strategic Management Journal*.

Ginzberg, E., and E. Reilly. *Effective Change in Large Organizations*. New York: Columbia University Press, 1957.

Gordon, G.; J.R. Kimberley; and A. MacEachron. "Some Considerations in the Design of Problem Solving Research on the Diffusion of Medical Technology." In W.J. Abernathy, A. Sheldon, and C.K. Prahalad, eds., *The Management of Health Care*. Cambridge, MA: Ballinger, 1975.

Gross, N.; J.B. Giacquinta; and M. Berstein. *Implementing Organizational Innovations: A Sociological Analysis of Planned Educational Change*. New York: Basic Books, 1971.

Hamel, G., and C.K. Prahalad. "Do You Really Have a Global Strategy?" *Harvard Business Review* (July-August 1985): 139–148.

Hout, T.; M.E. Porter; and E. Rudden. "How Global Companies Win Out." *Harvard Business Review* (September-October 1982): 98–108.

Kanter, R.M. *The Change Masters*. New York: Simon and Schuster, 1983.

Kaufman, H. *The Forest Ranger: A Study in Administrative Behavior*. Baltimore: Johns Hopkins University Press, 1960.

Kelly, P., and M. Kranzberg. *Technological Innovations: A Critical Review of Current Knowledge*. San Francisco: San Francisco University Press, 1978.

Lawrence, P.R., and J.W. Lorsch. *Organization and Environment*. Boston: Graduate School of Business Administration, Harvard University, 1967.

Lorange, P.; M. Scott Morton; and S. Ghoshal. *Strategic Control*. St. Paul: West Publishing Co., 1986.

Lorsch, J.W., and P.A. Lawrence. "Organizing for Product Innovation." *Harvard Business Review* (January-February 1965): 109–120.

Mansfield, E. *The Economics of Technological Change*. New York: W.W. Norton, 1968.

March, J.G., and H.A. Simon. *Organizations*. New York: Wiley, 1958.

Meurling, J. *A Switch in Time*. Chicago: Telephony Publishing Corp., 1985.

Mintzberg, H. *Power in and Around Organizations*. Englewood Cliffs, NJ: Prentice-Hall, 1983.

Mohr, L.B. "Determinants of Innovation in Organizations." *American Political Science Review* 63 (1969): 111–26.

———. *Explaining Organizational Behavior*. San Francisco, Jossey-Bass, 1982.

Myers, S., and D.G. Marquis. *Successful Industrial Innovations*. Washington, D.C.: National Science Foundation, NSF 69-17, 1969.

Nelson, R.R., and S.G. Winter. *An Economic Theory of Evolutionary Capabilities and Behavior*. Cambridge: Harvard University Press, 1982.

Normann, R. "Organizational Innovativeness: Product Variation and Reorientation." *Administrative Science Quarterly* 16, no. 2 (1971): 203–15.

Ouchi, W.G. "Markets, Bureaucracies, and Clans." *Administrative Science Quarterly* 25 (1980): 129–41.

Pascale, R.T., and A.G. Athos. *The Art of Japanese Management*. New York: Warner Books, 1981.

Peters, T.J., and R.H. Waterman. *In Search of Excellence*. New York: Harper & Row, 1982.

Pfeffer, J. *Power in Organizations*. Boston: Pitman, 1982.

Pfeffer, J., and G.R. Salancik. *The External Control of Organizations: A Resource Dependency Perspective*. New York: Harper and Row, 1978.

Porter, M.E. "Competition in Global Industries: A Conceptual Framework." In M.E. Porter, ed., *Competition in Global Industries*. Boston: Harvard Business School Press, 1986.

Prahalad, C.K. "The Strategic Process in a Multinational Corporation." Ph.D. diss., Graduate School of Business Administration, Harvard University, Boston, 1975.

Quinn, J.B. "Managing Innovations: Controlled Chaos." *Harvard Business Review* (May-June 1985): 73–84.

Roethlisberger, F.J. *The Elusive Phenomenon*. Boston: Division of Research, Graduate School of Business Administration, Harvard University, 1977.

Rogers, E.M., and F.F. Shoemaker. *Communication of Innovations: A Cross-cultural Approach*. New York: Free Press, 1971.

Ronstadt, R.C. *Research and Development Abroad by U.S. Multinationals*. New York: Praeger, 1977.

Rugman, A.M. *New Theories of the Multinational Enterprise*. New York: St. Martin's Press, 1982.

Sapolsky, H.M. "Organizational Structure and Innovation." *Journal of Business* 40 (1967): 497–510.

Schein, E.H. *Organizational Culture and Leadership*. San Francisco: Jossey-Bass, 1985.

Terpstra, V. "International Product Policy: The Role of Foreign R&D." *The Columbia Journal of World Business* (Winter 1977): 24–32.

Thompson, J.D. *Organizations in Action: Social Science Bases of Administrative Theory*. New York: McGraw Hill, 1967.

Urban, G.L., and J.R. Hauser. *Design and Marketing of New Products*. Englewood Cliffs, NJ: Prentice-Hall, 1980.

Van Maanen, J., and E.H. Schein. "Toward a Theory of Organizational Socialization." In B. Shaw, ed., *Research in Organizational Behavior*. JAI Press, 1979.

Vernon, R. "International Investment and International Trade in the Product Cycle." *Quarterly Journal of Economics* (May 1966): 190–207.

Wilson, J.Q. "Innovation in Organization: Notes toward a Theory." In J.D. Thompson, ed., *Approaches to Organization Design*. Pittsburgh: University of Pittsburgh Press, 1966.

Zaltman, G.; R. Duncan; and J. Holbeck. *Innovations and Organizations*. New York: Wiley, 1973.

DISCUSSION QUESTIONS

1. Describe the generic innovation process.
2. Compare and contrast the four different patterns of innovation process.
3. What organizational attributes are associated with an organization's ability to create innovations?
4. How do the attributes differ for the four patterns of the innovation process?

ACTIVITIES

Activity 13–1: AMERICAN OPTICAL CO.—SOFT CONTACT LENS DIVISION CASE

Step 1: Read the American Optical Co. case.

It is the spring of 1976, Floyd Sundue, Director of the fledgling Soft Contact Lens Division of the American Optical Corporation, is faced with a fundamental decision regarding the design of a new production facility. The conventional approach is to design such a facility as a single-flow shop. The specific manufacturing process provides him with a unique opportunity to implement a new concept—autonomous work groups. His past experience with organizations indicates the new facility could benefit from the approach.

As Floyd mulls over his notes, he knows a decision must be made quickly. The market for soft contact lenses has been growing rapidly. It has been dominated by Bausch and Lomb—the first company to obtain FDA approval for their product. Now, five years later, FDA approval for American Optical was imminent. The slow approval process had given Bausch and Lomb a virtual monopoly of the market. However, the market continued to grow at a rapid pace. Floyd knew he needed to get his product on the market quickly if he wanted to be a major producer of soft contact lenses.

HISTORY OF THE SOFT CONTACT LENS

The hydrophilic (water absorbing) material from which the lenses are produced was first developed by the Czechoslovakians. It was intended for the treatment of eye diseases such as glaucoma or to place drugs under the skin. In theory, the material would absorb the drug to be administered; then, once in place, it would be gradually released over an extended period of time. The purpose was to administer drugs to a patient.

In 1965, the Czechoslovak Academy licensed Flexible Lenses (a subsidiary of National Patent Corporation) to sell the material in Europe and the Americas. The licensee approached American Optical with the material but no agreement could be reached. Bausch and Lomb was then approached. They recognized the vast potential in using the material for the manufacture of a soft contact lens. Agreement was reached and, in 1971, Bausch and Lomb placed the first soft contact lens on the market. They were the undisputed market leader[1] in soft contact lens.

In the late sixties, there was another development with far-reaching implications for the industry. The Federal Food and Drug Administration (FDA) reviewed the material and classified it as a drug. This classification means that a prospective manufacturer must meet stringent requirements before receiving FDA approval for marketing the product. Specifically:

a. intensive clinical studies of the lens material and the procedure for regular cleaning suggested to the user
b. implementing procedures for recalling lenses distributed through various marketing channels
c. the process, facilities, and controls must conform to good manufacturing practices as interpreted by the FDA.

Approval of a New Drug Application or any significant alteration of approved materials or processes required three to four years. The earliest a company could enter the market was 1974, even if it had a new material patented and a manufacturing process developed. Bausch and Lomb had a significant time advantage over their competition; until 1974, they monopolized the market.

HISTORY OF AMERICAN OPTICAL

American Optical, located in Southbridge, Massachusetts, was founded about 1833 and went public about 1869. In 1967 Warner-Lambert purchased American Optical. At the time, American Optical revenues were about $148 million and net income was about $10 million.

In the early 1970s, Warner-Lambert decided to market the soft lens and, in 1973, purchased it from Griffin Laboratory of Buffalo and Toronto. Griffin Laboratory, a subsidiary of Frigitronics, had patent approval and appeared likely to receive FDA approval soon. Griffin's present production was being sold primarily to the Canadian market. American Optical dubbed it the SOFTCON lens.

Approval came in 1974. However, the approval only covered sales to the smaller therapeutic lens segment of the market. Patients requiring protection for an irritated eye could use the lens under close supervision. Examples are irritation due to an infected eyelid or as a "bandage" after eye surgery.

This was a disappointment. The major market segment was for corrective usage. These users would insert the lens in their eyes and be responsible for cleansing it daily without any supervision. The FDA had withheld approval because the daily cleaning and sterilization process was considered inadequate. Patents and the physical characteristics of the Griffin lens material prevented the company from adopting a similar heat-based process.

Dave Inman, President of the Optical Division of Warner-Lambert, initiated a search for another contact lens manufacturer while efforts to improve the SOFTCON cleaning process continued. He located Union Optical Company which appeared likely to receive FDA approval for corrective use soon. American Optical bought the right to market the lens for corrective use in early 1975. They called this lens AOSOFT.

This purchase reflected the importance which the AO management attached to quickly entering the soft contact lens market. The market had expanded from $8 million sales in 1971 to more than $55 million by 1974. Bausch and Lomb continued to dominate the market. A new competitor, Continuous Curve, was making lenses. The urgency of entering the market seemed evident, especially if AO was to have any significant share.

The responsibility for both manufacturing and marketing was assigned to Floyd Sundue. Floyd had wide exposure to numerous facets of business both as a consultant and as assistant to Inman. He was also experienced in implementing the concept of autonomous work groups.

DESCRIPTION OF THE PHYSICAL PROCESS

The American Optical process for producing soft lenses was based on the following steps (see Figure 13–9).

Figure 13–9 SOFT CONTACT LENS CUTTING & POLISHING

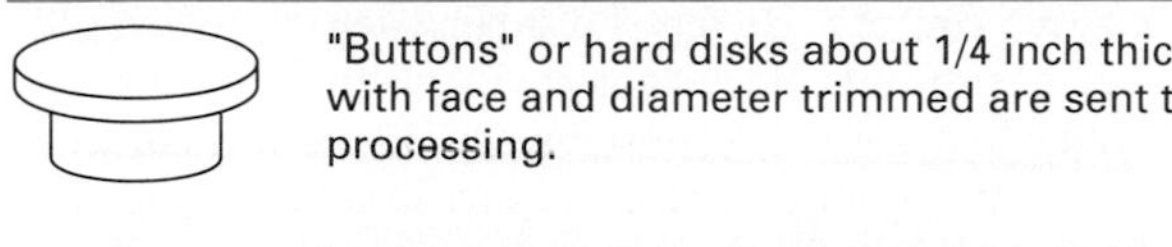

"Buttons" or hard disks about 1/4 inch thick with face and diameter trimmed are sent to processing.

The button is lathed on one side to the shape of the eye's cornea (base curve), the edge is beveled. Then, edge and base curve are both polished.

The front side is mounted and lathed to a specific curvature and thickness to fill the prescription of the patient. The original button now has a center thickness of 1/10 millimeter.

The front side is polished for an optically clear prescription lens.

The lens is hydrated in a saline solution to make it soft, and given a final inspection by the module.

The lens is placed in a vial, labeled and is sent to Quality Assurance for audit.

First, raw material was pulled from inventory. The chemicals were mixed and formed into rods. The rods were labeled and held until the Quality Assurance Department had taken samples and had given approval. Then small (approximately ½ inch long) buttons were cut and grouped into lots of approximately 50. The buttons were placed in jars. The buttons in each jar were cut to the same prescription specifications. Typically, two jars formed an order.

The initial step in cutting the lens was performed by a Base Curve Cutter. Here, the button was held securely in a chuck and the lathe cut the concave side of the lens which would be in direct contact with the eyeball. This was a critical operation, and the lathe needed to be set up exactly to the engineering specifications.

The second step was Bevel Grinding. Here the edge of the base curve was bevelled. Succeeding stations buffed the edge and polished the bevel. These operations contributed to a better fit on the eye. Then the base curve is polished for optical clarity.

After the bevelling and polishing operations, the button was mounted on a chuck. The chuck was a round tube with a convex end. Hot wax was used to fix the concave base curve to this end. The chuck held the base curve while the front curve was out on the lathe.

The Front Curve cutter cut the button to a specific curvature and thickness. At its thickest, the lens was about one-tenth of a millimeter. With such tight tolerances, the lathe had to be set up and operated to precisely engineered specifications.

The convex surface was then polished to get an optically clear lens. The lens then went through an ultrasonic vapor degreaser to remove it from the chuck and clean the wax off it. At this point, all the cutting and polishing operations required to make a prescription lens were completed. It was now necessary to soften the hard plastic lens.

Before being sent for softening, all lenses were thoroughly inspected at the Dry Inspection Station. Under a microscope the inspector could spot defects like pits, gouges, and scratches.

Next, the lenses were softened by placing them in a saline solution. The lenses absorbed the moisture until they were completely soft. The hydration process took between ten to twelve days.

During hydration the lens grew larger. Certain material and process defects only became apparent then. So, another inspection of all lenses was done under a microscope. Defective lenses were discarded.

The remaining lenses were free of any physical defects. However, even though they were all cut to the same prescriptive specifications, the margin of error was so small that a small percentage often differed from the required specifications. A significant fraction of the buttons in an order met the derived specifications. The remaining non-defective lenses were usable but met different prescriptive standards. Each lens had to be correctly labeled for physical characteristics. This required another inspection of all lenses which was done on a magnified projector. The lenses were each placed in a separate vial and labeled.

The final step was to sterilize the lens. This was done in an autoclave over a one-day period. The lens was then moved to a quarantine area to ensure that the sterilization was effective. After a couple of days in quarantine, it was moved to the finished good inventory racks and was ready for shipping.

PRESENT FACILITIES

American Optical had been waiting for FDA approval for some years. SOFTCON had therapeutic approval since 1974. Now it appeared that AOSOFT would receive approval for corrective use. As yet the demands on manufacturing had been light. While they waited for approval, the emphasis had been on improving productivity.

Processing was presently being done in leased facilities in Framingham, Massachusetts. Three experimental modules had been set up. The module layout is shown in Figure 13–10. Each module could make either AOSOFT or SOFTCON lenses with some changes to the equipment. Switching over required approximately two days.

Each module would operate for two shifts. Each of the six teams had eleven people with tasks broken down as shown below:

Operator Function	Task Breakdown
A	Base Curve Cutting
B	Bevel Grinding, Edge Buffing, Bevel Polishing, Base Curve Polishing
C	Measure, Mount & Inspect for Optical Clarity
D	Front Curve Cutting
E	Front Curve Polishing, Deblocking & Cleaning
F	Dry Inspection
G	Hydrating & Wet Inspection
H	Label Making, Vial Filling & Capping

The Rod Casting and Button Making operations were highly automated. Presently, one person was responsible for making all the buttons required. The small teams and their separate physical facilities were dictated by the experimental nature of the work. Floyd had seen an opportunity to implement the autonomous work group concept. He felt the experience gained would help in designing the larger facility which would be required when the corrective lens approval was received.

He organized each work group so it would have the full responsibility for decisions directly affecting their own work—including when to take breaks (e.g., lunch hours); hiring and firing personnel; planning the day's production; and assignment of tasks. Each team was responsible for the work they produced. Furthermore, each team member was responsible for checking the work of team members before them in the process sequence. This checking was in addition to the one-hundred percent inspections done as part of the process.

Teams were carefully selected to have a blend of experienced and entry-level operators who were compatible with each other. Some operators were interviewed on three separate occasions. Each member of the team went through a fourteen-week training period. Benefits of the product to society were demonstrated, and they were given a great deal of technical information about the process.

The results had been very gratifying; Paul Rivens, his Personnel Manager, had summarized them in a memorandum (Figure 13–11). Floyd placed a lot of emphasis on these results as he thought of the design of the new facility.

Floyd had also obtained estimates of process time and

Figure 13–10 MODULE FLOOR PLAN

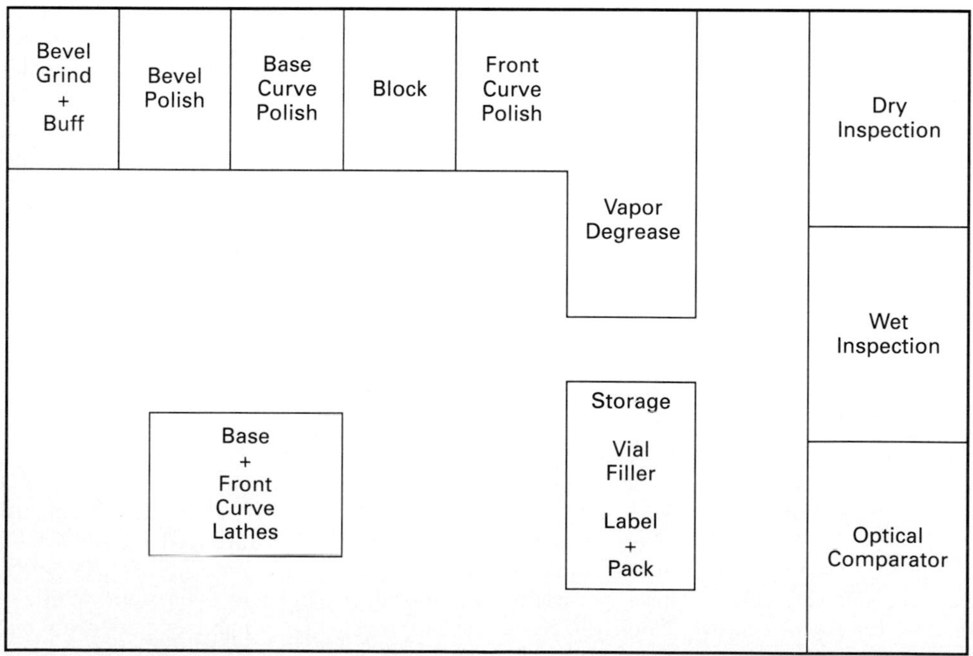

Figure 13–11 MEMORANDUM FROM RIVENS TO SUNDUE

TO: Floyd Sundue
FROM: Paul Rivens
DATE: February 1976
RE: Autonomous Work Groups

As you requested at our last staff meeting, these are my comments on the viability of the autonomous work group concept for the large-scale production of lenses. I am convinced that (a) this concept will work based on the results achieved with the test groups and (b) it must be implemented if we are to attract a stable well-motivated labor force in the Framingham area.

Test Group Results:
A pilot team with 11 members was formed in Framingham in 1974. Since then, five other teams have been hired and trained. The operating results have been good. After a fourteen-week training period, productivity has tripled and yield almost doubled when compared to the rates achieved at Griffin Labs.

The modules were set up as an easily distinguishable physical facility to reinforce the team's feelings of independence. Work locations were positioned so operators faced each other and could communicate and socialize easily. All efforts were made to provide a well-lighted and pleasant work space.

We found the proximity of the equipment encourages the operators to switch jobs. This reinforces their training. It also helps the team cover for absentees and to work with other operators in order to reach the production targets they set. It also provides the operators with an opportunity to break the routine of a repetitive, boring job.

Detractors at corporate offices say the socializing between team members and the job switching can be counter productive. The productivity and yield performance figures indicate that this is simply not true. The teams also show a willingness to impose and police standards of behavior. For example, the second shift supervisor asked operators to formulate such standards. They have compiled a code covering clothes, language, break times, etc. Morale and productivity continue to be high.

These tests have also given us greater insight into the functioning of work groups. This experience will enable us to form effective teams on an ongoing basis. For example, we asked our first test teams to select their own team leader. Three teams tried this and, in each case, the leader appeared incapable of leading, perhaps because the teams had chosen leaders they could manipulate. Subsequently, we selected the team leader, trained him in recruiting and supervisory skills, and built the team around him. This has proven to be an effective strategy.

Evidence of high morale is our low rates of absenteeism (5%) and turnover (10%). These rates are particularly significant as our labor is primarily entry-level and unemployment in the Framingham area is only 2.8 percent. As you know, when both factors are present, we would typically have high rates of turnover and absenteeism. This did not happen. Perhaps the pay structure (a base salary 10% above the area average with merit increases in the third, sixth, and ninth months) has contributed to this. I believe, however, that the main reason is the autonomous work group. The team members develop strong relationships as they work in the same module day after day trying to achieve common goals. They are reluctant to leave what has become an enjoyable and stimulating work environment.

The results support the high morale evident in the teams. The teams have identified with, and feel accountable for, the finished lens. So, they evidence considerable pride and satisfaction in meeting production targets with a quality product.

The motivation and stability of the teams must be of prime concern in an era of labor confrontation. The experience of the American industry confirms that conventional organizations cause employee alienation and low morale. The effects are high absenteeism, turnover, and sometimes acts of sabotage, and the election of an unfriendly union. Griffin Labs had set up a conventional flow shop. They had a union. They also had low productivity and yields.

The results of our test groups are extremely encouraging. Productivity is high and the work force appears well satisfied. I feel the concept has proven itself. Our new facility should be designed to house more such modules.

equipment capacity (Figure 13–12). These estimates were based on the performance of the six experimental teams. He noted that manufacturing now assumed a 150 percent increase in standard yield versus the old Griffin Laboratory standard. Although lower than the yields claimed by Rivens in his memorandum, productivity was clearly up.

Floyd had further reason to trust the increased productivity figures. He had organized a Quality Assurance function with one objective. They were to ensure that American Optical complied with every FDA requirement. This meant that in addition to sampling for product quality, adequate documentation was required on each batch as it went through the production process. If the FDA suspected the process was not properly followed, adequate documentation was necessary to convince them it was. If unavailable, the FDA could shut down the entire facility. These records also provided an independent check on productivity. They corroborated the figures in Rivens' memorandum.

Another piece of data Floyd had collected was the cost of equipment (Table 13–7). The equipment cost

Figure 13–12 EQUIPMENT CAPACITY

Base Curve Lathe: 95–105 lenses per day
Base Curve Polish: 175 lenses per day
Measure & Mount: 100–110 lenses per day
Front Curve Cut: 35–45 lenses per day
Front Curve Polish; Deblock & Clean: 100–110 lenses/day for all 3 lathes
Dry Inspection: 70 lenses/hour
Wet Inspection (Vertexometer): 2 orders*/day
Wet Inspection (J&L): 2 orders/day

*An order is 100 lenses at the first work station. As it is processed, defective lenses are discarded. Figures for wet inspection and for packing represent capacity assuming yield standards are met.

represented about half the total cost of installing a module. The other half was primarily the labor cost of installation.

THE COMPETITION

Other than Bausch and Lomb, there were two major competitors to American Optical for the soft contact lens market. These were Continuous Curve Contact Lenses, Inc. and the Milton Roy Corp. Continuous Curve had succeeded in obtaining the necessary approval in 1974. Milton Roy was due to get approval shortly. Other manufacturers were primarily small laboratories spread around the country. They made special lenses for therapeutic use and were a neglible factor in the corrective lens market.

Table 13–8 shows dollar sales over the past five years, with the 1976, 1977, and 1980 forecast. The present market of $94 million is expected to more than double by 1980. American Optical's target for 1980 is a 20% market share.

Bausch and Lomb has the timing advantage and consumer recognition. Their manufacturing process differs

Table 13–7 EQUIPMENT COSTS/MODULE

Item Description	Quantity	Cost/Item
Lathes	4	$5500.00
Polishers	4	950.00
Bevel Grinder	1	800.00
Vapor Degreaser	1	3500.00
Ultrasonic Cleaners	4	1200.00
Radius Gauges and Tools	1	800.00
Microscopes	3	1100.00
Vertexometer	2	1500.00
Optical Comparator	1	2500.00
Oven for hydrating solution	1	1000.00
Laminar Flow Booth for Packaging	1*	800.00
Vial Filler for Saline Solution	1	7000.00

*The Laminar Flow Booth can package 1200 lenses/day.

Table 13–8 SALES ($ MILLIONS)

Year	Bausch & Lomb	Continuous Curve	Milton-Roy Corporation	American Optical	
				AOSOFT	SOFTCON
1971	8				
1972	18				
1973	33				
1974	54	3.5			0.5
1975	70	5			1
*1976**	85	6	1		2
*1977**	100	11	3	7	2
*1980**	130			50	10

*Forecasted years

from American Optical's. It is a highly automated technique. They spin-cast the liquid monomer (hydrophilic material) in a revolving mold. The amount of plastic injected into the mold, the rotation speed, and the mold's design determine the shape of the lens. The result is a lens with an aspherical base curve. The lens is polished for optical clarity and hydrated to make it soft.

The American Optical management feels it has a superior product on several counts.

- It knows the hydrophilic material it uses has a higher moisture content than Bausch and Lomb's. Bausch and Lomb has a 38.6% moisture content compared to 42.5% for AOSOFT and 55% for SOFTCON. The higher moisture content is more gentle to the cornea. American Optical expects this will help obtain better physician and customer acceptance.
- American Optical cuts a spherical base curve on their lens versus the Bausch and Lomb aspherical base curve. The spherical curve conforms more closely to the spherical contours of the human eye. The AO lens would prove easier to fit.
- American Optical bevels the edge of the lens to provide a less ragged edge than the Bausch and Lomb lens. This would make it easier to wear, increasing customer acceptance.

Management is also encouraged by results in countries where soft contact lenses are already being sold. Lenses manufactured by both techniques are sold in Canada, France, Germany, and the United Kingdom. Doctors have expressed a definite preference for the lathe-cut lens over the spin-cast lens.

American Optical intends to take an aggressive marketing stance. A program to increase consumer recognition has been developed. The company will offer about 200 different types of AOSOFT lens. A large finished goods inventory will be maintained to satisfy customer orders expeditiously.

Floyd has devoted considerable time to developing the marketing strategy. He now feels he should concentrate on manufacturing. If manufacturing cannot produce enough lenses, the company's growth will be constrained.

EVALUATION OF ALTERNATIVES

The current facilities (3 modules for 6 teams) could produce about $6 million worth of lenses. The leased space provided no room for expansion. It was evident that new facilities would have to be built. With this in mind, American Optical had purchased a tract of land close to the leased facilities. They planned on the new facility starting production in 1977.

The conventional design of such facilities was the approach used by Griffin Laboratory. There would be a Base Curve Cutting Department, followed by a Bevel and Polish Department and so on. Each operation would be done in a specialized area. The present modular facility could continue primarily as a developmental group with the capability to supplement production if necessary.

The approach Floyd was leaning toward was to continue with the autonomous work group concept. Results, so far, had been excellent. True, they had been with experimental teams but other firms—Volvo, General Foods, etc.—had reported equally good results. If he selected this alternative, a large building could be constructed with separate modules within it. As increasing sales required increased production, more modules could be added.

There were, he recognized, some very tangible benefits associated with the conventional flow shop. Firstly, the capacity of each department could be better balanced. The equipment would be more fully utilized and capital cost would be lower. A rough calculation (Table 13–9) showed that better utilization could be achieved in the modules. But, he knew that two additional people were required to perform certain management tasks, minor maintenace, set up equipment, and handle material.

Secondly, less training time is required when an operator needs to know only one job. One of the strengths of a module was the variety of jobs it offered. The experimental groups had been trained on each job. Training over the 14-week period also showed workers how an autonomous work group operated.

Thirdly, set-up time would increase with the modular approach. Each team would set up its work at the beginning of a shift and clean up at the end. This meant an hour of lost production. In a conventional flow shop, the new shift would continue with the work left by the last shift. There would be less set-up and clean-up time. Floyd also recognized some very substantial intangible benefits to be obtained by using autonomous work groups.

Results of the experiment had shown, he felt, that the teams identified with and felt accountable for the end product. This was evident by their high morale. Absenteeism and turnover were low. The effects of low morale and employee alienation could be acts of sabotage or unionization with the intent to strike. He was well aware of the present atmosphere of labor confrontations as in the recent bitter strike at General Motors in Lordstown. This attitude could be expected to be widespread amongst the entry-level work force which American Optical was planning to hire. Yet, these workers had been making a quality product and appeared to derive satisfaction and pride from meeting their productivity targets. What is more, these targets were much higher than those achieved by the conventional flow shop of Griffin Laboratory. Though some of the increased productivity could be attributed to process improvements, he felt that the operator's attitude was the biggest contributor.

Another important feature which the work groups provided was manufacturing control. Since the operators were entry-level, they had little prior experience. The module concept made it easy to sequence jobs with each team. Further, if defects appeared on inspection, it would be relatively easy to trace it to a specific machine or operator. A conventional flow shop would re-

Table 13–9 UTILIZATION PERCENTAGES

Task	Capacity	% Utilization
Base Curve	100 lenses/day	100
*Base Curve Polish**	175 lenses/day	57
Measure and Mount	105 lenses/day	95
Front Curve	120 lenses/day	83
Front Curve Polish	105 lenses/day	95
Dry Inspection	70 lenses/hour	18
Vertexometer†	2 orders/day	50
J&L†	2 orders/day	50
Label and Pack	1 order/day	100

*One person can perform Base Curve Polish and Dry Inspection.
†One person can perform the Vertexometer and J&L functions.

quire each job to carry considerable documentation to perform the same function. The rapid identification and accurate tracing of process problems would increase yield substantially.

The modular design would also make it easier to alter manufacturing capacity. Forecasts of the soft contact lens market size had been notoriously inaccurate. For example, in 1974 the total industry sales were expected to peak at $100 million. Sales were already approaching that figure (Table 13–8) in 1976. A peak of $300 million, sometime in the early eighties, was now projected. Floyd felt this was very optimistic. He felt the $200 million sales in 1980 would be the peak. Given this wide range of potential sales, he felt the modular design offered the most flexibility.

Finally, the modular design made it easier for Quality Assurance because it generated data per the FDA requirements. It would be possible to meet FDA requirements with a conventional flow shop as well. However, a new reporting system would have to be devised and possibly more data collected.

CONCLUSION

As Floyd reviewed the alternatives open to him, he tended to favor the autonomous work group approach. But, he wondered, had he considered all the pros and cons? Was there some way he could quantify the intangible benefits? The experimental work groups had performed well; would the results continue to be as good? He knew the Executive Committee would favor the conventional flow shop approach. Should he supplement his efforts to convince them that the new concept was a preferable alternative with additional data?

NOTE

[1]National Patent filed suit in October 1972 seeking further royalty payments and the dissolution of the exclusive licensing agreement. The suit was still being contested.

Step 2: Prepare the case for class discussion.

Step 3: Answer the following questions, individually, in small groups, or with the entire class, as directed by your instructor:

Description

1. Describe the process for producing soft lenses.

Diagnosis

2. Why is American Optical considering the introduction of autonomous work groups?
3. Further explain the advantages and disadvantages of this work redesign using theories or concepts from the following areas: perception, motivation, communication, decision making, group dynamics, intergroup relations, leadership, power, and organization structure.

Prescription

4. Should management institute the new work design?

Action

5. What secondary consequences would the redesign have?
6. Should they renegotiate the contract?

Step 4: Discussion. Share your answers to the above questions, in small groups, with the entire class, or in written form. Then answer the following questions:

1. What symptoms suggest a problem exists?
2. What problems exist in the case?
3. What theories and concepts help explain the problems?
4. How can the problems be corrected?
5. Are the actions likely to be effective?

Activity 13–2: WORK SIMPLIFICATION AND JOB ENLARGEMENT ROLE PLAY

Step 1: Familiarize yourself with the activities of a bank teller, a dining-services worker, or a secretary.

Step 2: Redesign the job using work simplification techniques.

Step 3: Your instructor will select several pairs of students to role play the work redesign.

Step 4: Now redesign the job using job enlargement techniques.

Step 5: Your instructor will select several pairs of students to role play this work redesign.

Step 6: Discussion. Individually, in small groups, or with the entire class, answer the following questions:

Description

1. What did you observe?
2. Which way would you prefer to work? Why?

Diagnosis

3. How did the two redesigns differ? What advantages and disadvantages did each offer?
4. What problems still exist in the design of the jobs?

Activity 13–3: JOB REDESIGN PROBLEMS

Step 1: Read the following scenario:

There are twenty people in a word processing department reporting to one supervisor. They type a wide variety of work that is supplied by various departments and groups. Some jobs are small, while others involve lengthy manuscripts. Some work comes with a due date, and the remainder does not.

The work is supplied to the typists by their supervisor. She attempts to see that each person gets exactly one-twentieth of the work. The supervisor looks at the work before she gives it to the typists to make sure that it is legible. If it is not, she returns it to the originating department.

Usually, each typist has been able to process between thirty and forty pages a day. Because of the exactness of the work and the expense of skilled typists, the work is then sent to proofreaders for review to help keep errors to a minimum. However, the departments still complain about large numbers of errors in their manuscripts. Many due dates and schedules are not met. The department experiences high absenteeism and turnover.

Step 2: Diagnose the situation.

1. What symptoms exist?
2. What problems exist?

Step 3: Redesign the job using the following approaches:

1. job enrichment
2. job enlargement
3. work simplification

Step 4: In small groups share your job design. Decide which approach would be the most effective, and which the least effective.

Step 5: Discussion. With the entire class, share your group's conclusions. Then answer the following questions:

1. Compare and contrast the three methods of work redesign.
2. What problems does each solve? create?
3. What advantages and disadvantages does each offer?

Step 6: Read the scenario below.*

The customer complaint department in a telephone company included 104 young women and men who answered customer complaint letters and 16 others who handled complaints from customers over the telephone. The issues addressed by the complaints were quite complex. Management viewed these jobs as challenging and requiring a high degree of skill. Seventy percent of the group were college graduates.

Generally, the employees used form letters to answer complaints. All outgoing work crossed the supervisor's desk before being mailed. A verifier checked each letter for accuracy. Supervisors also signed the letters written by new employees for many months.

Turnover and absenteeism were high. Morale was low.

Step 7: Your task is to redesign the job to accomplish the following objectives: (1) improve the quality of service; (2) maintain or improve productivity levels; (3) reduce turnover; (4) lower costs; and (5) improve employee satisfaction.

Step 8: Your instructor will describe what actually happened and what resulted from those actions.

Step 9: Discussion. In small groups or with the entire class, answer the following questions:

1. Why was the program effective?
2. Would other approaches have worked?
3. What problems did this approach solve? create?

*This case is adapted from research reported in R.N. Ford and M.B. Gillette, "A New Approach to Job Motivation: Improving the Work Itself." In R. Ford, *Motivation Through the Work Itself.* New York: American Management Association, 1969.

Activity 13–4: TRW—OILWELL CABLE DIVISION CASE

Step 1: Read the TRW—Oilwell Cable Division case below.

It was July 5, 1983 and Bill Russell had been expecting the phone call naming him general manager he had just received from the corporate office of TRW in Cleveland. Bill had been the acting general manager of the Oilwell Cable Division in Lawrence, Kansas since January when Gino Strippoli left the division for another assignment. He had expected to be named general manager but the second part of the call informing him that he must lay off twenty people or achieve an equivalent reduction in labor costs was greatly disturbing to him. It was now 8:00 A.M. and at 8:15 A.M. Bill had called a meeting of all plant personnel to announce his appointment and, now, to also announce the impending layoffs. He was wondering in his own mind how to handle the tough decisions that lay before him.

TRW

TRW is a diversified, multinational manufacturing firm that in 1983 had sales approaching $5.5 billion (See Table 13–10). Its roots can be found in the Cleve-

Table 13–10 TRW FINANCIAL DATA FOR 1979–1983

	Statement of Consolidated Earnings ($ millions except per share data)				
	1983	1982	1981	1980	1979
Net sales	$5,493.0	$5,131.9	$5,285.1	$4,983.9	$4,560.3
Other income	64.6	69.1	52.9	42.4	45.3
	5,557.6	5,201.0	5,338.0	5,026.3	4,605.6
Cost of sales	4,285.1	4,011.0	4,116.4	3,876.3	3,534.6
Administrative and selling expenses	840.6	791.0	734.9	693.1	631.6
Interest expense	29.7	51.2	65.9	66.5	52.3
Other expenses	37.3	7.8	34.8	27.0	32.2
	5,192.7	4,861.0	4,952.0	4,662.9	4,250.7
Earnings before income taxes	364.9	340.0	386.0	363.4	354.9
Income taxes	159.7	143.7	157.2	158.9	166.4
Net earnings	205.2	196.3	228.8	204.5	188.5
Preference dividends	3.5	5.7	8.5	11.6	15.9
Earnings applicable to common stock	$ 201.7	$ 190.6	$ 220.3	$ 192.9	$ 172.6
Fully diluted earnings per share	$ 5.36	$ 5.20	$ 6.13	$ 5.49	$ 5.11
Primary earnings per share	5.53	5.49	6.60	6.15	5.86
Cash dividends paid per share	2.65	2.55	2.35	2.15	1.95
Fully diluted shares (millions)	38.3	37.8	37.3	37.3	36.9
Primary shares (millions)	36.5	34.7	33.4	31.4	29.5
Percent of sales					
Net sales	100.0%	100.0%	100.0%	100.0%	100.0%
Other income	1.2	1.3	1.0	0.8	1.0
	101.2	101.3	101.0	100.8	101.0
Cost of sales	78.0	78.2	77.9	77.8	77.5
Administrative and selling expenses	15.3	15.4	13.9	13.9	13.9
Interest expenses	0.6	1.0	1.2	1.3	1.1
Other expenses	0.7	0.1	0.7	0.5	0.7
	94.6	94.7	93.7	93.5	93.2
Earnings before income taxes	6.6	6.6	7.3	7.3	7.8
Income taxes	2.9	2.8	3.0	3.2	3.7
Net earnings	3.7	3.8	4.3	4.1	4.1
Preference dividends	0.0	0.1	0.1	0.2	0.3
Earnings applicable to common stock	3.7%	3.7%	4.2%	3.9%	3.8%

SOURCE: Reprinted from *1983 TRW Inc. Data Book* with permission of TRW Inc.

Figure 13–13 ORGANIZATIONAL STRUCTURE AT TRW

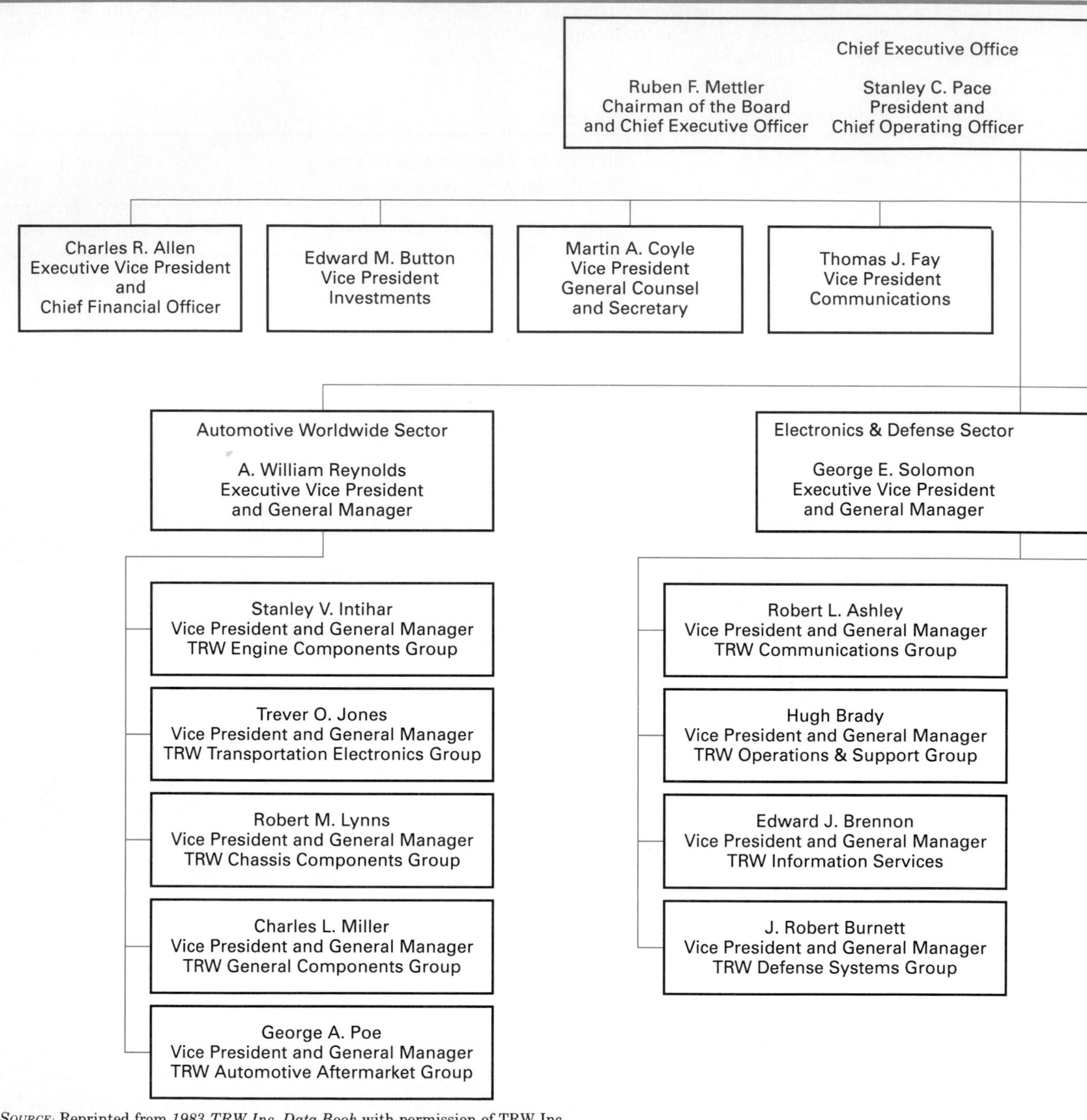

SOURCE: Reprinted from *1983 TRW Inc. Data Book* with permission of TRW Inc.

land Cap Screw Company which was founded in 1901 with a total investment of $2,500 and employment of 29. Today, through a growth strategy of acquisition and diversification, the company employs 88,000 employees at over 300 locations in 17 countries. The original shareholders investment of $2,500 in 1901 has grown

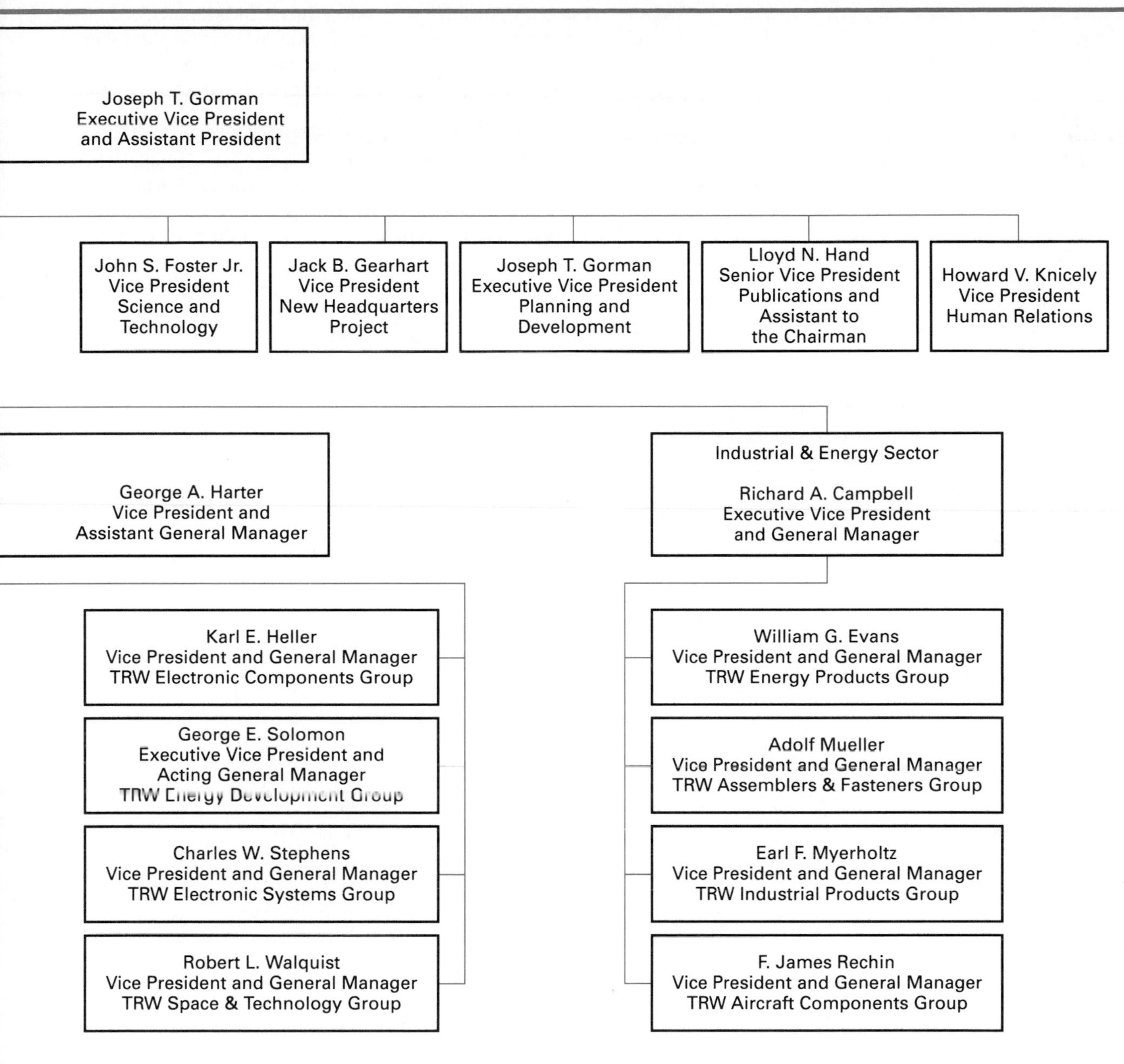

to over $1.6 billion in 1983. As quoted from the company's 1983 Data Book, "This growth reflects the company's ability to anticipate promising new fields and to pioneer in their development—automotive, industrial, aircraft, aerospace, systems, electronics, and energy. We grew with these markets and helped create them."[1]

The organization chart depicting TRW as it exists in 1983 is contained in Figure 13–13.

OILWELL CABLE DIVISION, LAWRENCE, KANSAS

The Oilwell Cable Division is part of the Industrial and Energy Segment of TRW. In 1983, this segment of TRW's business represented 24% of its sales and 23% of its operating profits. The pumps, valves, and energy services group, of which the Oilwell Cable Division is a part, accounted for 30% of the Industrial and Energy Segments net sales. The financial data for TRW by industry segment are contained in Tables 13–11 and 13–12.

The Oilwell Cable Division had its beginning as the Crescent Wire and Cable Company of Trenton, New Jersey. When TRW acquired Crescent, the company was losing money, occupied an outmoded plant, and had significant labor problems. In order to improve the profitability of the Crescent division, TRW decided to move its operations out of Trenton. The first decision was to move oilwell cable production to Lawrence, Kansas in 1976. The line was moved into a new building and all new equipment was purchased. Only Gino Strippoli, the plant manager, and three other employees made the move from Trenton to Lawrence.

The reason for choosing Lawrence as the new site for Crescent division was fourfold. Most importantly, Lawrence was considerably closer to the customer base of the division which was in Northeast Oklahoma. Second, Kansas was a right-to-work state and, given the labor problems of the Trenton plant, TRW was looking for a more supportive labor environment for its new operations. Third, the wage rates for the Lawrence area were very reasonable compared to Trenton. Finally, there was an already existing building that could house the oilwell cable production line in an industrial park in North Lawrence. In addition to the building, there was considerable acreage next to the building that would allow for future expansion.

By just moving the oilwell cable line to Lawrence, TRW hoped to be able to focus in on this product and make it more profitable before moving the other products from the Crescent plant in Trenton. By 1978, when the Oilwell Cable plant had reached division status, no further consideration was given to moving the rest of the Trenton plant. The remaining operations in Trenton were sold.

TEAM MANAGEMENT AT LAWRENCE

When Gino Strippoli was given the task of starting up operations in Lawrence, he saw a great opportunity to establish a new management system. With a new

Table 13–11 SEGMENTS OF BUSINESS BY INDUSTRY—TRW

	1983		1982		1981		1980		1979	
Net Sales										
Car & Truck										
Original equipment	$1,123		$1,052		$1,200		$1,291		$1,367	
Replacement equipment	472		483		490		461		432	
	1,595	29%	1,535	30%	1,690	32%	1,752	35%	1,799	39%
Electronics & Space Systems										
Electronic components	396		406		437		419		363	
Computer-based and analytical services	729		546		393		377		284	
Electronic systems, equipment, and services	951		767		772		648		552	
Spacecraft	628		486		430		355		302	
	2,604	47%	2,205	43%	2,032	38%	1,799	36%	1,501	33%
Industrial & Energy										
Fasteners, tools, and bearings	486		496		596		562		558	
Pumps, valves, and energy services	394		471		506		436		380	
Aircraft components	414		425		461		435		322	
	1,294	24%	1,392	27%	1,563	30%	1,433	29%	1,260	28%
Net Sales	$5,493	100%	$5,132	100%	$5,285	100%	$4,984	100%	$4,560	100%

Table 13–11 Continued

	1983		1982		1981		1980		1979	
Operating Profits										
Car & Truck	$ 116.8	27%	$ 129.2	30%	$ 146.0	30%	$ 149.4	31%	$ 192.7	44%
Electronics & Space Systems	214.2	50	170.0	40	123.3	25	133.3	28	88.9	20
Industrial & Energy	98.2	23	126.9	30	219.9	45	193.9	41	156.8	36
Operating Profit	429.2	100%	426.1	100%	489.2	100%	476.6	100%	438.4	100%
Company staff expense	(56.0)		(53.9)		(48.5)		(49.4)		(43.3)	
Interest income	15.1		15.4		12.6		1.4		3.1	
Interest expense	(29.7)		(51.2)		(65.9)		(66.5)		(52.3)	
Equity in affiliates	6.3		(14.0)		(1.4)		1.3		9.0	
Gain on debt exchange	—		17.6		—		—		—	
Earnings Before Income Taxes	$ 364.9		$ 340.0		$ 386.0		$ 363.4		$ 354.9	
Segment Assets										
Car & Truck	$ 968.6	33%	$1,029.7	35%	$1,101.3	38%	$1,148.1	40%	$1,157.2	43%
Electronics & Space Systems	1,113.7	37	1,000.6	34	888.3	31	865.1	31	779.9	29
Industrial & Energy	886.2	30	921.6	31	915.0	31	808.2	29	752.4	28
Segment Assets	2,968.5	100%	2,951.9	100%	2,904.6	100%	2,821.4	100%	2,689.5	100%
Eliminations	(102.0)		(83.2)		(61.7)		(77.9)		(72.2)	
Company staff assets	381.3		176.3		211.9		68.0		79.6	
Investment in affiliates	73.6		79.8		71.8		74.3		52.2	
Total Assets	$3,321.4		$3,124.8		$3,126.6		$2,885.8		$2,749.1	
Operating Margin										
Car & Truck	7.3%		8.4%		8.6%		8.5%		10.7%	
Electronics & Space Systems	8.2		7.7		6.1		7.4		5.9	
Industrial & Energy	7.6		9.1		14.1		13.5		12.4	
TRW segments	7.8		8.3		9.3		9.6		9.6	
Operating Return on Segment Assets										
Car & Truck	12.1%		12.5%		13.3%		13.0%		16.7%	
Electronics & Space Systems	19.2		17.0		13.9		15.4		11.4	
Industrial & Energy	11.1		13.8		24.0		24.0		20.8	
TRW segments	14.5		14.4		16.8		16.9		16.3	

Dollar amounts in millions

Source: Reprinted from *1983 TRW Inc. Data Book* with permission of TRW Inc.

plant, new equipment, and almost all new employees, the time seemed perfect to test the value of team management. Gino had long been a supporter of team involvement and now a golden opportunity was being presented to him to set up an experiment to test his ideas.

Team management is a form of worker participation whereby team members are responsible for task-related decisions concerning their areas of responsibility. Teams are formed along functional lines. In the case of the TRW-Lawrence plant, eleven teams exist ranging in membership from four to seventeen. The titles of the

Table 13–12 QUARTERLY FINANCIAL DATA—TRW

	1983				1982			
	Q4	Q3	Q2	Q1	Q4	Q3	Q2	Q1
Net Sales								
Car & Truck								
Original equipment	$ 288.9	$ 256.9	$ 298.4	$ 278.7	$ 226.5	$ 226.8	$ 300.0	$ 299.0
Replacement equipment	110.1	119.5	127.2	115.5	110.2	116.8	132.5	123.3
	399.0	376.4	425.6	394.2	336.7	343.6	432.5	422.3
Electronics & Space Systems								
Electronic components	104.2	102.5	98.2	90.9	84.4	101.7	112.3	107.0
Computer-based and analytical services	187.3	184.0	190.1	167.6	178.8	158.1	110.0	98.7
Electronic systems, equipment, and services	213.8	195.9	201.9	239.7	205.5	193.3	187.7	180.8
Spacecraft	143.9	148.2	162.2	173.8	93.6	123.8	149.8	119.1
	649.2	630.6	652.4	672.0	562.3	576.9	559.8	505.6
Industrial & Energy								
Fasteners, tools, and bearings	127.1	117.9	122.5	118.4	104.9	113.1	132.8	145.2
Pumps, valves, and energy services	106.9	93.6	96.1	97.0	106.3	114.0	118.3	132.0
Aircraft components	99.2	100.4	108.7	105.8	97.9	94.6	113.1	120.0
	333.2	311.9	327.3	321.2	309.1	321.7	364.2	397.2
Net Sales	$1,381.4	$1,318.9	$1,405.3	$1,387.4	$1,208.1	$1,242.2	$1,356.5	$1,325.1
Operating Profits								
Car & Truck	$ 27.2	$ 30.2	$ 34.2	$ 25.2	$ 20.7	$ 28.4	$ 49.4	$ 30.7
Electronics & Space Systems	50.1	56.5	54.2	53.4	46.1	47.4	44.3	32.2
Industrial & Energy	30.2	24.4	25.7	17.9	24.9	22.7	34.6	44.7
Operating Profit	107.5	111.1	114.1	96.5	91.7	98.5	128.3	107.6
Company staff expense	(15.0)	(13.5)	(14.2)	(13.3)	(12.2)	(14.5)	(13.7)	(13.5)
Interest income	5.5	3.9	3.5	2.2	3.2	4.5	3.8	3.9
Interest expense	(5.0)	(7.3)	(8.4)	(9.0)	(17.1)	(10.0)	(10.7)	(13.4)
Equity in affiliates	.4	3.3	4.1	(1.5)	(1.9)	(5.7)	(.3)	(6.1)
Gain on debt exchange	—	—	—	—		17.6		
Earnings Before Income Taxes	93.4	97.5	99.1	74.9	63.7	90.4	107.4	78.5
Income taxes	40.8	38.7	45.9	34.3	32.2	31.4	45.7	34.4
Net Earnings	$ 52.6	$ 58.8	$ 53.2	$ 40.6	$ 31.5	$ 59.0	$ 61.7	$ 44.1
Earnings Per Common Share								
Fully diluted	$ 1.37	$ 1.54	$ 1.39	$ 1.06	$ .81	$ 1.55	$ 1.66	$ 1.18
Primary	1.41	1.59	1.44	1.09	.83	1.65	1.76	1.25
Common dividends paid	.70	.65	.65	.65	.65	.65	.65	.60
Operating Margin								
Car & Truck	6.8%	8.0%	8.0%	6.4%	6.1%	8.3%	11.4%	7.3%
Electronics & Space Systems	7.7	9.0	8.3	7.9	8.2	8.2	7.9	6.4
Industrial & Energy	9.1	7.8	7.9	5.6	8.1	7.1	9.5	11.3
TRW segments	7.8	8.4	8.1	7.0	7.6	7.9	9.5	8.1
Effective income tax rate	43.7	39.7	46.3	45.6	50.6	34.7	42.6	43.8

Dollar amounts in millions except per share data

SOURCE: Reprinted from *1983 TRW Inc. Data Book* with permission of TRW Inc.

teams and brief descriptions of their make-up are shown in Table 13–13. Figure 13–14 depicts the current organization of the Oilwell Cable Division.

The five production teams listed in Table 13–13 are formed around the production process in use at TRW-Lawrence. Each of the teams meets on a weekly basis

1981				1980				1979			
Q4	Q3	Q2	Q1	Q4	Q3	Q2	Q1	Q4	Q3	Q2	Q1
$ 275.6	$ 273.3	$ 321.7	$ 328.7	$ 337.0	$ 279.4	$ 329.2	$ 345.7	$ 341.1	$ 315.9	$ 356.9	$ 362.?
108.5	123.8	130.4	127.6	115.2	110.4	125.4	109.7	108.5	112.2	118.9	92.?
384.1	397.1	452.1	456.3	452.2	389.8	454.6	455.4	449.6	428.1	475.8	445.?
107.5	113.2	107.3	108.8	99.9	106.2	105.7	107.1	94.9	91.7	97.1	79.?
104.3	85.0	98.5	105.4	99.5	101.5	97.0	78.8	79.4	72.3	71.9	60.?
185.5	203.0	201.3	182.7	178.0	156.2	162.5	151.3	155.9	131.6	143.2	121.?
109.7	110.7	103.6	105.8	100.4	88.8	83.6	82.0	83.9	78.4	72.9	67.?
507.0	511.9	510.7	502.7	477.8	452.7	448.8	419.2	414.1	374.0	385.1	328.?
139.4	143.9	156.6	156.0	137.9	131.4	146.3	146.3	142.3	135.4	144.3	136.?
122.9	127.6	132.2	123.0	114.8	116.0	106.6	98.6	101.5	95.9	100.5	82.?
118.4	110.2	113.5	119.5	117.6	103.6	110.4	104.0	87.6	78.2	83.2	72.?
380.7	381.7	402.3	398.5	370.3	351.0	363.3	348.9	331.4	309.5	328.0	291.?
$1,271.8	$1,290.7	$1,365.1	$1,357.5	$1,300.3	$1,193.5	$1,266.7	$1,223.5	$1,195.1	$1,111.6	$1,186.9	$1,064.?
$ 29.9	$ 34.8	$ 44.6	$ 36.7	$ 34.1	$ 33.6	$ 41.0	$ 40.7	$ 40.2	$ 42.2	$ 56.5	$ 53.?
(21.4)	73.1	38.4	33.2	33.5	33.7	35.5	30.6	24.9	22.5	25.3	16.?
45.6	54.6	62.8	56.9	50.0	50.4	50.1	43.4	41.7	38.4	46.4	30.?
54.1	162.5	145.8	126.8	117.6	117.7	126.6	114.7	106.8	103.1	128.2	100.?
(10.5)	(12.8)	(12.5)	(12.7)	(12.8)	(13.8)	(11.5)	(11.3)	(11.4)	(12.5)	(10.9)	(8.?)
5.6	5.4	1.2	.4	.6	.3	.2	.3	1.2	.2	.2	1.?
(14.0)	(16.3)	(18.4)	(17.2)	(17.7)	(17.3)	(17.3)	(14.2)	(14.4)	(13.4)	(12.6)	(11.?)
(1.9)	(1.9)	1.1	1.3	(3.0)	1.1	2.0	1.2	3.0	2.3	1.1	2.?
33.3	136.9	117.2	98.6	84.7	88.0	100.0	90.7	85.2	79.7	106.0	84.?
6.4	53.9	53.3	43.6	34.9	39.1	42.1	42.8	41.0	33.4	51.8	40.?
$ 26.9	$ 83.0	$ 63.9	$ 55.0	$ 49.8	$ 48.9	$ 57.9	$ 47.9	$ 44.2	$ 46.3	$ 54.2	$ 43.?
$ .72	$ 2.22	$ 1.72	$ 1.47	$ 1.32	$ 1.30	$ 1.57	$ 1.30	$ 1.20	$ 1.25	$ 1.47	$ 1.1?
.72	2.42	1.86	1.60	1.45	1.45	1.78	1.47	1.36	1.44	1.71	1.3?
.60	.60	.60	.55	.55	.56	.55	.50	.50	.50	.50	.4?
7.8%	8.8%	9.9%	8.0%	7.5%	8.6%	9.0%	8.9%	8.9%	9.9%	11.9%	12.1%
(4.2)	14.3	7.5	6.6	7.0	7.4	7.9	7.3	6.0	6.0	6.6	4.9
12.0	14.3	15.6	14.3	13.5	14.4	13.8	12.4	12.6	12.4	14.1	10.4
4.3	12.6	10.7	9.3	9.0	9.9	10.0	9.4	8.9	9.3	10.8	9.4
19.2	39.4	45.5	44.2	41.2	44.5	42.1	47.2	48.1	41.9	48.9	47.8

or as needed with exception of the resource team which meets every two weeks. The typical meeting lasts an hour and a half to two hours. There is no formal structure for the team meeting but most meetings would adhere to an agenda similar to the one described below:

Table 13–13 TEAM STRUCTURE—TRW

Team	Number of Teams	Composition
Management	1	Members of management
Resource	1	Management information systems, Design engineering, Process engineering, Employment, Accounting, Chemists, etc.
Technical	1	Non-exempt laboratory personnel
Administration	1	
Maintenance	1	Boiler, Electrical, Mechanical
Shipping and Receiving	1	
Production	5	Extruding, Armoring, Braiding

1. Scheduling manhours and overtime
2. Round-robin discussion/reporting from various plant committees (e.g., safety, gainsharing, etc.)
3. Area manager's comments regarding scrap, labor efficiency, and any new information since the last meeting.

Other decisions made by the team are listed in Figure 13–15 which illustrates the roles of the various levels of management at the Oilwell Cable Division. The figure also shows the relationships between levels. For instance, management has the responsibility for setting overall divisional goals and objectives and providing the resources necessary to the teams in order that these targets are attained.

The role of the area managers is one of being an intermediary. They are present at most teams to act as facilitators and to provide the teams information necessary to carry out their scheduling functions. In addition, the area managers fill a coordination function by meeting twice a week to discuss mutual problems and to discuss other items that should be presented at the weekly team meetings.

As can be seen in the figure, the teams are filling

Figure 13–14 ORGANIZATIONAL STRUCTURE AT THE OILWELL CABLE DIVISION

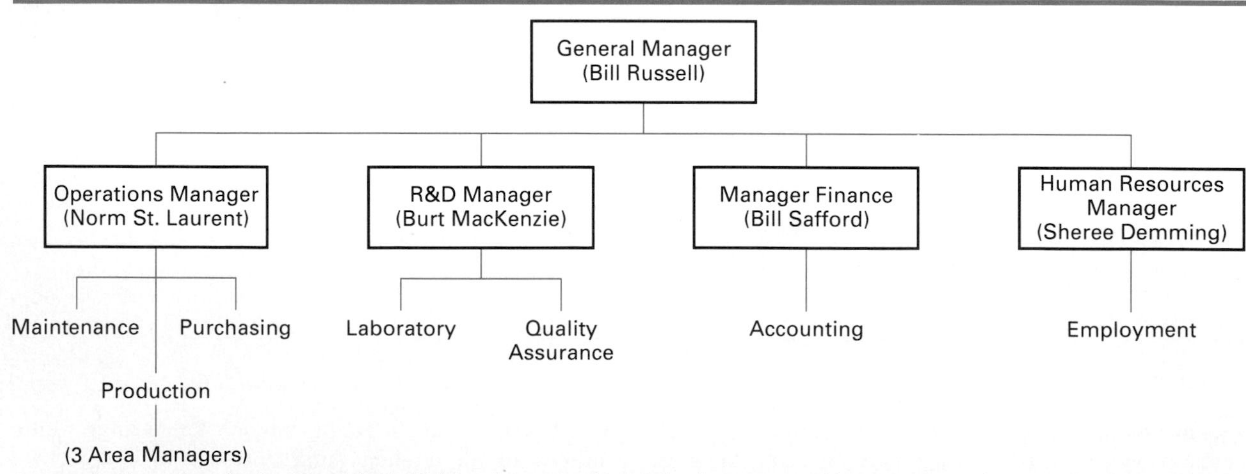

An organizational chart for the Oilwell Cable Division does not exist and the chart presented here represents the casewriters' depiction of the structure existing at TRW-Lawrence based on discussions with division personnel.

Figure 13–5 QUESTIONS FOR ASSESSING ORGANIZATIONAL READINESS FOR PARTICIPATION IN WORK REDESIGN

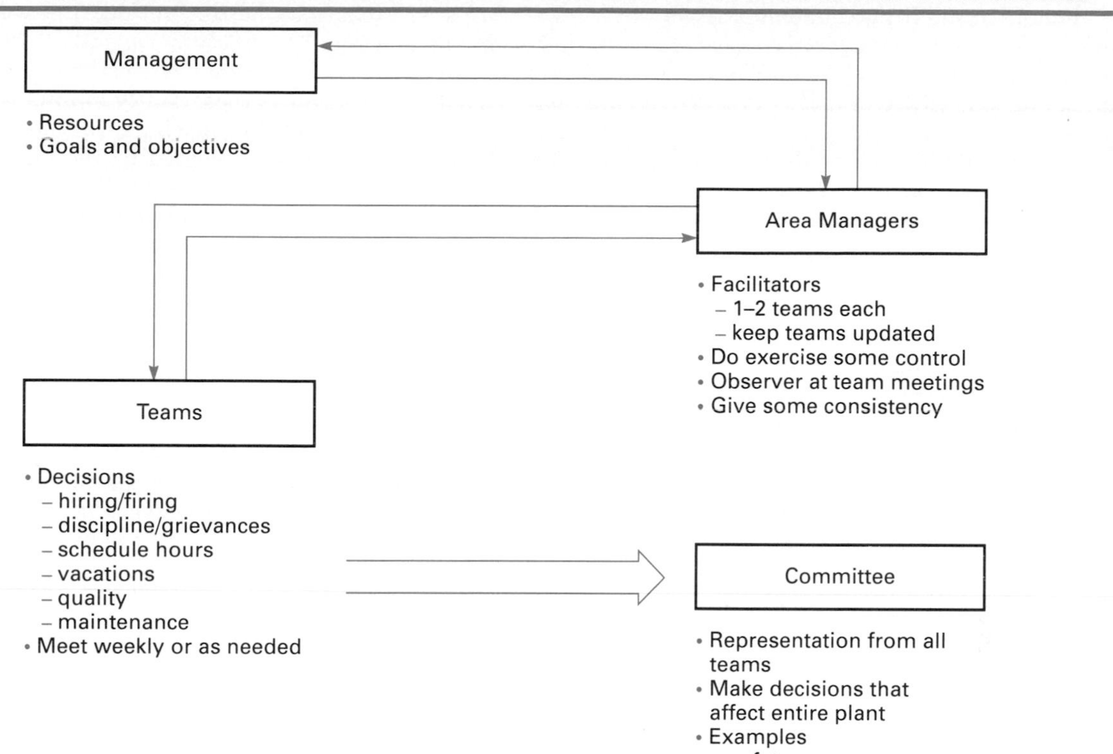

managerial roles and the decisions they make are more typical of those made by supervisory levels in more traditional plants. In essence, they, the team members, are given control over their work areas.

For decisions that affect the entire plant, a task force or a division-wide committee is established which includes representatives from all of the teams. Examples of some of these division-wide committees include safety, gainsharing, and benefits.

RESULTS FROM TEAM MANAGEMENT

After some initial start-up problems with the team management concept, the experiment started by Gino Strippoli in 1976 seems to now be a success. In a 1981 article in *Fortune* titled, "What Happens When Workers Manage Themselves?," Gino is quoted as saying: "In the beginning we considered it (team management) an experiment, but somewhere along the way we said, 'This is no longer an experiment; this is how we operate.' "[2]

The success of the experiment was not only written up in *Fortune* but also was the subject of several case studies.[3] But this success was not achieved easily. In the beginning, there was a good deal of mistrust among employees regarding management's motives. Also, when first starting up the Lawrence facility, there was only one union employee brought from Trenton. The rest of the people hired had little experience with the production process involved in making wire cable. As a result, there was a lot of frustration with a high level of turnover. The turnover rate of 12% in the first two years of operation compared to a national average of 3.8% at this time.[4]

But Gino was not to be deterred from seeing his experiment succeed. He realized that he was concentrating too heavily on team involvement concepts and not paying enough attention to technical concerns. A compensation scheme was developed that encouraged employees to master the various pieces of equipment in the plant. This action seemed to have the desired effect for the division became profitable for the first time in January, 1978.

In 1978, employment had dropped from a high of 132 to what seemed to be a more optimal level of 125. Turnover dropped from an excess of 12% to a range of 2–

4%, which was more in line with the national average for manufacturing firms. More impressive was the absentee rate which hovered in the range of 2½–3% during the period 1978–82. The national average during this period was closer to 6.5%.[5] Productivity was improving steadily as well. The Oilwell Cable Division now enjoyed the highest productivity of any plant in the oilwell cable industry.

It was not only the objective data which indicated that team management was succeeding but comments from employees at the Oilwell Cable Division seemed to confirm this as well. By and large, all employees rated TRW-Lawrence as a good company and preferred the team management concept to more traditional methods of management.

Some sample comments from the various levels of "management" verify this conclusion:

Team Members

". . . an excellent place to work."

"Team management gives employees a good deal of responsibility."

"Now at least we have some control over scheduling."

"The company gains as much as the employee because of the flexibility. Now there is little idle time."

"Team management gives the employee a feeling of equality."

"System allows for the maximum contribution of each member of the team."

Area Managers

"The plant is not a Utopia but I do feel better at the end of the day."

"Decision making is more difficult but team management results in easier implementation and better understanding by team members."

Management

"System allows for crossing over lines of responsibility. There is not the turf issue that exists in traditionally structured plants."

"Team management concept has resulted in an excellent labor climate. TRW-Lawrence is a good place to work and the workers here are receptive to change."

"The major benefit of the team management concept is flexibility while maintaining goal orientation."

This last statement is one of the real keys to team management—flexibility. Under such a management system idle time is greatly reduced as is the involvement of the plant manager in day-to-day operating problems. As noted by Strippoli, "I really feel for the first time that I am managing rather than putting out fires. The teams are putting out the fires way down in the organization."[6]

From the worker's point of view, the major benefit of team management is their ability to control their job. This control has resulted in a high level of commitment by the employees as evidenced by the numerous suggestions made by the teams which have resulted in significant improvements in quality and productivity.

Of course, the team management concept is not without its difficulties. As noted earlier, there are numerous problems with start up. It takes awhile for participants to become comfortable with the system and to accept the responsibility of managing themselves. In this case, this was a period of two years. However, after the settling-in period, productivity improved dramatically and has been maintained at that level through 1982. This achievement is illustrated in Figure 13–16.

In addition to start-up problems, the people who filled middle-management positions had great difficulty in adjusting to their new roles as facilitators as opposed to being bosses in the traditional sense. This is an area that is often overlooked in implementing participation schemes in factories. In the case of the Oilwell Cable Division, this inability to adapt to a new system resulted in four area managers leaving their positions. Plant management tried to deal with this problem by providing facilitator training for area managers. While the current area managers still express some frustration at not being able to simply "tell" workers what to do, they do feel the team management concept is a much more effective system than traditional supervisory systems and they would not want to go back to a traditional system.

All in all, Gino was very pleased with the experiment. At the end of 1982, he left the Lawrence facility for another assignment and Bill Russell, who had been Gino's operations manager, replaced him as the acting general manager.

THE OILWELL CABLE DIVISION'S MARKET

The basic product produced by the Oilwell Cable Division is wire that provides power to submersible pumps used in oil drilling. As a result, the demand for its product is directly dependent on the demand for submersible pumps, a demand which is a function of the price of crude oil. As the price of oil increases, the demand for pumps increases as it became economically feasible to drill deeper wells.

Drilling deeper wells also produces a need for cables that are able to withstand the harsher environments found in such wells. For example, these wells often require the use of lead jackets to protect the cables from the corrosive effects of hydrogen sulfide.

With the Iranian oil crisis of 1979 and the resultant

Figure 13–16 PRODUCTIVITY AT TRW-LAWRENCE (1978–1983)

Index 1978 = 100
*Represents first six months only

increase in oil prices, cable producers were able to sell pretty much all they were able to produce. Prices were determined on the basis of quality and delivery. Now, however, with the advent of an oil glut, demand for submersible pumps was dropping and the competitive factors in the market were determined more on the basis of price.

In all, TRW had ten competitors in the cable market. TRW was the market leader with a significant share of the market but, in 1982 and 1983, it was facing strong competition from both domestic and foreign producers. Foreign competition was becoming stronger because of the strength of the U.S. dollar.

Location was also a competitive factor that foreign competitors enjoyed especially with regard to oil and gas drilling in Southeast Asia and the Middle East. As the production of cable was basically a semi-continuous process, economies of scale were important. With this in mind, it was infeasible to build smaller plants nearer to a customer base that was widely dispersed. As noted earlier, one of the reasons for moving to Lawrence was so that TRW could be closer to its primary customers in Oklahoma.

By the end of June, 1983, the market for cable had fallen off dramatically. As Bill Russell reviewed the quarterly financial data (see Table 13–12) and he observed the idle equipment and employees in the plant, he knew he had to do something soon if he were to maintain market share and profitability.

THE LAYOFF DECISION

As Bill Russell prepared to meet with all personnel at the Lawrence facility, he wondered how he would handle the process of laying off 16% of the current workforce of 125. Two things particularly troubled him. First, his predecessor, Gino Strippoli, had implied that there would never be a layoff at the Oilwell Cable Division. Second, and perhaps more importantly, he had to decide whether the decision as to how to reduce labor costs was a decision he should make alone or one that the teams should undertake as their responsibility.

It was now 8:15 A.M. and Bill headed out to meet his employees.

ENDNOTES

1. *TRW 1983 Data Book,* TRW Inc., 23555 Euclid Avenue, Cleveland, Ohio 44117.
2. Charles G. Burck "What Happens When Workers Manage Themselves," *Fortune,* July 27, 1981, pp. 62–9.
3. See for instance, Anil Verma "Electrical Cable Plant," in Thomas A. Kochan and Thomas A. Barocci (Eds.) *Human Resource Management and Industrial Relations* (Boston: Little, Brown and Company, 1985, pp. 425–35) and Cal W. Downs and Mary Lee Hummert *Case History of TRW Oilwell Cable Division Team Management* (unpublished manuscript, University of Kansas, Lawrence, Kansas, 1984).
4. *Handbook of Labor Statistics,* U.S. Department of Labor, Bureau of Labor Statistics, December, 1983, p. 180.
5. *Ibid.,* p. 136.
6. Burck, *op. cit.,* p. 69.

Step 2: Prepare the case for class discussion.

Step 3: Answer the following questions, individually, in small groups, or with the entire class, as directed by your instructor:

Description

1. Describe the manufacturing process in Lawrence.

Diagnosis

2. Why is the Oilwell Cable Division considering introducing work redesign?
3. Further explain the advantages and disadvantages of the work redesign using theories or concepts from the following areas: perception, motivation, communication, decision making, group dynamics, intergroup relations, leadership, power, and organization structure.

Prescription

4. How should the team's responsibilities be changed?
5. Should the work be redesigned?

Action

6. What consequences would the redesign have?

Step 4: Discussion. Share your answers to the above questions, in small groups, with the entire class, or in written form. Then answer the following questions:

1. What symptoms suggest a problem exists?
2. What problems exist in the case?
3. What theories and concepts help explain the problems?
4. How can the problems be corrected?
5. Are the actions likely to be effective?

Activity 13–5: LONG-LIFE INSURANCE COMPANY

Step 1: Read the following scenario:

The group life insurance department of the Long-Life Insurance Company employs 100 people: 30 actuaries, 30 analysts, and 40 clerks. Together these employees set insurance rates, design and run computer programs to provide them with information required to set rates, answer qustions from other departments about existing policies, and maintain records about the purchase of life insurance by customers. All members of the department work from 9 to 6 with one hour for lunch between 12 and 1.

Recently the department has been experiencing increasing absenteeism among its workers. In addition, many complain that the mandatory lunch period often interrupts their train of thought. Other departments in the company complain that they frequently cannot obtain answers to questions since they do not necessarily work the same hours as those in the group department. The computer programmers have repeatedly stated that they could do more productive work if they spent several days a week at home where there are fewer interruptions and distractions.

Step 2: Individually or in small groups, design alternate work arrangements for the group life insurance department.

Step 3: Discussion. In small groups or with the entire class, share the plans you developed. Then answer the following questions:

1. What elements do these plans have in common?
2. What are the strengths and weaknesses of each plan?
3. What types of alternate work arrangements are feasible for the group life insurance department?
4. What problems might arise as a result of the implementation of these plans?

Activity 13–6: FINE FURNITURE, INC.

Step 1: Read the following scenario:

Fine Furniture, Inc., manufactures Scandinavian-style, high technology European-style, and Formica and lacquer contemporary bookcases and storage units. The company employs approximately 500 workers in its large manufacturing facility in southeastern United States. Many of these employees pride themselves on being craftspeople in various aspects of furniture manufacturing. Currently the company emphasizes high specialization of work functions. The manufacturing process is divided into many discrete tasks, each performed by a separate individual. One worker, for example, may cut the backs of the bookcases; another may insert the shelf pegs into the frames; still another might attach the doors to the storage units.

Workers often complain that they are not really using their skills in furniture building; and describe their jobs as mechanical and boring. They also complain that they feel as if each is "a small cog in a very large machine." Retailers who distribute Fine Furniture's products have noticed an increase in the number of defective pieces they have received and that production slowdowns have delayed product delivery from three to six months.

Manufacturing employees receive an hourly wage that ranges between ten and twenty dollars per hour, depending on their seniority and special skills. In peak production seasons, employees work overtime and can increase their earning by 25 to 50 percent. Employees are represented by a local of the International Teamsters Union, which has succeeded in negotiating a high-paying contract for its employees. Recently, however, employees have demonstrated some dissatisfaction with the union's lack of attention to ensuring job security. The introduction of automation to the manufacturing process has resulted in approximately 5 percent of the workforce receiving layoff notices in the past year.

Top management has informed both the union representatives and the manufacturing workforce that it intends to increase the amount of automation in the workplace, even introducing some new robotics that have successfully been used to manufacture furniture abroad.

Step 2: Individually or in small groups, design a QWL program for Fine Furniture.

Step 3: Discussion. In small groups or with the entire class, share the programs you developed. Then answer the following questions:

1. What elements do these programs have in common?
2. How will the programs address the problems at Fine Furniture?
3. What are the strengths and weaknesses of each program?
4. What should be the components of an effective QWL program?
5. What other options are available for improving the situation?

Activity 13–7: PLANNING FOR INNOVATION

Step 1: Read the following scenario:

Mason, Inc., is a Fortune 500 company that designs, develops, and manufactures personal grooming products. From 1950 to 1980 it was a leader in introducing new, profitable products into the marketplace. Its Research and Development Division grew from 20 to 150 professionals during that time. Since 1980, however, the company has relied on its past successes and has failed to introduce any significant innovative product into the marketplace. Top management wants to reestablish Mason's reputation as the #1 innovator in the industry.

Step 2: Individually or in small groups, offer a plan for encouraging innovation at Mason, Inc. Discuss staffing, rewards, organizational structure, work design, and any other facets of organizational behavior that apply.

Step 3: Discussion. In small groups or with the entire class, share the plans you developed. Then answer the following questions:

1. What elements do these plans have in common?
2. How well do the plans follow the innovation process?
3. Do the plans incorporate provisions for fulfilling the various roles required for innovation?
4. What are the strengths and weaknesses of each plan?
5. What should be the components of an effective plan?

CONCLUDING COMMENTS

The increased availability of sophisticated technology and automation in the work place has had a significant impact on the design of work. Work design approaches serve as both diagnostic frameworks and prescriptions for organizational change.

In this chapter, we described three major types of work design: (1) work simplification, (2) work enrichment, and (3) alternate work arrangements. We also looked at comprehensive quality-of-working-life programs. Each approach responds to problems of productivity and work satisfaction. In addition, we addressed the role of innovation in organizations, particularly as it relates to work redesign, and noted that transfer of work redesign initiatives from other countries to the United States often spurs innovation.

The activities of this chapter offered the opportunity to consider the impact of various work redesigns and the role of innovation in the workplace. They provided practice in redesigning work in a variety of situations, and proposing work simplification, job enrichment, alternate work arrangements, and QWL programs. The cases of American Optical and TRW—Oilwell Cable Division allowed a comparison of the relative impact of different redesign approaches.

Note, however, that the introduction of any redesign program can either increase or decrease organizational effectiveness. Choice of a program must consider the nature of the jobs, the workers, technology, management, and the organizational context of the jobs involved. The process of implementing the proposed changes is also a key to its effectiveness, as described in the next chapter.

ENDNOTES

[1]Reprinted from "Volvo's radical new plant: 'The death of the assembly line?' " August 28, 1989 issue of *Business Week* by special permission, copyright © 1989 by McGraw-Hill, Inc.

[2]H. Shaiken, *Work Transformed* (New York: Holt, Rinehart, and Winston, 1984).

[3]The description of work simplification is based, in part, on F.W. Taylor's prescriptions in *The Principles of Scientific Management* (New York: Harper, 1911).

[4]C. Perrow, The organizational context of human factors engineering, *Administrative Science Quarterly* 28 (1983): 521–541.

[5]F.E. Emery, The assembly line—Its logic and our future, *National Labour Institute Bulletin* 1 (1975): 1–19.

[6]A detailed description of the Lordstown situation is presented in a case by Hak-Chong Lee, which appeared in J.R. Gordon, *A Diagnostic Approach to Organizational Behavior* 1st ed. (Boston: Allyn and Bacon, 1983).

[7]*Ibid.*, p. 573.

[8]T. Cummings, Designing work for productivity and quality of work life, *Outlook* 6 (1982).

[9]J.D. Kilbridge, Reduced costs through job enlargement: A case, *Journal of Business* 33 (1960): 357–362.

[10]D. Wharton, Removing monotony from factory jobs, *American Mercury* (October 1954): 94.

[11]See, for example, J.D. Kilbridge, *op. cit.;* J.F. Biggane and P.A. Stewart, Job enlargement: A case study. In *Design of Jobs* 1st ed., ed. L.E. Davis and J.C. Taylor (New York: Penguin, 1972), pp. 264–276; G.E. Susman, Job enlargement: Effects of culture on worker responses, *Industrial Relations* 12 (1973): 1–15; E.F. Huse, *Organization Development* 2d ed. (St. Paul, Minn.: West, 1980).

[12]F. Herzberg and A. Zautra, Orthodox job enrichment: Measuring true quality in job satisfaction, *Personnel* (September-October 1976).

[13]J.R. Hackman, G. Oldham, R. Janson, and K. Purdy, A new strategy for job enrichment, *California Management Review* 17 (1975): 59; J.R. Hackman and G. Oldham, Development of the Job Diagnostic Survey, *Journal of Applied Psychology* 60 (1975): 161; J.R. Hackman and G. Oldham, *Work Design* (Reading, Mass.: Addison-Wesley, 1980).

[14]*Ibid.*

[15]*Ibid.*

[16]J. Woodward, *Industrial Organization: Theory and Practice* (London: Oxford University Press, 1965).

[17]E. Trist and K.W. Bamforth, Some social and psychological consequences of the long-wall method of coal getting, *Human Relations* 4 (1951): 3–38; A.K. Rice, *Productivity and Social Organization: The Ahmedabad Experiments* (London: Tavistock, 1958).

[18]Hak-Chong Lee, *op. cit.*

[19]T.G. Cummings, Self-regulating work groups: A sociotechnical synthesis, *Academy of Management Review* 3 (1978): 625–634.

[20]Huse, *op. cit.*, p. 247.

[21]Rice, *op. cit.;* Trist and Bamforth, *op. cit.*

[22]M. Fein, Job enrichment: A reevaluation, *Sloan Management Review* (Winter 1974): 69–88.

[23]T.D. Wall, N.J. Kemp, P.R. Jackson, and C.W. Clegg, Outcomes of autonomous workgroups: A long-term field experiment, *Academy of Management Journal* 29 (1986): 280–304.

[24]W.E. Reif and R.C. Tinnell, A diagnostic approach to job enrichment, *MSU Business Topics* (Autumn 1973): 29–37.

[25]J.W. Newstrom and J.L. Pierce, Alternative work schedules: The state of the art, *Personnel Administrator* 24 (1979): 19–23.

[26]*Ibid.*

[27]R.T. Golembiewski and C.W. Proehl Jr., A survey of the empirical literature on flexible workhours: Character and consequences of a major innovation, *Academy of Management Review* 3 (1978): 837–853.

[28]B. Shamir and I. Salomon, Work-at-home and the quality of working life, *Academy of Management Review* 10 (1985): 455–464.

[29]S.G. Schroeder, Alternate workstyles: A solution to productivity problems?, *Supervisory Management* 28 (July 1983): 24–30; W. Olsten, Effectively managing alternative work options, *Supervisory Management* 29 (April 1984): 10–15.

[30]Newstrom and Pierce, *op. cit.;* A.O. Elbing, H. Gadon, and J.R.M. Gordon, Flexible working hours: The missing link, *California Management Review* 7 (1975): 50–57.

[31]B. Stein, A. Cohen, and H. Gadon, Flextime: Work when you want to, *Psychology Today* 10 (1976): 40–43.

[32]J.A. Hollingsworth and F.A. Wrebe, Flextime: An international innovation with limited U.S. acceptance, *Industrial Management* 31 (March-April, 1989): 22–26.

[33]*Ibid.*

[34]Stein et al., *op. cit.*

[35]R.E. Walton, Quality of working life: What is it?, *Sloan Management Review* 15 (1973): 11–21.

[36]D.A. Nadler and E.E. Lawler III, Quality of work life: Perspectives and directions, *Organizational Design* (Winter, 1983).

[37]*Ibid.*

[38]R.H. Guest, Quality of work life—Learning from Tarrytown, *Harvard Business Review* 57 (1979): 76–87.

[39]See R. Zager and M.P. Rosow (eds.), *The Innovative Organization: Productivity Programs in Action* (New York: Pergamom, 1982).

[40]See L. Davis et al. (eds.), *The Quality of Working Life* (New York: Free Press, 1975); R.E. Walton and L. Schlesinger, Do supervisors thrive in participative work systems?, *Organizational Dynamics* 7 (Winter 1978): 25–38.

[41]H.C. Katz, *Shifting Gears: Changing Relations in the U.S. Automobile Industry* (Cambridge, Mass.: MIT Press, 1985).

[42]M. Edid, How power will be balanced on Saturn's shop floor, *Business Week* (5 August 1985): 65.

[43]*Ibid.*

[44]T.A. Kochan, H.C. Katz, and N.R. Mower, *Worker Participation and American Unions* (Kalamazoo, Mich.: Upjohn Institute for Employment Research, 1984).

[45]*Ibid.*

[46]See S.D. Goldstein, Organizational dualism and quality circles, *Academy of Management Review* 10 (1985): 509–526; G.W. Meyers and R.G. Scott, Quality circles: Panacea or Pandora's box?, *Organizational Dynamics* 13 (Spring 1985): 34–50; L.R. Smeltzer and B.L. Kedia, Knowing the ropes: Organizational requirements for quality circles, *Business Horizons* 28 (July-August 1985): 30–34; G.P. Shea, Quality circles: The danger of bottled change, *Sloan Management Review* 27 (Spring 1986): 33–46; R.P. Steel and R.F. Lloyd, Cognitive, affective, and behavioral outcomes of participation in quality circles: Conceptual and empirical findings, *Journal of Applied Behavioral Science* 24 (1988): 1–17, for further discussion of quality circles.

[47]T.R. Miller, The quality circle phenomenon: A review and appraisal, *SAM Advanced Management Journal* 54(1) (1989): 4–7, 12; E.E. Lawler III and S. Mohrman, Quality circles after the fad, *Harvard Business Review* (January-February 1985): 65–71.

[48]See I. Bluestone, How quality-of-worklife projects work for the United Auto Workers, *Monthly*

Labor Review (July 1980): 37–39; S.H. Fuller, How quality-of-worklife projects work for General Motors, *Monthly Labor Review* (July 1980): 39–41.

[49]J.W. Thacker and M.W. Fields, Union involvement in quality-of-work-life efforts: A longitudinal investigation, *Personnel Psychology* 40 (1987): 97–111.

[50]R.E. Walton, Work innovations in the United States, *Harvard Business Review* 57 (1979): 88–98.

[51]J.A. Pearce II and E.C. Ravlin, The design and activation of self-regulating work groups, *Human Relations* 40 (1987): 751–782.

[52]J. Simmons and W. Mares, *Working Together* (New York: Knopf, 1983).

[53]G.R. Bushe, Temporary or permanent middle-management groups? Correlates with attitudes in QWL change projects, *Group and Organization Studies* 12 (March 1987): 23–37.

[54]H.C. Katz, T.A. Kochan, and M.R. Weber, Assessing the effects of industrial relations systems and efforts to improve the quality of working life on organizational effectiveness, *Academy of Management Journal* 28 (1985): 509–526.

[55]K. Bradley and S. Hill, Quality circles and managerial interests, *Industrial Relations* 26 (Winter 1987): 68–82.

[56]E.R. Ruffner and L.P. Ettkin, When a circle is not a circle, *SAM Advanced Management Journal* 52 (Spring 1987): 9–15.

[57]*Ibid.*

[58]R.W. Griffin, Consequences of quality circles in an industrial setting: A longitudinal assessment, *Academy of Management Journal* 31 (1988): 338–358.

[59]R.E. Alie, The middle-management factor in quality circle programs, *SAM Advanced Management Journal* 51 (Summer 1986): 9–15.

[60]J.R. Kimberly, The organizational context of technological innovation. In D.D. Davis and Associates (eds.), *Managing Technological Innovation* (San Francisco: Jossey-Bass, 1986).

[61]See D.G. Marquis, The anatomy of successful innovations, *Innovation* (November 1969) by Technology Communications, Inc. Reprinted in *Managing Advanced Technology* vol. 1 (New York: American Management Association, 1972), pp. 35–48.

[62]E.B. Roberts and A.R. Fusfeld, Staffing the innovative technology-based organization, *Sloan Management Review* (Spring 1981): 19–34.

[63]T. Peters and R. Waterman, *In Search of Excellence* (New York: Harper & Row, 1982).

[64]M. Sashkin, Participation management is an ethical imperative, *Organizational Dynamics* 12 (Spring 1984): 4–22.

RECOMMENDED READINGS

Cantwell, J. *Technological Innovation and Multinational Corporations*. New York: B. Blackwell, 1989.

D.D. Davis and Associates. *Managing Technological Innovation*. San Francisco: Jossey-Bass, 1986.

M.I.T. Commission on Industrial Productivity. *Made in America: Regaining the Productive Edge*. Cambridge, Mass.: MIT Press, 1989.

Shetty, Y.K., and Buehler, V.M. (eds.) *Quality, Productivity, and Innovation*. New York: Elsevier, 1987.

Tushman, M.L., and Moore, W.E. (eds.) *Readings in the Management of Innovation* 2d ed. Cambridge, Mass.: Ballinger 1988.

Van de Ven, A.H., Angle, H.L., and Poole, M.S. (eds.) *Research on the Management of Innovation*. Cambridge, Mass.: Ballinger, 1989.

Von Hippel, E. *The Sources of Innovation*. New York: Oxford University Press, 1988.

14

Changing Organizations and Their Cultures

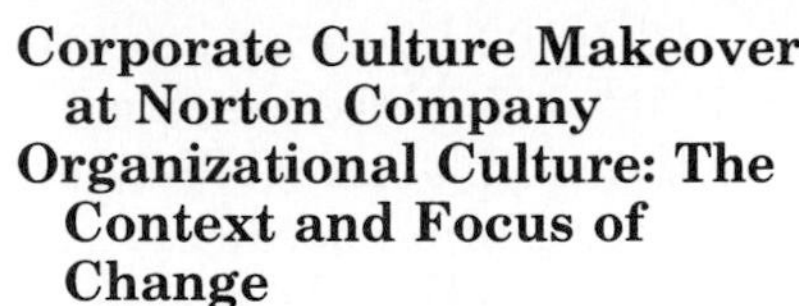

CHAPTER OUTLINE

LEARNING OBJECTIVES

After completing the reading and activities in Chapter 14, students will be able to

- define organizational culture and describe its components;
- compare and contrast the organizational cultures of two or more organizations;
- discuss crises as causes of change;
- compare and contrast the model of planned change and action research;
- offer a general approach to implementing action in organizations;
- discuss the different types of change agents and evaluate each type;
- list possible resistances to change and suggest ways of overcoming them;
- describe three types of intervention strategies and possible uses of each;
- offer ways of changing organizational culture and responding to crises in organizations; and
- describe the conditions under which organizational transformations occur.

Corporate Culture Makeover at Norton Company

Sometimes coffee chatter at Norton Co., the century-old Worcester abrasives company, sounds more like New Age talk than manufacturing talk.

Managers encourage "new conversation, not old conversation" and sprinkle their memos with phrases like "teamwork" and "taking charge."

Norton is in the midst of a corporate culture makeover.

The reworking is a conscious effort headed by Norton's top man and has already cost the company $200,000 in workshops and training sessions.

A painful restructuring in 1985 forced the firm to lay off 1,500 workers and take a $167.5 million write-off. John M. Nelson, chairman and chief executive officer, says he realized Norton needed to become an exceptional company to survive. The way to do that, he decided, was to create a more cooperative workplace. . . .

At Norton, a $1.4 billion manufacturer of abrasive paper and grinding wheels, cooperation is not just a buzzword. "One of the most important concepts is the need to break down organizational barriers and to think as one company and act as one company," says Deborah A. Kaufman, Norton's vice president who has overseen the corporate changeover. "What it really called for was a different attitude and mind-set of everybody who worked there."

A company of 16,000 employees worldwide, Norton was serious about the change. Nelson traveled to five continents, talking to small groups of managers about the need to work together. Norton hired consultants, staged a three-day workshop for 1,000 managers, held another review session a year later and designed posters outlining the company's ethics.

Norton says 8,000 managers have gotten the message. And they say apparently it is working.

For example, take Norton's maintenance supervisor, Paul D. Villiers. The 40-year-old manages a crew of 21 men who repair Norton's machinery. He attended the three-day workshop and returned to his men, offering them a more cooperative relationship and asking them to tell him what he was doing wrong as a manager.

The suggestions flowed: unlock the tool room so time is not wasted tracking down the supervisor for a key; streamline the 16-page work order; allow flextime so men can report to work as early as 2 A.M. when machines that need maintenance aren't being used.

Villiers listened and ended up saving 43 hours a week that had previously been squandered in cumbersome procedures.

"They like being treated as men with responsibility," says Villiers. "We have a lot of trust in this department. The tools are out there—they could rip me off tonight. There's a lot more harmony within the group now. The men are cross-training each other. It's almost like a buddy system."

Villiers' comments are part of what Norton managers routinely refer to as new conversation. The company downplays older conversation, when people might say: "I can't do that, it's not my job, it's not my department, it's the other department's job."

Instead, employees embrace new conversation, a dialogue that says: "What can I do to overcome this barrier? What can I do to work more cooperatively with the other person, the other department?"

"It's not unusual for people to say: " 'That's old conversation, let's talk new conversation,' " says Kaufman.[1]

What type of culture is the Norton Company trying to create? What issues must Norton's management consider in implementing this change? Assuming that the new culture is desirable, how can management ensure that the accompanying changes will be accepted and effective?

In this chapter, we consider primarily the action step of the diagnostic approach. The chapter first describes organizational culture, presenting its components and discussing its links to organizational effectiveness. The chapter continues with a general approach to changing organizations. It then looks at the technique of force field analysis, one way of diagnosing a situation to increase the likelihood of effective action. It next identifies the forces that influence change (including crises in organizations) and affect the selection of a change agent. The chapter discusses the selection and implementation of an appropriate intervention strategy, particularly addressing ways of changing organizational culture, responding to crises, managing long-term change, and dealing with ethical issues in implementation. The chapter concludes by offering approaches to evaluating and institutionalizing change; and discusses the transformation of organizations.

ORGANIZATIONAL CULTURE: THE CONTEXT AND FOCUS OF CHANGE

Culture, a concept borrowed by organizational theorists from anthropology,[2] is "a pattern of basic assumptions—invented, discovered, or developed by a given group as it learns to cope with its problems of external adaptation and internal integration—that has worked well enough to be considered valid and, therefore, to be taught to new members as the correct way to perceive, think, and feel in relation to these problems."[3] It can also be viewed as "a set of understandings or meanings shared by a group of people. The meanings are largely tacit among members, are clearly relevant to the particular group, and are distinctive to the group. Meanings are passed on to new group members."[4]

While these definitions can apply to civilizations, ethnic groups, occupations, or groups within organizations, in this section we consider their applications to organizations as a whole. Managers use culture to help define the implementation of an organization's business strategy; acceptable ways of interacting with external constituencies such as shareholders, the government, or customers; the types of people to hire and how to develop them; criteria of effective performance; unacceptable behaviors that lead to firing or demotion; acceptable interpersonal relationships within the company; and appropriate management style.[5]

How would you describe the corporate culture at Norton Company? The new culture emphasizes collaboration rather than competition, "new conversation, not old conversation." The basic assumptions there have changed: workers now ask how they can overcome barriers rather than saying that their jobs prevent them from acting proactively.

We can further assess culture by asking three questions.[6] First, what is the background of the founders, their successors, and current leaders? Second, how did a particular organization respond to and what did it learn from crises or other critical events? Third, who are viewed as deviants in the organization, and how does the organization respond to them? Although the introductory scenario lacks information to answer these questions for Norton, securing these data likely would reveal more about the organization's culture.

We can also understand an organization's culture by gathering data in two additional ways: analyzing the ways new members are socialized (see Chapter 3) or examining, jointly with organizational insiders, puzzling aspects of an organization.[7]

Components of Organizational Culture

Organizational culture can be broken down into three levels.[8] The first level is observable and consists of audible and visible patterns of behavior, technology, and art. The second level is less available to observation and refers to the way people interpret and make sense of the first level. The third level includes individuals' ideas and assumptions that affect behavior.

Compare the way two organizations might deal with their external environments and internal constituencies. The first creates a relatively participative, egalitarian, people-oriented culture, while the second builds an authoritarian, elitist, task-oriented culture.[9] What makes these cultures different? Figure 14–1 lists ways culture is embedded and transmitted, which we examine in more detail in the next sections.

Beliefs, Expectations, and Shared Values Basic organizational philosophy reflects the beliefs, expectations, and shared values of its leaders. Together these drive the organization toward its goals—profits or service, for example. Basic beliefs influence employee behavior and attitudes; they define success for employees and establish standards of achievement.[10] Slogans such as, "We'll find a way" (Continental Bank), "Quality is Job 1" (Ford Motor Company), and "Fly the Friendly Skies" (United Airlines) reflect corporate values, a key component of culture. At Norton, changing the corporate culture required management's changing the key values to focus on collaboration and teamwork rather than competition and individuality.

Heroes and Heroines Heroes and heroines personify corporate values. Leaders viewed in this way reinforce the basic values of an organization's culture by making success attainable and human, providing role models, symbolizing their company to the outside world, preserving what makes the company special, setting a standard of performance, and motivating employees.[11] Managers

Figure 14–1 HOW CULTURE IS EMBEDDED AND TRANSMITTED

1. Formal statements of organizational philosophy, charters, creeds, materials used for recruitment and selection, and socialization
2. Design of physical spaces, facades, buildings
3. Deliberate role modeling, teaching, and coaching by leaders
4. Explicit reward and status system
5. Stories, legends, myths, and parables about key people and events
6. What leaders pay attention to, measure, and control
7. Leader reactions to critical incidents and organizational crises
8. Organizational design and structures
9. Organizational systems and procedures
10. Criteria used for recruitment, selection, promotion, leveling off, retirement, and "excommunication" of people

Based on E.H. Schein, The role of the founder in creating organizational culture, *Organizational Dynamics* (Summer 1983).

can help create heroes or heroines, who reflect new or desired corporate values, as a way of expediting change.

Myths and Stories Myths, in this context, are stories about corporate heroes or heroines. What does the repeated telling of an Horatio Alger–like story about the advancement of a mailboy to CEO suggest about a company's values?[12] The themes of such stories provide clues to an organization's culture. An organization whose stories emphasize deference to authority and fitting in with others has a different culture than one whose themes focus on cooperation and participation.[13] Again, managers can encourage the relating of such stories as a way of embedding culture.

Rituals and Ceremonies Ceremonies such as retirement dinners or employee of the month awards contribute to corporate culture by dramatizing the organization's basic values. Often linked with a corresponding organizational story, such an event can provide a purpose and clues to new behavior patterns.[14] The award of a pin for twenty-five years of service shows that a company values loyalty. Such ceremonies can also act as rites of passage, which delineate entry into an organization's inner circle.

Physical Arrangements The selection and arrangement of offices and furnishings often reveal significant insights into corporate culture. Consider an investment firm that provides only a desk and telephone for its brokers. Now consider a firm that offers private office space to the same job holders. How might the organizational cultures of these two firms differ? How should top management at Norton design the physical layout of its plant and offices to enhance desired culture?

Other Elements In addition to the factors just examined above, both the society and the industry in which an organization operates provide a context for understanding its culture.[15] Consider, for example, the difference between United States and Japanese cultures and their implications for corporate culture. Many U.S. companies reflect a cultural orientation of individualism, whereas Japanese companies typically reflect their culture's collective orientation. Or compare U.S. to Scandinavian cultures, with their respective emphases on capitalism and socialism. In part because of these differences, Scandinavian automobile companies introduced teamwork and worker responsibility much earlier than was the case in the U.S., resulting in different corporate cultures in auto manufacturers. Some cultural systems accept change more rapidly than others; thus the state of the technological, economic, and social development of a nation affects its organizational cultures. In Arab cultures, for example, personal relationships and trust are most important and govern the relationship of subordinate to supervisor.[16] Consequently organizational change interventions must fit with the culture involved,[17] and managers in multinational companies must carefully diagnose national cultures before selecting and implementing change strategies.

The industry culture in which an organization operates can be defined by the natures of its product, stage in the life cycle of the industry (similar to organizational life cycles, described in Chapter 12), technology, and institutional structure (e.g., competitors and trade associations).[18] Some even argue that regional industry cultures exist too; that Massachusetts high-technology culture, for example, differs from California high-technology culture.[19]

Links to Organizational Effectiveness

Is one type of organizational culture more likely to result in organizational effectiveness than another type? Recent research suggests an affirmative answer to this question.[20]

As discussed in Chapter 11, William Ouchi compared American management practices to Japanese practices and called for U.S. organizations to adopt a hybrid of the two, which he called *Theory Z* management.[21] Theory Z management emphasizes long-term employment and job security, combined with slow evaluation and promotion policies. Evaluation of workers is highly personal, although there are many formal measures of organizational, group, and individual performance. The individual retains responsibility for decision making but must reach decisions through collective discussion. The organization offers a moderately specialized career path and encourages a concern for the entire individual, including his or her family. Ouchi notes that not all companies should adopt Theory Z management, but it offers a viable alternative to traditional American management, which is characterized by short-term evaluation, individual decision making and responsibility, rapid evaluation and promotion, formalized performance measures, specialized career paths, and limited consideration of workers' personal lives.

Others advocating long-time employment for U.S. companies point out the importance of recognizing that congruent employment practices such as slower promotion, more job diversity, and different employee selection procedures, must support it.[22] Effectively introducing Theory Z management requires building a cohesive top-management team, creating and communicating a strategic vision, building strong human resources management support systems within an organization, and creating a participative organizational structure that facilitates problem solving and consensus building.[23]

Culture can be a source of competitive advantage, particularly if it is considered valuable, rare, and difficult to imitate. IBM, Hewlett-Packard, Procter and Gamble, and McDonald's may have such cultures.[24] Thus managers should try to create an unusual culture as part of their strategic planning. Other researchers describe various attributes of successful and well-managed organizations, such as Eastman-Kodak, IBM, Procter & Gamble, Atlantic Richfield, Control Data, and Dayton-Hudson, as components of effective corporate culture.[25] These qualities include good pay and strong benefits, open communication, emphasis on quality, employee participation in decision making, employee sharing of profits through stock ownership or profit sharing plans, relative equality in the status of employees, relative job security, career-long training, individual freedom of expression, a bias for action, emphasis on risk taking and innovation, good labor–management relations, and use of simple and lean administrative structures. Figure 14–2 illustrates many of these principles in a summary of the corporate objectives of Hewlett-Packard, an organization frequently included in lists of top U.S. companies. Note that organizations must set realistic goals and values about the relationship between employee and employer, to ensure that they deliver what they promise.[26]

Organizational culture also has implications for individual performance, although care must be taken in assessing links between the two.[27] Culture

Figure 14–2 HEWLETT-PACKARD'S CORPORATE OBJECTIVES THAT PRESCRIBE ITS ORGANIZATIONAL CULTURE

Profit	To achieve sufficient profit to finance our company growth and to provide the resources we need to achieve our other corporate objectives.
Customer	To provide products and services of the greatest possible value to our customers, thereby gaining and holding their respect and loyalty.
Fields of interest	To enter new fields only when the ideas we have, together with our technical, manufacturing, and marketing skills, assure that we can make a needed and profitable contribution to the field.
Growth	To let our growth be limited only by our profits and our ability to develop and produce technical products that satisfy real customer needs.
Our People	To help HP people share in the company's success, which they make possible; to provide job security based on their performance; to recognize their individual achievements; and to ensure the personal satisfaction that comes from a sense of accomplishment in their work.
Management	To foster initiative and creativity by allowing the individual great freedom of action in attaining well-defined objectives.
Citizenship	To honor our obligations to society by being an economic, intellectual, and social asset to each nation and each community in which we operate.

Based on "Statement of Corporate Objectives." In S. Harris, Hewlett-Packard: Shaping the corporate culture, in Fombrun et al., *Strategic Human Resource Management* (New York: Wiley, 1984).

influences cooperation, decision making, control, communication, commitment, and perception in organizations.[28] It also allows individuals to justify their behaviors in terms of their organization's values.[29] Thus managers can use organizational culture to foster the type of individual performance they desire.

The fit of an individual's attitudes and behaviors with the culture has an effect on his or her performance in an organization. Because of this fact, researchers have analyzed the extent to which individuals hold the beliefs and values of their culture and the extent to which they behave in ways prescribed by the culture.[30] As shown in Figure 14–3, the so-called *good soldier* both conforms to the culture's values and behaves in ways prescribed by the culture. The *adapter* acts in prescribed ways, even though he or she holds different beliefs and values. A manager at Norton who does not believe in "new conversation" but acts collaboratively anyway would fall into this category. The *maverick* has congruent values and beliefs but acts in nonconforming ways. At Norton, a maverick might believe in the new approach to management but replace team activities with more individualistic performance efforts. Last, the *rebel* neither believes nor behaves in ways prescribed by the culture and thus is typically viewed as an outsider by other organizational members.

These four categories of individuals each have a different impact on organizations and must be managed differently. For example, if a manager wishes to perpetuate the status quo, he or she may use a good soldier as a role model to more junior workers. Managers might have an adapter lead a task force responsible for implementing new programs. A maverick could be encouraged to develop creative solutions to organizational problems. Managing a rebel and making him or her productive may challenge even the most creative and effective manager.

Diagnosing the fit between an individual and his or her corporate culture

Figure 14–3 INDIVIDUAL FIT WITH ORGANIZATIONAL CULTURE

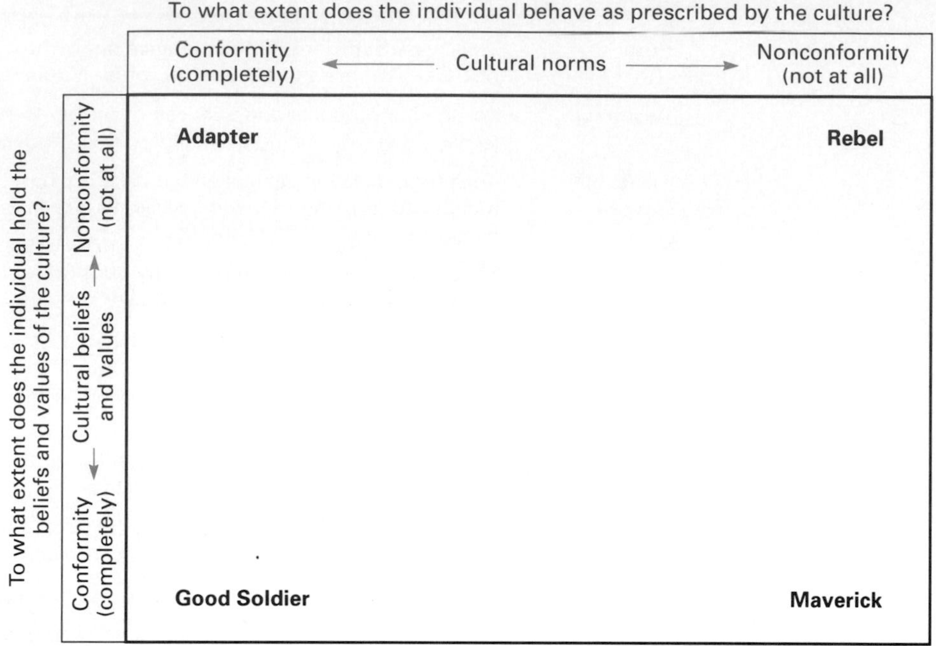

Reprinted with permission from V. Sathe, *Culture and Related Corporate Realities* (Homewood, Ill.: Irwin, 1985), p. 88.

helps predict whether the person can survive in the organization and suggests strategies for responding to misfits. For example, hiring a potential rebel for a conservative, stable organization may create too much turbulence for effective personal or organizational performance. Such diagnosis can also raise questions about the validity of existing culture and force organizational leaders to consider alternatives. A maverick might identify potential dysfunctions in a status-quo organization and motivate changes.

Certain conditions, shown in Figure 14–4, may call for a major change in an organization's culture. Clearly Norton's management felt that the conditions faced by their company warranted a change to a more collaborative culture. Yet careful assessment of the potential impact of such a change must precede its introduction; it is not always the answer. Alternatives to culture change should be examined if management can answer the following questions affirmatively[31]:

Figure 14–4 CONDITIONS THAT CALL FOR CULTURAL CHANGE IN AN ORGANIZATION

- Persistent organizational performance and/or morale problems
- A fundamental change in the organization's mission
- Deregulation and fierce international competition
- Major technological changes
- Major market changes
- Major changes in the social environment
- Acquisitions and mergers
- Organizational growth
- A family business moving to professional management
- A domestic organization expanding overseas

Based on V. Sathe, *Culture and Related Corporate Realities* (Homewood, Ill.: Irwin, 1985), p. 403

1. Can the desired results be obtained by behavior change without culture change?
2. Can the desired results be obtained by using the existing culture creatively?
3. Can the desired results be obtained by utilizing the latent potential of the prevailing culture?
4. Can the desired results be achieved via a culture change toward more intrinsically appealing beliefs and values rather than toward more alien ones?
5. What evidence is there that a major culture change can be successfully carried out in a reasonable period of time?

MODELS OF CHANGE

What is the first step you would take to ensure that the changes proposed for Norton Company would be effective? Is deciding to change a culture sufficient? Should you begin by diagnosing the situation, fleshing out a plan for dealing with the problems identified, presenting it to top management with a timetable for implementation, and then appearing the next day ready to begin? Or should you schedule a meeting with the organizational members involved, jointly agree on a diagnosis of the situation, brainstorm ways of improving it, meet repeatedly to detail plans for implementing change, and finally implement each step of the plans in sequence?

Model of Planned Change

The model of planned change used here consists of seven steps, shown in Figure 14–5.[32] Although this model was developed for a specific type of change program known as *organization development*, we consider it here as a more generic approach to action. It focuses on change by a consultant external to the organization involved, but it traces equally well the general approach an organization member—employee, manager, or staff consultant—could take to change his or her organization. The following sections describe the seven steps of the model—scouting, entry, diagnosis, planning, action, evaluation, and termination—in more detail.

Scouting A change agent (internal or external consultant, manager, or staff member) and a client obtain preliminary information about each other, without committing themselves formally to the project. More particularly, the change agent must assess the organization's readiness for change, as well as the fit of its needs with his or her abilities and interests. He or she also identifies a reasonable point or person of contact in the firm. In the case of Norton Com-

Figure 14–5 MODEL OF PLANNED CHANGE

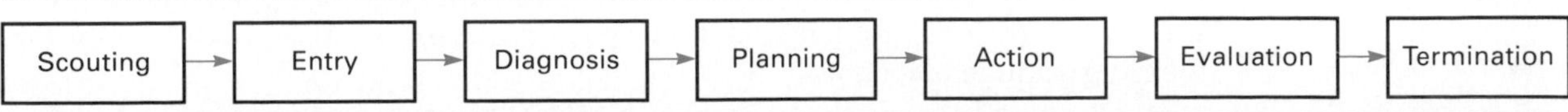

pany, John Nelson likely scouted the organization before deciding to change its culture. Scouting ends with a change agent's decision about whether to proceed with a change effort.

Entry A change agent next negotiates a contract with an organization through a bona fide representative. The agent must develop an effective working relationship with the officially assigned or unofficially chosen representative, sharing their expectations about the change process. At this stage, for example, John Nelson traveled throughout the world for Norton, talking to small groups of managers about the proposed cultural change. At these meetings, participants shared their feelings about the company and clarified all parties' commitment to action. Also at this stage a change agent must identify organizational members who will serve as the primary implementers of change. At Norton, Deborah Kaufman acted in this role.

Diagnosis This step involves problem definition, further goal specification, and evaluation of the resources available to effect the desired change. Note that the activities comprising this step correspond to those of diagnosis presented throughout this book.

Planning Here a change agent and client generate alternate strategies for meeting the objectives of the change. They outline the prescription for change, determine the steps in its implementation, and detail the nature, cost, timing, and personnel required for any new system. This step also requires anticipating and planning for all possible consequences of the change effort. At Norton, John Nelson could take major responsibility for planning action, or other managers may take the initiative during the planning stage and test any proposed action with the rest of the firm's managers and some employees. Alternatively, a task force of managers and employees might act as the planners and then meet with top management and other organizational members to determine the resources necessary for action.

Action In this step, a change agent—John Nelson, top management, or a group of other organizational members—implements the best strategy. For example, the change agents might form problem-solving groups or offer training to managers; necessary reallocation of decision making would also occur at this point.

Evaluation A change agent collects data about the nature and effectiveness of the change as it occurs; this is an integral part of any change process. The extent of evaluation needed depends on the significance or scope of the project. The results of the evaluation indicate whether the change process is complete or should return to an earlier stage to effect further change. Let us assume that measures of productivity indicate significant improvement as a result of the introduction of the new corporate culture. This outcome suggests that the change agent can institutionalize the change. If, instead, ineffective outcomes result, a change agent should return to an earlier stage—scouting, to determine whether a client is really committed to change; diagnosis, to determine the real nature of problems; or planning, to determine the best strategy for meeting change objectives.

Termination Either success or failure may terminate a project. In the first case, plans for continuing the change into the future, or for knowing when it will end, should be specified. Ensuring the institutionalization of effective changes should also occur as part of this step. This means establishing the change processes as permanent ways of operating. In the second case, a change agent may engage in face-saving activities or propose alternate methods for dealing with the problems identified earlier. Failure may also signal a need for other organizational changes, such as different staffing activities, a new reward system, or new technology.

Action Research Model

In some situations, an action research model of change, shown in Figure 14–6, might respond better than the model of planned change to a group's or organization's needs. In action research, a change agent collaborates extensively with a client group in gathering and feeding back data. Together they collect and discuss the data, and then use them for planning.[33] In implementing the collaborative culture at Norton Company, for example, the change agents (e.g., John Nelson, the CEO, and Deborah Kaufman, who oversaw the corporate changeover) and client (e.g., other managers) would gather data about its use as the new system is implemented, discuss the data to determine the system's assets and deficiencies, and then use these data to plan for ways to improve the system's functioning. A change agent often interviews key organizational members to identify and diagnose problems in a given organization. At the

Figure 14–6 AN ACTION RESEARCH MODEL FOR ORGANIZATION DEVELOPMENT

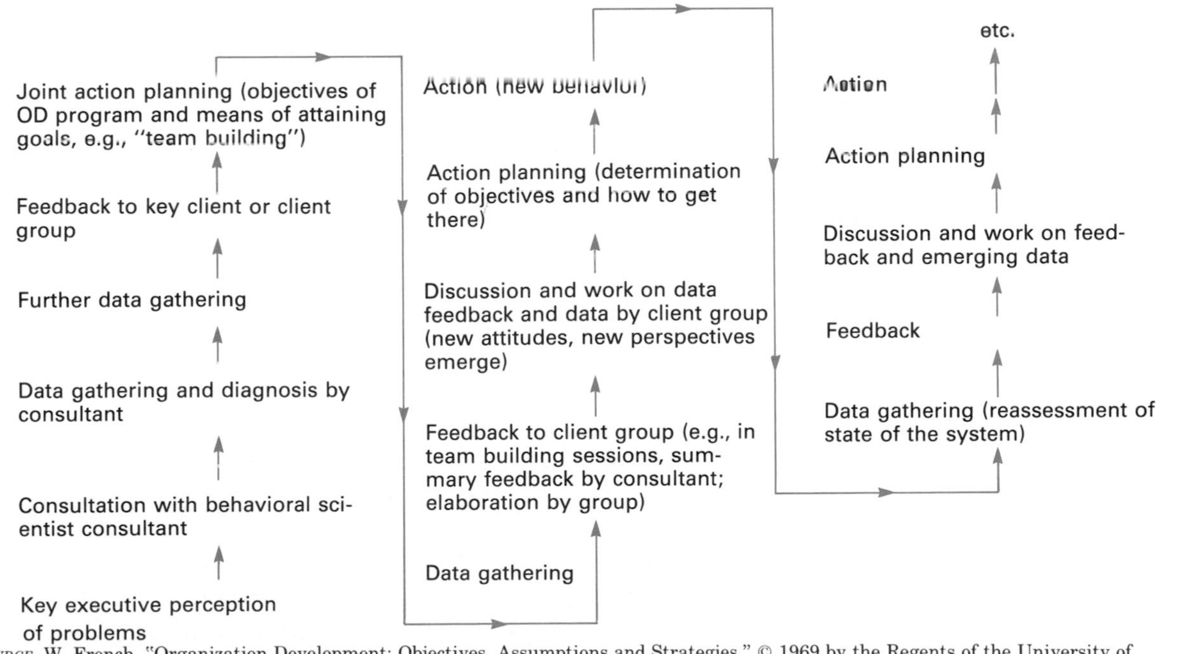

SOURCE: W. French, "Organization Development: Objectives, Assumptions and Strategies." © 1969 by the Regents of the University of California. Reprinted from CALIFORNIA MANAGEMENT REVIEW, volume XII, no. 2, p. 26 by permission of the Regents.

same time, he or she consciously or unconsciously sets the stage for action recommendations.

FORCE FIELD ANALYSIS

Within the context of the planned change model discussed above, we can use *force field analysis* to translate a prescription for change into action. Based on laws of physics, force field analysis views a problem as a product of forces working in different, often opposite, directions. Kurt Lewin translated the basic physical principle into its organizational application[34]: an organization, or any of its subsystems, maintains the status quo when the sum of opposing forces is zero. When forces in one direction exceed forces in the opposite one, the organization or subsystem moves in the direction of the greater forces.

To move an organization toward a different, desired state requires either (1) increasing the forces for change in that direction; (2) decreasing the forces against change in that direction; or (3) combining the two approaches in some way. Generally, reducing resistance forces creates less tension and fewer unanticipated consequences in a system than does increasing forces for change. At Norton, for example, reducing managers' resistance to the new culture would increase the likelihood of a successful changeover. Figure 14–7 shows what happens when a resistance force is eliminated. When the managers no longer resist change, the present state, shown by the solid vertical line, moves closer to the desired state, indicated by the dotted vertical line. In any case, a complete force field analysis looks at ways to alter all forces—both for and against change.

Force field analysis involves identifying the forces acting on the change and finding ways of overcoming resistance to change. Specifying the nature and feasibility of alternate actions involves identifying the appropriate change agent and intervention strategies. Determining the feasibility of these actions requires a consideration of implementation issues. Evaluation and institutionalization of the changes conclude the action.

What precipitated the change at Norton? Why did top management decide to change the culture?

Figure 14–7 FORCE FIELD ANALYSIS OF INTRODUCING A NEW CULTURE AT NORTON COMPANY

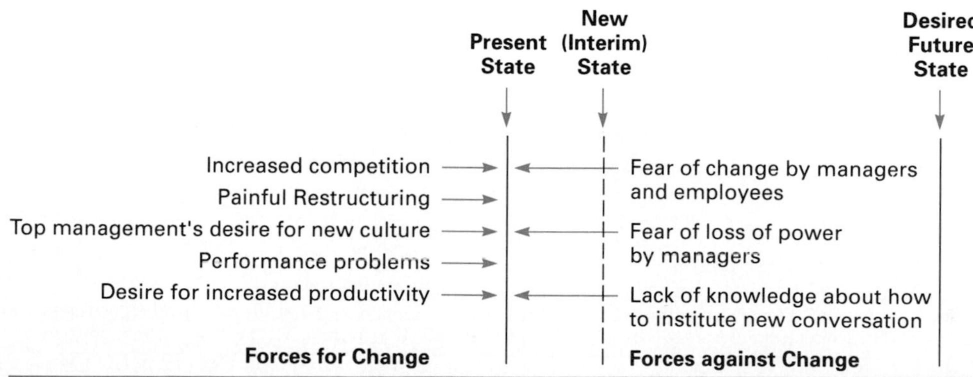

Identifying Forces for Change

Let us consider again the situation at Norton Company. Top management's prescription focused on changing the corporate culture to a more collaborative, team-oriented, proactive one. What forces for change—driving forces—existed? Increased global competition, a painful restructuring, and the need for improved productivity and achievement spurred the change.

Forces for Change Changes in an organization's environment, such as new laws or regulations, rapidly increasing competition, or an unpredictable rate of inflation, may require an organization to implement new structures or reward systems. New product development or product selection due to the availability of improved technology, changes in competition in the industry, or unusual requirements of a new client may also affect an organization. Similarly, changes in the work force, such as more educated workers, more women, or more technically trained management, may call for new forms of decision making or communication. Finally, organizational crises, such as bankruptcy or takeover attempts; reduced productivity, product quality, satisfaction, or commitment; or increased turnover or absenteeism may call for changes in intra- or interdepartmental relations. Frequently one or two specific events external to an organization precipitate change. Careful description of an organizational system should pinpoint the forces for change. Can you make a complete list of forces for change at Norton? Think about a situation you have faced yourself that called for change. What forces for change existed in that situation?

Crises in Organizations As mentioned above, change occurs as a response to a crisis in an organization. Crises provide strong forces for change. Consider the threat posed by a hostile takeover attempt. An organization immediately alters its structure and personnel to prevent such a crisis.

Crises can arise from potential bankruptcy, industrial accidents, product defects or tampering, major computer breakdowns, and myriad other causes. The Tylenol tampering, the Challenger explosion, the Union Carbide explosion in Bhopal, India, and the Chrysler bankruptcy were all major crises that captured the public's attention in the 1980s. Figure 14–8 illustrates the four types of events triggering corporate crises. Note that they can be categorized both according to severity and along a technical-social dimension.[35] Crises can be stimulated by events both inside and outside an organization: computer breakdowns threaten organizational functioning from the inside, hostile takeovers from the outside.

Identifying Forces against Change

Forces known as *resistance forces* counteract forces for change. Examples are middle managers who resist changes in their routines and supervisory activities or who are unwilling to relinquish their decision-making authority. Similarly, top management may be unwilling to allocate the resources required to change the culture. Identifying and then reducing resistance forces may be essential to making an individual or group receptive to change.

Forces against change more often occur within an organization than impinge from outside and stem from rigid organizational structures and rigid

Figure 14–8 FOUR TYPES OF CORPORATE-CRISIS TRIGGERING EVENTS

Technical/Economic

Cell 1 (Internal)	Cell 2 (External)
Major industrial accidents Product injuries Computer breakdown Defective, undisclosed information	Widespread environmental destruction Natural disasters Hostile takeover Societal crises (civil or political) Large scale systems failure
Cell 3	**Cell 4**
Failure to adapt/change Sabotage by insiders Organizational breakdown Communication breakdown On-site product tampering Illegal activities Occupational health diseases	Symbolic projection Sabotage by outsiders Terrorism, executive kidnapping Off-site product tampering Counterfeiting

Human/Organizational/Social

Reprinted with permission from P. Shrivastava and I.I. Mitroff, Strategic management of corporate crises, *Columbia Journal of World Business* 22 (Spring 1987): 7.

individual thinking. Specific forces against change include employees' distrust of a change event, fear of change, desire to maintain power, and complacency; lack of resources to support the change; conflicts between individual and organizational goals; and organizational inertia against changing the status quo. These forces frequently combine into significant resistance to change.

Resistance results from a variety of factors, as shown in Figure 14–9. First, it occurs when a change ignores the needs, attitudes, and beliefs of organizational members. If workers have high security needs, for example, they may perceive as threatening any increased automation in the work place. Second, individuals resist change when they lack specific information about it, as when they do not know when, how, or why it is occurring. Third, individuals may not perceive a need for change; they may feel that their organization is presently operating effectively and profitably. In these cases, change often is neither voluntary nor requested by organizational members. Fourth, organizational members frequently have a "we–they" attitude, which causes them to view a change agent as an enemy. Particularly when change is imposed by representatives of a distant corporate headquarters or an outside consulting firm, organizational members may feel inconsequential to the change. Fifth, members may view change as a threat to the prestige and security of their supervisors. They may perceive a change in procedures or policies as an implicit criticism of their supervisor's performance. Sixth, employees may perceive a change as a threat to their expertise, status, or security. The introduction of a new computer system, for example, may cause employees to feel that they lack sufficient knowledge to perform their jobs. An accompanying revision of the organization's structure may challenge their relative status in the organization. And introduction of a new reward system may threaten their feelings of job security.

Figure 14–9 SOURCES OF RESISTANCE TO CHANGE

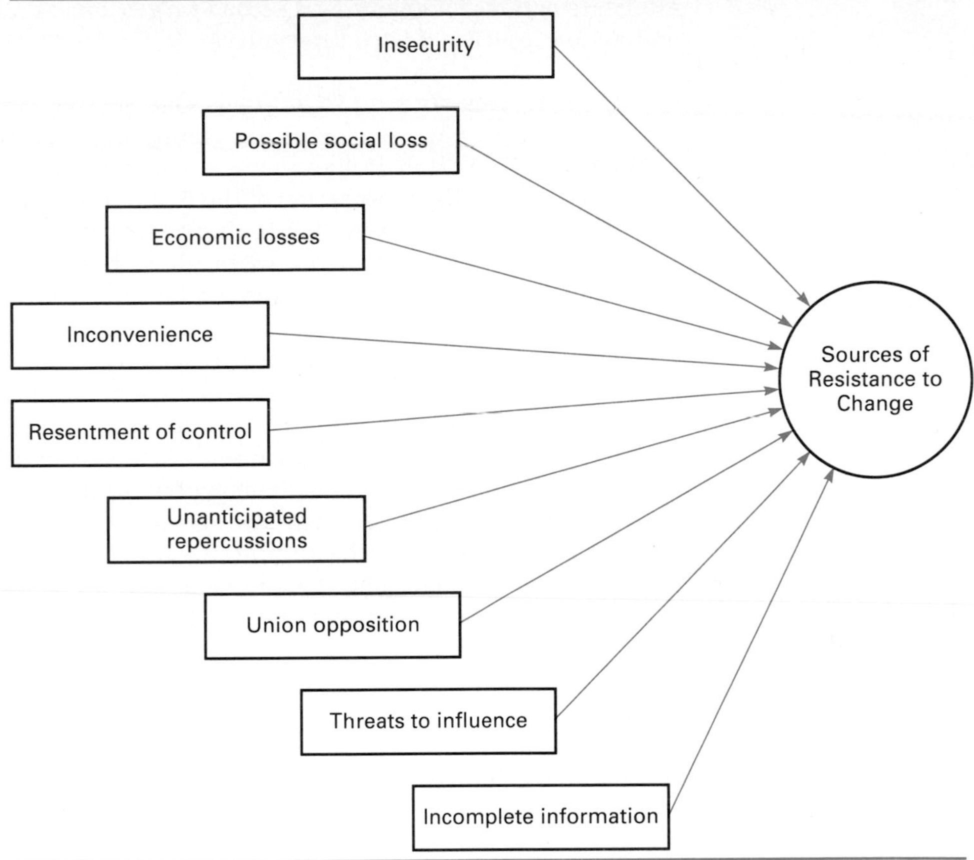

For effective change to occur, a change agent must confront each of these factors and overcome the resulting resistance to change.

Can you think of other forces against change in this situation? Think again about a situation that calls for changes. What forces against change existed in that situation? How do change agents deal with these forces?

Building an Action Plan

The next step of force field analysis involves identifying alternate actions for changing each force for and against change and then formulating a subset of them into an action plan. The approach described here is an analytical one. It must be supplemented with a consideration of individuals' psychological reactions to change and development of appropriate strategies for dealing with them.

Specifying Alternate Actions Consider possible reluctance of managers to reduce their involvement in decision making, a force resisting change in a firm. The following actions could reduce this reluctance: implementing the change slowly, educating the managers about the value of the change, or testing an experimental version of new procedures to increase worker participation in decision making. Table 14–1 lists these alternatives as well as alternate actions for changing a second target force. It also cites the feasibility and action priority of each alternative.

Overcoming Resistance to Change Overcoming resistance to change is a key issue for managers or external change agents. For example, when top management at Norton decides to implement changes to improve productivity, they must ensure the cooperation of the rest of the firm's members. Employees can sabotage change efforts, increasing their cost and decreasing their effectiveness. Resistance to change can result in behavior ranging from lowered productivity, increased absenteeism, and decreased motivation to slowdowns, strikes, and unionization.

A change agent must anticipate resistance to change and plan ways to overcome it, as shown in Table 14–2. In general, an agent can encourage participation of those affected by the change during the planning stage.[36] Employee participation in task forces, quality circles (see Chapter 13), and other vehicles that encourage their contribution to decision making should reduce resistance. An agent can also let his or her clients experience a need for change: highlighting the limitations of current work circumstances lets workers feel their inadequacy and develop the motivation for changes. A change agent should always maintain open and frequent communication with his or her client. This apprises individuals of the changes to expect and the reasons for them. To do so, the agent must schedule regular informational meetings for all employees affected by the change. An agent should also consider the needs of individual employees. Responding to needs whenever possible helps develop in the individuals a vested interest in the change. The more the agent

Table 14–1 EXAMPLE OF ANALYSIS OF TARGET FORCES AT NORTON COMPANY

Target Forces	Alternate Actions	Feasibility	Action Priority
Fear of change by managers and employees	Implement change slowly	Moderate; change can occur over a 12-month period	High
	Educate workers about the change	High; easy and relatively low cost	Medium
	Illustrate the benefits of the new system	High; easy and relatively low cost	High
	Pilot-test the system for small group	Moderate; time-consuming and pilot may be difficult to design	Medium-high
	Involve employees in planning the change	High; time-consuming but important to acceptance	Medium
Lack of knowledge about how to institute new system	Offer training in culture change	High; important to eventual implementation	High
	Provide new policies and procedures	High; important to system implementation	Medium

Table 14–2 Approaches for Dealing with Resistance to Change

Approach	Commonly Used in Situations	Advantages	Drawbacks
Education and communication	Where there is a lack of information or inaccurate information and analysis.	Once persuaded, people will often help with the implementation of change.	Can be very time-consuming if lots of people are involved.
Participation and involvement	Where the initiators do not have all the information they need to design the change and where others have considerable power to resist.	People who participate will be committed to implementing change.	Can be very time-consuming if participators design an inappropriate change.
Facilitation and support	Where people are resisting because of adjustment problems.	No other approach works as well with adjustment problems.	Can be time-consuming, and still fail.
Negotiation and agreement	Where someone or some group will clearly lose out in a change and where that group has considerable power to resist.	Sometimes it is a relatively easy way to avoid major resistance.	Can be too expensive in many cases if it alerts others to negotiate for compliance.
Manipulation and co-optation	Where other tactics will not work or are too expensive.	It can be a relatively quick and inexpensive solution to resistance problems.	Can lead to future problems if people feel manipulated.
Explicit and implicit coercion	Where speed is essential and the change initiators possess considerable power.	It is speedy and can overcome any kind of resistance.	Can be risky if it leaves people mad at the initiators.

can show individuals that the change will help them work better and be more satisfied with their work, the more he or she is increasing the likelihood of support for the change. Finally, where possible, a change agent should encourage voluntary change. Establishing a climate of innovation and experimentation can reduce an organization's tendency to maintain the status quo. Particularly when change is rewarded, individuals will feel more comfortable in changing.

Formulating an Action Plan Force field analysis concludes with a listing of each proposed action, in the order it will be performed. You can continue the analysis for Norton Co. begun in Figure 14–7 and Table 14–1 to develop a complete action plan yourself. Then try a similar analysis with an organi-

Figure 14–10 STEPS IN FORCE FIELD ANALYSIS

1. Identify forces for change.
2. Identify forces against change.
3. Brainstorm actions to reduce forces against change.
4. Brainstorm actions to enhance forces for change.
5. Assess feasibility of each action specified.
6. Prioritize actions.
7. Build an action plan from ranking of actions.
8. Develop timetable and budget for action plan.

zational change situation you have faced. Be sure to perform all the steps described above and summarized in Figure 14–10.

SELECTING A CHANGE AGENT

Who could make the changes in culture called for in the introductory scenario? Should top management direct the proposed changes themselves, or should they use an outside consultant to facilitate them? Figure 14–11 offers a typology of possible change agents. Clearly the use of *internal* versus *external* change agents presents some tradeoffs.

Internal Change Agents

Both Deborah Kaufman and John Nelson have first-hand knowledge of their organization, are known and immediately available to organizational members, and require almost no additional expenditures in fees or salary. However, because of their investment in the organization, insiders can be too close to and not objective enough in looking at a problem—or can be viewed as part of a problem. In addition, their services can be costly if measured in terms of time unavailable for other organizational projects.

Most frequently, the manager of the group involved in a change becomes the implementor of the changes. This selection occurs informally, primarily because he or she is closest to the situation, has greatest knowledge of it, and has control over it. Further, the manager is already on board, which can reduce the time required to begin the change. In addition, other organizational members already know the manager and have clear expectations about actions he or she might take.

External Change Agents

Consultants offer the opposite advantages and disadvantages. They tend to have more technical knowledge, diverse competencies, and objectivity. They may lack information about a particular situation, take longer to start implementing change, and add large out-of-pocket costs.

One study of the personality of change agents indicated that the most effective organization development (OD) consultants could be described as

Figure 14–11 TYPES OF CHANGE AGENTS

Change Generators

1. *Key change agents.* Those who convert an issue into a felt need. This is usually the role of a charismatic leader. An example is Lee Iacocca, whose methods, style, and values dominated the change process at Chrysler. Iacocca eventually became a symbol of U.S. pride and rebirth.
2. *Demonstrators.* These change agents demonstrate support for the change conceptualized by the key change agent. They are first in the line of confrontation to face those who prefer the status quo. The demonstrator's role is to provide visible, vocal support for the change.
3. *Patrons.* These individuals support the change process, financially or psychologically. For instance, a patron of change may provide the key change agent with a budget, a prestigious title, a promotion, or other symbols of support.
4. *Defenders.* This role entails defending the change at the grass roots—the lower levels of the organization. The manager-defender is caught up by the charisma of the key change agent, by becoming an adherent, and by spreading the word among the troops. Defenders may see how they can benefit from the change, or they may be pushed into defending the change by resisters.

Change Implementors

5. *External change implementors.* These individuals are invited from outside the organization to implement change. They may be consultants for organizational development efforts hired to articulate and implement the key change agent's vision. External change agents have the advantage of a fresh perspective and no vested interest in keeping things the way they are.
6. *External/internal change implementors.* These individuals develop internal implementors. Staff managers from headquarters, who are alien to the field organizations, may have the task of carrying the word from on high to the masses. They are external in the sense that they appear to come from outside. Yet they are long-standing members of the organization with the traditional supports.
7. *Internal change implementors.* These are managers who assume the responsibility to implement the change in their own organizations. Convinced of the need for change, they model other change agents to move their units in the desired direction, often translating or redefining the change to meet their own needs.

Change Adopters

8. *Early adopters.* These managers practice the new change. The first adopters show the highest commitment and become the prototypes for the change. Going beyond implementation, they maintain the change, making it the norm in their organization.
9. *Maintainers.* These managers are primarily concerned with meeting current business needs, doing their jobs to keep the organization going. However, they are willing to adopt the change in the process, because they see how it contributes to their own work. Their objective is to sustain the organization, and they realize that the change is one of the things that you have to do now and then to assure the organization's survival. An example is how managers readily take on new or added responsibilities in the wake of a reorganization of functions and reporting relationships.
10. *Users.* Managers become users when they make a habit of the change. Initially, they have the least commitment to the change, and they are probably the last adopters. Yet they are likely to benefit the most from the change. Without them, the change would never be successful.

London, M. *Change Agents: New Roles and Innovation Strategies for Human Resource Professionals.* San Francisco: Jossey-Bass, 1988, pp. 58–59. Used with permission of the publisher.

empathetic, sensitive, open, tolerant, flexible, patient, friendly, cooperative, and imaginative. They developed and used information to understand situations and identify behavior patterns. They acted in a self-reliant fashion, were bold, risk taking, and initiating. In contrast, the least effective consultants were suspicious, tense, directive, and impersonal. They stayed within bounds of known facts, focused on the practical, secured minimal information, and were more concerned with the how than the why of situations. They also were shy and aversive to risk.[37]

Table 14–3 summarizes the advantages and disadvantages of internal and external change agents, taking into account costs, knowledge, experiences, and objectivity. Selection of a change agent should include the steps shown in Figure 14–12. According to these guidelines, is John Nelson's choice of Deborah Kaufman as the primary change agent appropriate?

Table 14–3 ADVANTAGES AND DISADVANTAGES OF INTERNAL AND EXTERNAL CHANGE AGENTS

	Internal Agents	External Agents
Advantages	Possess better knowledge of the organization Are more quickly available Require lower out-of-pocket costs Are a known quantity Have more control and authority	Have more objective views of the organization Have more experience in dealing with diverse problems Can call on more individuals with diverse expertise Have more technical knowledge, competence, and skills available
Disadvantages	May be too close to the problem May hold biased views May create additional resistance if viewed as part of the problem Must be reassigned; not available for other work	Have less knowledge of the organization Require higher out-of-pocket costs Are an unknown quantity Have longer start-up time Reflect unfavorably on the image of management

SELECTING AN INTERVENTION STRATEGY

In this book we have identified three focuses of change in an organization: (1) behavioral, (2) structural, and (3) technological. The behavioral focus deals with changes in member knowledge, skills, and interactions, and changing member attitudes; it can also involve improving group behavior (see Chapter 5), communication (see Chapter 5), leadership skills (see Chapter 8), power relations (see Chapter 9), and intergroup behavior (see Chapter 10). The structural approach calls for redesigning organizations and jobs or work situations (see Chapters 11 and 12). The technological approach requires changing equipment, methods, materials, or techniques and changing the relationship between the worker and his or her job (see Chapter 13).

The term *organization development* was originally defined as "a long-range effort to improve an organization's problem-solving and renewal processes,

Figure 14–12 STEPS IN SELECTING A CHANGE AGENT

1. Determine the objectives of the change.
2. Consider the extent of help and involvement desired.
3. Consider the extent of help and involvement available in the organization.
4. Identify individuals with expertise congruent with the objectives.
5. Identify and specify relevant constraints: time, cost, effort, involvement, and other resources.
6. Communicate expectations, including needs, constraints, and personal biases, to the change agent.
7. Establish criteria for evaluating the change plan: cost, time, effort, or other resources needed; technical feasibility; likelihood of success; congruence between consultants' experience and proposed plan; ease of implementation; and likelihood of resistance.
8. Determine the tradeoffs in selecting various change agents (cost versus experience, for example).
9. Assess which change agents fit the organization's needs.

particularly through a more effective and collaborative management of organizational culture—with special emphasis on the culture of formal work teams—with the assistance of a change agent or catalyst; and the use of the theory and technology of applied behavioral science, including action.[38] In this chapter we use the term more generically, as a wide range of interventions for organizational change.

The choice of a specific intervention strategy depends on several criteria: (1) the target system, (2) the target group, (3) the depth of intervention desired, (4) the nature of the prescribed change mechanisms, and (5) the expertise of the change agent. In this section we offer an overview of these options rather than an in-depth analysis of each intervention strategy. Managers and consultants should consult additional sources to become expert in specific interventions.

The Target System

One typology of intervention strategies breaks them down into four possible target systems: (1) technical, (2) social, (3) administrative, or (4) strategic.[39] Low productivity may signal problems with the technical system. Providing capital improvements and offering training to workers can help resolve these problems.

Inadequate quality of working life may suggest problems with an organization's social system. Interventions that alter the reward system, integrate organizational values into change efforts, confront organizational power and politics, and improve communication address these problems.

An organization that responds slowly to both receiving and distributing information may have an ineffective system for administering the organization. Ensuring that a logical organization structure exists, communicating the structure to organizational members, clarifying policies, procedures, and standards, and maintaining a strong system for collecting and disseminating information can aid the effectiveness of the administrative system.

Management strength and competence reflect the health of a strategic system, which includes top management, planning, and management information. Choosing appropriate management styles, systematically evaluating the environment, adapting to changing conditions, building executive succession systems, and encouraging innovation are interventions that strengthen the strategic system.

The Target Group

The selection of the appropriate target for change depends on the nature of the problem diagnosed. Interventions can focus on a person, role, dyad or triad, team or group, intergroup interaction, or an entire organization.[40] Analysis of the forces for and against change also helps pinpoint the appropriate target. If, for example, one supervisor refuses to adopt a new policy, one target of change should be that individual. If, on the other hand, an organization lacks effective policies for dealing with unions, then the organization as a whole should be the target.

Too often, change agents misfocus interventions, addressing the wrong target. Consider a situation where some employees report late to work. Some organizations try to resolve this problem by instituting earlier official starting times. What is the target of this change? What might be the consequences of such a change? In this situation, the change should focus on the tardy individuals rather than on the entire organization.

Depth of Intervention

Similar assessment of the appropriate *depth* of intervention must occur. The extent to which change focuses on the core areas of personality or self, at the individual level, differentiates various intervention strategies.[41] Strategies can range from deep to surface interventions: from those that "touch the more deep, personal, private and central aspects of an individual or his relationship with others . . . [to those that] deal with more external aspects of the individual and which focus upon the more formal and public aspects of role behavior. . . ."[42]

Modification of reward systems, which interface with individual performance and motivation, is a moderately surface strategy. Processes that attempt to alter individual work style by focusing on feelings, attitudes, and perceptions exemplify deeper strategies. The deepest level of intervention—intrapersonal analysis—uses strategies to increase the individual's knowledge of his or her own attitudes, values, and conflicts as the first step in change.

Interventions should occur "at a level no deeper than that required to produce enduring solutions to the problems at hand. . . . The cost, skill demands, client dependency, and variability of outcome all increase with depth of intervention. . . . Further, as the depth of intervention increases, the effects tend to locate more in the individual and less in the organization."[43]

Practitioners should also classify change attempts as one of three different types.[44] First-order changes reinforce present understandings of situations. They include adjustments in structures, reward systems, or other organizational behaviors. Second-order changes modify the present understanding in a particular direction. A decline in productivity, once viewed as a technical problem, can now be handled as a QWL issue. Third-order changes give organizational members the capacity to change their understanding of a situation. Training organizational members to view a situation through new lenses offers more long-term possibilities for change.

Nature of the Change Mechanisms

The nature of the change mechanisms chosen also depends on the problem diagnosis and force field analysis. Figure 14–13 offers an array of such mechanisms. Change agents can provide feedback to organizational members about their or others' attitudes and behaviors as a way of spurring change. If a male manager learns, for example, that his subordinates view him as too autocratic, he might modify his leadership style. Change agents can also increase interaction and communication through altering an organization's structure, as described in Chapters 11 and 12. The introduction of project teams facilitates lateral communication; so does the implementation of QWL programs that encourage team collaboration and problem solving. Change agents might also alert management and workers to changing sociocultural norms. At Norton, Deborah Kaufman oversaw the corporate changeover to the norms of collaboration and "new conversation." In addition, some strategies encourage confrontation to resolve differences; confrontation meetings, process consultation

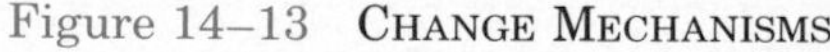

Figure 14–13 CHANGE MECHANISMS

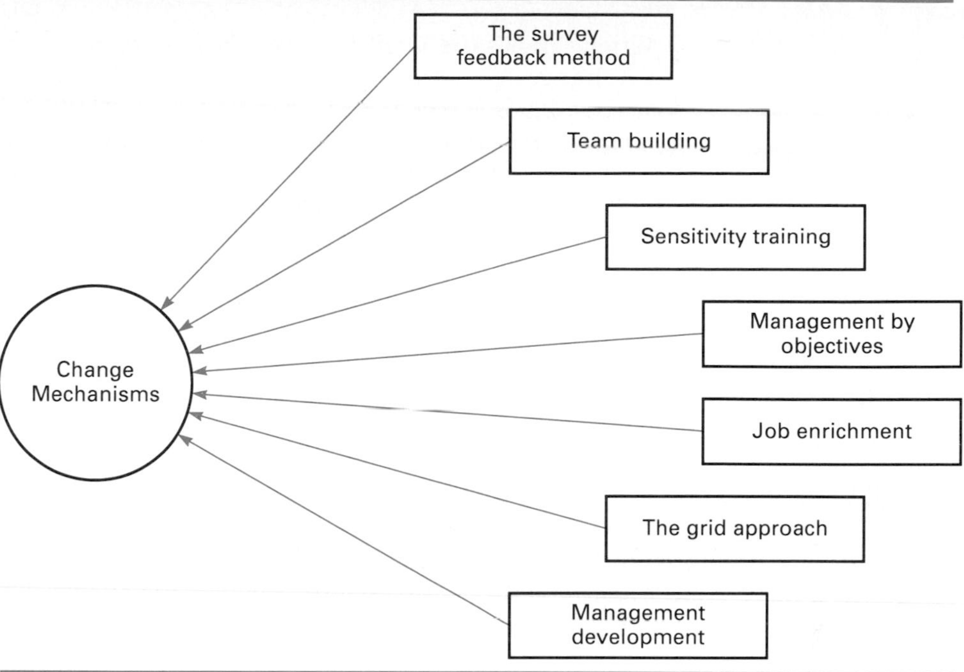

(where a consultant diagnoses the nature of communication, decision making, and other processes based on observations of group performance), and third-party facilitation can take this approach to change. Finally, change mechanisms can include education of workers through training and skill practice.

Problems based in individual performance frequently call for use of feedback and increased interaction as change mechanisms. Problems with conflict generally require confrontation and working for resolution of differences, or creation of an awareness of new norms emphasizing teamwork. Leadership dilemmas can be corrected by education of the leaders, including delivery of new knowledge and skill practice. While some change mechanisms respond best to specific types of problems, use of multiple mechanisms generally strengthens the action and resulting change.

Preferred change strategies vary among different countries. In Italy, for example, where managers' and consultants' values do not support dealing with emotionally charged issues in a group context, team building and third-party interventions are common, whereas t-groups (groups that meet in a neutral setting to share their feelings about themselves and others, to improve intrapersonal style and interpersonal relations), confrontation meetings, and process consultation are not.[45]

Expertise of the Change Agent

Of course, the precise change mechanism used depends to some extent on the expertise of the change agent. Organizational members, as well as external consultants, often have training or experience in performing certain types of interventions. Thus selection of a strategy should complement selection of a change agent.

IMPLEMENTING ORGANIZATIONAL CHANGES

Action follows the identification of target forces for change and the selection of a change agent and intervention strategy. Implementation must ensure that the strategies succeed. While careful preparation for change—description, diagnosis, and prescription—increases the chances of success, it does not guarantee effective action. Implementation requires an ongoing assessment of the reactions of organizational members to the change. Briefing sessions, special seminars, or other means of information dissemination must permeate the change effort. Implementation must include procedures for keeping all participants informed about change activities and effects.

The use of a broad-based steering committee to oversee the change may increase its likelihood of success.[46] Such a group, composed of representatives of top management, first-line supervisors, and rank-and-file employees, can advise on issues related to program budget as well as on organizational policies and priorities.

Further, the dynamic nature of organizational systems calls for flexibility in action: all efforts must include contingency plans for unanticipated costs, consequences, or resistance. A strong commitment to the change on the part of top management can buffer change efforts for such difficulties and ensure the transfer of needed resources to the action program.

Changing Organizational Culture

We can diagnose an organization's culture to determine its fit with organizational goals and ability to relate effectively to the organization's environment. If the fit is a poor one, can culture be changed?

We can follow five guidelines for instituting such changes.[47] Changing an organization's culture first requires a clear vision of the organization's future direction and the values and behaviors required to meet it. Second, top management must support the culture change. When two organizations merge, top management of the new venture will largely determine and must support its new culture. Third, top managers must model the new culture for subordinates in and through their own behavior. They must represent the desired values, expectations, and behaviors. Fourth, changes in an organization's structure, human resource systems, and management styles and practices must support the shift in culture. If an organization assumes an egalitarian, people-oriented culture, managers must encourage, measure, and reward worker participation in decision making. If an organization assumes a more authoritarian, production-oriented culture, managers must encourage, measure, and reward worker obedience to authority and "bottom-line" performance. Fifth and finally, members of the organization must be able to fit with the new culture. This may require selection and socialization of newcomers—and termination of misfits; the merger of two organizations or a radical cultural change in a single organization is likely to result in some employee casualties.

Some researchers have suggested that different processes may be required to change different cultures, depending on a given organization's stage of development, orientation, ability to change, experience with alternate cultural frameworks, and history.[48] Every view of change, however, calls for careful diagnosis of current culture by managers and other organizational members before designing and implementing change efforts.

Responding to Crises

Management should consider crisis management an integral part of their strategic planning so that they do not make short-sighted, inappropriate decisions under pressure.[49] Being prepared to deal with crises may necessitate establishing a multifaceted portfolio of technology, conducting periodic crisis audits to identify the potential for a catastrophe, and building crisis-management teams or units that can practice their coping skills far in advance of a disaster.[50]

The effectiveness of an organization's response to a crisis depends on several factors.[51] First, the organization's members must have or be able to secure adequate information and resources to cope with the emergency. Second, they must define emergency work, distinguishing it from regular work but maintaining functional roles while doing it. Third, an organization must demonstrate flexibility in operations and decision making so managers can deal readily with uncertainty and loss of autonomy and control. In addition, organizational members must think creatively and avoid groupthink (see Chapter 5) in a crisis.

Regardless of the mechanisms chosen, managers should conduct crisis management in five phases, summarized in Figure 14–14.[52] First, managers must be alert to crisis warnings, or events that signal the advent of a crisis. Repeated memoranda about the same mechanical difficulties in one type of aircraft might provide such a warning. Second, top management must prepare for and prevent a disaster. A crisis-management team can systematically watch for and respond to early warning signs. Next, management should have contingency plans for containing and limiting damage. Implementation of short- and long-term recovery mechanisms follows. Procedures for dealing with crises such as product tampering, computer breakdowns, or hostile takeover attempts should exist, and management should be able to implement them immediately. Finally, learning ways to improve crisis management should conclude an organization's response.

Managing Large-Scale Change

Managing large-scale organizational change might require a fairly elaborate approach. In general, the process includes four components: (1) pattern breaking, (2) experimenting, (3) visioning, and (4) bonding and attunement.[53] *Pattern breaking* involves freeing a system from structures, processes, and functions that are no longer useful. An organization that can relinquish approaches that

Figure 14–14 THE FIVE PHASES OF CRISIS MANAGEMENT

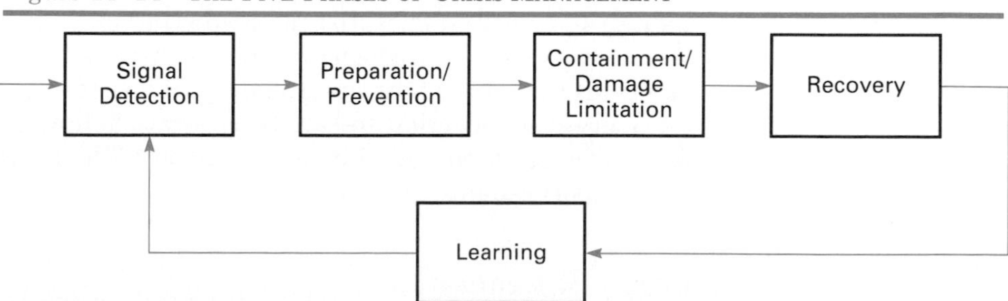

Reprinted with permission from I.I. Mitroff, Crisis management: Cutting through the confusion, *Sloan Management Review* 29 (Winter 1988): 19.

no longer work, whose managers are rewarded for weeding out unproductive products and processes, and is willing to challenge long-held traditions opens the organization to new options. At Norton, removing all structures and processes associated with the former, competitive, adversarial workplace was a first step in instituting change. *Experimenting,* by generating new patterns, encourages flexibility and yields new options. Training small groups of supervisors to institute teamwork at Norton illustrates this element. To experiment, organizations must have a philosophy and mechanisms in place that encourage innovation and creativity. *Visioning,* the third element, calls for the selection of a new perspective as the basis of the change. Visioning activities, such as building shared meaning throughout an organization and using current mission statements, generate support for and commitment to the planned changes. At Norton, the insistence on "new conversation" propelled the organization to the last component—*bonding and attunement.* Here management attempts to integrate all facets of the organizational change, to move members toward the new way of action by focusing them on important tasks and generating constructive interpersonal relationships.

Ethical Issues in Implementation

Change agents often confront problems of integrity in their interactions with organizations. Some managers may implement their personal agenda for change at the expense of solid diagnosis of the organization's needs. Others may promise more than they can deliver. Similarly, some consultants fail to build ways of institutionalizing the change into their process so that the organization must continue to rely on—and pay—them. Organizational leaders, as well as internal and external consultants, should ensure that selection and implementation of change strategies respond to well-documented organizational and individual needs. They must also ensure that a change process respects the rights of individuals in the workplace. Reading 14–1, "Ethical Dilemmas in Various Stages of Organizational Development," discusses ethical issues and responses in greater detail.

EVALUATING THE CHANGE PROCESS

Follow-up—both informal and formal—is critical to the success of any organizational improvement and should occur regularly as part of action. Weekly or special staff meetings are appropriate settings for follow-up discussions.[54] Table 14–4 offers a checklist for predicting the success of a planned change. It assesses client characteristics, the fit between consulting team and client, and characteristics of the environment. While the focus of the change strongly influences the collection and analysis of data, follow-up or evaluation generally focuses on four areas: (1) affective reactions, (2) learning, (3) behavioral changes, and (4) performance changes.[55]

Focus of Evaluation

Affective reactions are participants' attitudes about an intervention program. We can assess whether they liked a program; we can also determine whether

Table 14–4 DIAGNOSTIC TOOL FOR PREDICTING THE SUCCESS OF ORGANIZATIONAL PLANNED CHANGE

Client Characteristics	Rating	Consulting Team/Client Characteristics	Rating	Environmental Characteristics	Rating
Commitment of top management		Values fit		External stakeholders' current dissatisfaction	
Capable evangelist		Goals fit		External stakeholders' anticipated future dissatisfaction	
Supportive organization culture		Methodology fit		Common perception among internal stakeholders regarding the environment	
Flexible organization structure		Competence fit		Level of consensus between the consulting team and top management regarding the environment	
Readiness of employee population					

Reprinted, by permission of the publisher, from Y. Zeira and J. Avedisian, Organizational planned change: Assessing the chances for success, *Organizational Dynamics* (Spring 1989): 40.

they found it interesting, useful, or beneficial. Change agents or top management frequently use questionnaires or interviews to obtain data about the reactions of organizational members.

Learning refers to participants' understanding and retention of material covered in a change program. Did participants learn how to use the new computer system as a result of its introduction? Did they acquire additional information about other cultures or international business as a result of training programs? To evaluate learning, change agents can analyze the differences between scores on pre- and post-tests, follow-up interviews, or open-ended survey responses.

Behavioral changes include the participants' actions on the job. Do they interact differently with peers and subordinates? Do they use new or different techniques to accomplish their job activities? Figure 14–15 describes common behavior changes in a successful organization change effort.

Performance changes are reflected in objective organizational measures, such as productivity and quality rates, sales volume, profit, absenteeism, and turnover, as well as more subjective performance-appraisal ratings. We can assess whether the introduction of a new reward system increases worker output or whether a new quality-control system improves product quality, for example.

Data Collection

As noted above, collection of data about change efforts occurs in the same way as does description of a situation—the first phase of the diagnostic approach.

Figure 14–15 COMMON BEHAVIOR CHANGES IN SUCCESSFUL ORGANIZATION CHANGE EFFORTS (AS REPORTED BY PARTICIPANTS)

Question 1: Common behavior changes for individuals at all organizational levels

Communicating openly. Sharing intentions, motives, needs, feelings, and cognitions relevant to the work situation. Giving feedback that is descriptive rather than evaluative, and specific rather than general. Asking for and accepting feedback. Listening—including paraphrasing, summarizing, restating, asking for clarification, and checking out impressions. Directly confronting differences when they arise. Acting to produce structural and normative changes that lead to increased information sharing, such as loosening implicit or explicit guidelines as to who should talk to whom, and circulating minutes of meetings.

Collaborating. Solving problems as close to where they occur as possible. Discussing, planning, and readjusting organizational actions jointly and cooperatively. Holding more group and intergroup discussions and meetings. Involving critical outsiders to the organization in decisions that pertain to them. Making all the serious and creative decisions—particularly decisions where there are multiple stakeholders—in teams. Expanding influence skills beyond bargaining and authoritative commands to include softer means of influence such as seeding ideas, cajoling, and nudging. Moving away from "oneupmanship" and competition, and toward agreement and cooperation.

Taking responsibility. Figuring out for oneself what is necessary to be effective in one's job and taking initiative for getting whatever information, cooperation, services, or materials are needed from other relevant parties inside or outside of the organization. Asking for and taking responsibility and authority. Persisting in the struggle to make needed changes, especially in the face of frustration and ambiguity. Forming and offering more suggestions. Stating one's own contribution to a problematic situation rather than blaming others. Exhibiting behaviors that demonstrate movement along a continuum from monitoring one's own work to managing and prioritizing it to affecting the design of it to affecting its organizational context (e.g., policies and procedures) to affecting the goals and directions of the organization itself. Taking responsibility is also reflected in expressions of interest and excitement in the work and in *decreased* approval seeking, face saving, indifference, burnout, or "coasting."

Maintaining a shared vision. Developing and communicating written statements of philosophy. Holding meetings to develop clarity of values, purpose, and the means by which the purpose will be achieved. Talking about how organization values translate into daily work behavior. Changing organizational structure, policies, and practices to reflect stated values. Having and telling a "story," a shared history that gives meaning to the organization's activities. Creating rituals and ceremonies to reestablish and remember values. Setting, discussing, and reinforcing high standards.

Solving problems effectively. Defining problems from a win/win perspective, with an open-minded search for solutions that are mutually acceptable instead of pressing for one's own "right" answer. Taking problems out of a personal context and instead working on them vis a vis an agreed-upon superordinate goal. Keeping problem definition separate from solution seeking. Generating and simultaneously entertaining multiple explanations for a phenomenon. Generating and discussing multiple alternatives for resolving problems.

Respecting/supporting. Providing recognition for a job well done. Talking about what's going well versus what's deficient. Making use of an individual's assets versus trying to "correct" their shortcomings. Acknowledging people. Encouraging and rewarding people for taking time for themselves and their families. Equalizing status symbols. Helping; standing in for one another. Treating people equitably. Suspending judgment when things go wrong; allowing for goodness in others and not automatically attributing negative motives. An *absence* of disrespectful and nonsupportive behaviors such as racial, ethnic, and sexist jokes, "scapegoating," and stereotyping. An *absence* of discrimination based on race, sex, or ethnicity. An *absence* of aggressive or punitive behavior.

Processing/facilitating interactions. Stopping meetings or one-on-one discussions to examine the process when things are not going well. Assigning (and rotating) the task of observing group process. Reserving time at the end of meetings to critique what was done well/poorly, what facilitated making the decision and/or doing the task, and so on. Clarifying meeting goals and purposes. Rotating the chairperson role. Making group-facilitating rather than group-hindering interventions. Group members changing their roles in the group depending on what is needed for the group to function well. Effectively managing the process of meetings by consensually establishing relevant agendas, holding to them, and recording what is going on so people can understand and follow.

Inquiring. Taking multiple and numerous measures of the discrepancies between the organization's goals and its current state. Taking baselines and using surveys, audits, unobtrusive measures and control groups where possible to gain information about how the organization is functioning. Experimenting with changes in such a way that the outcome will allow causal inference and useful conclusions. Soliciting information from customers, regulators, and competitors. Looking for new ideas in books, articles, technical studies, speeches, and from one another. Frequently examining and questioning structure, practices, and policies to be sure they maximize achievement of the organization's goals.

Experimenting. Taking risks. Having a "bias for action" and not waiting for the perfect design or plan before trying things out. Allowing time to meet, talk, and try new behaviors. Accepting mistakes. Rewarding good tries. Having fewer re-

Figure 14–15 CONTINUED

strictions on how things get done. Eliminating symbols of conformity (e.g., three-piece suits) and structures/policies that demand conformity (e.g., timeclocks). Deemphasizing action plans, milestones, and measurable objectives. Acting as umbrellas over experimental programs. Backing/sheltering risk takers, especially when they fail. Defending against intrusions from higher levels. Working with those who are experimenting to demonstrate that experimentation is valued and represents an investment in the organization's future.

Question 2: Common behavior changes for managers

Generating participation. Linking planning and implementation in terms of time and who does it. Involving people when they have the necessary expertise, when the decision must be high quality, and when implementation depends on them. Using meetings, workshops, or a consultant to solicit input from people on proposed changes. *Not* dictating the exact way to accomplish a delegated task. Structuring the work in a way that opens possibilities for self-management by the job incumbent. Providing task and job designs that provide meaningful work, real responsibility for work outcomes, and reliable knowledge of results. Relaxing traditional authoritarian forms of control (e.g., over budgets and allocations of resources and people) and allowing workers to do more. Changing behavior *away from* unilateral edicts and imposing one's will as the basis for power and toward softer influence techniques. Facilitating more than directing.

Leading by vision. Continually articulating the organization's purpose, goals, values, and standards and the means by which they are to be carried out operationally. Setting up feedback mechanisms to find out if the vision is being implemented. Structuring the organization and devising policies to be consistent with stated purpose, values, and goals. Reinforcing behaviors that reflect organizational values. Creating ceremonial occasions to reinforce values and goals. Scheduling their own activities to reflect commitment to values and goals. "Role-modeling" behaviors that exemplify the organization's priorities and values.

Functioning strategically. Talking about underlying causes, interdependencies, and long-range consequences and acting accordingly. *Not* acting based on a single-function view of the organization. Having long time horizons. Resisting giving in to short term pressures for quick results in order to allow people to learn new behaviors. Deliberately and thoughtfully planning the markets and businesses in which the organization is engaged. Fitting the organizational structure to the organization's key objectives and to the nature of its businesses and markets. Planning for the skills and knowledge required for meeting future objectives. Creating a well thought out and well understood strategic design to guide operating plans and activities.

Promoting information flow. Clearly communicating the elements of the job that need to be accomplished in order to succeed (e.g., communicating standards, goals, tolerances to be worked within, and limits of authority). Being clear about feelings, needs, expectations, commitment, and loyalty issues. Establishing multiple channels for upward, sideways, and downward communication that complement the core chain of command lines (e.g., use of task forces, advisory groups, and unions). Enhancing mechanisms and influencing social norms to promote direct cross-unit communication.

Developing others. Teaching needed skills. Helping subordinates identify needs, interests, skills, aspirations, and talents. Rewarding desired behaviors with "strokes" or whatever rewards the manager controls. Delegating tasks based on subordinates' competencies and according to a developmental plan. *Not* doing subordinates' jobs for them. Relating subordinates to a larger context. Giving people accurate information regarding their performance. Providing personal growth experiences for subordinates. Judging subordinates by their end outputs, not the methods used to produce them. Processing successes and failures with subordinates to help them learn. Helping subordinates take advantage of opportunities and resources offered by the organization.

From *Journal of Applied Behavioral Science*, "Common Behavior Changes in Successful Organization Development Efforts," by J.I. Porras and S.I. Hoffer, 22 (4), 1986, pp. 486–487.

Data can be collected through the use of interviews, questionnaires, observation, or company records. In general, evaluation should use multiple methods to measure most accurately the impact of a change. It should use the most appropriate methods to compare actual performance or outcomes against objectives, standards, policies, or other plans and then to draw a summary conclusion about action effectiveness.

Figure 14–16 is a summary checklist for evaluating organizational improvement efforts. These evaluation questions highlight each facet of the diagnostic approach described in this book. Evaluation involves first describing the objectives of a change and its environmental context, including both in-

Figure 14–16 QUESTIONS FOR EVALUATING ORGANIZATIONAL IMPROVEMENT EFFORTS

Factor	Question
Outcomes	
Objectives	1. *What were the intended outcomes of the program and what were the actual outcomes?* It is necessary to determine why the program was initiated and its impact on "bottom line" outcomes such as productivity, turnover, absenteeism and satisfaction.
Environmental Context (External Factors)	
Labor market and characteristics of workforce	2. *How tight was the labor market and what were the characteristics of the available labor pool?* Ascertain unemployment level and characteristics of workforce when evaluating an organizational improvement program.
Social and political trends	3. *Were there changes occurring in society affecting workers and the organization?* The success of a program may be affected by how consistent it is with certain societal trends.
Economy and market	4. *What was the general state of the economy at the time of the improvement program?* Certain programs may work only in favorable economic conditions.
Environmental stability	5. *How much is the organization's immediate environment changing—and is the organizational structure appropriately matched?* A program may be greatly affected by the degree of congruence between an organization's structure and degree of environmental uncertainty that exists for the organization.
Internal Factors	
Product technology	6. *What is the product of the organization and the primary technology used to transform inputs into outputs?* Ascertain the match between technology, structure and kind of people involved and whether the program is congruent with them or tries to make them congruent with the program.
Structure	7. *Where on the mechanistic-to-organic structure continuum is the organization?* The program should be consistent with the organization's structure or explicitly attend to changing that structure.
Size	8. *How large is the organization and the plant or division within which the problem is taking place?* Size affects complexity of programs and the organizational resources available.
Organizational climate	9. *What are the prevailing norms and values in the organization regarding involvement in organizational improvement efforts?* Programs require changed behavior, thus changed climate—which requires program attention to resistance.
Guiding Assumptions and Models	
	10. *How explicit were the assumptions about organizations and change that guided the organizational improvement program?* Being explicit about assumptions increases the chance that all involved understand the program and that the assumptions are more carefully examined and tested.
	11. *How comprehensive and consistent with current organizational theory were the guiding assumptions and models?* The success of a program can be influenced both by internal logic and by failure to incorporate what we know about organizations and improvement.

Figure 14–16 CONTINUED

Factor	Question
Program Phases	
Initiation phase	12. *What was the reason for starting the program and who was initially involved?* Programs generally require a broadly shared "felt need" and involvement of affected people to succeed.
Entry and startup phase	13. *What were the initial activities at the start of the program and who was involved?* The pitfall to avoid is premature implementation; moving into a program without adequate diagnosis increases resistance stemming from lack of understanding and support. Prescription without diagnosis leads to malpractice.
Diagnostic phase	14. *What were the explicit diagnostic activities?*
	15. *What aspects of the organization were diagnosed and how?* Pitfalls include the "elephant problem" (sending eight blind men out to touch the organization and try to put the separate "felt" pieces together) and the "expert" problem, caused by outsiders who do a fancy diagnosis that no one understands.
Strategy planning phase	16. *How was the actual program planned and by whom?* The two dimensions to assess are (1) how available resources (internal and external consultants) were used, and (2) how the diagnostic model and data were used.
	17. *How explicit and detailed were the plans?* Lack of planning leads to seat-of-the-pants implementation of a program.
Implementation phase	18. *What was actually done, how, when, and by whom?* Two pitfalls are incomplete, patchwork implementation and *intervention interruptus,* or failing to carry the program through to completion.
Evaluation and corrective action phase	19. *Was there explicit evaluation and monitoring of the program and, if so, what was measured and how?* Political pressure resulting from overadvocacy of programs sets up forces against evaluation. Evaluative measures should be directly related to intended program outcomes.
	20. *What was done with the evaluation—did it result in corrective action or modification of the program?* Corrective action may fail because of lack of top-level organizational commitment and/or postimplementation letdown and regression when the novelty wears off.

SOURCE: Reprinted, by permission of the publisher, from "When Does Work Restructuring Work? Organizational Innovations at Volvo and GM," by Noel Tichy with Jay N. Nisberg, ORGANIZATIONAL DYNAMICS, Summer 1976.

ternal and external factors (see questions 1–9). An evaluator next reviews the diagnosis of an organizational problem by examining the guiding assumptions and models for the improvement effort (see questions 10 and 11). Third, evaluation includes monitoring a prescription for change by analyzing early program phases (see questions 12–15). Finally, evaluation focuses on the action itself, assessing strategy, planning, implementation, and follow-up (see questions 16–20).

INSTITUTIONALIZING ACTION IN ORGANIZATIONS

Action must extend beyond short-run changes for real organizational improvement to result. Getting the change to "stick" must be a significant goal of a change effort. How, for example, does the new culture at Norton Company become permanent? Certainly the way activities are performed in moving from prescription to action influences the permanency of a change. Accurate targeting of forces influencing change, followed by careful selection of change agents and intervention strategies, and concluding with effective action, contribute to long-range improvement.

In addition, mechanisms for continually monitoring changes must be developed and instituted. Permanent committees or task forces to observe ongoing implementation and outcomes of a change can serve the monitoring function. Formulation of new organizational policies based on a change can encourage its continuation. Most important of all, commitment to a change by all organizational members expedites its institutionalization.

MAKING EFFECTIVE ORGANIZATIONAL TRANSFORMATIONS

Even if managers and other organizational members diagnose a situation correctly and select appropriate prescriptions for improving it, the complementary action does not always result in the intended outcomes. Sometimes more basic changes—transformations of the organization itself—are required.

Transformation means fundamentally changing organizations to function better in today's competitive world.[56] Four types of changes can be called transformational: (1) changes in what drives an organization (e.g., marketing or production); (2) changes in the relationship between parts of an organization (e.g., between sales and operations); (3) changes in the way work is done; and (4) basic cultural changes.[57] Major researchers in the area agree with the following observations about transformation:

1. Transformation is a response to environmental and technological change by different types of organizations.
2. Transformation is a new model of organizations for the future.
3. Transformation is based on dissatisfaction with the old and belief in the new.
4. Transformation is a qualitatively different way of perceiving, thinking, and behaving.
5. Transformation is expected to spread throughout an organization at different rates of absorption.
6. Transformation is driven by line management.
7. Transformation is ongoing, endless, forever.
8. Transformation is orchestrated by inside and outside experts.
9. Transformation represents the leading edge of knowledge about organizational change.
10. Transformation generates some open communication and feedback throughout an organization.[58]

Transformational change, or "frame-breaking" change, differs from the more frequently observed, converging change, which involves fine-tuning in a company or making incremental modifications to minor shifts in the environment.[59] Frame-breaking change involves redefining an organization's mission, changing the distribution of power within an organization, reorganizing, altering patterns of interaction, and hiring new executives.[60]

Most organizations evolve through relatively long periods of incremental change and adaptation.[61] Periodically, however, reorientations occur—relatively short periods of discontinuous change, where an organization's strategy, power relations, structure, and controls need to be fundamentally re-created into a new configuration.[62] At these times, action effectiveness may decline unless an organization changes in substantial and significant ways.

Environmental pressures, global competition, and deregulation spur organizational transformations. Threats posed by the environment or some misfit between an organization and its environment can precipitate transformations. Organizational growth, pressure by specific constituencies, a real or perceived crisis, or atypical performance demands can also pressure an organization to change. And environmental catastrophes, environmental opportunities, managerial crises, or external or internal revolutions can trigger basic changes in organizations.

Such transitions refer to significant changes in the primary tasks or goals of an organization and its strategy to achieve them.[63] They often involve structural change, a new kind of leadership, and a network of supporters.[64] Eastman Kodak Company found itself stagnant and overly bureaucratic in the early 1980s. Its leadership responded to the resulting organizational ineffectiveness by changing the organizational structure, creating new alliances with customers, and facilitating new ideas and ventures in the middle 1980s.[65] Top management diversified the company extensively, through acquisitions, joint ventures, and new start-ups. They integrated the organization by thinking about issues laterally—across departments and functions. They developed synergies between worldwide R&D and global manufacturing, made quality a key ingredient of corporate culture, and changed the reward system to tie pay to performance.[66]

Transformational leaders (see Chapter 8) play a major role in transforming and revitalizing organizations. They must overcome resistance to change in the organization's technical, political, and cultural systems.[67] The four stages of transition these leaders direct are shown in Figure 14–17.

Another model of the transformation process suggests that it is a reframing of a situation by individuals involved.[68] It begins with a challenge to the original frame, typically motivated by a crisis. Preparation for reframing occurs next. Here different information about problems leads to new understandings of the situation. Then participants develop new and different frames or understandings. The transformation concludes with members adopting and accepting the new view or understanding. This model applies to all stages of an organization's life cycle, including emerging organizations whose survival may depend on their ability to deal with critical issues at a single point in time. Internal conditions, such as a surplus of resources, system readiness, sufficient information linkages, and a change agent with leadership and power, permit transitions of an organization. Did conditions at Norton call for an organizational transformation? Is one required now?

Figure 14–17 STAGES OF TRANSITION IN CHANGE

Stage 1: Shock

People experience impending change as threat. They shut down thinking and as many systems as possible (just as in physiological shock). People need warm blankets and rest, that is, time to recover, emotional support, information, and an opportunity to gather with others. Productivity is low. People cannot think and do not remember.

What to do: Help people look for common ground in shock, build support network, and give information again and again. Managers should give visible support. Do not involve people in planning. Provide safety, that is, clear organization expectations, reward systems, support systems, and available resources.

Stage 2: Defensive Retreat

Holding on, attempting to maintain old ways. A great deal of anger, refusal to let go of past. People and organizations can get stuck here or recycle back to Stage 1 as each element of change is introduced.

What to do: Help people identify what they are holding on to, and then how to maintain it in the new situation or how to let it go. Identify areas of stability: things that are not changing. Give information continually and consistently. Ask "what is risky" and provide safety in response to discomfort with risk taking.

Stage 3: Acknowledgment

Sense of grief and sadness over loss. Letting go, beginning to see the value of what is coming, and looking for ways to make it work by considering the pros and cons. Ability to take risks begins here. It takes the form of risk taking and exploring new ways to look at things and to do things. Can lead to high energy if managed well.

What to do: Involve people in exploring options and planning through use of careful decision-making process as a structure/support. Overtly encourage and support risk taking by pointing out ways that the organization will support it. Emphasize that everyone is learning.

Stage 4: Adaptation and Change

What is coming has arrived. Ready to establish new routines and to help others. Risk taking comes into full bloom at this stage relative to changing methods, products, whatever is called for.

What to do: Implement plans. Encourage and support risk taking using the supports and structures developed in stage 3. Establish feedback loops so that information travels in all directions, new learning occurs, and mid-course corrections can be made when necessary.

Moore, M., and Gergen, P. "Turning the Pain of Change into Creativity and Structure for the New Order." In R.H. Kilmann, T.J. Covin, and Associates, *Corporate Transformation: Revitalizing Organizations for a Competitive World,* San Francisco: Jossey-Bass, 1988, p. 376. Used by permission of the publisher.

Change and Strategic Management

Organizational transformations may be closely linked to the strategic management of an organization, which focuses on making and implementing decisions about an organization's future by defining the organizational mission, identifying strategic alternatives, and implementing strategic plans. Defining a mission requires top management to forecast technological and environmental focuses that will influence an organization in the future. Top managers must also consider internal and external social forces, such as the strengths and interactions of various work groups inside and outside an organization. They should also consider characteristics of the human resources in an organization—skills, values, and needs of the workers—in planning the future direction of an organization.

Identification of strategic alternatives follows the decision-making process described earlier. Managers must identify the best ways to move from the present to a desired state. The leadership and personality styles of top management,[69] location of power in an organization, and nature of existing jobs help determine the nature of an appropriate strategy. Increasingly, an assessment of organizational culture affects strategic planning. Thus merger, divestment, or joint-venture decisions must consider the compatibility of the cultures of the organizations involved. An analysis of an organization's stage in its life cycle (see Chapter 12) also provides data for strategic planning.

Implementation of a strategic plan may call for transforming an organization. Changing an organization's structure and reward system can facilitate or hinder strategy implementation. In addition, managerial processes, such as leadership, communication, and decision making, influence a plan's effectiveness.

SUMMARY

Organizational change is the final step of the diagnostic approach, following description, diagnosis, and prescription. Action involves scouting, entry, diagnosis, and planning activities, followed by evaluation and institutionalization of a change.

In this chapter, we examined each facet of the change process. We focused first on organizational culture and the way the change process can address and alter it. We looked at the components of organizational culture, described ways of analyzing it, and commented on its links to organizational effectiveness.

We outlined a seven-step model of planned change and then used force field analysis to diagram the change process. Action begins by identifying forces for and against change, then seeking ways to overcome resistance to change. Next comes selection of an internal or external change agent. This change agent then chooses the appropriate intervention strategy, taking into account the target system, target group, depth of intervention, prescribed change mechanisms, and his or her own expertise.

Finally we looked at ways of changing organizational culture and responding to crises. We also considered ethical issues associated with change. We considered ways of evaluating and then institutionalizing changes. We concluded with a discussion of transformational change of organizations. Figure 14–18 is a series of diagnostic questions regarding culture and organizational change.

Figure 14–18 Diagnostic Questions for Assessing Organizational Culture and Planned Change

- What type of culture exists in the organization?
- What components reinforce the culture?
- Are the seven steps of the planned change model implemented?
- Are forces for and against change identified?
- Are appropriate change agents selected?
- Does the organization have mechanisms for dealing with crises?
- Do the intervention strategies fit with the change situation?
- Are changes evaluated?
- Do mechanisms exist for institutionalizing changes?
- Is a transformational change required, and how can it be implemented?

READING

Reading 14–1: ETHICAL DILEMMAS IN VARIOUS STAGES OF ORGANIZATIONAL DEVELOPMENT

Louis P. White and Kevin C. Wooten

Increasingly, organizational change efforts are being utilized to solve many human, structural, and technological problems in contemporary organizations. This increased attention to the uses of organizational development (OD) has been accompanied by growth in the number of OD consultants as well as those who have long term needs for OD efforts. Practitioners in the field have increased in number and many organizations have sought OD programs and practitioners, but the professionalization of OD has not kept pace structurally and scientifically. Reviews of the OD literature (Alderfer, 1976, 1977; French & Bell, 1978; Friedlander & Brown, 1974; White & Mitchell, 1976) provide ample evidence of the tremendous growth in sophisticated techniques to conduct effective OD. At the same time, rapid increases in the use of OD to solve a myriad of organizational problems have caused some to ponder whether it is a religious movement (Harvey, 1974) or a new social technology (Havelock, 1972).

Within the last decade many efforts have been made to codify the evidence that OD efforts are effective, an indication that OD is developing as a science. With justification, however, the interdisciplinary approach to this developing science has given rise to scholarly critiques of what OD is as a discipline (Jones & Pfeiffer, 1977; Weisbord, 1977) and where OD is as a profession (Bowers, 1976; Burke, 1976). Simultaneously, a growing concern about professional ethics in the field has begun to emerge. The problem of ethical dilemmas in OD practice has been written about, but never really examined in terms of where in the OD process they occur. This may be due in part to lack of a systematic approach to the study and analysis of the ethical dilemmas faced by the interventionist and client systems.

Ethical problems and dilemmas faced by OD practitioners may leave OD's scientific and professional progression in a disadvantageous position unless agreement can be reached as to the types of ethical dilemmas and the points at which they are likely to be encountered. It is not the purpose or scope of this paper to prescribe behaviors to resolve ethical dilemmas or to discuss the ethical principles that surround various dilemmas. As used herein, "ethical dilemmas" are the result of behaviors and inappropriate actions or roles on the part of both change agents and client systems. Therefore, this paper approaches ethical problems and dilemmas as a mutual responsibility of change agents and client systems, dependent largely on the nature of their specific relationship.

Ethical dilemmas, as approached from the perspective that such problems are caused largely by the nature of the relationship between the change agent and the client system, is a term that requires fuller elaboration. Previous approaches to the definition of an ethical dilemma (Benne, 1959; Walton & Warwick, 1973) have centered around the various values held by change agents, and how these values have influenced their actions. Operationally, then, an ethical dilemma can be defined as any choice situation encountered by a change agent or client system that has the potential to result in a breach of acceptable behavior. A dilemma therefore is different from a breach of ethics. A breach of ethics is a verifiable act or conduct on the part of a professional that breaches a law, role, standard, or established norm.

MAJOR CATEGORIES OF ETHICAL DILEMMAS

Although a number of authors have addressed the area of professional ethics in organizational development, the literature is sparse concerning the specification of types of ethical dilemmas that occur. However, a review of the available literature from works in organizational development, management consulting, and training and development does yield some consistency in thought and form. Although ranging considerably in terminology, the dilemma categories described coincide remarkably. Generally, five types of ethical dilemmas in organizational development practice tend to be observed and described by practitioners and scholars alike. They are:

1. misrepresentation and collusion
2. misuse of data
3. manipulation and coercion
4. value and goal conflict
5. technical ineptness

Misrepresentation and collusion are a pervasive and widely occurring dilemma in organizational development practice. This dilemma, or choice situation, requires the change agent or client system to decide between options of fully representing all available information and including or excluding various parties involved in the change effort. Works by Shay (1965), Pfeiffer and Jones (1977), French and Bell (1978), and

Maidment and Losito (1980) have investigated its nature. This dilemma may occur for a variety of reasons. First, misrepresentation and collusion can occur when the change agent misrepresents his/her skill base, education, experience, certification, or specialized training, or when the client system misrepresents the organization's interest, need, or goal.

Another instance of misrepresentation and collusion occurs when the change agent or the client system attempts to exclude outside parties, such as other change agents or other parts of the client system, for personal goal or protection that negatively affects the OD effort. Collusion also may occur by inappropriately structuring the relationship between the change agent and the client systems. For example, lack of clarity concerning goals, values, needs, and change methods can result in poorly defined roles and subsequently a poorly defined change effort. Additionally, a lack of clarity or an agreement to collude among parties may result in an avoidance of unresolved issues. Moreover, collusion may occur through loss of objectivity by assimilating the change agent into the organizational culture.

The second major category of ethical dilemmas in organizational change is misuse of data (Pfeiffer & Jones, 1977; Shay, 1965; Walton & Warwick, 1973; Zaltman & Duncan, 1976). This dilemma or choice situation requires the change agent or client system to decide what information is used and how it is used. Misuse of data in organizational development occurs when the voluntary consent or confidentiality of the client system is violated or abridged. Misuse of data as a breach of ethics in organizational development also may occur in two other ways. It may occur when data are distorted, deleted, or not reported by either the client system or the change agent, or when the data are used to assess persons or groups punitively, resulting in personal, professional, or organizational harm. Data concerning personality traits, career interest, and market information are frequent examples.

Manipulation and coercion constitute the third major category of ethical dilemmas in organizational development (Huse, 1975; Lippitt & Lippitt, 1978; Pfeiffer & Jones, 1977; Walton & Warwick, 1973; Warwick & Kelman, 1973; Zaltman & Duncan, 1976). The dilemma presents itself in the form of a decision concerning the exercise of the "free will" of organizational participants. Basically, manipulation and coercion occur when the organizational development effort requires organizational members to abridge their personal values or needs against their will. Forced participation in a change effort, such as sensitivity training, is exemplary. Closely related are examples involving changes in personal attributes or the structure of organizational members affected.

The fourth major category of ethical dilemmas in organizational development is value and goal conflict (Benne, 1959; Lippitt & Lippitt, 1978; Pfeiffer & Jones, 1977; Warwick & Kelman, 1973; Zaltman & Duncan, 1976). The dilemma in this situation involves a decision concerning the appropriate mix of change agent and client system values and goals as they relate to the overall change effort. Value and goal conflict occurs when there is ambiguity or conflict concerning whose values will be maximized by the change effort or whose needs will be fulfilled by meeting such goals. Value and goal conflict also occurs when there is ambiguity in defining change goals or choosing an intervention target. Another form of this type of dilemma occurs when conflict or ambiguity results in the reluctance on the part of the change agent or client system to alter change strategies or when the change agent or client system withholds services or needed resources.

The fifth major type of ethical dilemma in organizational development is technical ineptness. Technical ineptness is the most widely written about type of ethical dilemma (Benne, 1959; French & Bell, 1978; Lippitt & Lippitt, 1978; Pfeiffer & Jones, 1977; Shay, 1965; Walton & Warwick, 1973; Warwick & Kelman, 1973; Zaltman & Duncan, 1976). The dilemma of technical ineptness involves decisions by change agents and client systems whether to diagnose and divulge their deficiencies in required skills or whether to provide options for overcoming these deficiencies. This breach of ethics may occur when there is a lack of knowledge or skill in the use of techniques and procedures to diagnose social systems problems effectively, formulate change targets, choose and utilize the proper change technology and strategy, or intervene in the social system at the appropriate depth and scope. Technical ineptness also may occur when there is an inability to evaluate effectively an intervention or terminate an organizational development relationship. This dilemma also may result from the inability or reluctance to reduce client dependency or to transfer monitoring of the change effort to internal parties.

AN ALTERNATIVE VIEW OF THE OD PROCESS

Isolation of ethical dilemmas at various stages of the OD process requires examination not only of the relationship between the change agent and the client system but also of how this relationship changes as OD progresses. Role theory has been used to explain a broad range of organizational behaviors (House & Rizzo, 1972; Tracy & Johnson, 1981) and may be extended to include behavioral exchanges occurring in the OD process.

Role theory as proposed by Katz and Kahn (1966) bridges both personal and social behavior by illustrating their interaction. This is accomplished by viewing the conduct of individuals in a behavioral or organizational context as a number of role systems. This method allows the investigator to analyze the behavior not only of the individuals but also of the social system.

Although many authors have generally discussed the various roles of the change agent or the role of the client (Argyris, 1970; Havelock, 1973; Lippitt, 1975; Steele, 1969) there have been recent efforts toward expanding and incorporating the idea into the notion of role systems. Mirvis and Seashore (1979), in discussing the ethical dilemmas of organizational research, used role theory to isolate clearly, for the first time, both a conceptual scheme and a pragmatic tool for investigating professional ethics. This argument can be broadened to include developing relationships between change agents and client systems. The role episode is illustrated in Figure 14–19. As shown, the role episode includes both a role sender and a role receiver, or a focal person. This role episode represents a continuous cycle of sending, receiving, responding, and the sending of new expectations. Related to organizational development, role sending and role receiving can be seen as a continuous cycle of role episodes on the part of change agents and client systems. The figure further shows that the role episode is comprised of four concepts: role expectations, sent role, received role, and role behavior. These concepts are described by Katz and Kahn as follows:

> Role expectations, which are evaluative standards applied to the behavior of any person who occupies a given organizational office or position; sent role, which consists of communications stemming from role expectations and sent by members of the role set as attempts to influence the focal person; received role, which is the focal person's perception of the role-sendings addressed to him, including those he sends himself; and role behavior, which is the response of the focal person to the complexity of information he has received (1966, p. 182).

A variety of authors (Blake & Mouton, 1976; Ford, 1974; Kaplan, 1978; Milstein & Smith, 1979; Schein, 1969) have dealt with the dynamic nature of the relationship between the change agent and the client system. Issues such as the nature of a change contract, depth of the intervention, and dependency and identification of the real client are well documented in the OD literature. These factors influence not only the relationship between the change agent and the client system but the change process as well. However, few change models elaborate fully on how the relationship between the change agent and the client system can and should change as the OD intervention progresses from start to finish. It is through a fuller analysis and illustration of how stages of an intervention and change relationship evolve that their mutuality may be appreciated fully. Figure 14–20 is an attempt to illustrate globally the role episode that should occur between the change agent and the client system at various stages of an OD effort.

Role theory provides a vehicle to illustrate the interaction process occurring between the change agent and client system. The model in Figure 14–19, when used in conjunction with the process relational model (Figure 14–20), can demonstrate that the actors in each of the 10 stages of the OD process confront specific questions of ethicality. The roles that each actor assumes are inextricably linked to the resolution of these choice behaviors congruent with the underlying ethical principle.

The process relational model illustrates 10 stages of OD that deal with the conceptual framework of most organizational change methodologies (i.e., diagnosis, intervention, evaluation, etc.). Moreover, it focuses more fully on the role relationship between the parties involved (i.e., initiation, clarification, termination, etc.).

Although this model is shown to be sequential—that is, the relationship between the client system and the interventionist progresses from one stage to the next—its sequential presentation is offered only to illustrate what should occur in the ideal form. Many organizational change techniques, methodologies, and practices, by their very structure and content, do not deal systematically with one or several of these important stages.

Figure 14–19 A MODEL OF THE ROLE EPISODE

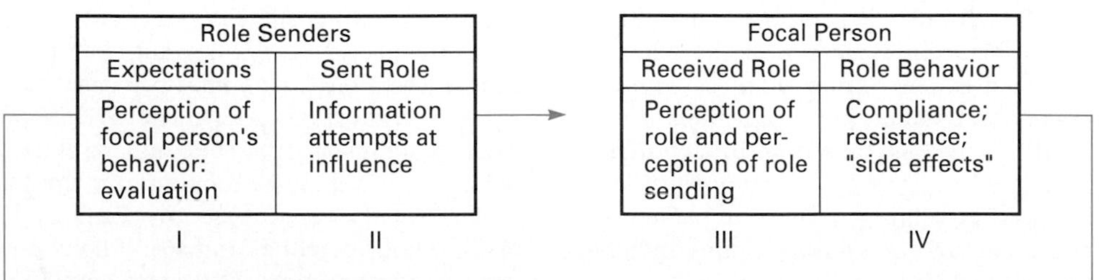

From D. Katz and R. Kahn, *The Social Psychology of Organizations*. Copyright © 1966 John Wiley & Sons, Inc. Reprinted by permission of John Wiley & Sons, Inc.

Figure 14–20 A Process Relational Model of Organizational Development

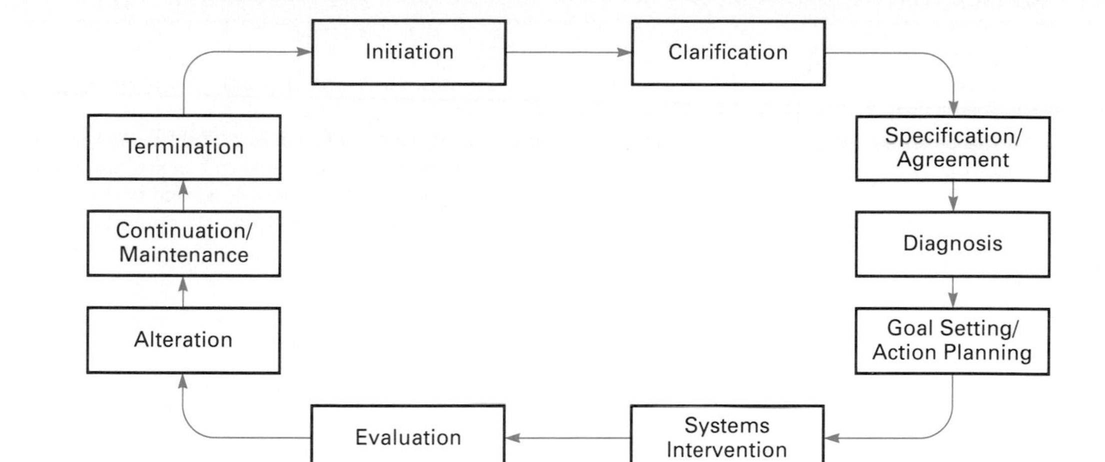

Implicit in this model is that these stages typically occur between the client system and the change agent, either consciously or unconsciously. On the conscious level, if each of these 10 stages is dealt with and worked through successfully between the client system and the change agent, there is a lower probability that ethical dilemmas will occur.

Also implicit in the process relational model is the change agent-client system relationship in any organizational change effort—a relationship that represents a collection of continuous interrelated activities in which both the change agent and the client system play their part or role in order to reach a predetermined outcome. Using the role system model developed by Katz and Kahn (1966), presented earlier, the behavior or role behavior of the change agent and client system during each stage of an organizational change effort can be studied as a role episode or series of role episodes.

ETHICAL DILEMMAS AT VARIOUS STAGES OF CHANGE

Of specific concern to most OD interventionists is the stage in the OD process at which specified dilemmas occur. Building on the notion that certain ethical dilemmas do tend to occur at various stages of OD, practitioners and consumers alike could deal with them more effectively by modifying and clarifying their role relationships. Although each organizational intervention and role relationship is situation specific, the OD literature and the experience of practitioners tend to indicate commonality of experience.

Table 14–5 depicts 10 stages of change, the appropriate role behaviors for change agents and client systems, and the possible ethical dilemmas that can occur at these various stages. Each of the 31 ethical dilemmas shown is a specific illustration of the five major categories of ethical dilemmas previously discussed. Implicit in the various dilemmas is the notion that ethical dilemmas are produced not only by change agents but by client systems as well. Also implicit in the table is the notion that several of the dilemmas mentioned are closely related to other dilemmas at the various stages of change. The utility of the table, therefore, is to isolate the occurrence of these dilemmas at specific stages of change, as the nature of the relationship between the client system and the change agent changes.

As shown, the stage of initiation often is impaired by various types of misrepresentation. Here, inaccurate information may be provided by either the change agent or the client system, resulting in either misrepresentation of the consultant's background or skill base or misrepresentation of organizational interest. As the role relationship moves into the stage of clarification, three different dilemmas may arise. Problems in determining who the real client is and the inappropriate determination of value orientations are of frequent mention. Additionally, the avoidance of reality testing on the part of both the change agent and the client system may occur if there is difficulty or a lack of effort in raising issues that might hamper the change effort.

In the specification/agreement stage the finite structuring of the relationship occurs. At this point the ethical dilemma involves the degree of specificity concerning the range of services to be offered, the fee structure, a tenable time frame, resources to be used, and accountability for services and resources. Similarly, inappropriate definition of the change problem may result in ambiguity concerning the problems to be addressed—whose problems they are and by what means they are to be dealt with. Collusion of parties also may occur in

Table 14–5 Organizational Development Change Stages, Appropriate Role Behaviors, and Possible Ethical Dilemmas

Stage	Purpose	Role of Change Agent	Role of Client System	Dilemmas
Initiation	First information sharing	To provide information on background, expertise, and experience	To provide information on possible needs, relevant problems, interest of management and representative groups	Misrepresentation of the consultant's skill base and background Misrepresentation of organizational interest
Clarification	Further elaboration of initiation stage	To provide details of education, licensure, operative values, optimum working conditions	To provide a detailed history of special problems, personnel, marketplace, internal culture, and organizational politics	Inappropriate determination of who the client is Avoidance of reality testing Inappropriate determination of value orientation
Specification/ agreement	Sufficient elaboration of needs, interest, fees, services, working conditions, arrangements	To specify actual services, fees to be charged, time frame, actual work conditions	To specify whose needs are to be addressed, goals, objectives, and possible evaluative criteria or end-state outcomes	Inappropriate structuring of the relationship Inappropriate definition of change problem Collusion to exclude outside parties
Diagnosis	To obtain an unfiltered and undistorted view of the organization's problems and processes pinpointing change targets and criterion	To collect data concerning organizational problems and processes, and to provide feedback	To assist change agent in data collection	Avoidance of problems Misuse of data Distortion and deletion of data Ownership of data Voluntary consent Confidentiality
Goal setting/ action planning	To establish the specific goals and strategies to be used	To agree mutually with the client system on the goals and strategies to be used	To agree mutually with the change agent on the goals and strategies to be used	Inappropriate choice of intervention goal and targets Inappropriate choice of operative means Inappropriate scope of intervention
Systems intervention	The intervention into ongoing behaviors, structures, and processes	To intervene at specific targets, at a specific depth	To invest the energy and resources required by planned intervention	Assimilation into culture Inappropriate depth of intervention Coercion vs. choice, freedom, and consent to participate Environmental manipulation
Evaluation	To determine the effectiveness of the intervention strategies, energy, and resources used, as well as the change agent-client system relationship	To gather data on specified targets and report findings to the client system	To analyze the evaluation data and determine effectiveness of the intervention	Misuse of data Deletion and distortion of data

Table 14–5 CONTINUED

Stage	Purpose	Role of Change Agent	Role of Client System	Dilemmas
Alteration	To modify change strategies, depth, level, goals, targets, or resources utilized if necessary	To make alteration to meet original goals, or to develop new mutual goals and strategies with client system	To make known needs and expectations, and to provide the context for a modification of the original agreement, if necessary	Failure to change and lack of flexibility Adoption of inappropriate strategy
Continuation/ maintenance	To monitor and maintain ongoing strategies, provide periodic checks, and continue intervention based on original or altered plans and strategies	To specify the parameters of the continuation of the maintenance of the relationship	To provide or allocate the resources required to maintain or continue the intervention	Inappropriate reduction of dependency Redundancy of effort Withholding of services
Termination	To have the change agent disenfranchise self from the client system and establish a long term monitoring system	To fulfill the role agreed on in previous stages and evaluate overall effectiveness from feedback from the client system	To determine the organization's state of health, and whether it has developed the adaptive change process	Inappropriate transition of change effort to internal sources Premature exit Failure to monitor change

the specification/agreement state, with change agents and client systems excluding outside competitions and influences.

As shown in the table, a wide variety of ethical dilemmas may occur in the diagnosis stage. Avoidance of diagnosing known problems occurs when the change agent and client system perceptually defend against their own inability or unwillingness to solve a problem. Of greater frequency in the diagnosis stage is the misuse, as well as the distortion and delegation, of data. Here misuse of data could result in personal, professional, and organizational harm. Delegation and distortion of data also may result in a misleading diagnosis, thereby rendering the intervention ineffective. Ownership of the data is a frequent dilemma as well, wherein survey feedback or process observation is not shared with all contributing members. Similarly, the question of voluntary consent of organizational members and insured confidentiality appears to be a frequent problem that has received much attention.

In the stage of goal setting/action planning, ethical problems include the choice of a change goal and targets, the choice of operative means, and the scope of the intervention. Here the major categories of collusion of parties, technical ineptness, and value of goal conflict are apparent. These dilemmas result in inappropriately choosing goals, targets, depth, and change method because of lack of skill, lack of objectivity, or differing needs and orientations.

In systems intervention, the assimilation into the organization's culture presents a range of ethical considerations for the change agent. These dilemmas result in the change agent's losing the objectivity of a third party position by incorporation of inappropriate values, adherence to inappropriate norms, or development of a psychological state incongruent with the activities to be addressed by the change effort. Table 14–5 also shows the dilemma of inappropriate depth. This dilemma results in change efforts that cannot provide for adequate or effective change.

Frequently mentioned in the OD literature is the notion of free will and consent to participate in OD activities. The table shows the dilemma for coercion to participate in OD activities. Here resides the potential for involuntary change or psychological or professional harm to organizational members. There also exists the possibility of environmental manipulation through the involuntary change in personal attributes, structure, or organizational process, without awareness or participation of organizational members.

As in the stage of diagnosis, the misuse, deletion, or distortion of data may occur in the evaluation stage. Here, evaluation data are distorted or deleted in a manner that results in personal, professional, or organizational harm. The misuse of evaluation data is frequent in cases in which the major motivation for collecting and reporting evaluation data is to advance the personal interest of change agents on internal parts of the client system.

The table also illustrates the stage of alteration as

beset by two dilemmas. These dilemmas are failure to change (or lack of flexibility) and the adoption of an inappropriate new strategy. Each can be seen to occur typically in an intervention in which alteration is necessary for full effectiveness of the intervention effort. Failure to change and a lack of flexibility can be caused by overadherence to the specifications of a contract, the lack of skill or expertise, or the lack of resources. Further, the adoption of an inappropriate new strategy may result from pressure to produce change in light of nonsupportive evaluation data.

As a change effort progresses into the latter stages, a variety of ethical dilemmas can be observed in the continuation/maintenance stage. The table illustrates three specific ethical dilemmas for this stage. Reducing dependency is a difficult issue for most change agents to encounter. The reduction of effort and withholding of change agent services from the client system also are difficult. Of specific ethical interest is the change agent's continued intense helping relationship or service.

In the termination stage of change, a variety of dilemmas may occur. Value and goal conflict, as well as technical ineptness, may result in the transition of change to inadequately prepared or unskilled internal parties, premature exit, or the failure to monitor change longitudinally. Of specific difficulty is the determination of (1) when internal sources are capable of responsibly carrying through the long term aspects of a change effort and (2) whether the internal parties have developed the necessary processes to diagnose and solve problems. Improper assessment of a client system can lead to premature exit on the part of the change agent, which may result in the broader issue of responsibility to the client. Moreover, a failure to monitor change is an issue that has long term implications not only for the effectiveness of the organization but also for the long run viability of the change method.

DISCUSSION

Through the use of role theory and an accompanying process relational model of OD, OD has been shown to be a highly integrative process. It involves an integration of technology, human interactions, and the ethical questions that arise as a result of these variables. A result of this analysis yields many more yet to be explored issues. Yet unanswered are questions such as "What are the underlying ethical principles that should serve the OD process?" and "What are the various ethical principles that apply to OD practice?" The models proposed may provide the necessary vehicles to address these types of substantive questions.

It can be said that a major distinguishing characteristic of OD as a profession is the high degree of heterogeneity of the change agent's education, training, and experience. Indeed, OD practitioners are drawn from fields ranging from business education to anthropology. The conceptualization presented herein provides a basis from which a systemic study of OD ethics can take place. For example, the ethical dilemmas shown in Table 14–5 can be analyzed and discussed in a way that would lead to the statement of the ethical principle underlying choice behaviors faced by the change agent and client system.

With the demand for and acceptance of OD programs and practitioners increasing rapidly, the ethical issues surrounding OD's practice should now receive increased attention. Its popularity in educational curriculum for practitioners serves as evidence for increased exposure by investigation and research. Because of the interdisciplinary values and backgrounds comprised in the OD field, ethical consonance among practitioners and consumers alike will require diligent effort. If OD is ever to be accepted as a legitimate science as well as a profession, then principles guiding the actions of those providing OD services must no longer be ignored.

REFERENCES

Alderfer, C.P. Change processes in organizations. In M.D. Dunnette (Ed.), *Handbook of industrial and organizational psychology*. Chicago, Ill.: Rand McNally, 1976, 1591–1638.

Alderfer, C.P. Organizational development. *Annual Review of Psychology,* 1977, 28, 197–233.

Argyris, C. *Intervention theory and method: A behavioral science view*. Reading, Mass.: Addison-Wesley, 1970.

Benne, K.D. Some ethical problems in group and organizational consultation. *Journal of Social Issues,* 1959, 15, 60–67.

Blake, R.R., & Mouton, J.S. *Consultation*. Reading, Mass.: Addison-Wesley, 1976.

Bowers, D.G. Organizational development: Promises, performance, possibilities. *Organizational Dynamics,* 1976, 4 (4), 50–62.

Burke, W.W. Organizational development in transition. *Journal of Applied Behavioral Science,* 1976, 12, 22–43.

Ford, C.H. Developing a successful client-consultant relationship. *Human Resource Management,* 1974, 13 (2), 2–11.

French, W.L., & Bell, C.H., Jr. *Organizational development*. Englewood Cliffs, N.J.: Prentice-Hall, Inc., 1978.

Friedlander, F., & Brown, L.D. Organizational development. *Annual Review of Psychology,* 1974, 25, 313–341.

Harvey, J.B. Organizational development as a religious movement. *Training and Development Journal,* 1974, 28 (3), 24–27.

Havelock, R.G. A critique: Has OD become a social technology? *Educational Technology,* 1972, 10 (2), 61–62.

Havelock, R.G. *The change agents' guide to innovation in education.* Englewood Cliffs, N.J.: Educational Technology Publications, 1973.

House, R.J., & Rizzo, R.J. Role conflict and ambiguity as critical variables in a model of organizational behavior. *Organizational Behavior and Human Performance,* 1972, 7, 467–505.

Huse, E. *Organizational development and change.* St. Paul, Minn.: West Publishing, 1975.

Jones, J.E., & Pfeiffer, J.W. On the obsolescence of the term organizational development. *Group and Organizational Studies,* 1977, 2, 263–264.

Kaplan, R.E. Stages in developing a consulting relationship: A case study of a long beginning. *Journal of Applied Behavioral Science,* 1978, 14, 43–48.

Katz, D., & Kahn, R.L. *The social psychology of organizations.* New York: John Wiley and Sons, Inc., 1966.

Lippitt, G.L. The trainer's role as an internal consultant. *Journal of European Training,* 1975, 4 (5), 14–23.

Lippitt, G.L., and Lippitt, R. *The consultant process in action.* La Jolla, Cal.: University Associates, 1978.

Maidment, R., & Losito, W. *Ethics and the consultant/trainer.* Madison, Wis.: American Society for Training and Development, Selected Paper No. 11, 1980.

Milstein, M.M., & Smith, D. The shifting nature of OD contracts: A case study. *Journal of Applied Behavioral Science,* 1979, 15, 179–191.

Mirvis, P.H., & Seashore, S.F. Being ethical in organizational research. *American Psychologist,* 1979, 34 (5), 44–48.

Pfeiffer, J.W., & Jones, J.E. Ethical considerations in consulting. In J.E. Jones, and J.W. Pfeiffer (Eds.), *The 1977 annual handbook for group facilitators.* La Jolla, Cal.: University Associates, 1977, 217–225.

Schein, E.H. *Process consultation: Its role in organization development.* Reading, Mass.: Addison-Wesley, 1969.

Shay, P.W. Ethics and professional practices in management consulting. *Advanced Management Journal,* 1965, 30 (1), 13–20.

Steele, F. Consultants and detectives. *Journal of Applied Behavioral Science,* 1969, 5, 187–202.

Tracy, L., & Johnson, T.W. What do the role conflict and role ambiguity scales measure? *Journal of Applied Psychology,* 1981, 66, 464–469.

Walton, R.E., & Warwick, D.P. The ethics of organizational development. *Journal of Applied Behavioral Science,* 1973, 9, 681–699.

Warwick, D.P., & Kelman, H.C. Ethics in social intervention. In G. Zaltman (Ed.), *Processes and phenomena of social change.* New York: Wiley Interscience, 1973, 377–449.

Weisbord, M.R. How do you know if it works if you don't know what it is? *O. D. Practitioner,* 1977, 9, 1–3.

White, S.E., & Mitchell, T.R. Organizational development: A review of research content and research design. *Academy of Management Review,* 1976, 1 (2), 57–73.

Zaltman, G., & Duncan, R. Ethics in social change. In G. Zaltman & R. Duncan (Eds.), *Strategies for planned change.* New York: John Wiley and Sons, 1976, 323–377.

DISCUSSION QUESTIONS

1. What types of ethical dilemmas may arise from organizational development practices?
2. What role do the change agent and client system play in these situations?
3. How do the dilemmas differ at various stages of change?

From L.P. White and K.C. Wooten, *Academy of Management Review* 8 (2) (1983): 690–697.

ACTIVITIES

Activity 14–1: THE CLASH OF CULTURES

Step 1: Read the following description of the merger between General Electric and Kidder, Peabody, & Co.:

New York—Executives at General Electric Co. thought they were too smart for it to happen to them.

The big conglomerate had watched as giants like Sears, Roebuck & Co. and Prudential Insurance Co. of America ran into myriad problems with the securities firms they had bought. Undeterred, GE stepped up with $600 million and in 1986 bought 80% of old-line, highly profitable Kidder, Peabody & Co.

True, Kidder hadn't been all that well managed. But then who knows more about management than GE does? GE also knew there were big cultural differences between its own organization men, proud of their in-house management school and generous pension plan, and the entrepreneurial prima donnas of Kidder, who chafed at any management controls and who made so much money they didn't need a pension plan. But these differences didn't seem to pose insurmountable problems either. GE had been running a highly successful commercial lending and leasing business for years, and finance guys are finance guys, right?

WELCOME TO WALL STREET

Thus began the education of General Electric, a frustrating and at times humiliating example of how a well-managed company can stumble when it enters a business it doesn't fully understand. . . .

Just about everything that could go wrong with the Kidder merger has. The cultures have clashed, and GE financial units and Kidder at times have competed with each other when they should have been cooperating. GE and Kidder leaders developed widely disparate views of what Kidder should be. Thus, there was confusion among Kidder executives and the impression among subordinates that the firm was rudderless.

Relations between the two organizations have been so awkward that when Kidder submitted a strategic plan to GE in October 1987, GE executives blessed the plan only because they thought an honest appraisal would devastate Kidder's morale. . . .

Many of Kidder's top producers have left within the past two years, complaining of paltry bonuses and the absence of strategic direction. Some who remain close their office doors part of the day, so they can talk to headhunters and complain to friends and competitors. Other Kidder people say privately that they are skeptical of any strategy promising more integration with GE.

Nonetheless, GE officials say they are optimistic. The culture differences are narrowing, they say. This month, for example, Kidder employees were extended a long-time GE perk: They can buy certain GE products—a refrigerator for instance—at a discount. . . .

GE put the 43-year-old Mr. Chapman in day-to-day command of Kidder. He was the one Kidder official GE thought could become a GE team player. He looked the part: a ruggedly handsome and personable former University of North Carolina football player who had worked as both an investment banker and a trader. He also had founded one of Kidder's most successful operations: trading financial futures.

But as Mr. Chapman readily admits, "I am a product of Kidder Peabody." He didn't like controversy, and his attempts to solve problems through compromise generally just left people angrier, Kidder officials say. As an ex-Marine and the son of a career Marine, Mr. Chapman had come to hate the rigid structure that life in the Marines imposed. He loved Kidder because it was freewheeling and unstructured. He couldn't—and wouldn't—become a GE guy. . . .

Kidder officials derisively referred to their GE counterparts as "credit clerks." And Kidder officials say GE Capital staffers would deliberately treat them as competitors.

GE Capital officials thought Kidder people were overly sensitive, overpaid and arrogant, and not nearly as talented as their counterparts at certain other investment banks. Sometimes Kidder would bid competitively for GE Capital business against other investment bankers and lose.

GE's Mr. Bossidy acknowledges such bad feelings existed on both sides, but he contends they were never "a consensus view."

The business philosophy of the two operations was very different, Kidder officials believed. While Kidder investment bankers generally act as agents to get the best terms for clients, GE Capital officers basically are lenders seeking the best terms for their own company. GE Capital people also are known as some of the toughest negotiators in the financial-services business. "Lenders of the last resort," Kidder bankers call them. . . .

Last week GE's chairman, Mr. Welch, met with Mr. Chapman to explain the decision to give Mr. Carpenter the top job at Kidder. According to Mr. Chapman, Mr. Welch asked him to stay on and added that if Mr. Chapman could make an effort to become an executive more in the GE mold, he would be a candidate to succeed Mr. Carpenter.

Instead, Mr. Chapman resigned. "I'm an outsider" at GE, he says. "I'm a Kidder person."

Step 2: Individually or in small groups, offer a plan for merging the companies successfully.

Step 3: Discussion. In small groups or with the entire class, share the plans you have developed. Then answer the following questions:

1. How were the two organizations different?
2. How could these differences be reconciled?
3. What strategies do the plans offer for doing this?
4. What elements do these plans have in common?
5. What are the strengths and weaknesses of each plan?
6. What problems might arise in their implementation?

Activity 14–2: FORCE FIELD ANALYSIS

Step 1: Choose an organizational problem you have experienced. Describe it in one paragraph.

Step 2: Analyze the problem using force field analysis.

Step 3: Discussion. Share your analysis with others, in small groups or with the entire class, answering the following questions:

1. What forces for change did you identify? forces against change?
2. How could each force be altered?
3. Which actions are most feasible?
4. Devise a plan of action.

Activity 14–3: BRIDGETON TEMPORARY SERVICES

Step 1: Your instructor will divide you into groups of four to six people; one group will represent management and the rest, competing consulting groups.

Step 2: Read the following description:

The Bridgeton Temporary Services provides bookkeeping and accounting services on a contract basis. Employees act as accounts payable clerks, accounts receivable clerks, general bookkeepers, computer programmers, and accountants. The seventy-five employees are each assigned to a supervisor who decides where each person will work. The supervisor also checks with the client for an evaluation of Bridgeton's employees. Employees report each day to the client, but must notify their supervisor at Bridgeton that they have arrived.

Employees have a variety of education, from high school diplomas to masters degrees. The firm also employs a number of working mothers with CPAs who do not want fulltime employment. Employees generally stay with Bridgeton ten to twelve months. Then they secure fulltime employment elsewhere, decide they do not wish to be employed at all, or obtain parttime employment with one of Bridgeton's clients. In addition to relatively high turnover, Bridgeton also suffers from high absenteeism. When questioned, the employees indicate that no one cares about them, that their pay is low, that their work frequently is uninteresting and below their capabilities, that they are moved among jobs too frequently, and that they frequently are not notified about their work assignment until thirty minutes before they are expected to be at the workplace. Many add that they feel someone is always looking over their shoulder. The company itself has more requests for temporary help than it can fill, yet it has been unable to secure enough workers. Some clients have complained about poor-quality work from some of the bookkeepers. Also, although revenues are increasing, profits have not kept pace.

Step 3: *The Management Group.* Assume that you are the top management of Bridgeton Temporary Services. You are concerned with the high rate of turnover and absenteeism in your company. You want to hire a group of consultants to diagnose your company's problem and to recommend a plan for solving it. Shortly they will ask for a preliminary meeting to gather information to use in formulating their consulting proposal. You should be prepared to provide them with your requirements and timetables, as well as with any constraints, financial or otherwise, that you see as relevant to their task. You must then develop guidelines for judging the various proposals presented. You expect, at a minimum, that each will include a diagnosis, change strategy, and plans for implementation, as well as the rationales on which these are based.

The Consulting Groups. Your group is interested in being hired as consultants to Bridgeton Temporary Services. The company's president is concerned with the high rate of turnover and absenteeism. The president has asked you to diagnose the company's problems and to recommend a plan for solving them. Specifically, the president wants you to answer the following questions:

1. What do you think the real problem is and why?
2. What solution(s) would you propose and why?
3. How would you implement your plan?
4. What reasons would you give for doing it this way?

You will have the opportunity to meet briefly with the top management of the firm in a short while to get answers to preliminary questions you have about the company. Then, on the date given by your instructor, you will offer your plan. The plan should include diagnosis, change strategy, and implementation.

Step 4: The management and consulting groups meet, independently and then together.

Step 5: The consulting teams present their proposals one at a time.

Step 6: The management team selects the consulting team they would like to hire and then describes its criteria for selection.

Step 7: Discussion. With the entire class, answer the following questions:

1. What group was hired? Why?
2. What symptoms existed?
3. What problems were identified?
4. What intervention strategies were proposed? Would they be effective?
5. What makes an effective consulting proposal?

Activity 14–4: JIM COOPER AND THE EDUCATION SCHOOL: A CASE OF CULTURAL CHANGE

Step 1: Read the case of Jim Cooper and the Education School.

Jim Cooper faced a dilemma. Appointed the new dean of the U.Va. School of Education in the spring of 1984, he had achieved a position and status of which many academics dream (especially in a university like U.Va., where the deans have very broad authority). However, he was taking over a school that was under the gun, to say the least. University committees had been formed to examine the role and performance of the Education School. Faculty morale was very low. There was a sense of isolation, from the rest of the University and from other faculty and students. Cooper found a faculty eager for change, but divided as to what direction was needed. The School's reputation had declined, as had student enrollment, and there was even a rumor that the provost was considering phasing the School out.

The Education School's decline was typical of the problems confronting schools of education across the country. The late 1960s and early 1970s were the "go-go" years for education, times of record enrollments reflecting the high value students placed on the teaching profession. All that changed during the next decade. Business, computer science, and engineering schools were on the rise, many liberal arts fields suffered, and education seemed to be hit the hardest. Education schools that had added many new faculty (U.Va.'s faculty doubled) now faced embarrassing questions from provosts and state legislatures. Those schools that didn't provide convincing answers got hurt, some losing one third or more of their funding.

FIRST STEPS

Cooper made some initial decisions that proved very valuable. He received a commitment from the provost that the School would not lose any faculty slots for the next three years. He obtained funding from the University to hold a two-day faculty retreat at the start of the school year. Within his first month on the job he also reorganized his administrative team, replacing two of the three associate deans. The word got out to the faculty very quickly: Cooper is a mover.

To call Jim Cooper a "mover" is accurate (by his own account he has a very low tolerance for inaction); it is only partially correct, however. Cooper moves quickly, but he also studies the situation closely. During his initial interviews and in subsequent visits to the University before he took over he met with the other academic deans, the president, faculty and grad students, and the secretary of education for Virginia. He asked people to identify the Education School's informal leaders, and he spent time learning about their views and forming relationships. Through all of these meetings he began to determine where his potential support lay, and what was on the agendas of other key people.

After he announced the selection of his new associate deans, he began planning the faculty retreat. He had taken part in a similar effort at another university, and knew that such a session could help him set his themes and gain active faculty involvement. He received help from others on the grounds who were experienced in helping organizations change, and the retreat idea took form. All 101 Education School faculty were asked to spend two days at Graves Mountain Lodge, to look at the School, at its future prospects, and to begin planning for needed changes. Jim found five experienced group facilitators to lead the faculty discussion, and all but five of the school's faculty attended.

Many faculty were skeptical about the retreat idea. Some years earlier similar (though less ambitious) efforts had been made, with little follow through. Jim knew this but he felt that a major statement was needed to let people know that this was not to be business as usual.

Most faculty felt that the retreat was a success, but they maintained their skepticism concerning long-term results. Jim had already decided that two days would be only a start, and at the retreat he announced that the faculty was to continue meeting in its small groups throughout the fall, in order to come up with written proposals concerning the changes needed in the school. The outside facilitators had agreed to continue in their role, and Jim and his associate deans deliberately stayed out of the sessions.

The retreat was successful for many reasons. Simply getting away together was a positive experience. The fact that the School had come up with the money was a statement about where Jim was coming from, about his values and priorities. The opportunity to relax and play together as well as work on School issues contributed to the positive climate.

These good feelings would not have been satisfying had Jim not made a personal statement about his aspirations for the School. He did so, and gave most faculty their first glimpse into his approach. In his talk he made reference to winning teams, and what it takes to create winning teams. The 12 points he listed are shown in Figure 14–21. These points, he was saying, were what he wanted and expected from all faculty and administrators in the School. Someone asked him for a copy of his points, and they were passed out to the faculty the following week.

In the speech Jim gave several examples to bring his points to life. One example was especially effective: he announced that the School would soon begin issuing "teacher warranties" on all of its graduates who go on and teach in Virginia schools. The School would offer to send a faculty member to work with any of its graduates who had difficulties in their first teaching year. This warranty caught the eye of the press, and it was picked up by the wire services as well as national news networks. While some faculty had concerns as to whether they could really help a poor teacher, there was agreement that the approach was creative and brought good publicity for the School.

FOLLOW THROUGH: LIFE AFTER THE RETREAT

The "retreat groups" continued meeting. Twice during the semester representatives from each group met with Jim and his staff to discuss the directions they were taking. Some focused on morale issues, others on a reorganization plan, physical plants needs, public relations problems, decision making procedures, and communications issues.

While the retreat groups were meeting, Jim continued announcing new initiatives. One was Project Excellence, a joint effort of the School and the Charlottesville and Albemarle public schools. Through this program the Education School provided funds to both school systems, which in turn awarded grants to teachers who proposed creative classroom approaches that couldn't be funded by regular school budgets. Innovations would be supported by grants of $50 to $500, and the city schools decided to add a matching grant to broaden their pool (see Figure 14–22).

That wasn't all. Jim decided that the public school teachers who supervised student teachers from the Education School needed more support and recognition, and closer ties with the School. He began the Clinical Instructor Project, which provided training and increased financial support for cooperating teachers. It also made them adjunct faculty members of the School,

Figure 14–21 JIM COOPER'S ASPIRATIONS FOR THE SCHOOL OF EDUCATION

Characteristics of a Team (School of Education) that I would like to belong to:

1. Sense of confidence and security in ourselves and in the School. Think of ourselves as winners.
2. Sense of pride in the importance of what we do and how we do it. A willingness to tell the world that we're good. (New teacher warranty.)
3. Sense of pride, not envy, in the accomplishments of our colleagues. Not a zero sum game.
4. A sense of trust in each other and the belief that no one, especially our colleagues, is out to get us.
5. Commitment to having fun. People rarely succeed at anything unless they enjoy it.
6. Increased communication among ourselves, especially across departments. Good news swapping. MIT study that indicates that if people are more than 10 meters apart, the probability of communicating at least once a week is only 8 or 9 percent. Must make special effort, especially since our building does not encourage communication.
7. An instructionally effective and physically attractive environment. School beautification plan.
8. Support for each other's ideas. "It is inherently easier to develop a negative argument than to advance a constructive one." Don't warn people, instead bolster them.
9. A willingness to take risks without guarantees, if the goal is a worthwhile one. "When in doubt, try it out." Demonstrate a bias toward action rather than sitting around waiting for someone else to take the necessary steps. Get your arms around almost any practical problem and knock it off. Don't just stand there, do something.
10. A willingness to give up some protected turf and privileges if in doing so the School will benefit. In the analogy for today, this means being willing to throw the block that will spring someone else into the clear.
11. A renewed commitment to meeting students' needs first, and professors' comforts second.
12. Strive to be "the best" at something. It doesn't much matter what it is as long as it helps the Redskins win.

Figure 14–22 UVA GRANT AIDS TEACHER PROJECTS

By Julie Young
of The Progress Staff

Teachers in the Charlottesville and Albemarle County schools will have a chance to try some special class projects this year with grant money being offered by the University of Virginia's School of Education.

Project Excellence, a joint project of the education school and the two local school systems, will provide money for creative classroom ventures that tight school budgets seldom allow, officials said Wednesday.

The project follows last week's proposal by new education dean James Cooper to place a warranty on UVa teaching graduates during their first year in school systems. Teachers with problems will be tutored on-site by their former UVa instructors under Cooper's proposal.

Project Excellence "is designed to support teachers in effecting a creative or stimulating classroom environment and help them carry out some ideas that promise to promote excellence in classroom instruction," said Mary P. Reese, assistant superintendent for personnel in the city schools.

Teachers have until next Wednesday to submit proposals on projects they would like to attempt this year, she said. Teachers might, for example, develop special prototype units in their subjects and use the grant money to have them copied, she said.

Innovative ideas ranging from $50 to $500 will be financed under the $3,000 grant—$1,500 from the University and a matching grant from the city school system's staff development budget, according to Mrs. Reese.

The University also will award $1,500 of the seed money to Albermarle County, but those funds will not be matched from the school budget, officials said.

Harold Burbach, associate dean of external relations and faculty affairs at the education school, said Wednesday the idea for the joint venture came from Robert F. McNergney, UVa's director of teacher education, who administered such a project successfully in another state.

"We want to attempt through ideas and involvement to build a stronger link with the public schools," Burbach said. The project "will enable us to work in a direct way with teachers through the school systems."

Literature on effective teaching indicates it is important for teachers to be given occasional bureaucratic loopholes, he said. The University has been a little negligent in the past in "translating that (literature) into effective practices in the classroom," he said.

The funds will "empower teachers directly, with no bureaucratic maze" standing between them and creative exploration, Burbach said.

"Teachers have got to be given the authority to do what they're expected to do," he said.

School officials said they hope the projects also will boost teacher morale, and will be refined and shared with other teachers once they have been carried out.

The University is attempting through such projects this year to promote a positive image for its education school in the second year of the nation's excellence movement.

"Educators typically have been on the defensive" as their practices have come under fire in recent years," Burbach said. "We've got to assert ourselves."

and gave them increased visibility and prestige. The General Assembly provided $98,000 to support and study the results of the project. In addition, Jim announced a warranty on the computer literacy of the school's graduates, similar in concept to the teacher warranty.

Jim wanted to make a statement early in his tenure about his directions. He also wanted to give faculty morale a quick boost. He knew that the retreat, successful as it was, soon would be only a pleasant memory if he didn't keep up the momentum. He worked to get media coverage of the School's initiatives, aware that the faculty (indeed, the whole University) was used to reading primarily negative statements about the Education School. The approach began working. Only the most cynical continued to say that this would be a process of all talk and no action.

By the second week of December each of the five retreat groups submitted its report, detailing the changes needed in the School. The faculty knew that the provost was expecting the School to come up with a new, simpler organization; he wasn't happy with the 8 departments and 24 programs offered. Thus, Jim and his staff focused first on the new organization plan for the school, and on January 24, 1985 Jim sent his Proposed Reorganization Plan to the faculty.

The proposal, a 45 page document with careful references to the suggestions from each retreat group (as well as a rationale, statement of principles, extensive documentation and explanation of new roles) suggested a simpler, leaner plan with just four departments. Aspects of the plan came directly from the retreat groups' proposals, and many faculty said they thought that Jim's proposal was as good as anything they would have offered. At the next faculty meeting, the new plan was endorsed by the faculty, unanimously.

INITIAL RESULTS, FUTURE DIRECTIONS

In the spring of 1985 it is much too early to determine the long-term effects that all of these changes will have on the U.Va. School of Education. Jim Cooper is actively recruiting some "heavyweights" in the education field to join the Education School faculty (he sees this as the best way to upgrade certain departments needing assistance). He is working on a national committee that is studying the state of the art in the teaching profession. He and his staff have submitted a grant proposal to develop an educational policy analysis center. They also expect to continue acting on other aspects of the retreat groups' proposals. The possibilities are great, as are Jim's energies and imagination.

What can be said concerning the *initial* results is that Jim Cooper and his staff have turned the School of Education around, in terms of morale, in terms of its previous lack of direction, in terms of its hopes for the future. A school that was fearing for its very life now has a renewed sense of life. Changes inevitably bring resistance and anger, and some of that has occurred. The primary feeling given off by the faculty, however, is one of optimism and a sense of direction. They aren't talking about phasing out the School of Education anymore.

Step 2: Prepare the case for class discussion.

Step 3: Answer the following questions, individually, in small groups, or with the entire class, as directed by your instructor:

Description

1. What conditions existed at the School of Education before the change?
2. What changes were implemented?

Diagnosis

3. Were the changes effective?
4. What problems remain or will occur as a result of the changes?

Prescription

5. What course of action or additional programs would you propose now?
6. Should other changes have been implemented?

Action

7. How does your plan of action compare to that actually implemented?
8. Which intervention strategies would have been more effective?
9. Were the changes evaluated?
10. Were the changes institutionalized?

Step 4: Discussion. In small groups, with the entire class, or in written form, share your answers to the above questions. Then answer the following questions:

1. What symptoms suggested a problem existed?
2. What problems existed in the case?
3. What theories and concepts help explain the problems?
4. How were the problems corrected?
5. Analyze the change process.
6. Was the change effective?

Activity 14-5: MANAGING AN ORGANIZATIONAL CRISIS

Step 1: Read the following scenario:

You are the vice president of marketing of a small manufacturing firm that processes baby food from local produce. Your firm sells the food to mothers who wish only the freshest products for their infants. Your products are stored in the refrigerator section of the grocery store and have a relatively short shelf life. Because of the concern about preservatives and healthful living, your company has grown significantly in the past five years.

Yesterday the local newspaper revealed that they had done a chemical analysis of a batch of your food and found traces of a compound that is known to cause cancer in mice. They warned the public to stop buying your product. You know that if you cannot reassure the public about the integrity of your product, the loss of sales will threaten your company's survival.

Step 2: Individually or in small groups, offer a plan for dealing with this crisis.

Step 3: Discussion. In small groups or with the entire class, share the plans you have developed. Then answer the following questions:

1. What were the key elements of the plans?
2. How did the plans differ?
3. How could these differences be reconciled?
4. What are the strengths and weaknesses of each plan?
5. What problems might arise in their implementation?
6. What are the components of an effective plan for dealing with the crisis?

Activity 14–6: ANALYSIS OF A PROBLEM SCENARIO

Step 1: Choose one scenario presented in the introduction to any chapter in this book.

Step 2: Repeat the diagnosis of the problem.

Step 3: Offer a prescription for change.

Step 4: Devise a plan of action that includes the following:

1. Describe the change process.
2. Select appropriate intervention strategies.
3. Select the change event.
4. Develop an evaluation procedure.

CONCLUDING COMMENTS

Managers and other change agents can use a variety of approaches to implement change in organizations. First they must understand the organization's culture. You offered a plan for merging two organizations with different cultures. In formulating the plan, you likely considered the differences in beliefs, values, heroes and heroines, rituals, and physical arrangements in the two companies.

Action involves identifying forces for and against change, overcoming resistance to change, and selecting the most appropriate change agent. You have performed these steps during a force field analysis of a problem situation you have faced, and also in acting as a consultant to the Bridgeton Temporary Services. Often implementing effective change means being prepared to deal with organizational crises. In Managing a Crisis you developed a plan for dealing with a major product defect that threatened the survival of your company.

You have also considered the application and effectiveness of various strategies for change. In your analysis of the School of Education case, you considered the effectiveness of one approach to action.

Planning for action in an organization of your choice requires an examination of the entire change process as well as proposals for evaluation strategies and methods of institutionalizing organizational improvements. In addition, the effectiveness of organizational change is likely to increase if there are well-defined boundaries to the change problems, employees perceive a set of issues as vital, salient, and important to improve, key parties are involved, participants receive training in problem solving and decision making, strong leadership functions, and rewards support the change. Finally, in this chapter we considered situations in which action, as we described it, may be inadequate. Sometimes more basic organizational transformation is required.

ENDNOTES

[1]Excerpted from The cooperative workplace, by Mary Sit, July 30, 1989. Reprinted courtesy of *The Boston Globe*.

[2]N.C. Morey and F. Luthans, Refining the displacement of culture and the uses of scenes and themes in organizational studies, *Academy of Management Review* 10 (1985): 219–229.

[3]E.H. Schein, *Organizational Culture and Leadership* (San Francisco: Jossey-Bass, 1985).

[4]M.R. Louis, Organizations as culture-bearing milieux. In L.R. Pondy et al. (eds.), *Organizational Symbolism* (Greenwich, Ct.: JAI, 1980).

[5]L. Schein, *A Manager's Guide to Corporate Culture* (New York: The Conference Board, 1989).

[6]V. Sathe, *Culture and Related Corporate Realities* (Homewood, Ill.: Irwin, 1985); E.H. Schein, SMR Forum: Does Japanese management style have a message for American managers?, *Sloan Management Review* (Fall 1981): 64–67.

[7]E.H. Schein, Coming to a new awareness of organizational culture, *Sloan Management Review* 25 (Winter 1984): 3–16.

[8]Sathe, *op. cit.*

[9]A.F. Buono, J.L. Bowditch, and J.W. Lewis III, When cultures collide: The anatomy of a merger, *Human Relations* 38 (1985): 484–485.

[10]T.E. Deal and A.A. Kennedy, *Corporate Cultures* (Reading, Mass.: Addison-Wesley, 1982).

[11]*Ibid.*

[12]L. Schein, *op. cit.*

[13]M. Elmes and D. Wilemon, Organizational culture and project leader effectiveness, *Project Management Journal* 19 (4) (1988): 54–63.

[14]S.L. Solberg, Changing culture through ceremony: An example from GM, *Human Resource Management* 24 (Fall 1985): 329–340.

[15]C.J. Fombrun, Corporate culture and competitive strategy. In C.J. Fombrun, N.M. Tichy, and M. Devanna (eds.), *Strategic Human Resource Management* (New York: Wiley, 1984).

[16]P.R. Harris and R.T. Moran, *Managing Cultural Differences* 2d ed. (Houston: Gulf, 1987).

[17]A.M. Jaeger, Organization development and national culture: Where's the fit?, *Academy of Management Review* 11 (1986): 178–190.

[18]Fombrun, *op. cit.*

[19]J. Weiss and A. Delbecq, High-technology culture and management, *Group and Organization Studies* 12(1) (1987): 39–54.

[20]W. Ouchi, *Theory Z: How American Business Can Meet the Japanese Challenge* (Reading, Mass.: Addison-Wesley, 1979); R. Pascale and A. Athos, *The Art of Japanese Management* (New York: Simon & Schuster, 1981); T. Peters and R. Waterman, *In Search of Excellence* (New York: Harper & Row, 1982); D.R. Denison, Bringing corporate culture to the bottom line, *Organizational Dynamics* 13 (Autumn 1984): 4–22.

[21]Ouchi, *op. cit.*

[22]T.J. Billesbach and J.M. Rives, Lifetime employment: Future prospects for Japan and the U.S., *SAM Advanced Management Journal* 30 (Autumn 1985): 26–30.

[23]C.W. Joiner Jr., Making the "Z" concept work, *Sloan Management Review* 26 (September 1985): 57–63.

[24]J.B. Barney, Organizational culture: Can it be a source of sustained competitive advantage?, *Academy of Management Review* 11 (1986): 656–665.

[25]Peters and Waterman, *op. cit.*, J. Moskowitz, Lessons from the best companies to work for, *California Management Review* 27 (Winter 1985): 42–47; J. O'Toole, Employee practices at the best managed companies, *California Management Review* 28 (1985): 35–66.

[26]B.H. Drake and E. Drake, Ethical and legal aspects of managing corporate cultures, *California Management Review* 30 (Winter 1988): 107–123.

[27]G.S. Saffold III, Culture traits, strength, and organizational performance: Moving beyond "strong" culture, *Academy of Management Review* 13 (1988): 546–558.

[28]Sathe, *op. cit.*

[29]Sathe, *op. cit.*

[30]Sathe, *op. cit.*

[31]Sathe, *op. cit.*, pp. 404–406.

[32]D.A. Kolb and A.L. Frohman, An organization development approach to consulting, *Sloan Management Review* (Fall 1970): 51–65.

[33]W. French, Organization development—Objectives, assumptions, and strategies, *California Management Review* 12 (1969): 23–34.

[34]K. Lewin, *Field Theory in Social Science* (New York: Harper & Row, 1951).

[35]P. Shrivastava and I.I. Mitroff, Strategic management of corporate crises, *Columbia Journal of World Business* 22 (Spring 1987): 5–12.

[36]L. Coch and J. French Jr., Overcoming resistance to change, *Human Relations* 1 (1948): 512–532.

[37]E.F. Hamilton, An empirical study of factors predicting change agents' effectiveness, *Journal of Applied Behavioral Science* 24(1) (1988): 37–59.

[38]W.L. French and C.H. Bell Jr., *Organization Development: Behavioral Science Interventions for Organization Improvement* 2d ed. (Englewood Cliffs, N.J.: Prentice-Hall, 1978), p. 14.

[39]K. Albrecht, *Organization Development: A Total Systems Approach to Positive Change in Any Business Organization* (Englewood Cliffs, N.J.: Prentice-Hall, 1983).

[40]M.B. Miles and R.A. Schmuck, The nature of organization development. In *Organization Development in Schools,* ed. R.A. Schmuck and M.B. Miles (La Jolla, Cal.: University Associates, 1976).

[41]R. Harrison, Choosing the depth of organization intervention, *Journal of Applied Behavioral Science* 6 (1970): 181–202.

[42]*Ibid.*

[43]*Ibid.*

[44]J.M. Bartunek and M. Moch, First-order, second-order, and third-order change and organizational development interventions, *Journal of Applied Behavioral Science* 23(4) (1987): 483–500.

[45]R.W. Bass and M.V. Mariono, Organization development in Italy, *Group and Organization Studies* 12(3) (1987): 245–256.

[46]W.L. French, A checklist for organizing and implementing an OD effort. In *Organization Development: Theory, Practice, and Research,* ed. W.L. French, C.H. Bell Jr., and R.A. Zawacki (Dallas: Business Publications, 1978).

[47]H. Schwartz and S. Davis, Matching corporate culture and business strategy, *Organizational Dynamics* (Summer 1981): 30–48.

[48]A.L. Wilkins and W.G. Dyer Jr., Toward culturally sensitive theories of cultural change, *Academy of Management Review* 13 (1988): 522–533; E.H. Schein, *Organizational Culture and Leadership* (San Francisco: Jossey-Bass, 1985).

[49]H. Kuklan, Managing crises: Challenges and complexities, *SAM Advanced Management Journal* 51 (Autumn 1986): 39–44.

[50]Shrivastava and Mitroff, *op. cit.*

[51]D.S. Mileti and J.H. Sorenson, Determinants of organizational effectiveness in responding to low-probability catastrophic events, *Columbia Journal of World Business* 22(1) (1987): 13–21.

[52]I.I. Mitroff, Crisis management: Cutting through the confusion, *Sloan Management Review* 29(2) (1988): 15–20.

[53]G. Barczak, C. Smith, and D. Wilemon, Managing large-scale organizational change, *Organizational Dynamics* 16 (Autumn 1987): 22–35.

[54]D.L. Lockwood and F. Luthans, Multiple measures to assess the impact of organization development interventions, *1980 Annual Handbook for Group Facilitators* (San Diego: University Associates, 1980), p. 461.

[55]W.F. Cascio and E.M. Awad, *Human Resources Management: An Information Processing Approach* (Reston, Va.: Reston, 1981).

[56]R.H. Kilmann, T.J. Covin, and Associates (eds.), *Corporate Transformation: Revitalizing Organizations for a Competitive World* (San Francisco: Jossey-Bass, 1988).

[57]R. Beckhard, The executive management of transformational change. In Kilmann et al., *op. cit.*

[58]Kilmann et al., *op. cit.*

[59]M.L. Tushman, W.H. Newman, and E. Romanelli, Convergence and upheaval: Managing the unsteady pace of organizational evolution. In K.S. Cameron, R.E. Sutton, and D.A. Whetton (eds.), *Readings in Organizational Decline: Framework, Research, and Prescriptions* (Cambridge, Mass.: Ballinger, 1988).

[60]*Ibid.*

[61]M.L. Tushman and E. Romanelli, Organizational evolution: A metamorphosis model of convergence and reorientation. In L.L. Cummings and B.M. Staw (eds.), *Research in Organizational Behavior* vol. 7 (Greenwich, Ct.: JAI Press, 1985).

[62]*Ibid.*

[63]J.R. Hackman, The transition that hasn't happened. In J.R. Kimberly and R.E. Quinn (eds.), *Managing Organizational Transitions* (Homewood, Ill.: Irwin, 1984).

[64]M. Beer, The critical path for change: Keys to success and failures in six companies. In Kilmann et al., *op. cit.*

[65]R.M. Kanter, *When Giants Learn to Dance* (New York: Simon & Schuster, 1989).

[66]*Ibid.*

[67]N. Tichy and D. Ulrich, Revitalizing organizations: The leadership role. In Kimberly and Quinn, *op. cit.*

[68]See J.M. Bartunek and M.R. Luis, The interplay of organization development and organizational transformation. In W.A. Pasmore and R.W. Woodman (eds.), *Research in Organizational Change and Development* vol. 2. (Greenwich, Ct.: JAI, 1988); J.M. Bartunek, The dynamics of personal and organizational reframing. In R. Quinn and K. Cameron (eds.), *Paradox and Transformation: Towards a Theory of Change in Organizations and Management* (Cambridge, Mass.: Ballinger, 1989).

[69]A. Szilagyi Jr. and D.M. Schweiger, Matching managers to strategies: A review and suggested framework, *Academy of Management Review* 9 (1984): 626–637.

RECOMMENDED READINGS

Beckhard, R., and Harris, R.T. *Organizational Transitions: Managing Complex Change* 2d ed. Reading, Mass.: Addison-Wesley, 1987.

Connor, P.E., and Lake, L.K. *Managing Organizational Change.* New York: Praeger, 1988.

Kilmann, R.H., Covin, T.J., and Associates (eds.) *Corporate Transformation: Revitalizing Organizations for a Competitive World.* San Francisco: Jossey-Bass, 1988.

London, M. *Change Agents.* San Francisco: Jossey-Bass, 1988.

Mohrman, A.M. Jr., et al. (eds.) *Large-Scale Organizational Change.* San Francisco: Jossey-Bass, 1989.

Quinn, R.E., and Cameron, K.S. (eds.) *Paradox and Transformation: Toward a Theory of Change in Organization and Management.* Cambridge, Mass.: Ballinger, 1988.

Sathe, V. *Culture and Related Corporate Realities.* Homewood, Ill.: Irwin, 1985.

Torbert, W. *Managing the Corporate Dream.* Homewood, Ill.: Irwin, 1987.

15

Increasing Organizational Effectiveness

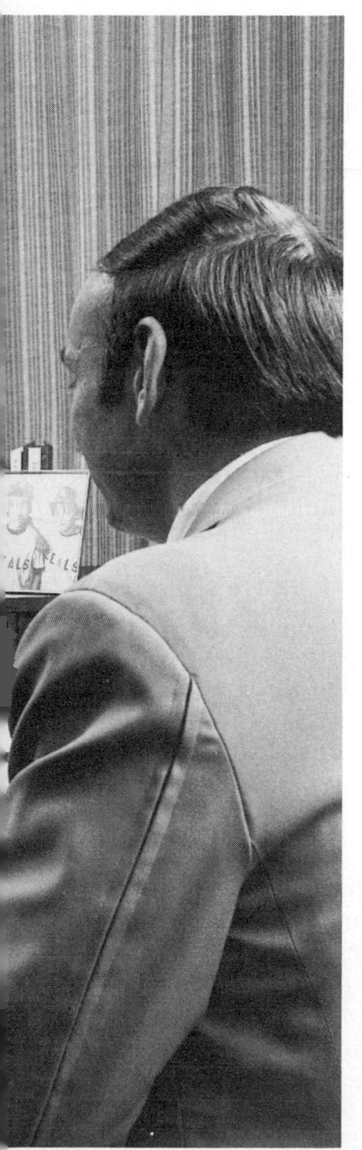

CHAPTER OUTLINE

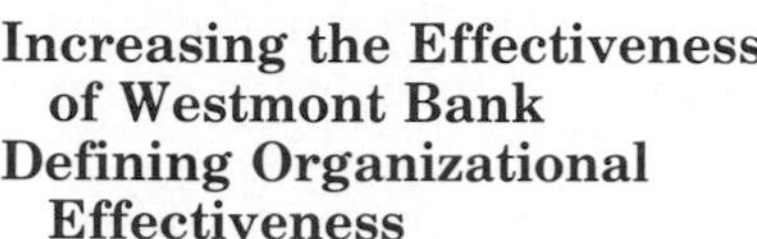

Increasing the Effectiveness of Westmont Bank
Defining Organizational Effectiveness
A Review of the Diagnostic Approach
- Description
- Diagnosis
- Prescription
- Action

Ensuring Organizational Effectiveness
SUMMARY
ACTIVITIES
CONCLUDING COMMENTS
ENDNOTES
RECOMMENDED READINGS

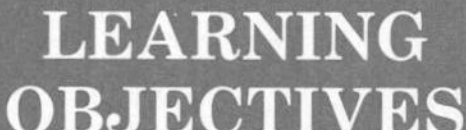

LEARNING OBJECTIVES

After completing the reading and activities in Chapter 15, students will be able to

- define organizational effectiveness and specify criteria of effective organizations;
- describe and apply the complete diagnostic approach; and
- show the significance of the diagnostic approach to organizational effectiveness.

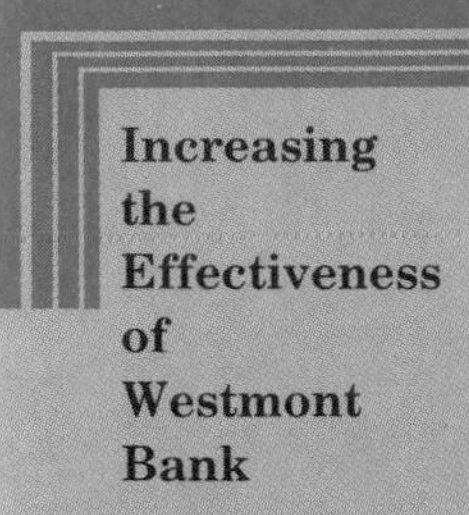

Increasing the Effectiveness of Westmont Bank

The corporate services sales department at Westmont Bank provides clients with cash management services designed to improve cash flow. Corporate services officers (CSOs) interview prospective clients to help them analyze their cash flow problems, determine which services can alleviate those problems, and work out appropriate processing procedures and pricing agreements. The CSOs also act as trouble-shooters between customers and the corporate operations department.

The corporate services sales team consists of one manager, four CSOs, two sales support assistants, and one market analyst. The team is very well developed in terms of task and personal roles. The personnel of this team has stayed fairly constant for the past few years; only one CSO and one support person have been there less than one year.

The team's tasks are highly structured, with some uncertainty existing in selling to large, influential companies. Each team member works hard to fulfill his or her well-defined roles. The markets assigned to sales officers are delineated with no overlap, although one officer fills in for another who is meeting with a client or handling problems.

Each sales support assistant supports two officers but helps the other when the work load is uneven. All team members share information about service procedures, pricing, and banking news. The objectives of this team are to develop new clients, sell products to existing clients, and make sure the needs of each client are met. Basically the sales team's orientation is the servicing of individual corporate customers.

The Operations Department is divided into several work groups, each defined by its product and structured strictly around task performance. The staff of each group includes clerks, supervisors, and operations managers, who perform the service; and product managers, who oversee procedures, request changes, and set the prices. One manager of corporate operations oversees all, tying them to upper management and the industry in general. The objectives of operations include increasing revenues and profitability, ensuring efficient service for the product, and keeping information about the competition and technological advances in the industry.

The manager of sales and the manager of corporate operations have very different styles. The sales manager encourages participation in decision making and delegates large amounts of authority to his staff. The manager of operations uses a more directive style. Product managers have significant control over their individual products but little authority is delegated beyond them.

The sales group tends to be flamboyant, highly ambitious, and people-oriented. Most are relatively young, with few family responsibilities. The operations staff is a mix of relatively unambitious clerks and reserved, highly ambitious, quantitatively-oriented product managers. The clerks tend to be older and less well educated than the product managers.

The bank has experienced an increasing rate of customer loss and a drop in new sales to large customers. Complaints about cooperation arise from both groups. Sales officers believe the product managers are too stubborn in not allowing lower pricing or specialized processing for important customers. CSOs continually demand a wide range of pricing, giving them flexibility to negotiate with prospects and beat the competition. They feel operations does not inform them soon enough of processing problems and disruptions to

service; they only find out when irate customers call. Product managers in turn distrust the salespeople. They complain that the CSOs are not discouraging prospects from requesting special processing. They believe the CSOs do not respect their pricing decisions and ask for too many price breaks. They state that their staff is constantly interrupted with questions about particular customers, slowing down the flow of work in the operations department.

The bank has recently been the target of a takeover attempt. This has created a push for greater productivity, with fewer staff members and less financial resources. Some realignment of reporting relationships has occurred, creating new stresses on the groups and their supervisors.[1]

How effectively does Westmont Bank function? How does management ensure that individual, group, and even organizational behavior result in an effective organization?

In this book, we have proposed the use of the diagnostic approach as an analytical tool for facilitating effective organizational functioning. The diagnostic approach assumes that effective behavior requires a combination of understanding complex circumstances and action. Since no single perspective can provide complete understanding of any situation,[2] we have examined and applied a series of perspectives to the analysis of organizational situations. We have also examined a variety of prescriptions for improving organizational performance, including interpersonal processes, work design, and organizational design. Throughout the book, we have discussed action strategies that accompany various diagnoses and prescriptions.

This chapter begins by defining organizational effectiveness. It continues by reviewing the diagnostic approach as a way of contributing to increased organizational effectiveness. The chapter concludes by discussing ways of ensuring and increasing organizational effectiveness, at Westmont Bank and other organizations.

DEFINING ORGANIZATIONAL EFFECTIVENESS

Researchers have argued that effectiveness serves as a central focus in all organizational analysis, acting as the goal of organization design and organization change.[3] Although some researchers suggest there are limitations in this definition,[4] many agree that the concept of organizational effectiveness reflects and represents a wide range of desirable organizational outcomes.

Organizational effectiveness has been defined and assessed in four major ways: (1) an organization's ability to accomplish its goals; (2) its ability to acquire needed resources from its external environment and thus achieve a competitive advantage; (3) the quality of an organization's internal processes and information; and (4) an organization's ability to at least minimally satisfy all of its strategic constituencies, including suppliers, consumers, members, and so on. Together these models can provide one set of guidelines for evaluating an organization's performance.[5]

There is a basic distinction between behavioral outcomes such as improved motivation, cohesion, adaptability, morale, and satisfaction; and business outcomes such as increased sales, profits, or service response time.[6] But certainly these two types of outcomes are interrelated and significant for Westmont Bank. Figure 15–1 is a partial listing of effectiveness criteria. Note that an organization cannot be judged effective unless many of these criteria are met. An effectiveness analysis can be refined and focused by asking six additional questions[7]:

1. What domain (e.g., organization–environment relations, production of outputs, morale, or input acquisition) should be the focus of evaluation?
2. Whose perspective, or which constituency's point of view, should be considered?
3. What level of analysis (e.g., individual, group, or organizational) should be used?
4. What time frame (short or long term) should be used?
5. What type of data (e.g., individual perceptions or organizational records) should be used?
6. What reference (e.g., comparison organizations, an organization's goals, improvement, or established standards) should be used?

Deficiencies in any measures of effectiveness signal dysfunctions in an organization and suggest that the *application of the diagnostic approach* should help diagnose the dysfunctions and contribute to increasing organizational effectiveness. Increased effectiveness necessitates recognition of the complexity of organizations, as well as the individuals and groups that comprise them. Thus this book has offered a multidimensional view of organizational behavior and members' attitudes. Increasing the quality of these behaviors and attitudes has positive consequences for many aspects of organizational effectiveness, including performance, adaptability, growth, and satisfaction, among others.

A REVIEW OF THE DIAGNOSTIC APPROACH

Let us consider the situation described in the introduction. We can apply the diagnostic approach to delineate its events and key interactions, increase our understanding of the situation, prescribe corrective action, identify issues related to implementation of the actions, and hypothesize their outcomes.

Before reading further you might perform this analysis yourself. Be sure to draw on all theoretical perspectives in the book to ensure a comprehensive analysis.

Description

The description of the situation presents one person's view of the bank: the case writer's. Does the case describe a well-functioning, effective organization? Interviews with members of the sales and operations departments, as well as

Figure 15–1 PARTIAL LISTING OF UNIVARIATE MEASURES OF ORGANIZATIONAL EFFECTIVENESS

- Overall effectiveness: The degree to which the organization is accomplishing all its major tasks or achieving all its objectives. A general evaluation that takes in as many single criteria as possible and results in a general judgment about the effectiveness of the organization.
- Quality: The quality of the primary service or product provided by the organization. This may take many operational forms, primarily determined by the *kind* of product or service provided by the organization.
- Productivity: The quantity of or volume of the major product or service that the organization provides. Can be measured at three levels: individual, group, and total organization. This is not a measure of efficiency; no cost/output ratio is computed.
- Readiness: An overall judgment concerning the probability that the organization could successfully perform some specified task if asked to do so.
- Efficiency: A ratio that reflects a comparison of some aspect of unit performance to the costs incurred for that performance. Examples: dollars per single unit of production, amount of down time, degree to which schedules, standards of performance, or other milestones are met. On occasion, just the total amount of costs (money, material, etc.) a unit has incurred over some period can be used.
- Profit or return: The return on the investment used in running the organization from the owners' point of view. The amount of resources left after all costs and obligations are met, sometimes expressed as a percentage.
- Growth: An increase in such things as manpower, plant facilities, assets, sales, profits, market share, and innovations. A comparison of an organization's present state with its own past state.
- Utilization of environment: The extent to which the organization successfully interacts with its environment, acquiring scarce, valued resources necessary for its effective operation. This is viewed in a long-term, optimizing framework and not in a short-term, maximizing framework. For example, the degree to which it acquires a steady supply of manpower and financial resources.
- Stability: The maintenance of structure, function, and resources through time, and more particularly through periods of stress.
- Turnover or retention: Frequency or amount of voluntary terminations.
- Absenteeism: The frequency of occasions of personnel being absent from the job.
- Accidents: Frequency of on-the-job accidents resulting in down time or recovery time.
- Morale: A predisposition in organization members to put forth extra effort in achieving organizational goals and objectives. Includes feelings of commitment. Morale is a group phenomenon involving extra effort, goals communality, and feelings of belonging. Groups have some degree of morale, while individuals have some degree of motivation (and satisfaction). By implication, morale is inferred from group phenomena.
- Motivation: The strength of the predisposition of an *individual* to engage in goal-directed action or activity on the job. This is not a feeling of relative contentment with various job outcomes as is satisfaction, but more akin to a feeling of readiness or willingness to work at accomplishing the job's goals.
- Satisfaction: The degree of feeling of contentment felt by a person toward his organizational role or job. The degree to which individuals perceive they are equitably rewarded by various aspects of their job situation and the organization to which they belong.
- Internalization of organizational goals: The acceptance of organizational goals by individuals and units within the organization. Their belief that the organization's goals are right and proper.
- Conflict-Cohesion: A bipolar dimension defined at the cohesion end by an organization in which the members like one another, work well together, communicate fully and openly, and coordinate their work efforts. At the other end lies the organization with verbal and physical clashes, poor coordination, and ineffective communication.
- Flexibility-Adaptation: The ability of an organization to change its standard operating procedures in response to environmental changes, to resist becoming rigid in response to environmental stimuli
- Evaluations by external entities: Evaluations of the organization or organizational unit by those individuals and organizations in its environment with which it interacts. Loyalty to, confidence in, and support given the organization by such groups as suppliers, customers, stockholders, enforcement agencies, and the general public.
- Climate*: The nature of the internal environment of the organization.
- Quality of working life*: The quality of the employee's relationship to his or her working environment.

*These dimensions were added by the author of this book.

SOURCE: Adapted from J.P. Campbell, "Research into the Nature of Organizational Effectiveness: An Endangered Species?" Unpublished manuscript. Minneapolis: University of Minnesota, 1973.

with other members of the organization, would expand the description by revealing additional factors influencing behavior in the situation. Collection of data by more formal procedures, such as the administration of questionnaires to measure attitudes or application of formal observation schedules to tabulate the frequency or nature of participant behavior, might provide additional information about the situation.

Diagnosis

The next step in the diagnostic approach involves the identification of key factors in the situation, followed by the application of theories or concepts to explain these factors. Clearly the increasing rate of customer loss, drop in new sales, and complaints from employees suggest that problems exist. Each chapter in this book has presented a series of diagnostic questions for addressing problems with various aspects of organizational behavior. Figure 15–2 gathers these questions together into a single (albeit long) diagnostic checklist. Let us use this list of questions to diagnose each area of organizational behavior in the situation at Westmont Bank.

Figure 15–2 THE DIAGNOSTIC CHECKLIST

Historical Factors

- Is there an appropriate division of labor?
- Is work done efficiently, and are workers sufficiently trained to do their jobs?
- Do employees have specified areas of responsibility?
- Is the work defined effectively?
- Do work groups operate effectively?
- Do managers perform organizing roles and have an appropriate span of control?
- Does the group have effective task and social leadership?
- Does management work with correct assumptions about employees?
- Is decision making effective?
- Is the interface of technology and individual workers effective?
- Does the organization's structure respond to the environmental contingencies?
- Is there a good fit between inputs and operations?
- Are there good fits between individuals, tasks, organizational arrangements, and the informal organization?

Perception

- What factors influence the perceptions of organizational members?
- What distortions of perception occur?

Attribution

- What factors influence the attributions of organizational members?
- What biases exist in these attributions?

Learning

- What behaviors are reinforced as part of the learning process?
- What cues encourage learning?
- What learning themes exist in the organization?
- How are these learning themes supported in the organization?

Attitude Formation

- What beliefs and values do individuals have?
- How do these beliefs and values influence individuals' attitudes?
- What functional and dysfunctional behavioral intentions result from the individuals' attitudes?

Personality

- Do the personality styles of participants fit with the situation?
- Do the personality styles of participants fit with other organizational members?

Individual Development

- Do organizational members experience problems in adult or career development?
- How compatible are the adult- and career-development stages of various organizational members?

Role Pressures

- Do individuals experience role conflict?
- Are roles clear, or ambiguous?
- Do the socialization processes used fit with situational requirements and reduce role ambiguity?
- How do managers and other employees deal with role pressures?

Motivation

- Do the rewards satisfy individuals' needs?
- Are rewards applied equitably and consistently after desired behaviors?
- Do individuals value the rewards they receive?
- Are rewards consistently applied in proportion to performance?
- Do individuals perceive that their efforts correlate with performance?
- Do individuals set goals that are specific, moderately difficult, yet accepted?
- Do individuals receive feedback about their goal accomplishment as part of the organization's reward system?

Figure 15–2 CONTINUED

- What type of reward system exists?
- Does it encourage desired outcomes, such as innovation, productivity, or attendance?
- Are benefits and incentive systems effective in motivating desired behaviors?

Group Dynamics

- Did the group form and develop effectively?
- What are the group's norms, roles, goals, and structural configuration?
- Does a good fit exist among them?
- Is the group's structure appropriate to the task, the people, and the information-processing needs?
- Does the group perform appropriate task and maintenance roles and avoid individual roles?
- Are individual and group goals appropriate and congruent?
- Does the group have the characteristics of an effective work team?
- Does the group practice strategies for team building?

Decision Making

- Do decision makers respond appropriately to routine versus nonroutine decisions?
- Do decision makers secure appropriate information before making a decision?
- Do organizational members make high-quality, accepted, ethical decisions?
- Do decision makers analyze the situation, set objectives, generate, evaluate, and select alternatives?
- Do ways of dealing with the limitations of the process exist?
- What barriers to decision making effectiveness exist?
- Is the group involved appropriately in decision making?
- What techniques can be used to overcome these barriers?

Communication

- What encoding and decoding errors occur in communication?
- How effective are downward, upward, and lateral communication?
- What special roles exist to facilitate communication?
- What factors affect the accuracy of communication?
- What barriers to communication exist?
- Does communication include feedback?
- What noise affects communication?
- Are the attitudes of the communicating parties compatible?
- How effective is nonverbal communication?
- Does communication lack cross-cultural sensitivity?
- Are interviews conducted effectively?
- Is the climate supportive or defensive?
- Do individuals use assertive, nonassertive, or aggressive communication?
- Do individuals use active listening techniques?

Leadership

- Do the managers have the traits required for leadership?
- Do the managers exhibit balanced managerial roles?
- Do the managers display the behaviors required for effective leadership?
- Do the leaders encourage the appropriate amount of participation in decision making?
- Does the leadership fit with the nature of the task, leader–member relationships, and the position power of the leader?
- Is leadership superfluous to the situational features and the followers' needs? Does it meet their needs?
- Do followers attribute attitudes to the leaders accurately?
- Are effective leader and subordinate behaviors reinforced?
- Do transformational leaders exist?

Power and Negotiation

- Who has power in the organization?
- From what sources does this power stem?
- Is the power properly placed?
- Are alliances, informal networks, or trade relations used to develop power?
- Is powerlessness overcome in the organization?
- What types of negotiations occur in the organization?
- Do negotiations tend to be distributive or integrative?
- What types of preparation for negotiations occur?
- Are interests identified, best alternative to a negotiated agreement determined, and base range identified?
- How effective are intercultural negotiations?

Conflict

- Is there conflict in the organization?
- What level of conflict exists?
- What stage of conflict exists?
- Are there mechanisms for effectively managing conflict and stress?
- Is there evidence of stress in the situation?
- What causes and results from stress in the situation?

Intergroup Relations

- What is the nature of the relationship between groups in the organization?
- What factors contribute to these relationships?
- How effective are intergroup relations?
- Are there mechanisms for effectively managing them?

Organization Structure and Design

- What division of labor and coordinating mechanisms are there?
- What structural configuration describes the organization?
- How would you describe the information processing?
- Does the informal organization reinforce or contradict the formal organization structure?
- Are the job groups relatively homogeneous and meaningful?
- Are unit groups of manageable size?
- Is there sufficient coordination among the groupings?
- Have groupings considered the impact of the organization's environment?

continued

Figure 15–2 CONTINUED

- How complex is the environment? Is decision making sufficiently decentralized?
- How unpredictable is the environment? Is the structure sufficiently organic and the information-processing mechanisms sufficient?
- How hostile is the environment? Is the structure temporarily centralized?
- Have groupings considered the impact of the organization's technology?
- How regulated is the technology? Is the structure sufficiently organic?
- How sophisticated is the technology? Is there sufficient support staff?
- Is the technology sufficiently buffered from the environment?
- Have groupings been designed to accomplish the organization's goals? Is the division of labor sufficiently specialized?
- Are there linkages among groups that might have different goals?
- Have groupings been designed to meet the needs and abilities of the work force? Is the structure sufficiently specialized to respond to differences in employee professionalism, expertise, group membership, and values?
- How old is the organization? Is the structure sufficiently elaborated?
- Does the structure make sense for the organization's age? Is the structure sufficiently elaborated?
- Does the structure make sense for the organization's stage of development?
- Do organizations at the entrepreneurial, collective, and elaborated stages have relatively organic designs?
- Do organizations at the formalization stage have more mechanistic structures?

Work Design

- Are the jobs sufficiently specialized?
- Are the jobs sufficiently enriched?
- Do alternate work arrangements exist? Are they effective?
- Do quality-of-working-life projects exist? Are they effective?
- Do work redesign efforts match workers' needs?
- Does innovation occur in the organization?
- Does a good quality innovation process exist?

Organizational Culture and Planned Change

- What type of culture exists in the organization?
- What components reinforce the culture?
- Are the seven steps of the planned change model implemented?
- Are forces for and against change identified?
- Are appropriate change agents selected?
- Does the organization have mechanisms for dealing with crises?
- Do intervention strategies fit with the change situation?
- Are changes evaluated?
- Do mechanisms for institutionalizing changes exist?
- Is transformational change required, and how can it be implemented?

Historical Perspectives Further diagnosis should address at least the interaction between groups and the structure of the organization. In addition, diagnosis should assess the fits between various parts of the organization.

Perception, Attribution, Learning, and Attitude Formation Perceptual distortions and attributional biases likely contribute to the problems in this case. The sales group may view the less-educated and less-ambitious operations staff as incompetent and lazy. The operations staff may view the sales staff as manipulative and uncooperative. Each may attribute the declining performance to the other group's personality rather than to situational causes or their own behavior. Learning dysfunctions and faulty attitude formation may also contribute to the problems, but they do not seem to be major causes.

Personality, Individual Development, and Role Pressures The scenario suggests that the possibility of a takeover has created stress for individuals. In addition, the ages of the various workers indicate that their career and personal developmental stages vary, creating diverse needs and problems. Some role conflict might also exist regarding the responsibility for setting acceptable prices.

Motivation The case provides limited information about the reward system. Certainly teamwork between sales and operations is not rewarded by the reward system. And we have no indication whether rewards are administered in proportion to performance. We also do not know if a goal-setting program exists or if individuals receive feedback about their goal accomplishment.

Group Dynamics No conscious effort was made to develop the two groups of workers into a single functioning team. Each department seems to be relatively independent and goal-focused. At the same time, norms dysfunctional to organizational goals have arisen because each group tries to make its position the dominant one. Each group's members feel they are not sufficiently involved in organizational decision making, even in situations where their acceptance of a decision is important.

Decision Making The data in the case are not sufficient to determine whether there are problems in decision making per se at Westmont Bank. Certainly questions exist about the appropriateness of the pricing decisions made by the operations group.

Communication Significant barriers to communication hinder both groups' performance. Encoding and decoding errors may occur, due to differences in the groups' background, goals, and technical facility. Insufficient face-to-face communication may limit the accuracy of transmission. Noise also interferes with the groups' functioning. The conflict between the groups likely contributes to or results from a defensive communication climate.

Leadership The case states that the sales and operations managers differ in style, but provides no further information about their effectiveness.

Power and Negotiation The struggle for power is being fought on personal and group levels and contributes to the conflict at Westmont. The professionals most deeply involved are highly ambitious, probably causing them to attempt to satisfy their personal need for power. The CSOs and product managers hold no legitimate power over one another, but likely rely on trade to affect their status within the organization. The product managers have expertise about their products and costs of production, and control over operational resources. They definitely hold a position of unsubstitutability and are therefore valued in the organization. The CSOs possess the power of charisma since they act as flamboyant persuaders. They are a source of information about clients and competition and are an unsubstitutable source of revenues for the product managers and the organization. Neither group seems able to negotiate effectively. They seem to use a distributive bargaining approach.

Conflict and Intergroup Relations The departments experience reciprocal interdependence, relying on each other for the resources to succeed. The operations group provides sales with services, which sales' clients use to maximize the productivity of their cash balances. The sales group provides operations with an outlet for their products and services and a way to add to their revenues. Because the groups' tasks are interdependent, the exchange of resources is continual and therefore increases the likelihood that conflict could occur, especially since their orientations to objectives and perceptions differ.

The major conflict is between the departments. They differ in resources, power, and status; and these differences contribute to their competitive attitudes. They seem to lack a superordinate goal. The sales team has formal objectives to increase the number of clients serviced. Each CSO has goals of both the number of services sold and the value of the sales; therefore each CSO wants to give special pricing or customized service to help make the sales. The product managers, in contrast, have as formal objectives increasing profitability of each service by reducing operating costs, improving the quality of service, and charging a sufficiently high price. Specialized pricing and customized service contradict operation's objectives.

Since the organization is not unionized, no union–management problems exist. The two employee groups do not act as planners and implementers, thus eliminating the possibility of this type of problem. But inaccurate perceptions deter them from experiencing effective working arrangements; the groups compete in a win–lose fashion. Conflict exists at the manifest stage, since regular confrontations occur between the two groups. To date, no mechanisms for resolving this conflict have been used. Each episode of conflict runs through four stages: frustration, conceptualization, behavior, and outcome. However, because no episode's behavior ever addresses the root of the conflict, the outcome usually leaves the unaddressed frustration to lead to new episodes.

Organizational Structure and Design The division of labor emphasizes horizontal differentiation. Coordination occurs primarily, although not adequately, through direct supervision. Authority rests with the department managers. No structural mechanism coordinates the two groups. The functional structure limits the organization's ability to respond quickly to a changing environment. The structure does not fit with the organization's goals. It lacks sufficient integrating roles.

Work Design The case suggests that the jobs in the two departments are reasonably enriched, although no alternate work arrangements exist. Introducing a quality-of-working-life program which combines representatives of the sales and operations departments into a problem-solving group would be appropriate.

Organizational Culture and Planned Change We can only deduce the nature of the organization's culture from the case description. The culture appears to be competitive rather than collaborative. This aggravates the conflict between sales and operations. Neither the organization's structure nor the reward system encourages collaboration. Little effort has been made to introduce planned change. (Issues of change for Westmont Bank are discussed later in this chapter.)

Prescription

The diagnosis just presented highlights problems with (1) perception and attribution, (2) communication, (3) intergroup relations and conflict, (4) power and negotiations, (5) organizational structure, and (6) organizational culture. Prescriptions must focus on each of these areas, as follows:

1. Management should help each group increase the accuracy of their perceptions and attributions of the other group.
2. Communication must be improved by reducing barriers.
3. A reduction in the competition between groups must occur; individuals must be encouraged to focus on common organizational, rather than merely departmental, goals. Conflict must be addressed.
4. Power between the groups must be equalized, and negotiating skills of the group members improved.
5. Integrating mechanisms must be added to the organizational structure.
6. The culture should become collaborative.

Action

What action must accompany the implementation of the prescriptions just listed? First, what forces for and against change are there? The workers might resist many of the prescriptions; historical precedents may prevent other changes. The manager or other change agent must prioritize the problems on which to act and the prescriptions to implement. Determining action priorities requires assembling the relative costs and benefits of various prescriptions, as well as prioritizing the severity of various problems that are to be addressed. Some prescriptions will meet such significant resistance as to preclude their implementation. Thus change agents must distinguish between what is actionable and what is ideal in any situation. This may require diagnosing the situation in somewhat different terms than originally, emphasizing now the feasibility of various action plans.

Implementation of both structural and interpersonal intervention strategies should improve organizational functioning and hence organizational effectiveness. Although the managers may seek advice from an outside consultant, they must take charge of the change effort themselves. Evaluation of the changes should follow. Finally, institutionalization of effective changes must occur.

What are the likely results of such changes? How does the diagnostic approach improve organizational functioning? In the next section, we conclude this chapter and the book by commenting on ways of ensuring and increasing organizational effectiveness.

ENSURING ORGANIZATIONAL EFFECTIVENESS

Managers and other organizational members have significant responsibility for ensuring organizational effectiveness. The leadership style they choose, their ability to communicate with peers, subordinates, and superiors, the quality of their decision making, and their skill in group work, for example, all contribute to organizational functioning. Understanding and choosing the appropriate individual and group behaviors are essential for employee productivity, satisfaction, adaptability, and other desirable outcomes. Using the diagnostic approach should help managers and other organizational members improve personal and organizational behavior.

If they are to be good diagnosticians, managers must quickly recognize threats to organizational growth and success. If profits and performance drop dramatically, a major alteration of an organization's culture, structure, and management style may be required. Downsizing an organization (described in Chapter 12) is one possibility; remaking the organization is another. Apple Computers, for example, responded to the threat of an industry-wide shakeout in the early 1980s by changing from a technical-superstar, entrepreneurial organization, to a market- and consumer-oriented one, and now focuses on new product concerns.[8]

Managers must develop new and creative strategies for responding to increasing environmental pressures. The emphasis on teamwork, the movement to more collaborative culture, and the call for visionary leadership are some of the factors that ultimately will stimulate the development of new organizational forms. The creation of new strategic partnerships, mega-organizations in the service sector due to mergers and acquisitions, and entrepreneurial departments within existing organizations should all contribute to increased organizational effectiveness.

The challenge for managers to increase and preserve organizational effectiveness never stops. Apparently effective, high-performing organizations can experience unanticipated problems and even decline (see the description of IBM in Chapter 12). Managers must be vigilant and use analytical tools such as the diagnostic approach to help ensure organizational effectiveness. They must understand the complexities of managing in a global economy and successfully develop and implement new competitive strategies, as well as manage an increasingly diverse work force. Improving individual, group, and organizational behavior and attitudes plays a major role in building effective organizations.

SUMMARY

This chapter concluded the book with a discussion of organizational effectiveness. It examined the nature of organizational effectiveness, including its multiple criteria. It reviewed and comprehensively applied the diagnostic approach to a situation in the corporate sales department of a large bank. It highlighted links between effective individual, group, and organizational behavior and organizational functioning. The chapter concluded with summary comments about the issues involved in ensuring and increasing organizational effectiveness.

ACTIVITIES

Activity 15–1: THE CONSOLIDATED LIFE CASE: CAUGHT BETWEEN CORPORATE CULTURES

Step 1: Read the Consolidated Life Case: Caught between Corporate Cultures.

PART I

It all started so positively. Three days after graduating with his degree in business administration, Mike Wilson started his first day at a prestigious insurance company—Consolidated Life. He worked in the Policy Issue Department. The work of the department was mostly clerical and did not require a high degree of technical knowledge. Given the repetitive and mundane nature of the work, the successful worker had to be consistent and willing to grind out paperwork.

Rick Belkner was the division's vice-president, "the man in charge" at the time. Rick was an actuary by training, a technical professional whose leadership style was laissez-faire. He was described in the division as "the mirror of whomever was the strongest personality around him." It was also common knowledge that Rick made $60,000 a year while he spent his time doing crossword puzzles.

Mike was hired as a management trainee and promised a supervisory assignment within a year. However, because of a management reorganization, it was only six weeks before he was placed in charge of an eight-person unit.

The reorganization was intended to streamline workflow, upgrade and combine the clerical jobs, and make greater use of the computer system. It was a drastic departure from the old way of doing things and created a great deal of animosity and anxiety among the clerical staff.

Management realized that a flexible supervisory style was necessary to pull off the reorganization without immense turnover, so they gave their supervisors a free hand to run their units as they saw fit. Mike used this latitude to implement group meetings and training classes in his unit. In addition he assured all members raises if they worked hard to attain them. By working long hours, participating in the mundane tasks with his unit, and being flexible in his management style, he was able to increase productivity, reduce errors, and reduce lost time. Things improved so dramatically that he was noticed by upper management and earned a reputation as a "superstar" despite being viewed as free spirited and unorthodox. The feeling was that his loose, people-oriented management style could be tolerated because his results were excellent.

A Chance for Advancement

After a year, Mike received an offer from a different Consolidated Life division located across town. Mike was asked to manage an office in the marketing area. The pay was excellent and it offered an opportunity to turn around an office in disarray. The reorganization in his present division at Consolidated was almost complete and most of his mentors and friends in management had moved on to other jobs. Mike decided to accept the offer.

In his exit interview he was assured that if he ever wanted to return, a position would be made for him. It was clear that he was held in high regard by management and staff alike. A huge party was thrown to send him off.

The new job was satisfying for a short time but it became apparent to Mike that it did not have the long-term potential he was promised. After bringing on a new staff, computerizing the office, and auditing the books, he began looking for a position that would both challenge him and give him the autonomy he needed to be successful.

Eventually word got back to his former vice-president, Rick Belkner, at Consolidated Life that Mike was looking for another job. Rick offered Mike a position with the same pay he was now receiving and control over a 14-person unit in his old division. After considering other options, Mike decided to return to his old division feeling that he would be able to progress steadily over the next several years.

Enter Jack Greely: Return Mike Wilson

Upon his return to Consolidated Life, Mike became aware of several changes that had taken place in the six months since his departure. The most important change was the hiring of a new divisional senior vice-president, Jack Greely. Jack had been given total authority to run the division. Rick Belkner now reported to Jack.

Jack's reputation was that he was tough but fair. It was necessary for people in Jack's division to do things his way and "get the work out."

Mike also found himself reporting to one of his former peers, Kathy Miller, who had been promoted to manager during the reorganization. Mike had always "hit it off" with Kathy and foresaw no problems in working with her.

After a week Mike realized the extent of the changes that had occurred. Gone was the loose, casual atmosphere that had marked his first tour in the division. Now, a stricter, task-oriented management doctrine was practiced. Morale of the supervisory staff had decreased to an alarming level. Jack Greely was the major topic of conversation in and around the division. People joked that MBO now meant "management by oppression."

Mike was greeted back with comments like "Welcome to prison" and "Why would you come back here? You must be desperate!" It seemed like everyone was looking for new jobs or transfers. Their lack of desire was reflected in the poor quality of work being done.

Mike's Idea: Supervisor's Forum

Mike felt that a change in the management style of his boss was necessary in order to improve a frustrating situation. Realizing that it would be difficult to affect his style directly, Mike requested permission from Rick Belkner to form a Supervisor's Forum for all the managers on Mike's level in the division. Mike explained that the purpose would be to enhance the existing management-training program. The Forum would include weekly meetings, guest speakers, and discussions of topics relevant to the division and the industry. Mike thought the forum would show Greely that he was serious about both his job and improving morale in the division. Rick gave the O.K. for an initial meeting.

The meeting took place and ten supervisors who were Mike's peers in the company eagerly took the opportunity to "Blue Sky" it. There was a euphoric attitude about the group as they drafted their statement of intent. It read as follows:

TO: Rick Belkner
FROM: New Issue Services Supervisors
SUBJECT: Supervisors' Forum

On Thursday, June 11, the Supervisors' Forum held its first meeting. The objective of the meeting was to identify common areas of concern among us and to determine topics that we might be interested in pursuing.

The first area addressed was the void that we perceive exists in the management-training program. As a result of conditions beyond anyone's control, many of us over the past year have held supervisory duties without the benefit of formal training or proper experience. Therefore, what we propose is that we utilize the Supervisors' Forum as a vehicle with which to enhance the existing management-training program. The areas that we hope to affect with this supplemental training are: a) morale/job satisfaction; b) quality of work and service; c) productivity; and d) management expertise as it relates to the life insurance industry. With these objectives in mind, we have outlined below a list of possible activities that we would like to pursue.

1. Further utilization of the existing "in-house" training programs provided for manager trainees and supervisors, i.e., Introduction to Supervision, E.E.O., and Coaching and Counseling.
2. A series of speakers from various sections in the company. This would help expose us to the technical aspects of their departments and their managerial style.
3. Invitations to outside speakers to address the Forum on management topics such as managerial development, organizational structure and behavior, business policy, and the insurance industry. Suggested speakers could be area college professors, consultants, and state insurance officials.
4. Outside training and visits to the field. This could include attendance at seminars concerning management theory and development relative to the insurance industry. Attached is a representative sample of a program we would like to have considered in the future.

In conclusion, we hope that this memo clearly illustrates what we are attempting to accomplish with this program. It is our hope that the above outline will be able to give the Forum credibility and establish it as an effective tool for all levels of management within New Issue. By supplementing our on-the-job training with a series of speakers and classes, we aim to develop prospective management personnel with a broad perspective of both the life insurance industry and management's role in it. Also, we would like to extend an invitation to the underwriters to attend any programs at which the topic of the speaker might be of interest to them.

cc: J. Greely
Managers

The group felt the memo accurately and diplomatically stated their dissatisfaction with the current situation. However, they pondered what the results of their actions would be and what else they could have done.

PART II

An emergency management meeting was called by Rick Belkner at Jack Greely's request to address the "union" being formed by the supervisors. Four general managers, Rick Belkner, and Jack Greely were at that meeting. During the meeting it was suggested the Forum be disbanded to "put them in their place." However, Rick Belkner felt that if "guided" in the proper direction the Forum could die from lack of interest. His stance was adopted but it was common knowledge that Jack Greely was strongly opposed to the group and wanted its founders dealt with. His comment was "It's not a democracy and they're not a union. If they don't like it here, then they can leave." A campaign was directed by the managers to determine who the main authors of the memo were so they could be dealt with.

About this time, Mike's unit had made a mistake on a case, which Jack Greely was embarrassed to admit to his boss. This embarrassment was more than Jack Greely cared to take from Mike Wilson. At the managers' staff meeting that day Jack stormed in and declared that the next supervisor to "screw up" was out the door. He would permit no more embarrassments of his division and repeated his earlier statement about "people leaving if they didn't like it here." It was clear to Mike and everyone else present that Mike Wilson was a marked man.

Mike had always been a loose, amiable supervisor. The major reason his units had been successful was the attention he paid to each individual and how they interacted with the group. He had a reputation for fairness, was seen as an excellent judge of personnel for new positions, and was noted for his ability to turn around people who had been in trouble. He motivated people through a dynamic, personable style and was noted for his general lack of regard for rules. He treated rules as obstacles to management and usually used his own discretion as to what was important. His office had a sign saying "Any fool can manage by rules. It takes an uncommon man to manage without any." It was an approach that flew in the face of company policy, but it had been overlooked in the past because of his results. However, because of Mike's actions with the Supervisors' Forum, he was now regarded as a thorn in the side, not a superstar, and his oddball style only made things worse.

Faced with the fact that he was rumored to be out the door, Mike sat down to appraise the situation.

PART III

Mike decided on the following course of action:

1. Keep the Forum alive but moderate its tone so it didn't step on Jack Greely's toes.
2. Don't panic. Simply outwork and outsmart the rest of the division. This plan included a massive retraining and remotivation of his personnel. He implemented weekly meetings, cross training with other divisions, and a lot of interpersonal "stroking" to motivate the group.
3. Evoke praise from vendors and customers through excellent service and direct that praise to Jack Greely.

The results after eight months were impressive. Mike's unit improved the speed of processing 60% and lowered errors 75%. His staff became the most highly trained in the division. Mike had a file of several letters to Jack Greely that praised the unit's excellent service. In addition, the Supervisors' Forum had grudgingly attained credibility, although the scope of activity was restricted. Mike had even improved to the point of submitting reports on time as a concession to management.

Mike was confident that the results would speak for themselves. However, one month before his scheduled promotion and one month after an excellent merit raise in recognition of his exceptional work record, he was called into his supervisor's, Kathy Miller's office. She informed him that after long and careful consideration the decision had been made to deny his promotion because of his lack of attention to detail. This did not mean he was not a good supervisor, just that he needed to follow more instead of taking the lead. Mike was stunned and said so. But, before he said anything else, he asked to see Rick Belkner and Jack Greely the next day.

The Showdown

Sitting face to face with Rick and Jack, Mike asked if they agreed with the appraisal Kathy had discussed with him. They both said they did. When asked if any other supervisor surpassed his ability and results, each stated Mike was one of the best, if not *the* best they had. Then why, Mike asked, would they deny him a promotion when others of less ability were approved? The answer came from Jack: "It's nothing personal, but we just don't like you. We don't like your management style. You're an oddball. We can't run a division with ten supervisors all doing different things. What kind of a business do you think we're running here? We need people who conform to our style and methods so we can measure their results objectively. There is no room for subjective interpretation. It's our feeling that if you really put your mind to it, you can be an excellent manager. It's just that you now create trouble and rock the boat. We don't need that. It doesn't matter if you're the best now, sooner or later as you go up the ladder, you will be forced to pay more attention to administrative duties and you won't handle them well. If we correct your bad habits now, we think you can go far."

Mike was shocked. He turned to face Rick and blurted out nervously, "You mean it doesn't matter what my results are? All that matters is how I do things?" Rick leaned back in his chair and said in a casual tone, "In so many words, Yes."

Mike left the office knowing that his career at Consolidated was over and immediately started looking for a new job. What had gone wrong?

EPILOGUE

After leaving Consolidated Life, Mike Wilson started his own insurance, sales and consulting firm, which specialized in providing corporate-risk managers with insurance protection and claims-settlement strategies. He works with a staff assistant and one other associate. After three years, sales averaged over $7 million annually, netting approximately $125,000 to $175,000 before taxes to Mike Wilson.

During a return visit to Consolidated Life, three years after his departure, Mike found Rick Belkner and Jack Greely still in charge of the division in which Mike had worked. The division's size had shrunk by 50 percent. All of the members of the old Supervisors' Forum had left. The reason for the decrease in the division's size was that computerization had removed many of the peoples' tasks.

Step 2: Prepare the case for class discussion.

Step 3: Answer the following questions, individually, in small groups, or with the entire class, as directed by your instructor:

Description

1. Describe the situation. What symptoms of problems exist?

Diagnosis

2. Diagnose the situation. What problems exist? What theories and concepts help explain the problems?

Prescription

3. Prescribe ways of improving the situation.

Action

4. Devise an action plan.

Step 4: Discussion. In small groups, with the entire class, or in written form, share your answers to the questions above.

Activity 15–2: CAROLINE MILLER (I) AND (II)

Step 1: Read the Caroline Miller case Parts (I) and (II).

CAROLINE MILLER (I)

Caroline Miller's career at the University had been outwardly smooth and successful in the nearly 10 years she had been active in its administration, but now she faced a personal decision. She was not satisfied with her future prospects in administering the women's education program and she was seriously concerned over whether she should continue. She had received several offers of jobs elsewhere and if she were to make a change, this seemed an opportune time. She thought about her accomplishments and disappointments in integrating women into the formerly all-male institution as she weighed the factors that would determine her decision.

Her staff work at the University had begun when she was approached by the Dean of the Graduate School, Frederick White, and was asked to accept a position in administration. Her children were at an age where she could consider doing more than the part-time teaching she had been engaged in, but despite her Ph.D. in biology she was not prepared to invest the time to combine a teaching and research career. She commented later, "I knew I related well to people, and I felt the Dean's office might offer me the opportunity I wanted." Her husband was an Associate Professor of French who knew that White prided himself on his open-mindedness in employing women. Dr. Miller spoke of White later: "In 1960 women administrators were not so common that White's tolerance could go unappreciated, and he enjoyed hearing that the women were grateful."

Shortly after her initial contact with him, he proposed a part-time position as an Assistant Dean in the Graduate School and she accepted eagerly, not asking for or receiving details as to status or duration of the job. He hired another woman in a similar position some months later, commenting with satisfaction that he had enough understanding of the family problems women had to contend with to allow the jobs to be held part-time. Actually, both women worked two-thirds time. Dr. Miller said of her feelings at this time,

> I was pleased with the arrangement because it meant I needn't feel guilty when I had to take time off for one reason or another, although I usually worked more hours than I was being paid for. I'd been there for some time before I began to notice the men employed full-time left the office most days at 4:00, and it took me even longer to realize that they were leaving to play handball.
>
> At that point I was at the salary level of an assistant professor, pro-rated, but it didn't occur to me to arrange for a "courtesy" faculty appointment, for which my Ph.D. and teaching experience would have qualified me.

During the next several years she learned to handle the routine of the Dean's office, processing students' admissions to the Graduate School, participating in the review of Ph.D. dissertations, handling fellowships and government training grants.

> I enjoyed the experience thoroughly in the first years, but when I had been following the same routine for seven years, I began to think about my own future again. I was ready for a more responsible job, especially after I ran the Associate Dean's office for several months while the Associate Dean was ill. I was pleased to find that I could do it competently and even calmly. It was hard now to remember my early "hangups" about contacting important people on the phone, and by then I had had superb management training from Ernie Stanford. I was very lucky to have worked with him and I'll always be grateful to him.

Stanford was a friendly, experienced Assistant Dean who knew his way around the University and had guided her early efforts with good humor and valuable advice. The Assistant Dean fulfilled varying duties, satisfying the exigencies of the University administration. The hierarchy among them was informal, with some hired on a long-term basis, generally paid more than the others—Stanford had been in this category.

> Although he had only a Bachelor's degree, Ernie was confident and capable, very much part of the University where he'd been an undergraduate. I sensed that he liked me and accepted me and did not feel threatened in spite of my Ph.D. and the fact that I was older than he. He greeted my first effort at draw-

ing up a budget with hoots of derision. "Where are your contingency funds?" he said. "Don't you know you must always see that you have little pockets of money for emergencies?" He taught me how to deal with the press, how to cut through red tape, and how to make decisions. I was always seeing both sides of every issue—not much help when you're trying to make a decision.

By the time she felt ready for advancement, Stanford had gone on to another University, but she commented later that she could imagine his disapproval of her if he had known that she had never secured a faculty appointment. She found that this lack blocked her access to the Associate Dean's job, a job that was now open and that she would have liked.

She arranged to speak to Dean White, explaining to him that she had learned a great deal, had derived pleasure and satisfaction from the job as Assistant Dean, especially in her contact with students and faculty, and felt she was ready for additional responsibility. She hoped he would consider her if a more challenging position opened somewhere in the University. Months went by but she heard nothing from Dean White.

Leaving a meeting one day that spring, she found herself walking with the Vice-Chancellor and asked him if Dean White had mentioned her job aspirations. She knew all significant administrative appointments went through the Vice-Chancellor's office. She was somewhat surprised to find that the Dean had not spoken to him about her, but soon forgot about it in the excitement of his next words. The meeting they had attended had been called to discuss the changes to be expected as the Undergraduate division of the University, like other men's colleges that year, began to plan for the admission of women to the undergraduate school. The Vice-Chancellor proposed that as the most qualified and experienced woman in the administration, she was the logical person to implement the plan. He thought they could probably arrange an Associate Deanship after the planning year in view of the unusual circumstances. She telephoned her husband, in California at a meeting, that evening to tell him how pleased she was. She responded to a call from the Chancellor's office a few days later.

He greeted me with his customary charm, told me how grateful he was that I was going to help him, and mentioned my new salary, which was much higher than the old one. I found I was to have my own office and my own secretary. The job would have to be on a full-time basis but my children were older now and that was not a problem. All this came at a time when I had wanted something new to do, but I could scarcely have hoped for so interesting and worthwhile a project. I hadn't been given a new title but I decided not to mention it.

The academic year passed quickly, she recalled later, though not without incident as she learned to cope with the business office and to manage her own budget. She felt the remodeling arrangements to house the women students had not been subject to adequate bidding and were likely to be expensive while they did not take into account enough of the women students' desires. The business office in turn thought her requests unreasonable. "Oh, we can't be bothered asking those women what they want," she was told. Overall, however, the housing problems were solved, admissions were processed, and she felt in the spring of 1967 that the University would be ready to receive the women in the fall. Except for her contacts in the business office, she found the men in the male-oriented undergraduate school surprisingly helpful to her and accepting of the new admission policy. She wondered occasionally why she never heard any objections but the issue of women on campus had, after all, been debated heatedly in the past and now seemed to be settled.

As the admission of women became imminent, the Chancellor discussed her personal situation with her for the coming year. He said he would like to make her an Associate Dean of the undergraduate school if that was all right with her. "I said it certainly was, but a few days later he called me to his office again."

He began the interview by telling her that her salary would be increased next year, that she had been doing a wonderful job, and he knew she would understand about one small difficulty. There had been, after all, only one Associate Dean. The man who presently held that title was understandably jealous of it, he was very valuable to Jim Clark, the undergraduate Dean, and he was threatening to leave if she were given a similar title. The Chancellor said he was sure she wouldn't mind if they went on calling her an Assistant Dean.

I think I succeeded in saying it pleasantly but I told him that I was afraid I did mind. I said I had been an Assistant Dean in the graduate school for six years, I was well-qualified, and I thought I deserved something more than that. I did not mention that my qualifications were more than those of the Associate Dean. The Chancellor smiled warmly, told me not to worry about it, and assured me—not for the last time—that he would work something out.

Shortly afterward he called to tell her that she would be known as Assistant to the Chancellor and Coordinator of Women's Education. "I stifled my impulse to comment that it wasn't a catchy title, and told him that it was acceptable." She was given a budget, was paid from the Chancellor's payroll, and retained her office in the undergraduate school. It occurred to her that a physical location nearer to the Chancellor's office, some blocks away, might be an advantage but he didn't mention it and it didn't seem worth bothering him about.

She realized that her special status put her in no clear administrative line but she would share the aura of the Chancellor's prestige and influence, which she was sure would be sufficient. Although her capacity was advisory and she had no decision-making authority, the Chancellor proposed that she be appointed to the important committees of the University which would effectively, he thought, allow her to participate in setting University policy. One of the most significant of these was the Administrative Council of the Undergraduate School.

> Shortly after my appointment to it had been made known, Dean Clark came in to see me and said, "Carrie, would you mind awfully giving us your slot on the Administrative Council?" He explained that it was too heavily weighted with administrators and that he really had to put more faculty members on it. I was aware that Clark was still annoyed with me for not having accepted the Assistant Deanship and that might have had something to do with it, but I found myself agreeing. Later I wondered whether Ernie wouldn't have told me to find someone else to drop from the Committee, but by then it was too late. Besides, I was involved in many other committees, and had the distinction of being the first woman to serve on another prestigious one made up of the Managers of each of the Residences.

Toward the end of that year, the value of the Managers' committee diminished when it was decided that it had grown too unwieldy and that much of the business ought to be handled in executive session. She was not chosen to be part of that small group and before long, her attendance became perfunctory.

She did insist on the formation of a standing committee of influential people concerned with the education of women, a committee that the Chancellor agreed was necessary and that he supported. Although its membership varied somewhat, it included a representative from the Chancellor's office, at least one Residence Manager, the Associate Dean of the undergraduate school, student representatives, and several faculty members personally invited by the Chancellor to serve. The committee proved prestigious and very useful. "After an issue or an idea had been thrashed out in this committee it emerged as a bona fide decision worthy of attention."

In Dr. Miller's view, one of the most pressing problems of the women students was the lack of women advisors living in the Residences. The male students traditionally had had the support of young faculty personnel who lived in the Residences, but the women had no female counterparts. Although her own budget was sufficient to pay the usual stipend to women chosen for such jobs, Residency funds supported the cost of their board and room. A discreet tug-of-war developed between Dr. Miller and the Managers. She was principally interested in choosing women who would have the welfare of her students in mind and serve as significant role models, while the Managers were equally firm about wanting women who could contribute their talents toward leading extra-curricular activities (dramatics, language tables, etc.).

Another struggle developed when she tried to correct the housing arrangements to provide some privacy for those women who didn't respond well to the crowded conditions forced on them. Although hundreds of women had been admitted to the University, they still made up a small proportion of the students. The men were eager to have them distributed throughout the dormitories and that was the arrangement made initially, putting twelve people where nine had been housed formerly. Many of the women students adapted readily, but others weren't able to share bathroom facilities with men without embarrassment and made their unhappiness known to Dr. Miller.

Through her Committee, she effected a compromise that would allow some women to elect to live in separate wings while others would continue to be distributed randomly. She was pleased with what seemed a sensible compromise, allowing the women an option, but the male students were not so delighted. They were openly opposed to the idea. "The Undergraduate Dean's office made itself popular with them by letting it be known that the compromise arrangement would be ignored. When rumors of this reached me, I tried to arrange further discussion meetings but was quietly rebuffed." The academic year was nearing an end but she made her feelings known by including a strongly worded section on the issue in her year-end report.

Her report to the Chancellor also strongly recommended an increase in the number of women in the student body. Since no significant building program was contemplated, it also suggested a reduction in the number of men to be admitted into the next freshman class. The reception to this idea was cool. The Chancellor issued a statement, indicating that there would not be a cutback in the number of new male undergraduates admitted. His statement went on to explain that further plans for including women in the Undergraduate School would be delegated to new committees.

Clark, the Undergraduate Dean, was due to resign that spring. He submitted a lengthy State-of-the-College report to the Chancellor and Dr. Miller received a copy of it, routinely circulated. Buried in it were comments on the space requirements of the Dean's office and Dr. Miller was startled to read that "the space occupied by the Coordinator of Women's Education is sorely needed by the Office of the Dean and should be returned to the Dean's use as soon as possible."

This latest irritation occurred as she was discussing yet again with the business office the need for additional security. Protests over the expense of additional lighting and locks persisted until one of the women students was raped months later. Each time expense was mentioned she explained that the women students were an asset. They had been absorbed into the existing college with very little additional outlay, while their board and room and tuition charges added to the income of the undergraduate school. No one ever seemed to listen to that argument. "How can you justify so much expense?" she was asked indignantly by the business manager.

As she thought over the priorities she ought to aim for that spring, as the first year in the new position neared an end, the need for more women among the student body seemed foremost, but she was not particularly concerned with pushing for it herself. She was confident that the male students would continue to exert pressure on the administration to admit more women students. She felt that her own mission ought to be the altering of the all-male image. To this end it would be necessary to have more women in faculty and administrative posts so that they would participate in the decision process. The number of women with faculty positions, when compared with the numbers who had matriculated at this University alone and been awarded Ph.Ds, proved to be shockingly low. In Psychology, for example, about a third of those receiving Ph.Ds in recent years had been women and even in earlier years (1955–66) they represented about one-fifth of those receiving the advanced degree. They made up 8% of the Psychology faculty, mostly at the Assistant Professor level. Over a third of those receiving advanced degrees in English were women, but women accounted for 11% of the English faculty, again mostly at lower levels. These two disciplines employed the bulk of women faculty members. There were none at all in Sociology, Political Science, Physics and Chemistry. Hoping to improve this situation, she was pleased with herself when she succeeded in setting up a Committee on the Status of Faculty Women, headed by a man who, she thought, had impeccable credentials. Charles Evans had been an early advocate of coeducation, his wife was active in the women's movement, and Dr. Miller was sure that requests emanating from his Committee for policies on part-time work or maternity leave would have great credibility. She felt they would not be written off as "not fitting into the academic scheme" as they might be if they came from a Committee chaired by a woman. The Committee met occasionally that summer and into the fall but she found that Evans didn't work very hard at it and mentioned fairly often that he really couldn't spare so much of his time. "I thought at the time that recommendations coming from the Committee would have credibility, if only there were some recommendations." When she saw her old friend, Ernie, at a meeting that winter and mentioned her disappointment, he shrugged and said, "Well, Carrie, old Charlie is a man after all." Then he said, "Who else is on your Affirmative Action Committee and how much trouble is the government giving you?" She found herself flushing in embarrassment as she said, "What? I didn't know we had such a thing." She didn't have to tell him she hadn't been asked to be a member of it. She soon found out that it had been meeting for six months.

Now into her third year as "coordinator," she found herself travelling all over the country, to the West and East Coasts, speaking to alumni groups. She was the recipient of VIP treatment. She was housed in deluxe hotel rooms and the Chancellor invariably introduced her as "one of our top administrators." He always smiled warmly as she spoke about full employment and the improved status of women. When she talked with him privately or with any of his other "top administrators," they agreed with her that her goal of more women on campus both as undergraduate and faculty was a clear necessity.

Later in April one of the many students with whom she maintained an easy relationship stopped in to see her in her office.

> In the course of her reading for her Government Policy assignment, the student had noticed a letter written to the House or Senate committee—she wasn't sure which—that was conducting hearings on Higher Education. It had been written by an influential professor at the University whose views were usually those of the Administration and it stated forcefully that the undergraduate school could not allow an equal number of women to be admitted without losing its identity and that some more sensible quota or goal would have to be maintained. Of course, no restriction on the numbers of women admitted to the graduate school would be specified.
>
> The student was indignant. "Since the grad school only recruits from well-known schools like this one," she said, "of course they're discriminating in both places! And then the boys resent us because we're smarter than they are. We sure have to be!" I'd learned a lot about administration by then and I hid my own indignation and promised the student I would look into it.

As she discussed the situation with her friends in the administration, especially with a psychiatrist who had been supportive of her efforts, she made an effort to see both sides as they explained that the professors of humanities in the undergraduate school felt threatened by the influx of women in a way that she had perhaps not been aware of in her orientation toward the sciences.

> They told me that, for whatever reasons, it looked as if fewer women would continue to find their way into science and engineering than into language and history, for example. There was no reason why equal numbers of men and women should not soon be competing for their faculty spots and I couldn't expect them to welcome that prospect.
>
> Complicating the issue further was the resistance to my attempts to alter the all-male image. My psychiatrist friend, Dr. Alec Weinman, said, "Look, Carrie, they like that image. Maybe that's what attracted them here in the first place and maybe it's part of why many of them have stayed when they could have had more money elsewhere. Women don't play handball!" He mentioned similar feelings among the alumni and said he supposed I had had pressure from them, but I denied it.
>
> In all my travels speaking to such groups I had heard no arguments at all except from a few crackpots and even they were always too gentlemanly to attack me publicly. The alumni were terrific. They were uniformly warm and supportive once women on campus had become a fait accompli. After all, they have daughters as well as sons. If you took the time to explain to them that you understood how they felt about the all-male University they had known, they would usually say, "Well, we weren't for this decision, but now that it's been made. . . ."

The Chancellor had been away from the University for an extended period and she had been unwilling to discuss her feelings with his surrogate, but when the Chancellor returned she confronted him with her dissatisfaction.

> I told him I really couldn't continue to rush around as the person who was responsible for integrating women if I was really a figurehead. I said I would have to have an active role or it was time for me to accept another job.

He promised to see that she was put on more influential committees and he asked her to write a report—to be presented at the annual meeting of the University trustees and administrative personnel—setting goals and timetables for the hiring of women to faculty positions.

> The Chancellor mentioned that he did have some doubts about setting goals. "Maybe we can hire many more women than those goals," he said, and I agreed, but argued that meanwhile it would be nice to have some minimum standards.
>
> I worked very hard on that report, with a minimum of cooperation from the Vice-Chancellor's office. For example, I needed to know the projected turnover in the faculty in order to set reasonable aims, and I had a very hard time getting the necessary data.
>
> Anyway, I prepared the report, brought it to the meeting, and then waited all through the meeting to be called on to present it. He never asked me to read it. I thought he had forgotten and I whispered a reminder to him. He mumbled something about circulating it later, but one of the trustees heard and said, "Oh, let's hear Carrie's report."

It wasn't until the report had been read that Dr. Miller sensed how deeply opposed some of the trustees and administrators were toward opening the faculty to women.

> I realized why the Chancellor had been reluctant to bring the question up for discussion, but I still wonder why he asked me to present the report at the meeting in the first place.
>
> I found that half those at the meeting were pretty much on my side and half were vehemently opposed. Those who were against hiring more women faculty members used the classic argument that merit should be the sole criterion for hiring, with the tacit understanding that women would lower the University standards. From the discussion at that meeting I got the impression that the idea of more women at the University had somehow incurred the wrath of a whole echelon of middle-management people who were important to the Chancellor. It wasn't clear to me—and perhaps not to them—why they were so threatened by it. Many of them were insecure men who later left.

It was at this point that Dr. Miller decided to ask for a leave of absence. Her husband had been asked to teach in California for a semester and she told the Chancellor she planned to use the time to think about her future role at the University while helping her friend, Dr. Weinman, in a short-term research project. She mentioned also that, as he had probably heard, she had had job offers elsewhere and it seemed only fair that she look at them during this leave. The Chancellor agreed to the leave of absence and after some discussion, a "caretaker" for her office for the coming year was decided on. He commented on her luck in finding a grant for her project because "of course, administrators are not allowed paid sabbaticals," and he promised to give her another raise upon her return. Although he had not yet put her on the committees he had mentioned when she had indicated her dissatisfaction some months earlier, he assured her that he would do so when she returned. Their parting interview was extremely cordial; he told her several times that she had been doing a wonderful job.

She explained later that she had been careful to tell him honestly that she felt her advisory position was not much good anymore, that the office was in fact counterproductive.

> I told him that my office was being used as a defusing agent . . . everyone foisted their problems on me but I really had no authority to do anything about them. I told him I thought the Residences should each be responsible for the men *and* women in them, that women were here to stay and that everyone had better get used to it. I tried, politely of course, to make it clear that I would like a new, clearly defined job with authority. I mentioned my interest in the Affirmative Action program again. He said he thought the job requirement for the person to run that program demanded a faculty position rather than an administrative one, but he would check into it. He mentioned that he was considering upgrading the student counseling service and wondered if I would be interested in running that office. He was aware that I had been pressing for a more effective career and counseling service. Properly funded and staffed, it seemed to me that running the counseling service might be interesting. I told him I'd like to hear more about it if upgrading would bring those specifics. "Well," he said, "of course, there's a new Vice-Chancellor coming on the scene next year, this is a time of budget cuts, and I can't make any commitments."

She left the Chancellor's office with the feeling that she should probably resign, but she wanted time to think about their conversation and to investigate her other options. His parting words were that he would work at finding the kind of position she wanted. She completed and sent him her Report on the first four years of women's education. It summed up the University's accomplishments but pointed out the areas in which the status of women at the University could be improved.

When she discussed the situation with her husband and mentioned that she would like to look around at the other job offers she had received, he commented that he was quite content in his own role at the University. He had always been helpful and encouraging to her, never resentful of household chores, though, she said, "He was always happier about doing things he volunteered to do rather than those he was asked to do, but that's understandable." She found, however, that the prospect of moving to another University because it might improve her own situation was a much more difficult problem than any that had faced them earlier. It would be possible to arrange a position for her husband similar to the one he held, but it was soon clear that he was not anxious to make a change. "You're just annoyed at them now and you're overreacting," her husband said. "You've got nothing to gain by resigning. Why not keep your options open?"

He agreed to go with her, however, to look at the job offer she thought most attractive, especially since it was on the East Coast. They were received warmly and a good deal of time was spent discussing her husband's prospective position, which was comparable to the one he had, but it was obvious that she was the one being actively recruited. They agreed to think about the offer, but by the time they left, she knew she wouldn't accept:

> I knew he didn't want to be asked as part of the deal, and it seemed best to drop the idea. Once I had been away from the University for a little while, it also seemed to me that my husband was probably right and I was overreacting. After all, the Chancellor kept assuring me that I was doing a great job, he gave me a raise every year. Surely his intentions were good and he would eventually support the changes I felt were necessary.

A few weeks later Dr. Miller wrote the Chancellor that she would be returning in March, that her project was going well, and that she would look forward to working with him again the following year. She mentioned the job possibilities they had discussed and indicated her confidence that he would have worked something out for her by the time of her return.

CAROLINE MILLER (II)

Dr. Miller returned to the University in early March. Although she had written him several times, she had not heard from the Chancellor during her absence; considering his busy schedule, that did not seem unusual.

> I was concerned, though, because while we'd been away I began getting letters from people back home saying they were surprised and sorry that I had resigned. I continued working on Weinman's project that spring and tried to contact the Chancellor's office several times without success. Meanwhile more people kept coming up to me and saying, "Caroline, why have you let us down like this? Why are you resigning?" I would assure them that I was only on a temporary project and would be returning, but I didn't seem to be convincing them.

She had been back at the University for a few weeks when, in a conversation with the Associate Dean of the Undergraduate School about her research project, he mentioned that the counseling service was being upgraded; it would have its own budget and a larger staff and he said they had been interviewing a number of women for the top job.

> I told him that that was a job that would interest me. Because of our past sensitive relationship when I hadn't wanted to serve as an assistant dean under him, it seemed best to confine my conversation about the job to him and not to approach the new Dean.

Not long afterward, she heard through the University "grapevine" that a woman recruited from outside the University had been named to head the Affirmative Action program. She had not previously held a faculty appointment and her academic qualifications were considerably less than Dr. Miller's. A few days later the University newspaper reported that the counseling service had been reorganized. In the future it would make special efforts to counsel and develop the abilities of women and minorities, and would be administered by two women. The woman appointed as deputy director had been an administrative assistant in one of the nonacademic campus organizations, and the woman in charge had had a minor administrative post at another university.

Dr. Miller had not been approached about either the Affirmative Action job or the counseling service and she thought it was time to see the Chancellor once more.

> I called his office and asked to have an appointment where there'd be time to talk to him. I didn't want to be squeezed between others. I had always had a very good relationship with his secretary and she said, "Oh, Dr. Miller, why don't you see him at home? I'll arrange to have you invited for cocktails." She did and a few days later I was greeted by the Chancellor, very cordially. We discussed my situation again, and he talked expansively about his plans for me but it did seem to me that he was talking about a lot of non-jobs. I finally smiled and said, very coolly, "But there's no job now, right?" He was a little embarrassed because he doesn't like jarring notes, but he said, "Well, I guess that's right."
>
> I waited about a week and then I wrote him a letter. I told him I had always been devoted to the University, and reminded him that he had given me the assignment of trying to change the University to make it a comfortable place for women. I said I had taken his charge seriously and that in the course of carrying it out I had undoubtedly antagonized some people, but if I hadn't, I couldn't effectively have brought about any change. I said I thought it was a pity that this now seemed to mark the end of my long affiliation with the University.

Two and half weeks went by and she had no answer from the Chancellor.

> There was no acknowledgment of my letter, no phone call. And everywhere I went—in the stores, wherever I was—people would say to me, "Carrie, why have you let us down like this? Why have you resigned?"
>
> Well, it really bothered me. I felt I was living a lie. Anyway, I had always had very good relationships with the students and when one of them, who happened to work on the University newspaper, came up to me with the refrain about why had I resigned, I found myself telling him that I hadn't, but that my office was being closed next year and that I hadn't been offered another job. He asked me if he could write it up for the newspaper and I said he could. We talked for quite a while.
>
> Early the following morning the telephone rang. It was the Chancellor and he was angry. "How could you do such a thing?," he said, "Don't you know this will prevent me from giving you a job anywhere in the University now, and I do want to give you a job?" I asked him what he wanted me to do. I said he knew it was true, and surely he didn't want me to retract the story.

Her husband was annoyed with her handling of the situation. Like the Chancellor, he was uncomfortable when events did not proceed smoothly. As she contemplated her future course of action, she wondered what she might have done differently.

> I realized my options were pretty limited. There was no job for me at the University, or in the little Midwestern town in which it was located, and it was clear that my husband didn't relish moving to another one. I would have to change fields and finding a new kind of job in a town dominated by the University would not be easy.

At the end of the year her old office of Coordinator of Women's Education was closed. The woman who had taken it over during Dr. Miller's leave and subsequent "resignation" issued a final report. Dr. Miller found that she was mentioned in it:

> It would be inappropriate to end this final report without giving full recognition to the outstanding leadership of Caroline Miller, whose imagination and energy helped to solve the many problems, large and small, that arose during the introduction of coeducation at the University. Her vision was instrumental in developing the means to achieve the goals as stated by the Trustees, and her forthright courage in pursuit of her convictions was crucial to the accomplishments of the Office for Women's Education.

Step 2: Prepare this case for class discussion.

Step 3: Answer the following questions, individually, in small groups, or with the entire class, as directed by your instructor:

Description
1. Describe the situation. What symptoms of problems exist?

Diagnosis
2. Diagnose the situation. What problems exist? What theories and concepts help explain the problems?

Prescription
3. Prescribe ways of improving the situation.

Action
4. Devise an action plan.

Step 4: Discussion. In small groups, with the entire class, or in written form, share your answers to the questions above.

This case was prepared by Sherrie S. Epstein for the Institute for Case Development and Research, Graduate School of Management, Simmons College, Boston, Massachusetts 02215.

Activity 15–3: ANNOTATED JOURNAL OF ORGANIZATIONAL EVENTS

Step 1: Select ten articles from daily newspapers or news magazines that illustrate organizational behavior principles.

Step 2: Write a one-page annotation of each article, incorporating relevant course concepts and applying the diagnostic approach where appropriate.

Step 3: Discussion. Share your analyses with the rest of the class, in small groups, with the entire class, or in written form.

Activity 15–4: ANALYSIS OF AN ORGANIZATIONAL NOVEL

Step 1: Select a contemporary novel about an organizational situation. (Your instructor may offer some choices or suggestions.)

Step 2: Read the novel.

Step 3: Describe the situation in the novel.

Step 4: Diagnose the situation.

Step 5: Prescribe ways for improving the situation.

Step 6: Devise an action plan.

Step 7: Discussion. Share your analysis with the rest of the class, in small groups, with the entire class, or in written form.

Activity 15–5: CASE ANALYSIS

Step 1: Choose a problematic situation you encountered in an organization of which you were a member.

Step 2: Describe the situation.

Step 3: Diagnose the situation.

Step 4: Prescribe ways of improving the situation.

Step 5: Devise an action plan.

Step 6: Discussion. Share your analysis with the rest of the class, in small groups, with the entire class, or in written form.

Activity 15–6: ORGANIZATIONAL ANALYSIS

Step 1: Choose an organization of which you were a member.

Step 2: Describe the interpersonal processes, organizational structure, and work design that characterized the organization.

Step 3: Diagnose any problems that existed in the organization.

Step 4: Prescribe ways of improving the situation.

Step 5: Devise an action plan.

Step 6: Discussion. Share your analysis with the rest of the class, in small groups, with the entire class, or in written form.

CONCLUDING COMMENTS

The activities of this chapter allowed you to apply the comprehensive diagnostic approach to the cases of Consolidated Life and Caroline Miller. You also applied organizational behavior concepts to understanding daily events reported in newspapers or news magazines. You analyzed a problem you have faced yourself in an organization, as well as problems in organizations as a whole. Your successful completion of the activities in this chapter reflect your ability to diagnose behavior in organizations and to suggest ways of increasing organizational effectiveness.

ENDNOTES

[1]Based in part on a case written by Kimberley Ann Sheehan at the Carroll School of Management, Boston College.

[2]See J.M. Bartunek, J.R. Gordon, and R.P. Weathersby, Developing complicated understanding in administrators, *Academy of Management Review* 8 (1983): 273–284.

[3]P.S. Goodman and J.M. Pennings, eds., *New Perspectives on Organizational Effectiveness* (San Francisco: Jossey-Bass, 1977); W.L. French, C.H. Bell, and P.A. Zawacki, eds., *Organization Development: Theory, Practice, and Research* (Dallas: Business Publications, 1978); R.H. Kilmann, L.R. Pondy, and D.P. Slevin, eds., *The Management of Organization Design: Research and Methodology* vol. II (Elsevir, Ill.: North-Holland, 1976).

[4]See, for example, J.P. Campbell, On the nature of organizational effectiveness. In P.S. Goodman and J.M. Pennings, *op. cit.;* and R.M. Steers, Problems in the measurement of organizational effectiveness, *Administrative Science Quarterly* 20 (1975): 546–558.

[5]S. Strasser, J.D. Eveland, G. Cummings, O.L. Deniston, and J.H. Romani, Conceptualizing the goal and system models of organizational effectiveness, *Journal of Management Studies* (July 1981): 323; K. Cameron, Critical questions in assessing organizational effectiveness, *Organizational Dynamics* (Fall 1980).

[6]J.P. Campbell, Research into the nature of organizational effectiveness: An endangered species, unpublished manuscript (Minneapolis: University of Minnesota, 1973).

[7]Cameron, *op. cit.*

[8]R.M. Kanter, *When Giants Learn to Dance* (New York: Simon & Schuster, 1989); G.P. Zachary, Apple's Gasee plans to resign as shake-up continues, *Wall Street Journal* (7 February 1990): B1.

RECOMMENDED READINGS

Cameron, K.S., Sutton, R.E., and Whetton, D.A. (eds.) *Readings in Organizational Decline: Framework, Research, and Prescription.* Cambridge, Mass.: Ballinger, 1988.

Campbell, J.P., Campbell, R.J., and Associates. *Productivity in Organizations: New Perspectives from Industrial and Organizational Psychology.* San Francisco: Jossey-Bass, 1988.

Kanter, R. *When Giants Learn to Dance.* New York: Simon & Schuster, 1989.

Steers, R.M. *Organizational Effectiveness: A Behavioral View.* Santa Monica, Cal.: Goodyear, 1976.

Torbert, W. *Managing the Corporate Dream.* Homewood, Ill.: Irwin, 1987.

Indexes

NAMES

SUBJECTS

continued

F

G

H

continued

K

L

M

N

O

P

S